BLOOMSBURY
ESSENTIAL
THESAURUS

BLOOMSBURY
ESSENTIAL
THESAURUS

A BLOOMSBURY REFERENCE BOOK
Created from the Bloomsbury Database of World English
www.bloomsbury.com/reference

First published in 2002
Reprinted 2004

Bloomsbury Publishing Plc, 38 Soho Square, London W1D 3HB

A CIP record for this title is available from the British Library

ISBN 0 7475 7616 5

10 9 8 7 6 5 4 3 2 1

All papers used by Bloomsbury Publishing are natural,
recyclable products made from wood grown in well-managed forests.
The manufacturing processes conform to the environmental
regulations of the country of origin.

Typeset by Selwood Systems, Midsomer Norton, Bath, United Kingdom
Printed in Great Britain by Clays Ltd, St Ives plc

Contents

General Editor
Susan Jellis

Editors
David Barnett
Korey Egge
Ros Fergusson
Jennifer Goss Duby
Barbara Kelly
Howard Sargeant

Project Coordinator
David Barnett

Project Assistants
Charlotte Regan
Joel Adams

Proofreaders
Sandra Anderson
Josephine M. P. Curtis
Ruth Hillmore
Susan Turner

Project Manager
Katy McAdam

Production Editor
Nicky Thompson

Database Manager
Edmund Wright

Keyboarders
Simon Arnold
Bernadette Crowley

Design
Nigel Partridge
Nathan Burton

BLOOMSBURY REFERENCE

Editor-in-Chief
Dr Kathy Rooney

Publisher
Nigel Newton

Dictionaries Publisher
Faye Carney

Production Director
Penny Edwards

US General Editor
*Encarta® World
English Dictionary*
Anne H. Soukhanov

How to Use the Thesaurus

The Thesaurus is arranged like a dictionary: you look up an entry word and immediately find alternatives for its common meanings. When there is more than one meaning of a word, each meaning is numbered. The first alternative, printed in **bold**, tells you exactly which meaning is being illustrated. The lists of alternatives are arranged for ease of use, with the more general alternatives towards the beginning of the list.

Alternatives that can be used only in more specific contexts are shown towards the end, often with a label, e.g. *informal* or *literary*, to indicate the type of language they belong to. Words used in informal contexts are labelled *infml* and those used in formal contexts are labelled *fml*.

You will sometimes also be offered words with opposite or contrasting meaning, introduced by the term *Opposite:*

Entry word for which alternatives are given

Part of speech of entry word

First alternative indicating the meaning

Word with opposite meaning to entry word

Each meaning distinguished by number

masses *n* 1 **common people**, crowd, multitude, commonality, hoi polloi *Opposite:* elite 2 *(infml)* **lots**, loads *(infml)*, tons *(infml)*, heaps *(infml)*, oodles *(infml)*

massif *n* **mountain range**, chain, sierra, ridge, line

massive *adj* 1 **bulky**, heavy, solid, weighty, hulking *Opposite:* slight 2 **huge**, enormous, gigantic, immense, colossal *Opposite:* tiny

Phrases entered in their alphabetical place

Label indicating that entry word belongs to informal usage

make a hash of *(infml)* *v* **muddle**, confuse, jumble, spoil, mix up

make allowances *v* **take into account**, bear in mind, consider, take into consideration, allow for

make amends *v* **compensate**, make reparations, make up for, pay back, recompense

At some entries there are also panels listing words that are not alternatives but *types of* the same thing, e.g. types of birds, or names for male or female animals.

gender *n* **sex**, sexual category, sexual characteristics, masculinity, femininity

WORD BANK
❑ **types of female animal** bitch, cow, dam, doe, ewe, filly, heifer, hind, jenny, lioness, mare, nanny goat, sow, tigress, vixen
❑ **types of male animal** billy goat, boar, buck, bull, bullock, colt, hart, jackass, ram, stag, stallion, steer, tom, tomcat, wether
❑ **types of male bird or female bird** capon, cob, cock, cockerel, drake, duck, gander, goose, hen, pen, rooster

Parts of objects, e.g. parts of an aircraft or the human body, are shown in the same way.

alimentary canal *n* **bowels**, guts, innards, insides, intestines

WORD BANK
❑ **parts of an alimentary canal** anus, appendix, bile duct, bladder, bowel, caecum, colon, duodenum, gallbladder, gullet, gut, intestine, kidney, large intestine, liver, oesophagus, pancreas, rectum, small intestine, spleen, stomach, throat

The notes shown after some entries help to discriminate between the meanings of closely related words by giving brief definitions for them.

accomplish *v* **achieve**, attain, realize, carry out, pull off *(infml)*

COMPARE AND CONTRAST CORE MEANING: bring something to a successful conclusion
accomplish succeed in doing something; **achieve** succeed in something, usually with effort; **attain** reach a specific objective; **realize** fulfil a specific vision or plan; **carry out** perform or accomplish a task or activity; **pull off** *(infml)* accomplish something, despite difficulties.

Test Your Word Power

Once – as a child – you were an expert, an accomplished virtuoso, at learning new words. Today, by comparison, you are a mere amateur.

Does this statement sound insulting? It may be – but if you are the average adult, it is a statement that is, unfortunately, only too true.

Educational testing indicates that children of ten who have grown up in families in which English is the mother tongue have recognition vocabularies of over twenty thousand words – *and that these same ten-year-olds have been learning new words at a rate of many hundreds a year since the age of four.* In astonishing contrast, studies show that adults who are no longer at school increase their vocabularies at a pace slower than twenty-five to fifty words annually.

So how do you assess your own vocabulary?

A Test of Vocabulary Range

Here are some brief phrases, each containing one word in *italics*; your task is to find the closest alternative definition for each italic word. To keep your score valid, avoid making wild guesses. The key to the correct answers will be found at the end of the test.

1. to *parry* a blow is to...
   - (a) fend it off
   - (b) fear it
   - (c) expect it
   - (d) invite it
   - (e) ignore it

2. a *prevalent* disease is...
   - (a) dangerous
   - (b) catching
   - (c) childhood
   - (d) fatal
   - (e) widespread

3. an *erudite* person is...
   - (a) very wise
   - (b) very knowledgeable
   - (c) impolite
   - (d) serious
   - (e) wrong

4. to *supersede* something is to...
   - (a) enforce it
   - (b) specify penalties for it
   - (c) replace it
   - (d) repeal it
   - (e) continue it

5. an *indefatigable* worker is...
   - (a) well-paid
   - (b) tired
   - (c) skilful
   - (d) untiring
   - (e) pleasant

6. a *loquacious* person is...
   - (a) miserable
   - (b) easily annoyed
   - (c) indecisive
   - (d) good at public speaking
   - (e) talkative

7. an *incorrigible* optimist is...
   - (a) happy
   - (b) impossible to change or reform
   - (c) foolish
   - (d) hopeful
   - (e) unreasonable

8. a notorious *demagogue* is a...
   - (a) believer in democracy
   - (b) firebrand
   - (c) someone who commits fraud
   - (d) liar
   - (e) spendthrift

9. living in *affluence* involves...
   - (a) difficult circumstances
   - (b) countrified surroundings
   - (c) fear
   - (d) wealth
   - (e) poverty

10. a *gourmet* is a...

(a) seasoned traveller
(b) greedy eater
(c) vegetarian
(d) connoisseur of good food
(e) skilful chef

11. to *simulate* interest is to...

(a) fake it
(b) feel it
(c) lose it
(d) stir it up
(e) ask for it

12. a *magnanimous* action is...

(a) puzzling
(b) generous
(c) foolish
(d) unnecessary
(e) wise

13. a *clandestine* meeting is...

(a) prearranged
(b) hurried
(c) important
(d) secret
(e) public

14. to *vacillate* is to...

(a) avoid something
(b) act indecisively
(c) administer an injection
(d) treat somebody
(e) scold somebody

15. a *circumspect* person is...

(a) restrained
(b) confident
(c) cautious
(d) honest
(e) intelligent

16. *diaphanous* material is...

(a) strong
(b) sheer and gauzy
(c) colourful
(d) expensive
(e) synthetic

17. a *taciturn* host is...

    (a) stingy
    (b) generous
    (c) disinclined to conversation
    (d) charming
    (e) gloomy

18. to *malign* somebody is to...

    (a) accuse somebody
    (b) help somebody
    (c) disbelieve somebody
    (d) denigrate somebody
    (e) introduce somebody

19. a *tendentious* statement is...

    (a) pompous
    (b) biased
    (c) misleading
    (d) formal
    (e) emotional

20. *vicarious* enjoyment is...

    (a) complete
    (b) unspoiled
    (c) experienced by identifying with another person
    (d) long-lasting
    (e) short-lived

21. a *placebo* is...

    (a) a calming drug
    (b) a substance that counteracts a poison
    (c) a drug that has no real effect
    (d) a sleeping pill
    (e) an anti-inflammatory drug

22. an *iconoclastic* attitude is...

    (a) adoring
    (b) sneering at tradition
    (c) troubled
    (d) difficult
    (e) religious

23. a *tyro* is a...

    (a) dominating personality
    (b) beginner
    (c) accomplished musician
    (d) dabbler
    (e) serious student

24. a *laconic* reply is...
    (a) immediate
    (b) assured
    (c) brief
    (d) unintelligible
    (e) angry

25. an *anomalous* situation is...
    (a) dangerous
    (b) intriguing
    (c) uncharacteristic
    (d) pleasant
    (e) unhappy

26. *perspicacity* is...
    (a) sincerity
    (b) astuteness
    (c) love
    (d) faithfulness
    (e) longing

27. an unpopular *martinet* is a...
    (a) candidate
    (b) supervisor
    (c) strict disciplinarian
    (d) military leader
    (e) discourteous snob

28. a *gregarious* person is...
    (a) outwardly calm
    (b) very sociable
    (c) completely untrustworthy
    (d) vicious
    (e) self-effacing and timid

29. an *inveterate* gambler is...
    (a) impoverished
    (b) successful
    (c) hardened
    (d) occasional
    (e) superstitious

30. a *surreptitious* glance is...
    (a) mysterious
    (b) staring
    (c) furtive
    (d) suspicious
    (e) sideways

Key:
1. parry = fend off
2. prevalent = widespread
3. erudite = very knowledgeable
4. supersede = replace
5. indefatigable = untiring
6. loquacious = talkative
7. incorrigible = impossible to change or reform
8. demagogue = firebrand
9. affluence = wealth
10. gourmet = connoisseur of good food
11. simulate = fake
12. magnanimous = generous
13. clandestine = secret
14. vacillate = act indecisively
15. circumspect = cautious
16. diaphanous = sheer and gauzy
17. taciturn = disinclined to conversation
18. malign = denigrate
19. tendentious = biased
20. vicarious = experienced by identifying with another person
21. placebo = drug with no real effect
22. iconoclastic = sneering at tradition
23. tyro = beginner
24. laconic = brief
25. anomalous = uncharacteristic
26. perspicacity = astuteness
27. martinet = strict disciplinarian
28. gregarious = very sociable
29. inveterate = hardened
30. surreptitious = furtive

Scoring:
Your **score** (one point for each correct choice): _____

The meaning of your score:
0–5:	below average
6–15:	average
16–24:	above average
25–30	excellent

A Test of Verbal Speed

Part 1

In no more than two minutes (time yourself, or have someone time you), decide whether the word in column B has the *same* (or *approximately the same*) meaning as the word in column A; the *opposite* (or *approximately opposite*) meaning; or whether the two words are merely *different*. Circle S for *same*, O for *opposite*, and D for *different*.

Column A	Column B			
1. sweet	bitter	S	O	D
2. big	threatening	S	O	D
3. danger	peril	S	O	D
4. love	hate	S	O	D
5. stand	rise	S	O	D
6. tree	branch	S	O	D
7. doubtful	certain	S	O	D
8. begin	start	S	O	D
9. strange	familiar	S	O	D
10. male	female	S	O	D
11. powerful	weak	S	O	D
12. beyond	under	S	O	D
13. go	get	S	O	D
14. growl	cry	S	O	D
15. open	close	S	O	D
16. chair	table	S	O	D
17. want	desire	S	O	D
18. idle	working	S	O	D
19. rich	luxuriant	S	O	D
20. building	structure	S	O	D

Part 2

In no more than three minutes (again, time yourself or have someone time you), write down as many *different* words as you can think of starting with the letter D.

Do not use various forms of a word, such as *do, doing, does, done, doer, etc.*

Key: *Part 1:* 1 – O, 2 – D, 3 – S, 4 – O, 5 – S, 6 – D, 7 – O, 8 – S, 9 – O, 10 – O, 11 – O, 12 – D, 13 – D, 14 – D, 15 – O, 16 – D, 17 – S, 18 – O, 19 – S, 20 – S

Part 2: Any English word starting with D is correct unless it is merely another form of a previous word on the list.

Scoring:

Part 1
Score 5 points for each correct answer. Maximum score: 100 points.
Your score on Part 1: _____

Part 2
Score 1 point for each word.
Your score on Part 2: _____

Total score on verbal speed: _____

The meaning of your verbal speed score:
0–50:   below average
51–99:   average
100–149:   above average
150–200:   excellent

A Test of Verbal Responsiveness

Part 1
Write in the blank column B a word starting with the letter P that has the *same*, or *approximately the same*, meaning as the word given in column A:

Example:
look   peer

Remember: Every answer *must* start with the letter P.

Column A	Column B
1. fragrance	_____
2. faultless	_____
3. maybe	_____
4. forgive	_____
5. own	_____
6. likely	_____
7. annoy	_____
8. good-looking	_____
9. suggest	_____
10. choose	_____

Part 2
Write in the blank column B a word starting with the letter G that is *opposite*, or *approximately opposite*, or in *contrast to* the word given in column A.

Example:
stop   go

Remember: Every answer *must* start with the letter G.

Column A	Column B
1. lose	_____
2. innocent	_____
3. specific	_____
4. rough	_____
5. take	_____
6. host	_____

7. cheerful   _____
8. clean   _____
9. stingy   _____
10. clumsy   _____

Key:
Part 1: If more than one answer is given, count as correct any word you have written that is the same as any one of the answers.
1. fragrance = perfume
2. faultless = perfect
3. maybe = perhaps, possibly
4. forgive = pardon
5. own = possess
6. likely = probable, possible
7. annoy = pester
8. good-looking = pretty
9. suggest = propose
10. choose = pick

Part 2: If more than one answer is given, count as correct any word you have written that is the same as any one of the answers.
1. lose   *Opposite* gain, get
2. innocent   *Opposite* guilty
3. specific   *Opposite* general
4. rough   *Opposite* gentle
5. take   *Opposite* give
6. host   *Opposite* guest
7. cheerful   *Opposite* gloomy, glum
8. clean   *Opposite* grubby, grimy
9. stingy   *Opposite* generous
10. clumsy   *Opposite* graceful

Scoring:
Score Parts 1 and 2 together. Write in the blank the total number of correct responses you gave: ____

The meaning of your verbal responsiveness score:
0–5:   below average
6–10:   average
11–15:   above average
16–20:   excellent

Vocabulary and Success

Now you know where you stand. If you are in the below average or average groups, you must consider, seriously, whether an inadequate vocabulary may be holding you back. If you scored above average or excellent, you have doubtless already discovered the unique and far-reaching value of a rich vocabulary, and you are eager to add still further to your knowledge of words. In either case, using this Thesaurus regularly will help you to build up a mental library of alternative and opposite terms and vary the words you use to express yourself, whether in speech or writing.

A

A1 *(infml)* adj **excellent**, first-rate, first-class, perfect, flawless *Opposite:* inferior

abandon v **1 dump**, discard, dispose of, throw out, throw away *Opposite:* keep **2 desert**, leave, forsake, leave behind, walk out on *(infml)* **3 end**, call off, cancel, give up, stop *Opposite:* continue ■ n **recklessness**, wildness, licence, intemperance, unrestraint *Opposite:* restraint

abandoned adj **1 discarded**, forsaken, dumped, neglected, cast off **2 empty**, deserted, derelict, vacant **3 wild**, uncontrolled, unrestricted, uninhibited, unrestrained *Opposite:* restrained

abandonment n **desertion**, leaving behind, leaving, rejection, neglect

abase *(literary)* v **lower**, demean, degrade, belittle, humiliate *Opposite:* respect

abase yourself *(literary)* v **grovel**, humble yourself, demean yourself, debase yourself, degrade yourself

abashed adj **embarrassed**, ashamed, mortified, disconcerted, dismayed *Opposite:* unabashed

abate *(fml)* v **decrease**, subside, grow less, decline, fade *Opposite:* rise

abatement *(fml)* n **1 reduction**, decline, lessening, diminution, decrease *Opposite:* increase **2 deduction**, discount, cut, reduction, decrease *Opposite:* increment

abbey n **religious foundation**, religious house, cloister, monastery, convent

abbreviate v **shorten**, cut, cut short, condense, abridge *Opposite:* lengthen

abbreviated adj **shortened**, condensed, abridged, truncated, curtailed *Opposite:* full-length

abbreviation n **short form**, contraction, ellipsis, acronym, shortening

ABC n **1 alphabet**, Roman alphabet, spelling system **2 basics**, fundamentals, essentials, rudiments, nitty-gritty *(infml)*

abdicate v **renounce**, relinquish, resign, step down, hand over *Opposite:* accept

abdication n **resignation**, handing over, renunciation, abandonment, relinquishment

abdominal adj **stomach**, belly, front, intestinal, gut

abduct v **kidnap**, make off with, seize, hold somebody against his or her will, capture

abduction n **kidnap**, seizure, kidnapping, carrying off, capture

abductor n **kidnapper**, hostage taker, captor, hijacker, snatcher *(US infml)*

aberrant adj **abnormal**, unusual, deviant, anomalous, peculiar *Opposite:* normal

aberration n **deviation**, abnormality, anomaly, irregularity, peculiarity

abet v **1 assist**, help, support, aid, back *Opposite:* hinder **2 encourage**, urge, connive, put up to, incite *Opposite:* deter

abhor v **detest**, hate, loathe, dislike, despise *Opposite:* adore

abhorrence n **hatred**, loathing, detestation, disgust, repugnance *Opposite:* adoration. *See* COMPARE AND CONTRAST *at* dislike.

abhorrent adj **repugnant**, objectionable, repulsive, detestable, hateful *Opposite:* desirable

abide v **1 put up with**, stand for, stand, bear, stomach **2** *(archaic)* **withstand**, endure, survive, resist, bear **3** *(archaic)* **live**, have your home, stay, dwell *(literary)*, lodge *(dated)*

abide by v **obey**, follow, keep to, conform to, stick to *Opposite:* defy

abiding adj **enduring**, remaining, surviving, long-lasting, unshakable *Opposite:* transient

ability n **aptitude**, skill, talent, competence, capacity

COMPARE AND CONTRAST CORE MEANING: the necessary skill, knowledge, or experience to do something

ability natural and acquired skills or knowledge; **skill** the ability to do something well gained through training or experience; **competence** ability measured against a standard; **aptitude** a natural tendency to do something well; **talent** an unusual natural ability to do something well; **capacity** mental or physical ability for something or to do something; **capability** the ability or potential to do something.

---

abject adj **1 extreme**, utter, absolute, wretched, dismal **2 humble**, servile, meek, submissive, subservient *Opposite:* confident

abjection n **1 wretchedness**, misery, desolation, despair, despondence *Opposite:* cheerfulness **2 humility**, humbleness, subservience, deference, servility *Opposite:* confidence

abjuration n **renunciation**, rejection, denial, repudiation, refrainment *Opposite:* affirmation

abjure v **renounce**, reject, repudiate, deny, disavow

ablaze adj **on fire**, blazing, burning, in flames, alight

able *adj* **1 capable**, competent, proficient, adept, skilled *Opposite*: incompetent **2 clever**, talented, intelligent, bright, gifted *Opposite*: incapable. *See* COMPARE AND CONTRAST *at* intelligent.

able-bodied *adj* **healthy**, fit, well, active, strong *Opposite*: weak

ablutions *(fml)* *n* **washing**, bathing, wash, cleanup, toilette

ably *adv* **capably**, well, skilfully, competently, with ease *Opposite*: incompetently

abnegate *(fml)* *v* **renounce**, reject, deny, repudiate, abjure *Opposite*: accept

abnegation *(fml)* *n* **rejection**, renunciation, repudiation, denial, abstention *Opposite*: acceptance

abnormal *adj* **irregular**, nonstandard, uncharacteristic, atypical, anomalous *Opposite*: normal

abnormality *n* **1 defect**, deformity, irregularity, malformation, malfunction **2 irregularity**, aberration, anomaly, deviation, oddity

aboard *adv* **1 on board**, on the ship, on the bus, on the train, on the plane **2** *(infml)* **involved**, participating, on the team, with us, on our side ■ *prep* **onto**, on, into, inside

abode *(literary)* *n* **house**, home, residence, place, dwelling *(fml)*

abolish *v* **put an end to**, eliminate, close down, bring to an end, stop *Opposite*: establish

abolition *n* **elimination**, ending, closing down, eradication, closure *Opposite*: establishment

abolitionist *n* **opponent**, objector, protester, eradicator, adversary *Opposite*: supporter

abominable *adj* **dreadful**, repulsive, offensive, detestable, monstrous

abominate *(fml)* *v* **hate**, loathe, detest, despise, dislike *Opposite*: love

abomination *n* **1 outrage**, disgrace, scandal, eyesore, atrocity **2** *(literary)* **hatred**, dislike, repugnance, loathing, revulsion *Opposite*: love

aboriginal *adj* **indigenous**, original, native, local, autochthonous *Opposite*: foreign. *See* COMPARE AND CONTRAST *at* native.

abort *v* **end**, abandon, call off, call a halt, cancel *Opposite*: continue

abortive *adj* **unsuccessful**, failed, fruitless, unproductive, futile *Opposite*: successful

abound *v* **1 thrive**, flourish, prosper, proliferate, be plentiful **2 brim**, overflow, throng, teem, swarm

abounding *adj* **many**, varied, multifarious, plentiful, abundant *Opposite*: scarce

about *prep* **concerning**, regarding, in relation to, on the subject of, on ■ *adv* **1 approximately**, roughly, in the region of, around, almost **2 around**, close, nearby, near, in the vicinity

about to *prep* **ready to**, on the verge of, on the point of, just going to, set to

about-turn *n* **1 turnaround**, reversal, shift, transformation, sea change **2 turn**, U-turn, 180° turn, revolution

above *prep* **1 more than**, greater than, higher than, beyond, exceeding *Opposite*: below **2 on top of**, over, higher than, atop *Opposite*: below

above all *adv* **especially**, in particular, primarily, principally, most of all

aboveboard *adj* **open**, fair, honest, forthright, straightforward *Opposite*: shady ■ *adv* **openly**, fairly, honestly, legally, lawfully *Opposite*: illegally

above-mentioned *adj* **said**, aforementioned *(fml)*, aforesaid *(fml)*

abrade *v* **graze**, scrape, roughen, chafe, grind down *Opposite*: smooth

abrasion *n* **scrape**, scratch, scuff, graze

abrasive *adj* **1 rough**, coarse, harsh, rasping, scratchy *Opposite*: smooth **2 rude**, sharp, harsh, brusque, argumentative *Opposite*: gentle

abreast *adv* **side by side**, alongside, shoulder to shoulder, beside, level ■ *adj* **well-informed**, in touch, up-to-date, up on, up with *Opposite*: ignorant

abridge *v* **shorten**, edit, condense, abbreviate, reduce *Opposite*: expand

abridged *adj* **shortened**, edited, condensed, reduced, abbreviated *Opposite*: complete

abridgement *see* abridgment

abridgment *n* **synopsis**, digest, condensation, précis, abstract

abroad *adv* **overseas**, away, out of the country

abrogate *(fml)* *v* **repeal**, revoke, rescind, retract, nullify. *See* COMPARE AND CONTRAST *at* nullify.

abrogation *(fml)* *n* **retraction**, repeal, annulment, abolition, rescindment

abrupt *adj* **1 sudden**, unexpected, unforeseen, rapid, hasty *Opposite*: gradual **2 curt**, short, brusque, terse, rude *Opposite*: polite

abscess *n* **boil**, pustule, swelling, eruption, blister

abscond *v* **run away**, escape, break out, make off, elope

absconder *n* **deserter**, runaway, escapee, fugitive, truant

absence *n* **1 nonappearance**, absenteeism, time off *Opposite*: presence **2 lack**, deficiency, want, dearth, privation *Opposite*: surplus

absent *adj* **1 missing**, gone, out, away *Opposite*: present **2 inattentive**, absent-minded, far away, preoccupied, vague *Opposite*: alert **3 lacking**, deficient, nonexistent, in short supply *Opposite*: present

absentee *n* **truant**, defaulter, runaway, absconder

absenteeism *n* **absence**, nonattendance, nonappearance, truancy, skiving *(infml)*

absently *adv* **inattentively**, vaguely, dreamily, distractedly, abstractedly *Opposite*: attentively

absent-minded *adj* **forgetful**, distracted, scatterbrained, preoccupied, vague *Opposite*: attentive

absent yourself *v* **excuse yourself**, send your apologies, stay away *Opposite*: attend

absolute *adj* **1 total**, complete, utter, unqualified, out-and-out **2 unconditional**, unlimited, supreme, unmodified, unadulterated *Opposite*: provisional **3 conclusive**, resolved, firm, fixed, definite *Opposite*: unconfirmed ■ *n* **given**, rule, principle, truth, fundamental

absolution *n* **forgiveness**, pardon, release, freedom, liberty *Opposite*: condemnation

absolutism *n* **totalitarianism**, despotism, dictatorship, tyranny, autocracy

absolve *v* **pardon**, forgive, clear, release, free *Opposite*: punish

absorb *v* **1 soak up**, attract, take in, take up, suck up *Opposite*: exude **2 understand**, learn, grasp, admit, take in **3 engross**, fascinate, engage, captivate, grip *Opposite*: bore

absorbed *adj* **engrossed**, wrapped up, fascinated, captivated, immersed *Opposite*: detached

absorbency *n* **porosity**, sponginess, permeability, penetrability, perviousness

absorbent *adj* **porous**, spongy, permeable, penetrable, pervious

absorbing *adj* **fascinating**, engrossing, captivating, gripping, enthralling *Opposite*: boring

absorption *n* **1 preoccupation**, fascination, interest, captivation, engagement **2 amalgamation**, incorporation, assimilation, combination, inclusion *Opposite*: rejection

abstain *v* **1 desist**, refrain, withdraw, withhold, go without *Opposite*: indulge **2 sit on the fence**, stay neutral, not take sides, hedge *Opposite*: vote

abstainer *n* **1 avoider**, shunner, teetotaller, withholder, refrainer **2 nonvoter**, hedger, fence sitter

abstemious *adj* **self-denying**, self-disciplined, moderate, ascetic, sober *Opposite*: unrestrained

abstemiousness *n* **sobriety**, self-denial, moderation, temperance, self-discipline *Opposite*: excess

abstention *n* **nonparticipation**, abstaining, refraining, holding back

abstinence *n* **self-denial**, self-restraint, self-discipline, moderation, asceticism *Opposite*: indulgence

abstinent *adj* **ascetic**, abstemious, sober, temperate, teetotal *Opposite*: indulgent

abstract *adj* **1 nonconcrete**, intellectual, mental, immaterial, intangible *Opposite*: concrete **2 theoretical**, conceptual, conjectural, hypothetical, speculative *Opposite*: practical ■ *n* **summary**, extract, précis, synopsis, abridgment ■ *v* **1 conceptualize**, theorize, hypothesize, intellectualize **2 summarize**, condense, shorten, précis, abridge *Opposite*: expand **3 extract**, take out, select, remove, separate

abstracted *adj* **inattentive**, preoccupied, vague, distant, distracted *Opposite*: alert

abstractedness *n* **preoccupation**, inattentiveness, inattention, pensiveness, distractedness *Opposite*: alertness

abstraction *n* **1 pensiveness**, preoccupation, dreaminess, vagueness, daydreaming *Opposite*: concentration **2 concept**, idea, thought, notion, construct *Opposite*: fact **3 removal**, extraction, withdrawal, deduction *Opposite*: inclusion

abstractly *adv* **theoretically**, conceptually, hypothetically, in theory *Opposite*: practically

abstruse *adj* **obscure**, perplexing, puzzling, complex, profound *Opposite*: simple. *See* COMPARE AND CONTRAST *at* **obscure**.

abstruseness *n* **complexity**, obscurity, difficulty, profundity, mysteriousness *Opposite*: simplicity

absurd *adj* **1 ridiculous**, ludicrous, farcical, nonsensical, illogical *Opposite*: reasonable **2 meaningless**, pointless, futile, empty, purposeless *Opposite*: meaningful

absurdity *n* **1 illogicality**, irrationality, silliness, ludicrousness, ridiculousness *Opposite*: logic **2 farce**, joke, nonsense, incongruity

absurdly *adv* **ridiculously**, ludicrously, farcically, nonsensically, preposterously *Opposite*: reasonably

absurdness *see* **absurdity**

abundance *n* **profusion**, plenty, richness, wealth, copiousness *Opposite*: scarcity

abundant *adj* **plentiful**, copious, rich, profuse, ample *Opposite*: scarce

a bundle of laughs *n* **good fun**, a barrel of monkeys, a barrel of laughs, a lot of fun, laugh (*infml*)

abuse *n* **1 mistreatment**, cruelty, ill-treatment, violence, maltreatment **2 misuse**, exploitation, manipulation, taking advantage, mishandling **3 insults**, verbal abuse, swearing, name-calling, foul language ■ *v* **1 exploit**, take advantage, misuse, manipulate **2 treat badly**, ill-treat, mistreat, maltreat, molest *Opposite*: look after **3 insult**, swear, shout abuse, hurl abuse, shout insults *Opposite*: compliment. *See* COMPARE AND CONTRAST *at* **misuse**.

abused *adj* **ill-treated**, physically abused, battered, badly treated, injured *Opposite*: looked after

abusive *adj* **1 rude**, insulting, unmannerly, foul, offensive *Opposite*: polite **2 violent**, cruel, vicious, sadistic, rough *Opposite*: gentle

abusiveness n **rudeness**, unpleasantness, impoliteness, nastiness, vulgarity

abut v **be next to**, adjoin, border, be adjacent to, touch

abutment n **support**, buttress, prop, strut, brace

abutting adj **adjoining**, next to, bordering, adjacent to, against

abuzz adj **alive**, throbbing, humming, pulsating, busy Opposite: still

abysmal adj **terrible**, awful, dreadful, horrible, appalling Opposite: superb

abyss n **gulf**, chasm, gorge, hole, void

academia n **academic world**, academic circles, university, university circles, academe (fml)

academic adj **1 educational**, school, college, university, scholastic **2 studious**, intellectual, scholarly, bookish, literary **3 theoretical**, speculative, abstract, moot, hypothetical Opposite: practical ■ n **researcher**, professor, college lecturer, don, scholar

academy n **school**, college, conservatory, conservatoire, arts school

a case in point n **working example**, instance, case, paradigm, illustration

accede v **1 agree**, assent, consent, comply, grant Opposite: reject **2 come into**, inherit, succeed, take over, enter upon

accelerate v **go faster**, speed up, increase speed, gather speed, pick up the pace Opposite: slow down

accelerated adj **speeded up**, faster, quicker, speedier, advanced Opposite: slower

acceleration n **1 increase of rate**, increase of velocity, spurt, burst of speed Opposite: deceleration **2 speeding up**, stepping up, hastening, hurrying, quickening Opposite: deceleration

accent n **1 pronunciation**, inflection, intonation, tone of voice, enunciation **2 emphasis**, stress, beat, accentuation, inflection ■ v **emphasize**, stress, accentuate, put stress on, give weight to

accentuate v **emphasize**, highlight, put emphasis on, stress, draw attention to Opposite: play down

accentuation n **1 prominence**, highlighting, attention, notice, emphasis **2 accent**, rhythm, stress, inflection, beat

accept v **1 receive**, take, agree to take, admit Opposite: refuse **2 consent**, agree, say yes, say you will, give a positive response Opposite: turn down **3 put up with**, endure, tolerate, bow, take **4 believe**, recognize, agree, admit, acknowledge Opposite: deny **5 take on**, undertake, acknowledge, assume, bear Opposite: reject

acceptability n **suitability**, adequacy, appropriateness, tolerability

acceptable adj **1 satisfactory**, suitable, good enough, adequate, up to standard Opposite: unacceptable **2 welcome**, pleasing, gratifying, agreeable, enjoyable Opposite: annoying

acceptably adv **well enough**, adequately, sufficiently well, suitably, tolerably Opposite: unreasonably

acceptance n **1 agreement**, assent, acquiescence, concurrence, accession Opposite: refusal **2 receipt**, taking, getting, reception, receiving Opposite: rejection **3 belief**, acknowledgment, credence, currency, agreement **4 recognition**, approval, tolerance, acknowledgment, toleration Opposite: disapproval

accepted adj **conventional**, established, customary, acknowledged, usual Opposite: unconventional

accepting adj **tolerant**, compliant, patient, long-suffering, uncomplaining Opposite: intolerant

access n **1 way in**, entrance, entry, approach, gate Opposite: exit **2 right of entry**, admission, right to use, admittance, entrée ■ v **get into**, gain access to, retrieve, call up, log on

accessibility n **convenience**, user-friendliness, openness, availability, approachability

accessible adj **1 nearby**, available, reachable, easily reached, handy Opposite: inaccessible **2 comprehensible**, understandable, user-friendly, easy to use, clear Opposite: obscure **3 approachable**, affable, genial, friendly, welcoming Opposite: unapproachable

accessibly adv **1 conveniently**, handily, suitably, helpfully, usefully Opposite: inconveniently **2 clearly**, simply, understandably, comprehensibly, straightforwardly Opposite: obscurely

accession n **1 attainment**, succession, taking over, taking office, appointment **2 agreement**, consent, concurrence, accord, assent

accessorize v **ornament**, decorate, beautify, trim, embellish

accessory n **1 addition**, decoration, fixture, fitment, attachment **2 accomplice**, partner, partner in crime, assistant, abettor

WORD BANK
❑ **types of accessory** ascot, bandanna, belt, bootlace, bow tie, braces, cravat, cummerbund, earmuffs, glove, handkerchief, hat, jewellery, mitt, mitten, muff, muffler, pashmina, sash, scarf, shawl, stole, tie, veil, wrap

accident n **1 chance**, coincidence, fortune, fate Opposite: design **2 crash**, collision, bump, smash, smash-up **3 mishap**, misfortune, calamity, catastrophe, disaster

accidental adj **unintentional**, unintended, inadvertent, chance, unplanned Opposite: deliberate

accidentally adv **by chance**, by accident, by mistake, unintentionally, inadvertently Opposite: purposely

accident-prone *adj* **ill-fated**, unfortunate, unlucky, ill-starred, doomed

acclaim *v* **praise**, sing the praises of, give approval, hail, commend *Opposite*: criticize ■ *n* **approval**, praise, commendation, acclamation, approbation *Opposite*: disapproval

acclaimed *adj* **praised**, admired, commended, celebrated, applauded

acclamation *n* **1 acclaim**, praise, commendation, approbation, approval **2 applause**, clapping, cheering, ovation, roar *Opposite*: jeering

acclimate *see* **acclimatize**

acclimatization *n* **adaptation**, becoming accustomed, getting used to, adjustment, accommodation

acclimatize *v* **get used to**, become accustomed, accustom, adapt, adjust

accolade *n* **tribute**, honour, compliment, award, praise

accommodate *v* **1 house**, lodge, put up, billet, quarter **2 contain**, have room for, hold, seat, have capacity for **3 get used to**, adapt, adjust, become accustomed to, familiarize **4 assist**, help, oblige, be of service, find ways to help

accommodating *adj* **helpful**, willing, obliging, compliant, cooperative *Opposite*: uncooperative

accommodation *n* **1 lodging**, housing, room, space, place **2 adjustment**, adaptation, alteration, change, modification

accompaniment *n* **supplement**, accessory, garnish, adjunct, complement

accompanist *n* **pianist**, instrumentalist, musician, player

accompany *v* **1 escort**, go with, go together with, go along with, come with, be an adjunct to, supplement, complement

accompanying *adj* **supplementary**, associated, complementary, additional, add-on

accomplice *n* **partner in crime**, assistant, accessory, collaborator, co-conspirator

accomplish *v* **achieve**, attain, realize, carry out, pull off (*infml*)

COMPARE AND CONTRAST CORE MEANING: bring something to a successful conclusion
accomplish succeed in doing something; **achieve** succeed in something, usually with effort; **attain** reach a specific objective; **realize** fulfil a specific vision or plan; **carry out** perform or accomplish a task or activity; **pull off** (*infml*) to accomplish something, despite difficulties.

---

accomplished *adj* **talented**, skilful, gifted, skilled, proficient

accomplishment *n* **1 completion**, execution, carrying out, finishing, realization **2 feat**, achievement, triumph, success, deed **3 talent**, skill, ability, expertise, capability

accord *v* **1 give**, allow, permit, render (*fml*), confer (*fml*) **2 agree**, concur, fit, match, correspond *Opposite*: clash ■ *n* **1 agreement**, treaty, settlement, pact, deal **2 consensus**, harmony, concurrence, unity, agreement *Opposite*: disagreement

accordance *n* **consensus**, agreement, accord, harmony, concord *Opposite*: disagreement

accordingly *adv* **1 appropriately**, suitably, correspondingly, fittingly *Opposite*: inappropriately **2 so**, for that reason, therefore, as a result, consequently

according to *prep* **1 as said by**, as stated by, on the word of **2 consistent with**, along with, in line with, in keeping with, in relation to *Opposite*: counter to

accost *v* **approach**, stop, confront, detain, hound

account *n* **1 report**, description, story, relation, narrative **2 explanation**, version, interpretation, justification, reason **3 bank account**, cheque account, current account, deposit account, savings account **4 arrangement**, credit, tally, balance, bill

accountability *n* **answerability**, responsibility, liability, culpability

accountable *adj* **answerable**, responsible, liable, held responsible, blamed

accountant *n* **bookkeeper**, auditor, chartered accountant, certified accountant, cost accountant

account for *v* **1 explain**, justify, give an explanation for, give a reason for, answer for **2 comprise**, make up, total, represent, constitute

accounts *n* **books**, balance sheet, financial statement

accoutrement *n* **accessory**, trapping, trimming, tool of the trade, equipment

accredit *v* **recognize**, sanction, endorse, authorize, certify

accreditation *n* **authorization**, endorsement, approval, certification, sanction

accredited *adj* **credited**, attributed, qualified, endorsed, official *Opposite*: unofficial

accretion *n* **1 accumulation**, buildup, increase, enlargement, addition *Opposite*: erosion **2 deposit**, layer, mass, lump, bump

accrual *n* **accumulation**, increase, buildup, accretion, addition *Opposite*: loss

accrue *v* **accumulate**, grow, mount up, build up, amass *Opposite*: dwindle

accumulate *v* **build up**, mount up, accrue, amass, collect *Opposite*: disperse. *See* COMPARE AND CONTRAST *at* **collect**.

accumulation *n* **1 buildup**, accretion, accrual, gathering, growth **2 collection**, stock, store, hoard, deposit

accumulative *adj* **1 acquisitive**, hoarding, materialistic, covetous, grasping **2 incremental**, increasing, rising, growing, mounting

accumulator *n* **collector**, saver, amasser, magpie (*infml*), squirrel (*infml*)

accuracy n **correctness**, accurateness, exactness, precision, truth *Opposite*: inaccuracy

accurate adj **precise**, correct, exact, true, truthful *Opposite*: inaccurate

accusation n **allegation**, indictment, claim, complaint, charge

accusatorial *(fml)* adj **1 critical**, judgmental, condemnatory, accusing, reproachful *Opposite*: complimentary **2 adversarial**, confrontational, argumentative, combative, antagonistic *Opposite*: amicable

accuse v **blame**, lay blame on, indict, point the finger, allege

accuser n **1 challenger**, confronter, criticizer, opponent, faultfinder **2 indicter**, litigant, petitioner, appellant, complainant **3 informer**, telltale, talebearer, whistleblower, sneak

accusing adj **reproachful**, condemning, reproving, critical, condemnatory

accustom v **get used to**, get used to, acclimatize, acclimate, become accustomed to

accustomed adj **1 familiarized**, inured, adapted, comfortable, habituated *(fml)* *Opposite*: unaccustomed **2 usual**, habitual, regular, familiar, customary *Opposite*: unusual

ace n **champion**, star, expert, winner, victor ■ adj *(infml)* **first-rate**, top, world-class, wonderful, excellent *Opposite*: lousy *(infml)*

acerbic adj **cutting**, bitter, caustic, acid, sour *Opposite*: mild

acerbity n **sharpness**, bitterness, sourness, acidity, acrimony

ache n **pain**, throbbing, aching, twinge, headache ■ v **1 hurt**, throb, be painful, sting, smart **2** *(fml)* **long**, desire, yearn, want, wish

achievable adj **attainable**, realizable, possible, reachable, doable *Opposite*: unrealistic

achieve v **attain**, realize, accomplish, reach, complete *Opposite*: fail. *See* COMPARE AND CONTRAST *at* **accomplish**.

achievement n **attainment**, accomplishment, success, feat, triumph *Opposite*: failure

achiever n **high-flier**, doer, self-starter, success, go-getter *(infml)* *Opposite*: loser

Achilles heel n **weakness**, flaw, failing, weak point, chink in somebody's armour

aching adj **painful**, achy, sore, tender, throbbing ■ n **1 ache**, pain, painful feeling, throbbing, throb **2** *(fml)* **longing**, desire, yearning, pining, itch

achy adj **painful**, aching, sore, tender, throbbing

acid adj **1 acidic**, tart, sour, bitter, sharp *Opposite*: sweet **2 cutting**, biting, caustic, acerbic, mordant *Opposite*: mild

acidic adj **acid**, tart, sour, bitter, sharp *Opposite*: sweet

acidity n **sourness**, sharpness, tartness, bitterness *Opposite*: sweetness

acidly adv **sharply**, cuttingly, tartly, sourly, acerbically *Opposite*: sweetly

acid test n **litmus test**, touchstone, trial, indicator

acknowledge v **1 admit**, recognize, accept, concede, grant *Opposite*: deny **2 greet**, salute, wave, nod, hail *Opposite*: ignore **3 reply**, answer, respond, react, return *Opposite*: ignore

acknowledged adj **recognized**, approved, known, accredited, accepted *Opposite*: denied

acknowledgment n **1 greeting**, salutation, nod, wave, salute **2 response**, reply, reaction, answer, retort **3 recognition**, acceptance, admission, confession, appreciation

acme n **peak**, summit, top, zenith, pinnacle *Opposite*: nadir

acolyte n **1 attendant**, assistant, aide, helper **2 follower**, devotee, disciple, adherent, supporter

acoustic adj **audio**, aural, auditory, audile, sound

acoustics n **audibility**, auditory range, sound quality

acquaint v **make aware**, inform, let know, let in on, make familiar with *Opposite*: keep from

acquaintance n **1 associate**, friend, contact, colleague, consociate *(fml)* *Opposite*: stranger **2 knowledge**, familiarity, understanding, awareness, conversance *Opposite*: ignorance **3 relationship**, contact, association, friendship, relations

acquiesce v **agree**, comply, accept, consent, assent *Opposite*: resist. *See* COMPARE AND CONTRAST *at* **agree**.

acquiescence n **agreement**, consent, compliance, submission, acceptance *Opposite*: resistance

acquiescent adj **agreeable**, compliant, yielding, accepting, submissive *Opposite*: resistant

acquire v **1 obtain**, get, get hold of, get your hands on, gain *Opposite*: lose **2 develop**, learn, pick up, take up, assimilate *Opposite*: drop. *See* COMPARE AND CONTRAST *at* **get**.

acquisition n **1 gaining**, attainment, achievement, getting hold of, procurement *Opposite*: loss **2 purchase**, possession, asset, gain

acquisitive adj **greedy**, covetous, grasping, avaricious, materialistic *Opposite*: generous

acquisitiveness n **greed**, hoarding, avarice, covetousness, materialism *Opposite*: generosity

acquit v **find not guilty**, clear, set free, free, release *Opposite*: convict

acquittal n **release**, discharge, freeing, clearing, exoneration *Opposite*: conviction

acquit yourself v **conduct yourself**, act, behave, perform, work

acreage n **land**, estate, property, domain, acres

acres n **1 land**, estate, domain, property, acreage **2** (*infml*) **expanse**, stretch, tracts, swathes, lots

acrid adj **1 pungent**, harsh, unpleasant, choking, bitter Opposite: pleasant **2 sharp**, cutting, caustic, bitter, vitriolic Opposite: mild

acrimonious adj **spiteful**, rancorous, discordant, hostile, unfriendly Opposite: amicable

acrimony n **bitterness**, spite, rancour, animosity, hostility Opposite: harmony

acrobat n **tumbler**, trapeze artist, circus performer, gymnast, funambulist

acrobatic adj **gymnastic**, athletic, lithe, supple, flexible

acrobatics n **1 gymnastics**, aerobics, physical exercises, callisthenics **2 agility**, skill, dexterity, nimbleness, quickness

acronym n **abbreviation**, short form, shortening, contraction, condensation

across adv **crossways**, crosswise, transversely, diagonally, from corner to corner

across-the-board adj **comprehensive**, sweeping, all-embracing, wide-ranging, far-reaching

act n **1 action**, deed, doing, undertaking, exploit **2 performance**, entertainment, turn, piece, item **3 pretence**, show, sham, con, feint **4 law**, piece of legislation, statute, decree, enactment ■ v **1 take action**, take steps, proceed, be active, perform **2 behave**, conduct yourself, perform, acquit yourself, comport yourself (*fml*) **3 pretend**, put on an act, put it on, play, fake **4 replace**, represent, act on behalf of, appear on behalf of, speak for **5 function**, work, take effect, produce a result, produce an effect **6 perform**, act out, be in, appear, play

acting n **drama**, the theatre, amateur dramatics, performing, the stage ■ adj **temporary**, substitute, stand-in, interim Opposite: permanent

action n **1 act**, deed, exploit, achievement, accomplishment Opposite: inaction **2 lawsuit**, suit, proceedings, charge, case **3 battle**, fighting, combat, conflict, engagement

actionable adj **indictable**, litigious, suable, chargeable, imputable Opposite: legal

action-packed adj **exciting**, thrilling, gripping, enthralling, suspenseful Opposite: dull

activate v **make active**, set in motion, set off, turn on, trigger Opposite: stop

activation n **start**, beginning, initiation, instigation, stimulation

active adj **1 lively**, vigorous, energetic, full of life, on the go Opposite: inactive **2 in force**, functioning, effective, in action, operating Opposite: defunct **3 working**, practising,

involved, committed, enthusiastic Opposite: half-hearted

actively adv **vigorously**, aggressively, energetically, enthusiastically, dynamically Opposite: half-heartedly

activeness n **liveliness**, animation, energy, vitality, vigour Opposite: passivity

activism n **direct action**, political action, social action, involvement, engagement

activist n **campaigner**, protester, objector, militant, advocate

activity n **1 pursuit**, interest, hobby, occupation, leisure interest **2 action**, movement, motion, bustle, commotion Opposite: inactivity

act on v **1 follow up on**, tackle, start in on, take action **2 have an effect on**, work, affect, perform

actor n **performer**, artist, thespian, artiste, player

act out v **1 enact**, perform, portray, act, play **2 work out**, work through, exorcize, express, purge

actress n **performer**, artist, thespian, artiste, player

actual adj **real**, genuine, authentic, concrete, tangible Opposite: imaginary

actuality n **1 fact**, certainty, reality, practicality, actual fact **2 real life**, the real world, here and now, reality

actually adv **in fact**, really, in point of fact, in reality, truly

actuate (*fml*) v **activate**, put into action, set in motion, trigger, start

act up v **cause trouble**, play up, be difficult, misbehave, malfunction Opposite: behave

acuity n **keenness**, acuteness, sharpness, alertness, awareness

acumen n **insight**, shrewdness, penetration, judgment, wisdom

acute adj **1 severe**, serious, critical, grave, important Opposite: moderate **2 perceptive**, shrewd, intelligent, canny, bright Opposite: obtuse **3 sensitive**, sharp, keen, heightened, finely tuned Opposite: dull **4 intense**, violent, strong, excruciating, piercing Opposite: mild

acutely adv **very**, intensely, highly, deeply, extremely Opposite: slightly

acuteness n **1 intensity**, severity, gravity, seriousness **2 sharpness**, keenness, sensitivity, perceptiveness Opposite: dullness

ad (*infml*) n **advertisement**, public notice, commercial, poster, billboard

adage n **saying**, saw, proverb, maxim, axiom

adamant adj **obstinate**, obdurate, unyielding, unbending, inflexible Opposite: amenable

adapt v **1 change**, alter, modify, adjust, vary Opposite: leave **2 become accustomed**, familiarize, get a feel for, get used to, acclimatize

adaptability n **flexibility**, adaptableness, malleability, compliance *Opposite*: inflexibility

adaptable adj **flexible**, malleable, pliable, adjustable, compliant *Opposite*: inflexible

adaptation n **1 alteration**, adjustment, acclimatization, modification, change **2 version**, edition, revision, reworking, variation

adapter n **electric plug**, connector, converter, device

add v **1 put in**, insert, adjoin, append, affix *Opposite*: delete **2 add up**, add together, tot up, total, combine *Opposite*: subtract **3 enhance**, complement, improve, increase, supplement *Opposite*: detract

added adj **additional**, extra, supplementary, further, other

addendum n **addition**, supplement, appendix, postscript, PS

addict n **devotee**, fan, aficionado, fanatic, buff

addiction n **habit**, compulsion, dependence, need, obsession

addition n **1 adding**, adding up, adding together, totalling, totting up *Opposite*: subtraction **2 supplement**, add-on, appendage, addendum, adjunct

additional adj **extra**, added, supplementary, other, further

additionally adv **as well**, in addition, moreover, furthermore, also

additive n **preservative**, stabilizer, improver, chemical, colourant

addle v **confuse**, befuddle, muddle, distract, bewilder

addled adj **1 confused**, muddled, bewildered, befuddled, perplexed *Opposite*: clear **2 spoiled**, rotten, decayed, off, putrid *Opposite*: fresh

addlepated (archaic) adj **confused**, muddled, bewildered, befuddled, perplexed *Opposite*: clear

add-on n **attachment**, addendum, adjunct, appendage, supplement ■ adj **supplementary**, accompanying, additional, extra, optional *Opposite*: essential

address n **speech**, talk, discourse, lecture, report ■ v **1 direct**, deliver, dispatch, refer, forward **2 speak**, lecture, talk, give a lecture, give a talk **3 tackle**, deal with, take in hand, attend, concentrate *Opposite*: ignore

adduce (fml) v **offer**, present, put forward, bring forward, give

add up v **1 add**, add together, total, combine, tally up *Opposite*: subtract **2 make sense**, hang together, be consistent, ring true, come together

add up to v **come to**, number, total, amount to, mount up to

adenoidal adj **nasal**, thick, muffled, indistinct

adept adj **skilful**, skilled, expert, proficient, adroit *Opposite*: inept

adeptness n **expertise**, proficiency, skill, adroitness, aptitude *Opposite*: ineptitude

adequacy n **1 sufficiency**, ampleness, abundance *Opposite*: insufficiency **2 competence**, capability, suitability, tolerability, appropriateness *Opposite*: inadequacy

adequate adj **1 sufficient**, ample, enough, plenty *Opposite*: insufficient **2 passable**, satisfactory, tolerable, acceptable, suitable *Opposite*: inadequate

adequately adv **sufficiently**, passably, tolerably, effectively, satisfactorily *Opposite*: inadequately

adhere v **1 stick to**, follow, keep to, stand by, abide by *Opposite*: abandon **2 stick**, stick on, hold fast, hold, hold on

adherence n **devotion**, obedience, observance, loyalty, faithfulness *Opposite*: disobedience

adherent n **supporter**, believer, devotee, advocate, fanatic *Opposite*: opponent

adhesion n **union**, sticking power, hold, grip, linkage *Opposite*: separation

adhesive n **glue**, paste, gum, epoxy resin

ad hoc adj **unplanned**, informal, impromptu, improvised, off-the-cuff *Opposite*: planned

ad infinitum adv **endlessly**, for ever, ceaselessly, repeatedly, infinitely

adjacent adj **neighbouring**, nearby, bordering, next, next door *Opposite*: distant

adjoin v **connect**, link up, attach, affix, be close to

adjoining adj **touching**, attached, connecting, abutting, contiguous (fml) *Opposite*: detached

adjourn v **1 suspend**, defer, delay, postpone, put off **2** (infml) **stop**, end, finish, break off, call it a day

adjournment n **suspension**, postponement, deferment, recess, break

adjudge v **1 judge**, find, regard as, consider, decide **2 pronounce**, rule, announce, declare, adjudicate

adjudicate v **arbitrate**, sit in judgment, pass judgment, referee, umpire

adjudication n **1 judgment**, arbitration, mediation, negotiation, intercession **2 settlement**, decision, judgment, decree, resolution

adjudicator n **judge**, arbitrator, referee, umpire, mediator

adjunct n **1 addition**, attachment, add-on, appendage, accessory **2 assistant**, aide, aide-de-camp, secretary, helper

adjure v **1 command**, order, instruct, charge, demand **2 appeal**, plead, beg, request, petition

adjust v **regulate**, alter, fiddle with, correct, fine-tune

adjustable adj **adaptable**, modifiable, changeable, variable, regulating *Opposite*: fixed

adjustment n **change**, alteration, modification, tuning, fine-tuning

adjutant n assistant, aide, aide-de-camp, secretary, personal assistant

ad-lib v improvise, do off the cuff, extemporize, make up on the spot, do cold ■ adj **off-the-cuff**, unplanned, informal, impromptu, improvised Opposite: rehearsed

administer v 1 **manage**, direct, run, order, control 2 **dispense**, give out, hand out, deal out, mete out

administrate v **control**, run, manage, direct, rule

administration n 1 **management**, direction, running, supervision, paperwork 2 **government**, executive, management, organization, presidency 3 **dispensation**, meting out, giving out, handing out, dealing out

administrative adj **managerial**, directorial, organizational, clerical, secretarial

administrator n **manager**, superintendent, commissioner, overseer, officer

admirable adj **estimable**, commendable, venerable, good, splendid Opposite: unworthy

admiration n **respect**, esteem, approbation, regard, approval Opposite: disapproval. See COMPARE AND CONTRAST at regard.

admire v regard, esteem, approve, think highly of, respect Opposite: disapprove

admired adj **respected**, venerated, esteemed, well-regarded, revered Opposite: despised

admirer n **fan**, devotee, follower, lover, aficionado

admiring adj **appreciative**, approving, complimentary, flattering, favourable Opposite: disapproving

admissibility n **acceptability**, tolerability, permissibility

admissible adj **allowable**, permissible, acceptable, tolerable Opposite: inadmissible

admission n 1 **admittance**, entrance, right of entry, access, permission Opposite: exclusion 2 **entrance fee**, entry fee, fee, charge, price 3 **confession**, declaration, profession, divulgence, disclosure Opposite: denial

admit v 1 **confess**, make a clean breast, acknowledge, own up, disclose Opposite: deny 2 **let in**, allow in, give access, permit, let pass Opposite: bar

admit defeat v pull out, withdraw, stop, call it a day, back out Opposite: persevere

admittance n **admission**, entry, access, right of entry, entrance Opposite: exclusion

admittedly adv **certainly**, definitely, indeed, undeniably, undoubtedly

admonish v **reprove**, caution, warn, reprimand, rebuke Opposite: praise

admonishment n **reprimand**, rebuke, reproach, caution, dressing-down Opposite: approval

admonition n **caution**, warning, reprimand, rebuke, reproach Opposite: approval

admonitory adj 1 **reproving**, reproachful, rebuking, condemnatory, critical Opposite: approving 2 **advisory**, cautionary, warning, deterrent, instructive

ad nauseam adv on and on, for ever, endlessly, interminably, ad infinitum

ado n **bustle**, activity, commotion, bother, excitement

adolescence n **teens**, youth, puberty, teenage years

adolescent n **teenager**, youth, youngster, juvenile, minor ■ adj **teenage**, young, youthful, juvenile, pubescent

adopt v **take on**, accept, assume, approve, take up Opposite: reject

adoption n **acceptance**, implementation, espousal, taking on, embracing Opposite: rejection

adoptive adj **legal**, step Opposite: natural

adorable adj **lovely**, gorgeous, delightful, lovable, delectable Opposite: detestable

adoration n 1 **esteem**, high regard, respect, admiration, adulation Opposite: hatred 2 **worship**, reverence, idolization, glorification, veneration

adore v 1 **love**, esteem, respect, admire, adulate Opposite: hate 2 **worship**, revere, idolize, glorify, venerate Opposite: revile 3 (infml) **like**, enjoy, love, be keen on, be partial to Opposite: dislike

adored adj **revered**, venerated, worshipped, idolized, cherished Opposite: hated

adoring adj **affectionate**, loving, doting, admiring, indulgent Opposite: cold

adorn v **decorate**, embellish, ornament, beautify, prettify Opposite: strip

adornment n **decoration**, embellishment, ornamentation, beautification, prettification

adrift adj **drifting**, floating, loose, free Opposite: fixed ■ adv **aimless**, wandering, drifting, at a loose end, lost Opposite: focused

adroit adj **skilful**, nimble, practised, able, dexterous Opposite: clumsy

adroitness n **skilfulness**, nimbleness, ability, dexterity, cleverness Opposite: clumsiness

adulate v **flatter**, put on a pedestal, elevate, praise, adore Opposite: disparage

adulation n **adoration**, praise, worship, hero worship, respect Opposite: disparagement

adulatory adj **praising**, flattering, fawning, sycophantic, obsequious Opposite: disparaging

adult adj **mature**, fully developed, grown-up, grown, fully-grown Opposite: immature

adulterate v **contaminate**, taint, make impure, spoil, pollute Opposite: purify

adulteration n **contamination**, debasement, pollution, tarnishing, corruption Opposite: purification

adulthood n **maturity**, parenthood, middle age, old age, later life Opposite: childhood

advance v 1 **go forward**, move forward, move

ahead, press forward, move on *Opposite*: retreat **2 improve**, enhance, take forward, increase, expand *Opposite*: regress ∎ *n* **1 development**, improvement, spread, progress, expansion *Opposite*: decline **2 loan**, early payment, down payment, fee, money up front

advanced *adj* **1 higher**, developed, sophisticated, complex, difficult *Opposite*: basic **2 later**, far along, well along, far ahead, well ahead *Opposite*: earlier **3 progressive**, forward-thinking, unconventional, cutting-edge, innovative *Opposite*: traditional

advancement *n* **progression**, progress, development, improvement, spread *Opposite*: decline

advantage *n* **benefit**, gain, lead, pro, improvement *Opposite*: disadvantage

advantageous *adj* **beneficial**, helpful, useful, to your advantage, valuable *Opposite*: disadvantageous

advent *n* **arrival**, start, beginning, coming on, dawn *Opposite*: departure

adventure *n* **escapade**, exploit, quest, venture, exploration

adventurer *n* **1 explorer**, traveller, voyager, buccaneer, swashbuckler **2 entrepreneur**, investor, speculator, trailblazer, pioneer

adventuresome *adj* **risk-taking**, carefree, daring, thrill-seeking, adventurous *Opposite*: unadventurous

adventurous *adj* **daring**, bold, audacious, brave, courageous *Opposite*: unadventurous

adversarial *adj* **confrontational**, argumentative, combative, antagonistic, oppositional *Opposite*: cooperative

adversary *n* **opponent**, challenger, rival, enemy, antagonist *Opposite*: supporter

adverse *adj* **1 opposing**, contrary, hostile, adversative, antagonistic *Opposite*: cooperative **2 unfavourable**, unpleasant, poor, difficult, unhelpful *Opposite*: favourable

adversity *n* **hardship**, difficulty, danger, misfortune, harsh conditions *Opposite*: privilege

advert *(infml)* *n* **advertisement**, public notice, commercial, poster, billboard

advertise *v* **1 promote**, publicize, market, present, push **2 announce**, broadcast, make known, make public, spread about *Opposite*: keep under wraps

advertisement *n* **commercial**, public notice, poster, billboard, announcement

advertiser *n* **publicist**, promoter, backer, supporter, advocate

advertising *n* **publicity**, promotion, marketing, publicizing, public relations

advice *n* **1 recommendation**, suggestion, guidance, opinion, counsel *(fml)* *Opposite*: warning **2 information**, guidance, instruction, assistance, intelligence

advisability *n* **wisdom**, prudence, sense, desirability, suitability *Opposite*: foolishness

advisable *adj* **sensible**, wise, prudent, worthwhile, desirable *Opposite*: unwise

advise *v* **1 recommend**, direct, guide, instruct, warn **2 inform**, let know, make aware, notify, instruct. *See* COMPARE AND CONTRAST *at* **recommend**.

advisedly *adv* **deliberately**, carefully, purposefully, on purpose, with intent *Opposite*: carelessly

adviser *n* **consultant**, counsellor, advice-giver, guru

advisory *adj* **advice-giving**, consultative, counselling, review

advocacy *n* **support**, encouragement, backing, sponsorship, promotion *Opposite*: opposition

advocate *n* **supporter**, backer, promoter, believer, activist *Opposite*: opponent ∎ *v* **support**, encourage, back, promote, recommend *Opposite*: discourage. *See* COMPARE AND CONTRAST *at* **recommend**.

aegis *n* **auspices**, sponsorship, guidance, protection, support

aeons *n* **a long time**, years, ages *(infml)*, donkey's years *(infml)*, eternity *(infml)*

aerate *v* **ventilate**, let breathe, expose, freshen *Opposite*: close up

aeration *n* **ventilation**, airing, freshening

aerial *adj* **midair**, airborne, above ground, in-flight, floating *Opposite*: terrestrial

aerobatics *n* **stunts**, manoeuvres, aerial tricks

aerobics *n* **exercises**, keep fit, callisthenics, workout

aerodrome *n* **airfield**, airport, landing strip, landing field, airstrip

aerodynamic *adj* **sleek**, smooth, slick, swept-back, clean

aerogram *n* **air letter**, airmail letter, aerogramme

aerogramme *see* aerogram

aeroplane *n* **aircraft**, plane, flying machine, crate *(dated infml)*

aerosol *n* **spray can**, spray, atomizer, mister

aerospace *n* **atmosphere**, upper atmosphere, space, troposphere, stratosphere

aesthete *n* **art lover**, aesthetician, connoisseur, cognoscente

aesthetic *adj* **artistic**, visual, appealing, beautiful

a few *pron* **a small number**, some, one or two, not many, handful *Opposite*: many

affability *n* **friendliness**, sociability, cordiality, joviality, gregariousness *Opposite*: unfriendliness

affable *adj* **genial**, pleasant, friendly, sociable, jovial *Opposite*: unfriendly

affair *n* **matter**, issue, concern, business, situation

affairs *n* **business**, matters, dealings, activities, concerns

affect *v* **1 influence**, involve, shape, concern, change **2 touch**, move, disturb, mark, distress **3 assume**, put on, imitate, fake, adopt

affectation *n* **1 showing off**, pretension, exaggeration, artificiality, affectedness *Opposite*: naturalness **2 mannerism**, way, quirk, show, trait

affected *adj* **pretentious**, artificial, exaggerated, unnatural, precious *Opposite*: natural

affectedness *n* **exaggeration**, pretension, artificiality, affectation, showing off *Opposite*: naturalness

affecting *adj* **moving**, touching, upsetting, distressing, disturbing

affection *n* **liking**, fondness, regard, warmth, attachment *Opposite*: dislike. *See* COMPARE AND CONTRAST *at* love.

affectionate *adj* **loving**, demonstrative, warm, friendly, kind *Opposite*: cold

affective *adj* **emotional**, sentimental, moving, touching, affecting

affianced *(fml) adj* **engaged**, attached, promised, spoken for, involved *Opposite*: unattached

affidavit *n* **sworn statement**, official declaration, affirmation, confirmation, proclamation

affiliate *v* **link**, connect, join, associate, belong to ■ *n* **associate**, partner, colleague, member

affiliation *n* **association**, relationship, connection, attachment, membership

affinity *n* **1 empathy**, sympathy, fellow feeling, attraction, kinship *Opposite*: indifference **2 similarity**, resemblance, likeness, correspondence *Opposite*: difference

affirm *v* **1 support**, confirm, encourage, sustain, uphold **2 assert**, insist, establish, state, verify

affirmation *n* **assertion**, confirmation, pronouncement, declaration, announcement *Opposite*: denial

affirmative *adj* **assenting**, positive, confirmatory, agreeing, favourable *Opposite*: negative

affix *v* **attach**, fix, fasten, stick, pin *Opposite*: remove

afflict *v* **trouble**, bother, affect, worry, distress

afflicted *adj* **distressed**, aggrieved, stricken, plagued, tormented

affliction *n* **1 suffering**, difficulty, burden, problem, hardship **2 illness**, sickness, disease, condition, disorder

affluence *n* **riches**, prosperity, comfortable circumstances, material comfort, privileged circumstances *Opposite*: poverty

affluent *adj* **rich**, wealthy, well-off, well-to-do, prosperous *Opposite*: poor

afford *v* **1 pay for**, have the funds for, manage to pay for, find the money for, come up with the money for **2** *(fml)* **give**, offer, present, allow, provide

affordable *adj* **reasonable**, within your means, inexpensive, cheap *Opposite*: expensive

afforest *v* **reforest**, plant *Opposite*: deforest

affray *n* **scuffle**, fight, brawl, disturbance, commotion *Opposite*: agreement

affront *n* **insult**, injury, slur, slight, outrage *Opposite*: compliment ■ *v* **offend**, insult, upset, outrage, slight *Opposite*: compliment

affronted *adj* **insulted**, injured, slighted, disrespected, upset *Opposite*: pleased

aficionada *n* **devotee**, enthusiast, adherent, fanatic, fan

aficionado *n* **devotee**, enthusiast, adherent, fanatic, fan

afire *see* aflame

aflame *adj* **1 on fire**, burning, in flames, ablaze, afire *Opposite*: extinguished **2 fired up**, enthusiastic, passionate, fired, excited *Opposite*: apathetic

afloat *adj* **flooded**, awash, inundated, under water, submerged *Opposite*: dry

aflutter *adv* **agitated**, excited, trembling, aquiver, nervous *Opposite*: calm

afoot *adj* **happening**, going on, occurring, taking place, up

aforementioned *(fml) adj* **above-mentioned**, said, aforesaid *(fml)*

aforesaid *(fml) see* aforementioned

afraid *adj* **frightened**, fearful, terrified, petrified, scared *Opposite*: unafraid

afresh *adv* **anew**, again, once again, once more, over

after *prep* **1 later than**, past, gone *Opposite*: before **2 behind**, following, to the rear of, next to *Opposite*: ahead of **3 in pursuit of**, in search of, in quest of, following, on the trail of **4 regarding**, considering, taking into account, with, bearing in mind **5 following**, subsequent to, later than *Opposite*: before **6 in the manner of**, in imitation of, in the style of, similar to, like ■ *adv* **afterwards**, subsequently, later, next *Opposite*: before ■ *conj* **when**, once, as soon as *Opposite*: before

after all *adv* **on balance**, finally, in the end, in spite of everything, nevertheless

aftercare *n* **1 post-operative care**, post-hospital care, home care, rehabilitation, recovery programme **2 support**, assistance, help, upkeep, maintenance

aftereffect *n* **repercussion**, reverberation, aftermath, aftershock, final outcome *Opposite*: precursor

afterglow *n* **warmth**, glow, serenity, exhilaration, feel-good factor

afterlife *n* **afterworld**, next world, life after death, eternal life, spirit world

aftermath *n* **result**, consequences, outcome, upshot, repercussion

afternoon *n* **after lunch**, p.m., early afternoon, midafternoon, late afternoon *Opposite*: morning

afters (infml) n **dessert**, pudding, sweet, sweet course, dessert course

afterthought n **addition**, postscript, extra, addendum, reflection Opposite: forethought

afterwards adv **later**, after that, subsequently, then, next Opposite: before

afterworld n **afterlife**, next world, life after death, eternal life, spirit world

again adv **once more**, another time, yet again, over, over again

against prep 1 **in opposition to**, not in favour, hostile, critical, opposed 2 **next to**, alongside, beside, touching, adjacent to 3 **in contradiction of**, contrary to, counter to, in contrast to, compared to

age n 1 **time of life**, stage, phase, stage of development 2 **era**, period, time, times, epoch ■ v **mature**, grow older, grow up, get on, advance in years

aged adj **old**, elderly, matured, ripened, hoary Opposite: young

age group n **generation**, cohort, age range, age bracket, contemporaries

ageless adj 1 **youthful**, fresh, unfading, unspoiled 2 **timeless**, endless, perpetual, everlasting, infinite

agency n 1 **organization**, bureau, society, charity, group 2 **activity**, action, work, intervention, help

agenda n **programme**, schedule, plan, outline, memo

agent n 1 **go-between**, manager, negotiator, mediator, representative 2 **cause**, means, driving force, instrument, vehicle

age-old adj **ancient**, old, long-standing, venerable, hoary Opposite: recent

ages (infml) n **aeons**, forever (infml), eternity (infml), centuries (infml), donkey's years (infml) Opposite: moment

agglomeration n **accumulation**, mass, collection, cluster, group

agglutinate v **adhere**, stick, clump, join, cling Opposite: separate

agglutination n **accretion**, cohesion, adhesion, clumping, joining

aggrandize v 1 **increase**, upgrade, expand, enlarge, develop Opposite: downgrade 2 (fml) **exaggerate**, overstate, puff up, build up, magnify Opposite: belittle

aggrandizement n 1 **enhancement**, enlargement, expansion, amelioration, improvement Opposite: deterioration 2 **empowerment**, enrichment, promotion, magnification, inflation Opposite: deflation 3 (fml) **exaggeration**, overstatement, braggadocio, glorification, embellishment Opposite: understatement

aggravate v 1 (infml) **annoy**, irritate, exasperate, provoke, make angry Opposite: soothe 2 **worsen**, exacerbate, exaggerate, heighten, intensify Opposite: alleviate

aggravated adj 1 **serious**, worse, intensified, heightened Opposite: alleviated 2 (infml) **annoyed**, angry, upset, put out, irritated Opposite: peaceful

aggravating (infml) adj **annoying**, irritating, infuriating, maddening, exasperating Opposite: pleasing

aggravation n 1 (infml) **bother**, trouble, difficulty, irritation, hassle (infml) 2 **worsening**, exacerbation, intensification, magnification, augmentation Opposite: alleviation

aggregate adj (fml) **collective**, total, combined, cumulative, amassed ■ n (fml) **total**, collection, mass, sum, whole ■ v **combine**, amass, gather, collect, accumulate Opposite: separate

aggregation n **combination**, accumulation, collection, accretion, mass

aggression n 1 **attack**, assault, invasion, onslaught, offensive Opposite: defence 2 **violence**, hostility, anger, belligerence, antagonism Opposite: friendliness

aggressive adj 1 **violent**, hostile, destructive, belligerent, antagonistic Opposite: peaceful 2 **forceful**, insistent, assertive, hard-hitting, uncompromising Opposite: mild

aggressiveness n 1 **violence**, belligerence, bellicosity, ferociousness, antagonism Opposite: friendliness 2 **fierceness**, insistence, forcefulness, determination, assertiveness Opposite: mildness

aggressor n **attacker**, invader, assailant, provoker, antagonist Opposite: defender

aggrieve (fml) v **distress**, upset, hurt, injure, pain

aggrieved adj 1 **hurt**, angry, upset, distressed, put out 2 **wronged**, mistreated, persecuted, maltreated, victimized

aghast adj **horrified**, amazed, shocked, horror-struck, astonished Opposite: unaffected

agile adj 1 **nimble**, supple, lithe, sprightly, alert Opposite: clumsy 2 **quick-thinking**, alert, clear-headed, bright Opposite: dull

agility n **nimbleness**, suppleness, quickness, dexterity, liveliness Opposite: clumsiness

agitate v 1 **disturb**, stir up, trouble, excite, rouse Opposite: calm 2 **campaign**, stir up opinion, protest, advocate, raise a fuss 3 **stir**, whisk, toss, shake up, disturb

agitated adj **restless**, disturbed, disconcerted, frantic, tense Opposite: calm

agitation n 1 **anxiety**, worry, nervousness, tension, distress Opposite: calm 2 **campaigning**, activism, demonstration, protest, stir

agitator n **campaigner**, protester, dissenter, activist

aglow adj **glowing**, shining, radiant, rosy, warm Opposite: pale

AGM n **annual general meeting**, annual meeting, open meeting, public meeting, meeting

agnostic n **doubter**, sceptic, doubting Thomas, questioner, nonbeliever *Opposite*: believer ■ adj **doubting**, sceptical, uncertain, unsure, unconvinced *Opposite*: believing

agnosticism n **doubt**, reservation, uncertainty, dissent, distrust *Opposite*: certainty

ago adv **before**, previously, back, past, since *Opposite*: ahead

agog adj **eager**, excited, impatient, keen, avid *Opposite*: uninterested

agonize v **worry**, struggle, strive, vacillate, wrestle

agonized adj **anguished**, tormented, suffering, tortured, in pain

agonizing adj **excruciating**, unbearable, painful, distressing, worrying

agony n **anguish**, pain, torture, suffering, distress *Opposite*: ecstasy

agrarian adj **agricultural**, farm, farming, land, rural *Opposite*: urban

agree v **1 be in agreement**, be in accord, concur, see eye to eye, coincide *Opposite*: differ **2 consent**, say yes, assent, acquiesce, accede *Opposite*: refuse **3 decide**, reach agreement, come to an agreement, come to an understanding, settle *Opposite*: disagree **4 correspond**, match, be the same, tie in, harmonize *Opposite*: differ

---

COMPARE AND CONTRAST CORE MEANING: accept an idea, plan, or course of action that has been put forward

agree be in agreement with somebody else about a course of action; **concur** agree or reach agreement independently on a specified point; **acquiesce** agree to or comply with something passively; **consent** give formal permission for something to happen; **assent** agree to something formally.

---

agreeable adj **1 pleasant**, pleasing, pleasurable, enjoyable, delightful *Opposite*: unpleasant **2 friendly**, affable, pleasant, courteous, delightful *Opposite*: disagreeable **3 amenable**, willing, in accord, compliant, happy *Opposite*: unwilling

agreeably adv **pleasantly**, enjoyably, delightfully, pleasingly, pleasurably *Opposite*: unpleasantly

agreed adj **decided**, settled, arranged, approved, fixed

agreement n **1 contract**, arrangement, covenant, treaty, promise **2 accord**, concord, conformity, harmony, union *Opposite*: disagreement

agribusiness n **farming industry**, farming, agro-industry, agricultural business, business

agricultural adj **1 agrarian**, farming, agronomic, farmed, cultivated **2 unindustrialized**, pastoral, rural, bucolic, undeveloped *Opposite*: urban

agriculture n **cultivation**, husbandry, crop growing, food production, agronomy

aground adj **beached**, ashore, stranded, stuck, grounded *Opposite*: afloat

ahead adv **1 in front**, to the front, in the lead, in advance, further on *Opposite*: behind **2 into the future**, in the future, to come, yet to be, forward *Opposite*: ago **3 early**, in advance, prematurely, up front, ahead of *Opposite*: late

ahead of prep **1 in front of**, before, beyond, up ahead of, in advance of *Opposite*: behind **2 before**, in advance of, earlier than, in front of, just before *Opposite*: after

aid v **help**, assist, support, abet, give support to *Opposite*: thwart ■ n **assistance**, help, support, relief, encouragement

aid and abet v **conspire**, collaborate, collude, connive, be in league with

aide n **assistant**, adviser, helper, supporter, personal assistant. *See* COMPARE AND CONTRAST *at* **assistant**.

aide-de-camp *see* **aide**

aide-mémoire (fml) n **1 summary**, outline, résumé, synopsis, digest **2 memory aid**, mnemonic, note, reminder, memorandum

ailing adj **1 underperforming**, failing, deteriorating, inadequate *Opposite*: thriving **2** (dated) **unwell**, ill, sick, unfit, laid up *Opposite*: well

ailment n **illness**, sickness, disease, disorder, complaint

aim v **1 aspire**, plan, intend, try, mean **2 point towards**, point, take aim, direct, mark ■ n **goal**, purpose, intention, object, objective

aimless adj **pointless**, meaningless, useless, worthless, purposeless *Opposite*: purposeful

aimlessness n **pointlessness**, purposelessness, senselessness *Opposite*: purposefulness

air n **1 atmosphere**, space, sky, heaven **2 appearance**, look, manner, tone, way of being **3 tune**, melody, song ■ v **1 declare**, express, vent, make public, proclaim *Opposite*: suppress **2 ventilate**, aerate, expose

airborne adj **flying**, aerial, floating, midair, in-flight

airbrush v **blend in**, touch up, cover up, colour, blend

air conditioner n **air cooler**, air exchanger, ventilator, dehumidifier, extractor *Opposite*: heater

air conditioning n **air-cooling system**, ventilation system, air-circulation system, air exchange system, climate control *Opposite*: heating

aircraft n **aeroplane**, plane, flying machine, airplane (US)

WORD BANK
❏ **types of civil aircraft** airliner, airship, autogiro, biplane, blimp, dirigible, executive jet, glider, hang glider, helicopter, jet, light aircraft, microlight, monoplane, paraglider, seaplane, skiplane, STOL, zeppelin
❏ **types of military aircraft** bomber, convertiplane,

fighter, fighter-bomber, helicopter gunship, stealth bomber, transport, VTOL

❏ **parts of an aircraft** aileron, air brake, autopilot, cabin, cockpit, ejector seat, fin, flight deck, flight recorder, fuselage, jet engine, joystick, landing gear, nose cone, nose wheel, propeller, rotor, rudder, tail, tailplane, tail rotor, turbofan, turbojet, turboprop, undercarriage, wing

airdrop *v* **parachute in**, airlift, send in, parachute, drop

airfare *n* **fare**, tariff, charge, ticket price, seat rate

airfield *n* **airstrip**, landing field, landing strip, aerodrome, airport

airily *adv* **lightheartedly**, lightly, carelessly, casually, easily *Opposite*: seriously

airiness *n* **1 lightheartedness**, buoyancy, animation, vivacity, cheerfulness *Opposite*: seriousness **2 spaciousness**, openness, freshness, lightness *Opposite*: closeness

airing *n* **1 ventilation**, aeration, exposure to air, drying, freshening **2 outing**, trip, excursion **3 exposure**, expression, disclosure, divulgence, ventilation

airless *adj* **stuffy**, close, muggy, unventilated, oppressive *Opposite*: airy

airlift *v* **fly**, transfer, winch, lift

airline *n* **air company**, commercial airline, scheduled carrier, carrier

airlock *n* **1 blockage**, obstruction, air bubble, occlusion, block **2 compartment**, cubicle, cell, chamber

airmail *v* **post**, send, dispatch, mail *(US)*

airplay *n* **airtime**, playing time, exposure, promotion, publicity

airport *n* **airfield**, aerodrome, airstrip, landing field, landing strip

airpower *n* **air strength**, airborne army, air force, air defence

air raid *n* **aerial attack**, aerial bombardment, air attack, bombing, air strike

airship *n* **dirigible**, zeppelin, blimp, aircraft

airshow *n* **aerobatics**, stunts, show, exhibition, fly-past

airsick *adj* **travel sick**, nauseous, queasy, sick, ill

airsickness *n* **travel sickness**, nausea, queasiness, sickness

airspace *n* **territory**, skies, boundaries, limits, flight exclusion zone

air strike *n* **aerial attack**, aerial bombardment, bombing, air raid, air offensive

airstrip *n* **runway**, landing strip, strip, landing field, airfield

airtight *adj* **1 sealed**, hermetically sealed, hermetic, impermeable **2 sound**, strong, unquestionable, unassailable, watertight *Opposite*: vulnerable

airwaves *n* **radio waves**, frequencies, frequency bands, radio frequencies, broadcasting frequencies

airway *n* **1 air route**, air corridor, flight lane, air lane, route **2 airline**, air transport company, air network

airworthiness *n* **safety**, soundness, reliability, working order

airworthy *adj* **flyable**, flightworthy, in working order, in good order, safe

airy *adj* **1 roomy**, ventilated, fresh, light, open *Opposite*: stuffy **2 unconcerned**, nonchalant, casual, light, carefree *Opposite*: serious

airy-fairy *(infml) adj* **vague**, unfocused, fanciful, unrealistic, impractical *Opposite*: practical

aisle *n* **passageway**, gangway, walkway, passage, corridor

ajar *adj* **half closed**, open, agape *(literary)*

a.k.a. *adj* **also known as**, better known as, otherwise known as, known to you and me as, alias

akin *adj* **similar**, of the same kind, parallel, like, analogous *Opposite*: unlike

alacrity *n* **promptness**, quickness, rapidity, speed, readiness *Opposite*: sluggishness

alarm *n* **1 fear**, apprehension, terror, fright, panic **2 alarm bell**, warning, distress signal, siren ■ *v* **frighten**, terrify, panic, distress, startle *Opposite*: calm

alarmed *adj* **worried**, upset, distressed, shocked, frightened *Opposite*: untroubled

alarming *adj* **disturbing**, upsetting, frightening, distressing, shocking *Opposite*: soothing

alarmist *n* **pessimist**, doom merchant, doomsayer, doomster *(infml)* ■ *adj* **pessimistic**, gloomy, panicky, exaggerated, hysterical *Opposite*: down-to-earth

alas *adv* **unfortunately**, sadly, regrettably, unhappily, unluckily

albatross *n* **millstone**, shackle, encumbrance, burden, impediment

albeit *conj* **although**, though, even though, even if, notwithstanding *(fml)*

album *n* **1 book**, folder, photograph album, photo album, autograph album **2 record**, LP, CD, tape, cassette

albumen *n* **egg white**, white, white of egg

alchemy *n* **pseudoscience**, experimentation, transformation

alcoholic *adj* **intoxicating**, inebriating, fermented, distilled, strong *Opposite*: nonalcoholic

alcove *n* **recess**, niche, bay, cubicle, nook

alert *adj* **attentive**, watchful, prepared, aware, vigilant *Opposite*: unprepared ■ *n* **warning**, signal, alarm, siren, red alert ■ *v* **warn**, forewarn, notify, draw somebody's attention to, tell

alertness *n* **attentiveness**, watchfulness, awareness, preparedness, vigilance *Opposite*: inattentiveness

alfresco *adv* **out of doors**, outdoors, outside, in the open air, on the lawn *Opposite*: indoors ■ *adj* **outdoor**, open-air, outside, patio, picnic *Opposite*: indoor

algorithm *n* **procedure**, process, system, set of rules

alias *adj* **also known as**, also called, otherwise known as, under the name of, a.k.a. ■ *n* **assumed name**, pseudonym, pen name, nom de plume, stage name

alibi *(infml)* *n* **explanation**, excuse, reason, defence, account

alien *n* **1 extraterrestrial**, creature from outer space, space invader, Martian, intelligent life form **2 foreigner**, stranger, immigrant, resident alien ■ *adj* **unfamiliar**, unknown, strange, outlandish, unusual *Opposite*: familiar

alienate *v* **estrange**, make unfriendly, disaffect, set against, distance *Opposite*: involve

alienated *adj* **estranged**, disaffected, isolated, withdrawn, separate *Opposite*: involved

alienation *n* **estrangement**, disaffection, unfriendliness, hostility, isolation *Opposite*: closeness

alight *v* **1 get off**, get out, descend, dismount **2 land**, perch, rest, stop, settle ■ *adj* **burning**, on fire, in flames, blazing, ablaze

align *v* **1 bring into line**, line up, make straight, make parallel, make even *Opposite*: disarrange **2 side with**, support, ally, affiliate, associate *Opposite*: distance

aligned *adj* **allied**, united, associated, affiliated, ranged

alignment *n* **1 position**, arrangement, placement, configuration, orientation *Opposite*: disorder **2 alliance**, association, coalition, grouping, affiliation

alike *adj* **similar**, comparable, the same, identical, like *Opposite*: different

alimentary canal *n* **bowels**, guts, innards, insides, intestines

---

WORD BANK

❑ **parts of an alimentary canal** anus, appendix, bile duct, bladder, bowel, caecum, colon, duodenum, gallbladder, gullet, gut, intestine, kidney, large intestine, liver, oesophagus, pancreas, rectum, small intestine, spleen, stomach, throat

---

alimony *n* **allowance**, maintenance, support, financial support, funding

alive *adj* **1 living**, animate, breathing *Opposite*: dead **2 energetic**, busy, active, perky, vibrant *Opposite*: inactive **3 thriving**, active, flourishing, successful, blooming *Opposite*: quiet **4 full**, packed, teeming, awash, swarming *Opposite*: dead **5 aware**, sensitive, tuned in, alert, interested *Opposite*: unaware. *See* COMPARE AND CONTRAST *at* living.

all *adv* *(infml)* **altogether**, completely, entirely, very, wholly ■ *pron* **1 every one**, each and every one, every single one, each *Opposite*: none **2 every bit**, the entire, the complete, the whole *Opposite*: none

all along *adv* **from the start**, right from the start, from the very beginning, from the word go, from the beginning

all and sundry *pron* **everyone**, everybody, one and all, every person, the whole world *Opposite*: nobody

allay *v* **dispel**, alleviate, calm, assuage, relieve *Opposite*: stimulate

all clear *n* **green light**, all-clear signal, nod, signal, permission *Opposite*: thumbs-down *(infml)*

all-comers *n* **everyone**, everybody, one and all, all, the general public

allegation *n* **claim**, accusation, assertion, contention, charge

allege *v* **claim**, assert, contend, charge, declare

alleged *adj* **supposed**, unproven, suspected, so-called, assumed *Opposite*: confirmed

allegiance *n* **loyalty**, commitment, adherence, faithfulness, duty *Opposite*: disloyalty

allegorical *adj* **metaphorical**, symbolic, emblematic, figurative, allegoric *Opposite*: literal

allegory *n* **parable**, fable, metaphor, symbol, extended metaphor

all-embracing *adj* **comprehensive**, complete, extensive, catholic, wide-ranging *Opposite*: narrow

all-encompassing *see* all-embracing

allergic *adj* **sensitive**, affected, sensitized, hypersensitive, averse *(fml)*

allergy *n* **1 reaction**, allergic reaction, sensitivity, hypersensitivity **2** *(infml)* **aversion**, dislike, antipathy, distaste, hate *Opposite*: liking

alleviate *v* **ease**, lessen, assuage, improve, lighten *Opposite*: aggravate

alleviation *n* **mitigation**, lessening, improvement, easing, assuagement *Opposite*: aggravation

all for *prep* **in favour of**, pro, for, in support of *Opposite*: against

alliance *n* **1 coalition**, grouping, association, union, cooperation **2 relationship**, partnership, bond, link, tie

allied *adj* **1 joined**, united, combined, amalgamated, aligned *Opposite*: unilateral **2 related**, associated, connected, akin, linked *Opposite*: unrelated

all in *adj* **1 total**, inclusive, overall, global, all-inclusive **2 exhausted**, weary, tired, tired out, worn out *Opposite*: fresh

all in all *adv* **all things considered**, on the whole, in general, generally speaking, when all is said and done

all-inclusive *adj* **comprehensive**, grand, complete, broad, all-embracing *Opposite*: incomplete

alliteration n **assonance**, consonance, sound repetition, sound pattern, resonance

alliterative adj **repetitive**, echoing, assonant, poetic

allocate v **assign**, allot, apportion, distribute, deal

allocation n **1 distribution**, provision, sharing out, apportionment, division **2 share**, portion, allotment, allowance

all-or-nothing adj **win-or-lose**, uncompromising, winner-take-all, rigid, zero-sum Opposite: flexible

allot v **assign**, designate, allocate, earmark, apportion

allotment n **1 vegetable garden**, vegetable patch, plot **2 share**, portion, part, allocation, allowance

all-out adj **maximum**, supreme, extreme, thoroughgoing, determined Opposite: half-hearted

allow v **1 let**, permit, agree, consent, tolerate Opposite: forbid **2 allocate**, set aside, make available, set a limit, allot **3** (fml) **accept**, admit, acknowledge, admit as true, grant Opposite: disallow

allowable adj **permissible**, acceptable, tolerable, admissible, suitable Opposite: unacceptable

allowance n **payment**, grant, stipend, pocket money, pin money

allowed adj **permitted**, allotted, authorized, approved, legitimate Opposite: prohibited

allow for v **take into account**, take into consideration, make allowance for, make allowances for, bear in mind

alloy n **1 blend**, amalgam, compound, mixture, composite **2 additive**, contaminant, adulterant, pollutant, ingredient. See COMPARE AND CONTRAST at mixture.

all-powerful adj **omnipotent**, invincible, supreme, almighty Opposite: weak

all-purpose adj **general purpose**, multipurpose, universal, overall, versatile Opposite: specialized

all-round adj **1 versatile**, multifaceted, exceptional, outstanding, talented **2 all-inclusive**, grand, inclusive, sweeping, large-scale Opposite: restricted **3 on all sides**, in every direction, everywhere, in all directions

all-star adj **star-studded**, celebrity, famous, prestigious, well-known Opposite: unknown

all-time adj **unsurpassed**, record, unprecedented, unparalleled, best Opposite: insignificant

allude v **refer**, make reference, make allusion, mention, indicate

allure n **attraction**, appeal, draw, magnetism, charm

alluring adj **appealing**, attractive, tempting, interesting, fascinating Opposite: repulsive

allusion n **reference**, mention, hint, suggestion, insinuation

allusive adj **indirect**, oblique, hinting, referential, suggestive Opposite: direct

alluvial adj **sedimentary**, silty, deposited, muddy, sandy

all-weather adj **year-round**, all-season, rain-or-shine, all-purpose, four-season

ally v **associate**, join, affiliate, align, connect ■ n **friend**, helper, supporter, assistant, partner Opposite: enemy

alma mater n **old school**, college, university, school, institution

almanac n **directory**, calendar, yearbook, handbook, manual

almighty adj **1 omnipotent**, invincible, all-powerful, supreme, omnipresent **2** (infml) **enormous**, massive, huge, immense, gigantic

almost adv **nearly**, not quite, just about, virtually, practically Opposite: exactly

alms n **charity**, donation, contribution, gift, offering

aloft adv **in the air**, in flight, airborne, on the wing, high up Opposite: below

alone adv **unaccompanied**, by yourself, on your own, single-handedly, unaided Opposite: accompanied ■ adj **lonely**, abandoned, deserted, isolated, forlorn

along prep **next to**, beside, by the side of, by, adjacent to

alongside prep **next to**, beside, at the side of, flanking, near ■ adv **abreast**, nearby, cheek by jowl, shoulder to shoulder, at close quarters

along with prep **with**, together with, in company with, in conjunction with, as well as Opposite: without

aloof adj **1 remote**, standoffish, proud, reserved, indifferent Opposite: friendly **2 separate**, remote, distant, set apart, away Opposite: close

aloofness n **1 unfriendliness**, coldness, detachment, remoteness, reserve Opposite: friendliness **2 distance**, remoteness, separateness, independence Opposite: closeness

aloud adv **1 audibly**, out loud, distinctly, noticeably, clearly Opposite: silently **2 loudly**, noisily, riotously, blusteringly, boisterously Opposite: quietly

alpha adj **important**, dominant, chief, primary, leading

alphabet n **writing system**, script, character set, letters, symbols

WORD BANK
❑ **types of alphabet** Arabic, Braille, cuneiform, Cyrillic, Greek, Hebrew, hieroglyphics, hiragana, ideogram, kanji, katakana, phonetic, pictogram, Roman, runic

alphabetic see **alphabetical**

alphabetical adj **arranged**, in order, listed, in a list, sequential

alpine *adj* **mountainous**, mountain, high-altitude, hilly, high

already *adv* **by now**, previously, before now, even now, by this time

also *adv* **1 in addition**, and, what's more, moreover, furthermore **2 too**, as well, likewise, similarly, correspondingly

also-ran *n* **loser**, failure, no-hoper *(infml)*, flop *(infml)*, dud *(infml)* *Opposite*: winner

altar *n* **table**, bench, slab, stand, platform

alter *v* **change**, modify, adjust, vary, amend *Opposite*: maintain. *See* COMPARE AND CONTRAST *at change*.

alteration *n* **modification**, adjustment, change, variation, amendment

altercate *v* **argue**, quarrel, disagree, dispute, squabble

altercation *n* **argument**, quarrel, disagreement, dispute, exchange

alter ego *n* **double**, shadow, doppelgänger, twin, clone

alternate *v* **1 interchange**, rotate, exchange, intersperse, substitute **2 fluctuate**, vary, swing, oscillate, vacillate ▪ *adj* **1 every other**, alternating, every second **2 alternative**, substitute, different, another, other *Opposite*: same

alternately *adv* **off and on**, in turn, by turns, one after the other, interchangeably *Opposite*: consecutively

alternation *n* **change**, interchange, repetition, rotation, fluctuation

alternative *n* **1 replacement**, substitute, substitution, change, another possibility **2 option**, choice, freedom of choice, discretion ▪ *adj* **1 other**, another, substitute, alternate, different **2 unconventional**, unorthodox, nonstandard, complementary, unusual *Opposite*: conventional

alternatively *adv* **on the other hand**, otherwise, instead, then again

although *conj* **though**, even though, even if, while, granting

altitude *n* **height**, elevation, height above sea level, loftiness, highness

altogether *adv* **1 in total**, all in all, all told, overall, in sum **2 totally**, completely, wholly, thoroughly, entirely **3 on the whole**, when all's said and done, overall, in general, mostly

altruism *n* **unselfishness**, self-sacrifice, humanity, selflessness, philanthropy *Opposite*: selfishness

altruistic *adj* **unselfish**, humane, selfless, philanthropic, noble *Opposite*: selfish

alumna *n* **graduate**, former student, ex-student, alum *(infml)*

alumnus *n* **graduate**, former student, ex-student, alum *(infml)*

always *adv* **1 at all times**, continuously, all the time, continually, constantly *Opposite*: never **2 forever**, for all time, for eternity, until the end of time, for ever and a day *Opposite*: temporarily

a.m. *adj* **morning**, before noon, before lunch, pre-lunch *Opposite*: p.m.

amalgam *n* **mixture**, mix, combination, blend, fusion. *See* COMPARE AND CONTRAST *at mixture*.

amalgamate *v* **merge**, join, combine, unite, integrate *Opposite*: separate

amalgamated *adj* **combined**, merged, joined, incorporated, united *Opposite*: separated

amalgamation *n* **1 combination**, mixture, mix, blend, fusion **2 merger**, union, incorporation, consolidation, unification

amanuensis *n* **secretary**, scribe, writer, copier, copyist

amass *v* **accumulate**, collect, gather, stockpile, hoard *Opposite*: distribute. *See* COMPARE AND CONTRAST *at collect*.

amateur *adj* **1 part-time**, unpaid, non-professional, leisure, recreational *Opposite*: full-time **2 unprofessional**, shoddy, slapdash, substandard, incompetent *Opposite*: skilful ▪ *n* **layperson**, nonprofessional, dilettante, dabbler *Opposite*: professional

amateurish *adj* **unprofessional**, shoddy, slapdash, clumsy, crude *Opposite*: skilful

amateurishness *n* **clumsiness**, ineptness, incompetence, unprofessionalism, shoddiness *Opposite*: professionalism

amaze *v* **astonish**, astound, shock, stun, startle

amazed *adj* **astonished**, astounded, shocked, stunned, startled

amazement *n* **astonishment**, wonder, admiration, shock, incredulity

amazing *adj* **astonishing**, astounding, remarkable, wonderful, incredible *Opposite*: unremarkable

ambassador *n* **diplomat**, envoy, representative, emissary, legate

ambience *n* **atmosphere**, feel, setting, environment, mood

ambient *adj* **surrounding**, background, local, neighbouring

ambiguity *n* **vagueness**, uncertainty, haziness, doubt, indistinctness *Opposite*: clarity

ambiguous *adj* **vague**, unclear, abstruse, equivocal, uncertain *Opposite*: clear

ambiguousness *n* **abstruseness**, opacity, obscurity, vagueness, uncertainty *Opposite*: clarity

ambit *n* **scope**, extent, range, realm, area

ambition *n* **1 drive**, determination, motivation, desire, spirit *Opposite*: apathy **2 goal**, aim, objective, aspiration, dream

ambitious *adj* **1 determined**, ruthless, striving, motivated, aspiring *Opposite*: unmotivated **2 grand**, impressive, bold, large-scale, elaborate *Opposite*: small-scale

ambitiously *adv* **1 determinedly**, ruthlessly, single-mindedly, energetically, pushily *(infml) Opposite:* unambitiously **2 optimistically**, overconfidently, unrealistically, idealistically, impractically *Opposite:* realistically

ambivalence *n* **uncertainty**, contradiction, unsureness, doubt, inconsistency *Opposite:* certainty

ambivalent *adj* **unsure**, undecided, in two minds, hesitant, uncertain *Opposite:* decisive

amble *v* **stroll**, saunter, wander, walk, mosey *(infml)* **dash**

ambush *n* **trap**, surprise attack, ensnarement, ambuscade *(literary)* ■ *v* **trap**, ensnare, lie in wait, take by surprise, waylay

ameliorate *(fml) v* **better**, perfect, amend, upgrade, enrich *Opposite:* deteriorate

amelioration *n* **improvement**, enhancement, enrichment, upgrading, amendment *Opposite:* deterioration

amenability *n* **acquiescence**, docility, willingness, responsiveness, pliability *Opposite:* stubbornness

amenable *adj* **agreeable**, open, acquiescent, willing, docile *Opposite:* stubborn

amend *v* **alter**, adjust, modify, revise, change *Opposite:* maintain

amendment *n* **alteration**, adjustment, modification, revision, change

amends *n* **compensation**, recompense, replacement, restitution, return

amenity *n* **1 facility**, convenience, comfort, service, feature **2 pleasantness**, attractiveness, niceness, agreeableness, affability *Opposite:* discomfort

amiability *n* **friendliness**, amicability, sociability, cordiality, agreeableness *Opposite:* unfriendliness

amiable *adj* **friendly**, sociable, agreeable, affable, kind *Opposite:* unfriendly

amicable *adj* **friendly**, good-natured, harmonious, agreeable, good-humoured *Opposite:* hostile

amid *prep* **1 in the middle of**, among, in the midst of, within, in **2 accompanied by**, along with, in the course of, during, at the same time as

amidst *see* **amid**

amiss *adv* **incorrectly**, inappropriately, mistakenly, wrongly, erroneously *Opposite:* correctly ■ *adj* **incorrect**, inappropriate, mistaken, wrong, erroneous *Opposite:* correct

amity *(fml) n* **friendship**, peace, good relations, goodwill, harmony *Opposite:* hostility

ammo *(infml) see* **ammunition**

ammunition *n* **bullets**, shells, missiles, bombs, grenades

amnesia *n* **loss of memory**, memory loss, forgetfulness, obliviousness, oblivion *Opposite:* recall

amnesty *n* **pardon**, reprieve, forgiveness, absolution, exoneration

among *prep* **1 in the middle of**, in the midst of, amid, amidst, surrounded by **2 with**, along with, amid, together with, in the company of **3 as well as**, including, in addition to

amongst *see* **among**

amoral *adj* **unprincipled**, unethical, dishonourable, unscrupulous, immoral *Opposite:* principled

amorality *n* **wickedness**, sinfulness, unscrupulousness, immorality *Opposite:* morality

amorous *adj* **ardent**, passionate, affectionate, loving, romantic *Opposite:* dispassionate

amorphous *adj* **formless**, shapeless, nebulous, vague, unstructured *Opposite:* defined

amortization *n* **repayment**, paying back, payback, paying off, remuneration

amortize *v* **pay back**, repay, pay off, remunerate

amount *n* **quantity**, sum, total, volume, expanse

amount to *v* **add up to**, total, come to, make, be equal to

ampersand *n* **and sign**, and, symbol, character

amphitheatre *n* **1 stadium**, arena, bowl, ring, dome **2 lecture theatre**, auditorium, lecture hall, lecture room

ample *adj* **enough**, sufficient, adequate, plenty, plentiful *Opposite:* insufficient

amplification *n* **1 intensification**, strengthening, magnification, augmentation, extension *Opposite:* reduction **2 elaboration**, clarification, development, expansion *Opposite:* obfuscation

amplify *v* **1 intensify**, increase, strengthen, magnify, enlarge *Opposite:* reduce **2 enlarge on**, go into detail, elaborate, add to, expand *Opposite:* abbreviate. *See* COMPARE AND CONTRAST *at* increase.

amplitude *n* **largeness**, scale, fullness, breadth, generosity

amply *adv* **sufficiently**, adequately, abundantly, thoroughly, fully *Opposite:* insufficiently

ampoule *n* **container**, vessel, bottle, flask

ampule *see* **ampoule**

amputate *v* **cut off**, chop off, remove, sever, separate

amulet *n* **charm**, good luck charm, talisman, lucky charm, juju

amuse *v* **1 make laugh**, make smile, charm, please, divert *Opposite:* depress **2 entertain**, keep busy, interest, absorb, engross *Opposite:* bore

amused *adj* **smiling**, laughing, pleased, tickled, entertained *Opposite:* annoyed

amusement *n* **1 laughter**, enjoyment, delight, fun, pleasure *Opposite:* sadness **2 entertainment**, pastime, hobby, distraction, diversion

amusement park *n* **funfair**, fair, theme park, amusements

amusements *n* **fun fair**, amusement arcade, amusement park, pier

amusing *adj* **funny**, humorous, entertaining, comical, witty *Opposite*: turgid

anachronism *n* **relic**, leftover, archaism, holdover, survival

anachronistic *adj* **out-of-date**, dated, old-fashioned, old, obsolete *Opposite*: contemporary

anaemic *adj* **weak**, feeble, lacklustre, insipid, pale *Opposite*: strong

anaesthetic *n* **painkiller**, local anaesthetic, general anaesthetic, sedative, analgesic ■ *adj* **painkilling**, numbing, deadening, sedating

anaesthetize *v* **deaden**, numb, freeze, sedate, put under

anaesthetized *adj* **knocked out**, out cold, under, asleep, sedated

analgesia *n* **1 numbness**, painlessness, insensibility, insensitivity, unawareness *Opposite*: pain **2 pain control**, pain relief, pain management, pain killing, numbing

analgesic *adj* **painkilling**, palliative, pain-relieving, deadening, anodyne ■ *n* **painkiller**, palliative, pain reliever, anodyne, anaesthetic

analogous *adj* **similar**, equivalent, parallel, corresponding, comparable *Opposite*: different

analogue *n* **equivalent**, similarity, referent, correspondent *(fml)*

analogy *n* **similarity**, likeness, equivalence, parallel, correspondence *Opposite*: contrast

analyse *v* **examine**, study, investigate, scrutinize, evaluate

analysis *n* **1 testing**, examination, assay, assessment **2 examination**, study, investigation, scrutiny, breakdown **3 psychoanalysis**, psychotherapy, psychiatry

analyst *n* **1 forecaster**, predictor, market analyst, city analyst, expert **2 psychoanalyst**, psychotherapist, psychiatrist

analytic *adj* **logical**, investigative, diagnostic, systematic, critical *Opposite*: illogical

analytical *see* analytic

anarchic *adj* **1 revolutionary**, radical, anarchistic, rebellious, anarchical **2 lawless**, chaotic, disordered, disorderly, out of control *Opposite*: orderly

anarchical *see* anarchic

anarchist *n* **revolutionary**, rebel, nihilist, radical

anarchistic *adj* **revolutionary**, antigovernment, anarchic, anarchical, rebellious

anarchy *n* **disorder**, chaos, lawlessness, revolution, mob rule *Opposite*: order

an arm and a leg *(infml)* *n* **king's ransom**, small fortune, fortune, packet *(infml)*, bomb *(infml)* *Opposite*: pittance

anathema *n* **bane**, scourge, canker, thorn in somebody's side, irritant

anatomical *adj* **functional**, structural, material, bodily, body

anatomy *n* **1 structure**, composition, makeup, framework, frame **2 analysis**, examination, investigation, review, study

ancestor *n* **1 forebear**, antecedent, forefather, predecessor, progenitor *Opposite*: descendant **2 forerunner**, precursor, antecedent, prototype, progenitor *Opposite*: successor

ancestral *adj* **family**, familial, inherited

ancestry *n* **lineage**, descent, origin, heritage, extraction

anchor *n* **newsreader**, commentator, presenter, announcer, broadcaster ■ *v* **fasten**, attach, fix, affix, secure *Opposite*: unfasten

anchorage *n* **port**, harbour, marina, dock, quay

anchorite *n* **hermit**, recluse, solitary

anchorman *see* anchorperson

anchorperson *n* **newsreader**, presenter, broadcaster, anchor, journalist

anchorwoman *see* anchorperson

ancient *adj* **1 antique**, early, earliest, prehistoric, primeval *Opposite*: modern **2 old-fashioned**, archaic, obsolete, outdated, antiquated *Opposite*: up-to-date

ancillary *adj* **auxiliary**, subsidiary, supplementary, additional, secondary *Opposite*: main

and *conj* **1 then**, after that, next, as a consequence, afterwards **2 in addition to**, as well as, with, along with, coupled with **3 furthermore**, moreover, also, what is more, in addition

and/or *conj* **either/or**, one or both, either or both

android *n* **robot**, automaton, bionic person, machine, humanoid

anecdotal *adj* **subjective**, circumstantial, hearsay, unreliable, untrustworthy *Opposite*: objective

anecdote *n* **story**, tale, sketch, narrative, narration

anew *adv* **again**, afresh, once again, once more, over

angel *n* **1 seraph**, archangel, cherub, messenger, spirit *Opposite*: demon **2 backer**, sponsor, guarantor, patron, benefactor. *See* COMPARE AND CONTRAST *at* backer.

angelic *adj* **innocent**, good, saintly, adorable, virtuous *Opposite*: wicked

anger *n* **annoyance**, irritation, fury, rage, wrath *Opposite*: calmness ■ *v* **annoy**, irritate, infuriate, incense, enrage *Opposite*: pacify

---

COMPARE AND CONTRAST CORE MEANING: a feeling of strong displeasure in response to an assumed injury

anger a strong feeling of grievance; **annoyance** mild anger and impatience; **irritation** impatience and exasperation; **resentment** aggrieved feelings caused by a sense of unfair treatment; **indignation** anger because something seems unfair or unreasonable; **fury** violent anger; **rage** sudden and extreme anger; **wrath** strong anger, often with a desire for revenge; **ire** *(literary)* strong anger.

angle n point of view, viewpoint, approach, position, slant ■ v slant, tilt, turn, twist, slope Opposite: level

angle for v fish for, seek, solicit, try for, try to get

angry adj annoyed, irritated, fuming, livid, irate Opposite: calm

angst n anguish, torment, anxiety, trouble, worry Opposite: happiness. See COMPARE AND CONTRAST at worry.

angst-ridden adj anguished, tormented, fearful, troubled, worried Opposite: content

anguish n suffering, torment, agony, torture, pain Opposite: contentment

anguished adj tormented, suffering, agonized, tortured, pained Opposite: content

angular adj bony, rawboned, rangy, lanky, gaunt Opposite: rounded

angularity n boniness, thinness, ranginess, lankiness, sharpness Opposite: roundness

animal n 1 creature, being, beast, mammal, organism 2 monster, beast, brute, swine ■ adj physical, bodily, visceral, instinctive, innate Opposite: spiritual

animate v liven up, enliven, rouse, bring to life, stir Opposite: put a damper on ■ adj living, alive, live, breathing, flesh-and-blood Opposite: inanimate. See COMPARE AND CONTRAST at living.

animated adj energetic, active, vibrant, vivacious, dynamic Opposite: lifeless

animation n 1 liveliness, energy, vibrancy, life, vigour Opposite: apathy 2 cartoon, moving picture, animatronics, computer graphics, simulation

animosity n hostility, hatred, loathing, ill feeling, ill will Opposite: goodwill. See COMPARE AND CONTRAST at dislike.

animus n 1 hostility, animosity, hatred, ill will, detestation Opposite: friendliness 2 temperament, personality, disposition, spirit, attitude

anklet n chain, bangle, band

annals n records, archives, chronicles, history, accounts

anneal v harden, strengthen, toughen, galvanize, forge

annex v take possession of, seize, take over, capture, invade Opposite: cede

annexation n capture, seizure, takeover, occupation, invasion Opposite: surrender

annexe n extension, new building, addition, wing, ancillary building

annihilate v 1 destroy, obliterate, extinguish, eradicate, exterminate Opposite: protect 2 (infml) defeat, rout, thrash, overwhelm, crush Opposite: lose

annihilation n total destruction, obliteration, extinction, eradication, extermination Opposite: protection

anniversary n birthday, centenary, bicentenary, wedding anniversary, centennial (US)

annotate v gloss, add footnotes, interpret, explain, make notes on

annotated adj glossed, marked, marked up

annotation n footnote, gloss, marginal note, explanation, note

announce v proclaim, make known, publicize, broadcast, declare Opposite: keep secret

announcement n statement, declaration, message, notice, proclamation

announcer n presenter, broadcaster, telecaster, reporter, newsreader

annoy v irritate, exasperate, vex, irk, get on your nerves, bother Opposite: please

---

COMPARE AND CONTRAST CORE MEANING: cause a mild degree of anger in somebody
annoy cause impatience or anger in somebody; **irritate** annoy somebody slightly; **exasperate** arouse anger or frustration in somebody; **vex** annoy somebody, especially causing upset or distress; **irk** annoy somebody by being tiresome or tedious.

---

annoyance n irritation, displeasure, exasperation, anger, infuriation Opposite: pleasure. See COMPARE AND CONTRAST at anger.

annoyed adj angry, irritated, infuriated, exasperated, aggravated Opposite: pleased

annoying adj maddening, irritating, infuriating, bothersome, exasperating Opposite: pleasing

annual adj yearly, twelve-monthly, once a year, once yearly, every twelve months

annuity n pension, allowance, income, grant, stipend

annul v cancel, call off, withdraw, end, dissolve Opposite: prolong. See COMPARE AND CONTRAST at nullify.

annulment n cancellation, withdrawal, dissolution, invalidation, deletion

anode n terminal, connection, contact

anodyne adj painkilling, palliative, pain-relieving, deadening, analgesic

anoint v smear, daub, rub, smooth, massage

anomalous adj irregular, uncharacteristic, strange, abnormal, inconsistent Opposite: usual

anomaly n irregularity, incongruity, difference, variance, abnormality

anonymity n 1 secrecy, obscurity, concealment, inconspicuousness, namelessness 2 indistinctness, blandness, insignificance, ordinariness, dullness Opposite: distinctiveness

anonymous adj 1 nameless, unidentified, unnamed, unsigned, unspecified Opposite: named 2 undistinguished, indistinctive, ordinary, everyday, run of the mill Opposite: distinctive

anonymously adv incognito, namelessly, in secret, secretly, in disguise

another adj **one more**, additional, a new, a different, a further

answer n **1 response**, reply, riposte, retort, rejoinder (fml) Opposite: question **2 solution**, key, way out, resolution, remedy Opposite: problem ■ v **1 reply**, respond, react, come back with, counter Opposite: challenge **2 solve**, satisfy, resolve, fulfil, lay to rest

COMPARE AND CONTRAST CORE MEANING: something said, written, or done in acknowledgment of a question or remark, or in reaction to a situation **answer** an acknowledgment of a question, letter, or situation; **reply** or **response** a spoken or written answer, or a reaction to a situation; **rejoinder** (fml) a sharp, critical, angry, or clever reply, usually spoken; **retort** a sharp spoken reply, often to criticism; **riposte** a quick or witty reply, usually spoken.

answerable adj **responsible**, accountable, liable, chargeable, subject to blame Opposite: unaccountable

answer back v **retort**, argue, counter, respond, riposte

answer for v **1 pay for**, suffer for, be punished for, make amends for, take the rap (slang) Opposite: get away with **2 be responsible for**, be accountable for, vouch for, take the responsibility for, be to blame for

antagonism n **1 resentment**, dislike, bitterness, hatred, antipathy Opposite: friendliness **2 rivalry**, opposition, aggression, hostility, enmity Opposite: cooperation

antagonist n **rival**, adversary, opponent, enemy, contender Opposite: friend

antagonistic adj **aggressive**, hostile, argumentative, unfriendly, incompatible Opposite: friendly

antagonize v **provoke**, irritate, annoy, upset, get your back up Opposite: mollify

ante n **bet**, wager, stake, payment, raise

antebellum adj **early nineteenth-century**, eighteenth-century, colonial, historical, Federalist

antecedent n **precursor**, forerunner, ancestor, predecessor, forebear

antecedents n **past history**, background, record, previous circumstances, qualifications

antedate v **predate**, go before, be earlier than, date from before, occur before

antediluvian adj **1 prehistoric**, ancient, old, primitive, primeval Opposite: modern **2** (infml) **antiquated**, out-of-date, obsolete, old-fashioned, archaic Opposite: up-to-date

antenatal adj **pre-birth**, pregnancy, prenatal (US) Opposite: postnatal

antenna n **feeler**, projection, tentacle, probe, protuberance

anterior adj **1 fore**, front, leading, foremost Opposite: anterior **2** (fml) **before**, earlier, sooner Opposite: posterior (fml)

anthem n **song of praise**, national hymn, sacred song, psalm, hymn

anthology n **collection**, compilation, album, omnibus, compendium

anthropomorphize v **humanize**, personify, make human, give a human face to, sentimentalize

anti (infml) adj **opposed**, against, antagonistic, ill-disposed, hostile Opposite: pro

anticipate v **1 expect**, foresee, await, wait for, predict **2 do in advance**, think ahead, look forward, jump the gun

anticipated adj **expected**, predicted, projected, estimated, awaited Opposite: unexpected

anticipation n **expectation**, expectancy, hope, eagerness, keenness

anticlimax n **letdown**, disappointment, deflation, comedown (infml), damp squib (infml) Opposite: climax

antics n **clowning**, tricks, pranks, larks, frolics

antidote n **cure**, remedy, solution, answer, corrective Opposite: poison

antipathetic adj **opposed**, hostile, antagonistic, conflicting, anti (infml) Opposite: sympathetic

antipathy n **opposition**, aversion, hostility, antagonism, hatred Opposite: support. See COMPARE AND CONTRAST at **dislike**.

antiquated adj **out-of-date**, old-fashioned, old, obsolete, archaic Opposite: modern. See COMPARE AND CONTRAST at **old-fashioned**.

antique adj **old**, traditional, aged, historic, old-fashioned Opposite: new

antiquity n **1 ancient times**, the distant past, olden days, olden times, time immemorial **2 relic**, remains, archaeological find, antique, artefact

antiseptic adj **1 sterile**, antibacterial, uncontaminated, clean, pure Opposite: infected **2 bland**, insipid, tame, uninteresting, colourless Opposite: colourful

antisocial adj **1 disruptive**, rebellious, harmful, inconsiderate, belligerent Opposite: constructive **2 unsociable**, unfriendly, disagreeable, shy, reserved Opposite: sociable

antithesis n **opposite**, direct opposite, exact opposite, contrast, converse Opposite: epitome

antithetic see **antithetical**

antithetical (fml) adj **opposite**, differing, contradictory, opposed, contrary

anxiety n **nervousness**, worry, concern, unease, apprehension Opposite: calmness. See COMPARE AND CONTRAST at **worry**.

anxious adj **1 worried**, concerned, uneasy, apprehensive, restless Opposite: calm **2 eager**, keen, enthusiastic, impatient, itching Opposite: indifferent

any adj **1 some**, one, several, a few Opposite: none **2 every**, each, whichever, whatever ■ adv **at all**, in the least, slightly, a little, somewhat

anybody *pron* **anyone**, any person, somebody, someone, everybody *Opposite*: nobody

anyhow *adv* **anyway**, in any case, at any rate, nevertheless, nonetheless

anyone *pron* **anybody**, any person, someone, somebody, everyone *Opposite*: no one

anyway *adv* **anyhow**, at any rate, in any case, nevertheless, nonetheless

anywhere *adv* **wherever**, where, somewhere, everywhere, someplace *(US infml)*

A-OK *(infml) adv* **excellent**, perfect, all right, just right, good

apace *adv* **quickly**, rapidly, swiftly, briskly, at a rate of knots *Opposite*: slowly

apart *adv* **separately**, not together, at a distance, to one side, away from each other *Opposite*: together

apart from *prep* **1 aside from**, except for, with the exception of, not counting, excluding *Opposite*: including **2 as well as**, in addition to, on top of, besides

apathetic *adj* **indifferent**, uninterested, listless, dispirited, lethargic *Opposite*: enthusiastic. *See* COMPARE AND CONTRAST *at* **impassive**.

apathy *n* **indifference**, unconcern, lethargy, laziness, boredom *Opposite*: interest

ape *v* **imitate**, mimic, copy, reproduce, simulate. *See* COMPARE AND CONTRAST *at* **imitate**.

aperture *n* **opening**, hole, space, crack, slit

apex *n* **top**, peak, summit, climax, zenith *Opposite*: base

aphorism *n* **saying**, maxim, adage, cliché, saw

apiece *adv* **each**, respectively, to each, for each, individually *Opposite*: collectively

aplomb *n* **assurance**, self-confidence, self-possession, composure, style *Opposite*: awkwardness

apocalypse *n* **catastrophe**, disaster, destruction, cataclysm, Armageddon

Apocalypse *n* **end of the world**, day of reckoning, Judgment Day, Armageddon

apocryphal *adj* **mythical**, fictional, untrue, legendary, invented *Opposite*: true

apologetic *adj* **sorry**, remorseful, contrite, repentant, rueful *Opposite*: unrepentant

apologist *n* **defender**, supporter, ally, protector, champion

apologize *v* **say sorry**, make an apology, ask for forgiveness, beg forgiveness, express regret

apology *n* **1 admission of guilt**, request for forgiveness, expression of regret, confession, act of contrition **2 poor substitute**, pathetic excuse, poor example, pretence, stopgap **3 defence**, excuse, explanation, justification

apostate *n* **renouncer**, defector, deserter, renegade

apostle *n* **1 advocate**, supporter, promoter, champion, proponent *Opposite*: detractor **2 disciple**, follower, missionary, messenger, devotee *Opposite*: leader

apotheosis *n* **high point**, acme, apogee, climax, limit *Opposite*: nadir

appal *v* **horrify**, shock, disgust, repel, sicken *Opposite*: please

appalled *adj* **horrified**, shocked, outraged, disgusted, repelled *Opposite*: delighted

appalling *adj* **1 horrifying**, shocking, disgusting, sickening, outrageous *Opposite*: appealing **2 awful**, terrible, dreadful, horrendous, inexcusable *Opposite*: wonderful

appallingly *adv* **extremely**, very, utterly, awfully, terribly *Opposite*: wonderfully

apparatus *n* **1 device**, gadget, gear, tackle, kit **2 system**, method, mechanism, arrangement, operation

apparel *n* **clothing**, clothes, garb, wear, kit

apparent *adj* **1 obvious**, clear, evident, plain, noticeable *Opposite*: unclear **2 seeming**, ostensible, deceptive, superficial, specious *Opposite*: actual

apparently *adv* **1 it seems that**, it appears that, in fact, rumour has it that, evidently **2 seemingly**, deceptively, speciously, ostensibly, outwardly *Opposite*: actually

apparition *n* **ghost**, spirit, spectre, phantom, ghoul

appeal *n* **1 plea**, petition, application, request, call **2 charm**, attractiveness, attraction, allure, influence *Opposite*: repulsion ■ *v* **1 request**, ask, plead, urge, petition **2 attract**, interest, fascinate, charm, tempt *Opposite*: repel

appealing *adj* **attractive**, tempting, interesting, pleasing, alluring *Opposite*: repulsive

appear *v* **1 come into view**, come into sight, become visible, emerge, come out *Opposite*: disappear **2 happen**, occur, be found, exist, surface **3 seem**, look, look as if, give the impression, give the idea **4 perform**, be seen, act, play, take part in **5 turn up**, show, be seen, arrive, roll up

appearance *n* **1 emergence**, development, arrival, growth, beginning *Opposite*: disappearance **2 look**, form, exterior, manifestation, outer shell **3 arrival**, entrance, advent, attendance, presence

appease *v* **1 mollify**, conciliate, pacify, placate, soothe *Opposite*: provoke **2 satisfy**, assuage, attenuate, calm, soothe *Opposite*: intensify

appeasement *n* **conciliation**, pacification, accession, mollification, placation *Opposite*: provocation

appeaser *n* **conciliator**, pacifier, gratifier, mollifier

appellation *(fml) n* **name**, designation, title, style, tag

append *v* **add**, add on, tag on, attach, affix *Opposite*: detach

appendage *n* **1 addition**, attachment, adjunct, add-on, accessory **2 extremity**, feeler, limb, member, projection

appendix n adjunct, add-on, supplement, PS, appendage

appertain (fml) v relate, belong, be associated with, be relevant to, have a bearing on

appetite n 1 **hunger**, craving, taste, need to eat, desire for food 2 **desire**, taste, enthusiasm, eagerness, keenness Opposite: aversion

appetizer n **taster**, sample, introduction, sneak preview, taste

appetizing adj 1 **delicious**, tasty, mouthwatering, enticing, tempting Opposite: revolting 2 **appealing**, inviting, attractive, desirable, enticing Opposite: unappealing

applaud v 1 **clap**, give a round of applause, give a standing ovation, show your appreciation, congratulate Opposite: boo 2 **approve**, support, admire, celebrate, congratulate Opposite: condemn

applause n 1 **clapping**, round of applause, ovation, hand, handclapping Opposite: jeering 2 **praise**, appreciation, approval, approbation, support Opposite: condemnation

appliance n 1 **domestic appliance**, laboursaving device, electrical equipment, machine, device 2 **application**, use, employment, utilization, purpose

---

WORD BANK
❑ **types of appliance** blender, coffeemaker, cooker, dishwasher, dryer, food processor, grill, hob, iron, juicer, microwave, microwave oven, minibar, mixer, percolator, range, rotisserie, smoke alarm, smoke detector, spin-dryer, stove, television, toaster, tumble dryer, washing machine, waste disposal

---

applicable adj **appropriate**, valid, related, pertinent, relevant Opposite: unrelated

applicant n **candidate**, interviewee, claimant, hopeful, aspirant. See COMPARE AND CONTRAST at candidate.

application n 1 **request**, claim, submission, bid, tender 2 **use**, function, purpose, relevance, appliance 3 **diligence**, concentration, hard work, effort, attention Opposite: negligence

applied adj **practical**, functional, useful, everyday, pragmatic Opposite: theoretical

apply v 1 **submit an application**, request, ask, go in, put in 2 **use**, operate, put into operation, employ, utilize 3 **be relevant**, relate, pertain, affect, concern 4 **put on**, rub on, spread over, smear, spread on Opposite: remove

apply yourself v **devote yourself**, work hard, concentrate, direct your efforts towards, attend to Opposite: neglect

appoint v 1 **employ**, sign up, hire, assign, take on Opposite: dismiss 2 (fml) **select**, choose, settle on, agree, pick Opposite: reject

appointed adj **chosen**, selected, agreed, fixed, prearranged

appointment n 1 **meeting**, date, scheduled time, engagement, rendezvous 2 **selection**, choice, choosing, nomination Opposite: dismissal 3 **job**, position, opening, office, post

apportion v **allocate**, allot, assign, divide up, distribute

apposite adj **appropriate**, apt, pertinent, relevant, suitable Opposite: inappropriate

appraisal n **assessment**, evaluation, judgment, review, consideration

appraise v **assess**, evaluate, judge, review, consider

appreciable adj **considerable**, substantial, significant, noticeable, palpable Opposite: insignificant

appreciate v 1 **be grateful for**, be thankful for, be glad about, be pleased about, value 2 **understand**, realize, be aware, recognize the value of, grasp 3 **increase in value**, go up in price, rise, escalate, soar Opposite: depreciate

appreciation n 1 **thanks**, gratitude, indebtedness, gratefulness, obligation Opposite: ingratitude 2 **approval**, admiration, positive reception, enjoyment, pleasure Opposite: disapproval 3 **understanding**, grasp, comprehension, perception, sense 4 **rise**, increase, escalation, growth, inflation Opposite: depreciation

appreciative adj 1 **grateful**, thankful, indebted, obliged, beholden Opposite: ungrateful 2 **approving**, enthusiastic, admiring, positive, favourable Opposite: disapproving

apprehend v **catch**, arrest, detain, take in for questioning, take into custody Opposite: release

apprehension n 1 **anxiety**, uneasiness, worry, trepidation, nervousness Opposite: confidence 2 **capture**, arrest, detention, seizure, taking Opposite: discharge

apprehensive adj **uneasy**, worried, nervous, fearful, hesitant Opposite: confident

apprehensiveness see apprehension

apprentice n **trainee**, learner, beginner, novice, student Opposite: expert. See COMPARE AND CONTRAST at beginner.

apprenticeship n **traineeship**, training, education, preparation, internship (US)

approach v 1 **move towards**, come up to, come near, draw near, come within reach of Opposite: retreat 2 **speak to**, talk to, get in touch with, contact, make contact with 3 **set about**, tackle, deal with, handle, manage 4 **approximate**, come close to, be similar to, come near to, move towards ■ n **method**, line of attack, tactic, line, slant

approachability n 1 **friendliness**, accessibility, openness, affability, cordiality Opposite: aloofness 2 **user-friendliness**, accessibility, availability, ease of use, usability Opposite: inaccessibility

approachable adj 1 **friendly**, amicable, sociable, open, open-minded *Opposite*: forbidding 2 **user-friendly**, accessible, usable, useful, helpful *Opposite*: inaccessible

approaching adj **imminent**, impending, pending, future, forthcoming

approbation n **approval**, consent, praise, admiration, esteem *Opposite*: disapproval

appropriate adj **suitable**, fitting, apt, apposite, right *Opposite*: inappropriate ■ v **take**, take over, misappropriate, seize, assume

appropriateness n **suitability**, correctness, aptness, appositeness, relevance

appropriation n **seizure**, assumption, annexation, adoption, arrogation *(fml)*

approval n 1 **appreciation**, admiration, liking, praise, esteem *Opposite*: disdain 2 **endorsement**, support, sanction, consent, agreement

approve v 1 **favour**, like, support, agree, accept *Opposite*: disapprove 2 **grant**, consent, sanction, allow, pass *Opposite*: reject

approved adj **accepted**, permitted, official, agreed, sanctioned

approving adj **positive**, favourable, appreciative, sympathetic, complimentary *Opposite*: disapproving

approximate adj **estimated**, rough, loose, near, inexact *Opposite*: exact

approximation n **estimate**, guess, calculation, guesstimate *(infml)*

apron n **bib**, pinafore, overall, pinny *(infml)*

apropos *(fml)* prep **regarding**, concerning, about, on the subject of, in relation to ■ adj **appropriate**, suitable, fitting, apt, apposite *Opposite*: inappropriate

apt adj 1 **appropriate**, suitable, fitting, apposite, pertinent *Opposite*: inappropriate 2 **prone**, likely, given to, inclined, tending 3 **quick**, capable, competent, able, skilled *Opposite*: inept

aptitude n **ability**, skill, talent, gift, capacity *Opposite*: inability. *See* compare and contrast *at* **ability, talent.**

aptly adv **appropriately**, fittingly, suitably, rightly, pertinently *Opposite*: inappropriately

aquatic adj **water**, marine, sea, river

aqueduct n **channel**, conduit, canal, watercourse, culvert

arbiter n 1 **arbitrator**, mediator, intermediary, negotiator, go-between 2 **authority**, influence, role model, leader, example

arbitrary adj **random**, chance, subjective, uninformed, illogical *Opposite*: systematic

arbitrate v **judge**, adjudicate, pass judgment, decide, settle

arbitration n **adjudication**, negotiation, mediation, settlement, intercession

arbitrator n **judge**, arbiter, mediator, go-between, intermediary

arbour n **bower**, retreat, nook, dell *(literary)*

arc n **curve**, arch, semicircle, sweep, bow

arcade n 1 **colonnade**, cloister, loggia, gallery, walkway 2 **precinct**, shopping centre, shopping arcade, shopping mall *(US)* 3 **video arcade**, amusement arcade, game parlor *(US)*

arcane adj **mysterious**, secret, esoteric, deep, hidden. *See* compare and contrast *at* **obscure.**

arch n 1 **arc**, curve, semicircle, bend, bow 2 **archway**, doorway, portico ■ v **curve**, bend, bow, arc *Opposite*: straighten ■ adj **playful**, mischievous, roguish, knowing, cunning

archaic adj **old**, ancient, dated, outdated, out-of-date *Opposite*: modern

arched adj **curved**, rounded, round, high, bowed

archenemy n **opponent**, enemy, rival, challenger, foe *(fml)* *Opposite*: ally

archetypal adj **typical**, model, representative, standard, archetypical *Opposite*: unconventional

archetype n **model**, epitome, prototype, original, classic

archetypical *see* **archetypal**

architect n 1 **designer**, draughtsman, draughtswoman, draughtsperson, planner 2 **originator**, inventor, founder, creator, engineer

architecture n **design**, planning, building, construction

archive n **record**, file, documentation, document, library

archly adv **playfully**, mischievously, roguishly, knowingly, cunningly

archness n **playfulness**, mischievousness, roguishness, cunning, coyness

archway n **arch**, arcade, pergola, portico, doorway

arctic *(infml)* adj **freezing**, cold, chilly, wintry, frozen *Opposite*: tropical

ardent adj **passionate**, enthusiastic, keen, fervent, zealous *Opposite*: dispassionate

ardour n **passion**, love, enthusiasm, zeal, fervour *Opposite*: indifference

arduous adj **difficult**, hard, laborious, gruelling, demanding *Opposite*: easy. *See* compare and contrast *at* **hard.**

arduousness n **difficulty**, laboriousness, strenuousness, onerousness, rigorousness *Opposite*: ease

area n 1 **part**, zone, extent, expanse, range 2 **neighbourhood**, locale, vicinity, part, quarter 3 **subject**, topic, field, question, matter

arena n **stadium**, ground, showground, sports ground, pitch

argot n **jargon**, slang, idiom, speech, dialect

arguable adj **debatable**, open to question, questionable, doubtful, dubious *Opposite*: certain

arguably adv **debatably**, questionably, perhaps, possibly, maybe Opposite: certainly

argue v 1 **quarrel**, dispute, fight, disagree, bicker Opposite: agree 2 **make a case**, contend, claim, say, maintain 3 **debate**, dispute, discuss, go over, explore. See COMPARE AND CONTRAST at **disagree**.

argument n 1 **quarrel**, fight, disagreement, dispute, row 2 **case**, line of reasoning, reason, contention, claim

argumentative adj **quarrelsome**, confrontational, contrary, belligerent, aggressive Opposite: peaceable

arid adj 1 **dry**, parched, bone dry, baked, waterless Opposite: humid 2 **boring**, dull, uninteresting, uninspiring, dry Opposite: exciting. See COMPARE AND CONTRAST at **dry**.

aridity n **dryness**, drought, desiccation, parchedness, aridness Opposite: humidity

aridness see **aridity**

arise v 1 **happen**, occur, take place, come up, begin 2 **result from**, be the result of, arise from, arise out of, be caused by

aristocracy n **nobility**, upper classes, peers of the realm, landed gentry, lords and ladies Opposite: lower class

aristocrat n **noble**, lord, lady, peer, grandee

WORD BANK
❑ **types of aristocrat** baron, baroness, baronet, count, countess, crown prince, duchess, duke, earl, knight, marchioness, marquess, prince, princess, viscount, viscountess

---

aristocratic adj 1 **noble**, titled, patrician, upper-class, blue-blooded Opposite: lower-class 2 **refined**, well-bred, patrician, noble Opposite: lowly

arm n 1 **limb**, appendage, member 2 **support**, armrest, rest 3 **division**, wing, branch, subdivision, offshoot ■ v **equip**, provide, supply, prepare, ready Opposite: disarm

---

WORD BANK
❑ **parts of an arm or hand** ball, cuticle, elbow, finger, fingernail, fingerprint, fingertip, fist, forearm, forefinger, funny bone (infml), hand, hangnail, heel, index finger, knuckle, little finger, middle finger, palm, pinkie (infml), ring finger, thumb, thumbnail, wrist

---

armada n **fleet**, flotilla, navy, squadron, task force

Armageddon n 1 **end of the world**, day of reckoning, Judgment Day, Apocalypse 2 **disaster**, destruction, catastrophe, cataclysm, apocalypse

armament n **arming**, mobilization, rearmament, deployment, buildup Opposite: disarmament

armaments n **arms**, weapons, weaponry, guns, missiles

armed adj **equipped**, fortified, prepared Opposite: unarmed

armed forces n **military**, services, forces, defence force, militia

armhole n **opening**, slit, hole

armistice n **truce**, peace agreement, settlement, ceasefire, resolution

armour n 1 **body armour**, bulletproof vest, flak jacket, breastplate, panoply 2 **protection**, reinforcement, defence, covering, cover

armoured adj **reinforced**, steel-clad, armour-plated, strengthened, bulletproof Opposite: unprotected

armour-plated adj **reinforced**, steel-clad, armoured, strengthened, bulletproof Opposite: unprotected

armoury n 1 **arsenal**, arms depot, magazine, ordnance depot, munitions store 2 **stock**, source, supply, resource

armrest n **support**, arm, rest

arms n **weapons**, weaponry, armaments, guns, missiles

army n 1 **military**, armed forces, defence force, militia, troops 2 **crowd**, throng, mass, host, multitude

aroma n **smell**, perfume, fragrance, scent, odour. See COMPARE AND CONTRAST at **smell**.

aromatic adj **perfumed**, fragrant, sweet-smelling, scented, pungent Opposite: odourless

around prep 1 **about**, all round, surrounding, covering, over 2 **close to**, near, in the vicinity, in the neighbourhood, in the environs 3 **all over**, throughout, here and there, about, round 4 **approximately**, about, in the region of, just about, roughly ■ adv 1 **in**, here, round, about, present 2 **from one place to another**, from place to place, about, everywhere, all over the place (infml) 3 **round here**, near here, nearby, about, round

arousal n **stimulation**, provocation, awakening, encouragement, excitement

arouse v **stimulate**, provoke, awaken, produce, stir Opposite: dampen

arraign v **accuse**, impeach, prosecute, bring before the court, have up (infml)

arraignment n **charge**, prosecution, legal process, legal action, indictment Opposite: exculpation (fml)

arrange v 1 **organize**, set up, coordinate, fix, fix up Opposite: cancel 2 **position**, put in order, place, assemble, put together Opposite: disarrange

arranged adj **decided**, agreed, set, settled, organized

arrangement n 1 **preparation**, plan, procedure, prearrangement, provision 2 **agreement**, understanding, bargain, pact, deal 3 **display**, array, composition, layout, assembly

arrant adj **complete**, total, outright, unmitigated, utter

array n 1 **collection**, selection, display, range,

arrangement 2 dress, clothing, regalia, finery, garb ■ *v* **1** *(fml)* **arrange**, display, organize, set out, exhibit **2** *(literary)* **clothe**, dress, deck out, drape, attire *(fml)*

arrears *n* **amount overdue**, amount outstanding, debts, sum unpaid *Opposite*: credit

arrest *v* **1** **take into custody**, seize, capture, detain, catch *Opposite*: release **2** *(fml)* **halt**, stop, block, prevent, obstruct **3** *(fml)* **attract**, engage, catch, hold, fix ■ *n* **capture**, seizure, detention, apprehension *Opposite*: release

arresting *adj* **impressive**, eye-catching, stunning, striking, interesting *Opposite*: uninteresting

arrival *n* **1** **entrance**, entry, coming, appearance *Opposite*: departure **2** **onset**, advent, occurrence, influx, coming *Opposite*: disappearance **3** **newcomer**, visitor, guest, incomer, caller

arrive *v* **1** **reach**, turn up, get there, land, disembark *Opposite*: depart **2** **work out**, reach, come to, come up with, attain **3** **succeed**, be successful, gain recognition, make your mark, make it *(infml)*

arrogance *n* **conceit**, haughtiness, egotism, pride, overconfidence *Opposite*: humility

arrogant *adj* **conceited**, haughty, egotistic, superior, proud *Opposite*: humble. *See* COMPARE AND CONTRAST *at* proud.

arrogate *(fml)* *v* **claim**, lay claim to, appropriate, misappropriate, assume *Opposite*: cede *(fml)*

arrogation *(fml)* *n* **appropriation**, misappropriation, assumption, takeover, annexation

arrow *n* **1** **projectile**, missile, dart, barb, shaft **2** **symbol**, sign, pointer, marker, indicator

arrowhead *n* **point**, tip, barb

arsenal *n* **1** **weapon store**, munitions store, magazine, armoury **2** **store**, battery, fund, cache, collection

arson *n* **fire raising**, pyromania, burning, incineration, ignition

arsonist *n* **fire raiser**, pyromaniac, burner, firebomber, incendiary

art *n* **1** **painting**, drawing, fine art, graphic arts, sculpture **2** **skill**, talent, knack, ability, virtuosity

artefact *n* **object**, objet d'art, manufactured object, article, manufactured article

arterial *adj* **major**, main, trunk, principal, through *Opposite*: subsidiary

artery *n* **route**, road, line, channel, pathway

artful *adj* **crafty**, devious, sly, deceitful, cunning *Opposite*: open

artfulness *n* **craftiness**, deviousness, slyness, cleverness, deceitfulness *Opposite*: straightforwardness

art-house *adj* **highbrow**, intellectual, sophisticated, esoteric, avant-garde *Opposite*: lowbrow

arthritic *adj* **stiff**, swollen, aching, sore, painful

article *n* **1** **piece of writing**, editorial, piece, item, commentary **2** **object**, item, piece, thing, artefact **3** **clause**, term, stipulation, condition, regulation

articles *n* **training**, traineeship, apprenticeship, tutelage, course

articulacy *n* **self-expression**, expressiveness, eloquence, fluency, articulateness

articulate *adj* **eloquent**, clear, coherent, fluent, lucid *Opposite*: inarticulate ■ *v* **1** **speak about**, express, state, put into words, convey *Opposite*: suppress **2** **enunciate**, pronounce, speak clearly, speak, say *Opposite*: mumble

articulated *adj* **1** **modular**, jointed, coupled, linked, connected *Opposite*: rigid **2** **spoken**, voiced, uttered, expressed, pronounced *Opposite*: unspoken

articulateness *n* **eloquence**, expressiveness, fluency, self-expression, coherence

articulation *n* **1** **enunciation**, pronunciation, speech, diction, delivery **2** **expression**, verbalization, communication, formulation

artifact *see* **artefact**

artifice *(fml)* *n* **1** **pretence**, ploy, trick, lie, sleight of hand **2** **deception**, deceit, cunning, trickery, artfulness

artificial *adj* **1** **false**, fake, mock, reproduction, synthetic *Opposite*: natural **2** **insincere**, false, put-on, pretend, fake *Opposite*: sincere

artificiality *n* **insincerity**, disingenuousness, affectedness, affectation, phoniness *Opposite*: sincerity

artillery *n* **weaponry**, arms, guns, armaments, weapons

artisan *n* **craftsperson**, skilled worker, craftworker, artist, artificer *(dated)*

artist *n* **1** **painter**, illustrator, drawer, sketcher, cartoonist **2** **performer**, entertainer, artiste

artiste *n* **performer**, entertainer, artist

artistic *adj* **creative**, imaginative, inventive, arty *(infml)*

artistry *n* **creativity**, originality, artistic ability, imagination, invention

artless *adj* **simple**, guileless, natural, unworldly, ingenuous *Opposite*: disingenuous

artlessness *n* **guilelessness**, naturalness, innocence, unaffectedness, inexperience *Opposite*: disingenuousness

artwork *n* **1** **work of art**, creation, representation, reproduction, painting **2** **illustrations**, pictures, photographs, diagrams, plates

arty *(infml)* *adj* **creative**, imaginative, inventive, artistic

arty-crafty *(infml)* *adj* **1** **overdecorative**, fanciful, pretentious, artistic **2** **rustic**, homespun, homemade, traditional, artistic *Opposite*: sophisticated

as *conj* **1 while**, when, during, whilst **2 because**, since, seeing that, being as, considering that

as a result of *prep* **because of**, by, through, by means of, on account of

ascend *v* **1 rise**, climb, soar, go up, come up *Opposite*: descend **2 climb**, go up, come up, mount, scale *Opposite*: descend

ascendancy *n* **dominance**, domination, predominance, pre-eminence, power *Opposite*: subordination

ascendant *adj* **1 rising**, dominant, ascending, prevailing, mounting *Opposite*: descendent **2 dominant**, controlling, governing, ruling, influential *Opposite*: subordinate

ascendency *see* ascendancy

ascension *(fml) n* **rise**, ascent, climb, mounting, scaling *Opposite*: descent

ascent *n* **1 climb**, rise, mounting, scaling, ascension *(fml) Opposite*: descent **2 gradient**, slope, incline, rake, angle

ascertain *v* **determine**, discover, find out, learn, make certain

ascetic *n* **abstainer**, celibate, puritan, penitent *Opposite*: hedonist ■ *adj* **austere**, abstinent, frugal, abstemious, spartan *Opposite*: hedonistic

asceticism *n* **austerity**, self-discipline, abstemiousness, self-denial, self-restraint *Opposite*: hedonism

ascribe *(fml) v* **1 assign**, credit, attribute, accredit, chalk up **2 put down to**, attribute, blame on, lay at the door of, charge

aseptic *adj* **clean**, sterile, pure, sterilized, uninfected *Opposite*: septic

asexual *adj* **1 genderless**, androgynous, neutral, sexless **2 vegetative**, somatic, parthenogenetic, nonsexual

as far as *conj* **to the extent that**, to the degree that, so far as, insofar as, as much as

ash *n* **residue**, cinders, slag, embers, powder

ashamed *adj* **1 embarrassed**, mortified, humiliated, abashed, humbled *Opposite*: proud **2 unwilling**, reluctant, hesitant, unhappy, sorry *Opposite*: pleased

ashen *adj* **pallid**, wan, pasty, white as a sheet, drained of colour *Opposite*: rosy

ashes *n* **ruins**, remains, vestiges, remnants, fragments

ashore *adv* **aground**, onto land, onto dry land, on shore

ashy *see* ashen

aside *adv* **1 sideways**, away, to the side, sidewise, to one side **2 disregarded**, ignored, excluded, set aside, apart **3 in reserve**, separately, away, to one side, up your sleeve ■ *n* **1 digression**, departure, tangent, interposition, parenthesis **2 whisper**, mumbled comment, remark, undertone, by-play

aside from *prep* **1 as well as**, in addition to, on top of, besides, over and beyond **2 barring**, excluding, ignoring, except, except for *Opposite*: including

asinine *adj* **silly**, foolish, unintelligent *Opposite*: intelligent

ask *v* **1 request**, inquire, solicit, question, query *Opposite*: answer **2 invite**, ask over, have over, summon, request **3 count on**, expect, demand, look for, require

askance *adv* **doubtfully**, suspiciously, sideways, dubiously, distrustfully

askew *adv* **crookedly**, awry, out of kilter, off centre, cockeyed *Opposite*: straight

ask for *v* **request**, provoke, solicit, inspire, demand *Opposite*: refuse

asking price *n* **price**, selling price, starting price, marked price, cost

aslant *adv* **obliquely**, at an angle, on a slope, diagonally, slantingly *Opposite*: straight ■ *adj* **slanting**, slant, slantwise, oblique, diagonal

asleep *adj* **1 sleeping**, slumbering, dead to the world, napping, sound asleep *Opposite*: awake **2 numb**, dead, benumbed, without feeling, lifeless

as long as *conj* **providing**, on condition that, given that, provided that, if

as of *(fml) prep* **from**, after, on or after, beginning, starting

aspect *n* **1 feature**, facet, characteristic, part, piece **2 position**, outlook, side, standpoint, viewpoint **3 appearance**, look, quality, bearing, air

as per *prep* **according to**, in accordance with, following, consistent with, in keeping with *Opposite*: counter

asperity *(fml) n* **severity**, brusqueness, gruffness, harshness, sharpness *Opposite*: affability

aspersion *n* **slander**, slur, slight, smear, accusation *Opposite*: praise

asphalt *n* **tar**, Tarmac, bitumen, blacktop *(US)*

asphyxia *n* **suffocation**, choking, lack of oxygen, oxygen deprivation, unconsciousness

asphyxiate *v* **suffocate**, smother, choke, stifle, strangle *Opposite*: resuscitate

asphyxiation *n* **suffocation**, choking, smothering, stifling, throttling

aspic *n* **jelly**, gel, mousseline

aspirant *n* **contender**, candidate, applicant, hopeful, seeker ■ *adj* **hopeful**, would-be, aspiring, wannabe *(infml)*. See COMPARE AND CONTRAST *at* candidate.

aspirate *v* **1 pronounce**, enunciate, articulate, sound, voice **2 remove**, extract, suck out, draw out, take out *Opposite*: inject

aspiration *n* **ambition**, goal, objective, aim, end

aspirational *adj* **ambitious**, self-improving, aspiring, hopeful, eager *Opposite*: unambitious

aspire v **seek**, aim, hope, desire, want

aspiring adj **hopeful**, would-be, ambitious, aspirant, wannabe *(infml)*

as regards prep **with regard to**, regarding, concerning, with reference to, as to

assail v 1 **attack**, assault, set about, lay into, beset *Opposite*: defend 2 **criticize**, attack, lay into, berate, revile *Opposite*: praise

assailant n **attacker**, mugger, accoster, assaulter, aggressor

assassin n **killer**, murderer, cutthroat, dispatcher, hired gun *(slang)*

assassinate v **kill**, murder, shoot, kill in cold blood, eliminate. *See* COMPARE AND CONTRAST *at* **kill**.

assassination n **foul play**, murder, killing, shooting, elimination

assault n 1 **attack**, beating, stabbing, mugging, battering 2 **offensive**, attack, onslaught, incursion, storming *Opposite*: retreat ■ v **attack**, mug, set about, assail, lay into *Opposite*: defend

assay v **examine**, assess, analyse, evaluate, test

assemblage n 1 **accumulation**, grouping, assembly, collection, meeting 2 **crowd**, throng, assembly, group, mass

assemble v 1 **bring together**, collect, pull together, draw together, accumulate *Opposite*: disband 2 **muster**, collect, meet, come together, convene *Opposite*: disperse 3 **put together**, build, fit together, make, compile *Opposite*: take apart. *See* COMPARE AND CONTRAST *at* **collect**.

assembly n 1 **gathering**, coming together, meeting, association, assemblage 2 **meeting**, congress, assemblage, gathering, muster 3 **legislative body**, legislature, council, government, representatives 4 **construction**, building, compilation, putting together, fabrication *Opposite*: destruction

assembly point n **meeting point**, meeting place, rendezvous, rallying point, muster station

assent v **agree**, acquiesce, concur, go along with, subscribe to *Opposite*: disagree ■ n **agreement**, acquiescence, concurrence, acceptance, approval *Opposite*: disagreement. *See* COMPARE AND CONTRAST *at* **agree**.

assert v 1 **declare**, state, insist on, proclaim, emphasize *Opposite*: deny 2 **stand up for**, profess, defend, maintain, uphold *Opposite*: renounce

assertion n **declaration**, statement, proclamation, claim, allegation *Opposite*: denial

assertive adj **self-confident**, self-assured, confident, firm, forceful *Opposite*: shy

assertiveness n **confidence**, forcefulness, insistence, decisiveness, boldness *Opposite*: shyness

assess v 1 **review**, consider, appraise, evaluate, judge 2 **calculate**, evaluate, value, rate, estimate

assessment n 1 **evaluation**, appraisal, judgment, review, consideration 2 **calculation**, estimation, valuation 3 **duty**, charge, impost, debt, bill

assessor n **evaluator**, appraiser, judge, inspector

asset n 1 **advantage**, strength, benefit, plus point, positive feature *Opposite*: drawback 2 **possession**, property, resource, holding

assets n **possessions**, property, resources, material goods, worldly goods

asset-stripping n **profit taking**, profitmaking, selling off, buying and selling, trading

assiduity n **diligence**, care, attention, application, industriousness *Opposite*: carelessness

assiduous adj **diligent**, persevering, industrious, painstaking, careful *Opposite*: lazy. *See* COMPARE AND CONTRAST *at* **careful**.

assiduousness n **diligence**, persistence, industriousness, attentiveness, tirelessness *Opposite*: laziness

assign v 1 **allocate**, allot, give, dispense, disperse 2 **appoint**, designate, delegate, send, transfer

assignation n **meeting**, tryst, rendezvous, appointment, date

assignment n 1 **task**, job, project, duty, obligation 2 **appointment**, duty, position, role, job 3 **transfer**, handing over, consignment, allocation, delegation

assimilate v 1 **integrate**, adapt, adjust, blend in, fit in 2 **incorporate**, take in, digest, absorb, understand *Opposite*: reject

assimilation n 1 **integration**, adjustment, acclimatization, accommodation, adaptation 2 **absorption**, incorporation, digestion, ingestion, inculcation

assist v **help**, aid, help out, lend a hand, give a hand *Opposite*: hinder

assistance n **help**, aid, support, backing, cooperation *Opposite*: hindrance

assistant n **helper**, aide, deputy, personal assistant, subordinate ■ adj **associate**, subordinate, secondary, junior

COMPARE AND CONTRAST CORE MEANING: somebody who helps another person in carrying out a task

assistant somebody who works to somebody else's instructions, often in a paid capacity; **helper** somebody who takes on an informal, often voluntary, role; **deputy** an officially designated chief assistant authorized to act on a superior's behalf; **aide** an assistant in military, political, or commercial contexts.

assisted adj **aided**, helped, abetted, supported, sponsored *Opposite*: unassisted

assizes n **court session**, judicial proceedings, court sitting, circuit court

associate v 1 **connect**, relate, link, correlate, bracket *Opposite*: separate 2 **mix**, socialize, spend time with, go around with, see *Opposite*: avoid **3 unite**, combine, join together, group together, join *Opposite*: disband ■ *n* **1 partner**, colleague, business partner, fellow worker, coworker **2 companion**, comrade, acquaintance, friend, ally ■ *adj* **subordinate**, secondary, junior, assistant

associated *adj* **related**, allied, linked, connected, accompanying

association *n* **1 organization**, union, alliance, society, company **2 friendship**, relationship, connection, fellowship, involvement **3 connotation**, overtone, suggestion, memory, reminder

assonance *n* **repetition**, recurrence, duplication, iteration, alliteration

as soon as *conj* **once**, the moment, the instant, the minute, immediately

assort *v* **classify**, separate, sort out, group, divide *Opposite*: disarrange

assorted *adj* **mixed**, various, miscellaneous, varied, multifarious *Opposite*: uniform

assortment *n* **variety**, collection, range, mixture, mixed bag

assort with *v* **associate**, mix with, socialize with, see, spend time with

assuage *v* **moderate**, ease, soften, lessen, appease *Opposite*: inflame

assume *v* **1 take for granted**, suppose, presume, presuppose, deduce **2 take up**, take responsibility, take on, take upon yourself, shoulder **3 feign**, affect, fake, simulate, put on. *See* COMPARE AND CONTRAST *at* **deduce**.

assumed *adj* **1 expected**, presumed, supposed, rumoured, implicit **2 false**, artificial, fake, phoney, bogus

assumed name *n* **alias**, pseudonym, pen name, nom de plume, stage name

assuming *adj* **presumptuous**, pretentious, arrogant, haughty, high and mighty *Opposite*: humble

assumption *n* **supposition**, statement, postulation, hypothesis, guess

assurance *n* **1 pledge**, declaration, word, guarantee, oath **2 self-confidence**, self-possession, self-reliance, confidence, poise *Opposite*: timidity

assure *v* **1 promise**, guarantee, give surety, pledge, swear **2 make certain**, ensure, guarantee, nail down, know for certain

assured *adj* **1 certain**, guaranteed, sure, confident, solid *Opposite*: uncertain **2 confident**, self-confident, self-assured, self-possessed, poised *Opposite*: diffident

asterisk *n* **symbol**, sign, mark, character, star ■ *v* **mark**, identify, label, indicate, specify

astern *adv* **1 behind**, aft, at the back, at the rear *Opposite*: forward **2 to the rear**, backwards, in reverse *Opposite*: ahead

astir *adj* **1 awake**, out of bed, up, up and about, aroused *Opposite*: asleep **2 active**, alive,

moving, stirring, live *Opposite*: inactive

as to *prep* **with regard to**, as regards, regarding, concerning, in respect of

astonish *v* **surprise**, amaze, astound, dumbfound, overwhelm

astonished *adj* **surprised**, amazed, astounded, dumbfounded, incredulous

astonishing *adj* **amazing**, surprising, astounding, shocking, bewildering *Opposite*: predictable

astonishment *n* **surprise**, amazement, wonder, bewilderment, shock

astound *v* **amaze**, astonish, surprise, shock, dumbfound

astounded *adj* **astonished**, surprised, amazed, stunned, dazed

astounding *adj* **amazing**, astonishing, surprising, shocking, beyond belief *Opposite*: unsurprising

astral *adj* **1 stellar**, astronomical, astrophysical, cosmological, celestial **2 immaterial**, spiritual, psychical, otherworldly, transcendent *Opposite*: material

astray *adv* **off course**, lost, off track, off target, off beam

astride *prep* **on both sides of**, spanning, straddling, across

astringency *n* **acerbity**, acidity, causticity, mordancy, sharpness *Opposite*: blandness

astringent *adj* **harsh**, severe, biting, caustic, acerbic *Opposite*: bland

astrologer *n* **fortune-teller**, seer, soothsayer, prophet, forecaster

astrological *adj* **zodiacal**, horoscopic, fortune-telling, prophetic, forecasting

astrology *n* **fortune-telling**, clairvoyance, soothsaying, forecasting, prediction

astronaut *n* **space traveller**, space pilot, cosmonaut, rocket pilot, spaceman

astronomical *adj* **1 astral**, planetary, cosmological, astrophysical, lunar **2** (*infml*) **exorbitant**, excessive, sky-high, through the roof, huge *Opposite*: affordable

astronomically (*infml*) *adv* **exorbitantly**, exceedingly, excessively, inordinately, extremely

astute *adj* **shrewd**, smart, perceptive, judicious, incisive *Opposite*: credulous

astuteness *n* **shrewdness**, good judgment, smartness, intelligence, wisdom *Opposite*: credulity

asunder (*fml*) *adv* **apart**, open, in pieces, in bits, in halves *Opposite*: together

as well *adv* **too**, also, additionally, in addition, on top

as well as *conj* **in addition to**, on top of, over and above, with, and

asylum *n* **1 place of safety**, refuge, haven, safe haven, sanctuary **2 protection**, security, refuge, sanctuary, shelter

asymmetric *adj* **unequal**, uneven, lopsided,

irregular, disproportionate *Opposite*: symmetrical

asymmetrical *see* **asymmetric**

asymmetry *n* **irregularity**, lopsidedness, unevenness, disproportionateness *Opposite*: symmetry

atavistic *adj* **primitive**, primeval, primal, ancient, ancestral

atheism *n* **unbelief**, doubt, freethinking, humanism, nonbelief *Opposite*: belief

atheist *n* **unbeliever**, doubter, sceptic, nonbeliever, agnostic *Opposite*: believer

atheistic *adj* **unbelieving**, nonbelieving, disbelieving, incredulous, irreligious *Opposite*: believing

athlete *n* **sportsperson**, contestant, participant, competitor, team member

athletic *adj* **fit**, sporty, healthy, in good shape, physical *Opposite*: unfit

athleticism *n* **fitness**, sportiness, litheness, agility, suppleness

atmosphere *n* **1 air**, sky, heavens, ether *(literary)* **2 ambience**, impression, feeling, feel, mood

WORD BANK
❏ **parts of the atmosphere** exosphere, ionosphere, mesosphere, ozone layer, stratosphere, thermosphere, tropopause, troposphere

atmospheric *adj* **impressive**, distinctive, moody, special, full of character

atmospherics *n* **interference**, disturbance, static, snow, hissing

atoll *n* **island**, isle, islet, coral reef, coral island

atom *n* **particle**, bit, tiny part, iota, jot

atomic *adj* **1 nuclear**, thermonuclear, fissionable **2 microscopic**, submicroscopic, minute, infinitesimal, minuscule *Opposite*: gigantic

atomizer *n* **spray**, spray can, vaporizer, aerosol

atonal *adj* **twelve-note**, twelve-tone, discordant, dissonant, inharmonious

atonality *n* **twelve-note scale**, twelve-tone scale, serialism, discordance, dissonance *Opposite*: tonality

atone *(fml)* *v* **compensate**, make up, make amends, redress, apologize

atonement *n* **compensation**, amends, penitence, penance, punishment

atrium *n* **hall**, foyer, entrance hall, entrance, vestibule

atrocious *adj* **1 bad**, terrible, dreadful, appalling, awful **2 brutal**, vicious, wicked, evil, cruel

atrociously *adv* **1 badly**, terribly, appallingly, fearfully, dreadfully *Opposite*: wonderfully **2 brutally**, viciously, wickedly, evilly, cruelly

atrociousness *n* **fearfulness**, dreadfulness, viciousness, wickedness, frightfulness

atrocity *n* **1 act of violence**, massacre, killing,

outrage, brutality **2 violence**, cruelty, viciousness, barbarity

atrophy *v* **waste away**, waste, wither, weaken, shrivel

attach *v* **1 fasten**, join, connect, fix, put together *Opposite*: detach **2 assign**, award, attribute, accord, ascribe *(fml)*

attaché *n* **diplomat**, public servant, civil servant, representative, envoy

attached *adj* **1 enclosed**, accompanying, supporting, supplementary **2** *(infml)* **emotionally involved**, devoted, fond of, close, friendly *Opposite*: uninvolved

attachment *n* **1 add-on**, accessory, extra, addition, supplement **2 bond**, affection, connection, regard, friendship

attack *v* **1 harm**, assault, harass, bother, molest *Opposite*: defend **2 criticize**, argue, confront, pounce on, disagree *Opposite*: support **3 infect**, occur, strike, hit, strike down **4 begin**, set to, deal with, tackle, pile in ■ *n* **1 bout**, dose, spell, occurrence, outbreak **2 violence**, assault, confrontation, act of violence, incident *Opposite*: defence **3 criticism**, condemnation, argument, disagreement *Opposite*: praise

attacker *n* **assailant**, aggressor, invader, enemy, foe *(fml)* *Opposite*: defender

attack the dignity of *v* **insult**, call names, abuse, give offence, offend

attain *v* **reach**, achieve, accomplish, conquer, manage *Opposite*: fall short. *See* COMPARE AND CONTRAST *at* **accomplish**.

attainable *adj* **within reach**, possible, achievable, realistic, reasonable *Opposite*: unattainable

attainment *n* **1 achievement**, accomplishment, realization, fulfilment, completion *Opposite*: failure **2 skill**, ability, talent, achievement, accomplishment

attar *n* **essence**, extract, essential oil, distillate, perfume

attempt *v* **endeavour**, make an effort, try, bid, make an attempt ■ *n* **effort**, try, go, shot, bid. *See* COMPARE AND CONTRAST *at* **try**.

attend *v* **1 be present**, go to, be there, grace with your presence, appear *Opposite*: miss **2 listen**, concentrate, focus, keep your mind on, pay attention *Opposite*: ignore

attendance *n* **1 presence**, attending, appearance, being present *Opposite*: non-attendance **2 turnout**, audience, number present, gate, crowd

attendant *adj* **associated**, linked, related, connected, consequent ■ *n* **1 assistant**, helper, aide, guide, employee **2 escort**, usher, bridesmaid, groomsman, pageboy

attend to *v* **deal with**, see to, tackle, turn your attention to, address *Opposite*: ignore

attention *n* **1 notice**, concentration, thought, awareness, consideration *Opposite*: inattention **2 care**, courtesy, consideration, kindness, devotion *Opposite*: neglect

attention-grabbing *adj* **eye-catching**, conspicuous, arresting, noticeable, striking *Opposite*: understated

attention to detail *n* **meticulousness**, thoroughness, care, carefulness, exactness *Opposite*: carelessness

attentive *adj* **1 considerate**, responsive, helpful, caring, thoughtful *Opposite*: inconsiderate **2 paying attention**, listening carefully, concentrating, observant, focused *Opposite*: inattentive

attentiveness *n* **1 care**, courtesy, thoughtfulness, consideration, kindness *Opposite*: neglect **2 concentration**, attention, focus, alertness *Opposite*: inattention

attenuate *v* **reduce**, decrease, lessen, diminish, dilute *Opposite*: intensify

attenuation *n* **reduction**, decrease, lessening, diminution, dilution *Opposite*: intensification

attest *v* **show**, bear out, prove, confirm, corroborate *Opposite*: refute

attestation *n* **confirmation**, corroboration, substantiation, verification, testimony *Opposite*: refutation

at the side of *prep* **beside**, next to, alongside, with, adjacent to

attic *n* **loft**, garret, roof space, upper floor *Opposite*: basement

attire *(fml)* *n* **clothing**, dress, clothes, outfit, garments

attitude *n* **1 view**, opinion, viewpoint, point of view, feeling **2 posture**, pose, position, bearing, stance **3** *(infml)* **boldness**, brashness, arrogance, insolence, defiance

attract *v* **1 draw**, bring together, pull, exert a pull on *Opposite*: repel **2 entice**, appeal, fascinate, charm, interest *Opposite*: put off

attraction *n* **magnetism**, lure, desirability, hold, charm *Opposite*: repulsion

attractive *adj* **1 appealing**, alluring, charming, pleasing, inviting *Opposite*: unattractive **2 good-looking**, beautiful, handsome, lovely, pretty *Opposite*: ugly. *See* COMPARE AND CONTRAST *at* **good-looking**.

attractively *adv* **nicely**, delightfully, charmingly, appealingly, prettily *Opposite*: unattractively

attractiveness *n* **1 good looks**, pleasant appearance, beauty, prettiness, charm *Opposite*: ugliness **2 magnetism**, charisma, draw, appeal, lure *Opposite*: repulsiveness

attribute *v* **ascribe**, put down to, lay at the door of, impute, blame on ■ *n* **quality**, characteristic, trait, property, feature

attribution *n* **credit**, acknowledgment, designation, ascription *(fml)*

attributive *adj* **prenominal**, preceding, modifying, qualifying

attrition *n* **abrasion**, erosion, slow destruction

attune *v* **adjust**, accustom, adapt, accommodate, acclimatize

atypical *adj* **different**, unusual, uncommon, strange, odd *Opposite*: typical

auction *n* **sale**, mart, Dutch auction, silent auction

audacious *adj* **1 daring**, bold, brave, fearless, courageous *Opposite*: cowardly *(fml)* **2 impudent**, bold, disrespectful, overconfident, cheeky *Opposite*: courteous

audaciousness *see* **audacity**

audacity *n* **1 boldness**, daring, courage, bravery, fearlessness *Opposite*: cowardice **2 impudence**, disrespect, boldness, rudeness, discourtesy *Opposite*: courtesy

audibility *n* **loudness**, noise, distinctness, discernibility, perceptibility *Opposite*: inaudibility

audible *adj* **perceptible**, clear, distinct, noticeable, loud *Opposite*: inaudible

audience *n* **1 spectators**, viewers, addressees, listeners, onlookers **2 meeting**, interview, consultation, appointment, hearing

audio *adj* **acoustic**, auditory, aural, audial

audiovisual *adj* **video**, filmed, film, cinematic, cinematographic

audit *n* **review**, check, inspection, examination, assessment ■ *v* **review**, inspect, examine, assess, appraise

audition *n* **test**, tryout, trial, interview ■ *v* **try out**, test, hear, interview

auditor *n* **1 examiner**, accountant, assessor, checker **2** *(fml)* **listener**, hearer, eavesdropper

auditorium *n* **hall**, theatre, amphitheatre, lecture hall

auditory *adj* **aural**, hearing, audio, acoustic

au fait *adj* **familiar**, at home with, at ease with, used to, accustomed *Opposite*: unaccustomed

augment *(fml)* *v* **increase**, enlarge, expand, extend, amplify *Opposite*: diminish. *See* COMPARE AND CONTRAST *at* **increase**.

augmentation *n* **increase**, growth, rise, expansion, intensification *Opposite*: decrease

augur *v* **foretell**, predict, portend, promise, prophesy

augury *n* **1 divination**, prediction, prophecy, forecasting, prognostication **2 portent**, omen, auspice, indication, prediction

august *(fml)* *adj* **imposing**, impressive, grand, majestic, dignified *Opposite*: humble

aura *n* **air**, atmosphere, force, appearance, quality

aural *adj* **auditory**, hearing, acoustic, audio

auspice *n* **omen**, portent, augury, sign, indication

auspices *n* **sponsorship**, patronage, backing, support, help

auspicious *adj* **favourable**, fortunate, promising, propitious, lucky *Opposite*: inauspicious

austere *adj* **1 stark**, severe, simple, basic,

sparse *Opposite*: comfortable **2 serious**, grim, severe, unsmiling, harsh *Opposite*: gentle **3 plain**, bare, simple, clean, undecorated *Opposite*: ornate

austerity n **1 severity**, strictness, sternness, gravity, soberness *Opposite*: levity **2 self-denial**, shortage, scarcity, economy *Opposite*: abundance **3 plainness**, starkness, bareness, simplicity, cleanness *Opposite*: opulence

autarchy n **autocracy**, absolute power, absolutism, despotism, tyranny *Opposite*: democracy

authentic adj **1 genuine**, original, authenticated, valid *Opposite*: fake **2 true**, reliable, dependable, trustworthy, faithful *Opposite*: false

authenticate v **validate**, confirm, verify, substantiate, endorse

authentication n **verification**, confirmation, substantiation, validation, certification

authenticity n **genuineness**, legitimacy, validity, reality, truth

author n **1 writer**, novelist, playwright, dramatist, poet **2 creator**, originator, inventor, source

authoritarian adj **strict**, demanding, totalitarian, despotic, absolute *Opposite*: liberal

authoritarianism n **totalitarianism**, dictatorship, oppression, absolutism, tyranny *Opposite*: democracy

authoritative adj **1 reliable**, trustworthy, dependable, respected, convincing *Opposite*: unreliable **2 commanding**, imposing, firm, confident, convincing *Opposite*: weak

authoritatively adv **with authority**, confidently, firmly, commandingly, convincingly

authoritativeness n **1 reliability**, trustworthiness, dependability, validity, credibility *Opposite*: unreliability **2 authority**, command, standing, position, weight

authority n **1 power**, right, ability, influence, weight **2 agency**, group, government department, board, corporation **3 confidence**, conviction, knowledge, experience **4 citation**, source, evidence **5 expert**, specialist, consultant, buff, expert witness

authority figure n **mentor**, person of influence, leader, role model, example

authorization n **approval**, consent, endorsement, sanction, agreement

authorize v **approve**, allow, sanction, permit, give permission *Opposite*: forbid

authorized adj **official**, lawful, legal, sanctioned, approved *Opposite*: unauthorized

authorship n **1 writing**, composition, invention, production, output **2 origin**, source, provenance, derivation, genesis

autobiographical adj **nonfictional**, factual, first-person, real-life, true to life *Opposite*: fictional

autobiography n **memoirs**, life story, life history

autochthonous adj **original**, native, indigenous, aboriginal. *See* COMPARE AND CONTRAST at **native**.

autocracy n **dictatorship**, monocracy, despotism, tyranny, absolutism *Opposite*: democracy

autocrat n **dictator**, absolute ruler, tyrant, despot

autocratic adj **1 despotic**, tyrannical, repressive, oppressive, monocratic *Opposite*: democratic **2 dictatorial**, domineering, bossy, overbearing, imperious

autograph n **signature**, name, inscription, dedication

automated adj **automatic**, mechanical, programmed, preset, mechanized *Opposite*: manual

automatic adj **1 mechanized**, automated, mechanical, programmed, preset *Opposite*: manual **2 involuntary**, reflex, unconscious, instinctive, programmed *Opposite*: voluntary **3 routine**, habitual, mechanical, regular, repeated *Opposite*: spontaneous

automation n **mechanization**, computerization, robotics

automaton n **robot**, android, machine

autonomous adj **self-governing**, sovereign, free, independent, separate *Opposite*: dependent

autonomy n **independence**, self-government, self-rule, sovereignty *Opposite*: dependence

autopsy n **postmortem**, dissection, analysis, debriefing, examination

autosuggestion n **self-suggestion**, self-hypnosis, autohypnosis, power of suggestion, self-deception

autumn n **1 season**, harvest time, equinox, Indian summer, fall *(US)* **2 end**, conclusion, close, culmination, decline

autumnal adj **seasonal**, equinoctial, fall *(US)* *Opposite*: spring

auxiliary adj **supplementary**, secondary, support, supporting, assisting *Opposite*: main

avail n **benefit**, advantage, reward, gain, purpose

availability n **obtainability**, handiness, convenience, readiness, accessibility *Opposite*: unavailability

available adj **obtainable**, accessible, on hand, to be had, existing *Opposite*: unavailable

avail yourself v **make use of**, use, benefit from, take, help yourself to

avalanche n **1 snow slip**, fall, slide **2 quantity**, increase, mass, flood, shower

avant-garde adj **new**, modern, experimental, unconventional, innovative *Opposite*: traditional

avarice n greed, greediness, materialism, covetousness, acquisitiveness *Opposite*: generosity

avaricious adj **greedy**, rapacious, grasping, acquisitive, covetous *Opposite*: generous

avariciousness *see* avarice

avenge v **retaliate**, punish, even the score, take vengeance, get even

avenger n **punisher**, retaliator, nemesis *(literary)*

avenue n **opportunity**, possibility, way, chance, opening

aver *(fml)* v **affirm**, state, claim, declare, assert *Opposite*: refute

average n **mean**, arithmetic mean, mode, median, norm ■ adj **regular**, normal, usual, typical, middling *Opposite*: extraordinary ■ v **be around**, be in the region of, be more or less, be close to

average down v **round down**, level down, bring down, lower, decrease

averagely adv **1 on average**, normally, typically, standardly, commonly *Opposite*: exceptionally **2 passably**, tolerably, adequately, unspectacularly, indifferently *Opposite*: exceptionally

average out v **equalize**, level out, balance out, even out

average up v **round up**, level up, bring up, raise, increase

averse *(fml)* adj **opposed**, antagonistic, loath, unenthusiastic, ill-disposed *Opposite*: favourable

aversion n **dislike**, hatred, loathing, repugnance, distaste *Opposite*: liking. *See* COMPARE AND CONTRAST *at* dislike.

avert v **1 prevent**, stop, ward off, avoid, forestall **2 turn away**, turn from, turn aside, divert, deflect

aviary n **birdcage**, coop, chicken coop, chicken run, hen house

aviation n **flying**, flight, aeronautics, air travel

aviator n **pilot**, flier, aeronaut, copilot

avid adj **keen**, enthusiastic, passionate, eager, devoted *Opposite*: indifference

avidity n **greed**, eagerness, voracity, covetousness, greediness *Opposite*: indifference

avidly adv **keenly**, enthusiastically, passionately, eagerly, devotedly *Opposite*: indifferently

avocation *(fml)* n **1 occupation**, job, vocation, calling, profession **2 hobby**, pastime, diversion, amusement, sport

avoid v **1 keep away**, stay away from, shun, steer clear, let alone **2 evade**, circumvent, get round, get out of, dodge *Opposite*: face **3 prevent**, forestall, avert, preclude *(fml)* *Opposite*: promote

avoidable adj **preventable**, unnecessary, needless, stoppable *Opposite*: inevitable

avoidance n **1 evasion**, escaping, evading, dodging, circumvention **2 prevention**, antici-pation, averting, forestalling, annulment *Opposite*: promotion **3 abstention**, refraining, refrainment, holding off, eschewal *Opposite*: indulgence

avow *(fml)* v **affirm**, state, declare, acknowledge, admit *Opposite*: deny

avowal *(fml)* n **affirmation**, statement, confirmation, declaration, acknowledgment *Opposite*: denial

avowed *(fml)* adj **affirmed**, stated, confirmed, declared, acknowledged *Opposite*: unspoken

avowedly *(fml)* adv **admittedly**, by your own admission, openly, self-confessedly, frankly

avuncular adj **kindly**, kind, kind-hearted, benign, friendly *Opposite*: unkindly

await v **1 lie in wait for**, wait on, expect, look forward to, look out for **2 lie ahead**, be in store, be to come, loom, near

awaited adj **anticipated**, expected, presumed, waited for *Opposite*: unexpected

awake adj **wide-awake**, conscious, wakeful, up, up and about *Opposite*: asleep

awaken v **1 wake**, wake up, rouse, get up, stir **2 rouse**, arouse, set off, stir, promote *Opposite*: suppress

awakening adj **developing**, growing, emerging, emergent, new ■ n **1 arousal**, wakening, emergence, stirring **2 awareness**, attention, recognition, realization, revival

award n **1 prize**, honour, reward, gift, grant **2 verdict**, decision, determination, judgment, settlement ■ v **give**, present, grant, endow, bestow *(fml)*

aware adj **1 conscious**, mindful, alert, attentive, responsive *Opposite*: oblivious **2 knowledgeable**, interested, concerned, informed, experienced *Opposite*: ignorant

---

COMPARE AND CONTRAST CORE MEANING: having knowledge of the existence of something
aware knowing something either intellectually or intuitively; **conscious** keenly aware of something and regarding it as important; **mindful** actively attentive, or deliberately keeping something in mind; **cognizant** *(fml)* having special knowledge about something; **sensible** *(fml)* keenly aware of something.

---

awareness n **1 consciousness**, mindfulness, alertness, responsiveness, attentiveness *Opposite*: oblivion **2 knowledge**, understanding, grasp, appreciation, familiarity *Opposite*: ignorance

awash adj **1 soaked**, flooded, drenched, waterlogged, saturated *Opposite*: dry **2 oversupplied**, full of, overflowing, packed, crammed *Opposite*: lacking

away adj **absent**, gone, left, missing, not here *Opposite*: present

awe n **1 wonder**, admiration, respect, amazement, surprise **2 fear**, terror, dread, fright, trepidation

awe-inspiring *adj* **overwhelming**, grand, breathtaking, splendid, tremendous

awesome *see* **awe-inspiring**

awestricken *see* **awestruck**

awestruck *adj* **impressed**, overwhelmed, stunned, enthralled, rapt *Opposite*: unimpressed

awful *adj* **dreadful**, terrible, appalling, unpleasant, horrible *Opposite*: wonderful

awfully *adv* **1 extremely**, very, really, terrifically, terribly **2 badly**, unpleasantly, dreadfully, terribly, appallingly *Opposite*: well

awfulness *n* **dreadfulness**, horror, misery, unpleasantness, terribleness

awkward *adj* **1 embarrassing**, tricky, problematic, difficult, thorny *Opposite*: straightforward **2 uncooperative**, difficult, stubborn, obstinate, obdurate *Opposite*: cooperative **3 unwieldy**, cumbersome, bulky *Opposite*: compact **4 clumsy**, inelegant, graceless, uncoordinated, ungainly *Opposite*: graceful **5 uncomfortable**, embarrassed, out of your depth, tongue-tied, self-conscious *Opposite*: comfortable

awkwardly *adv* **1 uncomfortably**, uneasily, with embarrassment, self-consciously, gauchely *Opposite*: comfortably **2 clumsily**, inelegantly, gracelessly, cumbersomely, gawkily (*infml*) *Opposite*: easily

awkwardness *n* **1 discomfort**, unease, embarrassment, uneasiness, self-consciousness *Opposite*: ease **2 clumsiness**, ineptness, inelegance, gracelessness, ungainliness *Opposite*: ease

awning *n* **canopy**, sunshade, sun shelter, blind

AWOL *adj* **absent without leave**, absent, missing, deserting, wanted *Opposite*: present

awry *adj* **1 crooked**, askew, skewed, off beam, out of kilter *Opposite*: straight **2 amiss**, wrong, muddled, incorrect, astray *Opposite*: right

axe *v* **1** (*infml*) **dismiss**, make redundant, let go, lay off, fire (*infml*) *Opposite*: employ **2 cut**, cut back, scale down, slim down, downsize

axiom *n* **maxim**, adage, saying, saw, proverb

axiomatic *adj* **self-evident**, goes without saying, obvious, manifest, clear

axis *n* **alliance**, partnership, bloc, league, federation

B

babble *v* **gabble**, mutter, prattle, chatter, blather (*infml*) ■ *n* **hum**, buzz, hubbub, drone, murmur

baby *n* **infant**, child, newborn, babe in arms, little one ■ *v* **pamper**, coddle, mollycoddle, cosset, overprotect

baby-faced *adj* **youthful**, boyish, girlish, childlike, wide-eyed *Opposite*: wizened

babyhood *n* **infancy**, childhood, early years, youth

babyish *adj* **childish**, infantile, immature, puerile, adolescent *Opposite*: mature

babysit *v* **look after**, child mind, protect, watch, mind

babysitter *n* **child minder**, minder, carer, sitter, childcare provider

bachelor *n* **unmarried man**, single man, eligible male, unattached man, confirmed bachelor

back *n* **backbone**, spine, spinal column, vertebral column, vertebrae ■ *adv* **behind**, to the rear, backwards, rearward *Opposite*: forwards ■ *v* **1 support**, provide for, finance, fund, help **2 go backwards**, reverse, move backwards, recede, back up *Opposite*: proceed

backache *n* **back pain**, back trouble, bad back, lumbago, sciatica

back away *v* **recoil**, shrink, draw back, shy away, back off *Opposite*: stay

backbiting *n* **spitefulness**, backstabbing, scandalmongering, cattiness, maliciousness

backbone *n* **1 spine**, spinal column, vertebral column, back, vertebrae **2 mainstay**, support, prop, spine, pillar **3 moral fibre**, strength of character, stamina, fortitude, courage

backbreaking *adj* **strenuous**, arduous, gruelling, exhausting, taxing *Opposite*: easy

backchat (*infml*) *n* **rudeness**, impudence, impertinence, disrespect, cheekiness *Opposite*: respect

backcloth *n* **backdrop**, scenery, set, stage set, background

backcomb *v* **brush**, comb, style, coif (*fml*), tease (*US*)

back down *v* **withdraw**, concede defeat, accept defeat, yield, admit defeat *Opposite*: stand your ground

backdrop *n* **1 backcloth**, scenery, set, stage set, scene **2 background**, setting, milieu, environment, framework

backer *n* **1 sponsor**, patron, guarantor, benefactor, angel **2 supporter**, promoter, champion, advocate, ally

COMPARE AND CONTRAST CORE MEANING: somebody who provides financial support

backer a person who gives moral or financial support; **angel** a person who provides financial support for an enterprise, e.g. a theatrical venture; **guarantor** a person who gives a legal undertaking to be responsible for somebody else's debts or obligations; **patron** a person who gives financial or moral support to a person, institution, or charity, especially in the arts; **sponsor** a person or organization that contributes money to help fund an event, usually in return for publicity, or gives money to a person taking part in a fundraising activity.

backfire v **go wrong**, boomerang, miscarry, fail, not go as planned

background n **1 upbringing**, circumstances, personal history, family, experience **2 backdrop**, setting, milieu, environment, surroundings *Opposite*: foreground

backhanded adj **indirect**, doubtful, oblique, insincere, snide

backhander (infml) n **bribe**, kickback, incentive, sweetener (infml), rake-off (infml)

backing n **support**, help, assistance, sponsorship, patronage

backlash n **reaction**, repercussion, counterattack, criticism, hostile response

backlog n **accumulation**, buildup, excess, surfeit, logjam

back off v **1 retreat**, pull back, move away, go backwards, recoil *Opposite*: advance **2 yield**, withdraw, admit you were wrong, backpedal, take back *Opposite*: insist

back out v **pull out**, withdraw, renege, go back on, cancel *Opposite*: continue

backpack n **rucksack**, knapsack, pack, bag, haversack

backpacker n **traveller**, hiker, walker, tourist, hitchhiker

back pain n **backache**, lumbago, back trouble, bad back, sciatica

backpedal v **backtrack**, back down, shift ground, go back on your word, recant

backroom adj **unobtrusive**, clandestine, secret, private, secretive *Opposite*: public

backside (infml) n **buttocks**, rump, behind, bottom, rear (infml)

backslide v **relapse**, go back to your old ways, lapse, revert, regress

backslider n **recidivist**, defaulter, transgressor, apostate, deserter

backstage adv **offstage**, behind the scenes, in the wings, in private, in secret

backstreet n **alley**, back alley, lane, side street *Opposite*: thoroughfare

back-to-back adj **consecutive**, end-to-end, nonstop, continuous, uninterrupted

backtrack v **1 retrace your steps**, go back over the same ground, turn back, begin again *Opposite*: move on **2 backpedal**, go into reverse, do a volte-face, do an about-turn, do a U-turn

back up v **1 corroborate**, substantiate, authenticate, vouch for, reinforce *Opposite*: contradict **2 copy**, duplicate, make a backup, keep a backup, keep a copy **3 move backwards**, reverse, go backwards, recede *Opposite*: advance

backup n **1 support**, encouragement, help, moral support, assistance **2 stand-by**, reserve, substitute, replacement, reinforcement **3 copy**, duplicate, replica, substitute, fill-in

backward adj **1 rearward**, to the rear, towards the back *Opposite*: forward **2 retrograde**, regressive, recessive *Opposite*: progressive **3 shy**, diffident, hesitant, reluctant, timid *Opposite*: confident

backward-looking adj **retrospective**, nostalgic, retrograde, traditional, conservative *Opposite*: forward-looking

backwards adv **1 towards the back**, back, rearward, towards the rear *Opposite*: forwards **2 the wrong way**, in reverse, back to front, the wrong way round

backwater n **backwoods**, the back of beyond, the middle of nowhere, sticks (infml), boondocks (US infml)

backwoods n **1 wilderness**, wilds, rough country, back country (US) **2 the middle of nowhere**, backwater, the back of beyond, sticks (infml), boondocks (US infml)

back yard n **courtyard**, patio, yard, terrace, porch

bacterial adj **microbial**, bacteriological, infective, infectious, contagious

bacteriological adj **microbiological**, biological, bacterial, pathological

bad adj **1 poor**, inferior, deficient, flawed, faulty *Opposite*: good **2 evil**, wicked, corrupt, immoral, depraved *Opposite*: good **3 naughty**, disobedient, troublesome, wayward, mischievous *Opposite*: good **4 harmful**, damaging, injurious, ruinous, dangerous *Opposite*: good **5 rotten**, off, decayed, decaying, decomposing *Opposite*: fresh **6 regretful**, penitent, remorseful, ashamed, apologetic *Opposite*: good **7 awful**, terrible, dreadful, appalling, shocking *Opposite*: good **8 adverse**, difficult, unhappy, testing, unpleasant *Opposite*: good **9 serious**, severe, grave, critical, life-threatening *Opposite*: slight

COMPARE AND CONTRAST CORE MEANING: indicating wrongdoing
bad applies to a whole range of wrongdoing from the most trivial to the most immoral or evil; **criminal** punishable as a crime under the law; **delinquent** antisocial or unlawful, or (fml) neglecting a duty, commitment, or responsibility; **mischievous** playfully naughty or troublesome, or (fml) causing or meant to cause serious trouble, damage, or hurt; **naughty** badly behaved or disobedient, or (infml) mildly indecent or sinful.

bad blood n **bad feeling**, ill feeling, bitterness, acrimony, antagonism *Opposite*: affection

baddie (infml) n **bad character**, rogue, villain, scoundrel, outlaw *Opposite*: hero

bad feeling n **spite**, rancour, spitefulness, bad blood, bitterness *Opposite*: affection

badge n **1 brooch**, pin, clasp **2 insignia**, emblem, symbol, mark, device

badger v **pester**, press, harass, plague, harry

bad habit n **weakness**, failing, flaw, character defect, vice *Opposite*: virtue

badinage n **banter**, repartee, teasing, joking, mockery

bad language n **swearing**, swearwords, vulgar language, profanities, coarse language

bad luck n **misfortune**, hard luck, ill luck, unluckiness, ill fortune *Opposite*: luck

badly adv **1 poorly**, deficiently, faultily, defectively, imperfectly *Opposite*: well **2 seriously**, severely, gravely, critically, desperately *Opposite*: slightly **3 naughtily**, disobediently, troublesomely, waywardly, mischievously

bad-mannered adj **rude**, ill-mannered, impolite, charmless, discourteous *Opposite*: well-mannered

bad manners n **rudeness**, impoliteness, incivility, discourtesy, discourteousness *Opposite*: courtesy

bad mood n **bad humour**, sulk, huff, bad temper, temper

badness n **evilness**, wickedness, immorality, evil, depravity *Opposite*: goodness

bad taste n **tastelessness**, vulgarity, showiness, crassness, crudeness *Opposite*: good taste

bad temper n **irritability**, petulance, sulkiness, ill temper, bad mood

bad-tempered adj **cross**, ill-tempered, ill-humoured, irascible, short-tempered *Opposite*: good-tempered

baffle v **confuse**, perplex, puzzle, stump, nonplus

baffled adj **puzzled**, perplexed, mystified, lost, stumped

bafflement n **bewilderment**, perplexity, confusion, puzzlement, bemusement *Opposite*: understanding

baffling adj **puzzling**, perplexing, mystifying, confusing, bewildering *Opposite*: obvious

bag n **container**, receptacle, sack, paper bag, plastic bag ■ v **1 take possession of**, grab, occupy, reserve, keep **2 catch**, shoot, snare, take, capture

WORD BANK
❏ **types of bag** bum bag, carrier, carrier bag, clutch bag, handbag, mailbag, nosebag, pocketbook, postbag, pouch, purse, reticule, satchel, shopper, shopping bag, shopping basket, shoulder bag, sporran, tote bag

bagatelle *(fml)* n **trifle**, trifling sum, nothing, a drop in the ocean, thing of no importance

baggage n **luggage**, bags, suitcases, cases, belongings

WORD BANK
❏ **types of baggage** attaché case, backpack, briefcase, carrycase, case, duffel bag, flight bag, haversack, holdall, kitbag, knapsack, luggage, overnight bag, pack, portmanteau, rucksack, suitcase, travel case, valise, vanity case, weekend bag

bagginess n **looseness**, formlessness, shapelessness, roominess, floppiness *Opposite*: tightness

baggy adj **loose**, loose-fitting, slack, shapeless, saggy *Opposite*: tight

bags n **luggage**, baggage, belongings, personal belongings, gear *(infml)*

bags of *(infml)* n **lots**, plenty, masses *(infml)*, loads *(infml)*, heaps *(infml)*

bail n **security**, surety, payment, financial guarantee, bond

bailiff n **1 steward**, agent, factor, estate manager, overseer **2 sheriff's officer**, law officer, legal officer, dispossessor, evictor

bail out v **1 stand surety**, obtain somebody's release, put up bail **2 escape**, run away, desert, flee, evacuate *Opposite*: stick out **3 help**, rescue, save, assist, aid

bait n **lure**, attraction, enticement, temptation, inducement ■ v **1 entice**, lure, tempt, attract, draw **2 taunt**, tease, torment, harass, provoke

bake v **1 cook**, heat, harden, dry out **2** *(infml)* **swelter**, overheat, scorch, burn, roast *Opposite*: freeze

baking adj **sweltering**, boiling, blazing, burning, blistering *Opposite*: freezing

baksheesh n **bribe**, handout, tip, gift, token

balance n **1 equilibrium**, poise, sense of balance, stability, steadiness *Opposite*: unsteadiness **2 weighing machine**, weighing scales, set of scales **3 remainder**, surplus, rest, what's left, residue ■ v **1 maintain equilibrium**, stay poised, keep upright, keep steady, poise *Opposite*: wobble **2 assess**, weigh up, weigh, consider, compare **3 equalize**, square, settle, even out, offset *Opposite*: weight

balanced adj **1 fair**, impartial, unbiased, unprejudiced, disinterested *Opposite*: biased **2 stable**, composed, well-adjusted, sensible, sane *Opposite*: unbalanced

balance out v **even out**, offset, compensate, make up, redress the balance *Opposite*: weight

balcony n **1 veranda**, terrace, loggia, lanai, gallery **2 circle**, upper circle, gallery, upper tier, the gods *(infml)*

bald adj **1 hairless**, balding, receding, thin on top, baldheaded *Opposite*: hirsute **2 bare**, worn, threadbare, smooth, patchy **3 plain**, blunt, frank, direct, straightforward *Opposite*: florid

balderdash n **rubbish**, nonsense, garbage, drivel, baloney *(infml)*

baldheaded adj **bald**, hairless, balding, receding, thin on top *Opposite*: hirsute

balding adj **bald**, baldheaded, hairless, receding, thin on top *Opposite*: hirsute

baldly adv **bluntly**, plainly, flatly, frankly, directly

baldness n 1 **hairlessness**, hair loss, bald-headedness, lack of hair Opposite: hairiness 2 **bluntness**, plainness, frankness, directness, straightforwardness Opposite: deviousness

bale n **bundle**, package, pack, roll, block

baleful adj **threatening**, menacing, malevolent, sinister, malignant Opposite: benevolent

balk see **baulk**

ball n **sphere**, orb, globe, globule, blob

ballad n **poem**, song, narrative, folk song, traditional song

ballast n **weight**, bulk, makeweight, stabilizer, balance

ball cock n **regulator**, controller, control, device

ballistic adj **airborne**, air-to-air, surface-to-air, flying

balloon n **hot-air balloon**, helium balloon, inflatable, dirigible ■ v **swell**, distend, inflate, expand, puff out Opposite: deflate

ballot n **vote**, secret ballot, poll, election, survey ■ v **canvass**, consult, survey, poll, assess opinion

ballyhoo n **uproar**, hullabaloo, commotion, ruckus, to-do (infml)

balm n 1 **ointment**, unguent, salve, oil, cream Opposite: irritant 2 **comfort**, relief, solace, consolation, palliative

balmy adj **mild**, clement, pleasant, temperate, gentle Opposite: wintry

baloney (infml) n **drivel**, balderdash, nonsense, rubbish, garbage

baluster n **post**, support, leg, upright, pole

balustrade n **railing**, handrail, guardrail, rail, banister

bamboozle (infml) v 1 **cheat**, deceive, con, trick, hoodwink 2 **confuse**, bewilder, puzzle, bemuse, perplex

ban v **forbid**, outlaw, prohibit, veto, bar Opposite: allow ■ n **prohibition**, veto, bar, injunction, embargo

banal adj **commonplace**, hackneyed, prosaic, predictable, ordinary Opposite: original

banality n **triteness**, predictability, ordinariness, dullness, triviality Opposite: originality

band n 1 **group**, combo, ensemble 2 **gang**, crowd, mob, group, crew (infml) 3 **stripe**, strip, belt, stretch, range

---

WORD BANK

❑ **types of band** big band, brass band, chamber orchestra, choir, dance band, duo, ensemble, jazz band, mariachi, octet, orchestra, pipe band, pop group, quartet, quintet, septet, sextet, sinfonietta, steel band, string band, string quartet, symphony orchestra, trio

---

bandage n **dressing**, binding, strapping, compress ■ v **dress**, bind, tie up, cover, bind up

bandanna n **scarf**, neckerchief, headscarf, headsquare, kerchief

bandit n **outlaw**, robber, thief, thug, gangster

banditry n **robbery**, theft, thieving, raiding, armed robbery

bandstand n **platform**, pavilion, stand, shelter, podium

band together v **join up**, unite, associate, get together, combine

bandwagon n **movement**, cause, trend, craze, fashion

bandy v **exchange**, toss around, throw around, mention, debate ■ adj **outward-curving**, bowed, bent, warped, convex Opposite: straight

bandy-legged adj **bowlegged**, bent, bowed, bandy

bandy words with v **argue**, dispute, bicker, wrangle, spar

bane n **nuisance**, curse, blight, bother, irritation Opposite: blessing

bang n 1 **explosion**, boom, crash, knock, thud 2 **knock**, hit, bump, blow, thump ■ v 1 **hit**, knock, thump, hammer, pound 2 **bump**, collide, crash, jolt, knock

banger (infml) n **wreck**, rattletrap (infml), heap (slang), jalopy (dated infml)

banish v 1 **expel**, send away, exile, deport, evict 2 **get rid of**, remove, dismiss, eliminate, discard

banishment n **expulsion**, exile, deportation, eviction, exclusion

banister n **handrail**, balustrade, guardrail, bar, rail

bank n 1 **set**, row, tier, series, group 2 **store**, depository, reservoir, stock, collection 3 **side**, edge, margin, embankment, border 4 **pile**, heap, mound, stack, mass ■ v 1 **deposit**, pay in, cash in, put in Opposite: withdraw 2 **have an account**, save, deposit, invest 3 **heap**, pile, mound, stack, mass Opposite: disperse 4 **tilt**, pitch, turn, lean, veer Opposite: level off

bank account n **account**, current account, deposit account, loan account, joint account

banker n **banking executive**, investment banker, merchant banker, financier

banking n **investment**, lending, funding, financial transactions, online banking

banknote n **note**, paper money, folding money (infml), bill (US), dollar bill (US) Opposite: coin

bank on v **count on**, depend on, rely on, trust, have confidence in Opposite: doubt

bankroll (infml) v **finance**, fund, back, pay, sponsor

bankrupt adj **insolvent**, penniless, ruined, broke (infml), bust (infml) Opposite: solvent ■ v **ruin**, destroy, liquidate, impoverish, make destitute

bankruptcy n **insolvency**, ruin, liquidation, economic failure, impoverishment

banned adj 1 **barred**, disqualified, debarred,

excluded, expelled *Opposite*: admitted **2 forbidden**, proscribed, prohibited, illegal, illicit *Opposite*: permitted

banner *n* **sign**, poster, flag, placard, streamer

banquet *n* **feast**, dinner, meal, formal meal, ceremonial meal

banshee *n* **spirit**, supernatural being, ghost, ghoul, spectre

banter *n* **teasing**, mockery, joking, repartee, wit ■ *v* **tease**, mock, joke, poke fun at, make fun of

baptism *n* **initiation**, introduction, debut, beginning, induction

baptize *v* **christen**, bless, immerse, sprinkle, initiate

bar *n* **1 rod**, pole, stick, staff, shaft **2 block**, slab, piece, ingot **3 obstruction**, hindrance, block, barrier, impediment **4 hostelry**, drinking place, watering hole *(infml)* ■ *v* **1 secure**, fasten, bolt, lock, barricade **2 obstruct**, close off, hinder, get in the way, block **3 ban**, exclude, keep out, debar, prohibit *Opposite*: admit ■ *prep* **excluding**, save, except, with the exception of, apart from

WORD BANK
❏ **types of bar or club** bodega, casino, country club, joint *(slang)*, local *(infml)*, nightclub, nightspot, pub, roadhouse *(dated)*, saloon, shebeen, speakeasy, tavern *(archaic)*, wine bar

barb *n* **1 point**, hook, tip, spur, spike **2 gibe**, insult, dig, taunt, cutting remark

barbaric *adj* **cruel**, brutal, vicious, ferocious, fierce *Opposite*: gentle

barbarism *n* **cruelty**, brutality, savagery, viciousness, ferociousness *Opposite*: gentleness

barbarity *n* **1 cruelty**, brutality, savagery, viciousness, ferociousness *Opposite*: gentleness **2 atrocity**, cruelty, outrage, assault, abuse

barbarous *adj* **cruel**, brutal, vicious, ferocious, fierce *Opposite*: gentle

barbecue *v* **grill**, flame, chargrill, sear, cook on a spit

barbed *adj* **1 pointed**, hooked, spiky, spiny, thorny **2 snide**, pointed, cutting, unkind, hurtful

barber *n* **gents' hairdresser**, gents' hair stylist, hairdresser, hair stylist, coiffeur *(fml)*

barbican *n* **tower**, keep, stronghold, turret, fortification

bard *(literary)* *n* **poet**, versifier, composer, wordsmith, songster

bare *adj* **1 naked**, nude, exposed, uncovered, undressed *Opposite*: covered **2 empty**, vacant, blank, clean, clear *Opposite*: full **3 stark**, barren, austere, severe, hard *Opposite*: lush **4 simple**, unadorned, plain, basic, unembellished *Opposite*: ornate **5 mere**, scant, meagre, measly *(infml)* ■ *v* **expose**, reveal, display, show, uncover *Opposite*:

cover. *See* COMPARE AND CONTRAST *at* **naked**.

barefaced *adj* **brazen**, blatant, unashamed, obvious, unabashed

barefoot *adj* **unshod**, shoeless, barefooted

barely *adv* **hardly**, scarcely, only just, just about *Opposite*: easily

bareness *n* **emptiness**, nakedness, starkness, austerity, plainness

bargain *n* **1 good deal**, good buy, steal *(infml)*, snip *(infml)*, giveaway *(infml)* **2 deal**, agreement, accord, arrangement, pact ■ *v* **haggle**, barter, negotiate, make a deal, trade ■ *adj* **cheap**, low, reduced, inexpensive, rock-bottom

bargain-basement *adj* **cheap**, cut-price, low-priced, reduced-price, bargain

bargain for *v* **expect**, count on, take into account, depend on, reckon with

bargain on *see* **bargain for**

barge *v* **rush**, push, elbow, burst, surge

barge in *v* **1 walk in**, storm in, push in, rush in, breeze in **2 interrupt**, butt in, cut in, break in, interject

barge into *v* **bump into**, collide with, clash with, smash into, knock into

bark *v* **howl**, yap, growl, yowl, snarl

barmy *(infml)* *adj* **irrational**, crazy *(infml)*, silly, batty *(infml)*, crackers *(infml)* *Opposite*: rational

barn *n* **outbuilding**, outhouse, shed, cowshed, byre

barney *(infml)* *n* **argument**, spat, row, quarrel, tiff

barnyard *n* **farmyard**, yard, court, forecourt

barometer *n* **weatherglass**, indicator, gauge, aneroid barometer, barograph

barometric *adj* **atmospheric**, air, meteorological

baron *n* **tycoon**, magnate, mogul, industrialist, captain of industry

baronial *adj* **grand**, impressive, opulent, stately, imposing *Opposite*: humble

baroque *adj* **1 ornate**, ornamental, decorative, elaborate, exaggerated *Opposite*: plain **2 flamboyant**, exaggerated, overdone, over-the-top *(infml)* *Opposite*: restrained

barrack *(infml)* *v* **heckle**, shout, interrupt, jeer

barracks *n* **quarters**, garrison, station, billet

barrage *n* **1 bombardment**, salvo, volley, fusillade **2 onslaught**, outpouring, hail, storm, flood *Opposite*: trickle **3 dam**, dike, bank, embankment

barred *adj* **1 striped**, banded, lined, stripy, streaked **2 grilled**, meshed, fenced, secure, solid **3 banned**, excluded, disqualified, debarred, not allowed *Opposite*: admitted

barrel *n* **tub**, cask, vat, butt, water butt

barren *adj* **1 desolate**, bleak, inhospitable, stark, harsh **2 infertile**, unproductive, sterile, unfruitful *Opposite*: fertile

barrenness n 1 **emptiness**, bleakness, bareness, loneliness, inhospitableness 2 **infertility**, sterility, unfruitfulness, unproductiveness *Opposite*: fertility

barricade n **blockade**, barrier, cordon, obstruction, fortification ■ v **secure**, obstruct, bar, fortify, block

barrier n 1 **obstacle**, difficulty, stumbling block, sticking point, impediment 2 **fence**, wall, barricade, blockade, block

barring prep **except for**, without, excluding, apart from

barrister n **lawyer**, attorney, counsellor, advocate, defender

barrow n 1 **cart**, handcart, stall, fruit stall, pushcart (US) 2 **wheelbarrow**, trolley, transporter, trailer, truck 3 **burial mound**, mound, tumulus, long barrow, tomb

barter v **exchange**, trade, switch, negotiate, bargain

base n 1 **foundation**, support, stand, pedestal, rest 2 **source**, origin, heart, starting point, root 3 **headquarters**, centre, main office, seat, station ■ v **found**, ground, build, create, construct ■ adj **dishonourable**, sordid, disreputable, squalid, immoral *Opposite*: honourable

baseless adj **unfounded**, untrue, unjustified, unsubstantiated, groundless *Opposite*: well-founded

baseline n 1 **starting point**, point of departure, reference point, reference line, starting position 2 **standard**, model, criterion, starting point, quality check 3 **reference**, control, check, set of data, set of values 4 **boundary**, boundary line, line, periphery, white line

basement n **cellar**, vault, crypt, lower ground floor *Opposite*: attic

baseness n **wickedness**, sordidness, vileness, immorality, ignobility *Opposite*: nobility

bash v 1 **thump**, punch, smash, whack, clout 2 **criticize**, condemn, find fault with, attack, knock ■ n 1 **punch**, hit, blow, thump, knock 2 **dent**, bump, smash, knock, prang (infml) 3 (infml) **attempt**, try, go, stab (infml), whirl (infml) 4 (infml) **party**, celebration, dance, ball, gala

bashful adj **shy**, timid, reserved, retiring, self-conscious *Opposite*: bold

bashfulness n **shyness**, modesty, self-consciousness, quietness, coyness *Opposite*: boldness

basic adj 1 **essential**, central, key, principal, main *Opposite*: trivial 2 **rudimentary**, straightforward, elementary, undeveloped, uncomplicated *Opposite*: complex

basics n **fundamentals**, essentials, necessities, nitty-gritty (infml), nuts and bolts (infml)

basin n 1 **sink**, hand basin, washbasin, washbowl 2 **bowl**, mixing bowl, dish

basis n **foundation**, base, root, source, starting point

bask v 1 **laze around**, lie, recline, lounge, stretch out 2 **enjoy**, savour, relish, soak up, luxuriate

basket n **carrier**, bag, hamper, picnic basket, linen basket

WORD BANK
❏ **types of basket** breadbasket, creel, hamper, laundry basket, linen basket, Moses basket, picnic basket, shopping basket, wicker basket

bas-relief n **moulding**, relief, basso-relievo, panelling, carving

bass adj **deep**, deep-toned, deep-voiced, low-pitched *Opposite*: high

baste v 1 **moisten**, drizzle, grease, cover, saturate 2 **thrash**, thump, clobber (infml), bash (infml), beat up (infml) 3 **sew**, stitch, tack, hem, seam

bastion n 1 **stronghold**, fortification, rampart, defence, bulwark 2 **mainstay**, support, defender, upholder, supporter

bat n 1 **racket**, paddle, willow, club 2 **batter**, player, batsman, batswoman, cricketer ■ v **flutter**, wink, flicker, flap, blink

batch n **lot**, consignment, group, set, bunch

bath n 1 **bathtub**, tub, hip bath 2 **immersion**, soak, steam bath, bubble bath, bed bath 3 **tank**, basin, reservoir, container ■ v **soak**, immerse yourself, have a bath, take a bath, wash

bathe v 1 **swim**, go for a dip, paddle 2 **immerse**, dip, soak, rinse, dunk

bather n **swimmer**, diver, snorkeller, paddler, skinny-dipper (infml)

bathetic adj 1 **anticlimactic**, disappointing, unsatisfying 2 **trite**, sentimental, unsatisfying, commonplace

bathos n **anticlimax**, letdown, comedown (infml)

baths n 1 **bathhouse**, Turkish bath, steam bath, sauna 2 **swimming pool**, pool, swimming baths

baton n **stick**, rod, wand, cane, pointer

batsman *see* **batter**

batswoman *see* **batter**

battalion n **throng**, crowd, mass, multitude, horde

batten v **fasten**, fix, close, secure, batten down *Opposite*: open

batter v 1 **pound**, bang, thump, thrash, hit 2 **assault**, maim, brutalize, attack, abuse ■ n **player**, bat, cricketer, batsman, batswoman

battered adj 1 **maltreated**, assaulted, abused, beaten, injured 2 **tattered**, tatty, decrepit, worn out, weather-beaten *Opposite*: pristine

battering n **pounding**, buffeting, hammering, beating, lashing

battery n **series**, set, sequence, succession, run

battle n 1 **fight**, clash, encounter, skirmish, engagement 2 **struggle**, crusade, fight, war, campaign ■ v 1 **fight**, go to war, attack, come to blows, engage **2 struggle**, wrestle, contend, fight, strive. *See* COMPARE AND CONTRAST *at* **fight**.

battleaxe *n* axe, hatchet, tomahawk, halberd

battle cry *n* whoop, war cry, yell, shout, cry

battlefield *n* **battleground**, combat zone, arena, theatre of war, front line

battleground *see* **battlefield**

battlements *n* ramparts, fortifications, walls, parapet, bulwark

batty *(infml) adj* irrational, eccentric, crazy *(infml)*, potty *(infml)*, barmy *(infml)* Opposite: rational

bauble *n* trinket, trifle, gewgaw, decoration, ornament

baulk *v* **1** recoil, draw back, hesitate, pull back Opposite: leap at **2 stop short**, pull up short, rein in

bawdy *adj* ribald, earthy, risqué, suggestive, indecent

bawl *v* **1 shout**, yell, roar, shriek, screech Opposite: whisper **2** *(infml)* **cry**, howl, wail, sob, weep

bawl out *(infml) v* **tell off** *(infml)*, haul over the coals, read the riot act to, take to task, give a talking-to *(infml)*

bay *n* **1** inlet, cove, natural harbour, haven *(literary)*, anchorage **2 compartment**, alcove, cubicle, recess, loading bay ■ *v* **woof**, bark, yap, yelp, howl

bay for *v* demand, insist on, be out for, cry for, shout for

bayonet *n* blade, knife, dagger, lance, spike ■ *v* stab, spear, impale, spike, knife

bazaar *n* **market**, marketplace, souk, open market, flea market

be *v* **1** exist, live, have being, be present, coexist **2 take place**, happen, occur, transpire, come about **3 be situated**, be located, remain, be there, be present

beach *n* seashore, seaside, coast, shore, coastline

beachcomber *n* scavenger, forager, explorer, collector, hoarder

beached *adj* stranded, aground, stuck, high and dry, run aground Opposite: afloat

beachhead *n* strategic position, foothold, base, position, foot in the door

beachwear *n* swimwear, leisurewear, sportswear

WORD BANK

❏ **types of beachwear** bathing costume *(dated)*, bathing trunks, bikini, cover-up, one-piece, swimming costume, swimming trunks, swimsuit, tankini, trunks, two-piece

beacon *n* **1 signal**, sign, alarm, warning, flare **2 bonfire**, fire, flare **3** *(literary)* **inspiration**, guiding light, encouragement, example, shining example

bead *n* drop, droplet, drip, blob, globule

beaded *adj* **1 decorated**, ornate, bead-trimmed, encrusted, sequinned **2 wet**, moist, dripping, soaked, drenched

beading *n* edging, border, trim, detail, moulding

beady *adj* **1 small**, round, shiny, bright, shining **2 beaded**, decorated, ornate, bead-trimmed, sequinned **3** *(infml)* **watchful**, unblinking, piercing, attentive, bright

beaked *adj* hooked, aquiline, Roman

beaker *n* cup, glass, mug, paper cup, plastic cup

beam *n* **1 girder**, rafter, joist, RSJ, timber **2 ray**, shaft of light, sunbeam, stream of light **3 smile**, grin, wide smile, big smile Opposite: scowl ■ *v* **1 smile**, grin, look happy Opposite: scowl **2 shine**, radiate, emit, send out, glow

beaming *adj* smiling, cheery, cheerful, sunny, genial Opposite: scowling

beanpole *n* support, stick, pole, post, cane

bear *v* **1 tolerate**, stand, put up with, stomach, accept **2 support**, take, stand, sustain, hold **3 assume**, accept, shoulder, carry, take **4 show**, display, exhibit, present, evince **5 carry**, convey, bring, take, transport **6 produce**, develop, yield, give birth to, bring forth

bearable *adj* manageable, tolerable, endurable, acceptable, sufferable Opposite: unbearable

bear a grudge *v* resent, begrudge, feel bitter about, have hard feelings about, feel aggrieved

beard *n* facial hair, whiskers, goatee, bush, stubble ■ *v* challenge, confront, accost, stand up to, face up to

bearded *adj* unshaven, hirsute, hairy, whiskery, bewhiskered Opposite: clean-shaven

bear down on *v* **1 advance on**, close in on, converge on, march on, charge Opposite: retreat **2 push down**, press down, thrust, press, lean on

bearer *n* **1 carrier**, bringer, deliverer, conveyor, transporter **2 holder**, possessor, owner, keeper, custodian

bear false witness *v* commit perjury, lie, equivocate, stretch the truth

bear fruit *v* succeed, be successful, show results, produce results, pay off Opposite: fail

bear hug *n* embrace, hug, cuddle, clinch, squeeze

bearing *n* **1 influence**, effect, impact, connection, relevance **2 manner**, behaviour, attitude, deportment, demeanour **3 compass reading**, direction, course, orientation, point of reference

bear in mind *v* remember, keep in mind, think of, consider, take into consideration Opposite: forget

bear out v **support**, verify, prove, substantiate, corroborate Opposite: undermine

bear the brunt v **receive the impact**, take the strain, receive the full force, bear the burden, bear the responsibility

bear up v **hold up**, hold out, cope, manage, get along Opposite: give in

bear with v **be patient with**, put up with, make allowance for, show forbearance, bear

beast n **1 creature**, animal, being, living thing, quadruped **2 monster**, fiend, ogre, animal, brute (literary)

beat v **1 defeat**, overcome, overwhelm, thrash, trounce **2 hit**, strike, bang, hammer, thump **3 throb**, palpitate, thump, pound, pulsate **4 whisk**, whip, blend, mix, combine **5 surpass**, break, smash, do better than, go one better than ■ n **1 stroke**, blow, hit, bang, thump **2 rhythm**, pulse, pulsation, throb, thump ■ adj (infml) **tired**, tired out, worn out, weary, exhausted Opposite: fresh. See COMPARE AND CONTRAST at defeat.

beat a hasty retreat v **depart**, leave, make off, run away, make a run for it

beat around the bush v **digress**, ramble, waffle, rabbit, bumble

beaten adj **1 compressed**, packed down, trodden, flattened, crushed **2 defeated**, conquered, crushed, vanquished

beaten-up adj **scruffy**, battered, tatty, tattered, worn out Opposite: pristine

beater n **whisk**, blade, attachment, paddle, stick

beatification n **sanctification**, canonization, sainting, elevation, blessing

beatify v **sanctify**, bless, consecrate, canonize, saint

beating n **1 thrashing**, whipping, thumping, pounding, hiding (infml) **2 defeat**, setback, thrashing, trouncing, pasting (infml)

beat it (infml) v **go away**, leave, be off, head off, clear off (infml) Opposite: stay

beat up (infml) v **attack**, assault, batter, mug, injure

beat-up (infml) adj **battered**, tattered, tatty, dilapidated, decrepit Opposite: pristine

beau n **1** (dated) **boyfriend**, admirer, steady (infml), suitor (fml), squire (dated) **2** (archaic) **fop**, peacock, poseur, dandy (infml), swell (dated infml)

beautification n **enhancement**, sprucing up, prettification, embellishment, improvement

beautiful adj **1 good-looking**, lovely, gorgeous, stunning, striking Opposite: ugly **2 lovely**, picturesque, scenic, delightful, charming Opposite: unattractive. See COMPARE AND CONTRAST at good-looking.

beautifully adv **1 attractively**, gorgeously, stunningly, handsomely, prettily Opposite: unattractively **2 well**, excellently, superbly, brilliantly, magnificently Opposite: poorly

beautify v **prettify**, smarten, enhance, remodel, spruce up

beauty n **1 loveliness**, attractiveness, good looks, prettiness, exquisiteness Opposite: unattractiveness **2 advantage**, attraction, benefit, upside, plus (infml) Opposite: drawback

beauty salon n **salon**, hair salon, beautician's

beaver (infml) v **work**, labour, toil, exert yourself, keep at Opposite: idle

becalmed adj **stuck**, at a standstill, stationary, at a halt, marooned Opposite: moving

because conj **since**, as, for

because of prep **owing to**, on account of, as a consequence of, due to, as a result of Opposite: despite

beck n **stream**, rivulet, burn, brook (literary)

beckon v **signal**, sign, summon, gesture, indicate Opposite: dismiss

become v **1 turn out to be**, turn into, develop, convert, grow into **2 suit**, befit, flatter, enhance, show off

become acquainted v **meet**, meet for the first time, be introduced to, make the acquaintance of, get to know

become aware of v **notice**, detect, discern, make out, sense Opposite: miss

become of v **happen to**, occur, be the outcome of, befall (literary)

becoming adj **1 flattering**, attractive, fetching, charming, pretty Opposite: unattractive **2 suitable**, appropriate, apt, fitting, befitting Opposite: inappropriate

bed n **1 plot**, flowerbed, patch, border **2 layer**, band, base, strip, seam **3 bottom**, floor, base, seabed, riverbed

---

WORD BANK

❑ **types of bed** bassinet, berth, bunk, bunk bed, camp bed, carrycot, cot, couchette, cradle, day bed, divan, double bed, four-poster, futon, hammock, king-size bed, Moses basket, queen-size bed, single bed, sofa bed, studio couch, trundle bed, twin bed, water bed

---

bedazzle (literary) v **amaze**, stun, impress, bewilder, daze

bedding n **bedclothes**, bedcovers, bed linen, covers

bedevil v **beset**, assail, torment, harass, trouble

bedlam n **chaos**, pandemonium, confusion, anarchy, disorder Opposite: order

bed linen see bedding

bedpan n **chamber pot**, pot, potty, commode

bedraggled adj **unkempt**, dishevelled, untidy, messy, scruffy Opposite: neat

bedridden adj **confined to bed**, flat on your back, laid up, incapacitated, disabled Opposite: active

bedrock n **1 rock layer**, substratum, solid rock,

base, foundation **2 basis**, base, core, heart, root

bedroom n dormitory, sleeping quarters, boudoir, room, dorm (infml)

bedside manner n rapport, style, approach, relationship, conduct

bedsit n flat, studio flat, bedsitter, studio apartment, studio

bedsore n ulcer, pressure sore, ulceration, sore, bruise

bedspread n coverlet, cover, quilt, throw, eiderdown

bedstead n bed, frame, base

bedtime n time for bed, sleep time, time to turn in (infml), time to hit the hay (infml), time to hit the sack (infml)

beefiness n muscularity, sturdiness, burliness, brawniness, stockiness

beef up (infml) v strengthen, improve, enhance, boost, reinforce Opposite: weaken

beefy adj muscular, brawny, heavy, hefty, burly Opposite: puny

beehive n apiary, hive, skep

beep v toot, peep, parp, bleep, beep-beep

beeper (infml) n pager, bleeper, monitor

beermat n coaster, mat, rest, bar cloth

beet n sugar beet, beetroot, chard, Swiss chard

beetle 1 n insect, bug, creepy-crawly (infml) **2** v (infml) hurry, scurry, scuttle, scud, dart

WORD BANK

❏ **types of beetle** cockroach, Colorado beetle, deathwatch beetle, dung beetle, flea beetle, Japanese beetle, ladybird, rhinoceros beetle, roach (infml), scarab, stag beetle, water beetle, weevil

befit v suit, become, be fitting, be suitable for, be appropriate

befitting adj becoming, suitable, appropriate, apt, fitting Opposite: unsuitable

before prep **1** in front of, facing, ahead of Opposite: behind **2** previous to, earlier than, sooner than, prior to, ahead of Opposite: after ■ adv beforehand, previously, earlier, in advance, in the past Opposite: afterwards

beforehand adv earlier, in advance, before, early, ahead of time Opposite: late

befriend v make friends with, take care of, look after, help, assist Opposite: shun

befuddle v confuse, muddle, mix up, bewilder, baffle Opposite: enlighten

befuddled adj confused, muddled, baffled, puzzled, perplexed Opposite: clear-headed

befuddlement n confusion, perplexity, bewilderment, bafflement, puzzlement Opposite: clarity

beg v ask for, request, plead, solicit, entreat

beget v cause, bring about, precipitate, create, bring

beg forgiveness v apologize, make an apology, express regret, say sorry

beggar n vagrant, tramp, homeless person, rough sleeper, street dweller ■ v defy, be beyond, confound, surpass, exceed

begin v **1** start, start on, commence, start in on, set in motion Opposite: finish **2** bring into being, instigate, initiate, inaugurate, activate **3** start the ball rolling, get down to, get to, get under way, set off Opposite: end

beginner n novice, learner, trainee, apprentice, student Opposite: old hand

COMPARE AND CONTRAST CORE MEANING: a person who has not acquired the necessary experience or skills to do something

beginner somebody who has just started to learn or do something; **apprentice** somebody who is being taught the skills of a trade over an agreed period of time by somebody fully trained; **greenhorn** somebody who lacks experience and may be naive or gullible; **novice** somebody with no previous experience or skill in the activity undertaken; **tyro** somebody who is raw and inexperienced.

beginning n start, opening, launch, establishment, creation Opposite: end

beg off v back out, bow out, duck out, cry off (infml)

begrudge v resent, envy, be envious, be jealous, be resentful

beg to differ v disagree, take issue with, demur, dissent, object Opposite: agree

beguile v entice, lure, charm, captivate, mesmerize

beguiling adj enticing, charming, mesmeric, fascinating, captivating

behave v **1** act, perform, conduct yourself, deport yourself, work **2** be good, obey the rules, do the right thing, toe the line, keep out of mischief Opposite: misbehave

behaviour n performance, actions, deeds, activities, manners

behavioural adj social, interactive, communicative, negotiating, developmental

behead v decapitate, cut off somebody's head, guillotine, execute, put to death

behind prep following, after, in the wake of, at the back of, at the rear of ■ adv at the back, at the rear, after, following, last Opposite: in front ■ adj behindhand, late, overdue, behind schedule, in arrears Opposite: early

behindhand adj late, behind, behind schedule, overdue, slow Opposite: early

beholden adj obliged, grateful, in somebody's debt, indebted, obligated

behove (fml) v be the duty of, be the bounden duty of, fall to, befit, be incumbent upon (fml)

being n **1** existence, life, actuality, presence, animation Opposite: nothingness **2** self, soul, mind, essence, spirit **3** life form, organism, creature, living being, human being

belabour v overemphasize, overdo, overstate, labour, stress

belated *adj* **late**, delayed, postponed, deferred, tardy *Opposite*: timely

belch *v* **bring up wind**, burp, hiccup, gulp, posset ■ *n* **burp**, hiccup, eructation

beleaguer *v* **1 harass**, annoy, pester, plague, badger **2 besiege**, surround, lay siege to, threaten, menace

beleaguered *adj* **under pressure**, harassed, fraught, careworn, stressed *Opposite*: care-free

belfry *n* **bell tower**, campanile, tower, spire, steeple

belie *v* **contradict**, disprove, give the lie to, call into question, deny *Opposite*: confirm

belief *n* **1 faith**, conviction, principle, creed, idea **2 confidence**, trust, certainty, credence, acceptance *Opposite*: distrust

believability *n* **credibility**, plausibility, acceptability, trustworthiness, authenticity

believable *adj* **credible**, authentic, realistic, plausible, convincing *Opposite*: unbelievable

believe *v* **1 trust**, have faith in, be certain of, have confidence in, accept as true *Opposite*: disbelieve **2 consider**, think, suppose, judge, imagine *Opposite*: doubt

believer *n* **supporter**, advocate, fan, devotee, follower *Opposite*: sceptic

belittle *v* **disparage**, demean, decry, deride, depreciate *Opposite*: praise

belittlement *n* **depreciation**, disparagement, derision, disdain *Opposite*: praise

belittling *adj* **demeaning**, disparaging, depreciating, condescending, patronizing *Opposite*: supportive

bell *n* **1 hand bell**, church bell, ship's bell, sleigh bell, school bell **2 buzzer**, doorbell, chime, alarm, alarm bell **3** *(infml)* **call**, ring, phone call, buzz *(infml)*, tinkle *(infml)*

bellicose *adj* **belligerent**, aggressive, warlike, pugnacious, combative *Opposite*: compliant

belligerence *n* **hostility**, pugnaciousness, bellicosity, pugnacity, aggression

belligerency *see* **belligerence**

belligerent *adj* **aggressive**, argumentative, quarrelsome, confrontational, pugnacious *Opposite*: cooperative

bellow *n* **roar**, shout, yell, bawl, holler *(US infml)* *Opposite*: whisper ■ *v* **shout**, roar, yell, bawl, thunder *Opposite*: whisper

belly *(infml)* *n* **stomach**, abdomen, middle, tummy *(infml)*, gut *(slang)*

bellyache *(infml)* *n* **1 upset stomach**, stomach ache, stomach pains, tummy ache *(infml)* **2 complaint**, grumble, moan *(infml)*, grouse *(infml)*, gripe *(infml)* ■ *v* **complain**, grumble, carp, whine, moan *(infml)*

bellybutton *(infml)* *n* **navel**, umbilicus, tummy button *(infml)*

belly flop *n* **fall**, flop, crash, dive

belly laugh *n* **guffaw**, laugh, chortle, horse-laugh, hoot

belong *v* **fit in**, fit, go, have its place, be in the right place

belongings *n* **possessions**, property, things, stuff, luggage

beloved *adj* **much-loved**, dearly loved, adored, favourite, darling *Opposite*: despised

below *prep* **less than**, under, not more than, beneath *(fml)* ■ *adv* **1 underneath**, under, lower, beneath *(fml)* *Opposite*: above **2 under**, underneath, lower than, further down, beneath *(fml)* *Opposite*: above

belt *n* **1 girdle**, tie, sash, cummerbund, strap **2 band**, ring, strip, ribbon, line ■ *v* **1 fasten**, buckle, secure, attach, belt up *Opposite*: undo **2** *(infml)* **hit**, thump, thrash, beat, strike **3** *(infml)* **dash**, rush, speed, hurry, race *Opposite*: dawdle

belt up *v* **fasten your belt**, secure your belt, put on your belt, buckle up

bemoan *v* **lament**, regret, mourn, complain, grumble *Opposite*: applaud

bemuse *v* **confuse**, daze, puzzle, perplex, stun

bemused *adj* **confused**, dazed, puzzled, perplexed, mystified *Opposite*: clear-headed

bench *n* **1 seat**, pew, stall, form, bleacher *(US)* **2 worktable**, counter, work surface, worktop, workbench

benchmark *n* **standard**, yardstick, level, target, point of reference

bend *n* **curve**, turn, crook, twist, curvature ■ *v* **1 turn**, bow, twist, crook, change direction *Opposite*: straighten **2 stoop**, bow, bend over, lean down, lean over *Opposite*: straighten up

bendable *adj* **bendy**, flexible, pliant, pliable, malleable *Opposite*: inflexible

bend over backwards *v* **do all you can**, put yourself out, pull out all the stops, do your utmost, go all out

bendy *adj* **flexible**, malleable, plastic, supple, bendable *Opposite*: stiff

beneath *(fml)* *prep* **under**, underneath, below, lower than, less than *Opposite*: over ■ *adv* **underneath**, under, below, lower *Opposite*: above

benediction *n* **approval**, sanction, blessing *Opposite*: malediction *(fml)*

benefactor *n* **sponsor**, patron, supporter, backer

beneficence *n* **generosity**, charity, benevolence, big-heartedness, magnanimity *Opposite*: parsimony

beneficent *adj* **1 charitable**, altruistic, generous, benevolent, humanitarian *Opposite*: self-seeking **2 beneficial**, helpful, useful, advantageous, valuable *Opposite*: deleterious

beneficial *adj* **helpful**, useful, valuable, advantageous, positive *Opposite*: detrimental

beneficiary n recipient, receiver, heir, payee, legatee Opposite: benefactor

benefit n 1 advantage, profit, help, assistance, use Opposite: detriment 2 subsidy, allowance, payment, grant 3 fundraiser, charity performance, charity event ■ v help, promote, profit, do good to, advance Opposite: harm

benefit from v profit from, enjoy, use, gain from, take advantage of

benevolence n kindness, compassion, generosity, munificence, goodwill Opposite: malevolence

benevolent adj kind, caring, compassionate, generous, giving Opposite: malevolent

benighted adj ignorant, unenlightened, unfortunate, disadvantaged Opposite: enlightened

benign adj kind, benevolent, caring, kindly, gentle Opposite: malignant

benignity n kindliness, gentleness, benevolence, compassion, warm-heartedness Opposite: malice

bent adj 1 twisted, curved, bowed, crooked, turned Opposite: straight 2 determined, set, fixed, resolved, decided ■ n inclination, gift, talent, flair. See COMPARE AND CONTRAST at **talent**.

bequeath v leave, give, donate, hand down, will Opposite: inherit

bequest n inheritance, legacy, gift, donation, settlement

berate v rebuke, shout at, harangue, criticize, scold Opposite: praise

bereaved adj mourning, bereft, in mourning, grieving, orphaned

bereavement n loss, grief, sorrow, mourning

bereft adj 1 bereaved, mourning, in mourning, grieving, orphaned 2 empty, starved, devoid, deprived, stripped

berserk adj irrational, mad, out of control, wild, off the deep end Opposite: rational

berth n mooring, dock, landing place, mooring place, wharf ■ v dock, moor, tie up, come in, land Opposite: put out

beset adj plagued, tormented, overwhelmed, overcome, harassed Opposite: free ■ v 1 harass, annoy, hamper, trouble, overwhelm Opposite: leave alone 2 (fml) surround, attack, overcome, overwhelm, assail

beside prep next to, at the side of, alongside, by, near

besides adv 1 as well, in addition, also, above and beyond, too 2 moreover, what's more, further, more to the point, anyway

besiege v surround, siege, lay siege to, encircle, blockade Opposite: defend

besieged adj overwhelmed, inundated, beleaguered, weighed down, plagued

besmirch v sully, defame, tarnish, damage, slander Opposite: praise

besotted adj infatuated, love-struck, head over

heels in love, fanatical, obsessed Opposite: repelled

bespeak v signify, signal, indicate, convey, reveal

bespoke adj custom-made, tailor-made, made to measure, customized, custom-built Opposite: off-the-shelf

best adj top, finest, greatest, unsurpassed, paramount Opposite: worst ■ v outdo, overcome, top, surpass, defeat

bestial adj inhuman, foul, degrading, cruel, brutish Opposite: humane

bestiality n cruelty, inhumanity, savagery, brutality, depravity Opposite: humanity

bestir yourself (fml) v motivate yourself, stir yourself, busy yourself, rouse yourself, get going

bestow (fml) v give, bequeath, donate, grant, present Opposite: withdraw. See COMPARE AND CONTRAST at **give**.

bestride v straddle, span, sit astride, stand astride, be astride

bestseller n hit, smash, success, winner, moneymaker Opposite: flop (infml)

bestselling adj successful, popular, blockbusting, hit, chart-topping

bet v 1 gamble, stake, wager, put money on, lay a wager 2 (infml) think, expect, anticipate, consider, believe ■ n 1 wager, gamble, stake, play, ante 2 option, alternative, candidate, choice, plan

betray v 1 be disloyal, give up, hand over, inform on, double cross Opposite: stand by 2 disclose, leak, tell, give away, reveal

betrayal n disloyalty, unfaithfulness, bad faith, duplicity, infidelity Opposite: loyalty

betrothal (fml) n engagement, promise, pact, compact, troth (archaic)

betrothed (fml) n fiancé, fiancée, husband-to-be, wife-to-be, girlfriend

better adj 1 improved, enhanced, superior Opposite: worse 2 healthier, improved, well, recovering, in good health Opposite: worse ■ v 1 (fml) improve on, top, outdo, outstrip, outshine 2 (fml) enhance, improve, change for the better, advance, ameliorate (fml) Opposite: worsen

betterment (fml) n furtherance, improvement, advancement, benefit, progress Opposite: deterioration

better-off adj rich, wealthy, affluent, comfortable, prosperous Opposite: poor

between prep 1 flanked by, sandwiched between, stuck between, amid, among 2 connecting, linking, joining, involving, concerning

bevelled adj oblique, slanting, sloping, chamfered, bias-cut

beverage (fml) n drink, hot drink, cold drink, liquid refreshment, brew (infml)

bewail (fml) v lament, bemoan, complain,

regret, grumble *Opposite*: applaud

beware *v* be careful, be cautious, be wary, look out, watch out

bewilder *v* confuse, puzzle, baffle, perplex, confound

bewildered *adj* confused, puzzled, dazed, bemused, befuddled *Opposite*: clear-headed

bewildering *adj* confusing, puzzling, baffling, mystifying, incomprehensible *Opposite*: clear

bewilderment *n* confusion, incomprehension, bafflement, puzzlement, perplexity *Opposite*: clarity

bewitch *v* enchant, fascinate, captivate, charm, mesmerize, intrigue *Opposite*: repel

beyond *prep* further than, past, away from, clear of, ahead of

biannual *adj* 1 twice-yearly, twice-a-year, six-monthly, semiannual 2 every other year, biennial, two-yearly, regular, periodic

bias *n* prejudice, partiality, preference, unfairness, predisposition *Opposite*: impartiality

biased *adj* prejudiced, unfair, partial, influenced, predisposed *Opposite*: unbiased

biblical *adj* scriptural, holy, bible, sacred, theological

bibliography *n* list, index, appendix, checklist, catalogue

bicameral *adj* two-tier, two-house, dual, bilateral, bipartite

bicentenary *n* 200th anniversary, 200th birthday, anniversary, bicentennial *(US)*

bicker *v* argue, dispute, quarrel, debate, squabble *Opposite*: agree

bicycle *n* cycle, two-wheeler, bike *(infml)*, push-bike *(infml)*

bid *v* 1 tender, offer, propose, submit, proffer 2 try, attempt, undertake, endeavour, seek 3 *(archaic)* order, call on, command, direct, tell ■ *n* 1 offer, proposal, proposition, tender, submission 2 attempt, try, effort, undertaking, endeavour

biddable *adj* compliant, acquiescent, docile, obedient, amenable *Opposite*: intractable *(fml)*

bidder *n* buyer, collector, dealer, purchaser, customer

bidding *n* request, command, order, will, call

bide your time *v* wait, be patient, wait and see, play the waiting game, hold back

biennial *adj* two-yearly, biannual, regular, periodic

bier *n* stand, rest, base, pedestal, table

biff *(infml)* *v* hit, punch, thump, knock, clout

bifurcate *v* divide, branch, split, fork, diverge *Opposite*: converge

bifurcation *n* fork, junction, split, divergence, branching *Opposite*: convergence

big *adj* 1 large, giant, immense, vast, great *Opposite*: small 2 spacious, capacious, roomy, large, deep *Opposite*: cramped 3 significant, considerable, substantial, sizable, large *Opposite*: insignificant 4 extensive, vast, immense, wide, great *Opposite*: narrow 5 older, elder, grown-up, adult, mature *Opposite*: little 6 bulky, large, cumbersome, massive, outsize *Opposite*: petite 7 tall, high, lofty, towering, soaring *Opposite*: short

bigamous *adj* polygamous, adulterous, two-timing *(infml)* *Opposite*: monogamous

bigamy *n* polygamy, adultery, two-timing *(infml)* *Opposite*: monogamy

big business *n* trade, commerce, industry, business sector, business world

big deal *(infml)* *n* major concern, serious issue, matter of life and death, federal case *(US)*

biggie *(infml)* *n* 1 big one, giant, colossus, monster, whopper *(infml)* 2 key player, major player, VIP, big gun, big shot *(infml)* *Opposite*: nobody

bighead *(infml)* *n* boaster, bragger, show-off *(infml)*, smart aleck *(infml)*, clever clogs *(infml)*

bigheaded *(infml)* *adj* conceited, egotistical, arrogant, vain, self-centred *Opposite*: modest

big-hearted *adj* kind, good-natured, supportive, helpful, kindly *Opposite*: mean-spirited

bigmouth *(infml)* *n* 1 gossip, gossipmonger, telltale, tattler, blabbermouth *(infml)* 2 boaster, bragger, braggart, know-all *(infml)*, bighead *(infml)*

big name *n* famous name, celebrity, star, superstar, VIP *Opposite*: unknown

bigot *n* chauvinist, extremist, dogmatist, fanatic, diehard

bigoted *adj* prejudiced, intolerant, chauvinistic, dogmatic, opinionated *Opposite*: open-minded

bigotry *n* prejudice, intolerance, chauvinism, narrow-mindedness, fanaticism *Opposite*: open-mindedness

big shot *(infml)* *n* key player, major player, VIP, big gun *(infml)*, bigwig *(infml)* *Opposite*: nobody

bigwig *(infml)* *see* big shot

bijou *adj* compact, tiny, cramped, small, poky *(infml)* *Opposite*: spacious

bike *(infml)* *n* bicycle, cycle, motorbike, motorcycle, push-bike *(infml)*

WORD BANK

❑ **types of bike** boneshaker, dirt bike, exercise bike, moped, motor scooter, mountain bike, penny-farthing, racing bike, rickshaw, scooter, scrambler, tandem, ten-speed, three-wheeler, trail bike, tricycle, two-wheeler, unicycle

❑ **parts of a bike** brake, chain, crossbar, derailleur, fork, frame, handlebars, mudguard, pedal, reflector, seat, spoke, tyre, wheel

biker *n* **motorcyclist**, scrambler, racer, rider, cyclist

bikini *n* **swimsuit**, two-piece, swimming costume, bathing costume *(dated)*, bathing suit *(US)*

bilateral *adj* **two-sided**, two-pronged, joint, mutual, consensual *Opposite*: unilateral

bilge *n* **1 hull**, keel, base, bottom **2 hold**, tank, interior, recesses, bowels **3 sludge**, mud, bilge water, silt, effluent **4** *(infml)* **nonsense**, rubbish, garbage, trash, drivel

bilingual *adj* **fluent**, multilingual, polyglot

bilious *adj* **nauseous**, sickly, queasy, sick, ill

bilk *(infml)* *v* **cheat**, trick, deceive, con, swindle

bill *n* **1 invoice**, statement, demand, receipt, damage *(infml)* **2 amount**, total, sum, fee, price **3 proposal**, measure, document, petition, proposition **4 beak**, mouth, mandible ■ *v* **charge**, invoice, debit, send the bill to

billboard *n* **sign**, hoarding, poster, advertisement, panel

billet *n* **accommodation**, quarters, boarding house, guest house, lodgings *(dated)* ■ *v* **accommodate**, quarter, house, station, shelter

billionaire *n* **multimillionaire**, magnate, tycoon, moneybags *(infml)*, fat cat *(slang)*

billionth *n* **tiny part**, morsel, particle, modicum, touch

billow *v* **1 catch the wind**, swell, bulge, balloon, fill *Opposite*: sag **2 roll upwards**, waft, rise, curl, flow *Opposite*: fall ■ *n* **puff**, cloud, swell, swirl, rush

billycan *n* **cooking pot**, pail, pan, pot, tin

bin *n* **1 rubbish bin**, wastepaper basket, waste bin, dustbin, litter bin **2 storage bin**, basket, container, silo, holder ■ *v* **throw away**, throw out, toss, discard, dispose of *Opposite*: keep

binary *adj* **two-part**, dual, double, twin, twofold

bind *v* **1 attach**, connect, join, combine, unite *Opposite*: undo **2 oblige**, force, require, compel, coerce ■ *n* **1 quandary**, tight situation, predicament, dilemma, muddle **2 nuisance**, drag, bore, annoyance, pain *(infml)*

binder *n* **folder**, file, ring binder, looseleaf folder

binding *n* **1 tie**, band, attachment, fastening, truss **2 edging**, cover, trim, stitching, strip ■ *adj* **compulsory**, obligatory, required, necessary, mandatory *Opposite*: voluntary

binge *n* **spree**, orgy, rampage, splurge *(infml)*, bender *(slang)* ■ *v* **overdo**, indulge, overindulge, gorge, pig out *(infml)* *Opposite*: diet

binoculars *n* **field glasses**, opera glasses, eyeglasses *(US fml)*

biochemical *adj* **chemical**, biological, living, organic, natural

biodegradable *adj* **recyclable**, decomposable, ecological, environmental, green

biographer *n* **writer**, author, autobiographer, historian, profiler

biographical *adj* **factual**, nonfiction, true, fact-based, realistic *Opposite*: fictional

biography *n* **life story**, life history, profile, memoir, life

biological *adj* **1 organic**, life, living, natural, biotic **2 natal**, birth, natural, genetic, true *Opposite*: adoptive

bionic *adj* **electronic**, automatic, robotic, electromechanical

biopic *n* **film**, movie, biography, documentary, life story

biopsy *n* **cell removal**, operation, surgery, culture, tissue removal

biorhythm *n* **cycle**, change, cyclical change, rhythm

biosphere *n* **environment**, planet, earth, land, sea

bipartisan *adj* **two-party**, dual-party, cross-party, joint, combined

bipartite *adj* **two-party**, two-part, mutual, shared, in common

biped *n* **two-legged animal**, human, primate, humanoid

birch *n* **cane**, rod, stick, switch, whip ■ *v* **whip**, flog, thrash, lash, strike

birdbath *n* **basin**, bowl, receptacle

birdbrained *(infml)* *adj* **silly**, foolish, stupid, asinine, witless *Opposite*: sensible

birdcage *n* **cage**, coop, pen, aviary, enclosure

birdlike *adj* **dainty**, petite, small-boned, delicate, slight *Opposite*: heavyset

birdseed *n* **seed**, grain, mixture, feed, chicken feed

birdsong *n* **call**, cry, song, trill, whistle

birdwatcher *n* **ornithologist**, bird lover, twitcher, birder

birth *n* **1 delivery**, labour, childbirth, nativity, parturition *(fml)* *Opposite*: death **2 beginning**, origin, dawn, start, onset *Opposite*: end ■ *adj* **natal**, natural, true, biological, genetic *Opposite*: adoptive

birthdate *see* **birthday**

birthday *n* **date of birth**, birthdate, anniversary

birthmark *n* **mark**, stain, discoloration, blemish, strawberry mark

birthplace *n* **origin**, source, home, home town, place of birth

birthright *n* **inheritance**, legacy, bequest, heritage, patrimony

birth sign *n* **sign of the Zodiac**, astrological sign, star sign

bisect *v* **cut in half**, intersect, divide, cut across, sever *Opposite*: join

bisection *n* **halving**, splitting, dissection, division, parting *Opposite*: union

bit *n* **1 piece**, morsel, crumb, fragment, speck **2 minute**, while, moment, second, a little while

bite v 1 **sink your teeth into**, nibble, gnaw, bite off, bite into 2 **wound**, nip, snap, attack, maul 3 **hurt**, sting, feel painful, nip, prick ■ n 1 **taste**, mouthful, nibble, chew, piece 2 **wound**, sting, puncture, bite mark 3 **sharp taste**, spiciness, tartness, piquancy, tang

bite-sized adj **small**, little, minute, tiny, petite Opposite: big

bite the bullet v **grasp the nettle**, take the bull by the horns, do it, face up to, go for it (slang) Opposite: avoid

bite the dust (infml) v 1 **fall down**, fall flat, take a fall, tumble, tumble down 2 **die**, pass away, kick the bucket (infml), croak (infml), expire (fml) 3 **fail**, go under, die a death, be unsuccessful, go bankrupt Opposite: succeed

biting adj 1 **cold**, freezing, piercing, cutting, stinging Opposite: hot 2 **sarcastic**, scathing, acerbic, mordant, satirical Opposite: sympathetic

bitingly adv **acidly**, acerbically, tartly, woundingly, cruelly Opposite: sympathetically

bits and bobs (infml) see **bits and pieces**

bits and pieces (infml) n 1 **belongings**, things, odds and ends, stuff, personal possessions 2 **knick-knacks**, leftovers, scraps, odds and ends, stuff

bitter adj 1 **sour**, acid, acidic, tart, astringent Opposite: sweet 2 **resentful**, embittered, sulky, cheated, angry Opposite: glad 3 **unpleasant**, acrimonious, antagonistic, nasty, hostile Opposite: amicable 4 **vicious**, rancorous, virulent, vehement Opposite: mild 5 **cold**, freezing, icy, biting, raw Opposite: hot

bitterly adv 1 **resentfully**, acrimoniously, sulkily, sullenly, cynically Opposite: gladly 2 **severely**, excessively, intensely, inordinately, desperately Opposite: slightly

bitterness n 1 **resentment**, acrimony, unpleasantness, sullenness, anger Opposite: friendliness 2 **sourness**, acidity, sour taste, astringency, bitter taste Opposite: sweetness

bittersweet adj **poignant**, nostalgic, affecting, touching, sentimental

bitty adj **disjointed**, fragmented, scrappy, fragmentary, disconnected Opposite: cohesive

bitumen n **tar**, asphalt, Tarmac, pitch, blacktop (US)

bivouac n 1 **camp**, encampment, temporary camp, mountaineering camp, military camp 2 **shelter**, awning, tent, pup tent, lean-to (US) ■ v **camp**, set up camp, pitch a tent

biweekly adv 1 **once every two weeks**, every other week, twice a month, every fortnight, once a fortnight 2 **twice a week**, semiweekly, every few days

bizarre adj **strange**, curious, inexplicable, out of the ordinary, unusual Opposite: ordinary

blab (infml) v **tell tales**, gossip, tattle, leak, tell

blabber v **chatter**, babble, go on, drivel, jabber

blabbermouth (infml) n **gossip**, telltale, chatterer, sneak, bigmouth (infml)

black adj **dark**, gloomy, obscure, dusky, murky Opposite: light

WORD BANK

❑ **types of black** blue-black, coal black, ebony, inky, jet black, pitch-black, raven, sable

black-and-blue adj **bruised**, aching, hurt, injured, battered

black-and-white adj **clear-cut**, straightforward, unambiguous, categorical, explicit Opposite: ambiguous

blackball v **exclude**, ban, keep out, reject, bar Opposite: invite

blackboard n **board**, slate, whiteboard, chalkboard (US)

blacken v 1 **darken**, make black, dirty, turn black, besmirch Opposite: lighten 2 **slander**, libel, defame, vilify, malign Opposite: praise

blackguard n **scoundrel**, rascal, rogue, villain, wretch (fml)

blackhead n **blocked pore**, spot, pimple, blemish, zit (slang)

blacklist v **ban**, debar, bar, exclude, shut out

blackly adv 1 **angrily**, menacingly, threateningly, belligerently, aggressively Opposite: optimistically 2 **hopelessly**, gloomily, lugubriously, dismally, dolefully Opposite: sunnily

blackmail n **extortion**, intimidation, bribery, corruption, extraction ■ v **extort**, extract, exact, hold to ransom, bribe

blackmailer n **extortionist**, coercer, criminal, crook (infml)

blackness n 1 **darkness**, duskiness, dimness, shadow, gloom Opposite: light 2 **hopelessness**, despondency, gloominess, depression, dolefulness Opposite: optimism 3 **anger**, fury, temper, aggression, belligerence Opposite: cheerfulness

black out v **faint**, pass out, lose consciousness, collapse, become unconscious Opposite: come to

blackout n 1 **fainting fit**, seizure, loss of consciousness, collapse 2 **power cut**, shutdown, power failure, power outage (US) 3 **embargo**, veto, clampdown, suppression, censorship

black-tie adj **formal**, dressy, ceremonial, posh (infml) Opposite: casual

blade n 1 **cutting edge**, knife-edge, edge, razor blade, knife blade 2 **vane**, fin, propeller, sail, oar

blame v 1 **hold responsible**, censure, accuse, point the finger at, hold accountable Opposite: exculpate (fml) 2 **criticize**, reproach, find fault with, condemn, think badly of Opposite: commend ■ n **responsibility**, guilt, culpability, fault, blameworthiness Opposite: commendation

blameless adj **innocent**, virtuous, righteous, faultless, irreproachable *Opposite*: guilty

blameworthy adj **responsible**, guilty, culpable, at fault, chargeable *Opposite*: innocent

blanch v **go pale**, grow pale, turn white, lighten, blench *Opposite*: redden

bland adj 1 **insipid**, weak, tasteless, mild, plain *Opposite*: tasty 2 **featureless**, ordinary, dull, lacklustre, humdrum *Opposite*: exciting

blandishment n **flattery**, cajolery, praise, fawning, soft words

blandness n 1 **tastelessness**, weakness, insipidness, mildness, plainness *Opposite*: tastiness 2 **dullness**, banality, flatness, triteness, insipidness *Opposite*: interest

blank adj 1 **empty**, vacant, bare, clean, clear *Opposite*: full 2 **outright**, complete, total, absolute, unqualified *Opposite*: partial 3 **uncomprehending**, impassive, vacant, empty, bemused *Opposite*: expressive ■ n **space**, void, gap, empty space, break

blanket n **coverlet**, cover, covering, throw, spread ■ adj **comprehensive**, extensive, complete, total, wholesale *Opposite*: partial ■ v **cover**, obscure, encase, drape, carpet *Opposite*: uncover

blankness n 1 **emptiness**, void, vacancy, bareness, barrenness 2 **lack of expression**, vacancy, indifference, emotionlessness, vacuousness *Opposite*: animation 3 **bewilderment**, confusion, obliviousness, incomprehension, lack of understanding *Opposite*: acuity

blank out v **block out**, blot out, suppress, wipe out, erase *Opposite*: acknowledge

blare v **ring out**, make a racket, boom, blast out, blare out

blare out *see* **blare**

blaring adj **deafening**, earsplitting, cacophonous, raucous, booming *Opposite*: quiet

blarney (*infml*) n **nonsense**, smooth talk, charm, drivel, flattery

blasé adj **nonchalant**, laid back, cool, relaxed, unmoved *Opposite*: concerned

blaspheme v **curse**, swear, issue oaths, use profanities, use foul language

blasphemer n **swearer**, curser, profaner, foul mouth, profaner

blasphemous adj **profane**, sacrilegious, irreligious, offensive, improper *Opposite*: pious

blasphemy n 1 **profanity**, sacrilege, wickedness, irreverence, violation *Opposite*: piety 2 **oath**, curse, profanity, swearword, imprecation (*fml*)

blast n **explosion**, detonation, flash, flare, gust ■ v 1 **blow up**, explode, detonate, demolish, blow away (*US slang*) 2 (*infml*) **blare**, resound, boom, make a racket, ring out 3 (*infml*) **criticize**, attack, lambaste, vilify, censure 4 **damage**, blight, disfigure, burn, blister. *See* COMPARE AND CONTRAST *at* **criticize**.

blast off v **take off**, lift off, launch *Opposite*: touch down

blastoff n **launch**, takeoff, liftoff *Opposite*: touchdown

blast out v **blare out**, ring out, make a racket, blare, boom

blatancy n **obviousness**, conspicuousness, ostentation, flagrancy, overtness *Opposite*: subtlety

blatant adj **obvious**, unconcealed, barefaced, unashamed, deliberate *Opposite*: furtive

blather (*infml*) v **chatter**, go on, babble, blabber, jabber ■ n **drivel**, prattle, chatter, babble, blabber

blaze v **burn**, be on fire, burst into flames, rage, glow ■ n 1 **fire**, inferno, conflagration, combustion 2 **glare**, glow, flash, brightness, intensity

blazing adj 1 **intense**, raging, mighty, heated, furious 2 **burning**, glowing, shining, radiating, blistering

blazon v **splash**, embellish, emblazon, display, show

bleach v **lighten**, peroxide, blanch, blench, whiten *Opposite*: colour

bleached adj **lightened**, faded, sun-bleached, washed-out, blanched

bleak adj 1 **hopeless**, unpromising, gloomy, doubtful, futile *Opposite*: promising 2 **unwelcoming**, austere, miserable, bare, drab *Opposite*: welcoming 3 **cold**, harsh, wintry, cheerless, miserable *Opposite*: warm 4 **forlorn**, miserable, dejected, disheartened, downhearted *Opposite*: cheerful

bleakly adv **forlornly**, dismally, hopelessly, drearily, despondently *Opposite*: cheerfully

bleakness n 1 **hopelessness**, despondency, sorrow, misery, sadness *Opposite*: hopefulness 2 **cheerlessness**, drabness, austerity, harshness, bareness *Opposite*: comfort

bleary adj **hazy**, watery, unfocused, fuzzy, blurry *Opposite*: clear

bleary-eyed adj **sleepy**, tired, half-awake, dozy, groggy *Opposite*: alert

bleat v **whine**, complain, nag, fuss, whinge (*infml*)

bleed v 1 **lose blood**, haemorrhage, shed blood 2 (*infml*) **extort**, exploit, drain, wring, deplete ■ n **blood loss**, haemorrhage, nosebleed

bleed dry (*infml*) v **drain**, suck dry, deplete, bring to its knees, exploit *Opposite*: replenish

bleeding n **blood loss**, haemorrhage, flow of blood, flow

bleep n **beep**, tone, sound, noise ■ v **call**, page, alert, signal, contact

bleeper n **pager**, monitor, beeper (*infml*)

blemish n **mark**, defect, imperfection, flaw, fault ■ v **damage**, tarnish, spoil, ruin, stain *Opposite*: restore. *See* COMPARE AND CONTRAST *at* **flaw**.

blemished *adj* marked, stained, imperfect, flawed, tarnished *Opposite*: unblemished

blench *v* 1 go pale, grow pale, lighten, blanch, whiten *Opposite*: redden 2 draw back, hesitate, falter, recoil, flinch

blend *v* mix, merge, combine, bring together, unify *Opposite*: separate ■ *n* mixture, merger, combination, assortment, amalgam. *See* COMPARE AND CONTRAST *at* mixture.

blender *n* mixer, food processor, chopper, liquidizer

bless *v* 1 sanctify, consecrate, hallow, extol, laud *Opposite*: curse 2 approve, sanction, support, endorse, back *Opposite*: decry

blessed *adj* 1 holy, sacred, sanctified, hallowed, consecrated *Opposite*: profane 2 welcome, providential, lucky, fortunate, pleasant *Opposite*: unfortunate

blessing *n* 1 consecration, sanctification, benediction, dedication 2 approval, sanction, permission, consent, approbation *Opposite*: veto 3 lucky thing, good thing, miracle, piece of good fortune, stroke of luck *Opposite*: disaster

blether *(infml)* *v* chatter, go on, babble, jabber, ramble ■ *n* drivel, prattle, chatter, gibberish, gossip

blight *n* disfigurement, stain, scar, blot, affliction ■ *v* ruin, disfigure, stain, scar, impair

blimpish *adj* bigoted, narrow-minded, prejudiced, intolerant, dogmatic *Opposite*: tolerant

blind *adj* sightless, unsighted, vision-impaired *Opposite*: sighted ■ *n* screen, window shade, canopy, awning, visor

blind alley *n* dead end, cul-de-sac, impasse

blind date *n* rendezvous, date, meeting, assignation, appointment

blindfold *n* bandage, cloth, covering, scarf, band

blinding *adj* 1 glaring, dazzling, bright, bedazzling, strong *Opposite*: soft 2 *(infml)* striking, extraordinary, outstanding, arresting, amazing *Opposite*: ordinary

blindness *n* 1 sightlessness, loss of sight, impaired vision *Opposite*: sight 2 thoughtlessness, carelessness, obliviousness, recklessness, rashness *Opposite*: thoughtfulness

blind spot *n* weakness, failing, failure, fault, flaw *Opposite*: strength

blink *v* 1 wink, bat an eyelid, flutter an eyelid, flicker an eyelid 2 flash, wink, flicker, twinkle, signal

blinkered *adj* inward-looking, insular, narrow-minded, narrow, limited

blip *n* problem, glitch, error, failure, breakdown

bliss *n* ecstasy, heaven, paradise, enjoyment, happiness *Opposite*: misery

blissful *adj* heavenly, wonderful, delightful, idyllic, perfect *Opposite*: miserable

blissfully *adv* supremely, wonderfully, ecstatically, delightfully, happily *Opposite*: miserably

blister *n* sore, swelling, eruption, burn, blood blister ■ *v* swell up, erupt, bubble, bulge, break out

blistering *adj* sweltering, baking, blazing, burning, searing *Opposite*: freezing

blithe *adj* casual, unconcerned, indifferent, unthinking, uncaring *Opposite*: thoughtful

blitz *n* 1 bombardment, blitzkrieg, saturation bombing, onslaught, offensive 2 *(infml)* onslaught, attack, crackdown, concerted effort, clear-out ■ *v* 1 *(infml)* crack down on, concentrate on, focus on, come down on, fall on 2 bombard, bomb, blast, barrage, hit 3 *(infml)* clean, clean up, tidy, whip round, clear away

blizzard *n* snowstorm, whiteout, storm, winter storm *(US)*

bloat *v* swell, inflate, blow up, expand, distend *Opposite*: contract

bloated *adj* swollen, distended, overstuffed, full, overfed

blob *n* splotch, globule, spot, splash, dash ■ *v* splotch, dot, dab, daub, smudge

bloc *n* alliance, coalition, union, federation, league

block *n* 1 chunk, hunk, lump, slab, wedge 2 building, apartment block, block of flats 3 wing, extension, unit, module, part 4 cellblock, toilet block, shower block, tower block 5 expanse, section, sector, zone, band ■ *v* obstruct, impede, hinder, jam, prevent *Opposite*: encourage. *See* COMPARE AND CONTRAST *at* hinder.

blockade *n* barrier, barricade, obstruction, line of defence, cordon ■ *v* deny access to, lay siege to, obstruct, defend, block

blockage *n* obstruction, impasse, jam, bottleneck, snarl-up

blockbuster *(infml)* *n* runaway success, hit, smash hit, chartbuster, bestseller *Opposite*: flop *(infml)*

blockbusting *adj* successful, sensational, outstanding, popular, record-breaking

blocked *adj* congested, impassable, choked up, jammed, gridlocked *Opposite*: clear

blocking *adj* obstructive, delaying, stalling, hindering, spoiling *Opposite*: cooperative

block off *v* 1 close off, block, close, cordon off, isolate *Opposite*: free 2 obstruct, obscure, hide, mask, cover *Opposite*: reveal

block out *v* blank out, blot out, suppress, wipe out, erase *Opposite*: acknowledge

block up *v* jam, fill, stop, obstruct, choke *Opposite*: free

bloke *(infml)* *n* man, fella *(infml)*, guy *(infml)*, lad *(infml)*, fellow *(dated)*

blond *adj* fair-haired, towheaded, light-coloured, pale, flaxen *Opposite*: dark

blonde see blond

blood n 1 gore, body fluid, plasma, lifeblood 2 family, relations, kin, relatives, kinfolks 3 lineage, ancestry, extraction, heritage, stock

bloodbath n massacre, slaughter, atrocity, scene of carnage

blood brother n best friend, friend, mate, ally, supporter Opposite: enemy

bloodcurdling adj terrifying, frightening, hair-raising, chilling, spine-tingling Opposite: comforting

bloodless adj 1 nonviolent, peaceful, non-aggressive, orderly, controlled Opposite: violent 2 pale, anaemic, white, pallid, wan Opposite: ruddy

bloodletting n quarrel, fight, dispute, argument, fracas

bloodline n descent, heritage, lineage, ancestry, background

blood lust n bloodthirstiness, hatred, cruelty, inhumanity, revenge

blood money n compensation, money, recompense, retribution, atonement

bloodshed n carnage, killing, violence, slaughter, murder

bloodshot adj red, inflamed, sore, pink Opposite: clear

bloodstream n flow, circulation, blood, arteries, veins

bloodsucker n parasite, leech, tick, mosquito, vampire

bloodsucking adj parasitical, leechlike, vampiric, vampirish

bloodthirstiness n ferociousness, viciousness, cruelty, barbarism, brutality

bloodthirsty adj cruel, gory, murderous, ferocious, vicious

bloody adj gory, blood-spattered, bleeding, wounded, injured

bloody-minded (infml) adj uncooperative, obstructive, stubborn, pigheaded, contrary Opposite: cooperative

bloody-mindedness (infml) n lack of cooperation, obstructiveness, stubbornness, obstinacy, pigheadedness Opposite: cooperation

bloom n coloration, tinge, tint, shadow, flush Opposite: pallor ■ v blossom, flower, come into flower, come into bud Opposite: wither

bloomer (infml) n error, blunder, mistake, gaffe, slip

blooming adj 1 flourishing, thriving, budding, up-and-coming, promising Opposite: struggling 2 blossoming, flowering, budding, in flower, in bloom

blossom n flower, flower head, bloom, bud ■ v 1 bloom, flower, bud, come into flower, come into bud Opposite: wither 2 flourish, thrive, grow, bloom, prosper Opposite: struggle 3 develop, grow, come out of your shell, mature, come out of yourself

blossoming adj developing, growing, prospering, maturing, thriving

blossom out v develop, grow, come out of your shell, come out of yourself, blossom

blot n spot, blemish, stain, mark, imperfection ■ v stain, tarnish, spoil, ruin, disfigure

blotch n blot, mark, blemish, spot, splodge

blotchy adj mottled, blemished, marked, spotty, spotted Opposite: plain

blot on the landscape n eyesore, scar, blemish, disfigurement, monstrosity

blot out v 1 conceal, hide, cover, eclipse, block Opposite: reveal 2 blank out, block out, forget, erase, put out of your mind Opposite: recall

blow v 1 whoosh, gust, waft, puff, bluster 2 move, propel, drive, carry, waft ■ n 1 knock, crack, jolt, swipe, strike 2 setback, upset, disappointment, shock, misfortune Opposite: boost

blow away v distribute, disperse, scatter, dispel, spread

blowback (infml) n reaction, response, repercussion, feedback

blow-by-blow adj thorough, step by step, detailed, full, complete Opposite: sketchy

blower (dated infml) n phone, telephone, mobile, line, dog and bone (slang)

blown-up adj 1 inflated, air-filled, hard, rigid, pumped-up Opposite: deflated 2 distended, swollen, bloated, enlarged, puffed-up Opposite: sunken 3 overdone, exaggerated, attention-grabbing, hyped, puffed-up Opposite: understated 4 bombed, wrecked, burned-out, ruined, demolished

blow out v extinguish, put out, snuff out, douse, dampen Opposite: ignite

blow somebody's cover v unmask, expose, uncover, make known, bring to light

blow the whistle v inform, report, turn in, expose, sneak

blow up v 1 destroy, explode, detonate, blast, demolish 2 inflate, pump up, fill, puff up, swell Opposite: deflate 3 enlarge, magnify, expand, increase, make larger Opposite: reduce 4 (infml) lose your temper, explode, be furious, flare up, hit the roof (infml) 5 (infml) exaggerate, overstress, embellish, embroider, make a mountain out of a molehill Opposite: play down

blowup n enlargement, magnification Opposite: reduction

blowy (infml) adj windy, breezy, blustery, gusty, squally Opposite: calm

blow your own trumpet (infml) v brag, boast, crow, show off, sing your own praises Opposite: deprecate

blow your top (infml) v flare up, lose your temper, fly into a rage, explode, hit the roof (infml) Opposite: calm down

blowzy adj 1 ruddy, red-faced, rubicund, coarse

complexioned 2 **unkempt**, bedraggled, messy, tousled, dishevelled *Opposite*: smart

blub *(infml) see* blubber

blubber *(infml)* v **sob**, weep, cry, snivel, whimper

bludgeon v 1 **beat**, hit, slam, strike, batter 2 **coerce**, compel, bully, bulldoze, steam-roller

blue *(infml) adj* **depressed**, down, sad, low, dejected *Opposite*: happy

---

WORD BANK

❏ **types of blue** azure, baby blue, cobalt blue, cornflower blue, cyan, electric blue, ice blue, indigo, lapis lazuli, midnight blue, navy blue, peacock blue, powder blue, Prussian blue, royal blue, sapphire, saxe blue, sky blue, slate blue, steel blue, turquoise, ultramarine

---

blue-blooded *adj* **aristocratic**, noble, high-class, well-bred, refined *Opposite*: common

blue-chip *adj* **top-class**, first-class, first-rate, top-grade, topnotch *(infml) Opposite*: second-rate

blue-collar *adj* **labouring**, manual, proletarian, working class *Opposite*: white-collar

blueprint *n* **plan**, drawing, design, proposal, outline

blues *(infml) n* **sadness**, melancholy, dejection, depression, despair *Opposite*: happiness

bluff v **trick**, con, fake, lie, pretend ■ *n* 1 **sham**, trick, con, pretence, fake 2 **cliff**, headland, hillside, hill, mound ■ *adj* **plain-spoken**, cheery, loud, hearty, forthright

bluffness *n* **cheeriness**, heartiness, directness, bluntness, plain-spokenness

blunder *n* **mistake**, gaffe, error, mix-up, misstep ■ *v* 1 **make a mistake**, get it wrong, slip up *(infml)*, foul up *(infml)*, mess up *(infml)* 2 **stumble**, stagger, lurch, flounder, trip. *See* COMPARE AND CONTRAST *at* mistake.

blundering *adj* **clumsy**, careless, awkward, lumbering, ungainly *Opposite*: dexterous

blunt *adj* 1 **dull**, rounded, dulled, blunted *Opposite*: sharp 2 **uncompromising**, straight-forward, direct, frank, honest *Opposite*: indirect ■ *v* **dampen**, dull, put a damper on, take the edge off, diminish *Opposite*: heighten

bluntly *adv* **frankly**, straightforwardly, hon-estly, directly, candidly *Opposite*: indirectly

bluntness *n* **candour**, frankness, directness, straightforwardness, honesty *Opposite*: mendacity

blur *v* **obscure**, cloud, make indistinct, hide, conceal *Opposite*: clarify ■ *n* 1 **blob**, smudge, smear, blot, blotch 2 **distortion**, fuzziness, haze, impression, shape ■ *v* **smudge**, smear, distort, confuse, shade *Opposite*: clear

blurred *adj* **blurry**, indistinct, unclear, hazy, distorted *Opposite*: distinct

blurry *see* blurred

blurt *v* **exclaim**, cry, utter, come out with, announce

blush *v* **go red**, flush, colour, go red in the face, redden *Opposite*: blanch

blusher *n* **makeup**, cosmetic, rouge *(dated)*

blushing *adj* **embarrassed**, self-conscious, red-faced, flushed, coy *Opposite*: bold

bluster *v* 1 **harangue**, threaten, bully, protest, rant 2 **blow**, gust, rage, puff, waft

blustery *adj* **windy**, gusty, stormy, squally, breezy *Opposite*: still

B movie *n* **supporting film**, short, B picture, B film, support

BO *(infml) n* **body odour**, smell, sweatiness, rankness, reek

board *n* 1 **plank**, slat, floorboard, timber, beam 2 **panel**, sheet, boarding 3 **committee**, panel, commission, management team, advisory group 4 **food**, meal, sustenance, nour-ishment, rations ■ *v* 1 **embark**, enter, go on board, go aboard, go into *Opposite*: dis-embark 2 **live**, room, be accommodated, stay, lodge *(dated)*

boarder *n* **lodger**, paying guest, resident, tenant, occupant

board up *v* **close**, shutter, secure, cover up

boardwalk *n* **walkway**, footpath, path, cause-way

boast *v* 1 **brag**, show off, crow, swank *(infml)*, fly your own kite *(infml)* 2 **have**, possess, pride yourself on, lay claim to, feature ■ *n* **claim**, assertion, brag, vaunt, pre-tension

boastful *adj* **arrogant**, proud, conceited, full of yourself, bragging *Opposite*: modest

boastfulness *n* **immodesty**, arrogance, conceit, self-importance, showing off *Opposite*: modesty

boasting *n* **boastfulness**, bragging, showing off, arrogance, self-aggrandizement *Oppo-site*: modesty ■ *adj* **boastful**, swaggering, arrogant, self-important, conceited *Oppo-site*: modest

boat *n* **craft**, ship, vessel

bob *v* 1 **move up and down**, nod, dip, bobble, jog 2 **curtsy**, bow, nod, duck, genuflect

bobbin *n* **reel**, spindle, spool, cylinder, roll

bobble *n* **ball**, pompom, tassel ■ *v* **move up and down**, nod, bob, jog, dip

bobbly *adj* **bumpy**, lumpy, rough, knobbly, tex-tured *Opposite*: smooth

bobby *(dated infml) n* **police officer**, constable, cop *(slang)*

bobsleigh *n* **toboggan**, sledge, sled *(US)*, bobsled *(US)*

bode *v* **augur**, portend, promise, predict, divine

bodge *(infml) v* **spoil**, damage, do badly, ruin, botch *(infml)*

bodily *adj* **physical**, corporal, corporeal,

fleshly, material *Opposite*: spiritual

body *n* **1 form**, figure, frame, physique, build **2 corpse**, dead body, cadaver, remains, carcass **3 organization**, group, association, federation, society **4 quantity**, corpus, amount, mass, area **5 bulk**, main part, essence, majority, mass

body blow *n* **setback**, blow, disappointment, upset, shock

body builder *n* **athlete**, weightlifter, muscle builder

body fluid *n* **saliva**, blood, urine, sweat, semen

bodyguard *n* **guard**, escort, attendant, guardian, protection officer

body language *n* **mannerisms**, stance, facial expression, movements, motion

boffin *(infml)* *n* **scientist**, expert, genius, researcher, inventor

bog *n* **swamp**, quagmire, mire, fen, fenland

bogey *n* **1 worry**, problem, concern, bother, annoyance **2 monster**, creature, beast, monstrosity, bogeyman

bogeyman *n* **monster**, creature, beast, monstrosity, bogey

boggle *(infml)* *v* **confuse**, baffle, perplex, astonish, overwhelm

boggy *adj* **marshy**, swampy, muddy, watery, wet *Opposite*: parched

bog-standard *(infml)* *adj* **basic**, standard, ordinary, simple, unadorned *Opposite*: superior

bogus *adj* **false**, fake, counterfeit, phoney, trick *Opposite*: genuine

bohemian *n* **free spirit**, freethinker, nonconformist, hippie, New Age traveller ■ *adj* **unconventional**, nonconformist, offbeat, alternative, carefree *Opposite*: conformist

boil *v* **1 simmer**, bubble, poach, cook, stew **2 rage**, fume, seethe, be angry, be irate **3** *(infml)* **overheat**, swelter, stew, bake, burn *Opposite*: freeze ■ *n* **ulcer**, sore, spot, swelling, abscess

boil down to *(infml)* *v* **amount to**, come down to, end up as, add up to, wind up as

boiler suit *n* **overalls**, coveralls, protective clothing, dungarees

boiling *adj* **hot**, sweltering, baking, steaming, torrid *Opposite*: freezing

boiling point *n* **crisis point**, danger level, flashpoint, high point, peak

boil over *v* **overflow**, bubble up, overheat, spill over, blow

boisterous *adj* **1 exuberant**, animated, spirited, rowdy, rambunctious *Opposite*: placid **2 wild**, turbulent, rough, stormy *Opposite*: calm

boisterousness *n* **1 exuberance**, high spirits, unruliness, roughness, riotousness *Opposite*: placidity **2 wildness**, turbulence, roughness, storminess *Opposite*: calmness

bold *adj* **1 brave**, daring, courageous, audacious, valiant *Opposite*: cowardly **2 confident**, forward, brash, brazen, self-assured *Opposite*: timid **3 conspicuous**, bright, vivid, flashy, showy *Opposite*: muted **4 black**, heavy, boldface *Opposite*: light

boldface *adj* **black**, heavy, bold *Opposite*: lightface

bold-faced *adj* **impudent**, brash, brazen, unconcerned, shameless *Opposite*: unassuming

boldness *n* **1 courage**, daring, bravery, bravado, valour *Opposite*: cowardice **2 confidence**, self-assurance, brashness, nerve, impudence *Opposite*: timidity

bole *n* **trunk**, stem, stalk

bollard *n* **post**, marker, pillar, stake, pole

bolster *v* **boost**, strengthen, reinforce, encourage, shore up *Opposite*: undermine

bolt *n* **bar**, pin, rod, catch, latch ■ *v* **1 fasten**, secure, lock, lock up, attach *Opposite*: unlock **2 run off**, make a dash for it, run, make a run for it, disappear **3 gulp**, wolf, gobble, devour, down *Opposite*: nibble

bolt from the blue *n* **surprise**, shock, upset, jolt, blow

bolthole *n* **hideaway**, refuge, sanctuary, den, place of safety

bomb *v* **1 bombard**, shell, blast, barrage, blitz **2** *(infml)* **fail**, flop, fall flat, sink without trace, disappoint *Opposite*: succeed

bombard *v* **1 bomb**, shell, open fire on, blast, barrage **2 assail**, shower, flood, inundate, overrun

bombardment *n* **1 attack**, offensive, assault, salvo, bombing **2 barrage**, flood, onslaught, blitz, volley

bombast *n* **pomposity**, pretentiousness, verboseness, affectation, grandiloquence *Opposite*: directness

bombastic *adj* **pompous**, pretentious, verbose, long-winded, grandiloquent *Opposite*: direct

bombshell *(infml)* *n* **shock**, surprise, bolt from the blue, blow, upset

bomb site *n* **area of devastation**, crater, ruins, battlefield, wasteland

bona fide *adj* **genuine**, authentic, true, real, valid *Opposite*: bogus

bonanza *n* **jackpot**, pot of gold, gold mine, stroke of luck, bonus

bonce *(infml)* *n* **head**, skull, cranium, nut *(infml)*, noddle *(dated infml)*

bond *n* **1 tie**, link, connection, union, attachment **2 promise**, pledge, oath, word ■ *v* **1 adhere**, stick, glue, fix, join **2 connect**, get on, become attached, relate, hit it off *(infml)* *Opposite*: clash

bondage *n* **slavery**, enslavement, captivity, oppression, servitude *Opposite*: freedom

bonded *adj* **fused together**, fused, stuck, glued, attached *Opposite*: split

bonding *n* **attachment**, closeness, tie, connection, love

bone of contention *n* **disagreement**, sticking point, difficulty, problem, obstacle

boner *(infml)* *n* **mistake**, blunder, error, gaffe, misstep

boneshaker *(infml)* *n* **wreck**, banger *(infml)*, rattletrap *(infml)*, jalopy *(dated infml)*, heap *(slang)*

bone up *(infml)* *v* **find out about**, research, look into, gen up *(infml)*, swot up *(infml)*

bonfire *n* **fire**, conflagration, blaze, beacon

bong *n* **bang**, blow, thud, crash, knock

bonhomie *n* **friendliness**, sociability, affability, geniality, amenability

bonk *(infml)* *v* **hit**, bang, knock, tap, slap ■ *n* **knock**, blow, slap, bang, tap

bonkers *(infml)* *adj* **irrational**, silly, crazy *(infml)*, daft *(infml)*, off the deep end *(infml)* *Opposite*: rational

bon mot *n* **witticism**, quip, joke, epigram, clever remark

bonny *adj* **good-looking**, lovely, pretty, handsome, attractive *Opposite*: unattractive

bonus *n* **1 extra**, addition, advantage, windfall, benefit **2 gratuity**, handout, pay supplement, reward

bon vivant *n* **pleasure-seeker**, lotus-eater, gourmet, epicure, gourmand *Opposite*: ascetic

bony *adj* **skinny**, scrawny, lanky, lean, thin *Opposite*: plump

boo *n* **catcall**, jeer, hoot, raspberry *Opposite*: cheer ■ *v* **jeer**, hoot, catcall, hiss, barrack *(infml) Opposite*: applaud

boob *(infml)* *n* **1 blunder**, mistake, error, gaffe, slip-up *(infml)* **2 fool**, dupe, sucker *(infml)*, mug *(slang)*, fall guy *(slang)* ■ *v* **make a mistake**, get it wrong, slip up *(infml)*, foul up *(infml)*, mess up *(infml)*

boo-boo *(infml)* *n* **blunder**, mistake, error, gaffe, slip-up *(infml)*

booby trap *n* **1 snare**, trap, trick, ruse, con **2 bomb**, tripwire, mine, explosive device

boogie *v* *(infml)* **dance**, jig, jive, bop *(infml)*, party *(infml)* ■ *n* **jig**, jive, bop *(infml)*, party *(infml)*

book *n* **volume**, tome, manuscript, paperback, hardback ■ *v* **reserve**, order, engage, put your name down for, sign up for

book in *v* **check in**, register, sign in, enlist, enrol *Opposite*: leave

booking *n* **reservation**, hold, option, deposit

bookish *adj* **studious**, serious, academic, scholarly, brainy

bookishness *n* **studiousness**, erudition, scholarliness, learning, learnedness

booklet *n* **brochure**, pamphlet, leaflet, flier

books *n* **records**, accounts, financial statements, balance sheet, profit and loss

bookworm *(infml)* *n* **avid reader**, book lover, bibliophile

boom *v* **1 roar**, rumble, thunder, bellow, resound **2 grow**, soar, rocket, increase, rise *Opposite*: collapse ■ *n* **1 growth**, increase, rise, upsurge, expansion *Opposite*: collapse **2 pole**, arm, bracket, beam ■ *adj* **prosperous**, flourishing, affluent, successful, thriving

boomerang *v* **rebound**, bounce back, return, ricochet, come back

booming *adj* **1 thriving**, prosperous, wealthy, flourishing, successful *Opposite*: failing **2 thunderous**, roaring, resounding, resonant, sonorous *Opposite*: quiet

boon *n* **advantage**, benefit, bonus, help, godsend *Opposite*: disadvantage

boor *n* **lout**, oaf, yob *(infml)*, yobbo *(infml)*, loudmouth *(infml)*

boorish *adj* **rude**, ill-mannered, impolite, coarse, rough *Opposite*: well-mannered

boorishness *n* **crudeness**, loutishness, uncouthness, incivility, rudeness *Opposite*: courteousness

boost *v* **1 increase**, improve, enhance, make better, further *Opposite*: reduce **2 encourage**, support, lift, uplift, give a boost to *Opposite*: discourage ■ *n* **improvement**, increase, enhancement, lift, helping hand *Opposite*: blow

booster *n* **injection**, inoculation, vaccination, immunization, shot *(infml)*

boost up *v* **1 increase**, improve, enhance, boost, add to *Opposite*: reduce **2 encourage**, support, lift, uplift, give a boost to *Opposite*: discourage

booth *n* **cubicle**, stand, closet, compartment, sukkah

bootlace *n* **shoelace**, cord, lace, strap, tie

bootleg *adj* **illegal**, pirated, stolen, illicit, unlicensed *Opposite*: legal

bootless *adj* **useless**, scant, feeble, inadequate, unsuccessful *Opposite*: successful

boot out *(infml)* *v* **dismiss**, get rid of, eject, evict, bounce *Opposite*: appoint

booty *n* **loot**, spoils, plunder, ill-gotten gains, valuables

bop *(infml)* *v* **1 dance**, jig, jive, boogie *(infml)* **2 hit**, bang, knock, tap, thump ■ *n* **1 jig**, dance, jive, boogie *(infml)* **2 disco**, dance, party, ball, rave *(slang)*

border *n* **1 frontier**, borderline, boundary **2 edge**, limit, boundary, margin, verge *Opposite*: centre **3 flowerbed**, bed, shrub border, herbaceous border ■ *v* **be next to**, touch, be bounded by, border on, run alongside

bordering *adj* **adjoining**, neighbouring, adjacent, next door, nearby

borderland *n* **boundary**, edge, frontier, limits, border *Opposite*: heartland

borderline *adj* **marginal**, disputed, uncertain, doubtful, unclear *Opposite*: clear-cut ■ *n* **frontier**, boundary, border

border on v **1 approach**, be close to, resemble, be similar to, verge on **2 be next to**, touch, be bounded by, border, adjoin

bore v **1 turn off** (infml), weary, send to sleep, bore to death, bore to tears Opposite: interest **2 drill**, perforate, penetrate, pierce, tunnel

bored adj **uninterested**, tired, bored rigid, bored stiff, bored to death Opposite: fascinated

boredom n **tedium**, monotony, dullness, tediousness, ennui Opposite: interest

borehole n **well**, hole, shaft

boring adj **uninteresting**, tedious, dull, dreary, mind-numbing Opposite: exciting

born adj **instinctive**, congenital, innate, intuitive, natural Opposite: trained

born-again adj **reinvigorated**, reborn, enthusiastic, avid, fervid

borough n **area**, district, municipality, division, township (US)

borrow v **1 use**, make use of, have access to, scrounge (infml), sponge (infml) Opposite: lend **2 copy**, plagiarize, derive, pirate, steal

borstal n **detention centre**, youth custody centre, prison, reformatory, jail

bosom (infml) adj **close**, best, dearest, special, firm Opposite: distant

boss n **manager**, supervisor, chief, head, person in charge Opposite: subordinate ■ v **give orders**, tell what to do, boss about, boss around, order around Opposite: obey

boss about see boss around

boss around v **give orders**, tell what to do, order about, order around, boss Opposite: obey

bossiness n **imperiousness**, officiousness, high-handedness, authoritarianism, overbearingness Opposite: meekness

bossy adj **domineering**, officious, dominant, high-handed, dictatorial Opposite: meek

botanic see botanical

botanical adj **vegetal**, plant, botanic

botch v **spoil**, damage, ruin, do badly, make a mess of ■ n (infml) **fiasco**, failure, disaster, flop (infml), cockup (infml)

botched adj **failed**, substandard, poor, ruined, inferior Opposite: first-rate

bother v **1 make an effort**, take the trouble, put yourself out, go to the trouble of, extend yourself **2 worry**, trouble, disturb, upset, unsettle **3 interrupt**, disturb, distract, trouble, pester ■ n **trouble**, difficulty, problem, nuisance, inconvenience

COMPARE AND CONTRAST CORE MEANING: interfere with somebody's composure
bother cause to feel worried, anxious, or upset, or disturb or interrupt; **annoy** irritate or harass; **bug** (infml) persistently cause trouble and annoy; **disturb** interrupt or distract in the process of doing something, or to upset the peace of mind of; **trouble** cause distress or inconvenience to; **worry** cause to be anxious.

bothered adj **worried**, concerned, troubled, anxious, apprehensive Opposite: untroubled

bothersome adj **troublesome**, inconvenient, worrisome, niggling, difficult

bothy n **hut**, cottage, cabin, house, shelter

bottle n **1 flask**, jug, carafe, flagon, decanter **2** (infml) **courage**, bravery, nerve, spirit, spine

bottleneck n **block**, blockage, restricted access, holdup, traffic jam

bottle out (infml) v **withdraw**, fail, refuse to do, lose courage, chicken out (infml)

bottle up v **contain**, repress, suppress, keep in check, keep inside

bottom n **1 base**, bed, foot, floor, substructure Opposite: top **2 end**, far end, foot, extremity, limit Opposite: top **3 underside**, underneath, bottom side, underbelly Opposite: top ■ adj **lowest**, bottommost, lowermost, nethermost (fml) Opposite: top

bottomless adj **unlimited**, unrestricted, endless, limitless, unending Opposite: restricted

bottom line n **1 fundamental issue**, key issue, fact of the matter, thing to bear in mind, crucial thing **2 lower limit**, threshold, floor, cutoff point, limit

bottommost adj **lowest**, last, bottom, final Opposite: topmost

boudoir n **bedroom**, dressing room, chamber (literary), bedchamber (literary)

bouffant adj **backcombed**, fluffy, full, puffed up, voluminous

bough n **branch**, limb, spur

boulder n **rock**, stone, sarsen

bounce v **1 rebound**, spring back, bound, spring up, recoil **2 spring**, jump, bound, bob, bobble **3 eject**, evict, throw out, remove, expel

bounce back v **recover**, improve, get better, pull through, perk up

bounciness n **1 liveliness**, spirit, vivacity, friskiness, playfulness Opposite: lethargy **2 elasticity**, springiness, resistance, resilience, pliability Opposite: firmness

bouncy adj **1 effervescent**, energetic, playful, lively, vivacious Opposite: lethargic **2 springy**, elastic, pliable Opposite: firm

bound adj **1 certain**, sure, guaranteed, destined, assured Opposite: unlikely **2 obliged**, compelled, forced, obligated, duty-bound Opposite: free ■ v **border**, border on, be next to, touch, be adjacent to ■ n **jump**, leap, spring, bounce, hop

boundary n **border**, frontier, borderline, edge, dividing line

bounded adj **1 surrounded**, bordered, enclosed, encircled, delimited **2 restricted**, hemmed in, limited, constrained, confined Opposite: free

boundless adj **unlimited**, endless, limitless, infinite, ceaseless Opposite: restricted

bounds n **limits**, boundaries, confines, restrictions, constraints

bounteous (literary) see bountiful

bountiful (literary) adj **1 generous**, giving, munificent, openhanded, liberal Opposite: parsimonious **2 plentiful**, generous, abundant, copious, profuse Opposite: scarce. See COMPARE AND CONTRAST at **generous**.

bounty n **reward**, price, prize, payment, gift

bouquet n **1 bunch**, spray, posy, arrangement, nosegay **2 smell**, aroma, scent, fragrance, perfume. See COMPARE AND CONTRAST at **smell**.

bourgeois adj **middle-class**, conventional, conformist, unadventurous, staid ■ n **conservative**, traditionalist, conformist, reactionary, conventional person

bout n **short period**, short time, session, spell, attack

bow n **1 arc**, curve, arch, sweep, bend **2 bob**, bend, curtsy, obeisance (fml) ■ v **1 bend**, bend over, lower, stoop, lean Opposite: straighten up **2 distort**, deform, arch, droop, sag Opposite: straighten

---

WORD BANK
❑ types of bow crossbow, Cupid's bow, longbow

---

bowdlerize v **censor**, edit, abridge, clean up, expurgate

bowed adj **curved**, bent, deformed, convex, hooked Opposite: straight

bowels n **guts**, entrails, viscera, innards (infml), insides (infml)

bower n **arbour**, retreat, grove, copse, den

bowl n **1 container**, vessel, dish, basin, mixing bowl **2 hollow**, depression, crater, basin, valley **3 ball**, wood, boule ■ v **1 career**, career, roll along, travel, speed **2 roll**, pitch, throw, lob, hurl

bowlegged adj **bandy-legged**, bandy, bent, bowed

bowl over v **1 astonish**, amaze, delight, overwhelm, take by surprise **2 knock down**, knock over, scatter, upturn, overturn

bow out v **back out**, beg off, duck out, cry off (infml)

bow tie n **tie**, cravat, dicky bow (infml), dicky (infml), necktie (US)

bow to v **accept**, yield, resign yourself to, recognize, acknowledge Opposite: reject

box n **1 container**, case, chest, packet, carton **2 rectangle**, square, frame, tick box, check box **3 cubicle**, stall, booth, compartment, enclosure ■ v **fight**, spar, punch, hit, thump

box in v **enclose**, surround, contain, shut in, trap

boxroom n **cubbyhole**, spare room, storeroom, glory hole (infml), closet (US)

boy n **young man**, lad, schoolboy, son, youngster

boycott v **refuse**, stay away from, impose sanctions, embargo, shun

boyfriend n **male friend**, date, escort, fiancé, partner Opposite: girlfriend

boyhood n **childhood**, youth, early years

boyish adj **youthful**, adolescent, childlike, fresh-faced, young

brace n **support**, strut, prop, stay, bracket

brace yourself v **prepare yourself**, ready yourself, make preparations, get ready for, prime yourself

bracing adj **invigorating**, stimulating, brisk, healthy, cold Opposite: soporific

bracket n **1 support**, strut, prop, stay, brace **2 group**, set, range, cohort, band ■ v **connect**, link, join, relate, associate Opposite: separate

brackish adj **salty**, saline, salted, briny, salt Opposite: fresh

brag v **boast**, crow, show off, swagger, talk big Opposite: underplay

braggart n **boaster**, egotist, show-off (infml), bigmouth (infml), loudmouth (infml)

bragging n **boasting**, boastfulness, showing off, arrogance, self-aggrandizement Opposite: modesty ■ adj **boastful**, arrogant, self-important, conceited, swaggering Opposite: modest

braid v **1 plait**, interweave, interlace, intertwine, weave Opposite: unravel **2 decorate**, trim, edge, fringe, bind Opposite: strip

brain n **1 intelligence**, mind, intellect, head, wits **2** (infml) **intellectual**, genius, intellect, prodigy, brainbox

brainchild n **idea**, invention, creation, innovation, breakthrough

brainless adj **foolish**, stupid, mindless, unintelligent, silly Opposite: sensible

brainpower n **intellect**, brains, capacity, ability, intellectual capacity

brains n **intelligence**, common sense, wits, intellect, brainpower Opposite: ignorance

brainstorm n **aberration**, fit, turn, disturbance, upset ■ v **think**, suggest, come up with, devise, dream up

brainteaser n **problem**, puzzle, riddle, challenge, conundrum

brainwash v **persuade**, indoctrinate, condition, convince, programme

brain wave (infml) n **bright idea**, inspiration, idea, breakthrough, innovation

brainy (infml) adj **intelligent**, clever, bright, quick, academic Opposite: unintelligent

braise v **cook**, stew, casserole, steam, simmer

brake v **decelerate**, slow down, reduce speed, put on the brakes, lose speed Opposite: accelerate ■ n **restraint**, constraint, curb, control, limitation Opposite: incentive

bran n **fibre**, dietary fibre, cellulose, roughage, bulk

branch n **1 bough**, limb, spur, twig **2 local office**, division, area office, subdivision, outlet Opposite: headquarters **3 division**, department, offshoot, wing, arm **4 area**, field, topic, domain, sphere **5 turning**, turn-off, arm, tributary, fork ■ *v* **split**, fork, divide, diverge, separate *Opposite*: converge

branch off *v* **split**, fork, divide, turn off, leave *Opposite*: merge

branch out *v* **diversify**, diverge, take a new direction, broaden, expand *Opposite*: consolidate

brand *n* **1 make**, product, brand name, trade name, trademark **2 type**, kind, sort, style, variety **3 identifying mark**, mark, marker, identification, label ■ *v* **1 mark**, imprint, stamp, label **2 call**, classify, label, name, describe

brandish *v* **wield**, wave, flourish, handle, flaunt

brand name *n* **trade name**, brand, label, make, trademark

brand-new *adj* **new**, unused, pristine, fresh, mint *Opposite*: old

brash *adj* **1 aggressive**, arrogant, self-confident, brazen, presumptuous *Opposite*: self-effacing **2 loud**, garish, vulgar, gaudy, bright *Opposite*: muted

brashness *n* **boldness**, brazenness, forcefulness, insolence, assertiveness *Opposite*: shyness

brass (*infml*) *n* **nerve**, impudence, self-assurance, self-confidence, cheek (*infml*) *Opposite*: bashfulness

brass tacks *n* **basics**, essentials, fundamentals, bare essentials, nuts and bolts (*infml*)

brassy *adj* **1 harsh**, loud, metallic, strident, grating *Opposite*: soft **2 brazen**, strident, overbearing, brash, arrogant *Opposite*: self-effacing

brat *n* **little monster**, imp, spoiled brat, terror (*infml*), holy terror (*infml*) *Opposite*: cherub

bratty *adj* **obnoxious**, spoiled, demanding, overindulged, selfish *Opposite*: well-behaved

bravado *n* **audacity**, boldness, daring, bluster, boasting *Opposite*: cowardice

brave *adj* **courageous**, valiant, heroic, bold, daring *Opposite*: cowardly ■ *v* **defy**, face, stand up to, confront, take on *Opposite*: shrink

brave out *v* **suffer**, face, bear, endure, stay the course *Opposite*: give up

bravery *n* **courage**, courageousness, valour, gallantry, daring *Opposite*: cowardice. *See* COMPARE AND CONTRAST *at* **courage**.

bravura *n* **boldness**, daring, spirit, nerve, guts (*slang*) *Opposite*: timidity ■ *adj* **brilliant**, magnificent, exceptional, dazzling, outstanding *Opposite*: nondescript

brawl *n* **scuffle**, fight, punch-up, clash, affray ■ *v* **fight**, scuffle, tussle, wrestle, clash

brawn *n* **strength**, muscle, brute force, power, burliness *Opposite*: weakness

brawny *adj* **muscular**, strong, powerfully built, hefty, burly *Opposite*: scrawny

bray *v* **1 whinny**, neigh, cry, call **2 grate**, rasp, bark, bellow, snort *Opposite*: murmur

braying *adj* **harsh**, loud, strident, jarring, grating *Opposite*: soft

brazen *adj* **bold**, barefaced, shameless, brash, unabashed *Opposite*: discreet

brazenness *n* **shamelessness**, boldness, barefacedness, flagrancy, impudence *Opposite*: discretion

brazen out *v* **face down**, stand your ground, face out, hold your own, stay the course *Opposite*: cave in

brazier *n* **stove**, barbecue, grill, hibachi, fire

breach *v* **1 get through**, break through, break, rupture, penetrate *Opposite*: block **2 break**, violate, contravene, infringe, flout *Opposite*: honour ■ *n* **1 opening**, break, hole, crack, fissure **2 violation**, contravention, infringement, defiance, betrayal *Opposite*: compliance **3 rift**, separation, division, rupture, estrangement *Opposite*: reconciliation

breach of the peace *n* **public disturbance**, public nuisance, nuisance, riot, fracas *Opposite*: order

bread *n* **food**, daily bread, sustenance, nourishment, rations

---

WORD BANK

❏ **types of bread** baguette, black bread, bloomer, brown bread, challah, chapati, ciabatta, cob, cottage loaf, crôuton, flat bread, focaccia, matzo, nan, pitta, poppadom, pumpernickel, puri, roti, rye bread, soda bread, sourdough, toast, tortilla, wheat bread, white bread, wholemeal

❏ **types of roll or bun** bagel, bap, brioche, bun, croissant, crumpet, muffin, roll

---

bread and butter *n* **1 livelihood**, living, income, maintenance, upkeep **2 mainstay**, lifeblood, backbone, basis, core

bread-and-butter *adj* **basic**, primary, fundamental, essential, important *Opposite*: superfluous

breadth *n* **1 width**, span, wideness, extent, size *Opposite*: depth **2 extensiveness**, extent, range, scope, span *Opposite*: narrowness **3 latitude**, room, freedom, space, leeway *Opposite*: restriction

breadthways *adj* **sideways**, side-to-side, widthways, breadthwise (*US*) ■ *adv* **across**, from side to side, breadthwise (*US*)

breadwinner *n* **wage earner**, worker, employee *Opposite*: dependant

break *v* **1 smash**, fracture, rupture, shatter, split *Opposite*: mend **2 break down**, stop working, fail, collapse, crash **3 infringe**, violate, contravene, breach, disobey *Opposite*: uphold **4 stop**, end, interrupt, disturb, break into **5 take a break**, break into, have a break, rest, stop **6 beat**, surpass, exceed, top, better **7 destroy**, shatter, crush, overwhelm, defeat **8 become known**, make public, become public, disclose, get round **9 decipher**, crack, decode, solve, unravel ■ n **1 disruption**, breakdown, discontinuity, interruption, pause **2 rest**, respite, coffee break, pause, lunch break **3 holiday**, time off, weekend break, trip, vacation **4 interruption**, pause, space, disruption, halt **5** (infml) **chance**, opportunity, opening, occasion, leg up

breakable adj **fragile**, delicate, brittle, frail, flimsy Opposite: sturdy

breakage n **breaking**, smashing, cracking, rupture, splintering Opposite: mending

break away v **secede**, separate, become independent, split, disaffiliate Opposite: join

breakaway n **separation**, rupture, severance, splitting up, breakup Opposite: fusion ■ adj **separate**, splinter, independent, autonomous, alternative Opposite: mainstream

break down v **1 stop working**, break, fail, go down, crash **2 lose control**, cry, be overcome, collapse, burst into tears **3 overcome**, defeat, destroy, knock down, smash down Opposite: build **4 analyse**, separate, dissect, break up, split **5 divide**, classify, categorize, split, separate Opposite: lump **6 decompose**, decay, putrefy, disintegrate, moulder

breakdown n **1 failure**, collapse, cessation, halt, interruption **2 analysis**, rundown, classification, dissection, summary

breaker n **wave**, roller, whitecap, white horse

break free v **escape**, break away, break with, separate, get away

break in v **1 tame**, train, discipline, domesticate, housetrain **2 force an entry**, break into, burgle, break and enter, force the lock **3 interrupt**, butt in, interject, interpose, cut in

break-in n **forced entry**, burglary, robbery, crime, felony

breaking n **contravention**, infringement, violation, breach, transgression Opposite: observance

breaking point n **verge of collapse**, limit, threshold, snapping point, crisis

break into v **1 break in**, force an entry, burgle, break and enter, break down the door **2 begin**, burst into, launch into, embark on, burst out Opposite: break off

breakneck adj **quick**, speedy, hurried, hasty, rapid Opposite: slow

break new ground v **be the first**, blaze a trail, lead the way, be in the vanguard, set a trend

break of day n **daybreak**, sunrise, daylight, first light, dawn Opposite: sundown

break off v **1 detach**, come off, snap off, come away, separate Opposite: attach **2 end**, terminate, stop, cease, finish Opposite: begin

breakoff n **discontinuation**, ending, interruption, suspension, stopping Opposite: continuation

break open v **open**, divide, come apart, burst, shatter

break out v **1 begin**, start, erupt, burst into, embark on Opposite: end **2 escape**, break loose, burst out, break free, emerge

breakout n **escape**, getaway, flight, running away, running off

break the ice v **get to know**, make friends, get acquainted, introduce yourself, set the ball rolling

break through v **burst through**, penetrate, come through, breach, wear down

breakthrough n **advance**, step forward, leap forward, new idea, innovation

break up v **1 divide**, fragment, disintegrate, crumble, fall apart Opposite: fuse **2 disperse**, separate, split up, keep apart, divide up Opposite: unite **3 separate**, tell somebody it's over, split up, end, finish

breakup n **1 disintegration**, fragmentation, division, crumbling, destruction Opposite: merger **2 ending**, end, splitting up, finish, separation

breakwater n **offshore barrier**, sea wall, harbour wall, causeway, pier

break with v **separate**, split, leave, part company, escape Opposite: associate

breath n **1 gasp**, sigh, pant, inhalation, exhalation **2 puff**, waft, current, draught, gush

breathe v **respire**, take breaths, inhale, exhale, suck in air

breathe new life into v **revitalize**, reinvigorate, revive, resurrect, rejuvenate

breather (infml) n **rest**, break, respite, sit-down (infml), time out (US)

breathing n **inhalation**, exhalation, panting, gasping, puffing ■ adj **living**, alive, conscious, sentient, aware

breathing space n **respite**, relief, space, recovery time, time

breathless adj **out of breath**, panting, gasping, puffing, winded

breathlessly adv **eagerly**, excitedly, with bated breath, on tenterhooks, anxiously Opposite: nonchalantly

breathtaking adj **out of this world**, wonderful, magnificent, spectacular, incredible Opposite: banal

breathy adj **wheezy**, hissing, gasping, panting, husky

breed n **type**, strain, class, kind, variety ■ v **1 reproduce**, have babies, propagate, procreate, multiply **2 raise**, rear, bring up, farm, produce **3 cause**, create, generate, bring about, produce

breeding n **upbringing**, education, background, social standing, refinement

breeding ground n **environment**, conditions, source, medium, place

breeze n **1 wind**, gust, gentle wind, light wind, waft Opposite: gale **2** (infml) **child's play**, cinch (infml), piece of cake (infml), doddle (infml), walkover (infml)

breezily *adv* **brightly**, cheerfully, cheerily, happily, merrily *Opposite*: seriously

breezy *adj* **1 blustery**, gusty, windy, brisk, windswept *Opposite*: still **2 cheerful**, cheery, jolly, lighthearted, flippant *Opposite*: serious

breviary *n* **missal**, prayer book, hymnal, book of psalms

brevity *n* **1 shortness**, briefness, quickness, swiftness, transience *Opposite*: length **2 conciseness**, succinctness, concision, pithiness, terseness *Opposite*: verbosity

brew *n* **1** *(infml)* **drink**, potion, infusion, cocktail, beverage *(fml)* **2 mixture**, mix, blend, combination, concoction ■ *v* **1 prepare**, make, infuse, steep, ferment **2 develop**, loom, threaten, grow, blow up

bribe *n* **inducement**, enticement, carrot, kickback, slush fund ■ *v* **induce**, corrupt, entice, suborn, persuade

bribery *n* **corruption**, inducement, enticement, subornation

bric-a-brac *n* **curios**, ornaments, stuff, jumble, knick-knacks

brick *n* **block**, slab, ingot, lump, piece

brickbat *n* **insult**, criticism, insinuation, suggestion, comment

brickwork *n* **fabric**, structure, bricks and mortar, masonry, stonework

bridal *adj* **wedding**, nuptial, marriage, honeymoon

bride *n* **wife**, wife-to-be, newlywed, spouse, partner

bridegroom *n* **husband**, husband-to-be, newlywed, spouse, partner

bridesmaid *n* **maid of honour**, attendant, matron of honour, flower girl

bridge *n* **bond**, tie, link, connection, conduit ■ *v* **link**, connect, join, span, tie together

---

WORD BANK
❏ **types of bridge** aqueduct, arch bridge, Bailey bridge, bascule bridge, beam bridge, cable-stayed bridge, cantilever bridge, drawbridge, flyover, footbridge, gangplank, humpback bridge, pontoon bridge, suspension bridge, swing bridge, viaduct, walkway

---

bridgehead *n* **foothold**, position, stepping stone, jumping-off point, vantage point

bridle *v* **1 bristle**, get angry, become annoyed, become indignant, prickle **2 curb**, restrain, control, rein in, keep in check *Opposite*: let loose

bridle path *n* **bridleway**, ride, path, track, trail

brief *adj* **1 short-lived**, transitory, fleeting, ephemeral, short-term *Opposite*: lasting **2 short**, concise, succinct, to the point, pithy *Opposite*: lengthy ■ *n* **1 synopsis**, summary, digest, abstract, outline **2 briefing**, instructions, guidelines, preparation, orders **3 task**, remit, mission, mandate, assignment

4 *(infml)* **legal representative**, lawyer, barrister, QC, attorney ■ *v* **inform**, tell, give instructions, prepare, instruct

briefcase *n* **document case**, attaché case, case, portfolio, music case

briefing *n* **meeting**, conference, seminar, press conference, updating session

brigade *n* **group**, team, crew, contingent, gang

bright *adj* **1 brilliant**, vivid, intense, dazzling, light *Opposite*: dark **2 intelligent**, quick, sharp-witted, clever, smart *Opposite*: unintelligent **3 cheerful**, happy, lively, optimistic, positive *Opposite*: gloomy. *See* COMPARE AND CONTRAST *at* **intelligent**.

brighten *v* **1 feel better**, brighten up, look up, perk up, cheer up **2 make brighter**, lighten, make lighter, brighten up, illuminate *Opposite*: darken **3 improve**, make better, enhance, animate, revivify

brighten up *v* **raise the spirits**, make brighter, brighten, lighten, make lighter *Opposite*: cast down

brightly *adv* **1 luminously**, lustrously, radiantly, glossily, glowingly *Opposite*: dully **2 sunnily**, perkily, cheerfully, cheerily, optimistically *Opposite*: gloomily

brightness *n* **1 illumination**, glare, intensity, brilliance, vividness *Opposite*: dullness **2 sunniness**, high spirits, cheerfulness, optimism, cheeriness *Opposite*: gloominess

brilliance *n* **1 brightness**, intensity, vividness, luminosity, radiance *Opposite*: dullness **2 cleverness**, wisdom, smartness, genius, talent *Opposite*: stupidity

brilliancy *see* **brilliance**

brilliant *adj* **1 luminous**, radiant, dazzling, sparkling, gleaming *Opposite*: dull **2 vivid**, bright, clear, intense, dazzling *Opposite*: faded **3 talented**, virtuoso, inspired, skilful, gifted *Opposite*: mediocre **4** *(infml)* **wonderful**, marvellous, superb, excellent, magnificent *Opposite*: awful

brim *n* **ridge**, edge, top, rim, lip

brimful *adj* **full to the top**, full, filled up, filled to the brim, overfull *Opposite*: empty

brimming *adj* **bursting**, teeming, overflowing, packed, filled

brine *n* **saline**, salt water, sea water

bring *v* **1 take along**, carry, fetch, convey, transport *Opposite*: take away **2 cause**, bring about, produce, lead to, result in **3 command**, earn, produce, make, bring in

bring about *v* **generate**, cause, produce, result in, end in *Opposite*: prevent

bring alive *v* **awaken**, bring to life, make real, animate, enliven

bring back *v* **1 evoke**, recall, bring to mind, summon up, reawaken **2 return**, replace, restore, reinstate, recapture *Opposite*: carry off

bring down *v* **1 overthrow**, topple, depose,

defeat, dethrone *Opposite*: elect **2 fell**, floor, topple, demolish, knock over *Opposite*: raise

bring down a peg *v* humble, chasten, force to eat humble pie, cut down to size, put in their place

bring down to earth *v* disillusion, disappoint, disenchant, enlighten, disabuse

bring forth *v* deliver, bear, give birth to, produce, yield

bring forward *v* **1** speed, advance, reschedule, move forward, change *Opposite*: delay **2 put on the table**, produce, present, offer, bring out *Opposite*: withdraw

bring home *v* make clear, clarify, illustrate, illuminate, underline

bring home the bacon *(infml)* *v* **1 be successful**, bring off, come up with the goods, come through, keep your end of the bargain *Opposite*: fail **2 provide**, keep a roof over your head, put food on the table, keep the wolf from the door, keep clothes on your back

bring in *v* **1** introduce, set up, establish, launch, start *Opposite*: end **2 recoup**, acquire, earn, make, take home *Opposite*: lose

bring into being *v* create, establish, found, institute, set up *Opposite*: destroy

bring into disrepute *v* discredit, dishonour, disgrace, shame, smear *Opposite*: honour

bring into line *v* standardize, coordinate, synchronize, make uniform, harmonize

bring off *v* succeed, carry off, achieve, accomplish, engineer *Opposite*: fail

bring on *v* cause, create, produce, make, start

bring out *v* **1** highlight, spotlight, show up, reveal, bring to the surface *Opposite*: suppress **2 introduce**, produce, release, put on sale, launch *Opposite*: withdraw

bring round *v* **1** sway, reason, get round, convince, persuade *Opposite*: deter **2 bring to**, rouse, awaken, wake up, revive *Opposite*: knock out

bring shame on *v* discredit, sully, tarnish, smear, stain *Opposite*: honour

bring to *v* bring round, rouse, awaken, wake up, revive *Opposite*: knock out

bring to a close *see* bring to an end

bring to an end *v* conclude, bring to a close, put a stop to, end, stop *Opposite*: start

bring together *v* **1** combine, mix, mix together, blend, pool *Opposite*: separate **2 gather**, amass, rally, compile, glean *Opposite*: distribute **3 reconcile**, integrate, unite, unify, link

bring to life *v* make real, animate, bring alive, anthropomorphize, give life to

bring to light *v* expose, unearth, disclose, uncover, publicize *Opposite*: hide

bring to mind *v* summon up, reawaken, rekindle, stir up, bring back

bring up *v* **1** mention, broach, raise, suggest, introduce *Opposite*: gloss over **2 raise**, rear,

care for, nurture, look after **3 vomit**, expel, spew, regurgitate, disgorge

bring up-to-date *v* inform, give the lowdown, look after, put in the picture, update *Opposite*: keep in the dark

brink *n* **1 verge**, threshold, edge, point, precipice **2 edge**, rim, lip, brim, border *Opposite*: centre

brinkmanship *n* strategy, tactics, politics, bluff, bluffing

briny *adj* salty, salt, saline, salted, brackish ■ *n* sea, ocean, deep, drink *(infml)*

brisk *adj* **1 energetic**, fast, quick, rapid, hurried *Opposite*: slow **2 abrupt**, curt, impatient, brusque, hurried *Opposite*: measured **3 refreshing**, cool, cold, invigorating, stimulating *Opposite*: warm

briskness *n* **1 speed**, rapidity, vigour, efficiency, urgency *Opposite*: tardiness **2 abruptness**, coldness, reserve, brusqueness, curtness *Opposite*: patience

bristle *n* stubble, hackle, hair, spine, spike ■ *v* **1 stiffen**, become erect, stand up, rise, prickle **2 bridle**, be resentful, get your hackles up, object, get angry **3 brim**, be full, teem, overflow, be thick with

bristly *adj* spiky, coarse, wiry, stubbly, sharp *Opposite*: smooth

brittle *adj* hard, stiff, inelastic, fragile, breakable *Opposite*: robust

brittleness *n* hardness, stiffness, fragility, weakness, frailty *Opposite*: robustness

broach *v* propose, present, submit, mention, raise

broad *adj* **1 spacious**, wide, large, big, extensive *Opposite*: narrow **2 comprehensive**, extensive, wide, far-reaching, wide-ranging *Opposite*: restricted **3 inexact**, rough, general, approximate, sketchy *Opposite*: precise **4 visible**, obvious, plain, clear, patent *Opposite*: subtle **5 distinctive**, distinct, thick, heavy, strong *Opposite*: slight ■ *n* lake, expanse of water, stretch of water, body of water, mere *(literary)*

broad-brush *adj* inclusive, comprehensive, broad, across-the-board, all-embracing *Opposite*: narrow

broadcast *v* **1 transmit**, air, show, televise, screen **2 air**, spread, disseminate, publicize, make known **3 scatter**, sow, distribute, disseminate, strew ■ *n* transmission, programme, show, airing, newscast

---

WORD BANK

❏ **types of broadcast** chat show, commercial, concert, current affairs, distance learning, docudrama, documentary, drama, game show, infomercial, infotainment, makeover programme, miniseries, news, newscast, news flash, newsreel, phone-in, play, quiz show, reality show, sitcom *(infml)*, soap *(infml)*, soap opera, sports, sportscast, telethon, travelogue

broadcaster n **presenter**, anchor, announcer, reporter, journalist

broaden v **widen**, extend, increase, make wider, become wider Opposite: narrow

broadly adv **approximately**, sketchily, generally, largely, roughly

broadly-based adj **wide**, broad, wide-ranging, extensive, sweeping

broad-minded adj **tolerant**, progressive, liberal, permissive, open-minded Opposite: narrow-minded

broad-mindedness n **liberality**, open-mindedness, tolerance, progressiveness, permissiveness Opposite: narrow-mindedness

broadness n **1 width**, breadth, wideness **2 scope**, breadth, span, range, extensiveness

broadsheet n **paper**, newspaper, quality newspaper, serious newspaper, heavyweight

broadside n **attack**, diatribe, tirade, onslaught, volley

brochure n **booklet**, catalogue, leaflet, pamphlet, information sheet

brogue n **accent**, burr, drawl

broil v **swelter**, burn, roast, bake, boil Opposite: freeze

broke (infml) adj **bankrupt**, penniless, poor, in the red, overdrawn Opposite: wealthy

broken adj **1 wrecked**, imperfect, fragmented, fractured, shattered Opposite: intact **2 inoperative**, malfunctioning, faulty, defective, out of order Opposite: working **3 beaten**, licked, defeated, dejected, crushed Opposite: triumphant

broken-down adj **1 inoperative**, malfunctioning, not working, broken, out of order Opposite: working **2 in poor condition**, dilapidated, run-down, falling apart, ramshackle

brokenhearted adj **sad**, grief-stricken, disappointed, desolate, despairing Opposite: overjoyed

broker n **trader**, agent, dealer, negotiator, stockbroker

bronze n **sculpture**, figure, statue, statuette, effigy

bronzed adj **tanned**, brown, suntanned, golden-brown, coppery

brooch n **pin**, badge, ornament, trinket, accessory

brood n **1 young**, clutch, litter, issue, family **2 children**, offspring, family, progeny, kids (infml) ■ v **ruminate**, worry, mope, dwell on, fret

broodily adv **thoughtfully**, pensively, meditatively, fretfully, sullenly Opposite: cheerfully

broodiness n **pensiveness**, glumness, fretfulness, sullenness, moroseness

brooding adj **ominous**, menacing, threatening, gloomy, dark

broodingly adv **glumly**, fretfully, sullenly, morosely, moodily Opposite: cheerfully

broody adj **1 sullen**, thoughtful, pensive, moody, glum Opposite: cheerful **2 maternal**, motherly, tender, caring

brook n **stream**, beck, rivulet, river, burn

broom n **brush**, sweeper, besom

broomstick n **handle**, broom handle, pole, stick, stave

brother n **comrade**, member, colleague, associate

brotherhood n **1 comradeship**, friendship, companionship, unity, loyalty **2 association**, society, union, guild, organization

brotherly adj **companionable**, fraternal, affectionate, kind, friendly

brouhaha n **commotion**, ruckus, brawl, rumpus, melee

brow n **summit**, top, crest, ridge, peak

browbeat v **intimidate**, badger, bully, dragoon, nag Opposite: coax

browbeaten adj **downtrodden**, oppressed, intimidated, bullied, subjugated Opposite: defiant

brown adj **tanned**, sunburnt, bronzed ■ v **fry**, grill, sear, toast, char

WORD BANK
❑ **types of brown** auburn, bay, bronze, burnt sienna, burnt umber, caramel, chestnut, chocolate, copper, hazel, henna, khaki, liver, mahogany, mocha, mousy, nut-brown, roan, russet, sorrel, tan, tawny, umber, walnut
❑ **types of light brown** beige, biscuit, buff, butterscotch, café au lait, camel, coffee, dun, ecru, fawn, flesh colour, honey, oatmeal

browse v **glance**, cruise, look, peruse, surf

bruise n **discoloration**, black eye, welt, bump, shiner (infml) ■ v **hurt**, damage, mark, injure, discolour

bruised adj **1 injured**, hurt, sore, black-and-blue, damaged Opposite: unhurt **2 wounded**, upset, hurt, offended, affected Opposite: unaffected

bruiser (infml) n **muscleman**, bodyguard, bouncer, tough, heavyweight

brunette adj **dark**, brown, raven (literary) Opposite: blond

brunt n **effect**, force, full force, impact, full impact

brush n **1 broom**, sweeper, besom **2 contact**, touch, stroke, graze, sweep **3 encounter**, meeting, confrontation, skirmish, disagreement ■ v **1 scrub**, clear, coat, groom, sweep **2 touch**, graze, scrape, sweep, stroke

brushed adj **fleecy**, fluffy, downy, furry, soft

brush off v **dismiss**, rebuff, snub, reject, give the cold shoulder to

brushoff (infml) n **turndown**, rebuff, snub, rejection, cold shoulder

brush up v **reread**, refresh, renew, revise, review

brushwood n **firewood**, twigs, branches, undergrowth, kindling

brusque adj **abrupt**, curt, offhand, rough, brisk Opposite: friendly

brusqueness n **roughness**, terseness, abruptness, offhandedness, lack of warmth Opposite: friendliness

brutal adj **1 ruthless**, cruel, vicious, fierce, pitiless Opposite: humane **2 harsh**, severe, rough, callous, insensitive Opposite: kind

brutality n **cruelty**, viciousness, violence, rough treatment, harshness Opposite: gentleness

brutalize v **1 coarsen**, harden, dehumanize, desensitize Opposite: humanize **2 abuse**, assault, maltreat, ill-treat

brute n **1 bully**, thug, beast, swine, monster **2** (literary) **animal**, beast, creature, monster

brutish adj **1 animal**, wild, violent, bestial **2 cruel**, ruthless, insensitive, pitiless, harsh Opposite: humane **3 loutish**, boorish, rough, unrefined, uncivilized Opposite: civilized

brutishly adv **cruelly**, harshly, unfeelingly, insensitively, callously Opposite: humanely

brutishness n **cruelty**, harshness, unkindness, unfeelingness, insensitivity Opposite: humanity

bubble v **fizz**, effervesce, boil, simmer

bubbly adj **1 effervescent**, foamy, sparkling, fizzy, fizzing Opposite: still **2 cheerful**, lively, sparkling, vivacious, bouncy Opposite: sad

buccaneer n **pirate**, adventurer, swashbuckler

buck n (infml) **blame**, liability, culpability, fault ■ v **1 jump**, rear, kick, kick out, bound **2 resist**, oppose, fly in the face of, go against, challenge

bucket n **pail**, container, vessel ■ v (infml) **pour**, pour with rain, pour down, teem, come down in torrents

buckets (infml) n **lots**, scores, loads (infml), tons (infml), heaps (infml)

buckle n **clasp**, clip, fastener, catch, fastening ■ v **1 fasten**, clip, clasp, secure, close Opposite: undo **2 collapse**, crumple, cave in, bulge, fold Opposite: straighten

buckle down (infml) v **get on with**, put your shoulder to the wheel, set to, get down to, knuckle down (infml)

buckshee (infml) adj **free**, complimentary, gratis, on the house ■ adv **free of charge**, free, gratis, for nothing, without paying

buck up v **1** (infml) **raise the morale of**, cheer up, raise the spirits of, hearten **2 improve**, get better, look up, liven up, pick up (infml) Opposite: take a turn for the worse **3** (infml dated) **hurry up**, get going, look lively, get a move on (infml), get your skates on (infml)

bucolic adj **rural**, pastoral, rustic, country, countrified Opposite: urban

bud n **sprout**, blossom, shoot, outgrowth ■ v **blossom**, flower, grow, bloom, open out

budding adj **promising**, potential, up-and-coming, nascent, burgeoning

budge v **move**, shift, dislodge, nudge, push

budget n **financial plan**, financial statement, accounts, finances, funds ■ adj **cheap**, economical, inexpensive, reasonable, low-priced Opposite: expensive ■ v **plan**, account, make financial arrangements, make provisions, cost

budgetary adj **financial**, economic, fiscal, commercial, monetary

buff n **fan**, enthusiast, expert, connoisseur, aficionado ■ v **polish**, rub, rub up, burnish, shine

buffalo (infml) v **intimidate**, coerce, threaten, inhibit, bully

buffer n **shock absorber**, bumper, cushion, barrier, shield ■ v **cushion**, shield, safeguard, defend, protect

buffet v **rock**, pound, batter, bang, knock

buffeting n **battering**, pounding, knocking, beating, pummelling

buffoon n **clown**, joker, comedian, fool, wag (dated)

buffoonery n **horseplay**, clowning, fooling around, frivolity, tomfoolery (infml)

bug n **1 insect**, fly, pest, creature, creepy-crawly (infml) **2** (infml) **germ**, microbe, virus, bacterium, infection **3** (infml) **fault**, error, mistake, problem, gremlin (infml) **4** (infml) **listening device**, hidden microphone, surveillance device, wiretap ■ v **1** (infml) **annoy**, irritate, infuriate, bother, madden **2 tap**, listen in on, keep under surveillance, spy on. See COMPARE AND CONTRAST at **bother**.

bugaboo see **bugbear**

bugbear n **worry**, problem, concern, bother, annoyance

bug-eyed (infml) adj **popeyed**, staring, big-eyed, wide-eyed, agog

buggy n **1 cart**, vehicle, truck, transporter **2 pushchair**, pram, perambulator (fml), stroller (US)

bugle v **announce**, herald, trumpet

build v **1 construct**, put up, erect, make, put together Opposite: destroy **2 put together**, create, make, join, assemble ■ n **shape**, size, figure, body, physique

build in v **incorporate**, include, integrate, add in Opposite: exclude

building n **structure**, construction, edifice, erection (fml)

WORD BANK

❑ **parts of a building** balcony, buttress, chimney, colonnade, doorway, elevation, escalator, exterior, façade, fire escape, frame, frontage, gable, guttering, landing, lift, porch, roof, smokestack, soffit, stairwell, veranda, vestibule, wall, window, wing

build up *v* **1 increase**, rise, develop, expand, enlarge *Opposite*: fall off **2 boost**, bolster, pump up, inspire, encourage *Opposite*: discourage

buildup *n* **1 accumulation**, backlog, accrual, collection, stockpile **2 hype**, publicity, puff, praise, flattery

built-in *adj* **1 integral**, fitted, fixed, en suite, in-built **2 natural**, inherent, innate, intrinsic, ingrained *Opposite*: acquired

built-up *adj* **urbanized**, urban, developed, residential, industrial

bulb *n* **corm**, rhizome, tuber, storage organ, underground part

WORD BANK
❑ **types of flower grown from a bulb** anemone, bluebell, crocus, cyclamen, daffodil, dahlia, freesia, gladiolus, hyacinth, iris, jonquil, lily, narcissus, snowdrop, tulip

bulbous *adj* **rounded**, spherical, bulging, globular, swollen

bulge *v* **stick out**, protrude, expand, be full to bursting, swell ■ *n* **protuberance**, swell, swelling, knot, lump

bulging *adj* **1 protruding**, protuberant, distended, swollen, swelling *Opposite*: flat **2** *(infml)* **full**, overfull, overfilled, overstuffed, crammed *Opposite*: empty

bulk *n* **1 size**, mass, volume, immensity, vastness **2 form**, body, weight, mass, hulk **3 greater part**, main part, largest part, majority, substance

bulkhead *n* **partition**, wall, dividing wall, screen, divider

bulkiness *n* **1 unwieldiness**, awkwardness, ungainliness, cumbersomeness, ponderousness **2 large size**, largeness, weight, bulk, mass *Opposite*: compactness

bulk large *v* **be prominent**, figure prominently, loom large, dominate, be important

bulk up *(infml)* *v* **build up**, increase, pad out, gain weight, gain muscle

bulky *adj* **1 unwieldy**, cumbersome, awkward, ungainly, ponderous *Opposite*: manageable **2 large**, huge, immense, massive, colossal *Opposite*: compact

bull *n* **papal decree**, decree, official statement, encyclical, instruction

bulldoze *v* **1 flatten**, raze, level, demolish, clear **2** *(infml)* **coerce**, bully, bludgeon, browbeat, steamroller

bulletin *n* **1 news report**, update, news item, news summary, press release **2 official statement**, communiqué, statement, announcement, press release **3 periodical**, journal, newsletter, newspaper, publication

bulletproof *adj* **1 toughened**, armoured, protective, reinforced, shatterproof **2** *(infml)* **invulnerable**, secure, invincible, unassailable, untouchable *Opposite*: vulnerable

bullheaded *(infml)* *adj* **obstinate**, headstrong, stubborn, wilful, intransigent

bullheadedness *(infml)* *n* **obstinacy**, stubbornness, wilfulness, intransigence, self-will

bullion *n* **gold**, gold bars, gold ingots

bullish *adj* **1 muscular**, strong, hulking, brawny **2** *(infml)* **optimistic**, confident, buoyant, cheerful, enthusiastic *Opposite*: pessimistic

bullishness *(infml)* *n* **confidence**, optimism, buoyancy, hopefulness, self-confidence *Opposite*: diffidence

bullnecked *adj* **stocky**, bullish, brawny, beefy, muscular

bullring *n* **arena**, ring, stadium, amphitheatre, sports stadium

bull's eye *n* **target**, centre, mark, middle, middle point

bully *n* **tormentor**, aggressor, persecutor, tyrant, oppressor ■ *v* **intimidate**, terrorize, persecute, torment, frighten

bullyboy *n* **thug**, bully, yob *(infml)*, hooligan *(infml)*, heavy *(slang)* ■ *adj* **aggressive**, intimidating, bullying, rough, threatening

bullying *n* **intimidation**, mistreatment, oppression, harassment, victimization

bully-off *n* **start of play**, start, kickoff, beginning, commencement *(fml)*

bulwark *n* **1 fortification**, embankment, earthwork, barricade, rampart **2 safeguard**, protection, defence, buttress, buffer

bumble *v* **1 mumble**, murmur, hesitate, mutter, stutter **2 stumble**, lumber, blunder, stagger, lurch

bumbling *(infml)* *adj* **awkward**, clumsy, blundering, lumbering, ungainly *Opposite*: graceful

bumf *(infml)* *n* **documents**, leaflets, pamphlets, brochures, papers

bump *v* **1 hit**, knock, bang, strike, wallop *(infml)* **2 jolt**, bounce, jounce, jar, jerk **3 collide**, slam into, crash into, knock, smash into ■ *n* **1 knock**, collision, smash, accident, crash **2 swelling**, lump, bruise, bulge, contusion *(fml)* **3 thud**, thump, bang, crash, blow

bumper *adj* **plentiful**, profuse, copious, extra-large, jumbo *Opposite*: meagre

bumpiness *n* **unevenness**, roughness, lumpiness *Opposite*: smoothness

bump into *v* **1 collide**, slam into, crash into, knock into, smash into **2 meet by chance**, run into, happen upon, happen on, meet

bumptious *adj* **full of yourself**, pleased with yourself, self-satisfied, self-important, smug *Opposite*: modest

bumptiousness *n* **self-importance**, conceitedness, arrogance, pompousness, brashness *Opposite*: modesty

bump up *(infml)* *v* **increase**, put up, boost, enhance, add to *Opposite*: decrease

bumpy *adj* **1 uneven**, rough, rutted, potholed *Opposite*: smooth **2 uncomfortable**, rough, bouncy, jarring, jerky *Opposite*: smooth

bunch *n* **1 group**, set, lot, mixture, collection **2 bouquet**, posy, spray, corsage **3** *(infml)* **gang**, gathering, team, set, group ■ *v* **crowd together**, huddle, form a group, gather, cluster *Opposite*: disperse

bundle *n* **package**, pack, parcel, packet, bale ■ *v* *(infml)* **hustle**, hurry, rush, push, shove

bundle up *v* **1 package**, pack, wrap, parcel, parcel up **2** *(infml)* **dress warmly**, wrap up, wrap up warmly

bung *n* **stopper**, plug, cork ■ *v* *(infml)* **throw**, toss, fling, lob, pass

bungle *(infml)* *v* **do badly**, make a mess of, make a dog's dinner of, mismanage, ruin *Opposite*: succeed

bungler *(infml)* *n* **blunderer**, incompetent, bumbler, botcher, muddler

bungling *(infml)* *adj* **clumsy**, incompetent, inept, blundering, maladroit *Opposite*: competent

bung up *(infml)* *v* **stop up**, block, close, clog, caulk *Opposite*: open

bunion *n* **swelling**, lump, enlargement, distension, bulge

bunk *n* **bed**, single bed, berth, couchette, bunk bed

bunker *n* **1 bin**, chest, container, box, store **2 underground shelter**, shelter, dugout, foxhole, ditch

bunkum *(infml)* *n* **nonsense**, humbug, drivel, gibberish, rubbish

bunting *n* **streamers**, decorations, flags, paper chains, ticker tape

buoy *n* **marker**, float, navigational aid ■ *v* **keep afloat**, hold up, sustain, maintain, prop up

buoyancy *n* **1 lightness**, weightlessness *Opposite*: heaviness **2 resilience**, resistance, flexibility, toughness **3 optimism**, cheerfulness, good spirits, enthusiasm, jauntiness *Opposite*: pessimism

buoyant *adj* **1 floating**, afloat, light **2 resilient**, resistant, flexible, tough **3 cheerful**, optimistic, happy, jaunty, carefree *Opposite*: morose

buoy up *v* **cheer**, uplift, encourage, boost, lift *Opposite*: depress

burble *v* **1 bubble**, ripple, babble, splash, murmur **2** *(infml)* **gush**, babble, ramble, go on about, blather

burden *n* **1 load**, weight, cargo **2 problem**, drain, encumbrance, affliction, liability **3** *(literary)* **theme**, topic, subject, subject matter ■ *v* **lumber** *(infml)*, weigh down, saddle, encumber, trouble. *See* COMPARE AND CONTRAST *at* subject.

burdened *adj* **loaded**, fraught, weighed down, laden, held back

burdensome *adj* **onerous**, heavy, taxing, troublesome, arduous

bureau *n* **1 government department**, agency,

office, department, unit **2 writing desk**, desk, writing table, escritoire

bureaucracy *n* **1 system of government**, government, administration, civil service, establishment **2 official procedure**, rules and regulations, formalities, paperwork, red tape *(infml)*

bureaucrat *n* **official**, public servant, civil servant, administrator, office holder

bureaucratic *adj* **1 administrative**, official, governmental, civil service, organizational **2 rigid**, inflexible, unbending, officious, involved

burgeoning *adj* **1 growing**, mushrooming, increasing, escalating, expanding *Opposite*: dwindling **2 budding**, promising, up-and-coming, nascent *Opposite*: fading

burgher *n* **citizen**, resident, inhabitant, denizen, voter

burglar *n* **thief**, robber, intruder, cat burglar, criminal

burglary *n* **1 breaking and entering**, theft, robbery, aggravated burglary, stealing **2 break-in**, theft, robbery, crime, housebreak *(US)*

burgle *v* **rob**, thieve, break in, loot, steal from

burial *n* **interment**, committal, entombment, funeral

burial chamber *n* **sepulchre**, tomb, mausoleum, vault, crypt

burial ground *n* **cemetery**, graveyard, churchyard, necropolis, garden of remembrance

burial place *n* **last resting place**, grave, tomb, crypt, mausoleum

buried *adj* **1 underground**, concealed, hidden, covered, dug in *Opposite*: dug up **2 suppressed**, hidden, covered up, repressed, forgotten *Opposite*: exposed

burlesque *n* **parody**, caricature, travesty, lampoon, skit ■ *v* **spoof**, mock, make fun of, lampoon, caricature

burliness *n* **brawniness**, heftiness, broad shoulders, muscularity, robustness *Opposite*: slimness

burly *adj* **brawny**, hefty, broad-shouldered, husky, muscular *Opposite*: slim

burn *v* **1 blaze**, be ablaze, flame, smoulder, glow **2 burn up**, burn down, burn away, gut, reduce to ashes **3 scorch**, singe, sear, char, scald **4 use up**, use, expend, consume **5 go red**, flush, blush, redden, colour **6 tingle**, sting, hurt, prickle, be on fire **7 corrode**, eat away, eat into **8 glow**, shine, twinkle, flare, glimmer **9** *(infml)* **race**, hurtle, tear, speed, scorch *Opposite*: dawdle ■ *n* **1 injury**, blister, scald, scorch **2 stream**, rivulet, beck, brook *(literary)*

burn down *v* **incinerate**, go up in flames, burn to the ground, burn to a crisp, reduce to ashes

burned-out *adj* **1 gutted**, destroyed, reduced to ashes, burnt down, burnt up **2 exhausted**, worn out, tired out, drained, unwell

burner *n* gas ring, ring, heat, flame, gas jet

burning *adj* **1 red-hot**, piping hot, boiling hot, fiery hot, sweltering *Opposite*: cold **2 on fire**, ablaze, blazing, flaming, smouldering *Opposite*: extinguished **3 strong**, ardent, fervent, all-consuming, passionate *Opposite*: weak **4 important**, vital, crucial, urgent, significant *Opposite*: insignificant **5 smarting**, stinging, tingly, prickly, painful **6 feverish**, febrile, flushed, hot, red *Opposite*: cool

burnish *v* polish, shine, buff, rub up, rub

burn out *(infml)* *v* exhaust, break down, wear out, tire, fatigue

burnout *n* exhaustion, stress, tension, weariness, poor health

burnt *adj* overcooked, well-done, cooked, seared, singed *Opposite*: rare

burn the candle at both ends *v* overdo things, wear yourself out, do too much, exhaust yourself, burn the midnight oil

burn the midnight oil *v* work late, stay up, work day and night, work overtime, burn the candle at both ends *Opposite*: slack

burnt-out *see* **burned-out**

burn up *v* incinerate, burn, burn down, reduce to ashes, burn to a crisp

burn your boats *see* **burn your bridges**

burn your bridges *v* pass the point of no return, cross the Rubicon, nail your colours to the mast, burn your boats

burr *n* **1 seed husk**, pod, pericarp, seed pod **2 accent**, twang, drawl, brogue, intonation

burrow *n* hole, warren, den, lair, hideaway ■ *v* **1 dig**, tunnel, excavate, channel, dig out **2 search**, dig, investigate, delve, scrabble **3 nestle**, snuggle, cuddle, nuzzle, cosy up

bursary *n* scholarship, grant, award, fund, exhibition

burst *v* **1 rupture**, split open, disintegrate, break open, fracture **2 erupt**, spout, gush, rush, break out *Opposite*: trickle ■ *n* spurt, eruption, gust, torrent, rupture *Opposite*: trickle

bursting *adj* **1 full**, overflowing, teeming, full to bursting, packed *Opposite*: empty **2** *(infml)* eager, desperate, keen, dying, longing *Opposite*: unwilling

burst in on *v* **1 interrupt**, intrude upon, intrude on, come upon, disturb **2 surprise**, take by surprise, catch unawares, take unawares, catch in the act

burst into tears *v* break down, dissolve in tears, break down and cry, burst out crying, lose control *Opposite*: laugh

burst out *v* **1 start**, begin, commence, burst into, break into **2 exclaim**, shout, cry, call out, say *Opposite*: whisper

bury *v* **1 inter**, put in the ground, lay to rest, entomb, put six feet under *Opposite*: exhume **2 hide**, conceal, cover, put out of sight, submerge *Opposite*: expose

bury the hatchet *v* make up, make peace, be reconciled, kiss and make up, resolve differences *Opposite*: fight

bus *v* transport, carry, take, convey, move

bush *n* **1 shrub**, plant, flowering shrub, hedging plant **2 scrubland**, wilds, outback, savanna, scrub

bushed *(infml)* *adj* exhausted, tired, worn-out, dead on your feet, all in *Opposite*: refreshed

bushes *n* undergrowth, scrub, shrubbery, greenery, underbrush *(US)*

bushy *adj* luxuriant, abundant, profuse, shaggy, thick *Opposite*: sparse

busily *adv* actively, energetically, briskly, industriously, vigorously *Opposite*: lazily

business *n* **1 commerce**, trade, industry, selling, production **2 company**, corporation, conglomerate, establishment, partnership **3 custom**, trade, dealings, transactions, sales **4 concern**, affair, problem, responsibility, interest **5 matter**, affair, issue, situation, event ■ *adj* commercial, occupational, corporate, professional *Opposite*: private

businesslike *adj* **1 efficient**, practical, professional, competent, systematic *Opposite*: unprofessional **2 unemotional**, objective, professional, detached, uninvolved *Opposite*: emotional

businessperson *n* business executive, executive, executive director, director, manager

busk *v* entertain, perform, sing, play

busker *n* street entertainer, street musician, entertainer, performer, musician

bust *n* sculpture, torso, statue, figure, model ■ *v* *(infml)* break, smash, shatter, burst, fracture *Opposite*: mend ■ *adj* *(infml)* not working, out of order, broken, ruined, had it *(infml)*

bustle *v* busy yourself, be on the go, be busy, hurry, rush around ■ *n* activity, movement, stir, hustle and bustle, commotion *Opposite*: calm

bustling *adj* busy, active, full of go, full of life, hurried *Opposite*: still

bust up *(infml)* *v* split up, break up, separate, part, break apart *Opposite*: make up

bust-up *(infml)* *n* argument, disagreement, fight, split

busy *adj* **1 active**, on the go, hard-working, hard at it, diligent *Opposite*: idle **2 full**, full of activity, demanding, hard, tiring *Opposite*: empty **3 engaged**, occupied, unavailable, taken *Opposite*: free

busybody *(infml)* *n* interferer, meddler, nuisance, gossip, scandalmonger

but *prep* **1 however**, although, nevertheless, on the contrary **2 other than**, except, excluding, bar, save for ■ *n* *(infml)* objection, proviso, provision, rider, condition

butch *adj* masculine, tough, strong, muscular, beefy

butcher *n* killer, murderer, slaughterer, exterminator, slayer *(fml or literary)* ■ *v* **1 slaughter**, murder, kill, exterminate, massacre **2** *(infml)* **make a mess of**, ruin, spoil, botch *(infml)*, make a hash of *(infml)*

butchery *n* **slaughter**, carnage, bloodshed, killing

butt *v* **ram**, hit, bump, strike, run into ■ *n* **1 object**, target, victim, scapegoat, stooge **2 handle**, stock, grip **3 end**, stub, stump, base, nub end **4 barrel**, tub, drum, cask, container

butte *n* **hill**, foothill, rise, mount, bluff

butterflies *(infml)* *n* **nervousness**, excitement, anxiety, tenseness, apprehension *Opposite*: confidence

butter up *(infml)* *v* **flatter**, curry favour, get on the right side of, sweet-talk *(infml)*, suck up to *(infml)* *Opposite*: insult

butt in *v* **1 interrupt**, break in, cut in, interfere, interject *Opposite*: mind your own business **2 squeeze in**, barge in, shove in, jump the queue, queue-jump

button *n* **push button**, switch, knob, key ■ *v* **fasten**, do up, close *Opposite*: undo

buttonhole *n* **flower**, spray, corsage ■ *v* *(infml)* **accost**, waylay, corner, grab, confront

button up *(infml)* *v* **be quiet**, keep quiet, be silent, say nothing, stop talking *Opposite*: blather *(infml)*

buttress *n* **support**, prop, reinforcement, flying buttress, structure ■ *v* **strengthen**, support, prop, prop up, reinforce

butty *(infml)* *n* **sandwich**, baguette, roll, bagel, wrap

buxom *adj* **plump**, rounded, ample, curvaceous, curvy

buy *v* **pay for**, purchase, acquire, procure, obtain *Opposite*: sell ■ *n* **purchase**, acquisition, bargain, deal

buyer *n* **purchaser**, consumer, shopper, bargain hunter, customer *Opposite*: seller

buy off *v* **bribe**, induce, corrupt, suborn, pay off *(infml)*

buy out *v* **acquire**, take over, purchase, take control of

buyout *n* **takeover**, merger, acquisition, purchase

buzz *n* **1** *(infml)* **telephone call**, call, ring, phone call, bell *(infml)* **2** *(infml)* **thrill**, high, kick, lift, jolt *Opposite*: downer *(infml)* **3** *(infml)* **gossip**, talk, word, rumour, whisper ■ *v* **hum**, drone, murmur, whine, whirr

buzzer *n* **signal**, bell, beeper *(infml)*, bleeper

buzzing *adj* **busy**, bustling, vibrant, full of life, lively *Opposite*: still

buzzword *(infml)* *n* **slogan**, catchword, saying, byword, catch phrase

by *prep* **1 with**, near, next to, beside **2 through**, via, in, by means of, as a result of **3 not later than**, before, sooner than

bye-byes *(infml)* *n* **sleep**, bed, land of nod *(infml)*, beddy-bye *(infml)*

bygone *adj* **past**, former, previous, long-gone, departed *(literary)* *Opposite*: future

bylaw *n* **regulation**, rule, ruling, statute, guideline

byline *n* **acknowledgement**, credit, heading, strap line

bypass *v* **go around**, avoid, get round, find a way round, sidestep

by-product *n* **side effect**, spin-off, consequence, result, derivative

byre *n* **cowshed**, shed, barn, milking parlour, stable

bystander *n* **onlooker**, passer-by, witness, eyewitness, spectator *Opposite*: participant

byword *n* **1 embodiment**, perfect example, epitome, shining example **2 catch phrase**, proverb, axiom, slogan, saying

byzantine *adj* **1 complex**, intricate, tortuous, convoluted, complicated *Opposite*: straightforward **2 devious**, scheming, underhand, deceitful, secretive *Opposite*: honest

C

cab *n* **1 taxi**, taxicab, black cab, hackney cab, hackney carriage **2 cabin**, compartment, cockpit

cabal *n* **1 faction**, section, unit, group, sect **2 plot**, scheme, conspiracy, connivance, collusion

cabaret *n* **1 show**, floor show, live entertainment, burlesque **2 nightclub**, club, bar, nightspot

caber *n* **log**, beam, pole, stick

cabin *n* **1 hut**, log cabin, cottage, bungalow, chalet **2 compartment**, cubicle, stateroom, room, berth

caboodle *(infml)* *n* **lot**, whole lot, entirety, totality, integrality

cache *n* **hoard**, store, accumulation, reserve, collection ■ *v* **hide**, hoard, store, secrete, reserve *Opposite*: discard

cachet *n* **status**, prestige, distinction, respect, reputation

cack-handed *(infml)* adj **clumsy**, awkward, gauche, maladroit, ham-handed *(infml)* Opposite: dexterous

cackle v **laugh**, hoot, screech, crow, guffaw

cacophonous adj **discordant**, unmusical, unmelodious, dissonant, inharmonious Opposite: melodious

cacophony n **discord**, discordance, dissonance, disharmony, unmusicality Opposite: melodiousness

cad *(dated)* n **rogue**, scoundrel, rake, rascal, blackguard Opposite: gentleman

CAD n **computer-aided design**, computer graphics, graphics, product design, drafting

cadaver n **corpse**, dead body, remains, body

cadaverous adj **bony**, skeletal, emaciated, wasted, gaunt Opposite: healthy

caddie n **assistant**, porter, carrier, transporter ■ v **transport**, assist, carry

caddish *(dated)* adj **dishonourable**, ungallant, rascally, rakish, ungentlemanly Opposite: gallant

caddy n **container**, tin, box, receptacle, carton

cadence n **1 tempo**, rhythm, pace, pulse, stroke **2 lilt**, intonation, accent, modulation, inflection

cadenza n **solo passage**, improvisation, solo, unaccompanied passage, showpiece

cadet n **trainee**, police cadet, army cadet, sea cadet

cadger *(infml)* n **scrounger** *(infml)*, borrower, moocher *(infml)*, sponger *(infml)*, ligger *(infml)*

cadre n **1 squad**, corps, unit, team, band **2 faction**, group, core, hard core, band

cage n **enclosure**, coop, pen, birdcage, crate ■ v **confine**, enclose, pen, coop up, impound Opposite: release

WORD BANK
❏ **types of pen or cage** apiary, aquarium, aviary, beehive, birdcage, chicken coop, chicken run, coop, cowshed, dovecote, henhouse, hutch, kennel, piggery, pigsty, pound, stable, stall, sty

caged adj **captive**, detained, confined, imprisoned, jailed Opposite: free

cagey *(infml)* adj **wary**, guarded, cautious, careful, reticent Opposite: reckless

caginess *(infml)* n **wariness**, caution, reticence, evasiveness, chariness Opposite: carelessness

cagoule n **waterproof jacket**, anorak, windcheater, parka, raincoat

cairn n **1 landmark**, marker, signpost, direction post, milestone **2 memorial**, monument, barrow, tomb, tombstone

cajole v **coax**, persuade, wheedle, entice, inveigle Opposite: compel

cake n **1 gateau**, pastry, fancy **2 bar**, block, slab, lump, tablet ■ v **cover**, coat, encrust, congeal, coagulate

WORD BANK
❏ **types of cake** angel food cake, barm brack, birthday cake, Black Forest gateau, brownie, carrot cake, cheesecake, Christmas cake, coffee cake, cruller, cupcake, Danish pastry, devil's food cake, doughnut, éclair, flapjack, fruitcake, gateau, gingerbread, key lime pie, macaroon, Madeira cake, madeleine, mince pie, muffin, pain au chocolat, petit four, seedcake, sponge cake, strudel, Swiss roll, torte, turnover, wedding cake

caked adj **covered**, coated, encrusted, layered

cakewalk *(infml)* n **child's play**, kid's stuff, easy victory, runaway victory, cinch *(infml)*

calamitous adj **disastrous**, dreadful, catastrophic, ruinous, tragic Opposite: beneficial

calamity n **disaster**, catastrophe, mishap, misfortune, tragedy

calcify v **harden**, set, solidify, fossilize, turn into stone Opposite: soften

calculable adj **1 quantifiable**, countable, finite, assessable, measurable Opposite: incalculable **2 predictable**, anticipated, expected, foreseeable, likely Opposite: unpredictable

calculate v **work out**, compute, estimate, weigh up, gauge

calculated adj **intended**, designed, planned, considered, premeditated Opposite: spontaneous

calculating adj **scheming**, manipulative, devious, shrewd, conniving Opposite: candid

calculation n **1 computation**, estimate, reckoning, sum, result **2 control**, cunning, scheming, intention, design Opposite: candidness

calendar n **diary**, schedule, year planner, timetable

calibrate v **standardize**, adjust, regulate, tune, bring into line

calibration n **1 standardization**, correction, adjustment, tuning, setting **2 graduation**, gradation, mark, measurement, degree

calibre n **1 quality**, ability, capacity, talent, competence **2 size**, bore, diameter, gauge, measure

call v **1 name**, describe, identify, entitle, label **2 shout**, cry out, scream, yell, call out **3 request**, summon, call on, invite, beckon **4 phone**, telephone, give a call, call up, phone up **5 visit**, call on, pay a visit, drop in, stop off **6 arrange**, convene, set up, organize, assemble ■ n **1 noise**, shout, cry, sound **2 song**, cry, birdsong **3 phone call**, telephone call, ring, buzz *(infml)*, bell *(infml)* **4 visit**, stop, halt **5 demand**, request, plea, appeal, bid **6 judgment**, verdict, decision, assessment, ruling

call a halt v **end**, stop, halt, bring to an end, close Opposite: start up

call a spade a spade v **be direct**, speak plainly, be blunt, speak your mind, lay it on the line *(infml)* Opposite: prevaricate

call attention to v make known, draw attention to, expose, publicize, highlight *Opposite*: conceal

call by v visit, stop by, come round, drop in, call in

call down v invoke, invite, request, appeal, pray

caller n visitor, guest, friend

call for v 1 order, demand, claim, clamour, request 2 need, require, justify, necessitate, cry out for

call forth v produce, cause, inspire, provoke, stimulate

calligraphy n handwriting, hand, writing, script, print

call in v 1 visit, drop in, drop by, come by, come round 2 phone, call, ring, telephone, give a call 3 recall, call back, pull in, take off the market 4 summon, invite in, call for, send for, bring in

calling n vocation, profession, occupation, business, line

call into question v query, question, dispute, challenge, doubt *Opposite*: accept

callisthenics n exercise system, keep fit, exercises, aerobics, step aerobics

call it a day v stop, finish, end, give up, break off *Opposite*: start up

call names v insult, abuse, hurl insults at, taunt, bait *Opposite*: compliment

call off v cancel, stop, abandon, suspend, shelve

call on v 1 ask, request, appeal to, urge, entreat 2 visit, drop in on, go to see, look up, look in on

callous adj heartless, unfeeling, cold-hearted, hardhearted, uncaring *Opposite*: warm-hearted

calloused adj hard, hardened, hard-skinned, rough, rough-skinned *Opposite*: soft

callousness n heartlessness, insensitivity, cruelty, coldness, cold-heartedness *Opposite*: warm-heartedness

call out v 1 summon, send for, call for, get, page 2 shout out, exclaim, call, yell, make a noise

call out for v demand, clamour, be in dire need of, require, request

callow adj inexperienced, immature, naive, adolescent, green *Opposite*: mature

call together v summon, convene, gather, collect, round up *Opposite*: disperse

call to mind v evoke, recall, recollect, suggest, call up *Opposite*: forget

call up v phone, call, telephone, give a call, give a ring

call-up n conscription, mobilization, recruitment, enlistment, muster *Opposite*: demobilization

call upon v 1 ask, request, appeal to, urge,

entreat 2 make demands on, demand, require, use, call for

callus n hard skin, corn, bump, lump, nodule

calm adj tranquil, peaceful, still, cool, composed *Opposite*: agitated ■ n peace, tranquillity, quietness, stillness, calmness *Opposite*: turbulence ■ v pacify, calm down, quieten, quieten down, soothe *Opposite*: excite

calmative adj calming, soothing, pacifying, quietening, relaxing *Opposite*: disturbing

calm down v settle down, relax, soothe, quieten, quieten down *Opposite*: agitate

calming adj soothing, reassuring, comforting, restful, sedative *Opposite*: disturbing

calmness n serenity, tranquillity, quietness, stillness, peace *Opposite*: restlessness

calumny (fml) n slander, defamation, denigration, libel, lies

calve v give birth, drop, reproduce, produce

camaraderie n friendship, companionship, solidarity, company, comradeship *Opposite*: enmity

cameo n character part, cameo role, appearance, role, part

camera-shy adj reclusive, retiring, reserved, private, aloof *Opposite*: extrovert

camouflage n concealment, disguise, smoke screen, cover-up, façade ■ v disguise, mask, hide, conceal, obscure

camp n 1 site, campsite, encampment, base camp, holiday camp 2 group, faction, followers, clique, supporters ■ v go camping, camp out, sleep out

campaign n movement, crusade, operation, drive, fight ■ v 1 fight, work, push, struggle, battle 2 electioneer, canvass, drum up support, solicit votes, stump

campaigner n activist, crusader, fighter, supporter, champion

campsite n encampment, camping area, campground (US)

campus n grounds, precincts, site, property, estate

canal n 1 waterway, channel, seaway 2 duct, tube, passage, vessel

canalize (fml) v direct, channel, funnel, guide, convey *Opposite*: diffuse

cancel v 1 call off, stop, abandon, withdraw, scratch *Opposite*: arrange 2 annul, revoke, stop, rescind, repeal *Opposite*: reinstate

cancel out v nullify, efface, undo, contradict, neutralize

cancer n 1 growth, tumour, malignancy, disease, melanoma 2 evil, blight, scourge, canker, plague

cancerous adj 1 tumorous, malignant, carcinomatous, carcinogenic, oncogenic *Opposite*: benign 2 harmful, pernicious, malign, malignant, noxious *Opposite*: beneficent

candelabrum *n* **candleholder**, candlestick, chandelier, lamp holder, lamp

candid *adj* **honest**, frank, open, truthful, sincere *Opposite*: guarded

candidacy *n* **application**, contention, entry, submission, candidature

candidate *n* **applicant**, contender, entrant, runner, aspirant

---

COMPARE AND CONTRAST CORE MEANING: somebody who is seeking to be chosen for something or to win something

candidate somebody who is being considered for a job, grant, or prize, standing for election, or taking part in an examination; **contender** a competitor, especially somebody who has a good chance of winning; **contestant** somebody who takes part in a contest or competitive event; **aspirant** somebody aspiring to distinction or advancement; **applicant** somebody who has formally applied to be a candidate for something; **entrant** somebody who enters a competition or examination.

---

candidness *n* **honesty**, frankness, openness, truthfulness, bluntness

candied *adj* **crystallized**, glacé, preserved, sugar-coated, sugared

candle *n* **taper**, nightlight, rush light, rush candle, rush

candlelight *n* **dim light**, soft light, low light, glow, glimmer

candlestick *n* **candleholder**, candelabrum, chandelier, sconce

can-do *(infml) adj* **positive**, willing, confident, ambitious, eager *Opposite*: diffident

candour *n* **frankness**, forthrightness, directness, candidness, outspokenness

candy-striped *adj* **striped**, stripy, pink-and-white striped

cane *n* **1 bamboo**, wicker, rattan **2 stick**, walking stick, staff ■ *v* **beat**, thrash, strike, hit, punish

canine *adj* **doggy**, dog-like, doggish ■ *n* **dog**, mongrel, cur, hound, pooch *(infml)*

WORD BANK
❑ **types of canine** coyote, dingo, dog, fox, jackal, wolf

canister *n* **container**, can, tin, flask, cylinder

canker *n* **evil**, cancer, scourge, blight, plague

canned *adj* **1 tinned**, preserved, conserved *Opposite*: fresh **2 prerecorded**, recorded, taped, reproduced, artificial *Opposite*: live

canniness *n* **shrewdness**, astuteness, sharpness, smartness, cleverness

cannonade *n* **barrage**, bombardment, hail, onslaught, pounding

cannonball *n* **projectile**, missile, ball, stone, grapeshot

canny *adj* **shrewd**, astute, sharp, smart, clever

canonical *adj* **official**, recognized, acknow-

ledged, established, undisputed *Opposite*: apocryphal

canonization *n* **1 making into a saint**, beatification, sanctification, consecration, hallowing **2 idolization**, glorification, adoration, worship, adulation

canonize *v* **1 make into a saint**, beatify, sanctify, consecrate, hallow **2 idolize**, glorify, adore, worship, venerate

canoodle *(infml) v* **carry on**, kiss and cuddle, pet, smooch, snog *(slang)*

canopy *n* **1 awning**, cover, covering, shelter, blind **2 top**, crown, roof, covering, cover

cant *n* **1 clichés**, platitudes, banalities, commonplaces, triteness **2 hypocrisy**, insincerity, false piety, humbug, lip service *Opposite*: sincerity **3 jargon**, slang, argot, patois, vernacular

cantankerous *adj* **grumpy**, irascible, irritable, crusty, quarrelsome

canter *n* **trot**, run, gallop, jog, sprint ■ *v* **run**, gallop, trot, jog, sprint

cantilever *n* **beam**, plank, girder

canto *n* **stanza**, verse, strophe, section, division

canton *n* **region**, district, area, borough, constituency

canvas *n* **1 painting**, oil painting, picture, old master, work of art **2 background**, backdrop, setting, context, scene

canvass *v* **1 campaign**, electioneer, drum up support, solicit votes, stump **2 test**, research, investigate, survey, poll

canvasser *n* **1 campaigner**, supporter, party worker **2 researcher**, investigator, examiner, pollster

canyon *n* **ravine**, gully, gorge, chasm, rift

cap *n* **1 cover**, lid, top, stopper, plug **2 restraint**, limit, control, restriction, check ■ *v* **1 cover**, top, stop, plug, stopper **2 surpass**, top, improve, better, outdo **3 limit**, regulate, control, restrain, restrict

capability *n* **ability**, capacity, competence, skill, resources. *See* COMPARE AND CONTRAST *at* **ability**.

capable *adj* **1 accomplished**, talented, skilled, gifted, clever *Opposite*: inept **2 able**, competent, proficient, efficient, qualified *Opposite*: incapable

capacious *adj* **roomy**, spacious, large, ample, big *Opposite*: cramped

capacity *n* **1 ability**, capability, skill, talent, aptitude **2 volume**, space, room, size, dimensions **3 role**, position, responsibility, function, office. *See* COMPARE AND CONTRAST *at* **ability**.

cape *n* **promontory**, peninsula, headland, outcrop, point

caper *n* **escapade**, adventure, jaunt, lark, antics ■ *v* **frolic**, cavort, jump, leap, dance

capital *n* **1 assets**, resources, funds, wealth, money **2 centre**, headquarters, hub

capitalist n entrepreneur, financier, industrialist, businessperson, investor ■ adj entrepreneurial, industrial, consumerist, consumer, commercial

capitalize v fund, finance, raise funding for, provide backing for

capitalize on v make the most of, maximize, take advantage of, use, utilize

capitation n 1 tax, poll tax, levy, toll, duty 2 fee, charge, payment, amount

capitulate v surrender, submit, yield, succumb, give way Opposite: resist. See COMPARE AND CONTRAST at yield.

capitulation n surrender, submission, defeat, retreat Opposite: resistance

caprice n whim, impulse, quirk, fancy, fad

capricious adj unpredictable, changeable, variable, impulsive, whimsical Opposite: predictable

capsize v overturn, turn over, roll over, keel over, turn turtle Opposite: right

capsule n 1 pod, container, case, casing, shell 2 pill, tablet, lozenge

captain n head, skipper, leader, chief, boss ■ v lead, skipper, manage, take charge, head

caption n slogan, subtitle, title, description, legend

captious adj 1 critical, pedantic, trivial, petty, nitpicking 2 confusing, misleading, devious, bewildering, disingenuous Opposite: clear

captivate v attract, charm, enchant, fascinate, entrance Opposite: repel

captivated adj enchanted, fascinated, charmed, entranced, spellbound Opposite: repulsed

captivating adj charming, attractive, appealing, fascinating, charismatic

captive n prisoner, detainee, internee, prisoner of war, hostage Opposite: escapee ■ adj 1 imprisoned, in prison, locked up, enslaved, confined Opposite: free 2 attentive, intent, fascinated, spellbound, rapt

captivity n imprisonment, custody, detention, confinement, internment Opposite: freedom

captor n abductor, imprisoner, kidnapper, hostage taker, jailer Opposite: liberator

capture v 1 take, seize, apprehend, arrest, pick up Opposite: release 2 imprison, detain, arrest, confine, take into custody Opposite: liberate 3 encapsulate, summarize, sum up, portray, describe 4 secure, attain, gain, acquire, obtain Opposite: lose 5 catch, seize, grab hold of, trap, ensnare ■ n imprisonment, detention, arrest, seizure, apprehension Opposite: release

capture your imagination v fascinate, excite, inspire, interest, enchant

car n 1 automobile, motor (slang), wheels (slang), auto (US) 2 railway carriage, cabin, carriage, coach, compartment

WORD BANK
❑ types of car all-terrain vehicle, compact, convertible, coupé, dragster, estate car, four-by-four, hatchback, hot rod (slang), limo, limousine, minivan, off-roader (infml), people carrier, racing car, runabout, saloon, sports car, stock car, stretch limo, three-wheeler

carafe n flask, decanter, bottle

caramelize v burn, heat, scorch, brown, broil (US)

carapace n case, shell, covering, sheath, outside

caravan n convoy, group, procession, parade, motorcade

carbohydrate n biological compound, simple carbohydrate, complex carbohydrate, starch, sugar

carbon copy n replica, duplicate, copy, facsimile, exact likeness Opposite: original

carbuncle n spot, blemish, boil, pustule, abscess

carcass n corpse, remains, cadaver, body, skeleton

carcinogenic adj cancer-causing, oncogenic, hazardous, toxic, poisonous

card n 1 greetings card, birthday card, anniversary card, postcard, picture postcard 2 pass, identification card, membership card, business card, calling card

cardboard n board, paper, card, packaging, packing ■ adj insubstantial, unconvincing, phoney, plastic, wooden Opposite: substantial

card-carrying adj official, paid-up, bona fide, listed, genuine

cardinal adj basic, fundamental, key, prime, serious Opposite: secondary

cardiovascular adj circulatory, cardiac, vascular, heart, blood

cardsharp n cheat, gambler, hustler, swindler, pro (infml)

care v be concerned, be interested, feel a concern, take an interest Opposite: disregard ■ n 1 upkeep, maintenance, repair, overhaul Opposite: neglect 2 attention, caution, precaution, carefulness, watchfulness 3 worry, concern, anxiety, trouble, unease Opposite: nonchalance 4 treatment, provision, support, attention Opposite: ill-treatment 5 supervision, guardianship, protection, custody, oversight (fml). See COMPARE AND CONTRAST at worry.

careen v swerve, sway, weave, lurch, swing

career n vocation, job, occupation, profession, calling ■ v rush, race, hurry, dash, speed

careerism n determination, single-mindedness, motivation, commitment, drive

careerist n professional, achiever, high flier, go-getter (infml) ■ adj single-minded, determined, motivated, focused, professional

care for v 1 **like**, feel affection for, love, have a soft spot for, cherish *Opposite*: dislike 2 **look after**, take care of, tend, supervise, oversee *Opposite*: ignore 3 (*fml*) **want**, desire, like to have, fancy, appreciate

carefree adj **untroubled**, happy-go-lucky, cheery, relaxed, cheerful *Opposite*: troubled

carefreeness n **lightheartedness**, cheerfulness, cheeriness, happiness, jollity *Opposite*: anxiety

careful adj 1 **cautious**, wary, vigilant, watchful, alert *Opposite*: reckless 2 **thorough**, meticulous, painstaking, particular, conscientious *Opposite*: careless 3 **prudent**, sensible, judicious, cautious, well thought-out *Opposite*: foolish 4 **protective**, sympathetic, sensitive, gentle, tender *Opposite*: rough

COMPARE AND CONTRAST CORE MEANING: exercising care and attention in doing something
careful a wide-ranging term, suggesting attention to detail and implying cautiousness in avoiding errors or inaccuracies; **conscientious** showing great care, attention, and industriousness in carrying out a task; **scrupulous** having or showing careful regard for what is morally right; **thorough** extremely careful and accurate; **meticulous** extremely careful and precise; **painstaking** involving or showing great care and attention to detail; **assiduous** undeviating in effort and care; **punctilious** very careful about the conventions of correct behaviour and etiquette; **finicky** concentrating too much on unimportant details; **fussy** tending to worry over details or trivial things.

carefulness n 1 **caution**, care, wariness, watchfulness, alertness *Opposite*: rashness 2 **attention to detail**, thoroughness, precision, care, meticulousness *Opposite*: carelessness 3 **prudence**, caution, judiciousness, wisdom, judgment *Opposite*: foolishness

careless adj 1 **slapdash**, happy-go-lucky, devil-may-care, casual, slipshod *Opposite*: careful 2 **uncaring**, thoughtless, offhand, inconsiderate, unthinking *Opposite*: considerate

carelessness n **sloppiness**, inattentiveness, inaccuracy, imprecision, negligence *Opposite*: care

caress v **stroke**, touch, pat, embrace, cuddle ■ n **touch**, stroke, pat, embrace, hug

caretaker n **concierge**, warden, porter, custodian, janitor

careworn adj **haggard**, drawn, beleaguered, worried, burdened *Opposite*: carefree

cargo n **load**, freight, consignment, shipment, goods

caricature n 1 **cartoon**, picture, drawing, sketch 2 **travesty**, misrepresentation, false impression, distortion, falsification

caricaturist n **artist**, cartoonist, humorist, satirist

caring adj **kind**, thoughtful, gentle, helpful, considerate *Opposite*: uncaring

carnage n **killing**, bloodshed, slaughter, massacre, bloodbath

carnal (*fml*) adj **physical**, fleshy, sensual, sexual *Opposite*: spiritual

carnival n **festival**, celebration, street party, fair, fete

carnivore n **flesh-eater**, meat-eater, predator, scavenger, insectivore

carnivorous adj **flesh-eating**, meat-eating, predatory, scavenging, insectivorous

carol n **song**, hymn, chant, chorus

carouse (*literary*) v **revel**, celebrate, drink, get drunk, raise the roof

carousel n 1 **merry-go-round**, roundabout, ride 2 **container**, cassette, cartridge, drum, magazine

carp v **complain**, grumble, find fault, nag, go on. *See* COMPARE AND CONTRAST *at* **complain**.

carpentry n **joinery**, woodwork, turning, carving, cabinetmaking

carpet n 1 **rug**, mat, runner, fitted carpet, carpet tiles 2 **covering**, layer, blanket, mass, spread ■ v (*infml*) **reprimand**, tell off, rebuke, criticize, blast (*infml*)

carpeting n **floor covering**, flooring, matting, carpet tiles

carping adj **critical**, nitpicking, complaining, dissatisfied, discontented ■ n **complaining**, nitpicking, faultfinding, dissatisfaction, whining

carport n **garage**, lean-to, shelter, porch, parking space

carriage n 1 **horse-drawn carriage**, coach, horse and carriage 2 (*fml*) **bearing**, posture, deportment, air, presence 3 **transportation**, delivery, carrying, haulage, conveyance

carriageway n **lane**, lane of traffic, roadway, road, thoroughfare

carried adj **approved**, accepted, passed, agreed, supported *Opposite*: rejected

carrier n 1 **transporter**, haulier, delivery service, carter, shipper 2 **shopping bag**, carrier bag, shopper

carrion n **flesh**, meat, tissue

carrot n **incentive**, inducement, bribe, bait, lure

carroty adj **orange**, red, auburn, ginger

carry v 1 **take**, bear, hold, support, clutch 2 **transmit**, transport, convey, transfer, bring 3 **contain**, include, involve, incorporate, hold 4 **have in stock**, stock, store, keep, supply 5 **approve**, accept, pass, agree, vote for

carrying adj **loud**, resonant, resounding, booming, ringing *Opposite*: quiet

carrying-on (*infml*) n **pranks**, goings-on (*infml*), doings (*infml*), high jinks (*infml*)

carry off v 1 **take away**, take off, remove, steal, abduct *Opposite*: bring back 2 **succeed**, manage, accomplish, achieve, do *Opposite*: fail

carry on v 1 **continue**, keep, keep on, keep at, go on *Opposite*: stop 2 **complain**, grumble, carp, nag, go on

carry-on (*infml*) n **fuss**, commotion, hullabaloo, palaver, to-do (*infml*)

carry out v **do**, perform, complete, achieve, succeed *Opposite*: neglect. See COMPARE AND CONTRAST *at* **accomplish, perform.**

carryout n **takeaway**, fast food, takeout (*US*)

carry over v **postpone**, defer, leave, reschedule, put back *Opposite*: expedite (*fml*)

carryover n **leftover**, legacy, inheritance, residue, remnant

carry the can (*infml*) v **take the blame**, accept responsibility, accept the blame, shoulder the blame, be the scapegoat

carsick adj **sick**, nauseous, ill, unwell, poorly (*infml*)

cart n 1 **farm cart**, wagon, dray, tumbrel, wain (*literary*) 2 **handcart**, barrow, wheelbarrow, trolley, pushcart (*US*) ▪ v **carry**, lug, heave, haul, drag

carte blanche n **free hand**, free rein, blank cheque, complete freedom, full authority

cartel n **interest group**, lobby, alliance, association, union

cart off v **remove**, drag off, take away, haul off, carry off

carton n **box**, cardboard box, container, pack, sachet

cartoon n 1 **animation**, animated film, animated movie 2 **drawing**, caricature, picture, comic strip

cartoonist n **artist**, animator, caricaturist, satirist, humorist

cartridge n **container**, holder, casing, unit, cassette

cartwheel v **turn**, somersault, go head over heels, roll, flip

carve v 1 **engrave**, inscribe, etch, cut, notch 2 **slice**, pare, cut in slices, whittle, cut up

carve out v **create**, make, establish, build, set up

carve up (*infml*) v **divide**, allocate, share out, apportion, distribute

carve-up (*infml*) n **division**, allocation, distribution, partitioning, share-out

carving n 1 **artefact**, model, statue, statuette, figure 2 **cutting**, engraving, etching, sculpting, fashioning

Casanova n **libertine**, Don Juan, gigolo, Romeo, ladies' man

cascade n **waterfall**, chute, cataract, force, falls ▪ v **flow**, pour, fall, drop, gush

case n 1 **circumstance**, situation, instance, event, occasion 2 **instance**, item, example, illustration, paradigm 3 **job**, project, commission, assignment, task 4 **court case**, legal action, lawsuit, suit, indictment 5 **argument**, reason, defence, justification, rationale 6 **container**, holder, box, casing, cover 7 **suit-**

case, overnight case, weekend case, briefcase, attaché case

casebook n **record**, log, diary, journal, notebook

case-hardened adj **unsympathetic**, unfeeling, hard, hardened, toughened *Opposite*: sensitive

cash n **money**, hard cash, ready money, coins, currency

cashier n 1 **treasurer**, banker, bursar 2 **bank clerk**, clerk, teller, official, assistant ▪ v **dismiss**, expel, drum out, court martial, boot out (*infml*)

cash in v **redeem**, trade in, sell, realize, bank

cash-in-hand adj **in cash**, cash, no questions asked, unofficially, off the record

cash in on v **take advantage of**, benefit from, do well from, exploit, make the most of

cashpoint n **cash dispenser**, cash machine, till, ATM, hole-in-the-wall (*infml*)

casing n **covering**, case, outside, exterior, skin

casino n **gaming club**, gambling den, nightclub, gaming house

cask n **barrel**, tub, drum, butt, vat

casserole n **cooking pot**, deep dish, covered dish, oven dish

cassette n 1 **cartridge**, tape, videotape 2 **case**, cartridge, holder, container, cover

cast v 1 **throw**, hurl, fling, toss, pitch 2 **produce**, generate, create, give rise to, engender 3 **mould**, form, shape, model ▪ n **company**, troupe, dramatis personae, actors, players. See COMPARE AND CONTRAST *at* **throw.**

cast about see **cast around**

cast an eye over v **scan**, skim, skim through, dip into, pick through *Opposite*: study

cast around v **search**, look for, seek, seek out, hunt out

cast a shadow over v **spoil**, hang over, darken, loom over, eclipse *Opposite*: brighten

cast aside v **get rid of**, put aside, throw away, toss aside, forget *Opposite*: keep

cast away v **give up**, throw away, cast off, discard, jettison *Opposite*: keep

castaway n **shipwrecked person**, survivor, exile

cast down v **discourage**, dishearten, depress, demoralize, disparage *Opposite*: cheer up

caste n **class**, social group, standing, background, social order

castigate (*fml*) v **criticize**, reprimand, chastise, scold, rebuke *Opposite*: praise. See COMPARE AND CONTRAST *at* **criticize.**

castigation (*fml*) n **criticism**, rebuke, reprimand, scolding, telling-off (*infml*) *Opposite*: praise

casting n 1 **forming**, manufacture, moulding 2 **object**, artefact, cast, moulding 3 **audition**, selection, screen test, interview, test

cast-iron adj 1 **inflexible**, rigid, unchangeable, immutable, fixed *Opposite*: flexible

2 guaranteed, definite, firm, sure, watertight

castle n **fortress**, fort, citadel, stronghold, bastion

castles in Spain see castles in the air

castles in the air n **flight of fancy**, fancy, dream, fantasy, notion Opposite: reality

cast off v **discard**, get rid of, reject, dispose of, abandon

castoff n **reject**, discard, hand-me-down, throwaway Opposite: purchase ■ adj **discarded**, rejected, unwanted, old, secondhand Opposite: new

cast out (fml) v **throw out**, evict, oust, eject, reject Opposite: install

castrate v **neuter**, sterilize, geld, spay

casual adj **1 unpremeditated**, unplanned, chance, unintentional, unintended Opposite: premeditated **2 seasonal**, informal, temporary, occasional, periodic Opposite: permanent **3 informal**, nonchalant, relaxed, calm, cool Opposite: formal **4 indifferent**, careless, offhand, blasé, cavalier Opposite: careful

casualness n **1 informality**, nonchalance, calmness, coolness, insouciance Opposite: formality **2 indifference**, carelessness, negligence, disregard, heedlessness Opposite: care

casualty n **injured person**, wounded person, dead person, fatality, loss

casuistry n **sophistry**, unsound reasoning, rationalization, excuse, twisting the facts

cat n **feline**, mouser, tom, big cat

WORD BANK
❑ **types of cat** Abyssinian, American shorthair, Birman, bobcat, British shorthair, Burmese cat, cheetah, Egyptian mau, jaguar, leopard, lion, lynx, Manx cat, Norwegian forest cat, ocelot, panther, Persian cat, puma, Siamese cat, tabby, tiger, tortoiseshell, wildcat

cataclysm n **catastrophe**, disaster, upheaval, calamity, debacle

cataclysmic adj **catastrophic**, disastrous, calamitous, dreadful, tragic

catacomb n **1 underground cemetery**, crypt, vault, tomb, mausoleum **2 tunnel network**, underground passage, labyrinth, warren, maze

catalogue n **1 list**, directory, index, file, register **2 set**, collection, list, litany, series ■ v **1 classify**, assemble, compile, arrange, categorize **2 enter**, record, insert, include, document **3 itemize**, list, enumerate, document, detail

cataloguing n **classification**, categorization, logging, sorting, taking down

catalyst n **promoter**, facilitator, stimulus, spur, incentive

cat-and-mouse adj **cruel**, sadistic, heartless, merciless, callous

catapult v **hurtle**, shoot, throw, project, propel

cataract n **waterfall**, cascade, falls, chute, torrent

catarrh n **mucus**, phlegm, discharge

catastrophe n **disaster**, calamity, upheaval, devastation, ruin Opposite: good fortune

catastrophic adj **disastrous**, shattering, calamitous, appalling, terrible Opposite: fortunate

catatonic adj **1 inert**, rigid, unresponsive, withdrawn, impassive **2** (infml) **unconscious**, asleep, comatose, inert, stupefied

catcall n **jeer**, hiss, boo, whistle, shout ■ v **taunt**, jeer, hiss, boo, shout

catch v **1 hold**, hold on to, gather, grasp, receive **2 grasp**, grab, hold, take, clutch Opposite: drop **3 snare**, ensnare, entrap, hook, net **4 capture**, arrest, apprehend, take prisoner, detain Opposite: release **5 contract**, become infected with, fall victim to, pick up, go down with **6 find**, discover, surprise, spot, notice **7 hear**, perceive, notice, become aware of, grasp **8 hit**, strike, knock, bump, bump into **9 stick**, get trapped in, snag, cling, entangle Opposite: free ■ n **1 fastening**, fastener, clasp, hook, latch **2** (infml) **snag**, drawback, problem, difficulty, hitch

catch-22 n **predicament**, no-win situation, dilemma, quandary, impossibility

catch a glimpse of v **spot**, notice, spy, glimpse, catch sight of

catchall adj **general**, universal, all-encompassing, wide-ranging, blanket

catch hold of v **take**, grab, clutch, seize, grasp

catching adj **infectious**, contagious, communicable, transmittable, easily spread

catch napping v **surprise**, take by surprise, catch out, catch on the hop, catch in the act

catch on (infml) v **1 become popular**, rise in popularity, become fashionable, be in fashion, take off (infml) Opposite: flop (infml) **2 understand**, be with you, follow you, comprehend, grasp Opposite: misunderstand

catch out (infml) v **expose**, trip up, wrong-foot, discover, catch

catch phrase n **catchword**, motto, slogan, tag

catch sight of v **spot**, notice, spy, glimpse, catch a glimpse of Opposite: miss

catch unawares v **surprise**, startle, creep up on, give somebody a shock, ambush

catch up v **draw near**, draw level, get closer to, become equal, pull alongside Opposite: fall behind

catchword n **catch phrase**, byword, motto, watchword, slogan

catchy adj **memorable**, attractive, likable, beguiling, haunting Opposite: forgettable

catechesis see catechism

catechism n **1 religious instruction**, religious education, religious teaching **2 dogma**, party line, mantra, article of faith, tenet **3 exam-**

ination, questioning, interrogation, dialectic

categorical *adj* **definite**, clear-cut, uncompromising, unconditional, unqualified *Opposite*: tentative

categorization *n* **1 classification**, cataloguing, labelling, tagging, grouping **2 category**, class, group, set, grouping

categorize *v* **classify**, sort out, catalogue, label, tag

category *n* **class**, sort, grouping, type, kind. *See* COMPARE AND CONTRAST *at* **type**.

cater *v* **provide**, supply, outfit, accommodate, gratify

caterwaul *v* **howl**, yowl, wail, squall, squeal

catgut *n* **cord**, line, thread, string, filament

catharsis *n* **release**, liberation, freeing up, cleansing, purification

cathartic *adj* **1 therapeutic**, liberating, releasing, emotional, intense **2 purifying**, cleansing, excretory, expulsive, purgative *(fml)*

catheter *n* **tube**, line, drip, drain, feed

catholic *adj* **wide-ranging**, broad, wide-reaching, all-embracing, extensive *Opposite*: narrow

catkin *n* **flower**, tassel, ament

catnap *n* **nap**, doze, rest, siesta, power nap ■ *v* **nap**, nod off, doze, sleep, catch some z's *(infml)*

cat-o'-nine-tails *n* **whip**, scourge, lash, birch

cattiness *n* **spitefulness**, nastiness, meanness, maliciousness, malevolence *Opposite*: kindness

cattle *n* **cows**, oxen, bulls, bullocks, steers

catty *adj* **spiteful**, nasty, venomous, mean, malicious *Opposite*: kind

catwalk *n* **1 stage**, walkway, runway, ramp, gangplank **2 bridge**, footbridge, walkway

caucus *n* **1 conclave**, assembly, committee, conference, convention **2 faction**, bloc, alliance, league, union

cauldron *n* **pan**, container, cooking pot, pot, vat

caulk *v* **seal**, waterproof, fill, block, plug

causal *adj* **fundamental**, underlying, contributory, contributing, connecting

causality *n* **cause and effect**, connection, interconnection, connectedness, causation

causation *n* **action**, connection, interconnection, relationship, causality

causative *adj* **causal**, instrumental, contributing, contributory, connective

cause *n* **reason**, grounds, source, root, origin *Opposite*: effect ■ *v* **make happen**, bring about, produce, set off, instigate *Opposite*: impede

cause offence *v* **be offensive**, shock, hurt somebody's feelings, offend, put somebody's nose out of joint

causeway *n* **walkway**, ramp, boardwalk, road, dike

caustic *adj* **1 corrosive**, acid, acidic, corroding, burning **2 sarcastic**, scathing, mordant, astringent, cutting *Opposite*: gentle. *See* COMPARE AND CONTRAST *at* **sarcastic**.

cauterize *v* **seal**, close, burn, sear, treat

caution *n* **1 carefulness**, thoughtfulness, attentiveness, attention, risk avoidance *Opposite*: carelessness **2 warning**, alert, notification, ultimatum, caveat ■ *v* **warn**, alert, notify, signal, give notice

cautionary *adj* **warning**, deterrent, admonitory, advisory, instructive

cautious *adj* **careful**, vigilant, guarded, wary, circumspect *Opposite*: reckless

---

COMPARE AND CONTRAST CORE MEANING: attentive to risk or danger

cautious aware of potential risk and behaving accordingly; **careful** taking reasonable care to avoid risks; **chary** cautiously reluctant to act; **circumspect** taking into consideration all possible circumstances and consequences before acting; **prudent** showing good judgment or shrewdness; **vigilant** alert and conscious of possible dangers; **wary** showing watchfulness or suspicion; **guarded** reluctant to share information with others; **cagey** (*infml*) secretive and guarded.

---

cautiousness *n* **caution**, carefulness, thoughtfulness, attentiveness, wariness *Opposite*: carelessness

cavalcade *n* **procession**, parade, column, line, convoy

cavalier *adj* **careless**, offhand, inconsiderate, high-handed, arrogant *Opposite*: polite

cavalry *n* **mounted troops**, horse regiment, horse soldiers

cave *n* **cavern**, grotto, hollow, pothole, fissure

caveat *n* **warning**, caution, admonition, qualification, stipulation

cave in *v* **1 collapse**, subside, fall in, fall down, topple **2 yield**, give in, surrender, give way, admit defeat *Opposite*: withstand

cave-in *n* **1 collapse**, fall, drop, slide, demolition **2 capitulation**, yielding, collapse, surrender, concession

cavern *n* **cave**, grotto, pothole, hollow, cavity

cavernous *adj* **1 vast**, spacious, deep, yawning, gaping *Opposite*: cramped **2 hollow**, echoing, resounding, sounding, resonant

caviar *n* **roe**, eggs, spawn

cavil *v* **quibble**, split hairs, be picky, complain, carp *Opposite*: accept

cavity *n* **hole**, space, hollow, crater, void

cavort *v* **frolic**, prance, caper, gambol, romp

caw *v* **call**, cry, croak, squawk

CB *n* **radio**, shortwave radio, citizens' band, telecommunication, walkie-talkie

CD player *n* **stereo**, personal stereo, hi-fi, CD, sound system

cease *v* **stop**, finish, end, come to an end, come to a close *Opposite*: start

ceasefire n truce, armistice, cessation of hostilities, end of hostilities, break in fighting

ceaseless adj unending, continual, constant, incessant, perpetual Opposite: sporadic

cease trading v go out of business, shut down, go bankrupt, close, fold

cede (fml) v yield, concede, give up, give, let go Opposite: resist

ceilidh n dance, barn dance, singsong, party, celebration

ceiling n limit, threshold, cutoff point, cap, check

celebrate v 1 enjoy yourself, have fun, have a good time, make merry, revel Opposite: lament 2 commemorate, observe, mark, keep, remember 3 praise, acclaim, commend, applaud, hail

celebrated adj famous, renowned, eminent, distinguished, illustrious Opposite: unknown

celebration n 1 festivity, party, festival, gala, fete Opposite: lamentation 2 commemoration, remembrance, observance, salutation, memorial

celebratory adj festive, triumphant, special, congratulatory, commemorative

celebrity n 1 superstar, star, personality, name, figure Opposite: nobody 2 fame, renown, notoriety, superstardom, prominence Opposite: obscurity

celestial adj 1 heavenly, holy, spiritual, godly, otherworldly 2 cosmic, astronomical, planetary, galactic, solar

celibate adj chaste, abstinent, self-restrained

cell n 1 lockup, prison cell, jail cell 2 group, sect, faction, cabal, caucus

cellulite n fat, fatty deposits, orange-peel skin, lumpiness, dimpling

cement n glue, adhesive, paste, epoxy resin ▪ v 1 join, stick, fix, glue, fasten together Opposite: separate 2 strengthen, reinforce, make stronger, prop up, fortify Opposite: undermine

cemetery n graveyard, burial ground, churchyard, garden of remembrance, mausoleum

cenotaph n war memorial, monument, memorial

censor v 1 edit, cut, remove, expurgate, bowdlerize 2 stifle, gag, repress, suppress, control

censored adj cut, expurgated, bowdlerized, changed, amended Opposite: complete

censorious adj disapproving, critical, severe, stern, hypercritical Opposite: approving

censorship n restriction, control, cutting, editing, bowdlerization

censure n criticism, disapproval, condemnation, denunciation, deprecation Opposite: approval ▪ v criticize, fault, reprimand, condemn, reproach Opposite: praise. See COMPARE AND CONTRAST at criticize, disapprove.

census n count, survey, poll, registration, tally

centenary n anniversary, birthday, centennial (US)

central adj 1 middle, mid, inner, innermost Opposite: outer 2 vital, dominant, essential, fundamental, chief Opposite: unimportant

centralism n control, concentration, monopolism, authoritarianism, centralization

centrality n importance, significance, criticality, supremacy, uniqueness Opposite: irrelevance

centralization n unification, integration, concentration, control, domination Opposite: decentralization

centralize v unify, consolidate, integrate, compact, concentrate Opposite: decentralize

centre n 1 midpoint, middle, halfway point, focus, focal point Opposite: edge 2 filling, inside, middle, core, layer Opposite: coating 3 heart, city centre, downtown (US) 4 complex, facility, development, building 5 focus, heart, core, bottom, root Opposite: periphery 6 cluster, concentration, focus, magnet, hotbed 7 middle ground, consensus, majority, middle course, happy medium Opposite: extreme 8 axis, pivot, pivotal point, fulcrum ▪ v 1 align, position, arrange, balance, adjust 2 focus on, turn on, concentrate on, home in on, target Opposite: ignore

centrepiece n centre of attention, focus, key feature, flagship, jewel in the crown

centrist adj middle-of-the-road, moderate, mainstream, reasonable, uncontroversial Opposite: extreme

century n period, era, time, span, epoch

CEO n chief executive officer, boss, chief, head, manager

ceramic adj earthenware, clay, pottery, terracotta, ironstone china

cereal n breakfast cereal, porridge, grits (US)

WORD BANK

❏ **types of cereal** barley, maize, millet, oat, rice, rye, sorghum, wheat

---

cerebral adj intellectual, rational, highbrow, logical, analytical Opposite: intuitive

ceremonial adj ritual, traditional, ritualistic, formal, official Opposite: informal ▪ n rite, ritual, ceremony, pomp, pageantry

ceremonious adj formal, solemn, dignified, grand, majestic Opposite: informal

ceremony n rite, ritual, formality, formal procedure, service

cert (infml) n certainty, foregone conclusion, cast-iron certainty, fait accompli, dead cert (infml)

certain adj 1 sure, convinced, positive, confident, firm Opposite: unsure 2 some, a number of, a few, several, selected Opposite: all

3 reliable, dependable, undeniable, guaranteed, clear *Opposite*: uncertain **4 particular**, specific, individual, precise, specified

certainly *adv* **1 surely**, positively, definitely, without doubt, undoubtedly *Opposite*: possibly **2 indeed**, absolutely, definitely, of course, emphatically

certainty *n* **1 foregone conclusion**, safe bet, cast-iron certainty, inevitability, cert *(infml)* **2 confidence**, conviction, faith, belief, assurance *Opposite*: uncertainty

certificate *n* **document**, licence, diploma, credential, documentation

certification *n* **guarantee**, warranty, documentation, authorization, accreditation

certified *adj* **official**, licensed, approved, authorized, accredited

certify *v* **confirm**, state, verify, endorse, attest

certitude *n* **conviction**, certainty, sureness, assurance, confidence *Opposite*: uncertainty

cessation *n* **end**, termination, close, stop, ending *Opposite*: start

cesspit *n* **tank**, pit, sewer, drain, gutter

chafe *v* **1 rub**, scrape, irritate, scratch, abrade **2 annoy**, bother, provoke, vex, irritate

chaff *v* **tease**, mock, make fun of, josh *(infml)*, pull somebody's leg *(infml)* ■ *n* **joking**, banter, repartee, teasing

chagrin *n* **humiliation**, mortification, vexation, irritation, disappointment

chain *n* **1 cable**, hawser, line **2 restraint**, shackle, manacle, fetter **3 group**, string, franchise, series **4 sequence**, series, string, succession, procession ■ *v* **bind**, manacle, shackle, lock up, restrain *Opposite*: unchain

chain reaction *n* **series of events**, train of events, knock-on effect, domino effect

chair *n* **chairperson**, presiding officer, president, head, leader ■ *v* **preside**, take the chair, lead, direct, oversee

chairperson *n* **presiding officer**, president, chair, head, leader

chalk *v* **write**, draw, mark, doodle, scribble

chalk up *v* **score**, mark up, gain, win, obtain

chalky *adj* **1 crumbly**, dry, powdery, fine, dusty **2 white**, pale, pallid, ghostly, deathly

challenge *v* **1 dare**, defy, throw down the gauntlet to, test **2 confront**, defy, brave, face up to *Opposite*: shirk **3 dispute**, contest, object to, question, argue *Opposite*: agree ■ *n* **test**, trial, task, contest, encounter

challenger *n* **contestant**, contender, competitor, opponent, pretender

challenging *adj* **1 demanding**, taxing, testing, difficult, tough *Opposite*: easy **2 stimulating**, thought-provoking, interesting, inspiring, exciting *Opposite*: routine **3 defiant**, disobedient, rebellious, insolent, impudent *Opposite*: compliant

chamber *n* **1 hall**, assembly room, meeting room, boardroom, legislative chamber **2 cavity**, hollow, compartment, space, slot

chamberlain *n* **official**, attendant, courtier, servant, manager

chameleon *n* **changeable person**, butterfly, trimmer, dilettante

champ *v* **chew**, munch, grind, masticate, chomp *(infml)* ■ *n* *(infml)* **champion**, winner, victor, title holder

champion *n* **1 winner**, victor, title holder, champ *(infml)* **2 defender**, supporter, backer, campaigner, advocate ■ *v* **defend**, support, back, campaign for, fight for

championship *n* **finals**, contest, challenge, title fight, battle

chance *n* **1 possibility**, probability, likelihood, prospect, risk **2 opening**, opportunity, option, occasion **3 gamble**, risk, hazard, venture, stake **4 luck**, fate, fortune, destiny, good fortune ■ *v* **risk**, hazard, gamble, try, attempt ■ *adj* **accidental**, coincidental, casual, fortuitous, unintended *Opposite*: planned

chancellor *n* **president**, leader, head of state, premier, prime minister

chance occurrence *n* **coincidence**, accident, twist of fate, quirk, happenstance

chance on *v* **stumble on**, happen on, strike on, hit on, come across

chancy *adj* **risky**, hazardous, dangerous, perilous, uncertain *Opposite*: safe

change *n* **1 alteration**, modification, variation, transformation, conversion **2 coins**, cash, loose change ■ *v* **1 alter**, modify, vary, adjust, amend **2 exchange**, replace, convert, substitute, transform

---

COMPARE AND CONTRAST CORE MEANING: make or become different

change make or become different in any way; **alter** change, especially to change an aspect of something; **modify** make minor changes or alterations, especially in order to improve something; **convert** change something from one form or function to another; **vary** change within a range of possibilities, or in connection with something else, with a suggestion of instability; **shift** change from one position or direction to another; **transform** make a radical change into a different form; **transmute** change into another form.

---

changeability *n* **1 unpredictability**, unsettledness, variableness, variability, irregularity *Opposite*: constancy **2 indecisiveness**, fickleness, unpredictability, flightiness, volatility *Opposite*: steadiness

changeable *adj* **variable**, unsettled, unpredictable, unreliable, unstable *Opposite*: constant

changed *adj* **altered**, different, transformed, reformed, rehabilitated *Opposite*: unchanged

change direction *v* **1 veer off**, swerve, turn,

bend, curve round **2 start afresh**, change course, change tack, have a rethink, turn over a new leaf

change for the better v **improve**, get better, look up, progress, pick up *(infml) Opposite*: deteriorate ■ *n* **improvement**, progress, development, upswing, upturn *Opposite*: deterioration

changeless *adj* **unchanging**, consistent, fixed, immutable, permanent *Opposite*: changing

changelessness *n* **permanence**, consistency, immutability, unalterability, invariability

change of heart *n* **about-turn**, volte-face, second thoughts, rethink, change of attitude

change over v **switch**, substitute, convert, transfer, change round

changeover *n* **move**, reversal, conversion, alteration, substitution

change round v **1 alter**, modify, amend, adjust, juggle *Opposite*: leave alone **2 exchange**, substitute, change, change over, reverse

change your mind v **have second thoughts**, come round, relent, back out, pull out

changing *adj* **altering**, varying, shifting, moving, fluctuating *Opposite*: changeless

channel *n* **1 canal**, conduit, waterway, strait, passage **2 ditch**, dike, groove, drain, trench **3 means**, outlet, conduit, path, way **4 station**, network, frequency ■ *v* **direct**, control, feed, conduct, route

chant *n* **song**, hymn, mantra, tune, carol ■ *v* **sing**, recite, repeat, vocalize, intone *(fml)*

chaos *n* **disorder**, confusion, bedlam, anarchy, pandemonium *Opposite*: order

chaotic *adj* **disordered**, muddled, confused, messy, untidy *Opposite*: orderly

chap *(infml) n* **guy** *(infml)*, bloke, gentleman, man, fella *(infml)*

chapel *n* **sanctuary**, oratory, chantry, side chapel, side altar

chaperon *n* **supervisor**, attendant, overseer, governess, escort ■ *v* **supervise**, oversee, escort, watch, look after

chaperone *see* chaperon

chaplain *n* **minister**, vicar, priest, pastor, rabbi

chapter *n* **1 section**, part, subdivision, division, segment **2 period**, episode, stage, phase, interval

char v **burn**, singe, scorch, carbonize, sear ■ *n* **domestic**, help, cleaner

character *n* **1 nature**, quality, temperament, personality, disposition **2 charm**, appeal, atmosphere, attractiveness, charisma **3 integrity**, strength, uprightness, rectitude, honour **4 eccentric**, personality, oddity, original **5 person**, individual, creature, sort, type

character assassination *n* **defamation**, slander, libel, affront, verbal abuse

character-building *adj* **challenging**, demanding, instructive, educative, empowering

characterful *adj* **individual**, distinctive, strong, upright, inspiring

characteristic *n* **trait**, feature, quality, attribute, point ■ *adj* **typical**, distinguishing, distinctive, individual, representative *Opposite*: uncharacteristic

characteristically *adv* **typically**, usually, normally, naturally, routinely *Opposite*: unusually

characterization *n* **description**, classification, account, portrayal, depiction

characterize v **1 describe**, portray, illustrate, depict, brand **2 typify**, set apart, distinguish, differentiate, exemplify

characterless *adj* **bland**, dull, soulless, uninteresting, insipid *Opposite*: interesting

characterlessness *n* **dullness**, soullessness, insipidness

charade *n* **pretence**, farce, sham, fake, travesty

charge v **1 accuse**, indict, allege, arraign, incriminate *Opposite*: absolve **2 attack**, rush, storm, assault, assail *Opposite*: retreat **3 rush**, dash, hurtle, stampede, hurry ■ *n* **1 cost**, price, expense, rate, amount **2 custody**, care, responsibility, control, trust **3 accusation**, indictment, allegation, arraignment, imputation **4 assault**, attack, advance, offensive, onslaught **5 order**, command, direction, instruction, injunction

chargeable *adj* **1 punishable**, criminal, indictable, imputable, actionable **2 taxable**, liable to tax, declarable, dutiable

charged *adj* **emotional**, exciting, electric, thrilling, stimulating *Opposite*: calm

chariness *n* **wariness**, caution, circumspection

charisma *n* **charm**, personality, appeal, magnetism, allure

charismatic *adj* **magnetic**, compelling, alluring, fascinating, captivating

charitable *adj* **1 generous**, giving, benevolent, altruistic, helpful *Opposite*: uncharitable **2 considerate**, understanding, accepting, sympathetic, tolerant *Opposite*: unforgiving

charity *n* **1 aid**, contributions, gifts, donations, help **2 aid organization**, charitable trust, charitable foundation, aid agency **3 kindness**, tolerance, humanity, compassion, generosity *Opposite*: unkindness

charlatan *n* **fake**, fraud, swindler, quack, counterfeit

charlatanism *n* **quackery**, trickery, pretence

charm *n* **1 attraction**, appeal, allure, charisma, magic **2 ornament**, keepsake, trinket, talisman, amulet ■ *v* **captivate**, enchant, beguile, hypnotize, mesmerize

charmed *adj* **1 lucky**, fortunate, enchanted, magical, fairy-tale *Opposite*: unlucky **2 delighted**, pleased, enchanted, thrilled, glad

charmer *n* **smooth talker**, enchanter, fascinator, smooth operator, ladies' man

charming *adj* **delightful**, amiable, attractive, appealing, charismatic *Opposite*: unattractive

charmless *adj* **unattractive**, unappealing, uninteresting, unsympathetic, unprepossessing *Opposite*: charming

chart *n* **diagram**, plan, graph, table, graphic representation ■ *v* **register**, record, project, plot, chronicle

charter *n* **contract**, deed, agreement, licence, grant ■ *v* **rent**, lease, hire, take on, commission

chary *adj* **wary**, cautious, suspicious, guarded, careful *Opposite*: reckless. *See* COMPARE AND CONTRAST *at* **cautious**.

chase *v* **1 pursue**, run after, hunt, hound, follow **2 race**, dash, rush, career, hurtle ■ *n* **pursuit**, hunt, hunting. *See* COMPARE AND CONTRAST *at* **follow**.

chaser *n* **pursuer**, follower, hunter, shadow, tail

chasm *n* **crater**, gulf, gap, abyss, gorge

chaste *adj* **innocent**, uncorrupted, virtuous, unblemished, unsullied *Opposite*: impure

chasten *v* **1 subdue**, suppress, restrain, tame, humble **2 punish**, reprimand, discipline, censure, chastise

chasteness *n* **pureness**, innocence, purity, virtuousness, faithfulness *Opposite*: immorality

chastise *v* **reprimand**, discipline, censure, punish, rebuke *Opposite*: praise

chastisement *(fml) n* **reprimand**, discipline, punishment, rebuke, scolding *Opposite*: praise

chastity *n* **purity**, innocence, virtue

chat *v* **talk**, converse, gossip, gab *(infml)*, natter *(infml)* ■ *n* **conversation**, one-to-one, heart-to-heart, tête-à-tête, talk

chattels *n* **possessions**, belongings, things, stuff, personal property

chatter *v* **babble**, rattle on, prattle, rant, gossip *Opposite*: shut up ■ *n* **talk**, gossip, chat, conversation *Opposite*: silence

chatterbox *(infml) n* **talker**, gossip, chatterer, tattler, blabbermouth *(infml)*

chatterer *see* **chatterbox**

chattily *adv* **conversationally**, informally, casually, easily

chattiness *n* **garrulity**, loquacity, communicativeness, informality

chatty *adj* **1 talkative**, garrulous, loquacious, forthcoming, gossipy *Opposite*: quiet **2 informal**, friendly, personal, casual, relaxed *Opposite*: formal. *See* COMPARE AND CONTRAST *at* **talkative**.

chat up *(infml) v* **flirt**, lead on, pick up *(infml)*, hit on *(US slang)*

chauffeur *n* **driver**, motorist, valet

chauvinism *n* **bigotry**, sexism, prejudice, narrow-mindedness, dogmatism

chauvinist *n* **bigot**, sexist, racist, homophobe, jingoist

chauvinistic *adj* **bigoted**, prejudiced, opinionated, dogmatic, narrow-minded

cheap *adj* **1 inexpensive**, economy, low-priced, economical, discounted *Opposite*: expensive **2 shoddy**, inferior, second-rate, substandard, common *Opposite*: superior **3 contemptible**, despicable, shameful, low, base *Opposite*: admirable **4 tightfisted**, miserly, mean, parsimonious, stingy *(infml) Opposite*: generous

cheapen *v* **denigrate**, demean, belittle, lower, degrade *Opposite*: elevate

cheaply *adv* **inexpensively**, economically, reasonably, modestly, competitively *Opposite*: expensively

cheapness *n* **1 tawdriness**, inferiority, shoddiness, tackiness *(infml) Opposite*: tastefulness **2 tightfistedness**, miserliness, meanness, parsimony, stinginess *(infml) Opposite*: generosity

cheapskate *(infml) n* **miser**, skinflint, killjoy, scrooge *(infml)*, meanie *(infml)*

cheat *v* **deceive**, trick, con, swindle, defraud ■ *n* **double-dealer**, rogue, cheater, charlatan, trickster

cheating *adj* **duplicitous**, double-dealing, dishonest, unprincipled, deceitful *Opposite*: honest ■ *n* **dishonesty**, deceit, deception, duplicity, chicanery

check *v* **1 test**, test out, prove, try, try out **2 make sure**, ensure, verify, confirm, certify **3 limit**, hold in, stop, impede, hold up *Opposite*: expedite *(fml)* ■ *n* **1 inspection**, examination, test, assessment, trial **2 safeguard**, curb, restraint, buttress, catch

checked *adj* **check**, patterned, crisscross, plaid, squared

checker *n* **inspector**, examiner, assessor, regulator, overseer

check in *v* **register**, sign in, sign up, sign on, enrol

check-in *n* **registration desk**, registration, reception desk, reception area, reception

checklist *n* **list**, specification, agenda, worksheet, spec *(infml)*

checkmate *n* **check**, mate, end, ending, victory *Opposite*: stalemate

check out *v* **1 leave**, depart, vacate, sign out, exit **2 inspect**, investigate, look into, explore, examine

check over *v* **look over**, reread, go through, go over, examine

checkpoint *n* **barrier**, turnpike, frontier, border, spot check

checkup *n* **examination**, medical, inspection, health check, once-over *(infml)*

check up on *v* **keep an eye on**, check on, spy on, watch, monitor *Opposite*: ignore

cheek *(infml) n* **nerve**, gall, impertinence, effrontery, audacity *Opposite*: humility

cheek by jowl *adv* **side by side**, on top of one another, close together, together, close

cheekiness *(infml)* *n* **impudence**, disrespect, effrontery, insolence, irreverence *Opposite*: respect

cheek-to-cheek *adv* **close**, close up, close together, together, intimately

cheeky *adj* **impudent**, audacious, bold, defiant, insolent *Opposite*: respectful

cheep *v* **chirp**, peep, tweet, twitter, sing

cheeping *n* **chirping**, tweeting, peeping, twittering, singing

cheer *n* **cheerfulness**, optimism, merriment, joyfulness, liveliness *Opposite*: gloom ■ *v* **applaud**, shout, root for, hail, praise *Opposite*: boo

cheerful *adj* **happy**, cheery, bright, smiling, joyful *Opposite*: sad

cheerfully *adv* **1 happily**, optimistically, merrily, joyfully, gleefully *Opposite*: sadly **2 gladly**, willingly, readily, with pleasure *Opposite*: grudgingly

cheerfulness *n* **happiness**, joyfulness, cheer, cheeriness, merriment *Opposite*: sadness

cheeriness *n* **cheerfulness**, happiness, joyfulness, liveliness, joviality *Opposite*: gloominess

cheering *adj* **heartening**, encouraging, positive, uplifting, promising *Opposite*: discouraging

cheerless *adj* **gloomy**, depressing, dismal, miserable, sad *Opposite*: bright

cheerlessness *n* **bleakness**, dreariness, gloominess, soullessness, wintriness *Opposite*: brightness

cheer on *v* **encourage**, root for, support, laud, egg on *Opposite*: discourage

cheer up *v* **perk up**, brighten, brighten up, liven, enliven *Opposite*: depress

cheery *adj* **happy**, joyful, smiling, cheerful, merry *Opposite*: gloomy

cheeseparing *adj* **mean**, miserly, mean-spirited, avaricious, tightfisted *Opposite*: generous ■ *n* **meanness**, miserliness, stinginess, mean-spiritedness, avarice *Opposite*: generosity

cheesy *(infml)* *adj* **tasteless**, cheap, tawdry, unpleasant, tacky *(infml) Opposite*: stylish

chemical *n* **substance**, element, compound

chemistry *n* **interaction**, attraction, understanding, empathy, sympathy

cheque *n* **payment**, form, order, draft, authorization

chequered *adj* **1 check**, checked, squared, patterned, crisscross **2 uneven**, inconsistent, up-and-down, variable, changeable *Opposite*: even

cherish *v* **treasure**, appreciate, relish, esteem, revere *Opposite*: neglect

cherished *adj* **valued**, precious, beloved, esteemed, appreciated *Opposite*: neglected

cherry-pick *v* **select**, choose, pick, handpick, pick and choose

cherub *n* **angel**, cupid, amoretto, putto

cherubic *adj* **1 holy**, divine, spiritual, saintly, blessed **2 angelic**, cute, innocent, attractive, lovable

chest *n* **upper body**, torso, rib cage, ribs, trunk

chestnut *(infml)* *n* **joke**, tired joke, anecdote, cliché, old favourite *(infml)*

chesty *adj* **wheezy**, rasping, phlegmy, congested

chevron *n* **V-shape**, V, stripe, badge, insignia

chew *v* **masticate**, chew up, gnaw, grind, crush

chew over *v* **meditate**, ponder, think about, ruminate on, consider

chew up *v* **1 damage**, crush, rip up, injure, destroy **2 chew**, grind, masticate, champ, munch

chewy *adj* **rubbery**, stringy, fibrous, gristly, leathery *Opposite*: tender

chic *adj* **stylish**, fashionable, well-dressed, attractive, smart *Opposite*: unfashionable ■ *n* **style**, elegance, panache, stylishness, modishness

chicanery *n* **deception**, trickery, verbiage, nonsense, underhandedness

chichi *adj* **contrived**, recherché, self-conscious, pretentious, affected

chicken *(infml)* *adj* **cowardly**, frightened, scared, reluctant, fearful *Opposite*: brave. *See* COMPARE AND CONTRAST *at* **cowardly**.

chicken feed *(infml)* *n* **small change**, next to nothing, small beer *(infml)*, small potatoes *(infml)*

chief *n* **ruler**, head, boss, captain, commander ■ *adj* **principal**, main, topmost, leading, foremost

chief executive *n* **CEO**, boss, leader, president

chiefly *adv* **primarily**, mainly, essentially, mostly, predominantly

chieftain *n* **tribal chief**, ruler, chief, overlord, lord

chieftainship *n* **leadership**, command, authority, rank, status

chilblain *n* **swelling**, inflammation, blister

child *n* **1 youngster**, young person, adolescent, youth, juvenile **2 offspring**, descendant, spawn, scion, son **3 baby**, infant, newborn, toddler, nursling **4 result**, product, outcome, creation. *See* COMPARE AND CONTRAST *at* **youth**.

childbearing *n* **reproduction**, pregnancy, gestation, childbirth, motherhood

childbirth *n* **giving birth**, delivery, labour, contractions, childbearing

childhood *n* **babyhood**, infancy, youth, upbringing, infanthood *Opposite*: adulthood

childish *adj* **1 immature**, irresponsible, silly, foolish, infantile *Opposite*: mature **2 childlike**, juvenile, innocent, ingenuous

childishness n **immaturity**, silliness, irresponsibility, pettiness Opposite: maturity

childlike adj **innocent**, naive, candid, unsophisticated, trusting Opposite: jaded

childproof adj **safe**, tamper-proof, secure

child's play n **piece of cake** (infml), picnic (infml), doddle (infml), walkover (infml), pushover (infml)

chill n **1 coldness**, coolness, low temperature, chilliness, nippiness Opposite: warmth **2 sudden fear**, anxiety, apprehension, wariness, shudder **3 gloom**, depression, pall, shadow **4 unfriendliness**, aloofness, detachment, coolness, coldness Opposite: warmth ■ adj **1 biting**, freezing, wintry, nippy, chilly **2 remote**, uninvolved, aloof, indifferent, chilly Opposite: warm ■ v **1 cool**, freeze, make colder, put on ice, refrigerate Opposite: warm **2 discourage**, depress, deter, dispirit, cast a shadow over Opposite: encourage

chilled adj **ice-cold**, freezing, frozen, refrigerated, cooled Opposite: hot

chilliness n **1 coolness**, coldness, frostiness, nippiness, low temperature Opposite: warmth **2 unfriendliness**, aloofness, stiffness, detachment, formality Opposite: friendliness

chilling adj **frightening**, alarming, unsettling, distressing, terrifying Opposite: reassuring

chill out (infml) v **1 calm down**, take it easy, stop worrying, lighten up (infml) **2 relax**, loosen up, rest, unwind, kick back (infml)

chilly adj **1 cold**, cool, nippy, chill, frosty Opposite: warm **2 frigid**, formal, supercilious, aloof, detached Opposite: welcoming

chime n **clang**, ding, ding-dong, sound, peal ■ v **strike**, peal, ring, sound, ring out

chime in v **1 butt in**, interrupt, interject, voice your opinion, speak up **2 agree**, be compatible, be consistent, be in line, be in agreement Opposite: contradict

chimera n **fantasy**, fancy, whimsy, illusion, mirage

chimerical adj **imaginary**, fantastical, illusory, unreal

chimes n **bells**, glockenspiel, carillon

china n **1 tableware**, crockery, porcelain **2 collectibles**, ornaments, figurines

chink n **narrow opening**, crack, crevice, slit, opening

chink in somebody's armour n **weak spot**, weakness, Achilles heel, flaw, failing

chinless adj **weak**, ineffectual, irresolute, inept, spineless Opposite: bold

chintzy (infml) adj **fussy**, quaint, cottagey, over-elaborate, twee

chinwag (infml) n **chat**, gossip, talk, conversation, natter (infml) ■ v **chatter**, talk, chat, gossip, converse

chip n **1 piece**, bit, crumb, flake, chunk **2 mark**, damage, imperfection, flaw, blemish **3 token**, counter, marker, playing piece, poker chip ■ v **1 break off**, fragment, hew, flake, pare **2 damage**, disfigure, mark, blemish, notch

chip away at v **weaken**, wear away, eat into, erode, diminish

chip in (infml) v **1 contribute**, help, participate, collaborate, take part **2 chime in**, butt in, interject, voice your opinion, say what you think

chip off the old block (infml) n **younger version**, mirror image, clone, living image, replica

chipper (infml) adj **1 cheerful**, high-spirited, lively, exuberant, good-humoured Opposite: glum **2 smartly dressed**, well-dressed, neat, trim, smart Opposite: scruffy

chipping n **chip**, piece, fragment, bit, shaving

chippings n **stones**, pebbles, gravel, shingle

chirpy (infml) adj **lively**, vivacious, alert, bright, effervescent Opposite: gloomy

chiselled adj **regular**, clean-cut, strong, delicate, fine-boned

chit (dated) n **receipt**, bill, tally, account, tab (US infml)

chitchat (infml) v **talk**, discuss, have a chat, gossip, babble ■ n **chatter**, gossip, chat, conversation, talk

chivalrous adj **1 courteous**, mannerly, gracious, polite, civil Opposite: discourteous **2 gallant**, courtly, brave, valiant, loyal Opposite: cowardly

chivalry n **1 courtesy**, courteousness, politeness, attentiveness, gentility Opposite: discourteousness **2 gallantry**, courtliness, loyalty, courage, bravery Opposite: cowardice

chivvy v **urge**, pester, harass, badger, pressure Opposite: discourage

chock n **wedge**, block, doorstop, chuck ■ v **brace**, steady, fix, block, stop Opposite: release

chock-a-block (infml) see chock-full

chock-full (infml) adj **packed**, jammed, crammed, full, crowded Opposite: empty

chocolate-box adj **pretty**, romanticized, twee, picturesque, soft-focus

choice n **1 selection**, choosing, pick, election, adoption **2 range**, selection, variety, set, group ■ adj **excellent**, high-quality, superior, special, prime

choke v **1 strangle**, throttle, stifle, suffocate, asphyxiate **2 obstruct**, clog, block, stop up, congest Opposite: free up (infml) **3 fill with emotion**, freeze up, weep, well up

choke back v **suppress**, hold back, fight back, stifle, repress Opposite: let out

choked (infml) adj **upset**, emotional, overcome, dismayed, disappointed

cholesterol n **fat**, saturated fat, saturated fatty acid, fatty acid, lipid

chomp (infml) v **chew**, munch, crunch, eat, masticate Opposite: nibble

choose v 1 **select**, pick, take, pick out, single out Opposite: reject 2 **decide**, want, prefer, desire, wish

choosy (infml) adj **particular**, hard to please, fussy, picky, fastidious Opposite: indifferent

chop v **cut**, slice, hack, axe, lop

chop down v **shorten**, decrease, cut back, cut down, lop off

choppy adj **rough**, stormy, wild, tempestuous Opposite: calm

chops (infml) n **jaw**, mouth, gob (slang)

chop up v **cut up**, chop, cut into pieces, slice, cube

choral adj **vocal**, harmonic, sung

chord n **harmony**, triad, arpeggio, major chord, minor chord

chore n 1 **task**, job, errand, odd job, assignment 2 **routine**, bore, hard work, imposition, inconvenience

choreograph v 1 **create**, compose, design, arrange, put together 2 **manoeuvre**, plan, direct, strategize, manage

choreography n 1 **composition**, dance routine, step design, step sequence, step arrangement 2 **manoeuvring**, direction, management, manipulation, strategy

chorister n **singer**, musician, treble

chortle n **laugh**, chuckle, gurgle, giggle, snigger ■ v **chuckle**, laugh, gurgle, giggle, snigger

chorus n **refrain**, chorus line, response, repeat, repetition ■ v **speak at once**, speak together, speak in unison

chosen adj **selected**, select, elect, preferred, special

christen v 1 **baptize**, name, bless, sanctify 2 **name**, nickname, call, dub, label 3 (infml) **launch**, inaugurate, debut

christening n 1 **baptism**, ceremony, rite, naming 2 (infml) **launch**, first use, inauguration, debut

Christian name n **first name**, given name, forename, personal name, praenomen

chronic adj 1 **long-lasting**, lingering, persistent, continuing, enduring Opposite: fleeting 2 **habitual**, persistent, ingrained, inveterate, established Opposite: occasional

chronicle n **record**, history, account, annals, journal ■ v **report**, record, recount, relate, narrate

chronological adj **sequential**, consecutive, linear

chronology n 1 **sequence of events**, order of events, time line, timetable, train of events 2 **account**, record, chronicle, narrative, history

chubbiness n **plumpness**, roundness, fleshiness, stoutness, fatness Opposite: slenderness

chubby adj **plump**, rotund, round, fleshy, stout Opposite: slender

chuck v 1 (infml) **throw**, hurl, toss, fling, pitch 2 (infml) **get rid of**, throw out, throw away, dispose of, discard Opposite: keep 3 (infml) **quit**, resign, walk off, leave, walk out 4 **tap**, pat lightly, pat, tickle ■ n **chock**, wedge, block, clamp. See COMPARE AND CONTRAST at **throw**.

chuck down (infml) v **rain hard**, teem, pour, rain cats and dogs (infml), bucket (infml) Opposite: drizzle

chuck in (infml) v **give up**, pack it in, throw in the towel (infml), call it quits (infml)

chuckle v **laugh**, laugh to yourself, chortle, laugh inwardly, giggle ■ n **laughter**, chortle, inward laughter, giggle, snigger

chuck out (infml) v **get rid of**, throw out, throw away, dispose of, discard

chuffed (infml) adj **pleased**, content, satisfied, happy, delighted

chug (infml) v **continue**, keep going, keep at it, persist, plug away (infml) Opposite: stop

chum (infml) n **friend**, associate, acquaintance, mate, pal (infml) Opposite: stranger

chumminess (infml) n **friendliness**, sociability, closeness, intimacy, matiness

chummy (infml) adj **friendly**, sociable, congenial, matey, close

chunk n **piece**, hunk, mass, lump, portion

chunky adj 1 **lumpy**, bumpy, coarse, rough Opposite: smooth 2 **solid**, heavy, hefty, weighty, substantial Opposite: lightweight 3 (infml) **stocky**, stout, fat, chubby, plump Opposite: slender

churchgoer n **worshipper**, congregant, communicant

churchyard n **graveyard**, burial ground, cemetery, necropolis, boneyard (infml)

churlish adj 1 **rude**, boorish, coarse, truculent, crass Opposite: polite 2 **ill-natured**, irritable, unpleasant, grumpy, sullen Opposite: pleasant

churn v **mix**, roil, agitate, shake, whip

churn out v **mass-produce**, manufacture, turn out, roll out, issue

chute n 1 **shaft**, slide, channel, sluice, raceway 2 **waterfall**, cascade, force, cataract, descent

chutzpah (infml) n 1 **boldness**, self-confidence, self-assurance, assertiveness, bravado 2 **gall**, boldness, nerve, impudence, cheek (infml)

C in C n **commander in chief**, field marshal, generalissimo, commander, leader

cinch n 1 (infml) **child's play**, piece of cake (infml), breeze (infml), walk in the park (infml), doddle (infml) 2 (infml) **sure bet**, certainty, dead certainty, sure thing (infml) 3 **girth**, restraint, belt, strap ■ v 1 **bind**, restrain, fix, tighten, gird (literary) 2 (dated infml) **guarantee**, assure, insure, settle, make certain

cinders n **embers**, ashes, residue, coals

cinema n **films**, movies, motion pictures, film, pictures (infml dated)

cinematic adj **filmic**, photographic, movie-like, filmmaking, moviemaking

cinematography n **photography**, shooting, film making, picture making, movie making

cipher n 1 **code**, secret message, symbols, cryptograph, encryption 2 **nobody**, non-entity, nothing, zero

circa prep **approximately**, about, around, roughly, round about Opposite: exactly

circadian adj **daily**, 24-hour, 24-hourly, diurnal, day by day

circle n 1 **ring**, loop, round, sphere, disc 2 **group**, gang, set, clique, crowd ■ v 1 **go around**, orbit, fly around, fly in a circle, circumnavigate 2 **encircle**, surround, ring, enclose, bound

circlet n **band**, coronet, tiara, diadem, crown

circuit n 1 **route**, track, trail, path 2 **tour**, trip, journey, route, round

circuitous adj 1 **indirect**, winding, meandering, roundabout, twisting Opposite: direct 2 **complicated**, convoluted, discursive, tangential, long-winded Opposite: straightforward

circuitry n **electrical system**, electric circuit, circuit board, motherboard, printed circuit

circular adj **spherical**, rounded, globular, round ■ n **leaflet**, flier, pamphlet, advertisement, handbill

circularity n **indirectness**, circuitousness, obliqueness, roundaboutness, convolutedness Opposite: directness

circulate v 1 **flow**, move, travel, pass 2 **pass around**, distribute, hand out, give out, send out Opposite: withhold 3 (infml) **mingle**, socialize, mix, meet people, be sociable

circulation n 1 **flow**, movement, passage, motion, rotation 2 **exchange**, flow, transmission, spread, dissemination 3 **distribution**, readership, sales

circumference n **perimeter**, boundary, bounds, limits, edge Opposite: middle

circumlocution n **periphrasis**, indirectness, roundaboutness, long-windedness, convolutedness Opposite: directness

circumlocutory adj **periphrastic**, indirect, meandering, roundabout, long-winded Opposite: direct

circumnavigate v **sail round**, orbit, circle, travel round, go around

circumscribe (fml) v **limit**, restrict, define, demarcate, mark out

circumscription (fml) n **restriction**, limit, limitation, constraint, restraint Opposite: freedom

circumspect adj **cautious**, prudent, careful, guarded, wary Opposite: reckless. See COMPARE AND CONTRAST at **cautious**.

circumspection n **care**, carefulness, caution, cautiousness, judiciousness Opposite: rashness

circumstance n 1 **condition**, situation, state of affairs, status quo, context 2 (fml) **event**, occurrence, incident, instance, happening

circumstantial adj **incidental**, contingent, indirect, inferred, conditional Opposite: concrete

circumvent v **avoid**, get round, evade, skirt, dodge

circumvention n **avoidance**, evasion, escape, sidestepping, dodging

circus (infml) n **show**, festival, spectacle, extravaganza, event

cirque n **corrie**, cwm, combe, hollow, valley

cistern n **water tank**, storage tank, tank, reservoir, container

citadel n **fortress**, stronghold, bastion, fort, castle

citation n **quote**, quotation, mention, reference, excerpt

cite (fml) v **quote**, mention, refer to, allude to

citified adj **oversophisticated**, sophisticated, cosmopolitan, slick, suave Opposite: countrified

citizen n **inhabitant**, national, resident, legal resident, voter

citizenry (fml) n **people**, population, community, public, electorate

citizenship n 1 **nationality**, residency, right of abode 2 **social responsibility**, public spirit, social conscience, civic duty

city n **metropolis**, municipality, conurbation, capital, town Opposite: hamlet ■ adj **urban**, metropolitan, town, municipal

COMPARE AND CONTRAST CORE MEANING: an urban area where a large number of people live **city** originally a town having a cathedral or having such a status conferred on it by the Crown; in the United States, a large municipal centre governed under a charter granted by the state; in Canada, a large municipal unit incorporated by the provincial government, but now used generally for any large urban area; **conurbation** an urban region formed or enlarged by the merging of adjacent cities and towns through expansion or development; **metropolis** a large or important city, sometimes the capital of a country, state, or region; **town** a populated area smaller than a city and larger than a village; **municipality** a city, town, or area with some degree of self-government.

city dweller n **urbanite**, citizen, burgher, townie (infml)

civic adj **public**, municipal, local, community, town Opposite: private

civil adj 1 **public**, political, municipal, civic, civilian 2 **courteous**, polite, respectful, well-mannered, accommodating Opposite: rude

civilian n **noncombatant**, private citizen, citizen, member of the public, neutral Opposite: martial

civility n politeness, courtesy, good manners, courteousness, respect *Opposite*: rudeness

civilization n 1 society, nation, culture, empire, polity 2 development, evolution, progress, cultivation, refinement

civilize v enlighten, educate, cultivate, improve, advance

civilized adj cultured, educated, refined, enlightened, polite *Opposite*: barbarous

civilizing adj humanizing, taming, educating, cultivating, refining

civil liberties *see* civil rights

civilly adv politely, respectfully, courteously, amicably, considerately *Opposite*: rudely

civil rights n human rights, rights, constitutional rights, privileges, civil liberties

civil servant n public servant, government employee, bureaucrat, official, administrator

clack v snap, click, clap, bang, rap

clad adj dressed, clothed, covered, attired (fml), arrayed (literary)

cladding n covering, layer, facing, casing, shell

claim v 1 maintain, assert, say, state, declare 2 ask for, call for, demand, apply for, request *Opposite*: deny 3 receive, obtain, take, pick up, retrieve ■ n 1 assertion, statement, accusation, declaration, allegation 2 demand, request, application, petition, call 3 right, entitlement, prerogative, privilege, due

claimant n applicant, plaintiff, pretender, petitioner, appellant

clairvoyance n psychic power, telepathy, prophecy, fortune-telling, palm reading

clairvoyant n psychic, mystic, spiritualist, telepathist, diviner ■ adj intuitive, psychic, telepathic, second-sighted, perceptive

clamber v climb, scramble, crawl, scale

clamminess n 1 dampness, wetness, moistness, dankness, sliminess *Opposite*: dryness 2 humidity, mugginess, closeness, heat, airlessness *Opposite*: freshness

clammy adj 1 damp, wet, moist, dank, slimy *Opposite*: dry 2 humid, muggy, close, sticky, sweaty *Opposite*: fresh

clamorous adj noisy, vociferous, loud, rowdy, boisterous *Opposite*: tranquil

clamour v 1 shout, scream, yell, cry, screech *Opposite*: whisper 2 demand, insist, appeal, cry out, bay ■ n 1 appeal, demand, call, request, cry 2 uproar, hullabaloo, din, commotion, noise

clamp v fasten, hold, compress, fix, brace

clamp down v shut down, take tough action, come down hard, restrict, limit *Opposite*: relent

clampdown n crackdown, restriction, curb, suppression, embargo

clam up (infml) v stop talking, choke, refuse to speak, remain silent, be unforthcoming *Opposite*: rattle on

clan n 1 tribe, family, relations, relatives, kinsfolk 2 (infml) clique, fraternity, band, coterie, set

clandestine adj secret, underground, covert, concealed, stealthy *Opposite*: open. *See* COMPARE AND CONTRAST *at* secret.

clang v clank, sound, toll, ring, reverberate

clanger (infml) n blunder, mistake, error, slip-up (infml), boob (infml)

clank n clang, clink, clatter, clash, bang

clannish adj cliquey, cliquish, unfriendly, unsociable, aloof *Opposite*: open

clap v applaud, give a standing ovation, put your hands together, give a round of applause, acclaim *Opposite*: boo ■ n slap, pat, tap, thrust, thwack

clapped-out (infml) adj worn out, dilapidated, rundown, decrepit, falling apart

clapping n applause, appreciation, ovation, acclamation, acclaim *Opposite*: jeering

claptrap (infml) n nonsense, rubbish, humbug, drivel, hogwash (infml) *Opposite*: sense

clarification n explanation, amplification, illumination, clearing up, explaining *Opposite*: obfuscation

clarify v 1 elucidate, make clear, explain, clear up, illuminate *Opposite*: confuse 2 refine, purify, cleanse, filter, process *Opposite*: cloud

clarity n clearness, lucidity, simplicity, precision, intelligibility *Opposite*: ambiguity

clash v 1 fight, conflict, disagree, quarrel, collide *Opposite*: agree 2 clatter, clank, clang, crash, bang 3 conflict, mismatch, jar, contravene *Opposite*: match ■ n 1 clank, clatter, clang, crash, bang 2 battle, encounter, brush, fight, skirmish 3 disagreement, quarrel, argument, row, fight. *See* COMPARE AND CONTRAST *at* fight.

clashing adj inharmonious, conflicting, jarring, incompatible, nonmatching *Opposite*: compatible

clasp v grasp, hold, clutch, embrace, hug *Opposite*: release ■ n fastener, hook, catch, hook and eye, popper

class n 1 group, set, tutorial group, tutor group, course group 2 lesson, period, session, lecture, seminar 3 category, type, sort, kind, genre 4 refinement, sophistication, elegance, style, flair *Opposite*: tackiness (infml) ■ v categorize, classify, rank, assign, group. *See* COMPARE AND CONTRAST *at* type.

class-conscious adj snobbish, classist, elitist, toffee-nosed (infml), stuck-up (infml) *Opposite*: egalitarian

classic adj 1 timeless, immortal, unforgettable, memorable, abiding 2 definitive, typical, characteristic, standard, model *Opposite*: atypical 3 simple, stylish, elegant, chic, understated ■ n masterpiece, landmark, benchmark, model, masterwork

classical adj traditional, conventional, orthodox, usual, typical Opposite: modern

classification n 1 **organization**, cataloguing, arrangement, sorting, ordering 2 **category**, class, group, grouping, set

classified adj **secret**, confidential, top secret, off the record, hush-hush (infml) Opposite: open

classify v **categorize**, order, organize, pigeon-hole, catalogue

classiness (infml) n **refinement**, sophistication, elegance, stylishness, class Opposite: tackiness (infml)

classless adj **egalitarian**, meritocratic, equal, open, free Opposite: class-conscious

classmate n **fellow student**, fellow pupil, contemporary, peer

classroom n **schoolroom**, teaching space, seminar room, tutorial room, lecture theatre

classy (infml) adj **refined**, sophisticated, elegant, stylish, chic Opposite: tacky (infml)

clatter v **rattle**, bang, clang, smash, clank

clause n **section**, article, part, division, passage

claustrophobic adj **enclosed**, confining, oppressive, suffocating, stifling

claw v **scrape**, scratch, scrabble, tear, graze ■ n **talon**, nail, hook

claw back v **recover**, regain, recoup, retrieve Opposite: lose

clay n **soil**, earth, dirt, mud

clean adj 1 **spotless**, dirt-free, unsoiled, fresh, sparkling Opposite: dirty 2 **pure**, wholesome, untainted, unadulterated, unpolluted Opposite: impure 3 **tidy**, neat, orderly, shipshape, immaculate Opposite: slovenly ■ v **scrub**, scour, wipe, cleanse, dust Opposite: soil

clean-cut adj **neat**, well-groomed, tidy, smart, well turned-out Opposite: untidy

cleaner n 1 **domestic**, home help, help, char, domestic worker (US) 2 **cleaning product**, detergent, stain remover, cleanser, soap

cleaning n **housework**, spring-cleaning, scrubbing, dusting, washing

cleanliness n **hygiene**, sanitation, purity, spotlessness Opposite: dirtiness

clean-living adj **abstemious**, teetotal, moderate, wholesome

cleanly adv **easily**, efficiently, effectively, neatly, simply

cleanness n **purity**, freshness, simplicity, clearness Opposite: dirtiness

clean out v 1 (infml) **bankrupt**, impoverish, reduce, drain, make somebody broke 2 **unclog**, flush, clear, clean, wash out Opposite: block up

cleanse v **rinse**, clean, rinse out, bathe, purify Opposite: soil

cleanser n 1 **cleaner**, cleaning product, detergent, stain remover, soap 2 **makeup remover**,

cleansing cream, lotion, cream, cold cream

clean-shaven adj **shaved**, smooth, smooth-shaven, hairless Opposite: bearded

cleansing n **cleaning**, washing, scrubbing, bathing, rinsing

clean up v 1 **smarten**, spruce up, tidy up, sanitize, clear up 2 **wipe out**, eradicate, eliminate, get rid of, do away with

cleanup n **crackdown**, clampdown, elimination, onslaught, attack

clear adj 1 **transparent**, translucent, see-through, sheer, filmy Opposite: opaque 2 **strong**, rich, pure, vibrant Opposite: indistinct 3 **unblemished**, perfect, pure, flawless, faultless 4 **well-defined**, sharp, distinct, clear-cut Opposite: indistinct 5 **ringing**, pure, bell-like, resounding Opposite: muffled 6 **obvious**, evident, patent, incontrovertible, out-and-out Opposite: unclear 7 **unambiguous**, understandable, comprehensible, lucid, self-evident Opposite: unclear 8 **unobstructed**, empty, free, free-flowing, open Opposite: blocked 9 **cloudless**, bright, sunny, fine, fair Opposite: cloudy ■ v 1 **evaporate**, dissipate, disappear, disappear, settle Opposite: form 2 **unblock**, free, unclog, empty Opposite: block 3 **tidy**, clear out, empty, straighten, clean up 4 **free**, vindicate, exonerate, absolve, acquit 5 (infml) **net**, earn, gain, take home, make Opposite: gross

clearance n **permission**, authorization, consent, approval, sanction Opposite: prohibition

clear-cut adj **precise**, distinct, definite, sharp, clear Opposite: ambiguous

clear-headed adj **lucid**, alert, coherent, perceptive, decisive Opposite: muddled

clearing n **glade**, clearance, dell (literary) Opposite: thicket

clearly adv **obviously**, evidently, undoubtedly, plainly, visibly Opposite: ambiguously

clearness n 1 **translucency**, transparency, flawlessness, luminousness, limpidity Opposite: opacity 2 **directness**, clarity, lucidity, comprehensibility, plainness Opposite: vagueness

clear off (infml) v **go away**, leave, depart, get going, head off Opposite: stay

clear out v 1 **leave**, depart, get going, head off, be off 2 **empty**, clear, clean up, turn out, throw out

clear-out n **clean-out**, throw-out, tidy, spring clean, tidy-up

clear-sighted adj **perceptive**, insightful, percipient, realistic, sensible Opposite: confused

clear up v 1 **tidy up**, straighten, clear, clean up, tidy 2 **resolve**, solve, clarify, explain, settle Opposite: complicate

cleave v **slice**, cut, slash, hew, chop Opposite: join

cleft n **fissure**, crevice, crack, gap, split

clemency *n* **mercy**, leniency, forgiveness, pity, compassion *Opposite*: heartlessness

clement *adj* **mild**, moderate, temperate, balmy, pleasant *Opposite*: inclement

clench *v* **compress**, grit, tighten, clasp, scrunch *Opposite*: relax

clergy *n* **priesthood**, ministry, ordained priests, clerics *Opposite*: laity

cleric *n* **priest**, minister, ecclesiastic

clerical *adj* **1 secretarial**, office, bookkeeping, accounting **2 religious**, ecclesiastical, church, priestly *(literary)*

clerk *n* **1 office worker**, counter clerk, bank clerk, accounts clerk, filing clerk **2 administrator**, official, recorder, clerk to the council, clerk to the governors

clever *adj* **1 bright**, intelligent, smart, knowledgeable, intellectual *Opposite*: foolish **2 ingenious**, shrewd, astute, adroit, crafty *Opposite*: inept **3 glib**, smart, slick, pert, flippant **4 skilful**, talented, quick, adroit, gifted *Opposite*: clumsy **5 useful**, handy, convenient, effective, ingenious *Opposite*: useless. *See* COMPARE AND CONTRAST *at* intelligent.

cleverness *n* **skill**, ingenuity, quickness, shrewdness, smartness *Opposite*: ineptness

cliché *n* **truism**, formula, line, platitude, prosaism

clichéd *adj* **corny**, hackneyed, trite, old, unoriginal *Opposite*: original

click *n* **clack**, tick, snap, clunk ■ *v* **1** *(infml)* **make sense**, sink in, become clear, fall into place **2** *(infml)* **get on**, be on the same wavelength, connect, relate to, hit it off *(infml)* *Opposite*: clash

client *n* **customer**, shopper, consumer, user, end user

clientele *n* **customers**, clients, regulars, patrons, custom

cliff *n* **precipice**, rock face, face, crag, overhang

cliffhanger *n* **crisis**, tiebreaker, knife-edge, nail-biter *(infml)*

climate *n* **1 weather**, temperature, environment, microclimate, macroclimate **2 atmosphere**, situation, ambience, surroundings, environment

climax *n* **peak**, high point, pinnacle, culmination, height *Opposite*: low point

climb *v* **1 scale**, go up, move up, mount, ascend *Opposite*: fall **2 rise**, soar, go up, rocket, escalate *Opposite*: descend ■ *n* **1 ascent**, scramble *Opposite*: descent **2 increase**, rise, upswing, hike *Opposite*: fall

climb down *v* **1 descend**, go down, get down, come down, dismount *Opposite*: ascend **2 back down**, retreat, make concessions, give way, backpedal *Opposite*: stand your ground

climbdown *n* **change of mind**, concession, U-turn, shift, retreat

climber *n* **1 mountaineer**, rock climber, alpinist **2 climbing plant**, trailer, creeper, vine

WORD BANK
❏ **types of climber** bougainvillea, bryony, clematis, convolvulus, grapevine, honeysuckle, ivy, jasmine, kudzu, liana, morning glory, passionflower, rattan, sarsaparilla, Virginia creeper, wisteria, woodbine

climbing *n* **mountaineering**, hiking, hill-walking, alpinism, rock climbing

clinch *v* **settle**, seal, close, tie up, decide ■ *n* **embrace**, hug, hold, bear hug, cuddle

cling *v* **1 clutch**, grasp, hug, hang on to, hold *Opposite*: let go **2 adhere**, grip, stick, hug, fit tightly **3 retain**, maintain, hold to, keep to *Opposite*: give up **4 latch onto**, be dependent on, depend on, hang on, attach

clingy *adj* **1** *(infml)* **clinging**, figure-hugging, tight-fitting, snug, close-fitting *Opposite*: baggy **2 dependent**, insecure, anxious, clinging *Opposite*: independent

clinic *n* **1 hospital**, health centre, surgery, consulting room, private clinic **2 workshop**, seminar, class, meeting

clinical *adj* **1 scientific**, medical, experimental, quantifiable, proven **2 detached**, disinterested, dispassionate, scientific, cold *Opposite*: personal

clink *v* **clank**, jingle, tinkle, chink, jangle

clip *v* **1 cut**, trim, shorten, shear, cut off **2 fasten**, attach, pin, staple, secure *Opposite*: undo ■ *n* **1 excerpt**, passage, extract, quotation, quote **2 fastener**, pin, staple, paperclip, clasp

clip-on *adj* **attachable**, fasten-on, hook-on, separable, removable

clipped *adj* **1 trimmed**, neat, cut back, tidy, cut **2 distinct**, short, brusque, concise, curt

clipping *n* **cutting**, extract, excerpt, article, feature

clippings *n* **trimmings**, parings, ends, offcuts, pieces

clique *n* **group**, in-group, faction, set, gang

cliquey *adj* **cliquish**, exclusive, clannish, unfriendly, unsociable *Opposite*: open

cloak *n* *(literary)* **screen**, cover, shroud, veil, façade ■ *v* **cover**, hide, conceal, shroud, veil *Opposite*: reveal

cloak-and-dagger *adj* **secret**, clandestine, undercover, covert, mysterious *Opposite*: aboveboard

cloakroom *n* **lavatory**, toilet, WC, powder room, rest room

clobber *(infml)* *v* **hit**, thump, beat, strike, punch ■ *n* **1 stuff**, tackle, things, belongings, gear *(infml)* **2 clothes**, outfit, clothing, kit *(infml)*, threads *(US slang)*

cloche *n* **cover**, cold frame, protection

clock *n* **1 timepiece**, timer, chronometer **2 regulator**, timer, device, control, meter

clock up v **achieve**, reach, score, attain, accomplish

clockwork n 1 **mechanism**, device, machinery 2 **regularity**, preciseness, accuracy, flawlessness, smoothness

clod n **lump**, clump, chunk, wad, hunk

clog v **block**, clog up, stop up, choke, obstruct *Opposite*: unblock

clogged adj **blocked**, obstructed, choked, congested

clog up v **block**, jam, obstruct, congest, stop up *Opposite*: unblock

cloister n 1 **quadrangle**, colonnade, arcade, portico, walkway 2 **monastery**, abbey, friary, convent, nunnery ■ v **seclude**, shelter, retreat, withdraw, closet

cloistered adj **secluded**, sheltered, confined, protected, insulated *Opposite*: accessible

clomp v **clump**, stomp, stamp, thump, bang *Opposite*: tiptoe

clone n **replica**, duplicate, genetic copy, twin, double ■ v **duplicate**, copy, make a replica of, replicate, emulate. *See* COMPARE AND CONTRAST *at* copy.

clonk v **knock**, bump, crash into, thump, bang

close adj 1 **near**, nearby, close by, adjacent, local *Opposite*: distant 2 **intimate**, familiar, dear, devoted, loving *Opposite*: distant 3 **careful**, rigorous, particular, keen, meticulous *Opposite*: lax 4 **compact**, tight, concentrated, dense, packed *Opposite*: loose 5 **similar**, faithful, precise, exact, literal 6 **silent**, secretive, taciturn, uncommunicative, quiet *Opposite*: open 7 **oppressive**, muggy, airless, sultry, heavy *Opposite*: fresh 8 **miserly**, tight, tightfisted, grudging, mean *Opposite*: generous ■ v 1 **shut**, lock, seal, close up, slam *Opposite*: open 2 **come together**, meet, join, unite, gather 3 **shut down**, close down, shut up shop, go out of business, stop trading *Opposite*: open 4 **block**, bar, plug, obstruct, seal off *Opposite*: unblock 5 **conclude**, end, finish, complete, terminate *Opposite*: start ■ n **end**, conclusion, finale, completion, finish *Opposite*: start

close call n **close thing**, close shave, near miss, narrow escape, lucky escape

close-cropped adj **short**, close-cut, trimmed, close-trimmed

closed adj 1 **shut**, locked, bolted, padlocked, fastened *Opposite*: open 2 **impassable**, inaccessible, blocked, obstructed, impenetrable *Opposite*: open 3 **settled**, concluded, terminated, decided, ended *Opposite*:

unfinished 4 **narrow-minded**, closed-minded, prejudiced, bigoted, intolerant *Opposite*: open 5 **exclusive**, restricted, private, limited, cliquish *Opposite*: open

closed book n **mystery**, puzzle, enigma, conundrum, riddle

close down v 1 **end**, shut down, pull the plug on, close, conclude *Opposite*: start 2 **shut**, go out of business, cease trading, come to an end, wind down *Opposite*: open

closedown n **closure**, closing down, shutting, shutting down, closing *Opposite*: inauguration

close-fisted (infml) adj **miserly**, tight, niggardly, parsimonious, tightfisted *Opposite*: generous

close-fitting adj **body-hugging**, tight-fitting, figure-hugging, clinging, tight *Opposite*: baggy

close in v **draw near**, bear down, move in, approach, creep up *Opposite*: move away

close-knit adj **close**, supportive, strong, caring, cohesive *Opposite*: loose

close-lipped *see* **closemouthed**

closemouthed adj **reticent**, tight-lipped, reserved, silent, close-lipped *Opposite*: forthcoming

closeness n 1 **nearness**, proximity, propinquity (fml) *Opposite*: remoteness 2 **intimacy**, familiarity, friendship, nearness, understanding *Opposite*: distance 3 **airlessness**, stuffiness, mugginess, sultriness, oppressiveness *Opposite*: freshness

close-run adj **near**, close, closely contested, neck and neck, hard-fought

close shave *see* **close call**

closet v **cloister**, seclude, confine, shut up, lock up ■ adj **secret**, private, clandestine, undeclared, unprofessed *Opposite*: open

close thing *see* **close call**

close up v 1 **shut**, close, lock, lock up, secure *Opposite*: open 2 **huddle together**, squeeze up, squash up, bunch up, move up

close-up n **detail**, zoom, camera shot, shot, photo

close your eyes to v **ignore**, overlook, disregard, turn a blind eye to, pay no attention to *Opposite*: notice

closing adj **final**, concluding, last, finishing, ultimate *Opposite*: opening

closing stages n **last part**, final stages, conclusion, end, finale

closure n 1 **end**, conclusion, finish, closing, shutting *Opposite*: opening 2 **finality**, resolution, conclusiveness, definiteness, inevitability

clot n **mass**, lump, accumulation, globule, blob ■ v **coagulate**, coalesce, thicken, congeal, set

cloth n 1 **material**, fabric, textile, stuff, yard goods 2 **rag**, duster, tablecloth, handkerchief, napkin

clothe v dress, fit out, cover, garb, cloak Opposite: undress

clothes n dress, garments, outfit, wardrobe, apparel

clothing see clothes

cloud n mist, fog, haze, bank of cloud, cloud cover ■ v veil, blur, obscure, shadow, make unclear Opposite: clarify

WORD BANK
❏ **types of cloud** altocumulus, altostratus, cirrocumulus, cirrus, cumulonimbus, cumulus, funnel cloud, mare's-tail, nimbus, rain cloud, storm cloud, stratocumulus, stratus, thundercloud

cloudburst n rainstorm, downpour, deluge, flood, shower

cloud-cuckoo-land n dream world, fantasy world, land of make-believe, dreamland, pipe dream

clouded adj 1 troubled, anxious, concerned, worried, apprehensive Opposite: untroubled 2 opaque, cloudy, murky, misty, hazy Opposite: clear

cloudiness n 1 muddiness, murkiness, dirtiness, mistiness, opacity Opposite: transparency 2 vagueness, confusion, ambiguousness, uncertainness, imprecision Opposite: clarity 3 darkness, gloominess, dullness, greyness Opposite: brightness

cloudless adj clear, blue, sunny, bright, brilliant Opposite: cloudy

cloud nine n seventh heaven, raptures, bliss, nirvana, delight Opposite: despair

cloudy adj 1 overcast, grey, gloomy, dull, hazy Opposite: bright 2 murky, muddy, opaque, milky, churned up Opposite: transparent 3 uncertain, unclear, vague, confused, imprecise Opposite: clear

clout n 1 (infml) influence, power, authority, weight, sway 2 thump, whack, smack, blow, cuff ■ v hit, strike, thump, smack, slap

clove n piece, segment, section, portion, fragment

clover n ease, good life, high life

cloverleaf n junction, intersection, crossroads, crossing, interchange

clown n (infml) joker, tease, fool, buffoon, prankster ■ v clown around, fool around, horse around, play the fool, lark about

clowning n joking, buffoonery, horseplay, playing around, fooling around Opposite: seriousness

cloy v nauseate, sicken, be too much, satiate, pall

cloying adj 1 syrupy, sticky, sickly, sugary, saccharine 2 sentimental, nauseating, sickly-sweet, sickening, heavy

club n 1 association, society, guild, organization, union 2 weapon, blunt instrument, stick, cudgel 3 nightclub, disco, discotheque, casino, private club ■ v batter, hit, bludgeon, bang, strike

WORD BANK
❏ **types of club** baton, blackjack, bludgeon, cosh, cudgel, mace, shillelagh, truncheon

cluck v 1 cackle, squawk, clack, make a commotion 2 fuss, coo, chuckle, tut, flap (infml)

clue n sign, hint, evidence, inkling, suspicion

clued-up (infml) adj well-informed, knowledgeable, au fait, competent, on the ball (infml) Opposite: clueless (infml)

clueless (infml) adj naive, inexperienced, impractical, incompetent, ignorant Opposite: well-informed

clump n bunch, cluster, mass, tuft, thicket ■ v clomp, plod, stomp, clatter, tramp

clumpy adj ungainly, awkward, cumbersome, unwieldy, chunky Opposite: dainty

clumsiness n awkwardness, ungainliness, ineptness, gaucheness, gaucherie Opposite: gracefulness

clumsy adj awkward, inept, ungainly, maladroit, gauche Opposite: graceful

clunk n clang, clank, clink, thud

clunky adj chunky, heavy, solid, bulky, awkward

cluster n bunch, group, collection, band, gathering ■ v gather, come together, bunch, group, collect Opposite: disperse

clutch v grasp, hold, grab, grip, hang on to

clutter n mess, litter, disorder, confusion, untidiness Opposite: order ■ v encumber, litter, strew, fill, cover Opposite: free

cluttered adj untidy, messy, disordered, muddled, jumbled Opposite: orderly

coach n trainer, teacher, instructor, tutor ■ v teach, train, prepare, instruct, tutor. See COMPARE AND CONTRAST at teach.

coaching n training, education, schooling, teaching, tutoring

coachload n busload, group, party, crowd, horde

coachwork n bodywork, exterior, outside, paintwork

coagulate v clot, congeal, thicken, coalesce, set Opposite: thin

coagulation n 1 clotting, thickening, setting, congealing, gelling 2 clot, lump, ball, mass, cake

coalesce v merge, unite, combine, amalgamate, fuse Opposite: separate

coalescence n union, combination, amalgamation, meld, merger Opposite: separation

coalfield n coalmine, seam, mine, pit, colliery

coalition n alliance, union, partnership, combination, league

coalmine n colliery, mine, pit, coalface, quarry

coarse adj 1 rough, uneven, abrasive, stiff, bristly Opposite: smooth 2 indelicate, tasteless, vulgar, uncouth, crude Opposite: polite

3 unrefined, crude, untreated, organic, unprocessed *Opposite*: refined

coarsen v **roughen**, harden, toughen, season, stiffen *Opposite*: soften

coast n **shore**, shoreline, coastline, beach, seashore *Opposite*: interior ■ v **glide**, cruise, drift, sail, freewheel *Opposite*: struggle

coastal adj **seaside**, littoral, sea, ocean, beach

coastline n **shoreline**, seashore, coast, shore, seaboard *Opposite*: interior

coast-to-coast adj **comprehensive**, extensive, complete, umbrella, blanket

coat n **1 fur**, wool, fleece, hide, skin **2 covering**, coating, layer, veneer, glaze ■ v **cover**, paint, smother, dip, smear

---

WORD BANK

❏ **types of jacket** anorak, blazer, blouson, bomber jacket, dinner jacket, DJ, double-breasted jacket, flak jacket, fleece, jacket, Nehru jacket, reefer jacket, safari jacket, single-breasted jacket, smoking jacket, sports jacket, tail coat, tails, waterproof jacket, windcheater

❏ **types of overcoat** cagoule, cape, cloak, duffel coat, frock coat, gabardine, greatcoat, mac (infml), mackintosh (dated), overcoat, parka, pea coat, poncho, raincoat, topcoat, trench coat

---

coated adj **covered**, caked, frosted, glazed, treated

coating n **covering**, veneer, varnish, glaze, layer

coat of arms n **crest**, emblem, badge, logo, design

coax v **wheedle**, persuade, cajole, charm, entice *Opposite*: browbeat

cobble n **cobblestone**, paving stone, paver, sett, stone ■ v **mend**, repair, patch, patch up, stitch

cobbled adj **paved**, cobblestoned, flagged

cobblestone n **cobble**, paving stone, paver, sett, stone

cobble together v **improvise**, rig, concoct, contrive, devise

cobwebs n **sluggishness**, tiredness, torpor, lethargy, listlessness *Opposite*: liveliness

cochineal n **colouring**, food dye, dye, food additive, additive

cock v **tilt**, lift, slant, angle, incline *Opposite*: lower

cock-a-doodle-doo n **crowing**, crow, cry, call

cock-a-hoop adj **elated**, delighted, thrilled, overjoyed, jubilant *Opposite*: dejected

cockeyed adj **1** (infml) **foolish**, absurd, madcap, ridiculous, silly *Opposite*: sensible **2 misaligned**, crooked, askew, awry, uneven *Opposite*: straight

cockpit n **arena**, battleground, boxing ring, floor, ring

cocksure adj **smug**, arrogant, conceited, confident, overconfident *Opposite*: modest

cocktail n **concoction**, mixture, brew, blend, combination

cockup (infml) n **blunder**, mess, mistake, error, mess-up (infml)

cocky (infml) adj **smug**, arrogant, boastful, brash, self-assured *Opposite*: modest

co-conspirator n **collaborator**, partner in crime, accomplice, partner, associate

cocoon n **sheath**, covering, shell, case, bubble ■ v **wrap**, cover, envelop, insulate, protect *Opposite*: expose

coda n **1 conclusion**, ending, end, close, finale *Opposite*: introduction **2 addendum**, postscript, addition, afterthought, adjunct

coddle v **pamper**, mollycoddle, indulge, baby, overprotect

code n **1 cipher**, cryptogram, encryption, cryptograph, enigma **2 program**, programming, data, instructions, machine code **3 system**, policy, convention, regulations, rules

code-named adj **alias**, known as, dubbed, identified, named

code of conduct n **agreement**, rules, guidelines, regulations, protocol

code of practice n **regulations**, rules, guidelines, principles, protocol

codex n **manuscript**, scroll, papyrus, palimpsest, parchment

codicil (fml) n **appendix**, supplement, addition, rider, add-on

codification n **systematization**, organization, categorization, classification, collation

codify v **organize**, collect, collate, arrange, order

codswallop (infml) n **nonsense**, rubbish, drivel, claptrap (infml), twaddle (infml)

coefficient n **number**, constant, factor, amount, quantity

coerce v **force**, press, pressure, compel, bully

coercion n **pressure**, compulsion, force, intimidation, bullying *Opposite*: volition

coercive adj **forced**, forcible, intimidating, bullying, strong *Opposite*: gentle

coexist v **1 live**, exist, cohabit, live together, coincide **2 harmonize**, synchronize, collaborate, cooperate, reconcile

coexistence n **1 cohabitation**, living together, co-occurrence, symbiosis, concomitance **2 harmony**, accord, cohabitation, coevolution, synchronization

coexistent adj **concurrent**, simultaneous, contemporaneous, coincident, concomitant

coextensive adj **coincident**, equivalent, equal, parallel, corresponding

coffee break n **time off**, break, rest, time out, breather (infml)

coffeemaker n **percolator**, espresso machine, coffeepot, filter, cafetière

coffer n **strongbox**, chest, moneybox, cash box, treasure chest

coffers n **funds**, reserves, assets, capital, resources

coffin (fml) n **box**, sarcophagus, cist, casket (US)

cog n **component**, part, gear, mechanism, cogwheel

cogency n **power**, strength, intensity, vigour, coherence

cogent adj **forceful**, convincing, persuasive, coherent, lucid Opposite: unconvincing. See COMPARE AND CONTRAST at **valid**.

cogitate (fml) v **think**, consider, reflect, deliberate, ponder

cogitation (fml) n **thought**, consideration, rumination, musing, reflection

cognate adj **similar**, alike, related, kindred, equivalent Opposite: different

cognition n **thought**, reasoning, understanding, perception, reason

cognitive adj **reasoning**, mental, intellectual, cerebral, perceptive

cognizance (fml) n **knowledge**, awareness, grasp, perception, understanding Opposite: ignorance

cognizant (fml) adj **knowing**, aware, conscious, acquainted, familiar Opposite: ignorant. See COMPARE AND CONTRAST at **aware**.

cognoscenti n **connoisseurs**, experts, specialists, authorities, pundits

cogwheel n **cog**, wheel, gearwheel, gear, flywheel

cohabit v **live together**, shack up (infml), live in sin (dated)

cohabitation n **living together**, sharing, living in sin (dated)

cohabitee n **partner**, domestic partner, significant other, spousal equivalent (US)

cohere (fml) v **1 adhere**, bind, stick, join together, stick together **2 conform**, match, tally, correspond, hang together Opposite: disagree

coherence n **consistency**, unity, rationality, logic, lucidity Opposite: inconsistency

coherent adj **1 consistent**, logical, sound, reasoned, reasonable Opposite: inconsistent **2 intelligible**, clear, comprehensible, articulate, lucid Opposite: unintelligible

cohesion n **sticking together**, unity, consistency, solidity, organization Opposite: disintegration

cohesive adj **unified**, consistent, solid, interconnected, organized Opposite: fragmented

cohort n **unit**, troop, regiment, legion, army

coiffure (fml) n **hairstyle**, haircut, hairdo (infml) ■ v **style**, arrange, dress, cut, coif (fml)

coil n **loop**, curl, spiral, twist, twirl ■ v **wind**, convolute, twine, curl, loop

coin n **currency**, money, coinage, denomination, change ■ v **invent**, think up, make up, create, devise

coincide v **accord**, agree, match, correspond, concur Opposite: differ

coincidence n **1 accident**, chance, luck, twist of fate, quirk **2** (fml) **concurrence**, correspondence, correlation, agreement, relationship

coincidental adj **1 accidental**, chance, unplanned, spontaneous, unexpected Opposite: intentional **2 concurrent**, corresponding, simultaneous, synchronous, correlated Opposite: separate

coincidentally adv **accidentally**, by accident, by chance, unpredictably, unexpectedly Opposite: intentionally

col n **pass**, saddle, gap, dip, passage

cold adj **1 chilly**, freezing, icy, frosty, bitter Opposite: hot **2 emotionless**, unfriendly, unemotional, unsympathetic, unkind Opposite: friendly ■ n **1 coldness**, chill, chilliness, frost, iciness Opposite: heat **2 common cold**, head cold, flu, influenza, chill

cold-blooded adj **pitiless**, hardhearted, cold, cold-hearted, callous Opposite: compassionate

cold-bloodedness n **pitilessness**, coldness, hardheartedness, cold-heartedness, callousness Opposite: compassion

cold-hearted adj **cold-blooded**, cruel, callous, ruthless, unfeeling Opposite: compassionate

cold-heartedness n **cold-bloodedness**, cruelty, callousness, ruthlessness, unfeelingness Opposite: compassion

coldness n **1 cold**, chilliness, frostiness, iciness, wintriness Opposite: warmth **2 emotionlessness**, unkindness, unfriendliness, aloofness, distantness Opposite: friendliness

cold shoulder n **rebuff**, rejection, snub, slight, brushoff (infml) Opposite: welcome

cold snap n **freeze**, frost, iciness, wintriness, cold spell

colic n **stomachache**, cramp, indigestion, irritable bowel syndrome, stitch

collaborate v **work together**, join forces, team up, work in partnership, pool resources

collaboration n **cooperation**, teamwork, partnership, association, alliance

collaborative adj **cooperative**, concerted, collective, joint, combined

collaborator n **1 colleague**, coworker, partner, team-mate, associate **2 traitor**, turncoat, spy, agent, double agent

collage n **collection**, combination, assortment, hotchpotch, medley

collapse v **1 fall down**, cave in, give way, crumple, subside **2 fail**, end, fold, break down, dissolve Opposite: boom **3 fold**, disassemble, fold up, put away, minimize Opposite: expand ■ n **1 failure**, ruin, downfall, breakdown, flop **2 illness**, breakdown, attack, crisis, crack-up (infml)

collapsible adj **folding**, foldup, stacking, foldaway, portable

collate v **order**, organize, collect, gather, assemble

collateral n **security**, surety, warranty, guarantee, insurance

collation n **1 ordering**, organization, collection, gathering, assembling **2 meal**, snack, buffet, spread (infml), repast (literary)

colleague n **coworker**, associate, assistant, partner, collaborator

collect v **1 gather**, amass, assemble, accumulate, garner Opposite: disperse **2 store**, hoard, amass, stockpile, squirrel

COMPARE AND CONTRAST CORE MEANING: bring dispersed things together
collect bring things together, or to make a collection of similar things as a hobby; **accumulate** obtain things over a period of time; **gather** bring together things from various locations; **amass** obtain a large number of things over an extended period; **assemble** bring things together in an orderly way; **stockpile** collect and store things in large amounts for future use; **hoard** collect and store things in large amounts, often secretly.

collected adj **calm**, composed, poised, placid, serene Opposite: flustered

collection n **1 group**, gathering, assortment, assembly, assemblage **2 compendium**, compilation, set, corpus, anthology

collective adj **shared**, cooperative, communal, joint, united Opposite: individual ■ n **cooperative**, colony, kibbutz, commune, farm

collectively adv **en masse**, cooperatively, communally, jointly, together Opposite: individually

collectivism n **communism**, socialism, syndicalism, Marxism, Leninism

collectivist adj **communist**, socialist, syndicalist, Marxist, Leninist

collector n **gatherer**, amasser, gleaner, hoarder, accumulator

college n **school**, university, academy, seminary, institution

collegial adj **1 shared**, reciprocal, mutual, interconnected, communal **2 collegiate**, scholastic, academic, educational, institutional

collegiate adj **academic**, university, scholastic, educational, institutional

collide v **hit**, strike, crash, bump, bump into

colliery n **coalmine**, shaft, seam, pit, mine

collision n **1 crash**, smash, accident, impact, pile-up (infml) **2 clash**, conflict, confrontation, disagreement, difficulty

colloquial adj **informal**, idiomatic, conversational, everyday, spoken Opposite: formal

colloquialism n **idiom**, popular expression, common term, vulgarism

colloquium n **seminar**, symposium, discussion, conference, debate

colloquy (fml) n **discussion**, meeting, conference, seminar, conversation

collude v **conspire**, plot, scheme, plan, connive

collusion n **conspiracy**, complicity, involvement, agreement, knowledge

cologne n **fragrance**, perfume, eau de toilette, scent, aftershave

colonial adj **foreign**, overseas, expatriate ■ n **expatriate**, settler, emigrant, émigré, migrant

colonialism n **expansionism**, colonization, imperialism, interventionism

colonialist adj **expansionist**, imperialist, interventionist, colonial

colonist n **settler**, immigrant, pioneer, migrant, explorer Opposite: native

colonization n **settlement**, establishment, foundation, occupation, annexation

colonize v **settle**, people, inhabit, take over, take possession of

colonizer n **settler**, immigrant, colonist, explorer, conqueror

colonnade n **arcade**, walkway, portico, porch, loggia

colony n **1 settlement**, outpost, dependency, protectorate, satellite **2 gathering**, group, collection, cluster, association

coloration n **pattern**, colouring, colour, pigmentation, shade

colossal adj **huge**, massive, immense, gigantic, enormous Opposite: tiny

colossus n **giant**, titan, leviathan, behemoth, juggernaut

colour n **hue**, tint, shade, dye, paint ■ v **1 tint**, dye, paint, shade, wash Opposite: bleach **2 blush**, go red, flush, redden Opposite: blanch **3 affect**, influence, modify, alter, tint

WORD BANK
❏ **types of colour** beige, black, blue, brown, green, grey, orange, pink, purple, red, white, yellow

colourant n **dye**, hair dye, hair colour, pigment, stain

colouration see coloration

coloured adj **tinted**, dyed, painted, highlighted, stained

colourful adj **1 bright**, multicoloured, rich, vivid, vibrant Opposite: dull **2 interesting**, vibrant, flamboyant, imaginative, lively Opposite: uninteresting

colouring n **complexion**, skin tone, skin colour, ruddiness, pallor

colourless adj **1 neutral**, monochrome, pale, pallid, drab Opposite: colourful **2 dull**, dreary, monotonous, uninteresting, prosaic Opposite: interesting

colours n **flag**, standard, ensign, insignia

column n **1 pillar**, post, support, pilaster, stake **2 line**, file, string, procession, queue **3 article**, feature, editorial, piece, op-ed

columnist n **writer**, journalist, newspaper columnist, magazine columnist, correspondent

coma n **unconsciousness**, blackout, stupor, oblivion, persistent vegetative state

comatose adj **1 unconscious**, passed out, blacked out, out for the count *(infml)* **2** *(infml)* **exhausted**, tired, spent, used up, all in *Opposite*: energetic

comb v **1 untangle**, unsnarl, disentangle, get knots out of, run through **2 search**, examine, scrutinize, explore, rake

combat n **battle**, fight, war, contest, struggle ■ v **1 fight**, battle, oppose, contest, contend **2 resist**, prevent, check, reduce, stop

combatant n **fighter**, soldier, enemy, warrior, participant

combative adj **argumentative**, antagonistic, aggressive, belligerent, confrontational *Opposite*: peaceable

combat zone n **battleground**, battlefield, front line, theatre of war, war zone

combination n **1 mixture**, grouping, blend, amalgamation, recipe **2 arrangement**, permutation, code, pattern, order. See COMPARE AND CONTRAST at mixture.

combine v **1 unite**, join, merge, coalesce, mingle *Opposite*: divide **2 mix**, blend, intermix, amalgamate, bring together *Opposite*: separate ■ n **1 syndicate**, cartel, bloc, trust, association **2 harvester**, thresher, reaper

combined adj **joint**, mutual, shared, collective, united *Opposite*: individual

combustible adj **flammable**, inflammable, explosive, burnable, ignitable *Opposite*: fireproof

combustion n **ignition**, fire, burning, incineration

come v **1 approach**, move towards, draw closer to, get nearer to, come up to *Opposite*: leave **2 arrive**, appear, turn up, get here, roll up *Opposite*: go **3 happen**, occur, take place, fall, befall *(literary)* **4 reach**, extend, stretch, go, touch **5 originate**, hail from, derive, come from, stem from

come about v **happen**, occur, take place, transpire, fall out

come across v **1 stumble across**, meet, find, happen upon, encounter **2 look**, appear, seem, strike, impress

come alive v **bloom**, thrive, blossom, take off, enliven

come along v **1 appear**, arrive, turn up, occur, materialize *Opposite*: disappear **2 progress**, make headway, proceed, advance, unfold **3 accompany**, chaperone, escort, tag along, follow

come apart v **tear**, fall apart, break, shatter, collapse

come at v **rush**, pounce on, attack, threaten, fly at

come back v **return**, reappear, flood back, rush back, revive *Opposite*: go away

comeback n **1 retaliation**, reply, retort, response, riposte **2 return**, revival, reappearance, recovery, reinstatement

come between v **interfere**, set against, meddle, alienate, disaffect *Opposite*: unite

come by v **obtain**, acquire, get, get hold of, get your hands on *Opposite*: lose

come clean *(infml)* v **bare**, reveal, confess, own up, tell the truth *Opposite*: keep secret

comedian n **humorist**, comic, standup, clown, wit

come down v **1 decrease**, drop, go down, dip, plunge *Opposite*: go up **2 lose status**, suffer reverses, know misfortune, have a run of bad luck, have a change of fortune

comedown *(infml)* n **disillusionment**, blow, disappointment, letdown, downer *(slang)* *Opposite*: boost

come down in favour of v **approve**, back, support, get behind, come down on the side of

come down in sheets *(infml)* v **pour**, sheet down, pelt down, come down in torrents

come down in torrents *see* come down in sheets

come down on v **take to task**, pick on, be hard on, scold, punish

come down on the side of v **support**, come down in favour of, favour, back, endorse *Opposite*: oppose

come down to v **signify**, amount to, mean, hinge on, boil down to *(infml)*

come down with v **contract**, sicken, incubate, take to your bed, catch *Opposite*: fight off

comedy n **funniness**, joking, amusement, entertainment, humour *Opposite*: tragedy

come first v **1 head**, top, be at the top, be at the head, be in the lead *Opposite*: lose **2 be your priority**, be your main concern, be the most important thing, be paramount, be the only thing that matters

come forward v **volunteer**, offer, put up your hand, step forward, reveal yourself *Opposite*: hold back

come from v **1 descend**, derive, issue, emanate, originate **2 originate from**, be from, hail from, live in, grow up in

come in v **1 finish**, cross the line, be placed, finish up, end up **2 land**, berth, enter, arrive, pull in *Opposite*: depart

come into v **inherit**, receive, be left, be bequeathed, take over

come into being v **come about**, begin life, develop, take form, take shape

come into bud v **blossom**, flower, bud, come to life, burgeon *(literary)*

come into contact with v **1 meet**, encounter, experience, come across, have dealings with **2 touch**, brush against, press against, rub up against, meet

come into flower v **blossom**, bloom, come into bloom, flower, come to life

come into sight v **appear**, emerge, come into view, become visible, heave into view (literary) Opposite: disappear

come off (infml) v **happen**, occur, take place, come about, succeed Opposite: fail

come on v **start**, begin, go on, occur, kick in (infml) Opposite: stop

come out v **emerge**, materialize, appear, surface, come to light

come out of v 1 **originate**, grow, develop, arise, have roots in 2 **survive**, live through, escape, endure, come through

come out on top v **succeed**, triumph, win, emerge triumphant

come out with v **utter**, confess, admit, make known, blurt Opposite: conceal

come over v 1 **affect**, engulf, flow over, sweep over 2 **visit**, stop by, drop round, drop in, come round

come round v 1 **visit**, stop by, call, call by, come over 2 **regain consciousness**, come to, revive, wake up, awaken Opposite: black out 3 **agree**, consent, comply, acquiesce, yield

comestible (fml) adj **edible**, eatable, digestible

comestibles (fml) n **food**, provisions, fare, groceries

come through v **survive**, endure, last, prevail, get through

come to v 1 **regain consciousness**, come round, awaken, wake up, revive Opposite: black out 2 **amount to**, total, add up to, equal, make

come to a close v **end**, finish, conclude, come to an end, stop Opposite: begin

come to a decision v **make up your mind**, reach a verdict, decide, make a choice, reach an agreement Opposite: prevaricate

come to a halt v **stop**, come to rest, come to a stop, stop in your tracks, stop dead Opposite: continue

come to an end v **finish**, end, conclude, stop, cease Opposite: continue

come to a standstill see **come to a halt**

come to blows v **fight**, exchange blows, start fighting, raise your fists, go for each other

come together v 1 **meet**, rendezvous, converge, gather together, congregate Opposite: disperse 2 **combine**, mingle, meld, unite, take shape Opposite: separate

come to grief v **fall flat**, go up in smoke, come to a bad end, collapse, fail Opposite: succeed

come to grips with v **cope with**, deal with, manage, handle, tackle

come to life v **awaken**, come to, revive, regenerate, breathe Opposite: flag

come to light v **leak out**, surface, emerge, come out, arise

come to naught see **come to nothing**

come to nothing v **end in failure**, fail, end in tears, fall apart, fall through Opposite: succeed

come to rest v **pause**, stop, come to a halt, come to a standstill, halt

come to terms with v **accept**, deal with, cope with, put behind you, get over

come up v **arise**, turn up, happen, occur, come about

come up against v **experience**, encounter, meet, run into, hit

come up for air v **take a break**, relax, break off, rest, take a breather (infml) Opposite: continue

come upon v **happen upon**, fall upon, come across, encounter, meet

comeuppance (infml) n **due**, punishment, just deserts, poetic justice, nemesis

come up to v **match**, meet, equal, satisfy, reach

come up with v **create**, produce, provide, supply, find

comfort n 1 **wellbeing**, ease, relief, security, relaxation Opposite: discomfort 2 **consolation**, reassurance, relief, cheer, solace Opposite: distress ■ v 1 **cheer**, cheer up, encourage, gladden, hearten Opposite: depress 2 **pacify**, soothe, console, reassure, calm Opposite: upset

comfortable adj 1 **relaxed**, at ease, contented, happy, easy Opposite: snug 2 **snug**, cosy, relaxing, restful, secure Opposite: uncomfortable 3 **well-off**, well-to-do, rich, wealthy, affluent Opposite: poor

comforted adj **consoled**, supported, reassured, cheered, heartened Opposite: distressed

comforter n **consoler**, reliever, comfort, support, ray of sunshine

comforting adj **heartening**, uplifting, reassuring, cheering, encouraging Opposite: upsetting

comfy (infml) adj **comfortable**, secure, snug, cosy, relaxing Opposite: uncomfortable

comic adj **amusing**, funny, humorous, droll, sidesplitting Opposite: tragic ■ n 1 **joker**, jester, comedian, standup, clown 2 **comic book**, magazine, funny book, funny paper, comic strip

comical adj **amusing**, funny, humorous, droll, hilarious Opposite: tragic. See COMPARE AND CONTRAST at **funny**.

comicality n **funniness**, drollness, hilariousness, humour, comicalness

comics n **funnies**, comic books, comic strips, cartoons, cartoon strips

coming adj **forthcoming**, pending, impending, approaching, imminent Opposite: past ■ n **emergence**, launch, arrival, appearance, approach Opposite: departure

comings and goings n **activity**, movements, toing and froing, goings-on (infml)

command n 1 **order**, directive, commandment, demand, charge 2 **knowledge**, facility, knack, grasp, expertise 3 **authority**, control, rule, domination, power ■ v 1 **order**, direct,

demand, charge, instruct *Opposite*: obey
2 control, dominate, rule, lead, be in
charge

commandant *n* **superior**, chief, commander,
chief officer, commanding officer

commandeer *v* **seize**, requisition, hijack, take,
appropriate *Opposite*: request

commandeering *n* **appropriation**, acquisition,
confiscation, seizure, sequestration

commander *n* **superior**, chief, commandant,
chief officer, commanding officer

commanding *adj* **impressive**, forceful, strong,
powerful, imposing *Opposite*: weak

commando *n* **SAS**, trooper, paratrooper

commemorate *v* **honour**, remember, celebrate,
observe, venerate *Opposite*: ignore

commemoration *n* **memorial**, tribute, honour,
remembrance, commemorative *(US)*

commemorative *adj* **memorial**, dedicatory,
celebratory, honouring

commence *v* **begin**, start, originate, inaugurate, instigate *Opposite*: terminate

commencement *(fml)* *n* **beginning**, start, origination, inauguration, instigation *Opposite*: end

commend *v* **1 praise**, speak well of, acclaim,
extol, laud *Opposite*: denigrate **2 entrust**,
convey, hand over, consign, commit *Opposite*: keep

commendable *adj* **praiseworthy**, admirable,
worthy, creditable, laudable *Opposite*: lamentable

commendation *n* **1 praise**, approval, recommendation, acclamation, approbation
Opposite: criticism **2 award**, citation, certificate, honour, special mention

commensurate *(fml)* *adj* **equal**, proportionate,
corresponding, appropriate, adequate *Opposite*: disproportionate

comment *n* **1 remark**, observation, statement,
aside, reference **2 judgment**, observation,
criticism, analysis, critique **3 explanation**,
interpretation, clarification, expansion,
commentary ■ *v* **observe**, remark, mention,
state, note

commentary *n* **1 comment**, explanation, observation, note, annotation **2 review**, essay,
report, treatise, thesis

commentate *v* **describe**, explain, report,
analyse, review

commentator *n* **critic**, observer, reporter,
analyst, reviewer

commerce *n* **trade**, business, market, buying,
selling

commercial *adj* **1 business**, business-related,
trade, industrial, mercantile *Opposite*: charitable **2 profitable**, saleable, marketable,
viable, moneymaking *Opposite*: unprofitable ■ *n* **advertisement**, infomercial, trailer,
ad *(infml)*, advert *(infml)*

commiserate *v* **sympathize**, pity, empathize,

show compassion, offer condolences

commiseration *n* **sympathy**, condolences, compassion

commission *n* **1 payment**, costs, percentage,
cut *(infml)* **2 task**, assignment, duty, job,
charge **3 committee**, authority, agency,
administration, board **4 formal order**,
command, directive, instruction, charge
5 authority, power, responsibility, position,
appointment ■ *v* **assign**, appoint, authorize,
contract, order

commissioner *n* **official**, officer, representative, administrator

commit *v* **1 obligate**, pledge, bind, promise,
oblige **2 earmark**, designate, dedicate,
reserve, devote **3 do**, perform, execute, carry
out, perpetrate **4 entrust**, give, consign,
place, hand over

commit hara-kiri *see* **commit suicide**

commitment *n* **1 promise**, pledge, vow, obligation, assurance **2 dedication**, loyalty, devotion, steadfastness, allegiance *Opposite*:
indifference **3 obligation**, duty, responsibility, liability, charge

commit suicide *v* **kill yourself**, take your own
life, end it all, fall on your sword, commit
hara-kiri

committed *adj* **devoted**, dedicated, loyal,
staunch, steadfast *Opposite*: uncommitted

committee *n* **group**, board, team, commission,
working group

commit to memory *v* **learn**, memorize, learn
by heart

commodious *adj* **spacious**, roomy, capacious,
sizable, ample *Opposite*: cramped

commodity *n* **product**, service, goods, article
of trade

common *adj* **1 shared**, mutual, joint, public,
communal *Opposite*: individual **2 everyday**,
usual, customary, familiar, normal *Opposite*: extraordinary **3 widespread**, frequent,
general, universal, familiar *Opposite*: rare
4 vulgar, coarse, ill-mannered, rough, low-
class *Opposite*: refined ■ *n* **green**, park, open
space, playing field, playground

common denominator *n* **shared quality**, shared
belief, commonality, common ground, unifying factor

commonly *adv* **usually**, normally, frequently,
generally, regularly *Opposite*: unusually

commonness *n* **ordinariness**, normalness, frequency, prevalence, regularity

commonplace *adj* **1 ordinary**, everyday, usual,
routine, common *Opposite*: extraordinary
2 dull, pedestrian, hackneyed, trite, stale
Opposite: original

common sense *n* **good judgment**, good sense,
practicality, realism, judgment

commonsense *adj* **sensible**, practical, down-
to-earth, realistic, commonsensical

commonsensical *see* **commonsense**

commonwealth n **nation**, people, nationality, state, country

commotion n **ruckus**, tumult, uproar, turmoil, hubbub Opposite: peace

communal adj **shared**, public, collective, joint, mutual Opposite: individual

commune n **community**, collective, collective farm, kibbutz, cooperative ■ v **communicate**, converse, empathize, connect, be in touch

communicable adj **infectious**, catching, transmissible, contagious, transmittable

communicant n **church member**, churchgoer, worshipper

communicate v 1 **converse**, talk, speak, be in contact, be in touch 2 **convey**, share, impart, transmit, reveal 3 **connect**, interconnect, lead into, link, join

communication n 1 **contact**, interaction, consultation, transfer, exchange 2 **message**, communiqué, announcement, statement, letter

communications n 1 **infrastructure**, public services, transportation, transport network, links 2 **telecommunications**, broadcasting, postal system, data lines, network

communicative adj **talkative**, open, forthcoming, outgoing, chatty Opposite: reticent

communion n **unity**, spiritual union, empathy, closeness, relationship

communiqué n **announcement**, statement, communication, press release, bulletin

communism n **collectivism**, socialism, communalism, Marxism, Trotskyism

communist n **socialist**, collectivist, communalist, Marxist, Trotskyist Opposite: capitalist

community n 1 **neighbourhood**, area, village, hamlet, commune 2 **kinship**, unity, identity, cooperation, convergence Opposite: isolation 3 **society**, public, people, population, group

commute v 1 **travel**, go back and forth, shuttle 2 **convert**, alter, exchange, transform, substitute

compact adj 1 **dense**, solid, packed in, packed together, compressed Opposite: loose 2 **small**, neat, trim, tiny, miniature Opposite: large ■ v **compress**, pack, squeeze, squash, tamp Opposite: loosen ■ n **contract**, pact, agreement, deal, treaty

compact disc player n **stereo**, personal stereo, hi-fi, CD, boom box

compactness n 1 **density**, solidity, compression, firmness Opposite: looseness 2 **smallness**, neatness, trimness, tininess, miniaturization Opposite: largeness

companion n 1 **friend**, mate, acquaintance, confidant, colleague 2 **escort**, attendant, chaperon, fellow traveller, arm candy (US slang)

companionability n **friendliness**, bonhomie, camaraderie, affability

companionable adj **friendly**, sociable, close, intimate, chummy (infml) Opposite: frosty

companionship n **company**, friendship, camaraderie, comradeship, esprit de corps Opposite: enmity

company n 1 **business**, corporation, firm, concern, enterprise 2 **companionship**, friendship, camaraderie, comradeship, esprit de corps Opposite: isolation 3 **group**, crowd, circle, set, party Opposite: individual 4 **visitors**, guests, friends, companions, invitees 5 **theatre company**, troupe, theatre group, ballet, touring company

comparable adj **similar**, analogous, akin, equal, equivalent Opposite: dissimilar

comparative adj **relative**, reasonable, fair Opposite: absolute

compare v 1 **evaluate**, contrast, assess, measure up, match up to 2 **liken**, associate, link, relate, equate 3 **equal**, match, measure up, parallel, compete

compare notes v **exchange information**, tell, relate, share, pass on

comparison n 1 **contrast**, judgment, assessment, evaluation, appraisal 2 **association**, link, relationship, similarity, likeness

compartment n **cubicle**, booth, partition, box, stall

compass n **scope**, range, area, extent, breadth

compassion n **sympathy**, empathy, concern, kindness, consideration Opposite: coldness

compassionate adj **sympathetic**, empathetic, feeling, concerned, kind Opposite: unfeeling

compassionless adj **unsympathetic**, unkind, unfeeling, uncaring, cold

compatible adj 1 **well-matched**, like-minded, well-suited, companionable, friendly Opposite: incompatible 2 **matching**, fitting, consistent, corresponding, harmonizing Opposite: incompatible

compatriot n **national**, fellow citizen, countryman, countrywoman Opposite: foreigner

compel v **force**, induce, require, coerce, oblige Opposite: cajole

compelling adj 1 **convincing**, persuasive, gripping, captivating, fascinating Opposite: unconvincing 2 **forceful**, powerful, urgent, undeniable, insistent

compendium n **collection**, anthology, digest

compensate v 1 **recompense**, reimburse, pay off, pay compensation, pay damages 2 **balance**, counterweigh, counteract, counterbalance, offset

compensation n 1 **recompense**, reimbursement, payment, damages, costs 2 **advantage**, reward, recompense, return, benefit

compete v 1 **contest**, contend, vie, strive, participate 2 **compare**, equal, measure up, rival, match

competence n **ability**, capability, skill, aptitude, proficiency Opposite: ineptitude. *See* COMPARE AND CONTRAST *at* **ability**.

competent adj able, capable, skilled, proficient, adept Opposite: inept

competition n 1 **rivalry**, opposition, antagonism, war, struggle Opposite: cooperation 2 **contest**, match, race, struggle, battle

competitive adj 1 **spirited**, aggressive, rivalrous, adversarial, cutthroat Opposite: passive 2 **reasonable**, modest, good, inexpensive, cheap Opposite: expensive

competitor n **contestant**, participant, entrant, player, opponent

compilation n 1 **gathering**, compiling, collecting, assembling, composing Opposite: dispersal 2 **collection**, set, anthology, assemblage, edition

compile v 1 **amass**, accumulate, collect, bring together, assemble Opposite: disperse 2 **list**, draw up, compose, set down, register

complacency n **satisfaction**, smugness, self-satisfaction, contentment, gratification Opposite: anxiety

complacent adj **satisfied**, self-satisfied, smug, gratified, content Opposite: anxious

complain v 1 **grumble**, grouse, carp, whine, moan (infml) 2 **protest**, object, criticize, find fault, pick holes in Opposite: praise

---

COMPARE AND CONTRAST CORE MEANING: indicate dissatisfaction with something

complain express discontent or unhappiness about a situation; **object** be opposed to something, or express opposition to it; **protest** express strong disapproval or disagreement; **grumble** disagree in a discontented way, possibly repeatedly or continually; **grouse** complain regularly and continually, often in a way that is not constructive; **carp** keep complaining or finding fault, especially about unimportant things; **gripe** (infml) to complain continually and irritatingly; **whine** complain in an unreasonable, repeated, or irritating way; **nag** find fault with somebody regularly and repeatedly.

---

complainer n **whiner**, objector, protester, grumbler, faultfinder

complaint n 1 **grievance**, criticism, protest, grumble, objection Opposite: praise 2 **illness**, condition, ailment, disorder

complaisant adj **acquiescent**, amenable, tractable, willing

complement n 1 **accompaniment**, foil, match, balance, counterpart 2 **quota**, set, allowance, quantity, number ■ v 1 **complete**, add, supplement, round out, make up for Opposite: detract 2 **balance**, set off, harmonize, match, be a foil for Opposite: clash

complementary adj **balancing**, opposite, matching, corresponding Opposite: clashing

complete adj 1 **whole**, comprehensive, wide-ranging, overall, thorough Opposite: partial 2 **finished**, completed, concluded, accomplished, fulfilled Opposite: unfinished 3 **absolute**, utter, downright, perfect, total ■ v 1 **finish**, finalize, conclude, end, bring to an end Opposite: start 2 **accomplish**, achieve, fulfil, carry out, realize

completed adj **finished**, accomplished, finalized, done, complete Opposite: unfinished

completely adv **totally**, wholly, entirely, fully, utterly Opposite: partially

completeness n **wholeness**, fullness, extensiveness, comprehensiveness, inclusiveness

completion n **conclusion**, close, achievement, accomplishment, end Opposite: start

complex adj 1 **complicated**, difficult, convoluted, involved, dense Opposite: simple 2 **multifaceted**, compound, composite, multipart, intricate Opposite: simple ■ n 1 (infml) **fixation**, psychosis, phobia, obsession, neurosis 2 **development**, centre, campus, facility, multiplex

complexion n 1 **skin**, face, colouring, appearance, features 2 **nature**, character, cast, tone, aspect

complexity n **difficulty**, intricacy, complication, complicatedness, density Opposite: simplicity

compliance n 1 **obedience**, acquiescence, agreement, submission, amenability Opposite: defiance 2 **conformity**, observance, accordance, fulfilment Opposite: non-compliance

compliant adj 1 **acquiescent**, obedient, biddable, yielding, amenable Opposite: defiant 2 **conforming**, in compliance, compatible Opposite: noncompliant

complicate v **make difficulties**, set hurdles, thwart, confound, confuse Opposite: simplify

complicated adj **complex**, difficult, intricate, byzantine, thorny Opposite: simple

complication n **difficulty**, snag, problem, impediment, obstacle Opposite: solution

complicity n **involvement**, collusion, collaboration, connivance, participation Opposite: detachment

compliment n **praise**, commendation, tribute, accolade, approval Opposite: criticism ■ v **flatter**, praise, admire, congratulate, approve Opposite: criticize

complimentary adj 1 **flattering**, admiring, kind, gracious, civil Opposite: critical 2 **free**, gratis, courtesy, on the house, free of charge

comply with v **obey**, fulfil, observe, conform, abide by Opposite: disobey

component n **constituent**, module, section, factor, element Opposite: whole

comportment (fml) n **behaviour**, conduct, bearing, deportment, carriage (fml)

compose v 1 **make up**, comprise, constitute, combine, unite 2 **arrange**, order, set out, marshal, organize Opposite: disturb 3 **create**, invent, make up, make, compile

composed adj **calm**, collected, self-possessed, serene, unruffled Opposite: flustered

composer n **creator**, originator, musician, writer, author

compose yourself v **calm yourself**, control yourself, calm down, get a hold of yourself, settle down Opposite: panic

composite adj **compound**, complex, multiple, multipart, multifactorial Opposite: simple ■ n **amalgam**, mixture, complex, compound, fusion

composition n 1 **constitution**, makeup, structure, components, constituents 2 **work of art**, creation, work, opus, masterpiece 3 **arrangement**, configuration, conformation, structure, alignment

composure n **equanimity**, calm, serenity, self-possession, tranquillity Opposite: agitation

compound n **mix**, mixture, complex, amalgam, composite ■ adj **multiple**, complex, composite, multifaceted, multifarious Opposite: simple. See COMPARE AND CONTRAST at **mixture**.

comprehend v 1 **understand**, know, realize, grasp, figure out 2 (fml) **include**, incorporate, bring in, add in, involve

comprehensible adj **understandable**, clear, logical, plain, coherent Opposite: unintelligible

comprehension n **understanding**, grasp, knowledge, command, conception

comprehensive adj **complete**, inclusive, full, all-inclusive, wide-ranging Opposite: incomplete

comprehensiveness n **inclusiveness**, completeness, all-inclusiveness, exhaustiveness, extensiveness

compress v **squeeze**, condense, pack together, squash, constrict Opposite: expand ■ n **pad**, wad, cold compress, ice pack, wrapping

comprise v **include**, encompass, contain, cover, consist of Opposite: exclude

compromise n **agreement**, settlement, arrangement, bargain, concession ■ v **cooperate**, bargain, negotiate, meet halfway, find the middle ground Opposite: confront

compulsion n 1 **urge**, impulse, desire, craving, force 2 **coercion**, force, pressure, obligation, duress

compulsive adj 1 **obsessive**, neurotic, habitual, uncontrollable, irrational Opposite: rational 2 **gripping**, compelling, mesmerizing, attention-grabbing, exciting Opposite: boring

compulsory adj **required**, obligatory, necessary, enforced, essential Opposite: optional

compunction n **regret**, scruple, reluctance, qualm, second thoughts

computation n **calculation**, reckoning, totalling, addition, subtraction Opposite: estimation

compute v **calculate**, work out, total, add, subtract Opposite: estimate

computer-aided design n **CAD**, computer graphics, graphics, product design, drafting

comrade n **friend**, companion, mate, pal (infml), chum (infml) Opposite: enemy

comradely adj **friendly**, companionable, brotherly

comradeship n **camaraderie**, brotherhood, friendship

con v 1 **swindle**, defraud, cheat, trick, do (infml) 2 (infml) **deceive**, hoodwink, trick, mislead, dupe ■ n 1 **negative**, disadvantage, minus, objection, downside Opposite: pro 2 **confidence trick**, fraud, ploy, con trick, rip-off (infml)

concave adj **curved in**, dished, hollow, sunken Opposite: convex

conceal v 1 **hide**, cover, secrete, screen, obscure Opposite: reveal 2 **suppress**, keep quiet, keep under wraps, sit on, censor Opposite: divulge

concealed adj 1 **hidden**, covered, buried, obscured, masked Opposite: visible 2 **secret**, cloaked, masked, veiled, disguised Opposite: open

concealment n **cover-up**, disguise, camouflage, suppression Opposite: revelation

concede v 1 **acknowledge**, grant, admit, accept, allow (fml) Opposite: deny 2 **yield**, give in, give up, admit defeat, compromise Opposite: stand firm

conceit n **self-importance**, pride, vanity, arrogance, superiority Opposite: modesty

conceited adj **self-important**, proud, vain, arrogant, high and mighty Opposite: modest. See COMPARE AND CONTRAST at **proud**.

conceitedness n **self-importance**, arrogance, narcissism, bigheadedness

conceivable adj **imaginable**, believable, possible, plausible, likely Opposite: implausible

conceive v 1 **imagine**, visualize, envision, envisage, think up 2 **create**, think up, dream up, make up, invent 3 **consider**, regard, think of, look on, perceive

concentrate v 1 **think**, focus, ponder, muse, deliberate Opposite: daydream 2 **converge**, come together, assemble, collect, cluster Opposite: disperse 3 **thicken**, strengthen, reduce, purify, distil Opposite: dilute ■ n **distillate**, essence, quintessence, reduction

concentrated adj 1 **strong**, thick, condensed, reduced Opposite: diluted 2 **focused**, intense, concerted, rigorous, strenuous Opposite: half-hearted

concentration n 1 **attentiveness**, attention, absorption, awareness, focus Opposite: distraction 2 **strength**, intensity, potency Opposite: dilution

concept n **idea**, notion, thought, impression, perception

conception n 1 **comprehension**, understanding, grasp, command 2 **idea**, notion, concept, thought, impression **3 beginning**, start, outset, origin, formation

concern v 1 worry, trouble, disturb, bother, upset Opposite: reassure **2 relate to**, affect, be about, have to do with, be connected with ■ n 1 anxiety, worry, apprehension, distress, alarm Opposite: reassurance **2 interest**, business, point, item, affair **3 company**, firm, business, enterprise, establishment

concerned adj worried, anxious, disturbed, alarmed, uneasy Opposite: carefree

concerning prep about, relating to, regarding, with reference to, as to

concert n recital, performance, show, gig (infml)

concerted adj 1 combined, collaborative, joint, mutual Opposite: solitary **2 concentrated**, intensive, rigorous, strenuous, determined Opposite: half-hearted

concession n 1 privilege, allowance, dispensation, indulgence, acknowledgment **2 reduction**, discount, allowance, markdown, decrease **3 yielding**, surrendering, granting, giving way, conceding

concierge n caretaker, janitor, doorman, doorkeeper, gatekeeper

conciliate v reconcile, appease, placate, pacify, make peace Opposite: provoke

conciliation n reconciliation, appeasement, pacification, reunion, mollification Opposite: provocation

conciliator n peacemaker, mediator, intermediary, arbitrator, arbiter Opposite: troublemaker

conciliatory adj appeasing, peacemaking, placatory, pacifying, assuaging Opposite: provocative

concise adj brief, short, to the point, succinct, terse Opposite: verbose

conciseness see concision

concision n succinctness, terseness, brevity, shortness, curtness Opposite: wordiness

conclave n meeting, assembly, council, congress, gathering

conclude v 1 deduce, assume, presume, decide, reckon Opposite: speculate **2 end**, close, finish, terminate, finish off Opposite: start **3 settle**, complete, close, clinch, arrange. See COMPARE AND CONTRAST at deduce.

concluded adj decided, settled, determined, resolved, clinched Opposite: unresolved

concluding adj closing, final, last, ultimate, ending Opposite: opening

conclusion n 1 deduction, assumption, inference, supposition, decision **2 end**, close, finish, termination, finale Opposite: start

conclusive adj decisive, beyond question, definite, convincing, irrefutable Opposite: inconclusive

concoct v 1 prepare, cook, make, put together, mix up **2 make up**, create, devise, invent, dream up

concoction n 1 mixture, brew, blend, potion, drink **2 invention**, creation, fabrication, fantasy, fiction

concomitance n accompaniment, coexistence, conjunction, combination, association Opposite: independence

concomitant adj 1 simultaneous, parallel, concurrent, coexistent, contemporaneous Opposite: independent **2 attendant**, associated, accompanying, connected, affiliated Opposite: unrelated

concord n 1 agreement, harmony, unity, accord, peace Opposite: conflict **2 treaty**, pact, agreement, settlement, compact

concourse n 1 open space, public space, forecourt, courtyard, square **2 crowd**, throng, horde, multitude, mass **3 gathering**, assembly, meeting, rally, muster

concrete adj 1 tangible, existing, actual, material, solid Opposite: abstract **2 specific**, particular, distinct, certain, definite Opposite: indeterminate

concubine n mistress, kept woman, hetaera, odalisque

concur v 1 agree, harmonize, be in accord, correspond, coincide Opposite: conflict **2 assent**, go along with, agree to, acquiesce, accept Opposite: resist **3 coincide**, synchronize, fall together, coexist Opposite: diverge. See COMPARE AND CONTRAST at agree.

concurrence n 1 agreement, accord, harmony, consensus, correspondence Opposite: conflict **2 simultaneity**, coexistence, concomitance, coincidence, synchronism

concurrent adj simultaneous, synchronous, parallel, coexisting, contemporaneous Opposite: separate

condemn v 1 censure, denounce, deprecate, criticize, attack Opposite: commend **2 rebuke**, reprove, reprimand, reproach, blame Opposite: commend **3 convict**, sentence, find guilty, doom, judge Opposite: absolve. See COMPARE AND CONTRAST at criticize, disapprove.

condemnation n 1 censure, disapproval, blame, denunciation, criticism Opposite: commendation **2 conviction**, sentence, judgment Opposite: absolution

condemnatory adj disapproving, critical, disparaging, reproving, denouncing Opposite: approving

condensation n 1 wetness, dampness, damp, humidity, water **2 concentration**, compression, reduction **3 abbreviation**, shortening, abridgment, summarization, cutting Opposite: expansion

condense v 1 concentrate, compress, compact, squeeze, pack Opposite: expand **2 abbreviate**, shorten, abridge, summarize, reduce Opposite: expand

condensed adj 1 shortened, reduced, summarized, edited, abbreviated Opposite: expanded **2 concentrated**, thickened, reduced, evaporated, thick *Opposite*: diluted

condescend *v* **1** patronize, humiliate, talk down, look down on, disdain *Opposite*: respect **2** deign, lower yourself, stoop, humble yourself, demean yourself

condescending *adj* patronizing, disdainful, superior, haughty, pompous *Opposite*: deferential

condescension *n* disdain, superciliousness, aloofness, haughtiness, arrogance *Opposite*: deference

condition *n* **1** state, form, order, repair, fitness **2** stipulation, clause, proviso, provision, requirement **3** disorder, illness, complaint, ailment ■ *v* acclimatize, get used to, prepare, train, get ready

conditional *adj* provisional, restricted, restrictive, qualified, uncertain *Opposite*: unrestricted

conditioned *adj* trained, broken in, inured, hardened, accustomed *Opposite*: untrained

conditioning *n* training, breaking in, taming, habituation (*fml*)

conditions *n* circumstances, situation, surroundings, setting, environment

condolence *n* sympathy, commiseration, pity, comfort, concern

condolences *n* commiserations, words of comfort, deepest sympathy

condone *v* overlook, excuse, disregard, forgive, ignore *Opposite*: oppose

conducive *adj* favourable, helpful, contributing, encouraging, advantageous

conduct *v* **1** manage, run, control, direct, organize **2** lead, show, direct, accompany, guide ■ *n* **1** behaviour, demeanour, way, manner, deportment **2** management, handling, organization, administration, running. *See* COMPARE AND CONTRAST *at* guide.

conduction *n* transmission, transference, transfer, conveyance, passage

conduct yourself *v* behave, act, acquit yourself, behave yourself, carry yourself

conduit *n* channel, canal, duct, tube, pipe

confab (*infml*) *n* chat, tête-à-tête, heart to heart

confederacy *n* union, league, association, alliance, confederation

confederate *n* partner, associate, ally, colleague, accomplice *Opposite*: rival ■ *adj* allied, united, joined, associated, affiliated *Opposite*: rival ■ *v* ally, unite, join, affiliate, associate *Opposite*: disconnect

confederation *n* association, league, union, coalition, confederacy

confer *v* **1** (*fml*) award, present, grant, give, bestow (*fml*) *Opposite*: withhold **2** discuss, consider, talk over, go over, thrash out. *See* COMPARE AND CONTRAST *at* give.

conference *n* **1** session, meeting, consultation, discussion, talks **2** symposium, seminar, convention, forum, meeting **3** league, association, alliance, union, federation

confess *v* **1** admit, own up, acknowledge, make a clean breast, come clean (*infml*) *Opposite*: deny **2** declare, profess, affirm, assert, make known *Opposite*: repress

confession *n* **1** admission, concession, revelation, acknowledgment *Opposite*: denial **2** declaration, affirmation, profession, assertion, statement

confidant *n* friend, soul mate, alter ego, sister, brother

confidante *n* friend, intimate, sister, soul mate

confide *v* unburden, disclose, reveal, divulge, tell *Opposite*: withhold

confidence *n* **1** self-assurance, sureness, self-confidence, poise, assurance *Opposite*: timidity **2** certainty, conviction, belief, faith, trust *Opposite*: doubt **3** secret, intimacy, classified information

confidence trick *see* con trick

confident *adj* **1** self-assured, poised, self-confident, self-possessed, cool *Opposite*: timid **2** definite, sure, certain, positive, convinced *Opposite*: unsure

confidential *adj* **1** private, secret, classified, off the record, restricted *Opposite*: unrestricted **2** intimate, private, close, personal **3** sound, stable, trusted, trustworthy, reliable *Opposite*: untrustworthy

confidentially *adv* behind the scenes, privately, in secret, just between you and me, behind closed doors *Opposite*: openly

configuration *n* shape, outline, formation, conformation, arrangement

configure *v* arrange, design, set up, construct, align

confine *v* **1** restrain, restrict, limit, narrow, keep *Opposite*: unleash **2** detain, quarantine, imprison, jail, lock up *Opposite*: release

confined *adj* **1** limited, restricted, curbed, restrained, hemmed in *Opposite*: free **2** constricted, restricted, small, cramped, enclosed *Opposite*: open

confinement *n* **1** (*dated*) labour, childbirth, giving birth **2** imprisonment, quarantine, internment, detention, captivity *Opposite*: freedom **3** limitation, scope, restriction, restraint, limit

confines *n* limits, boundaries, borders, limitations, margins

confirm *v* **1** corroborate, verify, substantiate, bear out, prove *Opposite*: refute **2** settle, check, authorize, approve, sanction **3** (*fml*) strengthen, firm up, fortify, reinforce, deepen *Opposite*: undermine

confirmation *n* **1** corroboration, verification, substantiation, authentication, evidence *Opposite*: denial **2** validation, authorization, approval, sanction, endorsement *Opposite*: refusal

confirmed *adj* **long-established**, established, dyed-in-the-wool, inveterate, deep-rooted

confiscate *v* **take away**, remove, sequester, seize, impound *Opposite*: restore

confiscation *n* **seizure**, repossession, appropriation, removal, sequestration *Opposite*: return

conflagration *n* **fire**, blaze, inferno, forest fire, brush fire

conflate *v* **combine**, amalgamate, consolidate, merge

conflation *n* **combination**, amalgamation, consolidation, merger

conflict *n* **1 battle**, fight, war, struggle, encounter *Opposite*: peace **2 opposition**, disagreement, difference, clash, argument *Opposite*: concord ▪ *v* **1 disagree**, oppose, clash, differ, be at odds *Opposite*: concur **2 fight**, quarrel, struggle, argue, scrap *Opposite*: agree. *See* COMPARE AND CONTRAST *at* **fight**.

conflicting *adj* **contradictory**, incompatible, at odds, inconsistent, differing *Opposite*: consistent

confluence *n* **meeting**, convergence, union, joining together, coming together *Opposite*: divergence

conform *v* **1 fit in**, imitate, follow, toe the line, obey *Opposite*: rebel **2 agree**, match, correspond, fit, coincide *Opposite*: contradict

conformism *n* **conventionality**, toeing the line, conformity, orthodoxy, traditionalism *Opposite*: dissidence

conformist *n* **yes man**, traditionalist, follower, sheep *Opposite*: rebel ▪ *adj* **conventional**, traditional, orthodox, obedient, unadventurous *Opposite*: rebellious

conformity *n* **1 toeing the line**, playing the game, conformism, conventionality, traditionalism *Opposite*: rebellion **2 agreement**, compliance, consistency, correspondence, accord *Opposite*: divergence

confound *v* **1 confuse**, muddle, mix up, mistake, misperceive *Opposite*: distinguish **2 stun**, amaze, puzzle, mystify, confuse

confounded *adj* **1** (*infml*) **annoying**, irritating, wretched, blasted (*infml*), darned (*infml*) **2 confused**, perplexed, mystified, baffled, puzzled

confrère (*fml*) *n* **colleague**, associate, collaborator, coworker

confront *v* **1 challenge**, oppose, antagonize, provoke, meet *Opposite*: appease **2 encounter**, handle, tackle, face up to, meet *Opposite*: duck

confrontation *n* **1 opposition**, argument, disagreement, quarrel, altercation *Opposite*: consensus **2 hostility**, war, battle, fight, clash

confrontational *adj* **argumentative**, quarrelsome, hostile, challenging, aggressive *Opposite*: amicable

confuse *v* **1 puzzle**, perplex, baffle, mystify, bewilder *Opposite*: enlighten **2 cloud**,

muddy the waters, complicate, blur, muddy *Opposite*: clarify **3 muddle**, mix up, misperceive, mistake, confound *Opposite*: distinguish

confused *adj* **1 puzzled**, perplexed, baffled, mystified, bewildered *Opposite*: enlightened **2 disordered**, disorderly, muddled, mixed up, in disarray *Opposite*: orderly

confusing *adj* **unclear**, puzzling, perplexing, baffling, mystifying *Opposite*: clear

confusion *n* **1 bewilderment**, perplexity, puzzlement, mystification, uncertainty *Opposite*: understanding **2 misperception**, misunderstanding, mix-up, muddle, mistake *Opposite*: clarity **3 disorder**, chaos, turmoil, upheaval, commotion *Opposite*: order **4 embarrassment**, awkwardness, disorientation, uncertainty, self-consciousness *Opposite*: confidence

congeal *v* **set**, clot, coagulate, thicken, solidify *Opposite*: liquefy

congealed *adj* **set**, dried, coagulated, clotted

congenial *adj* **agreeable**, friendly, affable, amiable, pleasant *Opposite*: hostile

congeniality *n* **affability**, bonhomie, geniality

congenital *adj* **1 inherited**, hereditary, inborn, inbred, genetic *Opposite*: acquired **2 ingrained**, established, long-established, habitual, inveterate

congest *v* **clog**, overfill, overcrowd, block, jam *Opposite*: clear

congested *adj* **1 overfilled**, jammed, choked, clogged, blocked *Opposite*: empty **2 obstructed**, clogged, mucous, stuffy, filled *Opposite*: clear

congestion *n* **1 overcrowding**, bottleneck, cramming, jamming, blocking *Opposite*: emptiness **2 blockage**, clogging, obstruction

conglomerate *n* **corporation**, multinational, company, firm, business

conglomeration *n* **1 composite**, accumulation, mass, collection, assembly **2 assortment**, potpourri, hotchpotch, collection, accumulation

congratulate *v* **commend**, toast, pat on the back, cheer, applaud *Opposite*: denigrate

congregate *v* **gather**, assemble, collect, meet, mass *Opposite*: disperse

congregation *n* **1 worshippers**, churchgoers, parishioners, flock **2 gathering**, crowd, throng, host, mass

congress *n* **assembly**, council, conference, meeting, convention

congressperson *n* **representative**, senator, legislator, lawmaker, deputy

congruent (*fml*) *adj* **corresponding**, consistent, matching, compatible, similar *Opposite*: disparate

conjectural *adj* **speculative**, tentative, unsubstantial, unsupported

conjecture *n* **guesswork**, estimation, guess,

surmise, inference ■ *v* **estimate**, imagine, guess, speculate, infer

conjoin *(fml)* *v* **link**, join, connect, couple

conjugal *adj* **marital**, matrimonial, married, wedded, spousal *Opposite*: unmarried

conjunction *n* **combination**, union, unification, coincidence, concurrence

conjure *v* **1 raise**, summon, call up, invoke, conjure up **2 mesmerize**, charm, trick, voodoo, spellbind

conjure up *v* **1 evoke**, create, recall, call up, bring to mind **2 raise**, conjure, summon, call up, invoke

conjuring *n* **magic**, illusion, sleight of hand, trickery

conked-out *(infml)* *adj* **asleep**, dead to the world, crashed-out *(slang)*

conk out *(infml)* *v* **1 fail**, break, wear out, malfunction, stall *Opposite*: start up **2 collapse**, pass out, doze off, nod off, fall asleep *Opposite*: wake up

connect *v* **1 attach**, join, link, fix, fasten *Opposite*: disconnect **2 associate**, relate, link, tie, link up *Opposite*: separate **3 get along**, get on, bond, click *(infml)*, hook up *(infml)*

connected *adj* **1 joined**, attached, fixed, united, tied *Opposite*: separate **2 linked**, associated, related, allied, coupled *Opposite*: unrelated

connection *n* **1 joining**, fitting together, assembly, linking, piecing together **2 bond**, tie, union, link, join **3 context**, association, relationship, correlation, relation

connections *n* **1 influence**, network, associates, acquaintances, links **2 relations**, relatives, associations, links, family

connive *v* **plot**, scheme, conspire, collude, plan

conniver *n* **manipulator**, schemer, plotter, intriguer, planner

conniving *adj* **devious**, scheming, conspiratorial, sly, crafty *Opposite*: ingenuous

connoisseur *n* **specialist**, expert, enthusiast, aficionado, buff

connotation *n* **implication**, association, suggestion, meaning, undertone

connote *v* **mean**, signify, suggest, intimate, imply

conquer *v* **1 seize**, take, take over, take control of, capture *Opposite*: surrender **2 defeat**, beat, overpower, overthrow, subjugate *Opposite*: lose **3 overcome**, surmount, get the better of, triumph over, master *Opposite*: give in. *See* COMPARE AND CONTRAST *at* **defeat**.

conquered *adj* **defeated**, beaten, vanquished, overpowered

conqueror *n* **defeater**, vanquisher, subjugator, captor, victor *Opposite*: vanquished

conquest *n* **1 defeat**, subjugation, overthrow, takeover, rout *Opposite*: surrender **2 victory**, success, triumph, win *Opposite*: defeat

conscience *n* **scruples**, principles, ethics, integrity, sense of right and wrong

conscience-stricken *adj* **guilty**, sorry, remorseful, guilt-ridden, contrite

conscientious *adj* **1 careful**, thorough, meticulous, painstaking, punctilious *Opposite*: careless **2 dutiful**, responsible, honourable, upright, upstanding *Opposite*: dishonest. *See* COMPARE AND CONTRAST *at* **careful**.

conscientiousness *n* **scrupulousness**, thoroughness, assiduousness, meticulousness, carefulness *Opposite*: carelessness

conscious *adj* **1 awake**, wide awake, sleepless, insomniac *Opposite*: unconscious **2 aware**, mindful, sentient, sensible, cognizant *(fml)* *Opposite*: unaware **3 deliberate**, intentional, premeditated, wilful, determined *Opposite*: unintentional. *See* COMPARE AND CONTRAST *at* **aware**.

consciously *adv* **deliberately**, intentionally, knowingly, determinedly, wilfully *Opposite*: unintentionally

consciousness *n* **awareness**, realization, perception, mindfulness, notice *Opposite*: unconsciousness

conscript *v* **call up**, recruit, enlist, enrol, draft *(US)* ■ *n* **recruit**, novice, draftee *(US)*, rookie *(US infml)*

conscription *n* **recruitment**, call-up, mobilization, enlistment, enrolment

consecrate *v* **sanctify**, bless, set apart, hallow, dedicate *Opposite*: desecrate

consecrated *adj* **hallowed**, sanctified, sacred, holy, blessed *Opposite*: desecrated

consecration *n* **sanctification**, dedication, blessing, hallowing *Opposite*: desecration

consecutive *adj* **successive**, uninterrupted, following, repeated, serial *Opposite*: alternate

consensus *n* **agreement**, accord, harmony, compromise, consent *Opposite*: disagreement

consent *v* **1 permit**, allow, approve, accept, sanction *Opposite*: forbid **2 agree**, comply, assent, acquiesce, accede *Opposite*: refuse ■ *n* **1 permission**, approval, assent, blessing, sanction *Opposite*: refusal **2 agreement**, accord, consensus, harmony. *See* COMPARE AND CONTRAST *at* **agree**.

consequence *n* **1** *(fml)* **importance**, significance, value, concern, import **2 result**, effect, outcome, end result, corollary

consequent *adj* **resulting**, resultant, consequential, following, subsequent

consequential *adj* **1 resulting**, resultant, consequent, following, subsequent **2 important**, significant, momentous, far-reaching, substantial *Opposite*: inconsequential

consequently *adv* **as a result**, so, therefore, subsequently, accordingly

conservation *n* **preservation**, upkeep, maintenance, protection, management *Opposite*: destruction

conservative *adj* **1 traditional**, middle-of-the-road, conventional, conformist, reactionary *Opposite*: avant-garde **2 cautious**, moderate, careful *Opposite*: speculative ■ *n* **traditionalist**, conformist, reactionary, fundamentalist, purist *Opposite*: progressive

conservatory *n* **1 greenhouse**, glasshouse, hothouse, garden room, porch **2 school of the arts**, music school, art school, school of dance, conservatoire

conserve *v* **1 preserve**, save, keep, protect, safeguard *Opposite*: destroy **2 store**, save, keep, eke out, be careful with *Opposite*: expend ■ *n* **jam**, marmalade, preserve

consider *v* **1 think through**, mull over, reflect, deliberate, contemplate **2 judge**, believe, think, regard, deem *(fml)* **3 respect**, bear in mind, care about, take into consideration, count *Opposite*: disregard

considerable *adj* **substantial**, significant, large, extensive, sizable *Opposite*: insignificant

considerably *adv* **significantly**, much, noticeably, by far, greatly *Opposite*: slightly

considerate *adj* **thoughtful**, kind, understanding, caring, sensitive *Opposite*: inconsiderate

consideration *n* **1 thought**, reflection, contemplation, attention, deliberation *(fml)* **2 respect**, concern, thoughtfulness, kindness, selflessness *Opposite*: thoughtlessness **3 matter**, factor, point, issue, fact **4 regard**, esteem, importance, significance, weight

considered *adj* **careful**, measured, well-thought-out, painstaking *Opposite*: rash

considering *prep* **bearing in mind**, allowing for, in view of, given, taking into account *Opposite*: excluding

consign *v* **1 entrust**, commit, hand over, give **2 relegate**, dispatch, condemn, banish, get rid of **3 deliver**, transfer, send, dispatch, ship

consignment *n* **batch**, delivery, shipment, load, package

consist *v* **1 reside**, lie, be based on, depend on, be defined by **2 contain**, be made up of, be made of, entail, involve

consistency *n* **1 constancy**, steadiness, reliability, uniformity, evenness *Opposite*: inconsistency **2 texture**, thickness, runniness, feel, makeup

consistent *adj* **1 reliable**, steady, dependable, constant, unswerving *Opposite*: inconsistent **2 coherent**, uniform, harmonious, even *Opposite*: incoherent

consistently *adv* **1 time after time**, time and again, again and again, repeatedly, every time *Opposite*: erratically **2 reliably**, steadily, dependably, constantly, unswervingly *Opposite*: inconsistently

consolation *n* **comfort**, solace, relief, support *Opposite*: grief

consolatory *adj* **comforting**, consoling, cheering, soothing

console *v* **comfort**, cheer up, soothe, calm, relieve *Opposite*: depress

consolidate *v* **1 combine**, unite, join, fuse, merge *Opposite*: split up **2 strengthen**, firm up, establish, confirm, enhance *Opposite*: weaken

consolidation *n* **1 alliance**, merging, union, link, association *Opposite*: split **2 strengthening**, firming, establishment, solidification, firming up *Opposite*: weakening

consoling *adj* **comforting**, soothing, cheering, calming

consort *n* **1** *(fml)* **companion**, partner, associate, spouse, wife **2 ensemble**, group, orchestra, band

consortium *n* **group**, grouping, association, conglomerate, syndicate

consort with *(fml)* *v* **associate**, accompany, mix, mingle, hang around

conspicuous *adj* **1 visible**, noticeable, obvious, exposed, on show *Opposite*: inconspicuous **2 eye-catching**, striking, prominent, outstanding, notable *Opposite*: unremarkable

conspicuously *adv* **noticeably**, obviously, clearly, evidently, blatantly *Opposite*: inconspicuously

conspicuousness *n* **obviousness**, plainness, prominence, overtness

conspiracy *n* **plot**, scheme, plan, intrigue, collusion

conspirator *n* **schemer**, plotter, conniver, collaborator, accomplice

conspiratorial *adj* **private**, shared, confidential, complicit, collusive

conspire *v* **1 plot**, connive, plan, scheme, work against **2 combine**, work together, unite, collaborate, collude

constancy *n* **1 faithfulness**, loyalty, fidelity, dependability, reliability *Opposite*: unfaithfulness **2 steadiness**, firmness, consistency, steadfastness, endurance *Opposite*: inconsistency

constant *adj* **1 continuous**, endless, relentless, continual, persistent *Opposite*: intermittent **2 frequent**, persistent, recurrent, incessant, recurring *Opposite*: occasional **3 steady**, stable, even, invariable, unvarying *Opposite*: irregular **4 faithful**, loyal, trustworthy, devoted, staunch *Opposite*: disloyal

constantly *adv* **continually**, continuously, always, regularly, frequently *Opposite*: intermittently

constellation *n* **group**, gathering, collection, assemblage, pattern

consternation *n* **dismay**, disquiet, alarm, anxiety, worry *Opposite*: composure

constituency *n* **1 area**, borough, ward, region **2 electorate**, voters, population, public, community

constituent n 1 **voter**, citizen, resident 2 **ingredient**, element, component, part ■ adj **basic**, essential, integral, component, fundamental

constitute v 1 **amount to**, represent, add up to, signify, total *Opposite*: fall short 2 **make up**, form, compose, represent 3 *(fml)* **set up**, establish, found, create, institute *Opposite*: disband

constitution n 1 **charter**, bill, instrument of government, statute 2 **health**, makeup, disposition, nature, condition 3 **establishment**, creation, formation, organization, foundation 4 **composition**, structure, makeup, components, constituents

constitutional adj **legitimate**, legal, lawful, statutory *Opposite*: unconstitutional

constrain v 1 **oblige**, compel, pressure, make, coerce 2 **limit**, restrain, hold back, confine, restrict

constrained adj **forced**, unnatural, inhibited, unspontaneous, embarrassed *Opposite*: natural

constraint n **restriction**, limitation, restraint, constriction, limit *Opposite*: freedom

constrict v 1 **tighten**, narrow, contract, compress, shrink *Opposite*: loosen 2 **limit**, restrict, constrain, narrow, control *Opposite*: extend

constricted adj **limited**, restricted, restrained, bound, confined *Opposite*: free

constriction n 1 **tightening**, contraction, narrowing, compression, shrinking *Opposite*: loosening 2 **restriction**, constraint, limitation, limit, condition

construct v 1 **build**, make, create, put up, erect *Opposite*: knock down 2 **compose**, put together, create, structure, piece together *Opposite*: take apart ■ n **concept**, hypothesis, theory, paradigm, idea

construction n 1 **creation**, assembly, manufacture, production, erection *Opposite*: destruction 2 **building**, edifice, structure, creation, erection *(fml)* 3 **interpretation**, understanding, comprehension, meaning, explanation

constructive adj **positive**, helpful, productive, useful, beneficial *Opposite*: unhelpful

construe v **interpret**, take, read, see, understand

consul n **diplomat**, ambassador, representative, emissary, envoy

consult v 1 **ask**, check, discuss, talk to, confer 2 **refer**, look up, turn to, check, access

consultant n **adviser**, mentor, counsellor, expert, specialist

consultation n **discussion**, dialogue, talk, session, meeting

consume v 1 **eat**, drink, devour, munch, feed on 2 **use**, use up, expend, spend, utilize *Opposite*: conserve 3 **destroy**, annihilate, burn up, incinerate, burn down

consumer n **buyer**, purchaser, shopper, customer, user

consummate v **complete**, carry out, achieve, accomplish, conclude ■ adj 1 **skilled**, skilful, expert, accomplished, talented *Opposite*: inept 2 **perfect**, excellent, complete, ideal, flawless *Opposite*: imperfect 3 **utter**, out-and-out, total, complete, absolute

consumption n 1 **depletion**, use, expenditure, utilization, spending *Opposite*: conservation 2 **ingesting**, feasting, feeding, eating, drinking

contact n 1 **interaction**, communication, dealings, connection, exchange 2 **connection**, acquaintance, friend, link, associate ■ v **get in touch**, make contact, drop a line, communicate, write

contagious adj **transmissible**, transmittable, spreadable, infectious, catching

contain v 1 **cover**, take in, comprise, encompass, hold *Opposite*: exclude 2 **check**, control, restrain, hold back, inhibit *Opposite*: unleash 3 **limit**, control, keep in check, delimit, restrict

contained adj **limited**, controlled, checked, confined, restricted *Opposite*: unbounded

contaminate v **soil**, pollute, foul, taint, infect *Opposite*: purify

contaminated adj **dirty**, dirtied, filthy, soiled, polluted *Opposite*: pure

contamination n **pollution**, adulteration, corruption, infection, uncleanness *Opposite*: decontamination

contemplate v 1 **look**, gaze, stare, watch, examine 2 **weigh**, muse, deliberate, consider, think 3 **anticipate**, expect, plan, think of, consider 4 **meditate**, muse, imagine, envisage, envision

contemplation n 1 **inspection**, observation, survey, review, scrutiny 2 **thought**, meditation, consideration, study, reflection

contemplative adj **thoughtful**, meditative, deep in thought, lost in thought, absorbed *Opposite*: unthinking

contemporaneity n **concurrence**, simultaneity, coexistence, contemporaneousness

contemporaneous adj **concurrent**, coexistent, concomitant, contemporary, simultaneous

contemporaneousness *see* **contemporaneity**

contemporaries n **age group**, generation, peers, coevals *(fml)*

contemporary adj **current**, modern, up-to-date, latest, present-day *Opposite*: old ■ n **peer**, colleague, classmate, coeval *(fml)*

contempt n **disdain**, dislike, disrespect, disapproval, scorn *Opposite*: admiration

contemptibility n **shamefulness**, reprehensibility, vileness, contemptibleness

contemptible adj **despicable**, disgraceful, shameful, detestable, distasteful *Opposite*: laudable

contemptibleness *see* **contemptibility**

contemptuous *adj* **scornful**, derisive, disdainful, disapproving, sneering *Opposite*: admiring

contemptuousness *n* **scornfulness**, disrespect, scorn, disdain, derision *Opposite*: admiration

contend *v* **1 argue**, assert, allege, insist, maintain **2 compete**, vie, challenge, run, put yourself forward **3 struggle**, resist, oppose, deal with, put up with

contender *n* **candidate**, nominee, competitor, contestant, challenger. *See* COMPARE AND CONTRAST *at* **candidate**.

contend with *v* **deal with**, cope with, face, experience

content *n* **substance**, matter, subject matter, theme, gist ▪ *adj* **gratified**, happy, satisfied, contented, pleased *Opposite*: unhappy ▪ *v* **gladden**, soothe, satisfy, please, make happy *Opposite*: dissatisfy

contented *adj* **happy**, satisfied, pleased, content, comfortable *Opposite*: unhappy

contention *n* **1 assertion**, position, argument, opinion, belief **2 argument**, disagreement, dispute, debate, conflict *Opposite*: harmony

contentious *adj* **1 controversial**, polemical, provocative, divisive, debatable *Opposite*: uncontroversial **2 argumentative**, combative, quarrelsome, antagonistic, disputatious *Opposite*: easygoing

contentment *n* **serenity**, gladness, satisfaction, happiness, pleasure *Opposite*: discontent

contest *n* **competition**, tournament, challenge, race, match ▪ *v* **challenge**, dispute, question, oppose, query *Opposite*: accept

contestant *n* **competitor**, contender, participant, participator, challenger *Opposite*: question master. *See* COMPARE AND CONTRAST *at* **candidate**.

context *n* **setting**, background, circumstances, situation, framework

contextual *adj* **background**, related, circumstantial, framing

contiguity *(fml)* *n* **proximity**, nearness, closeness, adjacency

contiguous *(fml)* *adj* **adjoining**, bordering, next to, adjacent, side by side

continent *n* **landmass**, mainland, land

contingency *n* **eventuality**, possibility, likelihood, exigency, emergency

contingent *adj* **depending**, liable, dependent, reliant, conditional ▪ *n* **commission**, legation, committee, party, group

continual *adj* **repeated**, frequent, recurrent, incessant, constant *Opposite*: intermittent

continuance *n* **extension**, protraction, extending, protracting, perpetuation *Opposite*: halting

continuation *n* **1 perpetuation**, progression, extension, drawing out, persistence *Opposite*: cessation **2 addition**, sequel, instalment, extension, carryover

continue *v* **1 prolong**, maintain, sustain, perpetuate, carry on *Opposite*: stop **2 last**, endure, linger, remain, stay *Opposite*: end **3 renew**, restart, resume, reprise, revive

continuing *adj* **ongoing**, current, enduring, remaining, unending *Opposite*: finished

continuity *n* **steadiness**, endurance, continuousness, permanence, stability *Opposite*: interruption

continuous *adj* **incessant**, unceasing, nonstop, unremitting, constant *Opposite*: intermittent

continuousness *n* **continuity**, constancy, permanence

contort *v* **distort**, twist, screw, warp, deform

contour *n* **outline**, delineation, silhouette, relief, curve

contract *n* **agreement**, bond, indenture, pact, convention ▪ *v* **1 diminish**, grow smaller, shrink, tighten, narrow *Opposite*: expand **2 become infected with**, catch, go down with, get, develop *Opposite*: fight off **3 sign**, commission, sign up, commit, engage

contraction *n* **1 reduction**, shrinkage, tightening, narrowing, retrenchment *Opposite*: expansion **2 tightening**, jerking, cramp, spasm, tic **3 shortening**, merging, combining, abbreviation, ellipsis

contractor *n* **worker**, independent, outworker, outside worker, freelancer

contract out *v* **delegate**, offer, subcontract, outsource, farm

contradict *v* **1 deny**, oppose, challenge, dispute, refute *Opposite*: confirm **2 disprove**, cancel, refute, dispute, undermine *Opposite*: support. *See* COMPARE AND CONTRAST *at* **disagree**.

contradiction *n* **1 illogicality**, flaw, inconsistency, incongruity, ambiguity **2 denial**, disagreement, challenge, negation, opposition *Opposite*: confirmation

contradictory *adj* **inconsistent**, contrary, self-contradictory, opposing, clashing *Opposite*: consistent

contraption *n* **gadget**, machine, device, apparatus, contrivance

contrarily *adv* **disobediently**, rebelliously, stubbornly, wilfully, defiantly *Opposite*: cooperatively

contrariness *n* **disobedience**, uncooperativeness, perversity, rebelliousness, wilfulness *Opposite*: cooperation

contrary *adj* **1 conflicting**, opposing, different, differing, divergent *Opposite*: similar **2 disobedient**, rebellious, obstinate, uncooperative, defiant *Opposite*: cooperative ▪ *n* **opposite**, inverse, other side of the coin, converse, reverse

contrast *n* **difference**, dissimilarity, distinction, disparity, gap *Opposite*: similarity ▪ *v* **1 compare**, juxtapose, analogize, weigh, distinguish **2 stand out**, stick out like a sore thumb, differ, diverge, conflict *Opposite*: agree

contrasting *adj* **conflicting**, opposing, complementary, different, distinct *Opposite*: similar

contravene *v* **break**, flout, breach, disobey, disregard *Opposite*: observe

contravention *n* **breaking**, flouting, breach, infringement, disobeying *Opposite*: observance

contribute *v* **1 donate**, pay, underwrite, subsidize, back **2 weigh in**, have a say, add, throw in, say **3 cause**, further, influence, impact, participate

contribution *n* **1 donation**, gift, giving, payment, subsidy **2 influence**, input, role, involvement, say

contributor *n* **donor**, sponsor, backer, giver, supplier

contributory *adj* **related**, influential, causal, causative, contributing

con trick *(infml)* *n* **swindle**, confidence trick, trick, rip-off *(infml)*

contrite *adj* **sorry**, repentant, remorseful, regretful, apologetic *Opposite*: impenitent

contriteness *see* contrition

contrition *n* **remorse**, repentance, penitence, regret, sorrow *Opposite*: shamelessness

contrivance *n* **1 gadget**, device, apparatus, machine, contraption **2 plot**, plan, plot, ruse, scheme

contrive *v* **design**, lay out, engineer, arrange, plan

contrived *adj* **forced**, artificial, unnatural, manufactured, affected *Opposite*: genuine

control *v* **1 operate**, work, run, use, utilize **2 restrain**, limit, restrict, hold back, rein in *Opposite*: release **3 manage**, command, supervise, run, direct **4 rule**, manipulate, influence, dominate, oppress **5 oversee**, monitor, regulate, inspect, watch over ■ *n* **1 switch**, regulator, controller, governor, circuit breaker **2 power**, jurisdiction, rule, domination, hegemony **3 skill**, manipulation, influence, handling, expertise **4 limit**, limitation, constraint, restriction, restraint

controllable *adj* **manageable**, governable, malleable, tractable, easy to deal with *Opposite*: uncontrollable

controlled *adj* **1 contained**, unflappable, under control, self-controlled, self-possessed *Opposite*: panicky **2 skilful**, accurate, measured, precise, meticulous *Opposite*: imprecise **3 regulated**, structured, planned, measured, delimited *Opposite*: free

controller *n* **1 supervisor**, manager, organizer, regulator, director **2 regulator**, switch, control, device, governor

control panel *n* **instrument panel**, console, dashboard, dash, instrumentation

controls *n* **instrument panel**, wheel, helm

controversial *adj* **contentious**, provocative, hotly debated, debatable, divisive *Opposite*: uncontroversial

controversy *n* **disagreement**, argument, debate, storm, hullabaloo *Opposite*: agreement

contumacious *(fml)* *adj* **insubordinate**, rebellious, disobedient, defiant, noncompliant *Opposite*: conformist

conundrum *n* **puzzle**, mystery, challenge, problem, riddle. *See* COMPARE AND CONTRAST *at* **problem**.

conurbation *n* **urban area**, built-up area, urban sprawl, city, metropolis. *See* COMPARE AND CONTRAST *at* **city**.

convalesce *v* **improve**, recover, recuperate, get better, rally *Opposite*: deteriorate

convalescence *n* **recuperation**, recovery, restoration, rehabilitation, R and R *Opposite*: deterioration

convalescent *adj* **convalescing**, recovering, recuperating, improving, getting better *Opposite*: deteriorating

convene *v* **call together**, assemble, summon, set up, organize *Opposite*: disband

convenience *n* **suitability**, expediency, ease, handiness, opportuneness *Opposite*: inconvenience

convenient *adj* **1 suitable**, expedient, opportune, fitting, appropriate *Opposite*: inconvenient **2 handy**, close at hand, adjacent, near, close *Opposite*: out-of-the-way

conveniently *adv* **suitably**, expediently, handily, opportunely, accessibly *Opposite*: inconveniently

convent *n* **nunnery**, religious foundation, religious community, cloister

convention *n* **1 gathering**, meeting, conference, congress, assembly **2 agreement**, pact, resolution, contract, settlement **3 rule**, principle, custom, practice, habit

conventional *adj* **1 conservative**, conformist, predictable, unadventurous, middle-of-the-road *Opposite*: adventurous **2 usual**, established, standard, normal, regular *Opposite*: unusual

conventionality *n* **conformism**, conservatism, orthodoxy, predictability *Opposite*: unconventionality

converge *v* **meet**, join, touch, unite, congregate *Opposite*: diverge

convergence *n* **meeting**, junction, union, coming together, conjunction *Opposite*: divergence

conversance *n* **familiarity**, acquaintance, awareness, knowledge

conversant *adj* **familiar**, up-to-date, au fait, well-informed, acquainted *Opposite*: unfamiliar

conversation *n* **talk**, chat, discussion, tête-à-tête, dialogue *Opposite*: monologue

conversational adj 1 **informal**, chatty, relaxed, casual, familiar Opposite: formal 2 **colloquial**, spoken, everyday, vernacular, informal

conversationalist n **talker**, communicator, gossip, raconteur, speaker

converse v **talk**, speak, communicate, chat, discuss ■ n **contrary**, opposite, reverse, inverse, antithesis Opposite: same ■ adj **opposite**, contrary, opposing, reverse, inverse Opposite: same

conversely adv **on the other hand**, equally, by the same token, on the contrary, in opposition

conversion n 1 **change**, adaptation, alteration, translation, renovation 2 **switch**, change, changeover, transfer, move

convert v 1 **change**, adapt, alter, renovate, remodel 2 **switch**, change, change over, transfer, go over 3 **win over**, bring round, talk round, convince, induce Opposite: dissuade ■ n **recruit**, follower, disciple, supporter, proselyte. See COMPARE AND CONTRAST at change.

convertible adj **adaptable**, exchangeable, alterable, translatable, changeable

convex adj **curved**, curving, arched, rounded, bowed Opposite: concave

convey v 1 **take**, carry, transport, bear, send 2 **communicate**, express, suggest, put across, get across

conveyance n 1 **means of transport**, transport, vehicle 2 **transportation**, transport, carriage, transference, transmission

convict v **find guilty**, sentence, imprison, condemn, detain Opposite: acquit ■ n **criminal**, offender, prisoner, felon, villain (slang)

conviction n 1 **certainty**, certitude, confidence, assurance, sincerity Opposite: doubt 2 **belief**, opinion, principle, faith, persuasion 3 **sentence**, verdict, condemnation, imprisonment Opposite: acquittal

convince v **persuade**, prove, sway, influence, induce Opposite: dissuade

convinced adj 1 **persuaded**, influenced, swayed, won over, converted Opposite: doubtful 2 **certain**, sure, positive, persuaded, confident Opposite: unsure 3 **committed**, strong, firm, staunch, wholehearted Opposite: weak

convincing adj 1 **persuasive**, plausible, believable, credible, compelling Opposite: unconvincing 2 **authentic**, realistic, believable, credible, lifelike Opposite: implausible 3 **undoubted**, substantial, resounding, considerable, conclusive Opposite: dubious. See COMPARE AND CONTRAST at valid.

convincingly adv **believably**, credibly, plausibly, persuasively, winningly Opposite: unconvincingly

convivial adj **pleasant**, welcoming, warm, friendly, hospitable Opposite: unfriendly

conviviality n **pleasantness**, welcome, warmth, friendliness, hospitality Opposite: unfriendliness

convoluted adj **intricate**, complex, complicated, long-winded, elaborate Opposite: straightforward

convoy n 1 **group**, band, party, company, line 2 **motorcade**, cavalcade, cortege, caravan, flotilla

convulse v **shake**, jerk, tremble, shudder, quiver

convulsion n **seizure**, fit, spasm, paroxysm, tremor

convulsive adj **jerky**, sudden, abrupt, violent, uncontrollable

co-occur v **coexist**, coincide, concur

cook v **heat**, boil, prepare, fry, roast ■ n **chef**, caterer, kitchen worker

WORD BANK
❏ **types of cook** baker, celebrity chef, commis chef, cordon-bleu chef, head chef, pastry chef, sous-chef

cooked adj **heated**, baked, prepared, roasted, microwaved Opposite: raw

cookery see cooking

cookie (infml) n **person**, character, individual, sort (infml), type (infml)

cooking n **cuisine**, catering, food service, home economics, cookery

cook up v 1 **prepare**, concoct, make, throw together (infml) 2 (infml) **invent**, think up, concoct, devise, plan

cool adj 1 **cold**, chilly, chill, nippy, fresh Opposite: warm 2 **calm**, unruffled, nonchalant, casual, imperturbable Opposite: uptight (infml) 3 **unfriendly**, unenthusiastic, offhand, icy, distant Opposite: friendly 4 (infml) **fashionable**, sophisticated, stylish, trendy (infml), hip (slang) Opposite: unfashionable ■ v 1 **make cold**, freshen, refrigerate, chill, cool off Opposite: warm 2 **wane**, dampen down, dampen, cool off, decrease Opposite: increase

cool bag see cool box

cool box n **cool bag**, chiller, cooler

cool down v 1 **turn cold**, cool, cool off, freshen Opposite: warm up 2 **calm down**, compose yourself, settle down, simmer down, back off Opposite: flare up

cooler n **chiller**, cool box, cool bag

WORD BANK
❏ **types of cooling appliance** air conditioner, air cooler, air exchanger, deepfreeze, freezer, fridge, fridge-freezer, refrigerator

coolness n 1 **cold**, coldness, chill, chilliness, freshness Opposite: warmth 2 **calmness**, level-headedness, detachment, aloofness, distance 3 **unfriendliness**, chill, chilliness, reserve, hostility Opposite: friendliness

cool off v 1 **turn cold**, cool, freshen, grow

chilly *Opposite*: warm up **2** *(infml)* **calm down**, compose yourself, settle down, simmer down, cool down *Opposite*: flare up

coop *n* pen, cage, run, enclosure, hutch

co-op *(infml)* *n* **cooperative**, collective, mutual society, friendly society

cooperate *v* **1** **collaborate**, work together, unite, liaise, band *Opposite*: compete **2** **oblige**, accommodate, help, aid, assist *Opposite*: hinder

cooperation *n* **collaboration**, assistance, help, support, teamwork *Opposite*: hindrance

cooperative *adj* **1** **obliging**, helpful, supportive, accommodating, willing *Opposite*: difficult **2** **joint**, two-way, mutual, shared, collaborative *Opposite*: individual ■ *n* **collective**, company, organization, association, enterprise

co-opt *v* **appoint**, designate, choose, bring on board, draft *Opposite*: discharge

coop up *v* **cage**, enclose, pen, house, imprison *Opposite*: let out

coordinate *v* **organize**, direct, manage, synchronize, harmonize

coordination *n* **1** **organization**, direction, management, logistics, harmonization *Opposite*: disorganization **2** **dexterity**, skill, adroitness, grace, proficiency *Opposite*: clumsiness

cope *v* **manage**, handle, deal with, survive, get through *Opposite*: founder

copied *adj* **imitated**, imitative, counterfeit, mock, imitation *Opposite*: original

copious *adj* **abundant**, plentiful, profuse, many, numerous *Opposite*: scant

coppice *see* copse

copse *n* **wood**, coppice, thicket, grove, covert

copy *n* **1** **reproduction**, duplicate, replica, facsimile, print *Opposite*: original **2** **item**, book, disk, version, publication **3** **text**, words, manuscript, typescript, file ■ *v* **1** **reproduce**, duplicate, clone, replicate, re-create **2** **imitate**, mimic, emulate, ape, simulate *Opposite*: originate

COMPARE AND CONTRAST CORE MEANING: make something that resembles something else to a greater or lesser degree
copy make an identical version of something; **reproduce** make a copy of something by technical means; **duplicate** create an identical version of something two or more times; **clone** make a near or exact reproduction, especially of a piece of equipment or an organism; **replicate** create an identical version of something repeatedly and exactly; **re-create** make something that appears to be the same as something that no longer exists, or that exists in a different place.

cord *n* string, twine, rope, cable, flex

cordial *adj* pleasant, affable, genial, friendly, affectionate *Opposite*: unfriendly

cordiality *n* pleasantness, geniality, affability, friendliness, affection *Opposite*: unfriendliness

cordless *adj* battery, battery-operated, free-style, hand-held, mobile

cordon *n* barrier, barricade, obstruction, obstacle, line

cordon off *v* close, bar, isolate, block off, barricade *Opposite*: open

core *n* **1** centre, heart, hub, nucleus, middle **2** essence, spirit, soul, heart, gist **3** sample, plug, extract ■ *adj* essential, central, fundamental, main, principal *Opposite*: peripheral

corner *n* **1** angle, crook, bend **2** turn, turning, curve, junction, bend *Opposite*: straight **3** place, spot, area, location, locality ■ *v* pin down, surround, trap, restrict, confront

cornerstone *n* foundation stone, keystone, foundation, basis

corner the market *v* dominate, monopolize, control, command, predominate

cornucopia *n* abundance, profusion, wealth, copiousness, plethora *Opposite*: dearth

corny *adj* unsophisticated, trite, banal, clichéd, hackneyed *Opposite*: original

corollary *n* consequence, result, effect, outcome, upshot

coronet *n* crown, tiara, diadem, circlet, wreath

corporate *adj* **1** business, company, commercial, trade **2** communal, shared, group, community, mutual *Opposite*: individual

corporation *n* company, business, firm, establishment, concern

corps *n* **1** force, troop, group, company, cadre **2** group, body, company, organization, league

corpse *n* dead body, cadaver, carcass, stiff *(slang)*

corpulence *n* obesity, plumpness, fleshiness, middle-age spread, spare tyre

corpulent *adj* obese, fat, fleshy, rotund, plump *Opposite*: slim

correct *v* **1** rectify, fix, put right, sort out, mark **2** modify, amend, alter, adjust, revise ■ *adj* **1** precise, right, accurate, exact, truthful *Opposite*: inaccurate **2** appropriate, suitable, proper, acceptable, approved *Opposite*: unsuitable

correction *n* alteration, improvement, rectification, modification, amendment

correctness *n* **1** precision, rightness, truth, accuracy, exactness *Opposite*: inaccuracy **2** appropriateness, suitability, acceptability, fittingness, uprightness *Opposite*: unsuitability

correlate *v* relate, associate, compare, link, draw a parallel *Opposite*: dissociate

correlation *n* association, connection, relationship, link, parallel

correspond *v* **1** agree, resemble, parallel, match, match up *Opposite*: conflict **2** communicate, keep in touch, write, drop a line, fax

correspondence n **1 letters**, mail, communication, messages, memos **2 agreement**, similarity, resemblance, association, connection *Opposite*: clash

correspondent n **1 communicator**, letter-writer, writer, pen friend, pen pal **2 foreign correspondent**, newspaperman, newspaperwoman, columnist, reporter

corresponding adj **consistent**, conforming, agreeing, matching, equivalent

corridor n **1 passage**, passageway, hall, hallway, walkway **2 strip**, access strip, air corridor, flight path

corroborate v **verify**, validate, document, support, agree *Opposite*: contradict

corrode v **rust**, disintegrate, destroy, decompose, decay

corroded adj **rusty**, rusted, tarnished, blemished, oxidized *Opposite*: pristine

corrosion n **erosion**, weathering, decay, rust, deterioration

corrosive adj **1 harsh**, scarring, eroding, destructive, acidic *Opposite*: gentle **2 sarcastic**, acerbic, harsh, bitter, biting *Opposite*: kind

corrugated adj **crenellated**, ridged, ribbed, grooved, wavy *Opposite*: smooth

corrupt adj **immoral**, unethical, dishonest, shady, fraudulent *Opposite*: honest ■ v **debase**, degrade, taint, pervert, warp

corrupted adj **debased**, degraded, sullied, despoiled, spoiled *Opposite*: pure *(literary)*

corruption n **1 dishonesty**, exploitation, bribery, sleaze, fraud *Opposite*: honesty **2 depravity**, perversion, immorality, harm, debasement *Opposite*: purity *(literary)*

corruptness n **dishonesty**, immorality, sleaziness, degenerateness

corsage n **bouquet**, spray, posy, flowers, arrangement

cosh v **hit**, bludgeon, club, strike

cosily adv **1 snugly**, warmly, pleasantly, comfortably, invitingly *Opposite*: bleakly **2 familiarly**, intimately, closely, warmly, lovingly *Opposite*: coldly

cosmetic adj **1 ornamental**, decorative, aesthetic *Opposite*: substantive **2 superficial**, skin-deep, surface, token, outer *Opposite*: in-depth

WORD BANK
❑ **types of cosmetic** blusher, concealer, eye shadow, eyeliner, face powder, foundation, kohl, lip gloss, lip pencil, lipstick, mascara, nail polish, powder, rouge *(dated)*

cosmetic surgery n **plastic surgery**, laser surgery, tuck, lift

WORD BANK
❑ **types of cosmetic surgery** Botox™ injection, breast enhancement, collagen injection, ear pinning, facelift, face peel, lipectomy, liposuction, nose job, rhinoplasty

cosmic adj **1 intergalactic**, interplanetary, interstellar, galactic, planetary *Opposite*: terrestrial **2 universal**, vast, enormous, huge, immense *Opposite*: tiny

cosmopolitan adj **multicultural**, multiethnic, pluralistic, diverse, international *Opposite*: provincial

cosmos n **universe**, space, outer space, ether, heaven

cosset v **shelter**, protect, spoil, mollycoddle, indulge *Opposite*: neglect

cost n **1 price**, charge, rate, fee, price tag **2 budget**, amount, outlay, expenditure, expense **3 effort**, suffering, detriment, loss, expense

co-star n **star**, film star, actor, lead, movie star *(US)* ■ v **1 perform**, collaborate, entertain, star, appear **2 feature**, showcase, spotlight, star

cost-cutting n **saving**, cutbacks, economizing, cutting back, belt-tightening

cost-effective adj **lucrative**, moneymaking, profitable, bankable, gainful *Opposite*: uneconomical

costly adj **1 expensive**, overpriced, inflated, highly priced, exorbitant *Opposite*: inexpensive **2 luxurious**, precious, valuable, lavish, rich *Opposite*: basic **3 damaging**, harmful, detrimental, disadvantageous, injurious *Opposite*: beneficial

costs n **price**, charges, budget, expenses, outlay

costume n **clothes**, clothing, regalia, dress, outfit

costume drama n **play**, spectacle, drama, historical drama, period piece

cosy adj **1 snug**, warm, pleasant, comfortable, inviting *Opposite*: inhospitable **2 familiar**, friendly, intimate, close, warm *Opposite*: cold **3 expedient**, convenient, self-serving, cliquey, clannish

cosy up v **ingratiate yourself**, curry favour with, make overtures, pander, insinuate *Opposite*: distance

coterie n **clique**, circle, band

cotton on *(infml)* v **comprehend**, understand, follow, grasp, realize

couch n **sofa**, settee, divan, chaise lounge, chesterfield ■ v **express**, phrase, put, dress up, word

cough up *(infml)* v **pay up**, pay, give, fork out *(infml)*, fork up *(infml)*

council n **assembly**, meeting, board, congress, body

counsel n *(fml or literary)* **advice**, guidance, direction, warning, guidelines ■ v **1** *(fml or literary)* **advise**, recommend, advocate, suggest, propose **2 support**, help, guide, aid, encourage

counselling n **therapy**, psychotherapy, psychoanalysis, analysis, treatment

counsellor n **therapist**, psychotherapist, psychoanalyst, analyst, social worker

count v **1 add up**, total, calculate, tot up, tally **2 consider**, regard, view, hold, esteem **3 make your mark**, weigh, amount to something, matter, be important ∎ n **1 calculation**, computation, reckoning, head count, bottom line **2 total**, sum total, sum, amount, tally

countable adj **calculable**, measurable, assessable, finite, quantifiable Opposite: incalculable

count against v **weigh against**, detract, diminish, hurt, backfire Opposite: help

countenance n **expression**, face, features, physiognomy, mien (fml) ∎ v (fml) **tolerate**, stand for, put up with, allow, approve

counter v **1 contradict**, dispute, refute, oppose, answer **2 counteract**, offset, foil, frustrate, thwart

counteract v **counter**, offset, respond, frustrate, thwart

counterattack n **attack**, revenge, counteroffensive, retaliation, defence

counterbalance v **tip the scales**, offset, balance, correct, compensate ∎ n **counterweight**, makeweight, ballast

counterfeit adj **fake**, forged, bootleg, phoney, bogus Opposite: genuine ∎ v **forge**, fake, copy, fabricate, imitate ∎ n **forgery**, copy, fake, imitation, reproduction Opposite: original

counterfeiter n **forger**, criminal, fraudster, imitator, faker

countermand v **cancel**, revoke, stop, reverse, annul

counterpart n **opposite number**, equal, equivalent, colleague

counter-revolutionary n **rebel**, insurgent, insurrectionist, anarchist, radical ∎ adj **antirevolutionary**, moderate, democratic, pacifist Opposite: revolutionary

counter to prep **against**, contrary to, in opposition to, at odds with, in conflict with Opposite: according to

countless adj **uncountable**, innumerable, myriad, limitless, immeasurable Opposite: few

count on v **depend on**, be sure of, rely on, trust, bank on

count out v **exclude**, weed out, leave out, omit, disregard Opposite: include

countrified adj **1 rustic**, rural, unspoiled Opposite: urban **2 unsophisticated**, unpolished, unfashionable, simple, rough Opposite: urbane

country n **1 republic**, state, nation, realm, kingdom **2 farmland**, woodland, grazing, pastures, wilderness Opposite: town **3 people**, inhabitants, residents, nation, population

countryman n **compatriot**, national, fellow citizen, inhabitant, native

countrywoman n **compatriot**, national, fellow citizen, inhabitant, native

count up v **total**, add up, count, calculate, tot up

county n **region**, section, province, district, shire

coup n **1 coup d'état**, overthrow, revolution, rebellion, putsch **2 feather in somebody's cap**, achievement, accomplishment, triumph, feat

coup de grâce n **deathblow**, last nail in the coffin, knockout punch, killer punch

coup d'état n **overthrow**, coup, revolution, rebellion, putsch

couple n **twosome**, pair, duo, dyad ∎ v **combine**, link, join, connect, pair Opposite: separate

coupled with prep **together with**, in addition to, on top of, as well as, besides

couplet n **verse**, distich, stanza, unit, rhyme

coupling n **1 link**, join, connection, connector, coupler **2 combination**, juxtaposition, pairing, blend, mixture

coupon n **voucher**, ticket, token, slip, form

courage n **1 bravery**, nerve, pluck, fearlessness, mettle Opposite: cowardice

COMPARE AND CONTRAST CORE MEANING: personal resoluteness in the face of danger or difficulties
courage the ability to show resoluteness and determination, whether physical, mental, or moral, against a wide range of difficulties or dangers; **bravery** extreme lack of fear; **fearlessness** resoluteness in the face of dangers or challenges; **nerve** coolness, steadiness, and self-assurance; **guts** (slang) strength of character and boldness; **pluck** resolution and willingness to continue struggling against the odds; **mettle** spirited determination.

courageous adj **brave**, daring, bold, spirited, plucky Opposite: cowardly

courageousness see courage

courier n **1 messenger**, carrier, biker, dispatch rider **2 holiday rep**, rep, agent, guide

course n **1 sequence**, progression, development, passage **2 direction**, route, path, track, road **3 option**, choice, possibility, route, avenue **4 lesson**, class, programme, module, curriculum ∎ v **flow**, pour, run, gush, stream Opposite: trickle

course of action n **strategy**, course, policy, plan, method

coursework n **assignments**, homework, reading, project, prep (infml)

court n **1 law court**, court of law, tribunal **2 courtyard**, square, yard, patio, piazza ∎ v **1** (dated) **date**, go out, see, pay court to (dated) **2 woo**, curry favour with, cosy up to, pander to, flatter Opposite: shun **3 risk**, invite, encourage, incite, attract Opposite: avoid

court case n **lawsuit**, suit, case, hearing, indictment

courteous adj **polite**, well-mannered, considerate, chivalrous, civil Opposite: rude

courteousness n **politeness**, good manners, courtesy, consideration, civility Opposite: rudeness

courtesy n **politeness**, good manners, courteousness, consideration, civility Opposite: rudeness

courthouse n **court**, law court, court of law, high court, crown court

courtier n **flatterer**, sycophant, self-seeker, creature, toady

courtly adj **courteous**, chivalrous, polite, civil, refined Opposite: rude

court order n **legal ruling**, order, sanction, interdict, veto

courtship n **wooing**, dating, relationship

courtyard n **patio**, yard, square, court, enclosure

cousin n **friend**, companion, colleague, partner, counterpart

cove n **bay**, inlet, harbour

covenant n **agreement**, contract, treaty, promise, pledge

cover v **1 conceal**, hide, cover up, obscure, disguise Opposite: expose **2 protect**, shield, guard, shelter, defend **3 wrap**, coat, cover up, envelop, swathe Opposite: reveal **4 deal with**, include, comprise, embrace, take in Opposite: overlook **5 travel**, cross, traverse, pass through, go through ■ n **1 covering**, wrapping, jacket, shell, case **2 shelter**, concealment, protection, hiding place, refuge

coverage n **attention**, treatment, reporting, exposure, handling

covered adj **enclosed**, roofed, sheltered, protected, shielded Opposite: exposed

covering n **cover**, casing, top, lid, layer

coverlet n **bedspread**, cover, throw, bedcover, counterpane (dated)

covert adj **secret**, clandestine, underground, concealed, hidden Opposite: open ■ n **copse**, wood, thicket, coppice, undergrowth. See COMPARE AND CONTRAST at **secret**.

covertness n **secrecy**, stealth, concealment, surreptitiousness, underhandedness Opposite: openness

cover up v **1 conceal**, hide, obscure, mask, disguise Opposite: expose **2 suppress**, keep under wraps, keep secret, paper over, hide Opposite: divulge

cover-up n **conspiracy**, plot, scheme, smoke screen, fig leaf

covet v **want**, long for, yearn for, crave, hanker after. See COMPARE AND CONTRAST at **want**.

coveted adj **sought-after**, longed for, wanted, fashionable, desired Opposite: scorned

covetous adj **envious**, jealous, greedy, avaricious, acquisitive Opposite: generous

covetousness n **envy**, enviousness, jealousy, avarice, avariciousness Opposite: generosity

cow v **intimidate**, scare, frighten, bully, overawe

coward n **sissy**, deserter, runaway, weakling, chicken (infml)

cowardice n **weakness**, fearfulness, spinelessness, fear, timidity Opposite: courage

cowardly adj **gutless**, spineless, craven, pusillanimous, faint-hearted Opposite: brave

COMPARE AND CONTRAST CORE MEANING: lacking in courage

cowardly lacking in courage, or caused by a lack of courage; **faint-hearted** timid and lacking in resolve; **spineless** seriously lacking willpower or strength of character; **gutless** seriously lacking in courage and determination; **pusillanimous** showing a contemptible degree of cowardice; **craven** showing a contemptible degree of cowardice and weakness of will; **chicken** (infml, often used by children and young people) cowardly.

cowboy n **1 cowhand**, cowman, herdsman, stockman, rancher **2** (infml) **fly-by-night**, dodgy operator, crook (infml)

cowed adj **intimidated**, browbeaten, scared, frightened, submissive Opposite: defiant

cower v **shrink**, cringe, tremble, recoil, shy away Opposite: stand your ground

cowl n **hood**, cover, cloak, top

coworker n **colleague**, fellow worker, collaborator, associate, workmate

cowshed n **barn**, stable, pen, stockyard, byre

cox v **steer**, direct, pilot, navigate, coxswain

coy adj **1 teasing**, playful, engaging, coquettish (literary) **2 shy**, bashful, timid, modest, reserved Opposite: brazen

crabbed see **crabby**

crabbiness n **bad-temperedness**, bad temper, irritability, grumpiness, cantankerousness Opposite: equanimity

crabby adj **grumpy**, bad-tempered, short-tempered, irritable, snappy Opposite: easygoing

crack v **1 break**, fracture, split, splinter, snap **2 break down**, go to pieces, lose control, collapse, crack up (infml) **3 bang**, bump, hit, whack, bash (infml) **4** (infml) **solve**, work out, figure out, fathom, decipher ■ n **1 fissure**, flaw, break, fracture, chink **2 weakness**, flaw, fault, imperfection, defect **3** (infml) **blow**, crash, bang, snap, pop **4** (infml) **quip**, dig, joke, aside ■ adj **expert**, top-flight, ace (infml)

crack a joke v **make a joke**, quip, joke, jest (literary)

crackbrained adj **eccentric**, irrational, foolish, stupid, crazed Opposite: rational

crack down (infml) v **clamp down**, tighten up, come down hard, get tough

cracked adj **1 fractured**, broken, split, splintered, cleft Opposite: intact **2** (infml)

irrational, eccentric, crazed, crackbrained, foolish *Opposite*: rational

cracking *(infml)* adj **1 fast**, furious, rapid, swift, outrageous *Opposite*: slow **2 excellent**, brilliant, great, fantastic, fabulous *Opposite*: terrible ■ adv **very**, extremely, especially, terribly, exceedingly

crackle v **crunch**, snap, pop, sizzle, crack

crack of dawn n **daybreak**, dawn, daylight, sunrise, first light *Opposite*: dusk

crackpot *(infml)* adj **impractical**, unrealistic, eccentric, wild, outlandish *Opposite*: realistic

crack up *(infml)* v **1 break down**, go to pieces, lose control, collapse, crack *(infml)* **2 break up**, laugh, guffaw, giggle, titter

crack-up *(infml)* n **1 breakdown**, collapse, crisis, meltdown, burnout **2 crash**, accident, wreck, smash, collision

cradle n **support**, frame, structure, framework, underpinning ■ v **hold**, embrace, support, cuddle, clasp *Opposite*: drop

craft n **1 skill**, dexterity, expertise, ability, craftsmanship **2 trade**, profession, art, job, calling **3 vehicle**, vessel, boat, aircraft, spacecraft **4 cunning**, deceit, slyness, wiliness, shrewdness *Opposite*: forthrightness ■ v **make**, fashion, create, manufacture, construct

craftiness n **cunning**, slyness, shrewdness, wiliness, guile *Opposite*: forthrightness

craftsmanship n **skill**, artistry, workmanship, expertise, technique

craftsperson n **craftworker**, artisan, artist

crafty adj **cunning**, sneaky, sly, shrewd, devious *Opposite*: forthright

crag n **cliff**, rock face, precipice, peak, scarp

craggy adj **1 rocky**, stony, rough, rugged, uneven *Opposite*: even **2 lined**, rugged, wrinkled, wrinkly, weathered *Opposite*: smooth

cram v **1 stuff**, pack, fill up, ram, shove *Opposite*: remove **2** *(infml)* **study**, revise, go over, review, memorize *Opposite*: forget

crammed adj **full**, packed, filled, crowded, cramped *Opposite*: empty

cramp n **spasm**, pain, contraction, shooting pain, twinge ■ v **restrict**, hamper, limit, constrict, constrain

cramped adj **overcrowded**, confined, restricted, close, poky *(infml)* *Opposite*: spacious

crane n **hoist**, derrick, winch, gantry

crank v **turn**, reel, wind, activate, move

crankiness *(infml)* n **eccentricity**, nonconformity, originality, idiosyncrasy, quirkiness

crank up v **start**, turn on, wind up, activate, get going *Opposite*: turn off

cranky *(infml)* adj **eccentric**, quirky, idiosyncratic, bizarre, strange *Opposite*: ordinary

cranny n **crevice**, crack, fissure, chink, cleft

crash n **1 collision**, accident, smash, smash-up, pile-up *(infml)* **2 failure**, breakdown, collapse, shutdown **3 bang**, smash, din, clatter, clang **4 bankruptcy**, failure, collapse, liquidation ■ v **1 collide**, run into, smash into, bump into, hurtle **2 break down**, collapse, fizzle, fail **3 boom**, bang, thunder, clash, clatter **4 go under**, go bankrupt, fold, collapse, fail *Opposite*: thrive

crash course n **training**, orientation, workshop, induction, immersion

crash-land v **collide**, crash, fall, smash, come down

crass adj **insensitive**, tactless, thoughtless, vulgar, obnoxious *Opposite*: sensitive

crassness n **insensitivity**, vulgarity, tactlessness, obnoxiousness, grossness *Opposite*: sensitivity

crater n **pit**, depression, hole, cavity, hollow *Opposite*: mound

crave v **1 desire**, long for, need, want, yearn for *Opposite*: dislike **2** *(archaic)* **ask**, beg, pray, request, entreat *Opposite*: reject. *See* COMPARE AND CONTRAST *at* **want**.

craven adj **cowardly**, gutless, spineless, weak, timorous *Opposite*: bold. *See* COMPARE AND CONTRAST *at* **cowardly**.

craving n **longing**, desire, passion, hunger, thirst *Opposite*: dislike

crawl v **1 creep**, edge, inch, wriggle, slither **2 skulk**, scuttle, creep, sneak, slink **3** *(infml)* **grovel**, ingratiate yourself, flatter, fawn, suck up *(infml)* *Opposite*: alienate **4 apologize**, eat humble pie, grovel, humiliate yourself, prostrate yourself

craze n **fad**, trend, fashion, enthusiasm, rage

crazed adj **irrational**, distraught, overwrought, wild, inflamed *Opposite*: rational

craziness *(infml)* n **foolishness**, stupidity, folly, idiocy, madness *Opposite*: reasonableness

crazy *(infml)* adj **1 foolish**, unwise, silly, senseless, irrational *Opposite*: sensible **2 fond**, keen, passionate, enthusiastic, devoted *Opposite*: lukewarm

creak v **squeak**, screech, scrape, grate, groan

creaky adj **1 squeaky**, rusty, grating, rasping **2** *(infml)* **stiff**, rigid, inflexible, tight, arthritic *Opposite*: supple

cream n **1 ointment**, salve, balm, unguent, emulsion **2 best**, elite, finest, cream of the crop, pick of the bunch *Opposite*: dregs ■ v **blend**, soften, mash, emulsify, combine

cream off v **skim off**, handpick, select, choose, pick out *Opposite*: reject

crease n **1 pleat**, fold, tuck, gather **2 crinkle**, crumple, wrinkle, rumple, pucker **3 furrow**, wrinkle, line, groove, crow's foot ■ v **1 fold**, pleat, tuck, gather **2 crumple**, wrinkle, scrunch, crinkle, rumple *Opposite*: smooth

creased adj **wrinkled**, wrinkly, crinkled, crinkly, lined *Opposite*: smooth

crease up (infml) v amuse, break up, have somebody in hysterics, tickle pink, tickle

create v 1 make, produce, generate, fashion, form Opposite: destroy 2 invent, design, originate, initiate, give rise to 3 establish, set up, found, start, get going 4 (infml) make a fuss, kick up a fuss, kick up a rumpus, complain, cry

creation n 1 formation, making, conception, construction, manufacture Opposite: destruction 2 nature, cosmos, universe, life, world 3 invention, handiwork, fabrication, innovation, concept

creative adj original, imaginative, inspired, artistic, inventive Opposite: unimaginative

creativeness see creativity

creativity n originality, imagination, inspiration, ingenuity, inventiveness

creator n maker, inventor, originator, architect, designer Opposite: destroyer

creature n 1 being, living being, person, man, woman 2 animal, beast, organism, insect, critter (slang)

crèche n playgroup, kindergarten, playschool, nursery

credence n credibility, authority, weight, belief, confidence

credential n qualification, diploma, recommendation, testimonial, certificate

credentials n identification, authorization, ID, permit, pass

credibility n trustworthiness, reliability, authority, standing, sincerity

credible adj 1 believable, convincing, plausible, likely, probable Opposite: implausible 2 trustworthy, reliable, sincere, dependable, sound Opposite: unreliable

credit n 1 praise, recognition, thanks, acclaim, glory Opposite: blame 2 standing, position, status, esteem, prestige 3 belief, confidence, trust, faith Opposite: disbelief ■ v 1 believe, accept, trust, have faith in, have confidence in Opposite: disbelieve 2 acknowledge, recognize, acclaim, pay tribute, praise

creditable adj admirable, praiseworthy, good, worthy, laudable Opposite: shameful

credo n creed, doctrine, ideology, principle, view

credulity n gullibility, naivety, innocence, trust, imprudence Opposite: astuteness

credulous adj gullible, naive, trusting, imprudent, unsuspecting Opposite: astute

credulousness see credulity

creed n faith, dogma, doctrine, credo, belief

creek n cove, bay, inlet, gulf

creep v 1 tiptoe, skulk, steal, sneak, slink Opposite: stomp 2 crawl, slither, inch, edge, worm 3 (infml) grovel, crawl, fawn, toady, flatter ■ n (infml) flatterer, toady, sycophant, bootlicker (infml), crawler (infml)

creeper n climber, trailer, vine, liana

creepiness (infml) n eeriness, scariness, weirdness, uncanniness, strangeness

creep up on v sneak up on, surprise, stalk, take by surprise

creepy (infml) adj eerie, disturbing, spine-chilling, uncanny, weird

creepy-crawly (infml) n insect, bug, beastie (infml)

cremate v incinerate, burn, consume, immolate (literary)

cremation n burning, incineration, immolation (fml)

crème de la crème n best, cream, pick, flower, elite

crenellated adj fortified, notched, indented

crescendo n increase, upsurge, swelling, buildup, climax

crescent adj semicircular, hemispherical, curved, arced, falcate

crest n 1 top, peak, summit, crown, apex Opposite: base 2 tuft, topknot, growth, cockscomb, comb 3 coat of arms, blazon, emblem, symbol, heraldry

crestfallen adj downcast, dejected, disappointed, deflated, subdued Opposite: confident

crevasse n fissure, cleft, crack, split, fracture

crevice n crack, fissure, chink, split, cleft

crew n 1 team, squad, staff, troop, company 2 (infml) group, gang, party, circle, crowd

crib (infml) v cheat, copy, plagiarize, steal, borrow

crick n pain, strain, discomfort, cramp, spasm ■ v strain, hurt, pull, cramp, wrench

crime n 1 offence, misdeed, felony, misdemeanour, transgression 2 corruption, wrongdoing, misconduct, lawbreaking, delinquency 3 wrong, sin, fault, transgression

crime novel n detective story, whodunit, thriller

criminal n offender, convict, prisoner, felon, lawbreaker ■ adj 1 illegal, wrong, against the law, illicit, unlawful Opposite: legal 2 scandalous, excessive, iniquitous, senseless, outrageous

criminality n delinquency, misconduct, wrongdoing, corruption, lawbreaking Opposite: honesty

criminalization n 1 outlawing, banning, interdiction, proscription (fml), illegalization (US) Opposite: legalization 2 corruption, delinquency, marginalization, alienation, deterioration Opposite: rehabilitation

criminalize v 1 outlaw, ban, forbid, proscribe, interdict Opposite: legalize 2 corrupt, marginalize, deprave, pervert Opposite: rehabilitate

criminal world n underworld, gangland, underbelly of society

crimp v 1 **fold**, crumple, crinkle, press, rumple 2 **pleat**, gather, fold, concertina, ruche *Opposite*: smooth 3 **interfere**, hamper, hinder, constrain, curb

cringe v 1 **recoil**, wince, flinch, shrink, shy away 2 **squirm**, blush, wince, be embarrassed

crinkle v **crumple**, crease, rumple, wrinkle, ruffle *Opposite*: straighten out ■ n **wrinkle**, fold, crease, line, pucker

crinkled adj **creased**, lined, wrinkled, crumpled, rumpled *Opposite*: straight

crinkly adj **wrinkled**, creased, furrowed, wavy, puckered *Opposite*: smooth

crippling adj **damaging**, debilitating, incapacitating, destabilizing, swingeing

crisis n 1 **disaster**, catastrophe, emergency, calamity, predicament 2 **turning point**, head, watershed, crossroads, defining moment

crisis point n **critical stage**, flashpoint, breaking point, crunch time

crisp adj 1 **crunchy**, brittle, hard, crusty, crispy *Opposite*: soggy 2 **snappy**, brusque, terse, curt, sharp 3 **cold**, cool, fresh, frosty, chilly *Opposite*: stuffy 4 **incisive**, decisive, confident, businesslike, efficient *Opposite*: hesitant

crispy adj 1 **crunchy**, brittle, hard, crusty, crisp *Opposite*: soggy

crisscross n **lattice**, network, grid ■ v **cross**, traverse, intersect, overlap, cross over

criterion n **standard**, principle, measure, norm, condition

critic n 1 **reviewer**, columnist, commentator, reporter, journalist 2 **evaluator**, appraiser, judge, commentator 3 **detractor**, opponent, enemy, censor, criticizer *Opposite*: supporter

critical adj 1 **unfavourable**, disparaging, disapproving, nitpicking, judgmental *Opposite*: favourable 2 **analytical**, judicious, diagnostic, serious, detailed 3 **significant**, decisive, vital, important, essential *Opposite*: insignificant 4 **dangerous**, serious, grave, life-threatening, perilous

critically adv **seriously**, gravely, dangerously, perilously, precariously *Opposite*: mildly

criticism n 1 **censure**, disapproval, reproach, disparagement, condemnation *Opposite*: praise 2 **analysis**, appreciation, assessment, evaluation, critique

criticize v 1 **assess**, analyse, dissect, evaluate, appraise 2 **disapprove**, censure, condemn, find fault with, castigate (fml) *Opposite*: praise

---

COMPARE AND CONTRAST CORE MEANING: express disapproval or dissatisfaction with somebody or something
criticize point out faults; **censure** make a formal, often public or official, statement of disapproval; **castigate** (fml) to criticize or rebuke severely; **blast** (infml) to criticize severely; **condemn** give an unfavourable judgment on somebody or some-

---

thing; **find fault with** criticize, often unfairly; **pick holes in** look for and find mistakes, particularly in an argument; **nitpick** find fault, often unjustifiably, with insignificant details.

---

critique n **analysis**, assessment, evaluation, account, review ■ v **assess**, evaluate, criticize, comment, review

croak n **cry**, caw, rasp, squawk ■ v 1 **call**, cry, squawk, caw, rasp 2 **grate**, gutturalize, rasp, growl 3 (infml) **grumble**, mutter, complain, moan, grouse (infml)

croaky adj **hoarse**, rasping, guttural

crockery n **tableware**, china, earthenware, plates, dishes

crony n **associate**, ally, supporter, accomplice, co-conspirator

cronyism n **favouritism**, job for the boys (infml), nepotism, patronage

crook n 1 (infml) **criminal**, offender, felon, robber, lawbreaker 2 **staff**, rod, stick, crosier

crooked adj 1 **bent**, curved, warped, twisted, kinked *Opposite*: straight 2 **uneven**, jagged, zigzag, oblique, askew *Opposite*: straight 3 (infml) **dishonest**, criminal, corrupt, fraudulent, illegal *Opposite*: honest

crookedness n **dishonesty**, shadiness, corruption, illegality, fraudulence *Opposite*: honesty

croon v **sing**, serenade, murmur, hum, warble

crop n **harvest**, yield, produce, cash crop, catch crop ■ v 1 **collect**, harvest, gather, pick, bring in 2 **cut**, shorten, clip, trim, shear

cropped adj **short-haired**, close-cropped, clipped

crop up (infml) v **appear**, happen, turn up, arise, emerge

crosier n **staff**, rod, stick, crook

cross n **symbol**, mark, sign ■ v 1 **traverse**, go across, crisscross, cut across, span 2 **thwart**, frustrate, impede, oppose, obstruct *Opposite*: assist ■ adj **irritated**, angry, irritable, annoyed, snappy

---

WORD BANK
❑ **types of cross** Celtic cross, cross of Lorraine, Greek cross, Latin cross, Maltese cross, St. Andrew's cross, St. Anthony's cross, St. George's cross, tau cross

---

crossbreed v **hybridize**, cross, interbreed, mongrelize

crosscheck v **validate**, substantiate, check, double-check, verify ■ n **validation**, substantiation, double-checking, verification

cross-country adj **off-road**, rough, outdoor, all-terrain

cross-cultural adj **multicultural**, multiracial, multiethnic, diverse, cosmopolitan

crosscurrent n **contrast**, divergence, deviation, rebellion, nonconformity

cross-examination n **questioning**, re-examination, interrogation, cross-questioning, probe

cross-examine v **question**, cross-question, interrogate, quiz, probe

cross-fertilization n 1 **pollination**, fertilization, cross-pollination Opposite: self-fertilization 2 **exchange**, interchange, interaction, synthesis, synergy

cross-fertilize v 1 **fertilize**, pollinate, cross-pollinate 2 **exchange**, interchange, interact, synthesize, share

crossfire n **clash**, disagreement, conflict, antagonism, flak

crossing n 1 **journey**, adventure, trip, voyage, passage 2 **intersection**, junction, overpass, flyover, level crossing

crossover n 1 **switch**, change, sea change, conversion, move 2 **overlap**, common ground, commonality

crosspatch (dated infml) n **curmudgeon**, malcontent, grouch (infml), grump (infml), pain (infml)

cross-purposes n **disagreement**, disparity, variance, contrast, frustration

cross-question v **cross-examine**, re-examine, interrogate, question, review

cross-questioning n **cross-examination**, re-examination, interrogation, review, double-checking

cross-reference n **citation**, reference, documentation, source, note

crossroads n 1 **junction**, intersection, crossing, roundabout 2 **turning point**, landmark, decision, moment of truth, crisis

cross section n 1 **view**, section, slice, layer, plane 2 **sample**, example, range, representation

cross swords v **clash**, argue, disagree, do battle, fight Opposite: agree

crossways see **crosswise**

crosswise adv **sideways**, diagonally, across, corner to corner, obliquely

crossword n **acrostic**, mind-bender, game, puzzle, cryptic crossword

crotchetiness (infml) n **grumpiness**, grouchiness, tetchiness

crotchety (infml) adj **grumpy**, bad-tempered, irritable, difficult, cantankerous Opposite: good-humoured

crouch v **squat**, bend, hunker, stoop, duck

crow v 1 **caw**, cry, call, squawk, screech 2 **gloat**, boast, brag, show off, swagger

crowd n 1 **troop**, throng, mass, multitude, swarm 2 **group**, set, gang, circle, clique ■ v 1 **throng**, flock, herd, assemble, gather 2 **overcrowd**, pack, cram, squeeze, squash

crowded adj **overcrowded**, packed, full, teeming, swarming Opposite: deserted

crown n 1 **circlet**, coronet, tiara, diadem 2 **trophy**, prize, garland, laurels, honour 3 **top**, peak, summit, pinnacle, head ■ v **cap**, top, round off, complete, finish off

crow's foot n **wrinkle**, line, laughter line

crucial adj **vital**, critical, central, decisive, key Opposite: trivial

crucible n 1 **container**, pot, receptacle, vat, kettle 2 **ordeal**, trial, test, baptism of fire 3 **hotbed**, hothouse, forcing ground, melting pot, ground zero

crucifixion n 1 **execution**, killing, punishment 2 **ordeal**, victimization, torment, agony, suffering

crucify v 1 **execute**, kill, hang, punish 2 **torment**, victimize, attack, savage, maul

crud (infml) n **nonsense**, gibberish, malarkey (infml), twaddle (infml)

crude adj 1 **raw**, unrefined, unprocessed Opposite: refined 2 **approximate**, rough, inaccurate, inexact, loose Opposite: precise 3 **unpolished**, basic, simple, rudimentary, makeshift Opposite: sophisticated 4 **vulgar**, indecent, rude, coarse, obscene Opposite: delicate

crudeness n 1 **primitiveness**, roughness, rawness, coarseness, simplicity Opposite: sophistication 2 **vulgarity**, crudity, coarseness, rudeness, offensiveness Opposite: delicacy

crudity n 1 **rudeness**, crudeness, coarseness, vulgarity, offensiveness Opposite: delicacy 2 **roughness**, coarseness, rawness, simplicity, rusticity Opposite: sophistication

cruel adj 1 **unkind**, merciless, nasty, pitiless, brutal Opposite: kind 2 **painful**, punishing, devastating, harsh, hard Opposite: pleasant

cruelty n **unkindness**, nastiness, brutality, malice, spite Opposite: kindness

cruise v 1 **voyage**, sail, journey, travel, boat 2 **coast**, skim, spin, travel, glide ■ n **voyage**, vacation, trip, journey, tour

crumb n **morsel**, scrap, titbit, bit, speck

crumble v 1 **smash**, beat, crush, grind, powder 2 **disintegrate**, dissolve, deteriorate, fall apart, fall down

crumbling adj **disintegrating**, decomposing, decaying, putrefying, caving in Opposite: solid

crumbly adj **brittle**, powdery, flaky, friable, crumbling Opposite: solid

crummy (infml) adj 1 **inferior**, shoddy, shabby, worthless, poor-quality Opposite: superior 2 **unwell**, sick, ill, sickly, miserable Opposite: healthy

crumple v **crease**, crinkle, rumple, crush, screw Opposite: smooth

crumpled adj **creased**, wrinkled, wrinkly, crinkly, lined Opposite: smooth

crunch v **munch**, chew, champ, chomp (infml) ■ n **crisis**, moment of truth, crunch time, critical situation, crux

crunchy adj crispy, crisp, brittle, crusty Opposite: soggy

crusade n cause, campaign, movement, battle, fight ■ v campaign, lobby, struggle, battle, apply yourself

crusader n campaigner, supporter, advocate, champion, activist

crush v 1 squash, squeeze, compress, press, mash 2 quell, suppress, put down, quash, subdue 3 defeat, rout, massacre, trounce, overwhelm 4 humiliate, devastate, mortify, put down, abash ■ n 1 (infml) infatuation, passion, affection, fondness, liking Opposite: dislike 2 press, squash, squeeze, crowd, throng. See COMPARE AND CONTRAST at love.

crushed adj crumpled, creased, wrinkled, crinkly, crinkled Opposite: smooth

crushing adj devastating, overwhelming, swingeing, severe, draconian Opposite: mild

crushingly adv triumphantly, exultantly, superciliously, haughtily, contemptuously

crust n coating, outside, outer layer, shell, top

crusted adj encrusted, caked, coated, covered, thick

crusty adj 1 crispy, crisp, hard, brittle, crunchy Opposite: soft 2 grumpy, bad-tempered, irritable, testy, cantankerous Opposite: good-humoured

crutch n 1 stick, support, prop, walking aid, staff 2 prop, support, aid, help, buttress

crux n root, bottom, heart, core, nub

cry v 1 weep, sob, snivel, whimper, shed tears Opposite: laugh 2 shout, exclaim, shout out, call, call out Opposite: whisper ■ n call, shout, exclamation, yell, scream Opposite: whisper

crying adj 1 in tears, tearful, teary, sobbing, weeping 2 desperate, deplorable, awful, horrible, terrible

cry out v 1 shout out, shout, cry, call, call out Opposite: whisper 2 need, be in need of, require, demand, call for

crypt n vault, tomb, catacomb, sepulchre, burial chamber

cryptic adj mysterious, enigmatic, puzzling, obscure, ambiguous Opposite: obvious. See COMPARE AND CONTRAST at obscure.

crystal n mineral, rock crystal, quartz

crystalline adj 1 crystal-like, glassy, sparkling 2 clear, transparent, crystal clear, limpid, translucent Opposite: opaque

crystallization n manifestation, representation, outward expression, illustration, summation

crystallize v form, take shape, fall into place, come together, shape up Opposite: disintegrate

cry your eyes out v weep, sob, blubber (infml)

cub n novice, beginner, learner, apprentice, trainee Opposite: old hand

cubbyhole n compartment, nook, cranny, pigeonhole, cupboard

cubicle n compartment, booth, partition, stall, workspace

cubist adj abstract, geometric, modern

cuckoo (infml) adj eccentric, strange, weird, unusual, bizarre Opposite: ordinary

cuddle v hug, embrace, clasp, hold, nuzzle ■ n embrace, hug, clasp, hold, clinch

cuddle up v snuggle up, curl up, cosy up

cuddly adj soft, lovable, fluffy, warm, endearing

cudgel v hit, bludgeon, whack, pound, batter

cue n signal, prompt, sign, indication, reminder ■ v prompt, signal, show, indicate, remind

cuff v buffet, slap, strike, hit, rap

cuisine n food, fare, cooking, gastronomy, cookery

cul-de-sac n dead end, no through road, impasse, blind alley

culinary adj cooking, gastronomic, cookery, food

cull v 1 discard, reject, remove, scrap, get rid of Opposite: retain 2 pick, select, choose, gather, harvest ■ n reject, scrap, discard, castoff, second

culminate v end, conclude, finish, terminate, climax Opposite: start

culmination n conclusion, finale, peak, height, zenith Opposite: inception (fml)

culpability n blameworthiness, liability, blame, guilt, fault Opposite: innocence

culpable adj guilty, in the wrong, to blame, blameworthy, responsible Opposite: innocent

culprit n offender, criminal, guilty party, perpetrator, wrongdoer

cult n 1 sect, religious group, religious persuasion, movement 2 fad, craze, trend, adoration, veneration ■ adj alternative, offbeat, out of the ordinary, unusual, trendy (infml) Opposite: mainstream

cultivate v 1 farm, grow, plant, plough, tend 2 promote, encourage, nurture, work on, foster Opposite: neglect

cultivated adj refined, educated, cultured, sophisticated, urbane Opposite: uncouth

cultivation n 1 farming, agriculture, husbandry, crop growing, agronomy 2 development, promotion, encouragement, nurturing, fostering Opposite: neglect 3 refinement, education, culture, sophistication, urbanity Opposite: uncouthness

cultivator n grower, farmer, gardener, planter, agronomist

cultural adj 1 national, social, ethnic, folk, traditional 2 artistic, literary, intellectual, educational, edifying

culture n 1 civilization, society, mores, traditions, customs **2 ethos**, philosophy, values, principles, beliefs **3 sophistication**, refinement, urbanity, civilization, cultivation *Opposite*: uncouthness **4 art, music, and literature**, arts, humanities, fine arts, performing arts

cultured *adj* **refined**, well-educated, learned, educated, erudite *Opposite*: uncouth

culvert *n* **duct**, channel, conduit, tunnel, main

cum *(infml)* *prep* **with**, together with, along with, in combination with, also used as

cumbersome *adj* **unwieldy**, awkward, weighty, bulky, clumsy *Opposite*: manageable

cumulative *adj* **increasing**, snowballing, swelling, accumulative, growing *Opposite*: diminishing

cunning *adj* **1 sly**, wily, crafty, sneaky, shrewd *Opposite*: guileless **2 ingenious**, inventive, resourceful, creative, innovative ■ *n* **1 slyness**, wiliness, craftiness, sneakiness, shrewdness *Opposite*: ingenuousness **2 skill**, cleverness, ingenuity, creativity, dexterity

cup *n* **1 mug**, beaker, demitasse, teacup **2 trophy**, chalice, goblet, prize

cupidity *(fml)* *n* **greed**, avarice, covetousness, materialism, conspicuous consumption *Opposite*: generosity

cupola *n* **dome**, vault, roof, ceiling

cur *n* **mongrel**, dog, hound, mutt *(slang)* *Opposite*: purebred

curable *adj* **treatable**, remediable, correctable, mendable, repairable *Opposite*: incurable

curate *n* **priest**, minister, cleric, ecclesiastic ■ *v* **create**, mount, install, stage

curative *adj* **healing**, remedial, restorative, therapeutic, palliative *Opposite*: injurious

curator *n* **warden**, custodian, keeper, steward, guardian

curb *n* **control**, limit, restriction, restraint, check ■ *v* **restrain**, control, limit, hold back, rein in *Opposite*: promote

curdle *v* **1 coagulate**, clot, thicken, congeal, gel *Opposite*: separate **2** *(infml)* **go sour**, go bad, go off, turn, sour

cure *v* **heal**, treat, make well, restore to health, alleviate *Opposite*: exacerbate ■ *n* **treatment**, therapy, medicine, medication, remedy ■ *v* **preserve**, smoke, dry, salt, pickle

cure-all *n* **panacea**, universal remedy, magic potion, magic bullet, antidote

curfew *n* **restriction**, time limit, deadline, guillotine, limitation

curio *n* **trinket**, antique, curiosity, souvenir, knick-knack

curiosity *n* **1 inquisitiveness**, interest, prying, nosiness *(infml)*, snooping *(infml)* *Opposite*: disinterest **2 oddity**, rarity, novelty, curio, strange thing

curious *adj* **1 inquisitive**, inquiring, interested, questioning, probing *Opposite*: uninterested **2 peculiar**, odd, strange, unusual, intriguing *Opposite*: ordinary

curl *v* **1 twist**, coil, bend, wave, crimp **2 swirl**, spiral, twirl, twist, curve ■ *n* **1 coil**, twist, whorl, spiral, eddy **2 ringlet**, wave, lock, kiss curl, spit curl *(US)*

curl up *v* **double up**, crouch, hug your knees, roll into a ball, go into the foetal position *Opposite*: straighten

curly *adj* **wavy**, coiled, twisted, frizzy, crimped *Opposite*: straight

curmudgeon *n* **malcontent**, grouch *(infml)*, grump *(infml)*, pain *(infml)*, misery *(infml)*

curmudgeonly *adj* **bad-tempered**, crabby, cantankerous, grumpy, testy *Opposite*: pleasant

currency *n* **1 money**, legal tender, coinage, coins, exchange **2 prevalence**, frequency, vogue, commonness, popularity

current *adj* **present**, existing, actual, in progress, recent *Opposite*: former ■ *n* **flow**, stream, undercurrent, tide, flux

curriculum *n* **course**, prospectus, programme, syllabus, core curriculum

curry favour *v* **ingratiate yourself**, cosy up, get in with, play up to, smarm *(infml)*

curse *n* **1 swearword**, oath, expletive, epithet, blasphemy **2 jinx**, spell, magic, setback, blow *Opposite*: blessing **3 scourge**, plague, blight, bane, misfortune ■ *v* **1 swear**, blaspheme, damn, use bad language, eff and blind *(slang)* *Opposite*: bless **2 plague**, afflict, trouble, blight, torment

cursed *adj* **1 damned**, afflicted, banned, anathematized, blighted *Opposite*: blessed **2** *(infml)* **annoying**, irritating, bothersome, vexatious, perturbing

cursor *n* **pointer**, arrow, marker, indicator

cursory *adj* **superficial**, hasty, brief, passing, quick *Opposite*: thorough

curt *adj* **abrupt**, brisk, brusque, rude, brief *Opposite*: civil

curtail *v* **limit**, restrain, restrict, hold back, cut back *Opposite*: extend

curtailment *n* **limitation**, restriction, curb, shortening, reduction *Opposite*: extension

curtain *n* **drape**, blind, screen, shutter, shade

curtain raiser *n* **prelude**, overture, prologue, preamble, lead-in

curtness *n* **brusqueness**, abruptness, shortness, briskness, snappiness *Opposite*: civility

curtsy *v* **genuflect**, bow, bob, kneel, stoop ■ *n* **bow**, genuflection, bob, obeisance *(fml)*

curvaceous *adj* **curvy**, rounded, curved, shapely, voluptuous

curvature *n* **curving**, bend, twist, warp, arc

curve *n* **arc**, bend, bow, arch, camber ■ *v* **bend**, bow, curl, coil, twist *Opposite*: straighten

curved *adj* **rounded**, curled, coiled, arched, bent *Opposite*: straight

curvilinear *see* **curved**

curviness *n* **roundedness**, sinuousness, shapeliness, curvaceousness

curving adj **1 curved**, curvy, bending, sinuous, snaking *Opposite*: straight **2 bent**, warped, twisted, bowed, crooked *Opposite*: straight

curvy adj **undulating**, wavy, rounded, curved, curvilinear *Opposite*: straight

cushion n **pillow**, bolster, pad, headrest, beanbag ■ v **1 protect**, shield, guard, support, bolster *Opposite*: expose **2 mitigate**, moderate, lessen, stifle, soften *Opposite*: exacerbate

cushy (infml) adj **easy**, comfortable, undemanding, cosy, jammy (infml) *Opposite*: difficult

cusp n **1 point**, tip, nib, end **2 crossover**, border, limit, edge, verge

cussed (infml) adj **annoying**, irritating, uncooperative, obstinate, stubborn *Opposite*: cooperative

cussedness (infml) n **pigheadedness**, stubbornness, obstinacy, wilfulness, perversity *Opposite*: cooperation

custodial adj **1 prison**, jail, secure, penal, residential **2 protective**, safeguarding, safekeeping, sheltered, supervisory

custodian n **1 guardian**, curator, keeper, defender, upholder **2 caretaker**, janitor, concierge, warden, night watchman

custody n **1 detention**, arrest, confinement, imprisonment, incarceration (fml) *Opposite*: liberty **2 protection**, keeping, safekeeping, care, charge

custom n **1 tradition**, practice, convention, institution, ritual *Opposite*: novelty **2 habit**, practice, routine, pattern, way **3 trade**, business, patronage, clientele, market. *See* COMPARE AND CONTRAST *at* **habit**.

customary adj **1 usual**, normal, habitual, expected, routine *Opposite*: exceptional **2 traditional**, conventional, time-honoured, established, long-established *Opposite*: unconventional **3 typical**, characteristic, usual, habitual, normal *Opposite*: uncharacteristic. *See* COMPARE AND CONTRAST *at* **usual**.

custom-built adj **specially made**, commissioned, bespoke, customized, personalized *Opposite*: off-the-peg

customer n **client**, buyer, shopper, purchaser, patron

customize v **modify**, tailor, adapt, alter, make to order

customized adj **modified**, tailored, adapted, personalized, custom-made *Opposite*: mass-produced

custom-made *see* **custom-built**

customs n **tax**, duty, levy, impost, toll

cut v **1 chop**, slice, carve, saw, hack *Opposite*: join **2 pierce**, score, nick, incise, engrave *Opposite*: seal **3 reduce**, decrease, limit, curtail, cut down *Opposite*: increase **4 edit**, shorten, censor, condense, chop *Opposite*: restore **5 stop**, discontinue, bring to an end, bring to a halt, finish *Opposite*: continue ■

n **1 scratch**, wound, slash, graze, incision **2 reduction**, decrease, cutback, decline, drop *Opposite*: increase **3** (infml) **share**, commission, percentage, kickback, rake-off (infml)

cut-and-dried adj **1 decided**, finished, settled, fixed, agreed *Opposite*: undecided **2 predictable**, obvious, open-and-shut, anticipated, expected *Opposite*: anomalous

cut back v **reduce**, curtail, curb, decrease, restrain *Opposite*: develop

cutback n **reduction**, cut, decrease, decline, drop

cut dead v **snub**, cold-shoulder, rebuff

cut down v **1 reduce**, decrease, cut back, ease up on, rein back *Opposite*: increase **2 fell**, chop down, bring down, hack down, lop **3** (infml) **kill**, strike down, slaughter, mow down, assassinate

cute adj **1 attractive**, pretty, delightful, charming, appealing *Opposite*: ugly **2 shrewd**, cunning, smart, sharp, quick

cuteness n **1 adorability**, lovability, attractiveness, appeal, charm *Opposite*: ugliness **2 shrewdness**, cunning, smartness, sharpness, quickwittedness

cutesy adj **mawkish**, saccharine, sugary, twee, chocolate-box *Opposite*: austere

cut-glass adj **upper-class**, plummy, public-school, posh (infml), county (infml) *Opposite*: broad

cut in v **interrupt**, break in, butt in, interject, move in

cutlery n **knives and forks**, tableware, silverware, silver, fighting irons

---

WORD BANK

❑ **types of cutlery** butter knife, cake slice, carving knife, chopstick, dessertspoon, fish knife, fork, knife, pastry fork, pastry slice, serving spoon, soupspoon, spoon, steak knife, tablespoon, teaspoon

---

cut loose (infml) v **get free**, get away, escape, make a break, break away

cut off v **1 remove**, sever, amputate, excise, detach *Opposite*: reconnect **2 stop**, disconnect, discontinue, bring to an end, halt *Opposite*: restore **3 isolate**, separate, keep apart, strand, detach *Opposite*: connect **4 interrupt**, stop, cut short, cut in, butt in

cutoff n **1 limit**, end point, end date, deadline, expiry *Opposite*: start **2 stoppage**, end, finish, halt, freeze *Opposite*: continuation

cut out v **1 remove**, take away, excise, extract, take out *Opposite*: put in **2 give up**, stop, renounce, forgo, do without **3 exclude**, ignore, overlook, isolate, marginalize *Opposite*: include

cutout n **1 shape**, template, stencil, outline, silhouette **2 safety device**, circuit breaker, safety switch, trip switch

cut-price adj **reduced**, cheap, bargain, budget, discount

cut short v break off, discontinue, call a halt, suspend, stop in full flow Opposite: extend

cutthroat adj merciless, pitiless, ruthless, unsparing, fierce Opposite: merciful

cutting adj 1 hurtful, wounding, unkind, acerbic, critical Opposite: kind 2 cold, biting, icy, sharp, keen Opposite: mild ■ n sprig, offshoot, scion

cutting edge n 1 vanguard, van, forefront, edge, leading edge Opposite: rearguard 2 sharp edge, razor edge, knife edge, blade, razor blade

cutting-edge adj leading-edge, front-line, pioneering, trailblazing, radical Opposite: old-fashioned

cuttingly adv harshly, abrasively, hurtfully, sharply, severely Opposite: kindly

cut up v chop, mince, slice, chop up, dice ■ adj (infml) distressed, upset, affected, distraught, heartbroken Opposite: happy

CV n curriculum vitae, qualifications, employment record, résumé (US)

cybernetics n artificial intelligence, information technology, AI, IT

cyberspace n Internet, World Wide Web, information superhighway, data superhighway, infobahn

cycle n series, sequence, set, round, rotation

cyclic see cyclical

cyclical adj recurring, returning, repeated, cyclical, recurrent Opposite: unique

cyclone n storm, windstorm, hurricane, typhoon, tornado

cylinder n 1 tube, roll, pipe 2 container, drum, canister, tank, bottle

cylindrical adj tubular, tube-shaped, cylinder-shaped, rod-shaped, rodlike

cynic n sceptic, doubter, detractor, disparager, misanthropist

cynical adj 1 sceptical, distrustful, suspicious, disparaging, negative Opposite: naive 2 sarcastic, mocking, scornful, sardonic, sneering Opposite: respectful

cynicism n scepticism, sarcasm, distrust, doubt, scorn Opposite: naivety

cyst n swelling, lump, polyp, nodule, growth

czar see tsar

D

dab v pat, wipe, apply, touch, tap ■ n bit, blob, spot, dash, drop

dabble v 1 experiment, try your hand, dip into, play at, potter 2 dip, paddle, splash, immerse

dab hand (infml) n expert, specialist, authority, whiz (infml), ace (infml)

dad (infml) n father, daddy (infml), pa (infml), papa (dated), pop (US infml)

daddy (infml) see dad

dado n panel, moulding, frieze, feature

daemon n 1 demigod, supernatural being, spirit 2 guardian spirit, inspiration, guiding force, inner spirit, muse

daft (infml) adj silly, foolish, eccentric, dippy (infml), daffy (infml) Opposite: sensible

daftness (infml) n silliness, foolishness, thoughtlessness, eccentricity, dimness Opposite: good sense

daily adv every day, each day, on a daily basis, day by day, day after day ■ adj everyday, day-to-day, regular, diurnal, circadian

daintiness n delicacy, elegance, gracefulness, refinement, prettiness Opposite: clumsiness

dainty adj pretty, delicate, graceful, refined, exquisite Opposite: clumsy

dais n platform, podium, pulpit, stage, stand

dale n valley, glen, dene, vale (literary) Opposite: hill

dally v linger, hang about, dawdle, loiter, hang around Opposite: hurry

dam n barrier, barrage, weir, wall, boom ■ v block, block up, stem, hold back, control

damage n 1 injury, harm, hurt, impairment, destruction Opposite: reparation 2 (infml) cost, price, bill, total, amount ■ v injure, harm, spoil, hurt, smash up Opposite: repair. See COMPARE AND CONTRAST at harm.

damaged adj injured, hurt, spoiled, dented, scratched Opposite: pristine

damages n compensation, costs, reparation, reimbursement, recompense

damaging adj harmful, destructive, negative, detrimental, hurtful Opposite: harmless

damn v 1 condemn, sentence, doom, consign, punish 2 criticize, denounce, censure, lambaste, pan (infml)

damning adj critical, negative, disapproving, unfavourable, condemning Opposite: complimentary

damp adj 1 dank, moist, humid, soggy, clammy Opposite: dry 2 half-hearted, indifferent, insipid, unenthusiastic, weak Opposite: enthusiastic ■ n moisture, dampness, humidity, clamminess, wetness *Opposite*: dryness ■ *v* **1 check**, curb, restrain, hinder, hamper *Opposite*: encourage **2 dampen**, moisten, humidify, wet *Opposite*: dry out

damp down *v* dampen, diminish, check, dull, curb *Opposite*: increase

dampen *v* **1 damp**, moisten, humidify, wet *Opposite*: dry out **2 damp down**, reduce, diminish, check, dull *Opposite*: increase

damper *n* **1 discouragement**, inhibition, hindrance, impediment, obstruction *Opposite*: spur **2 mute**, silencer, softener, muffler (*US*) **3 regulator**, stopper, control, controller

dampness *n* humidity, moisture, moistness, clamminess, wetness *Opposite*: dryness

dance *v* **1 twirl**, pirouette, sway, turn, bop (*infml*) **2 gambol**, prance, skip, caper, frolic ■ *n* **ball**, disco, rave (*slang*), hop (*dated infml*)

WORD BANK
❑ types of dance ballet, barn dance, belly dance, bop (*infml*), bossa nova, breakdance, cancan, cha-cha, Charleston, fandango, flamenco, foxtrot, jig, jitterbug, jive, lambada, limbo, lindy hop, line dancing, macarena, mambo, merengue, minuet, morris dancing, polka, quadrille, quickstep, rumba, salsa, samba, square dance, step dancing, strathspey, tango, tap dance, waltz

dandified (*dated*) *adj* dressed up, dressed to kill, overdressed, fashionable, natty *Opposite*: scruffy

dandle *v* **1 jiggle**, jog, bounce, dance, rock **2 pet**, stroke, caress, fondle, pamper

dandruff *n* scurf, scale, skin flake

dandy (*dated*) *n* fop, fashion plate, clotheshorse (*infml*), beau (*archaic*), coxcomb (*archaic*)

danger *n* **1 hazard**, risk, peril, threat, menace *Opposite*: safety **2 chance**, possibility, likelihood, risk

dangerous *adj* **1 unsafe**, hazardous, risky, treacherous, perilous *Opposite*: safe **2 grave**, serious, critical, grievous, alarming *Opposite*: safe

dangle *v* hang, hang down, swing, sway, suspend *Opposite*: stick up

dank *adj* damp, moist, chilly, clammy, humid *Opposite*: warm

dankness *n* wetness, dampness, moistness, humidity, clamminess *Opposite*: warmth

dapper *adj* neat, elegant, smart, trim, well-dressed *Opposite*: scruffy

dappled *adj* speckled, spotted, mottled, stippled, piebald

dare *v* **1 venture**, risk, gamble, face up to, have the courage **2 challenge**, defy, taunt, provoke, goad **3 presume**, venture, have the audacity, be so bold, take the liberty ■ *n* taunt, challenge, provocation, ultimatum, goad

daredevil *n* risk-taker, madcap, hothead, show-off (*infml*) *Opposite*: stick-in-the-mud (*infml*) ■ *adj* reckless, rash, madcap, hot-headed, bold *Opposite*: staid

daresay *v* guess, suppose, expect, assume, admit *Opposite*: deny

daring *adj* **1 bold**, brave, audacious, courageous, enterprising *Opposite*: cowardly **2 dangerous**, risky, unsafe, hazardous, treacherous *Opposite*: safe ■ *n* bravery, nerve, boldness, audacity, courage *Opposite*: cowardice

dark *adj* **1 dim**, shady, shadowy, murky, gloomy *Opposite*: bright **2 black**, brunette, brown, chestnut, sable *Opposite*: fair **3 gloomy**, depressing, bleak, sad, unhappy *Opposite*: cheery **4 sinister**, mysterious, threatening, evil, nefarious *Opposite*: good ■ *n* darkness, dusk, gloom, dimness, shadows *Opposite*: light

darken *v* blacken, dim, deepen, cast a shadow, grow dim *Opposite*: brighten

dark glasses *n* sunglasses, sunspecs (*infml*), shades (*infml*)

darkness *n* dark, night, dusk, gloom, dimness *Opposite*: light

darling *n* **1 sweetheart**, dear, love, dearest, beloved **2 favourite**, firm favourite, pet, the apple of somebody's eye ■ *adj* wonderful, gorgeous, lovely, adorable, dear *Opposite*: horrible

darn *v* sew, stitch, repair, mend, sew up *Opposite*: tear ■ *adj* (*infml*) very, extremely, exceptionally, extraordinarily

dart *n* arrow, barb, shaft, missile, projectile ■ *v* dash, scurry, whiz, rush, run *Opposite*: saunter

dash *n* **1 sprint**, rush, run, race, surge **2 trace**, splash, drop, pinch, soupçon **3 verve**, vigour, spirit, flair, panache ■ *v* **1 rush**, hurry, hasten, tear, race *Opposite*: amble **2** (*fml*) **knock**, throw, hurl, slam, fling **3** (*fml*) **smash**, break, shatter, crash, splinter **4 shatter**, ruin, crush, blight, destroy *Opposite*: bolster **5 frustrate**, confound, foil, shatter, discourage *Opposite*: encourage

dashing *adj* **1** (*dated*) **spirited**, confident, jaunty, flamboyant, bold *Opposite*: staid **2 elegant**, stylish, chic, debonair, fashionable *Opposite*: dowdy

dastardly *adj* low, shameful, dishonourable, mean, reprehensible *Opposite*: honourable

data *n* information, statistics, facts, figures, numbers

database *n* data bank, store, folder, list, archive

data processing *n* information retrieval, data handling, number-crunching (*slang*)

date *n* **1 day**, day of the week, year, time **2 time**, point in time, period, era, day **3 meeting**, rendezvous, appointment, blind date, engagement

dated *adj* old-fashioned, old, behind the times, unfashionable, passé *Opposite*: up-to-date

dateline *n* heading, subheading, subhead, identification

daub v smear, spread, slap, spatter, slop ■ n blot, blotch, spot, splotch, stain

daunt v put off, deter, discourage, intimidate, scare Opposite: encourage

daunting adj intimidating, unnerving, discouraging, frightening, overwhelming Opposite: heartening

dawdle v 1 loiter, delay, linger, plod, lag Opposite: hurry 2 waste time, hang around, hang about, dally, linger Opposite: hurry

dawdler n 1 straggler, stroller, wanderer, laggard, dallier Opposite: leader 2 idler, slacker, shirker, timewaster, shilly-shallier

dawdling n dilly-dallying, shilly-shallying, delaying, tarrying, loitering Opposite: haste ■ adj slow, sluggish, measured, leisurely, casual Opposite: hasty

dawn n 1 sunrise, crack of dawn, daybreak, first light, daylight Opposite: dusk 2 beginning, start, birth, emergence, dawning Opposite: end ■ v 1 begin, start, be born, emerge, originate Opposite: end 2 occur, cross your mind, register with, strike, become clear to

day n 1 daylight hours, daylight, daytime, sunlight hours Opposite: night 2 date, day of the week, calendar day 3 time, era, period, generation, epoch

daybreak n dawn, crack of dawn, first light, daylight, morning Opposite: dusk

daydream n reverie, fantasy, musing, contemplation, dream ■ v dream, have your head in the clouds, be miles away, be inattentive, fantasize Opposite: concentrate

daydreamer n idealist, dreamer, fantasist, visionary, woolgatherer

daydreaming n reverie, woolgathering, fantasizing, pensiveness, dreaminess Opposite: concentration

daylight n 1 day, daytime, sunshine, light of day, hours of daylight Opposite: nighttime 2 dawn, crack of dawn, sunrise, daybreak, first light Opposite: dusk

day out n outing, away day, trip, spree, jaunt

day room n lounge, recreation room, seating area, reception room, sitting room

days gone by n former times, earlier times, previous times, days of old, olden days Opposite: future

daytime n day, daylight, hours of daylight, morning, afternoon Opposite: nighttime

day-to-day adj everyday, commonplace, daily, routine, usual Opposite: unusual

day trip n excursion, outing, day out, trip, visit

day tripper n tourist, traveller, sightseer, holidaymaker, tripper (infml)

daze n confused state, stupor, trance, dream, daydream ■ v stun, shock, astonish, astound, surprise

dazzle v 1 blind, daze, confuse, overwhelm, bedazzle (literary) 2 amaze, astonish, astound, impress, overwhelm Opposite: bore ■ n glare, brightness, reflection, blaze, brilliance

dazzling adj 1 stunning, amazing, astounding, incredible, alluring Opposite: unimpressive 2 bright, glaring, glittering, blazing, luminous Opposite: dull

deactivate v neutralize, disable, switch off, turn off, disengage Opposite: activate

dead adj 1 lifeless, late, defunct, deceased (fml), departed (literary) Opposite: alive 2 numb, benumbed, stiff, insensitive, frozen Opposite: sensitive 3 boring, quiet, dull, uninteresting, deadly Opposite: exciting 4 finished, obsolete, over, ended, empty Opposite: current 5 silent, blank, quiet, down, inactive Opposite: live

---

COMPARE AND CONTRAST CORE MEANING: no longer living, functioning, or in existence

dead describes organisms that are no longer alive, physical objects that no longer function or exist, and abstract entities that are no longer valid or relevant; **deceased** (fml, restricted to people, especially in legal or other technical contexts, or as a euphemism) no longer living; **departed** (literary, restricted to people) no longer living; **late** (restricted to people) having died recently or within living memory; **lifeless** not living, or apparently not living; **defunct** no longer operative, valid, or functional, or no longer in existence; **extinct** no longer in existence, or no longer active.

---

deaden v soften, dull, muffle, dampen, mute Opposite: amplify

dead end n 1 cul-de-sac, blind alley, impasse, no through road, roadblock 2 block, stalemate, standstill, impasse, deadlock

deadened adj desensitized, unfeeling, insensitive, insensible, numb Opposite: sensitive

deadhead v take away, cut off, remove

dead heat n draw, tie, photo finish, drawn game, stalemate

deadline n time limit, limit, goal, aim, target Opposite: extension

deadlock n impasse, stalemate, gridlock, standstill, logjam

deadly adj 1 lethal, fatal, terminal, mortal, poisonous Opposite: harmless 2 (infml) boring, tedious, tiresome, dull, dead Opposite: interesting ■ adv completely, absolutely, extremely, very, perfectly Opposite: slightly ■ adj extreme, implacable, mortal, sworn, absolute

---

COMPARE AND CONTRAST CORE MEANING: causing death

deadly likely or designed to cause death; **fatal** describes accidents or illnesses that result in death; **mortal** causing, continuing until, or relating to death; **lethal** certain to or intended to cause death; **terminal** describes illnesses that result in death.

---

deadpan adj unsmiling, straight-faced, poker-faced, expressionless, blank *Opposite*: expressive

dead ringer *(infml) n* **double**, doppelgänger, image, spitting image *(infml)*, lookalike *(infml) Opposite*: opposite

deaf *adj* **1 hearing-impaired**, deafened, tone-deaf *Opposite*: hearing **2 unresponsive**, indifferent, oblivious, heedless, unmoved *Opposite*: mindful

deafening *adj* **loud**, earsplitting, ear-piercing, booming, thunderous *Opposite*: noiseless

deal *n* **transaction**, contract, agreement, arrangement, pact ■ *v* **1 distribute**, share out, give out, allocate, apportion *Opposite*: receive **2 trade**, do business, exchange, sell, transact business *Opposite*: buy

dealer *n* **trader**, merchant, seller, broker, supplier

dealership *n* **1 charter**, authorization, agreement, right, licence **2 premises**, showroom, offices, workplace, workshop

dealings *n* **transactions**, contact, communication, business, connections

deal out *v* **give out**, issue, distribute, mete out, administer *Opposite*: collect

deal with *v* **cope with**, manage, handle, see to, take care of *Opposite*: evade

dear *adj* **1 beloved**, cherished, prized, valued, precious *Opposite*: hated **2 expensive**, costly, extortionate, valuable, exorbitant *Opposite*: cheap ■ *n* **darling**, sweetheart, dearest, beloved, pet

dearest *n* **love**, sweetheart, pet, precious, sugar *(infml)*

dearly *adv* **greatly**, extremely, exceedingly, profoundly, sincerely

dearth *n* **lack**, shortage, scarcity, drought, famine *Opposite*: glut. *See* COMPARE AND CONTRAST *at* **lack**.

death *n* **1 passing**, bereavement, loss, demise *(fml)*, decease *(fml) Opposite*: birth **2 fatality**, casualty, loss of life, killing, murder *Opposite*: birth **3 end**, fall, downfall, ruin, collapse *Opposite*: beginning

deathblow *n* **body blow**, final blow, last straw, last nail in the coffin, end

death knell *n* **finish**, last nail in the coffin, end of the road, point of no return, last straw

deathless *adj* **eternal**, timeless, immortal, everlasting, undying *Opposite*: mortal

deathlike *adj* **skeletal**, gaunt, ashen, spectral, pallid

deathly *adj* **deadly**, deathlike, tomblike, deep, stony ■ *adv* **extremely**, intensely, deadly, intensively, absolutely *Opposite*: slightly

death mask *n* **effigy**, cast, head, model, sculpture

death rattle *n* **gurgle**, rattle, rasp, wheeze, croak

death toll *n* **fatalities**, death rate, mortality rate, fatality rate, loss of life

deathtrap *(infml) n* **safety risk**, hazard, minefield, pitfall, health hazard

death warrant *see* **death knell**

debacle *n* **disaster**, catastrophe, fiasco, shambles, tragedy *Opposite*: success

debar *v* **exclude**, expel, bar, ban, prohibit *Opposite*: admit

debark *v* **disembark**, alight, go ashore, land, get off *Opposite*: embark

debarkation *n* **disembarkation**, alighting, going ashore, landing, getting off

debase *v* **1 degrade**, impair, adulterate, sully, corrupt *Opposite*: purify **2 humiliate**, demean, degrade, shame, humble *Opposite*: glorify

debasement *n* **1 ruination**, adulteration, corruption, defilement, tarnishing *Opposite*: purification **2 humiliation**, degradation, disgrace, shame, disparagement *Opposite*: glorification

debatable *adj* **arguable**, dubious, controversial, doubtful, contentious *Opposite*: settled

debate *v* **1 discuss**, argue, dispute, deliberate, contest *Opposite*: conclude **2 ponder**, wonder, deliberate, weigh up, consider *Opposite*: decide ■ *n* **discussion**, argument, dispute, examination, consideration *Opposite*: conclusion

debater *n* **speaker**, orator, public speaker, disputant, arguer

debauched *adj* **decadent**, dissolute, degenerate, dissipated, immoral *Opposite*: moral

debauchery *n* **decadence**, dissoluteness, immorality, self-indulgence *Opposite*: morality

debilitate *v* **weaken**, incapacitate, enervate, drain, hamper *Opposite*: fortify

debilitated *adj* **weakened**, incapacitated, enervated, drained, hampered *Opposite*: fortified. *See* COMPARE AND CONTRAST *at* **weak**.

debilitating *adj* **weakening**, incapacitating, enervating, draining, devastating *Opposite*: refreshing

debility *n* **weakness**, incapacity, frailty, ineffectiveness, enfeeblement *Opposite*: strength

debit *n* **withdrawal**, subtraction, deduction, debt, charge *Opposite*: credit ■ *v* **deduct**, take out, withdraw, subtract, charge *Opposite*: credit

debonair *adj* **suave**, elegant, refined, charming, well-groomed *Opposite*: graceless

debouch *v* **emerge**, move out, spread out, exit, come out *Opposite*: confine

debrief *v* **question**, interrogate, interview, examine, quiz

debriefing *n* **interrogation**, questioning, interview, examination, probing *Opposite*: briefing

debris n **wreckage**, remains, fragments, rubble, waste

debt n **1 arrears**, liability, debit, balance, balance due *Opposite*: credit **2 obligation**, duty, responsibility, dues, liability

debtor n **borrower**, mortgagor, insolvent, defaulter, pledger

debug v **clear up**, correct, sort out, repair, fix *Opposite*: corrupt

debunk v **expose**, show up, deflate, demystify, discredit *Opposite*: perpetuate

debut n **entrance**, introduction, unveiling, presentation, inauguration *Opposite*: retirement

decade n **period**, era, time, epoch

decadence n **corruption**, debauchery, depravity, dissolution, self-indulgence *Opposite*: temperance

decadent adj **debauched**, corrupt, depraved, dissolute, degenerate *Opposite*: innocent

decamp v **run away**, run off, escape, flee, abscond *Opposite*: turn up

decant v **pour**, pour out, transfer, empty, empty out *Opposite*: fill

decanter n **carafe**, flask, vessel, bottle, pitcher

decapitate v **behead**, guillotine, execute, amputate, truncate

decapitation n **beheading**, amputation, killing, guillotining, execution

decay v **1 decompose**, rot, fester, perish, crumble **2 decline**, degenerate, deteriorate, fall off, dwindle *Opposite*: flourish ■ n **1 deterioration**, decline, degeneration, falling-off, falloff *Opposite*: growth **2 decomposition**, rot, rotting, putrefaction, corrosion

decayed adj **decomposed**, rotten, rotting, putrefied, perished *Opposite*: fresh

decaying adj **decomposing**, rotting, rotten, putrefying, crumbling *Opposite*: fresh

decease (fml) n **death**, passing, departure, release, demise (fml) *Opposite*: birth

deceased (fml) n **corpse**, cadaver, body, decedent (fml), departed (fml or literary) ■ adj **dead**, late, lifeless, defunct, extinct *Opposite*: alive. *See* COMPARE AND CONTRAST *at* **dead**.

deceit n **dishonesty**, treachery, deceitfulness, deception, trickery *Opposite*: honesty

deceitful adj **dishonest**, deceiving, fraudulent, untrustworthy, cunning *Opposite*: honest

deceitfully adv **dishonestly**, cunningly, fraudulently, deviously, treacherously *Opposite*: honestly

deceitfulness n **dishonesty**, deceit, treachery, lies, falseness *Opposite*: honesty

deceive v **1 mislead**, betray, trick, take in, lie to **2 cheat**, two-time, betray, play away (infml), cuckold (literary)

deceiver n **liar**, fraud, swindler, cheat, fraudster

deceiving adj **misleading**, lying, cheating, devious, deceptive *Opposite*: honest

decelerate v **slow down**, slow, slow up, brake, lose speed *Opposite*: accelerate

deceleration n **slowing down**, slowing up, slowing, braking, checking *Opposite*: acceleration

decency n **1 politeness**, decorum, decorousness, civility, courtesy *Opposite*: incivility **2 modesty**, respectability, uprightness, integrity, wholesomeness *Opposite*: decadence

decent adj **1 moral**, honest, virtuous, wholesome, demure *Opposite*: decadent **2 good**, right, proper, correct, suitable *Opposite*: inappropriate **3 reasonable**, respectable, adequate, sizable, generous *Opposite*: inadequate **4** (infml) **dressed**, clothed, clad, garbed, covered *Opposite*: undressed **5 respectable**, upright, polite, civilized, well-mannered

decentralization n **devolution**, subsidiarity, regionalization, delegation, reorganization *Opposite*: centralization

decentralize v **devolve**, regionalize, reorganize, disperse, distribute *Opposite*: centralize

deception n **1 dishonesty**, duplicity, deceptiveness, deceit, cheating *Opposite*: truthfulness **2 trick**, ruse, sham, fraud, con

deceptive adj **misleading**, illusory, deceiving, dishonest, false *Opposite*: reliable

deceptiveness n **falseness**, falsity, disingenuousness, deviousness, spuriousness *Opposite*: reliability

decide v **1 make a decision**, choose, come to a decision, make your mind up, settle on *Opposite*: equivocate **2 settle**, determine, conclude, resolve, decree *Opposite*: put off

decided adj **1 obvious**, definite, absolute, categorical, unquestionable *Opposite*: unclear **2 determined**, resolute, decisive, firm, sure *Opposite*: hesitant

decidedly adv **categorically**, definitely, absolutely, distinctly, particularly *Opposite*: possibly

decider n **game**, match, contest, trial, play-off

deciding adj **determining**, decisive, conclusive, key, pivotal *Opposite*: insignificant

decimal n **number**, fraction, unit

decimate v **devastate**, destroy, annihilate, ruin, cut a swath through

decimation n **devastation**, destruction, slaughter, annihilation, ruin

decipher v **decode**, decrypt, interpret, translate, make out *Opposite*: encode

decipherable adj **readable**, legible, intelligible, comprehensible, understandable *Opposite*: unintelligible

decision n **1 choice**, result, conclusion, verdict, pronouncement **2 determination**, resolve, firmness, willpower, strength of mind *Opposite*: indecision

decisive adj 1 **conclusive**, pivotal, key, critical, significant Opposite: insignificant 2 **strong-minded**, resolute, determined, certain, clear-sighted Opposite: uncertain

decisiveness n **resoluteness**, determination, conclusiveness, authoritativeness, positiveness Opposite: indecisiveness

deck n **level**, floor, surface, area, sun deck ■ v (infml) **hit**, knock down, knock over, floor, thump

deck hand n **sailor**, rating, seaman

declaim v **hold forth**, pronounce, proclaim, declare, utter Opposite: mutter

declamatory adj **dramatic**, formal, oratorical, rhetorical, theatrical Opposite: low-key

declaration n **statement**, announcement, assertion, speech, pronouncement

declare v **announce**, state, speak out, assert, affirm

declassification n **release**, publication, open access, derestriction, decontrol Opposite: restriction

declassify v **release**, publish, derestrict, open up, bring out Opposite: classify

decline v 1 **refuse**, turn down, reject, pass up, beg off Opposite: accept 2 **weaken**, fail, deteriorate, degenerate, fall off Opposite: improve ■ n **deterioration**, falling-off, falloff, decay, drop Opposite: improvement

declining adj **deteriorating**, decreasing, lessening, falling, diminishing Opposite: improving

decode v **decipher**, make out, make sense of, interpret, translate Opposite: encode

decoder n **cryptographer**, decipherer, interpreter, translator

décolleté adj **low-necked**, low-cut, plunging, low, revealing

decommission v **retire**, mothball, withdraw, take out, neutralize Opposite: introduce

decompose v **rot**, decay, crumble, fester, putrefy

decomposed adj **rotten**, disintegrated, decayed, perished, putrid Opposite: fresh

decomposing adj **rotting**, disintegrating, decaying, putrid, putrefying Opposite: fresh

decomposition n **decay**, rottenness, putrefaction, breakdown, disintegration Opposite: soundness

deconstruct v **critique**, criticize, decompose, review, analyse

decontaminate v **cleanse**, clean up, clean, purify, disinfect Opposite: contaminate

decontrol v **deregulate**, delimit, free, set free, loosen Opposite: control

decor n **decoration**, furnishings, colour scheme, interior decoration, scheme

decorate v 1 **beautify**, adorn, ornament, embellish, trim Opposite: strip 2 **paint**, smarten up, do up, spruce, do over (slang) 3 **honour**, award, garland, recognize, acknowledge

decorated adj **ornamented**, ornate, adorned, festooned, draped Opposite: plain

decoration n 1 **feature**, festoon, beading, border, carving 2 **beautification**, adornment, ornament, ornamentation, embellishment 3 **honour**, medal, award, sash, ribbon

decorative adj **ornamental**, pretty, attractive, pleasing to the eye, enhancing Opposite: ugly

decorous adj **well-mannered**, well-behaved, good, correct, modest Opposite: improper

decorum n **dignity**, propriety, sedateness, good behaviour, modesty Opposite: abandon

decoy n **lure**, trap, snare, trick, distraction ■ v **entice**, lure, lead astray, distract, entrap

decrease v 1 **reduce**, cut, diminish, cut down, contract Opposite: increase 2 **diminish**, decline, dwindle, subside, lessen ■ n **reduction**, cut, diminution, lessening, decline Opposite: increase

decreasing adj **diminishing**, declining, reducing, dwindling, shrinking Opposite: increasing

decree n **ruling**, verdict, announcement, pronouncement, declaration Opposite: request ■ v **command**, rule, pronounce, announce, dictate

decrepit adj 1 **dilapidated**, crumbling, decaying, falling to pieces, falling apart Opposite: pristine 2 (infml) **old**, feeble, frail, weak, infirm Opposite: vigorous. See COMPARE AND CONTRAST at **weak**.

decrepitude n 1 **decay**, dilapidation, ruin, shabbiness Opposite: soundness 2 (infml) **infirmity**, frailty, feebleness, weakness, debility

decriminalization n **legalization**, acceptance, allowance, toleration, sanction Opposite: criminalization

decriminalize v **make legal**, legalize, authorize, sanction, permit Opposite: outlaw

decry v **criticize**, complain, belittle, disparage, deprecate Opposite: praise

dedicate v 1 **give**, commit, devote, consecrate, pledge 2 **reserve**, devote, set aside, earmark, give over to

dedicated adj **committed**, devoted, steadfast, loyal, faithful Opposite: uncommitted

dedication n **devotion**, commitment, enthusiasm, keenness, perseverance

deduce v 1 **conclude**, assume, presume, suppose, gather 2 **infer**, reason, conclude, work out, figure out

COMPARE AND CONTRAST CORE MEANING: reach a logical conclusion on the basis of information **deduce** reach a conclusion using available knowledge; **infer** draw a conclusion from specific circumstances or evidence; **assume** take a premise or information as true without checking or confirming it; **reason** consider information and use it to reach a conclusion in a logical way; **conclude** form an opinion or make a judgment after much consideration; **work out** find a solution or explanation by careful thought or reasoning; **figure out** find a solution or reach a conclusion by careful thought or reasoning.

deduct v subtract, take away, take, remove, abstract Opposite: add

deduction n 1 inference, assumption, conclusion, presumption, judgment 2 subtraction, removal, withdrawal, abstraction, contribution Opposite: addition

deductive adj logical, inferential, reasonable, empirical, rational Opposite: illogical

deed n 1 action, feat, act, endeavour, exploit 2 document, title deed, title, charter, record

deem (fml) v think, believe, consider, estimate, suppose

deep adj 1 bottomless, profound, unfathomable, subterranean, cavernous Opposite: shallow 2 deep-seated, innate, inherent, entrenched, subconscious Opposite: superficial 3 low, rumbling, booming, sonorous, resonant Opposite: shrill 4 intense, profound, concentrated, potent, powerful Opposite: slight 5 profound, multifaceted, multilayered, mysterious, meaningful Opposite: transparent 6 hidden, secret, arcane, mysterious, silent Opposite: open

deepen v 1 intensify, extend, expand, concentrate, accumulate Opposite: weaken 2 dig out, excavate, hollow out, scoop out, extend Opposite: fill in

deeply adv intensely, profoundly, seriously, extremely, greatly Opposite: mildly

deepness n 1 depth, profundity, profoundness, bottomlessness, fathomlessness 2 lowness, resonance, sonority, low pitch

deep-rooted see deep-seated

deep-sea adj marine, oceanic, ocean

deep-seated adj innate, inherent, entrenched, subconscious, ingrained Opposite: superficial

de-escalate v scale down, cut back, reduce, decrease, slow Opposite: escalate

de-escalation n reduction, stepping down, scaling down, cutback, decrease Opposite: escalation

deface v spoil, ruin, mar, disfigure, mutilate Opposite: renovate

defacement n disfigurement, mutilation, vandalism, destruction, damage Opposite: restoration

de facto adv in effect, to all intents and purposes, in reality, actually, effectively ■ adj actual, genuine, effective, existing, real

defamation n insult, offence, slander, libel, slur Opposite: praise

defamatory adj insulting, offensive, slanderous, libellous, derogatory Opposite: complimentary

defame v insult, slander, libel, denigrate, malign Opposite: praise. See COMPARE AND CONTRAST at malign.

default n evasion, avoidance, nonpayment, defaulting, nonattendance ■ v fail to pay, evade, dodge, shirk, duck (infml) Opposite: pay

defaulter n 1 nonpayer, debtor, cheat, tax dodger (infml) 2 shirker, slacker, absentee, dodger (infml)

defeat n 1 overthrow, conquest, downfall, rout Opposite: victory 2 loss, reverse, setback, thrashing, beating Opposite: victory ■ v 1 beat, overcome, conquer, vanquish, trounce Opposite: lose 2 baffle, confound, foil, frustrate, thwart

COMPARE AND CONTRAST CORE MEANING: win a victory

defeat win a victory over an enemy or competitor, or to cause failure; **beat** defeat somebody in a contest, or to overcome a difficulty; **conquer** defeat decisively in battle, or to overcome a difficulty; **vanquish** defeat decisively in battle or competition; **overcome** win or succeed after a struggle; **triumph over** succeed against an adversary or against difficult odds; **thrash** gain an easy decisive victory in a sporting contest; **trounce** defeat an opponent convincingly.

defeatism n pessimism, resignation, despondency, despair, negativity Opposite: optimism

defeatist adj pessimistic, negative, fatalistic, resigned, despondent Opposite: optimistic ■ n pessimist, loser, fatalist, doomsayer, doommonger Opposite: optimist

defecate (fml) v excrete, eliminate waste, empty the bowels, have a bowel movement, evacuate

defecation n excretion, evacuation, elimination

defect n flaw, fault, imperfection, blemish, shortcoming ■ v desert, change sides, abscond, go over, turn traitor. See COMPARE AND CONTRAST at flaw.

defective adj faulty, imperfect, flawed, substandard, malfunctioning Opposite: perfect

defectiveness n faultiness, failure, inadequacy, unreliability, imperfection

defector n traitor, turncoat, renegade, convert, rebel Opposite: loyalist

defence n 1 protection, resistance, guard, security, cover Opposite: attack 2 justification, argument, vindication, plea, apology Opposite: accusation

defence force n army, armed forces, armed services, task force, fighters

defenceless adj unprotected, unarmed, exposed, unguarded, vulnerable Opposite: protected

defencelessness n vulnerability, helplessness, powerlessness, weakness, frailty Opposite: strength

defences n 1 resistance, immunity, protection, shield, safeguard 2 fortifications, ramparts, battlements, earthworks, emplacements

defend v 1 **protect**, guard, shield, safeguard, preserve Opposite: attack 2 **support**, stand up for, stick up for, stand for, represent Opposite: oppose. See COMPARE AND CONTRAST at **safeguard**.

defendant n **accused**, respondent, suspect, corespondent Opposite: accuser

defender n 1 **protector**, guard, warden, guardian, escort Opposite: attacker 2 **supporter**, champion, advocate, sponsor, upholder Opposite: opponent

defensible adj 1 **defendable**, impregnable, unassailable, invulnerable, secure Opposite: vulnerable 2 **justifiable**, valid, cast-iron, secure, rock-solid Opposite: indefensible

defensibly adv **excusably**, justifiably, explicably, forgivably, understandably Opposite: unjustifiably

defensive adj 1 **self-justifying**, self-protective, apologetic, touchy, distrustful Opposite: aggressive 2 **protective**, protecting, defending, shielding, fortified

defer v 1 **put off**, reschedule, put back, postpone, delay Opposite: bring forward 2 **bow to**, submit, be deferential, accede, comply

deference n **respect**, esteem, regard, reverence, admiration Opposite: disrespect

deferential adj **respectful**, admiring, reverent, polite, obsequious Opposite: disrespectful

deferment n **adjournment**, postponement, delay, stay, deferral

deferral n **postponement**, adjournment, delay, stay, deferment

defiance n **insubordination**, disobedience, insolence, rebelliousness, boldness Opposite: compliance

defiant adj **disobedient**, insolent, insubordinate, rebellious, bold Opposite: compliant

deficiency n 1 **lack**, shortage, absence, deficit, dearth Opposite: excess 2 **inadequacy**, defect, flaw, fault, imperfection. See COMPARE AND CONTRAST at **lack**.

deficient adj 1 **lacking**, poor, underprovided, undersupplied, short Opposite: abundant 2 **inadequate**, flawed, faulty, unsatisfactory, defective Opposite: perfect

deficiently adv **inadequately**, defectively, faultily, incorrectly, wrongly Opposite: perfectly

deficit n **shortfall**, shortage, arrears, discrepancy, debit Opposite: surplus. See COMPARE AND CONTRAST at **lack**.

defile v 1 (fml) **corrupt**, taint, besmirch, sully, spoil Opposite: purify 2 (fml) **dishonour**, desecrate, sully, violate, debase Opposite: respect ■ n **pass**, valley, gorge, gap

defiled (fml) adj 1 **corrupted**, tainted, besmirched, sullied, tarnished Opposite: untarnished 2 **dishonoured**, desecrated, sullied, violated, debased Opposite: respected

define v 1 **describe**, outline, express, state, explain 2 **characterize**, classify, identify, distinguish, specify 3 **mark out**, outline, delimit, demarcate, mark

defined adj **clear**, distinct, definite, well-defined, sharp Opposite: indistinct

defining moment n **turning point**, landmark, watershed, crossroads, moment of truth

definite adj 1 **exact**, specific, explicit, clear-cut, unambiguous Opposite: vague 2 **obvious**, recognized, significant, unquestionable, unmistakable Opposite: dubious 3 **fixed**, settled, agreed, final, assured Opposite: indefinite 4 **sure**, certain, positive, set on, determined Opposite: uncertain

definitely adv **certainly**, absolutely, positively, unquestionably, without doubt Opposite: possibly

definiteness n **certainty**, assurance, assuredness, conviction, finality Opposite: uncertainty

definition n 1 **meaning**, description, explanation, classification, characterization 2 **clarity**, sharpness, distinctness, focus, clearness Opposite: haziness

definitive adj 1 **conclusive**, final, decisive, ultimate, absolute Opposite: tentative 2 **authoritative**, conclusive, perfect, best, classic

deflate v 1 **let the air out**, go down, let down, collapse, shrink Opposite: inflate 2 **belittle**, disappoint, flatten, squash, quash Opposite: boost 3 **devalue**, depress, decrease, reduce, lower

deflated adj 1 **subdued**, humiliated, flattened, humbled, dispirited Opposite: exhilarated 2 **emptied**, flattened, shrunk, collapsed, let down Opposite: inflated

deflation n **depression**, devaluation, depreciation, reduction, decrease Opposite: inflation

deflect v 1 **bounce**, glance, ricochet, rebound, bend 2 **turn aside**, ward off, repel, redirect, sidetrack Opposite: attract

deflection n **refraction**, ricochet, rebound, glance, bend

deforest v **log**, denude, strip, clear-cut, desolate

deform v **distort**, bend, warp, buckle, bow

deformation n **distortion**, twist, buckle, bend, warp

deformed adj 1 **misshapen**, distorted, bent, warped, malformed 2 **abnormal**, corrupted, perverted, ruined, damaged

deformity n **disfigurement**, malformation, distortion, abnormality, misshapenness

defraud v **deceive**, swindle, cheat, trick, take advantage of

defray v **pay**, cover, meet, contribute, finance

defrock v **unfrock**, excommunicate, disqualify, drum out, expel

defrost v melt, thaw, thaw out, de-ice, unfreeze *Opposite*: freeze

deft adj skilful, adroit, neat, nimble, dexterous *Opposite*: clumsy

deftness n skill, dexterity, precision, handiness, swiftness *Opposite*: clumsiness

defunct adj 1 obsolete, invalid, redundant, outdated, out-of-date *Opposite*: current 2 dead, expired, extinct, gone (infml), deceased (fml) *Opposite*: alive. See COMPARE AND CONTRAST at dead.

defuse v resolve, calm, soothe, smooth out, neutralize *Opposite*: aggravate

defy v challenge, confront, disobey, rebel, resist *Opposite*: obey

degeneracy n depravity, wickedness, corruption, dissoluteness, decadence *Opposite*: morality

degenerate v deteriorate, collapse, relapse, worsen, reduce *Opposite*: improve ■ adj debased, decadent, immoral, debauched, corrupt *Opposite*: moral

degeneration n deterioration, collapse, disintegration, falling apart, worsening *Opposite*: regeneration

degenerative adj wasting, worsening, deteriorating, progressive

degradation n 1 humiliation, disgrace, shame, mortification, misery 2 squalor, filth, dilapidation, deprivation, poverty

degrade v 1 humiliate, shame, disgrace, mortify, demean *Opposite*: exalt (fml) 2 damage, destroy, reduce, cut down, worsen *Opposite*: upgrade 3 decay, decompose, disintegrate, break down, rot

degrading adj humiliating, debasing, demeaning, undignified, corrupting *Opposite*: ennobling

degree n 1 extent, quantity, intensity, magnitude, level 2 grade, gradation, mark, notch, step

dehumanize v desensitize, brutalize, degrade, debase *Opposite*: humanize

dehydrate v dry out, dry up, become dry, desiccate, parch

dehydrated adj dry, dried out, arid, parched, desiccated. See COMPARE AND CONTRAST at dry.

dehydration n dryness, drying out, drying up, desiccation, thirst

de-ice v unfreeze, melt, thaw *Opposite*: ice up

deification n elevation, veneration, adoration, beatification, exaltation (fml)

deify v idolize, worship, glorify, adore, venerate

deign v condescend, lower yourself, stoop, consent, agree

deity n divinity, god, goddess, godhead, divine being

dejected adj sad, disappointed, unhappy, miserable, depressed *Opposite*: cheerful

dejection n sadness, unhappiness, misery, gloom, depression *Opposite*: cheerfulness

dekko (infml) n look, glance, peek, shufti (infml), gander (infml)

delay v 1 postpone, put off, suspend, adjourn, defer *Opposite*: bring forward 2 procrastinate, hesitate, linger, dawdle, pause *Opposite*: hurry up 3 slow down, slow up, hold up, set back, obstruct *Opposite*: speed up ■ n 1 postponement, interruption, stay, suspension, adjournment 2 interval, wait, pause, break, lull

delayed adj late, behind, behind schedule, overdue, tardy *Opposite*: early

delectable adj 1 delicious, tasty, mouthwatering, appetizing, luscious *Opposite*: tasteless 2 delightful, charming, adorable, appealing, heavenly *Opposite*: unappealing

delectation (fml) n enjoyment, delight, pleasure, appreciation, entertainment

delegate n representative, agent, envoy, ambassador, deputy ■ v 1 hand over, farm out, pass on, give, assign *Opposite*: retain 2 designate, assign, appoint, allocate, deputize

delegation n 1 commission, deputation, mission, lobby 2 allocation, assignment, handing over, giving out, passing on *Opposite*: retention

delete v erase, remove, strike out, cross out, obliterate *Opposite*: insert

deleterious adj damaging, harmful, injurious, destructive, adverse *Opposite*: beneficial

deletion n removal, obliteration, erasure, loss, omission *Opposite*: addition

deliberate adj 1 intentional, purposeful, premeditated, conscious, calculated *Opposite*: accidental 2 careful, thoughtful, slow, cautious, unhurried *Opposite*: hasty ■ v think, reflect, consider, mull over, weigh up

deliberation n 1 (fml) reflection, thought, consideration, care, forethought *Opposite*: impulsiveness 2 discussion, debate, negotiation, planning, pondering

deliberative (fml) adj considered, premeditated, planned, calculated, thought through *Opposite*: casual

delicacy n 1 titbit, treat, luxury, dainty, fancy 2 sensitivity, tact, diplomacy, consideration, care *Opposite*: insensitivity 3 refinement, fastidiousness, subtlety, elegance, fineness *Opposite*: vulgarity 4 gracefulness, attractiveness, elegance, charm, grace *Opposite*: awkwardness 5 fragility, flimsiness, slenderness, frailty, weakness *Opposite*: sturdiness 6 precision, skill, care, deftness, adroitness *Opposite*: inaccuracy

delicate adj 1 fragile, frail, weak, slight, flimsy *Opposite*: robust 2 subtle, faint, slight, gentle, mild *Opposite*: overpowering 3 fine, precise, detailed, accurate, skilled *Opposite*: rough 4 refined, graceful, elegant, dainty, nice *Opposite*: inelegant 5 difficult, tricky, complicated, sensitive, awkward *Opposite*: straightforward **6 sensitive**, refined, thoughtful, considerate, sympathetic *Opposite*: tactless. *See* COMPARE AND CONTRAST *at* **fragile**.

delicateness *n* **fragility**, fragileness, frailty, vulnerability, feebleness *Opposite*: robustness

delicious *adj* **1 tasty**, appetizing, luscious, delectable, mouthwatering *Opposite*: tasteless **2 delightful**, lovely, wonderful, pleasant, enjoyable *Opposite*: unpleasant

deliciousness *n* **1 delectableness**, lusciousness, sweetness, tastiness, scrumptiousness *(infml) Opposite*: tastelessness **2 delightfulness**, charm, sweetness, attractiveness, pleasantness *Opposite*: unpleasantness

delight *n* **joy**, enjoyment, pleasure, happiness, glee *Opposite*: displeasure ■ *v* **1 please**, charm, amuse, thrill, gratify *Opposite*: disappoint **2 take pleasure in**, appreciate, revel in, relish, enjoy *Opposite*: dislike

delighted *adj* **pleased**, happy, charmed, enchanted, thrilled *Opposite*: unhappy

delightful *adj* **pleasant**, charming, lovely, wonderful, enjoyable *Opposite*: unpleasant

delimit *(fml) v* **set the limits of**, demarcate, define, restrict, mark out

delimitation *(fml) n* **demarcation**, definition, marking out, limitation, restriction

delineate *v* **1** *(fml)* **define**, describe, explain, portray, present **2 outline**, delimit, mark out, demarcate, define

delineation *n* **1** *(fml)* **description**, definition, explanation, setting down **2 demarcation**, definition, allocation, marking out, outlining

delinquency *n* **1 criminal behaviour**, crime, felony, lawbreaking, misbehaviour *Opposite*: uprightness **2** *(fml)* **negligence**, carelessness, recklessness, failure, irresponsibility *Opposite*: carefulness

delinquent *n* **criminal**, guilty party, felon, lawbreaker, wrongdoer ■ *adj* **1 criminal**, aberrant, antisocial, offending, felonious *Opposite*: law-abiding **2** *(fml)* **negligent**, careless, reckless, irresponsible, neglectful *Opposite*: dutiful

delirious *adj* **1 feverish**, fevered, hot, hallucinating, rambling *Opposite*: rational **2 elated**, ecstatic, transported, in seventh heaven, beside yourself *Opposite*: dejected

delirium *n* **1 fever**, hallucination, restlessness, confusion, frenzy *Opposite*: clarity **2 ecstasy**, elation, fervour, euphoria, excitement *Opposite*: dejection

deliver *v* **1 carry**, bring, transport, distribute, send *Opposite*: take away **2 produce**, provide, supply, dispense, serve **3** *(literary)* **set free**, release, rescue, save, liberate *Opposite*: capture **4 hand over**, give up, surrender, transfer, relinquish *Opposite*: keep

deliverance *(fml) n* **rescue**, release, liberation, relief, escape *Opposite*: capture

delivery *n* **1 distribution**, transfer, transport, sending, conveyance **2 manner of speaking**, presentation, approach, manner, technique **3 rescue**, release, liberation, relief, escape *Opposite*: capture

delta *n* **estuary**, outlet, mouth, channel

delude *v* **deceive**, take in, cheat, mislead, con

deluded *adj* **mistaken**, deceived, misled, duped, conned

deluge *n* **1 torrent**, flood, downpour, cloudburst, rainstorm **2 upsurge**, spate, flood, cascade, avalanche *Opposite*: trickle ■ *v* **1 overwhelm**, overload, overrun, swamp, bury **2 inundate**, flood, swamp, drown, soak *Opposite*: dry up

delusion *n* **1 illusion**, hallucination, vision, mirage, figment of the imagination *Opposite*: reality **2 misunderstanding**, misapprehension, misbelief, false impression, misconception

delusive *adj* **deceptive**, chimerical, misleading, specious, illusory *Opposite*: genuine

deluxe *adj* **sumptuous**, luxurious, luxury, exclusive, select *Opposite*: cheap

delve *v* **1 look into**, investigate, research, probe, explore **2** *(archaic)* **dig**, burrow, tunnel, scrabble, scratch ■ *n* **rummage**, hunt, dig, search, dive

demagogic *adj* **rabble-rousing**, inflammatory, manipulative, declamatory, agitating

demagogical *see* **demagogic**

demagogue *n* **firebrand**, agitator, manipulator, crowd pleaser, haranguer

demand *n* **1 request**, call, claim, petition, mandate *Opposite*: response **2 requirement**, need, pressure, exigency, claim ■ *v* **1 insist**, command, order, require, stipulate *Opposite*: request **2 ask**, inquire, question, query, want *Opposite*: answer **3 require**, need, want, call for, necessitate

demanding *adj* **1 difficult**, hard, challenging, tough, severe *Opposite*: easy **2 insistent**, self-centred, persistent, dissatisfied, discontented *Opposite*: satisfied

demarcate *v* **1 define**, mark out, delineate, draw, fix **2 separate**, distinguish, differentiate, isolate, discriminate *Opposite*: unite

demarcation *n* **separation**, differentiation, distinction, discrimination, segregation

demean *v* **degrade**, debase, humiliate, disgrace, humble *Opposite*: uplift

demeanour *n* **manner**, conduct, behaviour, character, deportment

demean yourself *v* **lower yourself**, swallow your pride, stoop low, go down on your knees, abase yourself *(literary)*

demented *(infml) adj* **irrational**, unreasonable, wild, frenzied, frantic *Opposite*: rational

demerger n **separation**, split, break, breakup, divergence *Opposite*: merger

demerit n **disadvantage**, failing, shortcoming, drawback, fault *Opposite*: merit

demijohn n **bottle**, flagon, magnum, jeroboam, rehoboam

demise *(fml)* n 1 **death**, passing, departure, decease *(fml)*, expiry *(fml or literary) Opposite*: birth 2 **end**, termination, finish, failure, ruin *Opposite*: creation

demo n 1 *(infml)* **sample**, showpiece, example, specimen, demonstrator 2 *(infml)* **demonstration**, presentation, display, show, exhibition 3 **protest**, demonstration, protest march, march, protest rally

demob *(infml)* v **demobilize**, discharge, dismiss, disband, release *Opposite*: mobilize ■ n **demobilization**, disbandment, discharge, release, dismissal

demobilization n **discharge**, release, disbandment, dismissal, retirement *Opposite*: mobilization

demobilize v **discharge**, dismiss, disband, release, retire *Opposite*: mobilize

democracy n 1 **social equality**, equality, egalitarianism, classlessness, consensus *Opposite*: inequality 2 **democratic system**, democratic state, democratic organization, representative form of government, republic *Opposite*: dictatorship

democrat n **egalitarian**, populist, republican, social democrat, constitutionalist *Opposite*: totalitarian

democratic adj 1 **self-governing**, self-ruled, independent, autonomous, elected *Opposite*: autocratic 2 **egalitarian**, free, classless, equal, open *Opposite*: repressive

demolish v 1 **knock down**, tear down, pull down, bulldoze, blow up *Opposite*: build 2 **destroy**, ruin, flatten, smash, wreck *Opposite*: preserve 3 *(infml)* **beat**, annihilate, defeat, rout, thrash 4 *(infml)* **disprove**, tear to pieces, dismantle, undermine, take apart *(infml) Opposite*: support 5 *(infml)* **devour**, wolf, gobble, eat, consume *Opposite*: nibble

demolition n **destruction**, pulling down, knocking down, annihilation, devastation *Opposite*: construction

demon n 1 **fiend**, evil spirit, devil, monster *Opposite*: angel 2 **fear**, anxiety, terror, torment, trouble 3 *(infml)* **expert**, genius, fiend, whiz *(infml)*, wizard *(infml)*

demonstrable adj 1 **obvious**, palpable, patent, evident, noticeable *Opposite*: imperceptible 2 **provable**, verifiable, self-evident, confirmable, comprehensible *Opposite*: doubtful

demonstrate v 1 **explain**, expound, display, operate, instruct 2 **prove**, validate, establish, reveal, make evident 3 **protest**, march, rally, lobby, support

demonstration n 1 **presentation**, display, illustration, explanation, exposition 2 **proof**, evidence, validation, establishment, revelation

demonstrative adj **affectionate**, warm, loving, friendly, emotional *Opposite*: reserved

demonstrator n 1 **protester**, supporter, activist, campaigner, lobbyist 2 **presenter**, instructor, tutor, teacher, trainer

demoralization n **discouragement**, deflation, undermining, depression, dejection *Opposite*: encouragement

demoralize v **dishearten**, undermine, dispirit, deflate, discourage *Opposite*: encourage

demoralized adj **disheartened**, dispirited, downhearted, discouraged, deflated *Opposite*: optimistic

demoralizing adj **disheartening**, discouraging, depressing, dispiriting, crushing *Opposite*: encouraging

demote v **downgrade**, relegate, move down, devalue, reduce *Opposite*: promote

demotion n **relegation**, downgrading, devaluation, reduction, lowering *Opposite*: promotion

demotivate v **discourage**, demoralize, dishearten, dispirit, deter *Opposite*: motivate

demotivation n **demoralization**, discouragement, disheartenment, deterrence, dissuasion *Opposite*: motivation

demur v **object**, protest, raise objections, baulk, express doubts *Opposite*: agree. *See* COMPARE AND CONTRAST *at* **object**.

demure adj 1 **modest**, sedate, decorous, reserved, shy *Opposite*: bold 2 **prim**, coy, prudish, strait-laced *Opposite*: pert

demystification n **clarification**, explanation, interpretation, revelation, decipherment *Opposite*: obfuscation

demystify v **clarify**, explain, elucidate, interpret, reveal *Opposite*: obscure

denial n 1 **disavowal** *(fml)*, refutation, rejection, rebuttal, contradiction *Opposite*: confirmation 2 **refusal**, deprivation, withholding, begrudging, turning down

denigrate v 1 **defame**, slander, libel, abuse, stigmatize *Opposite*: praise 2 **disparage**, vilify, pour scorn on, degrade, belittle *Opposite*: glorify

denigration n 1 **defamation**, slander, libel, abuse, stigmatization *Opposite*: commendation 2 **disparagement**, vilification, scorn, depreciation, belittling *Opposite*: glorification

denizen n **inhabitant**, resident, citizen, occupant, native

denotation n **meaning**, import, sense, signification, significance

denote v 1 **mean**, signify, stand for, represent, symbolize 2 **refer to**, allude to, imply, convey, express

denouement n **ending**, end, finale, conclusion, termination *Opposite*: opening

denounce v 1 **criticize**, censure, deplore, deprecate, condemn *Opposite*: support 2 **accuse**, point the finger at, blame, charge, inform. *See* COMPARE AND CONTRAST *at* disapprove.

dense adj 1 **crowded**, packed, packed in, full, jam-packed *(infml)* 2 **thick**, solid, impenetrable, compressed, condensed 3 **complicated**, complex, difficult, obscure, deep

denseness n 1 **crowdedness**, crowding, tightness, impenetrability, closeness 2 **thickness**, opacity, solidity, impenetrability, darkness 3 **complexity**, difficulty, complication, obscurity, opacity

density n **thickness**, compactness, mass, concentration, bulk

dent v 1 **knock**, hit, bump, bang, indent 2 **damage**, hurt, undermine, diminish, lessen ■ n 1 **hollow**, indentation, depression, dimple, cavity *Opposite*: lump 2 *(infml)* **blow**, knock, shock, setback, reversal *Opposite*: boost 3 *(infml)* **reduction**, hole, cut, dip, decrease

denude v **strip**, uncover, bare, remove, shed *Opposite*: cover

denunciate *(fml)* v **condemn**, criticize, accuse, censure, reprove *Opposite*: commend

denunciation n **condemnation**, criticism, accusation, censure, reproof *Opposite*: commendation

deny v 1 **repudiate**, refute, reject, contradict, disagree *Opposite*: agree 2 **refuse**, disallow, block, forbid, prevent *Opposite*: permit 3 **forgo**, renounce, disavow, reject, disown

deodorant n **roll-on**, deodorizer, spray

deodorize v **freshen**, scent, refresh, perfume, aromatize

depart v 1 **start out**, set out, move off, set off, leave *Opposite*: return 2 **deviate**, diverge, differ, vary, change *Opposite*: stick to 3 **pull out**, leave, go away, disappear, be off *Opposite*: arrive 4 *(fml)* **die**, pass on, pass away, succumb, expire *(fml)*

departed *(fml or literary)* adj **dead**, late, defunct, lamented *Opposite*: living. *See* COMPARE AND CONTRAST *at* dead.

departing n **leaving**, going away, withdrawal, departure, retreat *Opposite*: arriving

department n 1 **subdivision**, division, branch, sector, section 2 *(infml)* **responsibility**, area, speciality, realm, sphere

departure n 1 **leaving**, going away, parting, exit, exodus *Opposite*: arrival 2 **change**, deviation, divergence, digression, variation 3 **venture**, project, enterprise, endeavour, undertaking

depend v **be contingent**, hinge on, rest on, be subject to, hang on

dependability n **reliability**, steadiness, trustworthiness, loyalty, fidelity *Opposite*: unreliability

dependable adj **reliable**, trustworthy, loyal, faithful, steady *Opposite*: unreliable

dependence n 1 **reliance**, trust, confidence, belief, hope *Opposite*: independence 2 **need**, requirement, necessity, want 3 **addiction**, dependency, reliance, need, craving

dependency n 1 **territory**, colony, dependent state, dependent territory, adjunct 2 **dependence**, need, reliance, addiction, habit

dependent adj 1 **needy**, reliant, helpless, supported *Opposite*: independent 2 **reliant on**, in need of, at the mercy of, hooked on *(slang)* 3 **contingent**, conditional, determined, subject, related *Opposite*: independent

depend on v 1 **need**, require, rely on, be dependent on, lean on 2 **rely on**, count on, trust, be sure of, be certain of *Opposite*: mistrust

depict v **portray**, show, represent, describe, illustrate

depiction n **representation**, portrayal, description, illustration, delineation

deplete v **use up**, drain, exhaust, diminish, lessen *Opposite*: increase

depletion n **reduction**, exhaustion, diminution, lessening, running down *Opposite*: restoration

deplorable adj 1 **disgraceful**, terrible, awful, appalling, unacceptable *Opposite*: praiseworthy 2 **pitiful**, lamentable, execrable, woeful, appalling

deplore v 1 **censure**, condemn, criticize, deprecate, disapprove *Opposite*: praise 2 **lament**, bemoan, regret, be sorry, rue. *See* COMPARE AND CONTRAST *at* disapprove.

deploy v 1 **position**, arrange, set up, set out, install 2 **use**, employ, implement, utilize, adopt

deployment n 1 **placement**, disposition, positioning, distribution, arrangement 2 **utilization**, employment, implementation

depoliticize v **humanize**, personalize, socialize, neutralize *Opposite*: politicize

depopulate v **clear**, relocate, remove, clear out, evacuate *Opposite*: populate

depopulation n **clearance**, relocation, removal, evacuation, abandonment *Opposite*: settlement

deport v **expel**, extradite, banish, exile, transport

deportation n **exile**, banishment, extradition, repatriation, expulsion

deportee n **exile**, outcast, displaced person, refugee, evacuee

deportment n **manner**, gait, attitude, posture, bearing

depose v **overthrow**, oust, topple, throw out, remove *Opposite*: install

deposit v 1 **put**, put down, set down, leave, place *Opposite*: remove 2 **accumulate**, lay down, leave behind, build up, pile up 3 **pay in**, credit, put in, bank, consign *Opposite*: withdraw ■ n 1 **credit**, payment, sum *Oppo-*

site: withdrawal **2 security**, guarantee, pledge, surety **3 sediment**, residue, accretion, layer, accumulation

deposition *n* **1 statement**, testimony, admission, sworn testimony, confession **2 removal**, overthrow, unseating, ousting, dethronement **3 accumulation**, accretion, sedimentation, silting, buildup

depositor *n* **saver**, investor, account holder, creditor

depot *n* **yard**, maintenance yard, goods yard, garage, workshop

deprave *v* **lead astray**, corrupt, degrade, ruin, debase

depraved *adj* **debauched**, immoral, corrupt, evil, wicked *Opposite*: righteous

depravity *n* **debauchery**, immorality, corruption, wickedness, evil *Opposite*: righteousness

deprecate *v* **condemn**, censure, denigrate, denounce, deplore *Opposite*: approve

deprecating *adj* **condemnatory**, disapproving, derogatory, deprecatory, pejorative *(fml)* *Opposite*: approving

deprecation *n* **disapproval**, denigration, condemnation, censure, criticism *Opposite*: praise

deprecatory *adj* **1 disapproving**, derogatory, critical, denigrating, condemnatory *Opposite*: approving **2 apologetic**, sorry, repentant, contrite, remorseful *Opposite*: unrepentant

depreciate *v* **1 lessen**, devalue, deflate, decline, downgrade *Opposite*: appreciate **2 denigrate**, belittle, disparage, run down, criticize *Opposite*: commend

depreciation *n* **devaluation**, reduction, decrease, decline, downgrading *Opposite*: rise

depreciatory *adj* **belittling**, deprecatory, critical, denigrating, derogatory *Opposite*: complimentary

depredation *n* **plunder**, destruction, pillage, despoliation, attack

depress *v* **1 sadden**, dishearten, discourage, dispirit, demoralize *Opposite*: cheer up **2 press down**, push down, press, push, lower *Opposite*: release

depressant *n* **tranquillizer**, sedative, drug, narcotic, downer *(slang)* ■ *adj* **sedative**, tranquillizing, sedating, calming, narcotic

depressed *adj* **1 unhappy**, miserable, dejected, low, disheartened *Opposite*: happy **2 rundown**, deprived, poor, underprivileged, neglected *Opposite*: affluent

depressing *adj* **sad**, miserable, disheartening, discouraging, gloomy *Opposite*: cheering

depression *n* **1 downheartedness**, unhappiness, despair, sadness, gloominess *Opposite*: happiness **2 slump**, recession, decline, downturn, slide *Opposite*: boom **3 hollow**, dip, dent, impression, dimple *Opposite*: hump

depressive *adj* **gloomy**, depressing, cheerless, miserable, bleak *Opposite*: uplifting

deprivation *n* **lack**, deficiency, scarcity, denial, withdrawal *Opposite*: plenty

deprive *v* **divest**, rob, deny, take away, remove *Opposite*: provide

deprived *adj* **disadvantaged**, underprivileged, poor, destitute, depressed *Opposite*: privileged

depth *n* **1 deepness**, profundity, distance **2 intensity**, strength, power, vigour, concentration *Opposite*: weakness **3 complexity**, profundity, seriousness, gravity, wisdom *Opposite*: flippancy

deputation *n* **delegation**, commission, mission, lobby group

depute *v* **delegate**, hand over, relinquish, allot, transfer

deputize *v* **stand in**, represent, fill in, act, replace

deputy *n* **second-in-command**, assistant, agent, delegate, representative. *See* COMPARE AND CONTRAST *at* **assistant**.

derail *v* **disrupt**, upset, wreck, ruin, spoil

derange *v* **1 distress**, unsettle, upset, unhinge, shake **2 disorganize**, disrupt, disturb, dislocate, upset

derangement *n* **1 imbalance**, irrationality, madness, insanity, instability *Opposite*: sanity **2 disorder**, confusion, muddle, disorganization, disturbance *Opposite*: order

derby *n* **contest**, race, match, clash, sporting event

deregulate *v* **free**, relax, liberalize, decontrol, derestrict *Opposite*: regulate

derelict *adj* **dilapidated**, in ruins, rundown, ruined, neglected

dereliction *n* **1 neglect**, negligence, disregard, recklessness, carelessness *Opposite*: assiduousness **2 abandonment**, desertion, neglect, dilapidation, default

deride *v* **ridicule**, scoff, disparage, mock, scorn *Opposite*: admire. *See* COMPARE AND CONTRAST *at* **ridicule**.

derision *n* **disparagement**, scorn, disdain, mockery, ridicule *Opposite*: admiration

derisive *adj* **mocking**, scathing, sarcastic, irreverent, contemptuous *Opposite*: admiring

derisory *adj* **pitiful**, laughable, insulting, ridiculous, contemptible *Opposite*: generous

derivation *n* **origin**, root, source, beginning, seed. *See* COMPARE AND CONTRAST *at* **origin**.

derivative *adj* **unoriginal**, imitative, plagiaristic, copied, derived *Opposite*: original ■ *n* **offshoot**, by-product, result, end product, spin-off

derive *v* **1 get**, gain, obtain, draw, receive **2 originate**, stem, spring, arise, descend

derogatory *adj* **disparaging**, critical, insulting, offensive, depreciating *Opposite*: complimentary

derrick *n* **1 crane**, hoist, winch, elevator, lift **2 wellhead**, rig, gantry, oil platform, frame

desalinate *v* **purify**, desalt, detoxify, distil, refine

desalination *n* **purification**, detoxification, distillation, salt removal

descale *v* **clean out**, scrape, scour, flush, clean

descant *n* **harmony**, part, line, tune, air

descend *v* **1 go down**, move down, come down, slide down, fall down *Opposite*: ascend **2 slope**, decline, fall away, go downhill, drop away *Opposite*: ascend **3 derive**, originate, come from, stem, spring **4 lower yourself**, stoop, sink, resort, fall *Opposite*: rise **5 arrive**, drop in, appear, turn up, show up *Opposite*: leave **6 fall**, fall on, affect, come over, come upon

descendant *n* **successor**, offspring, progeny, child, heir *Opposite*: ancestor

descendent *adj* **descending**, down, downward, plunging, sinking *Opposite*: ascendant

descent *n* **1 fall**, drop, dive, tumble, plunge *Opposite*: ascent **2 decline**, deterioration, depreciation, degeneration, drop *Opposite*: improvement **3 ancestry**, parentage, lineage, origin, succession

describe *v* **1 explain**, portray, depict, illustrate, express **2 label**, refer to, define, designate, pronounce

description *n* **1 account**, report, explanation, portrayal, picture **2 type**, sort, kind, class, variety

descriptive *adj* **1 explanatory**, illustrative, narrative, informative, factual *Opposite*: imaginative **2 evocative**, expressive, vivid, graphic, eloquent

desecrate *v* **defile**, vandalize, insult, violate, outrage *Opposite*: consecrate

desecration *n* **violation**, defilement, vandalism, sacrilege, despoliation *Opposite*: consecration

deseed *v* **pit**, stone, core

desegregate *v* **integrate**, unify, unite, bring together, merge *Opposite*: segregate

desegregation *n* **integration**, unification, reunion, reconciliation, merging *Opposite*: segregation

deselect *v* **reject**, abandon, discard, cast off, remove *Opposite*: select

desensitize *v* **numb**, deaden, dull, soothe, pacify *Opposite*: sensitize

desert *n* **1 wasteland**, wilderness, barren region, arid region, waste **2 reward**, return, recompense, wages, just reward ■ *v* **1 abandon**, leave high and dry, leave, forsake, discard *Opposite*: support **2 abscond**, leave, go missing, go AWOL, run away *Opposite*: stay

deserted *adj* **1 empty**, isolated, uninhabited, desolate, solitary *Opposite*: inhabited **2 abandoned**, discarded, forsaken, cast off, ditched *(infml)*

deserter *n* **absconder**, runaway, fugitive, defector, traitor

desertion *n* **absconding**, abandonment, running away, disappearance, departure

deserve *v* **merit**, be worthy, earn, warrant, justify

deservedly *adv* **justly**, rightly, justifiably, reasonably, properly *Opposite*: unreasonably

deserving *adj* **worthy**, commendable, admirable, praiseworthy, justified *Opposite*: unworthy

desiccate *v* **dry up**, wither, dry out, dehydrate, parch

desiccated *adj* **dry**, dried, dried out, shrivelled, dehydrated *Opposite*: moist. *See* COMPARE AND CONTRAST *at* **dry**.

desiccation *n* **dryness**, dehydration, withering, shrivelling, drying

design *v* **1 create**, invent, conceive, originate, fabricate **2 plan**, intend, aim, devise, propose ■ *n* **1 project**, scheme, enterprise, plan, strategy **2 drawing**, blueprint, plan, sketch, outline **3 pattern**, motif, figure, shape, device **4 intention**, purpose, scheme, plan, object *Opposite*: serendipity

designate *v* **1 call**, label, title, entitle, term **2 assign**, select, choose, delegate, allocate **3 specify**, point out, indicate, choose, select ■ *adj* **in waiting**, elect, to be

designation *n* **title**, name, description, term, label

designedly *adv* **intentionally**, on purpose, purposely, deliberately, purposefully *Opposite*: accidentally

designer *n* **creator**, inventor, originator, engineer, stylist ■ *adj* **fashionable**, stylish, chic, expensive, exclusive *Opposite*: mass-produced

designing *adj* **scheming**, conniving, deceitful, wily, manipulative *Opposite*: ingenuous

desirability *n* **1 appeal**, attractiveness, attraction, allure, prestige **2 appropriateness**, aptness, rightness, suitability, advantage

desirable *adj* **1 wanted**, needed, necessary, required, looked-for *Opposite*: undesirable **2 attractive**, pleasing, enviable, pleasant, popular *Opposite*: undesirable

desire *v* **1 want**, wish for, long for, covet, crave **2** *(fml)* **request**, ask, require, appeal, entreat ■ *n* **wish**, want, longing, craving, yearning. *See* COMPARE AND CONTRAST *at* **want**.

desired *adj* **wanted**, anticipated, sought after, looked-for, favourite *Opposite*: unwanted

desirous *(fml) adj* **eager**, hopeful, wishing for, longing for, hoping for

desist *v* **cease**, stop, discontinue, give up, end *Opposite*: continue

desolate adj 1 **deserted**, isolated, bleak, abandoned, forsaken Opposite: populous 2 **unhappy**, forlorn, miserable, depressed, inconsolable Opposite: happy 3 **depressing**, gloomy, dismal, austere, forbidding Opposite: cheerful

desolation n 1 **barrenness**, isolation, bleakness, emptiness, dereliction 2 **unhappiness**, misery, despair, anguish, sadness Opposite: happiness

despair n **misery**, desolation, hopelessness, anguish, gloom Opposite: joy ■ v **lose hope**, give up hope, have no hope, see no light at the end of the tunnel, lose heart Opposite: hope

despairing adj **hopeless**, desolate, miserable, pained, despondent Opposite: hopeful

desperado n **criminal**, outlaw, gangster, bandit, villain

desperate adj 1 **frantic**, anxious, worried, distressed, distracted Opposite: calm 2 **reckless**, careless, rash, impulsive, dangerous Opposite: safe 3 **serious**, grave, extreme, critical, threatening Opposite: harmless 4 **eager**, dying, raring, bursting, impatient Opposite: loath 5 **hopeless**, wretched, irredeemable, deplorable, dreadful Opposite: hopeful

desperately adv 1 **frantically**, anxiously, frenziedly, hastily, distractedly Opposite: calmly 2 **very much**, badly, to a great extent, dreadfully, urgently Opposite: hardly

desperation n 1 **anxiety**, worry, fear, distraction, nervousness Opposite: calmness 2 **hopelessness**, despair, despondency, misery, anguish Opposite: hopefulness

despicable adj **appalling**, dreadful, contemptible, wicked, shameful Opposite: admirable

despise v **loathe**, scorn, look down on, hate, spurn Opposite: admire

despised adj **hated**, reviled, loathed, shunned, scorned Opposite: beloved

despite prep **in spite of**, regardless of, in the face of, even with, notwithstanding (fml) Opposite: because of

despoil v **rob**, plunder, sack, pillage, loot

despoilment n **despoliation**, vandalism, defacement, destruction, desecration

despoliation n **plundering**, pillage, sack, theft, robbery

despondency n **hopelessness**, sadness, misery, dejection, depression Opposite: cheerfulness

despondent adj **hopeless**, low, dejected, despairing, downhearted Opposite: cheerful

despot n **dictator**, tyrant, autocrat, oppressor, authoritarian

despotic adj **tyrannical**, dictatorial, autocratic, authoritarian, repressive Opposite: democratic

despotism n **tyranny**, dictatorship, absolutism, autocracy, authoritarianism Opposite: democracy

dessert n **sweet**, pudding, pud,(infml), afters (infml)

WORD BANK

❑ **types of dessert** baklava, banoffee pie, blancmange, bombe, cake, cassata, clafoutis, cobbler, crème brûlée, crème caramel, crumble, custard, flan, fruit salad, granita, ice cream, jelly, junket, meringue, mousse, pannacotta, pavlova, peach Melba, pie, profiteroles, pudding, sorbet, soufflé, sundae, syllabub, tart, tiramisu, zabaglione

---

destabilization n **weakening**, subversion, undermining, disruption, dislocation

destabilize v **undermine**, subvert, weaken, threaten, disrupt Opposite: strengthen

destination n 1 **journey's end**, terminus, last stop, end point, end of the road Opposite: starting point 2 **end**, purpose, target, aim, goal

destined adj **intended**, meant, fated, designed, certain

destiny n 1 **fate**, fortune, lot, luck, providence 2 **purpose**, vocation, intention, call, calling

destitute adj **poor**, penniless, impoverished, insolvent, needy Opposite: solvent

destitution n **poverty**, penury, hardship, need, insolvency Opposite: prosperity

destroy v 1 **obliterate**, annihilate, demolish, devastate, tear down Opposite: build 2 **ruin**, damage, break, break up, spoil Opposite: conserve 3 **abolish**, put an end to, get rid of, end, extinguish Opposite: sustain 4 **defeat**, crush, subdue, demolish, overcome

destroyed adj **demolished**, devastated, ruined, wrecked, smashed Opposite: intact

destroyer n **destructive force**, natural disaster, cause of death, killer, demolisher Opposite: creator

destruction n **obliteration**, annihilation, devastation, demolition, ruin Opposite: construction

destructive adj 1 **damaging**, devastating, harmful, detrimental, injurious 2 **unhelpful**, critical, negative, damaging, disparaging Opposite: constructive

destructiveness n 1 **harmfulness**, power, force, violence, ferocity 2 **criticism**, negativity, harshness, viciousness, hurtfulness Opposite: helpfulness

desultory adj **aimless**, casual, random, unfocused, haphazard Opposite: methodical

detach v **separate**, remove, disengage, disconnect, isolate Opposite: attach

detachable adj **removable**, separable, clip-on, hook-on, attachable Opposite: fixed

detached adj 1 **separate**, disconnected, standing apart, apart, removed Opposite: connected 2 **aloof**, indifferent, unemotional, unbiased, uninvolved Opposite: involved

detachment n 1 **aloofness**, remoteness, indifference, impassiveness, distance Opposite: involvement 2 **objectivity**, disinterest, disinterestedness, impartiality, fairness **3 disconnection**, separation, disengagement, disentanglement, extrication *Opposite*: connection **4 group**, unit, task force, detail, party

detail *n* **1 part**, feature, aspect, point, element **2 group**, unit, task force, detachment, party ■ *v* **1 list**, specify, describe, itemize, particularize **2 assign**, delegate, allocate, conscript, designate

detailed *adj* **full**, thorough, comprehensive, complete, exhaustive *Opposite*: sketchy

details *n* **particulars**, facts, information, minutiae, niceties

detain *v* **1 delay**, hold up, keep, keep back, impede *Opposite*: let go **2 arrest**, hold, keep in custody, capture, confine *Opposite*: release

detained *adj* **in custody**, in detention, under arrest, behind bars, in prison *Opposite*: free

detainee *n* **prisoner**, captive, internee, hostage, convict

detect *v* **notice**, sense, become aware of, perceive, spot

detectable *adj* **obvious**, visible, noticeable, measurable, demonstrable *Opposite*: undetectable

detection *n* **discovery**, uncovering, finding, recognition, exposure *Opposite*: concealment

detective *n* **investigator**, private detective, plain-clothes officer, private eye (*infml*), sleuth (*infml*)

detector *n* **sensor**, indicator, gauge, finder

détente *n* **rapprochement**, agreement, cooperation, compromise, accommodation *Opposite*: hostility

detention *n* **custody**, imprisonment, confinement, arrest, locking up *Opposite*: release

deter *v* **discourage**, put off, daunt, dissuade, prevent *Opposite*: encourage

detergent *n* **cleaner**, cleansing agent, cleanser, shampoo, washing-up liquid

deteriorate *v* **get worse**, worsen, decline, depreciate, go downhill *Opposite*: improve

deteriorating *adj* **worsening**, getting worse, falling, fading, waning *Opposite*: improving

deterioration *n* **worsening**, decline, weakening, drop, descent *Opposite*: improvement

determinant *n* **cause**, determining factor, factor, element, basis

determination *n* **strength of mind**, willpower, resolve, purpose, fortitude *Opposite*: weakness

determine *v* **1 decide**, settle, conclude, resolve, agree **2 find out**, verify, clarify, uncover, establish **3 influence**, affect, shape, mould, form **4 control**, regulate, govern, fix, limit

determined *adj* **strong-minded**, resolute, gritty, single-minded, unwavering *Opposite*: irresolute

determining *adj* **decisive**, causal, defining, influential, shaping *Opposite*: irrelevant

deterrence *n* **discouragement**, dissuasion, pre-emption, prevention, restriction *Opposite*: encouragement

deterrent *adj* **warning**, preventive, restrictive, restraining, limiting *Opposite*: encouraging ■ *n* **restraint**, disincentive, rein, curb, limit *Opposite*: incitement

detest *v* **hate**, loathe, despise, dislike, abhor *Opposite*: love

detestable *adj* **hateful**, despicable, repugnant, vile, revolting *Opposite*: lovable

detestation *n* **hatred**, hate, abhorrence, loathing, dislike *Opposite*: adoration

dethrone *v* **depose**, oust, unseat, overthrow, overwhelm *Opposite*: install

detonate *v* **explode**, blow up, set off, ignite, spark off

detonation *n* **explosion**, blast, ignition, report, bang

detour *n* **deviation**, diversion, roundabout route, alternative route, long way round

detoxication *see* detoxification

detoxification *n* **cleansing**, decontamination, purification, detoxication, reclamation *Opposite*: contamination

detoxify *v* **cleanse**, purify, clear, clean, depollute *Opposite*: contaminate

detract *v* **take away from**, diminish, lessen, reduce, weaken *Opposite*: bolster

detraction *n* **1** (*fml*) **slander**, abuse, disparagement, aspersion, denigration *Opposite*: praise **2 lessening**, reduction, subtraction, taking away, deduction *Opposite*: addition

detractor *n* **critic**, disparager, cynic, heckler, attacker *Opposite*: supporter

detriment *n* **disadvantage**, loss, harm, damage, injury *Opposite*: advantage

detrimental *adj* **harmful**, damaging, disadvantageous, unfavourable, negative *Opposite*: beneficial

detritus *n* **debris**, litter, waste, trash, rubbish

deuce *n* **tie**, draw, level pegging, even-steven (*infml*)

devaluation *n* **deflation**, depreciation, reduction, depression, devaluing *Opposite*: appreciation

devalue *v* **diminish**, lessen, undervalue, bring down, cheapen *Opposite*: overvalue

devastate *v* **1 destroy**, demolish, ravage, wreck, ruin *Opposite*: preserve **2 overwhelm**, overcome, shock, distress, upset *Opposite*: comfort

devastated *adj* **overwhelmed**, overcome, shattered, confounded, shocked *Opposite*: comforted

devastating *adj* **1 destructive**, harmful, damaging, ruinous, injurious **2 overwhelming**, shocking, upsetting, disturbing, distressing *Opposite*: comforting

devastatingly *adv* **terribly**, dreadfully, overwhelmingly, extraordinarily, hugely

devastation *n* **destruction**, damage, ruin, desolation, waste *Opposite*: preservation

develop *v* **1 grow**, mature, progress, advance, change **2 arise**, result, happen, stem, come **3 acquire**, pick up, foster, create, breed **4 expand**, enlarge, extend, increase, widen *Opposite*: contract **5 work out**, flesh out, expound, fill in, explain *Opposite*: outline **6 build on**, exploit, utilize, build **7 improve**, do up, renovate, refurbish, remodel

developed *adj* **technologically advanced**, industrialized, advanced, established, settled *Opposite*: developing

developer *n* **1 designer**, creator, inventor, brains, maker **2 buyer**, property developer, land developer, contractor, speculator

developing *adj* **emerging**, emergent, evolving *Opposite*: developed

development *n* **1 event**, happening, occurrence, change, incident **2 growth**, expansion, progress, advance, change *Opposite*: stasis **3 enhancement**, expansion, advancement, training, education

developmental *adj* **1 developing**, growing, evolving, changing, progressive *Opposite*: static **2 age-related**, age-linked, growth-related, hormonal, child-development

deviance *n* **nonconformity**, unconventionality, eccentricity, unorthodoxy, aberration *Opposite*: conformity

deviant *adj* **different**, divergent, nonstandard, aberrant, irregular *Opposite*: standard

deviate *v* **1 differ**, depart, diverge, stray, digress *Opposite*: conform **2 diverge**, move away, stray, depart, swerve *Opposite*: keep to

deviation *n* **1 difference**, departure, change, divergence, variation *Opposite*: normalization **2 nonconformity**, unconventionality, eccentricity, unorthodoxy, aberration

device *n* **1 machine**, tool, piece of equipment, mechanism, apparatus **2 expedient**, manoeuvre, stratagem, ruse, dodge **3 design**, emblem, logo, badge, crest

devious *adj* **1 deceitful**, tricky, scheming, designing, wily *Opposite*: straightforward **2 circuitous**, oblique, meandering, tortuous, winding *Opposite*: direct

deviousness *n* **guile**, cunning, artfulness, deceitfulness, untrustworthiness *Opposite*: straightforwardness

devise *v* **think up**, plan, figure out, work out, invent

devoid *adj* **empty**, barren, without, bereft, lacking *Opposite*: full

devolution *n* **decentralization**, delegation, transference, transfer *Opposite*: centralization

devolve *v* **transfer**, decentralize, give to, hand to, pass to *Opposite*: centralize

devote *v* **dedicate**, give, offer, apply, assign

devoted *adj* **1 committed**, loving, caring, affectionate, kind *Opposite*: uncaring **2 dedicated**, loyal, dutiful, faithful, staunch *Opposite*: uncommitted **3 keen**, enthusiastic, dedicated, ardent, fervent *Opposite*: unenthusiastic

devotee *n* **1 fan**, follower, supporter, aficionado, aficionada **2 disciple**, follower, believer, votary

devotion *n* **1 commitment**, attachment, love, fondness, affection *Opposite*: dislike **2 dedication**, care, attentiveness, support, loyalty *Opposite*: neglect **3 enthusiasm**, admiration, zeal, keenness, fervour *Opposite*: apathy **4** *(fml)* **piety**, devoutness, religious zeal, religious fervour, religious observance *Opposite*: impiety

devotional *adj* **religious**, worshipful, worshipping, prayerful, holy

devotions *n* **prayers**, holy rites, observances, supplications *(fml)*

devour *v* **1 consume**, demolish, dispose of, gulp, wolf **2** *(literary)* **overwhelm**, overcome, engulf, consume, destroy

devout *adj* **1 religious**, pious, spiritual, devoted, dedicated *Opposite*: uncommitted **2** *(fml)* **sincere**, heartfelt, deep, earnest, fervent *Opposite*: insincere **3 enthusiastic**, keen, ardent, zealous, fanatical *Opposite*: casual

devoutly *adv* **deeply**, keenly, seriously, intensely, profoundly

devoutness *n* **piety**, spirituality, religious fervour, religious zeal, piousness *Opposite*: impiety

dew *n* **droplets**, precipitation, condensation, dewdrops

dewdrop *n* **bead of moisture**, droplet, drop, drip

dewy *adj* **wet**, dew-covered, heavy with dew, damp, moist *Opposite*: dry

dewy-eyed *adj* **innocent**, naive, trusting, unrealistic, idealistic *Opposite*: down-to-earth

dexterity *n* **1 deftness**, skill, adroitness, handiness, legerdemain *Opposite*: clumsiness **2 ingenuity**, acuity, sharpness, quickness, resourcefulness *Opposite*: dullness

dexterous *adj* **1 deft**, adroit, handy, nimble-fingered, nimble *Opposite*: clumsy **2 quick-witted**, sharp, acute, resourceful, clever *Opposite*: dull

dextrous *see* dexterous

diadem *n* **crown**, tiara, circlet, coronet, wreath

diagnose *v* **make a diagnosis**, identify, analyse, spot, detect

diagnosis *n* **identification**, analysis, judgment, finding, verdict

diagnostic *adj* **analytic**, analytical, indicative, investigative, problem-solving

diagonal *adj* **slanting**, oblique, sloping, crossways, crosswise

diagram *n* **drawing**, figure, illustration, plan, map

diagrammatic *adj* **graphic**, illustrative, pictorial, visual, drawn *Opposite*: verbal

dial *n* **1 face**, gauge, indicator, disc, control panel **2 knob**, handle, control, button ▪ *v* **call**, telephone, phone, phone up, ring

dialect *n* **vernacular**, language, parlance, tongue, idiom

dialectic *n* **1 tension**, conflict, interaction, clash, opposition *Opposite*: harmony **2 discussion**, debate, investigation, examination, analysis

dialogue *n* **1 discussion**, exchange of ideas, channel of communication, discourse, interchange *Opposite*: silence **2** *(fml)* **conversation**, interview, chat, discussion, discourse *Opposite*: monologue

diamanté *adj* **glittery**, sparkly, glittering, sparkling, diamantine *Opposite*: dull ▪ *n* **rhinestones**, paste, strass

diameter *n* **width**, thickness, breadth, length, distance

diametrically *adv* **absolutely**, completely, utterly, totally, entirely *Opposite*: partially

diamond *n* **rhombus**, parallelogram, lozenge, equilateral

diaphanous *adj* **transparent**, delicate, gauzy, see-through, sheer *Opposite*: opaque

diarist *n* **memoirist**, writer, autobiographer, author, chronicler

diary *n* **1 appointment book**, personal organizer, PDA, personal digital assistant, calendar **2 journal**, record, log, chronicle, memoir

diaspora *n* **dispersion**, scattering, movement, displacement, migration *Opposite*: concentration

diatribe *n* **criticism**, attack, tirade, denunciation, harangue

dice *v* **1 cube**, cut up, chop, cut into cubes **2 gamble**, risk, stake, bet, wager

dice with death *v* **face danger**, sail close to the wind, play a dangerous game, cut it fine, play Russian roulette

dicey *(infml) adj* **risky**, dangerous, hazardous, chancy, uncertain *Opposite*: safe

dichotomy *n* **contrast**, opposition, irreconcilable difference, contradiction, gulf *Opposite*: harmony

dicker *(infml) v* **bargain**, haggle, argue, trade, wrangle

dicky *(infml) see* **bow tie**

dicky bow *(infml) see* **bow tie**

dictate *v* **1 speak**, say, say aloud, read out, read aloud **2 order**, state, command, decree, lay down **3 control**, determine, have a bearing on, influence, shape ▪ *n* **1 principle**, rule, standard, tenet, precept *(fml)* **2 command**, order, decree, prescription, injunction

dictation *n* **transcription**, notation, transcript

dictator *n* **tyrant**, ruler, despot, autocrat, authoritarian *Opposite*: democrat

dictatorial *adj* **tyrannical**, despotic, autocratic, authoritarian, overbearing *Opposite*: democratic

dictatorship *n* **1 regime**, government, rule, era, reign **2 despotism**, autocracy, totalitarianism, authoritarianism, tyranny *Opposite*: democracy

diction *n* **1 pronunciation**, enunciation, articulation, delivery, elocution **2 wording**, language, expression, phraseology, phrasing

dictionary *n* **lexicon**, vocabulary, glossary, phrase book, word list

dictum *(fml) n* **pronouncement**, dictate, saying, statement, maxim

didactic *adj* **educational**, instructive, informative, edifying, teaching

die *v* **1 pass away**, pass on, kick the bucket *(slang)*, croak *(slang)*, expire *(fml) Opposite*: live **2 stop**, give out, go dead, break down, fail *Opposite*: start

die away *v* **fade**, fade away, dwindle, fizzle, ebb *Opposite*: revive

die down *v* **subside**, decrease, lessen, diminish, decline *Opposite*: revive

diehard *adj* **intransigent**, reactionary, conservative, traditionalist, dyed-in-the-wool *Opposite*: progressive ▪ *n* **reactionary**, conservative, traditionalist, fogy, conformist *Opposite*: progressive

die of *v* **succumb**, fall victim, surrender, yield, submit *Opposite*: survive

die off *v* **die out**, become extinct, pass away, pass on, disappear *Opposite*: survive

die out *v* **become extinct**, disappear, vanish, die off, pass away *Opposite*: survive

diet *n* **1 food**, fare, nourishment, nutrition, sustenance **2 regime**, intake, supply, regimen **3 parliament**, legislature, assembly, council, congress ▪ *v* **slim**, starve, fast, cut back, cut down *Opposite*: binge

dietary *adj* **nutritional**, dietetic, eating, alimentary, alimental

dieter *n* **slimmer**, weight watcher, faster, starver, abstainer

differ *v* **1 be different**, be unlike, be at variance, vary, fluctuate *Opposite*: match **2 disagree**, argue, quarrel, fall out, wrangle *Opposite*: agree. *See* COMPARE AND CONTRAST *at* disagree.

difference *n* **1 dissimilarity**, disparity, distinction, differentiation, divergence *Opposite*: similarity **2 change**, alteration, variance, modification, transformation *Opposite*: consistency **3 argument**, dispute, disagreement, quarrel, contretemps *(fml)*

different *adj* **1 dissimilar**, diverse, unlike,

clashing, poles apart *Opposite*: similar **2 distinct**, separate, discrete, another *Opposite*: same **3 unusual**, special, singular, distinctive, atypical *Opposite*: run-of-the-mill

differential *n* **difference**, discrepancy, disparity, gap, variance

differentiate *v* **distinguish**, discriminate, tell apart, set apart, discern *Opposite*: blend

differentiation *n* **1 distinction**, discrimination, delineation, demarcation, separation *Opposite*: assimilation **2 difference**, diversity, variation, distinction, discrepancy *Opposite*: similarity

differently *adv* **in a different way**, another way, in your own way, otherwise, inversely *Opposite*: similarly

differing *adj* **opposing**, contradictory, contrary, divergent, different *Opposite*: similar

difficult *adj* **1 hard**, tricky, complicated, thorny, complex *Opposite*: straightforward **2 challenging**, hard, tough, trying, grim *Opposite*: easy **3 incomprehensible**, unintelligible, impenetrable, involved, complicated *Opposite*: simple **4 obstinate**, stubborn, recalcitrant, intractable, fractious *Opposite*: amenable. *See* COMPARE AND CONTRAST *at* hard.

difficulty *n* **1 complexity**, complicatedness, intricacy, adversity, complication **2 problem**, snag, obstacle, impediment, stumbling block **3 trouble**, effort, struggle, exertion, strain *Opposite*: ease

diffidence *n* **shyness**, hesitancy, reserve, timidity, reticence *Opposite*: brashness

diffident *adj* **shy**, hesitant, insecure, timid, reticent *Opposite*: brash

diffract *v* **bend**, deflect, curve, divert, spread

diffraction *n* **deflection**, bending, curving, diversion, spreading

diffuse *v* **disperse**, spread, disseminate, distribute, circulate *Opposite*: concentrate ■ *adj* **1 dispersed**, spread, disseminated, distributed, circulated *Opposite*: concentrated **2 wordy**, verbose, prolix, long-winded, drawn-out *Opposite*: concise *See* COMPARE AND CONTRAST *at* wordy.

diffusion *n* **dispersal**, dispersion, dissemination, distribution, circulation *Opposite*: concentration

dig *v* **1 break up**, plough, turn, hoe, till **2 excavate**, tunnel, hollow out, burrow, mine **3 prod**, nudge, push, shove, jab ■ *n* **1 poke**, prod, nudge, push, shove **2 gibe**, taunt, jeer, crack, insult *Opposite*: compliment

digest *v* **1 process**, assimilate, absorb, break down, consume **2 assimilate**, absorb, take in, take on board, grasp *Opposite*: ignore ■ *n* **1 abridgment**, résumé, summary, condensation, abstract **2 publication**, journal, magazine, periodical, book

digestible *adj* **edible**, palatable, eatable, consumable, comestible *(fml)* *Opposite*: indigestible

digestion *n* **assimilation**, ingestion, absorption, incorporation, breakdown

digestive *adj* **peptic**, gastric, intestinal, gastrointestinal, duodenal

digestive tract *see* alimentary canal

digger *n* **1 miner**, excavator, gravedigger, gold digger, prospector **2 excavator**, bulldozer, earthmover, crawler, backhoe

diggings *n* **excavation**, mine, quarry, pit, dig

dig into *v* **1 stick into**, push into, sink into, stab, prod **2 examine**, look at, delve into, investigate, go into *Opposite*: ignore

dig in your heels *v* **stand firm**, hold your ground, stand your ground, hold out, resist *Opposite*: give in

digit *n* **number**, numeral, figure, cipher, character

digital *adj* **numerical**, numerary, numeral, alphanumeric, cardinal

dignified *adj* **distinguished**, decorous, stately, noble, gracious *Opposite*: undignified

dignify *v* **distinguish**, honour, grace, glorify, venerate *Opposite*: degrade

dignitary *n* **notable**, VIP, worthy, celebrity, luminary *Opposite*: nobody

dignity *n* **1 self-respect**, self-esteem, pride, self-possession, self-worth *Opposite*: ignominy **2 formality**, gravity, solemnity, grandeur, decorum *Opposite*: informality **3 worthiness**, worth, nobility, nobleness, goodness *Opposite*: unworthiness

dig out *v* **1 uncover**, excavate, dig up, unearth, expose *Opposite*: bury **2** *(infml)* **retrieve**, find, discover, locate, reveal

digress *v* **deviate**, depart, wander, go off at a tangent, stray *Opposite*: focus

digression *n* **deviation**, departure, aside, parenthesis, detour *Opposite*: focus

digs *(dated infml)* *n* **lodgings** *(dated)*, lodging, accommodation, rooms, quarters

dig up *v* **1 unearth**, excavate, disinter, exhume, expose *Opposite*: bury **2** *(infml)* **bring to light**, dredge up, expose, reveal, find *Opposite*: hide

diktat *n* **command**, decree, edict, dictate, order

dilapidated *adj* **decrepit**, rundown, derelict, ramshackle, on its last legs *Opposite*: pristine

dilapidation *n* **disrepair**, dereliction, decrepitude, decay, ruin

dilate *v* **1 expand**, widen, open, enlarge, increase *Opposite*: contract **2 amplify**, expatiate, expand, dwell on, expound *Opposite*: abbreviate

dilation *n* **expansion**, opening, enlargement, increase, distension *Opposite*: contraction

dilatory *adj* **slow**, tardy, remiss, behindhand, slack *Opposite*: prompt

dilemma *n* **quandary**, tight spot, catch-22, predicament, impasse

dilettante *n* **amateur**, dabbler, abecedarian,

neophyte, novice *Opposite*: expert

diligence *n* **assiduousness**, meticulousness, conscientiousness, thoroughness, attentiveness *Opposite*: carelessness

diligent *adj* **industrious**, assiduous, painstaking, meticulous, conscientious *Opposite*: lazy

dilly-dally *v* **dawdle**, dally, delay, shilly-shally, drag your heels *Opposite*: hurry

dilute *v* **1 thin**, weaken, water down, adulterate *Opposite*: concentrate **2 reduce**, attenuate, temper, mitigate, water down *Opposite*: increase ■ *adj* **weak**, watered down, thinned, watery, insipid *Opposite*: concentrated

dilution *n* **1 thinning**, weakening, watering down, watering **2 reduction**, attenuation, enfeeblement, erosion, weakening *Opposite*: strengthening **3 concentration**, strength, intensity, potency

dim *adj* **1 badly lit**, murky, gloomy, shadowy, dusky *Opposite*: bright **2 soft**, faint, muted, weak, diffuse *Opposite*: strong **3 indistinct**, vague, blurred, blurry, hazy *Opposite*: clear ■ *v* **turn down**, lower, darken, reduce *Opposite*: turn up

dimension *n* **1 measurement**, length, height, width, breadth **2 aspect**, element, facet, feature, factor

dimensions *n* **size**, scope, extent, magnitude, proportions

diminish *v* **1 reduce**, lessen, make smaller, weaken, moderate *Opposite*: increase **2 shrink**, ebb, fade, fade away, fade out *Opposite*: grow

diminishing *adj* **lessening**, fading, waning, weakening, falling *Opposite*: increasing

diminution *n* **decrease**, reduction, lessening, attenuation, shrinking *Opposite*: growth

diminutive *adj* **small**, little, tiny, minuscule, miniature *Opposite*: huge

dimmer *n* **light switch**, dimmer switch, brightness control, regulator, rheostat

dimness *n* **1 softness**, faintness, weakness, diffuseness, dullness *Opposite*: brightness **2 murkiness**, gloom, gloominess, shadowiness, duskiness *Opposite*: brightness **3 indistinctness**, vagueness, blurriness, haziness, faintness *Opposite*: clearness

dimple *n* **hollow**, depression, pit, indentation, dent *Opposite*: bump

dimpled *adj* **1 dimply**, cleft, indented, dented, chubby *Opposite*: smooth **2 textured**, indented, dented, pocked, pockmarked *Opposite*: smooth

din *n* **noise**, hubbub, rumpus, racket *(infml)*, hullabaloo ■ *v* **drum into**, hammer, inculcate, instil, impress

dine *v* **eat**, feast, banquet, consume, ingest

diner *n* **patron**, customer, guest

ding *n* **ringing**, ring, dong, ding-dong, ding-a-ling ■ *v* **ring**, tinkle, dong, ding-dong

ding-dong *(infml)* *n* **argument**, spat, row, quarrel, tiff

dinge *n* **filth**, grime, mess, dirt, muck *(infml) Opposite*: cleanliness

dinginess *n* **1 dirtiness**, discoloration, griminess, dullness, dreariness *Opposite*: brightness **2 shabbiness**, drabness, squalidness, cheerlessness, seediness *Opposite*: neatness

dingy *adj* **1 dirty**, grimy, soiled, grubby, dull *Opposite*: clean **2 shabby**, drab, squalid, tatty, worn *Opposite*: bright

dinky *(infml)* *adj* **small**, compact, neat, natty, cute *Opposite*: hefty

dinnertime *n* **mealtime**, suppertime, lunchtime, tea-time

dinosaur *n* **relic**, museum piece, back number, fossil, has-been *(infml)*

WORD BANK

❏ **types of dinosaur** allosaurus, ankylosaur, apatosaurus, brachiosaurus, brontosaurus, cotylosaur, dicynodont, diplodocus, hadrosaur, ichthyosaur, iguanodon, megalosaur, mosasaur, oviraptor, pelycosaur, plesiosaur, pteranodon, pterodactyl, pterosaur, stegosaur, titanosaur, triceratops, tyrannosaur, velociraptor

dint *n* **indent**, dent, indentation, depression, hollow ■ *v* **dent**, damage, mark, spoil, blemish

dip *v* **1 plunge**, immerse, dunk, douse, bathe **2 drop**, drop down, descend, decline, sink *Opposite*: rise **3 slope**, incline, slant, descend, fall away *Opposite*: level ■ *n* **1 swim**, plunge, bathe **2 fall**, decline, drop, depression, falling off *Opposite*: rise **3 hollow**, depression, incline, slope, rise and fall

dip into *v* **skim**, flick through, flip through, glance, browse *Opposite*: study

diploma *n* **certificate**, qualification, credential

diplomacy *n* **1 international relations**, mediation, negotiation, peacekeeping **2 tact**, skill, subtlety, discretion, savoir-faire *Opposite*: tactlessness

diplomat *n* **1 civil servant**, envoy, representative, attaché, ambassador **2 tactician**, peacekeeper, negotiator, mediator, go-between

diplomatic *adj* **1 political**, ambassadorial, consular, embassy **2 tactful**, subtle, suave, discreet, sensitive *Opposite*: tactless

dipper *n* **ladle**, scoop, spoon

dire *adj* **terrible**, awful, dreadful, calamitous, horrible *Opposite*: wonderful

direct *v* **1 manage**, control, regulate, rule, oversee **2 aim**, point, turn, target, train **3 show the way**, guide, lead, put on the right track, point in the right direction **4** *(fml)* **order**, give orders, instruct, give instructions, command *Opposite*: request ■ *adj* **1 straight**, shortest, through, unswerving, undeviating

Opposite: circuitous **2 precise**, exact, absolute, complete, unequivocal *Opposite*: vague **3 straightforward**, honest, open, candid, frank *Opposite*: devious ■ *adv* **directly**, straight, nonstop, right, in a straight line *Opposite*: indirectly. *See* COMPARE AND CONTRAST *at* guide.

direction *n* **1 management**, control, government, guidance, leadership **2 way**, course, track, route, path **3 trend**, course, route, focus, aim

directional *adj* **manoeuvring**, steering, turning, reversing, guiding

directions *n* **instructions**, information, orders, guidelines, commands

directive *n* **order**, command, instruction, direction, edict

directly *adv* **1 in a straight line**, straight, right, unswervingly, nonstop *Opposite*: indirectly **2 completely**, diametrically, absolutely, wholly, unequivocally **3 openly**, honestly, frankly, straightforwardly, truthfully *Opposite*: ambiguously **4** *(fml)* **immediately**, quickly, at once, promptly, without delay

direct mail *n* **promotional mailing**, mail shot, circular, junk mail, unsolicited mail

directness *n* **honesty**, openness, straightforwardness, truthfulness, sincerity *Opposite*: deviousness

director *n* **manager**, leader, executive, boss, administrator

directorate *n* **board of directors**, executive, executive board, executive committee, board

director-general *n* **president**, head, director, chairperson, chief executive

directorship *n* **director's post**, management post, executive post, managerial position, presidency

directory *n* **listing**, phone book, catalogue, inventory, register

dirge *n* **elegy**, requiem, funeral hymn, lament, chant

dirt *n* **1 grime**, filth, mud, dust, muck *(infml)* **2 soil**, earth, clay, loam, mud **3 gossip**, scandal, filth, smut, lowdown *(infml)*

dirt-cheap *(infml)* *adj* **cheap**, reduced, cut-price, bargain, inexpensive *Opposite*: dear ■ *adv* **cheaply**, at a knockdown price, at bargain-basement prices, for a song, for next to nothing

dirtiness *n* **griminess**, filthiness, messiness, muddiness, grubbiness *Opposite*: cleanliness

dirty *adj* **1 filthy**, grimy, soiled, grubby, squalid *Opposite*: clean **2 dishonest**, illegal, corrupt, unfair, immoral *Opposite*: honest **3 dull**, muted, muddy, cloudy, murky *Opposite*: clear ■ *v* **soil**, stain, pollute, foul, defile *(fml)* *Opposite*: clean

COMPARE AND CONTRAST CORE MEANING: not clean

dirty stained or marked with dirt; **filthy** extremely or disgustingly dirty; **grubby** slightly dirty; **grimy** heavily ingrained with accumulated dirt; **soiled** stained or marked, especially during normal use; **squalid** insanitary and unpleasant; **unclean** dirty or impure, especially in moral or religious contexts.

dirty tricks *n* **unfair tactics**, foul play, deviousness, dishonesty, jiggery-pokery *(infml)*

dirty word *n* **swearword**, expletive, four-letter word, profanity, obscenity

disability *n* **incapacity**, infirmity, frailty, debility, ill health

disable *v* **incapacitate**, restrict, inactivate, deactivate, put out of action

disablement *n* **impairment**, incapacitation, deactivation, spiking *(infml)*

disabuse *v* **persuade out of**, disillusion, enlighten, set straight, shatter the illusions of

disadvantage *n* **difficulty**, drawback, shortcoming, weakness, hindrance *Opposite*: advantage

disadvantaged *adj* **deprived**, underprivileged, needy, destitute, poor *Opposite*: privileged

disadvantageous *adj* **detrimental**, damaging, hurtful, harmful, injurious *Opposite*: advantageous

disaffect *v* **estrange**, disillusion, disenchant, dissatisfy, alienate

disaffected *adj* **disillusioned**, dissatisfied, disgruntled, cynical, alienated *Opposite*: enthusiastic

disaffection *n* **disillusionment**, alienation, estrangement, dissatisfaction, cynicism *Opposite*: enthusiasm

disagree *v* **1 take issue with**, differ, demur, agree to differ, be at odds *Opposite*: agree **2 differ**, vary, diverge, deviate, contradict *Opposite*: agree **3 argue**, quarrel, wrangle, dispute, bicker *Opposite*: agree

COMPARE AND CONTRAST CORE MEANING: have or express a difference of opinion with somebody **disagree** have or put forward a different view or opinion; **differ** have different opinions about something; **argue** express disagreement, especially continuously or angrily; **dispute** have a heated argument; **take issue with** disagree strongly with; **contradict** argue against the truth or correctness of a statement or claim; **agree to differ** stop arguing and accept that the opposing viewpoints are irreconcilable; **be at odds** be in disagreement, especially over a period of time or about a particular issue.

disagreeable *adj* **1 displeasing**, distasteful, offensive, nasty, unpleasant *Opposite*: agreeable **2 bad-tempered**, unfriendly, unhelpful, difficult, contrary *Opposite*: pleasant

disagreement *n* **1 dispute**, difference of opinion, quarrel, argument, misunderstanding *Opposite*: agreement **2 difference**, divergence, incongruity, discrepancy, dissimilarity *Opposite*: agreement

disallow v 1 (fml) **reject**, refuse, deny, throw, disapprove Opposite: pass 2 **cancel**, prohibit, forbid, veto, bar Opposite: allow

disallowed adj **rejected**, forbidden, banned, excluded, vetoed Opposite: allowed

disappear v 1 **vanish**, fade, fade away, go, evaporate Opposite: appear 2 **cease to exist**, die out, die off, pass away, vanish Opposite: appear

disappearance n **vanishing**, evaporation, fading, loss, desertion Opposite: appearance

disappearing adj **vanishing**, waning, endangered, threatened, dying

disappoint v **let down**, disillusion, fail, dissatisfy, dishearten Opposite: please

disappointed adj **let down**, dissatisfied, disillusioned, upset, saddened Opposite: satisfied

disappointing adj **unsatisfactory**, unacceptable, second-rate, poor, below par Opposite: satisfactory

disappointment n 1 **dissatisfaction**, displeasure, distress, discontent, disenchantment Opposite: satisfaction 2 **setback**, failure, frustration, defeat, drawback

disapprobation (fml) n **disfavour**, condemnation, disapproval, dislike, displeasure Opposite: approval

disapproval n **condemnation**, displeasure, dissatisfaction, censure, discontentment Opposite: approval

disapprove v 1 **condemn**, censure, criticize, deplore, frown on Opposite: approve 2 (fml) **reject**, refuse, veto, turn down, deny Opposite: approve

COMPARE AND CONTRAST CORE MEANING: have an unfavourable opinion of something or somebody **disapprove** give a negative judgment based on personal standards; **frown on** express dislike or disapproval; **object** be opposed to something, or express opposition; **criticize** point out flaws or faults; **condemn** give an unfavourable judgment on somebody or something; **deplore** disapprove of something strongly; **denounce** criticize or condemn publicly and harshly; **censure** make a formal, often public or official, statement of disapproval.

disapproving adj **critical**, judgmental, negative, censorious, stern Opposite: approving

disarm v 1 **deactivate**, defuse, make safe, neutralize Opposite: arm 2 **win over**, charm, enchant, beguile, win the affection of Opposite: annoy

disarmament n **arms reduction**, nuclear disarmament, unilateral disarmament, decommissioning, demilitarization Opposite: rearmament

disarming adj **charming**, enchanting, attractive, appealing, captivating Opposite: unattractive

disarrange v **disorder**, disturb, jumble, dishevel, mix up Opposite: order

disarranged adj **disordered**, untidy, rumpled, messy, jumbled

disarray n 1 **confusion**, dismay, panic, alarm, hysteria Opposite: order 2 **mess**, disorder, chaos, confusion, untidiness Opposite: order

disassemble v **take apart**, take to bits, undo, take down, take to pieces Opposite: assemble

disassociate v 1 **dissociate**, separate, split, set apart, disentangle Opposite: associate 2 **distance**, detach, set apart, dissociate, draw back Opposite: implicate

disaster n 1 **tragedy**, ruin, adversity, catastrophe, calamity 2 (infml) **failure**, debacle, fiasco, shambles, farce Opposite: success

disastrous adj 1 **calamitous**, catastrophic, tragic, terrible, devastating 2 **unsuccessful**, unfortunate, luckless, doomed, unlucky Opposite: successful

disavow v **disown**, deny, renounce, reject, recant

disavowal (fml) n **repudiation**, denial, negation, renunciation, abjuration Opposite: avowal (fml)

disband v **break up**, split up, scatter, separate, part

disbar v **expel**, throw out, dismiss, banish, exclude

disbarment n **expulsion**, dismissal, banishment, exclusion, removal

disbelief n **incredulity**, doubt, distrust, mistrust, suspicion Opposite: faith

disbelieve v **distrust**, doubt, mistrust, suspect, be suspicious of Opposite: believe

disbeliever n **doubter**, agnostic, atheist, nonbeliever, sceptic Opposite: believer

disbelieving adj **unconvinced**, incredulous, suspicious, doubtful, distrustful Opposite: believing

disburse v **pay out**, pay, spend, expend, lay out

disbursement n **payment**, expenditure, expense, costs, distribution

discard v **throw away**, abandon, dispose of, remove, get rid of Opposite: keep

discarded adj **cast off**, thrown away, thrown out, rejected, dispensed with Opposite: kept

discern v 1 **make out**, notice, see, perceive, discover Opposite: miss 2 **understand**, perceive, distinguish, fathom, be aware of Opposite: miss 3 **distinguish**, tell the difference, separate, discriminate, differentiate

discernible adj **visible**, apparent, obvious, perceptible, noticeable

discerning adj **discriminating**, sharp, astute, judicious, sensitive Opposite: indiscriminate

discernment n **judgment**, acumen, discrimination, perspicacity, taste

discharge v 1 **emit**, send out, excrete, expel, ooze 2 **free**, release, set free, emancipate, liberate 3 **dismiss**, relieve of duty, let go, lay off, give somebody their cards Opposite:

retain **4** *(fml)* **pay off**, clear, settle, satisfy, liquidate ∎ *n* **1 emission**, flow, secretion, excretion, seepage **2 release**, liberation, emancipation, expulsion, ejection

disciple *n* **follower**, believer, supporter, devotee, partisan

disciplinarian *n* **tyrant**, martinet, despot, authoritarian, stickler

disciplinary *adj* **punitive**, corrective, penal, penalizing

discipline *n* **1 punishment**, correction, chastisement *(fml)*, castigation *(fml)* **2 regulation**, order, control, restraint, authority *Opposite*: chaos **3 self-control**, self-restraint, restraint, control, regulation **4 subject**, branch of learning, field ∎ *v* **1 punish**, chastise, correct, chasten, castigate *(fml)* **2 instruct**, educate, exercise, drill, prepare

disciplined *adj* **controlled**, self-controlled, orderly, well-ordered, methodical *Opposite*: undisciplined

disclaim *v* **deny**, disown, renounce, reject, repudiate

disclaimer *n* **1 rider**, proviso, qualification, provision, condition **2 repudiation**, denial, renunciation, negation, disassociation

disclose *v* **reveal**, unveil, divulge, make known, relate *Opposite*: conceal

disclosure *n* **revelation**, exposé, discovery, leak, confession

discoloration *n* **staining**, stain, tint, mark, streak

discolour *v* **fade**, stain, colour, darken, tarnish

discoloured *adj* **stained**, dirty, tarnished, faded, streaked

discomfit *(fml)* *v* **embarrass**, unsettle, disconcert, distress, rattle *Opposite*: relax

discomfiting *(fml)* *adj* **disconcerting**, embarrassing, unsettling, disturbing, distressing *Opposite*: reassuring

discomfiture *(fml)* *n* **embarrassment**, awkwardness, confusion, unease, disconcertment

discomfort *n* **1 ache**, pain, soreness, tenderness, irritation **2 uneasiness**, worry, distress, anxiety, embarrassment *Opposite*: calmness

discomposure *n* **agitation**, upset, uneasiness, embarrassment, discomfort

disconcert *v* **unsettle**, perturb, rattle, fluster, unnerve *Opposite*: relax

disconcerted *adj* **unsettled**, thrown off balance, confused, flustered, taken aback *Opposite*: calm

disconcerting *adj* **disturbing**, alarming, confusing, perplexing, bewildering *Opposite*: soothing

disconnect *v* **cut off**, detach, separate, divide, disengage *Opposite*: connect

disconnected *adj* **detached**, severed, disengaged, separated, divided *Opposite*: attached

disconnection *n* **1 stoppage**, interruption, cessation, cutting off, discontinuation *Opposite*: connection **2 separation**, severance, decoupling, disengagement, break *Opposite*: connection

disconsolate *adj* **unhappy**, dejected, gloomy, melancholy, sad *Opposite*: content

discontent *n* **dissatisfaction**, unhappiness, displeasure, disgruntlement, sadness *Opposite*: contentment

discontented *adj* **dissatisfied**, unhappy, disgruntled, malcontent, displeased *Opposite*: contented

discontentment *n* **dissatisfaction**, discontent, displeasure, unhappiness, irritation *Opposite*: contentment

discontinuation *n* **cessation**, termination, suspension, withdrawal, stoppage *Opposite*: continuation

discontinue *v* **stop**, cease, halt, end, suspend *Opposite*: continue

discontinued *adj* **obsolete**, finished, superseded, out-of-date, withdrawn

discontinuity *n* **break**, gap, cutoff, cutout, disjointedness *Opposite*: continuity

discontinuous *adj* **intermittent**, sporadic, broken, irregular, disjointed *Opposite*: continuous

discord *n* **1 disagreement**, conflict, dispute, argument, friction *Opposite*: accord **2 dissonance**, cacophony, disharmony, inharmoniousness, discordance *Opposite*: harmony

discordant *adj* **1 disagreeing**, conflicting, frictional, dissenting, acrimonious *Opposite*: amicable **2 dissonant**, jarring, harsh, inharmonious, cacophonous *Opposite*: harmonious

discount *n* **reduction**, money off, markdown, price cut, cut rate ∎ *v* **1 disregard**, overlook, ignore, disbelieve, pass over *Opposite*: accept **2 reduce**, mark down, lower, take off, deduct *Opposite*: put up

discounted *adj* **reduced**, on offer, cut-price, sale, on special offer

discourage *v* **1 dissuade**, oppose, hinder, inhibit, prevent *Opposite*: encourage **2 dispirit**, dishearten, cast down, depress, dismay *Opposite*: cheer

discouraged *adj* **disheartened**, dispirited, downcast, depressed, dejected *Opposite*: positive

discouragement *n* **1 disappointment**, dismay, despair, depression, low spirits *Opposite*: hopefulness **2 dissuasion**, caution, warning, opposition, deterrence *Opposite*: encouragement **3 deterrent**, hindrance, obstacle, impediment, damper *Opposite*: incentive

discouraging *adj* **disheartening**, depressing, dispiriting, gloomy, unpromising *Opposite*: encouraging

discourse *n* **1 dissertation**, treatise, homily,

sermon, address **2 dialogue**, conversation, discussion, communication, speech ▪ *v (fml)* **converse**, debate, compare notes, have a word, have a discussion

discourteous *adj* **rude**, ill-mannered, impolite, insolent, uncivil *Opposite*: polite

discourteousness *see* discourtesy

discourtesy *n* **rudeness**, impoliteness, disrespect, incivility, insolence *Opposite*: politeness

discover *v* **1 find out**, learn, determine, notice, realize **2 come across**, find, turn up, uncover, unearth

discoverer *n* **inventor**, originator, pioneer, innovator, creator

discovery *n* **1 find**, innovation, breakthrough, invention, finding **2 detection**, finding, unearthing, sighting, encounter

discredit *v* **1 slur**, demean, smear, insult, humiliate **2 question**, doubt, disbelieve, query, suspect

discreditable *adj* **shameful**, disreputable, ignominious, disgraceful, reprehensible *Opposite*: honourable

discreet *adj* **1 tactful**, prudent, circumspect, cautious, careful *Opposite*: tactless **2 inconspicuous**, subtle, unnoticeable, unobtrusive, understated *Opposite*: obvious

discrepancy *n* **inconsistency**, difference, incongruity, divergence, disagreement *Opposite*: correspondence

discrete *adj* **separate**, distinct, disconnected, detached, isolated

discretion *n* **1 carefulness**, prudence, caution, canniness, maturity *Opposite*: tactlessness **2 freedom of choice**, will, pleasure, option, choice

discretionary *adj* **optional**, flexible, open, elective, unrestricted *Opposite*: mandatory

discriminate *v* **distinguish**, tell apart, differentiate, separate, categorize

discriminating *adj* **discerning**, sharp, astute, selective, judicious

discrimination *n* **1 bias**, prejudice, unfairness, inequity, bigotry **2 taste**, judgment, good taste, discernment, insight **3 distinction**, difference, differential, contrast

discriminatory *adj* **biased**, prejudiced, unfair, bigoted, inequitable *Opposite*: non-discriminatory

discursive *adj* **expansive**, lengthy, conversational, long-winded, circumlocutory *Opposite*: concise

discursiveness *n* **expansiveness**, long-windedness, roundaboutness, verbosity, circumlocution *Opposite*: concision

discuss *v* **talk over**, deliberate, debate, converse, confer

discussion *n* **conversation**, debate, argument, dialogue, chat

discussion group *n* **class**, seminar, tutorial, round table, committee

disdain *n* **scorn**, contempt, derision, condescension, disparagement *Opposite*: respect ▪ *v* **despise**, scorn, spurn, hold in contempt, disparage *Opposite*: respect

disdainful *adj* **sneering**, scornful, derisive, condescending, aloof *Opposite*: respectful

disease *n* **illness**, sickness, ailment, infection, syndrome *Opposite*: health

diseased *adj* **unhealthy**, unwell, sickly, ill, sick *Opposite*: healthy

disembark *v* **come ashore**, go ashore, land, get off, arrive in port *Opposite*: embark

disembarkation *n* **arrival**, alighting, debarkation, landing, getting off

disembodied *adj* **ghostly**, spiritual, intangible, ethereal, immaterial *Opposite*: tangible

disembowel *v* **eviscerate**, gut, fillet, exenterate

disenchanted *adj* **disillusioned**, disappointed, dissatisfied, crestfallen, embittered *Opposite*: idealistic

disenchantment *n* **disillusionment**, disappointment, dissatisfaction, embitterment, bitterness *Opposite*: idealism

disenfranchise *v* **marginalize**, exclude, alienate, subjugate, disqualify *Opposite*: enfranchise

disenfranchisement *n* **marginalization**, exclusion, alienation, subjugation, disqualification *Opposite*: enfranchisement

disengage *v* **undo**, unfasten, unlock, untie, uncouple *Opposite*: fasten

disengagement *n* **1 withdrawal**, disentanglement, detachment, disconnection, extrication *Opposite*: engagement **2 release**, uncoupling, separation, extrication, withdrawal *Opposite*: attachment

disentangle *v* **unravel**, unscramble, untie, separate, straighten out *Opposite*: entangle

disequilibrium *n* **imbalance**, instability, uncertainty, flux, volatility *Opposite*: equilibrium

disestablish *v* **reform**, repudiate, renounce, re-evaluate, disclaim *Opposite*: establish

disfavour *n* **1 disrepute**, unpopularity, discredit, disgrace, obscurity *Opposite*: favour **2 distaste**, disdain, disapproval, displeasure, disapprobation *(fml)* *Opposite*: favour

disfigure *v* **mutilate**, scar, deface, mar, spoil *Opposite*: enhance

disfigurement *n* **scar**, mutilation, defacement, deformity, blemish *Opposite*: enhancement

disgorge *v* **expel**, eject, empty, pour out, spew *Opposite*: retain

disgrace *n* **shame**, discredit, scandal, ignominy, humiliation ▪ *v* **bring shame on**, discredit, bring into disrepute, shame, degrade

disgraced *adj* **discredited**, shamed, condemned, humiliated, fallen *Opposite*: popular

disgraceful *adj* **shameful**, shocking, outrageous, scandalous, discreditable

disgruntle v displease, irritate, anger, annoy, dissatisfy Opposite: satisfy

disgruntled adj discontented, dissatisfied, resentful, displeased, unhappy Opposite: contented

disguise v cover up, hide, conceal, mask, masquerade Opposite: reveal ∎ n mask, costume, camouflage, masquerade, cover

disguised adj camouflaged, masked, masquerading, cloaked, veiled Opposite: overt

disgust n revulsion, repugnance, abhorrence, repulsion, antipathy Opposite: attraction ∎ v sicken, repulse, revolt, repel, shock Opposite: please. See COMPARE AND CONTRAST at **dislike**.

disgusted adj sickened, revolted, repulsed, repelled, offended Opposite: charmed

disgusting adj revolting, repulsive, sickening, ghastly, filthy Opposite: attractive

dish n 1 plate, bowl, saucer 2 food item, course, recipe

WORD BANK
❏ types of cooked dish bruschetta, burritos, casserole, cassoulet, ceviche, chop suey, chow mein, couscous, curry, fajitas, falafel, fish cake, fondue, fricassee, frijoles, frittata, fry-up, goulash, gruel, Irish stew, kedgeree, lasagne, meat loaf, mixed grill, moussaka, nachos, nasi goreng, paella, pilau, pirozhki, pizza, quiche, ragout, ratatouille, risotto, sambal, satay, sauerkraut, stew, stir-fry, tacos, tagine, tamale, tempura, teriyaki, tofu, yakitori

disharmonious adj conflicting, discordant, tense, uneasy, bitter Opposite: harmonious

disharmony n conflict, disagreement, discord, tension, unrest Opposite: harmony

dishcloth n washing-up cloth, kitchen cloth, towel, drying-up cloth, dishrag (US)

dishearten v discourage, depress, sadden, cast down, dismay Opposite: buoy up

disheartened adj discouraged, depressed, saddened, dismayed, dejected Opposite: encouraged

disheartening adj intimidating, off-putting, daunting, dispiriting, depressing Opposite: encouraging

dishevelled adj unkempt, wild and woolly, tousled, ruffled, untidy Opposite: well-groomed

dishevelment n messiness, scruffiness, untidiness, unruliness Opposite: tidiness

dishonest adj lying, deceitful, false, untruthful, fraudulent Opposite: honest

dishonesty n deceit, deceitfulness, fraudulence, lying, untruthfulness Opposite: honesty

dishonour n disgrace, shame, discredit, ignominy, disrepute Opposite: honour ∎ v shame, disgrace, discredit, defame, bring into disrepute Opposite: honour

dishonourable adj disgraceful, disreputable, discreditable, shameful, ignominious Opposite: honourable

dish out (infml) v distribute, parcel out, allot, hand out, deal out

dishy (infml) adj good-looking, nice-looking, cute, attractive, handsome Opposite: ugly

disillusion v disenchant, bring down to earth, disappoint, let down, dishearten Opposite: inspire

disillusioned adj disenchanted, disappointed, disheartened, cynical Opposite: starry-eyed

disillusionment n disenchantment, disappointment, cynicism, letdown, discouragement Opposite: gratification

disincentive n deterrent, discouragement, hindrance, impediment, encumbrance Opposite: incentive

disinclination n reluctance, unwillingness, opposition, hesitation, aversion Opposite: inclination

disincline v put off, deter, discourage, dissuade, prevent Opposite: encourage

disinclined adj reluctant, unwilling, opposed, unenthusiastic, loath Opposite: inclined. See COMPARE AND CONTRAST at **unwilling**.

disinfect v sterilize, sanitize, purify, fumigate, cleanse Opposite: contaminate

disinfectant n antiseptic, sterilizer, purifier, bleach, sanitizer

disinformation n deception, falsehood, propaganda, half-truth, misinformation Opposite: truth

disingenuous adj dishonest, insincere, untruthful, deceitful, hypocritical Opposite: honest

disingenuousness n dishonesty, insincerity, untruthfulness, deceit, hypocrisy Opposite: honesty

disinherit v cut off, disown, leave penniless, cut out, divest Opposite: bequeath

disintegrate v crumble, fragment, break, collapse, split Opposite: combine

disintegration n breakdown, breakup, collapse, fragmentation, crumbling

disinter v 1 exhume, dig up, unearth Opposite: bury 2 (fml) uncover, unearth, bring to light, expose, reveal Opposite: cover up

disinterest n indifference, unconcern, apathy, disregard, heedlessness Opposite: interest

disinterested adj fair-minded, unbiased, impartial, without prejudice, neutral Opposite: biased

disinterestedness n impartiality, objectivity, fair-mindedness, neutrality, distance Opposite: bias

disinterment n 1 exhumation, digging up, unearthing Opposite: interment 2 (fml) exposure, unearthing, discovery, revelation, uncovering Opposite: concealment

disjoint v 1 split, separate, come apart, sever, divide Opposite: join 2 dislocate, dislodge, move, relocate, separate *Opposite*: retain

disjointed *adj* **rambling**, fragmented, incoherent, disorganized, disorderly *Opposite*: coherent

disjointedness *n* **disjunction**, disjuncture, incoherence, dislocation, disconnection *Opposite*: coherence

dislikable *adj* **disagreeable**, unpleasant, offensive, repugnant, horrible *Opposite*: likable

dislike *v* **hate**, detest, loathe, frown on, disapprove *Opposite*: like ■ *n* **distaste**, antipathy, aversion, hatred, hate *Opposite*: liking

---

COMPARE AND CONTRAST CORE MEANING: a feeling of not liking somebody or something **dislike** a feeling or attitude of disapproval; **distaste** mild dislike, mainly of behaviour and activities; **hatred** or **hate** intense dislike or hostility; **disgust** a feeling of horrified and sickened disapproval; **loathing** intense dislike; **repugnance** strong disgust, mainly of behaviour and activities; **abhorrence** a feeling of aversion or intense disapproval, mainly of behaviour and activities; **animosity** a feeling of hostility and resentment; **antipathy** a deep-seated dislike or hostility; **aversion** a strong feeling of dislike; **revulsion** a sudden violent feeling of disgust.

---

dislocate *v* **1 put out of place**, displace, put out of joint, disjoint, dislodge *Opposite*: replace **2 disrupt**, interrupt, disturb, upset, disorder *Opposite*: restore

dislocation *n* **1 displacement**, disarticulation, dislodgment **2 disruption**, interruption, disturbance, disorder, upset

dislodge *v* **remove**, get out, extricate, free, displace *Opposite*: wedge

disloyal *adj* **unfaithful**, treacherous, untrue, false, fickle *Opposite*: loyal

disloyalty *n* **unfaithfulness**, treachery, falseness, infidelity, betrayal *Opposite*: loyalty

dismal *adj* **miserable**, gloomy, depressing, dreary, dull *Opposite*: bright

dismay *v* **disappoint**, shock, sadden, depress, perturb *Opposite*: comfort ■ *n* **disappointment**, shock, consternation, apprehension, panic *Opposite*: comfort

dismayed *adj* **discouraged**, disheartened, demoralized, downcast, depressed *Opposite*: heartened

dismember *v* **tear limb from limb**, cut into pieces, cut up, dissect, tear apart

dismemberment *n* **taking apart**, mutilation, division, maiming, splitting off

dismiss *v* **1 discharge**, relieve of duty, give notice, give somebody the push, fire (*infml*) *Opposite*: retain **2 send away**, allow to go, release, send home *Opposite*: detain **3 reject**, set aside, think no more of, put out of your mind, shelve *Opposite*: dwell on

dismissal *n* **removal**, notice, discharge, release, sack *Opposite*: appointment

dismissive *adj* **flippant**, indifferent, unconcerned, trivializing, contemptuous *Opposite*: attentive

dismount *v* **get down**, get off, alight, climb down, descend *Opposite*: mount

disobedience *n* **defiance**, noncompliance, breaking the rules, insubordination, waywardness *Opposite*: obedience

disobedient *adj* **defiant**, noncompliant, rebellious, insubordinate, badly behaved *Opposite*: obedient

disobey *v* **defy**, refuse to comply, break the rules, contravene, violate *Opposite*: obey

disobliging *adj* **unhelpful**, uncooperative, unaccommodating, rude, unfriendly *Opposite*: obliging

disorder *n* **1 chaos**, disarray, confusion, mess, muddle *Opposite*: order **2 complaint**, illness, sickness, ailment, syndrome ■ *v* **disorganize**, disarrange, disturb, jumble, muddle *Opposite*: order

disordered *adj* **chaotic**, messy, muddled, topsy-turvy, higgledy-piggledy *Opposite*: well-ordered

disorderliness *n* **confusion**, messiness, muddle, chaos, disarray *Opposite*: orderliness

disorderly *adj* **1 unruly**, riotous, uncontrollable, rebellious, wild *Opposite*: orderly **2 muddled**, jumbled, confused, messy, unsystematic

disorganization *n* **inefficiency**, ineptitude, ineffectiveness, chaos, disorder *Opposite*: organization

disorganize *v* **muddle**, mix up, confuse, jumble, dislocate *Opposite*: organize

disorganized *adj* **muddled**, jumbled, confused, messy, unsystematic *Opposite*: organized

disorient *see* disorientate

disorientate *v* **confuse**, perplex, fox, befuddle, fuddle *Opposite*: orientate

disorientated *adj* **confused**, unsettled, bewildered, perplexed, thrown (*infml*) *Opposite*: clear-headed

disorientation *n* **puzzlement**, bafflement, stupefaction, bewilderment, confusion

disown *v* **renounce**, reject, wash your hands of, turn your back on, disclaim *Opposite*: acknowledge

disparage *v* **belittle**, laugh at, mock, ridicule, pour scorn on *Opposite*: praise

disparagement *n* **belittling**, mocking, ridicule, criticism, derision *Opposite*: praise

disparaging *adj* **critical**, unfavourable, disapproving, censorious, unsympathetic *Opposite*: approving

disparate *adj* **dissimilar**, unlike, different, incongruent, unrelated *Opposite*: similar

disparity *n* **difference**, inequality, discrepancy, disproportion, gap *Opposite*: parity

dispassion *n* **aloofness**, coolness, calmness, impassivity, serenity *Opposite*: enthusiasm

dispassionate *adj* **calm**, composed, unflustered, unemotional, detached *Opposite*: fiery

dispatch *v* **1 send off**, send out, post, mail, ship *Opposite*: keep **2 kill**, murder, assassinate, put to death, slaughter ■ *n* **message**, communication, notice, letter, report

dispatch rider *n* **courier**, messenger, deliverer

dispel *v* **dismiss**, chase away, drive out, disperse, scatter *Opposite*: attract

dispensable *adj* **expendable**, superfluous, unessential, unnecessary, replaceable *Opposite*: indispensable

dispensary *n* **chemist's**, pharmacy, drugstore (*US*)

dispensation *n* **indulgence**, allowance, special consideration, privilege, exemption

dispense *v* **give out**, hand out, distribute, allot, mete out *Opposite*: withhold

dispenser *n* **distributor**, slot machine, machine, vending machine

dispersal *n* **dispersion**, spreading, scattering, diffusion, distribution *Opposite*: concentration

disperse *v* **scatter**, go away, disband, break up, dissolve *Opposite*: concentrate

dispersion *n* **dispersal**, spreading, scattering, diffusion, distribution *Opposite*: concentration

dispirit *v* **dishearten**, discourage, dampen, depress, dismay *Opposite*: rouse

dispirited *adj* **disheartened**, discouraged, dejected, depressed, downhearted *Opposite*: cheerful

dispiriting *adj* **disheartening**, depressing, demoralizing, upsetting, saddening *Opposite*: uplifting

displace *v* **1 move**, relocate, shift, transfer, put out of place *Opposite*: restore **2 oust**, supplant, replace, supersede, succeed *Opposite*: restore

displacement *n* **movement**, dislocation, dislodgment, shift, supplanting

display *v* **1 show**, exhibit, put on show, present, put on view *Opposite*: conceal **2 flaunt**, parade, show off, strut, pose *Opposite*: conceal ■ *n* **show**, exhibition, presentation, demonstration, parade

displease *v* **anger**, annoy, irritate, upset, put out *Opposite*: please

displeased *adj* **annoyed**, dissatisfied, put out, irked, unhappy *Opposite*: pleased

displeasure *n* **anger**, annoyance, irritation, disapproval, discontentment *Opposite*: pleasure

disport (*archaic*) *v* **show off**, pose, swagger, strut, flaunt

disposable *adj* **throwaway**, one-use, non-refundable *Opposite*: reusable

disposal *n* **removal**, discarding, clearance, dumping, throwing away *Opposite*: retention

dispose *v* **1 incline**, influence, persuade, prompt, encourage **2 settle**, resolve, fix, decide, determine **3** (*fml*) **position**, place, set out, arrange, set

disposed *adj* **willing**, likely, liable, inclined, of a mind *Opposite*: unwilling

dispose of *v* **1 throw away**, throw out, dispense with, discard, get rid of *Opposite*: keep **2 transfer**, pass on, divest yourself of, relieve yourself of, sell *Opposite*: keep **3** (*fml*) **attend to**, determine, settle, sort out, sort **4 kill**, murder, execute, assassinate, dispatch **5** (*fml*) **consume**, demolish, get through, devour, use up

disposition *n* **nature**, character, temperament, temper, outlook

dispossess (*archaic or fml*) *v* **deprive**, divest, strip, rob, disinherit

dispossessed *adj* **evicted**, expelled, ejected, turned out, driven out

dispossession *n* **deprivation**, denial, withdrawal, removal

disproportion *n* **imbalance**, discrepancy, disparity, inequality, inconsistency *Opposite*: equality

disproportionate *adj* **uneven**, unequal, lopsided, inconsistent, top-heavy *Opposite*: corresponding

disproportionately *adv* **excessively**, unduly, unreasonably, extremely, too *Opposite*: slightly

disprove *v* **refute**, invalidate, contradict, challenge, negate (*fml*) *Opposite*: prove

disputable *adj* **arguable**, debatable, moot, questionable, uncertain *Opposite*: incontrovertible

disputation (*fml*) *n* **argument**, strife, conflict, debate, disagreement *Opposite*: agreement

disputatious (*fml*) *adj* **argumentative**, quarrelsome, awkward, difficult, contrary *Opposite*: conciliatory

disputative (*fml*) *adj* **argumentative**, quarrelsome, awkward, difficult, contrary *Opposite*: conciliatory

dispute *v* **1 argue**, debate, discuss, quarrel, wrangle *Opposite*: agree **2 challenge**, question, contest, query, doubt *Opposite*: accept ■ *n* **argument**, disagreement, quarrel, difference, clash *Opposite*: agreement. *See* COMPARE AND CONTRAST *at* **disagree**.

disqualification *n* **ineligibility**, banning, barring, disentitlement, debarment *Opposite*: entitlement

disqualified *adj* **ineligible**, banned, barred, debarred, prohibited *Opposite*: eligible

disqualify *v* **ban**, bar, debar, prohibit, exclude *Opposite*: allow

disquiet *n* **unrest**, uneasiness, concern, worry, anxiety *Opposite*: calmness

disquieting *adj* **worrying**, disturbing, alarming, unsettling, troubling *Opposite*: reassuring

disquisition (fml) n **essay**, tract, discussion, address, speech

disquisitional (fml) adj **verbose**, wordy, long-winded, rambling, digressive Opposite: concise

disregard v **ignore**, take no notice of, turn a blind eye to, discount, pay no attention to Opposite: heed ■ n **disrespect**, indifference, contempt, disdain, neglect Opposite: regard

disregarded adj **1 ignored**, omitted, overlooked, unheeded, unnoticed Opposite: acknowledged **2 snubbed**, slighted, marginalized, sidelined, dishonoured Opposite: respected

disrepair n **poor shape**, bad shape, bad condition, poor order, disorder

disreputable adj **notorious**, infamous, scandalous, disgraceful, seedy Opposite: reputable

disrepute n **disgrace**, ill repute, disrespect, disregard, discredit Opposite: esteem

disrespect n **disregard**, contempt, insolence, impertinence, impudence Opposite: respect ■ v **insult**, affront, belittle, disparage, denigrate Opposite: respect

disrespectable adj **dishonourable**, frowned on, disreputable, unpopular, infamous Opposite: respectable

disrespectful adj **rude**, impolite, bad-mannered, discourteous, insolent Opposite: respectful

disrobe (fml) v **strip**, undress, unclothe, uncover, divest (fml) Opposite: dress

disrupt v **disturb**, upset, interrupt, dislocate, disorder

disruption n **disturbance**, commotion, trouble, interruption, distraction

disruptive adj **troublesome**, unruly, disorderly, unsettling, disturbing

disruptiveness n **unruliness**, rowdiness, disorderliness, indiscipline, naughtiness

dissatisfaction n **displeasure**, discontent, disappointment, unhappiness, frustration Opposite: satisfaction

dissatisfied adj **disgruntled**, displeased, discontented, disappointed, unhappy Opposite: satisfied

dissatisfy v **disgruntle**, displease, disappoint, put out, frustrate Opposite: satisfy

dissect v **1 cut up**, cut apart, divide, dismember, slice up **2 scrutinize**, break down, examine, study, explore

dissection n **1 cutting up**, partition, division, separation, segmentation **2 examination**, analysis, investigation, scrutiny, observation

dissemble v **1 pretend**, mislead, act, put on an act, dissimulate **2** (fml) **disguise**, conceal, hide, suppress, mask Opposite: disclose

disseminate v **distribute**, broadcast, circulate, spread, publicize. See COMPARE AND CONTRAST at **scatter**.

dissemination n **distribution**, broadcasting, diffusion, propagation, spreading

dissension n **opposition**, disagreement, dissent, discord, rebellion Opposite: consent

dissent v **disagree**, oppose, rebel, dispute, differ Opposite: agree ■ n **opposition**, disagreement, dissension, discord, rebellion Opposite: consent

dissenter n **rebel**, dissident, nonconformist, insurgent, mutineer

dissertation n **thesis**, paper, study, critique, essay

disservice n **damage**, harm, wrong, injury, difficulty Opposite: service

dissidence n **disagreement**, unorthodoxy, nonconformity, independence, rebellion Opposite: conformism

dissident n **dissenter**, rebel, nonconformist, protester, insurgent Opposite: conformist ■ adj **rebel**, rebellious, dissenting, unorthodox, nonconforming Opposite: conformist

dissimilar adj **unlike**, different, diverse, unrelated, disparate Opposite: similar

dissimilarity n **difference**, variation, distinction, contrast, divergence Opposite: similarity

dissimulate v **disguise**, conceal, hide, suppress, mask Opposite: disclose

dissimulation (fml) n **concealment**, suppression, disguise, camouflage, dishonesty Opposite: disclosure

dissipate v **1 dispel**, disperse, dissolve, scatter, drive away **2 squander**, waste, fritter away, throw away, blow (slang)

dissipated adj **dissolute**, degenerate, debauched, self-indulgent, immoral Opposite: upright

dissipation n **debauchery**, indulgence, rakishness, overindulgence, degeneracy Opposite: uprightness

dissociate v **distance**, detach, divorce, separate, disconnect Opposite: associate

dissociation n **detachment**, separation, disconnection, severance, alienation Opposite: association

dissolute adj **degenerate**, depraved, immoral, debauched, self-indulgent Opposite: upright

dissoluteness n **decadence**, overindulgence, extravagance, self-indulgence, degeneracy Opposite: temperance

dissolution n **closure**, disbanding, termination, ending, suspension Opposite: inauguration

dissolve v **1 melt**, soften, liquefy, thaw, run Opposite: solidify **2 disband**, close, break up, suspend, end Opposite: inaugurate **3 disappear**, dissipate, dispel, disperse, melt away Opposite: appear

dissonance n **discord**, disagreement, dissension, conflict, difference Opposite: harmony

dissonant *adj* **discordant**, unmusical, harsh, inharmonious, cacophonous *Opposite*: harmonious

dissuade *v* **deter**, put off, discourage, advise against, persuade against *Opposite*: persuade

dissuasion *n* **discouragement**, deterrence, persuasion, opposition, warning *Opposite*: encouragement

dissuasive *adj* **discouraging**, opposing, inhibitive, hindering *Opposite*: encouraging

distance *n* **1 coldness**, aloofness, detachment, reserve, remoteness *Opposite*: warmth **2 space**, expanse, void, vastness, gap *Opposite*: closeness ■ *v* **dissociate**, move away, detach, separate, avoid *Opposite*: associate

distant *adj* **1 faraway**, remote, far-off, far-flung, outlying *Opposite*: near **2 vague**, faint, indistinct, hazy, obscure *Opposite*: clear **3 aloof**, cold, unfriendly, detached, reserved *Opposite*: warm

distaste *n* **aversion**, dislike, antipathy, disgust, disfavour *Opposite*: love. *See* COMPARE AND CONTRAST *at* **dislike**.

distasteful *adj* **repugnant**, offensive, disgusting, repulsive, objectionable *Opposite*: pleasant

distastefulness *n* **unpleasantness**, offensiveness, nastiness, repulsiveness *Opposite*: pleasantness

distend *v* **swell**, bloat, balloon, inflate, swell up *Opposite*: deflate

distended *adj* **swollen**, bloated, inflated, enlarged, expanded

distension *n* **swelling**, expansion, enlargement, tumescence, dilation

distil *v* **1 purify**, refine, condense, extract, concentrate *Opposite*: dilute **2 extract**, garner, glean, cull, collect *Opposite*: expand

distillate *n* **essence**, tincture, concentrate, extract, distillation

distillation *n* **1 concentration**, condensation, refinement, purification, extraction *Opposite*: dilution **2 essence**, epitome, embodiment, summation, condensation **3 distillate**, tincture, extract, concentrate

distinct *adj* **1 separate**, different, dissimilar, discrete, diverse *Opposite*: same **2 clear**, definite, well-defined, noticeable, marked *Opposite*: unclear

distinction *n* **1 difference**, division, dissimilarity, discrepancy, otherness *Opposite*: similarity **2 feature**, characteristic, idiosyncrasy, peculiarity, trait **3 merit**, excellence, note, worth, accolade *Opposite*: disgrace

distinctive *adj* **characteristic**, idiosyncratic, distinguishing, individual, typical *Opposite*: common

distinctiveness *n* **uniqueness**, individuality, particularity, individualism, singularity *Opposite*: sameness

distinctly *adv* **definitely**, clearly, noticeably, markedly, particularly *Opposite*: vaguely

distinguish *v* **1 differentiate**, tell apart, tell between, discriminate, decide *Opposite*: homogenize **2 make out**, discern, see, recognize, perceive **3 set apart**, single out, characterize, mark, classify

distinguishable *adj* **1 different**, unique, distinct, special, divergent **2 discernible**, obvious, noticeable, clear, evident *Opposite*: indistinguishable

distinguished *adj* **illustrious**, eminent, famous, famed, well-known *Opposite*: undistinguished

distinguishing *adj* **unique**, individual, personal, distinctive, characteristic *Opposite*: typical

distort *v* **1 misrepresent**, interfere with, twist, alter, garble **2 deform**, disfigure, twist, warp, alter *Opposite*: straighten

distorted *adj* **1 one-sided**, slanted, partial, inaccurate, partisan *Opposite*: accurate **2 twisted**, malformed, warped, bent, contorted *Opposite*: straight **3 unrecognizable**, grotesque, unnatural, monstrous, bizarre

distortion *n* **1 bend**, buckle, twist, deformation, warp **2 misrepresentation**, alteration, lie, falsehood, falsification

distract *v* **1 sidetrack**, divert, confuse, addle, befuddle **2 entertain**, amuse, divert, absorb, engross

distracted *adj* **1 unfocused**, abstracted, preoccupied, sidetracked, diverted *Opposite*: attentive **2 troubled**, agitated, anxious, perplexed, confused *Opposite*: calm

distracting *adj* **off-putting**, disturbing, diverting, disrupting

distraction *n* **1 interruption**, disruption, commotion, disturbance, interference **2 diversion**, entertainment, hobby, pastime, leisure activity **3 agitation**, anxiety, bewilderment, confusion, desperation

distraught *adj* **distressed**, beside yourself, out of your mind, hysterical, upset *Opposite*: calm

distress *n* **1 suffering**, pain, sorrow, anguish, agony *Opposite*: peace **2 trouble**, danger, rigour, difficulty, misfortune ■ *v* **upset**, disturb, trouble, bother, afflict *Opposite*: soothe

distressed *adj* **1 upset**, distraught, troubled, concerned, worried *Opposite*: content **2 in pain**, suffering, anguished, tormented, miserable

distressing *adj* **upsetting**, worrying, difficult, stressful, painful

distress signal *n* **call for help**, cry for help, alarm bell, alarm, call

distribute *v* **1 deal out**, hand out, share out, allocate, give out *Opposite*: amass **2 deliver**, supply, circulate, spread out, spread *Opposite*: retain. *See* COMPARE AND CONTRAST *at* **scatter**.

distributer *see* distributor

distribution *n* **1 sharing**, allocation, giving out, division, allotment **2 delivery**, supply, circulation, transportation, dispersal **3 spreading**, dispersal, dissemination, scattering

distributor *n* **supplier**, provider, wholesaler, broker, trader

district *n* **area**, locality, quarter, borough, ward

distrust *n* **suspicion**, disbelief, doubt, misgiving, cynicism *Opposite*: trust ■ *v* **disbelieve**, doubt, be suspicious of, mistrust, suspect *Opposite*: trust

distrustful *adj* **suspicious**, doubting, wary, nervous, disbelieving *Opposite*: trusting

disturb *v* **1 interrupt**, distract, bother, disrupt, annoy **2 upset**, worry, bother, concern, perturb **3 move**, transfer, shift, dislocate, remove **4 spoil**, unsettle, upset, meddle, tamper. *See* COMPARE AND CONTRAST *at* **bother**.

disturbance *n* **1 trouble**, commotion, riot, uproar, fracas **2 annoyance**, interruption, intrusion, bother, disruption

disturbed *adj* **1 troubled**, bothered, concerned, worried, distressed *Opposite*: unconcerned **2 unstable**, troubled, traumatized, unbalanced, unhinged *Opposite*: stable

disturbing *adj* **worrying**, troubling, alarming, upsetting, distressing *Opposite*: reassuring

disunite *v* **split**, divide, separate, undo, dissolve *Opposite*: unite

disunity *n* **disagreement**, discord, divergence, dissent, conflict *Opposite*: unity

disuse *n* **neglect**, abandonment, unemployment, dereliction *Opposite*: use

disused *adj* **empty**, abandoned, neglected, derelict, deserted *Opposite*: occupied

ditch *n* **channel**, trench, dike, drain, waterway ■ *v* (*infml*) **scrap**, get rid of, drop, split up with, discard

dither *v* **hesitate**, dally, dawdle, waste time, vacillate

ditherer *n* **vacillator**, dawdler, waverer, hesitater

dithering *n* **indecisiveness**, indecision, hesitation, irresolution, wavering *Opposite*: decisiveness

ditty *n* **song**, poem, rhyme, limerick, nursery rhyme

diurnal *adj* **1 day**, daytime, daylight *Opposite*: nocturnal **2 daily**, 24-hour, 24-hourly, circadian, quotidian (*fml*)

diva *n* **prima donna**, singer, chanteuse, soprano

divan *n* **settee**, couch, sofa

dive *v* **1 jump**, leap, drop, lunge, submerge *Opposite*: surface **2 plummet**, plunge, fall, nose-dive, crash *Opposite*: shoot up ■ *n* **1 lunge**, leap, drop, jump **2 plunge**, fall, nosedive, crash, free-fall **3** (*infml*) **dump** (*infml*), hole (*infml*), fleapit (*infml*)

diver *n* **swimmer**, deep-sea diver, snorkeller, frogman, scuba diver

diverge *v* **1 deviate**, move away, wander, depart, swerve *Opposite*: converge **2 differ**, disagree, vary, conflict *Opposite*: concur **3 digress**, ramble, stray, deviate

divergence *n* **1 deviation**, departure, discrepancy, disagreement, separation *Opposite*: convergence **2 difference**, difference of opinion, disagreement, variance, conflict *Opposite*: agreement

divergent *adj* **different**, differing, deviating, conflicting, contradictory *Opposite*: similar

diverse *adj* **1 varied**, miscellaneous, assorted, sundry **2 different**, dissimilar, unlike, distinct, separate *Opposite*: similar

diversely *adv* **varyingly**, variously, distinctly, separately, dissimilarly *Opposite*: similarly

diversification *n* **change**, divergence, variation, modification, broadening *Opposite*: specialization

diversify *v* **branch out**, expand, spread, broaden your horizons, vary *Opposite*: specialize

diversion *n* **1 distraction**, entertainment, pastime, hobby, leisure activity **2 change**, alteration, departure, digression, deviation

diversionary *adj* **distracting**, diverting, misleading, deflecting, deceptive

diversity *n* **variety**, assortment, multiplicity, range, mixture *Opposite*: uniformity

divert *v* **1 redirect**, deflect, reroute, switch **2 distract**, sidetrack, turn away, avert, deter *Opposite*: focus **3 entertain**, amuse, please, delight, gladden

divest *v* **strip**, rid, dissociate, separate, part from *Opposite*: give

divide *v* **1 split**, separate, partition, segregate, break up *Opposite*: join **2 share**, share out, divide up, deal out, distribute **3 cause a rift**, split up, break up, split, come between *Opposite*: unite ■ *n* **gulf**, rift, division, split, gap

dividend *n* **bonus**, extra, payment, share, surplus

divider *n* **partition**, separator, screen

dividing line *n* **distinction**, margin, borderline, border, watershed

divination *n* **prophecy**, prediction, forecast, foretelling, insight

divine *adj* **1 heavenly**, celestial, godly, godlike, deific (*fml*) *Opposite*: secular **2 great**, exquisite, delightful, lovely, pleasing ■ *v* **discover**, guess, presume, deduce, discern

divinity *n* **religion**, theology, religious studies, spirituality, mysticism

divisible *adj* **isolatable**, detachable, separable, dividable *Opposite*: inseparable

division *n* **1 separation**, splitting up, partition, dissection, detachment *Opposite*: union **2 sharing out**, distribution, allotment, allocation, apportionment **3 split**, rift, disagreement, discord, break *Opposite*: unity

4 boundary, partition, border, dividing line, demarcation **5 category**, classification, type, class, grouping **6 department**, section, group, branch, sector

divisive *adj* **discordant**, troublesome, disruptive, conflict-ridden, contentious

divisiveness *n* **disruptiveness**, dissension, disagreement, discord, disunity

divorce *n* **separation**, split, breakup, split-up, annulment *Opposite*: marriage ■ *v* **dissociate**, disconnect, separate, distance, detach *Opposite*: associate

divorced *adj* **separated**, removed, unconnected, split, detached *Opposite*: together

divot *n* turf, sod, clump, clod, piece

divulge *v* reveal, tell, make known, disclose, let drop

divvy *(infml)* v **divide up**, divide, share out, deal out, distribute

dizzily *adv* **dazedly**, woozily, lightheadedly, shakily, unsteadily *Opposite*: steadily

dizziness *n* **faintness**, giddiness, wooziness, vertigo, shakiness

dizzy *adj* **1 faint**, giddy, woozy, shaky, light-headed **2** *(infml)* **frivolous**, flippant, silly, lighthearted, flighty

DJ *n* **1 dinner jacket**, tuxedo, black tie, tux *(infml)* **2 disc jockey**, MC, radio presenter, broadcaster, deejay *(infml)*

do *v* **1 perform**, accomplish, act, carry out, complete **2 see to**, fix, prepare, sort out, look after **3 solve**, work out, resolve, figure out, puzzle out **4** *(infml)* **cheat**, trick, con, swindle, defraud ■ *n* *(infml)* **reception**, party, function, drinks party, cocktail party. *See* COMPARE AND CONTRAST *at* **perform**.

doable *adj* **achievable**, possible, workable, feasible, attainable *Opposite*: impossible

do a bunk *(infml)* v **disappear**, vanish, bolt, run away, scoot *(infml)* *Opposite*: hang about

do away with *v* **1 abolish**, dispense with, remove, dispose of, get rid of *Opposite*: retain **2** *(infml)* **kill**, murder, assassinate, finish off *(infml)*, do in *(infml)*

docile *adj* **quiet**, passive, unassuming, compliant, submissive *Opposite*: wild

docility *n* **quietness**, submissiveness, meekness, tameness, gentleness *Opposite*: fierceness

dock *n* **berth**, mooring, anchorage, wharf, quay ■ *v* **1 come in**, tie up, land, berth, moor **2 cut**, cut off, crop, stop, reduce *Opposite*: increase

docket *n* **1 tag**, sticker, label, marker, ticket **2 agenda**, programme, schedule, calendar, timetable ■ *v* **label**, tag, identify, disclose, declare

dockside *n* **wharf**, jetty, dock, quayside, quay

dockyard *n* **shipyard**, boatyard, dry dock

doctor *n* **1 medical practitioner**, physician, healer, doc *(infml)*, medic *(infml)* **2 academic**, scholar, expert, specialist, Doctor of Philosophy ■ *v* **1 amend**, modify, adjust, meddle with, rework **2 treat**, care for, look after, cure, heal

doctorate *n* **higher degree**, research degree, university degree, PhD, Doctor of Philosophy

doctrinaire *adj* **rigid**, inflexible, stern, strict, unbending *Opposite*: liberal

doctrine *n* **policy**, principle, set of guidelines, canon, dogma

document *n* **text**, file, article, essay, paper ■ *v* **record**, keep a record, detail, write down, provide evidence

documentation *n* **certification**, papers, credentials, documents, citations

dodder *v* **1 tremble**, shake, waver, quake, quiver **2 totter**, reel, teeter, stagger, wobble *Opposite*: stride

doddering *adj* **tottering**, reeling, teetering, staggering, wobbling

doddery *adj* **shaky**, unsteady, tottery, feeble, frail *Opposite*: steady

doddle *(infml)* *n* **child's play**, piece of cake *(infml)*, cinch *(infml)*, pushover *(infml)*, breeze *(infml)* *Opposite*: challenge

dodge *v* **1 move**, cut, duck, move away, side-step **2 avoid**, evade, shirk, elude, get out of

dodgy *(infml)* *adj* **1 dishonest**, suspect, unreliable, untrustworthy, doubtful *Opposite*: reliable **2 risky**, dangerous, hazardous, unsafe, chancy *Opposite*: safe

do down *(infml)* *v* **disparage**, smear, belittle, deride, pour scorn on

doer *n* **achiever**, dynamo, go-getter *(infml)*, live wire *(infml)*

doff *v* **take off**, lift, tip, tilt, remove *Opposite*: don

dog *n* **canine**, hound, doggy *(infml)*, mutt *(infml)*, pooch *(infml)* ■ *v* **1 follow**, pursue, chase, trail, track **2 bother**, beleaguer, harass, vex, plague

WORD BANK

❏ **types of large dog** Afghan hound, Alsatian, bloodhound, borzoi, boxer, bulldog, collie, dalmatian, Doberman pinscher, Great Dane, greyhound, guide dog, husky, Labrador, mastiff, Newfoundland, Old English sheepdog, Pyrenean mountain dog, retriever, Rottweiler, Saint Bernard, setter, sheepdog, wolfhound

❏ **types of small dog** affenpinscher, airedale, basenji, basset, beagle, Border terrier, bull terrier, cairn terrier, chihuahua, chow, corgi, dachshund, fox terrier, foxhound, Jack Russell, Pekingese, pomeranian, poodle, pug, Scottie, Sealyham, shar-pei, shih tzu, spaniel, terrier, whippet, Yorkshire terrier

dog-eared *adj* **damaged**, tattered, battered, well-read, worn *Opposite*: pristine

dogfight *n* **fight**, conflict, combat, encounter, raid

dogged adj **determined**, single-minded, unwavering, indefatigable, steadfast Opposite: half-hearted

doggedness n **perseverance**, persistence, single-mindedness, tenacity, resolve Opposite: apathy

doggerel n 1 **verse**, poetry, rhyme, limerick, ditty 2 **gibberish**, nonsense, prattle, rubbish, garbage

dogleg n **sharp bend**, angle, corner, curve, bend ■ v **bend**, turn, curve, swerve

dogma n **creed**, doctrine, philosophy, canon, belief

dogmatic adj **rigid**, inflexible, unbending, strict, intransigent Opposite: flexible

dogmatism n **intransigence**, inflexibility, strictness, presumption, arrogance Opposite: openness

dog-tired (infml) adj **exhausted**, worn out, shattered, tired, all in Opposite: fresh

do in (infml) v **kill**, murder, assassinate, finish off (infml), do away with (infml)

doings (infml) n **activities**, actions, events, happenings, deeds

doldrums n 1 **stagnation**, sluggishness, boredom, lethargy, lassitude Opposite: energy 2 **gloominess**, melancholy, dejection, despondency, pessimism Opposite: cheerfulness

doleful adj **unhappy**, miserable, sad, woeful, dejected Opposite: cheerful

dolefulness n **sadness**, unhappiness, misery, mournfulness, woefulness Opposite: cheerfulness

dole out (infml) v **share out**, dispense, distribute, allocate, allot Opposite: hoard

doll n **toy**, figurine, figure, model, puppet

dollar n **dollar bill**, buck (infml), big one (infml), greenback (US slang)

dollop (infml) n **blob**, spoonful, spoon, squirt, drop

doll up (infml) v **dress up**, smarten up, spruce up, titivate, smarten Opposite: tone down

dolly (infml) see **doll**

dolmen n **megalith**, obelisk, trilithon, monument, standing stone

domain n **area**, field, sphere, sphere of influence, province

dome n **vault**, cupola, roof, ceiling

domed adj **vaulted**, hemispherical, rounded, round

domestic adj 1 **home**, family, house, household, familial Opposite: public 2 **national**, local, internal, inland, native Opposite: international

domesticate v **tame**, break, bring under control, control, housetrain

domesticated adj **tame**, pet, trained, tamed, housetrained Opposite: wild

domestication n **taming**, training, house-training, subjugation

domesticity n **home life**, family life, home comforts, married life, creature comforts

domestic partner n **cohabitee**, partner, significant other, spousal equivalent (US)

domicile (fml) n **home**, residence, house, flat, quarters

dominance n **supremacy**, ascendancy, domination, power, authority Opposite: weakness

dominant adj 1 **domineering**, bossy, overbearing, officious, authoritarian Opposite: submissive 2 **leading**, main, central, foremost, prevailing Opposite: minor

dominate v 1 **control**, rule, lead, govern, direct 2 **overlook**, overshadow, tower above, tower over, dwarf

domination n **power**, control, command, authority, dominion

domineering adj **bossy**, dominant, overbearing, officious, authoritarian Opposite: meek

dominion n 1 **power**, authority, control, command, domination 2 **territory**, colony, province, region, protectorate

don v **put on**, throw on, get into, pull on, dress in Opposite: take off ■ n **university teacher**, lecturer, fellow, academic, tutor

donate v **give**, contribute, bequeath, provide, offer. See COMPARE AND CONTRAST at **give**.

donation n **gift**, contribution, payment, bequest, endowment

done adj **complete**, completed, ended, finished, through

donkey's years (infml) n **years**, aeons, for ever, ages (infml), yonks (slang)

donkeywork (infml) n 1 **hard work**, heavy labour, hard graft 2 **groundwork**, preparatory, work, preparation, research

donnish adj **academic**, bookish, dry, serious, intellectual

donor n **giver**, contributor, benefactor, patron, supporter

doodle v **draw**, sketch, scribble, squiggle ■ n **drawing**, sketch, scribble, picture, squiggle

doom n 1 **fate**, destiny, lot, kismet, portion (literary) 2 **disaster**, trouble, end, death, tragedy

doomed adj 1 **fated**, destined, damned, condemned, predestined 2 **hopeless**, disaster-prone, ruined, lost, damned

doom-laden adj **gloomy**, pessimistic, dismal, depressing, despairing Opposite: upbeat (infml)

doomsday n **end of the world**, end of time, Last Judgment, Judgment Day, Day of Judgment

doomy (infml) adj 1 **pessimistic**, despairing, gloomy, glum, melancholy Opposite: cheery 2 **ominous**, threatening, portentous, worrying, troubling Opposite: hopeful

door n **entrance**, gate, entry, exit, access

doorplate n **name plate**, sign, plaque, house sign, plate

doorstep n **entrance**, threshold, access, doorway, front doorstep

doorway n **entrance**, door, front entrance, entry, front door

doppelgänger n **double**, mirror image, shadow, twin, clone

dormant adj 1 **inactive**, asleep, sleeping, quiescent, quiet Opposite: active 2 **latent**, undeveloped, hidden, unexpressed

dosage n **amount**, quantity, dose, measure, prescription

dose n 1 **amount**, quantity, dosage, measure, prescription 2 (infml) **bout**, spell, period, attack, experience ■ v **treat**, give medicine to, dose up, medicate

doss n **sleep**, nap, catnap, siesta, snooze (infml)

dossier n **file**, record, report, folder, profile

dot n **spot**, point, mark, blotch, speck ■ v **speckle**, sprinkle, pepper, fleck, spot

doting adj **fond**, loving, devoted, affectionate, adoring

dotted adj **scattered**, sprinkled, spotted, speckled, spread

dotty adj 1 **unconventional**, odd, eccentric, idiosyncratic, strange Opposite: normal 2 **absurd**, impractical, illogical, foolish, nonsensical Opposite: practical 3 (infml) **crazy** (infml), fond, besotted, doting, infatuated

double adj **dual**, binary, twofold, duple, twin ■ adv **twice**, twofold, twice over, two times ■ n 1 **duo**, pair, duet, couple 2 **doppelgänger**, clone, alter ego, twin, stand-in ■ v 1 **increase twofold**, double up, amplify, magnify, expand Opposite: lessen 2 **bend**, fold, double up, bend over, fold up

double act n **pair**, twosome, duo, two-hander, couple

double agent n **spy**, mole, infiltrator, inside agent, secret agent

double-book v **overbook**, overfill, overextend, overstretch

double check n **second check**, reassessment, check, verification

double-check v **make sure**, ensure, reassure yourself, check, verify

double-cross v **betray**, con, let down, cheat, sell out ■ n **betrayal**, deception, swindle, trick, con

double-crosser n **swindler**, cheat, trickster, liar, fraudster

double-dealer n **swindler**, liar, cheat, fraudster, trickster

double-dealing n **duplicity**, betrayal, deceit, cheating, treachery Opposite: honesty ■ adj **duplicitous**, deceitful, double-faced, cheating, swindling Opposite: honest

double Dutch (infml) n **rubbish**, gibberish, gabble, nonsense, garbage

double-edged adj **ambiguous**, two-edged, disingenuous, ironic, sly Opposite: ingenuous

double-faced adj **insincere**, deceitful, dishonest, two-faced, false Opposite: honest

double-jointed adj **flexible**, supple, agile, lithe

double-quick (infml) adj **rapid**, swift, speedy, prompt, instant Opposite: slow ■ adv **rapidly**, swiftly, speedily, promptly, quickly Opposite: slowly

double talk n 1 **gibberish**, nonsense, trash, rubbish, garbage 2 **sophistry**, doublespeak, deceit, jargon, smoke and mirrors

double up v **bend**, fold, double, bend over, fold up

doubt v **disbelieve**, mistrust, suspect, have reservations, have doubts Opposite: believe ■ n **hesitation**, uncertainty, reservation, misgiving, distrust Opposite: certainty

doubter n **nonbeliever**, cynic, doubting Thomas, agnostic, pessimist Opposite: believer

doubtful adj 1 **unsure**, uncertain, hesitant, in doubt, dubious Opposite: certain 2 **unlikely**, unpromising, uncertain, insecure, shaky Opposite: probable 3 **unreliable**, dubious, suspect, questionable, untrustworthy Opposite: reliable

---

COMPARE AND CONTRAST CORE MEANING: feeling doubt or uncertainty

doubtful undecided or feeling hesitant; **uncertain** or **unsure** lacking certainty or confidence; **in doubt** still undecided and liable to change; **dubious** doubtful and, often, suspicious; **sceptical** questioning the truth or likelihood of something.

---

doubtfully adv **uncertainly**, hesitantly, distrustfully, doubtingly, suspiciously Opposite: confidently

doubtfulness n 1 **uncertainty**, hesitancy, indecision, doubt, distrust Opposite: certainty 2 **unlikelihood**, improbability, chance in a million, slim chance Opposite: likelihood

doubting adj **hesitant**, doubtful, distrustful, suspicious, unbelieving Opposite: trusting

doubtless adv **no doubt**, without a doubt, probably, almost certainly, without question Opposite: possibly

doughty (archaic) adj **brave**, determined, tough, spirited, indomitable Opposite: feeble

dour adj 1 **severe**, unfriendly, sour, stern, hardfaced Opposite: kindly 2 **determined**, stubborn, set, purposeful, resolute Opposite: indecisive

dourness n 1 **severity**, unfriendliness, sourness, sternness, grimness Opposite: kindness 2 **determination**, stubbornness, purpose, drive, resoluteness Opposite: indecision

douse v 1 **drench**, soak, wet, souse, cover 2 **quench**, extinguish, put out, smother, snuff Opposite: kindle

dovetail v **fit together**, slot in, join together,

come together, unite *Opposite*: separate

dowdiness n **drabness**, plainness, dullness, dreariness, frumpiness

dowdy adj **plain**, frumpy, drab, unfashionable, dreary *Opposite*: fashionable

dowel n **rod**, pin, peg

do without v **abstain**, deny yourself, go without, keep off, forgo

down prep **along**, through, the length of ■ adj **1 listed**, nominated, scheduled, timetabled, tabled **2 depressed**, unhappy, miserable, dejected, downhearted *Opposite*: happy **3 out of action**, inoperative, not working, out of order *Opposite*: working **4 behind**, losing, short *Opposite*: winning ■ v **1 put down**, lay down, throw down, set down, lay aside *Opposite*: pick up **2 knock down**, floor, overpower, overcome, defeat **3 consume**, eat, drink, gulp down, swallow

down-and-out adj **destitute**, penniless, homeless, on the streets, broke (infml) *Opposite*: well-heeled (infml)

downbeat adj **1 pessimistic**, gloomy, dark, bleak, negative *Opposite*: upbeat (infml) **2** (infml) **casual**, informal, relaxed, unpretentious, laid-back (infml)

downcast adj **sad**, pessimistic, dejected, depressed, down *Opposite*: cheerful

downer (infml) n **disappointment**, shame, pity, letdown, discouragement

downfall n **failure**, ruin, fall, end, demise (fml) *Opposite*: success

downgrade v **demote**, reduce, lower, relegate *Opposite*: upgrade

downhearted adj **sad**, pessimistic, dejected, disappointed, depressed *Opposite*: cheerful

downhill adj **easy**, simple, effortless, plain sailing, straightforward *Opposite*: uphill

download v **transfer**, copy, move, take

downmarket adj **low quality**, inferior, cheap, low cost, second-rate *Opposite*: upmarket

down payment n **payment**, instalment, deposit, disbursement

downplay v **tone down**, moderate, restrain, soften, modulate *Opposite*: highlight

downpour n **heavy shower**, deluge, rainstorm, cloudburst, torrent

downright adv **positively**, undeniably, unquestionably, undoubtedly, totally *Opposite*: questionably

downside n **negative aspect**, shortcoming, weakness, snag, stumbling block *Opposite*: advantage

downsize v **slim down**, cut back, economize, rationalize, trim *Opposite*: expand

downstairs adv **below**, down the stairs, down, down below

downswing n **fall**, slump, decline, dip, downturn *Opposite*: upswing

downtime n **stoppage**, lost time, idle time, interruption

down-to-earth adj **practical**, realistic, sensible, matter-of-fact, pragmatic *Opposite*: fanciful

downtrodden adj **browbeaten**, subjugated, broken, oppressed, demoralized

downturn n **slump**, recession, dip, decline, depression *Opposite*: upturn

downward adj **descending**, down, downhill, sliding, descendent *Opposite*: upward

downy adj **silky**, soft, velvety, furry, feathery *Opposite*: rough

dowry n **wedding gift**, present, grant, settlement, portion

doyen n **leading figure**, senior member, leading light, notable, leader

doyenne n **leading figure**, senior member, leading light, notable, leader

do your homework (infml) v **prepare**, research, plan, find out

doze v **nap**, sleep, slumber, snooze (infml), kip (infml) ■ n **nap**, slumber, sleep, snooze (infml), kip (infml)

dozens (infml) n **lots**, loads (infml), masses (infml), tons (infml), stacks (infml)

doze off v **fall asleep**, go to sleep, nod off, nod, drift off *Opposite*: wake up

dozily adv **sleepily**, tiredly, lethargically, sluggishly, drowsily *Opposite*: alertly

doziness n **sleepiness**, tiredness, lethargy, sluggishness, drowsiness *Opposite*: alertness

dozy adj **1 sleepy**, drowsy, tired, dozing, nodding *Opposite*: alert **2 silly**, foolish, dreamy, scatterbrained, daffy (infml)

drab adj **1 gloomy**, sombre, dull, grey, dingy *Opposite*: bright **2 uninteresting**, unexciting, monotonous, boring, dreary *Opposite*: interesting

drabness n **dullness**, plainness, dowdiness, dreariness, dinginess *Opposite*: brightness

draconian adj **harsh**, severe, strict, strong, austere *Opposite*: mild

draft n **outline**, sketch, summary, plan, rough copy ■ v **draw up**, prepare, sketch out, outline, write

drag v **1 pull**, haul, draw, heave, lug **2 dawdle**, lag, crawl, creep, loiter *Opposite*: fly. See COMPARE AND CONTRAST at **pull**.

dragging adj **slow**, tedious, tiresome, wearisome, uninteresting *Opposite*: interesting

draggy (infml) adj **1 sluggish**, slow, slow-moving, snail-paced, dawdling *Opposite*: brisk **2 tiresome**, tedious, dragging, wearisome, uninteresting *Opposite*: interesting

drag in v **bring in**, involve, allude to, mention, implicate *Opposite*: exclude

dragnet n **1 net**, mesh, trawl net, game net, trap **2 search**, hunt, pursuit, tracking operation, quest

dragoon v **coerce**, press, bully, intimidate, browbeat

drag out v extend, prolong, draw out, lengthen, stretch *Opposite*: cut short

drag up v return to, bring up, dredge up, revive, mention

drag your feet v hold back, hang back, drag your heels, take your time, stall

drain v use up, exhaust, consume, deplete, sap *Opposite*: replenish ■ n sewer, ditch, channel, culvert, conduit

drained adj exhausted, weak, weary, tired, worn out *Opposite*: energetic

draining adj exhausting, trying, wearing, tiring, gruelling

drama n 1 play, stage show, performance, production, spectacle 2 excitement, commotion, fuss, performance, crisis

dramatic adj 1 considerable, significant, radical, noticeable, spectacular *Opposite*: modest 2 affected, melodramatic, theatrical, histrionic, studied *Opposite*: natural

dramatics n histrionics, hysterics, excitement, commotion, fuss

dramatist n playwright, writer, author, scriptwriter

dramatization n staging, performance, production, adaptation

dramatize v exaggerate, sensationalize, play up, embellish, lay on *Opposite*: play down

drape v swathe, dress, wrap, cover, clothe

drapery n curtains, hangings, drapes, swags

drastic adj radical, severe, extreme, dire, sweeping *Opposite*: modest

draught n 1 current, flow, waft, breeze, breath 2 (dated) medicine, concoction, mixture, brew, tonic

draw v 1 sketch, illustrate, copy, depict, describe 2 pull, drag, haul, move, tow *Opposite*: shove 3 pull out, extract, withdraw, take out, unsheathe *Opposite*: put away 4 get, obtain, extract, derive, gain 5 attract, pull, lure, appeal, entice 6 finish equal, tie, equal, square, even ■ n 1 dead heat, tie, stalemate, deadlock, standoff 2 attraction, magnet, crowd puller, inducement, lure. *See* COMPARE AND CONTRAST *at* pull.

draw a veil over v conceal, keep quiet about, ignore, forget, hush up (infml) *Opposite*: expose

draw back v move away, draw away, withdraw, retreat, recoil *Opposite*: approach

drawback n disadvantage, problem, downside, negative, weakness *Opposite*: advantage

draw in v involve, implicate, engage, ensnare, hook

drawing n sketch, picture, illustration, diagram, portrayal

drawl n accent, twang, brogue, tones, pronunciation

drawn adj haggard, strained, pinched, tired, wan *Opposite*: relaxed

draw near v approach, get closer, come nearer, come up, creep up *Opposite*: move away

drawn-out adj protracted, lengthy, long, convoluted, interminable *Opposite*: swift

draw off v pour, siphon off, pull, drain off, suck up

draw on v use, employ, be inspired by, resort to, fall back on

draw out v prolong, extend, make last, lengthen, stretch *Opposite*: cut short

drawstring n tie, string, lace, belt

draw the short straw v get a raw deal, do badly, be unlucky, come off worst, lose out

draw up v draft, put together, assemble, prepare, write

dray n wagon, cart, low-loader, transporter, lorry

dread v fear, be afraid of, be terrified of, be frightened of, be worried about *Opposite*: look forward to ■ n terror, fear, trepidation, anxiety, dismay *Opposite*: confidence

dreadful adj terrible, awful, horrible, frightful, alarming *Opposite*: lovely

dreadfully adv extremely, very, terribly, awfully, really

dreadfulness n awfulness, horror, misery, ghastliness, gruesomeness

dream n 1 vision, daydream, reverie, nightmare, hallucination *Opposite*: reality 2 aspiration, wish, goal, hope, ambition 3 delight, joy, pleasure, marvel, ideal *Opposite*: nightmare ■ v fantasize, visualize, imagine, fancy, daydream

dreamer n visionary, idealist, romantic, fantasist *Opposite*: realist

dreaminess n 1 pensiveness, abstraction, vagueness, wistfulness, languor 2 perfection, beauty, exquisiteness, loveliness, gorgeousness

dreamland n paradise, heaven, nirvana, fairyland, fantasy world *Opposite*: real world

dreamlike adj unreal, fantastic, surreal, weird, bizarre *Opposite*: real

dream up v concoct, think up, invent, imagine, come up with

dream world n fantasy world, land of make-believe, fairyland, never-never land, cloud-cuckoo-land *Opposite*: real world

dreamy adj 1 pensive, vague, faraway, wistful, preoccupied *Opposite*: alert 2 wonderful, beautiful, superb, out of this world, fantastic *Opposite*: ordinary

dreariness n 1 dullness, monotony, tedium, boredom, routine *Opposite*: excitement 2 bleakness, misery, cheerlessness, grimness, gloominess *Opposite*: cheerfulness

dreary adj 1 dull, boring, monotonous, tedious, lifeless *Opposite*: interesting 2 bleak, cheerless, dismal, miserable, grim *Opposite*: cheerful

dredge v search, scour, comb, ransack, rummage

dredge up v unearth, dig up, drag up, bring up, uncover Opposite: bury

dregs n residue, sediment, silt, lees, deposit

drench v soak, wet, saturate, douse, steep Opposite: dry out

drenched adj soaked, sodden, wet, inundated, saturated Opposite: dry

dress v 1 wear, put on, dress up, clothe, slip into Opposite: undress 2 adorn, decorate, deck out, ornament, trim ■ n 1 frock, gown, robe 2 clothing, clothes, costume, garb, wear

WORD BANK
❏ types of dress ballgown, cheongsam, cocktail dress, evening dress, gymslip, kaftan, kimono, muumuu, pinafore, robe, sari, shalwar-kameez, sheath, shift, shirtdress, sundress, wedding dress

dress down v scold, reprimand, lecture, rebuke, censure Opposite: praise

dressed adj turned out, robed, garbed, outfitted, kitted out (infml) Opposite: undressed

dressing n bandage, covering, gauze

dressing gown n housecoat, negligée, wrap, peignoir, robe

dressmaking n couture, tailoring, sewing

dress rehearsal n practice, run through, trial, dummy run, rehearsal

dress sense n flair, stylishness, fashion sense, panache, chic

dress up v disguise, revamp, embellish, decorate, titivate

dressy adj elegant, fashionable, stylish, chic, classy (infml) Opposite: sloppy

dribble v 1 drool, salivate, slobber, slaver, drivel 2 trickle, ooze, drip, seep, leak Opposite: gush

dried adj dehydrated, dried out, dried up, desiccated, dry

drift v float, flow, glide, coast, waft ■ n gist, meaning, point, sense, idea

drifter n wanderer, tramp, vagabond, rolling stone, vagrant

drifting adj wandering, nomadic, homeless, itinerant, travelling Opposite: settled

driftwood n flotsam, jetsam, wreckage, refuse, waste

drill n practice, exercise, discipline, training, instruction ■ v 1 bore, make a hole, pierce, puncture, penetrate 2 train, coach, school, discipline, instruct. See COMPARE AND CONTRAST at teach.

drily adv ironically, humorously, wittily, subtly, wryly

drink v swallow, down, sip, gulp, slurp ■ n 1 thirst-quencher, liquid refreshment, soft drink, cold drink, hot drink 2 alcoholic drink, alcohol, liqueur, nip, tipple (infml) 3 mouthful, taste, gulp, swallow, sip

drinkable adj fit to drink, safe to drink, filtered, potable

drinking fountain n water spout, jet, tap, faucet (US)

drip v dribble, trickle, drop, leak, seep Opposite: gush ■ n drop, trickle, dribble, leak Opposite: stream

drip-dry adj noniron, wash-and-wear, crease-resistant, permanent-press, easy-care

dripping adj wet, soaked, drenched, sodden, saturated Opposite: dry

drive v 1 steer, handle, guide, direct, operate 2 take, run, chauffeur, transport 3 power, run, cause to move, set in motion 4 force, make, coerce, constrain, impel 5 push, propel, urge, goad, send 6 hammer, push, force, plunge, sink ■ n 1 energy, determination, ambition, initiative, motivation Opposite: lethargy 2 urge, desire, need, instinct, passion 3 campaign, crusade, push, fundraiser, appeal

drivel n nonsense, balderdash, gibberish, bunkum (infml), hogwash (infml)

driven adj ambitious, determined, obsessed, motivated, compelled Opposite: apathetic

driver n chauffeur, motorist, operator

drive up the wall (infml) v exasperate, infuriate, make your blood boil, enrage, irritate

driving adj 1 heavy, pouring, lashing Opposite: light 2 powerful, dynamic, energetic, motivating, forceful

drizzle n light rain, trickle, shower, sprinkle (US) Opposite: downpour ■ v rain, spit, spot, shower, trickle Opposite: pour

drizzly adj damp, wet, rainy, misty

droll adj amusing, funny, comic, witty, humorous Opposite: dull

drone v hum, buzz, whine, whirr, murmur

drool v dribble, salivate, slobber, slaver, drivel

droop v 1 sag, wilt, bow, hang down, flop 2 tire, tire out, wear out, flag, wilt Opposite: perk up

droopiness n 1 tiredness, fatigue, weariness, exhaustion, apathy Opposite: freshness 2 floppiness, limpness, lifelessness, slackness, bagginess Opposite: stiffness

droopy adj 1 tired, tired out, worn out, fatigued, weary Opposite: fresh 2 hanging, floppy, limp, dangling, sagging Opposite: upright

drop v 1 fall, go down, plunge, plummet, crash Opposite: rise 2 let fall, let go, release, throw down 3 drip, trickle, ooze, seep, dribble Opposite: pour 4 abandon, stop, shelve, give up, discontinue Opposite: maintain ■ n 1 descent, fall, plunge, decline, dip Opposite: ascent 2 droplet, drip, bead, globule, dewdrop 3 reduction, decrease, decline, fall, cut Opposite: increase

drop a line v write, get in touch, correspond, contact, send a letter

drop back v fall behind, fall back, slow down, lag behind, straggle

drop behind *see* **drop back**

drop in *v* **call**, call by, call in, come round, drop by

droplet *n* **drop**, drip, bead, dewdrop, globule

drop off *(infml)* *v* **1 go to sleep**, nod off, fall asleep, doze off, drift off *Opposite*: wake up **2 deliver**, unload, deposit, leave *Opposite*: pick up

drop out *v* **leave**, give up, quit, withdraw, stop *Opposite*: carry on

dropper *n* **dispenser**, measurer, tube, glass dropper, eye dropper

droppings *n* **dung**, muck, stools, faeces, manure

dross *n* **rubbish**, trash, garbage, scum, waste

drought *n* **dearth**, deficiency, scarcity, famine *Opposite*: abundance

drove *n* **throng**, horde, crowd, gaggle, multitude *Opposite*: trickle

droves *n* **multitudes**, hordes, crowds, scores, masses *(infml)*

drown *v* **1 go down**, go under, sink, die *Opposite*: float **2 drench**, overwater, soak, swamp, saturate *Opposite*: dry **3 cover**, mask, obscure, hide, overlie *Opposite*: amplify

drowse *v* **doze**, be sleepy, nap, have a nap, catnap *Opposite*: wake

drowsiness *n* **sleepiness**, lethargy, stupor, tiredness *Opposite*: wakefulness

drowsy *adj* **sleepy**, tired, dozy, lethargic, somnolent *Opposite*: awake

drub *v* **beat**, pound, thrash, defeat, hammer *(infml)*

drubbing *n* **beating**, thrashing, hammering *(infml)*, pasting *(infml)*, licking *(infml)*

drudge *n* **worker**, skivvy *(infml)*, menial *(fml)* *Opposite*: drone ■ *v* **work**, toil, labour, grind, plod

drudgery *n* **labour**, toil, work, chore, grind

drug *n* **medication**, medicine, painkiller

drum *n* **barrel**, cask, cylinder, container ■ *v* **pound**, beat, tap, thump, thud

drum into *v* **impress**, instil, drive into, teach, din in

drumming *n* **thudding**, pounding, beating, hammering, tapping

drum roll *n* **roll of drums**, tattoo, rattle, paradiddle, rumble

drum up *v* **gather**, stimulate, rally, foster, encourage *Opposite*: suppress

drunk *adj* **inebriated**, intoxicated, plastered *(infml)*, under the influence *(infml)*, smashed *(infml)* *Opposite*: sober

druthers *(infml)* *n* **preference**, free choice, first choice, fancy, cup of tea

dry *adj* **1 dehydrated**, dried out, dried up, arid, waterless *Opposite*: wet **2 thirsty**, dehydrated, parched, in need of a drink, gasping **3 deadpan**, wry, ironic, understated, droll *Opposite*: gushing **4 uninteresting**, dull,

tedious, boring, monotonous *Opposite*: interesting **5 teetotal**, abstinent, abstemious, temperate, prohibitionist ■ *v* **1 make dry**, rub, rub down, towel, wipe *Opposite*: wet **2 desiccate**, become dry, dry out, dry up, dehydrate *Opposite*: swell

COMPARE AND CONTRAST CORE MEANING: lacking moisture

dry having little or no moisture; **dehydrated** experiencing fluid loss, or preserved by drying; **desiccated** (used of products, especially food) free from moisture, or preserved by drying; **arid** (used of land) dry from lack of rain; **parched** dry from excessive heat or lack of rain; **shrivelled** dry, shrunken, and wrinkled; **sere** (*literary*) dry and withered.

dryad *n* **wood nymph**, fairy, naiad, pixie, nymph

dry-clean *v* **clean**, launder, wash, valet

dryer *n* **drying device**, hair dryer, tumble dryer, clothes dryer, clothes horse

dry-eyed *adj* **unemotional**, impassive, expressionless, unmoved, stoical *Opposite*: tearful

dry land *n* **solid ground**, shore, beach, terra firma *Opposite*: sea

dryness *n* **1 aridness**, aridity, dehydration, drought, desiccation *Opposite*: wetness **2 wryness**, irony, understatement, matter-of-factness, sarcasm

dry out *v* **1 air**, dry, dry off, tumble dry, tumble *Opposite*: damp **2 shrivel up**, curl up, dry up, wither, become dehydrated *Opposite*: soak

dry run *n* **rehearsal**, run-through, dummy run, trial run, trial

dry up *v* **1 desiccate**, become dry, dry out, dry, dehydrate *Opposite*: swell **2** *(infml)* **falter**, lose the thread, stop midstream, forget your lines, come to a halt *Opposite*: continue **3 fail**, run out, be used up, come to an end, disappear *Opposite*: continue

dual *adj* **double**, twin, twofold

dualism *n* **symmetry**, contrast, dichotomy, opposition, polarity

duality *n* **dichotomy**, division, dyad, contrast, opposition

dub *v* **call**, nickname, christen, hail as, label

dubbin *n* **polish**, wax, blacking, dressing, waterproofing

dubiety *(fml)* *n* **doubtfulness**, doubt, dubiousness, uncertainty, hesitancy *Opposite*: certitude

dubious *adj* **1 doubtful**, uncertain, unsure, undecided, unconvinced *Opposite*: certain **2 suspect**, untrustworthy, questionable, shady, unsavoury *Opposite*: trustworthy **3 ambiguous**, doubtful, debatable, uncertain, questionable *Opposite*: unambiguous. *See* COMPARE AND CONTRAST *at* **doubtful**.

dubiousness *n* **1 doubt**, doubtfulness, uncertainty, hesitancy, suspicion *Opposite*: certainty **2 fallibility**, unreliability, improbability, ambiguity, vagueness *Opposite*: reliability

duchy n **dukedom**, estate, territory, barony, principality

duck n **water bird**, waterfowl, diver ∎ v 1 **stoop**, bend, bow, bob, nod *Opposite*: straighten 2 **avoid**, evade, dodge, sidestep, circumvent *Opposite*: confront

duckboard n **walkway**, boardwalk, path, planking, catwalk

duck out v **back out**, pull out, drop out, withdraw, get out

duct n **channel**, canal, pipe, tube, vessel

ductile adj **pliable**, malleable, elastic, pliant, plastic. *See* COMPARE AND CONTRAST *at* pliable.

dud (infml) n **failure**, fiasco, letdown, disappointment, flop (infml) *Opposite*: success ∎ adj **useless**, worthless, ineffective, broken, no good *Opposite*: usable

due adj 1 **expected**, scheduled, appointed, anticipated, looked-for 2 **appropriate**, fitting, suitable, proper, right and proper *Opposite*: undue 3 **owing**, unpaid, outstanding, payable, owed *Opposite*: paid ∎ adv **directly**, exactly, direct, dead, straight *Opposite*: indirectly

duel n **contest**, fight, battle, gunfight, combat ∎ v **fight**, clash, battle, contest, struggle

duellist n **fighter**, combatant, opponent, gunfighter, contender

dues n **fees**, subscription, payment, charge, levy

duet n **duo**, double act, twosome, couple, pair

due to prep **because of**, owing to, by reason of, as a result of, attributable to

duff (infml) adj **useless**, inferior, broken, faulty, rotten *Opposite*: excellent

dugout n **bunker**, trench, foxhole, ditch, hollow

dulcet adj **melodious**, melodic, honeyed, soothing, pleasant *Opposite*: harsh

dull adj 1 **boring**, uninteresting, tedious, monotonous, dreary *Opposite*: interesting 2 **cloudy**, overcast, gloomy, leaden, dismal *Opposite*: bright 3 **dark**, dim, muted, faded, lacklustre *Opposite*: bright 4 **stupid**, obtuse, plodding, sluggish, unintelligent *Opposite*: bright ∎ v **deaden**, dampen, stultify, cloud, blunt *Opposite*: accentuate

dullness n 1 **tediousness**, tedium, monotony, dreariness, dryness *Opposite*: liveliness 2 **cloudiness**, gloom, half-light, gloominess, leadenness *Opposite*: brightness 3 **darkness**, dimness, drabness, dowdiness, dinginess *Opposite*: brightness

duly adv **accordingly**, suitably, fittingly, appropriately, properly *Opposite*: unduly

dumbfound v **astonish**, amaze, astound, surprise, stagger

dumbfounded adj **astonished**, amazed, astounded, thunderstruck, staggered

dummy n 1 **mannequin**, model, lay figure, figure, form 2 **copy**, replica, imitation, fake, mock-up *Opposite*: original ∎ adj **imitation**, fake, mock, pretend, replica *Opposite*: original

dummy run n **rehearsal**, run-through, dry run, trial run, trial

dump v 1 **put**, leave, abandon, tip, throw 2 **get rid of**, abandon, leave, dispose of, discard *Opposite*: keep 3 (infml) **abandon**, discard, leave, desert, walk out on (infml) *Opposite*: stand by ∎ n 1 **landfill**, junkyard, scrapyard, rubbish dump, tip 2 (infml) **eyesore**, mess, monstrosity, hovel, tip

dumper n **tipper**, fly-tipper, litterer, litter lout (infml), litterbug (infml)

dune n **bank**, sandbank, hill, mound, ridge

dung n **manure**, droppings, slurry, muck, fertilizer

dungeon n **prison**, cell, jail, vault, oubliette

dunk v **dip**, submerge, immerse, soak, steep

duo n **pair**, twosome, couple, double act, two of a kind

dupe v **fool**, trick, deceive, con, take in ∎ n **victim**, target, fool, sucker (infml), mug (slang)

duplicate v 1 **replicate**, copy, photocopy, reproduce, make two of 2 **repeat**, replicate, reproduce, copy, do again ∎ n **copy**, replacement, photocopy, spare, carbon copy *Opposite*: original ∎ adj **identical**, matching, replica, replacement, spare *Opposite*: original. *See* COMPARE AND CONTRAST *at* copy.

duplication n 1 **repetition**, replication, doubling, copying, photocopying 2 **replica**, duplicate, copy, print, facsimile *Opposite*: original

duplicitous adj **double-dealing**, two-faced, tricky, deceitful, dishonest *Opposite*: honest

duplicity n **deceit**, deception, dishonesty, disloyalty, unfaithfulness *Opposite*: honesty

durability n **toughness**, sturdiness, strength, robustness, resilience *Opposite*: flimsiness

durable adj **tough**, hard-wearing, sturdy, strong, robust *Opposite*: flimsy

duration n **length**, extent, period, time, interval

duress n **pressure**, force, threat, coercion, compulsion *Opposite*: persuasion

during prep **throughout**, through, in, in the course of

dusk n **twilight**, sunset, nightfall, sundown, evening *Opposite*: dawn

dusky adj **shadowy**, dark, darkish, dim, hazy *Opposite*: bright

dust n **powder**, dirt, sand, earth, soil ∎ v 1 **clean**, clean up, wipe, wipe down, wipe up 2 **sprinkle**, brush, cover, scatter, sift

dustbin n **bin**, litter bin, wheelie bin, wastepaper bin, rubbish bin

dust bowl n **desert**, waste, wasteland, wilderness

duster n **cloth**, rag, feather duster, dust cloth

dust jacket n **cover**, jacket, outer, dust cover, paper cover

dustpan *n* **pan**, scoop, shovel, receptacle, container

dustsheet *n* **dust cover**, cover, sheet, throw, cloth

dusty *adj* **dirty**, grimy, filthy, sandy, grubby *Opposite*: spotless

dutiful *adj* **obedient**, well-behaved, compliant, loyal, devoted *Opposite*: disobedient

duty *n* **1 responsibility**, obligation, onus, burden, calling **2 job**, task, function, responsibility, obligation **3 tax**, payment, levy, due, impost

duty-bound *adj* **constrained**, compelled, obliged, forced, obligated

duty-free *(infml)* *adj* **tax-free**, tax-exempt, untaxed, nontaxable

duvet *n* **quilt**, eiderdown, coverlet, comforter *(US)*

dwell *(literary)* *v* **reside**, live, have your home, stay, inhabit *Opposite*: leave

dweller *n* **inhabitant**, resident, occupant, occupier, tenant

dwelling *(fml)* *n* **house**, home, residence, place of abode, lodging

dwell on *v* **think about**, ponder, brood over, mull over, go on about *Opposite*: forget

dwindle *v* **decrease**, decline, diminish, fall off, drop *Opposite*: increase

dwindling *adj* **declining**, decreasing, diminishing, deteriorating, falling *Opposite*: burgeoning

dye *v* **colour**, stain, tint, change the colour of ■ *n* **1 colouring**, colour, stain, pigment **2 hair dye**, colour, tint, rinse, peroxide

dyed-in-the-wool *adj* **long-established**, confirmed, committed, dedicated, incorrigible

dying *adj* **1 last**, final, ultimate, closing, ending **2 disappearing**, failing, fading, vanishing, becoming extinct *Opposite*: thriving

dyke *n* **1 embankment**, dam, barrier, bank, wall **2 ditch**, watercourse, channel, drain, conduit

dynamic *adj* **active**, self-motivated, energetic, vibrant, forceful *Opposite*: lethargic

dynamics *n* **1 changing aspects**, subtleties, forces at work, dynamic forces, underlying forces **2 louds and softs**, dynamic range, changes in volume, dynamic contrast, crescendos

dynamism *n* **vitality**, vigour, energy, drive, enthusiasm *Opposite*: lethargy

dynamite *v* **blow up**, blast, explode, detonate, wreck

dynamo *n* **1 electric generator**, generator, motor, turbine **2** *(infml)* **extrovert**, live wire *(infml)*, go-getter *(infml)*, live one *(infml)*

dynastic *adj* **hereditary**, successional, imperial, sovereign, ruling

dynasty *n* **1 reign**, rule, empire, period, era **2 family**, house, line

dyspepsia *n* **indigestion**, heartburn, acid stomach, upset stomach, unsettled stomach

dysphemism *n* **1 offensiveness**, rudeness, vulgarity, obscenity, ribaldry *Opposite*: euphemism **2 obscenity**, swear word, expletive, oath, profanity *Opposite*: euphemism

dysphemistic *adj* **vulgar**, lewd, offensive, obscene, rude *Opposite*: euphemistic

E

each *pron* **every one**, each one, all, both ■ *adj* **every**, all, both, every single

eager *adj* **keen**, enthusiastic, excited, raring to go, ready *Opposite*: unenthusiastic

eagerness *n* **keenness**, enthusiasm, excitement, readiness, willingness *Opposite*: apathy

eagle-eyed *adj* **observant**, hawk-eyed, sharp-sighted, sharp-eyed, alert *Opposite*: unobservant

ear *n* **1 external ear**, outer ear, earhole, lug *(infml)*, shell-like *(infml)* **2 ability**, sensitivity, talent, knack, facility **3 attention**, hearing, heed, regard

WORD BANK

❑ **parts of an ear** anvil, auricle, cochlea, eardrum, hammer, incus, internal ear, malleus, middle ear, stapes, stirrup, tympanic membrane, tympanum, vestibule

earful *(infml)* *n* **scolding**, lecture, piece of your mind, reprimand, talking-to *(infml)*

earlier *adv* **before**, in advance, previously, formerly, beforehand *Opposite*: later ■ *adj* **previous**, former, past, prior *Opposite*: later

earliest *adj* **first**, initial, original *Opposite*: latest

early *adv* **1 early on**, at the beginning, before time, in advance, ahead of schedule *Opposite*: late **2 soon**, promptly, without delay, now, as soon as possible *Opposite*: later ■ *adj* **1 initial**, first, primary, premature *Opposite*: later **2 timely**, prompt, quick, speedy, immediate *Opposite*: tardy

early years *n* **babyhood**, infancy, childhood, youth, formative years *Opposite*: adulthood

earmark v **allocate**, assign, allot, set aside, put aside

earn v **1 make**, be paid, take home, receive, get **2 deserve**, work for, win, warrant, merit

earnest adj **1 serious**, solemn, grave, sober, intense Opposite: frivolous **2 sincere**, heart-felt, deep, intense, strong Opposite: superficial

earnestness n **sincerity**, seriousness, solemnity, intensity, feeling Opposite: facetiousness

earnings n **1 pay**, salary, wage, wages, income Opposite: expenditure **2 profit**, revenue, gain, return, dividend Opposite: loss

earphone see **earpiece**

earpiece n **receiver**, headset, headphones, earphone

earshot n **hearing range**, range, hearing distance, hearing

earsplitting adj **loud**, piercing, shrill, deafening, noisy Opposite: quiet

earth n **soil**, ground, dirt, mud, terrain

Earth n **world**, globe, planet

earthling n **human being**, human, earthly being, intelligent life-form, human life-form Opposite: extraterrestrial

earthly adj **1 worldly**, material, mortal, secular, everyday Opposite: heavenly **2 possible**, imaginable, conceivable

earthmover n **bulldozer**, digger, power shovel, excavator, steam shovel

earthquake n **tremor**, upheaval, trembling, shaking, seismic activity

earthshaking see **earthshattering**

earthshattering adj **momentous**, tremendous, remarkable, stunning, devastating Opposite: trivial

earthwards adv **towards the earth**, towards the ground, downwards, down, in a nose-dive Opposite: skyward

earthwork n **fortification**, rampart, bulwark, barrier

earthy adj **1 unpretentious**, down-to-earth, no-nonsense, simple, unsophisticated Opposite: refined **2 vulgar**, crude, gross, bawdy, rude

ease n **1 effortlessness**, simplicity, straight-forwardness, facility, easiness Opposite: difficulty **2 comfort**, luxury, affluence, wealth, opulence Opposite: hardship ■ v **1 relieve**, alleviate, reduce, lessen, mitigate Opposite: worsen **2 slide**, slip, edge, push gently, draw out **3 make easier**, facilitate, help, aid, assist Opposite: hinder

easel n **stand**, frame, tripod, support, mount

ease up v **relax**, slow down, slacken off, calm down, ease off

easily adv **1 with no trouble**, without difficulty, without problems, effortlessly, simply **2 without doubt**, by far, by a long shot, by a long way, by a long chalk

easy adj **1 simple**, trouble-free, straight-forward, effortless, uncomplicated Opposite: difficult **2 informal**, relaxed, calm, cool, tranquil Opposite: tense **3 comfortable**, affluent, luxurious, undemanding, leisurely Opposite: hard

easygoing adj **relaxed**, casual, tolerant, even-tempered, calm Opposite: anxious

easy-peasy (infml) adj **simple**, easy, straight-forward, effortless Opposite: difficult

eat v **1 consume**, have, gobble, wolf, munch Opposite: starve **2 have a meal**, dine, lunch, breakfast, snack

eat away v **erode**, corrode, eat into, wear away, wear down

eater n **consumer**, feeder, diner, devourer, guzzler (infml)

eatery (infml) n **restaurant**, self-service restaurant, cafeteria, bistro, eating place

eat into v **1 use up**, eat up, gobble up, reduce, consume **2 corrode**, rust, pockmark, attack, destroy

eat up v **1 consume**, down, gobble, guzzle (infml), scoff (infml) **2 absorb**, obsess, take over, consume, dominate **3** (infml) **lap up**, love, applaud, enthuse about, rave about (infml) Opposite: hate

eat your heart out (infml) v **brood**, dwell on, grieve, pine

eat your words (infml) v **apologize**, retract, say sorry, eat humble pie, take it all back Opposite: stand firm

eau de cologne n **perfume**, cologne, fragrance, scent, toilet water

eavesdrop v **listen in**, overhear, tap, spy, pry

eavesdropper n **listener**, nosy parker (infml), spy, observer

ebb v **1 recede**, go out, flow away, retreat, fall away Opposite: come in **2 fade**, diminish, recede, fail, disappear Opposite: surge ■ n **receding tide**, ebb tide, outgoing tide, falling tide Opposite: flow

ebb and flow v **fluctuate**, vacillate, vary ■ n **shift**, fluctuation, vacillation, variation, flux

ebullience n **joviality**, enthusiasm, liveliness, happiness, cheerfulness Opposite: lugubriousness

ebullient adj **jovial**, enthusiastic, lively, happy, bouncy Opposite: lugubrious

e-cash n **electronic cash**, digital cash, smart card

eccentric adj **odd**, unconventional, unorthodox, unusual, peculiar Opposite: conventional ■ n **oddity**, character, original, case (infml)

eccentricity n **1 oddness**, unconventionality, peculiarity, strangeness, weirdness Opposite: conventionality **2 quirk**, peculiarity, foible, idiosyncrasy, oddity

ecclesiastic n **clergyman**, clergywoman, priest, cleric, minister

ecclesiastical *adj* **church**, clerical, religious, apostolic, papal *Opposite*: secular

echelon *n* **level**, rank, grade, tier, class

echo *n* **reverberation**, resonance, repeat, boom, ricochet ■ *v* **1 reverberate**, resonate, resound, boom, rebound **2 repeat**, reiterate, copy, parrot, confirm

echoing *adj* **resounding**, reverberating, reflecting, ringing, resonant

eclectic *adj* **heterogeneous**, varied, wide-ranging, extensive, diverse *Opposite*: narrow

eclecticism *n* **extensiveness**, range, diversity, scope, variety

eclipse *v* **1 hide**, conceal, obscure, cover, darken **2 outdo**, overshadow, outshine, surpass, overwhelm

ecofriendly *adj* **biodegradable**, green, environmentally friendly, sustainable

ecological *adj* **environmentally friendly**, natural, biological, organic

ecologist *n* **environmentalist**, biologist, natural scientist, naturalist, conservationist

e-commerce *n* **e-business**, e-tailing, cyber-marketing, electronic transactions

economic *adj* **1 financial**, monetary, fiscal, pecuniary, commercial **2 profitable**, cost-effective, moneymaking, lucrative, efficient *Opposite*: uneconomic

economical *adj* **1 frugal**, parsimonious, thrifty, careful, sparing *Opposite*: wasteful **2 inexpensive**, cheap, cost-effective, low-cost, budget *Opposite*: expensive

economize *v* **cut back**, cut down, retrench, save, scrimp and save *Opposite*: spend

economy *n* **1 frugality**, thrift, cost-cutting, saving, parsimony *Opposite*: extravagance **2 saving**, cutback, retrenchment, reduction, scaling-down ■ *adj* **cheap**, budget, reduced, family, low-cost *Opposite*: expensive

WORD BANK
❏ **types of economic condition** austerity, boom, boom and bust, deflation, depression, downswing, downturn, hyperinflation, inflation, inflationary spiral, recession, recovery, reflation, slump, stagflation, upswing, upturn
❏ **types of economic system** collectivism, command economy, free enterprise economy, free market economy, market economy, mixed economy, new economy, planned economy, private economy, service economy

ecosystem *n* **natural environment**, biome, biota, ecology, environment

ecstasy *n* **1 joy**, delight, elation, bliss, rapture *Opposite*: misery **2 trance**, high, frenzy, state *(infml) Opposite*: stupor

ecstatic *adj* **1 overjoyed**, delighted, thrilled, elated, blissful *Opposite*: miserable **2 elated**, high, overexcited, frenzied, in a frenzy *Opposite*: calm

eddy *n* **whirlpool**, swirl, vortex, whirl, maelstrom

edge *n* **1 border**, rim, boundary, perimeter, periphery *Opposite*: centre **2 brink**, verge, threshold, point **3 sharpness**, bitterness, acidity, harshness, venom **4 advantage**, upper hand, superiority, control, authority ■ *v* **1 approach**, skirt, sidle, pick your way, creep **2 border**, frame, trim, fringe, enclose

edgeways *adv* **sideways**, side-on, crossways, across, laterally

edging *n* **border**, trim, fringe, hem, frill

edgy *adj* **nervous**, on edge, anxious, jumpy, jittery *Opposite*: relaxed

edible *adj* **eatable**, fit for human consumption, palatable, appetizing, comestible *(fml) Opposite*: poisonous

edict *n* **proclamation**, announcement, pronouncement, decree, statute

edification *n* **improvement**, education, enlightenment, instruction, elevation *Opposite*: obfuscation

edifice *n* **1 building**, construction, pile, structure, mansion **2 organization**, network, structure, association, group

edify *v* **enlighten**, inform, educate, instruct, improve *Opposite*: obfuscate

edifying *adj* **educational**, informative, illuminating, instructive, scholastic

edit *v* **1 rewrite**, revise, amend, rework, correct **2 oversee**, run, manage, be in charge of, direct

edited *adj* **1 amended**, corrected, revised, rewritten, redrafted *Opposite*: unedited **2 abridged**, concise, shortened, summarized, truncated *Opposite*: complete

edition *n* **version**, publication, copy, issue, impression

editor *n* **1 publishing supervisor**, publishing manager, editor in chief, managing editor, executive editor **2 subeditor**, copy editor, corrector, checker, cutter

editorial *n* **leader**, editorial column, viewpoint, perspective, essay

editorialize *v* **expound**, pontificate, spout, preach, sermonize

edit out *v* **delete**, remove, cut, omit, abridge

educate *v* **teach**, instruct, edify, tutor, train. *See* COMPARE AND CONTRAST *at* **teach**.

educated *adj* **1 well-informed**, well-read, learned, erudite, knowledgeable *Opposite*: uneducated **2 cultured**, cultivated, tasteful, sophisticated, refined *Opposite*: boorish

educated guess *n* **guess**, estimation, estimate, approximation, guesstimate

education *n* **teaching**, learning, schooling, tutoring, instruction

educational *adj* **instructive**, enlightening, didactic, edifying, informative

educator *n* **teacher**, instructor, lecturer, professor, educationalist

eerie *adj* **unnerving**, uncanny, weird, strange, peculiar

efface v **obliterate**, eradicate, destroy, wear away, rub out

effect n **1 result**, consequence, outcome, upshot, end product **2 influence**, weight, force, power, validity **3 impression**, meaning, sense, impact, purpose ■ v (fml) **achieve**, carry out, produce, bring about, realize

effective adj **1 successful**, efficient, productive, useful, helpful Opposite: ineffective **2 real**, actual, in effect, active, operative Opposite: nominal **3 operational**, operative, in force, in operation, in effect Opposite: inoperative

---

COMPARE AND CONTRAST CORE MEANING: producing a result

effective causing the desired or intended result; **efficient** capable of achieving the desired result with the minimum use of resources, time, and effort; **effectual** (fml) potentially successful in producing a desired or intended result; **efficacious** (fml) having the power to achieve the desired result, especially an improvement in somebody's physical condition.

---

effectively adv **1 efficiently**, successfully, productively, well, excellently Opposite: ineffectively **2 in reality**, to all intents and purposes, in point of fact, in all but name

effectiveness n **efficiency**, productiveness, efficacy, success, use Opposite: ineffectiveness

effects (fml) n **belongings**, property, personal property, possessions, things

effectual (fml) adj **effective**, worthwhile, successful, productive, helpful Opposite: ineffectual

effervesce v **hiss**, fizz, bubble, sparkle, froth

effervescence n **1 fizz**, bubbles, sparkle, froth, foam **2 vivacity**, vibrancy, vitality, animation, sparkle Opposite: languor

effervescent adj **1 fizzy**, sparkling, bubbly, aerated, bubbling Opposite: still **2 lively**, vibrant, bubbly, bouncy, sparkling Opposite: dull

efficacious (fml) adj **effective**, efficient, successful, productive, useful Opposite: ineffective

efficacy n **effectiveness**, efficiency, usefulness, productiveness, worth Opposite: ineffectiveness

efficiency n **competence**, efficacy, effectiveness, productivity, proficiency Opposite: inefficiency

efficient adj **1 well-organized**, effective, competent, capable, able Opposite: ineffective **2 inexpensive**, timesaving, labour-saving, economical, cost-effective Opposite: wasteful. See COMPARE AND CONTRAST at **effective**.

effigy n **image**, statue, icon, figure, figurine

effluent n **waste**, sewage, bilge water, seepage, runoff

effort n **1 exertion**, energy, determination, force, elbow grease (infml) Opposite: ease **2 attempt**, try, endeavour, go, shot

effortless adj **easy**, natural, unforced, graceful, unproblematic Opposite: strenuous

effortlessness n **ease**, naturalness, smoothness, simplicity, facility Opposite: difficulty

effrontery n **impudence**, nerve, gall, boldness, arrogance

effusion n **outpouring**, gush, rush, expression, declaration

effusive adj **gushing**, demonstrative, fulsome, vociferous, extravagant Opposite: reserved

e.g. adv **for example**, for instance, say, let's say, perhaps

egalitarian adj **equal**, classless, free, democratic, equal opportunities Opposite: class-conscious

egg n **reproductive cell**, ovum, egg cell, ovule ■ v **urge**, incite, spur, encourage, push Opposite: dissuade

egghead (infml) n **brainbox**, intellectual, boffin (infml), brain (infml), bookworm (infml)

egg on v **encourage**, urge, push, incite, spur Opposite: dissuade

eggshell n **protective covering**, shell, case, casing, covering

ego n **personality**, character, self, self-image, self-worth

egocentric see egotistical

egoism, egoist, egoistic see egotism, egotist, egotistical

egomaniac see egotist

egotism n **self-centredness**, selfishness, conceit, vanity, arrogance Opposite: altruism

egotist n **narcissist**, self-seeker, individualist, self-publicist, self-aggrandizer

egotistical adj **selfish**, conceited, vain, self-centred, self-important Opposite: altruistic

eiderdown n **quilt**, continental quilt, duvet, cover, bedspread

either adj **1 whichever**, either one, one or the other, any **2 each**, both Opposite: neither

eject v **1 expel**, emit, get rid of, spew, spout **2 expel**, banish, drive out, throw out, remove

eke out v **1 make something last**, spin out, make a little go a long way, draw out, use sparingly Opposite: squander **2 supplement**, complement, add to, pad out, make up Opposite: diminish **3 scrape**, scratch, scrape together, scratch out, make

elaborate adj **1 complex**, complicated, intricate, detailed, involved Opposite: straightforward **2 intricate**, sumptuous, extravagant, ornate, decorative Opposite: simple ■ v **1 expound**, expand, enlarge, go into detail, explain Opposite: condense **2 complicate**, work up, build on, develop, detail Opposite: simplify

elaboration n **amplification**, embellishment, explanation, expansion, development

elapse v **pass**, pass by, intervene, slip away, go by

elastic adj **1 stretchy**, expandable, flexible, supple, resilient Opposite: rigid **2 flexible**, adaptable, changeable, variable, mutable Opposite: inflexible. See COMPARE AND CONTRAST at **pliable**.

elasticated adj **stretchy**, elastic, expanding, expandable, stretchable Opposite: rigid

elate v **exhilarate**, thrill, excite, lift, uplift Opposite: dishearten

elated adj **ecstatic**, overjoyed, thrilled, delighted, euphoric Opposite: disheartened

elation n **ecstasy**, delight, euphoria, jubilation, excitement Opposite: despair

elbow v **prod**, jostle, nudge, shove, dig

elbowroom n **1 space**, room, room to spare, room to manoeuvre **2 scope**, freedom, leeway, room to manoeuvre, choice

elder n **leader**, head, chief

elderly adj **aging**, old, aged, mature, of advanced years Opposite: young

eldest adj **oldest**, first-born, first

elect v **1 vote for**, return, vote into office, pick, select **2 choose**, opt for, decide on, select, designate ■ adj **designated**, future, chosen, selected

elected adj **chosen**, designated, selected, voted, nominated

election n **1 vote**, poll, ballot **2 selection**, choice, appointment, designation, nomination

electioneer v **campaign**, whistle-stop, canvass, run

elective adj **1 voting**, chosen by election, filled by election, passed by vote Opposite: appointed **2 optional**, voluntary, free, selective, discretionary Opposite: compulsory

elector n **voter**, member of the electorate, voting member, constituent

electoral adj **democratic**, voting, election, polling, balloting

electorate n **people**, voters, registered voters, voting public, constituency

electric adj **1 electronic**, electrically powered, mains powered, battery-operated, plug-in **2 absorbing**, charged, exciting, thrilling, emotional Opposite: boring

electrical see **electric**

electricity n **current**, voltage, power, energy, electrical energy

electrified adj **1 electric**, electrically powered, wired-up, connected **2 excited**, captivated, thrilled, transfixed, awestruck Opposite: bored

electrify v **captivate**, transfix, thrill, excite, exhilarate Opposite: bore

electrifying adj **exciting**, stirring, thrilling, captivating, stimulating Opposite: boring

electrode n **conductor**, rod, anode, cathode, probe

electronic adj **1 electric**, microelectronic, electrical, automated, computer-operated **2 computerized**, high-tech, on-screen, online, computer

electronics n **microchip technology**, microelectronics, computer electronics, integrated circuit technology, semiconductor technology

elegance n **grace**, style, sophistication, chic, taste Opposite: inelegance

elegant adj **sophisticated**, stylish, graceful, chic, well-designed Opposite: inelegant

elegiac (fml) adj **mournful**, sad, melancholic, funereal, plaintive Opposite: cheerful

elegy n **funeral song**, dirge, requiem, poem, speech

element n **1 component**, part, section, division, portion **2 hint**, amount, quantity, touch, bit **3 factor**, cause, feature, component, ingredient **4 habitat**, environment, milieu, medium, domain

elemental adj **rudimentary**, basic, fundamental, essential, primary

elementary adj **basic**, simple, straightforward, uncomplicated, plain

elements n **rudiments**, basics, fundamentals, essentials, foundations

elephantine adj **1 ponderous**, lumbering, clumsy, slow, heavy Opposite: dainty **2 huge**, enormous, colossal, gigantic, massive Opposite: minute

elevate v **1 lift**, lift up, raise, uplift, hoist Opposite: lower **2 promote**, raise, advance, move up, further Opposite: demote

elevated adj **1 pre-eminent**, eminent, important, prominent, high Opposite: lowly **2 raised**, raised up, lifted, high, higher

elevation n **1 height**, altitude, rise Opposite: depth **2 promotion**, rise, advancement, boost Opposite: demotion

elevenses n **snack**, morning snack, midmorning snack, nibble, bite

eleventh-hour adj **ultimate**, last-minute, lastditch, final

elf n **pixie**, imp, sprite, fairy, gnome

elfin adj **sylphlike**, petite, dainty, tiny, waiflike

elicit v **1 provoke**, cause, produce, bring about, occasion **2 draw out**, draw, bring out, extract, obtain Opposite: repress

eligibility n **suitability**, aptness, entitlement, appropriateness, fitness Opposite: unsuitability

eligible adj **1 qualified**, entitled, suitable, fit, appropriate Opposite: ineligible **2 single**, unmarried, unattached, available

eliminate v **1 remove**, eradicate, abolish, get rid of, do away with Opposite: retain **2 destroy**, kill, exterminate, liquidate, wipe out *(infml) Opposite*: preserve **3 defecate**, urinate, excrete, expel, pass

elimination *n* removal, abolition, exclusion, rejection, eradication *Opposite*: preservation

elite *n* best, cream, cream of the crop, elect, crème de la crème *Opposite*: hoi polloi ■ *adj* **choice**, best, select, selective, leading *Opposite*: run-of-the-mill

elitism *n* **exclusiveness**, exclusivity, superiority, selectivity, selectiveness *Opposite*: equality

elitist *adj* **exclusive**, discriminatory, selective, superior, snobbish *Opposite*: egalitarian

elixir *n* **1 medicine**, tincture, solution, tonic, preparation **2 potion**, restorative, tonic, cureall, snake oil

ellipsis *n* **abbreviation**, contraction, elision, truncation, abridgment

elliptical *adj* **1 oval**, ovoid, ovate, egg-shaped, elongated **2 concise**, succinct, cryptic, indirect, oblique *Opposite*: verbose

elocution *n* **diction**, articulation, pronunciation, enunciation, delivery

elongate *v* **lengthen**, draw out, extend, stretch, prolong *Opposite*: shorten

elongated *adj* **lengthened**, stretched out, extended, drawn-out, prolonged *Opposite*: shortened

elope *v* **run away**, run off, escape, decamp, abscond *Opposite*: return

elopement *n* **flight**, escape, desertion, decampment, truancy *Opposite*: return

eloquence *n* **expressiveness**, articulateness, articulacy, persuasiveness, expression *Opposite*: inarticulacy

eloquent *adj* **expressive**, fluent, articulate, well-spoken, persuasive *Opposite*: inarticulate

else *adj* **different**, new, other, experimental ■ *adv* **1 as well**, besides, in addition, other, more **2 other**, otherwise, differently, different, new

elucidate *v* **explain**, clarify, explicate, expound, illuminate *Opposite*: confuse

elucidation *n* **clarification**, illumination, exposition, explanation, explication *Opposite*: obfuscation

elude *v* **1 escape**, flee, evade, get away, dodge **2 baffle**, confound, foil, puzzle, stump

elusive *adj* **indefinable**, subtle, intangible, vague, indescribable *Opposite*: obvious

elusiveness *n* **indefinability**, subtlety, intangibility, vagueness, tenuousness *Opposite*: accessibility

emaciated *adj* **thin**, wasted, skeletal, withered, shrunken *Opposite*: plump. *See* COMPARE AND CONTRAST *at* thin.

emaciation *n* **thinness**, skinniness, gauntness, scrawniness, scragginess *Opposite*: plumpness

e-mail *n* **electronic post**, electronic message,

communication, correspondence ■ *v* **send**, flame, spam, ping, chat

emanate *v* **1 originate**, come, stem, spring, derive **2 *(fml)* radiate**, emit, give off, give out, send out *Opposite*: absorb

emancipate *v* **liberate**, set free, free, release, unshackle *Opposite*: enslave

emancipation *n* **liberation**, freedom, release, deliverance *(fml)*, manumission *(fml)*

emasculate *(fml)* *v* **weaken**, enfeeble, undermine, enervate, unnerve *Opposite*: empower

emasculated *adj* **ineffectual**, powerless, helpless, impotent, weak *Opposite*: strong

embalm *v* **mummify**, conserve, preserve, fix, keep

embankment *n* **ridge**, bank, mound, defences, dam

embargo *n* **ban**, restriction, prohibition, restraint, block *Opposite*: permission ■ *v* **1 forbid**, prohibit, ban, stop, restrict *Opposite*: permit **2 confiscate**, sequestrate, seize, take away, expropriate

embark *v* **board**, get on, go aboard *Opposite*: disembark

embark on *v* **begin**, start, commence, engage in, set off on *Opposite*: abandon

embarrass *v* **humiliate**, mortify, shame, abash, show up *Opposite*: honour

embarrassed *adj* **uncomfortable**, self-conscious, ill at ease, nervous, ashamed *Opposite*: proud

embarrassing *adj* **awkward**, uncomfortable, uneasy, disconcerting, trying

embarrassment *n* **awkwardness**, blushes, humiliation, mortification, shame *Opposite*: pride

embassy *n* **consulate**, legation, mission, delegation, deputation

embed *v* **implant**, set in, insert, drive in, push in

embellish *v* **1 decorate**, adorn, embroider, beautify, ornament *Opposite*: simplify **2 exaggerate**, elaborate, overdo, aggrandize, enhance *Opposite*: understate

embellishment *n* **1 decoration**, adornment, ornamentation, embroidery, beautification **2 exaggeration**, elaboration, aggrandizement, enhancement, enlargement *Opposite*: understatement

ember *n* **cinder**, ash, coal

embezzle *v* **misappropriate**, misuse, appropriate, steal, cheat. *See* COMPARE AND CONTRAST *at* steal.

embezzlement *n* **misappropriation**, misuse, appropriation, theft, larceny *(dated)*

embezzler *n* **swindler**, fraud, thief, larcenist, fraudster

embitter *v* **disillusion**, poison, sour, estrange, alienate

embittered adj **disillusioned**, bitter, resentful, sour, disaffected *Opposite*: mellow

emblazon v **decorate**, adorn, embellish, ornament, illustrate

emblem n **symbol**, crest, logo, sign, badge

emblematic adj **symbolic**, representative, characteristic, illustrative, exemplary

emblematical *see* **emblematic**

embodiment n **personification**, example, quintessence, incarnation, epitome

embody v **exemplify**, symbolize, represent, personify, epitomize

embolden v **encourage**, hearten, buoy up, bolster, reassure *Opposite*: discourage

emboss v **stamp**, chase, tool, engrave, mark

embrace v **1 hug**, hold, enfold, cuddle, clasp *Opposite*: release **2 accept**, welcome, adopt, take up, support *Opposite*: reject **3 comprise**, contain, include, incorporate, involve *Opposite*: exclude ■ n **hold**, hug, cuddle, clinch, clasp *Opposite*: release

embroider v **1 sew**, stitch, cross-stitch, trim, decorate **2 elaborate**, embellish, exaggerate, overstate, inflate *Opposite*: understate

embroil v **involve**, entangle, enmesh, ensnare, entrap

embryo n **beginning**, rudiment, germ, kernel, seed

embryonic adj **developing**, emergent, nascent, primary, early *Opposite*: advanced

emcee (*infml*) n **MC**, master of ceremonies, compere, host, presenter ■ v **compere**, host, present, introduce

emend v **alter**, correct, amend, revise, rewrite

emerge v **1 come out**, appear, materialize, come into view, come into sight *Opposite*: disappear **2 come to light**, transpire, leak out **3 arise**, appear, occur, develop, begin

emergence n **appearance**, rise, advent, arrival, development *Opposite*: decline

emergency n **crisis**, disaster, tragedy, accident, danger ■ adj **spare**, extra, backup, alternative, reserve

emergent adj **developing**, up-and-coming, embryonic, growing, nascent *Opposite*: established

emigrant n **expatriate**, migrant, immigrant, settler, exile *Opposite*: native

emigrate v **trek**, migrate, travel, move away, leave *Opposite*: return

emigration n **migration**, expatriation, exile, relocation, exodus *Opposite*: return

eminence n **distinction**, renown, reputation, fame, importance *Opposite*: anonymity

eminent adj **well-known**, renowned, important, distinguished, famous *Opposite*: unknown

eminently adv **very**, highly, extremely, exceedingly, exceptionally

emir n **ruler**, commander, prince, leader, governor

emirate n **principality**, country, state, nation, land

emissary n **representative**, envoy, ambassador, messenger, agent

emission n **release**, production, discharge, emanation, secretion *Opposite*: absorption

emit v **produce**, release, give off, give out, send out *Opposite*: absorb

emollient adj **soothing**, palliative, placatory, calmative, calming *Opposite*: disruptive ■ n **balm**, lotion, moisturizer, ointment, salve *Opposite*: irritant

emolument (*fml*) n **payment**, remuneration, reward, fee, compensation. *See* COMPARE AND CONTRAST *at* **wage**.

emotion n **feeling**, sentiment, reaction, passion, excitement

emotional adj **1 moving**, touching, poignant, bittersweet, affecting **2 expressive**, open, demonstrative, emotive, sensitive *Opposite*: impassive

emotionless adj **impassive**, blank, unemotional, detached, cold *Opposite*: emotional

emotive adj **sensitive**, emotional, poignant, affecting, moving

empathize v **identify with**, understand, sympathize, commiserate, relate to *Opposite*: dismiss

empathy n **understanding**, sympathy, compassion, responsiveness, identification *Opposite*: indifference

emperor n **ruler**, tsar, sovereign, king, head of state *Opposite*: subject

emphasis n **stress**, importance, weight, accent, prominence

emphasize v **highlight**, stress, accentuate, call attention to, underline *Opposite*: understate

emphatic adj **1 forceful**, categorical, vigorous, definite, unequivocal *Opposite*: hesitant **2 resounding**, absolute, ringing, clear, evident *Opposite*: ambiguous

empire n **territory**, realm, kingdom, domain

empirical adj **experiential**, experimental, observed, pragmatic, practical *Opposite*: theoretical

empiricism n **pragmatism**, experimentation, observation, practicality

empiricist n **pragmatist**, observer, experimenter, realist, researcher *Opposite*: theorist

employ v **1 pay**, retain, use, hire, take on *Opposite*: dismiss **2 use**, utilize, make use of, occupy, spend *Opposite*: waste ■ n **employment**, service, pay, hire, engagement *Opposite*: unemployment. *See* COMPARE AND CONTRAST *at* **use**.

employed adj **working**, in a job, in employment, in work, engaged *Opposite*: unemployed

employee n **worker**, operative, servant, wage earner, member *Opposite*: employer

employer n **boss**, company, manager, owner, proprietor *Opposite*: employee

employment n 1 **service**, pay, hire, engagement, occupation *Opposite*: unemployment 2 **occupation**, job, profession, trade, work

emporium n **store**, retail store, department store, warehouse, bazaar

empower v 1 **authorize**, allow, sanction, permit, vest *Opposite*: forbid 2 **inspire**, embolden, encourage, galvanize, rouse *Opposite*: discourage

empowerment n 1 **authorization**, enabling, permission, consent, dispensation *Opposite*: embargo 2 **liberation**, enfranchisement, emancipation, inspiration, encouragement

empress n **ruler**, tsaritsa, tsarina, sovereign, queen *Opposite*: subject

emptiness n 1 **bareness**, barrenness, blankness, desolation, hollowness *Opposite*: fullness 2 **meaninglessness**, worthlessness, purposelessness, hollowness, futility *Opposite*: purpose

empty adj 1 **unfilled**, bare, blank, vacant, hollow *Opposite*: full 2 **idle**, futile, ineffectual, unproductive, insincere 3 **meaningless**, pointless, vain, hollow, futile *Opposite*: meaningful ■ v **drain**, clear, pour out, discharge, clear out *Opposite*: fill. *See* COMPARE AND CONTRAST *at* **vacant, vain.**

empty-handed adj **unsuccessful**, frustrated, thwarted, unrewarded, defeated *Opposite*: successful

empty-headed adj **stupid**, silly, vacuous, frivolous, inane *Opposite*: intelligent

emulate v 1 **imitate**, follow, copy, mimic, ape 2 **compete with**, vie with, contend with, rival, outdo. *See* COMPARE AND CONTRAST *at* **imitate.**

emulation n **imitation**, competition, rivalry, mimicry, simulation *Opposite*: originality

emulsify v **blend**, combine, beat together, stir together, mix *Opposite*: separate

emulsion n **suspension**, blend, mixture, cream, mix

enable v **allow**, permit, make possible, empower, qualify *Opposite*: prevent

enact v 1 **perform**, act out, play, portray, represent 2 **pass**, ratify, endorse, decree, sanction *Opposite*: reject

enactment n 1 **performance**, performing, acting out, portrayal, representation 2 **passing**, ratification, ratifying, endorsement, sanctioning

enamel n **coating**, varnish, veneer, glaze, lacquer ■ v **coat**, paint, varnish, lacquer, cover

enamoured adj **fond**, in love, charmed, taken with, captivated *Opposite*: repelled

en bloc adv **all together**, all at once, as one, collectively, en masse *Opposite*: separately

encamp v **set up camp**, set up, install, base, settle

encampment n **camp**, military camp, campsite, base camp, army camp

encapsulate v **sum up**, summarize, put in a nutshell, epitomize, condense *Opposite*: expand

encase v **cover**, enclose, sheathe, coat, wrap *Opposite*: uncover

encased adj **covered**, enclosed, sheathed, coated, wrapped *Opposite*: uncovered

enchant v **charm**, captivate, fascinate, enthral, entrance *Opposite*: disgust

enchanted adj **charmed**, enthralled, captivated, delighted, entranced *Opposite*: disgusted

enchanting adj **charming**, captivating, enthralling, alluring, delightful *Opposite*: disgusting

enchantment n **charm**, attraction, delight, fascination, allure

encircle v **surround**, enclose, ring, circle, enfold

enclave n 1 **region**, reserve, territory, commune, area 2 **group**, community, class, clique, clan (*infml*)

enclose v 1 **surround**, hem in, encircle, enfold, ring 2 **wall**, fence, hedge, pen, seal off 3 **include**, put in, attach, insert, add *Opposite*: leave out

enclosed adj **surrounded**, bounded, hemmed in, fenced, walled *Opposite*: open

enclosure n 1 **field**, arena, stockade, pen, paddock 2 **inclusion**, attachment, insertion, addition, insert

encode v **encrypt**, code, put into code, scramble, convert *Opposite*: decode

encompass v **include**, cover, take in, incorporate, involve *Opposite*: exclude

encore n **repeat**, extra, impromptu item, curtain call, reprise

encounter v 1 **meet**, come across, bump into, run into, come upon 2 **face**, confront, contend with, grapple with, combat *Opposite*: avoid ■ n 1 **meeting**, chance meeting, happenstance 2 **confrontation**, engagement, contest, argument, skirmish

encourage v 1 **inspire**, hearten, cheer, raise your spirits, buoy up *Opposite*: discourage 2 **support**, egg on, urge, animate, incite *Opposite*: discourage 3 **foster**, assist, help, aid, nurture *Opposite*: stifle

encouragement n **support**, backup, help, reassurance, inspiration *Opposite*: discouragement

encouraging adj **hopeful**, heartening, cheering, reassuring, promising *Opposite*: discouraging

encroach v **intrude**, infringe, invade, trespass, make inroads into *Opposite*: respect

encroachment n **infringement**, violation, advance, intrusion, invasion

encrusted adj **covered**, coated, thick, crusted, caked *Opposite*: bare

encrypt v **encode**, code, put into code, scramble, translate *Opposite*: decode

encumber v **burden**, hinder, hamper, impede, get in the way *Opposite*: facilitate

encumbrance n **burden**, hindrance, nuisance, impediment, handicap *Opposite*: help

encyclopaedia *see* **encyclopedia**

encyclopedia n **reference work**, compendium, compilation, fact file, information database

encyclopedic adj **comprehensive**, full, complete, in-depth, thorough *Opposite*: narrow

end n **1 finish**, conclusion, ending, closing stages, last part *Opposite*: beginning **2 extremity**, edge, side, tip, top *Opposite*: middle **3 purpose**, aim, reason, objective, goal **4 death**, downfall, decline, ruin, dissolution *Opposite*: birth **5 remnant**, leftover, stub, scrap, remainder *Opposite*: whole **6 consequence**, outcome, upshot, result, end result *Opposite*: cause ■ v **1 stop**, finish, conclude, close, terminate *Opposite*: begin **2 result**, finish, conclude, culminate, end up

endanger v **put in danger**, jeopardize, risk, compromise, threaten *Opposite*: protect

endangered adj **rare**, in danger of extinction, dying out, scarce, threatened *Opposite*: common

endear v **commend**, recommend, ingratiate, make appealing, insinuate *Opposite*: alienate

endearing adj **appealing**, attractive, charming, engaging, winning *Opposite*: unappealing

endearment n **kind word**, sweet nothing, compliment, blandishment, loving word *Opposite*: insult

endeavour v **try**, strive, attempt, make every effort, do your utmost *Opposite*: neglect ■ n **1 attempt**, effort, try, exertion, best shot **2 enterprise**, undertaking, bid, venture, foray

endemic adj **widespread**, prevalent, common, rife, rampant *Opposite*: rare

ending n **end**, finish, finale, conclusion, culmination *Opposite*: beginning

end it all v **commit suicide**, kill yourself, take your own life, do away with yourself, die by your own hand

endless adj **1 boundless**, infinite, limitless, without end, interminable *Opposite*: finite **2 eternal**, continual, continuous, nonstop, perpetual *Opposite*: temporary

endorse v **1 sanction**, approve, ratify, recommend, countersign *Opposite*: reject **2 support**, back, advocate, favour, subscribe to *Opposite*: denounce

endorsed adj **permitted**, recognized, sanctioned, recommended, authorized *Opposite*: disallowed

endorsement n **1 authorization**, commendation, confirmation, countersignature, ratification **2 backing**, support, advocacy, sanction, encouragement

endow v **award**, donate, give, bequeath, provide

endowment n **1 donation**, gift, bequest, legacy, award **2 natural gift**, talent, ability, capability, aptitude

end product n **outcome**, end result, result, upshot, product

end result n **outcome**, end product, result, upshot, product

end up v **finish up**, finish off, transpire, turn out, result in *Opposite*: start out

endurable adj **tolerable**, manageable, bearable, passable, sufferable *Opposite*: intolerable

endurance n **1 staying power**, strength, stamina, fortitude, resolution *Opposite*: weakness **2 stamina**, fortitude, tolerance, grit, guts *(slang)* **3 persistence**, perseverance, tenacity, continuance, survival

endure v **1 bear**, tolerate, undergo, put up with, go through *Opposite*: succumb **2 last**, continue, go on, persist, survive *Opposite*: perish

enduring adj **lasting**, continuing, durable, stable, long-term *Opposite*: short-lived

end user n **user**, purchaser, shopper, consumer, client *Opposite*: producer

endways adv **end on**, endways on, jutting out, end foremost, end uppermost *Opposite*: lengthways

endwise *see* **endways**

enemy n **opponent**, adversary, rival, opposition, competitor *Opposite*: friend

energetic adj **1 lively**, active, vigorous, brisk, animated *Opposite*: lethargic **2 strenuous**, vigorous, brisk, dynamic, challenging *Opposite*: easy

energize v **invigorate**, strengthen, boost, galvanize, electrify *Opposite*: enervate

energizing adj **invigorating**, stimulating, enlivening, revitalizing, reviving *Opposite*: draining

energy n **1 vigour**, liveliness, dynamism, vitality, drive *Opposite*: lethargy **2 power**, force, strength, momentum, resources

enervate v **weaken**, debilitate, sap the strength of, drain, fatigue *Opposite*: invigorate

enervating adj **exhausting**, weakening, enfeebling, fatiguing, draining *Opposite*: invigorating

enfeeble v **weaken**, debilitate, enervate, deplete, exhaust *Opposite*: strengthen

enfold v **enclose**, surround, wrap, wrap up, envelop

enforce v **1 apply**, carry out, impose, implement, make compulsory **2 coerce**, oblige, compel, require, insist on

enforced adj **compulsory**, obligatory, forced, imposed, required *Opposite*: optional

enforcement n **implementation**, application, execution, putting into practice, administration

enfranchise v **give somebody the vote**,

empower, emancipate, liberate, naturalize *Opposite*: disenfranchise

enfranchisement *n* **empowerment**, naturalization, suffrage, manumission *(fml) Opposite*: disenfranchisement

engage *v* **1 involve**, occupy, engross, absorb, take part **2 appoint**, take on, employ, hire, contract *Opposite*: dismiss **3 battle**, fight, combat, contest, encounter **4 hold**, keep, absorb, charm, attract *Opposite*: repel **5 connect**, slot in, fit into place, interlock, join *Opposite*: disengage

engaged *adj* **1 busy**, occupied, unavailable, in use, being used *Opposite*: free **2 spoken for**, involved, promised, tied up, betrothed *(fml) Opposite*: unattached

engagement *n* **1 appointment**, meeting, rendezvous, assignation, visit **2 employment**, job, position, situation, post **3 battle**, fight, encounter, conflict, action. *See* COMPARE AND CONTRAST *at* fight.

engaging *adj* **attractive**, appealing, charming, winning, fetching *Opposite*: unattractive

engender *v* **1 produce**, cause, create, bring about, stimulate **2** *(fml)* **beget**, give birth to, generate, propagate, spawn

engine *n* **machine**, motor, turbine, mechanism, generator

WORD BANK
❑ **parts of an engine** alternator, ball bearing, cam, camshaft, cog, cogwheel, coil, crank, crankshaft, cylinder, distributor, gasket, gear, gearbox, gearing, lever, manifold, piston, pump, radiator, seal, shaft, solenoid, spark plug, starter, sump, tappet, valve

---

engineer *v* **bring about**, cause, contrive, concoct, plot

engorge *v* **swell up**, swell, puff up, expand, blow up *Opposite*: deflate

engrave *v* **etch**, score, scratch, carve, incise

engraving *n* **1 etching**, lithograph, print, reproduction, woodcut **2 engraved design**, carving, etching, linocut, inscription

engross *v* **absorb**, captivate, hold your attention, hold, engage *Opposite*: bore

engrossed *adj* **absorbed**, captivated, enthralled, gripped, held *Opposite*: bored

engrossing *adj* **absorbing**, captivating, enthralling, gripping, interesting *Opposite*: uninteresting

engulf *v* **swallow up**, overcome, overwhelm, immerse, submerge

enhance *v* **improve**, add to, increase, boost, develop *Opposite*: impair

enhanced *adj* **improved**, greater, strengthened, heightened, boosted *Opposite*: diminished

enhancement *n* **improvement**, augmentation, development, enrichment, heightening *Opposite*: detraction

enigma *n* **paradox**, conundrum, problem, mystery, puzzle

enigmatic *adj* **mysterious**, inscrutable, puzzling, perplexing, obscure *Opposite*: straightforward. *See* COMPARE AND CONTRAST *at* obscure.

enjoin *(fml)* *v* **order**, command, instruct, direct, tell *Opposite*: forbid

enjoy *v* **1 like**, delight in, appreciate, revel in, relish *Opposite*: dislike **2 benefit from**, have, experience, be blessed with, possess *Opposite*: lack

enjoyable *adj* **pleasant**, agreeable, pleasing, entertaining, amusing *Opposite*: boring

enjoyment *n* **pleasure**, delight, satisfaction, gratification, fun *Opposite*: boredom

enjoy yourself *v* **be amused**, be delighted, let yourself go, play, party *(infml)*

enlarge *v* **1 increase**, expand, broaden, widen, lengthen *Opposite*: decrease **2 detail**, elaborate, expand, amplify, flesh out *Opposite*: compress. *See* COMPARE AND CONTRAST *at* increase.

enlargement *n* **expansion**, extension, amplification, increase, widening *Opposite*: decrease

enlighten *v* **tell**, inform, explain to, instruct, edify

enlightened *adj* **1 rational**, unprejudiced, reasonable, logical, open-minded *Opposite*: irrational **2 educated**, aware, informed, knowledgeable, wise *Opposite*: unaware

enlightening *adj* **informative**, instructive, edifying, helpful, educational *Opposite*: uninformative

enlightenment *n* **explanation**, illumination, clarification, insight, information *Opposite*: ignorance

enlist *v* **1 join**, join up, sign on, sign up, volunteer **2 recruit**, conscript, procure, solicit, count on *Opposite*: reject

enliven *v* **liven up**, cheer up, invigorate, wake up, cheer *Opposite*: put a damper on

en masse *see* en bloc

enmesh *v* **entangle**, tangle, trap, catch, catch up *Opposite*: disentangle

enmity *n* **hostility**, hate, hatred, ill will, animosity *Opposite*: goodwill

ennui *n* **boredom**, languor, world-weariness, tedium, weariness *Opposite*: excitement

enormity *n* **1 atrociousness**, horror, monstrousness, wickedness, heinousness *Opposite*: goodness **2 atrocity**, abomination, outrage, evil, horror *Opposite*: kindness **3 size**, extent, vastness, scale, immensity

enormous *adj* **huge**, vast, massive, giant, mammoth *Opposite*: tiny

enormously *adv* **extremely**, very, a lot, a great deal, hugely *Opposite*: slightly

enough *adj* **sufficient**, adequate, ample, plenty, abundant *Opposite*: insufficient

enquire *v* **ask**, find out, query, investigate, probe *Opposite*: reply

enrage *v* **infuriate**, anger, make your blood

boil, madden, incense *Opposite*: calm

enraged *adj* **furious**, infuriated, angry, beside yourself, fuming *Opposite*: calm

enrapture *(fml)* *v* **entrance**, delight, captivate, enchant, mesmerize *Opposite*: bore

enrich *v* **improve**, supplement, enhance, deepen, develop *Opposite*: diminish

enrichment *n* **enhancement**, improvement, augmentation, amelioration, upgrading *Opposite*: diminution

enrol *v* **register**, sign up, put your name down, join, join up

enrolment *n* **registration**, matriculation, signing up, admission, acceptance *Opposite*: resignation

ensemble *n* 1 **band**, company, troupe, group, corps 2 **outfit**, suit, costume, coordinates, rig-out *(infml)* 3 **collection**, assembly, aggregate, set, combination ■ *adj* **collaborative**, collective, joint, group, cooperative *Opposite*: solo

enshrine *v* **protect**, treasure, hallow, preserve, cherish

enshroud *v* **obscure**, hide, mask, shield, cover *Opposite*: expose

ensign *n* **flag**, pennant, banner, standard, colours

enslave *v* **subjugate**, dominate, subject, bind, yoke *Opposite*: liberate

ensnare *v* **enmesh**, embroil, catch, trap, entrap *Opposite*: set free

ensue *v* 1 **follow**, succeed, follow on, result, arise *Opposite*: precede 2 **result**, follow, proceed, arise, derive *Opposite*: precede

ensuing *adj* **resultant**, subsequent, succeeding, resulting, following *Opposite*: preceding

ensure *v* **make sure**, make certain, safeguard, guarantee, confirm

entail *v* **involve**, require, demand, need, necessitate

entangle *v* 1 **tangle**, twist, intertwine, snarl up, catch up *Opposite*: disentangle 2 **snare**, trap, catch, snag, enmesh *Opposite*: free

entanglement *n* **predicament**, tangle, muddle, morass, mess

enter *v* 1 **go in**, go into, come in, come into, cross the threshold *Opposite*: leave 2 **input**, insert, put in, record, register *Opposite*: delete 3 **submit**, put in, propose, hand in, state 4 **compete**, participate, take part, take up, try 5 **join**, sign up, agree to, enlist, enrol 6 **walk on**, come on, appear, make an entrance *Opposite*: exit

enter into *v* **become involved in**, take part in, join in, throw yourself into, participate in *Opposite*: withdraw

enter on *v* **start**, begin, enter upon, move into, start out on *Opposite*: finish

enterprise *n* 1 **business**, company, firm, corporation, organization 2 **venture**, project, activity, undertaking, endeavour 3 **initiative**,

innovativeness, creativity, inventiveness, originality *Opposite*: apathy

enterprising *adj* **innovative**, inventive, imaginative, resourceful, adventurous *Opposite*: unadventurous

entertain *v* 1 **amuse**, divert, distract, regale, interest *Opposite*: bore 2 **accommodate**, wine and dine, feed, invite, regale *Opposite*: visit 3 **consider**, think about, give thought to, contemplate, think over *Opposite*: reject

entertainer *n* **performer**, artiste, artist, talent, turn

WORD BANK

❑ **types of entertainer** actor, actress, busker, clown, co-star, comedian, comic, compere, conjurer, contortionist, dancer, DJ, double act, emcee *(infml)*, film star, impressionist, juggler, magician, mime, musician, popstar, rapper, singer, standup comedian, stooge, straight man, street entertainer, street musician, street performer, trapeze artist, ventriloquist

---

entertaining *adj* **amusing**, enjoyable, diverting, pleasurable, charming *Opposite*: dull

entertainment *n* 1 **entertaining**, performing, acting, show business, theatre 2 **amusement**, fun, diversion, distraction, enjoyment *Opposite*: boredom 3 **show**, production, concert, attraction, performance

enter upon *v* **start**, begin, enter on, move into, start out on *Opposite*: finish

enthral *v* **captivate**, charm, mesmerize, beguile, fascinate *Opposite*: bore

enthralled *adj* **fascinated**, engrossed, gripped, captivated, absorbed *Opposite*: bored

enthralling *adj* **fascinating**, beguiling, engrossing, gripping, captivating *Opposite*: boring

enthrone *(fml)* *v* **crown**, instate, ordain, swear in, consecrate *Opposite*: dethrone

enthuse *v* 1 **be enthusiastic**, be passionate, talk excitedly, show enthusiasm, be effusive 2 **stimulate**, galvanize, excite, spur to action, impassion *Opposite*: bore

enthusiasm *n* 1 **eagerness**, interest, passion, gusto, zeal *Opposite*: apathy 2 **craze**, interest, hobby, passion, mania

enthusiast *n* **fan**, fanatic, buff, aficionado, aficionada

enthusiastic *adj* **eager**, keen, passionate, fervent, excited *Opposite*: apathetic

entice *v* **lure**, tempt, induce, seduce, bribe *Opposite*: put off

enticement *n* **lure**, temptation, incentive, inducement, bribery *Opposite*: deterrent

enticing *adj* **tempting**, alluring, inviting, attractive, appealing *Opposite*: uninviting

entire *adj* 1 **whole**, complete, full, total, perfect *Opposite*: part 2 **absolute**, complete, total, thorough, unqualified *Opposite*: partial

entirety *n* **sum**, whole, wholeness, totality, entireness *Opposite*: part

entitle v **1 enable**, allow, permit, sanction, authorize *Opposite*: debar **2 title**, call, name, dub, label

entitled adj **1 permitted**, in your own right, eligible, allowed, enabled *Opposite*: barred **2 titled**, called, named, dubbed, labelled

entitlement n **right**, power, prerogative, privilege, claim

entity n **object**, thing, article, being, unit *Opposite*: nonentity

entourage n **staff**, associates, following, followers, train

entrails n **guts**, intestines, bowels, viscera, innards *(infml)*

entrance n **1 entry**, way in, doorway, door, opening *Opposite*: exit **2 arrival**, entry, appearance, entering, ingress *(fml) Opposite*: departure **3 admission**, entry, ticket, pass, admittance ■ v **captivate**, engross, fascinate, charm, delight *Opposite*: bore

entrance hall n **lobby**, foyer, reception area, hallway, vestibule

entrancing adj **captivating**, enchanting, enthralling, spellbinding, fascinating *Opposite*: boring

entrant n **applicant**, contestant, candidate, participant, competitor. *See* COMPARE AND CONTRAST *at* **candidate**.

entrap v **trick**, deceive, ensnare, trap, lure

entrapment n **trap**, frame, snare, trick, setup *(infml)*

entreat v **plead**, beg, pray, ask, request *Opposite*: demand

entreaty n **appeal**, plea, petition, request, supplication *(fml) Opposite*: demand

entrée n **1 starter**, hors d'oeuvre, first course, appetizer, antipasto **2 introduction**, induction, entrance, access, admittance *Opposite*: exclusion

entrench v **embed**, ensconce, ingrain, root, establish

entrepreneur n **businessperson**, trader, organizer, impresario, financier

entrepreneurial adj **business**, small-business, commercial, risk-taking, empire-building

entrust v **trust**, commend, delegate, assign, deliver *Opposite*: deprive

entry n **1 admission**, entrance, access, pass, ticket **2 entrance**, doorway, door, opening, access *Opposite*: exit **3 record**, item, note, account, statement **4 application**, submission, attempt, effort, go *Opposite*: withdrawal

entwine v **tangle**, entangle, twist, interweave, interlace *Opposite*: undo

enumerate v **1 detail**, list, spell out, itemize, name **2 count**, number, tally, compute, reckon *Opposite*: estimate

enunciate v **1 pronounce**, articulate, voice, utter, speak *Opposite*: mumble **2 express**, spell out, detail, state, put forward *Opposite*: suppress

enunciation n **1 pronunciation**, articulation, diction, speech **2 expression**, assertion, declaration, proclamation, clarification *Opposite*: suppression

envelop v **enclose**, encircle, encase, engulf, swathe *Opposite*: unwrap

envelope n **cover**, wrapper, covering, wrapping, casing

enviable adj **desirable**, fortunate, lucky, privileged, to die for *Opposite*: unenviable

envious adj **jealous**, green with envy, resentful, spiteful, covetous

environment n **1 nature**, ecosystem, earth, world, natural world **2 surroundings**, setting, situation, atmosphere, scene **3 background**, upbringing, circumstances, conditions, situation

environmental adj **ecological**, conservation, conservational, environmentally friendly, ecofriendly

environmentalist n **ecologist**, conservationist, preservationist, green

environs n **vicinity**, surroundings, locality, environment, neighbourhood

envisage v **imagine**, visualize, foresee, predict, see

envision *see* **envisage**

envoy n **representative**, diplomat, attaché, emissary, herald

envy n **jealousy**, greed, bitterness, resentment, spite *Opposite*: goodwill ■ v **covet**, desire, resent, begrudge, grudge

epaulette n **decoration**, insignia, strap, chevron

ephemeral adj **short-lived**, passing, fleeting, brief, momentary *Opposite*: lasting. *See* COMPARE AND CONTRAST *at* **temporary**.

ephemeralness n **brevity**, transitoriness, transience, fleetingness, temporariness *Opposite*: timelessness

epic n **classic**, historical fiction, costume drama, period piece, extravaganza *Opposite*: short story ■ adj **marathon**, heroic, classic, larger-than-life, impressive *Opposite*: minuscule

epicure n **gourmet**, gastronome, connoisseur, bon vivant, epicurean

epicurean adj **1 hedonistic**, decadent, pleasure-seeking, pleasure-loving, sensualist *Opposite*: ascetic **2 gastronomic**, gourmet, culinary ■ n **gourmet**, gastronome, connoisseur, bon vivant, epicure

epidemic n **1 plague**, outbreak, endemic, scourge, contagion **2 spate**, wave, rash, craze, increase *Opposite*: decrease ■ adj **widespread**, wide-ranging, prevalent, rampant, sweeping *Opposite*: restricted. *See* COMPARE AND CONTRAST *at* **widespread**.

epidermis n **skin**, hide, flesh, cuticle, integument

epigram n **witticism**, saying, axiom, ditty, rhyme

epilogue *n* **conclusion**, coda, speech, monologue *Opposite*: prologue

episode *n* **1 incident**, affair, chapter, event, occurrence **2 chapter**, part, section, scene, instalment **3 occurrence**, incidence, attack, outbreak, bout

episodic *adj* **1 serialized**, discontinuous, divided **2 sporadic**, intermittent, periodic, discontinuous, irregular *Opposite*: regular

epistle *(fml)* *n* **letter**, missive, communication, message, communiqué

epitaph *n* **inscription**, legend, caption, epigraph

epithet *n* **nickname**, description, label, sobriquet, appellation *(fml)*

epitome *n* **essence**, personification, embodiment, model, quintessence *Opposite*: antithesis

epitomize *v* **typify**, characterize, exemplify, personify, embody

epoch *n* **era**, age, time, period, date

epoch-making *adj* **historic**, crucial, important, momentous, earthshattering *Opposite*: insignificant

equable *adj* **composed**, calm, easygoing, unflappable, placid *Opposite*: jumpy

equal *adj* **1 identical**, equivalent, like, alike, the same *Opposite*: unequal **2 on a par**, even, uniform, level, on level pegging *Opposite*: unequal ■ *n* **match**, equivalent, counterpart, parallel, peer ■ *v* **1 come to**, amount to, equate, make, correspond **2 match**, rival, keep pace with, copy, meet

equality *n* **parity**, fairness, equivalence, likeness, equal opportunity *Opposite*: inequality

equalize *v* **match**, level, even out, align, line up *Opposite*: differentiate

equally *adv* **1 similarly**, likewise, in the same way, by the same token, alike *Opposite*: conversely **2 evenly**, uniformly, regularly, equivalently, alike *Opposite*: unequally

equanimity *n* **composure**, calmness, levelheadedness, equability, self-control *Opposite*: volatility

equate *v* **associate**, liken, link, connect, parallel *Opposite*: contrast

equation *n* **reckoning**, calculation, comparison, equivalence, equality

equestrian *adj* **riding**, equine, show jumping, horseracing, horsey

equidistant *adj* **halfway between**, midway between, between, in between, intermediate

equilateral *adj* **symmetrical**, regular, square, rectangular, triangular

equilibrium *n* **balance**, symmetry, steadiness, stability, evenness *Opposite*: imbalance

equip *v* **1 provide**, endow, fit out, outfit, kit out **2 prepare**, train, school, qualify, ground

equipment *n* **tools**, apparatus, tackle, utensils, paraphernalia

equitable *(fml)* *adj* **fair**, evenhanded, reasonable, justifiable, rightful *Opposite*: unfair

equity *(fml)* *n* **fairness**, evenhandedness, impartiality, justice, fair play *Opposite*: injustice

equivalence *n* **correspondence**, sameness, likeness, similarity, equality *Opposite*: difference

equivalent *adj* **equal**, corresponding, correspondent, alike, same *Opposite*: different ■ *n* **counterpart**, equal, opposite number, parallel, twin

equivocal *adj* **vague**, ambiguous, confusing, ambivalent, misleading *Opposite*: unambiguous

equivocate *v* **prevaricate**, vacillate, be evasive, quibble, beat about the bush *Opposite*: speak your mind

equivocation *n* **vagueness**, indirectness, ambiguity, prevarication, weasel words *(infml)* *Opposite*: directness

era *n* **age**, epoch, aeon, time, period

eradicate *v* **eliminate**, get rid of, destroy, exterminate, do away with *Opposite*: introduce

eradication *n* **abolition**, purge, annihilation, extermination, obliteration *Opposite*: introduction

erase *v* **rub out**, remove, delete, expunge, obliterate

erasure *n* **removal**, destruction, eradication, elimination, deletion

erect *v* **1 build**, construct, assemble, set up, raise *Opposite*: demolish **2 create**, set up, found, initiate, establish ■ *adj* **straight**, upright, vertical, rigid, stiff *Opposite*: prone

erection *n* **1 construction**, building, assembly, creation, formation **2** *(fml)* **structure**, building, construction, edifice, pile

erode *v* **wear away**, wear down, corrode, eat away, eat into

eroded *adj* **weathered**, worn, weather-beaten, corroded, eaten away

erosion *n* **corrosion**, attrition, destruction, loss *Opposite*: accretion

erotic *adj* **sexy**, sensual, stimulating, suggestive, arousing

err *(fml)* *v* **go wrong**, blunder, stumble, go astray, get something wrong

errand *n* **task**, duty, run, chore, job

errant *adj* **wayward**, sinful, naughty, misbehaving, delinquent *Opposite*: well-behaved

erratic *adj* **unpredictable**, unreliable, inconsistent, irregular, changeable *Opposite*: consistent

erroneous *adj* **mistaken**, flawed, wrong, specious, inaccurate *Opposite*: correct

error *n* **mistake**, fault, blunder, inaccuracy, miscalculation. *See* COMPARE AND CONTRAST *at* **mistake**.

ersatz *adj* **faux**, artificial, substitute, reproduction, imitation *Opposite*: genuine

erstwhile *adj* **former**, previous, past, old, earlier *Opposite*: current

erudite *adj* **scholarly**, knowledgeable, well-educated, well-read, cultured *Opposite*: uneducated

erudition *n* **knowledge**, learnedness, education, learning, culture *Opposite*: ignorance

erupt *v* 1 **explode**, blow up, break out, flare up, go off *Opposite*: subside 2 **explode**, lose your temper, hit the roof (infml), blow your top (infml), blow a fuse (infml) *Opposite*: hold back

eruption *n* **outbreak**, outburst, explosion, upsurge, epidemic

escalate *v* **intensify**, worsen, heighten, go from bad to worse, deteriorate *Opposite*: de-escalate

escalating *adj* **mounting**, rising, intensifying, ever-increasing, swelling *Opposite*: diminishing

escalation *n* **rise**, growth, boom, increase, climb *Opposite*: reduction

escalator *n* **moving staircase**, staircase, stairway, stairs

escapade *n* **adventure**, jaunt, antic, caper, spree

escape *v* 1 **flee**, run away, get away, break out, run off *Opposite*: be captured 2 **leak out**, leak, drip, seep, flow 3 **avoid**, evade, dodge, elude, shake off *Opposite*: face ■ *n* 1 **seepage**, leakage, leak, outflow, discharge 2 **flight**, getaway, break, breakout, escaping *Opposite*: capture 3 **diversion**, distraction, pastime, leisure activity, escapism

escapee *n* **runaway**, fugitive, absconder, deserter, fleer

escapism *n* **diversion**, distraction, entertainment, relaxation, daydreaming

escapist *adj* **diverting**, distracting, entertaining, relaxing, fantasy *Opposite*: realistic

escarpment *n* **cliff**, bluff, scarp, ridge, incline

eschew *v* **avoid**, shun, have nothing to do with, steer clear of, give a wide berth to *Opposite*: embrace

escort *n* **guide**, attendant, minder, bodyguard, chaperon ■ *v* **accompany**, guide, usher, lead, attend

esoteric *adj* **obscure**, mysterious, abstruse, impenetrable, cryptic *Opposite*: straightforward

ESP *n* **extra-sensory perception**, psychic powers, clairvoyance, second sight, telepathy

especial *adj* **special**, unusual, exceptional, extraordinary, outstanding *Opposite*: ordinary

especially *adv* 1 **particularly**, in particular, specially, above all, more than ever 2 **exceptionally**, remarkably, notably, markedly, outstandingly

espousal *n* **adoption**, backing, support, championship, promotion *Opposite*: opposition

espouse *v* 1 **take up**, adopt, support, back, advocate *Opposite*: oppose 2 (archaic) **marry**, wed, take your vows, walk down the aisle, get hitched (infml)

essay *n* **paper**, thesis, dissertation, composition, article ■ *v* (fml) **try**, endeavour, strive, have a shot, attempt

essence *n* 1 **spirit**, core, heart, quintessence, crux 2 **concentrate**, extract, tincture, distillate, concentration

essential *adj* 1 **necessary**, vital, indispensable, important, crucial *Opposite*: unnecessary 2 **fundamental**, basic, elemental, key, central *Opposite*: secondary ■ *n* **necessity**, requisite, prerequisite, requirement, must *Opposite*: extravagance. *See* COMPARE AND CONTRAST *at* **necessary**.

essentially *adv* 1 **fundamentally**, basically, in essence, in effect, really 2 **effectively**, more or less, broadly, in the main, for the most part

essentials *n* **basics**, fundamentals, prerequisites, rudiments, necessities *Opposite*: frills

establish *v* 1 **set up**, found, institute, start, create *Opposite*: close down 2 **ascertain** (fml), determine, find out, prove, confirm *Opposite*: disprove

established *adj* **recognized**, well-known, traditional, conventional, customary *Opposite*: new

establishment *n* 1 **founding**, formation, creation, setting up, institution *Opposite*: dissolution 2 **business**, firm, company, institution, concern 3 **authorities**, powers that be, the ruling classes, the established order, the system

estate *n* 1 **plantation**, land, park, lands, parkland 2 **area**, zone, industrial estate, business park, commercial centre 3 **assets**, property, holdings, worth, fortune

esteem *v* **appreciate**, cherish, hold dear, venerate, value *Opposite*: scorn ■ *n* **regard**, respect, admiration, high regard, reverence *Opposite*: contempt. *See* COMPARE AND CONTRAST *at* **regard**.

esteemed *adj* **respected**, valued, honoured, revered, admired *Opposite*: scorned

estimable *adj* **admirable**, worthy, deserving, laudable, venerable *Opposite*: unimpressive

estimate *n* 1 **quote**, price, estimation, valuation, costing *Opposite*: cost 2 **approximation**, estimation, guess, educated guess, evaluation ■ *v* **approximate**, guess, assess, reckon, value *Opposite*: calculate

estimated *adj* **projected**, assessed, valued, appraised, approximate

estimation *n* 1 **opinion**, assessment, inference, evaluation, view *Opposite*: fact 2 **educated guess**, approximation, estimate, guesstimate, evaluation

estranged *adj* **alienated**, separated, apart, at odds, on bad terms

estrangement *n* **separation**, hostility, rupture, distancing, disaffection *Opposite*: reconciliation

estuary *n* **river mouth**, bay, inlet, sound, creek *Opposite*: source

etc. *adv* **et cetera**, and so on, and so forth, and the like, and the rest

etch *v* **engrave**, scratch, scrape, cut, incise

etching *n* **engraving**, drawing, print, design, impression

eternal *adj* **everlasting**, undying, unending, never-ending, perpetual *Opposite*: transient

eternity *n* **1 time without end**, perpetuity, infinity, all time, ever and a day **2** (*infml*) **a long time**, aeons, forever (*infml*), ages (*infml*), donkey's years (*infml*)

ethereal *adj* **1 ghostly**, otherworldly, unearthly, spectral, shadowy *Opposite*: earthly **2 waiflike**, frail, delicate, airy, insubstantial *Opposite*: substantial

ethic *n* **moral belief**, ethos, idea, principle, code

ethical *adj* **moral**, principled, right, fair, decent *Opposite*: unethical

ethics *n* **principles**, morals, beliefs, moral code, moral principles

ethnic *adj* **cultural**, traditional, folkloric, racial, indigenous

ethnicity *n* **culture**, way of life, origin, background, traditions

ethos *n* **philosophy**, beliefs, principles, code, character

etiquette *n* **manners**, good manners, protocol, custom, propriety *Opposite*: bad manners

eulogize *v* **praise**, extol, laud, sing the praises of, praise to the skies *Opposite*: criticize

eulogy *n* **tribute**, acclamation, acclaim, praise, homage *Opposite*: criticism

euphemism *n* **neutral term**, understatement, rewording, bowdlerization, code word *Opposite*: dysphemism

euphemistic *adj* **inoffensive**, polite, bowdlerized, cleaned up, neutral *Opposite*: dysphemistic

euphoria *n* **elation**, ecstasy, jubilation, rapture, excitement *Opposite*: despair

euphoric *adj* **overjoyed**, elated, ecstatic, joyful, joyous *Opposite*: despairing

evacuate *v* **1 empty**, abandon, withdraw from, leave, vacate *Opposite*: fill **2 send away**, remove from, move out of, clear from *Opposite*: bring in

evacuation *n* **removal**, clearing, emptying, withdrawal, flight *Opposite*: influx

evacuee *n* **refugee**, émigré, emigrant, migrant

evade *v* **1 avoid**, dodge, escape, elude, shirk *Opposite*: confront **2 equivocate**, prevaricate, hedge, stonewall (*infml*), fudge (*infml*)

evaluate *v* **assess**, appraise, weigh up, gauge, estimate

evaluation *n* **assessment**, appraisal, estimation, calculation, valuation

evaluator *n* **assessor**, surveyor, inspector, judge

evanescent *adj* **short-lived**, fleeting, momentary, ephemeral, passing *Opposite*: permanent

evangelical *adj* **enthusiastic**, fervent, eager, zealous, keen *Opposite*: apathetic

evaporate *v* **vanish**, fade away, fade, disappear, melt away *Opposite*: solidify

evaporation *n* **vaporization**, drying up, loss, vanishing, disappearance

evasion *n* **1 avoidance**, dodging, elusion, circumvention, skirting **2 prevarication**, equivocation, hedging, stonewalling (*infml*), fencing (*infml*)

evasive *adj* **elusive**, slippery, shifty, indirect, oblique *Opposite*: direct

evasiveness *n* **indirectness**, equivocation, shiftiness, elusiveness, ambiguousness *Opposite*: directness

eve *n* **day before**, evening before, night before

even *adj* **1 smooth**, flat, level, straight, unfluctuating *Opposite*: uneven **2 constant**, steady, uniform, unvarying, unchanging *Opposite*: fluctuating **3 equal**, similar, level, on a par, just as *Opposite*: unequal

evenhanded *adj* **fair**, impartial, unbiased, just, equal *Opposite*: biased

evenhandedness *n* **fairness**, impartiality, justice, neutrality, equity (*fml*) *Opposite*: partiality

even if *conj* **though**, albeit, although, even though, in spite of the fact that

evening *n* **twilight**, sunset, dusk, nightfall, late afternoon *Opposite*: morning

evenness *n* **consistency**, sameness, symmetry, uniformity, flatness *Opposite*: irregularity

even out *v* **1 flatten**, level, smooth, square, align **2 balance out**, balance, level out, balance up, equalize *Opposite*: unbalance

event *n* **occasion**, happening, occurrence, incident, affair

even-tempered *adj* **calm**, unflappable, equable, placid, imperturbable *Opposite*: temperamental

eventful *adj* **exciting**, action-packed, lively, busy, hectic *Opposite*: dull

eventual *adj* **ultimate**, final, last, ensuing, subsequent *Opposite*: immediate

eventuality (*fml*) *n* **possibility**, prospect, case, contingency, outcome

eventually *adv* **finally**, ultimately, sooner or later, in the end, in due course *Opposite*: immediately

even up *v* **equalize**, stabilize, even out, redress

the balance, balance up *Opposite*: unbalance

ever *adv* **always**, forever, eternally, all the time, constantly *Opposite*: never

evergreen *adj* **immortal**, perennial, ever popular, classic, old time favourite *Opposite*: stale

---

WORD BANK

❏ **types of evergreen tree** bay, bo tree, boxwood, bunya, carob, cedar, cola, cypress, eucalyptus, fir, fir tree, gum tree, holly, juniper, kahikatea, kauri, larch, laurel, mahogany, mangrove, monkey puzzle, pine, redwood, sandalwood, sequoia, spruce, yew

---

everlasting *adj* **eternal**, endless, ceaseless, never-ending, perpetual *Opposite*: transient

ever-present *adj* **ubiquitous**, chronic, pervasive, omnipresent

every *adj* **each**, all, every single, every one

everyday *adj* **ordinary**, average, normal, unremarkable, common *Opposite*: extraordinary

everyone *n* **everybody**, all, all and sundry, one and all, each person *Opposite*: no one

everything *n* **all**, the whole thing, the lot, the whole lot, the whole shebang *(infml) Opposite*: nothing

everywhere *adv* **all over**, ubiquitously, far and wide, the world over, universally

evict *v* **throw out**, expel, turn out, eject, remove *Opposite*: install

eviction *n* **removal**, expulsion, ejection, throwing out, exclusion

evidence *n* **1 indication**, sign, signal, mark, suggestion **2 proof**, confirmation, facts, data, substantiation ■ *v* **show**, demonstrate, evince, make clear, prove

evident *adj* **obvious**, plain, apparent, clear, manifest *Opposite*: obscure

evidently *adv* **1 obviously**, clearly, plainly, manifestly, palpably **2 apparently**, seemingly, as far as we know, it would seem, as far as one can tell

evil *adj* **1 wicked**, malevolent, sinful, malicious, criminal *Opposite*: good **2 foul**, vile, nasty, horrible, unpleasant *Opposite*: pleasant ■ *n* **wickedness**, malevolence, sin, iniquity, vice *Opposite*: good

evildoer *n* **wrongdoer**, sinner, criminal, offender, delinquent *Opposite*: benefactor

evilness *n* **wickedness**, badness, evil, immorality, sinfulness *Opposite*: goodness

evince *v* **show**, display, reveal, exhibit, manifest *Opposite*: conceal

evocation *n* **recreation**, elicitation, recall, air, hint

evocative *adj* **reminiscent**, suggestive, redolent, haunting

evoke *v* **call to mind**, bring to mind, suggest, call up, induce *Opposite*: suppress

evolution *n* **development**, fruition, growth, progress, progression *Opposite*: regression

evolve *v* **develop**, grow, progress, advance, go forward *Opposite*: regress

ewer *n* **jug**, pitcher, vessel, bottle, container

ex *adj* **former**, sometime, onetime, erstwhile, lapsed *Opposite*: future

exacerbate *v* **make worse**, worsen, aggravate, impair, intensify *Opposite*: soothe

exact *adj* **1 correct**, precise, accurate, strict, faithful *Opposite*: approximate **2 careful**, meticulous, precise, particular, thorough *Opposite*: careless ■ *v* **demand**, obtain, extort, extract, wrest

exacting *adj* **demanding**, testing, challenging, rigorous, tough *Opposite*: easy

exactitude *n* **precision**, correctness, accuracy, meticulousness, exactness *Opposite*: carelessness

exactly *adv* **precisely**, just, absolutely, quite, in every respect *Opposite*: approximately

exactness *n* **precision**, accuracy, exactitude, correctness, meticulousness *Opposite*: vagueness

exaggerate *v* **overstress**, embellish, embroider, make a mountain out of a molehill, inflate *Opposite*: understate

exaggerated *adj* **overstated**, inflated, embroidered, embellished, blown up *Opposite*: understated

exaggeration *n* **overstatement**, hyperbole, embellishment, embroidery, overemphasis *Opposite*: understatement

exalt *(fml) v* **1 promote**, raise, elevate, intensify, boost **2 praise**, laud, acclaim, applaud, pay tribute to *Opposite*: disparage

exaltation *(fml) n* **1 adulation**, adoration, acclaim, acclamation, praise *Opposite*: condemnation **2 excitement**, rapture, exhilaration, happiness, joy *Opposite*: despair

exalted *(fml) adj* **high**, lofty, glorious, dignified, illustrious *Opposite*: lowly

exam *n* **test**, assessment, examination, paper

examination *n* **1 inspection**, scrutiny, checkup, investigation, analysis **2 test**, assessment, exam, paper

examine *v* **1 look at**, inspect, scrutinize, observe, study **2 consider**, think about, look into, investigate, research **3 test**, assess, grade, judge, question

examiner *n* **inspector**, auditor, surveyor, superintendent, assessor

example *n* **1 sample**, instance, case, case in point, specimen **2 model**, pattern, paradigm, standard, paragon

exasperate *v* **infuriate**, madden, frustrate, annoy, irritate *Opposite*: placate. *See* COMPARE AND CONTRAST *at* **annoy**.

exasperating *adj* **infuriating**, maddening, frustrating, vexing, annoying *Opposite*: calming

exasperation *n* **frustration**, irritation, enragement, annoyance, vexation

excavate *v* **dig**, mine, quarry, dig out, exhume *Opposite*: bury

exceed v **go beyond**, surpass, go above, go over, top *Opposite*: fall short

exceedingly adv **very**, exceptionally, remarkably, extremely, extraordinarily *Opposite*: slightly

excel v **shine**, stand out, outshine, outclass, surpass *Opposite*: fall behind

excellence n **fineness**, brilliance, superiority, distinction, quality *Opposite*: mediocrity

excellent adj **outstanding**, brilliant, exceptional, admirable, superb *Opposite*: poor

except prep **apart from**, but, excluding, with the exception of, aside from *Opposite*: including

exception n **exclusion**, omission, exemption, concession, allowance

exceptionable *(fml)* adj **offensive**, obnoxious, rude, objectionable, repugnant *Opposite*: inoffensive

exceptional adj **excellent**, brilliant, special, extraordinary, incomparable *Opposite*: ordinary

exceptionality n **rarity**, infrequency, extraordinariness, uniqueness, remarkableness *Opposite*: normality

exceptionally adv **very**, remarkably, extremely, extraordinarily, outstandingly *Opposite*: slightly

excerpt n **extract**, passage, quote, quotation, selection

excess n **1 surplus**, glut, overload, surfeit, overabundance *Opposite*: shortage **2 overindulgence**, intemperance, dissipation, inordinateness, prodigality *Opposite*: moderation ■ adj **extra**, additional, surplus, spare, superfluous

excesses n **extremes**, dissipation, intemperance, overindulgence, prodigality

excessive adj **extreme**, too much, unnecessary, unwarranted, undue *Opposite*: moderate

excessively adv **very**, extremely, overly, exceptionally, markedly *Opposite*: moderately

excessiveness n **extremeness**, exorbitance, extravagance, immoderateness *(fml)*, immoderation *(fml) Opposite*: moderation

exchange v **switch**, switch over, replace, trade, barter *Opposite*: keep ■ n **1 conversation**, argument, talk, chat, discussion **2 trade**, switch, barter, replacement, substitute

exchangeable adj **redeemable**, transferable, negotiable, commutable, interchangeable

exchange blows v **fight**, scuffle, go for each other, trade punches, brawl

excise v **delete**, remove, edit, cut out, expunge *Opposite*: insert

excision n **editing**, deletion, removal, cutting out, erasure *Opposite*: insertion

excitability n **nervousness**, edginess, volatility, fieriness, temper *Opposite*: coolness

excitable adj **nervous**, emotional, highly strung, edgy, impulsive *Opposite*: unflappable

excite v **1 stimulate**, enthuse, animate, motivate, enliven *Opposite*: bore **2 incite**, agitate, provoke, instigate, stir up *Opposite*: soothe

excited adj **1 happy**, enthusiastic, eager, animated, motivated *Opposite*: indifferent **2 agitated**, nervous, provoked, overwrought, hot and bothered *Opposite*: calm

excitement n **1 enthusiasm**, eagerness, anticipation, pleasure, exhilaration *Opposite*: indifference **2 agitation**, tension, unrest, ferment, restlessness *Opposite*: calm

exciting adj **thrilling**, exhilarating, stirring, stimulating, electrifying *Opposite*: boring

exclaim v **cry out**, cry, shout, call out, call *Opposite*: whisper

exclamation n **shout**, cry, yell, scream, howl *Opposite*: whisper

exclude v **1 keep out**, bar, reject, leave out, prevent *Opposite*: welcome **2 reject**, rule out, eliminate, discount, ignore *Opposite*: include

excluding prep **exclusive of**, not including, without, apart from *Opposite*: including

exclusion n **1 keeping out**, barring, rejection, leaving out, prohibiting *Opposite*: welcome **2 ban**, refusal, sanction, embargo, prohibition **3 rejection**, elimination, marginalization, prohibition, veto *Opposite*: inclusion

exclusive adj **1 high-class**, elite, select, restricted, limited *Opposite*: inclusive **2 sole**, complete, undivided, full, whole *Opposite*: partial

exclusiveness n **1 luxury**, sophistication, refinement, superiority, stylishness **2 selectiveness**, selectivity, exclusivity, elitism, snobbery

excommunicate v **exclude**, bar, debar, expel, eject *Opposite*: admit

excommunication n **exclusion**, barring, debarring, expulsion, ejection *Opposite*: admission

excoriate v **1 skin**, peel, pare, strip, flay **2** *(fml)* **criticize**, denounce, attack, berate, upbraid *Opposite*: commend

excrescence n **monstrosity**, eyesore, blot, growth, outgrowth

excruciating adj **1 agonizing**, painful, unbearable, awful, terrible *Opposite*: pleasant **2 embarrassing**, tedious, stultifying, irritating, infuriating *Opposite*: enthralling

exculpate *(fml)* v **free**, let off, excuse, clear, release *Opposite*: arraign

exculpation *(fml)* n **acquittal**, exoneration, discharge, pardon, clearing *Opposite*: arraignment

excursion n **1 trip**, jaunt, outing, junket, tour **2 group**, team, party, expedition **3** *(fml)*

digression, departure, detour, deviation, tangent

excusable *adj* **understandable**, forgivable, justifiable, explicable, pardonable *Opposite*: inexcusable

excuse *v* **1 forgive**, pardon, let off, acquit, absolve *Opposite*: blame **2 overlook**, make allowances for, pass over, tolerate, justify **3 exempt**, release, let off, free, relieve *Opposite*: oblige ■ *n* **justification**, reason, explanation, pretext, defence

excused *adj* **exempted**, released, exempt, let off, relieved *Opposite*: required

execrable *adj* **awful**, appalling, disgusting, repulsive, deplorable *Opposite*: excellent

execute *v* **1 carry out**, perform, implement, complete, accomplish **2 put to death**, kill, murder, hang, electrocute. *See* COMPARE AND CONTRAST *at* **kill, perform**.

execution *n* **1 putting to death**, capital punishment, the death sentence, killing, hanging **2 implementation**, performance, accomplishment, carrying out, completing

executive *n* **manager**, senior manager, director, administrator, official ■ *adj* **1 decision-making**, policymaking, managerial, management, administrative **2 expensive**, exclusive, high class, superior, select

executor *n* **doer**, prime mover, initiator, originator, architect

exemplary *adj* **1 admirable**, praiseworthy, excellent, perfect, ideal *Opposite*: shameful **2** *(fml)* **model**, archetypal, textbook, typical, classic

exemplify *v* **demonstrate**, typify, represent, illustrate, show

exempt *adj* **excused**, exempted, released, relieved, discharged *Opposite*: required ■ *v* **excuse**, free, let off, let go, release *Opposite*: oblige

exemption *n* **exception**, immunity, release, indemnity, exclusion *Opposite*: obligation

exercise *n* **1 physical activity**, working out, training, keep fit, drill *Opposite*: inactivity **2 move**, movement, drill, step, stretch **3** *(fml)* **implementation**, carrying out, use, application, employment *Opposite*: avoidance ■ *v* **1 work out**, train, keep fit, do exercises, drill **2 use**, put into effect, implement, apply, employ *Opposite*: avoid

exercises *n* **military exercises**, manoeuvres, drills, war games

exert *v* **bring to bear**, use, apply, exercise, make use of

exertion *n* **effort**, action, application, physical exertion, energy *Opposite*: ease

exert yourself *v* **make an effort**, try hard, push yourself, strive, labour

exhale *v* **breathe out**, blow out, puff out, let your breath out, respire *Opposite*: inhale

exhaust *v* **1 tire out**, wear out, drain, fatigue, weaken *Opposite*: refresh **2 use up**, use, wear out, consume, drain *Opposite*: renew

exhausted *adj* **tired**, worn out, shattered, fatigued, drained *Opposite*: refreshed

exhausting *adj* **tiring**, wearing, shattering, fatiguing, killing *Opposite*: refreshing

exhaustion *n* **tiredness**, fatigue, collapse, weariness, enervation *Opposite*: energy

exhaustive *adj* **thorough**, complete, comprehensive, in-depth, full *Opposite*: superficial

exhibit *v* **1 display**, show, unveil, put on a display, put on view *Opposite*: hide **2 show off**, parade, flaunt, expose, display ■ *n* **exhibition**, display, show, showcase, showing

exhibition *n* **1 display**, show, showing, demonstration, exposition **2 grant**, scholarship, bursary, award, fund

exhibitionist *n* **attention seeker**, braggart, extrovert, show-off *(infml)*

exhilarate *v* **excite**, elate, thrill, enliven, invigorate *Opposite*: bore

exhilarated *adj* **elated**, ecstatic, euphoric, overjoyed, delighted *Opposite*: indifferent

exhilaration *n* **excitement**, elation, high spirits, animation, happiness

exhort *v* **urge**, press, push, pressure, insist *Opposite*: forbid

exhortation *(fml)* *n* **appeal**, call, encouragement, urging, incitement

exhume *v* **dig up**, disinter, unearth, disentomb, disclose *Opposite*: bury

exigency *(fml)* *n* **need**, demand, requirement, emergency, necessity

exigent *(fml)* *adj* **1 urgent**, pressing, crucial, vital, important *Opposite*: unimportant **2 demanding**, tough, testing, challenging, taxing *Opposite*: easy

exile *n* **1 émigré**, tax exile, expatriate, deportee, refugee **2 banishment**, deportation, expulsion, separation, ostracism ■ *v* **banish**, send away, deport, expel, separate

exist *v* **1 be**, be real, be present, be existent, happen **2 live**, be, survive, continue living, stay alive

existence *n* **being**, life, reality, presence, survival

existent *(fml)* *adj* **existing**, current, present, extant, ongoing

existing *adj* **present**, current, in effect, prevailing, standing

exit *n* **1 way out**, door, outlet, egress *(fml)* *Opposite*: entrance **2 departure**, exodus, walking out, leaving, going away *Opposite*: arrival ■ *v* **go out**, leave, depart, go, walk out *Opposite*: enter

exodus *n* **mass departure**, departure, migration, emigration, flight *Opposite*: arrival

exonerate *v* **clear**, absolve, acquit, vindicate, forgive *Opposite*: blame

exoneration n 1 **pardon**, absolution, acquittal, vindication, exculpation *(fml)* Opposite: blame 2 **release**, freeing, liberation, exemption, discharge

exorbitant adj **excessive**, inflated, ridiculous, dear, overpriced Opposite: reasonable

exorcize v **get rid of**, get free of, banish, drive out, force out

exotic adj 1 **unusual**, out of the ordinary, novel, striking, interesting Opposite: ordinary 2 **foreign**, from abroad, tropical, alien, non-native Opposite: familiar

expand v **make bigger**, get bigger, enlarge, increase, develop Opposite: contract. See COMPARE AND CONTRAST *at* **increase**.

expandable adj **stretchy**, elastic, foldup, foldout, pullout

expand upon v **enlarge on**, elaborate on, give details, embellish, amplify

expanse n **area**, breadth, stretch, span, region

expansion n **growth**, development, increase, extension, spreading out Opposite: contraction

expansive adj 1 **communicative**, generous, magnanimous, friendly, open Opposite: reserved 2 **extensive**, spread-out, spacious, roomy, sizable Opposite: cramped

expansively adv 1 **at length**, extensively, widely, comprehensively, broadly Opposite: briefly 2 **effusively**, lavishly, openly, generously, jovially

expansiveness n 1 **effusiveness**, lavishness, openness, generousness, enthusiasm Opposite: reserve 2 **size**, large size, mass, extent, reach

expat *(infml) see* **expatriate**

expatriate n **émigré**, tax exile, emigrant, refugee, colonial Opposite: native

expect v 1 **wait for**, anticipate, look forward to, await, look ahead 2 **imagine**, suppose, guess, think, believe 3 **demand**, require, insist on, count on, anticipate

expectancy n **anticipation**, expectation, hope, suspense, bated breath

expectant adj 1 **eager**, hopeful, in suspense, hoping, on tenterhooks 2 **pregnant**, expecting, in the family way *(dated infml)*, in the club *(slang)*

expectation n **hope**, anticipation, expectancy, belief, prospect

expected adj **likely**, probable, foreseeable, predictable, awaited Opposite: surprising

expecting adj **pregnant**, expectant, in the club *(slang)*, in the family way *(dated infml)*

expectorant n **cough medicine**, linctus, cough mixture, medicine, cough syrup

expediency n 1 **convenience**, practicality, pragmatism, usefulness, feasibility 2 **appropriateness**, suitability, fitness, advisability, convenience Opposite: unsuitability

expedient adj 1 **appropriate**, fitting, suitable, advisable, necessary Opposite: inappropriate 2 **advantageous**, convenient, practical, useful, beneficial Opposite: altruistic ∎ n **measure**, means, method, manoeuvre, device

expedite *(fml)* v **speed up**, accelerate, hurry up, advance, further Opposite: impede

expedition n 1 **journey**, excursion, voyage, trip, outing 2 **team**, party, crew, group, company

expeditious adj **speedy**, prompt, quick, swift, hasty Opposite: slow

expel v 1 **dismiss**, fire, eject, oust, throw out 2 **drive out**, force out, push out, eject, flush out

expend v 1 **use up**, use, consume, spend, burn up Opposite: conserve 2 *(fml)* **spend**, disburse, pay out, lay out, pay Opposite: save

expendable adj 1 **consumable**, replaceable, throwaway, disposable, usable Opposite: durable 2 **dispensable**, disposable, superfluous, unessential, nonessential Opposite: indispensable

expenditure n **spending**, outgoings, expenses, payments, outflow Opposite: income

expense n 1 **cost**, expenditure, outlay, disbursement, outflow Opposite: income 2 **price**, rate, figure, amount, price tag 3 **sacrifice**, cost, detriment, disadvantage, loss

expenses n **expenditures**, outgoings, outlay, payments, costs Opposite: income

expensive adj 1 **costly**, dear, high-priced, steep *(infml)*, pricey *(infml)* Opposite: cheap 2 **luxurious**, exclusive, affluent, lavish, classy *(infml)* Opposite: cheap

experience n 1 **involvement**, knowledge, skill, practice, understanding Opposite: inexperience 2 **occurrence**, incident, episode, encounter, event ∎ v **feel**, go through, face, live through, undergo

experienced adj **knowledgeable**, skilled, practised, qualified, veteran Opposite: inexperienced

experiment n **trial**, test, investigation, research, experimentation ∎ v **test**, try out, investigate, try, trial

experimental adj **new**, tentative, untried, trial, speculative Opposite: proven

experimentation n **testing**, research, investigation, trialling

expert n **specialist**, authority, professional, connoisseur, doyen Opposite: amateur ∎ adj **skilled**, skilful, practised, proficient, professional Opposite: inexperienced

expertise n **skill**, knowledge, proficiency, capability, know-how *(infml)*

expertness n **skilfulness**, dexterity, knowledge, expertise, proficiency Opposite: inexperience

expiate v **make amends**, compensate, make up for, recompense, redress

expire v 1 **end**, run out, finish, terminate, conclude 2 *(fml)* **die**, pass away, pass on, perish, breathe your last *(literary)*

expiry n 1 **end**, ending, running out, finish, finishing *Opposite*: beginning 2 *(fml)* **death**, passing, end, dying, demise *(fml)*

explain v 1 **make clear**, describe, put in plain words, elucidate, clarify 2 **justify**, account for, defend, rationalize, vindicate

explanation n 1 **reason**, justification, rationalization, vindication, account 2 **description**, account, clarification, enlightenment, details

explanatory adj **descriptive**, instructive, illustrative, illuminating, clarifying

expletive n **swearword**, curse, oath, exclamation, obscenity

explicable adj **explainable**, understandable, reasonable, justifiable, rational *Opposite*: inexplicable

explicate v **explain**, elucidate, spell out, clarify, expound

explicit adj 1 **clear**, obvious, open, overt, plain *Opposite*: implicit 2 **definite**, precise, exact, specific, unequivocal *Opposite*: vague 3 **frank**, uninhibited, candid, open, graphic

explode v 1 **blow up**, go off, burst, erupt, burst out *Opposite*: implode 2 **get angry**, fly into a rage, hit the ceiling, hit the roof *(infml)*, blow up *(infml)* *Opposite*: calm down 3 **disprove**, prove wrong, discredit, invalidate, nullify *Opposite*: prove

exploit v 1 **take advantage of**, abuse, misuse, ill-use, manipulate 2 **use**, develop, make use of, take advantage of, utilize *Opposite*: waste ■ n **feat**, deed, adventure, activity, heroic act

exploitable adj 1 **gullible**, credulous, innocent, vulnerable *Opposite*: shrewd 2 **usable**, utilizable, consumable, available

exploitation n 1 **misuse**, abuse, mistreatment, taking advantage, manipulation 2 **use**, utilization, development, management, operation

exploitative adj **unfair**, unequal, abusive, manipulative *Opposite*: fair

exploration n 1 **examination**, investigation, survey, study, consideration 2 **travelling**, discovery, journeying, adventure, voyaging

exploratory adj **investigative**, examining, probing, tentative, experimental

explore v 1 **travel**, discover, reconnoitre, see the sights, sightsee 2 **investigate**, study, search, look at, survey

explorer n **traveller**, voyager, surveyor, pioneer, pathfinder

explosion n 1 **bang**, blast, detonation, eruption, burst 2 **outburst**, fit, eruption, paroxysm, burst 3 **upsurge**, leap, flood, outbreak, eruption *Opposite*: slump

explosive adj 1 **volatile**, unstable, unpredictable, dangerous *Opposite*: stable 2 **short-**tempered, quick-tempered, hotheaded, volatile, fiery *Opposite*: placid

WORD BANK

❑ **types of explosive material** dynamite, gelignite, gunpowder, napalm, nitroglycerine, plastic explosive, propellant, Semtex™, TNT

❑ **types of explosive weapon** A-bomb, antiballistic missile, atom bomb, ballistic missile, bomb, booby trap, bunker-buster, cruise missile, daisycutter, depth charge, firebomb, guided missile, hand grenade, hydrogen bomb, mine, missile, Molotov cocktail, nail bomb, neutron bomb, nuclear missile, nuclear warhead, nuclear weapon, petrol bomb, pipe bomb, smart bomb, torpedo, smoke bomb, warhead, time bomb, weapon of mass destruction

exponent n 1 **advocate**, proponent, promoter, fan, champion 2 **interpreter**, explainer, performer, practitioner

export v 1 **sell abroad**, sell overseas, send abroad, send overseas, ship *Opposite*: import 2 **spread**, transfer, carry across, pass on, disseminate

expose v 1 **open up**, reveal, uncover, bare, display *Opposite*: cover 2 **subject**, lay open to, put in danger, endanger, imperil *(fml)* 3 **blow the whistle on**, unmask, reveal, lay bare, bring to light *Opposite*: cover up

exposé n **disclosure**, revelation, leak, exposure, discovery

exposed adj **unprotected**, visible, uncovered, bare, out in the open *Opposite*: covered

exposition n 1 **description**, discussion, explanation, account, clarification 2 **exhibition**, fair, show, trade fair, display

expostulate v **disagree**, protest, object, reprove, remonstrate. *See* COMPARE AND CONTRAST *at* **object**.

exposure n 1 **contact**, experience, introduction, acquaintance, dealings 2 **revelation**, disclosure, revealing, unveiling, publicity *Opposite*: whitewash

expound v **explain**, expand on, talk about, develop, illustrate

express v 1 **state**, articulate, utter, voice, communicate 2 **squeeze out**, extract, press out, force out ■ adj 1 **fast**, rapid, direct, nonstop, prompt *Opposite*: slow 2 **precise**, explicit, definite, exact, specific *Opposite*: vague

expression n 1 **look**, face, air, appearance, countenance 2 **phrase**, idiom, turn of phrase, term, saying 3 **communication**, manifestation, illustration, example, demonstration 4 **extraction**, squeezing out, pressing out, forcing out

expressionless adj **straight-faced**, unresponsive, impassive, poker-faced, inexpressive *Opposite*: expressive

expressive adj 1 **communicative**, sensitive, open, easy-to-read, animated *Opposite*: impassive 2 **representative**, representing, demonstrating, signifying, indicative

expressively adv **meaningfully**, dramatically, emotionally, sensitively, vividly Opposite: blandly

expressivity n **articulacy**, eloquence, self-expression, fluency, clarity Opposite: inarticulacy

expressly adv **specifically**, particularly, explicitly, clearly, definitely

expropriate v **steal**, confiscate, seize, commandeer, appropriate

expulsion n **dismissal**, exclusion, throwing out, eviction, removal Opposite: admittance

expunge v **obliterate**, purge, erase, delete, rub out Opposite: insert

expurgated adj **cut down**, abridged, censored, edited, bowdlerized

exquisite adj 1 **beautiful**, gorgeous, delicate, attractive, superb Opposite: ugly 2 **excellent**, perfect, delightful, flawless, wonderful Opposite: flawed 3 **discriminating**, discerning, sensitive, fastidious, refined 4 **intense**, touching, moving, excruciating, poignant Opposite: dull

exquisiteness n **beauty**, delicacy, daintiness, perfection, attractiveness Opposite: ugliness

extant adj **existing**, in existence, present, living, surviving Opposite: lost. See COMPARE AND CONTRAST at **living**.

extemporaneous adj **extemporary**, extemporal, unrehearsed, impromptu, ad-lib Opposite: rehearsed

extempore adj **extemporaneous**, ad-lib, off-the-cuff, impromptu, unrehearsed Opposite: rehearsed ■ adv **extemporaneously**, ad lib, off the cuff, impromptu, spontaneously Opposite: rehearsed

extemporize v **ad-lib**, improvise, speak off the cuff, play it by ear, make it up as you go along Opposite: prepare

extend v 1 **spread**, spread out, range, cover, encompass 2 **continue**, reach, stretch, go on, run 3 **make bigger**, expand, enlarge, make longer, lengthen Opposite: curtail 4 **prolong**, stretch out, drag out, lengthen, postpone Opposite: cut short 5 **increase**, expand, widen, broaden, add to Opposite: decrease 6 **offer**, give, hold out, proffer, tender Opposite: withdraw. See COMPARE AND CONTRAST at **increase**.

extended adj **lengthy**, protracted, long, prolonged, stretched Opposite: cut short

extension n 1 **additional room**, addition, lean-to, wing, conservatory 2 **extra time**, delay, postponement, leeway, allowance 3 **expansion**, enlargement, lengthening, broadening, increase Opposite: contraction

extensive adj 1 **big**, large, huge, vast, massive Opposite: restricted 2 **wide**, widespread, wide-ranging, general, all-embracing Opposite: narrow

extensively adv 1 **significantly**, considerably, greatly, to a great extent, to a large extent

Opposite: insignificantly 2 **at length**, lengthily, widely, far, broadly Opposite: briefly

extensiveness n **breadth**, comprehensiveness, fullness, richness, vastness Opposite: narrowness

extent n 1 **size**, area, coverage, limit, boundary 2 **degree**, amount, level, range, scope

extenuating adj **mitigating**, explanatory, justifying, moderating, palliative

exterior adj **external**, outside, outdoor, peripheral, outward Opposite: interior ■ n 1 **outside**, façade, elevation, surface, shell Opposite: interior 2 **appearance**, look, aura, veneer, front

exterminate v **kill**, eliminate, annihilate, massacre, destroy

extermination n **extinction**, annihilation, execution, killing, slaughter Opposite: preservation

external adj **outside**, exterior, outdoor, peripheral, outward Opposite: internal

externalize v **express**, give voice to, utter, get off your chest, voice Opposite: internalize

externally adv **outwardly**, on the outside, on the exterior, on the surface, superficially Opposite: inwardly

extinct adj **nonexistent**, inexistent, died out, destroyed, vanished Opposite: living. See COMPARE AND CONTRAST at **dead**.

extinction n **death**, extermination, destruction, loss, annihilation Opposite: survival

extinguish v 1 **douse**, quench, snuff, stub out, smother Opposite: light 2 **end**, take away, destroy, snuff out, do away with 3 **eclipse**, overshadow, outshine, obscure, show up

extol (fml or literary) v **praise**, commend, eulogize, admire, worship Opposite: deprecate

extort v **extract**, obtain under duress, obtain by threat, wrest, wring

extortion n **coercion**, threats, blackmail, squeezing, force

extortionate adj **expensive**, exorbitant, inflated, high, overpriced Opposite: reasonable

extra adj **additional**, further, added, spare, second ■ adv 1 **more**, in addition, further, on top, spare 2 **especially**, particularly, ultra, exceptionally, more ■ n **optional extra**, addition, add-on, supplement, bonus

extract v 1 **take out**, remove, haul out, pull out, dig out Opposite: put in 2 **obtain**, winkle out, unearth, extricate, root out 3 **extort**, force, wrest, wheedle out, wring ■ n **excerpt**, cutting, quotation, citation, abstract

extraction n 1 **removal**, taking out, withdrawal, pulling out, drawing out Opposite: insertion 2 **origin**, birth, descent, ancestry, family

extracurricular adj 1 **additional**, supplementary, optional, secondary, extramural Opposite: regular 2 (infml) **extramarital**, adulterous, clandestine, illicit, improper

extradite v **deport**, expel, banish, transfer, repatriate

extradition n **repatriation**, handing over, deportation, expulsion, return

extra-large adj **outsize**, outsized, giant, jumbo, oversized Opposite: undersized

extramarital adj **adulterous**, illicit, clandestine, improper, extracurricular (infml)

extramural adj **external**, extracurricular, additional, optional, vocational Opposite: intramural

extraneous adj **1 irrelevant**, unrelated, unconnected, inappropriate, beside the point Opposite: pertinent **2 inessential**, unimportant, unnecessary, superfluous, peripheral Opposite: essential

extraordinaire adj **excellent**, extraordinary, superb, exceptional, remarkable Opposite: ordinary

extraordinarily adv **1 strangely**, oddly, unusually, bizarrely, abnormally Opposite: normally **2 extremely**, very, unusually, particularly, amazingly

extraordinary adj **1 strange**, odd, unusual, unexpected, astonishing Opposite: ordinary **2 special**, particular, exceptional, remarkable, great Opposite: normal

extrapolate v **infer**, generalize, induce, deduce, conclude

extrasensory adj **telepathic**, psychic, clairvoyant, mystic, mystical

extraterrestrial adj **celestial**, interplanetary, Martian, alien, interstellar Opposite: terrestrial ■ n **alien**, creature, creature from outer space, space invader, ET Opposite: earthling

extravagance n **1 profligacy**, overspending, wastefulness, excessiveness, lavishness Opposite: prudence **2 luxury**, indulgence, folly, nonessential, overindulgence Opposite: essential

extravagant adj **1 profligate**, wasteful, excessive, spendthrift, overgenerous Opposite: thrifty **2 exaggerated**, overstated, profuse, excessive, elaborate Opposite: restrained

extravaganza n **show**, musical, variety performance, gala, festival

extreme adj **1 great**, tremendous, severe, intense, acute Opposite: insignificant **2 radical**, fanatical, immoderate, zealous, excessive Opposite: moderate **3 farthest**, furthest, outermost, ultimate, maximum **4 dangerous**, life-threatening, thrilling, risky, exciting Opposite: safe ■ n **limit**, boundary, edge, end, pole

extremely adv **very**, tremendously, enormously, awfully, really Opposite: somewhat

extreme sport n **adrenaline sport**, alternative sport, Xtreme sport

extremism n **radicalism**, fanaticism, zealotry,

activism, intemperance Opposite: moderation

extremist n **radical**, fanatic, activist, revolutionary, rebel Opposite: moderate ■ adj **radical**, fanatical, revolutionary, rebel, terrorist Opposite: moderate

extremity n **1 edge**, limit, boundary, margin, extreme Opposite: centre **2 limb**, hand, foot, arm, leg

extricate v **get out**, extract, remove, disentangle, detach Opposite: engage

extrication n **disconnection**, detachment, disentanglement, disengagement, release Opposite: engagement

extroversion n **sociability**, friendliness, self-confidence, socialness, conviviality Opposite: introversion

extrovert n **outgoing person**, gregarious person, assertive person, socializer, befriender Opposite: introvert ■ adj **sociable**, outgoing, gregarious, friendly, social Opposite: introverted

exuberance n **enthusiasm**, excitement, liveliness, energy, high spirits Opposite: apathy

exuberant adj **enthusiastic**, excited, lively, energetic, high-spirited Opposite: lethargic

exude v **1 radiate**, give out, give off, display, show Opposite: absorb **2 secrete**, release, ooze, leak, discharge

exult v **revel**, take pride, gloat, glory, triumph Opposite: lament

exultant adj **jubilant**, overjoyed, triumphant, joyful, thrilled Opposite: miserable

exultation n **happiness**, triumph, joy, rejoicing, jubilation Opposite: misery

eye n **appreciation**, sense, taste, discrimination, discernment ■ v **look at**, stare at, gaze at, watch, observe

WORD BANK
❏ **parts of an eye** aqueous humour, cone, conjunctiva, cornea, eyeball, iris, lens, macula, optic nerve, pupil, retina, rod, vitreous humour

eyeball (infml) v **stare at**, glare at, have a good look at, look at, gaze at

eye-catching adj **striking**, noticeable, attention-grabbing, startling, arresting Opposite: unremarkable

eyeful (infml) n **look**, view, glance, squint (infml), gander (infml)

eyelet n **hole**, grommet, eyehole, perforation, loophole

eye opener n **revelation**, discovery, realization, surprise, shock

eyesight n **vision**, sight, sightedness, eye, view

eyesore n **blot on the landscape**, blot, monstrosity, blemish, fright

eyewitness n **witness**, observer, bystander, onlooker, looker-on

F

fable *n* tale, legend, parable, myth, story

fabled *adj* 1 **legendary**, wonderful, remarkable, extraordinary, famous *Opposite*: unknown 2 **fictitious**, mythical, imaginary, legendary, fairy-tale *Opposite*: factual

fabric *n* 1 **cloth**, material, textile, stuff, piece goods 2 **structure**, foundation, framework, basics, makeup 3 **brickwork**, stonework, masonry, structure, superstructure

WORD BANK
❏ **types of fabric from animals** alpaca, angora, astrakhan, baize, brocade, camel hair, cashmere, chenille, crepe de Chine, felt, flannel, fur, gabardine, horsehair, jersey, lambswool, leather, loden, mohair, pashmina, shahtoosh, silk, taffeta, tweed, vicuna, wool, worsted
❏ **types of fabric from plants** burlap, calico, canvas, chambray, cheesecloth, chintz, corduroy, cotton, cretonne, damask, denim, drill, flannelette, gauze, gingham, grosgrain, hessian, lawn, linen, madras, moleskin, muslin, organdy, poplin, sacking, sailcloth, seersucker, tarpaulin, terry, terry towelling, ticking, towelling, twill, velour, velvet, voile, winceyette
❏ **types of synthetic fabric** acrylic, chiffon, crêpe, fishnet, fleece, lamé, moquette, nylon, percale, polyester, PVC, rayon, sateen, satin, spandex, tulle, viscose

fabricate *v* 1 **invent**, make up, concoct, dream up, trump up 2 **construct**, make, manufacture, produce, engineer *Opposite*: destroy

fabricated *adj* **invented**, made-up, untrue, fictitious, fictional *Opposite*: genuine

fabrication *n* 1 **untruth**, lie, invention, falsehood, cock-and-bull story *Opposite*: truth 2 **construction**, manufacture, production, assembly, creation 3 **counterfeit**, forgery, fake, imitation. *See* COMPARE AND CONTRAST *at* lie.

fabulous *adj* 1 **excellent**, wonderful, tremendous, magnificent, marvellous *Opposite*: awful 2 **fictitious**, mythical, imaginary, legendary, fairy-tale *Opposite*: factual

façade *n* 1 **frontage**, portico, fascia, front 2 **pretence**, veneer, impression, front, face

face *n* 1 **countenance**, features, mug (*slang*), phiz (*slang*), phizog (*slang*) 2 (*infml*) **nerve**, gall, boldness, audacity, pluck 3 **expression**, look, appearance, air, aspect 4 **outside**, surface, aspect, façade, wall *Opposite*: back ■ *v* 1 **be opposite**, be in front of, stand in front of, stand facing, look toward 2 **confront**, tackle, meet, cope with, challenge *Opposite*: avoid 3 **accept**, admit, be realistic, realize, bite the bullet *Opposite*: deny

WORD BANK
❏ **parts of a face** brow, cheek, cheekbone, chin, chops (*infml*), eye, eyebrow, forehead, hairline, jaw, jawline, jowl, lips, mandible, mouth, nose, temple

faceless *adj* **impersonal**, featureless, unidentified, anonymous, nameless

facelift *n* 1 **plastic surgery**, cosmetic surgery, tuck 2 **renovation**, modernization, refurbishment, redecoration, restoration

face-off *n* **confrontation**, conflict, argument, showdown, challenge

face pack *n* **face mask**, facial, beauty treatment, mudpack

face-saving *adj* **dignified**, diplomatic, tactical, tactful, restorative *Opposite*: humiliating

facet *n* 1 **aspect**, feature, part, component, factor 2 **surface**, face, side, plane, façade

face the music *v* **accept responsibility**, face the storm, face up to your actions, take the flak, bite the bullet

facetious *adj* 1 **flippant**, silly, ill-timed, ill-judged, inappropriate *Opposite*: earnest 2 **lighthearted**, playful, humorous, witty, droll *Opposite*: serious

facetiousness *n* 1 **flippancy**, frivolousness, inappropriateness, silliness, inanity *Opposite*: earnestness 2 **lightheartedness**, wittiness, wit, drollness, humorousness *Opposite*: seriousness

face to face *adv* 1 **in person**, in the flesh, personally, head-on, person to person 2 **head on**, opposite, in confrontation, nose to nose, head to head

face up to *v* **accept**, admit, come to terms with, realize, confront *Opposite*: deny

facial *n* **beauty treatment**, face mask, face pack, makeover, massage

facile *adj* **superficial**, simplistic, flippant, trite, inane *Opposite*: profound

facilitate *v* **make easy**, ease, make possible, enable, smooth *Opposite*: impede

facilitation *n* **assistance**, help, furtherance, advancement, easing *Opposite*: obstruction

facilitator *n* **organizer**, architect, originator, prime mover, initiator

facilities *n* **amenities**, services, conveniences, restroom, toilet

facility *n* 1 **skill**, capability, capacity, talent, flair *Opposite*: inability 2 **service**, provision, resource, feature, advantage

facing prep **opposite**, in front of, fronting

facsimile n **copy**, duplicate, reproduction, replica, likeness

fact n 1 **truth**, reality, actuality, verity (fml) Opposite: fiction 2 **piece of information**, detail, point, circumstance, datum 3 **happening**, deed, occurrence, event, act

faction n 1 **section**, party, splinter group, bloc, division 2 **conflict**, division, disunity, schism, disharmony Opposite: agreement

factional adj 1 **sectarian**, dissenting, disaffected, separatist, schismatic Opposite: united 2 **dramatized**, fictionalized, drama-documentary, semirealistic, documentary

factious adj **divisive**, sectarian, schismatic, discordant, contentious Opposite: unifying

factitious adj **contrived**, artificial, simulated, affected, unnatural Opposite: genuine

fact of life n **reality**, practicality, fact, truth, actuality

factor n **influence**, thing, feature, aspect, reason

factory n **plant**, works, installation, industrial unit, manufacturing plant

WORD BANK
❑ types of **factory** assembly plant, brewery, cannery, distillery, forge, foundry, machine shop, mill, mint, pottery, sawmill, smithy, steelworks, sweatshop, water mill, workshop

facts n 1 **truth**, evidence, reality, actuality, proof 2 **particulars**, details, specifics, essentials, data

fact sheet n **information sheet**, information leaflet, booklet, brochure, handout

factual adj 1 **objective**, hard, verifiable, bona fide, authentic Opposite: subjective 2 **truthful**, accurate, realistic, honest, true-life Opposite: fictional

faculty n 1 **sense**, power, endowment, capability, function 2 **ability**, facility, gift, talent, knack Opposite: inability 3 **staff**, teaching body, teaching staff, teachers, professors

fad n **fashion**, craze, trend, whim, vogue

faddiness n **fussiness**, fastidiousness, pickiness, choosiness (infml), pernicketiness (infml)

faddy adj **fussy**, finicky, picky, particular, choosy (infml)

fade v 1 **become paler**, lighten, become lighter, lose colour, bleach Opposite: darken 2 **disappear**, weaken, die away, diminish, fade away Opposite: grow 3 **wane**, wither, die, waste away, wilt Opposite: flourish

fade away v 1 **disappear**, vanish, fade, evaporate, dwindle Opposite: persist 2 **waste away**, shrivel, wane, wither, atrophy Opposite: thrive

fading adj **disappearing**, declining, dying, vanishing, diminishing Opposite: growing

faff about (infml) see **faff around**

faff around (infml) v **waver**, hesitate, vacillate, shilly-shally, mess about (infml)

fail v 1 **be unsuccessful**, nose-dive, miss the mark, go belly up, fall flat Opposite: succeed 2 **fall short**, not make the grade, not be up to scratch, flunk (infml), fluff (infml) Opposite: pass 3 **stop working**, break down, crash, go down, stop 4 **go out of business**, go bankrupt, crash, fold, go under Opposite: thrive 5 **let down**, disappoint, neglect, forsake, desert Opposite: satisfy 6 **weaken**, fade, diminish, dwindle, decline Opposite: rally

failed adj **unsuccessful**, botched, disastrous, futile, abortive Opposite: successful

failing n **shortcoming**, flaw, weakness, weak point, fault Opposite: forte ■ prep **without**, in the absence of, lacking ■ adj **deteriorating**, worsening, weakening, fading, waning Opposite: strengthening. See COMPARE AND CONTRAST at **flaw**.

fail-safe adj **foolproof**, guaranteed, dependable, reliable, unfailing Opposite: unreliable

failure n 1 **disappointment**, letdown, catastrophe, fiasco, disaster Opposite: success 2 **breakdown**, stoppage, malfunction, crash, collapse 3 **bankruptcy**, closure, crash, collapse, insolvency

faint adj 1 **dim**, weak, faded, indistinct, feeble Opposite: bright 2 **dizzy**, giddy, woozy, unsteady, vertiginous 3 **slight**, diminished, muffled, soft, low Opposite: loud ■ v **pass out**, collapse, black out, fall down, lose consciousness Opposite: come to

faint-hearted adj **fearful**, apprehensive, hesitant, cowardly, shy Opposite: bold. See COMPARE AND CONTRAST at **cowardly**.

faintly adv 1 **dimly**, weakly, slightly, indistinctly, feebly Opposite: brightly 2 **slightly**, softly, barely, indistinctly, imperceptibly Opposite: loudly

faintness n 1 **dimness**, weakness, feebleness, indistinctness, haziness Opposite: brightness 2 **slightness**, quietness, weakness, feebleness, softness Opposite: loudness 3 **dizziness**, giddiness, wooziness, vertigo, lightheadedness

fair adj 1 **reasonable**, just, fair-minded, open-minded, impartial Opposite: biased 2 **light**, blond, fair-haired, flaxen, tow-headed Opposite: dark 3 **adequate**, passable, average, reasonable, decent 4 **pleasing**, attractive, good-looking, lovely, pretty Opposite: unattractive 5 **good**, bright, sunny, clear, cloudless Opposite: inclement ■ n 1 **travelling fair**, fairground, funfair, amusement park, theme park 2 **festival**, sale, fête, exposition, bazaar

fairground n **fair**, funfair, theme park, amusement park, playground

fair-haired adj **fair**, blond, flaxen, tow-headed Opposite: dark

fairly adv 1 **honestly**, justly, properly, legitimately, impartially Opposite: unfairly 2 **moderately**, rather, quite, reasonably, somewhat 3 **completely**, positively, literally, practically, absolutely

fair-minded *adj* fair, open-minded, even-handed, nondiscriminatory, impartial *Opposite*: prejudiced

fairness *n* justice, equality, evenhandedness, impartiality, fair-mindedness *Opposite*: unfairness

fairy *n* pixie, brownie, sprite, elf, leprechaun

fairyland *n* wonderland, dreamland, dream world, seventh heaven, heaven

fairy story *n* 1 myth, fairy tale, folktale, folk story, legend 2 **invention**, fabrication, lie, untruth, falsehood

fairy tale *n* 1 **invention**, fabrication, lie, untruth, falsehood 2 **fairy story**, folktale, folk story, myth, legend

fairy-tale *adj* 1 **mythical**, enchanted, magic, magical, imaginary *Opposite*: real 2 **fortunate**, happy, storybook, perfect, romantic *Opposite*: unhappy 3 **fabricated**, unbelievable, make-believe, made-up, highly coloured *Opposite*: truthful

faith *n* 1 **trust**, confidence, reliance, conviction, belief *Opposite*: disbelief 2 **loyalty**, devotion, faithfulness, commitment, dedication *Opposite*: disloyalty

faithful *adj* 1 **loyal**, devoted, trusty, trustworthy, staunch *Opposite*: faithless 2 **correct**, true, realistic, authentic, close *Opposite*: unrealistic

faithfulness *n* 1 **loyalty**, devotion, staunchness, dependability, reliability *Opposite*: faithlessness 2 **correctness**, closeness, realism, authenticity, accuracy *Opposite*: unreality

faithless *adj* **dishonest**, disloyal, untrustworthy, unfaithful, fickle *Opposite*: faithful

faithlessness *n* **dishonesty**, infidelity, inconstancy, fickleness, disloyalty *Opposite*: faithfulness

fake *n* **imitation**, copy, replica, simulation, mock-up *Opposite*: original ■ *adj* false, bogus, sham, phoney, counterfeit *Opposite*: genuine ■ *v* 1 falsify, copy, counterfeit, forge, replicate 2 **simulate**, feign, pretend, act, dissemble

faker *n* fraud, fake, liar, pretender, impostor

fall *v* 1 **drop**, go down, descend, plunge, plummet *Opposite*: ascend 2 **tumble**, fall over, fall down, drop, trip over 3 **decrease**, reduce, sink, come down *Opposite*: increase ■ *n* 1 **reduction**, decrease, drop, tumble, descent *Opposite*: increase 2 **waterfall**, rapids, cataract, cascade, white water

fall about *(infml) v* **laugh**, hoot, scream with laughter, guffaw, roar

fallacious *adj* **mistaken**, erroneous, misleading, deceptive, false *Opposite*: correct

fallacy *n* **misconception**, myth, error, mistake, delusion

fall apart *v* **disintegrate**, crumble, collapse, fall to pieces, fall to bits *Opposite*: come together

fall asleep *v* **nod off**, doze off, go to sleep, drop off *(infml) Opposite*: wake up

fall back *v* 1 **retreat**, withdraw, draw back, run away, regroup *Opposite*: advance 2 **drop behind**, fall behind, drop back, lag, lag behind *Opposite*: catch up

fallback *n* **replacement**, contingency, alternative, stand-in, substitute

fall back on *v* **resort to**, rely on, turn to, depend on, have recourse to

fall behind *v* 1 **drop back**, drop behind, fall back, lag, lag behind *Opposite*: keep up 2 **be delayed**, be late, be in arrears, default, fail to pay

fall by the wayside *v* **come to nothing**, fold, collapse, fail, abandon

fall down *v* 1 **collapse**, fall over, tumble, trip over, trip 2 **fail**, be unsuccessful, disappoint, go wrong, flop *(infml) Opposite*: succeed

fall flat *v* **fail**, miss the target, be a disaster, flop *(infml)*, bomb *(infml) Opposite*: succeed

fall for *v* 1 **fall in love with**, be attracted to, be taken with, be stuck on *(infml)*, take a shine to *(infml) Opposite*: go off 2 **be duped by**, be deceived by, be tricked by, be taken in by, believe *Opposite*: see through

fall foul of *v* **come into conflict with**, tangle with, have a brush with, come up against

fall guy *(infml) n* 1 **dupe**, stooge, fool, gull, sucker *(infml)* 2 **scapegoat**, whipping boy, victim, butt, sucker *(infml)*

fallibility *n* **imperfection**, frailty, weakness, shortcoming, failure *Opposite*: infallibility

fallible *adj* **imperfect**, mortal, weak, frail, human *Opposite*: infallible

falling *adj* **dwindling**, dropping, deteriorating, tumbling, sinking *Opposite*: rising

falling-out *n* **quarrel**, fight, row, disagreement, misunderstanding *Opposite*: reconciliation

fall into place *v* **work out**, shape up, make sense, come together, sort itself out

fall in with *v* 1 **meet**, come across, bump into, run into, get to know *Opposite*: avoid 2 **join**, join forces with, team up with, collaborate with, band together with 3 **agree with**, accept, support, go along with, comply with *Opposite*: reject

fall off *v* **decline**, go down, decrease, plunge, reduce *Opposite*: increase

falloff *n* **decrease**, decline, falling off, reduction, drop *Opposite*: increase

fall out *v* **quarrel**, argue, disagree, come to blows, row *Opposite*: make up

fallout *n* **consequence**, result, outcome, effect, knock-on effect

fall over *v* **tumble**, fall down, collapse, trip, trip over

fallow *adj* 1 **uncultivated**, unploughed, unplanted, unseeded, unused *Opposite*: cultivated 2 **inactive**, unproductive, idle, sterile, infertile *Opposite*: creative

fall short *v* **be deficient**, be wanting, be lacking,

prove inadequate, not make the grade *Opposite*: succeed

fall through v **fail**, go wrong, come to nothing, miscarry, misfire *Opposite*: succeed

fall to bits *see* **fall to pieces**

fall to pieces v **disintegrate**, come apart, crumble, fall apart, break up

false adj 1 **incorrect**, untruthful, untrue, wrong, dishonest *Opposite*: true 2 **mistaken**, erroneous, fallacious, misleading, deceiving *Opposite*: correct 3 **artificial**, bogus, sham, phoney, counterfeit *Opposite*: real

falsehood n 1 **lie**, untruth, tale, fiction, invention 2 **deception**, dishonesty, mendacity, deceit, deceitfulness. *See* COMPARE AND CONTRAST at **lie**.

false impression n **mistaken belief**, misconception, misreading, wrong idea, misapprehension

falseness n 1 **incorrectness**, dishonesty, deceit, deceitfulness, speciousness *Opposite*: honesty 2 **mistakenness**, erroneousness, wrongness, fallaciousness, deceptiveness *Opposite*: rightness

falsification n **fabrication**, distortion, forgery, misrepresentation, deception *Opposite*: correction

falsified adj **fabricated**, forged, untrue, counterfeit, false *Opposite*: true

falsify v **fabricate**, fake, forge, rig, misrepresent

falsity n **falseness**, spuriousness, hollowness, inaccuracy, deceptiveness *Opposite*: correctness

falter v 1 **hesitate**, pause, waver, stammer, stutter *Opposite*: continue 2 **fail**, weaken, fade, wane, abate (*fml or literary*) *Opposite*: rally 3 **stumble**, trip up, stagger, totter, sway. *See* COMPARE AND CONTRAST at **hesitate**.

faltering adj **hesitant**, tentative, halting, timid, uncertain *Opposite*: confident

fame n **renown**, celebrity, reputation, distinction, recognition *Opposite*: obscurity

famed adj **well-known**, famous, celebrated, renowned, eminent *Opposite*: unknown

familial adj **family**, ancestral, household, domestic, matrimonial

familiar adj 1 **well-known**, recognizable, common, customary, habitual *Opposite*: unfamiliar 2 **accustomed**, habitual, usual, recurring, everyday *Opposite*: unusual 3 **acquainted**, conversant, accustomed, used to, at home with 4 **friendly**, intimate, easy, informal, personal *Opposite*: formal

familiarity n 1 **knowledge**, understanding, acquaintance, awareness, ease *Opposite*: unfamiliarity 2 **intimacy**, informality, friendship, ease, closeness *Opposite*: formality

familiarization n **acquaintance**, getting used to, adjustment, adaptation, becoming accustomed

familiarize v **acquaint**, tell, explain, make clear, train

familiarize yourself v **get to know**, adapt, get used to, acclimatize yourself, acquaint yourself

familiarly adv **intimately**, closely, informally, cosily, casually *Opposite*: distantly

family n 1 **relations**, relatives, folks, children, family unit 2 **lineage**, descendants, dynasty, ancestors, line 3 **category**, genus, species, type, kind ■ adj **domestic**, household, everyday, intimate, private

family circle n **relatives**, relations, family, folks, people (*infml*)

family name n **surname**, last name, maternal name, paternal name, name

family tree n **ancestry**, pedigree, genealogy, ancestors, descendants

family unit n **family**, household, house, ménage (*fml*)

famine n **food shortage**, shortage, scarcity, dearth, want *Opposite*: abundance

famished adj **hungry**, ravenous, underfed, unfed, starving (*infml*) *Opposite*: sated

famous adj **well-known**, famed, celebrated, renowned, eminent *Opposite*: unknown

famously adv 1 **notably**, memorably, eminently, prominently, distinctively 2 **well**, excellently, superbly, like a house on fire, like nobody's business

fan n **admirer**, enthusiast, aficionado, aficionada, follower ■ v 1 **waft**, blow, cool, wave, percolate 2 **stir up**, stimulate, provoke, increase, fuel *Opposite*: defuse

fanatic n 1 **extremist**, zealot, radical, fundamentalist, crusader 2 **fan**, enthusiast, devotee, buff, follower ■ adj **fanatical**, obsessive, passionate, addicted, extreme *Opposite*: indifferent

fanatical adj **enthusiastic**, passionate, obsessive, dedicated, fervent *Opposite*: indifferent

fanaticism n **extremism**, radicalism, fervour, zeal, keenness *Opposite*: indifference

fanciful adj **imaginary**, fantastic, whimsical, unbelievable, out of this world *Opposite*: prosaic

fancy adj 1 **elaborate**, ornate, decorative, ornamental, intricate 2 **expensive**, upmarket, lavish, extravagant, posh (*infml*) *Opposite*: plain ■ v 1 (*infml*) **like**, want, be attracted to, wish for, desire 2 **imagine**, picture, think, conjure, believe ■ n **notion**, dream, hope, desire, fantasy

fancy-free adj **free**, at liberty, unfettered, unconstrained, at leisure *Opposite*: tied

fanfare n **display**, trumpet blast, salute, elaboration, flourish

fan out v **spread out**, separate, expand, broaden, disperse *Opposite*: assemble

fantasize v **daydream**, imagine, dream, picture, visualize

fantastic *adj* **1 excellent**, superb, great, marvellous, fabulous *Opposite*: awful **2 bizarre**, eccentric, imaginary, strange, fanciful *Opposite*: normal **3 incredible**, unbelievable, implausible, improbable, unlikely *Opposite*: plausible **4 large**, big, enormous, huge, great *Opposite*: tiny

fantasy *n* **1 dream**, daydream, image, fancy, hope **2 imagination**, unreality, fancy, caprice, power of invention *Opposite*: reality

fan the flames *v* **exacerbate**, aggravate, inflame, make worse, worsen *Opposite*: calm

far *adv* **1 far off**, far away, far afield, far and wide, distantly *Opposite*: close **2 much**, greatly, considerably, a lot, significantly *Opposite*: barely ■ *adj* **distant**, remote, far-off, faraway, far-flung *Opposite*: near

faraway *adj* **1 remote**, far-off, far-flung, outlying, distant *Opposite*: nearby **2 dreamy**, preoccupied, bemused, distant, in a world of your own *Opposite*: alert

farce *n* **shambles**, travesty, absurdity, circus, sham

farcical *adj* **absurd**, ridiculous, ludicrous, silly, nonsensical *Opposite*: solemn

fare *n* **1 price**, tariff, ticket, cost, fee **2 passenger**, customer, client, payer, rider **3 food**, menu, meal, dishes, provisions ■ *v* **do**, get on, manage, cope, get by

farewell *n* **goodbye**, sendoff, departure, valediction *(fml)*, leave-taking *(literary)* *Opposite*: greeting

far-fetched *adj* **unbelievable**, fantastic, implausible, incredible, fanciful *Opposite*: believable

far-flung *adj* **1 widespread**, extensive, sweeping, diffuse, wide-ranging *Opposite*: restricted **2 distant**, remote, far-off, faraway, outlying *Opposite*: nearby

far from *prep* **anything but**, unlike, different from, poles apart from *Opposite*: near

farm *n* **1 smallholding**, estate, plantation, ranch, spread **2 farmhouse**, farmstead, homestead, grange, ranch ■ *v* **cultivate**, work, till, plough, grow

farmer *n* **agriculturalist**, grower, market gardener, crofter, smallholder

farm hand *n* **farmworker**, labourer, seasonal worker, harvester

farming *n* **agribusiness**, agriculture, husbandry, cultivation, market gardening

farm out *v* **delegate**, subcontract, contract out, send out, hand out

farmstead *n* **homestead**, farm, ranch, grange

farmyard *n* **yard**, barnyard, cattle yard, stable yard

far-off *adj* **distant**, remote, far, faraway, far-flung *Opposite*: nearby

farrago *n* **hotchpotch**, potpourri, mishmash, medley, mixture

far-reaching *adj* **extensive**, sweeping, broad, across-the-board, comprehensive *Opposite*: limited

farsighted *adj* **wise**, visionary, farseeing, provident, prophetic *Opposite*: shortsighted

farsightedness *n* **foresight**, providence, prescience, forethought, wisdom *Opposite*: short-sightedness

farthest *adj* **furthest**, utmost, uttermost, outermost, furthermost

fascinate *v* **captivate**, charm, attract, enthral, mesmerize *Opposite*: repel

fascinated *adj* **captivated**, rapt, spellbound, charmed, involved *Opposite*: uninterested

fascinating *adj* **captivating**, charming, attractive, enthralling, mesmerizing *Opposite*: repellent

fascination *n* **captivation**, charm, attraction, appeal, allure

fashion *n* **1 style**, way, manner, mode, method **2 trend**, craze, fad, vogue, mode ■ *v* **shape**, mould, form, make, fit

fashionable *adj* **chic**, stylish, designer, up-to-the-minute, in *Opposite*: dated

fashion-conscious *adj* **chic**, stylish, fashionable, elegant, modish *Opposite*: old-fashioned

fast *adj* **1 quick**, speedy, rapid, swift, express *Opposite*: slow **2 sudden**, sharp, fleeting, momentary, short-lived *Opposite*: long-lasting **3 ahead**, gaining, in advance *Opposite*: slow **4 firm**, steadfast, constant, unwavering, faithful *Opposite*: fickle **5** *(infml)* **debauched**, wild, reckless, dissolute, profligate ■ *adv* **1 quickly**, speedily, rapidly, swiftly, promptly *Opposite*: slowly **2 firmly**, firm, tightly, tight, stable *Opposite*: loosely ■ *v* **abstain**, starve yourself, go without *Opposite*: feast ■ *n* **diet**, abstention, starvation, cleansing, hunger strike

fasten *v* **1 secure**, attach, fix, clip, clasp *Opposite*: detach **2 shut**, close, tie, tie up, do up *Opposite*: undo

fastener *n* **clasp**, fastening, tie, closure, popper

fastening *n* **clasp**, tie, closure, fastener, clip

fastidious *adj* **1 demanding**, fussy, finicky, faddy, picky *Opposite*: easygoing **2 delicate**, refined, particular, dainty, squeamish *Opposite*: slovenly

fastidiousness *n* **1 fussiness**, meticulousness, care, carefulness, neatness *Opposite*: carelessness **2 delicacy**, delicateness, daintiness, squeamishness *Opposite*: crudeness

fastness *n* **speediness**, swiftness, alacrity, speed, haste

fast track *n* **push**, boost, way forward, advancement, furthering

fast-track *v* **advance**, accelerate, forge ahead, progress, develop

fat n 1 **oil**, lard, grease, shortening (US) 2 **flab**, adipose tissue, padding, insulation, blubber (infml) ■ adj 1 **overweight**, plump, chubby, stout, portly Opposite: thin 2 **fatty**, greasy, oily, oleaginous, blubbery (infml) Opposite: lean 3 **thick**, hefty, sizable, big, large Opposite: slim 4 **rich**, wealthy, affluent, well-off, prosperous Opposite: poor

fatal adj 1 **deadly**, lethal, incurable, terminal, mortal 2 **ruinous**, disastrous, destructive, serious, grave Opposite: beneficial 3 **decisive**, critical, crucial, fateful, pivotal Opposite: unimportant. See COMPARE AND CONTRAST at **deadly**.

fatalism n **resignation**, passivity, acceptance, stoicism, pessimism

fatalistic adj **philosophical**, defeatist, resigned, stoic, stoical

fatality n 1 **death**, accident, casualty, loss, decease (fml) 2 **deadliness**, deathliness, lethalness, noxiousness, fatalness

fate n 1 **destiny**, fortune, providence, luck, doom 2 **outcome**, consequence, result, upshot, end

fated adj **predetermined**, destined, predestined, preordained, meant

fateful adj 1 **critical**, important, momentous, significant, crucial Opposite: insignificant 2 **ominous**, unfortunate, inauspicious, unlucky, ill-fated Opposite: lucky

father n 1 **dad** (infml), daddy (infml), pa (infml), pater (dated slang), pop (US infml) 2 **ancestor**, forefather, forebear, predecessor, progenitor Opposite: descendant 3 **founder**, originator, initiator, contriver, architect 4 **priest**, vicar, minister, padre, pastor ■ v 1 **beget**, sire, engender, procreate, spawn 2 **protect**, comfort, advise, look after, nurture

fatherhood n **paternity**, parenthood, kinship Opposite: motherhood

fatherland n **homeland**, native land, home, motherland, mother country

fatherliness n **protectiveness**, benevolence, affection, supportiveness, kindness

fatherly adj **paternal**, protective, concerned, caring, loving

fathom v 1 **sound**, measure, plumb, gauge, probe 2 **comprehend**, understand, work out, figure out, grasp

fathomable adj **comprehensible**, understandable, penetrable, graspable, intelligible Opposite: unfathomable

fathomless adj 1 **deep**, immeasurable, unfathomable, bottomless, inestimable Opposite: shallow 2 **incomprehensible**, immeasurable, unfathomable, obscure, incalculable Opposite: fathomable

fatigue n **exhaustion**, tiredness, weariness, weakness, lethargy Opposite: energy

fatigued adj **exhausted**, weary, tired, drained, worn-out Opposite: fresh

fatness n **obesity**, plumpness, chubbiness,
stoutness, portliness Opposite: thinness

fatten v **feed up**, stuff, plump, build up, feed Opposite: starve

fattening adj **calorific**, fatty, rich, greasy, oily Opposite: slimming

fatten up v **feed up**, stuff, build up, feed, fatten Opposite: starve

fatty adj **greasy**, fat, oily, blubbery (infml) Opposite: lean

fatuity (fml) n **unintelligence**, complacency, silliness, stupidity, childishness Opposite: sensibleness

fatuous adj **unintelligent**, complacent, unaware, silly, stupid Opposite: sensible

fatuousness n **unintelligence**, complacency, silliness, foolishness, stupidity Opposite: sensibleness

fault n 1 **responsibility**, liability, burden, culpability, accountability 2 **shortcoming**, failing, weakness, defect, flaw Opposite: strength 3 **blemish**, defect, imperfection, flaw, mark Opposite: bonus 4 **mistake**, error, blunder, slip, omission ■ v **blame**, criticize, condemn, find fault with, question Opposite: praise. See COMPARE AND CONTRAST at **flaw**.

faultfinder n **critic**, carper, complainer, grumbler, nitpicker

faultfinding n **criticism**, grumbling, nitpicking, whingeing (infml) ■ adj **critical**, reproachful, carping, damning, unfavourable Opposite: uncritical

faultless adj **flawless**, perfect, impeccable, immaculate, blameless Opposite: imperfect

faultlessness n **flawlessness**, perfection, purity, impeccability, immaculateness Opposite: imperfection

fault line n **crack**, rift, split, fissure, fault

faulty adj 1 **out of order**, defective, broken-down, broken, on the blink (infml) Opposite: perfect 2 **flawed**, imperfect, incorrect, incoherent, contradictory Opposite: sound

fauna n **animals**, creatures, wildlife, beasts

faux adj **fake**, artificial, unreal, reproduction, false Opposite: genuine

favour n 1 **good turn**, errand, kindness, courtesy, service Opposite: disservice 2 **approval**, regard, kindness, esteem, sympathy Opposite: disfavour 3 **gift**, trinket, token, present, keepsake ■ v 1 **prefer**, choose, support, back, approve Opposite: reject 2 **help**, assist, aid, advance, promote Opposite: hinder. See COMPARE AND CONTRAST at **regard**.

favourable adj 1 **advantageous**, helpful, beneficial, opportune, convenient Opposite: unfavourable 2 **promising**, auspicious, encouraging, propitious, bright Opposite: inauspicious 3 **approving**, positive, constructive, good, sympathetic Opposite: negative

favourite adj **chosen**, pet, beloved, favoured ■ n 1 **pet**, darling, beloved 2 **choice**, preference, pick

favouritism n preferentialism, preference, partiality, nepotism, bias Opposite: impartiality

fawn v flatter, grovel, toady, kowtow, crawl (infml)

fawning adj flattering, obsequious, smarmy, sycophantic, servile

fax n facsimile, message, document, transmission, copy ■ v send, transmit, convey, communicate, telex

faze v fluster, disconcert, disturb, put off, deter Opposite: encourage

fear n 1 fright, alarm, trepidation, terror, dread Opposite: assurance 2 worry, concern, anxiety, apprehension, misgiving ■ v dread, be afraid, be scared, be apprehensive, be frightened

fearful adj 1 frightening, terrifying, terrible, frightful, horrific 2 worried, afraid, scared, apprehensive, frightened Opposite: fearless 3 (infml) terrible, dreadful, appalling, awful, horrible Opposite: wonderful

fearfulness n 1 scariness, terribleness, frightfulness, horror, terror 2 apprehension, anxiety, awe, fear, dread Opposite: bravery 3 (infml) terribleness, atrociousness, dreadfulness, awfulness, horror

fearless adj courageous, brave, bold, unafraid, daring Opposite: cowardly

fearlessness n courage, bravery, boldness, heroism, valour Opposite: cowardice. See COMPARE AND CONTRAST at courage.

fearsome adj 1 frightening, formidable, terrifying, alarming, awesome 2 impressive, awesome, formidable, awe-inspiring, tremendous

feasibility n viability, possibility, probability, likelihood, practicability Opposite: impossibility

feasible adj viable, possible, practicable, achievable, reasonable Opposite: impossible

feast n 1 banquet, dinner, meal, buffet, spread (infml) 2 delight, treat, indulgence, pleasure, joy 3 celebration, festival, holiday, feast day, holy day ■ v eat, dine, indulge, partake, gobble Opposite: fast

feat n achievement, accomplishment, deed, exploit, act

feathery adj downy, fluffy, soft, light, plumy

feature n 1 facial feature, contour, lineament (literary) 2 characteristic, trait, mark, attribute, quality 3 article, piece, report, item, story ■ v 1 contain, include, present, introduce, bring out 2 perform, star, appear, act, turn up 3 highlight, star, include, showcase, show 4 figure, appear, participate, take part, play a part

featureless adj dull, drab, bland, uninspired, unremarkable Opposite: distinctive

febrile adj feverish, fevered, flushed, hot, delirious

feckless adj good-for-nothing, useless, hopeless, spineless, feeble Opposite: dynamic

fecklessness n uselessness, hopelessness, spinelessness, feebleness, irresponsibility Opposite: dynamism

fecund adj 1 productive, creative, prolific, industrious, fruitful 2 (fml) fertile, prolific, productive, fruitful, rich Opposite: infertile

fecundity n fertility, productiveness, fruitfulness, richness, prolificacy Opposite: infertility

federal adj central, centralized, national, state, civic Opposite: regional

federate v 1 unite, join, amalgamate, come together, merge Opposite: devolve 2 associate, unite, combine, join, confederate Opposite: disassociate

federation n 1 combination, union, association, confederation, amalgamation 2 alliance, coalition, confederation, grouping, partnership

fee n 1 payment, remuneration, salary, pay, stipend 2 charge, subscription, toll, tariff, cost. See COMPARE AND CONTRAST at wage.

feeble adj 1 weak, frail, delicate, shaky, thin Opposite: robust 2 unconvincing, ineffectual, poor, half-hearted, ineffective Opposite: convincing. See COMPARE AND CONTRAST at weak.

feebleness n 1 weakness, fragility, delicateness, frailty, shakiness Opposite: robustness 2 ineffectuality, weakness, half-heartedness, ineffectiveness Opposite: effectiveness

feed v 1 nourish, nurse, suckle, breast-feed, serve Opposite: starve 2 eat, consume, partake, devour, swallow 3 support, sustain, nourish, nurture, encourage ■ n feedstuff, food, fodder, forage, provender

feedback n response, reaction, comment, criticism, advice

feed into v 1 contribute, add to, supplement, enhance, add weight Opposite: draw on 2 connect, join up, flow into, lead into, merge

feel v 1 touch, finger, handle, sense, fondle 2 sense, experience, undergo, be aware of, bear 3 think, believe, consider, comprehend, understand ■ n 1 sensation, touch, texture, finish, sense 2 impression, atmosphere, air, feeling, ambience

feeler n sensor, antenna, whisker

feel for v sympathize, feel sorry for, pity, commiserate, empathize

feel-good adj optimistic, positive, satisfying, cheering, upbeat (infml)

feeling n 1 sensation, sense, sensitivity, touch Opposite: numbness 2 emotion, sentiment, mood, reaction, sense 3 affection, concern, regard, love, sympathy Opposite: antipathy 4 opinion, view, point of view, belief, impression 5 air, atmosphere, feel, ambience, mood 6 hunch, instinct, suspicion, intuition, idea

feel like v 1 want, desire, crave, wish, long for 2 seem, appear, resemble, look like

feel sorry for v pity, empathize with, feel for,

commiserate with, sympathize with

feign *v* **pretend**, put on, fake, simulate, make believe

feigned *adj* **put on**, artificial, insincere, pretend, fake *Opposite*: genuine

feint *n* **trick**, stratagem, ploy, ruse, gambit

feisty *(infml) adj* **lively**, spirited, energetic, aggressive, hearty *Opposite*: feeble

felicitations *(fml) n* **congratulations**, compliments, best wishes, blessings, greetings

felicitous *adj* **1 appropriate**, apt, suitable, apposite, well-chosen *Opposite*: inapposite **2 fortunate**, lucky, fortuitous, timely, happy *Opposite*: unfortunate

felicity *n* **1 happiness**, contentment, joy, pleasure, luck *Opposite*: unhappiness **2 appropriateness**, aptness, suitability, appositeness, fittingness *Opposite*: inappropriateness

feline *adj* **graceful**, slinky, subtle, elegant, stealthy

fell *v* **1 cut down**, chop down, hew **2 knock down**, knock out, floor, demolish *(infml)*, deck *(infml) Opposite*: set up

fellow *n* **1** *(dated)* **man**, boy, guy *(infml)*, chap *(infml)*, bloke *(infml)* **2** *(dated)* **companion**, colleague, associate, partner, comrade **3 member**, associate, researcher, academic

fellow feeling *n* **sympathy**, empathy, support, affinity, mutuality *Opposite*: hostility

fellowship *n* **1 communion**, companionship, camaraderie, comradeship, friendship *Opposite*: enmity **2 society**, association, college, affiliation, cooperative

felon *n* **criminal**, offender, lawbreaker, delinquent, villain *(infml)*

felony *n* **crime**, offence, misdemeanour, wrongdoing, lawbreaking

female *adj* **feminine**, womanly, ladylike, girlish *Opposite*: masculine ■ *n* **woman**, lady, girl *Opposite*: male

feminine *adj* **female**, womanly, ladylike, girlish *Opposite*: masculine

femininity *n* **femaleness**, feminineness, womanliness, girlishness *Opposite*: masculinity

feminism *n* **women's movement**, women's liberation, women's rights, women's suffrage, women's studies

feminist *n* **suffragist**, suffragette, activist, radical, campaigner

fen *n* **marsh**, wetland, fenland, bog, lowland

fence *n* **barrier**, boundary, hurdle, hedge, railing ■ *v* **1 enclose**, hedge, shut in, restrict, confine *Opposite*: open up **2 evade**, parry, feint, dodge, fight off

fencing *n* **1 fence**, railing, paling, barrier, palisade **2 repartee**, banter, wordplay, raillery, badinage

fender *n* **fireguard**, fire screen, guard, screen

fend for *v* **look after**, take care of, provide for, defend, support

fend for yourself *v* **take care of yourself**, look after yourself, support yourself, manage on your own, survive

fend off *v* **keep away**, repel, repulse, discourage, ward off *Opposite*: welcome

fenland *n* **marsh**, bog, fen, wetland, lowland *Opposite*: desert

feral *adj* **wild**, untamed, undomesticated, savage, uncontrollable *Opposite*: domesticated

ferment *v* **agitate**, inflame, stir up, incite, provoke ■ *n* **uproar**, tumult, confusion, excitement, commotion *Opposite*: peace

ferocious *adj* **1 fierce**, vicious, violent, cruel, brutal *Opposite*: gentle **2 intense**, strong, heated, raging, extreme *Opposite*: mild

ferociousness *see* ferocity

ferocity *n* **1 fierceness**, aggressiveness, viciousness, violence, brutality *Opposite*: gentleness **2 intensity**, strength, extremeness, severity *Opposite*: mildness

ferret *v* **hunt**, search, search out, rummage, dig out

ferret around *v* **look for**, search out, ferret about, delve, search around

ferret out *v* **1 discover**, uncover, find, reveal, unveil *Opposite*: conceal **2 track down**, flush out, uncover, hunt down, catch *Opposite*: hide

ferry *v* **transport**, carry, ship, convey, transmit

fertile *adj* **1 productive**, fruitful, prolific, generative, fecund *(fml) Opposite*: infertile **2 lush**, productive, abundant, rich, fruitful *Opposite*: barren

fertility *n* **fruitfulness**, richness, lushness, productiveness, fecundity *Opposite*: barrenness

fertilization *n* **1 insemination**, impregnation, pollination, artificial insemination, donor insemination **2 fertilizer application**, manuring, composting, top dressing, nourishment

fertilize *v* **1 inseminate**, impregnate, pollinate **2 manure**, feed, top-dress, compost, enrich *Opposite*: exhaust

fertilizer *n* **manure**, compost, top dressing, soil enricher, enricher

fervent *adj* **keen**, avid, ardent, eager, enthusiastic *Opposite*: indifferent

fervid *adj* **impassioned**, intense, heated, burning

fervour *n* **passion**, dedication, enthusiasm, eagerness, zeal *Opposite*: indifference

fester *v* **rankle**, irritate, gall, embitter, annoy

festival *n* **feast day**, holiday, celebration, anniversary, birthday

festive *adj* **celebratory**, cheerful, joyful, merry, happy *Opposite*: sad

festiveness *n* **merriness**, joyfulness, cheerfulness, happiness, jolliness *Opposite*: lugubriousness

festivities *n* **revels**, revelry, celebrations, merriment, partying

festivity n 1 **good cheer**, rejoicing, merriment, pleasure, enjoyment *Opposite*: sadness 2 **party**, event, do *(infml)*, gala, carnival

festoon n **garland**, decoration, swag, ornament, chain ■ v **decorate**, adorn, swathe, hang, drape *Opposite*: strip

festooned adj **garlanded**, wreathed, hung, decorated, draped *Opposite*: unadorned

fetch v 1 **get**, obtain, bring, carry, bring back 2 **sell for**, make, raise, get, draw

fetching adj **attractive**, eye-catching, handsome, good-looking, stylish *Opposite*: unattractive

fete *see* **fête**

fête n 1 **bazaar**, celebration, event, fair, gala 2 **holiday**, anniversary, jubilee, centenary, feast day ■ v **honour**, commemorate, lionize, entertain, praise

fetid adj **rotten**, putrid, foul, rank, fusty *Opposite*: fresh

fetish n 1 **obsession**, fixation, mania, craze, engrossment *Opposite*: aversion 2 **talisman**, charm, idol, image, totem

fetishize v **make a fetish of**, worship, idolize, be obsessed by, get hung up on *(slang)*

fetter n **shackle**, bond, chain, yoke, handcuff ■ v **tie**, bind, chain, restrain, hamper *Opposite*: unfetter

feud n **dispute**, argument, row, quarrel, bad blood *Opposite*: friendship ■ v **fight**, argue, dispute, quarrel, disagree

feudal adj **out-of-date**, outdated, old-fashioned, medieval, primitive *Opposite*: modern

fever n 1 **temperature**, infection, disease, illness, malaise 2 **passion**, fervour, excitement, agitation, vehemence

fevered adj **feverish**, agitated, restless, frenzied, fanatical *Opposite*: calm

feverish adj **excited**, agitated, nervous, heated, intense *Opposite*: tranquil

few adj **insufficient**, a small number of, hardly any, not many, only some *Opposite*: many

fey adj **whimsical**, fanciful, otherworldly, unworldly, fantastical

fiasco n **debacle**, disaster, mess, shambles, failure *Opposite*: success

fiat n 1 **official sanction**, sanction, authorization, permission, agreement 2 **order**, command, decree, edict, instruction

fib *(infml)* n **untruth**, white lie, lie, tall tale, falsification *Opposite*: truth ■ v **lie**, not tell the truth, misrepresent, perjure yourself, tell stories *Opposite*: come clean *(infml)*. *See* COMPARE AND CONTRAST *at* lie.

fibber *(infml)* n **liar**, deceiver, fabricator, prevaricator, perjurer

fibbing *(infml)* n **lying**, prevarication, falsification, escape

fibre n 1 **thread**, strand, string, filament, twine 2 **makeup**, composition, structure, character,

stuff 3 **grit**, strength, fortitude, backbone, character *Opposite*: weakness

WORD BANK
❏ **types of fibre** cane, coconut matting, coir, fibreglass, jute, kapok, matting, raffia, ramie, rattan, seagrass, sisal, straw, wicker

fibrous adj **tough**, leathery, stringy, rubbery, chewy *Opposite*: tender

fickle adj **inconsistent**, changeable, capricious, inconstant, indecisive *Opposite*: constant

fickleness n **inconsistency**, changeability, capriciousness, inconstancy, indecisiveness *Opposite*: constancy

fiction n 1 **creative writing**, works of fiction, literature, narrative, novels *Opposite*: nonfiction 2 **work of fiction**, novel, fantasy, story, short story 3 **falsehood**, fabrication, lie, untruth, misrepresentation *Opposite*: fact 4 **invention**, fantasy, imagination, nonsense, illusion *Opposite*: reality

fictional adj **imaginary**, imagined, illusory, unreal, false *Opposite*: real

fictionalization n **fictional account**, fictional version, account, narrative, story

fictionalize v **dramatize**, novelize, recount, adapt

fictitious adj **untrue**, fabricated, invented, made-up, false *Opposite*: factual

fiddle n *(infml)* **swindle**, fraud, cheat, hoax, con ■ v 1 **fidget**, play, play around, toy, pick at 2 **meddle**, tamper, interfere, mess, mess about *(infml)* 3 **tinker**, manipulate, adjust, tweak, jiggle *Opposite*: leave alone 4 *(infml)* **defraud**, swindle, cheat, con, hoax 5 *(infml)* **falsify**, doctor, tamper with, manipulate, fix

fiddling adj **petty**, unimportant, trifling, trivial, insignificant *Opposite*: significant ■ n *(infml)* **fraud**, deception, cheating, fixing, swindling

fiddly *(infml)* adj **tricky**, awkward, difficult, complex, detailed *Opposite*: easy

fidelity n **loyalty**, faithfulness, reliability, trustworthiness, dependability *Opposite*: infidelity

fidget v 1 **twitch**, squirm, fret, shuffle, jiggle *Opposite*: freeze 2 **fiddle**, play, play around, toy, jiggle *Opposite*: leave alone

fidgetiness n **twitchiness**, fretfulness, restlessness, jitteriness, uneasiness *Opposite*: stillness

fidgety adj **twitchy**, fretful, restless, squirmy, uneasy *Opposite*: still

field n 1 **meadow**, pasture, grassland, grazing, lea *(literary)* 2 **sports ground**, playing field, pitch, turf, arena 3 **subject**, area, topic, discipline, theme ■ v 1 **catch**, retrieve, pick up, go after, fetch 2 **deal with**, handle, tackle, take care of, see to *Opposite*: ignore

fielder n **player**, cricketer, baseball player, sportsperson, outfielder *Opposite*: batter

field test n **field trial**, test, trial, clinical trial, pilot

field-test *v* test, try out, study, put through its paces, trial

fieldwork *n* research, information-gathering, investigation, fact-finding, exploration

fiend *n* villain, evil person, brute, beast, monster *Opposite*: angel

fiendish *adj* 1 cruel, evil, brutal, monstrous, villainous *Opposite*: pleasant 2 cunning, ingenious, clever, crafty, devilish 3 impossible, tricky, difficult, hard, perplexing *Opposite*: straightforward

fiendishly *adv* 1 cruelly, brutally, wickedly, inhumanly, maliciously *Opposite*: pleasantly 2 extremely, excessively, extraordinarily, incredibly, impossibly

fierce *adj* 1 violent, ferocious, aggressive, brutal, severe *Opposite*: gentle 2 intense, violent, extreme, savage, ferocious *Opposite*: mild 3 strong, powerful, profound, deep, turbulent *Opposite*: mild

fiercely *adv* 1 violently, ferociously, aggressively, brutally, severely *Opposite*: gently 2 ferociously, intensely, strongly, brightly, hotly *Opposite*: feebly 3 extremely, exceedingly, very, passionately, resolutely *Opposite*: mildly

fierceness *n* 1 ferocity, brutality, violence, aggressiveness, sternness *Opposite*: gentleness 2 intensity, violence, strength, power, fury *Opposite*: mildness

fiery *adj* 1 burning, blistering, sweltering, blazing, flaming *Opposite*: icy 2 fierce, passionate, heated, angry, furious *Opposite*: mild

fiesta *n* feast, holiday, festival, carnival, celebration

fifth wheel *n* supernumerary, ghost at the feast, hanger-on *(infml)*, wallflower *(infml)*, gooseberry *(infml)*

fifty-fifty *adv* half and half, half each, two ways, equally, halfway

fight *v* 1 brawl, box, clash, scrap, wrestle 2 wage war, clash, struggle, battle, skirmish 3 dispute, oppose, struggle, contest, wrangle *Opposite*: accept ■ *n* 1 conflict, battle, engagement, skirmish, clash 2 scrap, tussle, brawl, fistfight, fisticuffs *(infml)* 3 argument, dispute, wrangle, clash, row *Opposite*: reconciliation 4 contest, match, bout, competition, round

COMPARE AND CONTRAST CORE MEANING: a struggle between opposing armed forces
fight a physical struggle between individuals or groups such as battalions or armies; **battle** a large-scale fight involving combat between opposing forces, warships, or aircraft as part of an ongoing war or campaign; **war** a state of hostilities between nations, states, or factions involving the use of arms and the occurrence of a series of battles; **conflict** warfare between opposing forces, especially a prolonged and bitter but sporadic struggle; **engagement** a hostile encounter involving military forces; **skirmish** a brief minor fight, usually one that is part of a larger conflict; **clash** a short fierce encounter, usually involving physical combat.

fight back *v* 1 retaliate, defend yourself, put up a fight, riposte, resist *Opposite*: attack 2 repress, control, hold back, suppress, push back *Opposite*: let out

fighter *n* boxer, wrestler, pugilist, prizefighter

fighting *adj* aggressive, belligerent, pugnacious, hostile, rebellious *Opposite*: pacifist ■ *n* combat, hostility, unrest, warfare, violence *Opposite*: peace

fight off *v* fend off, drive away, resist, repulse, repel *Opposite*: attack

fight shy of *v* avoid, evade, eschew, dodge *Opposite*: confront

figment *n* fabrication, creation, invention, illusion, fantasy

figurative *adj* metaphorical, symbolic, allegorical, nonliteral, emblematic *Opposite*: literal

figure *n* 1 number, numeral, character, symbol, digit 2 amount, cost, sum, quantity, total 3 shape, form, outline, stature, build 4 person, dignitary, celebrity, notable, individual 5 diagram, chart, picture, table, illustration ■ *v* 1 play a part, feature, appear, be included, be incorporated 2 reckon, guess, believe, think, suppose *Opposite*: doubt

figure of speech *n* expression, symbol, idiom, image, rhetorical expression

WORD BANK
❑ **types of figure of speech** alliteration, antonomasia, assonance, chiasmus, hendiadys, hypallage, hyperbaton, hyperbole, litotes, meiosis, metaphor, metonymy, oxymoron, personification, prosopopeia, simile, synecdoche, zeugma

figure out *v* work out, deduce, discover, fathom, decipher. *See* COMPARE AND CONTRAST *at* deduce.

figurine *n* statuette, figure, model, ornament, statue

filament *n* thread, strand, string, fibre, wire

filch *(infml)* *v* steal, rob, thieve, walk off with, snatch. *See* COMPARE AND CONTRAST *at* steal.

file *n* 1 folder, sleeve, dossier, heading, box file 2 report, dossier, profile, record, information 3 line, queue, row, column, procession ■ *v* 1 record, categorize, put on record, keep, file away 2 rub, rasp, scrape, sand, smooth 3 march, troop, parade, snake, walk in single file

filial *adj* familial, family, loving, devoted *Opposite*: parental

filigree *n* tracery, lacy pattern, lattice, latticework, lace

filing *n* shaving, particle, splinter, shard, shred

fill *v* 1 fill up, pack, stuff, cram, jam *Opposite*: empty 2 pervade, imbue, impart, permeate, saturate 3 plug, block, block up, seal, stop *Opposite*: clear 4 satisfy, fulfil, meet, satiate, provide for *Opposite*: fall short

filler *n* 1 padding, stuffing, wadding, filling, packing 2 plaster, grout, putty, caulking, pitch

fillet v **bone**, clean, prepare, gut, scale

fill in v 1 **complete**, fill out, write out, answer 2 **take somebody's place**, stand in, substitute, deputize, cover 3 **bring up to date**, put in the picture, give the latest, give the lowdown 4 **clog**, plug, choke, dam up, block

fill-in n **substitute**, stand-in, temp, replacement, temporary worker

filling n 1 **inside**, contents, guts, innards (infml) 2 **stuffing**, padding, bulk, wadding, packing ▪ adj **satisfying**, substantial, big, heavy, rich Opposite: meagre

filling station n **petrol station**, garage, service station, services, service area

fillip n **boost**, tonic, spur, stimulus, impetus Opposite: knock

fill out v 1 **complete**, fill in, write out, answer 2 **put on weight**, fatten up, bulk up, grow, develop Opposite: waste away

fill up v 1 **refill**, fill, replenish, load, stock up Opposite: empty 2 **satisfy**, satiate, stuff, bloat, fill

film n 1 **picture**, big screen, silver screen, flick (infml), movie (US) 2 **layer**, coat, coating, covering, sheet ▪ v **record**, video, tape, capture, shoot

film over v **mist over**, mist up, glaze over, steam up, cloud over Opposite: clear

filmy adj **light**, airy, translucent, transparent, diaphanous Opposite: solid

filter n **sieve**, strainer, colander, mesh, riddle ▪ v 1 **sort**, sort out, separate out, stream, categorize Opposite: mingle 2 **sift**, sieve, strain, clean, clarify 3 **seep**, ooze, trickle, penetrate, permeate

filth n 1 **dirt**, grime, rubbish, refuse, soil 2 **smut**, rudeness, lewdness, immorality, obscenity

filthiness n 1 **dirtiness**, griminess, dirt, grubbiness, foulness Opposite: cleanliness 2 **lewdness**, rudeness, immorality, smut, obscenity Opposite: decency

filthy adj 1 **dirty**, grimy, muddy, soiled, grubby Opposite: clean 2 **rude**, indecent, lewd, obscene, offensive Opposite: decent. See COMPARE AND CONTRAST at **dirty**.

filtration n **percolation**, separation, purification, clarification, categorization

fin n 1 **appendage**, flipper, paddle, dorsal fin, organ 2 **projection**, stabilizer, blade, paddle, propeller

finagle (infml) v **trick**, cheat, manipulate, engineer, wheedle

final adj 1 **last**, concluding, closing, ending, finishing Opposite: first 2 **conclusive**, definitive, absolute, decisive, irrevocable Opposite: provisional ▪ n **round**, match, game, decider, last leg

finale n **ending**, end, climax, culmination, finish Opposite: prelude

finalist n **qualifier**, contestant, challenger, runner-up, contender Opposite: also-ran

finality n **conclusiveness**, decisiveness, definiteness, inevitability, irrevocability Opposite: uncertainty

finalization n **completion**, conclusion, agreement, settlement, decision Opposite: commencement (fml)

finalize v **confirm**, settle, decide, firm up, complete Opposite: start

finally adv 1 **at last**, at length, at long last, ultimately, after all Opposite: initially 2 **conclusively**, completely, decisively, irrevocably, definitively Opposite: tentatively 3 **lastly**, in conclusion, to conclude, to finish, to end Opposite: firstly

finance n **money**, economics, business, investment, backing ▪ v **back**, invest in, pay for, fund, support

finances n **money**, funds, assets, cash, capital

financial adj **monetary**, fiscal, economic, pecuniary, monetarist

financier n **banker**, investor, backer, sponsor, investment banker

find v 1 **discover**, locate, come across, hit upon, unearth 2 **recover**, regain, get back, retrieve, discover Opposite: lose 3 **realize**, understand, get, obtain, attain ▪ n **discovery**, bargain, treasure trove, treasure, novelty

find fault with v **criticize**, nitpick, pick holes in, take to task, have a go at (infml) Opposite: praise. See COMPARE AND CONTRAST at **criticize**.

finding n 1 **discovery**, conclusion, result, verdict, outcome 2 **verdict**, ruling, result, sentence, decision

find out v 1 **discover**, learn, realize, observe, note 2 **catch**, expose, uncover, reveal, unmask

fine adj 1 **light**, slight, faint, thin, tenuous Opposite: heavy 2 (infml) **acceptable**, satisfactory, good, all right, okay (infml) Opposite: unsatisfactory 3 **tiny**, minute, light, delicate, small 4 **bright**, sunny, warm, beautiful, fair Opposite: dull 5 **delicate**, dainty, slender, refined, thin Opposite: coarse 6 **outstanding**, superb, excellent, superior, exceptional Opposite: poor 7 **subtle**, keen, sharp, skilled, refined Opposite: dull ▪ n **penalty**, punishment, payment, forfeit, levy ▪ v **penalize**, punish, levy, charge

fineness n 1 **excellence**, greatness, superiority, quality, distinction Opposite: poorness 2 **delicacy**, sheerness, thinness, narrowness, slenderness Opposite: thickness

finer points n **details**, minutiae, nuances, small print, nitty-gritty (infml)

finery n **regalia**, jewellery, evening dress, morning dress, dress uniform

finesse n 1 **skill**, flair, grace, poise, assurance Opposite: clumsiness 2 **subtlety**, delicacy, diplomacy, tact, discretion Opposite: tactlessness

finest adj **premium**, handpicked, optimum, best, supreme Opposite: worst

fine-tune v **adjust**, modify, tune, polish up, perfect

fine-tuning n **adjustment**, refinement, modification, perfection, tuning

finger n **1 digit**, limb, member, extremity **2 portion**, piece, slither, slice, bit *Opposite*: hunk ■ v **handle**, touch, feel, manipulate, toy with

fingerprint n **1 impression**, print, mark, pattern, thumbprint **2 characteristic**, identification, evidence, pattern, diagnostic

fingertip adj **sensitive**, delicate, fine, sensitized, hair-trigger

finicky adj **fastidious**, fussy, picky, particular, choosy *(infml)* *Opposite*: sloppy. *See* COMPARE AND CONTRAST *at* **careful**.

finish v **1 end**, stop, terminate, close, cease *Opposite*: start **2 use up**, drain, exhaust, polish off, empty *Opposite*: stock up **3** *(infml)* **destroy**, ruin, annihilate, defeat, exhaust **4 polish**, buff, rub, varnish, lacquer ■ n **1 end**, ending, close, conclusion, completion *Opposite*: start **2 surface**, texture, appearance, quality, varnish

finished adj **1 over**, ended, broken down, broken up, broken off **2 refined**, perfect, polished, elegant, professional *Opposite*: rough **3 polished**, buffed, varnished, glossed, gilded *Opposite*: unfinished **4 ruined**, wrecked, lost, destroyed, devastated

finish off v **1 complete**, conclude, finalize, bring to an end, wind up *Opposite*: start up **2 use up**, eat up, exhaust, finish off, polish off, demolish *(infml)* *Opposite*: stock up **3** *(infml)* **eliminate**, kill, exterminate, dispatch, dispose of

finite adj **limited**, restricted, determinate, fixed, set *Opposite*: infinite

fire n **1 blaze**, flames, bonfire, conflagration, inferno **2 combustion**, conflagration, ignition **3 passion**, ardour, fervour, excitement, enthusiasm *Opposite*: apathy ■ v **1 shoot**, set off, detonate, trigger, launch **2 excite**, arouse, inspire, enthuse, enliven **3** *(infml)* **dismiss**, let go, lay off, throw out, sack *(infml)* *Opposite*: take on

fire alarm n **bell**, siren, klaxon, buzzer, warning

firearm n **gun**, weapon, handgun, pistol, rifle

fireball n **ball lightning**, ball of fire, flash, lightning

firebrand n **troublemaker**, agitator, hothead, revolutionary, demagogue

firebreak n **clearing**, opening, strip, break, barrier

fire drill n **fire practice**, drill, rehearsal, evacuation, exercise

fire escape n **stairway**, ladder, escape hatch, staircase, emergency exit

fireguard n **1 fire screen**, screen, guard, fender, frame **2 firebreak**, clearing, strip, glade, opening

firelight n **glow**, glimmer, flame, flare, blaze

fireplace n **hearth**, inglenook, fire, fireside, chimney corner

firepower n **weapons**, arms, guns, armaments, munitions

fire practice n **fire drill**, drill, practice, rehearsal, evacuation

fireproof adj **incombustible**, nonflammable, flame-retardant, fire-retardant, fire-resistant *Opposite*: combustible

fireside n **hearth**, inglenook, fireplace, chimney corner

firetrap n **fire hazard**, danger, deathtrap *(infml)*

fire up v **1 get going**, initiate, start off, set off, launch **2 ignite**, fire, light, kindle, set alight **3 enthuse**, motivate, incite, stimulate, excite

firewood n **logs**, kindling, wood, fuel

firing n **gunfire**, fire, shooting, shots

firing line n **1 front line**, front, battlefield, vanguard **2 forefront**, vanguard, lead, cutting edge, leading edge

firm adj **1 solid**, compact, hard, rigid, dense *Opposite*: soft **2 secure**, stable, fixed, strong, safe *Opposite*: unstable **3 determined**, certain, definite, fixed, resolved *Opposite*: uncertain ■ v **harden**, stiffen, solidify, set, press down *Opposite*: soften ■ n **company**, business, partnership, multinational, corporation

firmly adv **1 tightly**, securely, steadily, powerfully, strongly *Opposite*: loosely **2 resolutely**, inflexibly, determinedly, decisively, definitely *Opposite*: irresolutely

firmness n **1 hardness**, rigidity, compactness, density, stiffness *Opposite*: softness **2 stability**, steadiness, strength, safety *Opposite*: instability **3 determination**, steadfastness, resolve, resolution, decisiveness *Opposite*: uncertainty

firm up v **1 settle**, conclude, tie up, confirm, establish **2 stabilize**, balance, steady, settle *Opposite*: destabilize

first adj **1 initial**, primary, original, opening, earliest *Opposite*: last **2 chief**, head, principal, leading, major *Opposite*: minor **3 fundamental**, basic, key, elementary, primary *Opposite*: advanced ■ adv **firstly**, initially, at the outset, in the beginning, to begin with *Opposite*: lastly

first aid n **emergency treatment**, medical treatment, medical care, resuscitation, mouth-to-mouth

first-class adj **best**, superb, first-rate, unrivalled, excellent *Opposite*: poor

firsthand adj **direct**, actual, immediate, personal *Opposite*: second-hand ■ adv **directly**, personally, from the horse's mouth, straight *Opposite*: indirectly

first light n **dawn**, daybreak, sunrise, daylight, morning *Opposite*: dusk

firstly adv **to start with**, initially, first of all, at the outset, first *Opposite*: lastly

first name *n* name, Christian name, given name, moniker *(slang)* Opposite: surname

first-rate *adj* best, superb, first-class, unrivalled, excellent Opposite: poor

firth *n* estuary, inlet, fjord, sound, creek

fish *v* **1 catch fish**, angle, go fishing, trawl, cast a line **2 search**, seek, trawl, probe, dig around

WORD BANK

❑ **types of flatfish** angelfish, brill, flounder, halibut, lemon sole, manta ray, plaice, pompano, ray, skate, sole, stingray, turbot

❑ **types of freshwater fish** bass, bream, carp, catfish, crappie, goldfish, grayling, guppy, loach, minnow, mullet, Nile perch, perch, pike, piranha, roach, stickleback, tench, tilapia, trout

❑ **types of sea fish** anchovy, anglerfish, cod, coley, dogfish, eel, haddock, hake, herring, John Dory, ling, mackerel, monkfish, pilchard, salmon, sardine, sea bream, shark, sprat, sturgeon, whitebait, whiting

❑ **types of tropical sea fish** barracuda, flying fish, kingfish, mahi-mahi, marlin, pomfret, sailfish, sawfish, snapper, swordfish, tuna

❑ **parts of a fish** air bladder, anal fin, dorsal fin, fin, gill, pectoral fin, pelvic fin, roe, scale, tail

fish for *v* search for, angle for, be after, invite, hope for

fishing *n* angling, casting, trawling, harpooning, whaling

fishnet *n* mesh, netting, net, tulle, gauze

fish out *(infml)* *v* pull out, take out, haul out, drag out, dig out Opposite: put in

fishy *(infml)* *adj* dubious, suspicious, irregular, underhand, shady Opposite: aboveboard

fission *n* breaking up, separation, splitting, division, schism Opposite: fusion

fissure *n* crack, split, crevice, fracture, cleft

fist *n* **1** *(infml)* **hand**, knuckle, paw *(infml)*, duke *(slang)*, mitt *(slang)* **2 fistful**, handful, bunch, wad

fistfight *n* brawl, scrap, scuffle, fisticuffs, skirmish

fistful *n* handful, bunch, fist, wad

fit *v* **1 measure**, tailor, size, take in, take up **2 match**, suit, correspond, tally **3 install**, put in, mount, fix, provide with ■ *adj* **1 appropriate**, fitting, right, proper, acceptable Opposite: unfit **2 healthy**, well, fine, in fine fettle, hale and hearty Opposite: unfit ■ *n* **convulsion**, spasm, seizure, attack, turn

fitful *adj* disturbed, sporadic, broken, restless, irregular Opposite: undisturbed

fit in *v* **1 conform**, blend in, integrate, go well with, assimilate **2 find time for**, squeeze in, manage, cope with, take on

fitness *n* **1 health**, strength, robustness, vigour, wellbeing Opposite: weakness **2 suitability**, appropriateness, aptness, qualification, capability Opposite: inappropriateness

fit out *v* equip, supply, set up, kit out, outfit

fitted *adj* **1 tailored**, close-fitting, formfitting, trim, snug Opposite: baggy **2 built-in**, fixed, permanent, attached, incorporated Opposite: freestanding

fitting *adj* suitable, appropriate, right, correct, proper Opposite: inappropriate

fittingness *n* suitability, appropriateness, rightness, correctness, properness Opposite: inappropriateness

fittings *n* accessories, decorations, furniture, equipment

WORD BANK

❑ **types of general fittings** ceiling rose, chimneypiece, dado, fender, fireplace, looking glass, mantel, mantelpiece, mirror, picture rail, radiator, skirting board, socket, wainscot

❑ **types of plumbing fittings** ball cock, basin, bath, bathtub, bidet, drinking fountain, hand basin, hot tub, nozzle, plumbing, rose, sauna, shower, sink, sitz bath, spa, spout, sprinkler, tank, tap, toilet, towel rail, tub, vanity unit, wash-hand basin, washbasin, washbowl, whirlpool bath

fit up *v* equip, supply, set up, kit out, fit out

five o'clock shadow *n* beard, stubble, bristles

fix *v* **1 mend**, repair, correct, put to rights, make right **2** *(infml)* **prepare**, make ready, get ready, cook, rustle up *(infml)* **3 agree**, arrange, establish, organize, set up Opposite: cancel **4 fasten**, attach, glue, stick, secure Opposite: detach **5** *(infml)* **rig**, manipulate, massage, arrange, fiddle *(infml)* ■ *n* **1** *(infml)* **dilemma**, predicament, tight spot, quandary, corner **2** *(infml)* **solution**, answer, resolution, remedy **3** *(infml)* **con**, fraud, swindle, trick, setup *(infml)* **4** *(slang)* **dose**, injection, shot *(infml)*, hit *(slang)*

fixated *adj* obsessed, absorbed, fanatical, engrossed, paranoid Opposite: indifferent

fixation *n* obsession, fascination, mania, passion, addiction

fixative *n* **1 preservative**, preserver, spray, varnish, coating **2 glue**, adhesive, cement, paste, gum

fixed *adj* **1 secure**, immovable, immobile, static, motionless Opposite: fluid **2 set**, unchanging, flat, preset, predetermined Opposite: variable **3 rigid**, inflexible, hard-and-fast, cast-iron Opposite: flexible

fixedness *n* secureness, immovability, immobility, motionlessness, stability Opposite: fluidity

fixture *n* **1 match**, game, meeting, contest, clash **2 accessory**, decoration, fitting

fix up *v* **1 arrange**, schedule, plan, make plans for, organize **2 repair**, renew, refurbish, renovate, redecorate

fizz *v* effervesce, sparkle, bubble, froth, foam ■ *n* effervescence, sparkle, bubbles, froth, foam

fizzle *v* **1 fizz**, hiss, sizzle, spit, sputter **2 fail**, fade away, peter out, tail off, disappear Opposite: flourish

fizzy *adj* **effervescent**, sparkling, bubbly, carbonated, foamy *Opposite*: still

fjord *n* **inlet**, sound, creek, firth

flab *n* **fat**, podginess, chubbiness, plumpness, corpulence

flabbergast *(infml)* *v* **amaze**, astonish, astound, dumbfound, stun

flabbergasted *(infml)* *adj* **amazed**, astonished, astounded, dumbfounded, dumbstruck

flabbiness *(infml)* *n* **flaccidity**, looseness, softness, slackness, floppiness *Opposite*: firmness

flabby *(infml)* *adj* **flaccid**, loose, soft, slack, saggy *Opposite*: firm

flaccid *adj* **limp**, soft, loose, drooping, sagging *Opposite*: firm

flag *n* **standard**, ensign, pennant, pennon, colours ▪ *v* **1 weaken**, tire, weary, wane, fade *Opposite*: rally **2 mark**, highlight, identify, label, signal

flagellate *v* **whip**, flog, scourge, lash, beat

flagellation *n* **whipping**, flogging, scourging, lashing, beating

flagging *adj* **weakening**, tiring, wearied, waning, fading *Opposite*: rallying

flagon *n* **bottle**, carafe, flask, canteen, carboy

flagpole *n* **flagstaff**, staff, pole, mast, post

flagrant *adj* **blatant**, scandalous, obvious, deliberate, brazen *Opposite*: covert

flagship *n* **1 warship**, man-of-war, ship of the line, capital ship, battleship **2 star**, leader, jewel, pearl, pièce de résistance ▪ *adj* **prize**, star, lead, top, leading

flagstaff *see* flagpole

flagstone *n* **paving stone**, kerbstone, slab, block, paver

flag-waving *n* **patriotism**, chauvinism, jingoism, nationalism, loyalism

flail *v* **1 thrash**, wave, whirl, flap, flounder **2 flog**, beat, batter, hit, strike

flail about *v* **flounder**, writhe, struggle, squirm, stagger

flair *n* **1 talent**, skill, aptitude, feel, gift *Opposite*: ineptitude **2 elegance**, stylishness, style, chic, panache *Opposite*: inelegance. *See* COMPARE AND CONTRAST *at* talent.

flak *(infml)* *n* **criticism**, condemnation, censure, disapproval, hostility *Opposite*: support

flake *n* **shaving**, fleck, sliver, chip, scale ▪ *v* **peel**, crumble, chip, come off, scale

flaky *adj* **1 peeling**, crumbling, crumbly, chipped, scaly **2** *(infml)* **unreliable**, undependable, irresponsible, flighty, forgetful *Opposite*: reliable

flamboyance *n* **showiness**, ostentation, flashiness, gaudiness, luridness *Opposite*: modesty

flamboyant *adj* **showy**, ostentatious, flashy, gaudy, lurid *Opposite*: understated

flame *n* **fire**, blaze, flare, spark, flicker ▪ *v* **burn**, blaze, light up, glow, flare

flameproof *adj* **nonflammable**, noninflammable, incombustible, fireproof, fire-retardant *Opposite*: inflammable

flaming *adj* **1 blazing**, burning, flaring, flickering, sparking *Opposite*: doused **2 intense**, angry, passionate, blazing, heated *Opposite*: calm

flammable *adj* **inflammable**, combustible, incendiary, igneous *Opposite*: fireproof

flan *n* **quiche**, tart, tartlet, pie, pastry

flank *n* **side**, edge, verge, margin, border ▪ *v* **border**, edge, line, skirt, fringe

flannel *(infml)* *v* **flatter**, beguile, sweet-talk *(infml)*, soft-soap *(infml)*, blarney *(infml)* ▪ *n* **flattery**, sweet talk *(infml)*, soft soap *(infml)*, blarney *(infml)*, weasel words *(infml)*

flap *v* *(infml)* **panic**, fret, dither, fluster, worry *Opposite*: calm down ▪ *n* **1** *(infml)* **panic**, fret, dither, fluster, state *(infml)* *Opposite*: calm **2 tab**, fold, lappet, lap, tail **3 flutter**, wave, flail, shake, wag

flare *v* **1 burn**, blaze, flame, flicker, flash **2 broaden**, splay, bell, widen, spread ▪ *n* **flash**, blaze, flicker, flame, burst

flared *adj* **widening**, wide, spreading, broadening, flaring *Opposite*: tapered

flare up *v* **erupt**, break out, explode, heat up, blaze *Opposite*: die down

flare-up *(infml)* *n* **outbreak**, eruption, flash, outburst, explosion

flash *v* **1 glint**, sparkle, twinkle, flare, flicker **2 pass quickly**, rush, speed, race, zoom *Opposite*: crawl **3** *(infml)* **flaunt**, show, show off, display, exhibit ▪ *n* **1 blaze**, spark, flare, flicker, sparkle **2 moment**, instant, second, twinkling, minute **3 news flash**, update, bulletin, announcement, report ▪ *adj* *(infml)* **showy**, ostentatious, flashy, gaudy, loud *Opposite*: understated

flashback *n* **memory**, recurrence, remembrance, recollection, hallucination

flash flood *n* **deluge**, downpour, cloudburst, spate, surge

flashpoint *n* **1 crisis**, breaking point, climax, turning point, crossroads **2 trouble spot**, hot spot, minefield, inferno, hornet's nest

flashy *adj* **showy**, ostentatious, glitzy, gaudy, loud *Opposite*: understated

flask *n* **bottle**, flagon, carafe, hip flask, decanter

flat *adj* **1 level**, even, smooth, plane, horizontal *Opposite*: uneven **2 unexciting**, dull, monotonous, tedious, boring *Opposite*: exciting **3 fixed**, set, preset, invariable, nonnegotiable *Opposite*: variable **4 categorical**, downright, absolute, out-and-out, emphatic *Opposite*: equivocal ▪ *n* **1 surface**, plane, level, face, blade **2 suite**, rooms, maisonette, studio, penthouse

flatly *adv* **1 categorically**, flat, absolutely,

unequivocally, emphatically *Opposite*: equivocally **2 dully**, monotonously, lifelessly, blandly, tediously *Opposite*: animatedly

flatmate n **cohabitant**, cohabitee, housemate, friend, roommate

flatness n **1 levelness**, evenness, smoothness, horizontalness, horizontality *Opposite*: unevenness **2 dullness**, monotony, monotonousness, tedium, boringness *Opposite*: excitement

flatten v **1 squash**, crush, level, even out, compress **2 knock over**, knock down, fell, poleaxe, crush

flatter v **compliment**, praise, cajole, sweet-talk *(infml)*, butter up *(infml)* *Opposite*: insult

flatterer n **toady**, sycophant, fawner, creep *(infml)*, crawler *(infml)* *Opposite*: critic

flattering adj **1 obsequious**, smooth, toadyish, sycophantic, unctuous *Opposite*: uncomplimentary **2 gratifying**, pleasing, satisfying, satisfactory, cheering *Opposite*: galling **3 becoming**, complimentary, kind, favourable, sympathetic *Opposite*: unbecoming

flattery n **sycophancy**, obsequiousness, toadyism, adulation, unctuousness *Opposite*: insult

flatulence n **pomposity**, pretentiousness, bombast, verbosity, grandiloquence *Opposite*: simplicity

flatulent adj **pompous**, pretentious, bombastic, verbose, grandiloquent *Opposite*: unpretentious

flaunt v **show off**, exhibit, display, parade, flourish *Opposite*: hide

flavour n **1 hint**, sense, feeling, feel, air **2 taste**, zest, tang, essence, aroma *Opposite*: tastelessness **3 additive**, seasoning, extract, spice, essence ■ v **1 season**, spice, lace, salt, ginger **2 characterize**, distinguish, mark, pervade, run through

flavourful adj **tasty**, tangy, appetizing, palatable, savoury *Opposite*: unappetizing

flavouring n **flavour**, additive, seasoning, extract, spice

flavourless adj **tasteless**, bland, insipid, flat, anodyne *(literary)* *Opposite*: tasty

flavoursome adj **tasty**, delicious, mouthwatering, appetizing, yummy *(infml)* *Opposite*: tasteless

flaw n **fault**, defect, blemish, imperfection, failing

COMPARE AND CONTRAST CORE MEANING: something that detracts from perfection

flaw an unintended mark or crack that prevents something from being totally perfect and detracts from its value, or a weakness in somebody's character or in a plan, theory, or system; **imperfection** a fault that makes a person or thing less than perfect; **fault** something that detracts from the integrity, functioning, or perfection of a thing, or a weakness in somebody's character, usually more serious than a flaw; **defect** a fault in a machine,

---

system, or plan, especially one that prevents it from functioning correctly, or a personal weakness; **failing** something that mars somebody or something in some way, especially an unfortunate feature of somebody's character; **blemish** a mark of some kind that detracts from the appearance of something, especially the complexion or skin, or a feature that detracts from somebody's otherwise undamaged reputation or record.

---

flawed adj **faulty**, defective, damaged, blemished, imperfect *Opposite*: perfect

flawless adj **perfect**, faultless, immaculate, impeccable, unblemished *Opposite*: imperfect

flawlessness n **perfection**, faultlessness, immaculateness, impeccability, spotlessness *Opposite*: imperfection

flaxen adj **fair-haired**, fair, blond, blonde, golden-haired

flay v **1 whip**, lash, thrash, flog, beat **2 criticize**, censure, condemn, pillory, lambaste *Opposite*: endorse

fleapit n **cinema**, venue, theatre, picture house *(dated)*

fleck n **speck**, spot, speckle, dot, flyspeck

flecked adj **marked**, speckled, dotted, streaked, splashed

fledgling n **novice**, beginner, learner, tyro, neophyte *Opposite*: expert ■ adj **inexperienced**, new, untried, young, inexpert *Opposite*: experienced

flee v **run away**, escape, fly, take flight, run off *Opposite*: remain

fleece *(infml)* v **swindle**, con, cheat, take for a ride, defraud

fleeciness n **woolliness**, downiness, fluffiness, furriness, fuzziness

fleecy adj **woolly**, fluffy, flocculent, soft, shaggy

fleet n **navy**, flotilla, armada, convoy, task force

fleeting adj **brief**, transitory, short-lived, momentary, passing *Opposite*: permanent. *See* COMPARE AND CONTRAST *at* **temporary**.

flesh n **1 tissue**, soft tissue, muscle **2 skin**, surface, epithelium, epidermis, dermis **3 meat**, beef, lamb, pork, ham **4 pulp**, pulpiness, meat **5 relatives**, family, relations, blood relatives, kin **6 body**, flesh and blood, physicality, corporeality, corpus **7 substance**, details, information, reality, solidness

flesh and blood n **family**, relations, relatives, kith and kin, flesh

flesh-and-blood adj **real live**, human, real, sentient, animate

fleshiness n **beefiness**, stoutness, portliness, heftiness, corpulence

fleshly adj **1 bodily**, corporeal, physical, corporal, human *Opposite*: psychological **2 carnal**, bodily, erotic, animal, voluptuous *Opposite*: ascetic **3 worldly**, secular, material, human, mundane *Opposite*: spiritual

flesh out v **amplify**, elaborate, pad, pad out, expand *Opposite*: condense

fleshy adj **plump**, ample, overweight, fat, corpulent *Opposite*: slender

flex v 1 **bend**, loosen up, activate, move, warm up *Opposite*: straighten 2 **contract**, tense, tighten, control *Opposite*: relax

flexibility n **suppleness**, litheness, elasticity, give, plasticity *Opposite*: rigidity

flexible adj 1 **supple**, lithe, elastic, plastic, stretchy *Opposite*: rigid 2 **adaptable**, accommodating, variable, compliant, open *Opposite*: intractable

flick n (infml) **film**, picture, big screen, silver screen, movie (US) ■ v **brush**, tap, glance, flip, graze

flicker v **sparkle**, glimmer, flash, waver, sputter ■ n 1 **glimmer**, spark, sparkle, twinkle, glint *Opposite*: beam 2 **trace**, ghost, impression, flash, glimmer

flickering adj **glimmering**, shimmering, intermittent, irregular, flashing

flick through v **look through**, dip into, leaf through, flip through, riffle *Opposite*: scrutinize

flier n **leaflet**, handout, advertisement, notice, insert

flight n 1 **trip**, journey, airlift, voyage, tour 2 **escape**, departure, getaway, breakout, evasion

flightiness n **capriciousness**, changeability, frivolity, volatility, erraticism *Opposite*: reliability

flight of fancy n **fantasy**, pipe dream, fancy, dream, daydream

flighty adj **unreliable**, capricious, changeable, erratic, undependable *Opposite*: dependable

flimsiness n **fragility**, weakness, delicacy, frailty, feebleness *Opposite*: sturdiness

flimsy adj 1 **fragile**, weak, delicate, insubstantial, slight *Opposite*: sturdy 2 **poor**, feeble, unconvincing, inadequate, weak *Opposite*: sound. *See* COMPARE AND CONTRAST *at* fragile.

flinch v **recoil**, start, cringe, shy away, baulk *Opposite*: stand your ground. *See* COMPARE AND CONTRAST *at* recoil.

fling v **throw**, toss, hurl, pitch, lob ■ n (infml) **romance**, love affair, affair, involvement, relationship. *See* COMPARE AND CONTRAST *at* throw.

flinty adj **hard**, unemotional, stern, inflexible, pitiless *Opposite*: soft

flip v **turn over**, toss, flick, spin, overturn ■ adj (infml) **flippant**, casual, joking, jokey, dismissive *Opposite*: serious

flip over v **tip**, tip up, upset, upturn, flip

flippancy n **levity**, facetiousness, glibness, offhandedness, impertinence *Opposite*: seriousness

flippant adj **facetious**, offhand, glib, dismissive, frivolous *Opposite*: serious

flip through v **leaf through**, browse, flick through, skim through, scan

flirt v 1 **trifle**, toy, play, seduce, lead on 2 **flick**, jerk, toss, flip, propel

flirtation n **romance**, fling, love affair, entanglement, liaison

flirtatious adj **playful**, coy, seductive, suggestive, kittenish

flirt with v **consider**, toy with, entertain, think about, trifle with

flit v **fly**, flutter, dart, skim, flash

float v 1 **sail**, swim, drift, glide, tread water *Opposite*: sink 2 **hover**, soar, drift, glide, hang *Opposite*: drop 3 **propose**, suggest, put forward, promote, offer *Opposite*: reject

floating adj **fluctuating**, detached, variable, moving, free *Opposite*: fixed

flock n **group**, set, cluster ■ v **gather**, collect, congregate, assemble, cluster *Opposite*: disperse

---

WORD BANK

❏ **types of flock** bevy (of quail/larks), brood (of chickens), cast (of hawks), charm (of finches), clutch (of chickens), colony (of gulls), covey (of partridges), exaltation (of larks) *(literary)*, flight (of doves/swallows), gaggle (of geese), herd (of swans), kettle (of hawks), mob (of emus), murmuration (of starlings) *(literary)*, muster (of peacocks), rookery (of penguins), siege (of herons), skein (of geese), watch (of nightingales) *(literary)*, wedge (of swans in flight), wisp (of snipe)

---

floe n **ice floe**, iceberg, ice field, icecap, ice sheet

flog v 1 **whip**, lash, beat, thrash, scourge 2 (infml) **sell**, vend, get rid of, trade, peddle *Opposite*: buy

flood n 1 **deluge**, overflow, downpour, torrent, tidal wave *Opposite*: drought 2 **abundance**, glut, excess, stream, rush *Opposite*: shortage ■ v **inundate**, submerge, overflow, swamp, saturate *Opposite*: ebb

flooded adj **underwater**, swamped, waterlogged, inundated, drowned

floodgate n **head gate**, sluicegate, water gate, lock, weir

floodlight n **illumination**, lighting, stream, flood, searchlight ■ v **light up**, illuminate, light, irradiate, spotlight

floodlit adj **illuminated**, lit up, lit, illumined *(literary)*

floodplain n **plain**, valley, delta, water meadow, fen

flood tide n 1 **inflow**, high tide, current 2 **groundswell**, swell, surge, wave, upsurge

floor n 1 **storey**, level, deck (US) 2 **bottom**, base, level, surface, flat ■ v **astonish**, stupefy, astound, stagger, confound

flooring n **parquet**, floorboards, terrazzo, tiles, floor tiles

floor manager n **supervisor**, overseer, manager, duty officer, line manager

floor plan n **layout**, plan, design, arrangement, allocation

flop v 1 **collapse**, slump, fall down, slacken, sag Opposite: stand up 2 (infml) **fail**, fold, close, crash, nose-dive Opposite: succeed 3 (infml) **collapse**, slump, fall down, slacken, sag Opposite: stand up ■ n (infml) **failure**, fiasco, dead loss, loser, dud (infml) Opposite: hit

floppiness n **limpness**, droopiness, looseness, slackness, softness Opposite: firmness

floppy adj **limp**, droopy, lank, loose, flappy Opposite: firm

flora n **plants**, flowers, vegetation, plant life

floral adj **flowery**, flowered, flower-patterned, floral-patterned

floral-patterned see **floral**

floret n **floweret**, bud, blossom, bloom, flower

florid adj 1 **ornate**, baroque, elaborate, fancy, flowery Opposite: plain 2 **ruddy**, red, sanguine, rosy, heightened Opposite: pallid

flotation n **launch**, initiation, debut, inauguration, introduction

flotilla n **fleet**, armada, convoy, task force, navy

flotsam n **debris**, refuse, driftwood, jetsam, wreckage

flounce v **prance**, storm, stomp, strut, swagger

flounder v 1 **splash**, struggle, thrash, wallow, stumble 2 **dither**, hesitate, falter, get into difficulties, waver

flour v **dust**, cover, coat, sprinkle, dredge

WORD BANK
❏ **types of flour** cornflour, cornmeal, meal, plain flour, polenta, rice flour, self-raising flour, wheatmeal, wholemeal

flourish v 1 **be successful**, succeed, thrive, grow, do well Opposite: decline 2 **shake**, show, flaunt, display, wave ■ n 1 **embellishment**, curl, curlicue, decoration, ornament 2 **grand gesture**, display, fanfare, show, bravado

flourishing adj **doing well**, thriving, successful, booming, healthy Opposite: declining

floury adj **starchy**, crumbly, crumbling, farinaceous, floured

flout v **disobey**, break, ignore, defy, contravene Opposite: obey

flow v 1 **run**, pour, flood, stream, gush 2 **spring**, arise, emerge, emanate, issue ■ n **movement**, current, stream, course, drift

flower n 1 **floret**, flower head, bud, blossom, bloom 2 **best**, pick, height, choicest, elite Opposite: worst ■ v 1 **bloom**, bud, blossom, open, come into bloom Opposite: fade 2 **develop**, come to fruition, flourish, peak, blossom Opposite: wane

WORD BANK
❏ **types of annual flower** aster, forget-me-not, lobelia, love-in-a-mist, marigold, nasturtium, pansy, petunia, poppy, stock, sunflower, sweet pea
❏ **types of perennial flower** African violet, aquilegia, begonia, buttercup, carnation, chrysanthemum, cowslip, daisy, delphinium, foxglove, fuchsia, geranium, lily of the valley, lotus, lovelies-bleeding, lupin, orchid, pelargonium, peony, pink, primrose, rose, snapdragon, sweet william, violet, wallflower
❏ **parts of a flower** androecium, anther, bract, calyx, carpel, corolla, fall, filament, floret, glume, gynoecium, involucre, lemma, lip, nectary, ovary, ovule, palea, pedicel, peduncle, perianth, petal, pistil, receptacle, sepal, spur, stamen, stigma, style, tepal

flowerbed n **plot**, garden plot, patch, border, herbaceous border

flowered adj **floral**, flowery, flower-patterned, floral-patterned

flowering n **peak**, high point, acme, blossoming, pinnacle Opposite: nadir

flower-patterned adj **floral**, flowery, flowered, floral-patterned

flowerpot n **plant pot**, planter, tub, jardinière, urn

flowery adj 1 **ornate**, ornamental, baroque, embellished, florid Opposite: plain 2 **floral**, flowered, flower-patterned, floriated

flowing adj **graceful**, smooth, curving, sinuous, elegant Opposite: jerky

fluctuate v **vary**, alter, ebb and flow, rise and fall, come and go

fluctuating adj **changing**, changeable, shifting, mutable, unstable Opposite: constant

fluctuation n **variation**, vacillation, rise and fall, oscillation, flux Opposite: steadiness

flue n **vent**, chimney, outlet, shaft, duct

fluency n **effortlessness**, eloquence, articulacy, ease, facility Opposite: hesitancy

fluent adj 1 **easy**, flowing, confident, assured, smooth Opposite: halting 2 **articulate**, eloquent, voluble, smooth-spoken, smoothtongued Opposite: tongue-tied

fluff v (infml) **do badly**, make a mess of, ruin, spoil, botch (infml) ■ n **fuzz**, lint, hair ■ v **fluff up**, plump up, ruffle, shake, pat

fluffiness n 1 **furriness**, fuzziness, hairiness, woolliness, fleeciness 2 **lightness**, airiness, softness, flimsiness, frothiness Opposite: heaviness

fluffy adj 1 **fleecy**, cottony, feathery, downy, furry 2 **frothy**, foamy, bubbly, soft, light

fluid n **liquid**, solution, water Opposite: solid ■ adj 1 **runny**, liquid, watery, liquefied, molten Opposite: solid 2 **effortless**, flowing, smooth, graceful, elegant Opposite: jerky 3 **changeable**, fluctuating, unstable, adaptable, flexible Opposite: constant

fluidity n **1 variability**, changeableness, changeability, flexibility, mutability *Opposite*: fixedness **2 smoothness**, gracefulness, grace, agility, flexibility *Opposite*: jerkiness

fluke *(infml)* n **stroke of luck**, accident, coincidence, lucky break, chance occurrence *Opposite*: mischance

flummox *(infml)* v **confuse**, perplex, baffle, stump, bewilder

flummoxed *(infml)* adj **confused**, perplexed, confounded, baffled, stumped

flunk *(infml)* v **fail**, be unsuccessful, not pass, do badly, bomb *(infml) Opposite*: ace *(infml)*

flunkey *(infml) see* **flunky**

flunky *(infml)* n **minion**, sidekick, assistant, helper, subordinate

fluorescent adj **glowing**, bright, shining, luminous, flaming

flurry n **1 burst**, spell, outbreak, bout, flood **2 wind**, gust, puff, squall, shower ■ v **fluster**, agitate, disturb, disconcert, perturb *Opposite*: soothe

flush v **1 redden**, blush, go red, colour, glow *Opposite*: pale **2 clear**, wash out, cleanse, rinse, swill ■ n **blush**, high colour, redness, rosiness, ruddiness *Opposite*: pallor ■ adj **1 even**, level, flat, true *Opposite*: uneven **2** *(infml)* **well off**, rich, in the money, in funds, rolling in it *(infml)*

flushed adj **red-faced**, rosy, red, blushing, glowing *Opposite*: pale

fluster v **disconcert**, agitate, confuse, upset, bother *Opposite*: soothe

flustered adj **harassed**, agitated, nervous, disconcerted, rattled *Opposite*: calm

flute n **groove**, channel, indentation, line, furrow *Opposite*: ridge

fluted adj **grooved**, channelled, corrugated, furrowed, lined *Opposite*: flat

flutter v **beat**, flap, wave, tremble, quiver ■ n **1 fluster**, excitement, flurry, agitation, confusion *Opposite*: composure **2** *(infml)* **bet**, wager, stake

flux n **fluidity**, mutability, fluctuation, instability, unrest *Opposite*: stability

fly v **1 hover**, soar, wing, take wing, take off **2 zoom**, tear, dash, hurry, race *Opposite*: dawdle **3 bolt**, run away, escape, flee, take flight *Opposite*: stand your ground

---

WORD BANK

❑ **types of flying insect** aphid, bee, blackfly, bluebottle, bumblebee, cicada, daddy longlegs, deer fly, dragonfly, firefly, fruit fly, gnat, grasshopper, greenfly, hornet, horsefly, locust, mayfly, midge, mosquito, tsetse fly, wasp, whitefly

---

flyaway adj **unmanageable**, unruly, uncontrollable, hard to handle, awkward *Opposite*: manageable

flyblown adj **1 maggoty**, wormy, infested, worm-eaten, festering **2 dirty**, filthy, contaminated, tainted, unclean *Opposite*: clean

fly-by-night adj **unscrupulous**, dubious, unreliable, shifty, questionable *Opposite*: reputable

flying adj **1 hovering**, airborne, soaring, in the air, on the wing **2 rapid**, brief, speedy, hurried, short

flying saucer n **UFO**, spaceship, spacecraft

fly in the face of v **challenge**, disagree with, go against, contradict, oppose *Opposite*: conform

fly in the ointment n **drawback**, complaint, impediment, snag, hitch

flyleaf n **front page**, first page, frontispiece, page, leaf

fly off the handle *(infml)* v **erupt**, explode, lose your temper, fly into a rage, hit the ceiling *(infml) Opposite*: calm down

flysheet n **flier**, handbill, handout, sheet, notice

fly the coop *(infml)* v **escape**, leave, run away, flee, bolt *Opposite*: remain

foal v **produce young**, produce offspring, breed, give birth, reproduce

foam n **bubbles**, froth, fizz, lather, suds ■ v **froth up**, effervesce, froth, bubble, fizz

foam at the mouth v **rage**, seethe, fume, boil, splutter

fob off v **1 foist**, palm off, dump, pass on, offload **2 mislead**, misinform, deceive, stall, pull the wool over somebody's eyes **3 cheat**, con, palm off, rip off *(infml)*, do *(infml)*

focal adj **principal**, pivotal, central, crucial, important *Opposite*: peripheral

focal point n **central point**, pivot, core, centre, focus *Opposite*: periphery

focus n **1 emphasis**, attention, effort, concentration, motivation **2 nub**, central point, core, spotlight, centre **3 focal point**, heart, hub, nucleus, meeting point ■ v **concentrate**, direct, converge, meet, come together

focused adj **motivated**, concentrated, fixated, attentive, absorbed

fodder n **food**, silage, hay, feed, feedstuff

foe *(fml)* n **adversary**, enemy, antagonist, rival, opponent *Opposite*: friend

foetid *see* **fetid**

fog n **1 mist**, vapour, smog, haze, miasma **2 muddle**, stupor, confusion, daze, haze *Opposite*: clarity ■ v **obscure**, cloud, bewilder, confuse, stupefy *Opposite*: sharpen

fogginess n **1 mistiness**, murkiness, haziness, cloudiness, gloom *Opposite*: brightness **2 obscurity**, confusion, doubtfulness, bewilderment, perplexity *Opposite*: clarity

foggy adj **1 hazy**, misty, cloudy, murky, smoggy *Opposite*: clear **2 unclear**, vague, confused, muddled, bewildered *Opposite*: precise

foghorn n **horn**, siren, hooter, klaxon

foible *n* **weakness**, fault, shortcoming, quirk, idiosyncrasy *Opposite*: strength

foil *v* **stop**, throw a spanner in the works, frustrate, thwart, outwit

foist *v* **force upon**, inflict upon, thrust upon, impose, palm off

fold *v* **1 double over**, bend, fold up, fold over, double *Opposite*: straighten **2 go out of business**, close, shut down, go bankrupt, collapse ■ *n* **crinkle**, crease, wrinkle, pleat, doubling

foldaway *see* **folding**

folded *adj* **doubled**, doubled over, doubled up, bent over, turned under *Opposite*: outspread

folding *adj* **portable**, foldup, foldaway, collapsible, hinged

fold up *v* **bend flat**, bend, collapse, double, fold over *Opposite*: unfold

foldup *see* **folding**

foliage *n* **leaves**, greenery, vegetation, undergrowth, shrubbery

foliage plant *n* **houseplant**, pot plant, greenery

folk *adj* **traditional**, popular, common, widespread, vernacular ■ *n* **people**, folks, the people, the population, everyone

folklore *n* **myth**, legend, oral tradition, mythology, tradition

folks *n* **1** (*infml*) **people**, folk, everyone, the silent majority, society **2** (*infml*) **everyone**, everybody, ladies and gentlemen, you guys, friends **3 relations**, relatives, nearest and dearest, family, kinsfolk

folk singer *n* **singer**, folkie, balladeer, troubadour

folksy *adj* **simple**, unsophisticated, unpretentious, wholesome, traditional

folktale *n* **tale**, story, legend, myth, ballad

follicle *n* **sac**, cavity, gland, hair follicle

follow *v* **1 pursue**, chase, stalk, trail, shadow *Opposite*: precede **2 monitor**, check on, keep an eye on, track, chart **3 come out of**, ensue, result, develop, arise **4 keep on**, go along, stay on, keep to, stick to **5 enjoy**, admire, support, keep up with, be keen on **6 obey**, abide by, keep to, respect, adhere to *Opposite*: break **7 understand**, see, comprehend, grasp, get the gist

---

COMPARE AND CONTRAST CORE MEANING: go after **follow** take the same route behind another person, for example by walking down the street or driving along the same road, deliberately or by chance, and not necessarily with the intention of closing the gap; **chase** try to reach, catch, or overtake another person who is in front; **pursue** make an effort to catch up with the person being followed; **tail** (*infml*) to follow secretly for purposes of surveillance; **shadow** follow secretly, used especially to talk about the activities of spies and detectives; **stalk** follow or try to get close to a person or hunted animal unobtrusively, especially obsessively to follow and criminally harass a person;

trail follow tracks or traces left by a person or animal no longer in sight.

---

follower *n* **supporter**, fan, admirer, hanger-on, devotee

following *adj* **next**, subsequent, succeeding, ensuing, resulting *Opposite*: previous

follow-on *adj* **resulting**, consequent, resultant, ensuing, secondary ■ *n* **side effect**, continuation, consequence, result, repercussion

follow through *v* **complete**, see through, bring to completion, bring to the end, finish off *Opposite*: drop

follow-up *n* **continuation**, addition, supplement, complement, development

folly *n* **irrationality**, foolishness, madness, stupidity, idiocy *Opposite*: prudence

foment *v* **foster**, stir up, stimulate, incite, generate *Opposite*: dampen

fond *adj* **loving**, tender, affectionate, caring, warm *Opposite*: uncaring

fondle *v* **massage**, touch, stroke, caress, pet

fondness *n* **liking**, affection, weakness, soft spot, partiality *Opposite*: dislike. *See* COMPARE AND CONTRAST *at* **love**.

fond of *adj* **devoted to**, taken with, attached to, keen on, partial to *Opposite*: indifferent

font *n* **1** (*literary*) **source**, supply, wellspring, fount, basis **2** (*literary*) **fountain**, spring, water source, well, source **3 typeface**, lettering, type style, type

food *n* **1 nourishment**, nutrition, nutriment, diet, sustenance **2 staple**, foodstuff, fare, provisions, groceries

foodie (*infml*) *n* **gourmet**, connoisseur, epicurean, bon vivant, bon viveur

food lover *see* **foodie**

foodstuff *n* **food**, staple, essential, ingredient, provisions

fool *n* **dolt** (*infml*), dope (*infml*), boob (*infml*), sucker (*infml*), mug (*slang*) ■ *v* **mislead**, trick, deceive, take in, con

fool about *v* **1 clown**, act the fool, play around, fool around, horse around **2 tamper**, meddle, fiddle, mess around (*infml*), fiddle around (*infml*)

fool around *v* **1 clown**, act the fool, play around, fool about, horse around **2 idle**, fiddle about, potter, muck about (*infml*), mess about (*infml*)

foolhardiness *n* **recklessness**, imprudence, stupidity, idiocy, foolishness *Opposite*: prudence

foolhardy *adj* **reckless**, rash, imprudent, foolish, unwise *Opposite*: sensible

foolish *adj* **1 stupid**, silly, unwise, imprudent, thoughtless *Opposite*: wise **2 ridiculous**, laughable, silly, ludicrous, absurd

foolishness *n* **irrationality**, stupidity, idiocy, silliness, imprudence *Opposite*: wisdom

foolproof *adj* **secure**, safe, infallible, fail-safe, perfect *Opposite*: risky

foot n base, bottom, end Opposite: top

footage n film, shots, tape, videotape, material

football n matter, point, problem, issue, hot potato

footer n addendum, title, footnote, note, text Opposite: header

footfall n footstep, step, tread, sound

foothill n hill, slope, base, foot, bottom Opposite: summit

foothold n position, base, purchase, grip, toehold

footing n 1 stability, equilibrium, purchase, foothold, grip 2 basis, position, foundation, base, support

footle (infml) v 1 fool around, idle, dawdle, potter, fiddle around (infml) 2 chatter, prattle, blabber, blather (infml), blab (infml) ■ n rubbish, nonsense, prattle, balderdash, bunkum (infml)

footlights n acting, the stage, the theatre, the limelight

footling (infml) adj trivial, unimportant, insignificant, trifling, inconsequential Opposite: important

footloose adj free, unattached, uncommitted, unrestricted, single

footnote n note, annotation, cross-reference, appendix, addendum

footpath n path, trail, track, pathway, walkway

footprint n footmark, footstep, print, imprint, impression

footrest n rail, bar, stool, footstool, foot rail

footsore adj tired, weary, exhausted, aching, sore

footstep n footfall, sound, step, tread, pace

footstool n footrest, stool, support, ottoman

footway see footpath

footwork n manoeuvring, cunning, skill, negotiation, horse-trading

fop n peacock, narcissus, poseur, poser (infml), dandy (dated)

foppish adj vain, affected, preening, narcissistic, self-obsessed

for prep 1 aimed at, intended for, designed for, meant for, used for 2 in favour of, in support of, pro Opposite: against

forage n 1 food, feed, fodder, silage 2 quest, search for, hunt, exploration, foray ■ v look for, search, seek, scavenge, rummage

for all prep despite, in spite of, even with, notwithstanding (fml)

foray n raid, incursion, venture, sortie, expedition

forbear (fml) v refrain, restrain yourself, abstain, hold back, withhold

forbearance (fml) n patience, self-control, restraint, tolerance, moderation Opposite: impatience

forbearing (fml) adj patient, long-suffering, forgiving, tolerant, lenient Opposite: impatient

forbid v prohibit, ban, bar, prevent, outlaw Opposite: allow

forbidden adj prohibited, banned, outlawed, illegal, illicit Opposite: permissible

forbidding adj 1 hostile, unfriendly, stern, harsh, unsympathetic Opposite: approachable 2 uninviting, unpleasant, dismal, depressing, bleak Opposite: welcoming 3 threatening, ominous, menacing, sinister, dangerous

force n 1 power, strength, energy, might, vigour Opposite: weakness 2 influence, weight, power, strength, intensity ■ v 1 compel, oblige, make, impose, coerce 2 push, shove, break down, break open, prise

forced adj 1 strained, unnatural, affected, put on, artificial Opposite: natural 2 involuntary, compulsory, required, obligatory, enforced Opposite: voluntary

force-feed v 1 feed up, fatten, fatten up, feed, nourish 2 teach, brainwash, programme, ram down somebody's throat, cram

forceful adj 1 powerful, vigorous, strong, dynamic, potent Opposite: weak 2 persuasive, convincing, compelling, valid, powerful Opposite: unconvincing

forcefulness n 1 strength, power, vigour, dynamism, influence Opposite: weakness 2 persuasiveness, validity, cogency, powerfulness, power

force out v drive out, expel, turn out, oust, evict

forces n armed forces, military, services, defence force

forcible adj 1 compulsory, violent, aggressive, armed Opposite: peaceful 2 effective, forceful, powerful, convincing, persuasive Opposite: weak

ford n shallows, crossing, passage, stepping stone ■ v cross, traverse, negotiate, cross over, wade

forearm v prepare, forewarn, prime, alert, tip off (infml)

forebear n ancestor, forerunner, antecedent, predecessor, grandparent Opposite: descendant

foreboding n premonition, presentiment, feeling, fear, intuition ■ adj ominous, menacing, threatening, sinister, forbidding Opposite: encouraging

forecast v predict, estimate, calculate, project, anticipate ■ n prediction, estimate, guess, calculation, conjecture

forecaster n forward planner, interpreter, analyst, prophet

foreclose (fml) v exclude, shut out, close out, ban, exile

forecourt n space, area, courtyard, concourse, square

forefront n 1 **front**, head, vanguard, lead, van *Opposite*: back 2 **foreground**, forepart, front, frontage, face *Opposite*: background

forego v 1 *(fml)* precede, come first, go before, herald, pave the way

foregoing adj **previous**, prior, preceding, earlier, former

foregone adj **inevitable**, predetermined, inescapable, unavoidable, fated *Opposite*: uncertain

foreground n **forefront**, front, centre, centre stage, focus *Opposite*: background

foreign adj 1 **alien**, external, extraneous, imported, overseas *Opposite*: indigenous 2 **strange**, unfamiliar, unknown, alien, exotic *Opposite*: familiar 3 **unrelated**, extraneous, irrelevant, external, unconnected *Opposite*: relevant

foreigner n **stranger**, foreign person, alien, immigrant, newcomer *Opposite*: national

foreknowledge n **premonition**, prescience, feeling, foresight, intuition *Opposite*: hindsight

foreleg n **front leg**, forelimb, limb, leg, appendage

foremost adj **chief**, leading, primary, prime, notable

forename n **first name**, given name, Christian name, nickname, pet name *Opposite*: surname

forerunner n 1 **portent**, indication, omen, sign, harbinger 2 **forebear**, ancestor, antecedent, precursor, predecessor

foresee v **expect**, foretell, prophesy, divine, predict *Opposite*: look back

foreseeable adj 1 **predictable**, probable, likely, imaginable, conceivable *Opposite*: unforeseeable 2 **near**, immediate, imminent, prospective, impending *Opposite*: far-off

foreshadow v **presage**, indicate, suggest, warn of, augur

foreshore n **shore**, beach, mudflat, sand, shingle

foresight n 1 **forethought**, prudence, far-sightedness, anticipation, sagacity *Opposite*: hindsight 2 **premonition**, insight, prescience, intuition, foreknowledge *Opposite*: hindsight

forest n **woods**, woodland, forestry, plantation, jungle

forestall v **prevent**, avert, obviate, hinder, thwart

foretaste n **sample**, token, indication, example, taste *Opposite*: recollection

foretell *(literary)* v **predict**, prophesy, presage, portend, forecast *Opposite*: review

forethought n **anticipation**, consideration, foresight, prudence, planning *Opposite*: afterthought

forever adv 1 **eternally**, for all time, in perpetuity, indefinitely, ad infinitum *Opposite*:

momentarily 2 *(infml)* **incessantly**, persistently, repeatedly, continually, endlessly *Opposite*: never

forewarn v **warn**, caution, alert, prime, forearm

forewarning n **warning**, notice, notification, word of warning, signal

foreword n **preface**, introduction, prelude, preamble, prologue *Opposite*: conclusion

forfeit n **penalty**, forfeiture, loss, penalization, punishment ■ v 1 **lose**, pay for, be deprived of, pay with, be stripped of 2 **surrender**, sacrifice, give up, part with, go without

forfeiture n **penalty**, forfeit, loss, penalization, punishment

forge n **furnace**, hearth, oven ■ v 1 **shape**, form, build, create, fashion 2 **counterfeit**, fake, falsify, copy, imitate

forge ahead v **take the lead**, come to the fore, make progress, make headway, move forward *Opposite*: lag

forged adj **fake**, counterfeit, false, spurious, phoney *Opposite*: genuine

forger n **counterfeiter**, falsifier, faker, coiner, imitator

forgery n **fake**, counterfeit, sham, phoney, imitation *Opposite*: original

forget v 1 **overlook**, disremember, fail to recall, be unable to remember, be unable to call to mind *Opposite*: remember 2 **stop thinking about**, put out of your mind, disregard, put behind you, turn your back on *Opposite*: attend to. *See* COMPARE AND CONTRAST *at* **neglect**.

forgetful adj 1 **absent-minded**, inclined to forget, vague, absent, oblivious *Opposite*: mindful 2 **inattentive**, neglectful, negligent, wandering, careless *Opposite*: attentive

forgetfulness n **absent-mindedness**, amnesia, obliviousness, insensibleness, vagueness

forgettable adj **unmemorable**, unremarkable, undistinguished, mediocre, ordinary *Opposite*: unforgettable

forgivable adj **pardonable**, excusable, allowable, defensible, justifiable *Opposite*: unforgivable

forgive v **pardon**, excuse, forgive and forget, let off, absolve *Opposite*: blame

forgiveness n 1 **pardon**, absolution, amnesty, exoneration, reconciliation *Opposite*: blame 2 **clemency**, pity, mercy, compassion, understanding *Opposite*: ruthlessness

forgiving adj **merciful**, lenient, magnanimous, sympathetic, compassionate *Opposite*: unforgiving

forgo v **do without**, sacrifice, pass by, waive, relinquish *Opposite*: take up

forgotten adj **lost**, gone, neglected, disregarded, buried *Opposite*: immortal

fork n **divide**, split, divergence, junction, branch

forked adj **split**, cleft, divided, branched, pronged *Opposite*: undivided

forlorn adj 1 **miserable**, sad, dejected, despondent, unhappy Opposite: cheerful 2 **desolate**, neglected, abandoned, lonely, lost Opposite: cherished

form n 1 **structure**, state, condition, nature, status 2 **type**, variety, kind, mode, manner 3 **document**, paper, questionnaire, pro forma, blank 4 **procedure**, method, system, arrangement, formula 5 **shape**, configuration, appearance, outline, look ■ v 1 **develop**, take shape, materialize, come into being, arise 2 **fashion**, shape, model, create, mould 3 **start**, found, create, bring into being, establish

formal adj 1 **official**, proper, prescribed, recognized, strict Opposite: informal 2 **conventional**, reserved, stiff, prim, starched Opposite: relaxed

formality n 1 **conventionalism**, reserve, stiffness, primness, correctness Opposite: informality 2 **procedure**, requirement, regulation, custom, ritual

formalization n **validation**, ratification, solemnization, reinforcement, celebration

formalize v **validate**, ratify, solemnize, reinforce, honour

format n **structure**, presentation, organization, arrangement, setup ■ v **arrange**, lay out, organize, configure, set up

formation n 1 **arrangement**, configuration, shape, structure, pattern 2 **creation**, development, construction, establishment, foundation

formative adj **influential**, determinative, seminal, decisive, developmental

formative years n **childhood**, early life, early years, early childhood, infancy Opposite: maturity

former adj **previous**, past, ex-, earlier, prior Opposite: current

formerly adv **previously**, before, in the past, once, earlier

formidable adj 1 **difficult**, tough, daunting, arduous, challenging Opposite: easy 2 **alarming**, frightening, dreadful, fearsome, redoubtable Opposite: encouraging 3 **awe-inspiring**, impressive, remarkable, astounding, awesome Opposite: uninspiring

formless adj **shapeless**, amorphous, unformed, unshaped, unstructured Opposite: distinct

formula n 1 **method**, plan, modus operandi, recipe, prescription 2 **cliché**, stock phrase, expression, phrase, formulation

formulaic adj 1 **prescribed**, standard, rigid, fixed, set 2 **unoriginal**, imitative, clichéd, overused, cookie-cutter Opposite: original

formulate v 1 **devise**, invent, prepare, put together, make 2 **express**, represent, present, frame, put into words

formulation n 1 **preparation**, design, construction, creation, invention 2 **representation**, guise, form, presentation, manifestation

forsake v 1 **abandon**, leave, disown, quit, desert Opposite: support 2 **renounce**, relinquish, give up, turn your back on, sacrifice

forsaken adj **abandoned**, cast off, discarded, deserted, jilted Opposite: supported

fort n **fortification**, fortress, stronghold, citadel, castle

forte n **strong point**, speciality, strong suit, gift, strength Opposite: failing

forth (fml) adv 1 **forwards**, ahead, onward Opposite: back 2 **out**, into view, into the open, into the world Opposite: back

forthcoming adj 1 **approaching**, impending, imminent, future, coming Opposite: distant 2 **available**, ready, offered, supplied, in the offing Opposite: unavailable 3 **helpful**, open, obliging, cooperative, informative Opposite: reticent

forthright adj **straightforward**, direct, frank, outspoken, plain-spoken Opposite: timid

forthrightness n **frankness**, candour, directness, candidness, outspokenness Opposite: timidity

forthwith adv **immediately**, without delay, at once, straightaway, right away Opposite: later

fortification n 1 **defences**, ramparts, buttresses, walls, earthworks 2 **strengthening**, defence, reinforcement, buttressing, building up Opposite: erosion

fortified adj 1 **defended**, protected, walled, garrisoned, secured Opposite: exposed 2 **reinforced**, strengthened, hardened, buttressed, toughened Opposite: unsupported 3 **encouraged**, heartened, invigorated, reinvigorated, stimulated Opposite: drained

fortify v 1 **defend**, protect, wall, garrison, secure Opposite: expose 2 **make stronger**, strengthen, reinforce, brace, support Opposite: weaken 3 **enrich**, boost, enhance, improve, mix Opposite: deplete 4 **give a boost to**, revive, refresh, reinvigorate, invigorate Opposite: drain 5 **build up**, boost, bolster, support, sustain Opposite: weaken

fortitude n **strength**, courage, resilience, staying power, grit Opposite: weakness

fortress n **stronghold**, fort, citadel, fortification, castle

fortuitous adj **accidental**, chance, casual, unexpected, unplanned Opposite: planned

fortunate adj 1 **privileged**, lucky, blessed, well-off, prosperous Opposite: unfortunate 2 **lucky**, providential, happy, opportune, auspicious Opposite: unfortunate. See COMPARE AND CONTRAST at lucky.

fortunately adv 1 **as luck would have it**, by chance, luckily, providentially, opportunely Opposite: unfortunately 2 **happily**, luckily, mercifully, thank goodness, thank heavens Opposite: unfortunately

fortune n 1 **wealth**, riches, affluence, opulence,

prosperity *Opposite*: poverty **2 packet** *(infml)*, bomb *(infml)*, mint *(infml)*, pile *(infml)*, tidy sum *(infml) Opposite*: pittance **3 luck**, chance, providence, accident, fate *Opposite*: design **4 destiny**, fate, kismet, karma, future *Opposite*: past

fortune-teller *n* clairvoyant, seer, soothsayer, psychic, medium

forty winks *(infml) n* **nap**, doze, sleep, siesta, catnap

forum *n* **1 opportunity**, medium, environment, setting, scene **2 meeting**, debate, discussion, round table, conference

forward *adj* **1 onward**, advancing, frontwards, headlong, headfirst *Opposite*: backward **2 presumptuous**, self-assured, bold, familiar, brazen *Opposite*: reticent ∎ *v* **1 send**, dispatch, post, send on, redirect **2 advance**, promote, further, progress, accelerate *Opposite*: hold back

forward-looking *adj* **progressive**, modern, forward-thinking, avant-garde, open-minded *Opposite*: backward-looking

forwardness *n* **boldness**, directness, brazenness, forthrightness, self-assurance *Opposite*: reticence

forwards *adv* **1 ahead**, frontwards, to the fore, up, onward *Opposite*: backwards **2 to the fore**, into view, into the open, up *Opposite*: backwards

forward-thinking *see* **forward-looking**

fossil *n* **relic**, remnant, vestige, remains

fossilization *n* **petrification**, preservation, calcification, hardening, solidification

fossilize *v* **turn into stone**, petrify, solidify, harden, calcify

foster *v* **1 look after**, take care of, care for, take in, bring up **2 promote**, further, advance, cultivate, forward *Opposite*: discourage ∎ *adj* **stand-in**, substitute, adoptive, temporary, short-term *Opposite*: natural

foster child *n* **child**, dependant, adoptee, ward, looked after child

foster parent *n* **guardian**, substitute parent, foster father, foster mother, carer

foul *adj* **1 unpleasant**, disgusting, offensive, distasteful, filthy *Opposite*: pleasant **2 vulgar**, obscene, lewd, uncouth, unwholesome *Opposite*: decent **3 inclement**, stormy, wet, unpleasant, rotten *Opposite*: fair **4 unclean**, stinking, polluted, tainted, soiled *Opposite*: clean **5 dishonest**, shady, criminal, treacherous, dishonourable *Opposite*: legitimate **6** *(infml)* **horrible**, rotten, unpleasant, nasty, dreadful *Opposite*: charming ∎ *v* **1 entangle**, tangle up, catch, ensnarl, snarl *Opposite*: free **2 pollute**, soil, make dirty, contaminate, taint

foul-mouthed *adj* **blasphemous**, crude, rude, dirty, vulgar *Opposite*: polite

foulness *n* **1 filth**, filthiness, squalor, pollution, dirt *Opposite*: cleanness **2 vulgarity**, obscenity, lewdness, profanity, uncouthness *Opposite*: decency

foul play *n* **1 deviousness**, unfairness, cheating, trickery, monkey business *(infml)* **2 criminal action**, treachery, dishonesty, villainy, violence *Opposite*: honesty

foul-smelling *adj* **smelly**, reeking, malodorous, fetid, rotten *Opposite*: sweet-smelling

foul-tasting *adj* **nasty**, disgusting, unpleasant, indigestible, revolting

foul-up *(infml) n* **blunder**, slip, mix-up, error, mistake *Opposite*: success

found *v* **originate**, set up, create, start, bring into being *Opposite*: close

foundation *n* **1 basis**, grounds, substance, groundwork, underpinning *Opposite*: superstructure **2 establishment**, institution, charity, institute, society

founder *n* **creator**, originator, initiator, organizer, forefather ∎ *v* **1 sink**, go down, plunge, wallow, submerge *Opposite*: float **2 fail**, break down, come to nothing, fall through, miscarry *Opposite*: succeed

foundling *(dated) n* **orphan**, waif, stray, urchin, outcast

fount *(literary) n* **source**, fountain, well, spring, wellspring

fountain *n* **1 cascade**, water feature, spout, jet, spring **2 source**, origin, cause, beginning, fountainhead

fountainhead *see* **fountain**

four-letter word *n* **swearword**, vulgarity, vulgarism, obscenity, expletive *Opposite*: euphemism

foursome *n* **group of four**, quartet, group, ensemble

fourth *n* **quarter**, twenty-five percent, fourth part

fox *v* **1 confuse**, baffle, muddle, puzzle, perplex *Opposite*: enlighten **2 deceive**, trick, outwit, fool, con

foxy *adj* **sly**, cunning, crafty, sharp, wily *Opposite*: naive

foyer *n* **lobby**, vestibule, reception area, hall, entrance hall

fracas *n* **quarrel**, row, fight, brawl, melee *Opposite*: calm

fraction *n* **1 part**, portion, segment, section, division *Opposite*: whole **2 little bit**, little, small part, tiny proportion, small percentage

fractional *adj* **slight**, small, tiny, minuscule, insignificant *Opposite*: great

fractionally *adv* **slightly**, marginally, just, a little, a fraction *Opposite*: greatly

fractious *adj* **irritable**, peevish, restless, complaining, grumpy *Opposite*: even-tempered

fracture *n* **break**, breakage, crack, rupture, fissure *Opposite*: repair ∎ *v* **crack**, break, rupture, splinter, split *Opposite*: mend

fragile adj 1 **delicate**, brittle, flimsy, breakable, frail Opposite: sturdy 2 **tenuous**, unstable, delicate, precarious, shaky Opposite: stable 3 **frail**, weak, delicate, infirm, feeble Opposite: strong

COMPARE AND CONTRAST CORE MEANING: easily broken or damaged
fragile not having a strong structure or not made of robust materials, and therefore easily broken or damaged; **delicate** similar to *fragile*, used especially of things that are beautiful or remarkable because of their fragility; **frail** easily broken or damaged, or physically weak and vulnerable to injury; **flimsy** too easily broken, torn, or damaged, especially used of badly or cheaply made goods, or of light and insubstantial clothing; **frangible** capable of being broken or easily damaged; **friable** easily reduced to tiny particles.

fragility n 1 **brittleness**, flimsiness, delicateness, delicacy, breakability Opposite: solidity 2 **tenuousness**, instability, delicacy, delicateness, precariousness Opposite: stability 3 **frailty**, weakness, feebleness, ill health, infirmity Opposite: strength

fragment n **piece**, portion, bit, splinter, sliver Opposite: whole ▪ v **break**, divide, break up, disintegrate, crumble Opposite: fuse

fragmentary adj **incomplete**, disconnected, bitty, scrappy, patchy Opposite: entire

fragmentation n **disintegration**, destruction, shattering, breaking up, crumbling Opposite: fusion

fragmented adj **disjointed**, uneven, scrappy, bitty, patchy Opposite: continuous

fragrance n 1 **smell**, scent, perfume, bouquet, aroma 2 **cologne**, scent, perfume, toilet water, eau de toilette. See COMPARE AND CONTRAST at smell.

fragranced adj **perfumed**, scented, sweet-smelling, fragrant

fragrant adj **perfumed**, aromatic, scented, sweet-smelling, fragranced Opposite: smelly

frail adj 1 **weak**, infirm, delicate, feeble, puny Opposite: robust 2 **flimsy**, insubstantial, fragile, delicate, spindly Opposite: sturdy. See COMPARE AND CONTRAST at fragile, weak.

frailness see frailty

frailty n 1 **infirmity**, weakness, feebleness, fragility, ill health Opposite: robustness 2 **shortcoming**, weakness, imperfection, failing, defect Opposite: strength

frame n 1 **structure**, framework, scaffold, skeleton, support 2 **edge**, surround, border, mount, setting 3 **body**, form, build, physique, skeleton ▪ v **enclose**, mount, border, edge, outline Opposite: inset

frame of mind n **mood**, mental state, mental condition, humour, temper

frame of reference n **context**, situation, standpoint, background, setting

framework n 1 **structure**, frame, scaffold,

skeleton, support 2 **outline**, agenda, basis, context, background

franchise n **permit**, licence, contract, authorization, charter ▪ v **license**, permit, contract, contract out, grant

frangible adj **breakable**, fragile, brittle, easily broken. See COMPARE AND CONTRAST at fragile.

frank adj **forthright**, free, honest, guileless, open Opposite: insincere

frankfurter n **hot dog**, sausage, wiener (US)

frankness n **honesty**, forthrightness, openness, bluntness, truthfulness Opposite: insincerity

frantic adj 1 **panicky**, hysterical, beside yourself, desperate, agitated Opposite: calm 2 **frenzied**, frenetic, hectic, feverish, wild Opposite: calm

fraternal adj 1 **sibling**, brotherly, brother's, familial, genealogical 2 **comradely**, brotherly, friendly, amicable, communal Opposite: hostile

fraternity n 1 **community**, network, group, world, clan (infml) 2 **brotherliness**, brotherhood, comradeship, mutual support, friendship Opposite: hostility

fraternization n **mixing**, socializing, intercourse, mingling, partying Opposite: avoidance

fraternize v **associate**, socialize, mix, hobnob, hang out (infml) Opposite: avoid

fraud n 1 **dishonesty**, deceit, deception, double-dealing, trickery Opposite: honesty 2 **impostor**, charlatan, hoaxer, swindler, cheat 3 **deception**, con, scheme, swindle, deceit

fraudster n **confidence trickster**, swindler, cheat, hoaxer, charlatan

fraudulence n **deceit**, duplicity, deceitfulness, illegitimacy, dishonesty Opposite: honesty

fraudulent adj **fake**, deceitful, untrue, duplicitous, dishonest Opposite: genuine

fraught adj 1 **full**, charged, filled, weighed down, laden Opposite: free 2 **tense**, anxious, nervous, troubled, apprehensive Opposite: calm

fray v **unravel**, ravel, wear, wear out, tatter Opposite: mend ▪ n **fight**, argument, quarrel, fracas, dispute

frayed adj **threadbare**, worn, tattered, ragged, unravelled

frazzled (infml) adj **exhausted**, weary, tired out, drained, fatigued Opposite: lively

freak n 1 **curiosity**, rarity, oddity, one-off, aberration 2 (infml) **enthusiast**, fanatic, fiend, buff, lover 3 **chance**, surprise, happenstance, accident, fluke (infml)

freakish adj **variable**, volatile, changeable, unpredictable, inexplicable Opposite: stable

freaky adj **weird**, strange, amazing, grotesque, unexpected Opposite: commonplace

freckle n **spot**, mark, patch, speckle, speck

freckled adj **speckled**, freckly, dappled, spotted, stippled

free *adj* **1 allowed**, at liberty, permitted, able, welcome *Opposite*: restricted **2 liberated**, unbound, released, emancipated, freed *Opposite*: imprisoned **3 unrestricted**, unregimented, unconventional, loose, unstructured *Opposite*: conventional **4 gratis**, free of charge, without charge, at no cost, complimentary **5 relaxing**, off, available, unoccupied, on holiday *Opposite*: working **6 open**, uninhibited, uncontrolled, spontaneous, honest *Opposite*: inhibited ■ *v* **1 release**, let go, set free, liberate, emancipate *Opposite*: imprison **2 exempt**, rid, unburden, excuse, pardon

free-and-easy *adj* **indulgent**, overindulgent, lax, overfamiliar, relaxed *Opposite*: uptight (*infml*)

freebie (*infml*) *n* **free sample**, handout, perk, free gift, free offer

freedom *n* **1 liberty**, autonomy, lack of restrictions, self-determination, independence *Opposite*: restriction **2 looseness**, inventiveness, nonconformity *Opposite*: conformity **3 frankness**, openness, abandon, free expression, candour *Opposite*: inhibition

free fall *n* **1 skydive**, jump, descent, drop, fall **2 decline**, descent, collapse, confusion, turmoil *Opposite*: upturn

free-fall *v* **1 skydive**, drop, plummet, fall, descend *Opposite*: soar **2 drop**, plummet, collapse, decline, fall apart

free-for-all (*infml*) *n* **brawl**, fight, brouhaha, riot, scuffle

free gift *n* **free sample**, free offer, giveaway (*infml*), freebie (*infml*)

freehand *adj* **without a pattern**, by eye, by hand, sketchy, free

freehanded *adj* **generous**, openhanded, unstinting, giving, liberal *Opposite*: stingy (*infml*)

freehold *n* **1 tenure**, ownership, right, occupancy **2 property**, estate, land, building, holding

freeholder *n* **property owner**, landowner, owner, holder, landlord

freeing *n* **release**, liberation, acquittal, emancipation, freedom *Opposite*: capture

freelance *adj* **self-employed**, temporary, irregular, casual, ad hoc *Opposite*: permanent

freeload (*infml*) *v* **live off others**, parasitize, take advantage, use others, sponge (*infml*)

freeloader (*infml*) *n* **slacker**, parasite, idler, hanger-on, user

freely *adv* **1 without restrictions**, at will, at liberty, easily, spontaneously **2 liberally**, generously, unreservedly, without restraint, without stinting *Opposite*: parsimoniously

free-range *adj* **unconfined**, free, loose, at large, uncaged *Opposite*: battery

free spirit *n* **individualist**, nonconformist, maverick, freethinker, rebel *Opposite*: conformist

freestanding *adj* **self-supporting**, unconnected, separate, detached, unattached *Opposite*: attached

freethinker *n* **individualist**, free spirit, nonconformist, nonbeliever, sceptic *Opposite*: conformist

freethinking *adj* **independent**, open-minded, enlightened, nonconformist, liberal *Opposite*: conformist

free time *n* **leisure**, leisure time, spare time, time off, recreation

free up *v* **1 make available**, empty, make space for, clear, liberate *Opposite*: occupy **2** (*infml*) **loosen**, unjam, unblock, unsnarl, unclog *Opposite*: snarl

freewheel *v* **1 coast**, sail, glide, cruise, roll along **2 take it easy**, drift, go with the flow, cruise *Opposite*: struggle

free will *n* **autonomy**, self-determination, choice, liberty, freedom *Opposite*: dependence

freeze *v* **1 turn to ice**, freeze up, ice up, ice over, solidify *Opposite*: thaw **2 refrigerate**, chill, cool, preserve *Opposite*: thaw **3 halt**, stop, stop in your tracks, stop dead, stiffen *Opposite*: relax **4 suspend**, stop, halt, hold, break off *Opposite*: resume **5 hold**, fix, restrict, stop, control ■ *n* **restriction**, halt, embargo, check, stoppage *Opposite*: resumption

freeze out (*infml*) *v* **exclude**, ostracize, ignore, shun, reject *Opposite*: welcome

freeze up *v* **ice over**, ice up, harden, solidify, freeze *Opposite*: thaw

freezing *adj* **cold**, subzero, icy, chilly, bitter *Opposite*: hot

freight *n* **1 cargo**, goods, merchandise, consignment, load **2 carriage**, shipping, conveyance, transport, transportation

frenetic *adj* **hectic**, bustling, busy, frantic, feverish *Opposite*: calm

frenzied *adj* **frantic**, hyperactive, hysterical, feverish, emotional *Opposite*: calm

frenzy *n* **1 fury**, turmoil, fever, rage, passion *Opposite*: calmness **2 whirl**, fit, tumult, rush, flurry

frequency *n* **incidence**, occurrence, regularity, rate of recurrence, rate

frequent *adj* **recurrent**, common, everyday, normal, numerous *Opposite*: infrequent ■ *v* **visit**, haunt, patronize, hang around, spend time at *Opposite*: avoid

fresco *n* **wall painting**, mural, frieze, wall, painting

fresh *adj* **1 at its best**, garden-fresh, crisp, moist, juicy *Opposite*: stale **2 new**, renewed, additional, replacement, other *Opposite*: old **3 clean**, bright, unmarked, unsullied, immaculate *Opposite*: soiled **4 wholesome**, crisp, pleasant, airy, refreshing *Opposite*:

musty **5 novel**, original, new, inventive, innovative *Opposite*: hackneyed **6 alert**, energetic, lively, vigorous, active *Opposite*: tired. *See* COMPARE AND CONTRAST *at* **new**.

freshen *v* **tidy**, neaten, dust, clean, air

freshen up *v* **wash**, shower, change, clean up, powder your nose *(infml)*

fresher *(infml) n* **first-year student**, first year, undergraduate, student, novice *Opposite*: finalist

fresh-faced *adj* **youthful**, young-looking, baby-faced, boyish, girlish

freshly *adv* **newly**, recently, just now, a moment ago, just this minute

freshness *n* **1 crispness**, juiciness, flavour, moistness *Opposite*: staleness **2 cleanness**, cleanliness, brightness, sparkle, brilliance *Opposite*: grubbiness **3 novelty**, originality, newness, inventiveness, innovation *Opposite*: tiredness

fret *v* **worry**, fuss, agonize, vex, trouble *Opposite*: calm down

fretful *adj* **worried**, restless, agitated, unsettled, distressed *Opposite*: calm

fretfulness *n* **anxiety**, restlessness, agitation, distress, unease *Opposite*: calmness

friable *adj* **crumbly**, powdery, workable, light *Opposite*: heavy. *See* COMPARE AND CONTRAST *at* **fragile**.

friary *n* **religious community**, monastery, religious foundation, fraternity, brotherhood

friction *n* **1 rubbing**, abrasion, contact, chafing, rasping **2 hostility**, conflict, tension, antagonism, disagreement *Opposite*: accord

friend *n* **1 comrade**, companion, mate, pal *(infml)*, chum *(infml) Opposite*: foe *(fml)* **2 acquaintance**, contact, colleague, associate, partner *Opposite*: stranger **3 ally**, helper, supporter, well-wisher, collaborator *Opposite*: rival

friendliness *n* **affability**, sociability, conviviality, amiability, approachability *Opposite*: reserve

friendly *adj* **1 affable**, sociable, approachable, outgoing, open *Opposite*: unfriendly **2 close**, familiar, intimate, congenial, amicable *Opposite*: frosty **3 beneficial**, helpful, favourable, welcoming, supportive *Opposite*: hostile

friendship *n* **1 bond**, relationship, alliance, attachment, acquaintance **2 companionship**, comradeship, camaraderie, closeness, familiarity *Opposite*: animosity

frieze *n* **decoration**, band, strip, panel, mural

fright *n* **1 fear**, terror, anxiety, foreboding, dread *Opposite*: composure **2 scare**, shock, start, turn, seizure

frighten *v* **scare**, terrify, alarm, startle, upset *Opposite*: soothe

frightened *adj* **scared**, afraid, terrified, alarmed, startled *Opposite*: calm

frightening *adj* **terrifying**, alarming, startling, fearsome, fearful *Opposite*: soothing

frightful *adj* **appalling**, horrible, unpleasant, dreadful, awful *Opposite*: pleasant

frightfully *adv* **terribly**, extremely, awfully, dreadfully, excessively

frightfulness *n* **awfulness**, atrociousness, severity, badness, hideousness *Opposite*: pleasantness

frigid *adj* **1 unfriendly**, standoffish, cold, distant, frosty *Opposite*: warm **2 cold**, frosty, chilly, icy, freezing *Opposite*: torrid

frigidity *n* **coldness**, frostiness, iciness, cold-heartedness, aloofness *Opposite*: warmth

frigidly *adv* **coldly**, icily, frostily, unemotionally, unfeelingly *Opposite*: warmly

frill *n* **1 decoration**, flounce, trimming, ruffle, ruche **2 extra**, add-on, luxury, decoration, accompaniment

frills *n* **accompaniments**, trappings, added extras, embellishments, add-ons *Opposite*: essentials

frilly *adj* **lacy**, ruched, gathered, pleated, fancy *Opposite*: plain

fringe *n* **1 tassel**, edging, edge, border, trimming **2 periphery**, edge, extreme, perimeter, border *Opposite*: centre ■ *adj* **1 peripheral**, outlying, marginal, far-flung, frontier *Opposite*: central **2 unconventional**, extreme, radical, marginal, extremist *Opposite*: mainstream

fringe benefit *n* **extra**, compensation, perk, privilege, reward

frisk *v* **1 play**, frolic, gambol, cavort, kick up your heels *Opposite*: plod **2 search**, pat down, body search, examine, inspect

friskiness *n* **playfulness**, excitability, excitement, liveliness, enthusiasm *Opposite*: lethargy

frisky *adj* **playful**, frolicsome, excitable, excited, lighthearted *Opposite*: lethargic

fritter away *v* **dissipate**, waste, squander, misspend, gamble away *Opposite*: conserve

frivolity *n* **1 playfulness**, perkiness, light-heartedness, merriment, gaiety *Opposite*: seriousness **2 triviality**, frivolousness, unimportance, inconsequentiality, superficiality *Opposite*: seriousness

frivolous *adj* **1 trivial**, silly, inconsequential, idle, shallow *Opposite*: serious **2 playful**, frolicsome, perky, lighthearted, silly *Opposite*: serious

frizz *v* **curl**, crimp, frizzle, perm, kink *Opposite*: straighten

frizzle *v* **1 burn**, shrivel, scorch, sear, dry up **2 frizz**, curl, perm, crimp, kink *Opposite*: straighten **3 sizzle**, fry, pan-fry, sauté, grill

frizzy *adj* **curled**, wiry, curly, kinky, frizzed *Opposite*: straight

frogmarch *v* **propel**, march, accompany, take, carry

frogspawn n eggs, spawn, tadpoles

frolic v play, skip, cavort, frisk, gambol Opposite: plod

frolicsome adj playful, frisky, frivolous, light-hearted, spirited Opposite: solemn

frond n leaf, branch, palm leaf, fern leaf

front n 1 façade, face, frontage, obverse, head Opposite: back 2 impertinence, cockiness, nerve, gall, temerity

frontage n front, façade, face, outlook, front part Opposite: rear

frontal adj forward, anterior, front, fore (literary) Opposite: posterior (fml)

front door n main entrance, main door, door, entrance, entry Opposite: back door

frontier n border, boundary, limit, edge, border line

frontispiece n illustration, print, picture, photograph, drawing

front line n 1 front, war zone, battle zone, combat zone, ground zero 2 forefront, cutting edge, leading edge, sharp end, vanguard

front-page adj headline, important, significant, momentous, attention-grabbing

frontrunner (infml) n leader, head, favourite, prime candidate, number one (infml) Opposite: also-ran

frontwards adv ahead, to the fore, forwards Opposite: backwards

frost n 1 ice, rime, hoar frost 2 cold, frostiness, iciness, coolness, frigidity Opposite: warmth

frosted adj ice-covered, frosty, iced, icy, snowy Opposite: thawed

frostily adv coldly, icily, coolly, frigidly, angrily Opposite: warmly

frostiness n 1 iciness, coldness, cold, chill, rawness Opposite: warmth 2 coldness, aloofness, frigidity, coolness, iciness Opposite: warmth

frosting n 1 icing, cake coating, decoration, royal icing, topping 2 dullness, opaqueness, opacity, matte finish, matte surface

frosty adj 1 icy, cold, chilly, freezing, frigid Opposite: warm 2 cold, unfriendly, cool, icy, frigid Opposite: friendly

froth n 1 foam, bubbles, lather, head, fizz 2 triviality, trivia, frivolity, superficiality, shallowness Opposite: substance ■ v to become foamy, foam, bubble, lather, lather up

frothiness n 1 foaminess, bubbliness, fizziness, fizz, soapiness 2 triviality, insubstantiality, lightness, frivolity, pettiness Opposite: seriousness

frothy adj 1 foamy, foam-covered, lathered, lathered up, bubbly 2 light, inconsequential, superficial, trivial, shallow Opposite: serious

frown v knit your brow, scowl, glare, glower, lower Opposite: smile ■ n scowl, glare, glower, grimace, puckered brow Opposite: smile

frown on v disapprove, take a dim view of, frown upon, condemn, dislike Opposite: favour. See COMPARE AND CONTRAST at disapprove.

frown upon see frown on

frowzy adj unkempt, dishevelled, frayed, messy, shabby Opposite: neat

frozen adj 1 ice-covered, cold, solid, freezing, iced up 2 immobile, stationary, unmoving, still, motionless Opposite: mobile

frugal adj thrifty, prudent, economical, sparing, penny-wise Opposite: profligate

frugality n thrift, stinginess, parsimony, prudence, economy Opposite: profligacy

fruit n 1 ovary, berry, pod, capsule, achene 2 produce, bounty, harvest, crop, yield 3 product, result, consequence, reward, fruition ■ v produce fruit, bear fruit, ripen, mature

WORD BANK

❑ **types of fruit** apple, apricot, avocado, banana, blackcurrant, cherry, citrus, damson, date, fig, grape, guava, kiwi fruit, kumquat, lychee, mango, melon, nectarine, olive, papaya, passion fruit, peach, pear, pineapple, plum, pomegranate, quince, raspberry, redcurrant, strawberry, watermelon

❑ **parts of a fruit** flesh, juice, kernel, peel, pip, pith, pulp, rind, seed, skin, stone

fruitful adj productive, fertile, rich, prolific, abundant Opposite: fruitless

fruitfulness n productivity, abundance, profitability, prosperity, fertility Opposite: fruitlessness

fruition n completion, maturity, readiness, realization, culmination

fruitless adj unsuccessful, futile, useless, unproductive, wasted Opposite: fruitful

fruitlessness n uselessness, futility, unproductiveness, failure, inadequacy Opposite: fruitfulness

fruity adj 1 rich, sweet, tangy, zesty, lemony 2 mellow, deep, rich, plummy, harmonious Opposite: shrill

frustrate v 1 thwart, prevent, foil, stop, block Opposite: promote 2 discourage, exasperate, irritate, upset, disturb Opposite: encourage

frustrated adj 1 unfulfilled, unsatisfied, irritated, upset, angry Opposite: satisfied 2 foiled, blocked, stymied, obstructed, hindered Opposite: successful

frustrating adj annoying, unsatisfying, exasperating, infuriating, maddening Opposite: satisfying

frustration n 1 prevention, hindrance, blocking, foiling, defeat Opposite: success 2 dissatisfaction, irritation, disturbance, annoyance, nuisance Opposite: satisfaction

fry v cook, sauté, stir-fry, fry up, deep-fry

frying pan n pan, skillet, omelette pan

fuddle v **confuse**, bewilder, stupefy, muddle, dull *Opposite*: clarify ■ n **muddle**, dither, mess, state *(infml)*

fuddy-duddy *(infml)* n **fogy**, reactionary, stick-in-the-mud *(infml)*, stuffed shirt *(infml)*

fudge *(infml)* n **nonsense**, rubbish, garbage, verbiage, waffle *(infml)* ■ v 1 **falsify**, alter, massage, doctor, fiddle *(infml)* 2 **prevaricate**, evade the issue, stall, beat about the bush, waffle *(infml)*

fuel n **energy source**, fossil fuel, alternative fuel, renewable fuel ■ v 1 **power**, fire, run, drive, operate 2 **stimulate**, increase, promote, fire, energize *Opposite*: quell

fug n **fog**, smog, haze, smoke, miasma

fuggy *adj* **stuffy**, stale, airless, suffocating, foggy *Opposite*: bracing

fugitive n **escapee**, deserter, absconder, outlaw, runaway ■ *adj* **brief**, fleeting, elusive, short, quick

fugue n **fugue state**, blackout, amnesia, memory loss

fulcrum n **pivot**, hinge, swivel, support, point

fulfil v 1 **achieve**, bear out, live up to, satisfy, justify 2 **carry out**, execute, follow, obey, complete *Opposite*: neglect 3 **satisfy**, meet, conform to, be in conformity with, accord with *Opposite*: fall short 4 **complete**, finish, go through with, get through, make it through *Opposite*: abandon 5 **supply**, fill, deliver, provide, furnish *(fml)* *Opposite*: renege 6 **succeed**, do proud, gain fulfilment, make good, fulfil your potential *Opposite*: fail. *See* COMPARE AND CONTRAST *at* perform.

fulfilled *adj* **satisfied**, content, happy, pleased, rewarded *Opposite*: frustrated

fulfilling *adj* **satisfying**, rewarding, pleasing, gratifying, enjoyable *Opposite*: frustrating

fulfilment n 1 **achievement**, realization, execution, completion, accomplishment *Opposite*: neglect 2 **contentment**, serenity, inner peace, self-actualization, nirvana *Opposite*: dissatisfaction

full *adj* 1 **occupied**, complete, bursting, packed, filled *Opposite*: empty 2 **complete**, broad, extensive, comprehensive, detailed *Opposite*: sketchy 3 **sonorous**, resonant, rich, deep, plummy *Opposite*: shrill 4 **satiated**, satisfied, bursting, sated, replete *Opposite*: hungry 5 **plump**, round, chubby, ample, broad *Opposite*: thin

full-blooded *adj* **vigorous**, hearty, thoroughgoing, forceful, robust *Opposite*: feeble

full-blown *adj* **complete**, full, full-scale, full-size, developed *Opposite*: incomplete

full-bodied *adj* **flavourful**, rich, intense, powerful, strong *Opposite*: insipid

full dress n **formal attire**, dress uniform, jacket and tie, evening dress, black tie

full-frontal *(infml)* *adj* **all-out**, unrestrained, wholehearted, uninhibited, concerted *Opposite*: half-hearted

full-length *adj* 1 **ankle-length**, floor-length, long *Opposite*: short 2 **head-to-toe**, whole-body, full, long, tall 3 **unabridged**, complete, uncut, unedited, unexpurgated *Opposite*: abridged

fullness n 1 **completeness**, richness, abundance *Opposite*: emptiness 2 **roundness**, plumpness, chubbiness, ampleness, pudginess *(infml)* *Opposite*: thinness

full of *adj* **alive with**, awash with, thick with, resplendent with, crammed with *Opposite*: lacking in

full-scale *adj* 1 **life-size**, full-size, complete, full 2 **total**, full-blown, unrestrained, all-out, unlimited *Opposite*: partial

full-size *adj* **normal**, standard, regular, ordinary

full-time *adj* **around-the-clock**, permanent, twenty-four-hour, day and night, 24/7 *Opposite*: part-time

full-timer n **full-time employee**, full-time worker, full-time member of staff *Opposite*: part-timer

fully *adv* **completely**, entirely, wholly, totally, altogether *Opposite*: partially

fully-fledged *adj* 1 **complete**, mature, well-developed, independent, self-sufficient 2 **qualified**, out-and-out, full, genuine, actual

fully-grown *adj* **mature**, adult, full-sized, full, well-developed *Opposite*: immature

fulminate v **rail**, rant and rave, rage, rant, thunder *Opposite*: praise

fulsome *adj* **flattering**, excessive, immoderate, effusive, overgenerous

fumble v 1 **grope**, scrabble, rummage, root, search 2 **mishandle**, botch up, blunder, muddle, muddle up ■ n **mistake**, error, blunder, botched job, mess

fume v **seethe**, rage, bristle, be angry, be furious ■ n 1 **emission**, vapour, miasma, smog, smoke 2 **stench**, smell, stink, reek, odour

fumigate v **sterilize**, disinfect, decontaminate, delouse, smoke

fumigation n **disinfection**, decontamination, smoking, delousing, cleansing

fuming *adj* **furious**, irate, incensed, enraged, seething

fun n **amusement**, excitement, enjoyment, entertainment, merriment *Opposite*: boredom ■ *adj* *(infml)* **amusing**, entertaining, enjoyable, exciting, pleasurable *Opposite*: boring

function n 1 **purpose**, meaning, role, job, occupation 2 **event**, gathering, meeting, affair, party ■ v **work**, perform, operate, run, go *Opposite*: malfunction

functional *adj* 1 **practical**, useful, handy, purposeful, efficient *Opposite*: useless 2 **operational**, operative, running, going, working *Opposite*: inoperative

functionary n **official**, representative, bureaucrat, lackey, employee

fund n 1 **supply**, stock, store, source, collection 2 **reserve**, account, supply, endowment, stock ■ v **finance**, support, back, sponsor, subsidize

fundamental adj 1 **basic**, primary, original, essential, elementary Opposite: secondary 2 **central**, essential, vital, ultimate, major Opposite: superfluous

fundamentally adv **at heart**, at bottom, basically, essentially, primarily Opposite: superficially

fundamentals n **basics**, rudiments, essentials, ground rules, brass tacks

funding n **backing**, support, finance, subsidy, money

fundraiser n 1 **campaigner**, crusader, supporter, representative, moneymaker 2 **appeal**, campaign, crusade, push, drive

funeral n **service**, memorial, interment, burial, cremation

funereal adj **gloomy**, melancholy, sorrowful, mournful, sad Opposite: cheerful

funfair n **fair**, fairground, theme park, amusement park, carnival (US)

fungal adj **fungiform**, mycological, fungoid, fungous

funky (infml) adj **up-to-date**, fashionable, unconventional, trendy (infml), cool (infml)

fun-loving adj **playful**, joyful, high-spirited, frivolous, exuberant Opposite: staid

funnel n **chimney**, pipe, flue, smokestack, conduit ■ v **channel**, direct, focus, guide, concentrate

funnily adv 1 **strangely**, curiously, surprisingly, oddly, unusually 2 **comically**, humorously, amusingly, hilariously, wittily

funniness n **humour**, comedy, comicalness, wit, wittiness Opposite: solemnity

funny adj 1 **amusing**, humorous, comic, comical, hilarious Opposite: serious 2 **strange**, odd, weird, curious, peculiar Opposite: normal 3 **quaint**, unconventional, eccentric, quirky, odd 4 **unwell**, sick, nauseous, off-colour, poorly (infml) Opposite: well ■ n (infml) **joke**, pun, witticism, bon mot, gag (infml)

COMPARE AND CONTRAST CORE MEANING: causing or intended to cause amusement
funny causing amusement or laughter, whether intentionally or not; **comic** used in the same way as *funny*, especially to describe books, poems, or plays; **comical** funny to the extent of being absurd, especially if this is unintentional; **droll** funny because it is whimsical or odd, or drily humorous; **facetious** supposed to be funny but ill-timed, inappropriate, or silly; **humorous** intended to make people laugh; **witty** using words in a clever, inventive, humorous way; **hilarious** extremely funny; **sidesplitting** very funny indeed, especially causing a great deal of uncontrollable laughter.

fur n **hair**, pelt, fleece, coat, fuzz

furious adj 1 **angry**, livid, fuming, irate, infuriated Opposite: calm 2 **energetic**, concerted, all-out, breakneck, violent

furiousness n 1 **anger**, rage, fury, wrath, crossness 2 **violence**, energy, vigour, ferocity, passion

furl v **roll up**, wrap up, curl, curl up, tie up Opposite: unfurl

furlough n **leave of absence**, leave, absence, holiday, R and R

furnace n **heater**, oven, kiln, boiler, blast furnace

furnish (fml) v **supply**, provide, equip, give, deliver Opposite: strip

furnished adj **equipped**, fitted out, well-appointed, well-found Opposite: unfurnished

furnishings n **furniture**, fittings, tables, chairs, cabinets

furniture n **fittings**, tables, chairs, cabinets, beds

furore n 1 **uproar**, outcry, commotion, controversy, protest 2 **excitement**, hysteria, hype, frenzy, ballyhoo

furred see furry

furriness n **hairiness**, fuzziness, woolliness, fleeciness, fluffiness Opposite: baldness

furrow n **channel**, groove, rut, undulation, gully ■ v **wrinkle**, crease, gather, draw, contract

furrowed adj **wrinkled**, crumply, creasy, wrinkly, crinkly Opposite: smooth

furry adj **hairy**, fuzzy, woolly, downy, furred

further adj **additional**, more, extra, added, supplementary ■ v **advance**, promote, foster, broaden, expand Opposite: prevent

furthermore adv **also**, in addition, besides, additionally, moreover

furthermost adj **farthest**, furthest, greatest, remotest, nethermost (fml)

furthest adj **farthest**, utmost, uttermost, outermost, furthermost

furtive adj **secretive**, stealthy, secret, sly, sneaky Opposite: open. See COMPARE AND CONTRAST at **secret**.

furtiveness n 1 **secrecy**, stealth, covertness, surreptitiousness, discreetness Opposite: openness 2 **sneakiness**, suspiciousness, guiltiness, slyness, craftiness Opposite: straightforwardness

fury n **anger**, rage, wrath, ferocity, ire (fml). See COMPARE AND CONTRAST at **anger**.

fuse v **combine**, blend, mingle, meld, coalesce Opposite: fragment

fusion n **synthesis**, union, combination, mixture, blend Opposite: fission

fuss n 1 **commotion**, excitement, bother, bustle, activity 2 **worry**, concern, bother, trouble, hassle (infml) 3 **protest**, controversy, argument, complaint, reaction ■ *v* **worry**, fret, stew, bother, niggle

fussiness *n* 1 **trivialness**, pedantry, obsessiveness, prissiness, hairsplitting 2 **meticulousness**, dogmatism, inflexibility, fastidiousness, exactness 3 **elaborateness**, frilliness, ornateness, overstatement

fusspot (*infml*) *n* **worrier**, neurotic, worryguts (*infml*)

fussy *adj* 1 **trivial**, pedantic, obsessive, prissy, assiduous 2 **picky**, particular, finicky, fastidious, selective *Opposite*: laid-back (*infml*) 3 **elaborate**, busy, frilly, ornate, overelaborate. *See* COMPARE AND CONTRAST *at* **careful**.

fusty *adj* 1 **stale**, mouldy, damp, fetid, musty *Opposite*: fresh 2 **stuffy**, antiquated, dull, boring, old-fashioned *Opposite*: trendy (*infml*)

futile *adj* **useless**, pointless, fruitless, unsuccessful, vain *Opposite*: useful

futility *n* **uselessness**, pointlessness, ineffectiveness, ineffectuality, vainness *Opposite*: usefulness

future *n* **prospect**, outlook, potential, time ahead, time to come *Opposite*: past ■ *adj* **forthcoming**, coming, imminent, yet to come, impending *Opposite*: past

futures *n* **stocks**, commodities, contracts, investments

futuristic *adj* **innovative**, revolutionary, ahead of its time, advanced, ultramodern *Opposite*: antiquated

fuzz *n* **down**, hair, fur, fluff

fuzziness *n* 1 **hairiness**, fluffiness, woolliness, down, wool 2 **blurriness**, nebulousness, haziness, vagueness, mistiness *Opposite*: clarity 3 **uncertainty**, vagueness, incoherence, ambiguity, indistinctness *Opposite*: certainty

fuzzy *adj* 1 **hairy**, furry, fluffy, downy, woolly 2 **blurry**, unclear, nebulous, hazy, vague *Opposite*: clear 3 **unsure**, ambiguous, unclear, indistinct, vague *Opposite*: clear

G

gab (*infml*) *v* **chatter**, chat, gossip, natter, prattle ■ *n* **chat**, chatter, talk, conversation, gossip

gabardine *n* **raincoat**, garment, mac (*infml*), mackintosh (*dated*)

gabble *v* **jabber**, rattle on, blabber, gibber, talk nineteen to the dozen ■ *n* **gibberish**, chatter, prattle, rubbish, nonsense

gabby (*infml*) *adj* **talkative**, chatty, garrulous, voluble, gushing *Opposite*: taciturn

gad *v* **socialize**, go partying, go clubbing, have a night on the town (*infml*), gallivant (*infml*)

gadabout *n* **pleasure-seeker**, fun lover, social butterfly, partygoer, raver (*infml*)

gadfly (*dated*) *n* **nuisance**, pest, irritator, tormentor, meddler

gadget *n* 1 **device**, tool, appliance, implement, contraption 2 **thingamajig** (*infml*), thingamabob (*infml*), gizmo (*infml*), doodah (*infml*), whatsit (*infml*)

gaffe *n* **blunder**, solecism, mistake, error, clanger (*infml*)

gaffer (*infml*) *n* **boss**, supervisor, owner, proprietor, manager *Opposite*: underling

gag *n* 1 **restraint**, curb, muzzle, tape, binding 2 **ban**, gagging order, injunction, restriction, interdiction 3 (*infml*) **joke**, one-liner, funny, shaggy dog story, quip ■ *v* 1 **muzzle**, stifle, muffle, restrain, curb 2 **suppress**, silence, interdict, prohibit, ban 3 **choke**, retch, suffocate, stifle, hyperventilate

gagging order *n* **restriction**, gag, injunction, prohibition, court order

gaggle *n* **crowd**, group, horde, throng, multitude

gaiety *n* **joyfulness**, lightheartedness, happiness, liveliness, merriment *Opposite*: misery

gaily *adv* **happily**, joyfully, cheerily, merrily, brightly *Opposite*: sadly

gain *v* 1 **get**, achieve, acquire, obtain, secure *Opposite*: lose 2 **increase**, add, put on, grow, expand *Opposite*: decrease ■ *n* 1 **achievement**, improvement, advantage, advance, increase *Opposite*: setback 2 **advantage**, profit, reward, benefit, return *Opposite*: loss. *See* COMPARE AND CONTRAST *at* **get**.

gain access *v* **get into**, enter, infiltrate, access, get permission

gainful *adj* **profitable**, advantageous, lucrative, rewarding, useful *Opposite*: unprofitable

gain ground *v* **progress**, advance, improve, expand, spread *Opposite*: fall back

gain on *v* **near**, close in on, approach, catch up on, close the gap

gainsay (*fml*) *v* **oppose**, contradict, argue, refute, deny *Opposite*: agree

gait *n* **walk**, step, pace, bearing, manner

gala *n* **festival**, celebration, party, ball, festivity

galactic *adj* 1 (*infml*) **huge**, enormous, immense, vast, extensive *Opposite*: infinitesimal 2 **celestial**, cosmic, planetary, astronomical, space *Opposite*: terrestrial

galaxy *n* **gathering**, assembly, meeting, cluster, collection

gale *n* **wind**, windstorm, storm, tempest, hurricane *Opposite*: breeze

gall *n* **1 audacity**, impudence, boldness, nerve, effrontery **2 sore**, irritation, lesion, wound, blister ■ *v* **irritate**, annoy, infuriate, anger, vex *Opposite*: please

gallant *adj* **1** *(literary)* **brave**, courageous, heroic, valiant, fearless *Opposite*: cowardly **2 courteous**, chivalrous, polite, gentlemanly, thoughtful *Opposite*: rude

gallantry *n* **1** *(literary)* **courage**, bravery, heroism, valour, daring *Opposite*: cowardice **2 courtesy**, thoughtfulness, chivalry, politeness, attentiveness *Opposite*: boorishness

gallery *n* **1 colonnade**, portico, arcade, galleria, corridor **2 balcony**, veranda, porch

galling *adj* **frustrating**, annoying, irritating, infuriating, exasperating *Opposite*: soothing

gallivant *(infml)* *v* **globetrot**, tour, travel around, gad, wander *Opposite*: stay put

gallons *n* **lots**, loads *(infml)*, tons *(infml)*, masses *(infml)*, heaps *(infml)* *Opposite*: handful

gallop *n* **sprint**, dash, charge, bolt, mad dash ■ *v* **dash**, career, hurtle, run, fly

gallows *n* **scaffold**, gibbet, gallows tree, crossbeam, arm

galore *adj* **abundant**, plentiful, copious, aplenty, plenteous *(literary)* *Opposite*: scant

galvanize *v* **stimulate**, spur, rouse, electrify, fire up *Opposite*: dampen

gambit *n* **stratagem**, manoeuvre, ploy, scheme, strategy

gamble *v* **1 bet**, wager, back, stake **2 risk**, stake, venture, hazard, chance *Opposite*: play safe ■ *n* **1 wager**, bet, stake, flutter *(infml)* **2 chance**, risk, hazard, venture, speculation

gamble away *v* **squander**, lose, fritter away, waste, throw away

gambler *n* **1 better**, high roller, wagerer, speculator, plunger *(infml)* **2 risk-taker**, adventurer, speculator, risker, chancer *(infml)*

gambling *n* **betting**, gaming, bookmaking

gambol *v* **frolic**, skip, hop, spring, leap

game *n* **1 pastime**, sport, diversion, amusement, entertainment **2 wild animals**, big game, game birds, game fish **3 match**, fixture, competition, contest, derby ■ *adj* **1 willing**, ready, up for, disposed, inclined *Opposite*: unwilling **2 brave**, spirited, plucky, gutsy *(infml)*, spunky *(infml)* *Opposite*: spiritless

WORD BANK
❑ **types of board game** backgammon, chess, Chinese chequers, dominoes, draughts, go, ludo, mahjongg, Monopoly™, pachisi, reversi, Scrabble™, snakes and ladders, solitaire

❑ **types of card game** baccarat, bridge, canasta, contract bridge, cribbage, euchre, gin rummy, hearts, patience, pinochle, poker, pontoon, rummy, whist

gamekeeper *n* **game warden**, breeder, keeper, handler, steward

gamely *adv* **bravely**, sportingly, spiritedly, stoically, determinedly *Opposite*: weakly

game plan *n* **plan**, strategy, scheme, stratagem, ploy

games *n* **sports**, competition, tournament, cup, sports event

gammy *(infml)* *adj* **sore**, stiff, painful, uncomfortable, aching

gamut *n* **range**, scale, length, scope, extent

gander *(infml)* *n* **look**, peek, glimpse, glance, dekko *(infml)*

gang *n* **1 mob**, band, ring, clique, posse *(slang)* **2 team**, squad, group, lineup, crew *(infml)*

gangland *n* **underworld**, criminal world, organized crime, vice, racketeering

gangling *adj* **lanky**, gangly, tall, rangy, awkward *Opposite*: elegant

ganglion *n* **swelling**, lump, knot, concentration, cyst

gangly *see* **gangling**

gangplank *n* **bridge**, walkway, footway, footbridge, gangway

gangrene *n* **infection**, decay, rot, decomposition, putrefaction ■ *v* **fester**, putrefy, decompose, decay, rot

gangrenous *adj* **infected**, festering, diseased, decaying, rotting *Opposite*: healthy

gangster *n* **criminal**, thug, hoodlum, racketeer, Mafioso

gang up on *v* **unite against**, join forces against, combine against, pick on, mob

gangway *n* **walkway**, footway, aisle, passage, passageway

gannet *(infml)* *n* **glutton**, gourmand, pig *(infml)*

gantry *n* **scaffold**, framework, support

gaol *see* **jail**

gap *n* **1 break**, opening, breach, slit, fissure **2 interval**, hiatus, pause, break, interruption *Opposite*: continuity **3 disparity**, difference, divergence, mismatch, inequality *Opposite*: parity **4 chasm**, gorge, ravine, canyon, rift

gape *v* **1 stare**, gaze, ogle, look hard, gawk *(infml)* **2 part**, separate, divide, yawn, break open. *See* COMPARE AND CONTRAST *at* **gaze**.

gaping *adj* **wide**, wide open, huge, yawning, cavernous *Opposite*: narrow

garage *n* **1 carport**, lockup, shed, outbuilding, parking garage **2 service station**, petrol station, gas station *(US)*

garb *n* **clothing**, dress, costume, apparel, outfit ■ *v* **clothe**, dress, do up, dress up, attire *(fml)*

garbage *n* **nonsense**, trivia, drivel, rubbish, hogwash *(infml)* *Opposite*: sense

garbed *adj* **arrayed**, clothed, dressed, robed, wearing

garble *v* **jumble**, confuse, muddle, mangle, distort

garbled *adj* **jumbled**, confused, muddled, distorted, mangled *Opposite*: clear

garden *n* **1 plot**, allotment, patch, bower, yard *(US)* **2 park**, gardens, public park, green, common ▪ *v* **plant**, cultivate, tend, work, grow

---

WORD BANK

❏ **types of garden** bog garden, cottage garden, flower garden, herb garden, Japanese garden, kitchen garden, knot garden, orchard, potager, rock garden, rose garden, vegetable garden, vegetable plot, water garden

❏ **parts of a garden** arboretum, arbour, bed, border, container, flowerbed, lawn, patio, pergola, planter, rockery, shrubbery, water feature, window box

---

gardener *n* **horticulturist**, landscape gardener, grower, planter, weeder

gargantuan *adj* **huge**, large, gigantic, enormous, vast *Opposite*: tiny

gargle *v* **1 rinse your mouth**, rinse, wash out, disinfect, freshen **2 gurgle**, bubble, burble, glug *(infml)*

gargoyle *n* **ornament**, decoration, carving, figurehead, effigy

garish *adj* **gaudy**, showy, lurid, vulgar, brash *Opposite*: tasteful

garland *n* **1 wreath**, chaplet, coronet, circlet, crown **2 festoon**, swag, drape, chain, lei

garment *n* **clothing**, vestment, costume, dress, frock *(dated)*

WORD BANK

❏ **parts of a garment** brim, buckle, button, buttonhole, coat-tail, collar, cuff, décolletage, drawstring, gusset, hem, lace, lapel, leg, lining, neck, neckband, neckline, pocket, sash, sleeve, strap, turn-up, waistband, zip

---

garner *v* **1 gather**, bring in, save, lay down, store *Opposite*: scatter **2 acquire**, get, gain, collect, bring together *Opposite*: squander

garnish *v* **enhance**, improve, set off, embellish, decorate ▪ *n* **1 accompaniment**, sauce, relish, trimming, savoury **2 embellishment**, decoration, adornment, ornament, trimming

garret *n* **attic**, loft, gable, penthouse, top storey

garrison *n* **barracks**, quarters, base, military base, casern. *See* COMPARE AND CONTRAST *at* **talkative**.

garrulous *adj* **talkative**, voluble, chatty, effusive, loquacious *Opposite*: taciturn. *See* COMPARE AND CONTRAST *at* **talkative**.

garrulousness *n* **verbosity**, volubility, chattiness, prattling, long-windedness *Opposite*: taciturnity

gas *n* **1 air**, vapour, fume, smoke **2** *(infml)* **chatter**, prattle, chitchat *(infml)*, gab *(infml)*, blather *(infml)* **3** *(infml)* **blast**, thrill, experience, trip *(infml) Opposite*: drag ▪ *v* *(infml)* **chat**, gossip, chitchat *(infml)*, natter *(infml)*, yak *(infml)*

gaseous *adj* **1 vaporous**, gassy, steamy, smoky, fumy **2 carbonated**, fizzy, bubbly, sparkling, effervescent *Opposite*: still **3** *(infml)* **talkative**, verbose, long-winded, chatty, chattering *Opposite*: tight-lipped

gash *n* **wound**, slash, cut, tear, laceration ▪ *v* **cut**, slash, wound, tear, lacerate

gasket *n* **seal**, washer, ring, liner, lining

gasp *n* **wheeze**, pant, huff, puff, breath

gasping *adj* **1 out of breath**, puffed, winded, breathless, panting **2 thirsty**, parched, dry, dehydrated, thirsting **3 desperate**, dying, longing, craving, yearning

gassy *adj* **1 carbonated**, fizzy, bubbly, sparkling, effervescent *Opposite*: still **2 vaporous**, gaseous, steamy, smoky, fumy **3** *(infml)* **talkative**, verbose, long-winded, chatty, gossipy *Opposite*: tight-lipped

gastric *adj* **stomach**, abdominal, intestinal, digestive, gastrointestinal

gastrointestinal *adj* **stomach**, abdominal, intestinal, digestive, gastric

gastronome *n* **gourmet**, food lover, connoisseur, epicure, foodie *(infml) Opposite*: glutton

gastronomic *adj* **culinary**, cooking, food, gourmet, epicurean

gastronomy *n* **cookery**, cooking, cuisine, food, gourmet food

gasworks *n* **gas plant**, power station, installation, power plant

gate *n* **1 entrance**, entry, door, gateway, opening **2 attendance**, crowd, turnout, audience **3 receipts**, takings, proceeds, revenue, take

gatecrash *v* **sneak in**, barge in, invade, intrude, crash *(infml)*

gatecrasher *n* **intruder**, interloper, trespasser, invader, partycrasher *(US) Opposite*: guest

gatepost *n* **support**, upright, post, frame, doorpost

gateway *n* **1 entry**, doorway, entrance, opening, access **2 opening**, first step, opportunity, access, way in

gather *v* **1 meet**, get together, collect, congregate, assemble *Opposite*: disperse **2 collect**, bring together, draw together, amass, pull together *Opposite*: distribute **3 harvest**, pick, collect, garner, pluck *Opposite*: scatter **4 understand**, conclude, assume, deduce, surmise *Opposite*: misunderstand **5 pleat**, fold, pucker, ruche, shirr *Opposite*: smooth ▪ *n* **fold**, pleat, pucker, wrinkle, ruck. *See* COMPARE AND CONTRAST *at* **collect**.

gathering *n* **meeting**, assembly, congregation, crowd, jamboree

gathering place *n* **meeting place**, centre, assembly point, forum

gather up v **pick up**, take up, draw up, scoop up, dredge up *Opposite*: put down

gauche adj **awkward**, uncouth, tactless, callow, graceless *Opposite*: poised

gaudiness n **showiness**, luridness, flamboyance, garishness, tawdriness *Opposite*: tastefulness

gaudy adj **garish**, flashy, kitschy, loud, showy *Opposite*: tasteful

gauge v **evaluate**, judge, assess, determine, measure ■ n **measurement**, estimate, assessment, measure, test

gaunt adj **thin**, skinny, lean, bony, emaciated *Opposite*: plump

gauntness n **thinness**, skinniness, leanness, boniness, scrawniness *Opposite*: plumpness

gauzy adj **thin**, delicate, filmy, see-through, gossamer *Opposite*: heavy

gawk (infml) v **stare**, gape, gaze, watch, goggle *Opposite*: ignore. *See* COMPARE AND CONTRAST *at* **gaze**.

gawkiness (infml) n **awkwardness**, clumsiness, inelegance, gracelessness, ungainliness *Opposite*: gracefulness

gawky (infml) adj **awkward**, clumsy, gangling, gangly, ungainly *Opposite*: graceful

gawp (infml) *see* **gawk**

gaze v **look**, stare, watch, contemplate, gape *Opposite*: ignore ■ n **stare**, look, contemplation, observation, scrutiny *Opposite*: glance

COMPARE AND CONTRAST CORE MEANING: look at somebody or something steadily or at length
gaze look for a long time with unwavering attention; **gape** look at somebody or something in surprise or wonder, usually with an open mouth; **gawk** or **gawp** (infml) stare stupidly or rudely; **ogle** look steadily at somebody for sexual enjoyment or to show sexual interest; **rubberneck** (infml) stare at somebody or something in an over-inquisitive or insensitive way; **stare** look at somebody or something directly and intently without moving the eyes away, as a result of curiosity or surprise or to express rudeness or defiance.

gazette n **newspaper**, paper, journal, periodical, newsletter

gear (infml) n 1 **kit**, stuff, things, paraphernalia, tackle 2 **clothes**, clothing, kit, outfit, togs (infml)

gear to v **adjust to**, align with, adapt to, tailor, modify

gear up v **get ready**, prepare, mobilize, ready yourself, psych yourself up (infml) *Opposite*: wind down

gel n **cream**, lotion, balm, ointment, salve ■ v 1 (infml) **come together**, take shape, crystallize, develop, form *Opposite*: fall apart 2 (infml) **see eye to eye**, relate, get on, get on like a house on fire, get along 3 **congeal**, thicken, coagulate, clot, harden *Opposite*: liquefy

gelatinous adj **viscous**, jellylike, gummy, gooey, sticky

geld v **castrate**, neuter, spay, sterilize, vasectomize

gem n 1 **jewel**, stone, precious stone, cut stone, gemstone 2 (infml) **treasure**, pearl, star, godsend, paragon

gemstone n **jewel**, stone, gem, precious stone, cut stone

WORD BANK
❑ **types of gemstone** agate, amethyst, aquamarine, beryl, bloodstone, carnelian, chalcedony, chrysoprase, diamond, emerald, garnet, jade, lapis lazuli, moonstone, mother-of-pearl, onyx, opal, pearl, ruby, sapphire, sard, topaz, tourmaline, turquoise

gender n **sex**, sexual category, sexual characteristics, masculinity, femininity

WORD BANK
❑ **types of female animal** bitch, cow, dam, doe, ewe, filly, heifer, hind, jenny, lioness, mare, nanny goat, sow, tigress, vixen
❑ **types of male animal** billy goat, boar, buck, bull, bullock, colt, hart, jackass, ram, stag, stallion, steer, tom, tomcat, wether
❑ **types of male bird or female bird** capon, cob, cock, cockerel, drake, duck, gander, goose, hen, pen, rooster

gene n **genetic factor**, inheritable factor, protein sequence, DNA segment

genealogical adj **hereditary**, ancestral, family, pedigree

genealogy n **family tree**, descent, lineage, pedigree, family

general adj 1 **overall**, universal, all-purpose, wide-ranging, broad *Opposite*: specific 2 **usual**, typical, conventional, customary, accustomed *Opposite*: unusual 3 **widespread**, common, blanket, across-the-board, sweeping *Opposite*: unique 4 **unspecific**, undefined, unclear, vague *Opposite*: specific

generality n 1 **generalization**, sweeping statement, simplification, oversimplification, overview *Opposite*: detail 2 **platitude**, cliché, banality, truism, axiom

generalization n **sweeping statement**, simplification, oversimplification, overview, generality *Opposite*: detail

generalize v **simplify**, oversimplify, take a broad view, make a sweeping statement *Opposite*: specify

generalized adj **widespread**, sweeping, comprehensive, general, global *Opposite*: isolated

generally adv **usually**, normally, in general, in the main, by and large *Opposite*: rarely

general public n **population**, populace, ordinary people, hoi polloi, rank and file *Opposite*: elite

generate v **make**, produce, create, cause, engender *Opposite*: prevent

generation n 1 age group, peer group, peers, cohort, compeers (fml) 2 age, era, epoch, period, aeon 3 production, making, creation, invention, initiation Opposite: destruction

generator n producer, maker, creator, originator, initiator

generic adj general, broad, common, basic, nonspecific Opposite: specific

generosity n kindness, big-heartedness, openhandedness, liberality, munificence Opposite: miserliness

generous adj 1 kind, big-hearted, liberal, openhanded, charitable Opposite: stingy (infml) 2 substantial, large, lavish, liberal, plentiful Opposite: meagre

COMPARE AND CONTRAST CORE MEANING: giving readily to others
generous willing to give money, help, or time freely; **liberal** free with money, time, or other assets; **magnanimous** very generous, kind, or forgiving; **munificent** very generous, especially on a grand scale; **bountiful** (literary) generous, particularly to less fortunate people.

genesis n origin, origins, beginning, start, birth

genetic adj hereditary, inherited, heritable, inherent, genomic Opposite: learned

genial adj friendly, amiable, warm, welcoming, hospitable Opposite: unfriendly

geniality n friendliness, warmth, cordiality, amiability, conviviality Opposite: hostility

genie n sprite, spirit, apparition, jinni, imp

genius n 1 mastermind, prodigy, intellect, virtuoso, whiz kid (infml) 2 brilliance, intellect, brains, virtuosity, intelligence Opposite: stupidity. See COMPARE AND CONTRAST at talent.

genocide n killing, slaughter, massacre, ethnic cleansing, liquidation

genre n type, sort, kind, category, field. See COMPARE AND CONTRAST at type.

gent (dated infml) n gentleman, man, bloke (infml), guy (infml), fellow (dated)

genteel adj 1 refined, proper, polite, courteous, discreet Opposite: vulgar 2 pretentious, snobbish, condescending, patronizing, affected Opposite: modest

gentility n refinement, propriety, manners, breeding, decorum Opposite: vulgarity

gentle adj 1 mild, calm, kind, tender, moderate Opposite: harsh 2 soft, light, soothing, mellow, restful Opposite: rough

gentleman n 1 man, male, chap (infml), guy (infml), bloke (infml) 2 nobleman, aristocrat, squire, grandee Opposite: cad

gentlemanly adj chivalrous, gallant, courteous, polite, civil Opposite: rude

gentleness n 1 mildness, calmness, kindness, tenderness, placidity Opposite: harshness 2 quietness, softness, lightness, smoothness, mellowness Opposite: harshness

gentrification n redevelopment, refurbishment, urban renewal, renovation, restoration Opposite: neglect

gentrify v redevelop, refurbish, renovate, restore, improve

gentry n upper class, nobility, aristocracy, elite, ruling class Opposite: working class

genuflect v 1 kneel, bow, curtsy, bend the knee, bob 2 bow to, defer to, kowtow, show respect for, grovel Opposite: disrespect

genuflection n kneeling, curtsy, bow, bob, dip

genuine adj 1 real, authentic, indisputable, true, unadulterated Opposite: fake 2 sincere, honest, frank, open, unaffected Opposite: false

genuineness n authenticity, realness, substance, legitimacy, validity

gen up (infml) v research, study, read up, revise, swot up (infml)

genus n type, kind, sort, species, class

geographic see geographical

geographical adj physical, topographical, terrestrial, earthly, environmental

geography n topography, natural features, characteristics, layout

geological division n eon, era, epoch, period

WORD BANK
❑ **types of eon (from oldest to most recent)** pre-Archaean, Archaean, Proterozoic, Phanerozoic
❑ **types of epoch (from oldest to most recent)** Palaeocene, Eocene, Oligocene, Miocene, Pliocene, Pleistocene, Holocene
❑ **types of era (from oldest to most recent)** Palaeozoic, Mesozoic, Cenozoic
❑ **types of period (from oldest to most recent)** Cambrian, Ordovician, Silurian, Devonian, Carboniferous, Permian, Triassic, Jurassic, Cretaceous, Tertiary, Quaternary

geometric adj regular, symmetrical, ordered, orderly, linear

geriatric adj elderly, aged, old, senior Opposite: young

germ n 1 microbe, microorganism, bacteria, virus, bug (infml) 2 origin, seed, embryo, rudiment, kernel

germane adj relevant, useful, connected, to the point, of interest Opposite: irrelevant

germ-free adj sterile, antiseptic, hygienic, sanitary, uninfected Opposite: contaminated

germinate v sprout, grow, develop, take root, evolve

germination n sprouting, propagation, incubation, growth, development

gestation n development, growth, incubation, maturation, pregnancy

gesticulate v gesture, wave, signal, motion, sign

gesticulation n sign, signal, gesture, wave, motion

gesture n 1 **sign**, signal, gesticulation, motion, wave 2 **act**, action, deed, token, intimation ■ v **gesticulate**, signal, shrug, nod, wave

get v 1 **obtain**, acquire, secure, procure, gain 2 **become**, grow, begin, have, attain 3 **catch**, contract, acquire, develop, be infected with 4 **cause**, make, induce, persuade, urge 5 **move**, step, progress, walk, climb 6 (infml) **understand**, comprehend, grasp, follow, perceive

COMPARE AND CONTRAST CORE MEANING: come into possession of something

get become the owner of something or succeed in finding and possessing it; **acquire** get possession of something, sometimes suggesting that time or effort was involved; **obtain** get something, especially by making an effort or having the necessary qualifications; **gain** get something through effort, skill, or merit; **procure** get something, especially with effort or special care; **secure** get something, especially after using considerable effort to persuade somebody to grant or allow it.

get across v **put across**, put over, convey, impart, communicate

get a grip (infml) v **calm down**, get hold of yourself, compose yourself, control yourself, chill out (infml)

get ahead v **advance**, climb the ladder, progress, make progress, prosper Opposite: fail

get ahead of v **pass**, pass by, be in front of, overtake Opposite: hold back

get along v **survive**, get by, manage, cope, live

get a move on (infml) v **speed up**, hurry up, get going, get moving, accelerate Opposite: slow down

get angry v **bristle**, bridle, explode, lose your cool, hit the roof (infml)

get a raw deal v **suffer**, draw the short straw, be hard done by, be put upon, come off badly

get at v 1 **reach**, find, contact, speak to, write to 2 **annoy**, tease, rub up the wrong way, irritate, get to

get away v **leave**, go away, escape, flee, depart

getaway n **escape**, exit, retreat, breakout, flight

get away from v **elude**, shake off, lose, escape from, outrun

get away with v **get off**, get off scot-free, escape, evade, elude Opposite: answer for

get a word in edgeways v **get a word in**, get a chance to speak, have your say, voice your opinion, say anything

get back v **retrieve**, recoup, repossess, regain, recuperate Opposite: lose

get back at v **get even**, turn the tables on, take revenge, get your own back, even the score

get behind v **support**, endorse, back, join forces, put in a good word for Opposite: oppose

get better v **recover**, recuperate, improve, turn the corner, bounce back Opposite: deteriorate

get bigger v **swell**, grow, inflate, mount, expand Opposite: shrink

get by v **survive**, manage, cope, scrape by, get on

get cracking (infml) v **get going**, make a start, get moving, get on, get a move on (infml)

get done v **accomplish**, achieve, complete, finish, do

get down v **descend**, get off, dismount, come down, climb down

get down to v **get to work**, begin, get on, start, concentrate Opposite: put off

get down to business v **get on with it**, get down to it, get down to brass tacks, get down to the nitty-gritty, stop beating about the bush

get even v **get your own back**, get back at, take revenge, turn the tables, even the score

get free of v **get rid of**, exorcize, escape, jettison, eliminate

get going v 1 **start**, make a start, get on, hurry up, stir 2 **start up**, turn on, activate, operate, power Opposite: turn off

get hitched (infml) v **get married**, marry, walk down the aisle, tie the knot (infml), wed (fml or literary)

get hold of v 1 **contact**, reach, find, get in touch with, talk to 2 **obtain**, find, acquire, search out, lay hands on

get in v 1 **arrive**, enter, appear, turn up (infml), show up (infml) Opposite: depart 2 **join**, be accepted, be included, make the grade, make the cut (US)

get in on the act (infml) v **take part**, join in, be included, be involved, jump on the bandwagon

get in the way v **obstruct**, hinder, impede, interfere, encumber

get into v 1 **gain entry**, enter, open, access, hack into Opposite: get out of 2 **put on**, slip into, don, change into, dress in Opposite: take off

get in touch with v **call**, get hold of, contact, reach, ring up

get into your stride v **get going**, get up to speed, get the hang of something, get off the ground

get involved v **interfere**, intervene, join in, be drawn in, put your oar in Opposite: hold back

get in with v **ingratiate yourself**, make friends with, curry favour, gain the favour of, associate with

get it (infml) v **understand**, see, get the drift, follow, comprehend Opposite: misunderstand

get it in the neck (infml) v **take the blame**, carry the can (infml), take the rap (slang)

get it off your chest v **bare your soul**, tell somebody, let it out, unburden yourself, share Opposite: bottle up

get it wrong v misunderstand, blunder, get the wrong idea, get the wrong end of the stick, boob (infml)

get less v subside, die down, lessen, reduce, fall Opposite: grow

get longer v lengthen, elongate, grow, extend, spread out Opposite: shorten

get lost v lose your way, lose your bearings, go astray, go wrong, take a wrong turning

get married v marry, walk down the aisle, get hitched (infml), tie the knot (infml), wed (fml or literary)

get moving v hurry up, speed up, get going, make a move, get a move on (infml)

get off v 1 leave, depart, exit, go, embark Opposite: arrive 2 dismount, get down, descend, come down, climb off Opposite: get on

get on v 1 deal with, handle, manage, accept, progress Opposite: mismanage 2 like, be compatible, work well with, relate, gel (infml) Opposite: dislike 3 board, climb on, mount, get on board, embark Opposite: get off 4 make a start, get going, begin, start, get down to Opposite: defer

get on your high horse v give yourself airs, put on airs, lord it, get all high and mighty

get on your nerves v annoy, irritate, bother, put your back up, irk

get out v leave, depart, quit, evacuate, retreat Opposite: enter

get out of v evade, avoid, dodge, duck, get round Opposite: participate

get over v 1 recover, live through, endure, survive, get beyond Opposite: succumb 2 come to terms with, accept, surmount, overcome, conquer 3 convey, communicate, impart, pass on, get across

get ready v prepare, steel, prime, brace, organize

get rid of v dispose of, discard, throw away, throw out, jettison Opposite: keep

get round v 1 become known, break out, circulate, get out, be revealed 2 avoid, go around, bypass, sidestep, evade

get smaller v shrink, shrivel up, narrow, deflate, recede Opposite: swell

get somewhere v make headway, make progress, make inroads, achieve something, make a breakthrough Opposite: fall behind

get the better of v defeat, beat, trounce, triumph over, get the upper hand

get the drift v understand, see, follow, get it (infml), get the message (infml)

get the hang of v learn, pick up, understand, master

get the message (infml) v understand, get the drift, take the hint, grasp, follow

get the most out of v maximize, make the most of, get the full benefit, exploit, milk (infml)

get the picture (infml) v understand, follow, see, grasp, get it (infml)

get the wrong end of the stick v misconstrue, misinterpret, make a mistake, misunderstand, misread

get the wrong idea v misunderstand, misread, misinterpret, misconstrue, misjudge

get thinner v narrow, taper, slim down, lose weight

get through v 1 survive, come through, endure, weather, ride out 2 use, consume, wear out, go through, expend 3 breach, break through, penetrate, cross, pass

get to v 1 annoy, irritate, bother, irk, affect 2 reach, make, arrive at, attain

get-together (infml) n meeting, gathering, social, assembly, rendezvous

get to know v become acquainted with, be introduced to, meet, become familiar with

get to your feet v stand up, rise, stand, get up, arise (literary)

get under way v begin, start, proceed, launch, commence Opposite: come to a halt

getup (infml) n outfit, clothes, costume, suit, dress

get-up-and-go (infml) n energy, vitality, verve, life, drive

get used to v become accustomed to, get into the habit, adjust, adapt, acclimatize

get your bearings v orient yourself, find your way, find your feet, adjust, adapt

get your own back v take revenge, get even, retaliate, get back at, avenge yourself

geyser n hot spring, spring, natural spring, fountain, jet

ghastly adj 1 horrifying, shocking, upsetting, distressing, grisly Opposite: pleasant 2 terrible, horrible, appalling, dreadful, nasty Opposite: pleasant 3 (infml) ill, sick, unwell, dreadful, bad Opposite: well

gherkin n pickled cucumber, dill pickle, pickle

ghostlike adj eerie, spectral, ghostly, supernatural, ethereal

ghostly adj ethereal, spectral, indistinct, supernatural, eerie

ghostwrite v cowrite, write, compose, author, coauthor

ghostwriter n cowriter, writer, composer, author, coauthor

ghoulish adj 1 morbid, macabre, dark, chilling, ghastly 2 cruel, savage, brutal, fiendish, bloodthirsty Opposite: gentle

GI n soldier, private, enlisted person, volunteer, conscript

giant adj huge, enormous, vast, large, massive Opposite: tiny

gibber v babble, rant, prattle, jabber, gabble

gibberish n nonsense, prattle, babble, gabble, rubbish Opposite: sense

gibe n jeer, taunt, sneer, remark, joke ■ v taunt, mock, tease, jeer, ridicule

giblets n guts, offal, innards (infml)

giddiness n 1 **dizziness**, unsteadiness, light-headedness, wooziness, shakiness *Opposite*: steadiness 2 *(dated)* **frivolity**, capriciousness, volatility, overexcitement, flightiness *Opposite*: seriousness

giddy adj 1 **dizzy**, unsteady, off-balance, light-headed, woozy *Opposite*: steady 2 *(dated)* **frivolous**, scatterbrained, capricious, volatile, excited *Opposite*: serious

gift n 1 **present**, donation, contribution, reward, bequest 2 **talent**, skill, ability, flair, knack. *See* COMPARE AND CONTRAST *at* **talent**.

gifted adj **talented**, skilled, bright, able, intelligent. *See* COMPARE AND CONTRAST *at* **intelligent**.

giftwrap v **wrap**, wrap up, package

gigantic adj **huge**, enormous, massive, vast, gargantuan *Opposite*: tiny

giggle v **titter**, snigger, chuckle, laugh, chortle ■ n **snigger**, titter, chuckle, laugh, chortle

giggly adj **silly**, hysterical, immature, tittering, sniggering *Opposite*: serious

gilded adj **golden**, gold-plated, gilt, gold

gild the lily v **overdo it**, get carried away, go too far, lay it on thick, over-egg the pudding

gilt n **gold**, gold leaf, gold plate ■ adj **golden**, gold-plated, gilded, gold

gimmick n **trick**, ploy, stunt, device, promotion

gingerly adv **cautiously**, tentatively, warily, delicately, carefully *Opposite*: boldly

ginormous *(infml)* adj **huge**, enormous, vast, massive, immense *Opposite*: tiny

girder n **beam**, joist, bar, rafter, crossbeam

girdle n **belt**, sash, cummerbund, tie, drawstring

gird your loins v **brace yourself**, get ready, grit your teeth, prepare yourself, steel yourself

girlfriend n **partner**, lover, sweetheart, fiancée, ladyfriend *(infml)* *Opposite*: boyfriend

girlhood n **childhood**, youth, infancy, early years, adolescence

girlish adj **youthful**, adolescent, childlike, young

girth n **circumference**, breadth, width, span, thickness *Opposite*: height

gist n **idea**, essence, substance, general picture, point *Opposite*: minutiae

give v 1 **provide**, offer, hand over, present, donate *Opposite*: take 2 **grant**, award, accord, bestow *(fml)*, confer *(fml)* *Opposite*: withhold 3 **impart**, convey, communicate, pass on, share *Opposite*: withhold 4 **perform**, put on, stage, produce, organize 5 **devote**, dedicate, give up, sacrifice, spend *Opposite*: withhold 6 **yield**, collapse, break, go, split *Opposite*: hold up

COMPARE AND CONTRAST CORE MEANING: hand over something to somebody

give hand over a possession to somebody else to keep or use; **present** give something in a formal or ceremonial way; **confer** *(fml)* give somebody an honour, privilege, or award, often at a formal ceremony; **bestow** *(fml)* present somebody with something, especially something unexpected or undeserved; **donate** give a contribution to a charitable organization or another good cause, or, in a medical context, give blood for blood transfusions or organs for transplant; **grant** agree to allow a request, favour, or privilege, especially at the discretion of a person in authority, or formally or officially give money.

give a beating v **attack**, assault, batter, hit, smack

give a boost v **strengthen**, boost, lift, encourage, boost up *Opposite*: deflate

give a lift v **encourage**, boost, boost up, strengthen, fortify *Opposite*: deflate

give a miss *(infml)* v **stay away from**, abstain from, hold back from, give a wide berth, avoid

give-and-take *(infml)* n **cooperation**, compromise, reciprocity, collaboration, teamwork *Opposite*: selfishness

give away v 1 **get rid of**, donate, offer, give, pass on *Opposite*: keep 2 **disclose**, reveal, let slip, betray, divulge *Opposite*: keep secret

giveaway n 1 **telltale sign**, clue, hint, indication, symptom 2 *(infml)* **gift**, special offer, free sample, trial offer, promotion ■ adj *(infml)* **bargain**, rock-bottom, low, introductory, special *Opposite*: exorbitant

give a wide berth v **steer clear**, keep well away, avoid, avoid like the plague, shun *Opposite*: seek out

give back v **return**, restore, hand back, repay, refund *Opposite*: keep

give chase *(fml)* v **pursue**, follow in hot pursuit, follow, go after, chase

give in v 1 **lose**, admit defeat, surrender, concede, submit *Opposite*: stand your ground 2 **hand over**, hand in, deliver, submit, present *Opposite*: withhold

give instructions v **direct**, inform, brief, instruct, tell

given adj **known**, assumed, agreed, specified, prearranged ■ prep **because of**, in view of, as a result of, taking into consideration, taking into account

given name n **first name**, Christian name, forename, name, moniker *(slang)*

given that conj **providing**, provided that, as long as, only if, assuming that

give off v **emit**, radiate, send out, discharge, exude

give out v 1 **hand out**, distribute, provide, offer, allot *Opposite*: keep 2 **declare**, announce, proclaim, pronounce, reveal *Opposite*: withhold 3 **emit**, send out, transmit, give off, radiate 4 **run out**, dry up, fail, come to an end, end *Opposite*: hold out 5 **fail**, collapse, break, yield, go *Opposite*: hold

give over *(infml)* v **stop**, cease, desist, pack in

(infml), lay off *(infml) Opposite:* continue

give over to v dedicate, devote, allocate, reserve, allot

give permission v consent, agree, allow, let, authorize *Opposite:* forbid

give somebody the slip v lose, shake off, get away from, escape from, avoid

give the cold shoulder to v ignore, rebuff, exclude, look straight through, send to Coventry

give the lie to v contradict, belie, rebut, refute, conflict with

give the once-over *(infml)* v examine, inspect, check out, scrutinize, look at

give up v 1 admit defeat, give in, surrender, concede, submit *Opposite:* stand your ground 2 hand over, part with, surrender, relinquish, give away *Opposite:* keep 3 stop, quit, leave off, renounce, abstain from *Opposite:* stick with 4 despair, abandon, lose hope, give up on 5 devote, dedicate, give, surrender, sacrifice *Opposite:* withhold 6 reveal, disclose, divulge, tell, let slip *Opposite:* keep secret

give up on v 1 stop, give up, quit, abandon, leave off 2 despair, abandon, lose hope, give up

give your word v promise, vow, swear, pledge, assure

gizmo *(infml)* n gadget, device, contraption, appliance, thing

glacial adj 1 icy, ice-cold, freezing, biting, bitter *Opposite:* tropical 2 hostile, unfriendly, icy, cold, cool *Opposite:* warm

glacier n ice field, icecap, ice floe, iceberg, floe

glad adj 1 delighted, happy, pleased, content, grateful *Opposite:* sad 2 willing, ready, prepared, happy, eager *Opposite:* unwilling

gladden v delight, please, cheer, bring joy to, hearten *Opposite:* sadden

glade n clearing, opening, gap, open space, dell *(literary)*

gladiator n 1 fighter, fencer, sword fighter, warrior, battler 2 campaigner, lobbyist, supporter, advocate, champion

gladness n happiness, cheerfulness, delight, joy, pleasure *Opposite:* sadness

glad rags *(infml)* n best clothes, finery, black tie, Sunday best, best bib and tucker *(infml)*

glamorize v 1 romanticize, idealize, exaggerate, embellish, dress up *Opposite:* understate 2 beautify, decorate, adorn, do up, dress up

glamorous adj stylish, fashionable, glitzy, dazzling, splendid *Opposite:* drab

glamour n 1 allure, charm, appeal, fascination, attraction *Opposite:* dullness 2 good looks, beauty, glitz, glitziness, style *Opposite:* drabness

glance v 1 look, peep, peek, glimpse, squint *Opposite:* gaze 2 glint, shine, gleam, glimmer,

gleam, glitter ■ n peep, look, glimpse, scan, squint *(infml) Opposite:* gaze

glance off v bounce off, ricochet, reflect, deflect, rebound

glancing adj sideways, sidelong, lateral, slanting, tangential

glare v 1 scowl, stare, glower, frown, look daggers 2 dazzle, flash, glimmer, glitter, shine 3 stand out, leap out, jump out, catch the eye, show ■ n 1 dirty look, stare, glower, scowl, frown 2 shine, brightness, dazzle, flash, shimmer *Opposite:* dullness

glaring adj 1 conspicuous, obvious, obtrusive, evident, blatant *Opposite:* inconspicuous 2 dazzling, brilliant, shimmering, bright, intense *Opposite:* dim 3 garish, brash, gaudy, loud, clashing *Opposite:* soft

glaringly adv blatantly, patently, flagrantly, clearly, extremely

glass n beaker, tumbler, wineglass, goblet, flute

glasses n spectacles, goggles, specs *(infml)*

WORD BANK
❑ **types of glasses** bifocals, dark glasses, monocle, pince-nez, shades *(infml)*, sunglasses, sunspecs *(infml)*

glassy adj 1 smooth, slippery, shiny, glossy, slick *Opposite:* dull 2 expressionless, glazed, dazed, blank, vacant *Opposite:* alert

glaze v varnish, finish, seal, coat, cover ■ n coating, varnish, finish, seal, cover

glazed adj 1 glassy, blank, fixed, expressionless, dull *Opposite:* alert 2 glossy, shiny, smooth, lustrous, varnished *Opposite:* dull

gleam v 1 shine, glow, beam, burn, blaze 2 flash, flicker, twinkle, shimmer, sparkle ■ n 1 glow, shine, beam, ray, blaze 2 flicker, flash, twinkle, shimmer, sparkle

gleaming adj shiny, polished, luminous, lustrous, glossy *Opposite:* dull

glee n 1 delight, happiness, pleasure, joy, elation *Opposite:* sadness 2 triumph, jubilation, smugness, exultance *Opposite:* despondency

gleeful adj 1 delighted, happy, pleased, joyful, elated *Opposite:* sad 2 triumphant, jubilant, smug, gloating, exultant *Opposite:* despondent

glen n valley, gorge, ravine, dale, vale *(literary)*

glib adj 1 persuasive, fluent, smooth, convincing, slick *Opposite:* hesitant 2 superficial, shallow, facile, casual, simplistic *Opposite:* profound

glibness n 1 persuasiveness, fluency, slickness, smoothness *Opposite:* hesitation 2 superficiality, shallowness, facileness, casualness *Opposite:* profoundness

glide v 1 slither, slide along, slip, skate 2 fly, soar, wheel, drift, coast

glimmer v twinkle, shine, gleam, flicker, glow

■ *n* **shine**, twinkle, gleam, flicker, glow

glimpse *n* 1 **look**, glance, peep, sight, peek (*infml*) 2 **hint**, sight, foretaste, indication, pointer ■ *v* **see**, catch sight of, glance at, peep at, look at

glint *v* **sparkle**, flash, wink, shine, twinkle ■ *n* **flash**, sparkle, shine, twinkle, spark

glisten *v* **gleam**, sparkle, glint, flash, reflect ■ *n* **sparkle**, gleam, glint, flash, shine

glistening *adj* **gleaming**, shining, sparkly, shiny, glittering

glitch *n* **hitch**, problem, malfunction, fault, anomaly

glitter *v* **gleam**, sparkle, shine, dazzle, shimmer ■ *n* 1 **sparkle**, gleam, shimmer, flash, twinkle 2 **tinsel**, sequins, spangles 3 **dazzle**, splendour, flashiness, glamour, showiness

glittering *adj* **impressive**, sparkling, dazzling, splendid, scintillating

glittery *adj* **shiny**, sparkly, shimmering, brilliant, dazzling

glitz *n* **glamour**, style, stylishness, glitziness, showiness

glitziness *n* 1 **glamour**, glitter, style, glitz, stylishness 2 **showiness**, tawdriness, flashiness, extravagance, tastelessness

glitzy *adj* **showy**, ostentatious, flashy, extravagant, swanky (*infml*)

gloat *v* **revel**, wallow, exult, smirk, delight

glob (*infml*) *n* **blob**, gobbet, drop, globule, lump

global *adj* 1 **worldwide**, international *Opposite*: local 2 **universal**, comprehensive, total, inclusive, overall

globally *adv* 1 **internationally**, worldwide, universally *Opposite*: locally 2 **altogether**, as a whole, generally, universally, totally

globe *n* 1 **sphere**, ball, orb 2 **earth**, world, planet

globetrot *v* **travel**, journey, tour, shuttle, backpack

globetrotter *n* **traveller**, tourist, backpacker, holidaymaker, journeyer

globular *adj* **spherical**, round, circular, bulbous, rotund

globule *n* **drop**, blob, bead, bubble, gobbet

gloom *n* 1 **darkness**, shade, murkiness, shadow, dimness *Opposite*: brightness 2 **pessimism**, despair, sadness, dejection, unhappiness *Opposite*: happiness

gloominess *n* 1 **dimness**, darkness, murkiness, shade, shadow *Opposite*: brightness 2 **despondency**, pessimism, gloom, depression, despair *Opposite*: happiness

gloomy *adj* 1 **dark**, depressing, dim, overcast, dull *Opposite*: bright 2 **depressed**, low, low-spirited, melancholy, miserable *Opposite*: cheerful

glorification *n* **adoration**, veneration, elevation, deification, praise *Opposite*: belittlement

glorify *v* **worship**, adore, lionize, deify, elevate *Opposite*: belittle

glorious *adj* **magnificent**, wonderful, splendid, celebrated, superb *Opposite*: shameful

glory *n* 1 **magnificence**, splendour, beauty, wonder, grandeur 2 **credit**, fame, praise, laurels, triumph *Opposite*: criticism

glory in *v* **enjoy**, lap up, wallow in, make the most of, revel in *Opposite*: despise

gloss *n* 1 **lustre**, polish, shine, brightness, sheen 2 **interpretation**, explanation, spin (*slang*) 3 **annotation**, commentary, footnote, explanation, comment

glossary *n* **lexicon**, dictionary, word list, vocabulary, thesaurus

glossiness *n* 1 **shininess**, smoothness, sheen, patina, lustre 2 (*infml*) **veneer**, surface, façade

gloss over *v* **skim over**, pass over, dismiss, evade, dodge *Opposite*: dwell on

glossy *adj* **sleek**, silky, silken, lustrous, shiny *Opposite*: dull

glow *n* **radiance**, ruddiness, light, luminosity, glimmering ■ *v* **burn**, blaze, flame, shine, smoulder

glower *v* **glare**, frown, scowl, look daggers, look hard

glowering *adj* **angry**, dark, scowling, sullen, surly

glowing *adj* 1 **bright**, shimmering, radiant, lustrous, shining *Opposite*: dull 2 **fulsome**, complimentary, flattering, appreciative, congratulatory *Opposite*: derogatory 3 **healthy-looking**, tanned, rosy, shining, radiant *Opposite*: pale

glue *n* **adhesive**, paste, superglue, cement, gum ■ *v* **paste**, stick, fasten, attach, join

gluey *adj* **sticky**, gummy, tacky, glutinous, thick

glum *adj* **gloomy**, down, morose, sad, low *Opposite*: cheerful

glumness *n* **pessimism**, unhappiness, misery, depression, dejection *Opposite*: cheerfulness

glut *n* **excess**, surplus, superfluity, flood, overabundance *Opposite*: shortage

glutinous *adj* **sticky**, gluey, gooey, tacky, gummy

glutton *n* **overeater**, gourmand, greedy guts (*infml*), gannet (*infml*), pig (*infml*)

gluttonous *adj* **greedy**, voracious, insatiable, excessive, desirous (*fml*)

gluttony *n* **greed**, greediness, excess, piggishness, rapaciousness

gnarled *adj* **knotted**, twisted, bent, knotty, crooked *Opposite*: straight

gnash *v* **grind**, clench, grit, grate, rasp

gnash your teeth *v* **be fuming**, be upset, grind your teeth, be frustrated

gnat *n* **midge**, mosquito, fly, firefly, insect

gnaw v **worry**, trouble, bother, cause anxiety, concern *Opposite*: comfort

gnome n **elf**, sprite, goblin, troll, leprechaun

go v 1 **leave**, go away, go off, depart, set off *Opposite*: come 2 **move**, move on, proceed, progress, make for 3 **work**, run, function, operate, move *Opposite*: stop 4 **reach**, extend, stretch, spread 5 **become**, get, grow, come to be 6 **die**, pass away, pass on, depart *(fml)*, expire *(fml) Opposite*: live ■ n 1 **energy**, liveliness, enthusiasm, spirit, verve *Opposite*: lethargy 2 **try**, attempt, turn, chance, shot 3 *(infml)* **energy**, life, zest, zip *(infml)*, oomph *(infml)*

go about v **get on with**, perform, carry out, accomplish, transact

goad v **provoke**, prod, push, stir, stimulate *Opposite*: calm ■ n 1 **stick**, prod, poker, rod, whip 2 **stimulus**, impetus, driving force, spur, stimulation. *See* COMPARE AND CONTRAST *at* motive.

go adrift v **wander**, drift, stray, go astray, deviate

go after v **try for**, aim for, target, go all-out for, bend over backwards

go against v **violate**, disobey, fly in the face of, infringe, buck *(infml)*

go-ahead *(infml)* n **permission**, consent, approval, green light, support

goal n 1 **objective**, aim, end, ambition, purpose 2 **goalmouth**, penalty area, box, area, goal line

go along with v **acquiesce**, concur, agree, grant, accept *Opposite*: refuse

go around v 1 **circulate**, spread, pass on, hand on, disseminate 2 **travel**, go from place to place, ride, walk, move 3 **revolve**, rotate, twirl, spin, twist

go around with *(infml)* v **accompany**, escort, tag along, spend time with, be together

go astray v **stray**, get lost, transgress, go off the rails, deviate

go away v 1 **leave**, get away, move, depart, be off *Opposite*: stay 2 **disappear**, vanish, fade, fade away, recede *Opposite*: stay

go back v **return**, turn back, revert, revisit, retrace your steps *Opposite*: advance

go back on v **change your mind**, backtrack, break your promise, have second thoughts, retract *Opposite*: keep your word

go back over v **reconsider**, re-examine, repeat, revise, return to

go backwards v **reverse**, retreat, regress, lose ground, fall back *Opposite*: advance

go bad v **decay**, go off, rot, decompose, putrefy

go bankrupt v **fail**, collapse, fold, go out of business, go to the wall

gobble v 1 **devour**, bolt, wolf, guzzle *(infml)*, scoff *(infml) Opposite*: nibble 2 *(infml)* **use up**, go through, run through, consume, eat into *Opposite*: conserve

gobbledegook *(infml)* n **nonsense**, jargon, gibberish, drivel, rubbish

go berserk v **lose control**, lose your temper, lose your cool, go mad, be beside yourself

go-between n **mediator**, intermediary, broker, arbitrator, messenger

go beyond v **surpass**, outdo, rise above, overtake, pass

goblet n **glass**, cup, chalice, wineglass

goblin n **elf**, sprite, imp, gnome, troll

go bust *(infml)* v **go bankrupt**, go under, shut down, fail, go out of business

go by v **pass**, pass by, elapse, lapse

god n **deity**, divinity, idol, spirit, supernatural being

goddess n **deity**, divinity, idol, spirit, supernatural being

godlike adj **divine**, superhuman, transcendent, heavenly, holy

godliness n 1 **religiousness**, holiness, devoutness, goodness, saintliness *Opposite*: wickedness 2 **divinity**, holiness, heavenliness, transcendence, sacredness

godly *(fml)* adj 1 **religious**, devout, holy, pious, saintly *Opposite*: wicked 2 **divine**, holy, heavenly, transcendent, godlike

go down v 1 **descend**, drop, sink, dive, plunge *Opposite*: go up 2 **deteriorate**, decline, slip, go downhill, get worse *Opposite*: improve 3 *(infml)* **lose**, be defeated, be beaten, go under, fail *Opposite*: win

go downhill v **deteriorate**, worsen, fail, get worse, go down *Opposite*: improve

go down with *(infml)* v **catch**, become ill with, contract, pick up, come down with

godsend n **blessing**, boon, stroke of luck, bonus, benefit *Opposite*: disaster

go easy on *(infml)* v 1 **treat gently**, indulge, sympathize, oblige, please *Opposite*: punish 2 **take it easy**, slow down, take it steady, avoid, stint *Opposite*: overdo

gofer *(infml)* n **runner**, messenger, minion, assistant, lackey

go for v 1 *(infml)* **try for**, go after, target, aim for, set your sights on 2 *(infml)* **like**, enjoy, prefer, follow, love *Opposite*: dislike 3 *(infml)* **choose**, pick, select, prefer, opt for *Opposite*: refuse 4 **attack**, lay into, set upon, assault, tear into

go forward v **advance**, progress, go on, move along, proceed *Opposite*: go back

go from bad to worse v **worsen**, take a turn for the worse, deteriorate, degenerate, go downhill *Opposite*: improve

go-getter *(infml)* n **achiever**, doer, self-starter, high-flier, live wire *(infml) Opposite*: layabout

go-getting *(infml)* adj **ambitious**, high-powered, determined, positive, single-minded

goggle v **stare**, gaze, gape, ogle, look

goggles n glasses, spectacles, specs (infml)

go hard v solidify, set, set hard, harden, stiffen Opposite: soften

go in v enter, set foot in, gain admittance, step in, access Opposite: leave

go in for v 1 enter, compete in, take part in, take up 2 like, prefer, follow, love, enjoy Opposite: dislike

going n 1 departure, exit, disappearance Opposite: arrival 2 conditions, circumstances, situation, case, setup ■ adj 1 successful, profitable, moneymaking, working Opposite: bankrupt 2 accepted, standard, valid, current, present 3 available, obtainable, ready, free, open Opposite: taken

going-over (infml) n 1 examination, inspection, check, investigation, analysis 2 overhaul, service, restoration, checkup, improvement 3 rebuke, reprimand, scolding, talking-to (infml), telling-off (infml)

going rate n market price, standard price, usual price, average price, price

goings-on (infml) n activity, comings and goings, affairs, business, toing and froing

go into v 1 discuss, go over, talk about, look into, examine Opposite: ignore 2 enter, go in, set foot in, gain admittance, step in Opposite: leave

go into detail v elaborate, enlarge on, amplify, expand, explain

go in with v partner, join, cooperate, merge, combine

gold n 1 treasure, bullion, ingots, gold plate, sovereigns 2 wealth, money, assets, resources, riches 3 (infml) first place, first prize, title, medal, trophy ■ adj gilded, gilt, gold-leaf, gold-plated, golden

gold brick n fake, fraud, fool's gold, counterfeit, swindle

golden adj 1 excellent, unique, first-rate, wonderful, superb 2 idyllic, best, peak, utopian, paradisaical 3 gold, gold-plated, gold-leaf, gilt, gilded 4 favoured, superior, special, elite, select

golden age n peak, pinnacle, apex, summit, zenith

golden mean n middle, midway, mean Opposite: extreme

golden opportunity n opportunity, advantage, chance, chance of a lifetime, good fortune

golden rule n standard, belief, tenet, code, guide

gold mine n moneymaker, treasure-trove, treasure house, money-spinner (infml)

gold-plated adj gilded, gilt, gold-leaf, golden, gold

gold standard n benchmark, system, yardstick, touchstone, criterion

go mad v lose your temper, blow up (infml), go off the deep end (infml), go haywire (infml), blow your top (infml)

go missing v disappear, vanish, abscond, escape, go AWOL

gone adj 1 (infml) dead, passed away, passed on, no more, deceased (fml) Opposite: alive 2 absent, away, left, disappeared, moved out Opposite: present 3 used up, spent, finished, consumed, depleted Opposite: remaining

gonfalon n pennant, banner, flag, standard, ensign

goo (infml) n 1 sludge, slush, slop, sticky stuff, gunge (infml) 2 slush, sentimentality, emotionalism, mush, corn (infml)

good adj 1 high-quality, first-class, superior, excellent, first-rate Opposite: poor 2 suitable, helpful, beneficial, sound, safe Opposite: useless 3 skilled, skilful, able, proficient, accomplished Opposite: bad 4 virtuous, decent, respectable, moral, upright Opposite: immoral 5 enjoyable, pleasant, nice, lovely, satisfactory Opposite: unpleasant 6 obedient, well-behaved, well-mannered, polite, well-brought-up Opposite: naughty 7 nice, lovely, clear, mild, pleasant Opposite: bad 8 effective, useful, valuable, right, appropriate Opposite: ineffective ■ n benefit, help, advantage, usefulness, profit

good cause n charitable organization, voluntary organization, deserving cause, charity, benefit

good deed n good turn, favour, kindness, service Opposite: sin

good faith n honesty, lawfulness, sincerity, probity, integrity

good fortune n luck, good luck, chance, a stroke of luck, lucky break Opposite: misfortune

good health n fitness, strength, healthiness, vigour, robustness Opposite: illness

goodhearted adj kind-hearted, kind, caring, generous, giving

good-humoured adj friendly, good-natured, good-tempered, easygoing, genial Opposite: ill-tempered

good judgment n judiciousness, acumen, astuteness, wisdom, perspicacity

good life n luxury, comfort, ease, life of ease, life of Riley

good-looking adj attractive, handsome, beautiful, lovely, pretty Opposite: unattractive

---

COMPARE AND CONTRAST CORE MEANING: having a pleasing facial appearance

good-looking having a pleasant personal, especially facial, appearance; **attractive** pleasing in appearance or manner, or sexually desirable; **beautiful** pleasing to the senses, especially pleasing to look at, and often used to describe women whose appearance is generally considered ideal or perfect; **handsome** with good facial features or a pleasing general appearance, generally used of men, but also of women who have strong but attractive features; **lovely** pleasing to look at, most often used of women; **pretty** with an attractive, pleasant face that is appealing, rather than outstandingly beautiful, most often used of women.

good looks *n* beauty, attractiveness, prettiness, handsomeness, loveliness

goodly *adj* large, substantial, fair, considerable, reasonable

good manners *n* propriety, manners, courtesy, decorum, etiquette *Opposite*: bad manners

good name *n* reputation, credit, standing, status, prestige

good-natured *adj* pleasant, cheerful, friendly, kind, happy *Opposite*: disagreeable

goodness *n* virtuousness, decency, kindness, honesty, integrity *Opposite*: badness

good offices *n* intervention, intercession, support, mediation, help

goods *n* 1 wares, stock, articles, produce, supplies 2 property, personal property, belongings, goods and chattels, things 3 merchandise, imports, exports, cargo, freight

good sense *n* prudence, reason, practicality, intelligence, nous (*infml*) *Opposite*: stupidity

good-sized *adj* sizable, generous, big, substantial, large *Opposite*: small

good taste *n* discernment, style, elegance, judgment, refinement *Opposite*: bad taste

good-tempered *adj* placid, good-natured, easygoing, good-humoured, amicable *Opposite*: bad-tempered

good thing *n* advantage, blessing, boon, benefit, plus (*infml*)

good turn *n* favour, kindness, good deed, service

goodwill *n* kindness, friendliness, helpfulness, benevolence, generosity *Opposite*: malice

good word *n* recommendation, testimonial, reference, character, defence

goody *n* 1 treat, perk, bonus, reward, extravagance 2 hero, winner, good guy (*US*) *Opposite*: baddie (*infml*) 3 titbit, sweet, snack, candy (*US*)

goody-goody (*infml*) *n* teacher's pet, goody two-shoes (*infml*), bluenose (*US dated infml*) ■ *adj* sanctimonious, smug, self-satisfied, self-righteous, prudish

gooey *adj* 1 sticky, viscous, thick, glutinous, gummy 2 (*infml*) slushy, corny, cloying, sentimental, mushy

goof (*infml*) *n* error, blunder, slip, gaffe, mistake ■ *v* 1 mistake, get it wrong, make a blunder, blunder, go wrong 2 mix up, muddle, botch (*infml*), mess up (*infml*), foul up (*infml*)

go off *v* 1 explode, blow up, go up, detonate 2 leave, go away, go, depart, set off *Opposite*: stay 3 go bad, decay, rot, decompose, putrefy

go off the deep end *v* lose your temper, lose your cool, go berserk, lose control, hit the roof (*infml*) *Opposite*: calm down

go on *v* 1 continue, last, keep on, keep up, persist *Opposite*: stop 2 occur, happen, take place, come about 3 blabber, chatter, prattle, blather (*infml*), blab (*infml*)

go on at (*infml*) *v* whine, complain, nag, criticize, grumble

go one better *v* surpass, outdo, top, crown, better

goose step *v* strut, stride, tramp, pace, walk

go out *v* 1 socialize, meet friends, party (*infml*), go out on the town (*infml*), paint the town red (*infml*) 2 ebb, recede, flow out

go out of business *v* go bankrupt, fold, close down, shut down, go belly up

go over *v* discuss, go into, examine, look at, study *Opposite*: ignore

go over the top *v* overdo it, get carried away, gild the lily, over-egg the pudding, go mad (*infml*)

gore *v* wound, pierce, stab, spear, stick ■ *n* blood, violence, bloodletting, slaughter, killing

gorge *n* valley, ravine, canyon, defile, gap ■ *v* 1 overeat, stuff, binge, glut, sate 2 devour, wolf, bolt, gobble, consume *Opposite*: nibble

gorgeous *adj* beautiful, magnificent, stunning, elegant, attractive *Opposite*: unattractive

gorgeousness *n* elegance, magnificence, beauty, splendour, exquisiteness

gorilla (*infml*) *n* thug, brute, bully, hoodlum, heavy (*slang*)

gormless (*infml*) *adj* stupid, unintelligent, dull, obtuse, brainless *Opposite*: bright

go round *v* visit, call on, look in, drop in, pop in

gory *adj* 1 bloody, bloodstained, blood-soaked 2 violent, gruesome, brutal, bloodthirsty, fierce *Opposite*: pleasant 3 disgusting, gruesome, grisly, unpleasant, ghastly *Opposite*: delightful

go-slow *n* stoppage, strike, slowdown (*US*)

gossamer *n* filaments, spider's web, cobwebs, threads (*US*) ■ *adj* delicate, flimsy, sheer, filmy, ethereal *Opposite*: robust

gossip *n* 1 rumour, hearsay, tittle-tattle, scandal, chitchat (*infml*) 2 chatter, chat, talk, conversation, chinwag (*infml*) 3 tattler, telltale, gossipmonger, scandalmonger, rumourmonger ■ *v* chatter, talk, converse, chat, natter (*infml*)

gossipmonger *n* tattler, telltale, gossip, scandalmonger, rumourmonger

go the distance *v* complete, finish, achieve, accomplish, carry out *Opposite*: give up

Gothic *adj* supernatural, melodramatic, eerie, grotesque, gloomy

go through *v* 1 experience, endure, undergo, bear, suffer 2 use, get through, run through, consume, utilize *Opposite*: keep 3 examine, look through, look over, go over, study

go through the roof v soar, rocket, rise, shoot up, spiral upwards *Opposite*: plummet

go to bed v retire, turn in *(infml)*, hit the hay *(infml)*, hit the sack *(infml)*

go to pieces v break down, crack, lose control, collapse, crumple

go to pot *(infml)* v deteriorate, disintegrate, fall apart, go downhill, go from bad to worse *Opposite*: improve

go to rack and ruin *(infml) see* **go to pot**

go to sleep v fall asleep, nod off, doze off, drift off, drop off *(infml) Opposite*: wake up

go to the dogs *(infml)* v go downhill, deteriorate, degenerate, decline, go from bad to worse *Opposite*: improve

go to the wall v go bankrupt, fold, go under, fail, close down

go to waste v be wasted, go down the drain, fall by the wayside, go to seed, go down the tube *(infml)*

gouge v scratch, score, scrape, mark, cut into ■ n score, scratch, gash, groove, hollow

gouge out v dig out, hollow out, press out, squeeze out, force out

go under v 1 collapse, go to the wall, fold, fail, go bust *(infml)* 2 lose consciousness, pass out, black out, faint

go up v explode, go off, detonate, blow up, ignite

go up in smoke v 1 burn, catch fire, burst into flames, burn to a crisp, burn to the ground 2 fail, fold, collapse, go wrong, go awry

gourmand n 1 glutton, overeater, greedy guts *(infml)*, gannet *(infml)*, pig *(infml)* 2 gastronome, food lover, connoisseur, gourmet, epicure

gourmet n gastronome, food lover, connoisseur, gourmand, epicure

govern v rule, preside over, oversee, administer, administrate

governess n tutor, teacher, instructor, schoolteacher, educator

government n administration, rule, management, direction, regime

governmental adj administrative, parliamentary, legislative, executive, constitutional

governor n director, ruler, manager, administrator, chief

governorship n administration, leadership, stewardship, directorship, captaincy

go wild *(infml)* v run riot, rampage, run amok, go on the rampage, run wild

go with v 1 *(infml)* date, go out with, see, socialize, go steady 2 adopt, accept, follow, run with, support

go without v not have, do without, be without, lack, want *Opposite*: have

gown n dress, robe, evening dress, wedding dress, ballgown

go wrong v 1 fail, break down, not work, not succeed, go awry *Opposite*: succeed 2 make a mistake, misjudge, blunder, slip up *(infml)*, goof *(infml)*

GP n family doctor, doctor, clinician, practitioner, medic *(infml)*

grab v 1 grasp, clutch, grip, take hold of, seize *Opposite*: let go 2 snatch, take, seize, remove, steal 3 *(infml)* affect, appeal, impress, attract, please

grab hold of v grab, grasp, grip, snatch, clutch

grace n 1 elegance, refinement, loveliness, beauty, polish *Opposite*: awkwardness 2 kindness, kindliness, decency, mercy, mercifulness *Opposite*: unkindness 3 blessing, prayer, thanks, thanksgiving ■ v 1 dignify, honour, favour, distinguish *Opposite*: demean 2 adorn, embellish, enhance, decorate, ornament *Opposite*: deface

graceful adj 1 elegant, beautiful, supple, agile, nimble *Opposite*: graceless 2 poised, dignified, polished, refined, stylish *Opposite*: awkward 3 flowing, fluid, smooth, easy on the eye, attractive *Opposite*: ugly

gracefulness n 1 elegance, grace, smoothness, fluidity, subtlety *Opposite*: inelegance 2 poise, dignity, refinement, grace, restraint *Opposite*: awkwardness

graceless adj 1 clumsy, ungainly, inelegant, awkward, maladroit *Opposite*: graceful 2 rude, impolite, ill-mannered, boorish, offensive *Opposite*: polite

gracelessness n 1 inelegance, awkwardness, clumsiness, ungainliness, unskilfulness *Opposite*: gracefulness 2 rudeness, impoliteness, mannerlessness, bad manners, boorishness *Opposite*: politeness

grace period n extra time, extension, overrun, overtime *(US)*

gracious adj 1 kind, polite, tactful, courteous, civil *Opposite*: rude 2 condescending, haughty, superior, patronizing, high and mighty *Opposite*: genuine 3 luxurious, elegant, comfortable, well-appointed, plush *(infml) Opposite*: modest 4 merciful, compassionate, lenient, humane, charitable *Opposite*: harsh

graciousness n kindness, courteousness, politeness, civility, affability *Opposite*: rudeness

gradation n nuance, degree, stage, progression, shift

grade n 1 score, mark, rating, ranking, evaluation 2 rank, position, status, standing, class ■ v classify, categorize, sort, arrange, order

gradient n slope, incline, ramp, hill, rise

gradual adj slow, measured, slow but sure, plodding, continuing *Opposite*: rapid

graduate v 1 progress, move up, advance, go forward, move on *Opposite*: fall back 2 mark off, measure off, divide up, regulate 3 arrange, order, categorize, classify, rank

graduation n 1 matriculation, qualification, completion, validation, attainment 2 award ceremony, graduation day, ceremony, passing out 3 mark, division, line, unit, step 4 calibration, division, measurement, marking up, marking out

graffiti n drawing, doodle, scrawl, scribble, writing

graft n 1 implant, insert, transplant, scion, slip 2 (infml) work, labour, toil, slog, grind ■ v 1 (infml) labour, strive, work, slog, slave 2 splice, attach, join, embed, implant

grain n 1 cereal, wheat, corn, barley, maize 2 seed, kernel, germ 3 particle, speck, fragment, crumb, bit 4 pattern, direction, configuration, arrangement, texture

grammar n syntax, sentence structure, language rules, parsing

grammatical adj 1 linguistic, syntactic, structural 2 correct, well-formed, right, proper, standard

gran (infml) see grandmother

granary n warehouse, barn, silo

grand adj 1 outstanding, impressive, imposing, majestic, magnificent Opposite: humble 2 ambitious, impressive, far-reaching, major, substantial Opposite: limited 3 distinguished, illustrious, celebrated, well-known, famous Opposite: ordinary 4 wonderful, fantastic, excellent, memorable, great Opposite: poor

granddad (infml) see grandfather

grandee n dignitary, notable, public figure, VIP, nob (infml) Opposite: upstart

grandeur n splendour, magnificence, sumptuousness, opulence, majesty Opposite: austerity

grandfather n granddad (infml), grandpa (infml), gramps (infml)

grandiloquence n pomposity, bombast, loftiness, fustian, rhetoric

grandiloquent adj pompous, lofty, haughty, bombastic, high-flown Opposite: plain

grandiose adj 1 pretentious, pompous, flamboyant, ostentatious, extravagant Opposite: modest 2 magnificent, lavish, splendid, impressive, stately Opposite: modest 3 elaborate, ambitious, complex, impenetrable, unfathomable Opposite: simple

grandiosity n 1 pretentiousness, pompousness, self-importance, affectedness, pomposity Opposite: unpretentiousness 2 magnificence, lavishness, splendour, impressiveness, stateliness Opposite: modesty 3 elaborateness, ambitiousness, complexity, impenetrability Opposite: simplicity

grandma (infml) see grandmother

grandmother n grandma (infml), nana (infml), gran (infml), granny (infml), nanny (infml)

grandness n magnificence, splendour, majesty, dignity, stateliness Opposite: simplicity

grandpa (infml) see grandfather

grange n farmhouse, country house, manor house, homestead, ranch

granny (infml) see grandmother

grant v 1 allow, permit, agree to, consent to, approve of Opposite: prohibit 2 give, accord, award, sign over, present ■ n funding, scholarship, endowment, contribution, donation. See COMPARE AND CONTRAST at give.

granular adj gritty, grainy, rough, coarse, granulated Opposite: smooth

granulated adj ground, coarse, grainy, gritty, rough

granule n grain, pellet, particle, morsel, crumb

grapevine n rumour mill, gossip, word of mouth, viral marketing, bush telegraph (infml)

graph n chart, diagram, grid, display

graphic adj 1 explicit, realistic, vivid, striking, detailed Opposite: sketchy 2 illustrative, pictorial, drawn, diagrammatic, decorative

grapple v 1 struggle, wrestle, seize, grab, grasp 2 contend, deal with, cope, face, handle

grasp v 1 take hold of, clutch, grab, seize, grip Opposite: let go 2 understand, comprehend, see the point of, follow, get ■ n 1 grip, hold, clutch, clasp, clench 2 understanding, comprehension, knowledge, awareness, perception 3 reach, scope, extent, range, capacity

grasping adj greedy, avaricious, covetous, selfish, acquisitive Opposite: generous

grass n grassland, meadow, pasture, prairie, sward

WORD BANK
❑ **types of grass** bamboo, beach grass, bluegrass, bulrush, couch grass, crab grass, esparto, fescue, Kentucky bluegrass, lyme grass, marram, meadow fescue, pampas grass, reed, rye-grass, spinifex, sugar cane, sword grass, timothy

grassland n plains, prairie, savanna, steppe, heath

grassroots n 1 masses, hoi polloi, rank and file, ranks, also-rans 2 basis, origin, foundation, base, root ■ adj popular, proletarian, public, common, ordinary

grassy adj green, verdant, lush

grate n grill, lattice, grille, trellis, grid ■ v 1 shred, scrape, rasp, file, grind 2 irritate, annoy, exasperate, vex, chafe Opposite: please

grateful adj thankful, appreciative, obliged, indebted, glad Opposite: ungrateful

gratefulness n thankfulness, appreciativeness, appreciation, gratitude, thanks Opposite: ingratitude

gratification n satisfaction, fulfilment, indulgence, enjoyment, delight Opposite: displeasure

gratify v please, satisfy, indulge, fulfil, oblige Opposite: displease

gratifying *adj* **rewarding**, satisfying, agreeable, heartwarming, acceptable *Opposite*: humiliating

grating *n* **grille**, grate, lattice, grid, screen ■ *adj* **1 rough**, harsh, raucous, strident, discordant *Opposite*: mellifluous **2 irritating**, annoying, infuriating, insensitive, vexing *Opposite*: pleasant

gratis *adj* **free**, free of charge, on the house, complimentary, for nothing

gratitude *n* **thanks**, thankfulness, appreciation, gratefulness, appreciativeness *Opposite*: ingratitude

gratuitous *adj* **1 unwarranted**, uncalled-for, wanton, unjustified, unnecessary *Opposite*: necessary **2 free**, gratis, complimentary, at no charge, on the house

gratuitously *adv* **unnecessarily**, pointlessly, unreasonably, needlessly, wantonly *Opposite*: necessarily

gratuity *n* **tip**, service charge, donation, token of appreciation, reward

grave *n* **tomb**, crypt, vault, burial chamber, mausoleum ■ *adj* **1 serious**, severe, weighty, momentous, crucial *Opposite*: minor **2 solemn**, serious, sombre, grim, earnest *Opposite*: cheerful **3 ominous**, foreboding, forbidding, fateful, dire *Opposite*: favourable

gravel *n* **stones**, pebbles, shingle, chippings

gravelly *adj* **1 croaky**, gruff, hoarse, rough, harsh *Opposite*: velvety **2 pebbly**, shingly, stony, rocky, gritty

gravely *adv* **1 grimly**, sternly, austerely, seriously, solemnly *Opposite*: cheerfully **2 fatally**, dangerously, critically, incurably, mortally

gravestone *n* **headstone**, marker, cenotaph, tombstone, memorial

graveyard *n* **cemetery**, churchyard, necropolis, burial ground, boneyard *(infml)*

gravitas *n* **seriousness**, gravity, sobriety, solemnness, sombreness

gravitate *v* **1 incline**, lean, move, drift, be attracted *Opposite*: repel **2 sink**, settle, drop, fall, descend *Opposite*: rise

gravitation *n* **movement**, attraction, gravity

gravity *n* **1 gravitation**, gravitational force, pull, draw **2 seriousness**, importance, significance, enormity *Opposite*: insignificance **3 solemnity**, grimness, sedateness, dignity, earnestness *Opposite*: cheerfulness

graze *v* **1 browse**, crop, nibble, forage, eat **2 scrape**, scratch, scuff, rub, skin **3 glance**, brush, skim, sweep, touch ■ *n* **scratch**, scrape, abrasion, lesion, scuff mark

grease *n* **fat**, lard, oil ■ *v* **lubricate**, oil, smear

greasiness *n* **fattiness**, griminess, sliminess, oiliness, oleaginousness

greasy *adj* **oily**, fatty, slippery, slimy, oleaginous

great *adj* **1 huge**, immense, enormous, vast, large *Opposite*: tiny **2 famous**, illustrious, eminent, distinguished, celebrated *Opposite*: ordinary **3 noble**, elevated, lofty, imposing, stately *Opposite*: lowly **4 wonderful**, fantastic, magnificent, excellent, incredible *Opposite*: awful **5 absolute**, utter, complete, downright, intense *Opposite*: slight **6 countless**, inordinate, prodigious, excessive, boundless *Opposite*: limited **7 important**, significant, momentous, critical, major *Opposite*: unimportant

greater *adj* **better**, superior, larger, bigger, more

greatest *adj* **most**, maximum, record, utmost, supreme

greatly *adv* **1 very much**, really, to a great extent, to the highest degree, deeply *Opposite*: hardly **2 importantly**, significantly, momentously, critically, seriously

greatness *n* **1 magnitude**, enormity, immensity, vastness, size **2 importance**, prominence, seriousness, significance, weightiness *Opposite*: insignificance **3 fame**, eminence, distinction, impressiveness, prominence *Opposite*: commonness

greed *n* **1 gluttony**, voracity, ravenousness, insatiability, hunger *Opposite*: moderation **2 avarice**, covetousness, materialism, acquisitiveness, greediness *Opposite*: generosity

greediness *see* **greed**

greedy *adj* **1 gluttonous**, voracious, ravenous, insatiable, hungry *Opposite*: moderate **2 avaricious**, covetous, grasping, materialistic, acquisitive *Opposite*: generous

greenery *n* **foliage**, vegetation, plants, leaves, greens (US)

greenfield *adj* **undeveloped**, green belt, out-of-town, rural, country *Opposite*: urban

greenhorn *n* **novice**, recruit, initiate, beginner, neophyte. *See* COMPARE AND CONTRAST *at* beginner.

greenhouse *n* **orangery**, glasshouse, hothouse, conservatory

green light *n* **permission**, clearance, consent, approval, stamp of approval *Opposite*: red light

greet *v* **1 welcome**, meet, make the acquaintance of, receive **2 address**, speak to, acknowledge, hail, salute *Opposite*: ignore **3 respond to**, react to, receive, meet, hail

greeting *n* **salutation**, welcome, welcoming, reception, acknowledgment

gregarious *adj* **outgoing**, sociable, social, extrovert, expressive *Opposite*: shy

gregariousness *n* **sociability**, friendliness, openness, unreservedness, conviviality *Opposite*: shyness

gremlin *(infml) n* **jinx**, malfunction, blip, glitch, bug *(infml)*

grid *n* **network**, lattice, net, web, gridiron

griddle *v* **grill**, sear, barbecue, cook

gridiron n grid, lattice, grating, framework, network

gridlock n 1 traffic jam, jam, holdup, tailback, snarl-up 2 deadlock, stalemate, standstill, logjam, impasse

grief n sorrow, heartache, anguish, misery, unhappiness Opposite: joy

grief-stricken adj grieving, distraught, traumatized, inconsolable, heartbroken Opposite: happy

grievance n 1 complaint, protest, criticism, objection, grumble 2 injustice, wrong, cause of distress, ill-treatment, unfairness

grieve v 1 mourn, feel sad, be sad, lament, be distressed Opposite: rejoice (literary) 2 hurt, afflict, pain, distress, upset Opposite: cheer

grievous adj 1 serious, significant, critical, dangerous, grave Opposite: slight 2 dreadful, awful, terrible, shameful, painful

grill v 1 (infml) question, interrogate, examine, press, probe 2 cook, barbecue, toast, brown, frizzle ■ n griddle, grate, barbecue, rotisserie. See COMPARE AND CONTRAST at question.

grille n grating, lattice, framework, grid, trellis

grim adj 1 depressing, bleak, dismal, gloomy, cheerless Opposite: hopeful 2 forbidding, ugly, unattractive, uninviting, grey Opposite: attractive 3 stern, serious, dour, severe, morose Opposite: kind 4 shocking, ghastly, horrible, horrific, gruesome Opposite: pleasant 5 (infml) ill, unwell, off-colour (infml), poorly, indisposed (fml) Opposite: well 6 (infml) shoddy, bad, awful, dire, appalling Opposite: excellent

grimace n scowl, frown, smirk, sneer, pout Opposite: smile ■ v frown, scowl, smirk, sneer, pout Opposite: smile

grime n filth, dirt, stain, soot, dust

griminess n dirtiness, dinginess, filthiness, grubbiness, dustiness Opposite: cleanliness

grimness n 1 bleakness, cheerlessness, dismalness, ominousness, gloominess Opposite: brightness 2 forbiddingness, ugliness, unattractiveness, greyness, dinginess Opposite: attractiveness 3 sternness, seriousness, dourness, severity, moroseness Opposite: kindness 4 gruesomeness, horror, hideousness, grisliness, dreadfulness Opposite: pleasantness

grimy adj dirty, grubby, smudged, soiled, filthy Opposite: clean. See COMPARE AND CONTRAST at dirty.

grin v smile, beam, smirk, laugh, chortle Opposite: frown ■ n beam, smile, smirk, laugh, chortle Opposite: frown

grin and bear it (infml) v put up with, take the rough with the smooth, take the bad with the good, weather, lump it (infml)

grind v 1 crush, break up, mill, pound, mince 2 grate, rasp, gnash, scrape Opposite: glide 3 sharpen, file, whet, abrade, polish Opposite: blunt ■ n (infml) toil, chore, slog, tedium, routine

grind down v 1 wear, erode, eat away, abrade, rub 2 oppress, tyrannize, persecute, harass, weaken Opposite: nurture

grinder n mill, mincer, crusher, pounder, pulverizer

grinding adj 1 crushing, oppressive, relentless, unending, never-ending 2 grating, crunching, earsplitting, screeching, squealing Opposite: pleasant

grip n 1 grasp, hold, clasp, clutch Opposite: release 2 control, rule, command, authority, clutches 3 understanding, comprehension, grasp, command, appreciation Opposite: ignorance ■ v 1 grasp, clasp, clutch, catch, seize Opposite: release 2 stick, adhere, cling, hang on, cleave to (literary) 3 overwhelm, fill, pervade, suffuse, swamp 4 fascinate, enthral, spellbind, transfix, mesmerize Opposite: bore

gripe (infml) v complain, grumble, protest, object, moan (infml) ■ n complaint, grumble, grievance, protest, objection Opposite: compliment. See COMPARE AND CONTRAST at complain.

gripped adj absorbed, engrossed, rapt, obsessed, enthralled Opposite: bored

gripping adj fascinating, spellbinding, enthralling, mesmerizing, transfixing Opposite: boring

grisliness n gruesomeness, ghastliness, grimness, hideousness, dreadfulness Opposite: pleasantness

grisly adj gruesome, ghastly, horrible, horrific, horrid Opposite: pleasant

gristle n cartilage, tendon, sinew

gristly adj tough, chewy, sinewy, stringy, leathery Opposite: tender

grit n 1 gravel, stones, pebbles, sand, shingle 2 determination, perseverance, tenacity, bravery, fortitude Opposite: cowardice ■ v clench, grind, gnash, grate

gritty adj 1 determined, persistent, resolute, courageous, persevering Opposite: cowardly 2 realistic, graphic, harsh, stark, uncompromising Opposite: romantic 3 grainy, coarse, rough, granular, sandy Opposite: smooth

grit your teeth v steel yourself, nerve yourself, brace yourself, persevere, hold on tight Opposite: knuckle under

grizzle (infml) v 1 cry, whine, moan, whimper, snivel 2 grumble, complain, moan, mutter, go on

grizzly adj fractious, irritable, crying, whiny, whining

groan v 1 moan, cry out, whimper, grunt, growl Opposite: laugh 2 (infml) grumble, complain, carp, moan, gripe (infml) 3 creak, squeak, squeal, screech, grind

groceries n food, shopping, provisions, rations, victuals

grogginess n tiredness, fatigue, sleepiness, unsteadiness, bleariness Opposite: alertness

groggy *adj* **tired**, sleepy, slow, unsteady, bleary *Opposite*: alert

groom *v* **1 prime**, train, coach, prepare, tutor *Opposite*: hinder **2 clean**, clean up, brush, comb, tidy

groove *n* **channel**, furrow, rut, trench, indentation *Opposite*: ridge

grope *v* **1 fumble**, feel, cast about, scrabble, flounder **2** (*infml*) **fondle**, touch, molest, caress, feel up (*infml*)

gross *adj* **1 aggregate**, combined, whole, overall, total *Opposite*: net **2 flagrant**, blatant, glaring, arrant, serious *Opposite*: minor **3 coarse**, vulgar, crass, rude, crude *Opposite*: polite **4 uncultured**, uncivilized, uncultivated, unsophisticated, unpolished *Opposite*: cultured **5 overweight**, obese, fat, heavy, stout *Opposite*: slim **6** (*infml*) **disgusting**, unpleasant, sickening, foul, nasty *Opposite*: pleasant ■ *v* **earn**, make, take, receive, bring in

grossly *adv* **1 wholly**, totally, completely, utterly, unacceptably *Opposite*: slightly **2 rudely**, coarsely, uncouthly, crassly, crudely *Opposite*: politely **3** (*infml*) **disgustingly**, revoltingly, nauseatingly, vilely, hideously *Opposite*: pleasantly

grotesque *adj* **1 distorted**, bizarre, misshapen, monstrous, gross (*infml*) *Opposite*: attractive **2 incongruous**, ridiculous, ludicrous, laughable, outrageous *Opposite*: fitting

grotto *n* **cavern**, pothole, hollow, cave

grotty (*infml*) *adj* **shabby**, rundown, dingy, tatty, grubby *Opposite*: spotless

grouch (*infml*) *n* **1 complaint**, grumble, whine, grouse (*infml*), moan (*infml*) *Opposite*: praise **2 grumbler**, complainer, malcontent, moaner (*infml*), whinger (*infml*) ■ *v* **complain**, grumble, sulk, gripe (*infml*), moan (*infml*)

grouchiness (*infml*) *n* **peevishness**, irritability, cantankerousness, crabbiness, bad temper *Opposite*: equanimity

grouchy (*infml*) *adj* **bad-tempered**, complaining, touchy, grumpy, crabby *Opposite*: eventempered

ground *n* **1 earth**, soil, land, field, dry land **2 playing field**, pitch, field, arena, stadium ■ *adj* **crushed**, pulverized, broken up, milled, minced ■ *v* **1 initiate**, prepare, coach, instruct, tutor **2 base**, substantiate, support, build, justify **3 punish**, deal with, chastise

groundbreaking *adj* **innovative**, pioneering, revolutionary, radical, trailblazing *Opposite*: outdated

grounding *n* **foundation**, basis, preparation, training, instruction

groundless *adj* **baseless**, unsupported, unjustified, unwarranted, unfounded *Opposite*: sound

ground plan *n* **1 floor plan**, plan, scale drawing, blueprint, diagram **2 outline**, sketch, blueprint, draft, preliminary design

ground rule *n* **fundamental**, axiom, stipulation, point of departure, modus operandi

grounds *n* **1 basis**, foundation, reason, justification, argument **2 estate**, land, park, parkland, gardens **3 dregs**, lees, sediment, residue, deposit

groundsheet *n* **tarpaulin**, sheeting, cover, throw, rug

groundswell *n* **1 swell**, wave, storm, squall, heavy sea **2 upsurge**, wave, outpouring, rise, swell

groundwork *n* **foundation**, basis, base, footing, underpinning

group *n* **1 collection**, cluster, set, assemblage, assembly *Opposite*: individual **2 grouping**, set, faction, crowd, company *Opposite*: individual **3 musical group**, band, trio, duo, quartet *Opposite*: soloist **4 alliance**, federation, consortium, amalgamation, confederation ■ *v* **1 classify**, categorize, arrange, sort, bracket **2 gather**, assemble, congregate, convene, cluster *Opposite*: disperse

groupie (*infml*) *n* **follower**, fan, enthusiast, supporter, aficionado

grouping *n* **1 alliance**, federation, consortium, assemblage, alignment **2 category**, class, set, type, group

grouse (*infml*) *v* **complain**, grumble, moan, gripe (*infml*), bellyache (*infml*) ■ *n* **complaint**, grumble, objection, protest, moan (*infml*). *See* COMPARE AND CONTRAST at **complain**.

grout *n* **mortar**, filling, plaster, cement, putty ■ *v* **fill**, mortar, plaster, cement, render

grouts *n* **dregs**, lees, residue, sediment, deposit

grove *n* **copse**, coppice, orchard, wood, stand

grovel *v* **1 plead**, beg, cringe, fawn, bow and scrape **2 crawl**, crouch, stoop, kneel, creep (*infml*) *Opposite*: stand up

grow *v* **1 develop**, grow up, mature, shoot up, sprout **2 expand**, enlarge, swell, extend, spread *Opposite*: shrink **3 increase**, multiply, intensify, escalate, strengthen *Opposite*: decrease **4 produce**, cultivate, nurture, breed, raise

growing *adj* **rising**, mounting, upward, budding, emergent *Opposite*: decreasing

growl *v* **roar**, snarl, bark, howl, rumble

grow less *v* **weaken**, wear off, fade, subside, decrease *Opposite*: increase

grown *adj* **grown-up**, fully-fledged, adult, developed, mature *Opposite*: immature

grown-up *adj* **adult**, mature, developed, grown, responsible *Opposite*: immature

growth *n* **1 growing**, development, evolution, progress, advance *Opposite*: decay **2 increase**, enlargement, expansion, augmentation, development *Opposite*: reduction **3 tumour**, cyst, lump, swelling, outgrowth

grow up *v* **1 grow**, develop, mature, evolve,

flourish **2 take shape**, arise, be born, develop, come about

groyne n **breakwater**, mole, barrier, bulwark, jetty

grub v **1 dig**, burrow, root out, excavate, pull up **2 search**, hunt, rummage, ferret, forage ■ n **1 larva**, maggot, caterpillar, bug, creepy-crawly *(infml)* **2** *(infml)* **food**, victuals, sustenance, feed, nourishment

grubbiness n **1 dirtiness**, griminess, filthiness, muddiness, sloppiness *Opposite*: cleanness **2 sordidness**, squalidness, seediness, contemptibleness, despicableness *Opposite*: purity

grubby adj **1 dirty**, grimy, soiled, filthy, muddy *Opposite*: clean **2 sordid**, squalid, seedy, contemptible, despicable *Opposite*: honourable. See COMPARE AND CONTRAST at **dirty**.

grudge n **complaint**, bitterness, resentment, dislike, hatred ■ v **resent**, hold against, begrudge, loathe, mind

grudging adj **reluctant**, unwilling, complaining, resentful, rancorous *Opposite*: willing

gruelling adj **arduous**, exhausting, demanding, taxing, tough *Opposite*: easy

gruesome adj **grisly**, ghastly, horrible, horrific, horrid *Opposite*: pleasant

gruesomeness n **grisliness**, ghastliness, horror, dreadfulness, hideousness *Opposite*: pleasantness

gruff adj **1 bad-tempered**, grumpy, angry, impatient, brusque *Opposite*: friendly **2 hoarse**, husky, gravelly, rasping, harsh *Opposite*: soft

gruffness n **1 grumpiness**, crustiness, abruptness, curtness, sternness *Opposite*: pleasantness **2 hoarseness**, huskiness, thickness, throatiness, harshness *Opposite*: softness

grumble v **complain**, protest, mutter, object, moan *(infml)* ■ n **complaint**, protest, objection, moan *(infml)*, grouse *(infml)*. See COMPARE AND CONTRAST at **complain**.

grumbler n **complainer**, whiner, groaner, grouch *(infml)*, moaner *(infml)*

grumpiness n **bad-temperedness**, irritability, cantankerousness, petulance, crabbiness *Opposite*: cheerfulness

grumpy adj **bad-tempered**, irritable, sullen, cantankerous, ill-tempered *Opposite*: cheerful

grunge *(infml)* n **filth**, grime, dirt, mess, muck *(infml)* *Opposite*: cleanliness

grungy *(infml)* adj **shabby**, dirty, scruffy, unkempt, dilapidated *Opposite*: clean

grunt v **speak indistinctly**, mumble, groan, snort

guarantee n **1 assurance**, promise, pledge, agreement, security **2 warranty**, certification, undertaking, contract, agreement ■ v **assure**, ensure, promise, pledge, warrant

guaranteed adj **certain**, definite, sure, cast-iron, fail-safe *Opposite*: uncertain

guarantor n **backer**, sponsor, underwriter, supporter, patron. See COMPARE AND CONTRAST at **backer**.

guard v **protect**, defend, safeguard, shield, watch over ■ n **1 protector**, sentinel, sentry, picket, lookout **2 safeguard**, security, protection, shield, fortification. See COMPARE AND CONTRAST at **safeguard**.

guarded adj **1 wary**, cautious, careful, circumspect, hesitant *Opposite*: open **2 protected**, secured, watched over, defended, safeguarded *Opposite*: unprotected. See COMPARE AND CONTRAST at **cautious**.

guardhouse n **prison**, jail, lockup, cells, detention centre

guardian n **1 guard**, sentinel, keeper, custodian **2 carer**, protector, godparent

guardianship n **protection**, custody, care, responsibility, supervision

guardrail n **handrail**, rail, banister, railing, paling

guerrilla n **freedom fighter**, rebel, insurgent, irregular, paramilitary

guess v **1 predict**, solve, fathom, work out, conjecture **2 deduce**, presume, speculate, suppose, estimate ■ n **deduction**, conjecture, supposition, presumption, speculation

guesstimate *(infml)* n **guess**, estimate, conjecture, projection, reckoning ■ v **estimate**, guess, reckon, conjecture, project

guesswork n **conjecture**, deduction, presumption, speculation, estimation

guest n **visitor**, caller, invitee, boarder, lodger *Opposite*: host

guesthouse n **hotel**, hostel, bed and breakfast, inn, boarding house

guestroom n **room**, bedroom, spare room

guff *(infml)* n **nonsense**, rubbish, rigmarole, stuff, stuff and nonsense *Opposite*: sense

guffaw v **laugh**, chuckle, chortle, roar, fall about *(infml)* ■ n **chuckle**, laugh, chortle, roar, belly laugh

guidance n **1 leadership**, direction, supervision, management, control **2 help**, assistance, advice, support, counselling

guidance counsellor n **adviser**, counsellor, therapist, mediator

guide v **1 direct**, steer, lead, conduct, escort **2 steer**, drive, pilot, direct, handle ■ n **1 leader**, director, attendant, chaperon, controller **2 tour guide**, courier, leader, escort, conductor **3 influence**, standard, model, ideal, guiding light **4 guidebook**, handbook, manual, instructions, vade mecum

---

COMPARE AND CONTRAST CORE MEANING: show somebody the way to a place

guide take somebody in the right direction or give a tour of a particular place; **conduct** take somebody to or around a particular place, especially when the person showing the way has some kind of authority or specialized knowledge; **direct**

show or indicate the way; **lead** show the way to others, usually by going ahead of them; **steer** encourage somebody to take a particular course; **usher** escort somebody to or from a place, especially a seat.

guidebook *n* **travel guide**, vade mecum, gazeteer, guide, manual

guideline *n* **advice**, recommendation, standard, guide, parameter

guild *n* **club**, union, society, association, league

guile *n* **cunning**, treachery, astuteness, slyness, wiliness *Opposite*: frankness

guileful *adj* **cunning**, treacherous, sly, astute, wily *Opposite*: naive

guileless *adj* **naive**, frank, candid, ingenuous, straightforward *Opposite*: guileful

guillotine *v* **behead**, decapitate, execute, kill

guilt *n* **1 remorse**, shame, self-reproach, conscience, contriteness **2 fault**, responsibility, blame, culpability, guiltiness *Opposite*: innocence

guiltless *adj* **innocent**, blameless, faultless, unimpeachable, irreproachable *Opposite*: guilty

guilt-ridden *adj* **guilty**, fearful, anguished, tormented *Opposite*: unashamed

guilty *adj* **1 culpable**, responsible, at fault, blameworthy, in the wrong *Opposite*: innocent **2 shamefaced**, remorseful, embarrassed, mortified, guilt-ridden *Opposite*: unashamed

guilty conscience *n* **guilt complex**, conscience, twinge, pang, guilt trip *(slang)*

guise *n* **1 appearance**, semblance, show, pretext, excuse **2 form**, appearance, shape, light, phase **3 costume**, disguise, dress, outfit, mask

gulf *n* **1 bight**, bay, inlet, sound, cove **2 hole**, abyss, chasm, gap, hollow

gullet *n* **crop**, maw, throat, craw, gorge

gullibility *n* **trustfulness**, innocence, credulity, unwariness, acceptance *Opposite*: shrewdness

gullible *adj* **naive**, susceptible, innocent, trusting, accepting *Opposite*: discerning

gully *n* **1 ravine**, gorge, valley, gap, chasm **2 channel**, ditch, furrow, rut, culvert

gulp *v* **swallow**, drink, toss down, guzzle *(infml)*, swig *(infml) Opposite*: sip ■ *n* **swallow**, drink, mouthful, swig *(infml)*, slug *(infml) Opposite*: sip

gulp back *v* **stifle**, suppress, restrain, hold back, fight back

gulp down *v* **wolf**, swill, swallow, down, gobble *Opposite*: sip

gum *n* **1 secretion**, exudate, resin, latex, juice **2 glue**, adhesive, paste, cement, epoxy resin ■ *v* **stick**, glue, paste, bond, cement *Opposite*: unstick

gummy *adj* **sticky**, gooey, gluey, tacky, adhesive

gumption *(infml) n* **1 common sense**, sense, shrewdness, practicality, presence of mind *Opposite*: stupidity **2 courage**, nerve, bravery, mettle, pluck

gun *n* **firearm**, handgun, shooter *(infml)*, piece *(slang)*

WORD BANK

❏ **types of gun** air pistol, air rifle, antiaircraft gun, automatic, bazooka, blunderbuss, cannon, carbine, flame-thrower, handgun, howitzer, machine gun, magnum, mortar, musket, pistol, revolver, rifle, sawn-off shotgun, semiautomatic, shotgun, submachine gun, Tommy gun *(infml)*

---

gun down *(infml) v* **kill**, assassinate, shoot, shoot down, mow down

gunfight *n* **gun battle**, shoot-out, firefight, fight, duel

gunfire *n* **firing**, shooting, gunshot, shots, bombardment

gunge *(infml) n* **slime**, dirt, mess, goo *(infml)*, gunk *(infml)*

gung ho *(infml) adj* **1 combative**, belligerent, militaristic, bellicose, aggressive *Opposite*: peaceable **2 enthusiastic**, eager, keen, zealous, ardent *Opposite*: reluctant

gungy *(infml) adj* **slimy**, dirty, filthy, messy, gunky *(infml) Opposite*: clean

gunk *(infml) n* **grease**, mess, filth, dirt, slime

gunky *(infml) see* **gungy**

gunman *n* **1 sniper**, murderer, assassin, killer, gangster **2 marksman**, markswoman, shot, crack shot, good shot

gunner *n* **soldier**, shooter, artilleryman, fusilier, rifleman

guns *n* **weapons**, ordnance, firepower, artillery, arms

gunshot *see* **gunfire**

gurgle *v* **1 bubble**, slosh, splash, ripple, murmur **2 babble**, burble, coo, warble, crow

guru *n* **1 spiritual leader**, religious teacher, maharishi, spiritual guide, spiritual adviser **2 leader**, authority, leading light, expert, pundit

gush *v* **1 pour**, flood, stream, surge, spurt *Opposite*: trickle **2 be effusive**, prattle, flatter, ooze, admire *Opposite*: criticize ■ *n* **flood**, flow, spurt, jet, stream *Opposite*: trickle

gushing *adj* **1 pouring**, flowing, overflowing, spouting, torrential *Opposite*: trickling **2 effusive**, voluble, enthusiastic, emotional, sentimental *Opposite*: reserved

gusset *n* **patch**, insert, inset, reinforcement, support

gust *n* **1 squall**, draught, flurry, breeze, blast *Opposite*: calm **2 burst**, explosion, expulsion, eruption, outburst ■ *v* **blow**, bluster, squall

gusto *n* **enjoyment**, delight, enthusiasm, passion, zest *Opposite*: apathy

gusty *adj* **windy**, breezy, squally, stormy, blustery *Opposite*: calm

gut *v* **1 disembowel**, eviscerate, clean, prepare, dress **2 ruin**, damage, destroy, burn, raze *Opposite*: build up **3 strip**, clear out, empty, empty out, plunder ■ *adj* **instinctive**, intuitive, emotional, automatic, unconscious *Opposite*: considered

gut feeling *n* **guess**, hunch, instinct, impression, intuition *Opposite*: fact

gutless *adj* **cowardly**, spineless, spiritless, weak, timid *Opposite*: plucky. See COMPARE AND CONTRAST *at* **cowardly**.

gut reaction *see* **gut feeling**

guts *n* **1 intestines**, bowels, stomach, viscera, entrails **2 interior**, recesses, bowels, inner workings, heart **3** *(infml)* **glutton**, gourmand, gannet *(infml)*, pig *(infml)*, greedy guts *(infml)*

gutsy *(infml) adj* **1 brave**, plucky, courageous, fearless, determined *Opposite*: cowardly **2 passionate**, impassioned, emotional, intense, fiery *Opposite*: insipid **3 greedy**, gluttonous, insatiable, voracious, piggish *Opposite*: ascetic

gutted *adj* **1 cleaned**, disembowelled, eviscerated, prepared, dressed **2** *(infml)* **devastated**, shattered, reeling, heartbroken, brokenhearted *Opposite*: pleased

gutter *n* **drain**, sewer, channel, trench, groove ■ *v* **flicker**, sputter, waver, drip, fade *Opposite*: flare

guttering *n* **gutters**, channels, trenches, grooves, sewers

guttural *adj* **harsh**, rough, rasping, throaty, deep *Opposite*: melodious

guv *(infml) n* **1 mate**, pal *(infml)*, chum *(infml)*, guvnor *(dated infml)*, man *(slang)* **2 boss**, superior, manager, chief, gaffer *(infml)*

guvnor *(dated infml) n* **1 mate**, pal *(infml)*, chum *(infml)*, guv *(infml)*, man *(slang)* **2 father**, pa *(infml)*, dad *(infml)*, pop *(infml)*, papa *(dated)* **3 boss**, superior, manager, chief, gaffer *(infml)*

guy *n* **1** *(infml)* **man**, gentleman, boy, bloke *(infml)*, chap *(infml)* **2 effigy**, figure, model, manikin, scarecrow ■ *v* *(infml)* **poke fun at**, imitate, tease, satirize, send up *Opposite*: respect

guyrope *n* **rope**, lashing, string, halyard, guy

guys *(infml) n* **people**, folks, gang, everybody

guzzle *(infml) v* **1 gulp**, gobble, wolf, stuff, swig *(infml)* *Opposite*: nibble **2 consume**, use, devour, burn up, use up *Opposite*: conserve

gym *(infml) see* **gymnasium**

gymkhana *n* **horse show**, riding show, equestrian show, showjumping competition, riding competition

gymnasium *n* **fitness centre**, exercise room, sports centre, leisure centre, sports club

gymnastic *adj* **1 athletic**, acrobatic, sporty, sporting **2 energetic**, athletic, lithe, supple *Opposite*: stiff

gymnastics *n* **physical exercises**, aerobics, calisthenics, keep fit, exercises

gymslip *n* **dress**, uniform, pinafore

gypsy *n* **nomad**, traveller, drifter, wanderer

gyrate *v* **rotate**, whirl, spin, revolve, twirl

gyration *n* **whirling**, twirling, spinning, turning, revolving

gyratory *adj* **spiral**, rotating, revolving, spinning, whirling *Opposite*: still

H

habit *n* **1 custom**, routine, tradition, convention, practice **2 tendency**, inclination, leaning, preference, fondness **3 addiction**, problem, dependency, weakness, fixation **4 uniform**, garb, apparel, outfit, garment

COMPARE AND CONTRAST CORE MEANING: established pattern of behaviour
habit an action or behaviour pattern that is regular, repetitive, often unconscious, and sometimes compulsive; **custom** the way somebody normally or routinely behaves in a situation, or a traditional practice in a particular community or group of people; **tradition** a long-established action or pattern of behaviour in a particular community or group of people, especially one that has been handed down from generation to generation; **prac-**
tice an established way of doing something, especially one that has developed through experience and knowledge; **routine** a typical pattern of behaviour that is regularly followed on a day-to-day basis, sometimes with the suggestion that this is monotonous and tedious; **wont** *(fml)* something that somebody does regularly or habitually.

habitable *adj* **inhabitable**, livable, fit for human habitation, comfortable, fit to live in *Opposite*: uninhabitable

habitat *n* **home**, locale, environment, surroundings, territory

habitation *n* **1 occupancy**, occupation, tenancy, residence **2 house**, home, lodging, residence, place **3 building**, structure, housing, construction, architecture

habitual *adj* **1 regular**, usual, routine, customary, normal *Opposite*: unusual **2 persistent**, frequent, chronic, long-term, ongoing *Opposite*: occasional **3 characteristic**, usual, customary, typical, expected *Opposite*: uncharacteristic. *See* COMPARE AND CONTRAST *at* usual.

habituate *v* **familiarize**, adjust, accustom, inure, acclimatize *Opposite*: disorientate

habituation *(fml)* *n* **familiarization**, adjustment, acclimatization, orientation, adaptation *Opposite*: disorientation

hack *v* **1 cut**, chop, slash, lacerate, scythe *Opposite*: splice **2** *(infml)* **cope**, manage, handle, deal with, succeed ■ *n* **1** *(infml)* **drudge**, slave, factotum, flunky *(infml)*, dogsbody *(infml)* *Opposite*: specialist **2** *(infml)* **journalist**, reporter, scribbler, writer, stringer

hackneyed *adj* **trite**, clichéd, tired, stale, everyday *Opposite*: original

haemorrhage *n* **loss**, outflow, outpouring, seeping away, depletion ■ *v* **lose**, flow away, seep away, pour out, drain away

haggard *adj* **worn**, fatigued, tired, faded, exhausted *Opposite*: fresh

haggle *v* **bargain**, barter, quibble, negotiate, wrangle

hail *n* **storm**, volley, burst, flood, barrage ■ *v* **1 greet**, welcome, address, speak to, call to *Opposite*: ignore **2 acclaim**, acknowledge, salute, uphold, confirm *Opposite*: reject **3 summon**, call, call over, flag down, wave *Opposite*: dismiss

hair *n* **1 tresses**, curls, mop, shock, mane *(literary or infml)* **2 coat**, fur, wool, pelt, fleece

haircut *n* **1 trim**, cut, clip, restyle **2 hairstyle**, style, hairdo *(infml)*, coiffure *(fml)*

hairdo *(infml)* *n* **haircut**, hairstyle, style, coiffure *(fml)*

hairdresser *n* **stylist**, barber, hair stylist, cutter, coiffeur *(fml)*

hairdressing *n* **hair gel**, styling gel, mousse, hair cream, styling spray

hairiness *n* **furriness**, shagginess, fuzziness, hirsuteness, fluffiness *Opposite*: baldness

hairless *adj* **bald**, receding, thin on top, bald as a coot, shaved *Opposite*: hairy

hair-raising *adj* **terrifying**, horrifying, extraordinary, spine-tingling, frightening *Opposite*: calming

hairsplitting *n* **quibbling**, nitpicking, cavilling, pettifoggery, equivocation

hairstyle *n* **haircut**, style, cut, hairdo *(infml)*, coiffure *(fml)*

WORD BANK
❑ **types of hairstyle** Afro, beehive, big hair *(infml)*, bob, bouffant, braids, bun, bunches, chignon, cornrow, cowlick, crew cut, crop, dreadlocks, flat top, French pleat, fringe, mohican, mullet, pageboy, pigtail, plait, pompadour, ponytail, quiff, ringlet, topknot

hairy *adj* **1 hirsute**, bearded, bushy, furry, shaggy *Opposite*: hairless **2** *(infml)* **dangerous**, hazardous, treacherous, risky, perilous *Opposite*: safe

halcyon *(literary)* *adj* **untroubled**, calm, peaceful, still, tranquil *Opposite*: turbulent

hale *adj* **healthy**, well, fit, robust, in good shape *Opposite*: unhealthy

half-baked *(infml)* *adj* **1 unplanned**, ill-considered, impulsive, ill-conceived *Opposite*: considered **2 impractical**, silly, unrealistic, idealistic, starry-eyed *Opposite*: sensible

half-hearted *adj* **unenthusiastic**, perfunctory, lukewarm, indifferent, lackadaisical *Opposite*: wholehearted

half-light *n* **twilight**, semi-darkness, dusk, gloom, gloominess

halfway *adv* **1 midway**, centrally, in the middle, between, in-between **2 almost**, nearly, mostly, partially, partly *Opposite*: completely ■ *adj* **middle**, central, intermediate, mid, midway

hall *n* **1 corridor**, passageway, hallway, foyer, entrance **2 gallery**, great hall, room, public room, ballroom **3 mansion**, dormitory, manor, tower, castle

hallmark *n* **1 seal**, stamp, trademark, symbol, logo **2 characteristic**, feature, trait, property, quality

hall of residence *n* **residence**, dormitory, student house, hall, dorm *(infml)*

hallow *v* **consecrate**, sanctify, bless, deify, revere *Opposite*: desecrate

hallowed *adj* **sacred**, holy, sanctified, blessed, consecrated *Opposite*: profane

hallucinate *v* **see things**, have delusions, have visions, fantasize, be delirious

hallucination *n* **vision**, illusion, figment of the imagination, phantasm, mirage

hallway *n* **corridor**, passageway, hall, foyer, entrance

halo *n* **corona**, aureole, nimbus, aura, radiance

halt *n* **standstill**, stop, close, break, pause *Opposite*: start ■ *v* **stop**, pause, cease, freeze, come to an end *Opposite*: begin

halter *n* **bridle**, rein, strap, lead, noose

halting *adj* **hesitant**, uncertain, tentative, stumbling, faltering *Opposite*: firm

halve *v* **1 bisect**, divide, cut in two, cut in half *Opposite*: double **2 split**, split fifty-fifty, go halves on, share, share out **3 decrease**, reduce, cut, slash, cut down *Opposite*: double

ham *v* **overact**, lay it on thick, overplay, overdo it, mug

ham-fisted *(infml)* *adj* **clumsy**, inelegant, inept, blundering, awkward *Opposite*: dexterous

ham-fistedness *(infml)* *n* **clumsiness**, ineptness, awkwardness, heavy-handedness

ham-handed *(infml)* *see* ham-fisted

ham-handedness (infml) see **ham-fistedness**

hamlet n **village**, settlement, homestead, community, colony Opposite: city

hammer v **1** (infml) **batter**, beat, assault, attack, brutalize **2** (infml) **defeat**, beat, thrash, trounce, walk over (infml) **3 strike**, pound, hit, knock, beat **4** (infml) **criticize**, disparage, condemn, censure, put down (infml) Opposite: praise

hammering n **1 pounding**, buffeting, battering, beating, lashing **2** (infml) **defeat**, beating, thrashing, trouncing, hiding (infml) Opposite: victory

hammer out v **1 beat**, pound, forge, shape, craft **2 accomplish**, establish, arrive at, reach, produce

hamper n **basket**, picnic basket, pannier ■ v **hinder**, obstruct, get in the way of, impede, slow down Opposite: facilitate. See COMPARE AND CONTRAST at **hinder**.

hamstrung adj **constrained**, restricted, thwarted, confined, cramped Opposite: liberated

hand n **1 pointer**, needle, indicator, arrow, finger **2 influence**, part, share, role, involvement **3 clap**, ovation, standing ovation, round of applause, burst of applause Opposite: boo **4 handwriting**, writing, script, scrawl, scribble ■ v **give**, hand over, offer, pass, tender Opposite: take

handbag n **bag**, shoulder bag, clutch bag, backpack, purse (US)

handbill n **leaflet**, flier, pamphlet, advertisement, circular

handbook n **manual**, instruction manual, guide, guidebook, instruction book

handcuff n **manacles**, chains, shackles, fetters, irons ■ v **chain**, manacle, shackle, fasten, tie up Opposite: release

hand down v **leave**, bequeath, pass down, transmit, will

handful n **1 some**, a few, one or two, not many, hardly any Opposite: many **2** (infml) **test**, trial, problem, nuisance, hard work

handicraft n **craft**, handcraft, handiwork, skill, art

WORD BANK

❏ **types of handicraft** appliqué, basketry, crochet, dressmaking, embroidery, knitting, lacemaking, macramé, needlepoint, needlework, quilting, sewing, smocking, stitching, tapestry, tatting, weaving

handily adv **1 conveniently**, closely, accessibly, nearby, in easy reach Opposite: inconveniently **2 skilfully**, dexterously, cleverly, neatly, ably Opposite: awkwardly

hand in v **1 submit**, give, give in, tender, offer Opposite: withhold **2 surrender**, return, give up, give back, hand over Opposite: withhold

handiness n **1 convenience**, proximity, closeness, accessibility Opposite: inconvenience **2 usefulness**, utility, efficacy, helpfulness,

practicality Opposite: uselessness **3 skilfulness**, skill, dexterity, practicality, cleverness Opposite: awkwardness

handiwork n **1 deed**, action, achievement, work, creation **2 handicraft**, craft, skill, talent, art

handkerchief n **tissue**, paper handkerchief, facial tissue, hankie (infml)

handle n **grip**, holder, handgrip ■ v **1 touch**, finger, feel, move, hold **2 control**, deal with, run, cope with, conduct **3 manage**, operate, conduct, supervise, take charge of **4 trade in**, sell, buy, deal in, import

handler n **trainer**, coach, manager, supervisor

handling n **treatment**, management, conduct, supervision, control

hand-me-down adj **second-hand**, castoff, recycled, used, worn Opposite: brand-new

hand out v **dispense**, distribute, administer, give away, give out Opposite: take in

handout n **1 windfall**, bonus, gift, donation, charity **2 document**, fact sheet, leaflet, brochure, pamphlet

hand over v **give up**, tender, surrender, entrust, relinquish Opposite: withhold

handover n **delivery**, abdication, assignment, conferral, bestowal

handpicked adj **select**, elite, exclusive, finest, top-quality Opposite: run-of-the-mill

handrail n **banister**, rail, railing, guardrail, balustrade

handset n **receiver**, earpiece, mouthpiece, phone, telephone

hands-off adj **detached**, remote, distant, non-interventionist, laissez-faire Opposite: hands-on

handsome adj **1 good-looking**, fine, attractive, striking, beautiful Opposite: ugly **2 generous**, substantial, sizable, attractive, liberal Opposite: ungenerous. See COMPARE AND CONTRAST at **good-looking**.

handsomely adv **generously**, substantially, sizably, attractively, well

hands-on adj **practical**, active, applied, proactive, energetic Opposite: hands-off

handspring n **somersault**, cartwheel, flip, flip-flop, vault

hand-to-hand adj **unarmed**, close-range, face-to-face, direct, bareknuckle

handwork n **handiwork**, handicraft, skill, art, craft

handwriting n **script**, writing, calligraphy, penmanship, scrawl

handy adj **1 convenient**, near, nearby, within reach, in easy reach Opposite: inconvenient **2 useful**, helpful, practical, clever, usable Opposite: useless **3 skilful**, dexterous, practical, clever, skilled Opposite: awkward

hang v **1 suspend**, dangle, droop, drape, hang down Opposite: take down **2 lynch**, suspend by the neck, execute, put to death, swing *(infml)* **3 droop**, flop, drape, sag, trail *Opposite*: stick up **4** *(infml)* **relax**, hang loose, chill out *(infml)*, hang out *(infml)*

hang about *v* **1 wait**, linger, loiter, dawdle, lie around *(infml)* **2 associate**, mix, socialize, spend time with, hang around

hang around *see* **hang about**

hang back *v* **hesitate**, drag your feet, drag your heels, linger, drop behind *Opposite*: forge ahead

hangdog *adj* **guilty**, dejected, furtive, intimidated, sheepish *Opposite*: chirpy *(infml)*

hang down *v* **sag**, dangle, droop, swing, hang *Opposite*: stick up

hanger *n* **coat hanger**, hook, peg, support, nail

hanger-on *n* **follower**, sycophant, disciple, proselyte, associate

hanging *n* **1 execution**, lynching, killing **2 wall hanging**, tapestry, drape, drapery, swag

hang on *v* **1 grip**, grasp, clutch, cling, hold on *Opposite*: let go **2 persevere**, keep it up, stick with it, stick it out, hold on *Opposite*: give up **3 depend on**, hinge on, follow from, turn on, rely on **4 wait**, linger, stay, hold on, remain *Opposite*: leave

hang out *v* **1 suspend**, dangle, drape, swing, hang up *Opposite*: take down **2** *(infml)* **spend time**, loiter, hang around, frequent, haunt **3** *(infml)* **associate**, mix, be friendly, hang around, interact **4** *(infml)* **relax**, hang around, loll around, hang about, laze about

hangout *(infml)* *n* **haunt**, den, retreat, meeting place, lair *(infml)*

hangover *n* **relic**, leftover, remnant, aftermath, aftereffect

hang together *v* **make sense**, add up, hold up, tell the complete story, give the full picture *Opposite*: fall apart

hang up *v* **1 suspend**, dangle, droop, drape, swing *Opposite*: take down **2 ring off**, put the phone down, disconnect, get off the phone, replace the receiver *Opposite*: pick up

hang-up *(infml)* *n* **anxiety**, worry, complex, inhibition, fixation

hank *n* **coil**, length, reel, skein, ball

hanker *v* **yearn**, crave, desire, long, ache

hankering *n* **yearning**, craving, longing, desire, ache *Opposite*: dislike

haphazard *adj* **random**, chaotic, slapdash, disorganized, messy *Opposite*: systematic

hapless *adj* **unfortunate**, unlucky, luckless, ill-fated, wretched *Opposite*: fortunate

haplessness *n* **misfortune**, bad luck, ill fortune, wretchedness, misery *Opposite*: luck

happen *v* **occur**, take place, go on, come about, ensue

happening *n* **occurrence**, event, incident, episode, phenomenon ■ *adj* *(infml)* **fashionable**, stylish, in, up-to-the-minute, edgy *Opposite*: old-fashioned

happenstance *n* **accident**, coincidence, chance, happenchance, fluke *(infml)*

happily *adv* **1 luckily**, fortunately, thankfully, as good luck would have it, opportunely *Opposite*: sadly **2 gladly**, willingly, cheerfully, freely, voluntarily *Opposite*: unwillingly **3 cheerfully**, contentedly, joyfully, gleefully, blissfully *Opposite*: sadly

happiness *n* **contentment**, pleasure, gladness, cheerfulness, joy *Opposite*: sadness

happy *adj* **1 content**, contented, pleased, glad, joyful *Opposite*: sad **2 lucky**, fortunate, favourable, opportune *Opposite*: unlucky

happy-go-lucky *adj* **carefree**, optimistic, easygoing, lighthearted, nonchalant *Opposite*: anxious

harangue *v* **berate**, lecture, criticize, rant, address ■ *n* **tirade**, diatribe, criticism, lecture, rant

harass *v* **annoy**, pester, bother, pursue, worry *Opposite*: leave alone

harassed *adj* **1 stressed**, under pressure, distraught, beleaguered, worried *Opposite*: relaxed **2 put upon**, pressured, persecuted, singled out, discriminated against

harassment *n* **pestering**, nuisance, annoyance, irritation, persecution

harbinger *n* **forerunner**, herald, portent, omen, indication

harbour *n* **port**, dock, anchorage, waterfront, wharf ■ *v* **1 believe**, entertain, hold, bear in mind, cherish **2 protect**, shelter, give refuge to, hide, conceal

hard *adj* **1 firm**, stiff, rigid, solid, tough *Opposite*: soft **2 difficult**, strenuous, laborious, tough, arduous *Opposite*: easy **3 problematical**, tricky, difficult, awkward, thorny *Opposite*: easy **4 intense**, fast, violent, brutal, fierce *Opposite*: gentle **5 cruel**, callous, harsh, severe, unkind *Opposite*: kind ■ *adv* **intensely**, fast, violently, fiercely, powerfully *Opposite*: gently

---

COMPARE AND CONTRAST CORE MEANING: requiring effort or exertion

hard requiring mental or physical effort or exertion to do or achieve; **difficult** requiring considerable planning or effort to accomplish; **strenuous** requiring physical effort, energy, stamina, or strength; **tough** needing a great deal of effort; **arduous** requiring hard work or continuous physical effort; **laborious** requiring unwelcome, often tedious, effort and exertion.

---

hard-bitten *adj* **tough**, hardened, cynical, stubborn, uncompromising

hard-boiled *(infml)* *adj* **unsentimental**, hardened, tough, cynical, case-hardened *Opposite*: sentimental

hard-core *adj* **uncompromising**, committed, dedicated, firm, staunch

harden v 1 **solidify**, set, freeze, consolidate, settle *Opposite*: soften 2 **toughen**, strengthen, reinforce, fortify, stabilize *Opposite*: weaken

hardened adj **hard-bitten**, toughened, tough, cynical, unsentimental

hardheaded adj **shrewd**, sharp, practical, no-nonsense, tough *Opposite*: impractical

hardhearted adj **callous**, cold, hard, insensitive, unfeeling *Opposite*: kind

hardheartedness n **callousness**, coldness, insensitivity, pitilessness, stoniness *Opposite*: kindness

hardiness n **toughness**, hardihood, stamina, durability, robustness *Opposite*: frailty

hardline adj **uncompromising**, inflexible, rigid, extreme, radical

hardly adv **barely**, only just, scarcely, by a hair's breadth, by the skin of your teeth

hardness n **rigidity**, stiffness, firmness, inflexibility, solidity *Opposite*: softness

hardship n **adversity**, privation, lack, poverty, destitution *Opposite*: comfort

hardware n **equipment**, apparatus, tackle, gear, kit

hard-wearing adj **durable**, long-lasting, strong, tough, resilient

hardy adj **robust**, resilient, enduring, tough, strong *Opposite*: frail

hark back v **go back to**, revisit, recall, relive, revive

harm n **damage**, hurt, injury, destruction, maltreatment *Opposite*: help ∎ v **hurt**, damage, spoil, injure, impair *Opposite*: help

COMPARE AND CONTRAST CORE MEANING: weaken or impair something or somebody
harm cause physical or mental impairment or deterioration; **damage** cause physical deterioration that makes an object less useful, valuable, or able to function, or impair something abstract such as a chance or somebody's reputation; **hurt** cause physical or mental pain or harm to people and animals; **injure** cause physical harm to a person or animal, usually causing at least a temporary loss of function or use, or impair something abstract such as somebody's reputation or pride; **wound** inflict physical harm on somebody, especially as a result of the use of a weapon, a violent incident, or a serious accident, or upset or offend somebody.

harmed adj **injured**, damaged, hurt, wounded, impaired *Opposite*: untouched

harmful adj **damaging**, injurious, destructive, detrimental, dangerous *Opposite*: harmless

harmless adj 1 **inoffensive**, innocuous, innocent, meaningless, bland *Opposite*: offensive 2 **safe**, risk-free, nontoxic, nonhazardous, sound *Opposite*: harmful

harmlessness n 1 **inoffensiveness**, naivety, innocence, wholesomeness, blandness *Opposite*: offensiveness 2 **innocuousness**, safety, mildness, nontoxicity

harmonious adj 1 **musical**, melodious, tuneful, pleasant-sounding, sweet *Opposite*: discordant 2 **agreeable**, congruous, balanced, matching, corresponding *Opposite*: discordant 3 **friendly**, cordial, affable, congenial, agreeable *Opposite*: hostile

harmonize v 1 **go with**, match, blend, complement, tone *Opposite*: jar 2 **bring into line**, synchronize, standardize, make uniform, make conform

harmonized adj **in line**, consistent, coordinated, matched, in step *Opposite*: uncoordinated

harmonizing adj **consistent**, toning, matching, agreeing, coordinating *Opposite*: clashing

harmony n **agreement**, accord, concord, synchronization, congruence *Opposite*: discord

harness v 1 **tie together**, strap on, yoke, bind, attach *Opposite*: separate 2 **control**, exploit, employ, channel, utilize

harp on v **complain**, go on, keep on, whine, grumble

harried adj **harassed**, put upon, bothered, agitated, stressed *Opposite*: calm

harrowing adj **disturbing**, upsetting, traumatic, distressing, frightening *Opposite*: relaxing

harry v **harass**, bother, pester, badger, annoy

harsh adj 1 **severe**, bleak, austere, inhospitable, stark *Opposite*: mild 2 **cruel**, unkind, unsympathetic, insensitive, callous *Opposite*: kind 3 **punitive**, exacting, strict, stern, severe *Opposite*: lenient 4 **discordant**, loud, blaring, raucous, jangly *Opposite*: pleasant

harshness n 1 **severity**, austerity, ruggedness, bleakness, starkness *Opposite*: gentleness 2 **callousness**, cruelty, ruthlessness, strictness, severity *Opposite*: gentleness

harvest n **crop**, yield, produce, return, fruitage *Opposite*: sowing ∎ v **reap**, gather, collect, bring in, pick *Opposite*: sow

hash v **chop**, cut up, mince, grind, shred

hassle (*infml*) n **bother**, annoyance, irritation, disturbance, stress ∎ v **harass**, irritate, annoy, bother, get on your nerves *Opposite*: leave alone

haste n **speed**, swiftness, rapidity, alacrity, rush *Opposite*: slowness

hasten v **hurry**, make haste, rush, speed up, speed

hastiness n **impulsiveness**, impetuosity, rashness, thoughtlessness, carelessness *Opposite*: carefulness

hasty adj **quick**, speedy, hurried, swift, rapid *Opposite*: slow

hatch v 1 **devise**, come up with, originate, formulate, plan 2 **give forth**, emerge, produce, break open, come out 3 **shade**, mark, crisscross, crosshatch, highlight

hate v **detest**, loathe, despise, abhor, revile *Opposite*: love ∎ n **hatred**, abhorrence, detestation, loathing, odium *Opposite*: love. See COMPARE AND CONTRAST at **dislike**.

hated *adj* **loathed**, detested, despicable, despised, unloved *Opposite*: loved

hateful *adj* **horrible**, detestable, vile, odious, unbearable *Opposite*: lovable

hatred *n* **hate**, abhorrence, detestation, loathing, odium *Opposite*: love. *See* COMPARE AND CONTRAST *at* **dislike**.

haughtiness *n* **arrogance**, conceit, pride, self-importance, overconfidence *Opposite*: modesty

haughty *adj* **supercilious**, proud, self-important, superior, high and mighty *Opposite*: humble

haul *v* **drag**, pull, tow, lug, tug *Opposite*: shove. *See* COMPARE AND CONTRAST *at* **pull**.

haul over the coals *v* **rebuke**, scold, reprimand, take to task, tell off *(infml)*

haunch *n* **1 upper leg**, hip, buttock, thigh, loin **2 side**, flank, hindquarter, thigh, rump

haunt *v* **1 walk**, roam, frequent, prowl, inhabit *Opposite*: leave **2 trouble**, disturb, worry, bother, preoccupy *Opposite*: soothe ■ *n* **meeting place**, rendezvous, stamping ground *(infml)*, hangout *(infml)*

haunted *adj* **1 eerie**, ghostly, weird, sinister, spooky *(infml)* **2 troubled**, preoccupied, worried, disturbed, anxious *Opposite*: relaxed

haunting *adj* **lingering**, melancholy, poignant, evocative, moving *Opposite*: forgettable

hauteur *n* **haughtiness**, arrogance, superiority, loftiness, snobbishness *Opposite*: humility

haut monde *n* **elite**, crème de la crème, high society, rich and famous, aristocracy *Opposite*: masses

have *v* **1 possess**, own, boast, exhibit, enjoy *Opposite*: lack **2 must**, need, ought to, should, require **3 receive**, obtain, grasp, get, gain *Opposite*: lose **4 consume**, take, partake, eat, drink *Opposite*: abstain **5 think of**, come up with, devise, develop, entertain **6 experience**, undergo, partake, engage in, take part in **7 be affected by**, suffer from, suffer with, be afflicted with, be ill with **8 organize**, carry out, arrange, hold, give **9 tolerate**, put up with, allow, permit, endure **10 produce**, bear, give birth to, bring forth

have a go at *(infml)* *v* **find fault with**, flay, criticize, get angry with, reprimand *Opposite*: praise

have a hand in *v* **partake in**, play a part in, play a role in, participate, be part of

have a horror of *v* **fear**, dread, be frightened of, be afraid of, be scared of

have in mind *v* **propose**, suggest, be thinking of, come up with, intend

have it in for *v* **persecute**, harass, bully, victimize, target *Opposite*: favour

haven *n* **1 refuge**, safe place, place of safety, sanctuary, shelter **2** *(literary)* **harbour**, port, anchorage, dock, port of call

have-nots *n* **disadvantaged**, poor, deprived, underprivileged, underclass *Opposite*: privileged

have on *v* **1 wear**, be dressed in, be clothed in, show off, flaunt **2** *(infml)* **tease**, kid, fool, joke, pull somebody's leg *(infml)*

haversack *n* **rucksack**, backpack, pack, knapsack, shoulder bag

have second thoughts *v* **change your mind**, go back on, reconsider, think better of, get cold feet

have to do with *v* **relate to**, concern, involve, be regarding, be in connection with

have up *(infml)* *v* **prosecute**, try, take to court, arrest, charge

have your eye on *v* **want**, desire, aim for, be after, hanker

havoc *n* **chaos**, destruction, disorder, turmoil, disaster *Opposite*: order

hawk *v* **sell**, peddle, vend, deal, market *Opposite*: buy

hawker *n* **dealer**, vendor, seller, marketer, salesperson *Opposite*: client

hawk-eyed *adj* **eagle-eyed**, sharp-eyed, sharp-sighted, observant, perceptive *Opposite*: unobservant

hawkish *adj* **aggressive**, belligerent, warmongering, warlike, militant *Opposite*: peaceable

hawser *n* **cable**, rope, chain, towline, tow

hay *n* **straw**, feed, fodder, dry feed, winter feed

hayrack *n* **rack**, trough, manger, feeder

haywire *(infml)* *adj* **wild**, out of order, erratic, nonfunctional, confused *Opposite*: functional

hazard *n* **danger**, threat, risk, peril, menace *Opposite*: safeguard ■ *v* **1 suggest**, proffer, put forward, propose **2 risk**, take a chance, chance, gamble, venture *Opposite*: protect

hazardous *adj* **dangerous**, unsafe, harmful, risky, lethal *Opposite*: safe

haze *n* **mist**, fog, miasma, cloud, vapour ■ *v* **become cloudy**, mist over, cloud over, darken *Opposite*: clear

haziness *n* **1 mistiness**, fogginess, cloudiness, obscurity, smokiness *Opposite*: clarity **2 confusion**, muddle, uncertainty, indistinctness, vagueness *Opposite*: clarity

hazy *adj* **1 misty**, foggy, cloudy, obscure, blurred *Opposite*: clear **2 unclear**, indistinct, muddled, confused, obscure *Opposite*: distinct

head *n* **1 skull**, cranium, dome, crown, nut *(infml)* **2 mind**, intelligence, intellect, sense, brain **3 boss**, leader, chief, president, controller **4 top**, peak, crown, promontory, apex *Opposite*: base **5 introduction**, beginning, start, opening, heading *Opposite*: end ■ *v* **1 come first**, lead, be first, precede, be foremost *Opposite*: follow **2 control**, rule, regulate, have control over, lead **3 go**, move, journey, advance, proceed

headache *(infml)* n **annoyance**, pain, bother, bore, nuisance *Opposite*: relief

headband n **hairband**, Alice band, sweatband, bandeau, circlet

header n 1 **shot**, pass, goal 2 **heading**, title, caption, slogan, legend *Opposite*: footer

headfirst adv **headlong**, head over heels, diving, pitching, plunging

headily adv 1 **exhilaratingly**, thrillingly, invigoratingly, excitingly, stimulatingly *Opposite*: dully 2 **pungently**, aromatically, strongly, richly, spicily *Opposite*: mildly 3 **impetuously**, impulsively, recklessly, rashly, hastily *Opposite*: cautiously

heading n 1 **title**, caption, headline, banner, header 2 **direction**, bearing, course, route, trajectory

headland n **promontory**, cape, peninsula, point, bluff

headline n **caption**, banner, title, heading, header

headlong adv 1 **headfirst**, head over heels, diving, pitching, plunging 2 **impetuously**, rashly, recklessly, hastily, hurriedly *Opposite*: carefully ▪ *adj* **impetuous**, rash, reckless, hasty, hurried *Opposite*: considered

head off v 1 **divert**, reroute, redirect, turn back, intercept 2 **forestall**, block, prevent, stop, avert *Opposite*: encourage 3 **leave**, go away, depart, take off, commence *Opposite*: remain

head office *see* **headquarters**

head of state n **premier**, president, leader, ruler, sovereign

head-on adv 1 **straight on**, straight ahead, frontally, directly, full steam ahead 2 **unflinchingly**, uncompromisingly, with guns blazing, confrontationally, bluntly *Opposite*: indirectly ▪ *adj* **face-to-face**, frontal, uncompromising, direct, confrontational *Opposite*: indirect

headpiece n **header**, heading, design, ornament, decoration

headquarters n **HQ**, control centre, nerve centre, head office, command centre

headset n **headphones**, receiver, earpiece, earphones

headship n **leadership**, direction, management, control, regime

head start n **advantage**, edge, lead, helping hand, help *Opposite*: disadvantage

headstone n **tombstone**, gravestone, stone, slab, memorial

headstrong adj **obstinate**, wilful, stubborn, inflexible, mulish *Opposite*: docile

head teacher n **principal**, head, headmaster, headmistress, rector

head-to-head adv **adjacent**, next to, end-to-end, in line, together ▪ *adj* **one-to-one**, face-to-face, direct, intimate, personal ▪ *n* **encounter**, meeting, discussion, dialogue, confrontation

headway n **progress**, movement, advance, progression, improvement

headwind n **breeze**, wind, gale, gust

heady adj 1 **exhilarating**, thrilling, invigorating, exciting, stimulating *Opposite*: dull 2 **pungent**, aromatic, strong, rich, spicy *Opposite*: mild 3 **impetuous**, imprudent, impulsive, reckless, rash *Opposite*: cautious

heal v 1 **cure**, restore to health, make well, nurse, mend *Opposite*: worsen 2 **make good**, settle, patch up, reconcile, set right *Opposite*: damage

healer n **doctor**, faith healer, naturopath, homeopath, therapist

healing n **recovery**, restoration, recuperation, therapy, treatment ▪ *adj* **curative**, remedial, therapeutic, medicinal, restorative

health n **wellbeing**, fitness, condition, healthiness, strength

healthful adj **healthy**, good for your health, good for you, beneficial, wholesome *Opposite*: unhealthy

healthiness n **health**, good condition, robustness, wellbeing, fitness

healthy adj 1 **fit**, well, strong, vigorous, in good physical shape *Opposite*: sick 2 **healthful**, good for your health, good for you, beneficial, nourishing *Opposite*: unhealthy

heap n **mound**, pile, stack, mountain, bundle ▪ *v* **pile up**, pile, layer, mound, mass

heaps *(infml)* n **lots**, loads *(infml)*, masses *(infml)*, tons *(infml)*, piles *(infml)* ▪ *adv* **a lot**, very much, a great deal, loads, lots

heap up v 1 **pile up**, pile, mound, mass, stack 2 **collect**, amass, gather, accumulate, stockpile

hear v 1 **make out**, catch, get, overhear, pick up 2 **gather**, learn, find out, understand, pick up 3 **listen to**, catch, get, pick up, receive 4 **understand**, pay attention to, attend to, heed, take notice of *Opposite*: miss 5 **sit in judgment**, try, judge, preside over, examine

hear from v **have news of**, have contact with, be in touch with, be contacted by, have a call from

hearing n 1 **earshot**, range, hearing distance, reach 2 **trial**, inquiry, investigation, examination, consideration

hear of v **consider**, conceive, tolerate, permit, admit

hearsay n **rumour**, gossip, tittle-tattle, idle talk, word of mouth *Opposite*: fact

heart n 1 **core**, heart of hearts, mind, sentiment, soul 2 **compassion**, sympathy, empathy, feeling, sensitivity *Opposite*: cruelty 3 **spirit**, courage, bravery, fortitude, pluck

heartache n **sorrow**, sadness, distress, anguish, despair *Opposite*: joy

heart attack n **1 cardiac arrest**, coronary, seizure **2** (infml) **shock**, fright, scare, turn, fit

heartbreak n **grief**, despair, anguish, sorrow, pain Opposite: joy

heartbreaking adj **tragic**, distressing, upsetting, sad, heartrending Opposite: uplifting

heartbroken adj **inconsolable**, forlorn, despairing, dejected, disconsolate Opposite: thrilled

heartburn n **stomach pain**, acid stomach, indigestion, colic, dyspepsia

hearten v **encourage**, inspire, raise your spirits, uplift, buoy Opposite: dishearten

heartening adj **encouraging**, promising, cheering, optimistic, reassuring Opposite: disheartening

heartfelt adj **sincere**, genuine, earnest, warm, cordial Opposite: superficial

hearth n **1 fireside**, fireplace, inglenook, grate **2 family life**, home sweet home, home, household

heartiness n **vigour**, enthusiasm, gusto, energy, cheerfulness

heartland n **centre**, core, hub, nucleus, focus Opposite: hinterland

heartless adj **callous**, cruel, unfeeling, cold-blooded, merciless Opposite: caring

heartlessness n **cruelty**, callousness, coldbloodedness, mercilessness, unkindness Opposite: kindness

heartrending adj **heartbreaking**, tragic, distressing, pitiful, pathetic Opposite: uplifting. See COMPARE AND CONTRAST at moving.

heart-searching n **soul-searching**, self-examination, self-analysis, introspection, deep thought

heart-to-heart adj **frank**, honest, open, candid, forthright ▪ n **talk**, tête-à-tête, one-to-one, chat, discussion

heartwarming adj **cheering**, positive, encouraging, heartening, pleasing Opposite: depressing

hearty adj **1 enthusiastic**, sincere, wholehearted, emphatic, vigorous Opposite: half-hearted **2 jovial**, cheerful, warm, genial, welcoming **3 strong**, sincere, abiding, deep, profound **4 substantial**, nourishing, filling, plentiful, abundant Opposite: meagre

heat n **1 warmth**, high temperature, temperature, hotness, warmness Opposite: coldness **2 passion**, emotion, fervour, ardour, intensity Opposite: indifference ▪ v **warm**, heat up, warm through, warm up, reheat Opposite: cool

heated adj **animated**, frenzied, impassioned, fiery, intense Opposite: calm

heater n **fire**, stove, radiator, electric fire, electric heater Opposite: air conditioner

heating n **1 warming**, warming up, heating up, reheating, microwaving **2 central heating**, heating system, solar heating, space heating Opposite: air conditioning

---

WORD BANK

❏ **types of heating appliance** boiler, electric fire, furnace, heater, heat pump, immersion heater, quartz heater, radiator, space heater, storage heater

---

heat wave n **hot spell**, Indian summer, drought, scorcher (infml), sizzler (infml)

heave v **1 haul**, drag, pull, yank, lug Opposite: push **2** (infml) **throw**, toss, pitch, fling, chuck (infml) **3 rise and fall**, throb, palpitate, swell, surge. See COMPARE AND CONTRAST at throw.

heaven n **1 bliss**, paradise, ecstasy, rapture, cloud nine Opposite: hell **2 air**, sky, cosmos, ether (literary), firmament (literary)

heavenly adj **1 divine**, holy, angelic, cherubic, saintly **2 wonderful**, blissful, delightful, lovely, fantastic Opposite: dreadful

heavenwards adv **upward**, skyward, up, into the air, into the sky Opposite: earthwards

heaviness n **weight**, bulk, mass, substance, solidity Opposite: lightness

heaving adj **crowded**, bursting at the seams, full to overflowing, busy, packed

heavy adj **1 weighty**, hefty, substantial, heavyweight Opposite: light **2 thick**, dense, full, viscous, compact Opposite: thin **3 demanding**, onerous, burdensome, tiring, tedious Opposite: easy **4 busy**, packed, tight, hectic, frenetic Opposite: light **5 powerful**, forceful, violent, hard, jarring Opposite: weak

heavy-duty adj **1 hard-wearing**, forceful, tough, durable, long-lasting Opposite: lightweight **2** (infml) **serious**, important, intensive, intense, high-level

heavy-handed adj **1 clumsy**, rough, careless, awkward, uncoordinated Opposite: dexterous **2 oppressive**, harsh, forceful, hard, severe

heavy-handedness n **1 clumsiness**, roughness, carelessness, awkwardness, gaucheness **2 oppressiveness**, harshness, forcefulness, severity, brutality

heavyset adj **stocky**, well-built, sturdy, solid, thickset Opposite: slight

heavyweight n **1 muscleman**, bodyguard, bouncer, heavy (slang) **2 big name**, leader, leading light, key player, colossus

heckle v **jeer**, interrupt, butt in, boo, shout down Opposite: cheer

heckler n **critic**, jeerer, interrupter, protester, troublemaker Opposite: supporter

heckling n **criticism**, jeering, interruption, protest, repartee

hectic adj **frantic**, frenzied, excited, confused, chaotic Opposite: calm

hector v **bully**, intimidate, harass, badger, hassle (infml)

hedge n **hedgerow**, privet, border, verge, windbreak ■ v 1 **ring**, fence, protect, encircle, surround 2 **evade**, prevaricate, stall, beat about the bush, fudge (infml)

hedgerow n **hedge**, border, verge, windbreak, shrubbery

hedonism n **pleasure-seeking**, high-living, intemperance, self-indulgence, profligacy Opposite: asceticism

hedonist n **pleasure-seeker**, rake, degenerate, sybarite, epicure Opposite: ascetic

hedonistic adj **self-indulgent**, pleasure-seeking, profligate, debauched, sybaritic Opposite: ascetic

heed v **pay attention to**, listen to, take note of, observe, notice Opposite: ignore ■ n **attention**, notice, note, regard, mindfulness Opposite: disregard

heedful adj **mindful**, vigilant, watchful, thoughtful, careful Opposite: heedless

heedless adj **neglectful**, oblivious, without regard, rash, reckless Opposite: careful

heedlessness n **thoughtlessness**, recklessness, carelessness, neglectfulness, rashness Opposite: carefulness

heel v **repair**, resole, mend, fix, reinforce

heel in v **dig in**, put in, bury, cover

heftiness n **robustness**, burliness, stoutness, heaviness, stockiness

hefty adj 1 **bulky**, large, robust, sturdy, stocky Opposite: slight 2 **heavy**, weighty, substantial, cumbersome, awkward

hegemony n **domination**, control, supremacy, dominion, power

height n 1 **tallness**, stature, altitude, loftiness, elevation Opposite: depth 2 **pinnacle**, summit, peak, top, apex Opposite: nadir

heighten v **intensify**, amplify, increase, enhance, add to

heinous adj **monstrous**, atrocious, odious, dreadful, shocking

heir n **successor**, inheritor, beneficiary, legatee, recipient

heirloom n **family treasure**, inheritance, valuable, gift, bequest

helideck see helipad

helipad n **landing pad**, landing strip, helideck, heliport, helistop

heliport, helistop see helipad

helix n **spiral**, coil, corkscrew, spring, ringlet

hell n 1 **Hades**, underworld, perdition, inferno, abyss Opposite: heaven 2 **torture**, misery, torment, agony, anguish

help v 1 **aid**, assist, help out, lend a hand, be of assistance Opposite: hinder 2 **relieve**, improve, ease, alleviate, amend Opposite: worsen 3 **avoid**, evade, dodge, stop, refrain from ■ n **assistance**, aid, benefit, support, service Opposite: hindrance

helper n **assistant**, aid, aide, collaborator, coworker. See COMPARE AND CONTRAST at assistant.

helpful adj 1 **useful**, beneficial, advantageous, of use, effective Opposite: useless 2 **obliging**, accommodating, supportive, caring, cooperative Opposite: unhelpful

helpfulness n 1 **usefulness**, effectiveness, utility, benefit, advantageousness Opposite: uselessness 2 **kindness**, neighbourliness, goodwill, concern, care Opposite: unhelpfulness

helping n **serving**, plateful, portion, ration, selection

helping hand n **help**, assistance, support, aid, boost

helpless adj **powerless**, weak, feeble, dependent, vulnerable Opposite: self-reliant

helplessness n **powerlessness**, weakness, feebleness, vulnerability, dependence Opposite: confidence

helpmate n **assistant**, associate, spouse, partner, coworker

help out v **help**, lend a hand, abet, aid, assist

help yourself v **use**, make use of, appropriate, take, have

helter-skelter adv **hurriedly**, in confusion, carelessly, haphazardly, pell-mell Opposite: calmly ■ adj **chaotic**, disorganized, confused, haphazard Opposite: ordered

hem v **edge**, turn up, shorten, lengthen, sew up Opposite: let down

hem in v **enclose**, close in, encircle, confine, restrict Opposite: release

hence (fml) adv 1 **therefore**, for this reason, consequently, that's why, and so 2 **from now on**, from this time, henceforth, later, in future

henceforth adv **from now on**, from this time, in future, hereafter (fml), henceforward (fml)

henhouse n **coop**, pen, barn, shelter, shed

herald n 1 **messenger**, crier, announcer, proclaimer, courier 2 (literary) **sign**, harbinger, indication, omen, portent ■ v 1 **proclaim**, announce, give out, publish, tout 2 **signal**, prefigure, foreshadow, presage, indicate

herculean adj **superhuman**, colossal, enormous, phenomenal, extraordinary Opposite: small

herd n 1 **people**, masses, mob, crowd, sheep 2 **group**, set, cluster ■ v 1 **round up**, steer, gather together, collect, drove 2 **shepherd**, usher, direct, guide, funnel

---

WORD BANK

❑ **types of herd** bale (of turtles), band (of gorillas), bevy (of roe deer), colony (of ants/sea lions), drove (of sheep), flock (of sheep), gam (of whales), gang (of elk), kennel (of dogs), leash (of foxes), litter (of cubs/kittens), mob (of kangaroos), pack (of wolves), pod (of porpoises/seals/walrus/whales), pride (of lions), rookery (of seals), school (of porpoises/whales), skulk (of foxes), troop (of kangaroos/monkeys)

---

here adv **at this time**, at this point, now, at this juncture

hereabouts adv **nearby**, near, around here, close

hereafter (fml) adv **after this**, in future, henceforth, from now on, from this time

hereditary adj 1 **genetic**, transmissible, inbred, inbred, innate 2 **inherited**, heritable, traditional, family

heresy n **dissent**, deviation, unorthodoxy, sacrilege, profanation (fml)

heretical adj **unorthodox**, profane, sacrilegious, dissenting, unconventional

herewith adv **with this**, together with this, enclosed, with, attached

heritable adj **inheritable**, transferable, transmissible, hereditary

heritage n **inheritance**, legacy, tradition, birthright, custom

hermaphrodite adj **androgynous**, epicene, intersexual

hermetic adj **airtight**, enclosed, closed

hermit n **recluse**, loner, solitary

hero n 1 **superman**, champion, conqueror, idol Opposite: loser 2 **male lead**, leading actor, leading man, star, protagonist

heroic adj **daring**, stout, valiant, brave, epic

heroics n **recklessness**, rashness, irresponsibility, going over the top, overdoing it Opposite: timidity

heroine n 1 **superwoman**, champion, conqueror, idol 2 **female lead**, leading actress, leading lady, star, protagonist

heroism n **valour**, bravery, courageousness, fearlessness, boldness

hero worship n **adulation**, idolization, idealization, admiration, glorification

hesitancy n **indecision**, caution, uncertainty, tentativeness, timidity Opposite: decisiveness

hesitant adj **cautious**, tentative, timid, shy, undecided Opposite: decisive. See COMPARE AND CONTRAST at **unwilling**.

hesitate v 1 **be uncertain**, be indecisive, vacillate, waver, falter 2 **be unwilling**, think twice, scruple, have qualms, be reluctant

COMPARE AND CONTRAST CORE MEANING: show uncertainty or indecision

hesitate be slow in doing something, or take a short break in an activity, as a result of uncertainty or reluctance; **pause** stop doing something briefly before carrying on, or wait intentionally for a short period before doing something; **falter** show a loss of confidence, especially speak or say something with a series of short stoppages, for example because of nervousness, fear, awkwardness, or incompetence; **stumble** speak or act hesitatingly, confusedly, or incompetently; **waver** become unsure or begin to change from a previous opinion; **vacillate** be indecisive or irresolute, changing between one opinion and another.

hesitation n 1 **uncertainty**, indecision, vacillation, wavering, faltering Opposite: decisiveness 2 **unwillingness**, qualms, reluctance, disinclination, hesitancy Opposite: willingness

heterogeneous adj **varied**, mixed, assorted, diverse, various Opposite: homogeneous

heuristic adj **experiential**, empirical, experimental, investigative, exploratory

hew v 1 **cut**, chop, fell, cleave, axe 2 **carve**, fashion, sculpt, shape, model

hex n **curse**, spell, jinx, voodoo

heyday n **prime**, zenith, glory days, peak, halcyon days (literary)

hiatus n **pause**, break, interruption, space, lull

hibernate v **lie dormant**, take cover, overwinter, hide, hide away

hiccup (infml) n **hitch**, glitch, interruption, delay, setback

hidden adj 1 **concealed**, out of sight, unseen, secreted, veiled 2 **unknown**, secret, mysterious, clandestine, covert

hidden agenda n **ulterior motive**, secret plan, motivation, driving force, impetus

hide v 1 **conceal**, put out of sight, hide from view, secrete, veil Opposite: flaunt 2 **go underground**, take cover, disappear, keep cover, hole up (slang) 3 **keep secret**, withhold, hold back, keep back, suppress Opposite: disclose

hideaway n **hiding place**, refuge, sanctuary, asylum, retreat

hidebound adj **narrow-minded**, prejudiced, conservative, conventional, parochial Opposite: broad-minded

hideous adj 1 **ugly**, unattractive, grotesque, repellent, unsightly Opposite: attractive 2 **revolting**, repugnant, repulsive, gruesome, shocking Opposite: pleasant. See COMPARE AND CONTRAST at **unattractive**.

hideousness n **ugliness**, repulsiveness, unsightliness, gruesomeness, dreadfulness

hideout n **safe house**, refuge, sanctuary, retreat, den

hidey-hole (infml) n **hiding place**, hideaway, safe house, safe place, shelter

hiding (infml) n **beating**, whacking, thumping, smacking, spanking

hiding place n **hideaway**, hole, place of escape, den, safe house

hierarchical adj **ranked**, graded, tiered, ordered, classified

hierarchy n **chain of command**, ladder, pecking order, grading, order

hieroglyph n **symbol**, pictograph, picture, ideogram, cipher

hifalutin (infml) see **highfalutin**

hi-fi n **sound system**, stereo system, stereo, CD player, cassette recorder

higgledy-piggledy adj **untidy**, topsy-turvy, in a mess, jumbled, confused Opposite: ordered

high *adj* **1 tall**, lofty, elevated, towering, soaring *Opposite*: low **2 in height**, from top to bottom, from head to foot, from top to toe, tall **3. above average**, great, extraordinary, elevated, extreme *Opposite*: normal **4 high-pitched**, shrill, piercing, penetrating, sharp *Opposite*: low-pitched **5 important**, eminent, prominent, high-ranking, superior *Opposite*: low ■ *n* **1 high point**, peak, climax, summit, high spot *Opposite*: low point **2** *(infml)* **thrill**, boost, tonic, lift, excitement

high achiever *n* **high flier**, success, star, winner, success story

highbrow *adj* **intellectual**, cultured, academic, scholarly, exclusive *Opposite*: lowbrow ■ *n* **intellectual**, academic, scholar, philosopher, sage *(literary)*

high-class *adj* **high-quality**, fancy, formal, elegant, superior *Opposite*: cheap

high court *n* **court**, principal court, supreme court *(US)*

highest *adj* **top**, topmost, utmost, ultimate, premier

highfalutin *(infml)* *adj* **pretentious**, pompous, affected, grandiose, snobbish *Opposite*: down-to-earth

high-flier *n* **high achiever**, success, winner, success story, star *Opposite*: plodder

high-flown *adj* **affected**, pretentious, grandiose, high-sounding, grandiloquent *Opposite*: down-to-earth

high-grade *adj* **high-quality**, quality, finest, superior, prime *Opposite*: low-grade

high ground *n* **1 upland**, highland, plateau, hillside, hilltop *Opposite*: lowland **2 principled stance**, moral stand, high road *(US)*

high-handed *adj* **bossy**, autocratic, dominant, undemocratic, domineering

high-handedness *n* **bossiness**, arrogance, imperiousness, inconsiderateness, overbearingness

high jinks *(infml)* *n* **mischief**, mischievousness, trouble, no good, nonsense

highland *n* **upland**, plateau, high ground, hilltop, moorland *Opposite*: lowland

high-level *adj* **sophisticated**, elevated, advanced, complex, top *Opposite*: unsophisticated

high life *n* **good life**, life of Riley, life of ease, lap of luxury, easy street

highlight *n* **high point**, climax, high spot, best part, best bit ■ *v* **emphasize**, draw attention to, underline, stress, focus on *Opposite*: downplay

highly *adv* **1 extremely**, very, exceedingly, very much, greatly *Opposite*: modestly **2 favourably**, approvingly, kindly, warmly, graciously *Opposite*: unfavourably

highly-strung *adj* **excitable**, edgy, tense, jittery, easily upset *Opposite*: laid-back *(infml)*

high-minded *adj* **principled**, worthy, moral, noble, upright *Opposite*: base

high-pitched *adj* **shrill**, high, piercing, penetrating, sharp

high point *n* **best moment**, high spot, best bit, climax, icing on the cake *Opposite*: low point

high-powered *adj* **successful**, dynamic, driven, ambitious, energetic

high-pressure *adj* **stressful**, difficult, relentless, pressured, intense *Opposite*: easy

high profile *n* **prominence**, conspicuousness, eminence, celebrity, notoriety *Opposite*: anonymity

high-profile *adj* **prominent**, prestigious, conspicuous, famous, eminent *Opposite*: discreet

high-rise *adj* **multistorey**, high, tall, big, lofty *Opposite*: low-rise ■ *n* **skyscraper**, block of flats, apartment block, tower block, office block

high society *n* **upper classes**, elite, polite society, beautiful people, upper crust *(infml)*

high-sounding *adj* **imposing**, high-flown, grandiloquent, grandiose, lofty

high-spirited *adj* **lively**, exuberant, merry, cheerful, vivacious *Opposite*: lethargic

high spirits *n* **liveliness**, exuberance, merriness, cheerfulness, vivacity *Opposite*: depression

high spot *n* **best moment**, high point, best bit, best part, climax

high-tech *adj* **advanced**, technological, computerized, digital, modern

high-up *(infml)* *n* **boss**, manager, director, big boss, bigwig *(infml)*

hijack *v* **1 take over**, seize, commandeer, capture, skyjack **2** *(infml)* **steal**, appropriate, take over, commandeer, borrow ■ *n* **takeover**, skyjacking, capture, seizure

hijinks *(infml)* *see* **high jinks**

hike *v* **ramble**, trek, walk, climb

hiker *n* **walker**, rambler, backpacker, trekker

hilarious *adj* **funny**, sidesplitting, comic, comical, humorous

hilariousness *n* **humour**, humorousness, uproariousness, comicalness, mirthfulness

hilarity *n* **amusement**, laughter, merriment, mirth, glee *Opposite*: sadness

hill *n* **1 mountain**, peak, mount, knoll, mound *Opposite*: valley **2 gradient**, slope, incline, rise *Opposite*: drop

hillock *n* **mound**, hump, hill, knoll

hilltop *n* **top**, summit, peak, pinnacle, brow *Opposite*: base

hilly *adj* **mountainous**, undulating, bumpy, alpine, craggy *Opposite*: flat

hind *adj* **back**, rear, rearmost, posterior *(fml)*, hindmost *(literary)* *Opposite*: fore *(literary)*

hinder v **hold back**, obstruct, impede, block, hamper *Opposite*: facilitate

---

COMPARE AND CONTRAST CORE MEANING: put difficulties in the way of progress
hinder delay or restrict the development or progress of something, either accidentally or by deliberate interference; **block** prevent movement through, into, or out of something, or prevent something from taking place; **hamper** restrict the free movement or action of somebody or something; **hold back** keep something from happening or restrain somebody from doing something; **impede** interfere with the movement, progress, or development of somebody or something; **obstruct** cause a serious delay in action or progress, or cause a major physical blockage in a road or passageway.

---

hindquarters n **back**, rear, rear legs, hind legs *Opposite*: front

hindrance n 1 **obstruction**, impediment, barrier, obstacle, encumbrance 2 **interference**, interruption, limitation, prevention, sabotage *Opposite*: assistance

hindsight n **reflection**, retrospection, perception, observation, remembrance *Opposite*: foresight

hinge n **pivot**, axis, fulcrum, joint, centre

hinge on v **depend on**, hang on, turn on, be dependent on, rest on

hint v **suggest**, intimate, insinuate, imply, mention ■ n 1 **suggestion**, clue, intimation, mention, indication 2 **tip**, advice, pointer, suggestion, clue 3 **trace**, tinge, suggestion, dash, taste

hinterland n **vicinity**, environs, surroundings, neighbourhood *Opposite*: heartland

hire v 1 **employ**, appoint, take on, contract, sign up *Opposite*: fire 2 **rent**, lease, let, charter, engage *Opposite*: purchase

hire out v **rent out**, rent, lend, lend out, lease

hirsute adj **hairy**, bearded, bushy, furry, long-haired *Opposite*: bald

hiss v 1 **jeer**, boo, hoot, mock, ridicule *Opposite*: cheer 2 **whisper**, murmur, rustle, whistle, susurrate

historic adj 1 **significant**, momentous, notable, famous, remarkable *Opposite*: insignificant 2 **past**, old, ancient, antique, historical *Opposite*: modern

historical adj **past**, old, ancient, antique, historic *Opposite*: modern

historically adv 1 **in history**, over all, factually, archaeologically 2 **traditionally**, generally, usually, as a rule, in the main

history n 1 **past**, times gone by, times past, olden times, antiquity *Opposite*: present 2 **account**, record, chronicle, narration, memoir

histrionic adj **theatrical**, dramatic, exaggerated, melodramatic, unrestrained *Opposite*: restrained

histrionics n **dramatics**, tantrums, hysterics, melodrama, drama

hit v 1 **strike**, punch, thump, slap, beat 2 **crash into**, strike, bang into, bump into, collide with 3 **affect**, afflict, damage, hurt, disadvantage ■ n 1 **blow**, knock, smack, slap, bump 2 **success**, winner, triumph, sensation, market leader *Opposite*: flop *(infml)*

hit-and-miss adj **haphazard**, random, unpredictable, unplanned, careless *Opposite*: planned

hit back v **retaliate**, get even, strike back, react, even the score

hitch n **snag**, catch, drawback, glitch, delay ■ v 1 **fasten**, hook, harness, join, tether *Opposite*: undo 2 **hitchhike**, get a lift, be given a lift, thumb a lift, put your thumb out

hitchhike v **hitch**, get a lift, be given a lift, thumb a lift, put your thumb out

hitherto adv **up till now**, up till then, until now, until then, till now

hit it off *(infml)* v **get on well**, connect, get on, make friends, take to each other *Opposite*: clash

hit on v **think of**, chance upon, discover, realize, arrive at

hit out v 1 **criticize**, attack, assail, condemn, lambaste 2 **strike out**, lash out, lunge, go for, attack

hit the hay *(infml)* v **go to bed**, say goodnight, get to sleep, get some rest, retire

hit the roof v **lose your temper**, be angry, fly into a rage, go berserk, see red *(infml)* *Opposite*: calm down

hit the sack *(infml)* *see* **hit the hay**

hit upon v **stumble on**, chance upon, discover, realize, arrive at

hive v **store**, put away, save, put aside, hoard *Opposite*: discard

hive off v **cream off**, skim off, transfer, separate, split off *Opposite*: merge

hoard v **save**, store, amass, stockpile, accumulate *Opposite*: throw away ■ n **store**, pile, mass, reserve, supply. *See* COMPARE AND CONTRAST *at* collect.

hoarder n **collector**, saver, accumulator, miser, squirrel *(infml)*

hoarding n **billboard**, notice board, advertisement, placard, poster

hoar frost n **frost**, ice, rime

hoarse adj **croaky**, gruff, gravelly, husky, rough *Opposite*: smooth

hoarseness n **croakiness**, gruffness, huskiness, roughness, harshness *Opposite*: smoothness

hoary adj 1 **overused**, old, ancient, age-old, stale *Opposite*: fresh 2 **white**, snow-white, whitened, snowy, grey

hoax n **trick**, deception, practical joke, joke, swindle ■ v **deceive**, trick, con, swindle, mislead

hoaxer n trickster, practical joker, fraudster, joker, swindler

hobble v limp, hop, shuffle, shamble, totter ■ n limp, shuffle, stagger, shamble, stumble

hobby n pastime, leisure pursuit, diversion, relaxation, sideline Opposite: job

hobbyhorse n favourite subject, pet topic, bee in your bonnet, obsession, idée fixe

hobgoblin n goblin, imp, elf, pixie, sprite

hobnob v socialize, mix, fraternize, associate, go around Opposite: shun

hobo n traveller, itinerant, vagrant, tramp, drifter

hoe v turn over, weed, dig, dig out, loosen

hog (infml) v monopolize, take over, help yourself, take the lion's share of, hang onto

hogwash (infml) n nonsense, gibberish, humbug, garbage, rubbish

hoi polloi n common herd, general public, masses, ordinary people, proletariat Opposite: aristocracy

hoist v lift, raise, pull, heave, erect ■ n winch, crane, lift, elevator, pulley

hoity-toity (infml) adj haughty, arrogant, snobbish, proud, disdainful Opposite: down-to-earth

hold v 1 grasp, clutch, grip, clasp, seize Opposite: release 2 fix, secure, fasten, bind, attach 3 embrace, hug, cuddle, enfold, squeeze 4 contain, accommodate, stow, carry, take in 5 detain, restrain, confine, shut in, imprison Opposite: let go 6 arrange, convene, call, conduct, have 7 possess, have, keep, retain, own 8 believe, think, maintain, presume, consider 9 sustain, maintain, continue, keep up, carry on 10 wait, hold on, hang on, stay on the line Opposite: hang up ■ n 1 grip, grasp, clasp, clutch, embrace 2 control, power, influence, claim, sway 3 storage space, storeroom, cargo bay, compartment, storage

holdall n bag, case, suitcase, portmanteau, carryall (US)

hold back v 1 restrain, inhibit, suppress, repress, hamper Opposite: let go 2 keep back, retain, keep, reserve, keep hold of Opposite: release. See COMPARE AND CONTRAST at **hinder**.

hold close v hug, embrace, hold tight, cuddle, enfold Opposite: release

hold down (infml) v keep, retain, maintain, manage, hang onto Opposite: lose

holder n 1 container, pouch, receptacle, vessel, box 2 owner, possessor, proprietor, controller, bearer

hold forth v speak out, harangue, preach, lecture, discourse Opposite: bottle up

hold in v 1 keep in check, restrain, keep back, hold back, control Opposite: release 2 restrain, keep the lid on, control, bridle, suppress Opposite: let out

holding n 1 land, field, property, farm, croft

2 stock, investment, share, property, interest

hold in high regard v revere, respect, venerate, idolize, esteem Opposite: despise

hold off v 1 refrain, desist, leave off, abstain, avoid Opposite: speed up 2 resist, fend off, keep away, keep off, repel Opposite: yield

hold on v 1 wait, hang on, be patient, wait a minute, hold your horses (infml) 2 grasp, grip, keep hold of, hold fast, stick to Opposite: let go 3 persist, persevere, keep on, stand your ground, stand firm Opposite: give up

hold onto v 1 retain, keep, hang onto, save, hoard Opposite: give up 2 grasp, clasp, clutch, grip, stick Opposite: release

hold out v 1 extend, give, present, offer, proffer Opposite: withdraw 2 endure, stand your ground, persist, stand firm, withstand Opposite: give in

hold out on v not tell, keep something from, hide something from, withhold something from Opposite: tell

hold over v defer, delay, postpone, put off, suspend Opposite: bring forward

hold sway v have authority, have influence, have power, be in power, be in control

hold the fort v look after things, take care of things, take over, take charge, mind things

hold up v 1 delay, slow down, slow up, impede, hinder Opposite: speed up 2 rob, raid, mug, do (slang), stick up (US infml) 3 survive, bear up, keep up, endure, keep going Opposite: give up 4 support, shore up, keep up, prop, sustain Opposite: bring down

holdup n 1 theft, raid, robbery, assault, mugging 2 delay, hitch, glitch, snag, stoppage

hold with v approve of, endorse, support, subscribe to, agree with Opposite: disapprove

hold your own v 1 match up, stand your ground, stand firm, look after yourself, take care of yourself 2 bear up, persevere, be stable, be comfortable, persist Opposite: succumb

hole n 1 cavity, hollow, void, chasm, gulf 2 aperture, gap, opening, crack, break 3 burrow, lair, retreat, run, sett 4 flaw, weakness, fault, error, defect Opposite: strength 5 (infml) hovel, slum, shack, pigsty (infml), fleapit (infml)

hole-and-corner adj secret, secretive, hidden, clandestine, private Opposite: public

hole-in-the-wall (infml) n restaurant, bar, bistro, café, dive (infml)

holey adj leaky, porous, perforated, worn, torn

holiday n 1 day off, day's leave, personal day (US) 2 leave, time off, break, sabbatical, hols (infml) Opposite: work 3 festival, anniversary, feast, saint's day, carnival ■ v be on holiday, stay, relax, sojourn (literary), vacation (US) Opposite: work

holidaymaker n traveller, sightseer, visitor,

tourist, day tripper *Opposite*: resident

holier-than-thou *(infml) adj* **self-righteous**, pious, smug, superior, sanctimonious *Opposite*: self-effacing

holiness *n* **sanctity**, sacredness, piety, godliness, religiousness

holistic *adj* **all-inclusive**, rounded, full, complete, general

holler *(infml) v* **shout**, yell, scream, shriek, howl *Opposite*: whisper

hollow *adj* **1 empty**, void, unfilled, vacant, unoccupied *Opposite*: solid **2 concave**, depressed, sunken, indented, cavernous *Opposite*: convex **3 resonating**, echoing, deep, low, dull *Opposite*: high-pitched **4 insincere**, empty, worthless, futile, vain *Opposite*: sincere ■ *n* **1 cavity**, recess, indentation, cup, nook *Opposite*: bulge **2 valley**, crater, dip, depression, basin *Opposite*: hill ■ *v* **excavate**, scoop, dig out, gouge, tunnel *Opposite*: fill. *See* COMPARE AND CONTRAST *at* vain.

hollowness *n* **1 void**, empty space, cavity, emptiness, concavity *Opposite*: solidity **2 insincerity**, emptiness, worthlessness, futility, vainness *Opposite*: sincerity

holy *adj* **1 sacred**, consecrated, hallowed, sanctified, blessed **2 saintly**, righteous, devout, religious, godly *Opposite*: irreligious

homage *n* **deference**, reverence, respect, service, duty *Opposite*: disrespect

home *n* **1 residence**, house, habitat, quarters, address **2 family**, household, family circle, family unit, background **3 birthplace**, place of birth, homeland, home town, native land **4 institution**, residence, residential home, children's home, rest home ■ *adj* **1 internal**, domestic, inland, interior, local *Opposite*: foreign **2 home-based**, household, homegrown, family, domestic *Opposite*: industrial ■ *adv* **homewards**, back home, in, home sweet home

homecoming *n* **return**, arrival, repatriation, visit, revisiting *Opposite*: emigration

home help *n* **domestic**, cleaner, maid, au pair, carer

home in *v* **focus**, zoom in, move in, aim, take aim *Opposite*: draw back

homeland *n* **native country**, mother country, native land, fatherland, motherland

homeless *adj* **on the streets**, living rough, dispossessed, destitute, vagrant *Opposite*: housed

homely *adj* **1 cosy**, simple, plain, ordinary, unpretentious *Opposite*: fancy **2 unattractive**, plain, unappealing, ugly, mousy *Opposite*: attractive. *See* COMPARE AND CONTRAST *at* unattractive.

home rule *n* **self-government**, autonomy, self-rule, independence, separatism

homesick *adj* **nostalgic**, sad, melancholy, pining, unsettled *Opposite*: content

homespun *adj* **plain**, simple, ordinary,

unsophisticated, down-to-earth *Opposite*: sophisticated

homestead *n* **farm**, farmstead, ranch, smallholding, croft

home town *n* **birthplace**, home, home base, back yard, home ground

home truth *n* **fact**, truth, bitter pill, criticism *Opposite*: lie

homework *n* **1 schoolwork**, exercise, lesson, study, assignment **2** *(infml)* **preparation**, reading, research, groundwork, reading up

homicidal *adj* **murderous**, destructive, killer, killing, bloodthirsty *Opposite*: harmless

homicide *n* **killing**, murder, slaughter, manslaughter, assassination

homily *n* **lecture**, sermon, talk, speech, discourse

hominid *n* **primate**, hominoid, anthropoid

hominoid *see* hominid

homogeneity *n* **1 sameness**, similarity, equality, consistency, regularity *Opposite*: dissimilarity **2 uniformity**, constancy, consistency, stability, regularity *Opposite*: variability

homogeneous *adj* **1 same**, similar, standardized, consistent, equal *Opposite*: heterogeneous **2 uniform**, consistent, constant, stable, regular *Opposite*: variable

homogeneousness *see* homogeneity

homogenize *v* **1 smooth**, emulsify, mix, beat, whip *Opposite*: separate out **2 standardize**, normalize, even out, regulate, make the same *Opposite*: distinguish

hone *v* **1 improve**, refine, enhance, polish, perfect *Opposite*: impair **2 sharpen**, whet, file, grind, polish *Opposite*: blunt

honest *adj* **1 upright**, trustworthy, moral, good, decent *Opposite*: immoral **2 truthful**, authentic, true, sincere, frank *Opposite*: untruthful

honestly *adv* **1 fairly**, justly, in all conscience, decently, reliably *Opposite*: immorally **2 really**, truly, truthfully, candidly, openly *Opposite*: untruthfully

honesty *n* **1 uprightness**, morality, trustworthiness, goodness, scrupulousness *Opposite*: immorality **2 sincerity**, truthfulness, integrity, frankness, candour *Opposite*: dishonesty

honeyed *adj* **1 ingratiating**, sugarcoated, cloying, flattering, fawning *Opposite*: sharp **2 melodious**, soft, dulcet, sweet, pleasing *Opposite*: harsh

honk *v* **beep**, hoot, toot, blare, blast

honorarium *n* **payment**, fee, grant, scholarship, exhibition. *See* COMPARE AND CONTRAST *at* wage.

honorary *adj* **1 nominal**, token, symbolic, titular **2 unpaid**, voluntary, unwaged, unsalaried, amateur *Opposite*: salaried

honour *n* **1 integrity**, decency, morality, righteousness, rectitude *Opposite*: baseness **2 respect**, admiration, esteem, regard, reverence *Opposite*: scorn **3 dignity**, distinction, nobility, pride, decorum **4 reputation**, image, good name, name, renown *Opposite*: disgrace **5 distinction**, award, tribute, credit, accolade *Opposite*: blot ■ *v* **1 keep**, stick to, fulfil, carry out *Opposite*: break **2 esteem**, respect, admire, take your hat off to, revere *Opposite*: disparage

honourable *adj* **1 moral**, upright, noble, worthy, right *Opposite*: immoral **2 respectable**, decent, admirable, praiseworthy, worthy *Opposite*: shameful

honoured *adj* **privileged**, pleased, flattered, grateful, thrilled *Opposite*: insulted

hoodlum *n* **gangster**, criminal, lawbreaker, thug, vandal

hoodwink *v* **trick**, deceive, dupe, delude, take in

hooey *(infml)* *n* **nonsense**, rubbish, humbug, gibberish, garbage *Opposite*: fact

hook *n* **peg**, hanger, nail, knob, catch ■ *v* **fasten**, attach, secure, join, tie *Opposite*: unhook

hook and eye *n* **fastener**, fastening, clasp, catch, clip

hooked *adj* **bent**, curved, bowed, curving, angular *Opposite*: straight

hook up *v* **1 connect**, link up, plug in, wire up, electrify *Opposite*: disconnect **2** *(infml)* **get together**, take up with, meet up, meet, pair off *Opposite*: part

hooligan *(infml)* *n* **criminal**, gangster, lawbreaker, thug, hoodlum

hoop *n* **ring**, loop, band, circle, round

hoot *v* **1 toot**, beep, honk, blare, blow **2 shout**, howl, whoop, roar, cry out

hop *v* **1 jump**, skip, leap, spring, bound ■ *n* **1 leap**, jump, skip, bound **2** *(infml)* **flight**, journey, trip, stage, leg **3** *(dated infml)* **dance**, party, disco, barn dance, social

hope *v* **want**, expect, trust, anticipate, wish *Opposite*: despair ■ *n* **1 confidence**, expectation, optimism, anticipation, faith *Opposite*: despair **2 likelihood**, prospect, possibility, promise, potential *Opposite*: impossibility **3 desire**, aspiration, dream, expectation, plan

hopeful *adj* **1 confident**, expectant, optimistic, positive, encouraged *Opposite*: pessimistic **2 promising**, encouraging, positive, rosy, propitious *Opposite*: discouraging **3 aspiring**, prospective, would-be, potential, budding ■ *n* **aspirant**, candidate, applicant, contender, seeker

hopefully *adv* **1 confidently**, expectantly, optimistically, positively, buoyantly *Opposite*: despairingly **2 with any luck**, with a bit of luck, all being well

hopefulness *n* **1 confidence**, hope, optimism, expectation, anticipation *Opposite*: despair **2 promise**, encouragement, positiveness, positivity, rosiness

hopeless *adj* **1 impossible**, desperate, unprom-

ising, fruitless, bleak *Opposite*: promising **2 despairing**, desperate, in despair, despondent, disheartened *Opposite*: positive **3 useless**, bad, pathetic, inept, incompetent *Opposite*: excellent

hopelessly *adv* **1 despairingly**, in despair, desperately, despondently, downheartedly *Opposite*: positively **2 terribly**, desperately, badly, completely, totally *Opposite*: slightly

hopelessness *n* **1 impossibility**, desperateness, fruitlessness, bleakness, futility *Opposite*: promise **2 despair**, desperation, despondency, bleakness, depression *Opposite*: hope **3 uselessness**, ineptness, ineptitude, incompetence, inability *Opposite*: excellence

horde *n* **throng**, crowd, mass, gang, group

horizon *n* **skyline**, distance, vanishing point, vista, prospect

horizontal *adj* **level**, flat, straight, plane *Opposite*: vertical

horn *n* **1 siren**, klaxon, hooter, alarm, buzzer **2 antler**, spine, barb, projection, tusk

horn of plenty *n* **cornucopia**, abundance, treasure chest, ready supply, never-ending supply *Opposite*: famine

horrendous *adj* **1 dreadful**, awful, terrible, dire, unbearable *Opposite*: wonderful **2** *(infml)* **outrageous**, exorbitant, sky-high, shocking, dreadful

horrible *adj* **unpleasant**, bad, awful, vile, nasty *Opposite*: pleasant

horribly *adv* **1 unpleasantly**, dreadfully, badly, terribly, unbearably *Opposite*: pleasantly **2 extremely**, greatly, very, totally, utterly

horrid *adj* **1 disgusting**, awful, dreadful, nasty, vile *Opposite*: pleasant **2 dreadful**, shocking, appalling, horrific, frightful

horridness *n* **1 nastiness**, beastliness, unpleasantness, hatefulness, meanness *Opposite*: pleasantness **2 disgustingness**, loathsomeness, vileness, dreadfulness, unpleasantness *Opposite*: attractiveness **3 dreadfulness**, frightfulness, terribleness, awfulness, horror

horrific *adj* **appalling**, dreadful, awful, horrendous, horrifying *Opposite*: wonderful

horrified *adj* **1 appalled**, shocked, aghast, sickened, disgusted *Opposite*: delighted **2 dismayed**, depressed, shocked, perplexed, disturbed

horrify *v* **1 appal**, disgust, revolt, shock, sicken *Opposite*: delight **2 dismay**, depress, shock, perplex, disturb

horrifying *adj* **1 horrific**, horrible, horrendous, terrible, sickening *Opposite*: delightful **2 shocking**, upsetting, disturbing, perplexing, perturbing

horror *n* **fear**, shock, revulsion, dismay, disgust *Opposite*: delight

horror-stricken *see* **horror-struck**

horror-struck *adj* **petrified**, scared stiff, terrified, horrified, stunned

hors d'oeuvre n **appetizer**, starter, entrée, crudités, first course

horse n **mount**, pony, charger, steed (literary)

WORD BANK
❏ **types of horse** Arabian horse, bronco, brood mare, carthorse, charger, cob, hack, hunter, mustang, pacer, packhorse, pony, racehorse, saddle horse, Shetland pony, shire horse, thoroughbred, trotter, warhorse, workhorse
❏ **parts of a horse** croup, fetlock, flank, foreleg, forelock, hindquarters, hock, hoof, mane, pastern, shank, withers

---

horse around v **fool around**, play around, clown, act the fool, cavort

horseman n **rider**, jockey, equestrian, huntsman, knight

horseplay n **rough-and-tumble**, boisterousness, play, fun, horsing around

horse sense (infml) n **common sense**, good sense, sense, wit, judgment

horseshoe n **1 lucky charm**, talisman, mascot, amulet, token **2 crescent**, curve, arc, loop, bend

horsewoman n **rider**, jockey, equestrian, huntswoman

horticultural adj **gardening**, garden, market garden, agricultural, nursery

horticulture n **gardening**, cultivation, propagation, agriculture, market gardening

hose n **tube**, pipe, line, hosepipe, garden hose
■ v **rinse**, water, spray, sluice, wash

hose down v **wash**, clean, sluice, rinse, hose Opposite: dry

hosepipe n **tube**, pipe, line, hose, garden hose

hospice n **nursing home**, hospital, rest home, sanatorium, clinic

hospitable adj **welcoming**, friendly, warm, open, generous Opposite: unfriendly

hospital n **infirmary**, sanatorium, rest home, hospice, sickbay

hospitality n **welcome**, friendliness, warmth, kindness, generosity Opposite: unfriendliness

host n **1 entertainer**, master of ceremonies, MC, presenter, compere **2 crowd**, swarm, cloud, congregation, mass ■ v **accommodate**, lay on, hold, present, introduce

hostage n **captive**, prisoner, detainee, victim

hostel n **1 inn**, hotel, bed and breakfast, guesthouse, motel **2 shelter**, refuge, boarding house, single room occupancy, dosshouse (slang)

hostess n **entertainer**, MC, presenter, compere, emcee (infml)

hostile adj **1 unfriendly**, aggressive, intimidating, antagonistic, unreceptive Opposite: friendly **2 adverse**, harsh, unwelcoming, unfavourable, unpleasant Opposite: pleasant

hostilities n **fighting**, warfare, conflict, battle, aggression

hostility n **aggression**, anger, unfriendliness, resentment, antagonism Opposite: friendliness

hot adj **1 warm**, burning, boiling, searing, fiery Opposite: cold **2 sweltering**, stifling, muggy, sultry, boiling Opposite: chilly **3 spicy**, peppery, piquant, pungent, fiery Opposite: bland **4 passionate**, fierce, angry, emotional, strong Opposite: dispassionate

hot air (infml) n **nonsense**, rubbish, drivel, stuff and nonsense, lies

hotbed n **breeding ground**, source, focus, hothouse, centre

hot-blooded adj **passionate**, volatile, hot-tempered, ardent, fierce Opposite: cold-blooded

hotchpotch n **jumble**, mixture, mishmash, mixed bag, miscellany

hotelier n **innkeeper**, landlord, landlady, proprietor, manager

hotfoot adv **immediately**, at once, without delay, instantly, urgently Opposite: slowly

hothead n **firebrand**, tearaway, madcap, loose cannon (slang)

hotheaded adj **impetuous**, volatile, rash, irascible, on a short fuse Opposite: prudent

hothouse n **greenhouse**, glasshouse, orangery, conservatory, winter garden

hotly adv **passionately**, fiercely, ardently, fervently, vehemently Opposite: dispassionately

hotness n **1 heat**, high temperature, temperature, warmness, warmth Opposite: coldness **2 overheating**, sweatiness, stickiness, warmness, warmth **3 spiciness**, heat, fieriness, piquancy, pepperiness Opposite: mildness

hot potato n **difficulty**, controversy, tricky problem, thorny problem, knotty problem

hotshot (infml) n **high-flier**, achiever, star, expert, go-getter (infml)

hot-tempered adj **excitable**, fiery, hot-blooded, volatile, quick-tempered Opposite: relaxed

hot up (infml) v **intensify**, liven up, quicken, increase, speed up Opposite: cool down

hot water (infml) n **trouble**, bother, difficulty, controversy, conflict

hound n **dog**, wolfhound, deerhound, basset hound, foxhound ■ v **pursue**, chase, harass, pester, persecute

hour n **1 60 minutes**, time, period, o'clock **2 time**, period, era, age, day

house n **1 residence**, home, address, building, pad (dated slang) **2 household**, family, dynasty, community, line **3 company**, firm, organization, business, establishment ■ v **1 accommodate**, lodge, shelter, give shelter to, take in **2 contain**, keep, store, hold, retain

---

WORD BANK
❏ **types of apartment** bedsit, flat, garden flat, loft, maisonette, penthouse, studio flat

---

❑ **types of house** bothy, bungalow, cabin, chalet, chateau, cottage, country house, detached house, farmhouse, grange, hacienda, homestead, igloo, lodge, manor, manor house, mansion, mobile home, palace, pied-à-terre, ranch, semidetached, shack, starter home, stately home, terraced house, timeshare, town house, villa

housecoat n robe, wrap, dressing gown, kimono, gown

house guest n visitor, guest, lodger, boarder

household n **family**, home, family circle, family unit, house ■ adj **domestic**, home, family, everyday, domiciliary Opposite: industrial

household name n **celebrity**, star, superstar, megastar, luminary Opposite: unknown

housekeeping n **housework**, chores, cleaning, tidying, tidying up

house of worship n **house of God**, church, cathedral, synagogue, mosque

houseplant n **pot plant**, plant, indoor plant, foliage plant

WORD BANK
❑ **types of houseplant** aspidistra, coleus, fern, moss, poinsettia, rubber plant, sansevieria, spider plant, yucca

housing n 1 **accommodation**, lodging, shelter, board, home 2 **cover**, covering, case, casing, frame

housing estate n estate, development, urban development, residential area, council estate

hovel n slum, shack, squat, fleapit (infml), dump (infml)

hover v 1 **float**, hang, drift, soar, fly Opposite: descend 2 **linger**, stay close, hang around, wait, remain Opposite: leave

how adv **in what way**, by what means, by what method, in what manner, just how

however adv **though**, but, on the other hand, yet, still Opposite: also

howl v **yowl**, bay, cry, wail, scream Opposite: murmur

howl down v **drown out**, shout down, boo, jeer, mock Opposite: cheer

howler (infml) n **blunder**, gaffe, error, malapropism, mistake

howling adj **violent**, whistling, gale-force, hurricane-force, breathtaking Opposite: gentle

hub n 1 **centre**, middle, boss, pivot Opposite: spoke 2 **core**, heart, focus, focal point, nucleus Opposite: periphery

hubbub n **noise**, hullabaloo, din, uproar, clamour Opposite: silence

huddle n **group**, cluster, knot, crowd, clump Opposite: scattering ■ v 1 **gather together**, crowd together, throng together, cluster, come together Opposite: scatter 2 **crouch**, bend, cower, nestle, hunch

hue n 1 **colour**, tint, tinge, tone, shade 2 **type**, kind, sort, description, manner

hue and cry n **uproar**, furore, commotion,

protest, public outcry Opposite: acceptance

huff n **sulk**, mood, bad mood, temper, fit of pique ■ v 1 **bluster**, grumble, complain, rant, gripe (infml) Opposite: calm down 2 **puff**, pant, wheeze, gasp, blow

huffy adj **touchy**, sensitive, moody, grumpy, sulky Opposite: good-natured

hug v **embrace**, hold close, enfold, cuddle, clasp ■ n **cuddle**, clinch, clasp, bear hug, embrace

huge adj 1 **enormous**, vast, gigantic, massive, giant Opposite: tiny 2 (infml) **incredible**, awesome, phenomenal, amazing, mindblowing (infml)

hugely adv **enormously**, immensely, overwhelmingly, vastly, tremendously Opposite: slightly

hulk n 1 **giant**, goliath, colossus, titan, ogre 2 **shell**, skeleton, frame, carcass, wreck

hulking adj **bulky**, vast, massive, colossal, enormous Opposite: dainty

hull n **body**, exterior, underside, keel, casing Opposite: interior

hullaballoo see hullabaloo

hullabaloo n **noise**, hubbub, din, uproar, clamour Opposite: silence

hum v 1 **drone**, whine, purr, buzz, whirr 2 (infml) **smell**, stink, reek, whiff (infml), pong (infml) ■ n 1 **whine**, drone, purr, buzz, whirr 2 (infml) **smell**, stink, odour, whiff (infml), pong (infml)

human n **person**, being, human being, individual, creature ■ adj **humanoid**, hominid, hominoid, anthropological, anthropoid Opposite: animal

human being n **person**, human, being, individual, creature

humane adj **compassionate**, caring, kind, gentle, humanitarian Opposite: cruel

humanitarian adj **caring**, charitable, benevolent, philanthropic, public-spirited Opposite: uncaring

humanity n 1 **humankind**, people, human race, mortality, homo sapiens 2 **kindness**, charity, compassion, sympathy, mercy Opposite: cruelty

humanize v 1 **anthropomorphize**, personify, personalize 2 **civilize**, cultivate, improve, soften, refine Opposite: brutalize

humanizing adj **civilizing**, improving, progressive, refining, softening Opposite: brutalizing

humankind n **human race**, humanity, people, mortality, homo sapiens

humanly adv **at all**, feasibly, physically, realistically, in any way

human race n **humankind**, humanity, people, mortality, homo sapiens

human rights n **basic rights**, civil liberties, civil rights, citizens' rights, inalienable rights

humble adj 1 **modest**, unassuming, retiring,

meek, self-effacing *Opposite*: arrogant **2 respectful**, subservient, servile, deferential, obliging *Opposite*: aloof **3 lowly**, poor, modest, simple, underprivileged *Opposite*: privileged ■ *v* **1 humiliate**, chasten, shame, bring down a peg, force to eat humble pie *Opposite*: glorify **2 degrade**, debase, demean, lower, reduce *Opposite*: exalt *(fml)*

humbled *adj* shamed, chastened, crestfallen, mortified, sheepish *Opposite*: proud

humbleness *n* **humility**, modesty, meekness, self-effacement, shyness *Opposite*: arrogance

humbling *adj* **1 chastening**, awe-inspiring, awesome, overwhelming *Opposite*: uplifting *(fml)* **2 mortifying**, embarrassing, shaming, sobering, crushing *Opposite*: heartening

humbug *n* **1 nonsense**, rubbish, gibberish, garbage, claptrap *(infml)* *Opposite*: fact **2 deception**, hypocrisy, lies, deceit, propaganda *Opposite*: sincerity

humdrum *adj* **dull**, boring, routine, unexciting, everyday *Opposite*: exciting

humid *adj* **moist**, damp, steamy, tropical, sticky *Opposite*: arid

humidify *v* **moisten**, dampen, saturate, impregnate *Opposite*: dry out

humidity *n* **moisture**, moistness, dampness, clamminess, stickiness *Opposite*: aridity

humiliate *v* **chasten**, embarrass, demean, degrade, disgrace *Opposite*: dignify

humiliated *adj* **chastened**, humbled, shamed, mortified, disgraced *Opposite*: proud

humiliating *adj* **chastening**, humbling, embarrassing, mortifying, shameful *Opposite*: gratifying

humiliation *n* **disgrace**, shame, mortification, embarrassment, dishonour *Opposite*: dignity

humility *n* **self-effacement**, unpretentiousness, humbleness, modesty, meekness *Opposite*: arrogance

humming *adj* **1 droning**, whining, purring, buzzing, whirring *Opposite*: silent **2** *(infml)* **smelly**, reeking, stinking, malodorous, stinky *(infml)*

hummock *n* **hillock**, mound, knoll, hill, rise *Opposite*: dip

humongous *(infml) adj* **enormous**, gigantic, colossal, massive, ginormous *(infml)* *Opposite*: tiny

humorist *n* **1 comedian**, comic, standup comedian, impressionist, entertainer **2 joker**, wit, satirist, punster, clown

humorous *adj* **funny**, amusing, entertaining, hilarious, comical *Opposite*: serious

humour *n* **1 funniness**, wit, comedy, comicality, comicalness *Opposite*: seriousness **2 wit**, wittiness, sparkle, drollness, sense of humour *Opposite*: dourness **3 comedy**, satire, black humour, spoof, slapstick ■ *v* **go along with**,

pacify, indulge, accommodate, please *Opposite*: oppose

humourless *adj* **1 sullen**, serious, po-faced, sour, dour *Opposite*: merry **2 unfunny**, unamusing, dull, straight, serious *Opposite*: funny

hump *n* **bulge**, bump, lump, swelling, protuberance *Opposite*: dip

humungous *see* **humongous**

hunch *n* **feeling**, gut feeling, sixth sense, premonition, intuition ■ *v* **bend**, huddle, stoop, crouch, lean forwards *Opposite*: straighten

hunger *n* **1 appetite**, emptiness, craving, hungriness, ravenousness **2 starvation**, food shortage, lack of food, malnutrition, famine *Opposite*: surfeit **3 craving**, desire, need, wish, yearning ■ *v* **crave**, yearn, long, desire, hanker *Opposite*: spurn

hungrily *adv* **1 ravenously**, greedily, voraciously, raveningly **2 eagerly**, impatiently, keenly, enthusiastically, excitedly *Opposite*: nonchalantly

hungry *adj* **1 famished**, ravenous, empty, ravening, voracious *Opposite*: full **2** *(infml)* **ambitious**, driven, thrusting, power-hungry, aggressive *Opposite*: content **3 avid**, eager, keen, thirsty *Opposite*: nonchalant

hunk *n* **chunk**, piece, lump, slab, wedge

hunker *v* **squat**, squat down, hunker down, crouch, crouch down *Opposite*: stand

hunky *(infml) adj* **muscular**, well-built, masculine, stocky, solid *Opposite*: puny

hunt *v* **1 chase**, pursue, stalk, follow, track *Opposite*: flee **2 seek out**, hunt down, track down, chase, pursue *Opposite*: evade **3 search**, seek, rummage, look, ferret about *Opposite*: find ■ *n* **search**, quest, chase, pursuit, expedition

hunt down *v* **find**, catch, track down, capture, get hold of *Opposite*: flee

hunted *adj* **panic-stricken**, alarmed, startled, frightened, unsettled *Opposite*: relaxed

hunter *n* **1 stalker**, predator, tracker, pursuer, chaser *Opposite*: prey **2 seeker**, searcher, quester, forager, scout *Opposite*: prey

hunting *n* **blood sport**, fox hunting, deer stalking, hare coursing, shooting

hurdle *n* **obstacle**, difficulty, problem, stumbling block, snag *Opposite*: aid ■ *v* **jump**, leap, jump over, leap over, clear

hurl *v* **throw**, fling, launch, toss, heave. *See* COMPARE AND CONTRAST *at* **throw**.

hurly-burly *n* **commotion**, chaos, turmoil, confusion, bustle *Opposite*: peace

hurricane *n* **storm**, gale, tempest, tropical storm, tornado

hurried *adj* **1 quick**, rushed, speedy, swift, sudden *Opposite*: leisurely **2 rushed**, pressurized, under pressure, harried, hassled *(infml)* *Opposite*: relaxed

hurry *v* **1 rush**, speed, hasten, run, dash *Oppo-*

site: delay **2 speed up**, accelerate, quicken, hasten, hustle *Opposite*: slow down ■ *n* **1 haste**, rush, dash, flurry, frenzy **2 urgency**, time pressure, panic, rush, haste

hurry up *v* **speed up**, accelerate, quicken, hasten, hustle *Opposite*: slow down

hurt *v* **1** injure, harm, wound, damage, mar *Opposite*: benefit **2 ache**, be sore, be painful, throb, trouble *Opposite*: soothe **3 offend**, upset, insult, injure, cause offence *Opposite*: comfort **4 impair**, damage, mar, spoil, ruin *Opposite*: improve ■ *n* **1 upset**, pain, distress, sadness, offence *Opposite*: gratification **2 injury**, damage, harm, pain, soreness *Opposite*: benefit ■ *adj* **upset**, offended, wounded, unhappy, indignant *Opposite*: gratified. *See* COMPARE AND CONTRAST *at* **harm**.

hurtful *adj* **upsetting**, unkind, cruel, spiteful, cutting *Opposite*: kind

hurting *adj* **sad**, aching, heartbroken, broken-hearted, down *Opposite*: happy

hurtle *v* **dash**, career, tear, race, plunge *Opposite*: plod

husband *n* **spouse**, partner, other half, significant other, mate *Opposite*: wife

hushed *adj* **quiet**, silent, muted, soft, whispered *Opposite*: loud

hush-hush *(infml) adj* **secret**, confidential, top-secret, cloak-and-dagger, clandestine *Opposite*: public

hush money *(infml) n* **bribe**, pacifier, incentive, sweetener *(infml)*, backhander *(infml)*

hush up *(infml) v* **cover up**, suppress, conceal, keep quiet, keep secret *Opposite*: reveal

husk *n* **shell**, casing, pod, covering, skin *Opposite*: kernel

huskiness *n* **throatiness**, hoarseness, dryness, roughness, gruffness *Opposite*: clearness

husky *adj* **throaty**, hoarse, dry, rough, gruff *Opposite*: clear

hustle *v* **1 propel**, jostle, manhandle, push, shove **2** *(infml)* **hurry**, hurry up, get going, get cracking, get a move on *(infml) Opposite*: slow down

hustle and bustle *n* **commotion**, chaos, turmoil, confusion, hurly-burly *Opposite*: calm

hut *n* **shed**, lean-to, cabin, shelter, shack

hutzpah *see* **chutzpah**

hybrid *n* **cross**, crossbreed, mix, amalgam, mixture

hydroplane *v* **skid**, slide, swerve, aquaplane, slew

hygiene *n* **cleanliness**, sanitation, sanitariness, cleanness, sterility

hygienic *adj* **clean**, sterile, disinfected, sanitary, germ-free *Opposite*: unhygienic

hymn *n* **song**, chant, carol, chorus, anthem ■ *v* **praise**, celebrate, eulogize, extol, laud *Opposite*: criticize

hype *n* **publicity**, propaganda, buildup, excitement, puff ■ *v* **publicize**, advertise, build up, tout, push

hyper *(infml) adj* **1 hyperactive**, restless, frenzied, agitated, overactive *Opposite*: placid **2 excitable**, hotheaded, on the edge, highly strung, volatile *Opposite*: calm

hyperactive *adj* **restless**, agitated, frenzied, overactive, manic *(infml) Opposite*: placid

hyperbole *n* **exaggeration**, overstatement, overemphasis, magnification, inflation *Opposite*: understatement

hypercritical *adj* **overcritical**, censorious, nit-picking, finicky, pedantic *Opposite*: lenient

hypersensitive *adj* **touchy**, oversensitive, thin-skinned, easily offended, easily hurt *Opposite*: thick-skinned

hypnotic *(infml) adj* **fascinating**, mesmerizing, entrancing, spellbinding, compelling *Opposite*: uninteresting

hypnotize *v* **fascinate**, mesmerize, spellbind, entrance, enthral *Opposite*: bore

hypocrisy *n* **insincerity**, double standard, pretence, duplicity, two-facedness *Opposite*: sincerity

hypocrite *n* **charlatan**, fraud, phoney, double-dealer, pretender

hypocritical *adj* **insincere**, two-faced, duplicitous, deceitful, phoney *Opposite*: genuine

hypothesis *n* **theory**, premise, suggestion, supposition, proposition

hypothesize *v* **imagine**, conjecture, put forward, assume, theorize

hypothetical *adj* **theoretical**, imaginary, supposed, conjectural, proposed *Opposite*: real

hysteria *n* **panic**, hysterics, frenzy, madness, emotion *Opposite*: calm

hysterical *adj* **1 panic-stricken**, out of control, agitated, overexcited, feverish *Opposite*: composed **2 uncontrollable**, frenzied, intense, violent, unrestrained *Opposite*: controlled **3** *(infml)* **hilarious**, uproarious, highly amusing, sidesplitting, comical *Opposite*: sad

hysterically *adv* **1 frantically**, feverishly, frenziedly, frenetically, agitatedly *Opposite*: calmly **2 uncontrollably**, violently, wildly, frenziedly, unrestrainedly *Opposite*: quietly **3** *(infml)* **uproariously**, hilariously, sidesplittingly, riotously, screamingly *Opposite*: mildly

hysterics *n* **1** *(infml)* **fits**, fits of laughter, stitches, laughter **2 hysteria**, panic, frenzy, agitation, distraction *Opposite*: calmness

I

ice *n* frost, snow, hoar frost, rime, black ice ■ *v* **1** freeze up, freeze, freeze solid, freeze over, ice over *Opposite*: thaw **2** decorate, finish off, frost, embellish, adorn **3** chill, cool, cool down *Opposite*: heat

icebreaker *n* opener, starter, opening, introduction

ice-cold *adj* freezing, frozen, icy, subzero, chilled *Opposite*: boiling

ice cream *n* ice, cone, ice-cream cone, sherbet, sorbet

iced *adj* chilled, cool, refrigerated, frozen, cold *Opposite*: hot

ice over *v* freeze, freeze over, freeze up, harden, solidify *Opposite*: thaw

ice pack *n* compress, cold compress, wrapping, poultice

ice up *v* freeze, freeze over, freeze up, ice over, frost up *Opposite*: thaw

iciness *n* coldness, coolness, frostiness, unfriendliness, hostility *Opposite*: warmth

icing *n* **1** frosting, decoration, glaze, glazing, ganache **2** freezing, freezing over, freezing up

icky *(infml) adj* **1** nasty, unpleasant, horrid, uncomfortable, horrible **2** sticky, gooey, tacky, messy, disgusting **3** sentimental, too much, saccharine, over-the-top *(infml)*, sloppy *(infml)*

icon *n* **1** idol, star, model, symbol, embodiment **2** image, likeness, representation, sign, picture

iconoclast *n* revolutionary, radical, free thinker, subversive, individualist *Opposite*: conservative

iconoclastic *adj* radical, revolutionary, subversive, individualistic, freethinking *Opposite*: conservative

icy *adj* **1** freezing, frozen, frosty, ice-cold, subzero **2** unfriendly, frosty, hostile, distant, aloof *Opposite*: warm

ID *n* identification, identity card, passport, papers, documents

idea *n* **1** opinion, belief, view, viewpoint, outlook **2** suggestion, design, plan, scheme, proposal **3** concept, impression, notion, understanding, perception **4** plan, inspiration, solution, brainchild, notion **5** aim, objective, plan, object, goal **6** gist, précis, outline, sketch, overview

ideal *n* **1** epitome, model, archetype, essence, stereotype **2** principle, standard, belief, value ■ *adj* best, model, ultimate, idyllic, supreme

idealism *n* **1** naivety, romanticism, impracticality, optimism *Opposite*: realism **2** perfectionism, fundamentalism, commitment, principle, morality

idealist *n* **1** perfectionist, fundamentalist, crusader, zealot, fanatic **2** romantic, optimist, dreamer *Opposite*: realist

idealistic *adj* **1** naive, unrealistic, romantic, impractical, optimistic *Opposite*: realistic **2** uncompromising, principled, committed, unswerving, unwavering

idealize *v* romanticize, put on a pedestal, view through rose-tinted spectacles, venerate, overemphasize

idealized *adj* perfect, flawless, faultless, ideal, unrealistic

ideally *adv* **1** in an ideal world, preferably, if possible, if at all possible **2** perfectly, supremely, superlatively, well

idée fixe *n* obsession, pet topic, hobbyhorse, fixation, bee in your bonnet

idem *adv* the same, the same thing, the same as before

identical *adj* same, indistinguishable, equal, matching, alike *Opposite*: different

identifiable *adj* recognizable, distinguishable, perceptible, discernible, detectable

identification *n* **1** recognition, classification, naming, detection, discovery **2** ID, documentation, proof of identity, papers, credentials **3** empathy, sympathy, affinity, rapport, bonding

identify *v* **1** recognize, classify, name, find, categorize **2** equate, connect, relate, link, associate

identify with *v* empathize with, sympathize with, relate to, feel for, have sympathy for

identity *n* individuality, uniqueness, distinctiveness, self, character

identity card *n* pass, card, passport, ID card *(infml)*

ideological *adj* conceptual, philosophical, moral, political, ethical

ideology *n* philosophy, belief, creed, dogma, line

idiolect *n* speech pattern, turn of phrase, style, dialect, idiom

idiom *n* **1** expression, phrase, set phrase, turn of phrase, saying **2** language, dialect, speech, style, vernacular

idiomatic *adj* natural, fluent, colloquial, vernacular, native *Opposite*: stilted

idiosyncrasy *n* **quirk**, peculiarity, eccentricity, foible, habit

idiosyncratic *adj* **characteristic**, personal, individual, distinctive, eccentric

idle *adj* **1 inactive**, inoperative, unoccupied, at rest, still *Opposite*: working **2 lazy**, indolent, shiftless, workshy, slothful *Opposite*: diligent **3 frivolous**, futile, pointless, worthless, vain **4 unfounded**, baseless, groundless, frivolous, meaningless **5 empty**, hollow, ineffectual, impotent, meaningless ■ *v* **1 laze**, laze around, hang around, sit around, sit about **2 turn over**, run, tick over *(infml)*. See COMPARE AND CONTRAST *at* **vain**.

idle away *v* **while away**, fritter away, waste, pass, spend

idleness *n* **laziness**, sloth, inertia, indolence, apathy *Opposite*: activity

idler *n* **slacker**, loafer, malingerer, timewaster, shirker *Opposite*: workaholic

idly *adv* **1 lazily**, indolently, shiftlessly, slothfully *(fml)* *Opposite*: diligently **2 frivolously**, futilely, pointlessly, worthlessly, uselessly *Opposite*: seriously

idol *n* **1 hero**, star, pin-up, obsession, ideal **2 icon**, graven image, statue, carving, sculpture

idolater *n* **fan**, admirer, fanatic, devotee, hero-worshipper

idolatry *n* **worship**, hero worship, adoration, admiration, veneration *Opposite*: denigration

idolization *see* **idolatry**

idolize *v* **worship**, hero-worship, adore, look up to, admire *Opposite*: denigrate

idyll *n* **nirvana**, honeymoon, honeymoon period, heaven, paradise *Opposite*: nightmare

idyllic *adj* **1 peaceful**, calm, tranquil, restful, relaxing *Opposite*: nightmarish **2 picturesque**, scenic, unspoiled, beautiful, charming

i.e. *adv* **that is to say**, that is, namely, viz, to be precise

if *n* **1 doubt**, uncertainty, question mark, unknown, unknown quantity **2 stipulation**, condition, rider, proviso, qualification

iffy *(infml) adj* **1 risky**, chancy, shaky, suspicious, dubious *Opposite*: reliable **2 unsure**, undecided, doubtful, hesitant, up in the air *Opposite*: certain

ignite *v* **1 catch fire**, catch light, go up in flames, burst into flames, flare up *Opposite*: go out **2 set fire to**, light, put a match to, set light to, set alight *Opposite*: put out **3 stir up**, stir, inflame, fan the flames of, kindle *Opposite*: dampen

ignition *n* **explosion**, detonation, eruption, burst, blastoff

ignoble *adj* **dishonourable**, shameful, despicable, immoral, dastardly *Opposite*: honourable

ignominious *adj* **humiliating**, embarrassing, shameful, disgraceful, reprehensible *Opposite*: honourable

ignominy *n* **humiliation**, embarrassment, shame, disgrace, infamy *Opposite*: honour

ignorance *n* **unawareness**, unfamiliarity, obliviousness, inexperience, witlessness *Opposite*: knowledge

ignorant *adj* **unaware**, uninformed, ill-informed, unfamiliar, oblivious *Opposite*: aware

ignore *v* **pay no attention to**, take no notice of, close your eyes to, pay no heed to, disregard *Opposite*: notice

ignored *adj* **overlooked**, unnoticed, disregarded, discounted, unheeded *Opposite*: noted

ilk *n* **type**, like, sort, kind, class

ill *adj* **1 unwell**, sick, under the weather, laid up, in poor health *Opposite*: well **2 unkind**, unfriendly, hostile, harsh, mean *Opposite*: good **3 harmful**, adverse, detrimental, unfavourable, unpropitious *Opposite*: good **4 wicked**, evil, immoral, bad, iniquitous *Opposite*: good ■ *adv* **1 unkindly**, hostilely, harshly, cruelly, unpleasantly *Opposite*: well **2 unfavourably**, adversely, unpropitiously, inauspiciously, ominously *Opposite*: well **3 hardly**, barely, scarcely *Opposite*: well ■ *n* **harm**, evil, misfortune, trouble, mischief *Opposite*: good

ill-advised *adj* **foolish**, foolhardy, misguided, rash, reckless *Opposite*: well-advised

ill-assorted *adj* **incompatible**, mismatched, unsuited, incongruous, antagonistic *Opposite*: compatible

ill-bred *adj* **rude**, impolite, boorish, bad-mannered, ill-mannered *Opposite*: well-bred

ill-conceived *adj* **doomed**, impractical, vague, ill-judged, half-baked *(infml)*

ill-considered *adj* **careless**, reckless, irresponsible, rash, hasty *Opposite*: prudent

ill-defined *adj* **imprecise**, vague, hazy, unclear, nebulous *Opposite*: clear

ill-disguised *adj* **obvious**, blatant, clear, apparent, plain *Opposite*: concealed

ill-disposed *adj* **hostile**, unfriendly, cold, cool, antagonistic *Opposite*: well-disposed

illegal *adj* **against the law**, unlawful, illicit, illegitimate, prohibited *Opposite*: legal. See COMPARE AND CONTRAST *at* **unlawful**.

illegality *n* **1 unlawfulness**, illicitness, illegitimacy, impropriety, wrongfulness *Opposite*: legality **2 crime**, misdemeanour, offence, felony, infraction

illegible *adj* **unreadable**, indecipherable, scrawled, scribbled, spidery *Opposite*: legible

illegitimate *adj* **unlawful**, illegal, illicit, prohibited, banned *Opposite*: legitimate

ill-fated *adj* **doomed**, ill-starred, unlucky,

unfortunate, hapless *Opposite*: lucky

ill-favoured *adj* **unattractive**, ugly, repulsive, repellent, hideous *Opposite*: good-looking

ill feeling *n* **animosity**, hostility, ill will, antagonism, enmity *Opposite*: friendliness

ill-founded *adj* **illogical**, false, inaccurate, trumped-up, unreliable *Opposite*: reliable

ill-gotten *adj* **illegal**, illicit, fraudulent, contraband, unlawful

ill health *n* **infirmity**, illness, sickness, disease, frailty *Opposite*: good health

ill humour *n* **bad mood**, mood, bad temper, foul mood, sulk

illiberal *adj* **1 intolerant**, bigoted, narrow-minded, reactionary, parochial *Opposite*: liberal **2** (*fml*) **mean**, parsimonious, miserly, niggardly, tight *Opposite*: generous

illicit *adj* **illegal**, unlawful, illegitimate, dishonest, criminal *Opposite*: legal. *See* COMPARE AND CONTRAST *at* **unlawful**.

illiterate *adj* **uneducated**, untaught, unschooled, untrained, uninformed *Opposite*: literate

ill-judged *adj* **misguided**, injudicious, inappropriate, unwise, imprudent *Opposite*: prudent

ill-mannered *adj* **rude**, bad-mannered, impolite, discourteous, disrespectful *Opposite*: well-mannered

ill-natured *adj* **unpleasant**, disagreeable, ill-tempered, bad-tempered, irascible *Opposite*: good-natured

illness *n* **1 disease**, sickness, complaint, ailment, infection **2 ill health**, sickness, disease, infirmity, disability *Opposite*: good health

illogical *adj* **1 irrational**, unreasoned, unscientific, specious, unsound *Opposite*: logical **2 unreasonable**, senseless, absurd, ludicrous, nonsensical *Opposite*: logical

illogicality *n* **1 irrationality**, speciousness, unsoundness, inconsistency, contradiction **2 unreasonableness**, senselessness, absurdity, ludicrousness, nonsensicality

ill-omened *adj* **inauspicious**, unlucky, unfortunate, ominous, fateful *Opposite*: blessed

ill-starred *adj* **unlucky**, doomed, ill-fated, unfortunate, hapless *Opposite*: lucky

ill-tempered *adj* **bad-tempered**, short-tempered, irascible, irritable, grumpy *Opposite*: good-tempered

ill-timed *adj* **inopportune**, mistimed, untimely, inconvenient, intrusive *Opposite*: opportune

ill-treat *v* **abuse**, harm, mistreat, misuse, ill-use *Opposite*: look after. *See* COMPARE AND CONTRAST *at* **misuse**.

ill-treated *adj* **abused**, harmed, mistreated, maltreated, ill-used *Opposite*: cherished

ill-treatment *n* **abuse**, harm, maltreatment, mistreatment, cruelty *Opposite*: care

illuminate *v* **1 light up**, light, brighten, lighten,

irradiate *Opposite*: darken **2 clarify**, elucidate, explain, clear up, illustrate *Opposite*: confuse

illuminating *adj* **enlightening**, revealing, informative, instructive, educational *Opposite*: confusing

illumination *n* **1 light**, lighting, lights, brightness, brilliance **2 enlightenment**, clarification, explanation, insight, knowledge *Opposite*: confusion

illuminations *n* **lights**, Christmas lights, coloured lights, decorations, fairy lights

ill-use *v* **abuse**, harm, mistreat, maltreat, treat badly *Opposite*: look after

ill-used *adj* **mistreated**, maltreated, badly treated, abused, hurt *Opposite*: cherished

illusion *n* **1 fantasy**, daydream, figment of your imagination, chimera, mirage *Opposite*: reality **2 impression**, semblance, appearance, feeling, sensation **3 delusion**, misapprehension, deception, misconception, magic

illusive *see* **illusory**

illusory *adj* **deceptive**, false, imagined, misleading, unreal *Opposite*: real

illustrate *v* **exemplify**, demonstrate, show, point up, prove

illustration *n* **1 picture**, drawing, figure, diagram, photograph **2 example**, demonstration, instance, case in point, exemplification

illustrative *adj* **descriptive**, explanatory, graphic, expressive, demonstrative

illustrious *adj* **distinguished**, celebrated, renowned, famous, eminent *Opposite*: obscure

ill will *n* **animosity**, hostility, ill feeling, antagonism, enmity *Opposite*: goodwill

image *n* **1 picture**, representation, drawing, icon, figure **2 impression**, picture, idea, concept, notion **3 copy**, twin, double, duplicate, carbon copy **4 appearance**, look, persona, aura, air

imagery *n* **images**, pictures, descriptions, metaphors, similes

imaginable *adj* **conceivable**, possible, thinkable, supposable, presumable *Opposite*: unimaginable

imaginary *adj* **fantasy**, make-believe, made-up, unreal, invented *Opposite*: real

imagination *n* **1 mind's eye**, mind, head, thoughts, dreams **2 resourcefulness**, ingenuity, creativity, inventiveness, vision

imaginative *adj* **creative**, inventive, original, ingenious, artistic *Opposite*: unimaginative

imaginativeness *n* **creativeness**, inventiveness, originality, ingeniousness, resourcefulness

imagine *v* **1 picture**, envisage, visualize, see, conjure up **2 make up**, dream, dream up, invent, make believe **3 suppose**, think, expect, assume, presume

imagined *adj* **fictional**, imaginary, abstract, unreal, illusory *Opposite*: real

imbalance *n* **inequity**, disparity, unevenness, disproportion, inequality *Opposite*: balance

imbibe *(fml) v* **drink**, down, swallow, take in, absorb

imbroglio *n* **mess**, embarrassment, entanglement, complication, enmeshment

imbue *v* **instil**, fill, permeate, infuse, saturate

imitate *v* **1 reproduce**, copy, duplicate, replicate, rip off *(infml)* **2 mimic**, copy, ape, emulate, take off *(infml)*

COMPARE AND CONTRAST CORE MEANING: adopt the behaviour of another person

imitate copy another's behaviour, voice, or manner, sometimes in order to make fun of him or her; **copy** do exactly what somebody else does; **emulate** try to equal or surpass somebody else who is successful or admired; **mimic** imitate somebody in a deliberate and exaggerated way, especially to amuse people; **take off** *(infml)* imitate somebody to amuse people; **ape** imitate somebody in an absurd or grotesque way.

---

imitation *n* **1 simulation**, reproduction, replication, copy, facsimile **2 impersonation**, impression, skit, parody, sendup *(infml)* ■ *adj* **mock**, fake, simulated, artificial, pretend *Opposite*: real

imitative *adj* **unoriginal**, derivative, plagiarized, copied, second-hand *Opposite*: original

imitator *n* **1 follower**, sheep, copier, clone, imitation *Opposite*: original **2 impersonator**, impressionist, mimic, double, actor

immaculate *adj* **1 spotless**, perfect, neat and tidy, clean, tidy *Opposite*: messy **2 perfect**, flawless, faultless, pristine, pure *Opposite*: flawed

immanent *(fml) adj* **inherent**, intrinsic, innate, ingrained, internal

immaterial *adj* **irrelevant**, unimportant, of no importance, of no consequence, inconsequential *Opposite*: relevant

immature *adj* **1 young**, undeveloped, small, unformed, juvenile *Opposite*: mature **2 childish**, babyish, infantile, juvenile, adolescent *Opposite*: mature

immaturity *n* **1 adolescence**, infancy, reproductive immaturity, youth, babyhood *Opposite*: maturity **2 childishness**, irresponsibility, naivety, ingenuousness, silliness *Opposite*: maturity **3 naivety**, inexperience, greenness, rawness, awkwardness *Opposite*: maturity

immeasurable *adj* **vast**, beyond measure, endless, infinite, incalculable *Opposite*: slight

immeasurably *adv* **extremely**, infinitely, vastly, incalculably, inestimably *Opposite*: slightly

immediate *adj* **1 instant**, direct, instantaneous, abrupt, fast **2 direct**, close, near, proximate

Opposite: distant **3 urgent**, current, pressing, high priority, burning

immediately *adv* **1 right away**, straightaway, at once, without delay, instantly *Opposite*: later **2 directly**, closely, nearly, proximately *Opposite*: distantly ■ *conj* **as soon as**, the moment, the instant, the minute, the second

immemorial *adj* **ancient**, age-old, old, centuries old, timeworn

immense *adj* **huge**, vast, enormous, massive, gigantic *Opposite*: tiny

immensely *adv* **hugely**, vastly, enormously, immeasurably, greatly

immensity *n* **hugeness**, vastness, enormity, sheer size, extent

immerse *v* **1 submerge**, dip, plunge, duck, dunk **2 engross**, throw yourself into, absorb yourself in, engage, occupy

immersed *adj* **engrossed**, wrapped up, absorbed, deep, occupied *Opposite*: distracted

immersion *n* **1 involvement**, engagement, absorption, entanglement, preoccupation **2 dipping**, soaking, wetting, dunking, steeping

immigrant *n* **settler**, émigré, migrant, refugee, colonist *Opposite*: emigrant

immigrate *v* **settle**, arrive, colonize, discover, found *Opposite*: emigrate

immigration *n* **migration**, settlement, arrival, entry, colonization

imminent *adj* **impending**, forthcoming, pending, looming, about to happen *Opposite*: distant

immobile *adj* **1 motionless**, stationary, still, stock-still, inert *Opposite*: mobile **2 fixed**, immovable, secure, steady, permanent *Opposite*: mobile

immobility *n* **stillness**, motionlessness, immovability, fixity, stasis *Opposite*: mobility

immobilize *v* **stop**, halt, restrain, arrest, bring to a halt *Opposite*: mobilize

immoderate *adj* **excessive**, extreme, intemperate, extravagant, unrestrained *Opposite*: moderate

immoderateness *(fml) see* **immoderation**

immoderation *(fml) n* **excess**, intemperance, extravagance, prodigality, abandon *Opposite*: moderation

immodest *adj* **boastful**, arrogant, conceited, ostentatious, bombastic *Opposite*: modest

immodesty *n* **arrogance**, conceit, boastfulness, pretentiousness, ostentatiousness *Opposite*: modesty

immolate *(literary) v* **1 sacrifice**, offer up, slaughter, make an offering of, kill **2 give up**, sacrifice, renounce, do without, forgo

immoral *adj* **wicked**, depraved, corrupt, dissolute, dishonest *Opposite*: moral

immorality *n* **wickedness**, sin, depravity, corruption, dissoluteness *Opposite*: morality

immortal *adj* **1 eternal**, everlasting, undying, perpetual, enduring *Opposite*: mortal **2 memorable**, well-known, famous, illustrious, unforgettable *Opposite*: forgotten

immortalize *v* **commemorate**, celebrate, preserve, make immortal, memorialize

immovable *adj* **1 fixed**, immobile, secure, steady, permanent *Opposite*: movable **2 resolute**, unbending, rigid, stubborn, obstinate *Opposite*: irresolute

immune *adj* **1 resistant**, protected, invulnerable, safe, insusceptible *(fml) Opposite*: susceptible **2 exempt**, excepted, absolved, excused, not liable *Opposite*: liable **3 impervious**, invulnerable, untouchable, untouched, unaffected *Opposite*: vulnerable

immune system *n* **body's defences**, natural defences, immune response, white blood cells, natural resistance

immunity *n* **1 resistance**, protection, invulnerability, imperviousness, insusceptibility *(fml) Opposite*: susceptibility **2 exemption**, exception, liberty, freedom, protection *Opposite*: liability

immunization *n* **vaccination**, inoculation, injection, shot *(infml)*, jab *(infml)*

immunize *v* **vaccinate**, inoculate, inject, protect, jab *(infml)*

immure *(literary) v* **imprison**, confine, shut away, shut up, hold captive *Opposite*: free

immutable *adj* **unchanging**, irreversible, fixed, absolute, unchangeable *Opposite*: mercurial

imp *n* **1 elf**, goblin, pixie, sprite, fairy **2 mischief**, urchin, rascal, scamp *(infml)*, scallywag *(dated infml)*

impact *n* **1 crash**, collision, shock, bang, blow **2 influence**, impression, effect, bearing, power

impacted *adj* **wedged**, stuck, jammed, squeezed, obstructed

impair *v* **damage**, harm, spoil, weaken, worsen *Opposite*: enhance

impaired *adj* **reduced**, lessened, decreased, weakened, diminished *Opposite*: unimpaired

impairment *n* **damage**, injury, hurt, loss, weakening *Opposite*: enhancement

impale *v* **spear**, pierce, stab, bayonet, spike

impalpable *(fml) adj* **intangible**, shadowy, vague, unclear, indefinable *Opposite*: palpable

impart *v* **communicate**, inform, tell, convey, divulge

impartial *adj* **neutral**, fair, unbiased, independent, objective *Opposite*: biased

impartiality *n* **neutrality**, fairness, independence, objectivity, detachment *Opposite*: bias

impassable *adj* **blocked**, impenetrable, closed, obstructed, inaccessible *Opposite*: open

impasse *n* **stalemate**, standoff, deadlock, gridlock, bottleneck

impassioned *adj* **emotional**, ardent, fervent, passionate, heated *Opposite*: impassive

impassive *adj* **1 expressionless**, blank, inexpressive, poker-faced, deadpan *Opposite*: expressive **2 unemotional**, unmoved, stolid, stoic, phlegmatic *Opposite*: impassioned

---

COMPARE AND CONTRAST CORE MEANING: showing no emotional response or interest

impassive showing no outward sign of emotion, especially on the face; **apathetic** not taking any interest in anything, or not bothering to do anything; **phlegmatic** generally unemotional and difficult to arouse; **stolid** solemn, unemotional, and not easily excited or upset; **stoic** showing admirable patience and endurance in the face of adversity without complaining or getting upset; **unmoved** showing no emotion, surprise, or excitement when this would normally have been expected.

---

impatience *n* **1 annoyance**, irritation, edginess, intolerance, displeasure *Opposite*: patience **2 eagerness**, keenness, anxiety, hurry, haste *Opposite*: patience

impatient *adj* **1 annoyed**, irritated, edgy, intolerant, exasperated *Opposite*: patient **2 eager**, keen, raring, anxious, in a hurry *Opposite*: patient

impeach *v* **indict**, accuse, arraign, charge, inculpate *(fml)*

impeccable *adj* **perfect**, flawless, faultless, unimpeachable, above reproach *Opposite*: flawed

impecunious *adj* **poor**, impoverished, penniless, poverty-stricken, destitute *Opposite*: wealthy

impede *v* **obstruct**, hinder, hamper, slow down, delay *Opposite*: facilitate. *See* COMPARE AND CONTRAST *at* **hinder**.

impediment *n* **1 obstacle**, obstruction, barrier, hurdle, hindrance **2 impairment**, disablement, weakness, disorder, inhibition

impel *v* **1 compel**, urge, force, drive, coerce *Opposite*: hold back **2** *(fml)* **propel**, force, drive, throw, push

impend *(fml) v* **loom**, approach, be on the horizon, be imminent, be in the offing *Opposite*: recede

impending *adj* **imminent**, looming, in the near future, approaching, coming *Opposite*: far-off

impenetrability *n* **1 impassability**, impermeability, density, denseness, thickness **2 incomprehensibility**, complexity, opacity, intricacy, obscurity *Opposite*: lucidity

impenetrable *adj* **1 impassable**, dense, tightly packed, thick, solid **2 incomprehensible**, unfathomable, indecipherable, inscrutable, unsolvable *Opposite*: understandable

impenitent *adj* **unrepentant**, unremorseful,

unapologetic, defiant, shameless Opposite: remorseful

imperative adj **1 necessary**, vital, crucial, essential, urgent Opposite: unimportant **2** (fml) **commanding**, domineering, bossy, imperious, overbearing Opposite: subservient ■ n **priority**, essential, requirement, necessity, obligation Opposite: option

imperceptible adj **slight**, gradual, subtle, invisible, undetectable Opposite: obvious

imperceptibly adv **slightly**, gradually, invisibly, subtly, little by little Opposite: obviously

imperfect adj **faulty**, defective, deficient, damaged, flawed Opposite: perfect

imperfection n **1 fault**, defect, deficiency, blemish, flaw **2 faultiness**, inadequacy, limitation, deficiency, failure Opposite: perfection. See COMPARE AND CONTRAST at **flaw.**

imperial adj **grand**, majestic, imposing, regal, stately

imperialism n **expansionism**, colonialism, empire-building, colonization, interventionism

imperil (fml) v **endanger**, put in danger, risk, put at risk, jeopardize Opposite: protect

imperious adj **domineering**, authoritative, commanding, arrogant, superior Opposite: humble

imperiousness n **haughtiness**, overbearingness, arrogance, superiority, bossiness Opposite: humility

imperishability n **durability**, resilience, stability, endurance, hardiness

imperishable adj **1 permanent**, durable, indestructible, resilient, stable **2** (literary) **enduring**, eternal, everlasting, permanent, immortal Opposite: transient

impermanence n **transience**, transitoriness, evanescence, ephemerality, temporariness Opposite: permanence

impermanent adj **temporary**, transitory, passing, transient, evanescent Opposite: permanent

impermeability n **watertightness**, airtightness, waterproofness, protection, impenetrability Opposite: permeability

impermeable adj **resistant**, impervious, waterproof, water-resistant, rainproof Opposite: permeable

impersonal adj **1 objective**, cool, detached, measured, careful Opposite: personal **2 anonymous**, faceless, soulless, featureless, grey **3 unfriendly**, cool, cold, aloof, frosty Opposite: friendly

impersonate v **1 mimic**, imitate, ape, copy, satirize **2 pretend to be**, pose as, masquerade as, personate, pass off

impersonation n **1 impression**, parody, caricature, takeoff (infml), sendup (infml) **2 imitation**, masquerade, personation, pretence, imposture (fml)

impertinence n **impudence**, insolence, disrespect, impoliteness, brazenness Opposite: respect

impertinent adj **impudent**, insolent, disrespectful, impolite, brazen Opposite: respectful

imperturbable adj **calm**, cool, unflappable, collected, composed Opposite: excitable

impervious adj **1 unreceptive**, unbending, unyielding, unwavering, rigid Opposite: responsive **2 impermeable**, solid, resistant, waterproof, water-resistant Opposite: permeable

imperviousness n **1 obduracy**, unyieldingness, rigidity, inflexibility Opposite: responsiveness **2 impermeability**, resistance, invulnerability, watertightness, solidity Opposite: permeability

impetuosity n **impulsiveness**, rashness, hastiness, hotheadedness, recklessness Opposite: consideration

impetuous adj **impulsive**, rash, hasty, hotheaded, unthinking Opposite: considered

impetuousness see **impetuosity**

impetus n **1 push**, motivation, incentive, energy, stimulus **2 force**, momentum, impulsion, thrust, forward motion Opposite: inertia

impiety n **irreverence**, sin, wickedness, transgression, immorality Opposite: piety

impinge (fml) v **impose**, intrude, interrupt, encroach, impact

impious adj **sinful**, irreverent, wicked, immoral, irreligious Opposite: pious

impish adj **mischievous**, naughty, wicked, playful, puckish

impishness n **mischievousness**, naughtiness, wickedness, playfulness, puckishness

implacability n **pitilessness**, mercilessness, relentlessness, ruthlessness, cruelty Opposite: kindness

implacable adj **pitiless**, merciless, relentless, ruthless, cruel Opposite: kind

implant v **establish**, embed, plant, insert, instil

implantation n **embedding**, establishment, grafting, attaching, joining

implausibility n **improbability**, unlikelihood, inconceivability, doubtfulness, questionability Opposite: plausibility

implausible adj **unlikely**, improbable, unbelievable, incredible, fantastic Opposite: plausible

implement n **tool**, device, gadget, instrument, contrivance ■ v **carry out**, put into practice, apply, realize, execute

implementation n **carrying out**, application, putting into practice, operation, execution Opposite: proposal

implicate v **1 connect**, involve, associate, link, incriminate Opposite: clear **2** (fml) **imply**, suggest, assume, hint at, point to

implication n 1 **insinuation**, inference, suggestion, innuendo, hint 2 **involvement**, association, connection, link, part 3 **consequence**, repercussion, outcome, result

implicit adj 1 **understood**, implied, unspoken, tacit, hidden Opposite: explicit 2 **unreserved**, absolute, total, complete, utter Opposite: qualified

implicitly adv 1 **indirectly**, covertly, tacitly, obliquely, subtly 2 **unreservedly**, absolutely, totally, completely, wholly

implied adj **indirect**, understood, implicit, unspoken, tacit

implode v **collapse**, fail, cave in, fall in, subside Opposite: explode

implore (fml) v **beg**, plead, pray, appeal, entreat

imploring (fml) adj **pleading**, desperate, longing, heartfelt, suppliant (fml)

implosion n **collapse**, falling-in, subsidence, cave-in, disintegration Opposite: explosion

imply v 1 **suggest**, hint at, point to, indicate, insinuate 2 **involve**, entail, mean, denote

impolite adj **rude**, ill-mannered, bad-mannered, boorish, disrespectful Opposite: polite

impoliteness n **rudeness**, bad manners, loutishness, boorishness, disrespect Opposite: politeness

impolitic adj **unwise**, inappropriate, misguided, ill-advised, ill-judged Opposite: wise

imponderable adj **unknown**, unquantifiable, incalculable, indeterminable, inestimable ■ n **unknown**, mystery, enigma, paradox, uncertainty

import v **bring in**, introduce, trade in, smuggle Opposite: export ■ n 1 **introduction**, importation, ingress (fml) Opposite: export 2 **significance**, importance, meaning, consequence (fml)

importance n 1 **significance**, meaning, weight, magnitude, import Opposite: triviality 2 **rank**, position, standing, status, reputation

important adj 1 **significant**, vital, imperative, central, chief Opposite: trivial 2 **high-ranking**, eminent, worthy, notable, prominent Opposite: insignificant

importantly adv **significantly**, notably, crucially, critically, vitally

importation n **import**, introduction, ingress (fml) Opposite: export

importer n **trader**, shipper, carrier, haulier, distributor

importunate (fml) adj **persistent**, demanding, unrelenting, annoying, overeager

importune (fml) v **bother**, pester, badger, harass, plague

importunity (fml) n 1 **persistence**, insistence, obstinacy, doggedness, stubbornness 2 **demand**, request, entreaty, appeal, petition

impose v 1 **enforce**, levy, exact, execute, carry out 2 **inflict**, force, foist, dump, insist 3 **intrude**, be in the way, be a nuisance, disturb, trespass

imposing adj **impressive**, striking, grand, magnificent, stately Opposite: unimpressive

imposition n **burden**, nuisance, annoyance, bother, obligation

impossibility n **unfeasibility**, impracticality, hopelessness, ridiculousness, unlikelihood Opposite: possibility

impossible adj 1 **irresolvable**, irresoluble, unfeasible, impracticable, unattainable Opposite: possible 2 **unbearable**, terrible, dreadful, intolerable, insufferable Opposite: manageable

impossibly adv **dreadfully**, terribly, hopelessly, unbearably, ridiculously Opposite: reasonably

impostor n **deceiver**, imitator, impersonator, pretender, fake Opposite: the real McCoy (infml)

imposture (fml) n **deception**, impersonation, pretence, masquerade, imitation

impotence n **ineffectiveness**, incapability, ineffectualness, feebleness, powerlessness Opposite: strength

impotent adj **powerless**, weak, helpless, unable, incapable Opposite: powerful

impound v **confiscate**, seize, lock up, take away, hold Opposite: release

impoverish v **deprive**, ruin, bankrupt, diminish, weaken Opposite: enrich

impoverished adj **needy**, poor, penniless, disadvantaged, underprivileged Opposite: rich

impoverishment n 1 **destitution**, failure, disadvantage, poverty, insolvency Opposite: prosperity 2 **diminishment**, ruination, decline, depletion, degeneration Opposite: enrichment

impracticability n **unworkability**, impossibility, impracticality, impracticableness, unworkableness Opposite: feasibility

impracticable adj **unviable**, useless, unrealistic, unfeasible, unpractical Opposite: viable

impractical adj 1 **unpractical**, unreasonable, unviable, unfeasible, unworkable Opposite: practical 2 **unrealistic**, idealistic, starry-eyed, not down to earth, clueless (infml) Opposite: realistic

impracticality n **unviability**, unfeasibility, impracticableness, inconvenience, hopelessness Opposite: practicality

imprecate (fml) v **curse**, revile, call down, execrate (literary or fml), maledict (literary)

imprecation (fml) n 1 **oath**, insult, swearword, expletive, curse 2 **swearing**, cursing, blasphemy, profanity, cussing (infml)

imprecise adj **sketchy**, vague, inexact, rough, inaccurate Opposite: precise

imprecision n fuzziness, roughness, sketchiness, inaccuracy, inexactitude Opposite: accuracy

impregnable adj **unassailable**, invincible, secure, unconquerable, impenetrable Opposite: vulnerable

impregnate v **saturate**, soak, steep, infuse, permeate Opposite: dry out

impresario n **manager**, producer, promoter, agent, entrepreneur

impress v 1 **excite**, move, amaze, influence, affect Opposite: disappoint 2 **emphasize**, stress, drive home, drum into, din into Opposite: gloss over

impression n 1 **feeling**, idea, notion, thought, sense Opposite: certainty 2 **imprint**, dent, mark, print, hollow 3 **mark**, impact, effect, influence, reaction 4 **impersonation**, imitation, parody, takeoff (infml), sendup (infml)

impressionable adj **susceptible**, suggestible, vulnerable, receptive, sensitive Opposite: unreceptive

impressionist n **impersonator**, mimic, imitator, comic, entertainer

impressionistic adj **ill-defined**, rough, loose, unfocused, imprecise Opposite: detailed

impressive adj **imposing**, inspiring, striking, remarkable, notable Opposite: unimpressive

impressiveness n **grandeur**, splendour, magnificence, brilliance, eminence

imprint n 1 **impression**, print, mark, indentation, print, mark, indentation, hollow 2 **stamp**, inscription, name, print, printer's mark 3 **hallmark**, emblem, stamp, seal, sign 4 **indication**, mark, impression, effect, sign ■ v **impress**, fix, establish, drive home, drum into

imprison v **confine**, detain, intern, lock up, lock away

imprisoned adj **confined**, jailed, captive, restrained, trapped Opposite: free

imprisonment n **custody**, captivity, detention, term, internment

improbability n **unlikelihood**, implausibility, dubiousness, doubtfulness, questionability Opposite: probability

improbable adj **unlikely**, doubtful, implausible, questionable, dubious Opposite: likely

impromptu adj **unprepared**, unrehearsed, unplanned, spontaneous, spur-of-the-moment Opposite: prepared

improper adj 1 (fml) **indecorous**, inappropriate, unsuitable, out of place, unfitting Opposite: fitting 2 **rude**, shocking, indecent, inappropriate, unacceptable Opposite: proper 3 **dishonest**, irregular, shady, illegal, criminal Opposite: honest

impropriety n **rudeness**, indecency, unseemliness, immodesty, indecorum Opposite: propriety

improve v 1 **look up**, perk up, get better, rally, mend Opposite: worsen 2 **better**, enhance,

ameliorate, enrich, upgrade Opposite: deteriorate 3 **correct**, adjust, touch up, titivate, amend

improved adj **better**, enhanced, amended, upgraded, developed Opposite: deteriorated

improvement n 1 **amendment**, correction, development, upgrade, enhancement Opposite: deterioration 2 **recovery**, recuperation, rally, progress, advance Opposite: decline

improve on v **better**, go one better, top, beat, exceed

improvident adj **imprudent**, careless, reckless, negligent, irresponsible Opposite: prudent

improvisation n 1 **inventiveness**, invention, creativeness, lateral thinking 2 **extemporization**, ad-libbing, standup

improvise v 1 **ad-lib**, extemporize, create, make up, invent Opposite: orchestrate 2 **contrive**, concoct, invent, create, devise

improvised adj **unpremeditated**, ad hoc, unplanned, makeshift, spontaneous Opposite: prepared

imprudence n **profligacy**, carelessness, indiscretion, rashness, injudiciousness Opposite: prudence

imprudent adj **foolish**, impulsive, indiscreet, irresponsible, rash Opposite: prudent

impudence n **impertinence**, boldness, insolence, nerve, effrontery Opposite: respect

impudent adj **bold**, brazen, insolent, rude, disrespectful Opposite: respectful

impugn (fml) v **question**, dispute, call into question, doubt, query

impulse n 1 **instinct**, desire, urge, whim, compulsion Opposite: aversion 2 **propulsion**, motive power, drive, stimulus, pressure 3 **tick**, pulse, nerve, pulsation, beat

impulsion n 1 **push**, propulsion, thrust, momentum, impetus 2 **desire**, yen, compulsion, instinct, whim Opposite: aversion

impulsive adj **unwary**, thoughtless, impetuous, imprudent, precipitate Opposite: cautious

impulsively adv **unwarily**, thoughtlessly, on impulse, impetuously, spontaneously Opposite: deliberately

impulsiveness n **precipitateness**, suddenness, thoughtlessness, impetuosity, spontaneity Opposite: deliberation (fml)

impunity n **exemption**, freedom, licence, liberty, latitude

impure adj **contaminated**, adulterated, mixed, tainted, polluted Opposite: pure

impurity n **contamination**, pollution, adulteration, uncleanness, infection Opposite: purity

imputation n **accusation**, assertion, attribution, reproach, complaint

impute v 1 **credit**, chalk up, attribute, accredit, assign 2 **complain**, accuse, implicate, allege, assert

in prep **inside**, within, around Opposite: outside ■ adv **around**, inside, accessible, available, at home Opposite: out ■ adj **cutting-edge**, fashionable, popular, now, in vogue Opposite: out

inability n **incapability**, incapacity, powerlessness, helplessness, failure Opposite: ability

inaccessibility n 1 **unreachability**, remoteness, distance, isolation, unapproachability Opposite: approachability 2 **unattainability**, unavailability, unaffordability, impossibility, confidentiality Opposite: accessibility 3 **difficulty**, obscurity, obscureness, obliqueness, impenetrability Opposite: lucidity

inaccessible adj 1 **unreachable**, out-of-the-way, unapproachable, hard to find, remote Opposite: approachable 2 **difficult**, obscure, esoteric, abstruse, oblique Opposite: simple

inaccuracy n 1 **imprecision**, inexactness, mistakenness, wrongness, erroneousness Opposite: precision 2 **error**, mistake, slip, flaw, blunder. See COMPARE AND CONTRAST at **mistake**.

inaccurate adj **imprecise**, inexact, mistaken, erroneous, wrong Opposite: precise

inaction n 1 **failure to act**, indecision, procrastination, fumbling, delay Opposite: decisiveness 2 **inactivity**, laziness, idleness, inertia, apathy Opposite: energy

inactivate v **deactivate**, put out of action, incapacitate, disable, turn off Opposite: set in motion

inactive adj 1 **motionless**, stationary, unmoving, immobile, stopped Opposite: moving 2 **idle**, dormant, out of action, unused, inoperative Opposite: working 3 **sedentary**, lazy, slothful, indolent, sluggish Opposite: energetic

inactivity n 1 **motionlessness**, immobility, stillness Opposite: motion 2 **idleness**, dormancy, inoperativeness Opposite: activity 3 **sedentariness**, laziness, sloth, indolence, sluggishness Opposite: energy

in addition to prep **as well as**, along with, on top of, besides, over and above

inadequacy n 1 **insufficiency**, meagreness, scantiness, lack, shortage Opposite: sufficiency 2 **fault**, failure, failing, incompetence, defectiveness Opposite: asset

inadequate adj 1 **insufficient**, scarce, derisory, laughable, poor Opposite: sufficient 2 **incompetent**, lacking, deficient, ineffective, inefficient Opposite: capable

inadmissible adj **unacceptable**, prohibited, excluded, barred, disallowed Opposite: acceptable

inadvertence n 1 **carelessness**, inattention, negligence, thoughtlessness, laxity 2 **oversight**, omission, error, mistake, blunder

inadvertency see inadvertence

inadvertent adj **unintentional**, careless, unintended, involuntary, unplanned Opposite: intentional

inadvisable adj **ill-advised**, imprudent, unwise, foolish, injudicious Opposite: wise

inalienable (fml) adj **unchallengeable**, absolute, immutable, unassailable, incontrovertible Opposite: disputable

in all adv **ultimately**, altogether, all in all, as a whole, all told

inane adj **silly**, unintelligent, absurd, ridiculous, stupid Opposite: sensible

inanimate adj 1 **lifeless**, dead, nonliving, inorganic, inert Opposite: alive 2 **inactive**, dull, unresponsive, apathetic, listless Opposite: spirited

inanity n 1 **meaninglessness**, senselessness, stupidity, ridiculousness, absurdity Opposite: logic 2 **silliness**, foolishness, frivolousness, stupidity, ridiculousness Opposite: sensibleness

inapplicability n **unsuitability**, inappropriateness, irrelevance, inaptness, wrongness Opposite: suitability

inapplicable adj **unsuitable**, irrelevant, inappropriate, inapposite, inapt Opposite: suitable

inapposite adj **unsuitable**, out of place, inappropriate, inapt, unfitting Opposite: suitable

inappositeness n **unsuitability**, inappropriateness, inaptness, wrongness, irrelevance Opposite: suitability

inappreciable adj **insignificant**, imperceptible, negligible, unimportant, immaterial Opposite: significant

inappreciably adv **insignificantly**, imperceptibly, negligibly, immaterially, microscopically Opposite: significantly

inappropriate adj **unsuitable**, unfitting, untimely, inapt, wrong Opposite: fitting

inappropriateness n **unsuitability**, impropriety, wrongness, incorrectness, unseemliness Opposite: appropriateness

inarticulacy n 1 **incoherence**, hesitation, lack of fluency, stumbling, stuttering Opposite: eloquence 2 **unintelligibility**, incomprehensibility, inaudibility, indistinctness, unclearness Opposite: clarity

inarticulate adj 1 **tongue-tied**, incoherent, mumbling, hesitant, faltering Opposite: eloquent 2 **garbled**, muttered, incoherent, unintelligible, incomprehensible Opposite: clear

inasmuch as conj **because**, insofar as, considering that, since, as

inattention n **inattentiveness**, daydreaming, woolgathering, distraction, abstraction Opposite: concentration

inattentive adj **careless**, distracted, abstracted, daydreaming, woolgathering Opposite: careful

inattentiveness n **carelessness**, inattention,

daydreaming, distraction, abstraction *Opposite*: attention

inaudibility *n* **quietness**, faintness, imperceptibility, noiselessness, silence *Opposite*: audibility

inaudible *adj* **quiet**, low, faint, soft, silent *Opposite*: perceptible

inaugural *adj* **opening**, initial, first, introductory, foundational

inaugurate *v* **1 swear in**, install, induct, instate, initiate *Opposite*: dismiss **2 open**, launch, dedicate, initiate, unveil *Opposite*: close **3 initiate**, establish, put in place, set up, start up *Opposite*: terminate *(fml)*

inauguration *n* **1 induction**, investiture, installation, swearing in, inaugural ceremony *Opposite*: dismissal **2 opening**, launch, opening ceremony, initiation ceremony, start *Opposite*: closure **3 initiation**, creation, introduction, setting up, conception *Opposite*: closedown

inauspicious *adj* **unpromising**, discouraging, ill-starred, ill-fated, ominous *Opposite*: promising

inauthentic *adj* **false**, imitation, fake, forged, counterfeit *Opposite*: genuine

in between *prep* **between**, next to, sandwiched by, in the middle of, amid

in-between *adj* **intermediate**, separating, isolating, halfway, indeterminate ■ *adv* **meanwhile**, in the interval, in the intervening time, between times, at the same time

inborn *adj* **innate**, natural, instinctive, intuitive, inherited *Opposite*: acquired

inbound *adj* **incoming**, arriving, inward bound, coming in, heading towards

inbred *adj* **congenital**, inherited, hereditary, ingrained, deep-seated *Opposite*: acquired

in brief *adv* **briefly**, in a few words, in short, to sum up, in a word

in-built *adj* **1 innate**, natural, inborn, inherent, instinctive *Opposite*: learned **2 incorporated**, integral, intrinsic, included, integrated *Opposite*: add-on

incalculable *adj* **1 countless**, without number, innumerable, infinite, multitudinous *Opposite*: finite **2 unpredictable**, unforeseeable, indeterminable, uncertain, haphazard *Opposite*: predictable

incalculably *adv* **greatly**, infinitely, immeasurably, inestimably, immensely

incandesce *v* **glow**, radiate, shine, luminesce, fluoresce

incandescence *n* **glow**, luminosity, light, luminescence, fluorescence

incandescent *adj* **glowing**, radiant, luminous, shining, bright

incantation *n* **chant**, invocation, prayer, spell, charm

incapable *adj* **1 unable**, powerless, inept, inexpert, unqualified *Opposite*: able **2 helpless**, weak, vulnerable, feeble, frail *Opposite*: strong

incapacitate *v* **debilitate**, injure, harm, disable, lay up *Opposite*: enable

incapacitated *adj* **debilitated**, injured, harmed, disabled, laid up *Opposite*: fit

incapacity *n* **1 inability**, ineffectiveness, incapability, powerlessness, weakness *Opposite*: ability **2 disability**, infirmity, frailty, ill health

incarcerate *(fml)* *v* **imprison**, jail, lock up, hold prisoner, intern *Opposite*: free

incarceration *(fml)* *n* **imprisonment**, confinement, custody, captivity, internment *Opposite*: freedom

incarnate *adj* **personified**, in person, in the flesh, alive, embodied

incarnation *n* **personification**, embodiment, manifestation, avatar, living form

in case *conj* **just in case**, in the event, lest, if, whether or no

incautious *adj* **careless**, rash, reckless, impetuous, impulsive *Opposite*: careful

incendiary *adj* **1 inflammable**, combustible, flammable **2 inflammatory**, provocative, rabble-rousing, aggressive, stirring *Opposite*: conciliatory ■ *n* **1** *(fml)* **troublemaker**, agitator, demagogue, activist, firebrand **2 arsonist**, pyromaniac, burner, firebomber, fire raiser

incense *v* **enrage**, anger, exasperate, infuriate, annoy *Opposite*: calm

incensed *adj* **enraged**, angry, exasperated, infuriated, irate *Opposite*: calm

incentive *n* **inducement**, enticement, motive, motivation, encouragement *Opposite*: disincentive. *See* COMPARE AND CONTRAST *at* MOTIVE.

inception *(fml)* *n* **beginning**, start, inauguration, initiation, foundation *Opposite*: culmination

incessant *adj* **nonstop**, never-ending, ceaseless, continuous, continual *Opposite*: sporadic

inch *v* **creep**, crawl, shuffle, edge

in charge *adj* **in command**, in control, at the helm, responsible, giving the orders

inchoate *(fml)* *adj* **undeveloped**, incipient, immature, beginning, budding *Opposite*: mature

incidence *n* **occurrence**, frequency, rate, commonness, prevalence

incident *n* **1 event**, occurrence, occasion, happening, episode **2 confrontation**, clash, skirmish, fight, episode

incidental *adj* **related**, accompanying, secondary, subsidiary, supplementary *Opposite*: essential

incidentally *adv* **by the way**, by the by, while we're on the subject, before I forget, parenthetically

incinerate *v* **burn**, burn up, set fire to, cremate, reduce to ashes

incinerator *n* furnace, brazier, kiln, oven, burner

incipient *adj* **emerging**, initial, embryonic, budding, early *Opposite*: final

incise *v* cut, slit, notch, score, carve

incision *n* cut, slit, opening, notch, scratch

incisive *adj* keen, perceptive, insightful, sharp, penetrating *Opposite*: dull

incite *v* provoke, inflame, rouse, goad, spur *Opposite*: quell

incitement *n* provocation, stimulation, agitation, encouragement, goad *Opposite*: deterrent

incivility *n* rudeness, impoliteness, discourteousness, discourtesy, lack of respect *Opposite*: politeness

inclement *adj* intemperate, extreme, severe, bad, foul *Opposite*: pleasant

inclination *n* **1** feeling, predisposition, disposition, leaning, proclivity *Opposite*: antipathy **2** slope, slant, incline, gradient, pitch

incline *v* **1** dispose, persuade, prejudice, bias, lean *Opposite*: deter **2** slant, slope, tilt, rise, fall ■ *n* slope, slant, gradient, rise, ascent

inclined *adj* **1** motivated, persuaded, tending, disposed, apt *Opposite*: averse *(fml)* **2** leaning, sloping, slanting, tilting, orientated

include *v* **1** contain, comprise, take in, consist of, take account of *Opposite*: omit **2** bring in, incorporate, add in, enter, involve *Opposite*: reject

included *adj* contained within, counted in, comprised, encompassed, involved *Opposite*: omitted

including *prep* counting, as well as, with, together with, plus *Opposite*: excluding

inclusion *n* presence, addition, enclosure, insertion, annexation *Opposite*: absence

inclusive *adj* comprehensive, wide-ranging, all-encompassing, complete, broad *Opposite*: restricted

incognito *adv* in disguise, disguised, undercover, anonymously, secretly *Opposite*: openly

incoherence *n* unintelligibility, inarticulateness, disjointedness, illogicality, confusedness *Opposite*: coherence

incoherent *adj* **1** disjointed, confused, jumbled, illogical, all over the place *(infml)* *Opposite*: clear **2** inarticulate, unintelligible, incomprehensible, garbled, mumbled *Opposite*: articulate

incombustible *adj* fireproof, flameproof, fire-resistant, flame-resistant, fire-retardant *Opposite*: flammable

income *n* profits, proceeds, returns, revenue, earnings *Opposite*: expenditure

incomer *n* settler, immigrant, colonist, migrant, newcomer

income tax *n* tax, toll, duty, excise, tariff

incoming *adj* **1** inbound, inward bound, homeward bound, arriving, entering *Opposite*: outgoing **2** new, next, succeeding, newly appointed, newly elected *Opposite*: outgoing

incommensurate *adj* disproportionate, unequal, inadequate, insufficient, lacking parity *Opposite*: proportionate

incommode *(fml)* *v* inconvenience, trouble, disturb, bother, put out

incommodious *(fml)* *adj* **1** cramped, restricted, confined, tiny, small *Opposite*: roomy **2** inconvenient, troublesome, awkward, annoying, bothersome

incommunicado *adj* not in contact, out of touch, not in communication, not able to communicate, unwilling to communicate

incomparable *adj* unequalled, unrivalled, unparalleled, unsurpassed, unmatched *Opposite*: ordinary

incompatibility *n* **1** mismatch, unsuitability, discordancy, inharmoniousness, irreconcilability **2** inconsistency, illogicality, irreconcilability, incongruity, mismatch *Opposite*: consistency

incompatible *adj* mismatched, unsuited, discordant, dissenting, irreconcilable *Opposite*: like-minded

incompetence *n* ineptitude, unskilfulness, inability, ineffectiveness, stupidity *Opposite*: ability

incompetent *adj* inept, useless, unskilled, ineffectual, hopeless *Opposite*: able

incomplete *adj* **1** imperfect, partial, unfinished, inadequate, half-finished *Opposite*: entire **2** unfinished, undeveloped, curtailed, shortened, deficient *Opposite*: finished

incomprehensible *adj* unintelligible, unfathomable, impenetrable, inexplicable, inconceivable *Opposite*: understandable

incomprehension *n* disbelief, incredulity, incredulousness, perplexity, blankness *Opposite*: understanding

inconceivable *adj* unimaginable, unthinkable, beyond belief, unbelievable, incredible *Opposite*: imaginable

inconclusive *adj* indecisive, questionable, unconvincing, unsatisfying, unsettled *Opposite*: decisive

in confidence *adv* in secret, confidentially, between ourselves, in private, privately *Opposite*: openly

incongruity *n* oddness, strangeness, absurdity, inappropriateness, inaptness *Opposite*: consistency

incongruous *adj* odd, strange, out of place, incompatible, inappropriate *Opposite*: consistent

in conjunction with *prep* together with, combined with, along with, with, in addition to *Opposite*: apart from

in consequence *(fml)* *adv* accordingly, as a

result, consequently, therefore, so

inconsequence n **unimportance**, irrelevance, insignificance, triviality, inconsequentiality *Opposite*: importance

inconsequential adj **unimportant**, trivial, petty, negligible *Opposite*: important

inconsequentiality n **unimportance**, insignificance, triviality, frivolity, inconsequence *Opposite*: importance

inconsiderable adj **small**, minor, tiny, paltry, negligible *Opposite*: sizable

inconsiderate adj **selfish**, thoughtless, insensitive, uncharitable, unkind *Opposite*: caring

inconsistency n **1 discrepancy**, contradiction, variation, variance, irregularity **2 changeability**, unpredictability, unreliability, fickleness, capriciousness *Opposite*: consistency

inconsistent adj **1 conflicting**, contradictory, incompatible, incongruous, paradoxical *Opposite*: consistent **2 unpredictable**, variable, unreliable, erratic, changeable *Opposite*: constant

inconsolable adj **grief-stricken**, brokenhearted, devastated, desolate, despairing *Opposite*: ecstatic

inconspicuous adj **unobtrusive**, discreet, unremarkable, ordinary, modest *Opposite*: obvious

inconstant adj **changeable**, variable, irregular, unpredictable, fluctuating *Opposite*: unchanging

incontestable adj **indisputable**, incontrovertible, irrefutable, unquestionable, indubitable *Opposite*: arguable

incontrovertible adj **undeniable**, unquestionable, irrefutable, incontestable, indisputable *Opposite*: questionable

inconvenience n **1 troublesomeness**, tiresomeness, inopportuneness, untimeliness, awkwardness *Opposite*: benefit **2 problem**, trouble, bother, difficulty, nuisance ■ v **disrupt**, put out, trouble, bother, disturb *Opposite*: help

inconvenient adj **troublesome**, tiresome, inopportune, problematic, untimely *Opposite*: beneficial

in cooperation with prep **together with**, in association with, in collaboration with, alongside, in conjunction with

incorporate v **1 include**, integrate, assimilate, fit in, add in *Opposite*: exclude **2 merge**, combine, feature, contain, include *Opposite*: divide

incorporated adj **combined**, united, unified, merged, fused *Opposite*: separate

incorporation n **combination**, amalgamation, integration, assimilation, merger *Opposite*: separation

incorporeal (fml) adj **intangible**, ethereal, spiritual, unreal, disembodied *Opposite*: tangible

incorrect adj **1 erroneous**, wrong, mistaken, untrue, inaccurate *Opposite*: right **2 improper**, unfitting, inappropriate, unseemly, unbecoming *Opposite*: proper

incorrectness n **1 erroneousness**, error, fallacy, wrongness, mistakenness *Opposite*: correctness **2 impropriety**, inappropriateness, unsuitability, unseemliness, indecorousness *Opposite*: propriety

incorrigible adj **irredeemable**, habitual, inveterate, dyed-in-the-wool, persistent *Opposite*: tractable

incorruptible adj **1 moral**, principled, just, straight, honourable *Opposite*: venal **2 imperishable**, everlasting, immortal, indestructible, unchanging *Opposite*: perishable

increase v **enlarge**, extend, expand, amplify, swell *Opposite*: decrease ■ n **upsurge**, surge, rise, growth, intensification *Opposite*: decrease

---

COMPARE AND CONTRAST CORE MEANING: make larger or greater

increase become or cause to become larger in number, quantity, degree, or scope; **expand** become or cause to become larger or more extensive; **enlarge** become or cause to become larger generally, or broaden in scope and detail; **extend** make larger in terms of length, area, period of time, or other existing limits; **augment** (fml) add to something in order to make it larger or more substantial; **intensify** become or cause to become greater in strength or degree; **amplify** become or cause to become louder, or greater in intensity or scope.

---

incredible adj **1 unbelievable**, implausible, improbable, far-fetched, absurd *Opposite*: believable **2 amazing**, astonishing, extraordinary, staggering, unbelievable *Opposite*: unremarkable **3** (infml) **excellent**, superb, tremendous, prodigious, phenomenal *Opposite*: mediocre

incredibly adv **1 unbelievably**, implausibly, inconceivably, absurdly, improbably *Opposite*: believably **2** (infml) **very**, extremely, unbelievably, amazingly, really

incredulity n **disbelief**, amazement, astonishment, doubt, scepticism *Opposite*: belief

incredulous adj **disbelieving**, sceptical, unbelieving, doubtful, doubting *Opposite*: believing

increment n **increase**, addition, rise, growth, boost *Opposite*: cut

incriminate v **implicate**, impeach, give away, lay the blame on, convict *Opposite*: exonerate

in-crowd (infml) n **inner circle**, beau monde, high society, clique, elite

incrustation n **coating**, crust, layer, covering, accumulation

incubate v **hatch**, gestate, raise, rear, nurture

incubation n **development**, gestation, cultivation, nurture, growth Opposite: destruction

inculcate v impress upon, teach, drum into, instruct, drill into

incumbency (fml) n 1 tenure, period of office, term of office, term, time 2 post, position, office, appointment 3 duty, obligation, responsibility, office, task

incumbent adj (fml) obligatory, mandatory, compulsory, binding, unavoidable Opposite: optional ■ n official, office holder, occupant, appointee, officer

incur v 1 experience, suffer, sustain, bring upon yourself, lay yourself open to Opposite: avoid 2 sustain, meet with, encounter, experience, suffer

incurable adj 1 terminal, fatal, deadly, inoperable, untreatable Opposite: curable 2 irredeemable, inveterate, incorrigible, hopeless, undying Opposite: redeemable

incurious adj uninterested, indifferent, unmoved, unconcerned, detached Opposite: inquisitive

incursion n 1 raid, night raid, attack, sortie, invasion Opposite: retreat 2 (fml) intrusion, invasion, spread, infiltration, arrival

in custody adj under arrest, in prison, in detention, detained, remanded

indebted adj obligated, obliged, grateful, thankful, in somebody's debt Opposite: ungrateful

indebtedness n obligation, gratitude, appreciation, thankfulness, gratefulness Opposite: ingratitude

indecency n 1 offensiveness, coarseness, crudeness, lewdness, obscenity Opposite: decency 2 impropriety, unsuitability, unseemliness, indecorousness, indelicacy Opposite: propriety

indecent adj 1 offensive, coarse, rude, crude, obscene Opposite: decorous 2 improper, unsuitable, unseemly, indecorous, unbecoming Opposite: proper

indecipherable adj 1 illegible, incomprehensible, unintelligible, unreadable, indistinct Opposite: legible 2 impenetrable, inscrutable, obscure, unfathomable, enigmatic Opposite: clear

indecision n irresolution, hesitancy, indecisiveness, uncertainty, vacillation Opposite: decisiveness

indecisive adj 1 irresolute, in two minds, vacillating, wavering, hesitant Opposite: decisive 2 inconclusive, indefinite, indeterminate, tentative, unclear Opposite: conclusive

indecisiveness n 1 irresolution, hesitancy, hesitation, vacillation, uncertainty Opposite: decisiveness 2 indefiniteness, inconclusiveness, woolliness, vagueness, indeterminacy Opposite: certainty

indecorous adj impolite, rude, shocking, inappropriate, unseemly Opposite: polite

indecorum n impoliteness, bad behaviour, rudeness, offensiveness, impropriety Opposite: politeness

indeed adv 1 in reality, in fact, actually, in truth, as a matter of fact 2 certainly, really, to be sure, undeniably, definitely

indefatigable adj untiring, unflagging, unrelenting, remorseless, unfaltering Opposite: half-hearted

indefensible adj 1 inexcusable, unpardonable, unforgivable, unjustifiable, unwarrantable Opposite: excusable 2 invalid, untenable, unsustainable, shaky, weak Opposite: valid 3 unprotected, exposed, vulnerable, undefended, unfortified Opposite: impregnable

indefinable adj indescribable, inexpressible, vague, indefinite, obscure

indefinite adj 1 unlimited, unfixed, unspecified, unknown, indeterminate Opposite: specified 2 unclear, imprecise, vague, hazy, woolly Opposite: precise 3 vague, uncertain, undecided, unclear, noncommittal Opposite: certain

indefinitely adv until further notice, for the foreseeable future, for life, forever, ad infinitum

indelible adj 1 permanent, fixed, ineradicable, fast, stubborn Opposite: temporary 2 unforgettable, deep-seated, deep-rooted, lasting, enduring Opposite: temporary

indelibly adv permanently, ineradicably, lastingly, forever, for good Opposite: temporarily

indelicacy n tactlessness, offensiveness, tastelessness, crudeness, unseemliness Opposite: politeness

indelicate adj tactless, offensive, improper, unseemly, impolite Opposite: polite

indemnify v 1 insure, underwrite, cover, assure, protect 2 reimburse, compensate, repay, pay, refund

indemnity n 1 insurance, protection, cover, life assurance, security 2 compensation, reimbursement, remuneration, reparation, payment

indent v 1 hollow out, dent, depress, stave in, scoop 2 notch, serrate, nick, pink, incise

indentation n 1 hollow, dent, depression, scoop, gouge 2 notch, groove, serration, nick, incision

indenture n contract, arrangement, pact, deal, agreement

independence n 1 self-government, sovereignty, autonomy, self-rule, self-determination Opposite: subjection 2 self-sufficiency, self-reliance, self-determination, freedom, autonomy Opposite: helplessness 3 individuality, freedom, liberation, unconventionality Opposite: conventionality 4 impartiality, objectivity, disinterest, neutrality, disinterestedness Opposite: partiality

independent adj 1 self-governing, sovereign,

autonomous, self-determining, self-regulating *Opposite*: dependent **2 self-sufficient**, self-reliant, autonomous, self-supporting, self-contained *Opposite*: dependent **3 free**, liberated, individual, individualistic, unconventional *Opposite*: conventional **4 impartial**, detached, objective, dispassionate, neutral *Opposite*: partial

in-depth *adj* painstaking, detailed, exhaustive, thorough, comprehensive *Opposite*: superficial

indescribable *adj* **1 indefinable**, inexpressible, unutterable, incommunicable, unspeakable **2 extreme**, great, tremendous, intense, dramatic

indestructible *adj* **1 abiding**, durable, everlasting, imperishable, eternal *Opposite*: perishable **2 unbreakable**, nonbreaking, resistant, shatterproof, rock-solid *Opposite*: fragile

indeterminable *adj* **1 unknowable**, indefinable, indescribable, impalpable *(fml)* *Opposite*: knowable **2 unresolvable**, unanswerable, uncountable *Opposite*: answerable

indeterminate *adj* **1 unknown**, unpredictable, undefined, unspecified, unstipulated *Opposite*: known **2 vague**, imprecise, uncertain, unclear, inexact *Opposite*: definite

index *n* **1 catalogue**, directory, guide, file, key **2 indication**, indicator, symbol, pointer, sign

indicate *v* **1 point to**, point at, point out, show, point towards **2 denote**, signify, be a sign of, imply, suggest **3 make known**, demonstrate, show, display, express **4 signal**, wink, flash

indication *n* **sign**, suggestion, signal, hint, warning

indicative *adj* revealing, symptomatic, telling, telltale, suggestive

indicator *n* pointer, needle, gauge, dial, display

indict *v* accuse, impeach, summons, prosecute, arraign *Opposite*: exonerate

indictable *adj* criminal, unlawful, illegal, chargeable, felonious

indictment *n* **1 accusation**, impeachment, summons, prosecution, arraignment *Opposite*: exoneration **2 condemnation**, denunciation, criticism, comment, censure *Opposite*: praise

indifference *n* **1 apathy**, coldness, coolness, unconcern, disinterest *Opposite*: concern **2 unimportance**, insignificance, inconsequence, meaninglessness, irrelevance *Opposite*: importance

indifferent *adj* **1 uncaring**, uninterested, unresponsive, apathetic, unsympathetic *Opposite*: concerned **2 average**, mediocre, moderate, undistinguished, middling *Opposite*: exceptional

indigence *(fml)* *n* **poverty**, need, penury, deprivation, destitution *Opposite*: wealth

indigenous *adj* native, original, aboriginal, homegrown, local *Opposite*: immigrant. *See* COMPARE AND CONTRAST *at* **native**.

indigent *(fml)* *adj* poor, needy, impoverished, poverty-stricken, penniless *Opposite*: wealthy

indigestible *adj* **1 heavy**, rich, tough, inedible, stodgy *(infml)* *Opposite*: edible **2 incomprehensible**, impenetrable, unreadable, complex, obscure *Opposite*: readable

indigestion *n* heartburn, stomachache, upset stomach, colic, gastritis

indignant *adj* angry, furious, vexed, irate, outraged *Opposite*: mollified

indignation *n* anger, resentment, outrage, annoyance, exasperation *Opposite*: delight. *See* COMPARE AND CONTRAST *at* **anger**.

indignity *n* humiliation, shame, disgrace, mortification, embarrassment *Opposite*: glory

indirect *adj* **1 circuitous**, roundabout, rambling, circumlocutory, tortuous *Opposite*: straight **2 unintended**, unplanned, secondary, ancillary, subsidiary *Opposite*: intended **3 devious**, oblique, implicit, tacit, implied *Opposite*: overt

indiscernible *adj* **imperceptible**, invisible, inaudible, unnoticeable, undetectable *Opposite*: perceptible

indiscipline *n* disorderliness, rowdiness, unruliness, insubordination, disruptiveness *Opposite*: control

indiscreet *adj* **1 careless**, injudicious, imprudent, incautious, unthinking *Opposite*: careful **2 tactless**, undiplomatic, unsubtle, garrulous, indelicate *Opposite*: tactful

indiscretion *n* **1 carelessness**, injudiciousness, imprudence, lack of caution, recklessness *Opposite*: carefulness **2 tactlessness**, garrulousness, indelicateness, nosiness *(infml)* **3 transgression**, impropriety, peccadillo, misdeed, lapse

indiscriminate *adj* **1 unselective**, undiscriminating, undiscerning, uncritical, broad *Opposite*: selective **2 haphazard**, random, arbitrary, wholesale, blanket *Opposite*: planned

indispensable *adj* **necessary**, essential, crucial, vital, required *Opposite*: unnecessary. *See* COMPARE AND CONTRAST *at* **necessary**.

indisposed *(fml)* *adj* **1 sick**, unwell, ill, laid up, under the weather *Opposite*: well **2 unwilling**, disinclined, reluctant, loath, loth *Opposite*: willing

indisposition *n* **1 illness**, complaint, condition, problem, debility *Opposite*: health **2 reluctance**, unwillingness, disinclination, refusal, resistance *Opposite*: willingness

indisputable *(fml)* *adj* **indubitable**, unquestionable, undeniable, incontrovertible, irrefutable *Opposite*: debatable

indissoluble *adj* binding, unbreakable, enduring, everlasting, eternal *Opposite*: temporary

indistinct *adj* **1 unclear**, hazy, dim, misty, blurred *Opposite*: clear **2 inaudible**, imperceptible, faint, soft, low *Opposite*: audible **3 vague**, imprecise, inexact, indefinite, indeterminate *Opposite*: definite

indistinctive *adj* **ordinary**, dull, everyday, unexceptional, unmemorable *Opposite*: unique

indistinctness *n* **1 blurriness**, haziness, fuzziness, mistiness, dimness *Opposite*: clarity **2 unclearness**, inarticulacy, faintness, softness *Opposite*: audibility

indistinguishable *adj* **1 undifferentiated**, homogeneous, identical, the same, interchangeable *Opposite*: separable **2 vague**, blurry, hazy, fuzzy, misty *Opposite*: clear **3 inaudible**, inarticulate, unintelligible, faint, soft *Opposite*: clear

individual *n* **person**, human being, entity, character, personality ■ *adj* **1 separable**, singular, separate, discrete, distinct **2 particularized**, special, private, exclusive, particular *Opposite*: collective **3 unusual**, distinctive, original, idiosyncratic, individualistic *Opposite*: ordinary

individualism *n* **uniqueness**, egoism, individuality, independence, selfishness *Opposite*: conformity

individualist *n* **free spirit**, nonconformist, eccentric, rebel, maverick *Opposite*: conformist

individuality *n* **independence**, uniqueness, eccentricity, personality, distinctiveness *Opposite*: conformity

individualize *v* **adapt**, modify, customize, personalize, convert

individually *adv* **separately**, independently, alone, on your own, by yourself *Opposite*: together

indivisible *adj* **inseparable**, united, amalgamated, blended, conjoined *(fml) Opposite*: separable

indoctrinate *v* **instruct**, programme, train, teach, coach

indoctrination *n* **instruction**, programming, propaganda, brainwashing, training

indolence *n* **laziness**, idleness, lethargy, sloth, inactivity *Opposite*: energy

indolent *adj* **lazy**, lethargic, idle, sluggish, slothful *Opposite*: energetic

indomitable *adj* **unconquerable**, strong, resolute, determined, stubborn *Opposite*: submissive

indoor *adj* **inside**, interior, covered, enclosed, internal *Opposite*: outdoor

indoors *adv* **inside**, in, within, at home, in the house *Opposite*: outside

indubitable *adj* **unquestionable**, definite, certain, positive, undoubted *Opposite*: questionable

induce *v* **1 persuade**, encourage, tempt, make, bring *Opposite*: dissuade **2 bring on**, bring about, provoke, stimulate, produce *Opposite*: deter

inducement *n* **stimulus**, incentive, encouragement, carrot, enticement *Opposite*: disincentive. *See* COMPARE AND CONTRAST *at* **motive**.

induct *v* **1 inaugurate**, swear in, initiate, welcome, receive **2 introduce**, initiate, train, instruct, educate

induction *n* **1 bringing on**, stimulation, generation, production, provocation **2 inauguration**, instalment, investiture, reception, swearing in **3 introduction**, initiation, training, instruction, orientation

indulge *v* **treat**, spoil, pamper, pander, cosset *Opposite*: deny

indulgence *n* **1 treat**, luxury, extravagance, pleasure *Opposite*: necessity **2 tolerance**, lenience, understanding, clemency, sympathy *Opposite*: strictness

indulgent *adj* **permissive**, kind, lenient, tolerant, generous *Opposite*: strict

industrial *adj* **1 manufacturing**, engineering, trade, business, work **2 developed**, built-up, industrialized, mechanized, manufacturing

industrial action *n* **strike**, stoppage, work-to-rule, go-slow, general strike

industrial espionage *n* **espionage**, spying, intelligence gathering, surveillance, bugging

industrial estate *n* **trading estate**, science park, enterprise zone, industrial zone, industrial development

industrialist *n* **manufacturer**, entrepreneur, magnate, mogul, captain of industry

industrialization *n* **industrial development**, economic development, development, economic growth, progress

industrialize *v* **change**, mechanize, develop, mass-produce, automate

industrialized *adj* **industrial**, developed, technologically advanced, manufacturing, commercial *Opposite*: agrarian

industrial tribunal *n* **hearing**, court, tribunal

industrious *adj* **diligent**, hard-working, busy, productive, conscientious *Opposite*: indolent

industriousness *n* **diligence**, hard work, application, conscientiousness, productiveness *Opposite*: indolence

industry *n* **1 manufacturing**, business, commerce, trade, engineering **2** *(fml or literary)* **hard work**, diligence, productiveness, conscientiousness, activity *Opposite*: indolence

inebriated *adj* **drunk**, intoxicated, plastered *(infml)*, smashed *(infml)*, under the influence *(infml) Opposite*: sober

inedible *adj* **uneatable**, indigestible, unpalatable, revolting, bad *Opposite*: edible

ineffable *(fml) adj* **indescribable**, inexpressible, unutterable, beyond words, overwhelming

ineffective *adj* **unsuccessful**, unproductive, useless, vain, futile *Opposite*: successful

ineffectiveness *n* **unsuccessfulness**, unproductiveness, uselessness, futility, hopelessness *Opposite*: success

ineffectual *adj* **incompetent**, indecisive, weak, feeble, useless *Opposite*: competent

ineffectuality *n* **incompetence**, indecisiveness, inadequacy, uselessness, feebleness *Opposite*: competence

inefficiency *n* **1 unproductiveness**, wastefulness, laxness *Opposite*: efficiency **2 disorganization**, incompetence, inadequacy, ineptitude, ineffectiveness *Opposite*: competence

inefficient *adj* **1 unproductive**, wasteful, uneconomical, lax, timewasting *Opposite*: efficient **2 incompetent**, inept, disorganized, ineffectual, inadequate *Opposite*: competent

inelastic *adj* **inflexible**, rigid, unbendable, stiff, unyielding *Opposite*: stretchy

inelegance *n* **1 unsophistication**, lack of style, tastelessness, bad taste, vulgarity *Opposite*: stylishness **2 clumsiness**, awkwardness, gracelessness, coarseness, roughness *Opposite*: grace

inelegant *adj* **1 unstylish**, unsophisticated, tasteless, vulgar, unpolished *Opposite*: stylish **2 clumsy**, awkward, ungainly, maladroit, graceless *Opposite*: graceful

ineligible *adj* **unqualified**, disqualified, barred, disallowed, banned *Opposite*: entitled

inept *adj* **incompetent**, inexpert, clumsy, useless, hopeless *Opposite*: competent

ineptitude *n* **incompetence**, clumsiness, uselessness, ineffectiveness, lack of ability *Opposite*: competence

ineptness *see* ineptitude

inequality *n* **disparity**, dissimilarity, variation, difference, discrimination *Opposite*: parity

inequitable *adj* **unfair**, unjust, unbalanced, undemocratic, unequal *Opposite*: fair

inequity *(fml)* *n* **unfairness**, injustice, discrimination, inequality, bias *Opposite*: fairness

ineradicable *adj* **indelible**, enduring, lasting, ingrained, stubborn *Opposite*: fleeting

inert *adj* **1 motionless**, still, lifeless, immobile, unmoving *Opposite*: moving **2 sluggish**, slow, inactive, passive, torpid *Opposite*: active

inertia *n* **apathy**, inactivity, torpor, lethargy, inaction *Opposite*: activity

inescapable *adj* **inevitable**, unavoidable, bound to happen, certain, patent *Opposite*: avoidable

inessential *adj* **unnecessary**, unneeded, superfluous, redundant, dispensable *Opposite*: necessary

inestimable *adj* **incalculable**, immeasurable, great, fathomless, enormous *Opposite*: measurable

inevitability *n* **unavoidability**, predictability, certainty, inescapability, irrevocability

inevitable *adj* **unavoidable**, predictable, expected, foreseeable, to be expected *Opposite*: avoidable

inevitably *adv* **unavoidably**, inescapably, without doubt, certainly, predictably

inexact *adj* **imprecise**, inaccurate, vague, rough, approximate *Opposite*: precise

inexactness *n* **imprecision**, vagueness, uncertainty, roughness, approximation *Opposite*: precision

in excess of *prep* **more than**, beyond, above, over and above, exceeding *Opposite*: below

inexcusable *adj* **unpardonable**, unforgivable, uncalled-for, intolerable, indefensible *Opposite*: excusable

inexhaustible *adj* **everlasting**, infinite, unlimited, never-ending, bottomless *Opposite*: limited

inexorability *(fml)* *n* **inevitability**, unavoidability, inescapability, relentlessness, certainty

inexorable *adj* **1** *(fml)* **unstoppable**, inevitable, unavoidable, inescapable, unchangeable **2 adamant**, obstinate, obdurate, unyielding, unbending

inexorableness *(fml)* *see* inexorability

inexpedient *adj* **1 inconvenient**, impractical, inopportune, untimely, ill-timed *Opposite*: convenient **2** *(fml)* **inadvisable**, inappropriate, unwise, unsuitable, injudicious *Opposite*: advisable

inexpensive *adj* **cheap**, low-cost, low-priced, economical, budget *Opposite*: costly

inexperience *n* **greenness**, rawness, innocence, immaturity, naivety *Opposite*: experience

inexperienced *adj* **green**, inexpert, raw, new, innocent *Opposite*: seasoned

inexpert *adj* **unskilled**, clumsy, inept, inexperienced, untrained *Opposite*: skilled

inexplicable *adj* **unaccountable**, mysterious, incomprehensible, unfathomable, bizarre *Opposite*: explicable

inexplicit *adj* **imprecise**, vague, ambiguous, hazy, sketchy *Opposite*: precise

inexpressible *adj* **indescribable**, beyond words, overwhelming, deep, indefinable

inexpressive *adj* **emotionless**, impassive, soulless, deadpan, unemotional *Opposite*: animated

inextricable *adj* **complicated**, complex, tricky, involved, knotty *Opposite*: simple

inextricably *adv* **indissolubly**, inseparably, indistinguishably, intimately, indivisibly

infallibility *n* **1 perfection**, rightness, flawlessness, correctness, exactitude *Opposite*: inaccuracy **2 dependability**, soundness, reliability, trustworthiness, steadiness *Opposite*: fallibility

infallible adj 1 **perfect**, right, correct, exact, accurate Opposite: imperfect 2 **dependable**, unfailing, foolproof, reliable, sound Opposite: unreliable

infallibly adv **dependably**, unfailingly, without fail, reliably, always Opposite: unreliably

infamous adj 1 **notorious**, disreputable, ill-famed, ill-reputed, dishonourable Opposite: reputable 2 **abominable**, villainous, wicked, iniquitous, loathsome Opposite: illustrious

infamy n 1 **notoriety**, ill repute, ill fame, shame, disrepute Opposite: esteem 2 **disgrace**, scandal, outrage, abomination, atrocity Opposite: good deed

infancy n 1 **babyhood**, childhood, early years, youth, immaturity Opposite: adulthood 2 **beginning**, early stages, embryonic stage, initial stages, first phase Opposite: conclusion

infant n **baby**, child, newborn, babe in arms, toddler Opposite: adult

infantile adj 1 **childish**, babyish, immature, puerile, juvenile Opposite: mature 2 **childhood**, juvenile, infant, baby, youthful Opposite: adult

infatuated adj **in love**, lovesick, obsessed, besotted, captivated Opposite: disenchanted

infatuation n **passion**, obsession, craze, love, fascination Opposite: disenchantment. See COMPARE AND CONTRAST at **love**.

in favour of prep **for**, all for, supporting, on the side of, supportive of Opposite: against

infect v 1 **contaminate**, pollute, taint, poison, blight Opposite: cleanse 2 **pervert**, corrupt, deprave, debase, defile (fml) Opposite: redeem 3 **influence**, affect, afflict, touch, inspire

infected adj 1 **contaminated**, polluted, tainted, poisoned, impure Opposite: pure 2 **ill**, diseased, sick, infested, disease-ridden Opposite: healthy 3 **septic**, festering, weeping, pussy, pus-filled Opposite: healthy 4 **affected**, influenced, touched, inspired, moved Opposite: untouched

infection n 1 **contagion**, contamination, pollution, taint, poison 2 **disease**, illness, virus, blight, bug (infml) 3 **corruption**, perversion, depravity, debasement, debauchery (fml)

infectious adj 1 **communicable**, catching, transferable, transmittable, transmissible 2 **irresistible**, compelling, captivating, alluring, contagious

infective adj **infectious**, communicable, catching, transferable, transmittable

infer v 1 **conclude**, deduce, suppose, gather, understand 2 **imply**, suggest, insinuate, hint

inference n 1 **conclusion**, deduction, supposition, conjecture, presumption 2 **implication**, extrapolation, corollary, interpretation, reading

inferior adj 1 **lower**, junior, secondary, subordinate, subsidiary Opposite: superior 2 **mediocre**, lesser, lower, substandard, poorer Opposite: superior ■ n **junior**, subordinate, underling, vassal, menial (fml) Opposite: superior

inferiority n 1 **lowliness**, humbleness, subordination, subservience, subsidiarity Opposite: superiority 2 **mediocrity**, weakness, inadequacy, shoddiness, meanness Opposite: superiority

inferiority complex n **inadequacy**, anxiety, phobia, depression, obsession

inferno n 1 **conflagration**, blaze, fire, firestorm, flames 2 **hellhole**, hell, underworld, perdition, fire and brimstone Opposite: heaven

infertile adj **sterile**, unproductive, barren, unfruitful, childless Opposite: fertile

infertility n **sterility**, barrenness, childlessness, aridity, unproductiveness Opposite: fertility

infest v **overrun**, fill, invade, infiltrate, pervade

infestation n **plague**, invasion, swarm, influx, infiltration

infidelity n **unfaithfulness**, faithlessness, disloyalty, betrayal, adultery Opposite: faithfulness

infighting n **rivalry**, internal strife, competitiveness, backbiting, squabbling

infiltrate v **penetrate**, permeate, gain access to, break into, creep into

infiltration n **penetration**, permeation, access, intrusion, insinuation

infiltrator n **mole**, spy, secret agent, double agent, subversive

infinite adj 1 **immeasurable**, never-ending, endless, countless, unbounded Opposite: limited 2 **extreme**, stupendous, great, immense, large Opposite: slight

infinitely adv **markedly**, a great deal, substantially, enormously, by a long way Opposite: slightly

infinitesimal adj **tiny**, minute, minuscule, microscopic, insignificant Opposite: huge

infinity n **eternity**, immensity, endlessness, infinitude, boundlessness

infirm adj **unwell**, sick, ill, frail, in poor health Opposite: healthy. See COMPARE AND CONTRAST at **weak**.

infirmary n **hospital**, sanatorium, sickbay, hospice, medical centre

infirmity n **ill health**, illness, frailty, disability, weakness Opposite: health

inflame v 1 **arouse**, anger, fan, provoke, stir up Opposite: calm 2 **exacerbate**, aggravate, fuel, intensify, increase Opposite: diminish

inflamed adj **reddened**, swollen, irritated, tender, sore

inflammable adj **flammable**, combustible, ignitable, incendiary Opposite: nonflammable

inflammation n **irritation**, swelling, soreness, tenderness, redness

inflammatory adj **provocative**, seditious, rabble-rousing, fiery, stirring Opposite: placatory

inflatable adj **blow-up**, pump-up, expandable

inflate v 1 **blow up**, pump up, fill with air, expand, fill Opposite: deflate 2 **exaggerate**, amplify, embellish, magnify, overestimate Opposite: understate 3 **increase**, go up, drive up, escalate, boost Opposite: deflate

inflated adj **exaggerated**, overstated, overblown, puffed up, magnified Opposite: understated

inflation n **price rises**, rise, increase, price increases Opposite: deflation

inflationary adj **price-raising**, price-increasing, spiralling

inflect v **change**, modulate, vary, adjust, modify

inflection n **modulation**, nuance, variation, variety, accent

inflexibility n 1 **stubbornness**, obstinacy, intransigence, rigour, dogmatism Opposite: tractability 2 **rigidity**, stiffness, hardness, firmness, tautness Opposite: flexibility

inflexible adj 1 **unbending**, stubborn, obstinate, uncompromising, strict Opposite: tractable 2 **rigid**, stiff, hard, unbendable, firm Opposite: bendable

inflict v **impose**, exact, mete out, wreak, perpetrate Opposite: remove

in-flight adj **onboard**, mid-flight, airborne, midair

inflow n **influx**, arrival, invasion, incursion, introduction Opposite: outflow

influence n 1 **effect**, inspiration, impact, stimulus, encouragement 2 **power**, sway, authority, weight, control ■ v 1 **sway**, manipulate, persuade, induce, win over 2 **affect**, motivate, inspire, shape, have an effect on

influential adj **powerful**, important, significant, persuasive, dominant Opposite: ineffectual

influenza n **flu**, cold, virus, infection, respiratory tract infection

influx n **arrival**, invasion, incursion, flood, entry Opposite: outflow

info (infml) n 1 **information**, data, statistics, facts, figures 2 **news**, report, tidings, word, communication

infomercial n **commercial**, advertisement, promotional film, ad (infml), promo (infml)

inform v 1 **tell**, notify, let know, update, bring up-to-date Opposite: keep in the dark 2 **blow the whistle on**, betray, sneak on, denounce, tell on Opposite: keep mum (infml)

informal adj 1 **relaxed**, casual, familiar, easy, comfortable Opposite: ceremonious 2 **unofficial**, off-the-record, unauthorized, unsanctioned, confidential Opposite: official 3 **colloquial**, idiomatic, vernacular, everyday, familiar Opposite: formal

informality n **casualness**, familiarity, ease, unpretentiousness, lack of formality Opposite: formality

informally adv 1 **casually**, nonchalantly, easily, unceremoniously, offhandedly Opposite: ceremoniously 2 **unofficially**, off the record, confidentially Opposite: officially

informant n 1 **source**, guide, interpreter, adviser, tipster 2 **informer**, sneak, spy, mole, grass (slang)

information n 1 **data**, statistics, facts, figures, material 2 **news**, report, tidings, word, communication

information processing n **data processing**, data handling, data manipulation, data analysis, data transmission

information retrieval n **data storage and retrieval**, data storage, data retrieval, data processing, computer processing

information sheet n **newsletter**, brochure, leaflet, bulletin, communiqué

information superhighway n **Internet**, World Wide Web, infobahn, the Net (infml), the Web (infml)

information technology n **IT**, computing, telecommunications, computer technology, electronic technology

informative adj **educational**, revealing, edifying, enlightening, useful Opposite: uncommunicative

informed adj **knowledgeable**, well-versed, conversant, up-to-date, educated Opposite: ignorant

informer n **informant**, sneak, spy, mole, grass (slang)

infraction n **breach**, violation, infringement, contravention, transgression

infrastructure n 1 **substructure**, organization, structure, setup, arrangement 2 **public services**, communications, public transport, power supplies, water supplies

infrequency n **rarity**, irregularity, uncommonness, paucity, scarcity Opposite: frequency

infrequent adj **rare**, uncommon, occasional, intermittent, sporadic Opposite: frequent

infringe v 1 **disobey**, disregard, breach, break, violate Opposite: obey 2 **encroach on**, intrude on, interfere with, trespass, invade Opposite: respect

infringement n 1 **breach**, violation, contravention, transgression, flouting Opposite: compliance 2 **encroachment**, intrusion, invasion, interference, trespass

in front of prep 1 **before**, ahead of, facing, opposite Opposite: behind 2 **in the presence of**, with, in the company of, before, watched by

infuriate v **enrage**, madden, incense, make your blood boil, annoy Opposite: calm

infuriated adj **enraged**, exasperated, furious, angry, incensed Opposite: calm

infuriating *adj* **maddening**, annoying, irritating, exasperating, galling *Opposite*: calming

infuse *v* **1 pervade**, fill, permeate, suffuse, imbue **2 instil**, impart, introduce, inculcate, imbue **3 steep**, soak, brew, immerse, saturate *Opposite*: drain

infusion *n* **brew**, tea, distillation, fermentation, drink

ingenious *adj* **1 inventive**, clever, imaginative, resourceful, original *Opposite*: unimaginative **2 effective**, cunning, inspired, clever, nifty (*infml*)

ingenuity *n* **inventiveness**, cleverness, resourcefulness, imagination, originality

ingenuous *adj* **1 innocent**, unworldly, artless, unsophisticated, naive *Opposite*: artful **2 honest**, direct, frank, open, straightforward *Opposite*: dishonest

ingenuousness *n* **1 innocence**, unpretentiousness, unworldliness, gullibility, simplicity *Opposite*: artfulness **2 openness**, straightforwardness, directness, honesty, frankness *Opposite*: dishonesty

ingest *v* **absorb**, swallow, take in, consume, eat *Opposite*: vomit

inglenook *n* **hearthside**, fireside, nook, corner, recess

inglorious *adj* **shameful**, dishonourable, disgraceful, humiliating, unsuccessful *Opposite*: glorious

ingoing *adj* **incoming**, new, inward *Opposite*: outgoing

ingot *n* **slab**, nugget, lump, brick, block

ingrain *v* **impress**, etch, drill in, fix, root

ingrained *adj* **deep-seated**, in-built, entrenched, fixed, deep-rooted *Opposite*: superficial

ingratiate *v* **insinuate yourself**, toady, get in with, grovel, curry favour *Opposite*: alienate

ingratiating *adj* **sycophantic**, insinuative, obsequious, smarmy, deferential *Opposite*: proud

ingratitude *n* **rudeness**, unmannerliness, lack of appreciation, ungratefulness, thanklessness *Opposite*: gratitude

ingredient *n* **element**, component, part, constituent, factor

ingress (*fml*) *n* **entry**, entrance, opening, door, admission

in-group *n* **clique**, gang, faction, circle, elite

ingrowing *adj* **ingrown**, impacted, malformed, deformed

inhabit *v* **live**, reside, populate, occupy, squat

inhabitable *adj* **habitable**, civilized, usable, hospitable, livable *Opposite*: uninhabitable

inhabitant *n* **occupant**, resident, citizen, native, denizen

inhabited *adj* **populated**, populous, tenanted *Opposite*: uninhabited

inhalation *n* **breath**, gulp, gasp, pant, mouthful

inhale *v* **breathe in**, gasp, gulp, huff, pant *Opposite*: exhale

inhaler *n* **bronchodilator**, nebulizer, spray

in hand *adj* **1 under control**, receiving attention, under consideration, under deliberation, being dealt with *Opposite*: pending **2 unused**, remaining, spare, superfluous, available

inharmonious *adj* **1 discordant**, clashing, harsh, jarring, unmusical *Opposite*: harmonious **2 argumentative**, clashing, incompatible, disagreeable, antagonistic *Opposite*: cordial

inherent *adj* **characteristic**, essential, innate, natural, intrinsic *Opposite*: acquired

inherit *v* **receive**, accede to, come into, succeed to, take over *Opposite*: bequeath

inheritance *n* **heirloom**, tradition, legacy, bequest, birthright

inhibit *v* **1 slow**, stop, hold back, restrain, hinder **2 constrain**, hinder, prevent, impede, obstruct

inhibited *adj* **self-conscious**, reserved, introverted, repressed, subdued *Opposite*: uninhibited

inhibition *n* **reserve**, shyness, embarrassment, self-consciousness, reticence *Opposite*: spontaneity

inhospitable *adj* **1 unwelcoming**, unfriendly, unreceptive, uncongenial, uninviting *Opposite*: hospitable **2 harsh**, forbidding, bleak, desolate, barren *Opposite*: inviting

inhuman *adj* **1 cruel**, vicious, cold-blooded, inhumane, brutal *Opposite*: kind **2 cold-hearted**, unfeeling, insensitive, merciless, callous *Opposite*: sensitive **3 otherworldly**, weird, strange, unearthly, eerie *Opposite*: earthly

inhumane *adj* **cold-hearted**, cold-blooded, cruel, callous, brutal *Opposite*: humane

inhumanity *n* **cruelty**, cold-heartedness, mercilessness, viciousness, ruthlessness *Opposite*: humanity

inimical *adj* **1 unfavourable**, contrary, opposed, adverse, detrimental *Opposite*: favourable **2 hostile**, unfriendly, unwelcoming, cold, ill-disposed *Opposite*: friendly

inimitable *adj* **unique**, matchless, unmatched, incomparable, peerless *Opposite*: common

iniquitous *adj* **wicked**, heinous, sinful, bad, evil *Opposite*: good

iniquity *n* **wickedness**, evil, sin, vice, immorality *Opposite*: goodness

initial *adj* **first**, early, original, preliminary, opening *Opposite*: final

initialize *v* **reset**, prime, prepare, set, make ready *Opposite*: disable

initiate *v* **1 start**, introduce, originate, begin, open *Opposite*: finish **2 instruct**, induct, admit, introduce, teach *Opposite*: expel

initiation n 1 **beginning**, start, opening, instigation, launch Opposite: end 2 **introduction**, admission, induction, admittance, instruction Opposite: expulsion

initiative n 1 **inventiveness**, creativity, wits, enterprise, resourcefulness 2 **plan**, proposal, scheme, idea, programme 3 **pole position**, upper hand, advantage, edge, lead

initiator n **motivator**, inventor, originator, author, creator

inject v 1 **vaccinate**, inoculate, give a jab (infml), give a shot (infml) 2 **bring**, add, introduce, insert, instil Opposite: remove

injection n 1 **inoculation**, dose, vaccination, booster, jab (infml) 2 **addition**, instillation, instilment, insertion, introduction Opposite: removal

in-joke n **private joke**, running joke, witticism

injudicious adj **ill-advised**, unwise, foolish, imprudent, careless Opposite: judicious

injudiciousness n **indiscretion**, imprudence, foolishness, rashness, impulsiveness Opposite: prudence

injunction n **ban**, sanction, embargo, restriction, order

injure v **damage**, harm, hurt, wound, cut Opposite: heal. See COMPARE AND CONTRAST at **harm**.

injured adj **hurt**, incapacitated, wounded, battered, bruised Opposite: unscathed

injurious adj **harmful**, distressing, damaging, adverse, detrimental Opposite: beneficial

injury n **wound**, damage, grievance, wrong, hurt

injury time n **extra time**, extension, overtime (US)

injustice n **discrimination**, unfairness, inequality, bias, prejudice Opposite: justice

in keeping with prep **consistent with**, suitable for, in accordance with, in line with, according to

inkling n **suspicion**, hint, clue, hunch, feeling Opposite: certainty

inkwell n **jar**, inkstand, pot, container, well

inlaid adj **decorated**, veneered, enamelled, ornamented, mosaic

inland adj **interior**, internal, upcountry, inward, central Opposite: coastal ■ adv **within**, inwards, inshore, upcountry, inside

inlay n 1 **enamel**, tile, piece, ornament, inset 2 **pattern**, decoration, ornament, mosaic, enamelling

inlet n **bay**, cove, creek, fjord, tidal creek

in line with prep **in agreement with**, according to, in keeping with, corresponding to, consistent with

inmate n **prisoner**, internee, patient, convict, jailbird (slang)

in memoriam prep **in memory of**, in remembrance of, as a memorial to, in commemoration of, for

inmost see **innermost**

innards (infml) n **entrails**, guts, intestines, bowels, viscera

innate adj **essential**, inborn, native, distinctive, natural

inner adj 1 **innermost**, inward, internal, inside, central Opposite: outer 2 **private**, secret, intimate, deep, hidden Opposite: public

inner city n **city centre**, centre, town centre, downtown (US)

inner-city adj **city**, metropolitan, town, central, inner Opposite: suburban

innermost adj **deepest**, private, secret, intimate, inmost Opposite: outermost

innings n **runs**, turn, batting, score, round

innocence n 1 **blamelessness**, goodness, guiltlessness, incorruptibility, virtue Opposite: guilt 2 **naivety**, inexperience, unworldliness, unsophistication, gullibility Opposite: experience

innocent adj 1 **blameless**, acquitted, guiltless, cleared, not guilty Opposite: guilty 2 **harmless**, unknowing, unintended, unintentional, inoffensive Opposite: malicious 3 **virtuous**, untouched, unsullied, chaste, immaculate Opposite: tainted 4 **unsophisticated**, unworldly, artless, harmless, naive Opposite: worldly

innocuous adj **inoffensive**, harmless, innocent, safe, mild Opposite: offensive

innovate v **invent**, modernize, originate, revolutionize, transform Opposite: stagnate

innovation n **novelty**, invention, revolution, modernization, origination Opposite: stagnation

innovative adj **groundbreaking**, advanced, state-of-the-art, pioneering, inventive Opposite: outdated

innuendo n **insinuation**, ambiguity, double entendre, inference, intimation

innumerable adj **countless**, uncountable, numerous, incalculable, immeasurable

inoculate v **immunize**, vaccinate, inject, protect, give a shot (infml) Opposite: infect

inoculation n **vaccination**, injection, booster, immunization, jab (infml)

inoffensive adj **innocuous**, harmless, bland, dull, safe Opposite: offensive

inoperable adj 1 **incurable**, untreatable, terminal, grave, fatal Opposite: operable 2 **impracticable**, unworkable, unfeasible, impossible, unachievable Opposite: doable

inoperative adj **out of action**, out of use, broken, broken down Opposite: operative

inopportune adj **ill-timed**, unfortunate, inconvenient, mistimed, untimely Opposite: opportune

in order to conj **so as to**, to, with the intention of, with the purpose of, with the aim of

inordinate adj **excessive**, undue, unwarranted, immoderate, unreasonable *Opposite*: moderate

inorganic *adj* **mineral**, inanimate, inert, lifeless *Opposite*: organic

in particular *adv* **specifically**, especially, specially, particularly, above all *Opposite*: generally

input *n* **contribution**, effort, say, participation, involvement ■ *v* **enter**, key, key in, record, store

inquest *n* **investigation**, inquiry, examination, postmortem, autopsy

inquire *v* **ask**, query, request, question, find out

inquire into *v* **investigate**, go into, delve into, look into, probe into

inquiring *adj* **1 inquisitive**, interested, curious, questioning, analytical *Opposite*: incurious **2 searching**, questioning, penetrating, probing, prying

inquiry *n* **1 review**, postmortem, autopsy, investigation, examination **2 request**, question, query, interrogation, quiz

inquisition *n* **inquiry**, inquest, investigation, examination, interrogation

inquisitive *adj* **1 curious**, inquiring, interested, questioning, probing *Opposite*: indifferent **2 prying**, intrusive, prurient, meddlesome, officious *Opposite*: incurious

inquisitiveness *n* **1 curiosity**, interest, keenness, desire for knowledge, thirst for knowledge *Opposite*: indifference **2 prurience**, meddlesomeness, prying, questioning, officiousness *Opposite*: indifference

inquisitor *n* **cross-examiner**, examiner, investigator, interrogator, questioner

inquisitorial *adj* **interrogational**, cross-examining, investigative, interviewing, questioning

inquorate *adj* **insufficient**, inadequate, not enough, too few, under strength

insalubrious *(fml) adj* **unhealthy**, unsavoury, unwholesome, harmful, unhygienic *Opposite*: healthy

ins and outs *n* **details**, fine points, particulars, facts, minutiae

insane *adj* **1 of unsound mind**, mentally disordered, mentally ill, deranged *Opposite*: sane **2 foolish**, silly, stupid, irrational, impractical *Opposite*: sensible

insanitary *adj* **unhygienic**, dirty, unclean, contaminated, unhealthy *Opposite*: hygienic

insanity *n* **foolishness**, stupidity, irrationality, folly, senselessness *Opposite*: common sense

insatiability *n* **voraciousness**, greed, greediness, gluttony, ravenousness

insatiable *adj* **voracious**, greedy, avid, ravenous, unquenchable

inscribe *v* **1 engrave**, carve, etch, cut, scratch *Opposite*: erase **2 list**, enter, record, register, enrol *Opposite*: delete **3 dedicate**, autograph, address, sign, assign

inscription *n* **1 writing**, caption, label, engraving, legend **2 dedication**, autograph, signature, personal note, initials

inscrutability *n* **mystique**, mystery, mysteriousness, enigma, incomprehensibility *Opposite*: clarity

inscrutable *adj* **enigmatic**, sphinx-like, unfathomable, mysterious, impenetrable *Opposite*: transparent

insect *n* **bug**, fly, pest, creature, creepy-crawly *(infml)*

WORD BANK
❏ **parts of an insect** abdomen, antenna, feeler, proboscis, thorax, wing
❏ **types of stage of insect development** caterpillar, chrysalis, glowworm, grub, imago, larva, maggot, nit, pupa, silkworm, woodworm

insecure *adj* **1 unconfident**, anxious, self-doubting, uncertain, timid *Opposite*: confident **2 vulnerable**, unprotected, unguarded, undefended, at risk *Opposite*: secure **3 shaky**, rickety, unstable, unsteady, loose *Opposite*: steady

insecurity *n* **lack of confidence**, anxiety, uncertainty, timidity, self-doubt *Opposite*: confidence

insensate *adj* **unconscious**, comatose, inert, anaesthetized, numbed *Opposite*: animate

insensible *adj* **1 unconscious**, comatose, inert, insentient, numb *Opposite*: conscious **2 unaware**, unresponsive, insensitive, oblivious, numb *Opposite*: sensitive **3 imperceptible**, indiscernible, unnoticeable, indistinguishable, inappreciable *Opposite*: obvious

insensitive *adj* **1 tactless**, thoughtless, inconsiderate, uncaring, unsympathetic *Opposite*: sensitive **2 numb**, unfeeling, insensate, insensible, dead *Opposite*: sensitive **3 unresponsive**, oblivious, unmoved, inured to, indifferent *Opposite*: responsive

insensitivity *n* **selfishness**, thoughtlessness, inconsiderateness, tactlessness, inattentiveness *Opposite*: sensitivity

insentient *adj* **lifeless**, inert, inanimate, insensate, unconscious *Opposite*: sentient

inseparable *adj* **1 close**, devoted, intimate, joined at the hip, in each other's pocket *Opposite*: distant **2 indivisible**, indissoluble, inextricable, united, conjoined *(fml) Opposite*: independent

insert *v* **1 introduce**, implant, inject, put in, place in *Opposite*: take out **2 add**, include, enclose, append, incorporate *Opposite*: extract ■ *n* **supplement**, pullout, addition, enclosure, inset

insertion *n* **1 addition**, inclusion, incorporation, enclosure, attachment *Opposite*: extraction **2 supplement**, pullout, addition, inset, insert

in-service *adj* **work-related**, occupational, professional, vocational, job-related

inset v insert, put in, add, include, incorporate *Opposite*: extract ■ *n* **supplement**, insert, pullout, insertion, inclusion

inshore adv **landwards**, coastwards, ashore, shorewards

inside adv **indoors**, in, within, in the interior, at home *Opposite*: outside ■ *adj* **1** confidential, privileged, secret, private, exclusive **2** inner, innermost, inmost, inward *Opposite*: outer **3** indoor, interior, internal *Opposite*: outside **4** *(infml)* locked up, imprisoned, put away *(infml)*, banged up *(infml)*, doing time *(slang)* ■ *n* interior, inner recesses, inner parts, contents *Opposite*: outside ■ *prep* in, within, surrounded by, contained by *Opposite*: outside

insides *(infml) n* internal organs, guts, entrails, bowels, viscera

insidious adj sinister, treacherous, crafty, sneaky, deceptive *Opposite*: harmless

insight *n* vision, understanding, awareness, intuition, perception

insightful adj perceptive, astute, shrewd, understanding, discerning *Opposite*: unperceptive

insightfulness *n* perspicacity, perceptiveness, astuteness, discernment, sensitivity

insignia *n* emblem, crest, badge, sign, symbol

insignificance *n* unimportance, irrelevance, inconsequentiality, triviality, paltriness *Opposite*: significance

insignificant adj unimportant, irrelevant, immaterial, inconsequential, trivial *Opposite*: significant

insincere adj dishonest, two-faced, hypocritical, disingenuous, deceitful *Opposite*: sincere

insincerity *n* dishonesty, disingenuousness, hypocrisy, deceit, mendacity *Opposite*: sincerity

insinuate *v* **1** imply, suggest, hint, intimate, indicate *Opposite*: declare **2** ingratiate yourself, worm your way in, wheedle, cosy up, curry favour *Opposite*: insult

insinuation *n* suggestion, implication, hint, intimation, allusion *Opposite*: statement

insipid adj **1** dull, bland, characterless, trite, tame *Opposite*: exciting **2** bland, tasteless, unappetizing, flavourless, watery *Opposite*: tasty

insipidness *n* **1** dullness, blandness, feebleness, characterlessness, colourlessness **2** tastelessness, lack of flavour, blandness, wateriness, weakness *Opposite*: tastiness

insist *v* **1** maintain, claim, assert, contend, swear *Opposite*: deny **2** require, demand, press for, stipulate, enforce

insistence *n* persistence, resolve, firmness, perseverance, doggedness

insistent adj **1** adamant, firm, persistent, unrelenting, resolute *Opposite*: half-hearted

2 incessant, repeated, persistent, relentless, unrelenting *Opposite*: occasional

insofar as conj inasmuch as, insomuch as, to the extent that, to the degree that, because

insolence *n* impudence, impertinence, rudeness, audacity, disrespect *Opposite*: respect

insolent adj impudent, rude, disrespectful, brazen, impertinent *(fml) Opposite*: respectful

insolubility *n* mysteriousness, indecipherability, intricacy, difficulty, impenetrability *Opposite*: solubility

insoluble adj inexplicable, mysterious, insolvable, unfathomable, indecipherable *Opposite*: solvable

insolvency *n* bankruptcy, liquidation, indebtedness, ruin, collapse *Opposite*: solvency

insolvent adj bankrupt, ruined, in debt, in receivership, broke *(infml) Opposite*: solvent

insomnia *n* sleeplessness, wakefulness, restlessness

insomuch as conj insofar as, inasmuch as, to the extent that, to the degree that, because

insouciance *n* carefreeness, nonchalance, indifference, happiness, unconcern *Opposite*: worry

inspect *v* look at, review, examine, scrutinize, look over *Opposite*: ignore

inspection *n* review, examination, scrutiny, assessment, check

inspector *n* examiner, superintendent, overseer, assessor, supervisor

inspiration *n* **1** stimulus, spur, motivation, stimulation, encouragement *Opposite*: disincentive **2** creativeness, inventiveness, brilliance, vision, creativity **3** insight, flash, idea, revelation, brain wave *(infml)*

inspirational adj stimulating, inspiring, stirring, rousing, moving *Opposite*: boring

inspire *v* stimulate, motivate, stir, move, encourage *Opposite*: bore

inspired adj **1** brilliant, outstanding, superb, exceptional, dazzling *Opposite*: uninspired **2** stimulated, stirred, moved, encouraged, motivated *Opposite*: uninspired

inspiring adj inspirational, stirring, rousing, moving, exciting *Opposite*: uninspiring

in spite of prep despite, regardless of, in the face of, notwithstanding *(fml)*

instability *n* unpredictability, variability, uncertainty, unsteadiness, volatility *Opposite*: stability

install *v* **1** connect, fit, put in, set up, fix *Opposite*: remove **2** ordain, establish, inaugurate, instate, induct *Opposite*: oust **3** settle in, settle, settle down, ensconce, position

installation *n* **1** connection, fitting, setting up, fixing, putting in *Opposite*: removal **2** system, mechanism, machinery, equipment, apparatus **3** appointment, ordination, inauguration, investiture, instatement *Opposite*: removal

instalment n 1 **payment**, segment, portion, part, section 2 **part**, episode, chapter

instance n **example**, case, case in point, occurrence, illustration

instant adj 1 **prompt**, immediate, sudden, swift, instantaneous Opposite: gradual 2 **prepared**, precooked, premixed, powdered, microwavable 3 **urgent**, pressing, immediate ■ n **moment**, second, split second, the twinkling of an eye, minute

instantaneous adj **prompt**, rapid, sudden, immediate, instant Opposite: gradual

instantly adv **promptly**, right away, instantaneously, immediately, directly Opposite: gradually

instate v **appoint**, ordain, inaugurate, establish, install Opposite: oust

instead adv **in its place**, as an alternative, as a substitute, as a replacement

instead of prep **in place of**, rather than, as opposed to, in preference to

instigate v **bring about**, prompt, initiate, start, activate Opposite: stifle

instigation n 1 **start**, beginning, initiation, establishment, commencement (fml) Opposite: end 2 **initiation**, prompting, urging, encouragement, provocation Opposite: discouragement

instigator n **initiator**, prime mover, mastermind, troublemaker, ringleader

instil v 1 **impart**, inculcate, drum into, drive into, impress upon 2 **drip**, pour, infuse, inject, introduce

instinct n 1 **nature**, character, makeup, predisposition, disposition 2 **drive**, reflex, feeling, impulse, urge Opposite: reason 3 **feeling**, intuition, gut feeling, sixth sense, sense 4 **talent**, knack, gift, flair, ability

instinctive adj 1 **involuntary**, automatic, reflex, natural, unconscious Opposite: conscious 2 **natural**, intuitive, innate, inherent, inborn Opposite: learned

instinctively adv **impulsively**, mechanically, on impulse, automatically, unconsciously

institute v **introduce**, establish, set up, bring about, found ■ n **organization**, institution, establishment, foundation, association

institution n 1 **establishment**, organization, body, association, society 2 **tradition**, custom, convention, ritual 3 **introduction**, establishment, setting up, foundation, creation

institutional adj 1 **official**, recognized, formal, established, organized Opposite: unofficial 2 **utilitarian**, uniform, dull, functional, ordinary Opposite: unique

institutionalized adj **established**, existing, long-standing, traditional, entrenched Opposite: innovative

instruct v 1 **teach**, train, coach, tutor, educate 2 **command**, order, tell, give orders to, charge. See COMPARE AND CONTRAST at **teach**.

instruction n 1 **teaching**, training, lessons, tuition, education 2 **order**, command, direction, directive

instructive adj **informative**, educational, useful, helpful, enlightening

instructor n **teacher**, coach, tutor, trainer, mentor

instrument n 1 **tool**, gadget, device, utensil, apparatus 2 **means**, channel, vehicle, method, medium

instrumental adj **contributory**, active, involved, helpful, influential Opposite: tangential

instrumentalist n **musician**, player, performer

instrumentation n 1 **arrangement**, composition, musical arrangement, music, score 2 **instrument panel**, equipment, instruments, controls, console

insubordinate adj **disobedient**, defiant, rebellious, mutinous, unruly Opposite: obedient

insubordination n **disobedience**, defiance, rebelliousness, mutiny, unruliness Opposite: obedience

insubstantial adj **flimsy**, light, slight, weak, frail Opposite: weighty

insubstantiality n **weakness**, fragility, thinness, flimsiness, lightness Opposite: robustness

insufferable adj **excruciating**, unbearable, intolerable, insupportable, unendurable

insufficiency n 1 **lack**, deficiency, dearth, absence, shortage 2 **inadequacy**, deficiency, unfitness, failure, inefficiency Opposite: adequacy

insufficient adj **inadequate**, deficient, lacking, in short supply, scarce Opposite: surplus

insular adj **inward-looking**, blinkered, narrow-minded, narrow, limited Opposite: open-minded

insularity n **narrow-mindedness**, narrowness, parochialism, intolerance, small-mindedness Opposite: openness

insulate v 1 **lag**, wad, line, fill, pad 2 **cloister**, protect, shield, cut off, isolate Opposite: expose

insulation n 1 **lining**, lagging, wadding, padding, filling 2 **protection**, isolation, separation, segregation, sequestration Opposite: exposure

insulator n **insulation**, padding, sound-proofing, lagging

insult v **offend**, affront, abuse, slur, slight Opposite: praise ■ n **affront**, offence, slight, slur, rudeness Opposite: compliment

insulting adj **abusive**, offensive, rude, insolent, wounding Opposite: polite

insuperable adj **insurmountable**, impossible, unbeatable, challenging, overwhelming Opposite: easy

insupportable adj **unbearable**, intolerable, unendurable, insufferable, unspeakable Opposite: bearable

insurance n **cover**, indemnity, assurance, protection, coverage

insurance policy n **1 document**, contract, cover, agreement, guarantee **2 safety net**, safeguard, precaution, protection, provision

insure v **protect**, cover, assure, indemnify, underwrite

insurer n **underwriter**, broker, guarantor

insurgence see **insurgency**

insurgency n **uprising**, rebellion, revolt, insurrection, revolution

insurgent n **rebel**, insurrectionary, revolutionary, guerrilla, mutineer ■ adj **mutinous**, rebellious, rebel, insurrectionary

insurmountable adj **unbeatable**, insuperable, unassailable, invincible, impossible Opposite: easy

insurrection n **uprising**, rebellion, revolt, insurgency, revolution

intact adj **complete**, whole, unbroken, in one piece, integral Opposite: broken

intake n **1 consumption**, eating, drinking, ingestion **2 entry**, entrants, students **3 opening**, pipe, tube, aperture, inlet Opposite: outlet

intangibility n **1 imperceptibility**, immateriality, immaterialness, untouchability, insubstantiality Opposite: tangibility **2 indescribability**, elusiveness, vagueness, subtlety, abstractness

intangible adj **1 imperceptible**, immaterial, insubstantial, incorporeal (fml), impalpable (fml) Opposite: concrete **2 unquantifiable**, elusive, vague, ethereal, subtle

integer n **whole number**, number, numeral, digit, figure Opposite: fraction

integral adj **1 essential**, vital, important, basic, fundamental **2 connected**, internal, central, at the heart of Opposite: unimportant **3 complete**, whole, intact, undivided, unbroken

integrate v **1 mix**, fit in, join in, assimilate, take part **2 put together**, mix, incorporate, add, join together Opposite: separate **3 open up**, desegregate, combine, mix, assimilate

integrated adj **1 combined**, united, joined, unified, cohesive Opposite: separated **2 open**, desegregated, multiethnic, multicultural, multilingual Opposite: segregated

integration n **addition**, mixing, incorporation, combination, amalgamation

integrity n **honesty**, truth, truthfulness, honour, veracity Opposite: dishonesty

intellect n **intelligence**, brainpower, brain, brains, mind Opposite: emotion

intellectual adj **knowledgeable**, intelligent, highbrow, academic, cerebral ■ n **philosopher**, thinker, academic, scholar, highbrow

intelligence n **1 brain**, cleverness, aptitude, intellect, brains Opposite: stupidity **2 information**, news, reports, communication, word

intelligence quotient n **IQ**, mental ability, aptitude

intelligent adj **1 clever**, bright, smart, quick, able Opposite: stupid **2 sensible**, rational, wise, logical, perceptive Opposite: irrational

COMPARE AND CONTRAST CORE MEANING: having the ability to learn and understand easily
intelligent quick to learn and understand; **bright** showing an ability to think, learn, or respond quickly, especially used of younger people; **quick** alert, perceptive, and able to respond quickly; **smart** showing intelligence and mental alertness but sometimes suggesting insolent intelligence; **clever** having sharp mental abilities, sometimes suggesting showy or superficial cleverness; **able** capable or talented, also used in educational circles of children who are intelligent; **gifted** talented, especially artistically or creatively, also used in educational circles of children who are exceptionally intelligent.

intelligentsia n **intellectuals**, academics, highbrows, cognoscenti, literati (fml)

intelligible adj **comprehensible**, understandable, clear, plain, lucid Opposite: unintelligible

intemperance n **self-indulgence**, overindulgence, excess, hedonism, gluttony Opposite: moderation

intemperate adj **self-indulgent**, uncontrolled, unrestrained, inordinate, immoderate Opposite: moderate

intend v **mean**, aim, propose, plan, have in mind

intended adj **1 envisioned**, future, planned, proposed, projected **2 planned**, intentional, deliberate, on purpose, premeditated Opposite: accidental ■ n (dated) **fiancé**, fiancée, husband-to-be, wife-to-be, girlfriend

intense adj **penetrating**, strong, powerful, forceful, concentrated Opposite: moderate

intensely adv **forcefully**, powerfully, strongly, deeply, extremely Opposite: mildly

intensification n **strengthening**, increase, rise, escalation, spiralling Opposite: reduction

intensify v **strengthen**, deepen, step up, exaggerate, increase Opposite: weaken. See COMPARE AND CONTRAST at increase.

intensity n **strength**, concentration, power, force, passion Opposite: moderation

intensive adj **concentrated**, rigorous, exhaustive, severe, thorough Opposite: easy

intensive care n **monitoring**, nursing, specialist care, 24-hour care, one-to-one care

intent n (fml) **intention**, aim, goal, target, objective ■ adj **1 concentrated**, absorbed, focused, directed, fixed **2 intending to**, bent on, determined, resolved, set on

intention n **aim**, purpose, goal, target, objective

intentional adj **deliberate**, planned, intended, premeditated, calculated Opposite: accidental

intently *adv* **closely**, fixedly, carefully, keenly, attentively *Opposite*: abstractedly

intentness *n* **attentiveness**, concentration, focus, attention, close attention *Opposite*: abstraction

inter *v* **bury**, entomb, lay to rest

interact *v* **interrelate**, act together, cooperate, relate, intermingle

interaction *n* **communication**, contact, interface, dealings, relations

interactive *adj* **communicating**, collaborating, cooperating, collaborative, cooperative

interbreed *v* **breed**, reproduce, multiply, mate, produce

intercalate *v* **insert**, introduce, interpolate, add, interpose *Opposite*: extrapolate

intercede *v* **intervene**, mediate, plead, negotiate, arbitrate

intercept *v* **cut off**, catch, interrupt, stop, seize

interception *n* **capture**, seizure, interruption, interference, intervention

intercession *n* **intervention**, mediation, arbitration, negotiation

interchange *v* **switch**, trade, exchange, substitute, trade off ■ *n* **1 trading**, exchange, transaction, substitution, trade-off **2 crossroads**, junction, intersection

interchangeable *adj* **substitutable**, identical, the same, compatible, transposable *Opposite*: incompatible

intercommunicate *v* **talk**, communicate, converse, discuss, contact

interconnect *v* **join**, intersect, connect, interrelate, interlock

intercontinental *adj* **international**, transnational, global, worldwide, large-scale *Opposite*: national

intercourse *n* **dealings**, contact, communication, interaction, association

intercut *v* **interpose**, insert, alternate, interweave, interject

interdependent *adj* **symbiotic**, dependent, reliant, codependent

interdict *n* **order**, court order, ban, prohibition, veto ■ *v* **ban**, prohibit, forbid, veto, embargo *Opposite*: permit

interest *n* **1 attention**, notice, curiosity, concentration, awareness *Opposite*: indifference **2 hobby**, activity, pursuit, pastime, leisure activity **3 concern**, importance, significance, relevance, note **4 good**, advantage, benefit, gain, profit ■ *v* **attract**, draw, appeal, fascinate, be of interest *Opposite*: bore

interested *adj* **absorbed**, attentive, involved, concerned, attracted *Opposite*: indifferent

interest group *n* **1 alliance**, association, cartel, trade union, pressure group **2 club**, association, group, society

interesting *adj* **stimulating**, thought-provoking, motivating, exciting, fascinating *Opposite*: boring

interface *n* **border**, boundary, line, crossing point, edge

interfere *v* **1 pry**, intrude, meddle, disturb, intervene **2 delay**, inhibit, restrict, affect, get in the way

interference *n* **1 meddling**, intrusion, prying, interfering, intervention **2 restriction**, obstruction, hindrance, obstacle, delay

interfering *adj* **intrusive**, meddlesome, prying, inquisitive, meddling

intergalactic *adj* **interstellar**, interplanetary, space

intergovernmental *adj* **interstate**, international, diplomatic, foreign, high-level

interim *adj* **temporary**, provisional, short-term, intervening, acting *Opposite*: permanent ■ *n* **interlude**, pause, break, interval, pause in the action

interior *n* **inside**, centre, core, heart *Opposite*: outside ■ *adj* **internal**, inner, central, inland, inside *Opposite*: peripheral

interior decoration *n* **decoration**, furnishings, decorating scheme, colour scheme, interior design

interject *v* **butt in**, exclaim, interrupt, interpose, cut in

interjection *n* **1 exclamation**, outburst, cry, utterance, shout **2 interruption**, interpolation, introduction, addition, insertion

interlace *v* **interweave**, intertwine, interlock, entwine, knit

interlard *v* **interpose**, insert, introduce, intersperse, interweave

interleave *v* **slot in**, put in, enclose, interweave, add

interlink *v* **interweave**, intertwine, interlace, interconnect, knit

interlock *v* **mesh**, dovetail, link, join, interconnect

interlocutor *n* **speaker**, talker, discusser, panelist, converser

interloper *n* **1 intruder**, trespasser, gatecrasher, persona non grata, impostor **2 meddler**, busybody (*infml*), snoop (*infml*), nosy parker (*infml*)

interlude *n* **interval**, break, rest, pause, interim

intermediary *n* **intercessor**, arbitrator, negotiator, go-between, mediator ■ *adj* **intermediate**, middle, midway, in-between, transitional

intermediate *adj* **middle**, midway, in-between, transitional, halfway *Opposite*: extreme

interment *n* **burial**, entombment, committal, funeral, funeral rites *Opposite*: disinterment

intermesh *v* **join**, interlink, knit, mesh, interconnect

interminable *adj* **endless**, ceaseless, everlasting, perpetual, never-ending *Opposite*: finite

intermingle *v* **intermix**, mingle, interact, combine, fuse

intermission *n* **intermezzo**, interval, break, interlude, pause

intermittent *adj* **spasmodic**, periodic, sporadic, occasional, irregular *Opposite*: constant. *See* COMPARE AND CONTRAST *at* periodic.

intermix *v* **meld**, intermingle, mix, mingle, blend *Opposite*: separate

intern *v* **imprison**, detain, confine, hold, jail *Opposite*: release ■ *n* **medical student**, doctor, student doctor, med student, medic *(infml)*

internal *adj* **1 interior**, inner, inside *Opposite*: external **2 domestic**, in-house, home, intramural *Opposite*: external

internalize *v* **1 adopt**, affect, take on, assume, co-opt **2 stew**, mull over, bottle up, suppress *Opposite*: externalize

international *adj* **global**, worldwide, intercontinental, universal, transnational *Opposite*: domestic

internecine *adj* **1 internal**, inner, civil, domestic **2 destructive**, devastating, decimating, deadly, injurious

internee *n* **prisoner**, captive, detainee, hostage, inmate

Internet *n* **World Wide Web**, information superhighway, cyberspace, the Net *(infml)*, the Web *(infml)*

WORD BANK

❑ **types of Internet facilities and activities** bot, browser, bulletin board, chat room, cookie, home page, instant messaging, ISP, newsgroup, portal, robot, router, search engine, service provider, URL, web page, web site, webcast, webconferencing, webzine

---

internment *n* **imprisonment**, captivity, confinement, custody, detention *Opposite*: release

interpersonal *adj* **relational**, social, personal, interactive *Opposite*: solitary

interplanetary *adj* **space**, planetary, interstellar, intergalactic, astronomical

interplay *n* **chemistry**, interaction, relationship, interchange, back-and-forth

interpolate *v* **1 insert**, interpose, intercalate, incorporate, include **2 interrupt**, interject, interpose, throw in, cut in

interpose *v* **1 interrupt**, cut in, throw in, interpolate, interject **2 intervene**, interfere, intercede, meddle, butt in

interpret *v* **1 explain**, clarify, account for, elucidate, make clear **2 take to mean**, understand, read, construe, infer *Opposite*: misread **3 translate**, decode, decipher, unravel, figure out

interpretation *n* **clarification**, understanding, reading, explanation, analysis

interpretative *adj* **explanatory**, revelatory, informational, informative, revealing

interpreter *n* **1 translator**, linguist, transcriber, polyglot, explainer **2 performer**, portrayer, exponent, promoter, medium

interpretive *see* **interpretative**

interracial *adj* **mixed**, of mixed race, multicultural, multiethnic, integrated *Opposite*: segregated

interregnum *n* **interval**, pause, lag, lapse, wait

interrelate *v* **interconnect**, relate, connect, link up, correlate

interrogate *v* **question**, cross-examine, quiz, interview, debrief. *See* COMPARE AND CONTRAST *at* question.

interrogation *n* **questioning**, examination, cross-examination, grilling, interview

interrogative *adj* **questioning**, curious, inquisitive, inquiring, probing

interrogator *n* **questioner**, interviewer, investigator, examiner

interrupt *v* **1 butt in**, barge in, interject, disturb, intrude **2 break off**, cut short, disrupt, break up, stop

interruption *n* **break**, pause, disruption, stoppage, disturbance *Opposite*: continuity

intersect *v* **cross**, interconnect, meet, traverse, overlap

intersection *n* **1 connection**, meeting, node, joint, joining **2 junction**, crossroads, fork, interchange, roundabout

intersperse *v* **mix together**, combine, intermingle, sprinkle, scatter

interstate *adj* **regional**, national, federal, political, administrative

interstellar *adj* **interplanetary**, space, star, intergalactic, stellar

interstice *n* **space**, gap, crack, opening, aperture

intertwine *v* **interweave**, entwine, interlace, link, interleave *Opposite*: divide

interval *n* **1 intermission**, break, pause, interlude, recess **2 gap**, space, distance, hiatus, separation

intervene *v* **1 intercede**, arbitrate, mediate, interfere, get involved *Opposite*: hold back **2 happen**, occur, take place, ensue, succeed

intervention *n* **interference**, involvement, intrusion, intercession, interposition

interview *n* **meeting**, talk, consultation, conference, discussion ■ *v* **question**, interrogate, talk to, converse with, put questions to

interviewee *n* **applicant**, candidate, hopeful, aspirant, contender *Opposite*: interviewer

interviewer *n* **1 examiner**, assessor, questioner, interrogator, evaluator *Opposite*: interviewee **2 presenter**, questioner, correspondent, personality, journalist

interweave *v* **intertwine**, interlace, mingle, intermingle, entwine

intestate *adj* **without a will**, unrepresented, unaccounted for, voiceless, unheard

intestinal *adj* **duodenal**, colonic, abdominal, stomach, bowel

in that *conj* **because**, as, since, given that

in the face of prep **despite**, in spite of, regardless of, notwithstanding *(fml)*

in the light of prep **taking into consideration**, in view of, considering, taking into account, with regard to

in the name of prep **on behalf of**, for, for the benefit of, for the sake of, on the authority of

intimacy n 1 **familiarity**, closeness, understanding, confidence, caring Opposite: distance 2 **quietness**, seclusion, privacy, informality, friendliness Opposite: formality

intimate adj 1 **close**, dear, near, warm, friendly Opposite: distant 2 **cosy**, quiet, informal, friendly, warm Opposite: formal 3 **personal**, confidential, private, secret, innermost Opposite: public 4 **thorough**, detailed, in-depth, profound, firsthand Opposite: superficial ■ v **suggest**, hint, insinuate, imply, indicate

intimately adv 1 **closely**, warmly, familiarly, confidentially, personally Opposite: distantly 2 **quietly**, informally, cosily, warmly, comfortably Opposite: formally 3 **thoroughly**, very well, fully, in detail, closely Opposite: superficially

intimation n **hint**, allusion, insinuation, suggestion, warning

intimidate v **threaten**, frighten, bully, coerce, terrorize

intimidated adj **daunted**, scared, frightened, overwhelmed, unsettled Opposite: relaxed

intimidating adj **threatening**, unapproachable, frightening, daunting, menacing Opposite: approachable

intimidation n **coercion**, pressure, bullying, threats, terrorization

into *(infml)* adj **addicted to**, interested in, obsessed by, mad about, keen on

intolerable adj **unbearable**, insufferable, impossible, unendurable, insupportable Opposite: bearable

intolerance n **bigotry**, prejudice, narrow-mindedness, fanaticism, narrowness Opposite: tolerance

intolerant adj **bigoted**, prejudiced, narrow-minded, fanatical, blinkered Opposite: tolerant

intonation n 1 **pitch**, inflection, lilt, cadence, timbre 2 **chanting**, chant, incantation, invocation, intoning

intone v 1 **say**, utter, speak, articulate, pronounce 2 *(fml)* **chant**, sing, croon, drone, hum

intoxicating adj 1 *(fml)* **alcoholic**, strong, powerful, heady, mind-altering Opposite: soft 2 **exciting**, invigorating, stimulating, exhilarating, fascinating Opposite: dull

intoxication n **alcoholism**, drunkenness, inebriation, intemperance, heavy drinking

intractability n 1 *(fml)* **unmanageability**, uncontrollability, obstinacy, stubbornness, pigheadedness Opposite: tractability 2 **difficulty**, knottiness, complexity, awkwardness, unwieldiness Opposite: simplicity

intractable adj 1 *(fml)* **stubborn**, obstinate, obdurate, wilful, headstrong Opposite: easygoing 2 **difficult**, problematic, troublesome, awkward, knotty Opposite: easy. See COMPARE AND CONTRAST at **unruly**.

intramural adj **internal**, inner, in-house, college, school Opposite: extramural

intransigence n **inflexibility**, stubbornness, narrow-mindedness, obstinacy, unyieldingness Opposite: flexibility

intransigent adj **inflexible**, stubborn, obdurate, obstinate, uncompromising Opposite: flexible ■ n *(fml)* **conservative**, dinosaur, diehard, reactionary, extremist Opposite: progressive

intravenous adj **venous**, vein, arterial, blood, circulatory

in-tray n **tray**, pigeonhole, in-box *(US)*

intrepid adj **fearless**, brave, bold, courageous, heroic Opposite: cowardly

intricacies n **details**, ins and outs, workings, particulars, minutiae

intricacy n **complexity**, difficulty, obscurity, sophistication, convolutedness

intricate adj **complicated**, complex, involved, difficult, elaborate Opposite: simple

intrigue n 1 **plotting**, conspiracy, manoeuvring, trickery, scheming 2 **conspiracy**, plot, deception, scheme, stratagem ■ v **interest**, fascinate, charm, attract, captivate

intriguing adj **interesting**, fascinating, exciting, stimulating, absorbing Opposite: uninteresting

intrinsic adj **basic**, essential, inherent, fundamental, central Opposite: acquired

introduce v 1 **present**, make known to, acquaint with, familiarize, announce 2 **host**, present, preside over, lead, head 3 **bring in**, set up, initiate, usher in, pioneer Opposite: conclude 4 **make somebody aware of**, bring to somebody's attention, acquaint somebody with, turn somebody on to, get somebody into

introduction n 1 **foreword**, opening, preface, prologue, preamble Opposite: conclusion 2 **outline**, overview, primer, summary, starter 3 **institution**, presentation, insertion, ushering in

introductory adj 1 **preliminary**, initial, opening, starting, early Opposite: final 2 **basic**, entry-level, preliminary, first, simple

introspection n **self-examination**, contemplation, brooding, meditation, self-analysis

introspective adj **self-examining**, self-absorbed, inward-looking, contemplative, brooding

introversion n **introspection**, self-absorption, contemplation, navel-gazing, shyness Opposite: extroversion

introvert *n* **recluse**, hermit, loner, homebody (*infml*), shrinking violet (*infml*) *Opposite*: extrovert ■ *adj* **introverted**, shy, withdrawn, reclusive, reserved *Opposite*: extrovert

introverted *adj* **shy**, withdrawn, reclusive, reserved, reticent *Opposite*: extrovert

intrude *v* **encroach**, break in, interrupt, interfere, impose

intruder *n* **interloper**, burglar, trespasser, prowler, stalker

intrusion *n* **disturbance**, interruption, imposition, interference, invasion

intrusive *adj* **invasive**, indiscreet, interfering, insensitive, upsetting *Opposite*: discreet

intuit *v* **sense**, perceive, discern, feel, understand

intuition *n* **1 instinct**, perception, insight, sixth sense, awareness **2 hunch**, feeling, inkling, suspicion, sense

intuitive *adj* **1 instinctive**, spontaneous, innate, in-built, instinctual *Opposite*: cerebral **2 perceptive**, sensitive, shrewd, discerning, insightful

intuitively *adv* **instinctively**, automatically, by instinct, spontaneously, naturally

intuitiveness *n* **instinct**, perceptiveness, perception, insightfulness, insight

inundate *v* **1 flood**, deluge, drown, immerse, submerge *Opposite*: drain **2 overwhelm**, snow under, swamp, overburden, beseige

inundation *n* **1 deluge**, flood, sea, stream, shower *Opposite*: trickle **2 flood**, blizzard, sea, wave, barrage

inure *v* **harden**, toughen, accustom, season, acclimatize

inurement *n* **hardening**, toughening, acclimatization, seasoning, desensitization

invade *v* **1 attack**, occupy, enter, conquer, annex **2 overrun**, infect, infest, plague, colonize

invader *n* **attacker**, aggressor, raider, intruder, assailant

invalid *adj* **1 null and void**, unacceptable, unenforceable, illegal, worthless *Opposite*: valid **2 unsound**, untrue, unfounded, illogical, untenable *Opposite*: valid **3 infirm**, enfeebled, debilitated, disabled, sick *Opposite*: well ■ *n* **convalescent**, patient, sick person

invalidate *v* **overturn**, cancel, annul, nullify, undo *Opposite*: validate. *See* COMPARE AND CONTRAST *at* **nullify**.

invalidation *n* **annulment**, undoing, overthrow, nullification, cancellation *Opposite*: validation

invalidity *n* **1 unsoundness**, inaccuracy, baselessness, irrationality, falsehood *Opposite*: validity **2 illegality**, inoperativeness, ineffectiveness, unsoundness, voidness *Opposite*: legality

invaluable *adj* **priceless**, irreplaceable, vital, instrumental, precious *Opposite*: worthless

invaluableness *n* **pricelessness**, irreplaceability, helpfulness, importance, value *Opposite*: worthlessness

invariable *adj* **constant**, set, unchanging, inflexible, consistent *Opposite*: erratic

invasion *n* **attack**, assault, incursion, raid, foray *Opposite*: withdrawal

invasive *adj* **1 aggressive**, offensive, hostile, warlike, bellicose **2 intrusive**, disturbing, interfering, insensitive, imposing *Opposite*: discreet

invective (*fml*) *n* **diatribe**, tirade, attack, broadside, counterblast *Opposite*: eulogy

inveigh *v* **protest**, complain, fulminate, criticize, rail

inveigle *v* **persuade**, entice, charm, cajole, trick

invent *v* **1 create**, devise, formulate, originate, conceive **2 make up**, think up, concoct, fabricate, contrive

invented *adj* **false**, made-up, fictitious, imaginary, pretend *Opposite*: real

invention *n* **1 device**, innovation, contraption, gadget, design **2 creation**, discovery, development, brainchild, origination **3 fabrication**, forgery, falsehood, deceit, lies *Opposite*: truth **4 creativity**, imagination, ingenuity, inventiveness, resourcefulness

inventive *adj* **creative**, imaginative, ingenious, resourceful, original *Opposite*: unimaginative

inventiveness *n* **ingenuity**, resourcefulness, originality, creativity, imagination

inventor *n* **discoverer**, originator, creator, architect, author

inventory *n* **1 list**, record, account, register, catalogue **2 supply**, range, array, stock, accounting

inverse *adj* **opposite**, converse, reverse, contrary, counter *Opposite*: same ■ *n* **reverse**, opposite, other, contrary, converse

inversion *n* **1 reversal**, overturn, downturn, upturn **2 reverse**, transposition, antithesis, contrary, converse

invert *v* **turn over**, upset, capsize, overturn, reverse *Opposite*: right

invest *v* **1 capitalize**, put in, devote, advance, finance **2 endow**, provide, supply, empower, authorize **3** (*fml*) **appoint**, ordain, instate, inaugurate, establish

investigate *v* **examine**, look into, explore, inspect, study

investigation *n* **study**, examination, analysis, research, survey

investigative *adj* **analytical**, exploratory, undercover, fact-finding, research

investigator *n* **detective**, private detective, private investigator, agent, private eye (*infml*)

investiture *n* **installation**, inauguration, swearing-in, instatement, admission

investment *n* **1 savings**, speculation, venture,

investor *n* **1 saver**, shareholder, depositor, stakeholder, financier **2 backer**, sponsor, patron, guarantor, security

inveterate *adj* **chronic**, confirmed, hardened, ingrained, incurable *Opposite*: occasional

invidious *adj* **unpleasant**, discriminatory, unenviable, unfair, undesirable *Opposite*: pleasant

in view of *prep* **considering**, bearing in mind, taking into consideration, taking into account, in consideration of *(fml) Opposite*: notwithstanding *(fml)*

invigilate *v* **supervise**, monitor, inspect, observe, check

invigilator *n* **supervisor**, inspector, monitor, overseer, scrutineer

invigorate *v* **energize**, revitalize, refresh, stimulate, enliven *Opposite*: exhaust

invigorated *adj* **strengthened**, fortified, energized, refreshed, restored *Opposite*: weakened

invigorating *adj* **bracing**, brisk, stimulating, refreshing, revitalizing *Opposite*: enervating

invincibility *n* **strength**, insuperability, invulnerability, impregnability, indomitability *Opposite*: vulnerability

invincible *adj* **unbeatable**, invulnerable, unconquerable, indomitable, impregnable *Opposite*: vulnerable

inviolable *adj* **unbreakable**, sacred, sacrosanct, firm, unchallengeable

inviolate *adj* **1 unaltered**, unchanged, unbroken, intact, entire *Opposite*: altered **2 pure**, unsullied, untouched, whole, intact *Opposite*: contaminated

invisibility *n* **hiddenness**, inconspicuousness, indiscernibility, faintness, indistinctness *Opposite*: visibility

invisible *adj* **1 imperceptible**, unseen, indistinguishable, indiscernible, undetectable *Opposite*: visible **2 hidden**, concealed, disguised, unnoticed, obscured *Opposite*: obvious **3 imaginary**, nonexistent, intangible, shadowy, insubstantial *Opposite*: palpable

invitation *n* **1 offer**, request, call, summons, bidding **2 encouragement**, inducement, provocation, incitement, enticement *Opposite*: discouragement

invite *n* *(infml)* **invitation**, request, call, summons, offer ■ *v* **1 ask**, request, call, summon, bid *(archaic) Opposite*: blackball **2 provoke**, incite, induce, attract, encourage *Opposite*: forbid

inviting *adj* **attractive**, appealing, alluring, tempting, welcoming *Opposite*: unappealing

invocation *n* **prayer**, call, request, entreaty, petition

invoice *n* **bill**, account, statement, demand, proof of purchase *Opposite*: receipt ■ *v* **bill**, debit, charge

invoke *v* **1 cite**, quote, use, refer, mention **2 appeal**, call upon, call up, beg, summon **3 evoke**, call to mind, conjure up, incite, arouse

involuntarily *adv* **unwillingly**, reluctantly, unhappily, against your will, compulsorily *Opposite*: willingly

involuntary *adj* **1 compulsory**, obligatory, forced, unwilling, reluctant *Opposite*: willing **2 instinctive**, spontaneous, reflex, unintentional, automatic *Opposite*: intentional

involve *v* **1 contain**, include, take in, comprise, consist of **2 concern**, have to do with, affect, interest, encompass **3 implicate**, draw in, mix up, get into, embroil **4 engage**, engross, absorb, grip, occupy *Opposite*: bore **5 imply**, mean, entail, necessitate, require

involved *adj* **1 complicated**, complex, intricate, elaborate, knotty *Opposite*: simple **2 concerned**, caught up, mixed up, occupied, implicated *Opposite*: uninvolved

involvement *n* **1 attachment**, interest, concern, enthusiasm, commitment *Opposite*: detachment **2 participation**, association, connection, contribution, engrossment

invulnerable *adj* **untouchable**, invincible, unassailable, safe, impenetrable *Opposite*: vulnerable

inward *adj* **1 inner**, innermost, inmost, private, deep *Opposite*: external **2 internal**, interior, inner, inner-directed, innermost *Opposite*: outer **3 incoming**, ingoing, entering, inward bound, inflowing *Opposite*: outward

inwardly *adv* **secretly**, privately, to yourself, silently, deeply *Opposite*: openly

inwards *adv* **within**, inwardly, inside, in *Opposite*: outwards

iota *n* **jot**, bit, scrap, speck, grain *Opposite*: lot

IQ *n* **intelligence quotient**, level of intelligence, intelligence, intellect, brains

irascible *adj* **quick-tempered**, irritable, petulant, hot-tempered, short-tempered *Opposite*: easygoing

irate *adj* **angry**, incensed, furious, mad, irritated *Opposite*: calm

ire *(literary) n* **fury**, rage, anger, wrath, annoyance *Opposite*: calmness. *See* COMPARE AND CONTRAST *at* anger.

iridescent *adj* **lustrous**, rainbow-like, shimmering, shimmery, colourful *Opposite*: monochrome

irk *v* **annoy**, vex, displease, trouble, bother *Opposite*: please. *See* COMPARE AND CONTRAST *at* bother.

irksome *adj* **annoying**, irritating, exasperating, tiresome, tedious *Opposite*: pleasant

iron *v* **press**, smooth out, iron out, smooth, flatten *Opposite*: crumple ■ *adj* **firm**, hard, strong, determined, tough *Opposite*: soft

iron curtain n obstacle, impediment, hurdle, line, border

ironic adj **1 caustic**, dry, biting, sarcastic, satirical **2 incongruous**, paradoxical, poignant, peculiar, odd. See COMPARE AND CONTRAST at **sarcastic**.

ironical see **ironic**

iron out v sort out, resolve, smooth over, clear up, settle

ironwork n wrought iron, metalwork, ironmongery, ironware, iron object

irony n **1 satire**, dryness, causticness, sardonicism, sarcasm Opposite: sincerity **2 paradox**, incongruity, fatefulness, dramatic irony, contrariety

irradiate v **1 light up**, light, illuminate, brighten, cast light on Opposite: darken **2 enlighten**, clarify, inform, instruct, inspire Opposite: obfuscate

irradiation n **1 radioactivity**, radiation, contamination, X-ray, treatment **2 preservation**, treatment, sterilization, purification

irrational adj illogical, unreasonable, foolish, ridiculous, absurd Opposite: rational

irrationality n illogicality, unreasonableness, foolishness, ludicrousness, absurdity Opposite: sense

irreconcilable adj incompatible, irresoluble, conflicting, opposing, opposed Opposite: compatible

irrecoverable adj **1 irretrievable**, gone, lost, given up, written off (infml) **2 irreparable**, beyond repair, irreversible, irredeemable, irremediable

irredeemable adj hopeless, unalterable, absolute, complete, incorrigible Opposite: redeemable

irreducible adj complex, complicated, involved, intricate, difficult

irrefutable adj indisputable, certain, unquestionable, overwhelming, unassailable Opposite: disputable

irregular adj **1 uneven**, unequal, asymmetrical, unbalanced, rough Opposite: even **2 erratic**, variable, random, haphazard, intermittent Opposite: regular **3 improper**, unacceptable, abnormal, wrong, unsuitable Opposite: proper

irregularity n **1 unevenness**, inequality, variability, randomness, haphazardness Opposite: regularity **2 indiscretion**, abnormality, wrongdoing, misdeed, anomaly

irrelevance n **1 insignificance**, unimportance, inappropriateness, worthlessness, triviality Opposite: relevance **2 inconsequence**, side issue, detail, technicality, red herring

irrelevant adj immaterial, neither here nor there, unrelated, inappropriate, extraneous Opposite: relevant

irreligious adj ungodly, unspiritual, nonreligious, blasphemous, sacrilegious Opposite: devout

irremediable adj irreparable, irreversible, irredeemable, beyond repair, irrevocable

irreparable adj beyond repair, irreversible, irretrievable, severe, lasting

irreplaceable adj unique, inimitable, matchless, exceptional, rare Opposite: common

irrepressible adj uncontrollable, out of control, wild, unruly, disorderly Opposite: contained

irreproachable adj blameless, faultless, flawless, perfect, impeccable Opposite: blameworthy

irresistible adj **1 overwhelming**, overpowering, uncontrollable, compelling, strong Opposite: weak **2 desirable**, tempting, appealing, enticing, alluring Opposite: unappealing

irresolute adj indecisive, vacillating, unsure, weak, undetermined Opposite: determined

irresolution n indecision, indecisiveness, vacillation, weakness, hesitancy Opposite: determination

irrespective adv regardless, nevertheless, nonetheless, heedlessly, notwithstanding (fml)

irrespective of prep regardless of, despite, no matter, in spite of, heedless of Opposite: considering

irresponsibility n recklessness, carelessness, inattention, negligence, rashness Opposite: responsibility

irresponsible adj reckless, careless, negligent, rash, foolish Opposite: responsible

irretrievable adj irreparable, irreversible, irrevocable, severe, irrecoverable

irreverence n disrespect, mockery, derision, impertinence, impudence Opposite: respect

irreverent adj disrespectful, mocking, derisive, rude, impudent Opposite: respectful

irreversible adj irreparable, irretrievable, irrevocable, unalterable, irremediable Opposite: temporary

irrevocable adj binding, irreversible, final, unalterable, unchangeable Opposite: flexible

irrevocably adv irreversibly, forever, permanently, once and for all, for all time

irrigate v water, flood, wet, moisten, hose down Opposite: dry out

irritability n touchiness, bad temper, petulance, cantankerousness, tetchiness (infml) Opposite: equanimity

irritable adj bad-tempered, short-tempered, ill-tempered, cross, petulant Opposite: easygoing

irritant n nuisance, annoyance, aggravation, irritation, bane Opposite: balm

irritate v **1 annoy**, infuriate, bother, exasperate, aggravate (infml) Opposite: soothe **2 inflame**, rub, chafe, sting, hurt Opposite: soothe. See COMPARE AND CONTRAST at **annoy**.

irritated adj annoyed, cross, angry, exasperated, wound up (infml) Opposite: unperturbed

irritating *adj* annoying, exasperating, irksome, infuriating, frustrating *Opposite*: soothing

irritation *n* 1 annoyance, frustration, impatience, exasperation, aggravation *(infml) Opposite*: calmness 2 nuisance, bother, irritant, bane, pain *(infml)* 3 inflammation, soreness, tenderness, itchiness, rash. *See* COMPARE AND CONTRAST *at* anger.

island *n* isle, islet, atoll, desert island, key *Opposite*: mainland

islander *n* inhabitant, local, resident, occupant, native

island-hop *v* travel around, tour, sail around, sail, cruise

isle *n* island, islet, atoll, desert island, key

islet *see* isle

ism *(infml) n* doctrine, ideology, belief, belief system, creed

isolate *v* cut off, separate, segregate, detach, set apart *Opposite*: include

isolated *adj* 1 remote, cut off, inaccessible, lonely, secluded *Opposite*: nearby 2 lonely, alone, solitary, insular, friendless 3 one-off, exceptional, unique, solitary, unrepeated *Opposite*: common

isolation *n* separation, segregation, remoteness, loneliness, seclusion *Opposite*: inclusion

isolationism *n* separateness, remoteness, seclusion, independence, standoffishness

isometrics *n* exercise, body building, workout, keep fit

isotope *n* element, form, variant, version

issue *n* 1 subject, matter, question, topic, problem 2 copy, number, edition, back number, back copy 3 production, release, distribution, circulation, publication 4 progeny, offspring, children, young, descendants ■ *v* 1 supply, give out, hand out, deliver, distribute 2 announce, broadcast, send out, make, declare 3 publish, release, broadcast, disseminate, distribute *Opposite*: withdraw 4 emanate, emerge, issue forth, gush, flow 5 originate, stem, spring, arise, rise

isthmus *n* strip, neck, bridge, peninsula, spit

IT *n* information technology, computer science, data processing, information processing, data retrieval

italic *adj* sloping, slanted, oblique *Opposite*: roman

itch *v* 1 irritate, prickle, scratch, tickle, crawl *Opposite*: soothe 2 long, desire, wish, hanker, yearn ■ *n* 1 itchiness, tickle, irritation, prickling, tingling 2 desire, longing, wish, eagerness, hankering

itchiness *n* irritation, tickle, inflammation, tingling, prickliness

itching *adj* eager, longing, dying, keen, burning *Opposite*: reluctant

itchy *adj* prickly, tickly, scratchy, uncomfortable, irritated

item *n* 1 thing, article, piece, entry, point 2 *(infml)* couple, pair, twosome, match, duo

itemize *v* list, detail, enumerate, record, document

iterate *v* repeat, restate, reiterate, go over, retell

iteration *n* repetition, restatement, reiteration, rehearsal, duplication

itinerant *adj* peripatetic, roving, wandering, nomadic, roaming *Opposite*: settled

itinerary *n* route, schedule, journey, circuit, tour

itsy-bitsy *(infml) adj* tiny, little, small, minute, minuscule *Opposite*: huge

ivory tower *n* seclusion, isolation, retreat, remoteness, academic world *Opposite*: real world

J

jab *v* stab, prod, thrust, dig, poke ■ *n* 1 prod, stab, thrust, dig, poke 2 *(infml)* injection, immunization, inoculation, vaccination, booster

jabber *v* chatter, babble, prattle, gabble, ramble

jacket *n* cover, covering, casing, sheathing, sheath

jack in *(infml) v* stop, give up, resign, abandon, leave *Opposite*: take up

jackknife *v* turn, skid, swerve, veer, swivel

jackpot *n* prize, bonanza, winnings, windfall, rollover

jack up *v* 1 lift, lift up, raise, raise up, put up *Opposite*: lower 2 increase, raise, put up, hike up, boost *Opposite*: slash

jaded *adj* 1 bored, world-weary, jaundiced, cynical, fed up *(infml) Opposite*: enthusiastic 2 tired, weary, exhausted, worn-out, lacklustre *Opposite*: fresh

jagged *adj* 1 uneven, rough, ragged, crude, irregular *Opposite*: even 2 sharp, pointed, pointy, rough, serrated *Opposite*: smooth

jaggedness *n* 1 unevenness, raggedness, roughness, irregularity, bumpiness *Opposite*: evenness 2 sharpness, pointedness, pointiness, roughness, serration *Opposite*: smoothness

jail *n* prison, lockup, open prison, dungeon, borstal ■ *v* imprison, lock up, lock away, put behind bars, confine *Opposite*: free

jailbreak *n* breakout, escape, getaway, exodus, flight

jailer *n* prison officer, guard, governor, keeper, prison guard *Opposite*: liberator

jalopy *(dated infml)* *n* wreck, banger *(infml)*, tin lizzie *(infml)*, rattletrap *(infml)*, heap *(slang)*

jam *v* 1 push, squash, cram, stuff, pack 2 fill, fill up, throng, pack, block 3 stop, seize, seize up, grind to a halt, stick ■ *n* 1 traffic jam, gridlock, bottleneck, logjam, roadblock 2 *(infml)* predicament, mess, quandary, pickle *(infml)*, fix *(infml)*

jamb *n* upright, post, support, column, doorpost

jamboree *n* celebration, party, carnival, fête, garden party

jammed *adj* 1 stuck, wedged, stuck fast, lodged, caught *Opposite*: free 2 blocked, congested, thronged, packed, crammed *Opposite*: deserted

jammy *(infml)* *adj* lucky, fortunate, comfortable, easy *Opposite*: unlucky

jam-packed *(infml)* *adj* crowded, full, full up, packed, filled to capacity *Opposite*: empty

jangle *v* rattle, jingle, clank, clink, clatter

jar *n* pot, container, vessel, crock, urn ■ *v* 1 shake, jolt, jerk, bump, hit 2 irritate, grate, annoy, irk, get on somebody's nerves *Opposite*: harmonize

jargon *n* 1 terminology, slang, argot, parlance, language 2 nonsense, verbiage, cant, mumbo jumbo *(infml)*, waffle *(infml)*

jarring *adj* 1 irritating, grating, annoying, unpleasant, unbearable *Opposite*: calming 2 disturbing, unsettling, shocking, destabilizing, uncomfortable *Opposite*: reassuring 3 clashing, incongruous, uncharacteristic, discordant, inharmonious *Opposite*: harmonious

jaundiced *adj* cynical, pessimistic, sceptical, unenthusiastic, jaded

jaunt *n* outing, trip, excursion, break, day out

jauntiness *n* cheerfulness, jolliness, gaiety, dash, spryness

jaunty *adj* carefree, cheerful, cheery, jolly, spry

javelin *n* spear, projectile, missile, lance, harpoon

jaw *n* chin, jawbone, jawline, jowl, mouth

jawbone *n* jaw, chin, maxilla, mandible

jaywalk *v* cross, cross over, walk across, stroll across, go across

jaywalker *n* pedestrian, walker, crosser, traverser, stroller

jazz up *(infml)* *v* enhance, spice, spice up, liven up, enliven

jealous *adj* 1 envious, covetous, resentful, green with envy, green 2 protective, suspicious, wary, watchful, mistrustful *Opposite*: trusting

jealousy *n* 1 envy, covetousness, resentment, resentfulness, desirousness *(fml)* 2 protectiveness, suspicion, suspiciousness, wariness, watchfulness

jeer *v* boo, hiss, heckle, catcall, taunt *Opposite*: applaud ■ *n* hiss, boo, taunt, catcall, hoot

jeer at *v* insult, taunt, sneer, mock, deride *Opposite*: cheer

jeering *n* derision, mockery, name-calling, mocking, taunting *Opposite*: applause ■ *adj* derisive, scornful, mocking, sardonic, contemptuous

jejune *adj* 1 boring, undemanding, uninteresting, lightweight, insubstantial *Opposite*: interesting 2 childish, immature, adolescent, unsophisticated, crude *Opposite*: mature

jell *v* 1 solidify, set, congeal, firm, harden *Opposite*: liquefy 2 take shape, shape up, crystallize, come together, firm up *Opposite*: disintegrate 3 bond, get on, be compatible, be on the same wavelength, click *(infml)* *Opposite*: clash

jellied *adj* gelatinous, set, solid, congealed

jellify *v* set, gelatinize, congeal, jell, gel *Opposite*: liquefy

jelly *n* 1 gelatin, aspic, gel 2 petroleum jelly, lubricant, ointment ■ *v* set, thicken, jellify, gelatinize, congeal *Opposite*: liquefy

jemmy *v* lever, open, force, prise, crowbar

jeopardize *v* put at risk, risk, put in danger, endanger, expose

jeopardy *n* danger, risk, threat, peril, hazard

jerk *v* 1 yank, tug, pull, wrench, haul 2 lurch, jolt, shudder, judder, bump 3 twitch, shudder, tremble, shake ■ *n* 1 pull, tug, yank, wrench, haul 2 jolt, bump, shudder, judder, lurch 3 spasm, twitch, shudder, tremble, shake

jerkin *n* jacket, body warmer, tunic, waistcoat, gilet

jerkiness *n* bumpiness, jumpiness, bounciness, lurching, shuddering *Opposite*: smoothness

jerky *adj* irregular, spasmodic, erratic, fitful, bumpy *Opposite*: smooth

jerry-build *v* throw up, fling up, throw together *(infml)*, knock together *(infml)*

jerry-built *adj* poor, shoddy, jerry-rigged, cheap and nasty, flimsy

jerry can *n* can, container, canister

jest *(literary)* *n* joke, prank, hoax, quip, spoof ■ *v* banter, joke, kid, tease, quip

jester *n* fool, clown, comedian, entertainer, comic

jet *n* spurt, spout, fountain, squirt, stream

jetsam *n* odds and ends, flotsam, debris, detritus, rubbish

jet set *(infml) n* **glitterati**, high society, rich and famous, beautiful people, idle rich *Opposite:* hoi polloi

jettison *v* **throw away**, throw out, get rid of, abandon, discard *Opposite:* keep

jetty *n* **dock**, breakwater, quay, landing stage, pier

jewel *n* 1 **gemstone**, gem, precious stone, semi-precious stone, crystal 2 **ornament**, trinket, accessory

jib *v* **baulk**, stop short, pull up, recoil, retreat

jibe *see* **gibe**

jiffy *(infml) n* **moment**, second, minute, flash, instant

jig *v* **jerk**, skip, hop, caper, leap

jiggle *v* **wiggle**, waggle, shake, joggle, rattle

jigsaw *n* **puzzle**, jigsaw puzzle, picture puzzle, Chinese puzzle, tangram

jigsaw puzzle *see* **jigsaw**

jilt *v* **reject**, turn down, break up, split up, walk out *Opposite:* stick by

jingle *n* **tune**, song, refrain, chorus, ditty ■ *v* **tinkle**, rattle, ring, clink, clank

jingoism *n* **chauvinism**, patriotism, nationalism, xenophobia, hostility

jingoistic *adj* **chauvinistic**, patriotic, nationalistic, xenophobic, hostile

jinx *n* **curse**, plague, evil eye, spell, bad luck

jinxed *adj* **unlucky**, luckless, hapless, unfortunate, star-crossed *Opposite:* lucky

jitters *(infml) n* **nervousness**, agitation, uneasiness, anxiety, apprehension *Opposite:* calmness

jittery *adj* **nervous**, jumpy, on edge, edgy, fidgety *Opposite:* calm

job *n* 1 **occupation**, work, line, line of work, trade 2 **task**, duty, responsibility, chore, assignment 3 **position**, post, appointment, vacancy, role

jobbing *adj* **casual**, occasional, freelance, part-time, temporary *Opposite:* regular

jobless *adj* **unemployed**, out of work, laid off, unwaged, on benefit *Opposite:* employed

job-sharing *n* **part-time work**, work-sharing, sharing

jockey *n* **rider**, equestrian, steeplechaser, showjumper, competitor ■ *v* 1 **ride**, race, steeplechase, showjump, compete 2 **manoeuvre**, compete, contend, fight, struggle 3 **manipulate**, cajole, trick, deceive, talk into

jocular *adj* **funny**, joking, jokey, jovial, playful *Opposite:* solemn

jocularity *n* **wittiness**, comicality, humour, playfulness, jokiness *Opposite:* solemnity

jog *v* 1 **trot**, run, train, exercise, keep fit 2 **nudge**, prod, bump, push, bang

jogger *n* **runner**, sprinter, cross-country runner, harrier, athlete

joggle *v* **shake**, wiggle, waggle, jiggle, jerk

joie de vivre *n* **vitality**, enthusiasm, liveliness, exuberance, high-spiritedness *Opposite:* lethargy

join *v* 1 **fasten**, connect, link, unite, stick *Opposite:* separate 2 **connect**, link up, merge, bring together, unite *Opposite:* disengage 3 **sign up**, enrol, enlist, join up, go in with *Opposite:* leave ■ *n* **joint**, seam, connection, intersection, link

joined *adj* 1 **bonded**, fixed together, hinged, hitched, linked *Opposite:* detached 2 **associated**, allied, affiliated, twinned, connected *Opposite:* independent

joinery *n* **woodwork**, cabinetmaking, furniture making, carving, carpentry

join forces *v* **team up**, collaborate, get together, come together, rally *Opposite:* split

join in *v* **participate**, become involved, take part, enter into, take a turn *Opposite:* leave

joint *adj* **combined**, dual, shared, multiparty, united *Opposite:* individual ■ *n* **join**, linkage, link, junction, intersection

join together *v* **merge**, amalgamate, integrate, dovetail, associate *Opposite:* split

join up *v* 1 **enlist**, enrol, sign up, join, subscribe *Opposite:* quit 2 **meet up**, link, team up, come together, get together

joist *n* **beam**, spar, truss, support

joke *n* 1 **witticism**, shaggy dog story, tall story, pun, anecdote 2 **laughing stock**, butt, object of ridicule, fool, buffoon 3 **prank**, trick, practical joke, stunt, hoax ■ *v* **kid**, pretend, clown, play the fool, pull somebody's leg *(infml)*

joker *n* **clown**, fool, buffoon, comedian, comic

jokey *adj* **amusing**, good-humoured, light-hearted, flippant, funny *Opposite:* serious

joking *adj* **jokey**, playful, flippant, light-hearted, facetious *Opposite:* serious ■ *n* **clowning**, teasing, raillery, fooling around, fooling about

jollification *n* **festivity**, revelry, celebration, merrymaking, party

jolliness *see* **jollity**

jollity *n* **cheerfulness**, fun, hilarity, joviality, jolliness *Opposite:* seriousness

jolly *adj* **cheerful**, happy, fun, jovial, bright *Opposite:* sad ■ *adv (dated infml)* **very**, really, tremendously, hugely, terrifically

jolt *v* **shake**, jerk, bump, joggle, nudge ■ *n* 1 **bump**, shake, jerk, joggle, bounce 2 **shock**, surprise, bolt from the blue, blow, reminder

josh *(infml) v* **tease**, make fun of, chaff, ridicule, mock

jostle *v* **push**, knock, bump, elbow, shove

jot *n* **iota**, atom, bit, speck, tittle

jot down *v* **write down**, make a note of, scribble down, put on paper, put down

jotter *n* **notepad**, notebook, pad, personal organizer, writing pad

journal *n* 1 **periodical**, magazine, paper,

weekly, monthly **2 diary**, log, chronicle, record, register

journalism n **reporting**, reportage, broadcasting, commentary, fourth estate

journalist n **correspondent**, reporter, broadcaster, newsreader, columnist

journalistic adj **reporting**, editorial, newspaper, current affairs

journey n **trip**, voyage, expedition, ride, flight ▪ v **travel**, tour, go, trek, voyage

joust v **fight**, tilt, compete, battle, engage Opposite: agree

jovial adj **cheerful**, jolly, good-humoured, fun-loving, breezy Opposite: glum

joviality n **cheerfulness**, jollity, jolliness, cheeriness, bonhomie Opposite: glumness

jovialness see **joviality**

jowl n **jaw**, chin, jawbone, jawline, muzzle

joy n **1 happiness**, delight, enjoyment, bliss, ecstasy Opposite: sadness **2 delight**, jewel, treasure, pearl, angel

joyful adj **1 happy**, elated, ecstatic, thrilled, pleased Opposite: sad **2 wonderful**, blissful, pleasurable, fantastic, enjoyable Opposite: unpleasant

joyfulness n **happiness**, enjoyment, bliss, ecstasy, merriment Opposite: sadness

joyless adj **miserable**, cheerless, depressing, bleak, desolate Opposite: happy

joylessness n **cheerlessness**, misery, gloom, unhappiness, bleakness Opposite: happiness

joyous adj **happy**, merry, blissful, festive, cheerful Opposite: glum

joyousness n **happiness**, pleasure, bliss, joyfulness, jubilation Opposite: glumness

joyrider n **carjacker**, car thief, speeder, twoccer (slang), hot-rodder (slang)

joyriding n **carjacking**, car theft, speeding, hot-rodding (slang)

JP n **Justice of the Peace**, magistrate, justice, judge, arbitrator

jubilant adj **triumphant**, proud, thrilled, ecstatic, delighted Opposite: disappointed

jubilation n **elation**, triumph, joyousness, euphoria, delight Opposite: disappointment

jubilee n **anniversary**, celebration, commemoration, festival, festivity

judder v **shake**, vibrate, shudder, quiver, tremble ▪ n **shudder**, vibration, quiver, tremor, jerk

judge n **1 magistrate**, justice, justice of the peace, judge advocate **2 arbitrator**, adjudicator, moderator, umpire, referee **3 evaluator**, critic, reviewer, arbiter, expert ▪ v **1 arbitrate**, adjudicate, mediate, referee, umpire **2 assess**, evaluate, weigh, weigh up, look at **3 consider**, reckon, think, believe, maintain **4 estimate**, guess, consider, say, assess **5 condemn**, criticize, sneer at, belittle, pass judgment on

judgment n **1 verdict**, ruling, decision, finding, sentence **2 discernment**, good sense, shrewdness, wisdom, common sense **3 opinion**, view, considered opinion, feeling, thoughts

judgmental adj **critical**, hypercritical, condemnatory, negative, disapproving Opposite: complimentary

judicial adj **legal**, court, justice, official

judiciary n **judges**, bench, courts, magistrates

judicious adj **sensible**, wise, careful, shrewd, astute Opposite: foolish

judiciousness n **wisdom**, prudence, shrewdness, sense, care Opposite: foolishness

jug n **pitcher**, ewer, carafe, crock

juggernaut n **giant**, titan, leviathan, behemoth, goliath

juggle v **1 fit in**, manage, cope with, run, deal with **2 manipulate**, falsify, alter, misrepresent, tamper with

juice n **extract**, sap, liquid, fluid, liquor

juiciness n **succulence**, ripeness, lusciousness, moistness Opposite: dryness

juicy adj **1 succulent**, luscious, thirst-quenching, moist, ripe Opposite: dry **2** (infml) **titillating**, scandalous, salacious, exciting, sensational Opposite: dull

jumble v **mix up**, muddle, clutter, disarrange, shuffle Opposite: tidy ▪ n **1 muddle**, heap, clutter, hotchpotch, mishmash **2 unwanted items**, odds and ends, second-hand goods, castoffs, junk (infml)

jumbled adj **untidy**, topsy-turvy, muddled, chaotic, disorderly Opposite: orderly

jumbo adj **oversize**, outsize, huge, enormous, giant-sized Opposite: tiny

jump v **1 bound**, leap, hop, skip, soar **2 be startled**, be surprised, start, get a fright, be frightened **3** (infml) **obey**, do as you are told, conform, toe the line, play the game ▪ n **1 leap**, bound, hop, skip, spring **2 obstacle**, hurdle, fence, wall, hedge **3 start**, jolt, jerk, lurch, jar

jump back v **rebound**, recoil, bounce back, ricochet

jumper n **athlete**, high jumper, long jumper, hurdler, steeplechaser

jump in v **make a start**, take the plunge, get going, leap in, take the bull by the horns

jumpiness n **1 jitteriness**, anxiety, nervousness, agitation, edginess Opposite: calmness **2 jerkiness**, erraticism, unsteadiness, suddenness, abruptness Opposite: smoothness

jump-start v **1 kick-start**, start up, get going, set in motion, bump-start **2 stimulate**, trigger, set off, start up, kick-start ▪ n **1 kick-start**, bump-start, push-start, startup, start **2 stimulus**, momentum, spur, drive, impetus

jumpy adj **1 jittery**, anxious, nervous, worried, tense Opposite: calm **2 jerky**, erratic, unsteady, sudden, abrupt Opposite: smooth

junction n connection, intersection, seam, link, joint

juncture n 1 **point in time**, stage, moment, occasion, interval 2 *(fml)* **join**, connection, joint, link, seam

jungle n 1 **tropical forest**, rain forest, forest, wilderness, bush 2 **tangle**, muddle, maze, jumble, mess

junior adj **low-ranking**, subordinate, inferior, lower, low-grade Opposite: senior ■ n **subordinate**, underling, beginner, trainee, novice Opposite: old hand

junk *(infml)* n 1 **rubbish**, scrap, debris, litter, refuse 2 **second-hand goods**, jumble, unwanted items, castoffs, odds and ends ■ v **discard**, throw away, throw out, get rid of, scrap Opposite: keep

junket n **trip**, excursion, visit, outing, spree

junk food n **snack food**, convenience food, fast food, TV dinner

junk mail n **fliers**, leaflets, brochures, direct mail, mailshot

junta n 1 **military government**, military rule, regime, martial law, government 2 **cabal**, faction, clique, gang, band 3 **council**, committee, legislative body, assembly, forum

jurisdiction n 1 **authority**, dominion, influence, power, control 2 **area**, state, extent of power, territory, province

juror n **jury member**, assessor, estimator, judge, adjudicator

jury n **adjudicators**, judges, bench, panel, board

just adv 1 **a minute ago**, a moment ago, a second ago, only this minute, in the past few minutes 2 **at this moment**, now, immediately, presently, in a minute 3 **only**, merely, simply, solely, purely 4 **barely**, hardly, scarcely, slightly 5 **simply**, really, truly, definitely, emphatically 6 **exactly**, precisely, absolutely,

emphatically, completely ■ adj 1 **fair**, impartial, objective, unbiased, unprejudiced Opposite: unfair 2 **correct**, moral, ethical, good, appropriate Opposite: unjust 3 **reasonable**, valid, sensible, sound, balanced

just deserts n **what you deserve**, what was coming to you, just reward, comeuppance *(infml)*

justice n 1 **fairness**, reasonableness, impartiality, evenhandedness, righteousness Opposite: unfairness 2 **validity**, legitimacy, rightfulness, acceptability, reasonableness 3 **judge**, magistrate, justice of the peace, judge advocate

justifiable adj **defensible**, admissible, justified, reasonable, correct Opposite: indefensible

justification n **defence**, reason, reasoning, explanation, validation

justified adj **warranted**, defensible, vindicated, correct, right Opposite: unwarranted

justify v 1 **defend**, validate, explain, rationalize, excuse 2 **align**, adjust, straighten up, line up

justly adv 1 **fairly**, impartially, rightly, reasonably, honestly Opposite: unfairly 2 **correctly**, morally, deservedly, reasonably, justifiably Opposite: unjustly

just reward see just deserts

jut v **stick out**, protrude, overhang, poke out, project

juvenile adj 1 **youthful**, young, immature, adolescent, fresh-faced Opposite: mature 2 **childish**, infantile, babyish, puerile, immature Opposite: grown-up ■ n **youngster**, adolescent, young person, teenager, youth Opposite: adult

juxtapose v **put side by side**, put together, put next to, put beside, put adjacent to

juxtaposition n **collocation**, association, apposition, comparison, contrast

K

kaleidoscope n 1 **complex pattern**, phantasmagoria, display, mixture, medley 2 **series**, web, set, chain reaction, domino effect

kaleidoscopic adj **colourful**, variegated, multicoloured, many-coloured, motley Opposite: monochromatic

kangaroo *(infml)* v **jerk**, jump, leap, bump, jolt Opposite: glide

kaolin n **clay**, kaolinite, argil, potter's clay, potter's earth

kaput *(infml)* adj **broken**, ruined, wrecked, finished, ended Opposite: working

karaoke n **singing**, singsong, karaoke night, music, entertainment

karma n 1 **destiny**, fate, kismet, fortune, providence 2 *(infml)* **atmosphere**, aura, feeling, ambience, vibrations *(infml)*

kebab n **skewer**, brochette, grill stick

keel v **capsize**, turn upside down, upset, overturn, turn over Opposite: right

keel over *(infml)* v 1 **collapse**, fall over, faint,

pass out, lose consciousness *Opposite*: come to **2 capsize**, keel, turn upside down, upset, overturn *Opposite*: right

keen *adj* **1 eager**, enthusiastic, willing, fanatical, dedicated *Opposite*: indifferent **2 acute**, quick, clever, perceptive, alert *Opposite*: dull **3 sensitive**, responsive, finely honed, finely tuned, well-developed *Opposite*: insensitive **4 intense**, strong, acute, deep, powerful *Opposite*: mild **5** *(literary)* **sharp**, sharpened, whetted, bright, steely *Opposite*: blunt **6 icy**, bitter, cold, chilly, wintry *Opposite*: mild **7 competitive**, low, cheap, attractive, affordable *Opposite*: prohibitive ■ *v* **cry out**, wail, howl, weep, sob

keenness *n* **1 enthusiasm**, eagerness, zeal, passion, willingness *Opposite*: reluctance **2 fondness**, attraction, devotion, partiality, liking *Opposite*: aversion **3 acuteness**, perception, quickness, cleverness, perceptiveness *Opposite*: dullness **4 intensity**, intenseness, strength, acuteness, depth *Opposite*: mildness **5** *(literary)* **sharpness**, razor-sharpness, brightness, steeliness *Opposite*: bluntness **6 iciness**, bitterness, coldness, chill, wintriness *Opposite*: mildness **7 competitiveness**, lowness, cheapness, attractiveness, affordability

keen on *adj* **partial to**, taken with, fond of, wild about, gone on *(infml)*

keen-sighted *adj* **sharp-sighted**, sharp-eyed, eagle-eyed, hawk-eyed

keep *v* **1 hold onto**, hang onto, save, retain, have *Opposite*: let go **2 hide**, conceal, repress, withhold, hold back *Opposite*: let out **3 maintain**, hold, sustain, preserve, conserve *Opposite*: abandon **4 store**, hold, stash, stack, shelve *Opposite*: get rid of **5 continue**, go on, carry on, keep on, persist in *Opposite*: stop **6 honour**, fulfil, carry out, comply with, obey *Opposite*: break **7 detain**, delay, hold up, hold back, keep back *Opposite*: release **8 take care of**, care for, tend, look after, watch over **9 stay**, remain, be, keep yourself *Opposite*: become **10 own**, look after, care for, farm, rear

keep abreast *v* **stay current**, keep up, keep up to date, be well-informed, stay in touch

keep an eye on *v* **1 watch closely**, keep a close watch on, observe, spy on, watch **2 look after**, watch over, keep in check, mind, take care of

keep a secret *v* **not tell a soul**, be discreet, keep quiet, be the soul of discretion, keep mum *(infml)* *Opposite*: spill the beans *(infml)*

keep a straight face *v* **show no emotion**, have a poker face, look blank, dissemble, keep a stiff upper lip *(infml)*

keep at *v* **persevere**, persist, soldier on, keep your nose to the grindstone, stick to *Opposite*: give up

keep at bay *v* **hold off**, keep away, ward off, stave off, fend off *Opposite*: encourage

keep away *v* **hold off**, ward off, keep at bay, stave off, fend off *Opposite*: encourage

keep back *v* **1 withhold**, keep secret, suppress, omit, hide *Opposite*: reveal **2 reserve**, conserve, hold on to, save, withhold *Opposite*: use up **3 restrain**, curb, control, restrict, limit

keep count *v* **record**, note, keep a record of, note down, keep a note of *Opposite*: lose track of

keep down *v* **1 oppress**, suppress, repress, subjugate, subdue *Opposite*: liberate **2 limit**, curb, restrain, control, check

keeper *n* **custodian**, warder, guard, guardian, caretaker

keep fit *n* **physical exercise**, exercise, working out, aerobics, gymnastics ■ *v* **keep in shape**, exercise, work out, train, keep in trim

keep from *v* **1 withhold**, omit, hide, conceal, keep back *Opposite*: reveal **2 prevent**, restrain, stop, deter, prohibit *Opposite*: allow **3 protect**, shield, shelter, save, cushion *Opposite*: expose

keep going *v* **persevere**, carry on, persist, hold up, last *Opposite*: stop

keep in *v* **hold in**, repress, withhold, hold back, retain *Opposite*: let out

keep in check *v* **control**, restrict, restrain, curb, limit

keeping *n* **charge**, custody, possession, care, trust

keep in mind *v* **bear in mind**, remember, recall, retain *Opposite*: forget

keep in the dark *v* **keep in ignorance**, withhold information from, keep something back from, hold something back from, conceal something from *Opposite*: inform

keep mum *(infml)* *v* **keep quiet**, not tell a soul, be discreet, keep secret, keep under wraps *Opposite*: spill the beans *(infml)*

keep off *v* **1 hold off**, hold back, separate, shut out, ward off *Opposite*: encourage **2 abstain**, do without, go without, avoid, not touch *Opposite*: indulge

keep on *v* **continue**, persist, persevere, carry on, go on *Opposite*: give up

keep on at *(infml)* *v* **nag**, badger, pester, harp on, harass *Opposite*: give up on

keep out *v* **exclude**, shut out, bar, ban, deny entry *Opposite*: admit

keepsake *n* **memento**, reminder, souvenir, gift, token

keep secret *v* **withhold**, suppress, sit on, keep from, keep under wraps *Opposite*: let slip

keep the ball rolling *v* **continue**, keep things moving, keep things going, keep up the momentum, maintain momentum *Opposite*: stop

keep the lid on *v* **keep under control**, contain, control, suppress, restrain

keep to *v* **obey**, comply with, abide by, stick to, adhere to

keep track of *v* **follow**, keep an eye on, keep up with, monitor, keep up to date with *Opposite*: lose track of

keep under control *v* **keep in check**, restrain, contain, keep the lid on, suppress

keep under wraps *v* **keep secret**, keep to yourself, keep back, keep quiet, hide *Opposite*: reveal

keep up *v* **1** continue, sustain, maintain, carry on, persevere *Opposite*: stop **2 stay beside**, keep abreast, keep pace, stay even, match *Opposite*: fall behind **3 stay in touch**, keep in touch, keep in contact, keep abreast, keep up to date *Opposite*: lose touch

keep your chin up *v* **make the best of things**, take the bad with the good, look on the bright side, make the best of a bad job, not let things get the better of you *Opposite*: go under

keep your cool *(infml)* *v* **stay calm**, keep your head, calm down, simmer down, cool off

keep your word *v* **be as good as your word**, keep your promise, deliver on a promise, be true to your word, keep your side of the bargain *Opposite*: go back on

keg *n* **barrel**, cask, tub, firkin, drum

ken *n* **knowledge**, acquaintance, understanding, awareness, comprehension

kennel *n* **house**, hut, shelter

kerfuffle *(infml)* *n* **commotion**, disturbance, disorder, agitation, hubbub

kernel *n* **1 pip**, pit, stone *Opposite*: husk **2 core**, nub, root, heart, essence

kettle *n* **pot**, pan, cauldron, steamer, fish kettle

kettle of fish *n* **mess**, predicament, difficulty, problem, quagmire

key *n* **1 skeleton key**, master key, passe-partout, passkey, latchkey **2 pitch**, register, tone, scale, note **3 button**, knob, control **4 solution**, answer, explanation, means, secret ■ *adj* **important**, main, crucial, significant, vital *Opposite*: unimportant ■ *v* **input**, keyboard, enter, key in, type

keyboard *n* **control panel**, console, controls ■ *v* **type**, key, key in, input, enter

keyboarder *n* **keyboard operator**, typist, typesetter, data entry clerk *(US)*

keyhole *n* **hole**, aperture, spyhole, peephole, opening

key in *v* **key**, type, input, enter, typeset

keynote *n* **theme**, essence, idea, gist, core ■ *adj* **important**, crucial, major, essential, defining

key player *n* **leading light**, principal, kingpin *(infml)*, big cheese *(infml)*

keystone *n* **foundation**, basis, bedrock, underpinning, grounding

kibbutz *n* **collective**, commune, cooperative, community, settlement

kick *v* **1 boot**, strike, hack, put the boot in **2 dribble**, punt, place-kick, kick off **3 jolt**, jerk, recoil, flex, reflex **4** *(infml)* **give up**, quit,

end, cease, stop *Opposite*: take up ■ *n* **1 recoil**, rebound, return, reaction, reflex **2** *(infml)* **thrill**, boost, pleasure, excitement, frisson

kick back *(infml)* *v* **relax**, take it easy, lounge, loaf, veg out *(infml)*

kickback *n* **bribe**, softener, payment, reward, inducement

kick in *v* **1 break down**, smash, demolish, flatten, destroy **2** *(infml)* **take effect**, come on-stream, get going, get underway, start *Opposite*: run out

kick in the teeth *n* **setback**, blow, shock, betrayal, letdown *Opposite*: boost

kick off *(infml)* *v* **start**, begin, start the ball rolling, get underway, commence *Opposite*: end

kickoff *(infml)* *n* **start**, beginning, opening, initiation, commencement *(fml)* *Opposite*: end

kick out *(infml)* *v* **throw out**, sling out, eject, force out, make redundant *Opposite*: appoint

kick-start *v* **1 start up**, start, get going, turn over, crank up *Opposite*: stop **2 restart**, start, revive, resuscitate, jump-start ■ *n* *(infml)* **fillip**, shot in the arm, spur, stimulus, boost

kick up a fuss *v* **protest**, rampage, make a scene, make a fuss, complain *Opposite*: smooth over

kid *n* *(infml)* **child**, teenager, adolescent, youngster, toddler *Opposite*: adult ■ *v* **1 tease**, joke, poke fun at, make fun of, mock **2** *(infml)* **fool**, trick, delude, hoodwink, con. *See* COMPARE AND CONTRAST *at* youth.

kidder *n* **joker**, tease, trickster, clown, prankster

kiddy *(infml)* *n* **youngster**, child, baby, tot *(infml)*, kid *(infml)*

kidnap *v* **abduct**, take hostage, capture, take prisoner, hijack *Opposite*: release

kid's stuff *n* **child's play**, piece of cake, pushover, doddle *(infml)*

kill *v* **1 murder**, assassinate, execute, put to death, slaughter *Opposite*: revive **2** *(infml)* **switch off**, shut down, deactivate, disconnect, cut *Opposite*: start up

---

COMPARE AND CONTRAST CORE MEANING: deprive of life

kill cause the death of a person or animal; **murder** take the life of another person deliberately and not in self-defence in a serious criminal act; **assassinate** murder a public figure by a sudden violent attack; **execute** take somebody's life as part of a judicial or extrajudicial process; **put to death** deliberately take somebody's life, especially in accordance with a legal death sentence; **slaughter** kill farm animals for food, or kill a person or large numbers of people brutally; **slay** *(fml or literary)* kill a person or animal; **put down** *or* **put to sleep** kill a sick or injured animal, especially when done by a vet.

killer n **1 murderer**, assassin, slaughterer, executioner, exterminator **2 disease**, destroyer, natural disaster, predator

killing n **murder**, assassination, butchery, slaughter, carnage

killjoy n **spoilsport**, party pooper (infml), sourpuss (infml), wet blanket (infml), misery (infml) Opposite: merrymaker

kill off v **put an end to**, stop, halt, destroy, end Opposite: set up

kill time v **pass the time**, waste time, wait, loiter, twiddle your thumbs

kill yourself v **commit suicide**, end it all, take your own life, top yourself (slang)

kill yourself laughing v **laugh your head off**, double over, have hysterics (infml), split your sides (infml), crease up (infml)

kiln n **oven**, furnace, forge

kilt v **pleat**, gather, fold, crease, smock

kimono n **dressing gown**, negligée, peignoir, bathrobe, robe

kin n **family**, relatives, relations, nearest and dearest, kith and kin

kind adj **caring**, nice, generous, gentle, compassionate Opposite: inhumane ■ n **type**, sort, class, variety, category. See COMPARE AND CONTRAST at type, generous.

kind-hearted adj **kind**, caring, sympathetic, nice, gentle

kind-heartedness n **kindness**, sympathy, compassion, benevolence, thoughtfulness Opposite: cruelty

kindle v **1 encourage**, stimulate, stir up, fire up, promote Opposite: quench **2 spark**, light, set alight, burn, ignite Opposite: douse

kindliness n **kindness**, compassion, sympathy, amiability, gentleness Opposite: cruelty

kindly adj **friendly**, sympathetic, generous, caring, kind ■ adv **gently**, compassionately, sympathetically, benevolently, kind-heartedly Opposite: cruelly

kindness n **compassion**, gentleness, sympathy, kind-heartedness, benevolence Opposite: cruelty

kind of (infml) adv **rather**, somewhat, fairly, in a way, quite

kindred adj **associated**, close, like, alike, allied Opposite: dissimilar ■ n **1 kinship**, family, kin, blood, ties **2 family**, relations, relatives, kinsfolk, nearest and dearest

king n **1 monarch**, sovereign, ruler, rajah, tsar Opposite: subject **2 ruler**, chief, head, leader, dictator **3 leader**, star, superstar, luminary, leading light

kingdom n **realm**, empire, monarchy, territory, domain

kingly adj **magnificent**, stately, grand, majestic, regal

kingpin (infml) n **key player**, leading light, principal, superstar, linchpin

kingship n **monarchy**, sovereignty, crown, power, authority

king-size adj **extra-large**, outsize, enormous, huge, giant Opposite: miniature

kink n **bend**, twist, crook, hook, bow

kinky adj **1 unusual**, strange, idiosyncratic, quirky, unnatural Opposite: conventional **2 crinkled**, crinkly, twisty, knotted, twisted Opposite: straight

kinsfolk n **family**, relatives, relations, kindred, kith and kin

kinship n **1 relationship**, connection, tie, link, bond **2 relatedness**, understanding, empathy, affiliation, affinity

kinsman (fml) n **relative**, relation, family member

kinswoman (fml) n **relative**, relation, family member

kiosk n **booth**, stall, stand, hut

kip (infml) n **nap**, sleep, doze, forty winks (infml), snooze (infml)

kismet n **fate**, fortune, luck, destiny, doom

kiss v **1 peck**, smooch (infml), canoodle (infml), osculate (fml), neck (dated) **2 touch**, brush, glance, graze, caress ■ n **1 caress**, light touch, contact, graze, pat **2 peck**, embrace, smacker (infml), smooch (infml), canoodle (infml)

kiss-and-tell (infml) adj **revealing**, exposing, divulging, sensational, scandalous

kit n **1 tackle**, tools, equipment, implements, supplies **2 set of clothes**, dress, strip, apparel, costume **3 belongings**, things, stuff, baggage, luggage

kitbag n **canvas bag**, knapsack, backpack, rucksack, duffel bag

kitchen n **kitchenette**, galley, scullery

kith and kin n **relatives**, family, relations, kinsfolk, flesh and blood

kit out v **equip**, prepare, provide, fit out, supply

kitsch n **1 vulgarity**, tastelessness, sentimentality, ostentation, showiness Opposite: tastefulness **2 trash**, frippery, junk (infml), tack (infml) ■ adj **tasteless**, in poor taste, vulgar, common, loud Opposite: tasteful

kittenish adj **1 playful**, frisky, lively, coltish, frolicsome Opposite: staid **2 flirtatious**, coy, frisky, cute, coquettish (literary)

kitty n **1** (infml) **cat**, kitten, puss (infml), pussy (infml), pussycat (infml) **2 fund**, pool, stake, ante, pot (US infml)

klaxon n **horn**, siren, alarm, signal

knack n **ability**, skill, talent, flair, aptitude. See COMPARE AND CONTRAST at talent.

knapsack n **bag**, shoulder bag, rucksack, backpack, daypack

knead v **massage**, rub, work, mould, manipulate

knee-deep *adj* **involved**, occupied, engrossed, absorbed, immersed *Opposite*: uninvolved

knee-jerk *(infml) adj* **1 unthinking**, automatic, reflex, habitual, immediate *Opposite*: considered **2 predictable**, prejudging, prejudiced, biased, dyed-in-the-wool *Opposite*: unpredictable

kneel *v* go down on your knees, genuflect, kneel down, kowtow *Opposite*: rise

knees-up *(infml) n* **party**, celebration, festivity, fiesta, bash *(infml)*

knell *n* toll, ring, peal, sound, ringing

knick-knack *n* trinket, ornament, curio, souvenir, object

knife *v* stab, spear, stick, wound, lacerate

WORD BANK
❏ **types of knife** bread knife, butcher's knife, carving knife, clasp knife, cleaver, flick knife, jackknife, paperknife, paring knife, penknife, steak knife, table knife

knife-edge *n* **critical point**, decisive point, turning point, watershed, crisis

knight *n* **cavalier**, caballero, knight-errant, adventurer

knit *v* **1 heal**, mend, set, join, meld **2 unite**, join, interweave, weave, interlace

knob *n* **1 handle**, doorknob, dial, button, handhold **2 lump**, bump, bulge, protuberance, protrusion

knobbly *adj* **lumpy**, bumpy, ridged, bony, protuberant *Opposite*: smooth

knock *v* **1 hit**, bump, collide, bang, thump **2** *(infml)* **criticize**, disparage, condemn, censure, belittle *Opposite*: praise ■ *n* **1 blow**, collision, hit, bump, bang **2** *(infml)* **setback**, blow, upset, misfortune, kick in the teeth

knock about *(infml) v* **1 beat**, hit, mistreat, abuse, batter **2 spend time**, kick about *(infml)*, hang about *(infml)*, hang out *(infml)*, hang around *(infml)*

knockabout *adj* **1 physical**, slapstick, boisterous, rowdy, rough *Opposite*: decorous **2 sturdy**, stout, strong, solid, substantial *Opposite*: flimsy ■ *n* **1 slapstick**, physical comedy, visual comedy, clowning, buffoonery **2** *(infml)* **game**, informal game, friendly, friendly game, knock-up

knock back *(infml) v* **down**, gulp, swallow, drink, put back

knock down *v* **1 floor**, fell, knock over, hit, strike **2 destroy**, demolish, dismantle, bulldoze, pull down *Opposite*: build **3 reduce the price of**, discount, mark down, lower, reduce *Opposite*: put up

knockdown *adj* **cheap**, reduced, low, rock-bottom, bargain *Opposite*: inflated

knocker *n* **1 door fixture**, knob, handle, bell, doorbell **2** *(infml)* **critic**, faultfinder, detractor, carper, caviller *Opposite*: admirer

knock off *(infml) v* **1 stop work**, finish, call it a day, down tools, leave *Opposite*: start **2 deduct**, take off, discount, subtract, reduce *Opposite*: add **3 mass-produce**, churn out, knock out, turn out, rattle off

knockoff *(infml) n* **copy**, fake, forgery, reproduction, counterfeit *Opposite*: original

knock-on effect *n* **consequence**, outcome, result, upshot, conclusion

knock out *v* **1 make unconscious**, hit, floor, fell, knock down **2 eliminate**, put out, defeat, overcome, beat **3 surprise**, amaze, astound, impress, overwhelm

knockout *(infml) n* **big success**, hit, sensation, triumph, winner *Opposite*: flop *(infml)*

knock over *v* **1 upset**, topple, overturn, tip over, spill **2** *(infml)* **surprise**, amaze, astound, impress, overwhelm

knock together *(infml) v* **assemble**, improvise, make up, concoct, cobble together

knock up *(infml) v* **improvise**, assemble, make up, concoct, knock together *(infml)*

knoll *n* **hill**, hillock, hummock, mound, mount

knot *n* **1 tie**, loop, reef knot, granny knot **2 lump**, bump, bulge, protuberance, nub **3 cluster**, huddle, clutch, band, collection ■ *v* **join**, tie, bind, tether, secure *Opposite*: untie

knotted *adj* **tied**, tense, secured, taut, tangled *Opposite*: relaxed

knotty *adj* **tricky**, awkward, complicated, complex, thorny *Opposite*: simple

know *v* **1 understand**, be aware of, be knowledgeable about, comprehend, appreciate **2 experience**, go through, undergo **3 be acquainted with**, be familiar with, distinguish, see, have knowledge of

knowable *adj* **intelligible**, comprehensible, understandable, coherent, identifiable *Opposite*: unknowable

know-all *(infml) n* **smart aleck** *(infml)*, clever Dick *(infml)*, clever clogs *(infml)*, smartypants *(infml)*, wiseacre *(infml)*

know backwards *v* **know well**, know back to front, know inside out, know like the back of your hand

know-how *(infml) n* **knowledge**, experience, expertise, savoir-faire, proficiency

knowing *adj* **1 meaningful**, significant, expressive, eloquent, perceptive *Opposite*: innocent **2 deliberate**, intentional, intended, conscious, calculating *Opposite*: unconscious

knowledge *n* **1 acquaintance**, familiarity, awareness, understanding, comprehension *Opposite*: ignorance **2 information**, facts, data, gen *(infml)* **3 wisdom**, learning, education, scholarship, erudition

knowledgeable *adj* **well-informed**, au fait, conversant, familiar, informed *Opposite*: ignorant

known *adj* **recognized**, identified, acknowledged, accepted, branded *Opposite*: unknown

knuckle *n* **protuberance**, projection, lump, prominence, bulge

knuckle down *(infml)* *v* **work hard**, apply yourself, get down to it, get your head down, buckle down *(infml)*

knuckle under *v* **give in**, give up, admit defeat, concede defeat, concede *Opposite*: continue

kohl *n* **eyeliner**, eye pencil, mascara

kosher *(infml)* *adj* **1 genuine**, authentic, true, real, bona fide *Opposite*: fake **2 lawful**, acceptable, legitimate, aboveboard, proper *Opposite*: unlawful

kowtow *v* **1 kneel**, bow, genuflect, prostrate oneself, salaam *Opposite*: stand up **2 grovel**, be servile, be obsequious, show deference, bow and scrape *Opposite*: lord it over ■ *n* **bow**, genuflection, prostration, salaam, homage

kudos *n* **glory**, praise, credit, fame, admiration *Opposite*: discredit

L

laager *n* **camp**, encampment, settlement, defensive position, shelter

lab *(infml)* *n* **workroom**, workshop, test bed, test centre, laboratory

label *n* **1 tag**, ticket, sticker, marker, sticky label **2 make**, brand name, trade name, trademark, mark **3 description**, categorization, classification, characterization ■ *v* **1 put a label on**, mark, identify, stamp **2 consider**, regard, describe, categorize, class

laboratory *n* **workroom**, workshop, test bed, test centre, research laboratory

laborious *adj* **arduous**, backbreaking, strenuous, hard, tough *Opposite*: easy. See COMPARE AND CONTRAST at **hard**.

laboriousness *n* **difficulty**, arduousness, hardness, toughness, tedium *Opposite*: ease

labour *n* **1 work**, toil, hard work, manual labour, efforts **2 workers**, workforce, employees, labour force, hands *Opposite*: management **3 task**, job, chore, effort, exertion **4 childbirth**, delivery, giving birth, contractions, confinement *(dated)* ■ *v* **1 strive**, strain, grind away, endeavour, keep at it *Opposite*: idle **2 struggle**, exert, grapple, wrestle, agonize **3 malfunction**, strain, complain, play up, seize up **4 drag yourself**, stagger, plod, trudge, trail *Opposite*: skip **5 overemphasize**, go on, dwell on, exaggerate, drive home *Opposite*: skim

laboured *adj* **tortured**, tortuous, forced, strenuous, arduous *Opposite*: effortless

labourer *n* **manual worker**, blue-collar worker, hand, workhand, worker

labour force *n* **workforce**, workers, labour, hands, staff

labour under *v* **suffer from**, struggle with, be disadvantaged by, be burdened with, be swayed by

labyrinth *n* **maze**, warren, web, tangle, jumble

labyrinthine *adj* **complex**, convoluted, intricate, complicated, tortuous *Opposite*: straightforward

lace *n* **tie**, shoelace, bootlace, cord ■ *v* **1 do up**, tie up, lace up, fasten *Opposite*: undo **2 spike**, mix, fortify

lacerate *v* **slash**, tear, cut, score, scratch

laceration *n* **cut**, slash, graze, scratch, tear

lack *n* **shortage**, absence, want, dearth, deficiency *Opposite*: surplus ■ *v* **be short of**, not have, be deficient in, want for, need *Opposite*: have

---

COMPARE AND CONTRAST CORE MEANING: an insufficiency or absence of something

lack a complete absence of a particular thing; **shortage** a lack of something that is needed or required; **deficiency** a shortfall in the amount of something necessary, e.g. a particular nutrient in the human body, or an inadequacy in the supply or performance of something; **deficit** the amount by which something falls short of a target amount or level; **want** *or* **dearth** a scarcity or absence of something.

---

lackadaisical *adj* **apathetic**, careless, indifferent, relaxed, half-hearted *Opposite*: enthusiastic

lackey *n* **minion**, lapdog, sycophant, toady, creature

lacking *adj* **missing**, not there, wanting, absent *Opposite*: present

lacking in *adj* **short of**, without, not having, bereft of, devoid of *Opposite*: full of

lacklustre *adj* **dull**, lifeless, dreary, unexciting, uninspiring *Opposite*: dazzling

laconic *adj* **terse**, brief, short, concise, economical *Opposite*: long-winded

lacquer *n* **polish**, varnish, gloss

lacy *adj* **delicate**, lacelike, net, filigree, fine

lad *n* **1 boy**, young man, youngster, youth, teenager *Opposite*: lass **2** *(infml)* **man**, guy *(infml)*, fella *(infml)*, bloke *(infml)*, chap *(infml)* Opposite: lass

ladder *n* **1 stepladder**, folding ladder, loft ladder, roof ladder, steps **2 ranking**, tree, table, pecking order, hierarchy ▪ *v* **run**, rip, tear, snag

laddie *(infml)* see **lad**

laddish *(infml) adj* **male**, masculine, macho, sexist, chauvinist

laden *adj* **weighed down**, burdened, overloaded, loaded Opposite: empty

la-di-da *(infml) adj* **affected**, pretentious, snobbish, put-on, full of airs and graces Opposite: common

lady *n* **woman**, female, matron

lag *v* **1 drop back**, drop behind, fall back, fall behind, trail Opposite: lead **2 insulate**, wrap, wad, protect, pad ▪ *n* **interval**, wait, delay, intermission, pause

laggard *n* **straggler**, dawdler, shirker, slacker, idler Opposite: leader

lagging *n* **insulation**, wadding, padding, sleeve, skin

lagoon *n* **1 inlet**, creek, cove, bay **2 lake**, pond, pool, loch, lough

lah-di-dah *(infml)* see **la-di-da**

laid-back *(infml) adj* **relaxed**, easygoing, easy, phlegmatic, cool Opposite: tense

lair *(infml) n* **hideout**, den, haunt, retreat, hideaway

laird *n* **landowner**, lord, landlord, property owner, owner

laissez-faire *n* **noninterventionism**, nonintervention, noninvolvement, laxity Opposite: intervention ▪ *adj* **noninterventionist**, unrestrictive, permissive, freewheeling, lax Opposite: proactive

laity *n* **1 laypeople**, flock, congregation, worshippers Opposite: clergy **2 nonprofessionals**, outsiders, amateurs, uninitiated

lake *n* **pond**, lagoon, loch, tarn, water

lakeside *n* **shore**, waterside, water's edge, bank, land

lama *n* **monk**, priest, brother, father, clergyman

lambaste *v* **attack**, upbraid, reprimand, criticize, reprove Opposite: praise

lambent *adj* **brilliant**, scintillating, witty, sharp, rapier-like Opposite: leaden

lament *v* **mourn**, grieve, weep, cry for, bemoan Opposite: celebrate ▪ *n* **lamentation**, cry, dirge, crying, weeping Opposite: celebration

lamentable *adj* **regrettable**, deplorable, inexcusable, execrable, appalling Opposite: laudable

lamentation *n* **lament**, dirge, cry, weeping, crying Opposite: celebration

laminate *v* **cover**, seal, coat, protect, enclose

laminated *adj* **plastic-coated**, coated, covered, bonded, composite

lampoon *v* **ridicule**, satirize, make fun of, parody, caricature ▪ *n* **satire**, parody, skit, sketch, caricature

lamppost *n* **streetlight**, streetlamp, light

lance *n* **spear**, weapon, bayonet, javelin ▪ *v* **cut**, pierce, prick, slice into, slice open

land *n* **1 earth**, ground, terrain, countryside **2 property**, plot, parcel, lot, acreage **3 homeland**, nation, country, territory ▪ *v* **1 arrive**, set down, alight, come down, touch down Opposite: take off **2 acquire**, get, annex, gain, obtain Opposite: lose

landed *adj* **property-owning**, landowning, wealthy, propertied, rich Opposite: landless

landfall *n* **1 arrival**, landing, touchdown, docking, mooring **2 land**, dry land, mainland, terra firma, shore

land forces *n* **army**, ground forces, troops, infantry, soldiers

landholder *n* **landowner**, landlord, property-owner, proprietor, owner

landing *n* **1 arrival**, alighting, touchdown, docking, mooring **2 mooring**, pier, jetty, quay, landing stage **3 mezzanine**, half floor, top of the stairs

landing field see **landing strip**

landing stage *n* **jetty**, quay, mooring, landing

landing strip *n* **runway**, airstrip, airfield, aerodrome, landing field

landlady *n* **1 property owner**, landowner, landholder, proprietor, owner Opposite: tenant **2 licensee**, proprietor, manager, hotelier, innkeeper

landless *adj* **dispossessed**, evicted, ousted, powerless Opposite: landed

landline *n* **cable**, line, phone line, wire, link

landlocked *adj* **closed in**, blocked-in, noncoastal, interior Opposite: coastal

landlord *n* **1 property owner**, landowner, landholder, proprietor, owner Opposite: tenant **2 licensee**, proprietor, manager, hotelier, innkeeper

landmark *n* **1 marker**, sight, attraction, sign, signpost **2 breakthrough**, milestone, revolution, innovation, benchmark ▪ *adj* **milestone**, breakthrough, momentous, revolutionary, innovative Opposite: run-of-the-mill

landmass *n* **continent**, land, landform, island, mainland

land on your feet *v* **come out on top**, succeed, get lucky, come through unscathed, find yourself Opposite: fail

landowner *n* **property owner**, landlord, owner, proprietor, landlady Opposite: tenant

landscape *n* **1 scenery**, countryside, land, site, scene **2 painting**, picture, watercolour, oil painting, drawing **3 background**, backdrop, circumstances, situation, setting ▪ *v* **design**, model, form, shape, plan out

landslide *n* **1 avalanche**, landslip, rock fall,

mudslide **2 victory**, rout, win, success, triumph

landslip n **landslide**, avalanche, rock fall, mudslide

landward adj **inland**, inward, inward-looking, inner, innermost

landwards adv **inland**, ashore, inwards, in

land with (infml) v **saddle with**, burden, dump with, encumber, load

lane n **traffic lane**, right-hand lane, right lane, fast lane, slow lane

language n **1 tongue**, idiom, dialect, parlance, lingo (infml) **2 communication**, speech, talking **3 words**, vocabulary, writing, prose, poetry

COMPARE AND CONTRAST CORE MEANING: communication by words

language the human use of spoken or written words as a communication system, or the particular system of communication prevailing in a specific country, nation, or community; **vocabulary** the body of words that make up a particular language; **tongue** a particular language used by a specific country, nation, or community; **dialect** a form of a language spoken in a particular region or by members of a particular social class or profession; **slang** words and expressions used instead of standard terms in casual speech or writing, or by a particular group of people; **jargon** terms associated with a particular specialized activity, profession, or culture, especially terms that are not generally understood by outsiders; **parlance** the style of speech or writing used by people in a particular context or profession; **lingo** (infml) the way of speaking associated with a particular, usually specialized, group of people; **-speak** a suffix added to nouns to describe the language used by a particular group of people or in a particular context, suggesting that this way of speaking or writing is obscure or difficult to follow; **-ese** a suffix added to nouns to describe the language associated with a group of people, especially when it resembles jargon.

languid adj **unhurried**, relaxed, languorous, lazy, indolent Opposite: vigorous

languish v **1 suffer**, weaken, fail, flag, deteriorate Opposite: thrive **2 decline**, fail, sink, teeter, fade away Opposite: thrive **3 pine**, pine away, long for, grieve

languor n **tiredness**, listlessness, lethargy, sluggishness, dreaminess Opposite: vigour

languorous adj **tired**, listless, lethargic, languid, sluggish Opposite: vigorous

laniard see **lanyard**

lank adj **limp**, lifeless, dull, thin, floppy

lanky adj **gangling**, gangly, long-legged, leggy, angular Opposite: rotund

lanyard n **rope**, cord, line, cable, halyard

lap n **1 circuit**, tour, round, circle **2 stage**, leg, part, segment, section ■ v **lick up**, slurp, lap up, drink

lapdog n **minion**, toady, sycophant, lackey, creature

lap of luxury n **bed of roses**, life of Riley, life of ease, Easy Street

lapse n **1 error**, slip, failure, mistake, blunder **2 interval**, space, break, delay, pause ■ v **1 decline**, tumble, descend, drop, fall Opposite: rise **2 slip**, tail off, trail off, drift, falter Opposite: start up **3 come to an end**, end, fail, give up, stop Opposite: renew

lapsed adj **failed**, onetime, former, erstwhile, recent Opposite: current

lapse into v **1 slide into**, slip into, fall into, drift into, resort to Opposite: choose **2 revert**, regress, backslide, relapse, fall back Opposite: progress

lap up v **1 lick up**, slurp up, lap **2 enjoy**, soak up, bask in, love, glory in Opposite: hate **3 swallow**, fall for, believe, be fooled by, take in Opposite: disbelieve

larceny (dated) n **theft**, stealing, robbery, thieving, embezzlement

larder n **pantry**, cold-room, storeroom, room, cupboard

large adj **1 big**, huge, great, sizable, immense Opposite: tiny **2 well-built**, outsized, hefty, bulky, ample Opposite: small **3 sizable**, considerable, not inconsiderable, significant, substantial Opposite: insignificant

large-hearted adj **generous**, giving, kind, kindly, kind-hearted Opposite: mean-spirited

largely adv **mainly**, in the main, mostly, for the most part, principally Opposite: particularly

largeness n **size**, bulk, expansiveness, mass, extent Opposite: smallness

larger-than-life adj **flamboyant**, confident, impressive, exaggerated, overstated Opposite: understated

large-scale adj **major**, important, significant, extensive, sweeping Opposite: small-scale

largesse n **1 generosity**, charity, liberality, munificence, benevolence Opposite: miserliness **2 gifts**, handouts, aid, assistance, donations

lark n **game**, joke, prank, caper, high jinks (infml)

lark about v **fool about**, play the fool, fool around, mess about (infml), mess around (infml) Opposite: behave

lark around see **lark about**

lash n **1 hit**, whip, blow, stroke, whiplash **2 cat-o'-nine-tails**, cat, whip, belt, switch ■ v **1 smash**, pound, beat, impact, bump **2 criticize**, lambaste, upbraid, condemn, slate (infml) **3 whip**, flog, flay, thrash, strike **4 shake**, jerk, thrash, twitch, thump **5 tie**, bind, fasten, knot, secure Opposite: loosen

lashings n **lots**, plenty, loads (infml), heaps (infml), piles (infml) Opposite: little

lash out v **1** (infml) **spend**, fritter, squander, run through, shell out Opposite: save **2 attack**, strike out, hit out, let fly, flail around **3 criti-**

cize, lambaste, berate, hit out, tear into *Opposite*: praise

lass *n* girl, miss, young woman, daughter, lassie *(infml) Opposite*: lad

lassie *see* lass

lassitude *n* weariness, listlessness, apathy, lethargy, fatigue *Opposite*: liveliness

lasso *n* noose, rope, loop, tether, riata

last *adj* **1** previous, latter, past, preceding, latest *Opposite*: next **2** final, end, ultimate, closing, concluding *Opposite*: first **3** remaining, surviving, extant, final, sole remaining *Opposite*: original ■ *v* keep, stay fresh, keep going, carry on, go on *Opposite*: die out

last-ditch *adj* eleventh-hour, desperate, emergency, frantic, frenzied

lasting *adj* permanent, long-lasting, long-term, lifelong, eternal *Opposite*: temporary

lastly *adv* finally, last of all, to finish, to conclude, to end *Opposite*: firstly

last minute *n* eleventh hour, final moment, last ditch, last gasp

last-minute *adj* late, tardy, delayed, overdue, belated *Opposite*: prompt

last name *n* surname, family name, name, patronymic, matronymic *Opposite*: given name

last out *v* survive, live, go on, continue, persist *Opposite*: fail

last resort *n* last chance, only hope, last-ditch effort, fallback

last straw *n* final straw, limit, end, breaking point, deciding factor

latch *n* fastener, handle, bolt, key, bar

latch on *(infml) v* understand, grasp, comprehend, get *(infml)*, catch on *(infml)*

latch onto *v* **1** stay with, stick to, fasten onto, befriend, take up with *Opposite*: abandon **2** take to, discover, get into, go in for, pursue

late *adj* **1** delayed, tardy, overdue, belated, unpunctual *Opposite*: early **2** later, delayed, deferred, postponed *Opposite*: early **3** late-night, nighttime, evening, twilight *Opposite*: early **4** dead, much lamented, late lamented, deceased *(fml)*, dear departed *(fml or literary) Opposite*: living **5** last-minute, eleventh-hour, last-ditch, final *Opposite*: early ■ *adv* **1** belatedly, unpunctually, tardily, behind schedule, behind time *Opposite*: early **2** at the last minute, too late, late on, finally, at the end *Opposite*: early **3** at night, in the small hours, in the dead of night, in the evening, after dark *Opposite*: early **4** recently, until recently, lately, of late, latterly. *See* COMPARE AND CONTRAST *at* dead.

latecomer *n* straggler, dawdler, laggard

lately *adv* recently, of late, these days, latterly, currently

latency *n* dormancy, inactivity, potential, expectancy, underdevelopment *Opposite*: expression

lateness *n* tardiness, unpunctuality, delay, belatedness, deferment *Opposite*: promptness

latent *adj* **1** hidden, covert, buried, concealed, invisible *Opposite*: manifest **2** dormant, inactive, lurking, embryonic, underlying

later *adv* later on, in a while, shortly, soon, afterwards *Opposite*: earlier

lateral *adj* side, on the side, adjacent, crossways, horizontal

latest *adj* newest, up-to-the-minute, hottest, state-of-the-art, modern *Opposite*: outdated

latex *n* sap, fluid, liquid

lather *n* **1** foam, suds, froth, bubbles, soapsuds **2** *(infml)* agitation, anxiety, panic, dither, pother *Opposite*: calmness ■ *v* soap, lather up, soap up

latitude *n* **1** parallel, position, location, coordinate *Opposite*: longitude **2** leeway, freedom, autonomy, liberty, room *Opposite*: restriction

latter *adj* last, final, concluding, second, end *Opposite*: former

latter-day *adj* modern, modern-day, contemporary, current *Opposite*: former

latterly *adv* **1** recently, lately, up till now, currently, of late *Opposite*: formerly **2** at the end, towards the end, in the last part, finally *Opposite*: initially

lattice *n* frame, mesh, framework, web, matrix

laud *v* praise, applaud, extol, acclaim, glorify *Opposite*: criticize

laudable *adj* admirable, praiseworthy, creditable, worthy, commendable *Opposite*: despicable

laudatory *adj* admiring, congratulatory, praising, complimentary, approving *Opposite*: damning

laugh *v* chuckle, chortle, guffaw, giggle, snigger *Opposite*: cry ■ *n* **1** chuckle, chortle, guffaw, giggle, hoot **2** *(infml)* fun, joke, teasing, giggle, lark

laughable *adj* pathetic, pitiful, derisory, inadequate, ridiculous *Opposite*: impressive

laugh at *v* sneer, jeer, mock, make fun of, ridicule *Opposite*: respect

laughing stock *n* figure of fun, joke, fool, buffoon, butt

laugh off *v* downplay, trivialize, shrug off, joke about, dismiss *Opposite*: face up to

laugh out of court *v* ridicule, mock, make fun of, scoff at, pour scorn on

laughter *n* happiness, amusement, hilarity, mirth, merriment *Opposite*: sadness

launch *v* **1** dispatch, send off, send, shoot, fire **2** open, start, begin, commence, initiate **3** introduce, present, inaugurate, unveil, reveal **4** hurl, throw, toss, fling, propel ■ *n* presentation, introduction, promotion, unveiling, inauguration

launching pad n **takeoff point**, springboard, start, base, foundation

launch into v **embark on**, get going on, break into, begin, commence

launch out v 1 **start**, start afresh, start anew, start out, begin *Opposite*: finish 2 *(infml)* **treat yourself**, indulge yourself, spend money like water, go mad, splash out *Opposite*: stint

launder v 1 **wash**, clean, dry-clean, valet 2 **legalize**, filter, clean, decontaminate

laundry n **washing**, wash, clean washing, dirty washing

laurels n **success**, glory, honour, achievements

lavish adj 1 **abundant**, plentiful, sumptuous, copious, prolific *Opposite*: scanty 2 **extravagant**, profligate, wasteful, unrestrained, excessive *Opposite*: frugal ■ v **heap**, pour, smother, cover, load *Opposite*: deprive

law n 1 **rule**, regulation, decree, act, edict 2 **principle**, theory, formula, rule

law-abiding adj **honest**, straight, upright, upstanding, peaceable *Opposite*: crooked *(infml)*

law and order n 1 **law enforcement**, keeping the peace, order, orderliness, policing *Opposite*: crime 2 **stability**, harmony, peace, peace and quiet, peacefulness *Opposite*: unrest

lawbreaker n **criminal**, felon, wrongdoer, convict, offender

lawful adj **legal**, legalized, legitimate, official, endorsed *Opposite*: unlawful. *See* COMPARE AND CONTRAST *at* **legal**.

lawgiver *see* **lawmaker**

lawless adj **unruly**, anarchic, uncontrolled, unregulated, ungovernable *Opposite*: law-abiding

lawlessness n **anarchy**, chaos, disorder, unruliness, mayhem *(infml) Opposite*: order

lawmaker n **legislator**, policymaker, lawgiver

lawsuit n **court case**, proceedings, litigation, process

lawyer n **legal representative**, notary, solicitor, barrister, trial lawyer

lax adj 1 **lenient**, soft, tolerant, permissive, accepting 2 **negligent**, slack, careless, slipshod, sloppy *Opposite*: strict 3 **limp**, loose, flaccid, relaxed, floppy *Opposite*: tense

laxity n 1 **leniency**, tolerance, permissiveness, softness, forbearance *(fml) Opposite*: severity 2 **carelessness**, negligence, sloppiness, slackness, indifference *Opposite*: vigilance

laxness *see* **laxity**

lay v **put down**, place, rest, put, arrange *Opposite*: pick up ■ adj **untrained**, amateur, nonprofessional, uninitiated, unqualified *Opposite*: professional

lay about v **strike out**, hit out, thrash about, flail around, hit

layabout n **slacker**, shirker, timewaster, idler, lounger *Opposite*: go-getter *(infml)*

lay bare v **reveal**, explain, show, expose, display *Opposite*: cover up

lay before v **set before**, present, put before, submit, set out *Opposite*: withdraw

lay bets v **bet**, gamble, wager, stake money on .

lay claim to v **appropriate**, claim, stake a claim to, demand, insist on *Opposite*: renounce

lay down v 1 **put down**, lay aside, put aside, give up, surrender *Opposite*: take up 2 **decree**, set down, put down, formulate, rule

lay down the law v **order**, boss, order around, boss around, dictate to

layer n 1 **level**, tier, seam, gradation, stratum *(fml)* 2 **coating**, coat, sheet, film, deposit

layette n **baby clothes**, babywear, baby linen, nursery equipment

lay in v **store**, acquire, hoard, save, stock up *Opposite*: use up

lay into v 1 *(infml)* **criticize**, attack, lambaste, get at, round on *Opposite*: praise 2 **hit**, attack, beat, thump, thrash *Opposite*: protect

lay it on v **exaggerate**, embroider, embellish, overdo, pile on *Opposite*: understate

lay it on the line *(infml)* v **be honest**, be direct, be blunt, be straight, be clear *Opposite*: lie

lay off v 1 **dismiss**, suspend, make redundant, sack, let go *Opposite*: take on 2 *(infml)* **stop**, cease, desist, discontinue, cut out *Opposite*: continue

layoff n 1 **dismissal**, redundancy, downsizing, rationalization, streamlining 2 **unemployment**, career break, inactivity, rest, joblessness *Opposite*: employment

lay on v **provide**, supply, make available, organize, cater

lay out v 1 **explain**, present, describe, outline, set out 2 **design**, plan, arrange, organize, prepare

layout n **plan**, design, arrangement, outline, draft

lay to rest v **bury**, entomb, inter *(fml)*

laze v **idle**, lounge, loaf, bask, relax *Opposite*: toil

laze about *see* **laze**

laze around *see* **laze**

laziness n **idleness**, lethargy, indolence, languor, sluggishness *Opposite*: energy

lazy adj **indolent**, idle, lethargic, languid, sluggish *Opposite*: energetic

lazybones *(infml)* n **layabout**, slacker, shirker, loafer, idler *Opposite*: worker

leach v **leak**, filter, percolate, trickle, seep

lead v 1 **guide**, indicate, direct, escort, pilot *Opposite*: follow 2 **be in charge of**, run, control, command, direct 3 **be in the lead**, take the lead, be the forerunner, be in front, have an advantage *Opposite*: trail

■ *n* **1 leader**, spearhead, leading light, trailblazer, groundbreaker **2 advantage**, advance start, head start, flying start **3 precedent**, example, style, pattern, model **4 clue**, tip, indication, information, hint **5 leash**, chain, tether, restraint, rope ■ *adj* **principal**, chief, main, central, prime. *See* COMPARE AND CONTRAST *at* **guide**.

lead astray *v* **mislead**, misinform, lead on, hoodwink, delude

leaden *adj* **1 steely**, ashen, dull, grim, dark *Opposite*: bright **2 heavy**, ponderous, weighty, sluggish, stodgy *(infml) Opposite*: light **3 laboured**, slow, sluggish, dragging, crawling *Opposite*: quick **4 lifeless**, dull, dreary, flat, monotonous *Opposite*: lively

leader *n* **1 guide**, director, organizer, mentor, guru *Opposite*: disciple **2 spearhead**, leading light, trailblazer, groundbreaker, lead **3 head**, chief, manager, superior, principal *Opposite*: underling

leadership *n* **management**, control, guidance, headship, direction

lead-in *n* **introduction**, preamble, preface, prelude, preliminary *Opposite*: conclusion

leading *adj* **prominent**, foremost, important, principal, chief *Opposite*: secondary

leading article *n* **editorial**, leader, opinion, view, comment

leading edge *n* **forefront**, cutting edge, sharp end, vanguard, avant-garde

leading light *n* **big name**, top name, star, superstar, celebrity *Opposite*: unknown

lead off *v* **begin**, start, start off, commence, open *Opposite*: end

lead on *v* **entice**, lure, tempt, seduce, attract

lead the way *v* **blaze a trail**, set a trend, originate, break new ground, break through

lead time *n* **notice**, run-up, advance notice, warning, notification

lead to *v* **cause**, bring about, make possible, initiate, set in motion

lead up to *v* **1 prepare for**, prepare the way, prepare the ground, sow the seeds, gear up **2 approach**, come to, get to, get round to

leaf *n* **1 foliage**, greenery, sprig, spray, frond **2 page**, sheet, folio, side **3 sheet**, foil, plate, lamina, film **4 flap**, foldout, projection, section, piece

leaflet *n* **booklet**, brochure, pamphlet, flier, handbill

leaf through *v* **look through**, flick through, skim, browse, flip

leafy *adj* **green**, verdant, lush, luxuriant, rank *Opposite*: bare

league *n* **association**, group, union, confederation, club

leak *n* **1 escape**, seepage, leakage, outflow, drip **2 disclosure**, betrayal, giveaway, revelation, release ■ *v* **1 seep**, escape, pour out, trickle, drip **2 disclose**, reveal, give away,

betray, uncover *Opposite*: keep under wraps *(infml)*

leakage *n* **leak**, escape, seepage, outflow, drip

leak out *v* **emerge**, get out, slip out, come out, come to light

leakproof *adj* **watertight**, waterproof, sealed, hermetic, rainproof *Opposite*: leaky

leaky *adj* **1 leaking**, holey, sieve-like, dripping, drippy *Opposite*: watertight **2** *(infml)* **unsecured**, unsafe, indiscreet, loose, lax *Opposite*: secure

lean *v* **1 bend**, bend over, bend forwards, incline, tilt **2 rest**, prop, support, place, put **3 tend**, incline, be disposed, favour, prefer ■ *adj* **thin**, slender, slim, wiry, sinewy *Opposite*: stout. *See* COMPARE AND CONTRAST *at* **thin**.

leaning *n* **inclination**, tendency, bent, affinity, preference *Opposite*: aversion

lean on *v* **1 depend on**, rely on, trust, count on **2** *(infml)* **intimidate**, pressurize, put pressure on, oblige, coerce

leap *v* **1 jump**, bound, dive, soar, fly **2 increase**, rise, shoot up, go up, jump *Opposite*: drop ■ *n* **1 bound**, jump, dive, spring, hop **2 rise**, increase, jump, hike, climb *Opposite*: drop

leap at *v* **jump at**, seize, grab, clutch, accept *Opposite*: baulk

leapfrog *v* **1 jump**, vault, leap, bound, spring **2 advance**, shoot ahead, get ahead, pull ahead, catapult **3 overtake**, pass, leave behind, outstrip, leave standing **4 circumvent**, evade, avoid, sidestep, bypass

leap out at *v* **stand out**, stick out, jump out, hit somebody in the face, impact

learn *v* **1 study**, absorb, pick up, acquire, cram *(infml) Opposite*: teach **2 find out**, hear, discover, realize, gather

learned *adj* **erudite**, educated, scholarly, academic, cultured *Opposite*: uneducated

learner *n* **beginner**, apprentice, student, pupil, novice *Opposite*: expert

learning *n* **knowledge**, education, erudition, scholarship, culture *Opposite*: ignorance

lease *v* **rent**, rent out, hire, hire out, let

lease out *see* **lease**

leash *n* **lead**, chain, tether, string, rope

least *adj* **smallest**, slightest, tiniest, minimum *Opposite*: most

leastways *(infml) adv* **in any case**, anyway, at least, at any rate, in spite of

leastwise *see* **leastways**

leave *v* **1 go away**, depart, go, run off, abscond *Opposite*: stay **2 put down**, set down, put, put away, place *Opposite*: remove **3 bequeath**, pass on, hand down, donate, entrust *Opposite*: withhold **4 result in**, cause, bring about, effect *(fml)* **5 delay**, defer, put off, avoid, hold off *Opposite*: bring forward **6 abandon**, desert, renounce, forsake, ditch *(infml) Opposite*: stand by **7 set aside**, allow, give, permit, assign ■ *n* **1 holiday**, sabbatical, time off, leave of absence, vacation **2** *(fml)* **permission**, consent, authority, authorization, dispensation

leave alone *v* **let alone**, let be, leave well enough alone, pay no attention, ignore *Opposite*: harass

leave be *see* **leave alone**

leave behind *v* **1** overtake, outstrip, outpace, surpass, leave standing *Opposite*: fall behind **2 put behind you**, escape, evade, get away from, put to one side *Opposite*: suffer **3** abandon, get rid of, cast off, leave, forget *Opposite*: retain

leave cold *v* **bore**, do nothing for, bore rigid, bore stiff, bore to tears *Opposite*: inspire

leave in peace *see* **leave alone**

leave much to be desired *v* **be unsatisfactory**, disappoint, let down, not make the grade, fall short *Opposite*: pass muster

leave no stone unturned *v* **do all you can**, do your utmost, pull out all the stops, spare no effort, try everything

leave of absence *n* **sabbatical**, time off, time out, leave

leave off *v* **stop**, desist, cease, refrain, discontinue *Opposite*: carry on

leave out *v* **omit**, exclude, count out, ignore, overlook *Opposite*: include

leavings *n* **leftovers**, scraps, remnants, remains, castoffs

lecherous *adj* **lewd**, lustful, lascivious, libidinous, lusty

lectern *n* **bookstand**, reading stand, reading desk, stand, bookrest

lecture *n* **1 talk**, address, sermon, speech, homily **2 reprimand**, dressing-down, scolding, tongue-lashing, ticking-off *(infml)* ■ *v* **1 teach**, address, instruct, talk, hold forth **2 harangue**, criticize, scold, reprove, censure

lecturer *n* **1 speaker**, public speaker, speechmaker, orator, presenter **2 teacher**, professor, instructor, academic, don

ledge *n* **1 shelf**, sill, niche, ridge, rack **2 outcrop**, ridge, sill, shelf, foothold

ledger *n* **book**, account book, record book, record, register

lee *n* **shelter**, cover, protection, shadow, shade

leer *v* **smirk**, ogle, eye, sneer, stare ■ *n* **sneer**, grimace, smirk, evil eye, stare

leery *(infml) adj* **suspicious**, wary, doubting, doubtful, circumspect *Opposite*: confident

lees *n* **dregs**, remains, leftovers, remnants

leeward *adj* **protected**, sheltered, shielded *Opposite*: upwind

leeway *n* **scope**, flexibility, margin, freedom, latitude

left-hand *adj* **left**, leftward, port *Opposite*: right-hand

left-handed *adj* **anticlockwise**, right to left, circular, round, helical *Opposite*: right-handed

leftover *n* **relic**, hangover, vestige, remnant, remainder

leftovers *n* **scraps**, remains, what's left, table scraps, leavings

left-wing *adj* **progressive**, reformist, leftist, socialist, communist *Opposite*: right-wing

left-winger *n* **progressive**, reformist, leftist, socialist, communist *Opposite*: right-winger

leg *n* **1 limb**, foreleg, member, extremity, hind leg **2 pole**, foot, support, stand, base **3 stage**, phase, lap, step, part

WORD BANK

❏ **parts of a leg or foot** ankle, big toe, calf, haunch, heel, instep, knee, lap, little toe, shin, sole, thigh, toe, toenail

legacy *n* **1 bequest**, inheritance, heirloom, heritage, birthright **2 relic**, hangover, vestige, remnant, remainder ■ *adj* **superseded**, obsolete, discontinued, outdated, antiquated *Opposite*: up-to-date

legal *adj* **lawful**, permissible, permitted, allowed, authorized *Opposite*: illegal

COMPARE AND CONTRAST CORE MEANING: describes something that is permitted, recognized, or required by law
legal permitted, recognized, or required by law; **lawful** a less common word meaning legal; **decriminalized** no longer categorized as a criminal offence; **legalized** previously categorized as illegal and now declared legal; **legitimate** complying with the law, or under the law; **licit** *(fml)* a rarely used word meaning legal.

legalese *n* **jargon**, cant, mumbo jumbo *(infml)*, gobbledegook *(infml)*

legality *n* **validity**, lawfulness, rightfulness, legitimacy *Opposite*: illegality

legalization *n* **ratification**, authorization, certification, validation, endorsement *Opposite*: criminalization

legalize *v* **decriminalize**, authorize, sanction, allow, permit *Opposite*: prohibit

legate *n* **representative**, envoy, ambassador, emissary, diplomat

legend *n* **1 fable**, myth, tale, lore, folklore **2 star**, celebrity, big name, icon, personality *Opposite*: unknown

legendary *adj* **1 fabled**, mythical, mythological, imaginary, fabulous *Opposite*: real-life **2 famous**, renowned, well-known, celebrated, great *Opposite*: unknown

legible *adj* **clear**, readable, intelligible, decipherable, understandable *Opposite*: illegible

legion *n* **multitude**, host, team, crowd, throng

legislate *v* **enact**, pass, establish, lay down the law, decree

legislation *n* **1 lawmaking**, lawgiving, legislature, regulation **2 laws**, legal code, body of law, bill, rule

legislative *adj* **lawmaking**, parliamentary, governmental, judicial, jurisdictive

legislature *n* **government**, parliament, administration, senate, assembly

legit *(slang) see* **legitimate**

legitimacy *n* **1 legality**, lawfulness, validity, rightfulness, justice **2 acceptability**, rightfulness, correctness **3 sincerity**, genuineness, realness, authenticity, validity

legitimate *adj* **1 lawful**, rightful, valid, legal, legit *(slang)* *Opposite*: unlawful **2 reasonable**, acceptable, justifiable, logical, valid *Opposite*: unreasonable **3 genuine**, sincere, real, valid, authentic *Opposite*: spurious

leg-pull *(infml)* *n* **joke**, practical joke, deception, trick, tease

legroom *n* **room**, space, freedom, elbowroom *(infml)*

legume *n* **leguminous plant**, pulse, pea, bean

legwarmer *n* **sock**, stocking, legging, gaiter, puttee

legwork *(infml)* *n* **research**, preparation, homework, groundwork, spadework

lei *n* **garland**, wreath, chaplet, coronet, circlet

leisure *n* **free time**, spare time, time off, leisure time, R and R *Opposite*: work

leisure centre *n* **sports centre**, gymnasium, sports club, swimming pool, gym *(infml)*

leisured *adj* **rich**, wealthy, affluent, moneyed, propertied *Opposite*: poor

leisurely *adj* **unhurried**, easy, relaxed, restful, relaxing *Opposite*: frantic

leisurewear *n* **sportswear**, casualwear, casual clothes, casuals, mufti

leitmotif *n* **motif**, theme, strand, element, topic

lemming *n* **conformist**, sheep, imitator, follower, copycat *(infml)* *Opposite*: nonconformist

lemon *n* **1 lemonade**, bitter lemon, fruit juice, squash, cordial **2** *(infml)* **failure**, dud *(infml)*, nonstarter *(infml)*, washout *(infml)*, flop *(infml)* *Opposite*: winner

lemony *adj* **lemon-flavoured**, lemon, citrus *Opposite*: sweet

lend *v* **1 loan**, advance, give, offer *Opposite*: borrow **2 provide**, offer, give, impart, add *Opposite*: take away

lend a hand *v* **help**, help out, give somebody a hand, do your bit, assist *Opposite*: hinder

lend an ear *v* **listen**, pay attention, hang on the words of, listen up *(slang)*

lender *n* **giver**, moneylender, financier, creditor, investor

length *n* **1 distance**, span, measurement, extent, dimension **2 duration**, time, time span, extent **3 piece**, strip, segment, section, bit

lengthen *v* **grow**, increase, extend, elongate, stretch *Opposite*: shorten

lengthways *adv* **lengthwise**, along, end to end, sideways, laterally *Opposite*: endways

lengthwise *see* **lengthways**

lengthy *adj* **long**, long-lasting, extensive, prolonged, protracted *Opposite*: brief

lenience *see* **leniency**

leniency *n* **clemency**, mercy, compassion, humanity, tolerance *Opposite*: severity

lenient *adj* **compassionate**, merciful, humane, tolerant, indulgent *Opposite*: severe

leonine *adj* **impressive**, imposing, majestic, proud, dignified

leotard *n* **one-piece**, body, body stocking, all-in-one, bodysuit *(US)*

leper *n* **outcast**, untouchable, pariah, outsider, exile

leprechaun *n* **sprite**, elf, imp, pixie, dwarf

lèse majesté *see* **lese majesty**

lese majesty *n* **1 disrespect**, disregard, dishonour, contempt, disdain *Opposite*: respect **2 treason**, high treason, sedition, betrayal, treachery *Opposite*: loyalty

lesion *n* **wound**, injury, cut, graze, scratch

less *adj* **a smaller amount of**, not as much of, a lesser amount of, a reduced amount of *Opposite*: more ■ *prep* **minus**, take away, with a reduction of, excluding *Opposite*: plus

lessen *v* **diminish**, decrease, decline, tail off, ease off *Opposite*: increase

lesser *adj* **smaller**, slighter, minor, reduced *Opposite*: greater

lesson *n* **1 class**, lecture, session, tutorial, seminar **2 example**, message, moral, warning, object lesson

lest *(fml)* *conj* **in case**, for fear that, so as not to

let *v* **1 allow**, give permission, permit, agree to, consent to *Opposite*: forbid **2 rent**, rent out, lease, lease out, hire ■ *n* **1** *(fml)* **problem**, difficulty, hindrance, impediment, complication **2 lease**, tenancy, occupancy, rent, agreement

let alone *see* **let be**

let be *v* **leave alone**, leave in peace, leave be, leave off, leave well enough alone *Opposite*: pester

let down *v* **1 lower**, drop, sink, let fall, move down *Opposite*: raise **2 deflate**, empty, drain *Opposite*: inflate **3 disappoint**, fail, abandon, betray, disillusion **4 lengthen**, extend, let out, expand, enlarge *Opposite*: take up

letdown *n* **disappointment**, anticlimax, failure, disillusionment, discouragement *Opposite*: success

let drop *v* **disclose**, reveal, divulge, let slip, let out

let fly *v* **1 lose your temper**, explode, rage, hit the roof *(infml)*, see red *(infml)* *Opposite*: keep your cool *(infml)* **2 throw**, fling, toss, hurl, pitch

let go *v* **release**, liberate, set free, free, set loose *Opposite*: retain

lethal *adj* **deadly**, fatal, mortal, poisonous, toxic. *See* COMPARE AND CONTRAST *at* **deadly**.

lethargic *adj* **sluggish**, tired, weary, exhausted, lacklustre *Opposite*: energetic

lethargy *n* **sluggishness**, tiredness, weariness, exhaustion, fatigue *Opposite*: energy

let in *v* **admit**, allow in, open the door to, show in, receive *Opposite*: keep out

let in for *(infml)* *v* **involve in**, entangle in, ensnare in, mix up in, entrap in *Opposite*: get out of

let in on *v* **make aware of**, tell, acquaint with, reveal to, disclose to *Opposite*: keep from

let into *v* **1 let in on**, fill in on, share, tell, inform of *Opposite*: keep from **2 admit to**, welcome into, usher into, take into, show into **3 accept into**, receive into, allow into, enlist into, enrol into

let know *v* **tell**, inform, advise, alert, warn *Opposite*: keep in the dark

let loose *v* **let out**, let go, set free, set loose, release *Opposite*: confine

let off *v* **1 excuse**, pardon, release, free, acquit *Opposite*: punish **2 fire**, explode, detonate, set off, shoot

let on *v* **1 admit**, disclose, divulge, reveal, declare *Opposite*: conceal **2 pretend**, make out, claim, profess, act *Opposite*: come clean *(infml)*

let out *v* **1 emit**, give, utter, release, produce *Opposite*: suppress **2 free**, let go, release, set free, let loose *Opposite*: keep in **3 enlarge**, expand, extend, widen, broaden *Opposite*: take in **4 let slip**, reveal, divulge, disclose, blurt out *Opposite*: conceal

let-out *n* **loophole**, escape clause, way out, technicality, window

let pass *v* **1 ignore**, let go, overlook, let ride, pay no attention to *Opposite*: pick up on *(infml)* **2 let through**, let by, let past, stand aside for, make way for *Opposite*: bar

let ride *v* **ignore**, close your eyes to, turn a blind eye to, let go, let pass *Opposite*: stop

let slip *v* **1 reveal**, disclose, divulge, give away, let out *Opposite*: hold back **2 let go**, lose, lose track of, lose sight of, take your eyes off *Opposite*: keep an eye on

letter *n* **1 communication**, note, message, memo, dispatch **2 character**, symbol, sign, capital, capital letter

letterbox *n* **post office box**, postbox, mailbox (US)

letter card *n* **note card**, notelet, note, card

lettered *adj* **educated**, knowledgeable, cultured, cultivated, literary *Opposite*: uneducated

lettering *n* **writing**, print, calligraphy, letters, inscription

letters *n* **literature**, culture, cultivation, knowledge, education

let the cat out of the bag *v* **talk**, let on, tell a

secret, tell, spill the beans *(infml)* *Opposite*: keep mum *(infml)*

let through *v* **make way for**, stand aside for, clear the way for, let pass, let past *Opposite*: block

let up *v* **ease off**, ease, ease up, lessen, slacken *Opposite*: intensify

let-up *(infml)* *n* **respite**, break, rest, relief, interval *Opposite*: intensification

let up on *v* **ease up on**, ease off on, slack off on, soften up on, spare

let your hair down *(infml)* *v* **relax**, have a good time, enjoy yourself, let yourself go, have fun

let yourself go *v* **1 unwind**, relax, mellow, let your hair down, throw caution to the winds **2 give up**, lose heart, go downhill, lose your self-respect, go to the dogs *(infml)*

levee *n* **1 embankment**, earthwork, bank, wall, rampart **2 reception**, royal reception, royal function, court reception, court function

level *adj* **1 flat**, smooth, flat as a pancake, even, dead flat *Opposite*: bumpy **2 horizontal**, parallel with the ground, even, flat *Opposite*: slanted **3 equal**, neck and neck, side by side, close, near ■ *n* **1 height**, altitude, stage, point, plane **2 intensity**, quantity, concentration, amount, degree ■ *v* **1 flatten**, smooth, steamroll, press flat, even out **2 aim**, direct, point, turn **3 demolish**, knock down, raze, blow up, raze to the ground *Opposite*: rebuild

level crossing *n* **railway crossing**, crossing, grade crossing (US)

level-headed *adj* **sensible**, calm, sound, even-tempered, reliable *Opposite*: rash

level-headedness *n* **composure**, equanimity, calmness, good sense, reliability *Opposite*: rashness

levelly *adv* **1 calmly**, steadily, sensibly, evenly, equably *Opposite*: excitedly **2 smoothly**, flatly, evenly *Opposite*: unevenly

level off *v* **stabilize**, even out, settle, settle down, smooth out

level out *v* **settle down**, stabilize, settle, even out, even up

level pegging *n* **equality**, parity, same score, tie, draw *Opposite*: inequality

lever *n* **handle**, control, regulator, knob

leverage *n* **influence**, power, force, control, weight

leviathan *n* **giant**, colossus, behemoth, monster

levitate *v* **float**, rise up, ascend, drift up, soar *Opposite*: sink

levitation *n* **defiance of gravity**, rising, raising, hovering, floating

levity *n* **lightheartedness**, cheerfulness, humour, lightness, flippancy *Opposite*: gravity

levy *v* **impose**, tax, collect, put, charge ■ *n* **tax**, rates, toll, duty, tariff

lewd *adj* **salacious**, obscene, crude, vulgar, indecent

lexical *adj* **verbal**, word, vocabulary, philological, etymological

lexicon *n* **1 vocabulary**, vocabulary list, word list, glossary, dictionary **2 language**, lexis, idiolect

ley *n* **1 grassland**, pasture, pastureland, pasturage, grazing **2 path**, pathway, footpath, bridle path, track

liability *n* **1 legal responsibility**, obligation, accountability, responsibility, charge **2 disadvantage**, problem, burden, millstone, jinx

liable *adj* **1 legally responsible**, accountable, answerable, responsible *Opposite*: unaccountable **2 likely**, apt, predisposed, prone *Opposite*: unlikely

liaise *v* **act as a go-between**, communicate, link, bridge, mediate

liaison *n* **link**, connection, contact, cooperation, relationship

liar *n* **deceiver**, fast talker, perjurer, fibber *(infml)*, storyteller *(infml)*

libation *n* **1 drink**, alcoholic drink, potion, brew *(infml)*, bevvy *(slang)* **2 offering**, oblation, offertory, sacrifice, tribute

libel *n* **defamation**, vilification, slander, smear, denigration *Opposite*: praise ■ *v* **defame**, vilify, sully, tarnish, malign *Opposite*: praise. *See* COMPARE AND CONTRAST *at* **malign**.

libellous *adj* **defamatory**, vilifying, slanderous, unfounded *Opposite*: admiring

liberal *adj* **1 open-minded**, broad-minded, moderate, noninterventionist, freethinking *Opposite*: narrow-minded **2 generous**, copious, abundant, profuse, substantial *Opposite*: meagre. *See* COMPARE AND CONTRAST *at* **generous**.

liberalism *n* **tolerance**, broad-mindedness, open-mindedness, moderation, freethinking *Opposite*: narrow-mindedness

liberalize *v* **relax**, slacken, loosen, ease up, open *Opposite*: tighten

liberate *v* **release**, free, set free, unshackle, unfetter *Opposite*: imprison

liberated *adj* **unconventional**, open-minded, freethinking, modern, enlightened *Opposite*: unenlightened

liberation *n* **freedom**, liberty, release, discharge, emancipation *Opposite*: captivity

liberator *n* **deliverer**, saviour, emancipator, releaser *Opposite*: captor

liberty *n* **1 freedom**, independence, autonomy, emancipation, liberation *Opposite*: captivity **2 right**, freedom, authorization, authority, permission *Opposite*: suppression

libidinous *adj* **lustful**, lecherous, lusty, lascivious, salacious

library *n* **collection**, archive, books, papers, records

librettist *n* **libretto writer**, lyricist, songwriter, writer, author

licence *n* **1 certificate**, authorization, warrant, pass, card **2 excess**, abandon, lawlessness, unrestraint, immoderation *(fml)* **3 freedom**, liberty, carte blanche, authority, permission

license *v* **certify**, permit, allow, authorize, accredit

licensed *adj* **approved**, qualified, certified, accredited, registered

licentiate *n* **licence holder**, licensee, certified professional, qualified practitioner

licentious *adj* **immoral**, degenerate, decadent, dissipated, depraved

licit *adj* **lawful**, legitimate, legal, valid, right *Opposite*: illegal. *See* COMPARE AND CONTRAST *at* **legal**.

lick *(infml)* *v* **defeat**, conquer, get the better of, overcome, thrash

lickety-split *(infml)* *adv* **quickly**, fast, at high speed, at a rate of knots, at a lick *(infml)* *Opposite*: sluggishly

licking *(infml)* *n* **trouncing**, thrashing, drubbing, hammering *(infml)*, pasting *(infml)*

lick your lips *v* **relish**, salivate, drool, anticipate, await

lid *n* **top**, cover, cap, closure

lido *n* **1 outdoor pool**, outdoor swimming pool, open-air pool, public swimming pool **2 public beach**, bathing beach, beach

lie *v* **1 recline**, stretch out, lounge, lie down, slouch **2 be positioned**, be arranged, be placed, be situated, sit **3 remain**, rest, stay, be, stop **4 tell lies**, tell untruths, perjure yourself, tell stories, be economical with the truth *Opposite*: tell the truth ■ *n* **untruth**, falsehood, fabrication, white lie, fib *(infml)* *Opposite*: truth

---

COMPARE AND CONTRAST CORE MEANING: something that is not true

lie a false statement made deliberately; **untruth** something that is presented as being true but is actually false; **falsehood** a lie or an untruth; **fabrication** an invented statement, story, or account devised with intent to deceive; **fib** *(infml)* an insignificant harmless lie; **white lie** a minor harmless lie, usually told to avoid hurting somebody's feelings.

---

lie about *see* lie around

lie around *(infml)* *v* **1 laze**, laze about, lounge around, flop about, sit around **2 be scattered about**, be all over the place, clutter up the place, be distributed, litter

lie back *v* **recline**, stretch out, lounge, sprawl, relax

lie down *v* **recline**, rest, stretch out, relax, lounge *Opposite*: stand up

lie-down *(infml)* *n* **sleep**, nap, rest, doze, snooze *(infml)*

lie in *(infml)* *v* **sleep late**, stay in bed, get up late, rise late

lie-in *(infml)* *n* **late sleep**, late rise, rest, doze, long sleep

lie in wait v lurk, hide, conceal yourself, ambush, prowl

lie off v remain near, remain close, stay near, stay close, lie near

lie of the land (infml) n general state, general situation, prospect, state of affairs, picture

life n 1 existence, being, living Opposite: death 2 lifetime, life span, life cycle, life expectancy, natural life 3 verve, vivacity, animation, energy, excitement

life-and-death adj critical, crucial, vital, pivotal, paramount Opposite: unimportant

lifeblood n essential, essence, quintessence, sine qua non, necessity

life cycle n life span, development, maturation, growth

life expectancy n life span, lifetime, allotted span, natural life

lifeguard n rescuer, beach attendant, swimming pool attendant, pool attendant, lifesaver (infml)

lifeless adj 1 dead, unconscious, unresponsive, unmoving, inert Opposite: alive 2 unexciting, dull, uninteresting, tedious, listless Opposite: animated. See COMPARE AND CONTRAST at dead.

lifelike adj realistic, natural, believable, convincing, credible Opposite: unrealistic

lifeline n salvation, link, help, support, helping hand

lifelong adj enduring, all-time, permanent, ultimate, lasting Opposite: temporary

life-or-death see life-and-death

life-size adj full-scale, full-size, actual size Opposite: miniature

life span n natural life, lifetime, life cycle, life expectancy, life

lifestyle n way of life, standard of living, existence, routine, life

life's work n achievement, accomplishment, success, attainment

life-threatening adj dangerous, serious, severe, grave, incurable

lifetime n 1 life, time, life span, natural life, life cycle 2 era, generation, time, period, epoch 3 (infml) days, eternity (infml), forever (infml), ages (infml), donkey's years (infml)

lift v 1 winch up, haul up, elevate, boost, raise 2 revoke, cancel, take back, relax, rescind Opposite: impose 3 lighten, buoy up, brighten, elate, uplift 4 (infml) steal, walk off with, help yourself, pocket, take ■ n boost, revitalization, tonic, encouragement, kick (infml)

ligature n 1 cord, string, rope, tie, line 2 (fml) bond, connection, link, linkage, union

light n 1 glow, beam, brightness, luminosity, daylight Opposite: darkness ■ adj 1 bright, sunny, sunlit, well-lit Opposite: dark 2 pastel, subtle, neutral, fair, pale Opposite: deep 3 weightless, buoyant, fluffy, insub-

stantial, frothy Opposite: heavy 4 gentle, delicate, soft, noiseless, featherlike Opposite: heavy 5 nimble, graceful, dainty, elegant, agile Opposite: awkward 6 carefree, happy, cheerful, untroubled, joyful Opposite: oppressive 7 easy, manageable, undemanding, simple, effortless Opposite: demanding 8 entertaining, lightweight, fun, frivolous, amusing Opposite: sombre ■ v set alight, set on fire, ignite, strike, set fire to Opposite: extinguish

WORD BANK
❑ **types of light** arc lamp, chandelier, floodlight, fluorescent lamp, footlights, headlight, hurricane lamp, lamp, lamppost, lantern, LED, light bulb, neon light, nightlight, penlight, searchlight, spotlight, streetlamp, streetlight, sunlamp, torch, torchlight, traffic light, uplighter

light-coloured adj pale, light, pastel, subtle, fair

lighten v 1 ease, lessen, alleviate, reduce, lift Opposite: overload 2 cheer up, improve, lift, refresh, buoy up Opposite: depress

lighten up (infml) v relax, take it easy, loosen up, unwind, cool it (infml)

lightface adj faint, light Opposite: boldface

light-fingered adj thieving, kleptomaniacal, larcenous, dishonest, sticky-fingered (infml)

light-footed adj nimble, graceful, dainty, elegant, agile Opposite: clumsy

lightheaded adj dizzy, faint, giddy, woozy, unsteady

lighthearted adj 1 carefree, happy-go-lucky, happy, cheerful, cheery Opposite: troubled 2 cheerful, jokey, cheery, funny, bright Opposite: gloomy 3 enjoyable, entertaining, amusing, diverting, fun Opposite: serious

lighting n illumination, light, lights

light into (infml) v attack, tear into, set upon, lay into, let have it Opposite: defend

lightly adv 1 gently, softly, delicately, imperceptibly, quietly Opposite: heavily 2 flippantly, frivolously, jokily, informally, casually Opposite: seriously 3 nimbly, gracefully, trippingly, adeptly, dexterously Opposite: awkwardly

light-minded adj frivolous, silly, foolish, vacuous, inane Opposite: serious-minded

lightness n 1 weightlessness, buoyancy, fluffiness, frothiness, flimsiness Opposite: heaviness 2 nimbleness, precision, grace, agility, dexterity Opposite: clumsiness

lightning n flash of lightning, forked lightning, sheet lightning, lightning bolt, lightning strike ■ adj fast, quick, speedy, whirlwind, sudden Opposite: slow

light out (infml) v run away, run off, leave in a hurry, cut and run, run for it

lights out n 1 bedtime, time for bed, sleep time, bye-byes (infml) 2 signal, taps, bugle call, curfew, last post Opposite: reveille

light up v **1 illuminate**, light, cast light on, shed light on, shine a light on *Opposite*: darken **2 shine**, glow, gleam, beam, burn *Opposite*: darken **3 cheer up**, brighten up, perk up, liven up, brighten

lightweight adj **frivolous**, trivial, insubstantial, inconsequential, unimportant *Opposite*: serious ■ n **person of little consequence**, small fry, little man, little guy, pawn

likable adj **pleasant**, nice, affable, agreeable, amiable *Opposite*: unpleasant

like prep **similar to**, akin to, approximating to, in the vein of, reminiscent of *Opposite*: unlike ■ adj **similar**, comparable, alike, corresponding, identical *Opposite*: dissimilar ■ v **be fond of**, love, be keen on, enjoy, be partial to *Opposite*: dislike

likelihood n **probability**, possibility, prospect, chance, chances

likely adj **1 probable**, possible, expected, prospective, to be expected *Opposite*: unlikely **2 liable**, apt, prone, tending, having a tendency to

like-minded adj **in agreement**, concurring, compatible, in accord, of one mind *Opposite*: incompatible

liken v **compare**, equate, relate, associate *Opposite*: contrast

likeness n **1 similarity**, resemblance, correspondence **2 portrait**, image, reproduction, picture, rendering

likewise adv **similarly**, the same, equally, also, as well

liking n **taste**, fondness, partiality, love, penchant *Opposite*: dislike. *See* COMPARE AND CONTRAST *at* **love**.

lilt n **intonation**, inflection, rise and fall, cadence, stress

lily-livered *(dated)* adj **cowardly**, faint-hearted, spineless, weak, chicken *(infml)* *Opposite*: courageous

limb n **1 extremity**, appendage, member **2 branch**, bough, spur

limber adj **lithe**, supple, agile, nimble, lissom *Opposite*: stiff

limber up v **warm up**, loosen up, exercise, practise, prepare

limelight n **attention**, public interest, public eye, fame, renown

limit n **1 boundary**, bounds, border, edge, perimeter **2 threshold**, cutoff point, check, cap, constraint ■ v **control**, regulate, restrain, curb, constrain *Opposite*: deregulate

limitation n **drawback**, inadequacy, imperfection, weakness, weak point

limited adj **incomplete**, imperfect, partial, inadequate, restricted *Opposite*: boundless

limited company n **limited liability company**, public limited company, joint-stock company, company, corporation

limited edition n **special edition**, limited printing, limited issue, limited print run, deluxe edition

limiter n **regulator**, controller, control, restraint, check

limitless adj **boundless**, unbounded, immeasurable, infinite, vast *Opposite*: limited

limits n **bounds**, restrictions, confines, parameters, boundaries

limp v **hobble**, shuffle, shamble, stagger, wobble ■ adj **floppy**, wilted, flaccid, lifeless, drooping *Opposite*: stiff

limpid adj **1 transparent**, clear, translucent, diaphanous, see-through *Opposite*: opaque **2 lucid**, clear, crystal clear, clear as day, understandable *Opposite*: obscure

limpness n **floppiness**, flaccidity, droopiness, lifelessness, sagginess *Opposite*: stiffness

limy adj **lime-flavoured**, lime, citrus

linchpin n **keystone**, cornerstone, hub, essential, kingpin *(infml)* *Opposite*: accessory

line n **1 row**, column, procession, lineup, queue **2 streak**, stripe, contour, mark, stroke **3 boundary**, limit, border, edge, frontier **4 link**, route, track, connection, course **5 string**, cable, rope, thread, twine **6 ancestry**, family, lineage, descent, race **7 edge**, profile, contour, outline, silhouette **8 policy**, attitude, method, approach, ideology **9 area**, occupation, field, interest, speciality ■ v **coat**, cover, face, reinforce, pad

lineage n **ancestry**, family, line, heredity, extraction

linear adj **1 in lines**, lined, line **2 straight**, rectilinear, direct, undeviating, right

lined adj **1 wrinkled**, creased, wizened, furrowed, crinkled *Opposite*: smooth **2 ruled**, feint *Opposite*: plain

line manager n **manager**, production manager, sales manager, boss, superior

line of attack n **stratagem**, tactic, technique, method, modus operandi

line officer n **combat officer**, frontline officer, fighting officer, field officer, officer

line of sight n **sightline**, line of vision, view

line of work n **profession**, career, job, occupation

liner n **lining**, pool liner, facing, bin liner, insert

line up v **1 assemble**, queue, gather together, collect, align **2 form ranks**, fall into line, marshal, order, align **3 plan**, organize, arrange, prepare, set up **4 arrange**, collect, order, organize, place *Opposite*: disarrange

lineup n **1 team list**, roster, team, listing, side **2 schedule**, listing, programme **3 group**, team, alliance, association, league

linger v **remain**, stay behind, hang on, loiter, stay *Opposite*: leave

lingerie n **underwear**, underclothes, underclothing, undergarments, undies *(infml)*

lingering adj **1 drawn-out**, spun-out, slow, protracted, long-drawn-out *Opposite*: quick

2 lasting, remaining, persistent, enduring, haunting

lingo *(infml)* *n* **language**, speech, idiom, vernacular, jargon

linguistic *adj* **language**, verbal, philological, dialectal, etymological

liniment *n* **ointment**, cream, unguent, rub, salve

lining *n* **coating**, liner, insert, facing

link *n* **connection**, relation, association, relationship, linkage ■ *v* **connect**, relate, associate, bring together, link up *Opposite*: separate

linkage *n* **connection**, relation, association, relationship, link

linked *adj* **related**, connected, accompanying, allied, associated *Opposite*: unrelated

linkup *n* **connection**, association, link, linkage, bond *Opposite*: separation

lionhearted *adj* **brave**, courageous, stouthearted, bold, audacious *Opposite*: cowardly

lionize *v* **glorify**, idolize, praise, fete, celebrate *Opposite*: censure

lion's share *n* **largest part**, bulk, most, majority, mass

lip *n* **edge**, rim, brim, brink

lip-smacking *adj* **delicious**, delectable, tasty, flavourful, flavoursome

liquefy *v* **dissolve**, soften, melt, run, thaw *Opposite*: solidify

liquescent *adj* **melting**, runny, gooey, liquefying *Opposite*: solid

liquid *n* **fluid**, water, juice, solution, liquor ■ *adj* **runny**, fluid, gooey, watery, melted *Opposite*: solid

liquidate *v* **1 settle**, clear up, pay, honour, pay off **2 shut down**, sell out, sell off, bankrupt, wind up **3 kill**, murder, execute, eliminate, assassinate

liquidation *n* **insolvency**, bankruptcy, closing, winding up, selling out

liquidator *n* **receiver**, official receiver, sequestrator, administrative receiver, overseer

liquidity *n* **1 liquidness**, fluidity, fluidness, wateriness *Opposite*: solidity **2 assets**, liquid assets, convertible assets, resources, financial assets

liquidize *v* **purée**, blend, pulverize, mash, pulp

liquor *n* **1 alcohol**, spirits, strong drink **2 liquid**, fluid, solution, juice

lissom *adj* **1 lithe**, supple, flexible, willowy, svelte *Opposite*: stiff **2 agile**, nimble, lively, quick, light *Opposite*: awkward

lissome *see* lissom

list *n* **1 catalogue**, register, record, roll, listing **2 tilt**, slant, slope, gradient, lean ■ *v* **1 record**, catalogue, register, itemize, enumerate **2 slant**, tilt, incline, lean, bank

listed *adj* **registered**, recorded, itemized, enumerated *Opposite*: unlisted

listen *v* **lend an ear**, pay attention, take note, attend, pin your ears back *(infml)* *Opposite*: ignore

listener *n* **hearer**, radio listener, audience member, audiophile, eavesdropper

listen in *v* **eavesdrop**, monitor, wiretap, bug, snoop *(infml)*

listening post *n* **observation post**, lookout post, surveillance post, sentry post

listen up *(infml)* *v* **listen**, pay attention, attend, heed, pay heed *Opposite*: ignore

listing *n* **1 citation**, item, entry **2 list**, catalogue, register, record, roll

listings *n* **schedule**, programme, guide

listless *adj* **languid**, lethargic, indolent, enervated, limp *Opposite*: energetic

litany *n* **1 prayers**, liturgical prayers, petitions, invocations, responses **2 list**, listing, catalogue, series, recital

lite *adj* **low-fat**, slimming, light, diet, low-calorie *Opposite*: fattening

literacy *n* **1 reading ability**, the three Rs, literateness **2 knowledge**, learning, mastery, nous, savvy *(infml)*

literal *adj* **1 factual**, truthful, honest, exact, accurate *Opposite*: figurative **2 word for word**, verbatim, accurate, exact, correct *Opposite*: inaccurate

literary *adj* **1 fictional**, mythical, legendary, storybook, fictitious *Opposite*: historical **2 bookish**, erudite, scholarly, well-read, literate

literate *adj* **well-educated**, well-read, knowledgeable, cultured, erudite *Opposite*: illiterate

literati *(fml)* *n* **1 intellectuals**, intellects, highbrows, intelligentsia, academics **2 authors**, writers, poets, playwrights, editors

literature *n* **1 writings**, works, collected works, texts, books **2 information**, sources, reading matter, brochures, pamphlets

lithe *adj* **supple**, flexible, lissom, agile, nimble *Opposite*: stiff

litigable *adj* **responsible**, liable, accountable, answerable, actionable

litigate *v* **take proceedings**, sue, contest, file, petition

litigation *n* **court case**, proceedings, lawsuit, legal action, legal process

litmus test *n* **acid test**, proof, confirmation, test, measure

litter *n* **1 waste**, rubbish, debris, refuse, trash *(US)* **2 disorder**, confusion, jumble, clutter, untidiness **3 offspring**, young, progeny, brood, family ■ *v* **drop litter**, scatter, spoil, strew, clutter *Opposite*: clean up

litterbug *(infml)* *see* litter lout

litter lout *(infml)* *n* **litterer**, fly-tipper, dumper, litterbug *(infml)*

little adj **1** small, slight, petite, diminutive, tiny Opposite: large **2** unimportant, trivial, slight, petty, trifling Opposite: major ■ pron bit, touch, spot, some, pittance Opposite: lot ■ adv **not very**, not much, not sufficiently, insufficiently, inadequately Opposite: well

little folk see little people

little green man n alien, Martian, extraterrestrial

little people n supernatural beings, imaginary beings, fairies, elves, pixies

littoral adj coastal, shoreline, seaside Opposite: inland ■ n shore, coast, seaside, shoreline, beach

liturgy n church service, mass, ritual, religious ceremony, rite

livable adj **1** habitable, functional, civilized, comfortable, agreeable Opposite: uninhabitable **2** bearable, endurable, acceptable, tolerable, worthwhile Opposite: intolerable

live v **1** exist, be alive, be in this world, survive, subsist Opposite: die **2** reside, stay, have your home, inhabit, settle ■ adj living, animate, conscious, breathing, aware Opposite: dead

liveable see livable

lived-in adj **1** homely, comfortable, relaxed, dishevelled, laid-back (infml) **2** careworn, haggard, worn, lined, tired

live down v get over, recover from, shake off, forget

livelihood n **1** living, income, source of revenue, means of support, maintenance **2** employment, occupation, trade, business, work

liveliness n energy, sparkle, vigour, joie de vivre, vivacity Opposite: lethargy

lively adj energetic, vigorous, sparkling, active, vivacious Opposite: lethargic

liven v perk up, cheer up, boost, quicken, energize Opposite: depress

liven up v enliven, stimulate, revive, cheer up, perk up

live off v rely on, depend on, impose on, sponge (infml), mooch (infml)

live on v **1** remain, continue, survive, persist, prevail Opposite: die away **2** survive on, get by on, exist on, subsist on, eke out a living

liveried adj uniformed, costumed, dressed up, caparisoned

liverish adj irritable, bad-tempered, moody, irascible, ill-humoured

livery n **1** (literary) insignia, colours, corporate colours, racing colours **2** uniform, dress, costume, vestments, regalia

livestock n animals, cattle, stock

live through v survive, come through, get through, experience, undergo Opposite: succumb

live up to v match, achieve, reach, come up to, meet

live wire (infml) n doer, activist, high-flier, extrovert, go-getter (infml)

live with v tolerate, put up with, bear, endure, manage

livid adj **1** discoloured, bruised, purple, black-and-blue, contused **2** furious, enraged, up in arms, beside yourself, incensed Opposite: delighted

living adj alive, breathing, existing, live, active Opposite: dead ■ n livelihood, income, living wage, source of revenue, subsistence

---

COMPARE AND CONTRAST CORE MEANING: having life or existence

living not dead, or, of inanimate things, still in existence; **alive** not dead; **animate** used especially to distinguish living animals and plants from inanimate objects such as rocks, water, or buildings; **extant** still in existence.

---

living thing n creature, being, living being, life form, organism

load n weight, cargo, freight, consignment, shipment ■ v **1** fill, pack, stack, load up, pile Opposite: unload **2** put in, insert, slot in, pop in (infml) Opposite: eject **3** burden, encumber, weigh down, overload, oppress Opposite: alleviate

loaded adj **1** laden, weighed down, encumbered, burdened, overloaded Opposite: empty **2** biased, leading, deceptive, trick, manipulative Opposite: innocent

loads (infml) n many, much, lots, tons (infml), heaps (infml) Opposite: handful

load up v fill up, stack, pack, pile, fill Opposite: unload

loaf v be idle, be unoccupied, hang about, laze, loiter

loafer n idler, slacker, shirker, sloth, loiterer

loan n advance, credit, finance, mortgage ■ v lend, advance, give a loan, give an advance, allow Opposite: borrow

loath adj wary, unwilling, reluctant, chary, against Opposite: eager. See COMPARE AND CONTRAST at unwilling.

loathe v hate, dislike, detest, despise, scorn Opposite: adore

loathing n hate, hatred, antipathy, repugnance, dislike Opposite: love. See COMPARE AND CONTRAST at dislike.

loathsome adj hateful, despicable, disgusting, repugnant, detestable Opposite: delightful

lob v **1** throw, toss, fling, pitch, hurl **2** hit, knock, strike, bat, whack ■ n toss, throw, pitch, hit, ball

lobby n **1** entrance hall, foyer, reception area, vestibule, atrium **2** pressure group, interest group, ginger group, campaign group, special interest group ■ v petition, press your case, try to influence, apply pressure, sway opinion

lobby group n pressure group, campaign group, interest group, lobby, alliance

lobe n **part**, section, portion, hemisphere

local adj **1 restricted**, limited, confined, narrow, insular Opposite: universal **2 home**, neighbouring, neighbourhood, community, district Opposite: national **3 native**, indigenous, resident, homegrown Opposite: foreign ■ n **resident**, inhabitant, citizen, native Opposite: stranger

locale n **location**, place, setting, site, spot

locality n **1 area**, district, region, neighbourhood, zone **2 position**, place, site, spot, setting

localize v **1 restrict**, confine, limit, focus, contain **2 pinpoint**, locate, identify, find exactly, narrow down

localized adj **contained**, limited, restricted, confined, local Opposite: generalized

locally adv **nearby**, close by, in the vicinity, in the neighbourhood

locate v **1 find**, trace, discover, track down, detect Opposite: lose **2 place**, put, position, situate, set

location n **site**, place, position, spot, setting

loch n **1 lake**, tarn, water, lough, broad **2 inlet**, fjord, firth, creek, sea loch

lock n **1 security device**, padlock, mortise lock, safety catch, combination lock **2 curl**, strand, tuft, wisp, ringlet ■ v **1 fasten**, bolt, secure, lock up, padlock Opposite: unlock **2 fix in place**, lodge, wedge, secure, confine Opposite: free **3 brace**, clench, stiffen, tighten Opposite: flex **4 link**, clasp, intertwine, join, unite

lock away v **1 imprison**, lock up, jail, send to prison, sentence to prison Opposite: release **2 shut away**, keep safe, secure, seal up, hide away Opposite: bring out

lock horns v **argue**, row, disagree, fight, contest

lock on v **home in on**, track, follow, shadow

lock up v **imprison**, put in jail, put in prison, put behind bars, confine Opposite: release

lockup n **jail**, prison, detention centre, reformatory, slammer (slang)

locomotion n **movement**, motion, propulsion, kinetic energy, kinesis Opposite: immobility

locomotive n **train**, engine, steam engine, tank engine

lodge n **1 small house**, cabin, cottage, chalet, hunting lodge **2 hotel**, inn, resort, motel ■ v **1 stay**, live, board, be a lodger, take lodgings **2 accommodate**, board, billet, put up, quarter **3 fix in place**, embed, implant, stick, catch

lodger n **tenant**, boarder, paying guest, co-tenant, lessee

lodging n **accommodation**, room, space, place to stay, housing

lodgings (dated) n **rooms**, quarters, accommodation, digs (dated infml)

loftiness n **1 haughtiness**, superior manner, disdain, arrogance, condescension Opposite: humility **2 grandeur**, nobility, dignity Opposite: baseness **3 height**, elevation, altitude

lofty adj **1 supercilious**, superior, disdainful, lordly, arrogant Opposite: humble **2 grand**, elevated, noble, admirable, distinguished Opposite: base **3 tall**, high, towering, soaring, high-ceilinged Opposite: low

log n **record**, journal, notes, minutes, logbook ■ v **make a note of**, chart, record, note down, note

logbook n **record**, record book, log, journal, report

loge n **box**, enclosure, box seat (US)

logic n **reason**, judgment, sense, common sense, lucidity

logical adj **1 plausible**, reasonable, obvious, sensible, understandable Opposite: implausible **2 rational**, reasonable, sound, commonsense, commonsensical Opposite: illogical

log in v **gain access**, open up, start, switch on, sign in

logjam n **1 deadlock**, standstill, standoff, stalemate, impasse **2 traffic jam**, holdup, tailback, buildup, snarl-up

logo n **symbol**, sign, emblem, badge, insignia

log off v **leave**, quit, exit, log out, close down Opposite: log on

log on v **gain access**, open up, start, switch on, sign in Opposite: log off

log out see **log off**

loiter v **1 amble**, stroll, wander, drift, dally **2 wait**, linger, lurk, skulk, hang around

loll v **1 lie**, lounge, lie back, sprawl, slouch **2 droop**, hang down, dangle, sag, flop

lollop v **1 bound**, bounce, bumble, stride, lope **2 relax**, take it easy, lounge, veg out (infml), lie about (infml)

lolly (infml) n **1 money**, cash, ready money, readies (infml), dosh (infml) **2 ice lolly**, ice, lollipop

lone adj **1 solitary**, single, single-handed, solo Opposite: accompanied **2 only**, sole, unique, singular **3 isolated**, lonely, separate, distinct, discrete

loneliness n **aloneness**, solitude, isolation, seclusion Opposite: companionship

lonely adj **1 forlorn**, lost, alone, friendless, without a friend in the world **2 isolated**, solitary, secluded, cut off, deserted

loner n **recluse**, hermit, lone wolf, outsider

long adj **1 extended**, extensive, elongated, lengthy, stretched Opposite: short **2 time-consuming**, protracted, lengthy, slow, prolonged Opposite: brief ■ v **long for**, want, yearn, crave, desire. See COMPARE AND CONTRAST at **want**.

long-ago adj **past**, old, historic, early, pre-historic *Opposite*: modern

long-drawn-out adj **protracted**, prolonged, lengthy, drawn-out, dragged-out *Opposite*: brief

long-established adj **age-old**, time-honoured, timeworn, ancient, old *Opposite*: new

longevity n **long life**, permanence, durability, endurance

long haul (*infml*) n **1 ordeal**, marathon, trial, struggle, endurance test **2 trek**, hike, distance, way, schlep (*US infml*)

longing n **desire**, wish, yearning, hunger, craving

longitude n **position**, meridian, coordinate, location *Opposite*: latitude

long-lasting adj **long-term**, continuing, enduring, long-standing, long-running *Opposite*: short-lived

long-life adj **UHT**, tinned, canned *Opposite*: fresh

long-lived adj **long-lasting**, long-standing, prolonged, abiding, long-term *Opposite*: short-lived

long-lost adj **lost**, gone, forgotten, missing

long-range adj **long-term**, future, distant, far-off

long shot n **slim chance**, long odds, poor prospect, remote possibility, outside chance

long-standing adj **established**, age-old, ancient, enduring, ongoing

long-suffering adj **forgiving**, resigned, tolerant, accommodating, patient *Opposite*: intolerant

long-term adj **lasting**, long-standing, enduring, continuing, durable *Opposite*: short-term

long-winded adj **long-drawn-out**, rambling, interminable, wordy, prolix *Opposite*: concise. *See* COMPARE AND CONTRAST *at* wordy.

loofah n **sponge**, scrubber, exfoliator

look v **1 observe**, watch, see, view, regard **2 examine**, inspect, scrutinize, pore over, study **3 seem**, appear, come across, seem to be **4 explore**, investigate, examine, consider, discuss **5 focus on**, gaze, stare, glare, glance ■ n **appearance**, expression, air, aspect, guise

look after v **care for**, take care of, see to, watch over, guard *Opposite*: neglect

look ahead v **look forward**, project, plan, anticipate, think about *Opposite*: look back

lookalike (*infml*) n **double**, twin, doppelgänger, mirror image, duplicate

look back v **1 remember**, reminisce, recall, recollect, relive *Opposite*: look ahead **2 review**, check, return, revisit

look daggers v **glare**, glower, scowl, give somebody a dirty look

look down on v **scorn**, disdain, despise, frown on, abhor *Opposite*: look up to

looked-for adj **anticipated**, expected, awaited, foreseen, hoped-for *Opposite*: unexpected

looker n **observer**, watcher, spectator, viewer, onlooker

look for v **search for**, seek, hunt for, rummage

look forward to v **anticipate**, hope for, expect, await, wait for *Opposite*: dread

looking glass n **mirror**, glass, hand mirror, shaving mirror

look into v **investigate**, go into, check out, research, study

look like v **resemble**, be like, be similar to, mimic, seem like

look on the bright side v **be positive**, be optimistic, make the best of something, make the best of a bad job, make the best of things *Opposite*: despair

look out v **1 watch out**, beware, take care, pay attention, be alert **2 look over**, look on to, look out on, give on to, front

lookout n **1 guard**, sentry, sentinel, watch **2 viewpoint**, vantage point, lookout tower, crow's nest, belvedere

look over v **inspect**, examine, check, peruse, scan

lookover (*infml*) n **inspection**, examination, scan, check, scrutiny

look-see (*infml*) n **look**, glance, glimpse, peep, peek

look through v **ignore**, take no notice of, give the cold shoulder, snub, cut *Opposite*: acknowledge

look up v **1 search**, hunt, research, find, consult **2 get better**, improve, take a turn for the better, mend, recuperate *Opposite*: worsen **3 visit**, call on, contact, get in touch, locate

look up to v **admire**, respect, esteem, worship, adore *Opposite*: look down on

loom n v **1 appear**, emerge, come out, materialize, show *Opposite*: recede **2 hang over**, approach, come up, threaten, menace *Opposite*: recede

looming adj **impending**, pending, forthcoming, coming up, approaching

loop n **ring**, coil, twist, circlet, hoop ■ v **wind**, twist, coil, entwine, encircle

loophole n **dodge**, get-out, gap, ambiguity, excuse

loose adj **1 movable**, slack, wobbly, unfastened, free *Opposite*: fixed **2 floppy**, relaxed, supple, slack, droopy *Opposite*: tight **3 loose-fitting**, baggy, unrestricting, flowing, roomy *Opposite*: tight **4 free**, freed, at liberty, unchained, untied *Opposite*: secure **5 assorted**, diverse, free, miscellaneous, eclectic **6** (*dated*) **irresponsible**, lax, slack, relaxed, free *Opposite*: strict

loose-fitting adj **loose**, baggy, voluminous, roomy, ample *Opposite*: tight

loose-limbed adj **supple**, lissom, agile, lithe, elastic *Opposite*: stiff

loosen v **come loose**, work loose, untie, undo, release Opposite: tighten

looseness n **1** bagginess, shapelessness, roominess, ampleness Opposite: tightness **2** (dated) **irresponsibility**, laxity, slackness, freeness, carelessness Opposite: strictness

loosen up v **1 warm up**, limber up, stretch, exercise, prepare **2 relax**, take it easy, kick back (infml), let your hair down (infml), chill out (infml)

loot n **1 booty**, spoils, plunder, swag (slang) **2** (infml) **money**, cash, wealth, assets, dosh (infml) ■ v **burgle**, plunder, ransack, pillage, rob

looter n **robber**, raider, plunderer, burglar, thief

lop v **1 cut**, chop, hack, sever, crop Opposite: graft **2 cut off**, chop off, slice off, remove, amputate Opposite: attach **3 deduct**, take off, subtract, discount, reduce Opposite: add

lope n **pace**, stride, step, gait, tread ■ v **stride**, move, walk, lollop, yomp (infml)

lopsided adj **uneven**, askew, crooked, cock-eyed, wonky (infml) Opposite: even

lopsidedness n **unevenness**, crookedness, skewedness, imbalance, disproportionateness Opposite: evenness

loquacious adj **talkative**, garrulous, chatty, voluble, verbose Opposite: silent. See COMPARE AND CONTRAST at **talkative**.

lore n **wisdom**, tradition, teachings, knowledge, experience

lose v **1 misplace**, be unable to find, mislay, drop, miss Opposite: find **2 be defeated**, be beaten, go under, fail, suffer defeat Opposite: win **3 shake off**, evade, give somebody the slip, leave behind, get away from **4 waste**, squander, exhaust, use up, consume Opposite: save

lose consciousness v **faint**, black out, pass out, swoon, collapse Opposite: come to

lose control v **lose your temper**, get carried away, go berserk, hit the roof (infml), lose it (infml) Opposite: keep your cool (infml)

lose heart v **become despondent**, become demoralized, give up, give in, lose motivation Opposite: take heart

lose it (infml) see **lose control**

lose out (infml) v **miss out**, get the worst of it, come off second best, fail to benefit, miss the boat Opposite: gain

loser n **failure**, also-ran, underdog, dud (infml), has-been (infml) Opposite: achiever

lose the thread v **get off the point**, lose the point, digress, go off at a tangent, deviate Opposite: follow

lose touch v **lose contact**, drift apart, lose track of, be out of the loop (infml) Opposite: keep up

lose track of v **misplace**, lose sight of, lose, be unable to follow, mislay Opposite: keep track of

lose weight v **diet**, go on a diet, slim, watch your weight, count the calories

lose your bearings v **get lost**, lose your way, stray, become disorientated, go wrong

lose your cool (infml) v **lose control**, go off the deep end, go berserk, lose your head, lose your rag (infml) Opposite: keep your cool (infml)

lose your footing v **stumble**, trip, trip up, fall over, slip

lose your nerve v **go to pieces**, break down, get flustered, give up, fall apart Opposite: keep your cool (infml)

lose your patience v **flare up**, snap, hit the roof (infml), lose your cool (infml), lose it (infml) Opposite: keep your cool (infml)

lose your rag (infml) see **lose your temper**

lose your temper v **fly into a rage**, explode, hit the roof (infml), go mad (infml), fly off the handle (infml) Opposite: keep your cool (infml)

lose your way v **lose your bearings**, get lost, become disorientated, stray, go wrong

losing adj **behind**, trailing, bringing up the rear, down Opposite: winning

loss n **1 deprivation**, removal, withdrawal, forfeiture, depletion **2 bereavement**, passing, passing away, death, demise **3 deficit**, debit, deficiency, shortfall Opposite: profit **4 damage**, harm, injury, cost, hurt **5 defeat**, beating, thrashing, trouncing, hammering (infml) Opposite: victory

lossmaking adj **uneconomic**, running at a loss, unprofitable, not viable, inefficient Opposite: profitable

loss of consciousness n **blackout**, faint, fainting fit, swoon, collapse

lost adj **1 misplaced**, mislaid, missing, gone, nowhere to be found Opposite: found **2 off-course**, disorientated, adrift, astray **3 confused**, bewildered, bemused, at sea, stumped **4 forlorn**, vulnerable, abandoned, alone, aimless **5 deep in thought**, spellbound, entranced, rapt, engrossed

lot n **1 batch**, set, assortment, grouping, bundle **2 ration**, share, slice, proportion, percentage **3 fate**, destiny, luck, kismet, fortune

loth see **loath**

lotion n **oil**, ointment, liniment, unguent, rub

lots n **plenty**, many, heaps (infml), bags (infml), loads (infml) Opposite: a few

lottery n **1 draw**, sweepstake, raffle, lotto, bingo **2 risk**, gamble, chance, fortune, luck Opposite: certainty

lotus-eater n **lazy person**, hedonist, dreamer, daydreamer, idler

louche adj **disreputable**, shady, dubious, immoral, suspect Opposite: respectable

loud adj **1 noisy**, deafening, piercing, strident, thunderous Opposite: quiet **2 vociferous**, rowdy, boisterous, raucous, noisy *Opposite*: gentle **3 lurid**, flamboyant, brash, flashy, gaudy *Opposite*: muted

loudmouthed *(infml)* *adj* **blustering**, loud, noisy, vociferous, voluble *Opposite*: quiet

loudness *n* **volume**, noise, decibels, level, intensity *Opposite*: quietness

lough *n* **1 lake**, tarn, broad, water, loch **2 inlet**, fjord, firth, creek, sea loch

lounge *n* **living room**, drawing room, sitting room, family room, salon ■ *v* **sprawl**, recline, laze, loaf, loll

lounger *n* **reclining seat**, recliner, sunbed, folding chair, deck chair

lousy *(infml)* *adj* **1 awful**, rotten, miserable, dreadful, abysmal *Opposite*: great **2 useless**, worthless, stupid, second-rate, mean *Opposite*: great

lout *n* **bully**, thug, rogue, boor, hoodlum

loutish *adj* **coarse**, impolite, rough, uncouth, rude *Opposite*: genteel

loutishness *n* **uncouthness**, rudeness, incivility, vulgarity, boorishness *Opposite*: politeness

lovable *adj* **endearing**, adorable, enchanting, attractive, delightful

love *v* **feel affection for**, adore, worship, be in love with, be devoted to *Opposite*: hate **2 like**, enjoy, appreciate, be keen on, be partial to *Opposite*: dislike ■ *n* **1 affection**, fondness, passion, liking, tenderness *Opposite*: hatred **2 darling**, dear, dearest, sweetheart, honey *(US infml)*

COMPARE AND CONTRAST CORE MEANING: a strong positive feeling towards somebody or something

love an intense feeling of tender affection and compassion, especially strong romantic or sexual feelings between people; **liking** a feeling of enjoying something or or finding it pleasant, or personal taste or choice; **affection** fond or tender feelings towards somebody or something; **fondness** a feeling of affection or preference; **passion** intense or overpowering emotion, either love for somebody, usually of a strong sexual nature, or strong liking or enthusiasm for something; **infatuation** an intense but short-lived, often unrealistic love for somebody, usually of a romantic or sexual nature; **crush** *(infml)* a temporary romantic infatuation, especially in teenagers and young people.

---

loved *adj* **precious**, treasured, respected, important, adored *Opposite*: detested

loved ones *n* **family**, nearest and dearest, relations, relatives, kin

loveless *adj* **harsh**, hard, unhappy, unkind, cruel *Opposite*: loving

loveliness *n* **beauty**, attractiveness, good looks, exquisiteness, charm *Opposite*: ugliness

lovely *adj* **1 beautiful**, attractive, pretty, good-looking, gorgeous *Opposite*: ugly **2 pleasant**, agreeable, delightful, perfect, wonderful *Opposite*: unpleasant. *See* COMPARE AND CONTRAST *at* **good-looking.**

lovesick *adj* **infatuated**, sentimental, overly affectionate, obsessed, pining

loving *adj* **affectionate**, tender, fond, devoted, caring *Opposite*: cold

low *adj* **1 near to the ground**, close to the ground, low down, short, small *Opposite*: high **2 depleted**, at a low level, down, short, in short supply *Opposite*: high **3 soft**, muted, soothing, muffled, subdued *Opposite*: loud **4 sad**, miserable, unhappy, down, depressed *Opposite*: cheerful ■ *n* **low point**, slump, depression, depths, nadir *Opposite*: peak

lowbrow *adj* **popular**, mass-market, philistine, undemanding, middle-of-the-road *Opposite*: highbrow

lowdown *(infml)* *n* **facts**, fundamentals, basics, ins and outs, particulars

lower *adj* **inferior**, subordinate, lesser, junior, poorer *Opposite*: superior ■ *v* **1 let down**, drop, let fall, hand down, sink *Opposite*: raise **2 lessen**, drop, cut, bring down, decrease *Opposite*: raise

lower class *n* **working class**, masses, hoi polloi, lower classes, proletariat *Opposite*: upper class

lower-class *adj* **working-class**, blue-collar, plebeian, popular *Opposite*: aristocratic

lowermost *adj* **lowest**, bottommost, deepest, bottom, last

lower yourself *v* **deign**, condescend, cheapen yourself, stoop, humiliate yourself

low-grade *adj* **low-quality**, inferior, cheap, substandard, second-rate *Opposite*: premium

low-key *adj* **simple**, unglamorous, unspectacular, understated, subdued *Opposite*: elaborate

lowland *n* **plain**, fen, flat, valley, swamp *Opposite*: high ground

lowliness *n* **humbleness**, meekness, submissiveness, inferiority, commonness *Opposite*: eminence

lowly *adj* **humble**, poor, deprived, ordinary, modest *Opposite*: exalted *(fml)*

low-lying *adj* **low**, lowland, sea-level, below sea level, coastal *Opposite*: high

low-minded *adj* **coarse**, common, vulgar, base, uncouth *Opposite*: refined

low-pitched *adj* **low**, deep, throaty, gruff *Opposite*: high-pitched

low point *n* **low**, all-time low, nadir, rock bottom *Opposite*: high point

low-rise *adj* **double-storey**, single-storey, small, low *Opposite*: high-rise

loyal *adj* **faithful**, trustworthy, devoted, reliable, dependable *Opposite*: disloyal

loyalist *n* **stalwart**, partisan, supporter, devotee, advocate *Opposite*: rebel

loyalty *n* **faithfulness**, allegiance, constancy,

fidelity, devotion *Opposite*: disloyalty

lozenge *n* pastille, tablet, pill

lubricate *v* oil, grease, loosen

lucid *adj* **1 articulate**, clear, well-spoken, silver-tongued, smooth-tongued *Opposite*: incoherent **2 rational**, sane, sober, clear-headed, compos mentis *Opposite*: delirious **3 luminous**, shining, luminescent, limpid, translucent *Opposite*: dull

lucidity *n* **1 intelligibility**, perspicuity, fluency, eloquence, lucidness *Opposite*: ambiguousness **2 rationality**, lucidness, clarity, reason, sanity *Opposite*: confusion **3 luminousness**, luminescence, limpidness, lucidness, translucence *Opposite*: dullness

lucidness *see* lucidity

luck *n* **1 good fortune**, good luck, stroke of luck, windfall, blessing *Opposite*: misfortune **2 chance**, fate, fortune, destiny, providence

luckless *adj* hapless, unlucky, unfortunate, jinxed, ill-fated *Opposite*: lucky

lucky *adj* fortunate, blessed, auspicious, propitious, providential *Opposite*: unlucky

---

COMPARE AND CONTRAST CORE MEANING: relating to advantage or good fortune
lucky bringing or experiencing success or advantage, especially when this seems to happen by chance; **fortunate** bringing or experiencing unexpectedly great success or advantage; **happy** resulting in something pleasant or welcome; **providential** happening at a favourable time; **serendipitous** favourable and happening entirely by chance.

---

lucky break *n* opportunity, opening, chance, blessing, boon

lucky charm *n* amulet, mascot, good luck charm, juju, talisman

lucky dip *n* raffle, draw, lottery, tombola, lotto

lucrative *adj* profitable, rewarding, worthwhile, beneficial, well-paid *Opposite*: unprofitable

ludicrous *adj* absurd, ridiculous, preposterous, nonsensical, comical *Opposite*: sensible

ludicrousness *n* absurdity, ridiculousness, unreasonableness, foolishness, nonsensicalness *Opposite*: sensibleness

lug *v* drag, heave, cart, carry, haul

luggage *n* baggage, bags, cases, suitcases, stuff

luggage compartment *n* hold, boot, locker, trunk (*US*)

lugubrious *adj* sad, mournful, gloomy, depressing, doleful *Opposite*: cheerful

lugubriousness *n* moroseness, gloominess, melancholy, depression, sadness *Opposite*: cheerfulness

lukewarm *adj* **1 tepid**, warm, cool, hand-hot **2 unenthusiastic**, half-hearted, cool, unexcited, indifferent *Opposite*: enthusiastic

lull *v* soothe, calm, reassure, quieten, settle down *Opposite*: rouse ■ *n* quiet, calm, stillness, silence, pause *Opposite*: storm

lullaby *n* cradlesong, song, ditty, child's bedtime song, serenade

lumbago *n* backache, back pain, bad back

lumber *v* **1** (*infml*) **burden**, encumber, weigh down, land, impose *Opposite*: relieve **2 trudge**, shamble, hobble, plod, clump

lumbering *adj* awkward, clumsy, unwieldy, hulking, graceless *Opposite*: dainty

luminary *n* celebrity, star, achiever, personality, personage *Opposite*: nobody

luminosity *n* glow, light, brilliance, radiance, shine

luminous *adj* glowing, shining, brilliant, bright, radiant *Opposite*: dull

lump *n* **1 bump**, swelling, protuberance, knob, inflammation *Opposite*: dent **2 piece**, chunk, morsel, block, section ■ *v* **1 group**, collect, combine, join, amalgamate *Opposite*: split **2** (*infml*) **put up with**, deal with, take, endure, bear

lumpy *adj* **1 clumpy**, uneven, bumpy, knobbly **2 cumbersome**, awkward, lumbering, unwieldy, graceless *Opposite*: graceful

lunge *n* swipe, grab, swing, thrust, stab ■ *v* **1 attack**, dive, spring, leap, charge **2 grab**, swipe, swing, thrust, stab

lurch *v* **1 pitch**, stagger, rock, tilt, list **2 totter**, stagger, stumble, sway, reel

lure *v* entice, tempt, attract, decoy, draw in ■ *n* bait, trap, decoy, enticement, temptation

lurid *adj* **1 shocking**, explicit, sensational, vivid, juicy (*infml*) *Opposite*: bland **2 loud**, garish, gaudy, bright, colourful *Opposite*: dull

luridness *n* **1 explicitness**, sensationalism, vividness, juiciness (*infml*) **2 garishness**, brightness, vividness, gaudiness, colourfulness

lurk *v* lie in wait for, loiter, prowl, hang about, skulk

luscious *adj* juicy, moist, delicious, succulent, sweet *Opposite*: dry

lusciousness *n* juiciness, succulence, moistness, palatability, sweetness *Opposite*: dryness

lush *adj* **1 verdant**, abundant, green, flourishing, thriving *Opposite*: arid **2 luxurious**, lavish, opulent, sumptuous, deluxe *Opposite*: downmarket

lushness *n* **1 greenness**, abundance, fertility, leafiness, luxuriance *Opposite*: aridity **2 luxury**, lavishness, sumptuousness, opulence, richness

lust *n* desire, envy, covetousness, longing, yearning ■ *v* yearn, desire, long, hanker, hunger

lustful *adj* lecherous, libidinous, lascivious, passionate, amorous

lustre *n* sheen, shine, patina, gleam, glint *Opposite*: dullness

lustreless *adj* dull, mat, drab, faded, unpolished *Opposite*: shiny

lustrous *adj* **shiny**, glossy, radiant, gleaming, shimmering *Opposite*: dull

lusty *adj* **hearty**, healthy, vigorous, forceful, robust *Opposite*: feeble

luxuriance *n* **lavishness**, luxury, extravagance, abundance, richness

luxuriant *adj* **1 lush**, flourishing, thriving, exuberant, rank *Opposite*: sparse **2 abundant**, lavish, plentiful, copious, ample *Opposite*: meagre

luxuriate *v* **enjoy**, wallow, indulge, bask, relish

luxurious *adj* **1 deluxe**, sumptuous, opulent, expensive, lavish *Opposite*: simple **2 extravagant**, indulgent, decadent, prodigal, epicurean *Opposite*: simple

luxuriousness *n* **expensiveness**, luxury, sumptuousness, magnificence, fulsomeness

luxury *n* **1 treat**, extra, extravagance, indul-gence, bonus *Opposite*: necessity **2 lav-ishness**, comfort, sumptuousness, opulence, magnificence

lying *adj* **deceitful**, dishonest, two-faced, insincere, untruthful *Opposite*: truthful ■ *n* **dishonesty**, deceit, duplicity, falseness, untruthfulness *Opposite*: truthfulness

lynch *v* **hang**, string up, murder, mob, assassinate

lynchpin *see* linchpin

lyric *adj* **1 poetic**, romantic, emotional, expressive, inspired **2 musical**, melodic, harmonious, tuneful, lilting

lyrical *adj* **poetic**, romantic, emotional, expressive, inspired

lyricism *n* **poeticality**, expressiveness, eloquence, floweriness

lyrics *n* **words**, lines, libretto

M

ma *(infml) n* **mother**, mum *(infml)*, mummy *(infml)*, mam *(infml)*, mama *(infml)*

macabre *adj* **ghoulish**, ghastly, grisly, chilling, gruesome

macadam *n* **asphalt**, tar, bitumen, Tarmac, blacktop *(US)*

macerate *v* **1 soften**, soak, steep, marinate, marinade **2 break up**, separate, soak, mash, pulp **3 waste away**, starve, fast, slim down, lose weight

Machiavellian *adj* **cunning**, unscrupulous, tricky, amoral, devious *Opposite*: honest

machinate *v* **plot**, scheme, conspire, intrigue, hatch

machination *n* **intrigue**, plotting, manoeu-vring, scheming, planning

machine *n* **1 mechanism**, engine, appliance, apparatus, contraption **2 system**, machinery, structure, procedure, mechanism **3 automaton**, robot, cyborg, android

machine-gun *v* **shoot**, kill, fire at, blaze, strafe ■ *adj* **staccato**, rapid, abrupt, fast, quick *Opposite*: slow

machinery *n* **1 mechanism**, moving parts, workings, works, cogs **2 machines**, apparatus, tackle, gear, technology **3 organization**, system, procedure, machine, structure

machinist *n* **machine operator**, operator, factory worker, operative, technician

machismo *n* **manliness**, masculinity, masculineness, maleness, virility

macho *adj* **manly**, masculine, virile, laddish

macro *n* **instruction**, command, key code, function, short cut

macrobiotic *adj* **wholefood**, vegan, vegetarian, organic, wholegrain

macrocosm *n* **system**, structure, formation, composition, whole *Opposite*: microcosm

mad *adj* **1 angry**, furious, livid, irate, infuriated *Opposite*: calm **2 uncontrolled**, frenzied, frenetic, panic-stricken, frantic *Opposite*: calm **3 passionate**, wild about, mad on, keen on, infatuated with *Opposite*: indifferent

madcap *adj* **silly**, zany, chaotic, wild, crazy *(infml) Opposite*: sensible

madden *v* **infuriate**, enrage, annoy, anger, irritate *Opposite*: pacify

maddened *adj* **infuriated**, incensed, annoyed, angered, enraged *Opposite*: calm

maddening *adj* **infuriating**, annoying, irritating, exasperating, frustrating *Opposite*: pleasing

made-to-measure *adj* **tailor-made**, custom-made, customized, custom-built, bespoke *Opposite*: off-the-peg

made-to-order *see* made-to-measure

made-up *adj* **pretend**, invented, concocted, fictional, fictitious *Opposite*: real

madly *adv* **1 intensely**, extremely, strongly, deeply, very **2 wildly**, frantically, frenetically, rashly, riotously *Opposite*: calmly

madness *n* **folly**, foolishness, stupidity, foolhardiness

maelstrom *n* **tumult**, turbulence, flurry, whirl, turmoil

maestro *n* **genius**, talent, virtuoso, marvel, expert *Opposite*: amateur

mafia *n* **clique**, gang, coterie, faction, set

magazine *n* **1 periodical**, publication, glossy magazine, journal, weekly **2 arsenal**, depot, repository, ordnance, stockpile

magic *n* **1 enchantment**, sorcery, witchcraft, voodoo, augury **2 conjuring**, tricks, trickery, illusion, sleight of hand **3 mystery**, charm, appeal, allure, attraction ■ *adj* **1 enchanted**, magical, fairylike, charmed, dreamlike **2 supernatural**, magical, paranormal, mysterious, miraculous *Opposite*: normal **3 thrilling**, magical, enchanting, delightful, wonderful *Opposite*: mundane **4 powerful**, special, key, all-important, famous

magical *adj* **1 enchanted**, magic, fairylike, charmed, dreamlike **2 supernatural**, magic, paranormal, mysterious, miraculous *Opposite*: normal **3 thrilling**, magic, enchanting, delightful, wonderful *Opposite*: mundane

magician *n* **1 conjurer**, illusionist, entertainer, escape artist, performer **2 sorcerer**, wizard, warlock, enchanter, necromancer *(literary)* **3 genius**, virtuoso, expert, wizard, marvel

magisterial *adj* **1 commanding**, authoritative, majestic, stately, dignified *Opposite*: lightweight **2 overbearing**, arrogant, superior, domineering, imperious *Opposite*: diffident **3 authoritative**, expert, able, knowledgeable, scholarly

magistrate *n* **law officer**, justice of the peace, judge, JP, justice

magma *n* **molten rock**, lava, tuff, igneous rock, pumice

magnanimity *n* **nobility**, high-mindedness, fairness, generousness, generosity *Opposite*: pettiness

magnanimous *adj* **generous**, benevolent, big-hearted, openhanded, altruistic *Opposite*: petty. *See* COMPARE AND CONTRAST *at* **generous**.

magnate *n* **tycoon**, mogul, entrepreneur, industrialist, baron

magnet *n* **1 magnetic body**, lodestone, horseshoe magnet, electromagnet, bar magnet **2 lure**, draw, attraction, crowd puller, inducement

magnetic *adj* **attractive**, charming, compelling, alluring, captivating *Opposite*: repellent

magnetism *n* **1 magnetic field**, attraction, pull **2 charisma**, appeal, allure, charm, magic

magnetize *v* **attract**, charm, influence, draw, fascinate *Opposite*: repel

magnification *n* **exaggeration**, intensification, enlargement, increase, amplification *Opposite*: reduction

magnificence *n* **splendour**, glory, brilliance, radiance, majesty

magnificent *adj* **superb**, wonderful, splendid, glorious, brilliant *Opposite*: unimpressive

magnify *v* **1 enlarge**, blow up, expand, amplify, increase *Opposite*: shrink **2** *(fml)* **worship**, praise, extol, laud, glorify

magnitude *n* **1 greatness**, size, extent, degree, amount **2 importance**, significance, enormity, weight, consequence *(fml)* *Opposite*: triviality

magnum *n* **bottle**, jeroboam, demijohn

magpie *(infml)* *n* **1 chatterer**, babbler, prattler, talker, gossip **2 collector**, hoarder, saver, accumulator, squirrel *(infml)*

maharishi *n* **religious teacher**, guru, mahatma, prophet, evangelist *Opposite*: follower

maiden *n* **girl**, lass, young woman, young lady, damsel *(literary)* ■ *adj* **first**, earliest, initial, original

mail *n* **letters**, correspondence, packages, parcels, post

mailbag *n* **1 postbag**, sack, bag, satchel, shoulder bag **2 correspondence**, feedback, mail, letters, postbag

mailer *n* **envelope**, padded envelope, carton, mailing tube, container

mailing list *n* **distribution list**, register, circulation list, newsgroup, address book

mail order *n* **home shopping**, electronic shopping, cybershopping, online shopping, teleordering

mailshot *n* **advertisement**, circular, leaflet, letter, brochure

maim *v* **wound**, injure, hurt, mutilate, damage

main *adj* **major**, chief, key, foremost, core *Opposite*: minor

mainland *n* **landmass**, continent, land *Opposite*: island

main line *n* **rail route**, principal route, major route

mainline *adj* **main**, chief, central, inter-city, principal *Opposite*: local

mainly *adv* **mostly**, largely, chiefly, for the most part, primarily

mainspring *n* **driving force**, motive force, motivating force, chief reason, chief motive

mainstay *n* **cornerstone**, linchpin, keystone, foundation, basis

mainstream *adj* **normal**, typical, conventional, ordinary, middle-of-the-road *Opposite*: unconventional

maintain *v* **1 uphold**, keep, keep up, continue, sustain *Opposite*: destroy **2 argue**, claim, insist, assert, hold *Opposite*: deny **3 look after**, care for, take care of, keep up, keep in good condition *Opposite*: neglect

maintenance *n* **1 preservation**, upholding, protection, continuation, continuance *Opposite*: destruction **2 repairs**, upkeep, looking after, care, keep *Opposite*: neglect **3 alimony**, allowance, child support, child maintenance, grant

majestic *adj* **1 impressive**, superb, grand, wonderful, splendid *Opposite*: modest **2 regal**, royal, grand, stately, imposing *Opposite*: humble

majesty *n* **magnificence**, splendour, dignity, grandeur, illustriousness

major adj 1 main, chief, key, foremost, leading Opposite: minor 2 **significant**, important, weighty, substantial, crucial Opposite: trivial 3 **serious**, grave, life-threatening Opposite: minor

majority n 1 **bulk**, preponderance, mass, greater part, lion's share 2 **margin**, difference, gap, advantage, lead 3 **adulthood**, maturity, manhood, womanhood, adult years Opposite: childhood ■ adj **mainstream**, popular, common, widely held, middle-of-the-road Opposite: minority

make v 1 **create**, fashion, compose, craft, build Opposite: destroy 2 **put together**, assemble, make up, put up, cobble together 3 **manufacture**, produce, fabricate, churn out, yield Opposite: consume 4 **cause**, bring about, create, give rise to, occasion 5 **cook**, prepare, concoct, produce, create 6 **earn**, bring in, get, take home, get paid Opposite: spend 7 **force**, compel, pressurize, pressure, command Opposite: ask 8 **become**, turn into, change into, be 9 **appoint**, elect, designate, nominate, name 10 **achieve**, get into, get on to, succeed, progress to Opposite: miss 11 **form**, make up, constitute, comprise, be 12 **manage**, accomplish, find time for, fit in, finish 13 **reach**, get to, make it to, get as far as, arrive at ■ n **sort**, type, kind, style, variety

make a beeline for v **make straight for**, go directly to, head for, target

make a big thing of v **make a mountain out of a molehill**, make a point of, make a show of, make a big deal out of (infml) Opposite: play down

make a clean breast of things v **admit**, confess, own up, tell all, tell the truth

make a difference v **have an effect**, matter, be important, change things

make a dog's breakfast/dinner of v **make a mess of**, make a pig's ear of, botch (infml), bungle (infml), foul up (infml)

make a fool of v **con**, deceive, dupe, fool, mislead

make a fool of yourself v **appear foolish**, embarrass yourself, expose yourself to ridicule, humiliate yourself, make an exhibition of yourself

make a fuss v **complain**, fuss, make a scene, kick up a fuss, make a mountain out of a molehill

make a fuss of v **make much of**, indulge, spoil, cosset, coddle Opposite: ignore

make a hash of (infml) v **muddle**, confuse, jumble, spoil, mix up

make allowances v **take into account**, bear in mind, consider, take into consideration, allow for

make amends v **compensate**, make reparations, make up for, pay back, recompense

make a mess of v **do badly**, make a dog's dinner of, manage badly, mishandle, mismanage

make a mountain out of a molehill v **exaggerate**, make a big thing of, make a fuss, make too much of, overstate

make a name for yourself v **succeed**, rise to fame, make it to the top, become known, gain respect

make an effort v **attempt**, endeavour, put yourself out, try, work hard

make an exhibition of yourself v **make a fool of yourself**, expose yourself to ridicule, embarrass yourself, behave foolishly, show off

make a note of v 1 **mark**, memorize, notice, observe, remark upon 2 **write down**, jot down, take down, keep a record of

make a point of v 1 **let people know about**, make a big thing of, make a fuss, make a show of, make a song and dance about (infml) 2 **make sure to**, not forget to, take care to, remember to, make an effort to

make a scene v **be angry**, carry on, make an exhibition of yourself, make a fuss, throw a tantrum

make a splash v **make an impression**, impress, get noticed, make an impact, turn heads

make a stab at (infml) v **attempt**, try, strive, endeavour, have a go at (infml)

make a start v **begin**, get going, jump in, start, get cracking (infml) Opposite: procrastinate

make a statement v **say something**, send a message, catch the eye, turn heads, make an impact

make available v **free up**, find, set aside, release, provide Opposite: refuse

make believe v **pretend**, imagine, fantasize, daydream, muse

make-believe n **fantasy**, pretence, roleplaying, play-acting, story Opposite: reality ■ adj **pretend**, imaginary, fantasy, made-up, invented Opposite: real

make better v **cure**, heal, treat, alleviate, relieve

make certain v **check**, double-check, ensure, make sure, be in no doubt

make clear v **clarify**, elucidate, spell out, explain, give details Opposite: obscure

make contact v **speak to**, approach, communicate, touch base, get in touch Opposite: drop

make contacts v **meet people**, exchange cards, introduce yourself, make friends, network

make do v **manage**, put up with, cope, accept, tolerate

make ends meet v **cope**, manage, pay your bills, break even, get by

make enquiries see make inquiries

make for v 1 **head for**, head towards, go towards, proceed towards, aim for 2 **produce**, create, bring about, give rise to, generate

make friends v **befriend**, take up with, get

in with, get to know, become acquainted *Opposite*: repel

make fun of *v* **mock**, poke fun at, laugh at, tease, ridicule *Opposite*: respect

make good *v* **succeed**, arrive, be somebody, do well, become successful *Opposite*: fail

make happen *v* **cause**, bring about, realize, make real, produce

make headway *v* **make progress**, progress, get somewhere, get on, make ground

make inquiries *v* **research**, investigate, explore, look into, inspect

make inroads *v* **1 produce a result**, have an effect on, get somewhere, make something happen, make headway **2 encroach**, creep up on, dent, overstep, infringe

make it *(infml)* *v* **succeed**, achieve, accomplish, attain, manage *Opposite*: give up

make known *v* **publicize**, announce, communicate, proclaim, broadcast

make light of *v* **play down**, make little of, minimize, underestimate, understate *Opposite*: overstate

make mincemeat of *v* **defeat heavily**, thrash, rout, overwhelm, overpower

make much of *v* **make a fuss of**, mollycoddle, baby, pet, pat

make off *v* **run away**, run off, decamp, make a break for it, make a run for it *Opposite*: come back

make off with *v* **appropriate**, run away with, steal, remove, pilfer *Opposite*: return

make out *v* **1 distinguish**, see, hear, perceive, pick out **2 understand**, work out, decipher, decode, figure out **3 fill in**, write out, make, compose, draw up **4 imply**, suggest, give the impression, make somebody believe, insinuate **5 get by**, get on, manage, fare, do

makeover *n* **1 transformation**, change, restyling, cosmetic treatment, beautification **2 renovation**, restoration, transformation, alteration, conversion

make progress *v* **1 make headway**, progress, advance, get somewhere, forge ahead *Opposite*: stall **2 recover**, get well, get better, improve, be on the mend *Opposite*: deteriorate

make public *v* **publicize**, publish, release, put out, reveal

maker *n* **creator**, manufacturer, fabricator, producer, architect *Opposite*: destroyer

make sense *v* **add up**, fit, seem sensible, seem right

make sense of *v* **understand**, decode, decipher, follow, grasp *Opposite*: misunderstand

makeshift *adj* **rough-and-ready**, crude, temporary, improvised, provisional *Opposite*: permanent

make short work of *v* **make short shrift of**, do quickly, dash through, rush through, dash off *(infml)*

make somebody's acquaintance *v* **meet for the first time**, meet, get to know, become acquainted, bump into

make somebody's blood boil *v* **anger**, annoy, exasperate, irritate, enrage *Opposite*: delight

make somebody's hackles rise *v* **anger**, antagonize, get up somebody's nose, annoy, get somebody's back up *Opposite*: placate

make sure *v* **validate**, confirm, certify, take care, ensure *Opposite*: assume

make the best of a bad job *see* **make the best of things**

make the best of things *v* **take the bad with the good**, look on the bright side, keep your chin up, keep smiling, take the rough with the smooth *Opposite*: complain

make the grade *v* **meet the standards**, be good enough, measure up, hit the mark, satisfy *Opposite*: fail

make the most of *v* **capitalize on**, take advantage of, maximize, profit from, make hay while the sun shines *(infml)* *Opposite*: squander

make tracks *(infml)* *v* **leave**, depart, go away, make a move, hit the road *Opposite*: stay

make up *v* **1 prepare**, make ready, get ready, set up, put together **2 contribute**, add, supply, come up with, provide *Opposite*: deduct **3 form**, comprise, constitute, add up to, make **4 invent**, concoct, forge, fabricate, think up **5 top up**, subsidize, complete, supplement, round up **6 be reconciled**, make peace, forgive and forget, kiss and make up, bury the hatchet *Opposite*: fall out **7 compensate**, make amends, make good, recompense, redeem

makeup *n* **1 cosmetics**, face paint, greasepaint, powder and paint, maquillage **2 composition**, constitution, structure, formation, construction **3 temperament**, character, personality, nature, disposition

make up your mind *v* **decide**, come to a decision, resolve, determine

make use of *v* **utilize**, use, draw on, take advantage of, avail yourself of. *See* COMPARE AND CONTRAST *at* use.

make waves *v* **kick up a fuss**, create a stir, rock the boat, dissent, revolt

makeweight *n* **1 counterpoise**, weight, counterbalance, ballast, counterweight **2 extra**, complement, supplement, compensation, reinforcement

make your mark *v* **succeed**, arrive, make an impact, make an impression, make your presence felt

make yourself known *v* **introduce yourself**, say who you are, identify yourself, give your name, come forward

make yourself useful *v* **help out**, be of service, lend a hand, assist, rally round *Opposite*: hinder

make your way *v* **go**, move, head, wend your way, pick your way

making n **creation**, manufacture, production, construction, assembly

makings n **1 ingredients**, requirements, components, elements, materials **2 qualities**, potential, wherewithal, what it takes, assets

maladjusted adj **disturbed**, neurotic, unstable, confused, alienated Opposite: well-adjusted

maladjustment n **instability**, disturbance, confusion, alienation, estrangement Opposite: stability

maladroit adj **awkward**, clumsy, inept, gauche, ungainly Opposite: dexterous

maladroitness n **clumsiness**, insensitivity, awkwardness, ineptitude, gaucheness Opposite: gracefulness

malady n **sickness**, illness, disease, disorder, condition

malaise n **1 sickness**, illness, disease, disorder, condition **2 dissatisfaction**, discontent, unease, disquiet, anxiety

malcontent n **complainer**, mischief-maker, protester, rebel, whiner ■ adj **discontented**, disgruntled, dissatisfied, unhappy, complaining Opposite: content

male adj **masculine**, mannish, manlike, manly, virile Opposite: feminine ■ n **man**, boy, guy (infml), bloke (infml), fella (infml) Opposite: female

malediction (fml) n **curse**, spell, blight, charm, hex Opposite: blessing

malefactor (fml) n **lawbreaker**, wrongdoer, criminal, outlaw, offender

malevolence n **wickedness**, malice, ill will, evil, spite Opposite: benevolence

malevolent adj **malicious**, spiteful, wicked, nasty, mean Opposite: benevolent

malformation n **deformity**, defect, fault, abnormality, distortion

malformed adj **misshapen**, deformed, abnormal, crooked, distorted Opposite: perfect

malfunction v **act up**, break down, crash, fail, play up Opposite: function ■ n **fault**, breakdown, failure, error, blip

malice n **hatred**, spite, malevolence, meanness, nastiness Opposite: kindness

malicious adj **hateful**, spiteful, malevolent, mean, nasty Opposite: kind

malign v **criticize**, defame, vilify, denigrate, disparage Opposite: praise ■ adj **harmful**, hurtful, damaging, destructive, negative Opposite: benign

COMPARE AND CONTRAST CORE MEANING: say or write something damaging about somebody **malign** criticize somebody in a spiteful and false or misleading way; **defame** make an attack on somebody's good name or reputation with a view to damaging or destroying it; **slander** in legal terms, make spoken false accusations about somebody that are damaging to the person's reputation; **libel** in legal terms, make false damaging accusations about somebody in writing, signs, or pictures; **vilify** make viciously defamatory statements about somebody.

malignancy n **1 spite**, malevolence, menace, evil, malice Opposite: kindness **2 melanoma**, tumour, disease, growth, cancer

malignant adj **1 evil**, malevolent, hateful, spiteful, malicious Opposite: kind **2 cancerous**, spreading, harmful, fatal, life-threatening Opposite: benign

malinger v **shirk**, duck, sidestep, go AWOL, play hooky (infml)

malleability n **1 bendiness**, ductility, flexibility, plasticity, pliability Opposite: rigidity **2 impressionability**, pliability, manipulability, compliance, acquiescence Opposite: inflexibility

malleable adj **1 soft**, supple, flexible, bendy, pliable Opposite: rigid **2 impressionable**, compliant, acquiescent, manipulable, biddable. See COMPARE AND CONTRAST at **pliable**.

malnourished adj **underfed**, undernourished, underweight, starving, famished Opposite: well-fed

malnutrition n **undernourishment**, malnourishment, underfeeding, starvation, famine

malodorous adj **foul-smelling**, fetid, reeking, smelly, stinking Opposite: fragrant

malpractice n **misconduct**, negligence, abuse, dereliction, mismanagement

maltreat v **hurt**, injure, harm, damage, misuse. See COMPARE AND CONTRAST at **misuse**.

maltreatment n **mistreatment**, abuse, ill-treatment, harm, damage

mama (infml) n **mother**, mummy (infml), mum (infml), mam (infml), mammy (infml)

mamma (infml) see **mama**

mammal n **animal**, marsupial, placental mammal, marine mammal

WORD BANK

❏ **types of large mammal** alpaca, bactrian camel, bear, bison, boar, buffalo, camel, dromedary, elephant, giraffe, hippopotamus, llama, panda, polar bear, rhinoceros, wart hog

❏ **types of marine mammal** dolphin, dugong, grampus, manatee, narwhal, porpoise, sea lion, seal, walrus, whale

❏ **types of small mammal** anteater, armadillo, badger, ferret, hare, hedgehog, hyrax, marten, mink, mongoose, otter, pine marten, polecat, porcupine, rabbit, raccoon, skunk, sloth, stoat, weasel, wolverine

mammon n **ambition**, greed, loot, money, riches

mammoth adj **enormous**, huge, massive, immense, epic Opposite: tiny

man n **gentleman**, male, fella (infml), guy (infml), bloke (infml) Opposite: woman ■ v **operate**, staff, crew, work, manage

manacle n **handcuff**, chain, shackle, bond, fetter ■ v **bind**, chain, chain up, fetter, handcuff Opposite: release

manage v **1 achieve**, accomplish, succeed, be

able to, bring about *Opposite*: fail **2 cope**, fare, get on, do, get by *Opposite*: give up **3 run**, direct, administer, supervise, be in charge **4 handle**, deal with, control, cope with **5 control**, discipline, master, dominate, boss

manageable *adj* **1 feasible**, doable, practicable, viable, possible *Opposite*: unmanageable **2 controllable**, handy, user-friendly, adaptable, easy to use *Opposite*: unwieldy

management *n* **1 organization**, running, administration, supervision, managing **2 directors**, managers, executives, employers, board

manager *n* **boss**, director, executive, administrator, supervisor

managerial *adj* **executive**, management, supervisory, directorial, decision-making

mandarin *n* **bureaucrat**, official, public servant, civil servant, manager

mandate *n* **1 order**, command, directive, decree, dictate **2 authority**, authorization, consent, permission, support **3 term of office**, reign, tenure, stay ■ *v* **assign**, authorize, command, delegate, instruct

mandatory *adj* **obligatory**, compulsory, required, forced, binding *Opposite*: optional

mandible *n* **jaw**, jawbone, maxilla, mouth, mouthpart

mane *(literary or infml)* *n* **tresses**, curls, shock, head of hair, locks *(literary)*

man-eating *adj* **carnivorous**, ferocious, fierce, wild, aggressive

man friend *(infml)* *n* **male companion**, boyfriend, partner

manful *adj* **brave**, strong, resolute, bold, determined *Opposite*: cowardly

manger *n* **trough**, feeding-box, container, crib

mangle *v* **crush**, mash, smash, contort, twist

mangy *(infml)* *adj* **dirty**, shabby, disgusting, filthy, foul *Opposite*: pristine

manhandle *v* **push**, shove, jostle, hustle, move

manhood *n* **1 maturity**, independence, adulthood **2 strength**, courage, determination, virility, boldness *Opposite*: unmanliness **3 men**, menfolk, males

mania *n* **obsession**, desire, love, craze, passion

maniac *n* **enthusiast**, fanatic, zealot, fiend, freak *(infml)*

manic *(infml)* *adj* **overexcited**, agitated, hectic, frenzied, busy *Opposite*: calm

manicure *v* **trim**, file, shape, cut, clip

manifest *adj* **apparent**, unmistakable, clear, plain, obvious *Opposite*: unclear ■ *v* **make plain**, establish, demonstrate, display, reveal

manifestation *n* **sign**, indication, index, indicator, appearance

manifesto *n* **declaration**, statement, policy, guidelines, proposal

manifold *adj* **various**, diverse, many, multiple, assorted *Opposite*: uniform

manipulate *v* **1 operate**, work, use, deploy, employ **2 influence**, control, bias, direct, sway **3 manoeuvre**, direct, control, stage-manage, engineer

manipulation *n* **1 operation**, handling, management, use, guidance **2 running**, control, exploitation, persuasion, scheming **3 falsification**, forgery, alteration, misuse, tampering **4 osteopathy**, massage, movement, flexing, rubbing

manipulative *adj* **scheming**, calculating, controlling, devious, unscrupulous

manipulator *n* **Machiavelli**, exploiter, schemer, Svengali, wheeler-dealer *(infml)*

mankind *n* **1** *(dated)* **men**, menfolk, manhood, males **2 human race**, humankind, humanity, human beings, people

manliness *n* **masculinity**, machismo, manhood *Opposite*: unmanliness

manly *adj* **virile**, mannish, male, masculine, macho

man-made *adj* **artificial**, synthetic, manufactured, substitute, imitation *Opposite*: natural

manna *n* **1 food**, sustenance, victuals, fodder, provisions **2 godsend**, blessing, boon, gift, help

mannequin *n* **dummy**, model, figure, tailor's dummy, dressmaker's dummy

manner *n* **1 way**, means, method, style, custom **2 type**, kind, sort, class, category **3 behaviour**, conduct, demeanour, bearing, comportment *(fml)*

mannered *adj* **affected**, artificial, put-on, false, simpering *Opposite*: natural

mannerism *n* **1 gesture**, trait, characteristic, gesticulation, habit **2 affectation**, show, act, display, pretence

mannerly *adj* **well-behaved**, polite, refined, well-mannered, respectful *Opposite*: rude

manners *n* **1 etiquette**, protocol, good manners **2 conduct**, deportment, manner, behaviour, demeanour

manoeuvre *n* **1 move**, movement, operation, exercise **2 ploy**, trick, plot, tactic, plan ■ *v* **manipulate**, plot, contrive, plan, scheme

manqué *adj* **failed**, near, would-be, unfulfilled, unsuccessful *Opposite*: successful

mansard *n* **attic**, loft, roof, eaves, rafters

manse *n* **vicarage**, rectory, parsonage, residence, church house

manslaughter *n* **murder**, homicide, killing, assassination, slaying

mantle *(fml)* *n* **responsibility**, function, role, position, duty

mantra *n* **chant**, intonation, repetition, refrain, hymn

manual *adj* **physical**, labour-intensive, blue-collar *Opposite*: mental ■ *n* **instruction booklet**, guide, handbook, guidebook, instruction manual

manufacture v build, assemble, construct, produce, create ■ n **production**, making, creation, building, assembly

manufactured adj **factory-made**, mass-produced, industrial, man-made, synthetic

manufacturer n **builder**, producer, constructor, creator, industrialist

manufacturing n **production**, manufacture, making, assembly, construction

manure n **dung**, compost, guano, muck, fertilizer

manuscript n **document**, copy, text, script

many adj **a lot of**, lots of, numerous, countless, several Opposite: a few

many-sided adj **multifaceted**, complex, complicated, deep, multidimensional Opposite: one-dimensional

map n **plan**, chart, atlas, record, drawing ■ v **chart**, plot, plan, record, draw

map out v **work out**, plan, devise, outline, arrange

map reading n **route-planning**, routing, direction-finding, orienteering, navigation

mar v **deface**, ruin, mutilate, damage, disfigure Opposite: repair

marathon adj **lengthy**, epic, long-drawn-out, gruelling, difficult

maraud v **raid**, plunder, ransack, loot, pillage

marauder n **raider**, robber, bandit, pillager, plunderer

marble n **glass ball**, agate, cat's eye

marbled adj **veined**, streaked, mottled, lined, shot through

march v **1 parade**, file, step, troop, process **2 stride**, stomp, storm, sweep, flounce ■ n **1 hike**, trek, walk, tramp, trudge **2 protest**, picket, mass lobby, rally, demonstration

marcher n **demonstrator**, protester, walker, campaigner, supporter

marchpast n **parade**, review, muster, procession

margin n **1 boundary**, border, brim, sideline, edge **2 surplus**, room, leeway, allowance, scope

marginal adj **1 negligible**, minimal, low, minor, slight Opposite: major **2 irrelevant**, insignificant, unimportant, borderline, fringe Opposite: central

marginalization n **relegation**, sidelining, demotion, downgrading, disregarding

marginalize v **relegate**, sideline, demote, downgrade, disregard Opposite: include

marginally adv **slightly**, a little, a touch, a bit (infml), a tad (infml)

marina n **harbour**, port, dock, quay, yacht haven

marinade n **1 dressing**, sauce, flavouring, juices, infusion **2 see marinate**

marinate v **steep**, soak, infuse, immerse, douse

marine adj **1 saltwater**, seawater, sea, aquatic **2 nautical**, oceangoing, naval, seafaring, seagoing

mariner n **sailor**, seafarer, seadog, old salt, tar (archaic infml)

marital adj **conjugal**, nuptial, wedded, spousal, matrimonial

maritime adj **1 nautical**, naval, oceanic, seafaring, seagoing **2 seaside**, coastal, shoreline, littoral

mark n **1 spot**, scratch, dent, stain, smear **2 sign**, indication, feature, characteristic, symbol **3 score**, point, assessment, evaluation, grade ■ v **1 stain**, scratch, smudge, smear, blot **2 indicate**, denote, show, demonstrate, evidence **3 celebrate**, commemorate, keep, observe, solemnize **4 correct**, assess, evaluate, score, grade (US)

markdown n **discount**, price cutting, reduction, concession Opposite: mark-up

marked adj **clear**, apparent, evident, noticeable, conspicuous

marker n **indicator**, sign, indication, symbol, pointer

market n **marketplace**, souk, bazaar, arcade, fair ■ v **sell**, promote, advertise, peddle, trade

marketable adj **in demand**, sought-after, wanted, vendible, merchantable

marketing n **advertising**, selling, presentation, publicizing, promotion

marketplace n **1 bazaar**, market, souk, flea market, open market **2 trading floor**, sphere, arena, market

marking n **pattern**, coloration, design

mark out v **1 outline**, demarcate, sketch, delimit, delineate **2 distinguish**, differentiate, single out, identify, characterize

mark-up n **price increase**, rise, hike, profit, profit margin Opposite: markdown

maroon v **abandon**, leave high and dry, leave, cast aside, cast adrift

marooned adj **stranded**, deserted, abandoned, isolated, stuck

marque n **make**, label, trademark, brand

marquee n **tent**, pavilion, canvas, shelter, erection (fml)

marquetry n **inlay**, pattern, design, veneer

marred adj **blemished**, flawed, stained, disfigured, tarnished Opposite: unblemished

marriage n **1 wedding**, matrimony, wedding ceremony, marriage ceremony, nuptials (fml) Opposite: divorce **2 union**, fusion, combination, coming together, alliance Opposite: separation

marriageability n **eligibility**, suitability, availability, fitness

marriageable adj **eligible**, suitable, available, adult, grown-up

married adj **wedded**, matrimonial, nuptial, conjugal, marital

marry v get married, join in matrimony, walk down the aisle, tie the knot (infml), get hitched (infml)

marsh n bog, swamp, quagmire, swampland, marshland

marshal n officer, deputy, law officer, sheriff (US) ■ v 1 assemble, position, gather together, collect, shepherd Opposite: disperse 2 arrange, order, sort out, put in order, organize Opposite: muddle

marshland n bog, swamp, swampland, marsh, wetland

marshy adj boggy, swampy, soggy, muddy, peaty Opposite: dry

mart n auction, sale, market, store, trading place

martial adj 1 military, soldierly, warlike, battle-hardened, fighting Opposite: civilian 2 warlike, fierce, aggressive, belligerent, hostile Opposite: peaceful

martial law n state of emergency, militarism, junta, dictatorship, emergency powers

Martian n alien, extraterrestrial, ET, space-man, invader Opposite: terrestrial

martinet n disciplinarian, stickler, despot, hardliner, perfectionist Opposite: softy (infml)

martyr n 1 sacrifice, sacrificial victim, victim, scapegoat, ransom (literary) 2 idealist, witness, believer, supporter 3 sufferer, invalid, patient

martyrdom n 1 death, killing, slaughter, torture, ritual murder 2 suffering, misery, pain, sacrifice, torment

marvel n 1 wonder, miracle, spectacle, sight, curiosity 2 genius, prodigy, phenomenon, wunderkind, whiz (infml) ■ v be amazed, be surprised, be impressed, admire, wonder Opposite: deride

marvellous adj 1 amazing, impressive, remarkable, magnificent, superb Opposite: ordinary 2 great, brilliant, wonderful, fantastic, fabulous

mascot n symbol, charm, talisman, amulet, periapt Opposite: hex

masculine adj male, manly, mannish, macho, virile Opposite: feminine

masculinity n maleness, manliness, mannishness, manhood, boyhood Opposite: femininity

mash n purée, pulp, mush ■ v pulp, squash, pound, crush, smash

mask n cover, disguise, guise, façade, front ■ v hide, conceal, disguise, cover, camouflage Opposite: expose

masked adj 1 disguised, incognito, camouflaged, concealed, screened Opposite: exposed 2 undetectable, imperceptible, latent, hidden, invisible Opposite: detectable

masonry n stonework, brickwork, building materials, granite, sandstone

masque n 1 performance, allegory, theatricals, play, opera 2 masquerade, dance, ball, masked ball

masquerade n 1 pretence, deception, cover-up, subterfuge, ruse 2 masked ball, masque, ball, dance ■ v pretend to be, impersonate, pose, disguise yourself, make believe

mass n 1 form, figure, frame, physique, build 2 quantity, corpus, amount, area, reservoir 3 bulk, main part, essence, majority, better part ■ v gather, assemble, group, congregate, collect Opposite: disperse ■ adj general, widespread, common, universal, wholesale

massacre n extermination, annihilation, carnage, butchery, mass slaughter ■ v slaughter, murder, exterminate, butcher, mow down

massage n manipulation, pressure, kneading, rubbing, reflexology ■ v 1 knead, manipulate, rub, rub down 2 falsify, manipulate, alter, amend, misrepresent

masses n 1 common people, crowd, multitude, commonality, hoi polloi Opposite: elite 2 (infml) lots, loads (infml), tons (infml), heaps (infml), oodles (infml)

massif n mountain range, chain, sierra, ridge, line

massive adj 1 bulky, heavy, solid, weighty, hulking Opposite: slight 2 huge, enormous, gigantic, immense, colossal Opposite: tiny

massively (infml) adv enormously, immensely, hugely, tremendously, vastly Opposite: slightly

mass-produce v churn out, turn out, manufacture, process, knock out

mass-produced adj high-street, off-the-peg, ready-to-wear, off-the-shelf, ready-made Opposite: personalized

master n 1 controller, ruler, leader, chief, boss Opposite: underling 2 expert, virtuoso, maestro, genius, prodigy Opposite: novice 3 teacher, guru, tutor, instructor, guide Opposite: pupil ■ adj chief, principal, main, major, leading Opposite: secondary ■ v 1 conquer, gain control of, overcome, subdue, get the better of 2 become skilled at, become proficient at, grasp, learn, understand Opposite: fail

masterful adj 1 expert, skilled, proficient, skilful, accomplished Opposite: incompetent 2 authoritative, commanding, imposing, assured, forceful Opposite: weak

masterly adj skilled, skilful, proficient, talented, gifted Opposite: incompetent

mastermind n brains, architect, organizer, instigator, brain (infml) ■ v plan, engineer, oversee, organize, devise Opposite: carry out

masterpiece n work of art, magnum opus, tour de force, stroke of genius, masterwork

masterwork see masterpiece

mastery n 1 expertise, skill, knowledge, proficiency, command **2 control**, power, supremacy, authority, command

masthead *n* title, banner, strip, logo, header

masticate *v* chew, munch, crunch, champ, grind

mastication *n* chewing, munching, eating, grinding, champing

mat *n* **1 rug**, carpet, doormat, bathmat, floorcovering **2 table mat**, place mat, doily, coaster, pad ■ *v* tangle, entwine, entangle, intertwine, knot *Opposite*: disentangle

match *n* **1 competition**, bout, contest, game, tie **2 equal**, counterpart, equivalent, pair, partner ■ *v* **1 be alike**, correspond, be identical, tally, fit *Opposite*: differ **2 go with**, complement, harmonize, accord, coordinate *Opposite*: clash

matching *adj* **1 corresponding**, identical, similar, alike, same *Opposite*: different **2 toning**, harmonizing, complementary, coordinative, coordinating *Opposite*: clashing

matchless *adj* peerless, outstanding, unrivalled, unparalleled, incomparable *Opposite*: ordinary

matchmaker *n* marriage broker, go-between, fixer, intermediary, cupid

mate *n* **1 friend**, companion, comrade, pal (*infml*), chum (*infml*) *Opposite*: rival **2 helper**, assistant, colleague, partner, coworker ■ *v* breed, reproduce, couple (*fml*), copulate (*fml*)

material *n* **1 substance**, matter, raw material, stuff **2 data**, information, ideas, facts, notes **3 fabric**, textile, stuff, cloth, yard goods ■ *adj* **1 physical**, substantial, solid, factual, quantifiable *Opposite*: insubstantial **2 significant**, relevant, pertinent, important, central *Opposite*: immaterial

materialism *n* acquisitiveness, avariciousness, avarice, covetousness, avidity *Opposite*: detachment

materialistic *adj* money-orientated, grasping, acquisitive, avaricious, covetous *Opposite*: spiritual

materialization *n* appearance, arrival, advent, embodiment, manifestation *Opposite*: disappearance

materialize *v* **1 come into existence**, happen, occur, exist, take shape *Opposite*: evaporate **2 appear**, turn up, show up, arrive, reveal yourself *Opposite*: disappear

materially *adv* significantly, considerably, substantially, importantly, essentially *Opposite*: slightly

materials *n* resources, supplies, ingredients, constituents, equipment

maternal *adj* **1 motherly**, parental, nurturing, protective, guiding **2 caring**, devoted, kind, tender, gentle *Opposite*: uncaring

maternity *n* motherhood, childbearing, parenthood

matey *adj* friendly, comradely, companionable, warm, amiable *Opposite*: unfriendly

mathematical *adj* **1 arithmetical**, numerical, arithmetic, geometric, algebraic **2 exact**, precise, scientific, accurate, measured *Opposite*: random

mathematics *n* calculation, reckoning, maths, algebra, arithmetic

matinée *n* afternoon showing, show, performance, presentation

matriarch *n* mother, matron, grandmother, older woman, materfamilias (*fml*) *Opposite*: patriarch

matriculate *v* **1 admit**, register, enrol, enlist, inscribe *Opposite*: strike off **2 be admitted**, sign up, join, be enrolled, register *Opposite*: drop out

matriculation *n* admission, registration, admittance, enrolment, enlistment *Opposite*: expulsion

matrimonial *adj* marital, wedded, married, nuptial, conjugal

matrimony *n* marriage, wedlock, wedding, ceremony, service *Opposite*: divorce

matrix *n* **1 substance**, medium, carrier, solution, base **2 situation**, environment, milieu, conditions, background **3 template**, mould, format, pattern, mint

matron *n* older woman, mature woman, middle-aged woman, matriarch, doyenne

matronly *adj* full-figured, plump, portly, stout, well-rounded

matte *adj* dull, lustreless, nonglossy, muted *Opposite*: glossy

matted *adj* tangled, entwined, entangled, dishevelled, intertwined

matter *n* **1 subject**, topic, theme, issue, affair **2 trouble**, problem, difficulty, worry, concern **3 substance**, stuff, stock, staple, material ■ *v* be of importance, be important, count, signify, be significant. *See* COMPARE AND CONTRAST at subject.

matter-of-fact *adj* **1 down-to-earth**, straightforward, rational, unemotional, realistic **2 factual**, unvarnished, down-to-earth, literal, unembroidered *Opposite*: fictional

matting *n* floorcovering, tatami, mats, coconut matting, rush matting

mattress *n* futon, air mattress, air bed, pallet, pad

maturation *n* maturing, ripening, mellowing, development, growth

mature *adj* **1 grown-up**, adult, fully-grown, middle-aged, older *Opposite*: immature **2 experienced**, responsible, prudent, wise, sensible *Opposite*: naive **3 established**, developed, advanced, settled, matured *Opposite*: undeveloped **4 ripe**, mellow, ready, strong, sweet *Opposite*: young ■ *v* grow up, develop, ripen, mellow, age

matured *adj* mature, ripe, ripened, mellowed, aged *Opposite*: young

maturely adv **wisely**, sensibly, responsibly, prudently Opposite: immaturely

maturity n **1 adulthood**, prime of life, middle age, old age Opposite: youth **2 ripeness**, mellowness, development, age Opposite: youth **3 wisdom**, experience, responsibility, reliability, sensibleness Opposite: inexperience

maudlin adj **oversentimental**, mawkish, slushy, mushy, syrupy Opposite: unemotional

maul v **1 claw**, attack, ill-treat, paw, mangle **2 criticize**, attack, savage, slate (infml), slam (infml)

mauling n **criticism**, disparagement, censure, barrage, blast

mausoleum n **tomb**, vault, sepulchre, crypt, resting place

maverick n **nonconformist**, eccentric, individualist, rebel, odd one out Opposite: conformist

mawkish adj **oversentimental**, slushy, mushy, syrupy, overemotional Opposite: unemotional

mawkishness n **sentimentality**, tearfulness, mushiness, slushiness, weepiness (infml) Opposite: detachment

maxi adj **large**, mega, big, jumbo, king-size Opposite: mini

maxim n **1 saying**, adage, proverb, saw, aphorism **2 rule**, tenet, guideline, truth, principle

maximal adj **best**, greatest, most, utmost, highest Opposite: minimal

maximization n **expansion**, growth, enlargement, extension, intensification

maximize v **1 make the most of**, make best use of, exploit, take full advantage of, capitalize on Opposite: minimize **2 increase**, expand, amplify, make bigger, boost Opposite: minimize

maximum n **1 most**, greatest, highest, utmost Opposite: minimum **2 limit**, ceiling, greatest extent, top figure, upper limit Opposite: minimum

maybe adv **perhaps**, possibly, it could be, perchance (literary), mayhap (archaic) Opposite: definitely

mayday n **SOS**, distress signal, emergency call, distress call, 999 call

mayhem (infml) n **chaos**, disorder, confusion, turmoil, havoc Opposite: order

maypole n **column**, post, pole, support

maze n **1 labyrinth**, warren, web, network **2 confusion**, muddle, jumble, mess, intricacy Opposite: order

MC n **master of ceremonies**, host, toastmaster, moderator, presenter (infml)

meadow n **field**, pasture, paddock, grazing land, lea (literary)

meagre adj **small**, slight, insufficient, inadequate, sparse Opposite: plentiful

meagreness n **insufficiency**, inadequacy, scantness, sparseness, stinginess (infml) Opposite: abundance

meal n **food**, bite, snack, something to eat

WORD BANK
❏ **types of meal** banquet, barbecue, breakfast, brunch, buffet, clambake, continental breakfast, dinner, elevenses, English breakfast, high tea, lunch, luncheon, picnic, ready-made meal, snack, supper, takeaway, tea, titbit, TV dinner
❏ **parts of a meal** afters (infml), antipasto, aperitif, appetizer, canapé, delicacy, dessert, entrée, hors d'oeuvre, main course, meze, nibbles, pudding, side dish, starter, sweet, sweet course, tapas, pud (infml)

mealtime n **breakfast time**, lunchtime, dinnertime, suppertime, tea-time

mealy-mouthed adj **hypocritical**, insincere, euphemistic, indirect, devious Opposite: frank

mean v **1 denote**, signify, indicate, stand for, represent **2 intend**, propose, aim, plan, want **3 entail**, involve, require, lead to, necessitate ■ adj **1 miserly**, tightfisted, parsimonious, ungenerous, stingy (infml) Opposite: generous **2** (archaic) **humble**, lowly, poor, simple, underprivileged **3 nasty**, unkind, cruel, callous, vile Opposite: kind **4 paltry**, derisory, meagre, miserable, scanty Opposite: plentiful **5 poor**, shabby, squalid, humble, lowly Opposite: comfortable **6 middle**, mid, average, normal, standard Opposite: extreme ■ n **average**, norm, median, middle, midpoint Opposite: extremity

COMPARE AND CONTRAST CORE MEANING: referring to somebody or something below normal standards of decency
mean unkind or malicious; **nasty** showing spitefulness, malice, or ill-nature; **vile** despicable or shameful; **low** without principles or morals; **base** lacking proper social values or moral principles; **ignoble** dishonourable and contrary to the high standards of conduct expected.

mean business v **be serious**, mean what you say, mean it, be determined, be deadly serious

meander v **1 wind**, zigzag, twist and turn, twist, snake **2 wander**, roam, amble, ramble, stroll Opposite: rush

meandering adj **twisting**, winding, twisty, tortuous, snaking Opposite: straight

meanie (infml) n **miser**, skinflint, penny pincher (infml), scrooge (infml), cheapskate (infml)

meaning n **1 sense**, connotation, denotation, import, gist **2 significance**, importance, implication, worth, value Opposite: insignificance

meaningful adj **1 expressive**, evocative, telling, eloquent, speaking **2 significant**, important, consequential, momentous, deep Opposite: meaningless

meaningfulness *n* meaning, importance, significance, seriousness, relevance *Opposite*: meaninglessness

meaningless *adj* **1** empty, worthless, throwaway, hollow, pointless *Opposite*: meaningful **2** unimportant, trivial, inconsequential, irrelevant, insignificant *Opposite*: significant

meaninglessness *n* emptiness, insignificance, futility, purposelessness, worthlessness *Opposite*: importance

mean it *v* be in earnest, not be joking, be deadly serious, mean business, mean what you say

meanness *n* **1** nastiness, unkindness, cruelty, callousness, spitefulness *Opposite*: kindness **2** miserliness, niggardliness, parsimoniousness, tightfistedness, close-fistedness *(infml) Opposite*: generosity

means *n* **1** way, method, process, measures, channel **2** income, earnings, resources, revenue, funds

mean-spirited *adj* ungenerous, uncharitable, harsh, mean, unkind *Opposite*: generous

meant *adj* **1** inevitable, preordained, fated, predestined, destined *Opposite*: accidental **2** intended, designed, planned, aimed, targeted *Opposite*: unexpected

meantime *n* interim, intervening time, period in-between, the time being

mean well *v* have good intentions, have your heart in the right place, try to do the right thing, try hard, have the best intentions

meanwhile *adv* in the meantime, for the meantime, in the interim, in the intervening time, for now

measly *(infml) adj* meagre, ungenerous, mean, derisory, paltry *Opposite*: ample

measurable *adj* **1** quantifiable, assessable, gaugeable, computable, calculable *Opposite*: indeterminate **2** considerable, appreciable, noticeable, detectable, perceptible *Opposite*: imperceptible

measurably *adv* noticeably, evidently, significantly, demonstrably, obviously *Opposite*: insignificantly

measure *n* **1** amount, degree, quantity, portion, ration **2** measuring device, gauge, meter, counter ■ *v* gauge, calculate, compute, determine, assess

measured *adj* **1** deliberate, calculated, precise, exact, careful *Opposite*: unthinking **2** slow, unhurried, unrushed, restrained, stately *Opposite*: hurried

measurement *n* dimension, size, extent, quantity, amount

WORD BANK

❏ **types of metric unit** centigram, centilitre, centimetre, decagram, decalitre, decametre, decigram, decilitre, decimetre, gram, hectare, hectogram, hectolitre, hectometre, kilogram, kilolitre, kilometre, litre, metre, microgram, micrometre, milligram, millilitre, millimetre, tonne

❏ **types of nonmetric unit** acre, barrel, bushel, degree Fahrenheit, dram, fluid dram, fluid ounce, foot, furlong, gallon, gill, inch, mile, ounce, peck, pint, pound, quart, rod, ton, yard

❏ **types of SI unit** becquerel (radioactivity), coulomb (electric charge), degree Celsius (temperature), farad (capacitance), gray (radiation dose), henry (inductance), hertz (frequency), joule (energy), lumen (luminous flux), lux (illuminance), newton (force), ohm (electric resistance), pascal (pressure), siemens (electric conductance), sievert (radiation effects), tesla (magnetic flux density), volt (electric potential), watt (power), weber (magnetic flux)

measure up *v* hit the mark, satisfy, deliver, fulfil requirements, do *Opposite*: fall short

measuring device *n* gauge, measure, meter, counter

WORD BANK

❏ **types of measuring device** altimeter, anemometer, aneroid barometer, balance, barograph, barometer, callipers, clock, compass, dipstick, dividers, dropper, Geiger counter, measuring tape, micrometer, mileometer, pipette, protractor, quadrant, rule, scale, speedo, speedometer, spirit level, statoscope, tachometer, tape, tape measure, theodolite, thermometer, weather vane, weighbridge, weighing machine, weighing scales, wind gauge, windsock

meat *n* **1** flesh, food, carrion **2** substance, heart, gist, pith, kernel

WORD BANK

❏ **types of cut** best end, breast, brisket, chop, chuck, chump, cutlet, drumstick, flank, foreshank, hock, joint, leg, loin, neck, rasher, rib, round, scrag end, shoulder, side, silverside, sparerib, steak, topside, wing

❏ **types of meat** beef, chicken, duck, gammon, goat, goose, grouse, hare, lamb, mutton, partridge, pheasant, pork, rabbit, turkey, veal, venison, wild boar

❏ **types of processed meat** bacon, beefburger, bratwurst, bresaola, burger, chorizo, foie gras, frankfurter, ground beef, ground meat, ham, hamburger, jerky, liver sausage, meat loaf, meatball, merguez, mince, minced beef, minced meat, mincemeat, mortadella, pancetta, parma ham, pastrami, pâté, patty, pepperoni, rissole, salami, sausage, saveloy

❏ **types of steak** Chateaubriand, fillet, porterhouse steak, rump, sirloin, T-bone steak, tenderloin

meaty *adj* **1** brawny, burly, muscular, fleshy, hunky *(infml) Opposite*: weedy **2** substantial, profound, deep, weighty, solid *Opposite*: lightweight

mecca *n* focus, focal point, magnet, hub, centre

mechanical *adj* **1** motorized, powered, power-driven, machine-driven, automated *Opposite*: manual **2** automatic, perfunctory, unconscious, unthinking, reflex

mechanics *n* workings, technicalities, procedure, mechanism, process

mechanism n 1 **device**, instrument, apparatus, machine, machinery 2 **means**, method, system, procedure, process

mechanistic adj **automatic**, mechanical, machine-like, automatous, robotic

mechanization n **automation**, computerization, streamlining, modernization, systematization

mechanize v **automate**, power, systematize, industrialize, program

mechanized adj **automated**, mechanical, industrialized, automatic, computerized

medal n **award**, decoration, honour, distinction, laurel

medallion n **medal**, decoration, pendant, ornament

medallist n **champion**, winner, victor, runner-up

meddle v **interfere**, butt in, stick your nose in, intrude, put your oar in

meddler n **troublemaker**, nuisance, gossip, interferer, busybody (infml)

meddlesome adj **interfering**, intrusive, meddling, officious, prying Opposite: detached

meddling n **interference**, inquisitiveness, intrusion, prying, intrusiveness ■ adj **interfering**, meddlesome, inquisitive, intrusive, prying Opposite: uninterested

media n **mass media**, television, radio, newspapers, magazines

median n **mean**, midpoint, middle, norm, standard

mediate v **arbitrate**, intercede, facilitate, intermediate, referee Opposite: provoke

mediation n **arbitration**, intercession, conciliation, intervention, negotiation Opposite: provocation

mediator n **go-between**, intermediary, third party, arbitrator, negotiator

medic (infml) n **doctor**, medical student, houseman, physician, registrar

medical adj **medicinal**, remedial, health, homeopathic, curative ■ n **checkup**, physical, health check, examination

WORD BANK
❏ **types of complementary therapy** acupressure, acupuncture, Alexander technique, Ayurvedic medicine, Bach flower remedy, chiropractic, colour therapy, cranial osteopathy, flotation, herbal medicine, homeopathy, hydrotherapy, hypnotherapy, iridology, kinesiology, massage, music therapy, naturopathy, neurolinguistic programming, osteopathy, Pilates, reflexology, reiki, shiatsu, T'ai Chi, yoga
❏ **types of medical procedure** amniocentesis, amputation, anesthesia, angioplasty, appendectomy, biopsy, booster, bypass, Caesarean section, CAT scan, checkup, chemotherapy, diagnosis, dialysis, endoscopy, facelift, graft, hysterectomy, immunization, keyhole surgery, laparoscopy, manipulation, mastectomy, operation, physiotherapy, plastic surgery, radiotherapy, resuscitation, sedation, tracheotomy, transfusion, ultrasound scan, vaccination, vasectomy, X-ray
❏ **types of medical specialty** anaesthetics, cardiology, dermatology, endocrinology, gastroenterology, general medicine, geriatrics, gynaecology, haematology, infectious diseases, internal medicine, neurology, obstetrics, oncology, ophthalmology, paediatrics, psychiatry, radiology, rheumatology, surgery

medicament n **medicine**, remedy, treatment, pharmaceutical, curative

medicated adj **medicinal**, antiseptic, antibacterial, antiviral, analgesic

medication n **drug**, pharmaceutical, pill, tablet, capsule

medicinal adj **medicated**, remedial, healing, therapeutic, curative

medicine n **drug**, remedy, medication, treatment, prescription

medieval adj **old-fashioned**, out-of-date, primitive, feudal, unenlightened Opposite: modern

mediocre adj **middling**, average, unexceptional, ordinary, middle-of-the-road Opposite: excellent

mediocrity n **patchiness**, unevenness, poorness, weakness, averageness Opposite: excellence

meditate v **contemplate**, ponder, think, consider, deliberate

meditation n **thought**, consideration, contemplation, reflection, rumination

meditative adj **thoughtful**, reflective, contemplative, pensive, introspective Opposite: active

medium adj **average**, intermediate, middle, middling, standard Opposite: extraordinary ■ n **means**, vehicle, channel, mode, method

medley n **mixture**, combination, assortment, mix, jumble

meek adj 1 **mild**, quiet, humble, gentle, docile Opposite: overbearing 2 **timid**, compliant, weak, cowed, fearful Opposite: assertive

meekness n 1 **humbleness**, quietness, docility, humility, submissiveness 2 **timidity**, submissiveness, fearfulness, compliance, weakness Opposite: assertiveness

meet v 1 **come across**, encounter, bump into, run into, chance on Opposite: avoid 2 **be introduced to**, make somebody's acquaintance, get to know, greet, become acquainted with 3 **gather**, get together, come together, convene, assemble Opposite: disperse 4 **experience**, encounter, come across, endure, go through 5 **touch**, contact, connect, join, converge Opposite: separate

meeting n 1 **business meeting**, conference, assembly, summit, seminar 2 **encounter**, introduction, reunion, appointment, engagement

megalith n **prehistoric monument**, standing stone, menhir, dolmen, sarsen

megalomania n **power lust**, overbearingness, tyranny, totalitarianism, autocracy

megalomaniac n **tyrant**, dictator, autocrat, despot ■ adj **power-hungry**, power-crazy, self-important, tyrannical, dictatorial

megaphone n **loudhailer**, voice amplifier, bullhorn (US)

melancholic adj **dejected**, sad, unhappy, miserable, forlorn Opposite: cheerful

melancholy adj **sad**, downhearted, miserable, down, low Opposite: cheerful ■ n **sadness**, unhappiness, dejection, sorrow, the blues Opposite: cheerfulness

meld v **mix**, merge, blend, fuse, combine Opposite: separate ■ n **combination**, mix, mixture, blend, amalgamation

melee n **1 fight**, commotion, brawl, fracas, uproar **2 muddle**, jumble, mix, confusion, mixture

mellifluous adj **pleasant**, soothing, sweet, melodious, honeyed Opposite: jarring

mellow adj **1 smooth**, rich, full, warm, soft Opposite: harsh **2 mature**, full-flavoured, ripe, aged, strong Opposite: young **3 easygoing**, good-humoured, tolerant, approachable, genial Opposite: uptight (infml) ■ v **1 calm down**, ease up, settle down, relax, soften **2 mature**, soften, develop, ripen, improve Opposite: deteriorate

mellowness n **1 smoothness**, richness, warmth, fullness, mellifluousness Opposite: harshness **2 ripeness**, sweetness, fullness, matureness, maturity Opposite: rawness **3 geniality**, equanimity, amiability, warmth, affability

melodic see melodious

melodious adj **tuneful**, harmonious, musical, easy on the ear, mellow Opposite: discordant

melodiousness n **tunefulness**, musicalness, pleasantness, euphoniousness, euphony Opposite: cacophony

melodrama n **1 fuss**, drama, scene, storm in a teacup, exaggeration **2 play**, drama, tragedy, stage show, act

melodramatic adj **histrionic**, overdramatic, overemotional, exaggerated, sensational Opposite: low-key

melody n **tune**, song, air, phrase, strain

melt v **1 thaw**, thaw out, dissolve, soften, liquefy Opposite: freeze **2 disappear**, dissolve, fade, vanish, evaporate Opposite: materialize

meltdown (infml) n **collapse**, breakdown, failure, disaster, disintegration Opposite: success

melting adj **tender**, sweet, loving, sentimental, soft Opposite: harsh

melting pot n **mixture**, mix, mishmash, blend, hotchpotch

member n **1 associate**, affiliate, fellow, adherent, participant **2 limb**, appendage, organ, extremity, leg **3 part**, constituent, component, element, portion

membership n **1 association**, affiliation, involvement, connection, relationship Opposite: exclusion **2 members**, associates, affiliates, fellows, adherents

membrane n **skin**, film, sheath, casing, tissue

memento n **souvenir**, reminder, vestige, keepsake, token

memo n **memorandum**, note, minute, letter, message

memoir n **1 account**, biography, history, chronicle, description **2 essay**, article, report, paper, thesis

memoirs n **autobiography**, journal, life story, life history, diary

memorabilia n **collectables**, collector's items, souvenirs, mementos, ephemera

memorability n **importance**, note, momentousness, uncommonness, impressiveness Opposite: inconsequence

memorable adj **unforgettable**, notable, remarkable, outstanding, impressive Opposite: forgettable

memorandum n **memo**, note, minute, letter, message

memorial n **monument**, cenotaph, statue, bust, plaque

memorize v **learn by heart**, learn by rote, learn, commit to memory, remember Opposite: forget

memory n **1 reminiscence**, recollection, recall, remembrance, retention **2 commemoration**, remembrance, celebration, memorial

menace n **1 threat**, danger, hazard, peril, jeopardy Opposite: reassurance **2** (infml) **thorn in the flesh**, nuisance, troublemaker, annoyance, bother ■ v **1 endanger**, threaten, jeopardize, hang over, loom over **2 threaten**, intimidate, terrorize, frighten, alarm Opposite: reassure

menacing adj **threatening**, ominous, frightening, alarming, intimidating Opposite: reassuring

menagerie n **zoo**, zoological gardens, city farm, farm park

mend v **1 repair**, fix, put right, put back together, restore Opposite: break **2 stitch**, sew, sew up, patch, patch up Opposite: rip **3 improve**, amend, rectify, reform, transform **4 recover**, get better, get well, recuperate, heal Opposite: deteriorate ■ n **patch**, darn, repair

mendacious adj **1 untruthful**, dishonest, deceitful, unreliable, lying Opposite: truthful **2 untrue**, misleading, false, spurious, untruthful Opposite: true

mendaciously adv **untruthfully**, dishonestly, deceitfully, falsely, unreliably Opposite: truthfully

mendacity n **lies**, deception, deceit, falsehood, fabrication Opposite: truthfulness

mendicant adj **homeless**, vagrant, vagabond, begging, penniless ■ n (fml) **beggar**, vagrant, tramp, down-and-out, homeless person

mending n **sewing**, darning, stitching, fixing, patching

menfolk n **kinsmen**, men, boys, husbands, sons

menial adj **unskilled**, boring, tedious, basic, lowly Opposite: skilled

menswear n **men's clothing**, sportswear, outerwear

mental adj **psychological**, cerebral, rational, intellectual, spiritual Opposite: physical

mentality n **attitude**, approach, outlook, mindset, state of mind

mention v **talk about**, state, say, cite, bring up Opposite: conceal ■ n **reference**, indication, discussion, remark, comment

mentor n **adviser**, counsellor, guide, tutor, teacher Opposite: pupil

menu n **bill of fare**, carte du jour, tariff, blackboard, set menu

mercantile adj **merchant**, commercial, trade, trading, business

mercenary n **soldier of fortune**, soldier, legionnaire, freedom fighter, dog of war ■ adj **acquisitive**, grasping, greedy, avaricious, covetous Opposite: altruistic

merchandise n **goods**, products, produce, commodities, stock ■ v **sell**, retail, trade in, deal in, handle

merchant n **1 retailer**, seller, vendor, shopkeeper, tradesperson **2 wholesaler**, dealer, trader, supplier, broker

merciful adj **1 compassionate**, kind, lenient, humane, generous Opposite: hardhearted **2 thankful**, fortunate, welcome, lucky, happy Opposite: unfortunate

merciless adj **cruel**, hardhearted, pitiless, harsh, heartless Opposite: kind

mercilessness n **cruelty**, hardheartedness, pitilessness, harshness, heartlessness Opposite: kindness

mercurial adj **changeable**, unpredictable, lively, active, impulsive Opposite: consistent

mercy n **1 compassion**, pity, clemency, kindness, leniency Opposite: cruelty **2 blessing**, relief, kindness, stroke of luck, piece of luck Opposite: blow

mere adj **1 ordinary**, simple, sheer, plain, unadorned **2 scant**, meagre, paltry, mean, miserable

merely adv **just**, only, simply, purely

meretricious adj **1** (fml) **superficial**, flashy, vulgar, tawdry, showy **2 specious**, plausible, deceptive, insincere, glib Opposite: genuine

merge v **1 combine**, unite, come together, join, amalgamate Opposite: separate **2 blend**, meld, blur, fuse, unify Opposite: separate

merger n **1 amalgamation**, union, combination, joining, fusion Opposite: separation **2 blend**, meld, blur, fusion, union Opposite: separation

merit n **1 value**, worth, quality, excellence, distinction **2 advantage**, good point, pro, plus point, asset Opposite: disadvantage **3 ability**, accomplishment, capability, aptitude, skill Opposite: worthlessness ■ v **deserve**, warrant, earn, call for, be worthy of

meritorious adj **commendable**, praiseworthy, estimable, admirable, laudable Opposite: despicable

merriment n **cheerfulness**, happiness, fun, high spirits, jollity Opposite: misery

merry adj **cheerful**, happy, cheery, jolly, joyful Opposite: miserable

merry-go-round n **whirl**, round, series, succession, string

merrymaker n **partygoer**, party guest, life and soul of the party, social butterfly, reveller Opposite: killjoy

merrymaking n **celebration**, revels, partying, jollification, jollity Opposite: misery

mesa n **butte**, hill, mound, tor, peak

mesh n **net**, web, network, netting, webbing ■ v **interlock**, interconnect, engage, fit together, enmesh Opposite: separate

mesmeric adj **fascinating**, absorbing, compelling, compulsive, mesmerizing Opposite: boring

mesmerize v **hypnotize**, fascinate, absorb, entrance, enthral Opposite: bore

mesmerizing see mesmeric

mess n **1 untidiness**, muddle, chaos, confusion, clutter Opposite: order **2 tight spot**, tight corner, predicament, quandary, dilemma **3 canteen**, refectory, dining room, dining hall, restaurant

mess about (infml) see **mess around**

message n **1 communication**, memo, memorandum, note, letter **2 meaning**, significance, point, lesson, moral

mess around (infml) v **1 waste time**, fool around, play, mess about (infml), muck about (infml) Opposite: behave **2 relax**, laze around, lounge around, loll around, rest up **3 tamper**, fiddle, meddle, interfere, mess **4 hang around**, associate, go around, go out, spend time **5 joke**, have a laugh, fool around, play the fool, act the fool **6 mistreat**, treat badly, treat unfairly, fool with, muck about (infml) **7 potter**, tinker, dabble, fiddle, mess about (infml)

messenger n **courier**, envoy, go-between, emissary, herald

messiah n **champion**, liberator, leader, defender, saviour

messiness n 1 **untidiness**, disorderliness, scruffiness, dirtiness, scrappiness *Opposite*: neatness 2 **unpleasantness**, acrimony, bitterness, awkwardness, nastiness

mess up (*infml*) v 1 **spoil**, ruin, wreck, scupper, blunder 2 **make untidy**, muddle up, mix up, make a mess, clutter *Opposite*: tidy up 3 **upset**, confuse, put out, put somebody off their stride, throw (*infml*) *Opposite*: sort out

mess-up (*infml*) n **muddle**, mix-up, mess, confusion, muddle-up

messy adj 1 **untidy**, muddled, chaotic, cluttered, in disarray *Opposite*: neat 2 **unpleasant**, acrimonious, bitter, awkward, complicated *Opposite*: amicable

metabolism n **breakdown**, absorption, digestion, uptake, use

metabolize v **break down**, absorb, digest, take up, make use of

metallic adj 1 **metal**, iron, steel, copper, brass 2 **shiny**, reflective, glossy, glittering, polished *Opposite*: dull 3 **tinny**, brassy, ringing, clanging, sharp *Opposite*: soft

metamorphose v **change**, transform, transmute, mutate, alter

metamorphosis n **transformation**, change, mutation, conversion, alteration

metaphor n **symbol**, image, figure of speech, allegory, comparison

metaphorical adj **figurative**, symbolic, allegorical, emblematic, representational *Opposite*: literal

metaphysical adj **abstract**, theoretical, philosophical, hypothetical, conjectural

meteoric adj **dramatic**, sudden, swift, spectacular, impressive *Opposite*: gradual

meteorological adj **climatological**, climatic, atmospheric, weather, weather-related

meteorology n **weather forecasting**, climatology, weather prediction, weathercasting

mete out v **give out**, deal out, allocate, impose, exact

meter n **measuring device**, gauge, counter

method n 1 **means**, way, process, system, procedure 2 **orderliness**, organization, order, form, structure

methodical adj **systematic**, logical, disciplined, precise, orderly *Opposite*: haphazard

methodological adj **procedural**, organizational, working, running, operational

methodology n **organizing system**, practice, procedure, organization, policy

meticulous adj **careful**, scrupulous, thorough, particular, painstaking *Opposite*: careless. *See* COMPARE AND CONTRAST *at* **careful**.

meticulously adv **exactly**, accurately, precisely, squarely, methodically *Opposite*: carelessly

meticulousness n **care**, thoroughness, strictness, diligence, perfectionism *Opposite*: carelessness

métier n **vocation**, occupation, profession, calling, sphere

metre n **rhythm**, beat, tempo, pulse, pattern

metropolis n **city**, conurbation, capital, metropolitan area, megalopolis. *See* COMPARE AND CONTRAST *at* **city**.

metropolitan adj **city**, urban, municipal, civic

mettle n **courage**, bravery, determination, spirit, grit. *See* COMPARE AND CONTRAST *at* **courage**.

mettlesome adj **lively**, spirited, high-spirited, courageous, plucky *Opposite*: lethargic

mew v **cry**, miaow, sob, whimper, yowl

mezzanine n **mezzanine floor**, entresol, storey, level

miaow v **cry**, purr, mew, caterwaul, whimper

miasma n **mist**, fog, haze, cloud, murk

microbe n **microorganism**, germ, bug (*infml*)

microbiological adj **biological**, bacteriological, fungal, viral, microparasitic

microcosm n **small-scale version**, version in miniature, miniature copy, miniature *Opposite*: macrocosm

micromanage v **interfere**, intervene, nitpick, breathe down somebody's neck, control

microorganism n **microbe**, germ, bug (*infml*)

microscopic adj **tiny**, minute, infinitesimal, minuscule, atomic *Opposite*: gigantic

microscopically adv **meticulously**, minutely, closely, carefully, painstakingly

microwave v **heat**, heat up, warm, warm up, warm through

mid adj **middle**, median, medium, midway, central *Opposite*: extreme

midair adj 1 **air**, airborne, in-flight, mid-flight, midcourse 2 **in the air**, up in the air, in the sky, overhead, above the ground

midday n **noon**, noontime, twelve noon, lunchtime, the middle of the day

middle n 1 **centre**, heart, focus, core, hub *Opposite*: circumference 2 **midpoint**, halfway point, median, mean, norm ■ adj 1 **central**, mid, internal, intermediate, inside 2 **median**, average, intermediate, medium, middling

middlebrow (*infml*) adj **unintellectual**, conventional, unchallenging, middle-of-the-road, mediocre

middleman n 1 **trader**, distributor, wholesaler, retailer, broker 2 **intermediary**, agent, go-between, mediator, negotiator

middle-of-the-road adj **normal**, mainstream, majority, standard, typical

middling adj 1 **usual**, typical, ordinary, average, run-of-the-mill *Opposite*: unusual 2 **adequate**, all right, tolerable, fair, passable *Opposite*: exceptional

midnight n **twelve o'clock**, twelve midnight, middle of the night, night, nighttime *Opposite*: noon

midpoint n **centre**, middle, nucleus, median, mean

midriff n **waist**, stomach, belly, middle, abdomen

midst n **middle**, centre, heart, focus, core

midstream adv **halfway through**, midway, in the middle, in full flow

midsummer n **middle of the summer**, summertime, summer solstice, dog days, the height of summer Opposite: midwinter

midway adj **central**, middle, mid, halfway ■ adv **halfway**, in the middle, midstream, in full flow, halfway through

midwinter n **middle of winter**, wintertime, winter solstice, the winter months, the depths of winter Opposite: midsummer

mien (fml) n **appearance**, bearing, expression, manner, look

miff (infml) v **irritate**, upset, annoy, vex, peeve (infml)

miffed (infml) adj **annoyed**, displeased, put out, chagrined, bothered

might n **strength**, power, force, capacity, valour

mightily adv **tremendously**, greatly, extremely, awfully, decidedly Opposite: slightly

mighty adj 1 **powerful**, strong, forceful, potent, great Opposite: weak 2 **huge**, enormous, vast, expansive, massive Opposite: insignificant

migrant n 1 **wanderer**, traveller, nomad, itinerant, wayfarer (literary) Opposite: resident 2 **refugee**, immigrant, emigrant, asylum seeker ■ adj **migratory**, travelling, wandering, drifting, itinerant Opposite: resident

migrate v **travel**, journey, wander, drift, roam

migration n **relocation**, immigration, emigration, exodus, movement

migratory adj **travelling**, wandering, drifting, migrant, itinerant

mild adj 1 **gentle**, kind, soft, easygoing, meek Opposite: harsh 2 **weak**, bland, tasteless, insipid, flat Opposite: strong 3 **slight**, unimportant, insignificant, trifling, trivial Opposite: serious 4 **warm**, balmy, pleasant, clement, temperate Opposite: harsh

mildly adv 1 **gently**, kindly, meekly, placidly, calmly Opposite: harshly 2 **slightly**, a little, somewhat, a touch, insignificantly Opposite: considerably

mild-mannered adj **gentle**, kind, polite, good-natured, placid Opposite: fierce

mildness n **gentleness**, kindness, leniency, tenderness, warmth Opposite: harshness

mileage n 1 **distance**, travelling distance, range, extent, way 2 (infml) **benefit**, profit, advantage, usefulness, assistance

milepost n **marker**, sign, mark, indicator, signpost

miles (infml) n **a long way**, a great distance, miles and miles, miles away, a long way away ■ adv **much**, very much, lots, a lot, far

milestone n 1 **sign**, signpost, indicator, mark, marker 2 **landmark**, highlight, high point, achievement, record

milieu n **setting**, environment, scene, background, surroundings

militancy n **aggressiveness**, combativeness, belligerence, forcefulness, violence

militant adj **confrontational**, aggressive, radical, revolutionary, combative Opposite: peaceable ■ n **activist**, revolutionary, radical, fighter, supporter

militarism n **belligerence**, aggression, aggressiveness, pugnaciousness, bellicosity

militarist adj **bellicose**, aggressive, warmongering, martial, military Opposite: pacific

militaristic see militarist

militarized adj **mobilized**, armed, battle-ready, prepared, organized

military adj **armed**, martial, soldierly, fighting Opposite: civilian ■ n **services**, forces, armed forces, military establishment, army

militate v **influence**, inspire, affect, work, act on

militia n **territorial army**, reservists, local militia, paramilitaries, mercenaries

milk (infml) v **exploit**, drain, tap, take advantage of, cash in on

milky adj **cloudy**, chalky, creamy, pale, translucent Opposite: clear

millennial adj **utopian**, idealistic, visionary, romantic, optimistic

millennium n **epoch**, era, age, period, time

millionaire n **tycoon**, mogul, magnate, billionaire, baron Opposite: pauper

millions n **many**, lots, masses, loads (infml), heaps (infml)

millstone n **burden**, weight, dead weight, albatross, shackle

mime v 1 **act out**, represent, simulate, express, symbolize 2 **mimic**, satirize, caricature, parody, ape

mimetic adj **imitative**, derivative, copied, representational, simulated Opposite: original

mimic v 1 **caricature**, ape, satirize, parody, mock 2 **imitate**, impersonate, represent, mirror, simulate ■ n **impersonator**, impressionist, imitator, caricaturist, parodist. See COMPARE AND CONTRAST at imitate.

mimicry n **imitation**, impersonation, impression, parody, caricature

minaret n **turret**, tower, spire

mince v **shred**, cut up, chop up, crumble, hash ■ n **mincemeat**, minced meat, minced beef, ground beef, ground meat

mincemeat n **mince**, minced meat, minced beef, ground beef, ground meat

mincing adj **affected**, foppish, dainty, prim, fussy

mind n 1 **brain**, intellect, wits, brains, brainpower 2 **attention**, concentration, thoughts, awareness, observance 3 **point of view**, mentality, opinion, thinking, view 4 **thinker**, intellect, intellectual, brain (infml), egghead (infml) ■ v **1 pay attention**, take care, beware, heed, be careful **2 object**, care, take offence, demur, resent Opposite: approve **3 look after**, tend, care for, attend to, take care of

mind-bending see mind-boggling

mind-blowing (infml) adj **astonishing**, amazing, incredible, inconceivable, astounding Opposite: unexceptional

mind-boggling (infml) adj **overwhelming**, complex, difficult, complicated, puzzling Opposite: simple

minded (fml) adj **inclined**, of a mind to, intent, set, prepared Opposite: disinclined

minder n **1** (infml) **guard**, guardian, escort, lookout, attendant **2 child minder**, carer, sitter, babysitter

mindful adj **watchful**, aware, wary, heedful, alert Opposite: unwary. See COMPARE AND CON-TRAST at aware.

mindless adj **1 tedious**, dull, boring, monotonous, mechanical Opposite: enthralling **2 senseless**, gratuitous, unnecessary, pointless, needless

mindlessly adv **1 automatically**, mechanically, unconsciously, unthinkingly, robotically Opposite: deliberately **2 senselessly**, stupidly, thoughtlessly, carelessly, foolishly Opposite: thoughtfully

mind-numbing adj **boring**, dull, tedious, tiresome, wearisome Opposite: interesting

mindset n **attitude**, outlook, mind, mentality, way of thinking

mind your own business v **keep your nose out of it**, keep off, keep out of it, keep yourself to yourself, mind your own beeswax (US) Opposite: snoop

mine n **1 pit**, excavation, colliery, coalfield, coalmine **2 source**, repository, fund, gold mine, store Opposite: dearth ■ v **extract**, excavate, quarry, dig, dig out

minefield n **problem**, trial, test, ordeal, hazard

miner n **tunneller**, sapper, coalminer, collier, driller

mingle v **1 mix**, blend, fuse, join, unite Opposite: separate **2 circulate**, associate, intermingle, socialize, mix

mingy (infml) adj **mean**, ungenerous, inadequate, sparse, stingy (infml) Opposite: generous

mini (infml) adj **small**, miniature, baby, diminutive, tiny Opposite: maxi

miniature adj **small-scale**, small, tiny, minute, little Opposite: enormous

miniaturization n **reduction**, shrinking, contraction, diminishment Opposite: enlargement

miniaturize v **reduce**, scale down, shrink, contract, diminish Opposite: enlarge

minibar n **bar**, fridge, cupboard, cooler, cocktail cabinet

minibreak (infml) n **long weekend**, weekend, holiday, break, vacation

minimal adj **1 negligible**, trifling, slight, nominal, token Opposite: significant **2 least**, smallest, minimum, tiniest, minutest Opposite: maximum

minimalism n **simplicity**, plainness, cleanness, austereness, starkness Opposite: elaboration

minimalist adj **simple**, uncluttered, understated, discreet, plain Opposite: baroque

minimize v **1 minimalize**, diminish, curtail, lessen, reduce Opposite: maximize **2 play down**, make light of, reduce, dismiss, shrug off Opposite: exaggerate

minimum n **least**, bare minimum, smallest amount, iota, jot Opposite: maximum ■ adj **smallest**, least, lowest, tiniest, minutest Opposite: maximum

minion n **follower**, assistant, hanger-on, underling, crony Opposite: superior

miniseries n **series**, serial, soap, drama, serialization

minister n **priest**, vicar, rector, parson, reverend ■ v (fml) **attend**, look after, care for, tend, nurse Opposite: neglect

ministerial adj **governmental**, parliamentary, cabinet, official, legislative

ministration (fml) n **care**, support, attention, nurture, aid Opposite: neglect

ministry n **office**, bureau, department, agency, organization

minnow n **small fry**, little man, little guy, nobody, sprat

minor adj **1 slight**, small, negligible, inconsequential, trivial Opposite: major **2 lesser**, inferior, junior, secondary, lower Opposite: major ■ n **juvenile**, youth, adolescent, child, teenager Opposite: adult

minority n **section**, faction, interest group, pressure group, subgroup ■ adj **alternative**, underground, marginal, sectional, smaller Opposite: majority

minstrel n **musician**, troubadour, wandering minstrel, player, entertainer

mint n (infml) **fortune**, millions, billions, pile (infml), packet (infml) Opposite: pittance ■ v **cast**, issue, imprint, make, strike

minus prep **1 less**, take away, excluding, reduced by, with the subtraction of Opposite: plus **2 without**, lacking, excluding, exclusive of, with the exception of Opposite: including ■ n **1 deficiency**, loss, drop, fall, decrease Opposite: addition **2 disadvantage**, detriment, handicap, hindrance, drawback Opposite: plus

minuscule adj **tiny**, minute, microscopic, infinitesimal, little Opposite: gigantic

minute n **moment**, instant, second, flash, sec (infml) Opposite: ages (infml) ■ v **record**, summarize, write down, précis, transcribe ■ adj **1 miniature**, tiny, minuscule, microscopic, infinitesimal Opposite: enormous

2 close, detailed, thorough, exhaustive, painstaking *Opposite*: cursory

minuteness *n* **smallness**, tininess, shortness, compactness

minutes *n* **notes**, record, proceedings, transcript, transcription

minutiae *n* **details**, niceties, intricacies, particulars, ins and outs *Opposite*: gist

miracle *n* **wonder**, phenomenon, marvel, sensation, vision

miraculous *adj* **amazing**, astounding, astonishing, incredible, unbelievable *Opposite*: mundane

mirage *n* **hallucination**, optical illusion, illusion, vision, delusion *Opposite*: reality

mire *n* **swamp**, marsh, mud, sludge, slush

mirror *n* **glass**, hand mirror, shaving mirror, looking glass *(dated)* ■ *v* **1 reflect**, echo, copy, parallel, emulate **2 represent**, symbolize, illustrate, typify, signify

mirror image *n* **double**, twin, copy, replica, likeness

mirth *n* **laughter**, hilarity, humour, jollity, fun *Opposite*: sadness

mirthful *adj* **joyful**, merry, gleeful, jovial, cheery *Opposite*: mirthless

mirthless *adj* **cheerless**, dour, gloomy, grim, dismal *Opposite*: cheerful

misadventure *n* **accident**, mishap, misfortune, disaster, calamity

misaligned *adj* **askew**, skewed, awry, cockeyed, crooked *Opposite*: straight

misalliance *n* **mismatch**, inequality, bad match, disparity, mésalliance

misanthropic *adj* **cynical**, pessimistic, distrustful, disdainful, sardonic *Opposite*: philanthropic

misanthropy *n* **cynicism**, pessimism, distrust, disdain, sardonicism *Opposite*: philanthropy

misapplication *n* **misuse**, abuse, misemployment, mishandling, exploitation

misapply *v* **misuse**, abuse, misemploy, mishandle, mismanage

misapprehend *v* **mistake**, misunderstand, misinterpret, misconstrue, misjudge

misapprehension *n* **misunderstanding**, misinterpretation, wrong idea, false impression, misconception *Opposite*: comprehension

misappropriate *v* **steal**, embezzle, pocket, take, help yourself *Opposite*: reimburse. *See* COMPARE AND CONTRAST *at* steal.

misappropriation *n* **embezzlement**, misuse, stealing, dishonesty, fraud

misbegotten *adj* **ill-conceived**, bad, inappropriate, foolish, deplorable

misbehave *v* **be naughty**, be bad, play up, act up, behave badly *Opposite*: behave

misbehaviour *n* **naughtiness**, misconduct, mischief, disobedience, waywardness

miscalculate *v* **misjudge**, underestimate, overestimate, get it wrong, overvalue

miscalculation *n* **error**, mistake, inaccuracy, blunder, slip

miscarriage *(fml)* *n* **failure**, lapse, breakdown, insufficiency, mistake

miscarriage of justice *n* **wrongful conviction**, unfair ruling, injustice, judicial error, mistake

miscarry *(fml)* *v* **fail**, founder, backfire, go wrong, go amiss

miscellaneous *adj* **various**, varied, assorted, mixed, diverse *Opposite*: homogeneous

miscellany *n* **assortment**, collection, selection, grouping, medley

mischance *n* **misfortune**, ill fortune, bad luck, ill luck, misadventure

mischief *n* **1 misbehaviour**, naughtiness, trouble, disobedience, waywardness **2 harm**, damage, trouble, disruption, injury **3 troublemaker**, nuisance, rascal, scamp *(infml)*, monkey *(infml)*

mischief-maker *n* **meddler**, troublemaker, gossip, ringleader, instigator

mischievous *adj* **1 naughty**, playful, impish, roguish, badly behaved *Opposite*: well-behaved **2** *(fml)* **harmful**, damaging, malicious, wicked, negative *Opposite*: harmless. *See* COMPARE AND CONTRAST *at* bad.

mischievousness *n* **1 naughtiness**, bad behaviour, impishness, playfulness, disobedience **2** *(fml)* **malice**, hatred, harm, animosity, spite

misconceive *v* **misunderstand**, misapprehend, misinterpret, get the wrong impression, get the wrong idea *Opposite*: understand

misconceived *adj* **ill-conceived**, ill-thought-out, flawed, misguided, inappropriate

misconception *n* **fallacy**, delusion, misapprehension, misconstruction, mistaken belief *Opposite*: fact

misconduct *n* **bad behaviour**, misbehaviour, delinquency, transgression, wrongdoing

misconstruction *n* **misinterpretation**, misunderstanding, misreading, false impression, misjudgment *Opposite*: understanding

misconstrue *v* **misinterpret**, misunderstand, misread, get the wrong idea about, get the wrong impression about *Opposite*: understand

miscount *v* **lose count**, miscalculate, make a mistake, underestimate, overestimate

misdeed *n* **misdemeanour**, crime, offence, wrong, transgression

misdemeanour *n* **1 petty larceny**, crime, offence, malfeasance **2 misdeed**, wrongdoing, lapse, transgression, foul

misdirect *v* **1 point in the wrong direction**, lead astray, send off course, send on a wild goose chase *Opposite*: direct **2 misallocate**, misuse, misapply, waste, misemploy

miser n 1 hoarder, accumulator, saver, collector, squirrel (infml) 2 skinflint, pinchpenny, penny pincher (infml), cheapskate (infml), scrooge (infml) Opposite: spendthrift

miserable adj 1 unhappy, sad, depressed, down, despondent Opposite: happy 2 depressing, cheerless, wretched, desolate, gloomy Opposite: cheery 3 inadequate, paltry, derisory, miserly, mean Opposite: generous 4 gloomy, dull, grey, overcast, dreary Opposite: bright

miserliness n parsimoniousness, greed, greediness, tightfistedness, avariciousness Opposite: generosity

miserly adj 1 mean, tightfisted, parsimonious, tight, niggardly Opposite: generous 2 paltry, derisory, mean, miserable, meagre Opposite: generous

misery n 1 unhappiness, sadness, depression, desolation, gloom Opposite: happiness 2 deprivation, destitution, distress, poverty, privation 3 (infml) grumbler, whiner, wet blanket (infml), grouch (infml), moaner (infml)

misfire v go wrong, backfire, fail, fall through, not come off Opposite: succeed

misfit n oddity, eccentric, loner, odd one out, nonconformist Opposite: conformist

misfortune n disaster, calamity, trial, tribulation, misadventure Opposite: opportunity

misgiving n scruple, qualm, doubt, niggle, suspicion

misguided adj mistaken, foolish, ill-advised, unwise, erroneous Opposite: wise

mishandle v 1 mismanage, make a mess of, misapply, misuse, botch (infml) 2 abuse, mistreat, exploit, ill-treat, rough up (infml)

mishap n accident, calamity, misfortune, disaster, catastrophe

mishear v hear wrong, get wrong, pick up wrong, not get, be mistaken

mishit v miss, nick, clip, hit a foul, slice ■ n error, slice, hook, miss, nick

mishmash n hotchpotch, jumble, muddle, miscellany, mixture

misinform v mislead, deceive, lie to, lead on, lead astray

misinformation n propaganda, dishonesty, distortion, fabrication, bending of the truth Opposite: fact

misinterpret v misconstrue, misunderstand, misread, get the wrong idea about, get the wrong impression about Opposite: understand

misinterpretation n misunderstanding, misconception, misapprehension, misreading, confusion Opposite: understanding

misjudge v miscalculate, underestimate, overestimate, be wrong about, get the wrong idea

misjudgment n 1 poor judgment, error of judgment, error, miscalculation, slip 2 wrong impression, misinterpretation, misconstruction, false reading, prejudice Opposite: understanding

mislaid adj lost, missing, nowhere to be found, gone astray, misplaced

mislay v lose, misplace, be unable to find, miss, put in the wrong place Opposite: find

mislead v give the wrong impression, misinform, deceive, lie, delude

misleading adj deceptive, ambiguous, confusing, false, disingenuous Opposite: truthful

mismanage v mishandle, make a mess of, misuse, manage badly, botch (infml)

mismanagement n mishandling, misconduct, negligence, malpractice, maladministration Opposite: efficiency

mismatch n incongruity, discrepancy, gap, disparity, misalliance Opposite: harmony

mismatched adj incompatible, unequal, uneven, unjust, one-sided

misnomer n misleading term, inaccurate term, poor description, loose term, contradiction

misplace v lose, be unable to put your hands on, drop, leave behind Opposite: find

misplaced adj 1 inappropriate, erroneous, misdirected, out-of-place, inapt Opposite: appropriate 2 mislaid, nowhere to be found, missing, lost, gone astray

misprint n typographical error, error, mistake, blunder, oversight

mispronounce v say wrong, distort, mangle, make a mess of, stumble through Opposite: articulate

mispronunciation n distortion, error, misstatement, slip, blunder

misquote v put words in somebody's mouth, misreport, misrepresent, misattribute, quote out of context

misread v misjudge, misinterpret, misunderstand, misconstrue, get the wrong idea Opposite: interpret

misrepresent v parody, pervert, twist, distort, pass off

misrepresentation n parody, caricature, distortion, falsification, twisting

misrule n 1 misgovernment, mishandling, corruption, maladministration, mismanagement 2 lawlessness, anarchy, unruliness, chaos, turmoil Opposite: order

miss v 1 overlook, fail to spot, let pass, fail to notice, fail to see Opposite: see 2 skip, fail to attend, escape, avoid, forget Opposite: attend 3 forego, lose, pass up, let pass, let go Opposite: take up 4 pine for, long for, yearn for, wish for, grieve for ■ n 1 omission, oversight, delinquency, neglect, mistake 2 failure, false step, error, slip, miscue

missal n service book, prayer book, liturgical book, breviary, Psalter

misshapen adj distorted, twisted, deformed, malformed, warped Opposite: shapely

missing adj lost, absent, gone astray, misplaced, mislaid Opposite: present

mission n 1 assignment, task, job, work, undertaking 2 calling, vocation, purpose, goal, aim 3 delegation, deputation, task force, legation, embassy

missionary n 1 evangelist, proselytizer, preacher, minister, priest 2 campaigner, champion, crusader, proselytizer, propagandist

missive n letter, communiqué, note, communication, memo

miss out v 1 omit, leave out, disregard, miss, exclude Opposite: include 2 fail to benefit, forgo, miss the boat, miss an opportunity, miss a chance Opposite: benefit

misspelling n spelling mistake, wrong spelling, misspelt word, slip, error

misspend v squander, fritter away, waste, throw away, misuse Opposite: save

misspent adj wasted, squandered, frittered away, misused, thrown away Opposite: profitable

misstep n mistake, slip, gaffe, blunder, error

miss the boat v miss an opportunity, miss a chance, miss out, fail to benefit, forego

miss the point v misunderstand, misinterpret, misconstrue, fail to understand, misread Opposite: understand

mist n haze, fog, vapour, smog, spray

mistake n 1 blunder, gaffe, slip, lapse, miscalculation 2 error, fault, inaccuracy, oversight, misspelling ■ v 1 misunderstand, misjudge, misinterpret, misconstrue, confuse Opposite: understand 2 confuse with, take for, mix up with, confound, mix Opposite: recognize

---

COMPARE AND CONTRAST CORE MEANING: something incorrect or improper

mistake an unwise decision or an error resulting from a lack of care; **error** something that unintentionally deviates from a recognized standard or guide; **inaccuracy** something that is incorrect because it has been measured, calculated, copied, or conveyed incorrectly; **slip** a minor mistake or oversight, especially one caused by carelessness; **blunder** a serious or embarrassing mistake, usually the result of carelessness or ignorance; **faux pas** (literary) an embarrassing mistake that breaks a social convention.

---

mistaken adj wrong, incorrect, false, erroneous, faulty Opposite: correct

mistime v misjudge, miss the boat, anticipate, jump the gun, pre-empt Opposite: coordinate

mistiness n 1 haziness, murkiness, duskiness, cloudiness, fogginess Opposite: clearness 2 vagueness, indistinctness, obscurity, opacity, lack of clarity Opposite: clarity

mist over v mist, mist up, fog over, become hazy, become clouded Opposite: clear

mistreat v abuse, misuse, ill-treat, harm, mishandle Opposite: pamper. See COMPARE AND CONTRAST at misuse.

mistreated adj abused, neglected, wronged, injured, victimized Opposite: pampered

mistreatment n maltreatment, exploitation, abuse, ill-treatment, neglect Opposite: pampering

mistress n 1 lover, concubine, courtesan, kept woman, ladyfriend (infml) Opposite: wife 2 owner, trainer, keeper, rider 3 expert, specialist, queen, doyenne, leading exponent Opposite: novice 4 teacher, schoolmistress, governess, instructress, schoolteacher Opposite: pupil 5 manager, employer, controller, proprietor, owner Opposite: servant

mistrial n invalid trial, unfair trial, miscarriage of justice, travesty, injustice

mistrust n suspicion, distrust, doubt, wariness, uncertainty Opposite: trust ■ v distrust, doubt, suspect, be wary of, be suspicious of Opposite: trust

mistrustful adj distrustful, wary, suspicious, doubtful, sceptical Opposite: trusting

misty adj 1 hazy, foggy, murky, cloudy, steamy Opposite: clear 2 indistinct, vague, obscure, dim, opaque Opposite: clear

misty-eyed adj 1 tearful, emotional, teary, teary-eyed, close to tears Opposite: dry-eyed 2 sentimental, nostalgic, romantic, weepy (infml), soppy (infml) Opposite: unsentimental

misunderstand v get the wrong idea, misinterpret, misread, misconstrue, get the wrong impression Opposite: understand

misunderstanding n 1 mistake, mix-up, confusion, misinterpretation, misconstruction 2 quarrel, row, argument, difference of opinion, disagreement Opposite: agreement

misunderstood adj unacknowledged, unrecognized, unappreciated, undervalued, misjudged Opposite: valued

misuse n misappropriation, misapplication, waste, ill use, mismanagement ■ v 1 waste, misappropriate, squander, misapply, mishandle 2 abuse, exploit, mistreat, maltreat, ill-treat Opposite: cherish

---

COMPARE AND CONTRAST CORE MEANING: treat somebody or something wrongly or badly

misuse put something to an inappropriate use or purpose, or treat a person or animal badly or harshly; **abuse** use in a wrong or inappropriate way something that should be used responsibly, for example a power, privilege, or a substance such as alcohol or a drug. It is also used to refer to cruel or violent treatment of a person or animal, especially on a regular or habitual basis; **ill-treat** or **maltreat** behave cruelly towards a person or animal, or treat something roughly and carelessly; **mistreat** treat a person badly, inconsiderately, or unfairly, not necessarily in a way involving physical cruelty, or treat something roughly and carelessly.

mite *(dated)* *n* **jot**, bit, scrap, speck, grain

mitigate *v* **alleviate**, lessen, ease, allay, moderate *Opposite:* aggravate

mitigating *adj* **justifying**, extenuating, modifying, qualifying, vindicating *Opposite:* aggravating

mitigation *n* **1 extenuation**, vindication, justification, qualification, moderation **2 alleviation**, easing, improvement, lessening, relief *Opposite:* intensification

mix *v* **1 mix up**, mingle, intermingle, blend, intersperse *Opposite:* separate **2 combine**, blend, unite, merge, join *Opposite:* separate out **3 fraternize**, mingle, associate, get together, socialize **4 go together**, accord, agree, fit, harmonize *Opposite:* clash ■ *n* **combination**, mixture, blend, assortment, fusion

mixed *adj* **1 varied**, diverse, assorted, sundry, miscellaneous *Opposite:* uniform **2 cosmopolitan**, integrated, international, interracial, multiracial *Opposite:* segregated

mixed bag *n* **ragbag**, assortment, combination, jumble, variety

mixed-up *(infml)* *adj* **1 confused**, muddled, bewildered, puzzled, perplexed *Opposite:* clear **2 disturbed**, maladjusted, confused, troubled, rebellious *Opposite:* well-adjusted

mixture *n* **combination**, mix, blend, amalgam, concoction

COMPARE AND CONTRAST CORE MEANING: something formed by mixing materials
mixture a number of elements or ingredients brought together; **blend** something formed by putting together two or more different kinds of things, especially in a skilled way, to form a new whole in which the original elements lose their distinctness; **combination** something formed by the association of two or more things that retain their distinctness; **compound** a technical word for a chemical formed from two or more elements, also used generally to describe anything composed of two or more separate parts; **alloy** a technical word for a metal such as steel that is formed by combining two or more different metallic elements; **amalgam** a technical word for an alloy formed by combining mercury with another metal, also used generally to describe something that is a mixture of two or more elements or characteristics.

---

mix up *v* **1 confuse**, misunderstand, muddle, confound, mistake *Opposite:* straighten out **2 mix**, combine, merge, blend, fuse *Opposite:* separate ■

mix-up *n* **mistake**, muddle, misunderstanding, confusion, error

mnemonic *n* **memory aid**, reminder, prompt, cue, aide-mémoire *(fml)*

mo *(infml)* *n* **tick** *(infml)*, sec *(infml)*, half a tick *(infml)*, half a sec *(infml)*, moment

moan *v* **1 groan**, sigh, whine, whimper, wail **2** *(infml)* **complain**, grumble, whinge *(infml)*, whine, gripe *(infml)* ■ *n* *(infml)* **complaint**, grumble, gripe *(infml)*, whinge *(infml)*, grouse *(infml)* *Opposite:* compliment

moaner *(infml)* *n* **grumbler**, complainer, whiner, wailer, objector

moat *n* **ditch**, trench, fosse, channel, dyke *Opposite:* bank

mob *n* **1 crowd**, horde, mass, multitude, throng **2** *(infml)* **masses**, populace, plebs, hoi polloi, rabble *Opposite:* elite ■ *v* **1 besiege**, descend on, crowd round, surround, swarm around *Opposite:* avoid **2 attack**, jostle, pester, set upon, set about *Opposite:* defend

mobile *adj* **1 active**, flexible, limber, supple, agile *Opposite:* immobile **2 expressive**, changing, changeable, lively, communicative *Opposite:* inexpressive **3 movable**, portable, transportable, itinerant, peripatetic *Opposite:* fixed **4 upwardly mobile**, successful, ambitious, aspiring, rising *Opposite:* unambitious

mobility *n* **1 flexibility**, freedom of movement, agility, suppleness, movement *Opposite:* stasis **2 progress**, social mobility, upward mobility, success, promotion

mobilization *n* **enlistment**, deployment, armament, organization, utilization *Opposite:* demobilization

mobilize *v* **rally**, assemble, muster, drum up, gather together *Opposite:* demobilize

mock *v* **1 ridicule**, tease, make fun of, laugh at, poke fun at *Opposite:* praise **2 mimic**, imitate, parody, ape, simulate ■ *adj* **fake**, pretend, simulated, imitation, artificial *Opposite:* genuine. *See* COMPARE AND CONTRAST *at* **ridicule**.

mocker *n* **ridiculer**, derider, scorner, scoffer, caricaturist

mockery *n* **1 ridicule**, scorn, derision, contempt, disdain *Opposite:* respect **2 travesty**, charade, farce, sham, caricature *Opposite:* exemplar *(literary)*

mocking *adj* **scornful**, derisive, contemptuous, disdainful, sardonic *Opposite:* respectful

mock-up *n* **replica**, copy, model, sample, dummy

mode *n* **form**, style, manner, method, means

model *n* **1 replica**, mock-up, representation, copy, reproduction **2 type**, sort, style, kind, version **3 example**, paradigm, pattern, standard, prototype ■ *v* **1 demonstrate**, show, exhibit, display, show off **2 sculpt**, mould, form, shape, fashion ■ *adj* **perfect**, classical, prototypical, typical, archetypal *Opposite:* atypical

moderate *adj* **1 reasonable**, modest, sensible, restrained, judicious *Opposite:* excessive **2 average**, medium, normal, balanced, middling *Opposite:* extraordinary ■ *v* **1 curb**, control, tone down, play down, diminish *Opposite:* intensify **2 arbitrate**, mediate, referee, facilitate, umpire

moderately adv **reasonably**, rather, somewhat, fairly, comparatively Opposite: excessively

moderation n **restraint**, control, self-control, temperance, fairness Opposite: excess

moderator n **mediator**, go-between, arbiter, arbitrator, referee

modern adj 1 **contemporary**, current, up-to-date, up-to-the-minute, recent Opposite: old-fashioned 2 **state-of-the-art**, latest, cutting-edge, leading-edge, novel Opposite: outdated 3 **progressive**, enlightened, forward-looking, avant-garde, advanced Opposite: traditional. See COMPARE AND CONTRAST at **new**.

modern-day adj **contemporary**, modern, current, recent, present-day Opposite: past

modernism n **innovation**, innovativeness, novelty, originality, modernization Opposite: traditionalism

modernistic adj **ultramodern**, modern, radical, futuristic, avant-garde Opposite: traditional

modernity n **modernism**, innovation, innovativeness, freshness, newness Opposite: traditionalism

modernization n **transformation**, upgrading, innovation, reconstruction, renewal

modernize v **update**, renovate, streamline, revolutionize, reform

modernizer n **innovator**, pacesetter, trendsetter, new broom, visionary

modest adj 1 **self-effacing**, humble, reserved, discreet, unpretentious Opposite: arrogant 2 **shy**, meek, diffident, quiet, reserved Opposite: overbearing 3 **unexceptional**, ordinary, humble, unpretentious, plain Opposite: showy 4 **moderate**, reasonable, acceptable, small, low Opposite: excessive

modesty n **humility**, reserve, reticence, diffidence, shyness Opposite: arrogance

modicum n **little**, bit, degree, scrap, ounce

modification n **change**, alteration, adjustment, amendment, reform

modified adj **adapted**, altered, changed, improved, revised Opposite: unmodified

modify v 1 **alter**, change, adapt, adjust, amend Opposite: maintain 2 **lessen**, reduce, restrain, moderate, curb Opposite: intensify. See COMPARE AND CONTRAST at **change**.

modish adj **fashionable**, stylish, in, chic, up-to-the-minute Opposite: unfashionable

modular adj **linked**, flexible, integrated, prefabricated, segmental

modulate v 1 **adjust**, alter, amend, vary, modify 2 **moderate**, curb, control, tone down, play down Opposite: intensify

modulation n 1 **adjustment**, change, alteration, swing, variation 2 **inflection**, intonation, accent, lilt, cadence Opposite: flatness

module n **unit**, component, part, element, section

modus operandi n **method**, formula, technique, way, protocol

modus vivendi n 1 **compromise**, arrangement, settlement, deal, bargain 2 **practice**, way of life, lifestyle, standard of living, habit

moggy (infml) n **cat**, puss (infml), pussy (infml)

mogul n **tycoon**, entrepreneur, magnate, industrialist, dynast

moist adj **damp**, wet, humid, soggy, clammy Opposite: dry

moisten v **dampen**, wet, moisturize, humidify, sprinkle Opposite: dry

moistness n **dampness**, humidity, wetness, clamminess, sogginess Opposite: aridity

moisture n **damp**, dampness, wetness, humidity, moistness Opposite: dryness

moisturize v 1 **nourish**, soothe, oil, condition, treat Opposite: dry 2 **moisten**, dampen, wet, humidify, spray

moisturizer n **cold cream**, cream, lotion, conditioner, night cream

molasses n **syrup**, treacle, golden syrup, black treacle, blackstrap molasses

mole n **spy**, infiltrator, secret agent, undercover agent, plant

molecule n **particle**, bit, iota, speck, shred

molest v 1 **assault**, mistreat, abuse, attack, feel up (infml) 2 **bother**, pester, annoy, torment, harass

mollify v **pacify**, calm, placate, appease, calm down Opposite: enrage

mollycoddle v **pamper**, fuss over, spoil, overprotect, cosset

molten adj **melted**, liquefied, liquid, fluid, heated Opposite: solid

moment n 1 **instant**, second, minute, split second, flash Opposite: age 2 (fml) **importance**, significance, weight, import, substance

momentarily adv **for a moment**, briefly, temporarily, fleetingly, transitorily

momentary adj **brief**, fleeting, passing, temporary, transitory Opposite: interminable

momentous adj **important**, significant, historic, earthshattering, crucial Opposite: insignificant

momentum n **impetus**, thrust, energy, force, drive Opposite: brake

monarch n **ruler**, sovereign, crowned head, emperor, king Opposite: subject

monarchism n **royalism**, imperialism, elitism, tsarism, traditionalism Opposite: republicanism

monarchist n **royalist**, loyalist, counter-revolutionary, traditionalist, imperialist Opposite: revolutionary

monarchy n **realm**, kingdom, dominion, domain, empire Opposite: republic

monastery n **religious foundation**, religious community, cloister, friary, abbey

monastic adj **austere**, reclusive, simple, spartan, frugal

monetary adj **financial**, fiscal, economic, monetarist, pecuniary

money n 1 **cash**, currency, ready money, ready cash, coinage 2 **capital**, funds, riches, means, wherewithal

moneybags (infml) n **millionaire**, multi-millionaire, billionaire, tycoon, mogul

money box n **piggy bank**, cash box, collecting box, safe

moneyed adj **wealthy**, rich, affluent, prosperous, comfortable

moneylender n **lender**, financier, banker, pawnbroker, loan shark

moneymaker n 1 **tycoon**, speculator, magnate, investor, mogul 2 **hit**, success, gold mine, profit centre, money-spinner (infml)

moneymaking adj **profitable**, commercial, economic, fruitful, lucrative

money-spinner (infml) n **hit**, moneymaker, cash cow (slang), going concern, success

money-spinning (infml) adj **economic**, profitable, lucrative, fruitful, worthwhile

mongrel n **dog**, cur, hound, crossbreed, pye-dog Opposite: pedigree

monitor n 1 **screen**, display, VDU, television set 2 **observer**, supervisor, overseer, inspector, invigilator ■ v **observe**, keep an eye on, supervise, scrutinize, examine

monk n **holy man**, religious, monastic, friar, abbot

monkey (infml) n 1 **fool**, laughing stock, dupe, ass, butt 2 **mischief**, rogue, rascal, scamp (infml), scallywag (dated infml)

monkey around v **fool around**, joke, play the fool, clown around, lark

monkey business (infml) n **tricks**, mischief, trouble, pranks, high jinks (infml)

monkey with v **tamper**, meddle, interfere, fiddle, tinker

monkish adj **reclusive**, austere, withdrawn, cloistered, simple Opposite: worldly

monochromatic adj 1 **unicolour**, homochromous, self-coloured, homochromatic, shaded 2 **dull**, indistinct, neutral, uniform, toneless Opposite: colourful

monochrome adj 1 **unicolour**, homochromous, homochromatic, self-coloured, monochromatic 2 **neutral**, colourless, dull, indeterminate, toneless Opposite: colourful

monocle n **eyeglass**, glass, lens

monogamous adj **faithful**, exclusive, committed, married, steady Opposite: bigamous

monogamy n **exclusivity**, fidelity, commitment, marriage, coupledom Opposite: bigamy

monogram n **initials**, signet, logo, seal, stamp ■ v **mark**, initial, sign, seal, identify

monograph n **book**, article, paper, essay, thesis

monolith n **standing stone**, menhir, megalith, sarsen, stone

monolithic adj **colossal**, monumental, massive, uniform, immovable

monologue n 1 **soliloquy**, speech, prologue, epilogue, aside Opposite: dialogue 2 **harangue**, rant, speech, running commentary, lecture Opposite: conversation

monopolistic adj **anticompetitive**, unchallenged, controlling, autocratic, exploitative Opposite: competitive

monopolization n **control**, domination, appropriation, takeover, expropriation Opposite: cooperation

monopolize v **control**, dominate, take over, corner, exploit Opposite: share

monopoly n **control**, domination, cartel, corner, trust (US)

monosyllabic adj **uncommunicative**, curt, gruff, brief, short Opposite: verbose

monosyllable n **word**, syllable, grunt, squeak Opposite: polysyllable

monotheism n **theism**, deism Opposite: polytheism

monotone n **drone**, whine, chant, intonation, mutter

monotonous adj **dull**, repetitious, uninteresting, repetitive, boring Opposite: varied

monotony n 1 **tedium**, dullness, boredom, flatness, dreariness Opposite: excitement 2 **uniformity**, repetitiousness, sameness, repetitiveness, predictability Opposite: variety

monsoon n **rainy season**, wet season, rains

monster n 1 **fiend**, ogre, beast, brute 2 **giant**, behemoth, leviathan, whopper (infml), biggie (infml) ■ adj **huge**, enormous, giant, monstrous, gigantic Opposite: small

monstrosity n **eyesore**, blot on the landscape, atrocity, sight, horror

monstrous adj 1 **atrocious**, outrageous, horrific, immoral, evil 2 **huge**, enormous, giant, monster, gigantic Opposite: small 3 **hideous**, grotesque, gruesome, ugly, horrible Opposite: lovely

monstrously adv **preposterously**, shockingly, offensively, unbelievably, prodigiously Opposite: unexceptionally

montage n **mosaic**, tableau, medley, mixture, pastiche

monthly adj 1 **regular**, periodic, frequent, once-a-month, scheduled Opposite: occasional 2 **month-long**, 30-day, period, season, medium-term ■ adv **regularly**, once a month, periodically, frequently, at monthly intervals Opposite: irregularly ■ n **magazine**, publication, periodical, journal, bulletin

monument n 1 **headstone**, marker, tombstone, gravestone 2 **memorial**, testimonial, testament, tribute

monumental adj 1 **colossal**, epic, immense, massive, enormous Opposite: small 2 **historic**, classic, significant, important, epic Opposite: minor

mooch *(infml)* v **wheedle**, beg, sponge *(infml)*, cadge *(infml)*, scrounge *(infml)*

moocher *(infml)* n **scrounger**, taker, sponger *(infml)*, cadger *(infml)*, freeloader *(infml)*

mood n **1 frame of mind**, disposition, temper, attitude, temperament **2 temper**, bad temper, sulk, the doldrums, anger **3 atmosphere**, feel, air, feeling, ambience

moodiness n **sulkiness**, changeableness, sullenness, grumpiness, glumness *Opposite*: cheeriness

moody adj **temperamental**, morose, sulky, sullen, glum *Opposite*: predictable

moon v **1 wander**, drift, meander, amble, dawdle **2** *(literary)* **fantasize**, dream, daydream, languish, pine

moonbeam n **ray**, moonlight, shaft of light, moonshine, glint *Opposite*: sunbeam

moonlight *(infml)* v **do work on the side**, do two jobs, supplement your income, have a second job, have a night job

moonscape n **wasteland**, desert, wilderness, barren land, waste

moonshine n **1** *(infml)* **poteen**, bootleg alcohol, home-brew, firewater *(dated slang)*, white lightning *(US)* **2 nonsense**, fantasy, silliness, fiction, gibberish

moonshot n **rocket launch**, launch, lunar expedition, lunar exploration, mission

moonstruck *(infml)* adj **dazed**, confused, irrational, distracted, in a daze *Opposite*: alert

moor n **heath**, moorland, common, upland, fell ■ v **tie**, fix, secure, chain, attach *Opposite*: untie

mooring n **anchorage**, berth, tie-up, bay, reserved space

moot adj **debatable**, arguable, doubtful, controversial, unresolved *Opposite*: established ■ v **propose**, put forward, suggest, bring up, introduce

mop v **wipe**, clean, swab, dust, mop up

mope v **brood**, languish, pine, sulk, pout

moppet *(infml)* n **child**, toddler, little one, tot *(infml)*, kid *(infml)*

mop up v **1 wipe up**, clear up, mop, wipe, swab **2** *(infml)* **finish off**, dispose of, see to, deal with, polish off

moraine n **glacial deposit**, debris, rubble, residue

moral adj **ethical**, good, right, honest, decent *Opposite*: immoral ■ n **message**, meaning, significance, rule, maxim

morale n **confidence**, self-esteem, spirits, self-confidence, assurance *Opposite*: aimlessness

moralist n **1 moralizer**, censor, preacher, critic, philosopher **2 virtuous person**, upright person, puritan, saint, prude

moralistic adj **moralizing**, didactic, strait-laced, serious, upright

morality n **1 ethics**, morals, principles, standards, scruples **2 goodness**, decency, probity, honesty, integrity *Opposite*: wickedness

moralize v **preach**, lecture, sermonize, criticize, nag

moralizing n **lecturing**, sermonizing, instruction, remonstration, admonishment ■ adj **lecturing**, critical, preaching, exhorting, hectoring *Opposite*: unprincipled

morals n **ethics**, morality, standards, scruples, principles

morass n **1 bog**, marsh, mire, swamp, wetland **2 mess**, chaos, muddle, quagmire, mire

moratorium n **suspension**, freeze, halt, pause, cessation

morbid adj **1 morose**, gloomy, dark, moody, melancholic *Opposite*: cheerful **2 gruesome**, dark, sinister, macabre, perverse

morbidity n **illness**, injury, disease, ill health, indisposition *Opposite*: health

mordant adj **caustic**, astringent, acerbic, penetrating, sarcastic *Opposite*: gentle

more adj **additional**, extra, supplementary, added, further *Opposite*: less

moreish *(infml)* adj **tasty**, delectable, tempting, delicious, yummy *(infml)* *Opposite*: bland

moreover adv **furthermore**, what is more, in addition, besides, also

mores n **customs**, values, habits, traditions, patterns

morgue n **mortuary**, undertaker's, chapel of rest, funeral home *(US)*

moribund adj **1 dying**, failing, expiring, on your last legs, at death's door *Opposite*: well **2 declining**, on the way out, waning, past its best, on its last legs *Opposite*: thriving

morning n **dawn**, daybreak, sunrise, break of day, first light *Opposite*: evening

morose adj **miserable**, glum, depressed, down, low *Opposite*: cheery

morph v **transform**, alter, switch, convert, adapt

morphology n **shape**, form, contours, formation

morsel n **scrap**, crumb, bit, piece, fragment *Opposite*: chunk

mortal adj **1 earthly**, worldly, human, corporeal, finite *Opposite*: immortal **2 deadly**, fatal, lethal, life-threatening, terminal **3 extreme**, great, grave, severe, serious *Opposite*: mild ■ n **human being**, human, person, individual, soul. *See* COMPARE AND CONTRAST *at* deadly.

mortality n **humanity**, death, transience, impermanence

mortally adv **1 fatally**, lethally, incurably, terminally **2 extremely**, severely, seriously, greatly, very *Opposite*: mildly

mortgage n **loan**, bank loan, advance, secured loan, debt ■ v **pledge**, forfeit, offer as security, use as a guarantee, pawn

mortification n **shame**, degradation, indignity, embarrassment, chagrin

mortified adj **ashamed**, embarrassed, humiliated, horrified, offended *Opposite*: proud

mortify v **degrade**, humiliate, take down, embarrass, crush

mortifying adj **humiliating**, shameful, embarrassing, degrading, chastening *Opposite*: uplifting

mortuary n **morgue**, undertaker's, chapel of rest, funeral home *(US)*

mosaic n **medley**, assortment, mixture, variety, montage

mosey *(infml)* v **saunter**, wander, amble, stroll, dawdle *Opposite*: rush

mossy adj **moss-covered**, moss-grown, moss-topped, overgrown, green

most pron **the majority**, nearly everyone, nearly all, a good number, a large amount *Opposite*: few ■ adv **very**, highly, extremely, really, truly *Opposite*: fairly

mostly adv **1 for the most part**, above all, mainly, generally, on the whole **2 usually**, more often than not, normally, typically, commonly *Opposite*: rarely

mote n **speck**, particle, jot, iota, bit *Opposite*: mass

mothball v **1 postpone**, delay, put on the back burner, put aside, put on ice **2 shut up**, pack away, decommission, put into storage, put out of commission *Opposite*: open up

moth-eaten adj **tattered**, threadbare, tatty, dog-eared, worn *Opposite*: brand-new

mother v **look after**, care for, protect, nurse, tend *Opposite*: neglect

motherhood n **maternity**, parenthood, kinship *Opposite*: fatherhood

motherland n **mother country**, native country, birthplace, homeland, fatherland

motherly adj **maternal**, protective, caring, loving, kind *Opposite*: uncaring

motif n **1 design**, pattern, image, decoration, shape **2 theme**, idea, subject, topic, keynote

motion n **1 movement**, action, activity, change, mobility *Opposite*: stillness **2 gesture**, wave, signal, sign, gesticulation **3 proposal**, suggestion, proposition, submission, recommendation ■ v **signal**, indicate, wave, gesture, beckon

motionless adj **stationary**, immobile, still, stock-still, static *Opposite*: moving

motionlessness n **stillness**, calm, immobility, paralysis, rigidity *Opposite*: mobility

motion picture n **film**, picture, feature film, video, flick *(infml)*

motivate v **1 cause**, prompt, provoke, induce, spur *Opposite*: deter **2 inspire**, stimulate, encourage, egg on, persuade *Opposite*: discourage

motivated adj **interested**, driven, inspired, moved, stirred *Opposite*: unmotivated

motivating adj **stimulating**, interesting, inspiring, galvanizing, encouraging *Opposite*: uninspiring

motivation n **1 incentive**, inspiration, enthusiasm, impetus, stimulus *Opposite*: disincentive **2 reason**, cause, motive, purpose, rationale

motivator n **instigator**, persuader, promoter, cheerleader, stimulus

motive n **reason**, motivation, spur, incentive, inducement *Opposite*: deterrent

COMPARE AND CONTRAST CORE MEANING: something that prompts action

motive the reason for doing something or behaving in a particular way; **incentive** something external, often some kind of reward, that inspires extra enthusiasm or effort; **inducement** something external that persuades or attracts somebody to a particular course of action, especially something that is offered as a reward; **spur** something such as the hope of a reward or the fear of punishment that encourages action or effort or energy; **goad** a stimulus that motivates somebody or stirs somebody into action, often against his or her will.

motiveless adj **unprovoked**, gratuitous, wanton, senseless, unwarranted *Opposite*: justified

motley adj **assorted**, miscellaneous, diverse, varied, mixed *Opposite*: uniform

motocross n **scramble**, cross-country race, motorcycle race, trail biking, motorcycle racing

motor n **engine**, petrol engine, diesel engine, internal combustion engine, electric motor ■ adj **motorized**, motor-powered, petrol-powered, diesel-powered, electrically powered ■ v **1** *(fml)* **drive**, travel, proceed, journey, ride **2** *(infml)* **zoom**, speed, tear along, race, zip *(infml)* *Opposite*: dawdle

motorcade n **convoy**, procession, parade, file, escort

motorist n **driver**, car driver, car user, car owner, chauffeur *Opposite*: passenger

motorized adj **motor**, motor-powered, petrol-powered, diesel-powered, electrically powered

mottled adj **dappled**, spotted, spotty, blotchy, speckled *Opposite*: plain

motto n **slogan**, saying, maxim, aphorism, adage

mould n **1 cast**, container, form, die, tin **2 frame**, pattern, template, stencil, outline **3 conformation**, character, type, variety, vein **4 mildew**, fungus, fungal growth, decay, rust ■ v **1 shape**, fashion, style, sculpt, form **2 influence**, change, guide, form, shape **3 cling**, hug, follow, fit around, wrap around

moulder v **rot**, gather dust, disintegrate, crumble, decay

mouldiness n **decay**, disintegration, mustiness, mildew, rottenness

moulding n **decoration**, detail, cornice, beading, dado

mouldy adj **1 mildewed**, festering, fungal, decaying, decayed Opposite: fresh **2 stale**, neglected, dirty, musty, fusty Opposite: fresh **3 boring**, dull, dreary, drab, insipid Opposite: exciting

moult v **shed**, cast, peel, slough, scale

mound n **1 knoll**, hillock, embankment, bank, hill Opposite: valley **2 pile**, stack, mass, bundle, mountain

mount v **1 prepare**, set up, produce, launch, arrange **2 rise**, mount up, increase, accumulate, grow Opposite: decrease **3 get on**, climb on, jump on, board, go on Opposite: dismount **4 climb**, ascend, go up, climb up, clamber up Opposite: descend **5 frame**, box, encase, inset, affix ■ n **1 base**, stand, support, pedestal, plinth **2 horse**, mule, ass, donkey, pony

mountain n **1 peak**, mount, crag, fell, massif Opposite: valley **2 pile**, mass, stack, bundle, mound

mountaineer n **climber**, alpinist, rock climber

mountainous adj **1 hilly**, high, steep, precipitous, rocky Opposite: flat **2 huge**, enormous, immense, monumental, gigantic Opposite: tiny

mountainside n **slope**, shoulder, gradient, incline, hillside

mountaintop n **peak**, summit, pike, crest, hilltop Opposite: bottom

mounted adj **1 on horseback**, equestrian, astride, straddling, riding Opposite: on foot **2 attached**, fixed, affixed, screwed on, displayed Opposite: loose

mounting adj **rising**, increasing, growing, swelling, escalating Opposite: decreasing

mourn v **grieve**, lament, grieve for, grieve over, weep for Opposite: rejoice (literary)

mourner n **bereaved person**, funeral-goer, griever, widow, widower

mournful adj **sad**, sorrowful, sombre, woeful, doleful Opposite: cheerful

mournfulness n **sadness**, sombreness, melancholy, gloominess, despondency Opposite: cheerfulness

mourning n **grief**, bereavement, sorrow, sadness, lamentation Opposite: rejoicing

mouth n **1 maw**, trap (infml), gob (slang), cakehole (slang) **2 entrance**, opening, door, doorway, aperture **3 estuary**, outlet, bay, inlet **4** (infml) **insolence**, impertinence, rudeness, cheek (infml), backchat (infml) ■ v **say**, mime, state, utter, reply

WORD BANK
❏ **parts of a mouth** adenoids, denture, gum, lip, palate, roof, soft palate, taste bud, tongue, tonsils, tooth, uvula

mouthful n **1 bite**, taste, piece, spoonful, forkful (infml) **2 harangue**, sermon, lecture, tirade, earful (infml)

mouthpiece n **spokesperson**, representative, agent, ambassador, delegate

mouth-to-mouth n **artificial respiration**, kiss of life, resuscitation, cardiopulmonary resuscitation, CPR

mouthwash n **gargle**, rinse, breath freshener, mouth spray

mouthwatering adj **delicious**, delectable, lip-smacking, luscious, tasty Opposite: revolting

movable adj **1 portable**, transportable, transferable, mobile, detachable Opposite: fixed **2 changeable**, variable, mutable, impermanent, adjustable Opposite: fixed

move v **1 reposition**, shift, budge, shove, stir **2 go**, progress, transport, walk, step **3 relocate**, transfer, redeploy, change, shift Opposite: stay put **4 cause**, provoke, persuade, encourage, prod **5 affect**, touch, stir the emotions, impress, upset ■ n **1 movement**, action, motion, gesture, transfer **2 attempt**, effort, step, action, activity **3 shift**, realignment, rearrangement, repositioning, relocation

move ahead v **progress**, move on, press forward, go on, move forward Opposite: retreat

move along v **1 proceed**, hasten, go on, advance, press on **2 move aside**, move over, make way, make room, shift Opposite: stay put

move away v **retreat**, back off, diverge, distance, deviate

move back v **recoil**, recede, shrink back, retreat, regress Opposite: advance

move fast v **streak**, zoom, speed, tear, whiz

move forward v **advance**, progress, push on, go ahead, proceed Opposite: fall back

move heaven and earth v **do your utmost**, pull out all the stops, make every effort, move mountains, leave no stone unturned

move in on v **approach**, surround, converge, come closer, draw near Opposite: retreat

move into v **enter**, start, enter on, begin, set the ball rolling Opposite: back out

movement n **1 motion**, mobility, locomotion, circulation Opposite: stillness **2 move**, action, motion, gesture, lift **3 drive**, programme, crusade, undertaking, measure **4 pressure group**, association, society, lobby, faction **5 progress**, advance, development, improvement, headway Opposite: stagnation

movements n **actions**, activities, travels, schedule, arrangements

move on v **1 leave**, depart, go, make off, set off Opposite: stay put **2 progress**, get going, go on, take the next step, uproot Opposite: backtrack

move out v **leave**, depart, go, relocate, move on Opposite: stay

move over v **move aside**, make way, make room, shift, step aside Opposite: stay put

mover n 1 **motivator**, driving force, agent, doer, goer 2 **initiator**, proposer, presenter, introducer, advocate *Opposite*: seconder

move towards v **come closer**, draw near, move in on, approach, converge *Opposite*: move away

move up v **go up**, rise, increase, progress, advance *Opposite*: drop

moving adj **touching**, poignant, affecting, pathetic, heartrending

---

COMPARE AND CONTRAST CORE MEANING: arousing emotion

moving causing deep feelings, especially of sadness or compassion; **pathetic** arousing feelings of compassion and pity, often centred on somebody who is vulnerable, helpless, or unfortunate; **pitiful** arousing compassion and pity, or arousing contempt or derision; **poignant** causing strong, often bittersweet feelings of sadness, pity, or regret; **touching** causing feelings of warmth, sympathy, and tenderness; **heartwarming** inspiring warm or kindly feelings, usually by showing life and human nature in a positive and reassuring light; **heartrending** causing intense sadness or distress, especially in sympathy with somebody else's unhappiness or hardship because it involves suffering or tragic events.

---

moving parts n **mechanism**, machinery, workings, components, gears

mow v **cut**, scythe, cut down, shear, trim

mow down v 1 **shoot**, kill, slaughter, massacre, butcher 2 **knock down**, run over, knock over, floor, topple

much adv 1 **significantly**, noticeably, considerably, greatly, substantially 2 **often**, frequently, over and over again, time and again, repeatedly ■ adj **a good deal of**, a great deal of, lots of, abundant, ample

much-loved adj **adored**, favourite, preferred, chosen, desired

muck n 1 **manure**, sewage, waste, sludge, dung 2 (infml) **dirt**, mess, grime, mud, filth

muck about (infml) v **fool about**, lark about, mess about (infml), mess around (infml), waste time

muckiness (infml) n **filthiness**, muddiness, dirtiness, grubbiness, griminess

muckraker n **scandalmonger**, gossipmonger, troublemaker, mudslinger, slanderer

muckraking n **scandalmongering**, dishing the dirt, mudslinging, slander, libel

muck up (infml) v **spoil**, ruin, damage, make a mess of, botch (infml)

mucky (infml) adj **dirty**, muddy, messy, grubby, grotty (infml) *Opposite*: clean

mucous adj **self-lubricating**, slimy, slippery, lubricated

mucus n **slime**, secretion, saliva, lubricant, phlegm

mud n **mire**, sludge, dirt, muck (infml)

muddiness n 1 **dirtiness**, grubbiness, filthiness, griminess, muckiness (infml) *Opposite*: cleanness 2 **cloudiness**, murkiness, dullness, opacity, thickness *Opposite*: clarity

muddle v 1 **mix up**, jumble, disorder, disorganize, disarrange *Opposite*: disentangle 2 **confuse**, bewilder, baffle, puzzle, perplex *Opposite*: clarify ■ n **disorder**, jumble, confusion, mix-up, chaos *Opposite*: order

muddled adj 1 **jumbled**, scrambled, mixed up, topsy-turvy, upside down *Opposite*: ordered 2 **confused**, befuddled, bewildered, bemused, perplexed *Opposite*: clear

muddleheaded adj 1 **baffled**, mixed up, confused, befuddled, bewildered *Opposite*: clear-headed 2 **inept**, illogical, impractical, random, ineffective *Opposite*: logical

muddle up v **mix up**, jumble, disorder, disorganize, disarrange

muddy adj 1 **mud-spattered**, dirty, grubby, grimy, filthy *Opposite*: clean 2 **cloudy**, murky, unclear, opaque, thick *Opposite*: clear

mud flap n **mudguard**, flap, shield, guard, cover

mudpack n **face mask**, facial, face pack, treatment, beauty treatment

mudslinger n **slanderer**, defamer, denigrator, character assassin, attacker

mudslinging n **defamation**, backbiting, slander, denigration, character assassination *Opposite*: praise

muff v 1 **miss**, drop, fumble, mishit, mishandle 2 **get wrong**, mishandle, botch (infml), bungle (infml), mess up (infml)

muffle v **deaden**, dampen, quieten, silence, mute *Opposite*: amplify

muffled adj **stifled**, muted, inaudible, soft, lowered *Opposite*: loud

mufti n **casuals**, civilian clothes, ordinary clothes, street clothes, casual wear *Opposite*: uniform

mug v **attack**, assault, rob, ambush, hold up

mugger n **robber**, assailant, thug, attacker, assaulter

mugginess n **humidity**, closeness, clamminess, oppressiveness, warmth *Opposite*: freshness

mugging n **attack**, assault, bag-snatch, robbery, ambush

muggy adj **humid**, close, sultry, clammy, oppressive *Opposite*: fresh

mug shot n **photo**, photograph, close-up, police photo, passport photo

mug up (infml) v **learn**, study, absorb, cram (infml), swot (infml)

mulch n **covering**, protection, insulation, organic matter, leaves ■ v **cover**, protect, insulate, dress, top dress

mulish adj **stubborn**, obstinate, defiant, headstrong, obdurate *Opposite*: amenable

mulishness n **stubbornness**, obstinacy, defiance, obduracy, determination *Opposite*: amenability

mulled *adj* **spiced**, flavoured, warmed, sweetened, warm

mull over *v* **ponder**, consider, contemplate, think over, think about

multicolour *adj* **colourful**, rainbow, variegated, many-hued, polychrome

multicultural *adj* **diverse**, multiethnic, multiracial, inclusive, all-inclusive

multifaceted *adj* **multilayered**, complex, complicated, many-sided, polygonal *Opposite*: simple

multifarious *adj* **diverse**, varied, assorted, mixed, miscellaneous *Opposite*: homogeneous

multilateral *adj* **1 many-sided**, polygonal, multifaceted, multidimensional **2 mutual**, all-party, multiparty, joint, bilateral *Opposite*: unilateral

multilingual *adj* **polyglot**, trilingual, bilingual

multimedia *n* **1 hypermedia**, software, interactive program, program **2 collage**, combination, montage, assemblage, construction

multimillionaire *n* **millionaire**, magnate, billionaire, tycoon, mogul

multinational *adj* **international**, cosmopolitan, transnational, global, worldwide *Opposite*: national ■ *n* **conglomerate**, corporation, transnational, international business, international company

multipartite *adj* **multiple**, multifarious, multifaceted, composite, compound

multiple *adj* **manifold**, numerous, many, several, various *Opposite*: few

multiplex *n* **multiscreen cinema**, cinema complex, picture house *(dated)*

multiplication *n* **increase**, growth, development, reproduction, duplication *Opposite*: decrease

multiplicity *n* **array**, diversity, variety, large quantity, range *Opposite*: dearth

multiply *v* **increase**, grow, reproduce, swell, proliferate *Opposite*: decrease

multipurpose *adj* **versatile**, flexible, adaptable, multiuse *Opposite*: dedicated

multiracial *adj* **interracial**, multicultural, multiethnic, inclusive, all-inclusive *Opposite*: exclusive

multistorey *adj* **high-rise**, multilevel, tall, high, towering *Opposite*: low-rise

multitude *n* **1 crowd**, horde, host, mass, throng *Opposite*: handful **2 variety**, assortment, array, collection, wealth *Opposite*: few

mum *(infml)* *n* **mother**, mummy *(infml)*, mama *(infml)*, ma *(infml)*, mammy *(infml)* ■ *adj* **silent**, tight-lipped, mute, quiet, dumb *Opposite*: communicative

mumble *v* **mutter**, murmur, drone, intone, gabble *Opposite*: enunciate

mumbled *adj* **muttered**, murmured, muffled, inaudible, slurred *Opposite*: enunciated

mumbo jumbo *(infml)* *n* **jargon**, gibberish, doublespeak, cant, technobabble *Opposite*: sense

mummify *v* **1 embalm**, preserve, wrap up, prepare, dress **2 shrivel**, dry out, dry up, wrinkle, wither *Opposite*: flourish

mummy *n* **1 mummified body**, body, cadaver, corpse

munch *v* **chew**, masticate, crunch, grind, eat

mundane *adj* **ordinary**, dull, routine, everyday, commonplace *Opposite*: exotic

mundaneness *n* **ordinariness**, routine, tedium, flatness, unimaginativeness *Opposite*: excitement

municipal *adj* **civic**, public, community, urban, metropolitan *Opposite*: private

municipality *n* **city**, metropolis, town, borough, burg *(US)*. See COMPARE AND CONTRAST at **city**.

munificence *n* **generosity**, largesse, benevolence, kindness, philanthropy *Opposite*: miserliness

munificent *adj* **generous**, liberal, magnanimous, unstinting, unsparing *Opposite*: miserly. See COMPARE AND CONTRAST at **generous**.

munitions *n* **weaponry**, ammunition, arms, guns, armaments

mural *n* **wall painting**, fresco, frieze, painting

murder *n* **homicide**, manslaughter, assassination, killing, slaying ■ *v* **kill**, assassinate, execute, put to death, slaughter. See COMPARE AND CONTRAST at **kill**.

murderer *n* **killer**, assassin, butcher, slaughterer, executioner

murderous *adj* **1 fatal**, lethal, mortal, deadly, homicidal **2** *(infml)* **difficult**, testing, arduous, rigorous, exhausting *Opposite*: easy

murk *n* **gloom**, darkness, shadows, dark, dimness *Opposite*: light

murkiness *n* **darkness**, fogginess, mistiness, cloudiness, gloom *Opposite*: brightness

murky *adj* **dark**, gloomy, foggy, misty, cloudy *Opposite*: clear

murmur *v* **1 whisper**, mutter, mumble, purr, croon *Opposite*: bray **2 complain**, grumble, grouch, mutter, grouse *(infml)* *Opposite*: praise

muscle *n* **1 sinew**, brawn, musculature, thew *(archaic)* **2 influence**, power, authority, force, control **3** *(infml)* **strength**, vigour, power, force, elbow grease *(infml)*

WORD BANK

❏ **types of muscle or tendon** abdominals, Achilles tendon, biceps, diaphragm, hamstring, pectoral, quadriceps, sinew, smooth muscle, sphincter, striated muscle, tendon, triceps

muscle in *(infml)* *v* **intrude**, intervene, barge in, butt in, interfere

muscular *adj* **brawny**, beefy, well-built, burly, well-developed *Opposite*: puny

muse v **think**, ponder, consider, mull over, deliberate

museum n **gallery**, exhibition hall, arts centre, academy, institution

mush n **1 pap**, purée, mash, paste, slop **2 sentimentality**, sentimentalism, slush, sugariness, slop (infml)

mushroom v **grow**, increase, expand, flourish, swell Opposite: decline

mushy adj **1 soggy**, soft, squashy, squishy, squidgy Opposite: firm **2 oversentimental**, mawkish, maudlin, syrupy, romantic

music n **melody**, tune, harmony, composition, song

WORD BANK

❑ **types of musical form** anthem, aria, bagatelle, ballad, cantata, canticle, capriccio, chorale, coloratura, concerto, étude, fantasia, fugue, hymn, intermezzo, madrigal, mass, nocturne, oratorio, overture, prelude, requiem, rondo, scherzo, sinfonia, sonata, song, suite, symphony, tone poem, waltz

❑ **types of musical register** alto, baritone, bass, countertenor, falsetto, mezzo-soprano, soprano, tenor

❑ **types of musical term** a cappella, adagio, allegro, andante, appassionato, arpeggio, capriccioso, con brio, con moto, crescendo, diminuendo, forte, fortissimo, grave, larghetto, largo, legato, lentissimo, lento, moderato, pianissimo, piano, pizzicato, rubato, sotto voce, staccato

❑ **types of classical music** Baroque, chamber music, comic opera, early music, opera, operetta, Romantic, twelve-tone

❑ **types of dance music** acid house, acid jazz, big beat, boogie, broken beat, disco, drum 'n' bass, funk, garage, hard core, hip hop, house, jungle, ragga, ragamuffin, rap, rave, reggae, rock steady, ska, speed garage, techno, trance, two step

❑ **types of electronic music** ambient, breakbeat, breaks and beats, chillout, downtempo, dub, electro, electronica, new age, trip hop

❑ **types of jazz music** bebop, boogie-woogie, cool jazz, dixieland, honky-tonk, jazz, jazz funk, jazz fusion, jazz rock, jive, modal jazz, New Orleans jazz, ragtime, swing, trad jazz

❑ **types of pop and vocal music** bluegrass, blues, britpop, country and western, doowop, easy listening, folk, gangsta rap, gospel, lounge, Motown, new wave, northern soul, pop, R&B, rap metal, rockabilly, soul, spiritual

❑ **types of rock music** grunge, heavy metal, indie, metal, punk, rock, rock 'n' roll, thrash metal

❑ **types of world music** afrobeat, bhangra, calypso, flamenco, Latin, mento, raga, rai, roots, salsa, yodel

musical adj **melodic**, harmonious, melodious, tuneful, easy on the ear Opposite: discordant

musician n **performer**, instrumentalist, player, artiste, composer

musing n **thinking**, reflection, reverie, daydream, consideration ■ adj **thoughtful**, reflective, pensive, contemplative, absorbed

musk n **perfume**, scent, smell, fragrance, aroma

musky adj **pungent**, perfumed, scented, odorous, aromatic

must v **have to**, have got to, be obliged to, ought to, should ■ n **necessity**, obligation, duty, essential, requirement Opposite: option

muster v **gather**, gather together, congregate, collect, get together Opposite: disperse ■ n **gathering**, assembly, meeting, congregation, congress

mustiness n **dankness**, staleness, mouldiness, stuffiness, fustiness Opposite: freshness

musty adj **mildewed**, stale, mouldy, fusty, stuffy Opposite: fresh

mutable adj **changeable**, alterable, changing, variable, fluctuating Opposite: fixed

mutant adj **distorted**, misshapen, malformed, transformed, altered

mutate v **change**, alter, transform, transmute, metamorphose

mutation n **change**, alteration, transformation, transmutation, metamorphosis

mute adj **silent**, speechless, voiceless, unspeaking, quiet Opposite: vocal

muted adj **subdued**, hushed, soft, quiet, gentle Opposite: loud

mutilate v **maim**, injure, hurt, disfigure, harm

mutilation n **disfigurement**, defacement, damage, injury, maiming

mutineer n **rebel**, insurgent, rioter, radical, insurrectionist

mutinous adj **rebellious**, revolutionary, seditious, subversive, disobedient Opposite: obedient

mutiny n **rebellion**, revolt, sedition, uprising, insubordination

mutter v **1 mumble**, murmur, drone, burble, slur Opposite: speak up **2 complain**, grouch, grumble, murmur, grouse (infml) Opposite: praise

mutual adj **joint**, shared, common, communal, reciprocated

muzzle v **silence**, gag, hush, stifle, suppress

muzzy adj **1 vague**, fuzzy, out of focus, blurred, bleary Opposite: clear **2 fuzzy**, woozy, groggy, bleary, shaky Opposite: clear-headed

myopia n **1 short-sightedness**, poor sight, near-sightedness (US) **2 bigotry**, prejudice, bias, intolerance, narrow-mindedness

myopic adj **1 short-sighted**, owlish, nearsighted (US) **2 narrow-minded**, bigoted, parochial, prejudiced, intolerant Opposite: broad-minded

myriad adj **countless**, innumerable, numberless, numerous, many Opposite: few ■ n **multitude**, mass, host, army, crowd Opposite: few

mysterious adj **1 strange**, unexplained, inexplicable, unsolved, odd **2 secretive**, enigmatic, shadowy, furtive, cryptic *Opposite*: open

mysteriousness *n* **strangeness**, oddness, weirdness, curiousness, inexplicableness *Opposite*: normality

mystery *n* **1 problem**, puzzle, conundrum, enigma, riddle **2 secrecy**, obscurity, ambiguity, inscrutability, vagueness ■ *adj* **unknown**, anonymous, unidentified, secret, clandestine ■ *n* **whodunit**, detective novel, thriller, crime novel

mystic *n* **spiritualist**, medium, shaman, sorcerer, wizard ■ *adj* **mystical**, spiritual, supernatural, magical, cabalistic

mystical *adj* **spiritual**, mystic, magical, supernatural, magic

mystification *n* **bewilderment**, confusion, perplexity, bafflement, puzzlement

mystified *adj* **puzzled**, confused, bewildered, baffled, perplexed *Opposite*: enlightened

mystify *v* **puzzle**, confuse, bewilder, confound, baffle

mystifying *adj* **mysterious**, baffling, inexplicable, puzzling, confusing

mystique *n* **air of mystery**, air of secrecy, aura, charisma, magic

myth *n* **1 legend**, fable, saga, fairy story, fairy tale **2 falsehood**, fiction, illusion, invention, fabrication *Opposite*: fact

WORD BANK

❑ **types of mythical being** Abominable Snowman, Bigfoot, bogey, bogeyman, bugaboo, daemon, demon, dryad, giant, gnome, goblin, gremlin (*infml*), hobgoblin, leprechaun, naiad, nymph, ogre, sasquatch, sylph, troll, wood nymph, yeti

mythic *see* **mythical**

mythical *adj* **1 legendary**, mythological, fabled, fabulous, storybook *Opposite*: factual **2 imaginary**, untrue, fictitious, fictional, made-up *Opposite*: real

mythological *adj* **mythical**, mythic, fabulous, fairy-tale, fabled *Opposite*: factual

mythology *n* **myths**, legends, folklore, tradition, mythos

N

nab *v* **1** (*infml*) **arrest**, seize, capture, detain, catch **2 steal**, walk off with, rip off (*infml*), swipe (*infml*), lift (*infml*)

nadir *n* **lowest point**, all-time low, depths of despair, depths, base *Opposite*: zenith

naff (*infml*) *adj* **tasteless**, unfashionable, unstylish, ridiculous, crass *Opposite*: fashionable

nag *v* **1 badger**, pester, plague, harass, harry **2 criticize**, find fault, carp, grumble, complain **3 irritate**, annoy, worry, trouble, torment. *See* COMPARE AND CONTRAST *at* **complain**.

nagging *adj* **irritating**, niggling, troublesome, distressing, irksome

nail *n* **pin**, spike, tack, peg ■ *v* **tack**, pin, fix, fasten, attach

nail-biting *adj* **nerve-racking**, tense, exciting, stressful, anxious *Opposite*: relaxing

nail down *v* **pin down**, get an agreement on, get a decision on, settle, confirm

naive *adj* **1 simple**, trusting, innocent, childlike, inexperienced *Opposite*: suspicious **2 unsophisticated**, gullible, wet behind the ears, green, foolish *Opposite*: shrewd

naivety *n* **innocence**, ingenuousness, candour, artlessness, naturalness *Opposite*: sophistication

naked *adj* **1 bare**, nude, undressed, unclothed, with nothing on *Opposite*: clothed **2 uncovered**, unprotected, exposed, unsheathed, unwrapped *Opposite*: covered **3 open**, undisguised, unadorned, unadulterated, unvarnished *Opposite*: hidden

COMPARE AND CONTRAST CORE MEANING: devoid of clothes or covering

naked not covered or concealed, especially not covered by clothing on any part of the body; **bare** without the usual furnishings or decorations, or not covered by clothing; **nude** not wearing any clothes at all, especially in artistic contexts; **undressed** not wearing any or many clothes, used especially when clothes have just been removed or are about to be put on.

nakedly *adv* **openly**, blatantly, starkly, obviously, overtly *Opposite*: covertly

nakedness *n* **1 nudity**, bareness, state of undress **2 defencelessness**, helplessness, exposure, vulnerability **3 blatancy**, obviousness, openness, overtness, starkness *Opposite*: covertness

namby-pamby (*infml*) (*insult*) *adj* **feeble**, soft, spineless, ineffectual, pathetic (*infml*) *Opposite*: tough

name *n* **1 first name**, Christian name, forename, surname, family name **2 designation**, term, tag, title, label **3 reputation**, renown, character, respectability, fame *Opposite*: notoriety **4 celebrity**, star, big name, public figure, VIP *Opposite*: nobody ■ *v* **1 call**, christen, baptize, nickname, label **2 identify**, specify, refer to, mention, cite *Opposite*: conceal

3 nominate, appoint, assign, choose, suggest *Opposite*: reject

name-calling *n* **abuse**, insults, foul language, swearing, invective *(fml)*

named *adj* **called**, baptized, christened, entitled, titled *Opposite*: nameless

name-drop *v* **boast**, brag, show off, vaunt, swank *(infml)*

name-dropper *n* **boaster**, bragger, braggart, show-off *(infml)*, bigmouth *(infml)*

nameless *adj* **1 anonymous**, unknown, unidentified, unnamed, unspecified *Opposite*: named **2 indescribable**, awful, dreadful, horrible, ghastly

namely *adv* **that is**, that is to say, viz, specifically, explicitly

nameplate *n* **plate**, sign, plaque, notice, panel

naming *n* **identification**, designation, nomenclature, christening, baptism

nanny *n* **1 child minder**, au pair, carer, minder, caretaker (US) **2** *(infml)* **grandmother**, nana *(infml)*, nan *(infml)*, granny *(infml)*, gran *(infml)*

nanosecond *n* **moment**, split second, second, instant, trice

nap *n* **1 doze**, catnap, siesta, sleep, rest **2 pile**, surface, finish, weave, texture ■ *v* **sleep**, catnap, have a siesta, doze, drowse

napkin *n* **serviette**, bib, paper towel, table linen, napery *(archaic)*

narcissism *n* **self-love**, self-absorption, egotism, conceit, self-importance *Opposite*: selflessness

narcissistic *adj* **vain**, self-absorbed, egotistic, egotistical, selfish *Opposite*: selfless

nark *(infml)* *v* **1 provoke**, incense, drive mad *(infml)*, aggravate *(infml)*, madden *Opposite*: please **2 complain**, grumble, whine, whinge *(infml)*, carp

narrate *v* **relate**, recount, tell, describe, recite

narration *n* **1 telling**, recitation, relating, unfolding, recounting **2 tale**, account, description, chronicle, history

narrative *n* **1 tale**, account, description, chronicle, history **2 plot**, story line, sequence of events

narrator *n* **storyteller**, speaker, raconteur, teller of tales, relator *Opposite*: listener

narrow *adj* **thin**, fine, slim, slender, slight *Opposite*: wide ■ *v* **1 get thinner**, get smaller, taper, contract, tighten *Opposite*: widen **2 restrict**, limit, narrow down, confine, focus *Opposite*: broaden

narrow down *v* **focus**, restrict, limit, confine, concentrate *Opposite*: broaden

narrow escape *n* **close call**, near miss, close shave, lucky escape, near thing *(infml)*

narrowing *n* **tapering**, contraction, thinning, reduction, tightening

narrowly *adv* **1 only just**, barely, hardly, scarcely, by a hair's breadth **2 closely**, intently, carefully, attentively, assiduously

narrow-minded *adj* **bigoted**, blinkered, insular, intolerant, prejudiced *Opposite*: broad-minded

narrow-mindedness *n* **bigotry**, insularity, prejudice, bias, intolerance *Opposite*: broad-mindedness

narrowness *n* **thinness**, fineness, slimness, slightness, constriction *Opposite*: width

narrow squeak *see* **narrow escape**

nascent *adj* **budding**, promising, embryonic, emerging, blossoming *Opposite*: moribund

nastiness *n* **spite**, meanness, malice, viciousness, cruelty *Opposite*: kindness

nasty *adj* **1 spiteful**, mean, malicious, vicious, cruel *Opposite*: kind **2 foul**, horrid, horrible, revolting, offensive *Opposite*: pleasant **3 severe**, painful, horrible, serious, grave *Opposite*: slight **4** *(infml)* **obscene**, offensive, indecent, vulgar, crude **5** *(infml)* **difficult**, tricky, hard, complicated, knotty. *See* COMPARE AND CONTRAST *at* **mean**.

nation *n* **1 state**, country, land, realm, homeland **2 people**, population, inhabitants, residents, populace

national *adj* **1 nationwide**, countrywide, state, general, coast-to-coast *Opposite*: local **2 state**, public, nationalized, state-run, state-owned *Opposite*: private ■ *n* **resident**, citizen, inhabitant, subject, native *Opposite*: visitor

nationalism *n* **1 independence**, autonomy, home rule, self-rule, self-government **2 patriotism**, chauvinism, jingoism, xenophobia

nationalist *n* **separatist**, autonomist, separationist

nationalistic *adj* **patriotic**, jingoistic, chauvinistic, xenophobic

nationality *n* **people**, population, race, ethnic group

nationalize *v* **make public**, take over, municipalize *Opposite*: privatize

nationalized *adj* **state-owned**, publicly owned, public sector, state, national *Opposite*: private

nationally *adv* **countrywide**, all over the country, on a national scale, nationwide, generally *Opposite*: locally

nation-state *n* **state**, country, land, nation, sovereign state

nationwide *adj* **countrywide**, general, national, state, coast-to-coast *Opposite*: local ■ *adv* **nationally**, countrywide, all over the country, on a national scale, generally *Opposite*: locally

native *adj* **1 innate**, natural, inborn, instinctive, inherent *Opposite*: acquired **2 indigenous**, local, aboriginal, resident, autochthonous *Opposite*: foreign ■ *n* **inhabitant**, resident, local, citizen, subject *Opposite*: foreigner

COMPARE AND CONTRAST CORE MEANING: originating in a particular place
native born or originating in a particular place; **aboriginal** existing in a region from the earliest known times; **indigenous** originating in and typical of a region or country; **autochthonous** originating where currently found, especially used of rocks and minerals that were formed in their present position, or flora, fauna, or inhabitants descended from those present in a region from earliest times.

native land n **land of origin**, land of birth, birthplace, native country, motherland

nativity n **origin**, birth, genesis, conception, dawn Opposite: demise (fml)

natter (infml) v **have a chat**, chat, chatter, gossip, talk ■ n **chat**, conversation, gossip, talk, chinwag (infml)

natty adj **smart**, fashionable, trim, dapper, chic Opposite: unfashionable

natural adj 1 **usual**, normal, ordinary, accepted, expected Opposite: unusual 2 **physical**, biological, environmental, ecological, geographical Opposite: technological 3 **innate**, native, inborn, instinctive, effortless Opposite: learned 4 **unaffected**, unpretentious, spontaneous, genuine, artless Opposite: affected 5 **untreated**, unprocessed, pure, raw, crude Opposite: artificial 6 **biological**, physical, birth, true, actual Opposite: adoptive

naturalistic adj **realistic**, real, true-to-life, natural, lifelike

naturalize v 1 **accept**, adopt, enfranchise 2 **adapt**, become established, grow wild, grow naturally, acclimatize

naturally adv 1 **of course**, obviously, logically, as expected, unsurprisingly Opposite: surprisingly 2 **innately**, inherently, instinctively, intuitively, effortlessly 3 **unaffectedly**, unpretentiously, spontaneously, genuinely, artlessly Opposite: pretentiously 4 **in nature**, physically, biologically, geographically, geologically Opposite: artificially

naturalness n **unaffectedness**, spontaneity, genuineness, artlessness, sincerity Opposite: affectedness

natural resource n **raw material**, mineral, mineral deposit, reserve, resource

natural world n **environment**, nature, biosphere, ecosphere

nature n 1 **Mother Nature**, countryside, natural surroundings, wildlife, flora 2 **class**, kind, sort, type, description 3 **character**, personality, temperament, disposition, spirit

naughtiness n **disobedience**, bad behaviour, wickedness, ill-discipline, waywardness Opposite: obedience

naughty adj **disobedient**, bad, badly behaved, wicked, ill-disciplined Opposite: good. See COMPARE AND CONTRAST at **bad**.

nausea n 1 **biliousness**, queasiness, sickness, vomiting, unsettled stomach 2 (literary) **revul-**

sion, repugnance, repulsion, abhorrence, disgust

nauseate v 1 **sicken**, turn your stomach, make you feel sick Opposite: please 2 (literary) **disgust**, repel, revolt, upset, put off Opposite: attract

nauseating (literary) adj **disgusting**, sickening, repellent, revolting, repulsive Opposite: pleasant

nauseous adj 1 **sick**, bilious, queasy, unwell, nauseated Opposite: well 2 **disgusting**, sickening, repellent, revolting, repulsive Opposite: pleasant

nautical adj **maritime**, seafaring, sailing, marine, naval

naval see **nautical**

navel n **umbilicus**, tummy button (infml), bellybutton (infml)

navel-gazing n **self-analysis**, reflection, rumination, brooding, self-absorption

navigable adj 1 **passable**, negotiable, crossable, traversable Opposite: impassable 2 **manoeuvrable**, controllable, seaworthy, sturdy, steerable

navigate v 1 **find the way**, plot a course, plot a route, map read, follow the map 2 **sail across**, circumnavigate, steer, pilot, take the helm

navigation n **direction finding**, steering, course plotting, map reading, celestial navigation

navigational adj **directional**, direction-finding, course-plotting, route-finding

navigator n **guide**, autopilot, skipper, pilot, direction finder

navvy (dated) n **manual worker**, labourer, manual labourer, worker, hand

navy n **fleet**, armada, flotilla, merchant navy, merchant marine (US)

near prep 1 **close to**, by, next to, in close proximity to, in the vicinity of Opposite: far from 2 **like**, close to, similar to, resembling, approaching 3 **on the verge of**, approaching, nearing, close to, bordering on ■ adv 1 **nearby**, close, close by, close at hand, in close proximity 2 **almost**, nearly, virtually, practically, just about ■ adj **close**, nearby, neighbouring, adjacent, adjoining Opposite: far ■ v **approach**, reach, draw up to, draw near to, go up to Opposite: leave

nearby adj **close**, near, neighbouring, adjacent, adjoining Opposite: distant ■ adv **near**, close, close by, close at hand, in close proximity

nearly adv **closely**, approximately, almost, near, virtually

near miss n **lucky escape**, close thing, close call, close shave, narrow escape

nearness n **immediacy**, imminence, proximity, closeness, juxtaposition Opposite: distance

nearside adj **passenger**, kerbside, inside

near thing (infml) see **near miss**

neat adj 1 **well-ordered**, in order, straight, arranged, tidy Opposite: untidy 2 **well-organized**, organized, methodical, systematic, careful Opposite: disorganized 3 **straight**, undiluted, unmixed, full-strength, pure Opposite: diluted 4 **simple**, ingenious, elegant, clever, convenient 5 **graceful**, effortless, practised, precise, deft Opposite: clumsy 6 **natty**, trim, compact, well-designed, elegant Opposite: cumbersome

neaten v order, tidy, tidy up, arrange, sort out Opposite: mess up (infml)

neatness n 1 **tidiness**, orderliness, carefulness, efficiency, precision Opposite: messiness 2 **ingeniousness**, elegance, cleverness, effectiveness, handiness Opposite: ineffectiveness 3 **gracefulness**, effortlessness, preciseness, deftness, skilfulness Opposite: clumsiness 4 **simplicity**, elegance, nattiness, trimness, compactness

nebulous adj unclear, vague, imprecise, hazy, unformulated Opposite: precise

necessary adj **essential**, indispensable, needed, vital, requisite (fml) Opposite: optional

COMPARE AND CONTRAST CORE MEANING: describes something that is required
necessary important in order to achieve a desired result, or required by authority or convention; **essential** of the highest importance for achieving something; **vital** extremely important to the survival or continuing effectiveness of something; **indispensable** absolutely essential, or extremely desirable or useful; **requisite** (fml) necessary for a particular purpose; **needed** required or desired.

necessitate v require, demand, need, call for, dictate

necessitude n need, necessity, demand, requirement, want

necessity n 1 **essential**, requirement, prerequisite, basic, necessary Opposite: luxury 2 **need**, requirement, inevitability, obligation, stipulation

neck n **narrow part**, stem, shank, shaft ■ v (dated infml) **kiss**, cuddle, hug, smooch (infml), embrace

neckerchief (dated) n bandanna, cravat, scarf, tie, band

necklace n chain, string, choker, band, necklet

necklet see necklace

necropolis n cemetery, burial ground, graveyard, resting place, churchyard

nectar n liquid, juice, sap, fluid, syrup

née adj formerly, previously, originally

need v 1 **demand**, require, call for, want, necessitate 2 **have to**, must, should, ought ■ n 1 **essential**, necessity, requirement, want, prerequisite Opposite: option 2 **privation**, poverty, want, hardship, neediness Opposite: luxury. See COMPARE AND CONTRAST at **necessary**.

needed adj **necessary**, desired, required, wanted. See COMPARE AND CONTRAST at **necessary**.

needful adj 1 (fml or archaic) **necessary**, obligatory, compulsory, mandatory, essential 2 (fml) **requiring**, necessitating, demanding, calling for, needing

neediness n need, poverty, want, penury, destitution

needle n 1 **pointer**, indicator, hand 2 **spine**, spike, prickle, barb, pine needle ■ v (infml) **irritate**, provoke, annoy, pester, niggle

needless adj unnecessary, pointless, uncalled-for, useless, unneeded Opposite: necessary

needlessness n uselessness, unhelpfulness, fruitlessness, impracticality, pointlessness Opposite: usefulness

needy adj **poor**, in need, deprived, disadvantaged, destitute

ne'er-do-well (dated) n layabout, waster, idler, slacker, shirker

nefarious adj wicked, evil, despicable, immoral, reprehensible Opposite: reputable

negate (fml) v 1 **refute**, contradict, disprove, disavow, deny Opposite: affirm 2 **invalidate**, cancel, reverse, render null and void, nullify Opposite: validate. See COMPARE AND CONTRAST at **nullify**.

negation n 1 **denial**, annulment, nullification, repudiation, cancellation Opposite: affirmation 2 **opposite**, contrary, absence, lack, antithesis Opposite: confirmation

negative adj 1 **unenthusiastic**, unconstructive, unhelpful, pessimistic, downbeat (infml) Opposite: encouraging 2 **bad**, undesirable, adverse, harmful, damaging Opposite: positive ■ n rejection, rebuff, veto, no, refusal Opposite: approval

negatively adv 1 **in the negative**, with a no, with a refusal, with a denial Opposite: affirmatively 2 **damagingly**, harmfully, destructively, undesirably, adversely Opposite: positively 3 **offputtingly**, discouragingly, unenthusiastically, unconstructively, unhelpfully Opposite: encouragingly

negativity n unconstructiveness, unhelpfulness, pessimism, disapproval Opposite: enthusiasm

neglect v 1 **abandon**, desert, forget, forsake, ignore Opposite: look after 2 **omit**, forget, overlook, ignore, disregard ■ n **negligence**, abandonment, desertion, disregard, inattention Opposite: care

COMPARE AND CONTRAST CORE MEANING: fail to do something
neglect fail to give the proper or required care and attention to somebody or something, or fail to do something, especially because of carelessness, forgetfulness, or indifference; **forget** fail, or fail to remember, to give due attention to somebody or something; **omit** fail to do something, either deliberately or accidentally; **overlook** fail to notice or check something as a result of inattention, preoccupation, or haste.

neglected adj **deserted**, abandoned, unkempt, uncared for, mistreated Opposite: looked after

neglectful adj **negligent**, careless, slipshod, remiss, lax Opposite: attentive

negligée n **nightdress**, nightgown, dressing gown, peignoir, nightie (infml)

negligence n **neglect**, inattention, disregard, laxity, slackness Opposite: attention

negligent adj 1 **neglectful**, careless, inattentive, slipshod, remiss Opposite: careful 2 (literary) **nonchalant**, relaxed, casual, informal, easy Opposite: formal

negligible adj **insignificant**, tiny, small, slight, unimportant Opposite: significant

negligibly adv **not noticeably**, just, insignificantly, trivially, marginally Opposite: significantly

negotiable adj 1 **open to discussion**, unfixed, flexible, open-ended, up for grabs (infml) Opposite: non-negotiable 2 **transferable**, exchangeable, convertible, assignable, movable 3 **passable**, navigable, crossable, traversable, accessible Opposite: impassable

negotiate v 1 **talk**, discuss, confer, consult, bargain 2 **sell**, transfer, exchange, convert, convey 3 **get past**, pass, navigate, go around, cross

negotiation n **arbitration**, mediation, discussion, cooperation, diplomacy

negotiations n **talks**, discussions, conference, consultation, dialogue

negotiator n **speaker**, representative, envoy, delegate, mediator

neighbourhood n **area**, district, region, locality, quarter

neighbouring adj **nearby**, local, adjoining, surrounding, bordering Opposite: distant

neighbourliness n **friendliness**, kindness, helpfulness, consideration, sociability Opposite: unfriendliness

neighbourly adj **helpful**, kind, pleasant, sociable, friendly Opposite: antisocial

nemesis (literary) n 1 **avenger**, retaliator, revenger, vindicator 2 **punishment**, vengeance, retribution, fate, doom

neologism n **new word**, coinage, buzzword (infml)

neonatal adj **newborn**, new, brand-new

neophyte n **novice**, beginner, recruit, learner, trainee

nepotism n **favouritism**, preferential treatment, partiality, bias, preference

nerve n 1 **courage**, bravery, spirit, audacity, bravado Opposite: cowardice 2 **boldness**, impudence, insolence, effrontery, bravado. See COMPARE AND CONTRAST at courage.

nerve centre n **hub**, centre of operations, control room, headquarters, HQ

nerve-racking adj **worrying**, anxious, tense, stressful, scary (infml)

nerves (infml) n **anxiety**, worry, tension, stress, mental strain

nerve-wracking see nerve-racking

nerviness n **edginess**, anxiety, jumpiness, tenseness, uneasiness Opposite: calmness

nervous adj **anxious**, worried, edgy, jumpy, panicky Opposite: calm

nervousness n **anxiety**, edginess, jumpiness, tenseness, uneasiness Opposite: calmness

nervy (infml) adj **nervous**, anxious, worried, edgy, jumpy Opposite: calm

nest egg n **savings**, reserve, capital, fund, store

nestle v 1 **cosy up**, cuddle up, huddle, nuzzle, settle 2 **cushion**, place, lie, soften, shelter

net n **mesh**, web, netting, lattice, grid ■ v 1 (infml) **catch**, achieve, obtain, procure 2 **earn**, make, gain, make a profit of, profit ■ adj **remaining**, disposable, clear, after deductions, left Opposite: gross

nether (fml) adj **rear**, hind, hinder, back, after

nether world (fml) n **hell**, inferno, purgatory, underworld, perdition

netting n **mesh**, net, web, fabric, meshwork

nettle (infml) v **irritate**, annoy, infuriate, bother, exasperate

network n **net**, system, grid, web, link

neurological adj **nervous**, nerve, neural

neurosis n **quirk**, complex, obsession, inhibition, idiosyncrasy

neurotic adj **anxious**, fearful, phobic, fixated, disturbed Opposite: rational

neuter v **spay**, sterilize, castrate, fix

neutral adj 1 **unbiased**, impartial, disinterested, dispassionate, middle-of-the-road Opposite: biased 2 **drab**, indistinct, indeterminate, pale, light-coloured Opposite: colourful

neutrality n **impartiality**, detachment, objectivity, noninvolvement, disinterest Opposite: bias

neutralization n **cancelling out**, nullification, off-setting, frustration, counteraction Opposite: activation

neutralize v **counteract**, counterbalance, defuse, deactivate, nullify

never adv 1 **not ever**, not once, on no occasion, at no time Opposite: always 2 **certainly not**, under no circumstances, by no means, in no way, not at all

never-ending adj **endless**, everlasting, continual, continuous, nonstop

nevertheless adv **yet**, but, however, nonetheless, on the other hand

new adj 1 **novel**, newfangled, original, innovative, fresh Opposite: old 2 **recent**, latest, up-to-the-minute, contemporary, up-to-date Opposite: outmoded 3 **brand-new**, pristine, newborn, in mint condition, newfound Opposite: used 4 **another**, additional, extra, further, different 5 **inexperienced**, new to the job, just starting out, wet behind the ears, green *Opposite*: experienced

COMPARE AND CONTRAST CORE MEANING: never experienced before or having recently come into being

new recently invented, discovered, made, bought, experienced, or not previously known or encountered; **fresh** excitingly or refreshingly different from what has been done or experienced previously; **modern** of the latest kind, or characterized by up-to-date ideas, techniques, design, or equipment; **newfangled** puzzlingly or worryingly new or different, especially because it seems gimmicky or overcomplicated; **novel** new and different, often in an interesting, unusual, or inventive way; **original** unique and not copied or derived from anything else.

newborn *adj* **1 new**, brand-new, neonatal **2 newfound**, new, brand-new, fresh, recent *Opposite*: established ■ *n* **baby**, infant, child, neonate, babe *(literary)*

newcomer *n* **1 new arrival**, stranger, Johnny-come-lately *(infml)* **2 novice**, recruit, beginner, neophyte, trainee *Opposite*: old hand

newfangled *adj* **novel**, new, innovative, up-to-date, up-to-the-minute *Opposite*: old-fashioned. *See* COMPARE AND CONTRAST *at* **new**.

newly *adv* **1 recently**, lately, freshly, just now, just this minute **2 afresh**, anew, again, once more

newlyweds *n* **just marrieds**, wedding couple, happy couple, bride and groom

newness *n* **novelty**, innovation, originality, freshness, inventiveness

news *n* **1 information**, reports, intelligence, gossip, rumour **2 news bulletin**, news broadcast, newscast, news summary, news flash

newscast *n* **news**, news bulletin, news broadcast, news summary, news flash

newsletter *n* **information sheet**, newssheet, bulletin, circular

newspaper *n* **1 paper**, broadsheet, daily, weekly, tabloid **2 newsprint**, printing paper, coarse paper

newsprint *n* **newspaper**, printing paper, coarse paper

newsreader *n* **presenter**, broadcaster, anchor, anchorperson

newsreel *n* **news film**, documentary, news report, news bulletin, news footage

newsroom *n* **news studio**, broadcasting studio, TV studio

newssheet *n* **newsletter**, bulletin, press release, information sheet, data sheet

newsstand *n* **kiosk**, stand, stall, booth

newsworthy *adj* **interesting**, exciting, remarkable, out of the ordinary, extraordinary *Opposite*: unremarkable

newsy *adj* **chatty**, gossipy, friendly, interesting, informative

next *adv* **after that**, then, afterwards, after, thereafter *Opposite*: first

next-door *adj* **adjacent**, adjoining, neighbouring, flanking, next

next of kin *n* **close relative**, blood relation, blood relative, spouse, partner

nexus *n* **connection**, link, tie, relationship, node

nib *n* **tip**, point, end

nibble *v* **chew**, nip, peck, gnaw, bite *Opposite*: chomp *(infml)* ■ **bite**, morsel, titbit, crumb, speck

nibbles *n* **snacks**, finger food, canapés, appetizers, hors d'oeuvres

nice *adj* **1 enjoyable**, agreeable, pleasant, good, lovely *Opposite*: unpleasant **2 polite**, considerate, friendly, courteous, charming *Opposite*: nasty **3 respectable**, proper, refined, virtuous, genteel *Opposite*: improper **4 attractive**, lovely, pleasant, delightful, appealing *Opposite*: unattractive **5 precise**, exact, fine-drawn, meticulous, narrow *Opposite*: broad **6 discriminating**, painstaking, particular, scrupulous, precise

nice-looking *adj* **good-looking**, pretty, lovely, attractive, handsome *Opposite*: unattractive

nicely *adv* **1 suitably**, effectively, satisfactorily, accurately, carefully *Opposite*: unsatisfactorily **2 agreeably**, kindly, well, politely, courteously *Opposite*: unpleasantly **3 carefully**, meticulously, finely, subtly, narrowly *Opposite*: broadly

nicety *n* **1 distinction**, precision, detail, small point, refinement **2 delicacy**, tactfulness, particularity, finesse, polish

niche *n* **1 alcove**, bay, nook, cubbyhole, recess **2 place**, position, slot, function, role

nick *n* **1 incision**, groove, mark, notch, cut **2** *(slang)* **prison**, jail, custody ■ *v* **1 score**, incise, mark, cut, scratch **2** *(slang)* **misappropriate**, steal, walk off with, make off with, make away with. *See* COMPARE AND CONTRAST *at* **steal**.

nick-nack *see* **knick-knack**

nickname *n* **name**, pet name, epithet, sobriquet, diminutive ■ *v* **label**, call, name, designate, dub

nifty *adj* **1 good**, quick, clever, skilful, neat *Opposite*: clumsy **2 smart**, attractive, well-designed, neat, natty *Opposite*: unattractive **3 useful**, handy, convenient, effective, ingenious *Opposite*: useless

niggardly *adj* **1 ungenerous**, mean, miserly, tight, parsimonious *Opposite*: generous **2 miserable**, meagre, wretched, insufficient, paltry

niggle *v* **1 criticize**, cavil, carp, nag, nitpick **2 trouble**, bother, nag, annoy, irritate ■ *n* **1 complaint**, grumble, objection, grievance, criticism **2 doubt**, anxiety, twinge, misgiving, concern

niggling *adj* **1 trivial**, petty, unimportant, inconsequential, insignificant *Opposite*: important **2 irritating**, awkward, finicky, troublesome, difficult

nigh *adj* **imminent**, close, near, at hand, approaching *Opposite*: remote

night *n* **1 nighttime**, hours of darkness, dark, darkness, nightfall *Opposite*: day **2 early hours**, small hours, middle of the night

nightcap *n* **1 drink**, bedtime drink, hot drink, hot toddy **2 sleeping cap**, hat, cap

nightclothes *n* pyjamas, nightwear, sleepwear (US)

nightdress *n* nightgown, nightshirt, negligée, nightie (infml)

nightfall *n* **dusk**, twilight, evening, sunset, end of the day *Opposite*: daybreak

nightlife *n* nightspots, social life, entertainment, club scene, discos

nightly *adj* **night**, evening, nocturnal ■ *adv* **every night**, night by night, once a night, through the night

nightmare *n* **dream**, bad dream, hallucination, vision, incubus ■ *adj* **traumatic**, frightening, dreadful, terrible, horrendous *Opposite*: wonderful

nightmarish *adj* **nightmare**, frightening, terrifying, horrendous, terrible *Opposite*: lovely

nightspot *n* bar, nightclub, disco, club

nighttime *n* **night**, evening, dark, hours of darkness, middle of the night *Opposite*: daytime

nightwear *n* sleepwear, nightclothes, pyjamas

nihilism *n* negativism, pessimism, nothingness, emptiness, anarchism

nihilist *n* pessimist, existentialist, anarchist, revolutionary, radical

nihilistic *adj* **negativistic**, pessimistic, existentialist, destructive, anarchic

nil *n* **nothing**, zero, none, null, nullity

nimble *adj* **sprightly**, lithe, deft, agile, quick *Opposite*: awkward

nimbleness *n* **sprightliness**, litheness, agility, quickness, dexterity *Opposite*: awkwardness

nimbus *n* **circle of light**, halo, corona, aura, radiance

nip *v* **1 squeeze**, compress, grasp, grab, grip **2** (infml) **race**, hurry, dash, rush, run *Opposite*: dawdle **3 peck**, nibble, snap, gnaw, bite ■ *n* **1 pinch**, tweak, grasp, grab, squeeze **2 sip**, drink, swallow, tot, swig (infml) **3 peck**, bite, nibble, snippet, clipping

nip in the bud (infml) *v* **stop**, prevent, hinder, block, thwart *Opposite*: encourage

nipper *n* **1 pincer**, claw, gripper, appendage **2** (infml) **baby**, child, little one, toddler, rug rat (US infml)

nippy *adj* **1 cold**, chilly, freezing, biting, icy *Opposite*: warm **2 quick**, fast, speedy, rapid, swift *Opposite*: slow

nirvana *n* **1 enlightenment**, spiritual enlightenment, state of grace **2 bliss**, heaven, joy, paradise, pleasure *Opposite*: hell

nitpick *v* **cavil**, complain, quibble, find fault, criticize. *See* COMPARE AND CONTRAST *at* criticize.

nitpicker *n* **faultfinder**, critic, carper, nagger, pedant

nitpicking *n* **criticism**, faultfinding, carping, hairsplitting, quibbling ■ *adj* **critical**, faultfinding, carping, finicky, fussy

nitty-gritty (infml) *n* **essentials**, brass tacks, fundamentals, basics, crux of the matter

no *adv* **on no account**, not at all, certainly not, definitely not, by no means ■ *n* **rejection**, negative, denial, rebuff, refusal ■ *adj* **not any**, not one, not at all

nob (infml) *n* **VIP**, grandee, toff (infml), big shot (infml), bigwig (infml)

no ball *n* **foul throw**, misthrow, foul ball (US)

nobble (infml) *v* **1 persuade**, win over, sway, convince, influence **2 coerce**, affect, force, intimidate, bribe **3 dope**, incapacitate, fix, tamper with, drug **4 accost**, waylay, confront, approach, detain

nobility *n* **1 aristocracy**, upper class, landed gentry, upper crust (infml) *Opposite*: hoi polloi **2 dignity**, graciousness, decency, goodness, nobleness *Opposite*: baseness

noble *adj* **1 honourable**, principled, moral, decent, upright *Opposite*: unprincipled **2 magnificent**, impressive, imposing, fine, splendid *Opposite*: unimpressive **3 aristocratic**, patrician, blue-blooded, titled, upper-class ■ *n* **aristocrat**, peer, nobleman, noblewoman, patrician *Opposite*: commoner

nobleness *n* **honourableness**, honour, morality, magnanimity, dignity

nobody *pron* **not one person**, not a single person, no one, not a soul *Opposite*: everybody ■ *n* **nonentity**, mediocrity, unknown, upstart, nothing *Opposite*: somebody

nocturnal *adj* **nighttime**, night, nightly *Opposite*: diurnal

nod *v* **move**, bow, bob, jiggle, dip ■ *n* **permission**, affirmation, signal, sign, gesture

noddle (dated infml) *n* **head**, nut (infml), bonce (infml), skull (infml), noggin (dated infml)

node *n* **1 bulge**, protuberance, lump, swelling, bump **2 meeting point**, join, connection, intersection, point

nod off *v* **doze off**, fall asleep, drift off, doze, catnap *Opposite*: wake up

nod to *v* **acknowledge**, greet, signal to, salute

nodule *n* **node**, knot, knob, lump, bump

no end (infml) *pron* **a lot**, a great deal, very much, enormously, greatly

no-frills *(infml)* *adj* **basic**, utilitarian, unadorned, economy, generic *Opposite*: luxury

noggin *(dated infml)* *n* **head**, noddle *(dated infml)*, bonce *(infml)*, skull *(infml)*, nut *(infml)*

noise *n* **sound**, din, clamour, clatter, blast *Opposite*: silence

noiseless *adj* **soundless**, silent, muted, hushed, quiet *Opposite*: noisy

noisome *adj* **foul**, offensive, disgusting, repulsive, repellent *Opposite*: pleasant

noisy *adj* **loud**, deafening, earsplitting, piercing, raucous *Opposite*: quiet

nomad *n* **wanderer**, traveller, itinerant, migrant, drifter

nomadic *adj* **itinerant**, travelling, roaming, wandering, roving

nom de plume *n* **pen name**, pseudonym, alias, assumed name, nom de guerre

nomenclature *n* **1 classification**, taxonomy, codification, categorization, organization **2 terminology**, vocabulary, language, terms, jargon

nominal *adj* **1 supposed**, ostensible, so-called, in name only, titular *Opposite*: actual **2 small**, trifling, token, minimal, insignificant *Opposite*: great

nominate *v* **1 propose**, put forward, suggest, name, submit *Opposite*: reject **2 appoint**, elect, designate, choose, select *Opposite*: reject

nomination *n* **1 proposal**, suggestion, recommendation, submission **2 choice**, selection, appointment, nominee, candidate

nominee *n* **candidate**, entrant, applicant, nomination, contender

nonaggression *n* **pacifism**, peaceful coexistence, nonviolence, inaction *Opposite*: aggression

nonalcoholic *adj* **soft**, lite, low-alcohol *Opposite*: alcoholic

nonaligned *adj* **neutral**, independent, unallied, unconnected, unrelated *Opposite*: aligned

nonalignment *n* **neutrality**, independence, autonomy, self-determination, impartiality *Opposite*: alignment

nonattendance *n* **1 truancy**, playing truant, skiving *(infml)*, bunking off *(infml)*, wagging *(slang)* *Opposite*: attendance **2 absence**, default, absenteeism, nonappearance *Opposite*: presence

nonbeliever *n* **disbeliever**, unbeliever, doubter, sceptic, agnostic *Opposite*: believer

nonchalance *n* **indifference**, detachment, disinterest, calmness, dispassion *Opposite*: interest

nonchalant *adj* **casual**, imperturbable, offhand, cool, calm *Opposite*: concerned

noncombatant *n* **civilian**, citizen, conscientious objector *Opposite*: soldier

noncommittal *adj* **guarded**, evasive, vague, wary, tactful *Opposite*: definite

noncompliance *n* **nonconformity**, refusal, failure, denial, defiance *Opposite*: compliance

noncompliant *adj* **disobedient**, recalcitrant, rebellious, uncooperative, dissenting *Opposite*: cooperative

nonconformist *adj* **unconventional**, eccentric, alternative, rebellious, radical *Opposite*: conformist ■ *n* **rebel**, dissenter, maverick, radical, eccentric *Opposite*: conformist

nonconformity *n* **1 unconventionality**, originality, eccentricity, idiosyncrasy, individuality *Opposite*: conformity **2 noncooperation**, noncompliance, divergence, variation, difference *Opposite*: conformity

noncooperation *n* **defiance**, disobedience, insubordination, rebellion, rebelliousness *Opposite*: cooperation

nondescript *adj* **unremarkable**, ordinary, unexceptional, dull, uninteresting *Opposite*: special

nondiscriminatory *adj* **fair**, equal, unbiased, evenhanded, just *Opposite*: discriminatory

none *pron* **1 no one**, nobody, not a soul, not a single person *Opposite*: everyone **2 not any**, nothing, not a bit, not an iota, not a hint *Opposite*: some

nonentity *n* **nobody**, unknown, mediocrity, nothing *Opposite*: somebody

nonessential *adj* **luxury**, extra, supplementary, additional, dispensable *Opposite*: essential ■ *n* **extra**, luxury, perk *Opposite*: essential

nonetheless *adv* **however**, nevertheless, even so, on the other hand

nonevent *n* **failure**, anticlimax, disappointment, letdown, flop *Opposite*: success

nonexistence *n* **1 absence**, lack, want, dearth, deficiency **2 nothingness**, unreality, fictionality *Opposite*: existence

nonexistent *adj* **missing**, unreal, fictional, imaginary, absent *Opposite*: existent *(fml)*

nonfiction *adj* **factual**, true-life, reference, fact-based *Opposite*: fiction

nonflammable *adj* **noninflammable**, fireproof, flameproof, fire-retardant, fire-resistant *Opposite*: inflammable

nonintervention *n* **inaction**, noninvolvement, noninterventionism, laissez-faire, abstention *Opposite*: intervention

noninterventionist *adj* **laissez-faire**, noninterfering, nonaligned, nonpartisan, neutral

noniron *adj* **crease-resistant**, easy-care, drip-dry, wash-and-wear, permanent-press

nonjudgmental *adj* **indulgent**, lax, easygoing, relaxed, lenient *Opposite*: judgmental

nonmember *n* **outsider**, visitor, guest *Opposite*: member

nonnegotiable *adj* **1 firm**, immutable, unchanging, inflexible, fixed *Opposite*: negotiable **2 nontransferable**, unmarketable, nonsalable, nonexchangeable, nonconvertible

no-no *(infml)* *n* **taboo**, forbidden thing, breaking of convention, social restriction

no-nonsense *adj* **straightforward**, plain, practical, down-to-earth, plain-speaking *Opposite*: airy-fairy *(infml)*

nonpareil *adj* **unparalleled**, peerless, best, unequalled, unique *Opposite*: common

nonpartisan *adj* **unbiased**, impartial, unprejudiced, independent, neutral *Opposite*: partisan

nonpayment *n* **defaulting**, evasion, default, avoidance *Opposite*: payment

nonplus *v* **unnerve**, befuddle, stump, bewilder, mystify

nonplussed *adj* **confused**, baffled, bewildered, puzzled, stumped

nonprofessional *adj* **amateur**, blue-collar, manual, lay *Opposite*: professional

nonprofitmaking *adj* **charitable**, public, state, not-for-profit *Opposite*: profitmaking

nonproliferation *n* **limitation**, reduction, control, prevention *Opposite*: proliferation

nonresident *adj* **transient**, visiting, commuting, holidaying, vacationing *(US)* *Opposite*: resident ■ *n* **visitor**, transient, guest, holidaymaker, tourist *Opposite*: resident

nonsense *n* **rubbish**, drivel, gibberish, noise, babble *Opposite*: sense

nonsensical *adj* **ridiculous**, stupid, senseless, absurd, illogical *Opposite*: sensible

nonspecific *adj* **generic**, general, broad, broad-based, broad-spectrum *Opposite*: specific

nonstandard *adj* **unusual**, out of the ordinary, atypical, special, modified *Opposite*: standard

nonstarter *(infml)* *n* **hopeless case**, loser, failure, nonrunner, dud *(infml)* *Opposite*: winner

nonstick *adj* **coated**, protected, surfaced, covered

nonstop *adj* **continuous**, never-ending, uninterrupted, around-the-clock, constant *Opposite*: intermittent

nontoxic *adj* **harmless**, safe, nonhazardous, innocuous, risk-free *Opposite*: toxic

nonviolence *n* **pacifism**, passivity, non-aggression, civil disobedience *Opposite*: aggression

nonviolent *adj* **peaceful**, nonaggressive, pacific, peaceable, passive *Opposite*: violent

nook *n* **corner**, alcove, cranny, niche, recess

noon *n* **midday**, twelve noon, noontime, noonday *(literary)*

noonday *(literary) see* **noon**

no one *pron* **not one person**, not a single person,

nobody, not a soul *Opposite*: everyone

noose *n* **1 loop**, lasso, halter, rope, riata **2 snare**, trap, booby trap, trick, con

norm *n* **standard**, average, custom, rule, model *Opposite*: exception

normal *adj* **usual**, standard, ordinary, typical, customary *Opposite*: abnormal

normality *n* **routine**, regularity, status quo, normalcy *(US)*

normalization *n* **regularization**, standardization, stabilization, regulation, control *Opposite*: deviation

normalize *v* **regularize**, standardize, regulate, put on a normal footing, control *Opposite*: destabilize

normally *adv* **1 usually**, in general, as a rule, on the whole, by and large *Opposite*: rarely **2 as normal**, as usual, naturally, unexceptionally, conventionally *Opposite*: abnormally

nose *n* **snout**, muzzle, beak, proboscis, conk *(slang)* ■ *v* *(infml)* **poke around**, watch, sneak, pry, snoop *(infml)*

nosebleed *n* **bloody nose**, blood, blood loss, haemorrhage

nosedive *n* **1 dive**, fall, drop, plunge, tumble *Opposite*: ascent **2 decrease**, fall, deterioration, drop, crash *Opposite*: increase

nose-dive *v* **1 plummet**, drop, plunge, dive, tumble *Opposite*: ascend **2 decrease**, deteriorate, plummet, drop, slump *Opposite*: rocket

nosegay *n* **posy**, spray, bouquet, bunch, sprig

nosh *(infml)* *n* **snack**, food, rations, tuck, goodies ■ *v* **eat**, munch, champ, eat up, consume

no-show *n* **absentee**, nonattender, dropout

nosh-up *(infml)* *n* **big meal**, feast, binge, blowout *(slang)*

nostalgia *n* **homesickness**, reminiscence, wistfulness, longing, melancholy

nostalgic *adj* **sentimental**, wistful, misty, longing, yearning *Opposite*: expectant

nostrum *n* **remedy**, plan, scheme, big idea, solution

nosy *(infml) adj* **inquisitive**, curious, interfering, prying, meddlesome

notability *n* **1 famous person**, celebrity, dignitary, VIP, notable *Opposite*: nobody **2 significance**, importance, relevance, import, weight

notable *adj* **noteworthy**, distinguished, outstanding, prominent, extraordinary *Opposite*: insignificant ■ *n* **celebrity**, dignity, VIP, personality, somebody *Opposite*: nobody

notarize *v* **authenticate**, certify, endorse, validate, rubber stamp

notary *n* **lawyer**, solicitor, legal official, legal clerk, attorney *(US)*

notation *n* **1 representation**, symbolization,

system, code, cipher **2 note**, footnote, jotting, memo, annotation

notch *n* **1 nick**, indentation, cut, mark, slash **2 level**, degree, step, stage, rung

not counting *prep* **apart from**, excluding, aside from, besides, except

note *n* **1 letter**, memo, memorandum, message, communication **2 footnote**, annotation, gloss, comment, addendum **3 tone**, edge, tinge, shade, hint ▪ *v* **1 notice**, take note of, take notice of, take in, observe *Opposite*: disregard **2 mention**, observe, state, say, remark **3 make a note of**, note down, write down, record, jot down

noted *adj* **renowned**, well-known, famous, distinguished, celebrated

notelet *n* **card**, note card, letter card

notepad *n* **writing pad**, pad of paper, memo pad, pad, jotter

notepaper *n* **writing paper**, writing pad, stationery, headed paper, letterhead

noteworthy *adj* **of note**, notable, striking, remarkable, important *Opposite*: insignificant

nothing *pron* **nought**, nil, zero, zilch *(infml)* ▪ *n* **nonentity**, nobody, unknown

nothingness *n* **oblivion**, nothing, emptiness, void, vacuum

notice *n* **1 sign**, poster, announcement, advertisement, bill **2 warning**, notification, announcement, communication ▪ *v* **become aware of**, see, take in, observe, perceive *Opposite*: close your eyes to

noticeable *adj* **obvious**, clear, visible, perceptible, conspicuous *Opposite*: inconspicuous

noticeboard *n* **display board**, information board, bulletin board *(US)*

notification *n* **announcement**, notice, warning, statement, report

notify *v* **inform**, alert, advise, warn, report

notion *n* **1 idea**, view, concept, belief, conception **2 impulse**, urge, whim, fancy, instinct

notional *adj* **1 theoretical**, estimated, speculative, academic, hypothetical **2 imaginary**, unreal, fancied, fanciful, whimsical *Opposite*: real

not mince words *v* **be direct**, speak plainly, call a spade a spade, be blunt, speak your mind *Opposite*: prevaricate

notoriety *n* **disrepute**, infamy, dishonour, bad reputation, bad name

notorious *adj* **1 infamous**, disreputable, dishonourable, tarnished *Opposite*: reputable **2** *(archaic)* **famous**, renowned, eminent, familiar, recognized *Opposite*: unknown

notoriously *adv* **particularly**, especially, extremely, very

notwithstanding *(fml)* *prep* **despite**, in spite of, aside from, excluding, setting aside ▪

adv **nevertheless**, all the same, nonetheless, anyhow

nought *n* **zero**, nothing, nil, zilch *(infml)*

nourish *v* **1 nurture**, give food to, sustain, suckle, feed **2 encourage**, promote, cultivate, support, foster

nourishing *adj* **nutritious**, wholesome, beneficial, healthful *Opposite*: unhealthy

nourishment *n* **food**, sustenance, diet, nutrition

nous *n* **1** *(infml)* **common sense**, good sense, sense, wisdom, horse sense **2 intellect**, ability, intelligence, rationality, reason

novel *n* **book**, narrative, work of fiction, tale, story ▪ *adj* **original**, new, fresh, different, innovative *Opposite*: well-worn. *See* COMPARE AND CONTRAST *at* **new**.

novelist *n* **writer**, author, story writer

novella *n* **short story**, short novel, novelette, tale, fable

novelty *n* **innovation**, originality, newness, freshness, uniqueness

novice *n* **beginner**, learner, trainee, apprentice, greenhorn *Opposite*: old hand. *See* COMPARE AND CONTRAST *at* **beginner**.

now *adv* **1 at the present**, at the moment, at this time, currently, presently *Opposite*: then **2 immediately**, right away, straightaway, at once, instantly *Opposite*: later

nowadays *adv* **these days**, today, now, at the present time, at the moment *Opposite*: formerly

noxious *adj* **1 harmful**, toxic, poisonous, deadly, lethal *Opposite*: harmless **2 nasty**, unpleasant, offensive, foul, horrible *Opposite*: pleasant

nozzle *n* **spout**, jet, control valve, spigot, outlet

nuance *n* **tone**, gradation, distinction, tinge, hint

nub *n* **crux**, crucial point, essence, core, heart

nuclear *adj* **atomic**, nuclear-powered, fissile, fissionable

nucleus *n* **centre**, basis, core, heart, nub

nude *adj* **unclothed**, in the nude, undressed, in a state of undress, stripped *Opposite*: clothed. *See* COMPARE AND CONTRAST *at* **naked**.

nudge *v* **push**, bump, elbow, shove, jolt ▪ *n* **prod**, push, shove, bump, jolt

nudity *n* **bareness**, nakedness, undress, deshabille

nugatory *adj* **trifling**, petty, insignificant, trivial, unimportant *Opposite*: significant

nugget *n* **piece**, bit, chunk, lump, hunk

nuisance *n* **irritation**, annoyance, bother, trouble, irritant *Opposite*: boon

null *adj* **1 invalid**, null and void, void, unacceptable, unsound *Opposite*: valid **2 worthless**, valueless, unimportant, insignificant, useless *Opposite*: useful

null and void *adj* **invalid**, void, null, unacceptable, flawed *Opposite*: valid

nullify v **invalidate**, annul, cancel out, abolish, negate (fml) Opposite: validate

COMPARE AND CONTRAST CORE MEANING: put an end to the effective existence of something
nullify make something legally invalid or ineffective, or cancel something out; **abrogate** (fml) end an agreement or contract formally and publicly; **annul** declare something officially or legally invalid or ineffective; **repeal** end a law officially; **invalidate** deprive something of its legal force or value, e.g., by failing to comply with certain terms and conditions; **negate** (fml) render something ineffective, e.g., by doing something that counterbalances its force or effectiveness.

numb adj **1 frozen**, anaesthetized, dead, deadened, unfeeling **2 emotionless**, shocked, dazed, disoriented, distressed Opposite: animated ■ v **deaden**, freeze, anaesthetize, stun, dull

number n **1 figure**, numeral, digit, integer **2 amount**, quantity, sum ■ v **come to**, add up to, total, amount to, run to

numberless adj **countless**, innumerable, numerous, endless, myriad Opposite: few

number one adj **1 first**, top, leading, best, most important **2** (infml) **excellent**, high quality, first-rate, top, top quality ■ n **1** (infml) **important person**, key player, linchpin, leader, prime candidate **2** (infml) **chief executive officer**, managing director, chief executive, boss, chief

numbing adj **1 deadening**, freezing, anaesthetizing **2 shocking**, distressing, dazing, upsetting, traumatic

numbness n **1 deadness**, unresponsiveness, lack of sensation Opposite: sensation **2 emotionlessness**, impassiveness, coldness, detachment, shock

numeracy n **mathematical ability**, numerical competence, skill, proficiency, expertise

numeral n **number**, figure, digit, cipher

numerate adj **mathematically competent**, good with numbers, proficient, accomplished, competent

numerical adj **mathematical**, arithmetic, arithmetical, statistical

numerous adj **many**, frequent, plentiful, abundant, several Opposite: few

numinous (fml) adj **mystic**, magical, magic, supernatural, transcendent

nunnery n **convent**, monastery, abbey, religious foundation, religious community

nuptial adj **marriage**, wedding, bridal, matrimonial, marital

nuptials (fml) n **wedding**, marriage, happy day

nurse v **1 care for**, look after, take care of, tend, foster Opposite: neglect **2 harbour**, cherish, nurture, have, foster

nursery n **1 nursery school**, day nursery, playgroup, kindergarten **2 plant sales outlet**, garden centre, plant market

nurture v **1 care for**, look after, take care of, raise, rear **2 cultivate**, cherish, develop, support, encourage

nut (infml) n **1 skull**, cranium, dome, crown, bonce (infml) **2 enthusiast**, fan, aficionado, aficionada, buff

WORD BANK
❏ **types of nut** acorn, almond, brazil nut, cashew, chestnut, cob, cobnut, coconut, cola nut, groundnut, hazelnut, hickory nut, horse chestnut, macadamia nut, monkey nut, peanut, pecan, pine nut, pistachio, walnut

nutrition n **nourishment**, diet, food, sustenance

nutritional adj **nutritious**, nourishing, nutritive, dietary, alimentary

nutritious adj **nourishing**, healthy, wholesome, healthful, beneficial Opposite: unhealthy

nutritive adj **1 nutritional**, dietary, dietetic, alimentary, food **2 nutritious**, nourishing, healthy, wholesome, healthful Opposite: unhealthy

nuts and bolts (infml) n **basics**, brass tacks, nitty-gritty (infml), practicalities, fundamentals

nutshell n **husk**, casing, shell

nuzzle v **nestle**, cuddle, burrow, snuggle, push

nymph n **fairy**, sprite, spirit, dryad, elf

O

oaf n **bumbler**, buffoon, lummox (infml), klutz (US slang)

oar n **paddle**, scull, sweep, blade

oasis n **retreat**, refuge, haven, sanctuary, escape

oath n **1 promise**, pledge, vow, word, assurance **2 curse**, swearword, expletive, four-letter word, imprecation (fml)

obduracy n **obstinacy**, stubbornness, inflexibility, mulishness, pigheadedness Opposite: compliance

obdurate adj **1 obstinate**, stubborn, inflexible,

unyielding, unbending *Opposite*: compliant **2 hardhearted**, callous, unfeeling, heartless, pitiless *Opposite*: warm-hearted

obedience *n* **compliance**, agreement, submission, respect, duty *Opposite*: disobedience

obedient *adj* **compliant**, dutiful, submissive, respectful, biddable *Opposite*: disobedient

obeisance *n* **1** *(fml)* **bow**, curtsy, bob, nod, genuflection **2 homage**, respect, deference, duty, loyalty

obelisk *n* **pillar**, column, pylon, needle, tower

obese *adj* **fat**, overweight, heavy, stout, plump *Opposite*: underweight

obesity *n* **plumpness**, fatness, stoutness, portliness, corpulence *Opposite*: thinness

obey *v* **do as you are told**, submit, follow, comply with, act upon *Opposite*: disobey

obfuscate *v* **obscure**, complicate, confuse, muddy, cloud *Opposite*: clarify

obfuscation *n* **complication**, mystification, confusion, muddying, clouding *Opposite*: clarification

obituary *n* **tribute**, article, announcement, eulogy, epitaph ■ *adj* **funerary**, funereal, memorial, epitaphic, death

object *n* **1 thing**, article, item, entity, body **2 purpose**, objective, aim, point, idea ■ *v* **oppose**, protest, challenge, expostulate, demur *Opposite*: approve

---

COMPARE AND CONTRAST CORE MEANING: indicate opposition to something

object be opposed or averse to something, or express opposition to it; **protest** express strong disapproval of or disagreement with something, or refuse to obey or accept something, often by making a formal statement or taking action in public; **demur** raise objections in a hesitant or tentative way; **remonstrate** reason or argue forcefully with somebody about something; **expostulate** express disagreement or disapproval vehemently, or attempt to dissuade somebody from doing something.

---

objectify *v* **1 actualize**, realize, represent, portray, reify **2 diminish**, reduce, simplify, trivialize

objection *n* **1 opposition**, protest, protestation, hostility, demurral *Opposite*: approval **2 doubt**, concern, problem, worry, niggle *Opposite*: confidence

objectionable *adj* **offensive**, obnoxious, horrible, unpleasant, intolerable *Opposite*: inoffensive

objective *adj* **1 impartial**, detached, neutral, unbiased, unprejudiced *Opposite*: subjective **2 factual**, actual, tangible, fact-based, demonstrable *Opposite*: subjective ■ *n* **object**, purpose, aim, point, idea

objectivity *n* **impartiality**, detachment, independence, neutrality, fairness *Opposite*: subjectivity

objet d'art *n* **work of art**, masterpiece, creation, piece, ornament

obligate *v* **compel**, oblige, force, make, require *Opposite*: request

obligation *n* **1 debt**, contract, commitment, promise, agreement **2 duty**, responsibility, requirement, compulsion, commitment *Opposite*: option

obligatory *adj* **1 required**, statutory, mandatory, binding, the law *Opposite*: discretionary **2 compulsory**, required, necessary, essential, de rigueur *(fml)* *Opposite*: optional

oblige *v* **1 compel**, obligate, force, make, require *Opposite*: request **2 gratify**, please, indulge, accommodate, help *Opposite*: disappoint

obliged *adj* **grateful**, thankful, appreciative, gratified, indebted

obliging *adj* **helpful**, kind, considerate, willing, agreeable *Opposite*: unhelpful

oblique *adj* **1 slanting**, slanted, tilted, sloping, leaning *Opposite*: upright **2 indirect**, implicit, implied, roundabout, circuitous *Opposite*: direct

obliqueness *n* **1 tilt**, inclination, slant, steepness, lean **2 indirectness**, circuitousness, circumlocution, obscureness, opaqueness *Opposite*: directness

obliterate *v* **destroy**, demolish, eliminate, eradicate, annihilate *Opposite*: create

obliteration *n* **destruction**, annihilation, eradication, elimination, abolition *Opposite*: creation

oblivion *n* **1 forgetfulness**, unconsciousness, stupor, insensibility, obliviousness *Opposite*: awareness **2 obscurity**, extinction, the past, the annals of history, nothingness *Opposite*: existence

oblivious *adj* **unaware**, unconscious, unmindful, ignorant, insensible *Opposite*: conscious

obnoxious *adj* **loathsome**, hateful, horrible, insufferable, intolerable *Opposite*: delightful

obscene *adj* **1 indecent**, lewd, explicit, offensive, crude *Opposite*: decent **2 disgusting**, nauseating, sickening, offensive, rude *Opposite*: decent **3 tasteless**, foul-mouthed, crude, loutish, boorish

obscenity *n* **1 indecency**, lewdness, offensiveness, explicitness, crudeness *Opposite*: decency **2 offensiveness**, atrocity, tastelessness, vulgarity, rudeness *Opposite*: tastefulness **3 curse**, swearword, four-letter word, expletive, cuss word *(US infml)*

obscurantism *n* **conservatism**, traditionalism, dogmatism, reaction, illiberalism *Opposite*: liberalism

obscurantist *adj* **reactionary**, conservative, backward-looking, traditionalist, old-fashioned *Opposite*: liberal ■ *n* **conservative**, reactionary, traditionalist, diehard, dogmatist *Opposite*: liberal

obscure *adj* **1 incomprehensible**, unclear,

vague, ambiguous, abstruse *Opposite*: clear **2 indistinct**, faint, shadowy, murky, blurry *Opposite*: clear **3 unknown**, little-known, minor, unseen, unheard of *Opposite*: famous ■ *v* **1 confuse**, disguise, conceal, complicate, obfuscate *Opposite*: clarify **2 darken**, cloak, mask, hide, shroud *Opposite*: disclose

COMPARE AND CONTRAST CORE MEANING: difficult to understand
obscure difficult to understand because it is expressed in a complicated way or because it involves areas of knowledge or study that are not known to most people; **abstruse** not easy to understand, often because it involves specialist knowledge or is expressed in specialist language; **recondite** requiring a high degree of scholarship or specialist knowledge to be understood; **arcane** requiring information that is secret or known only to a few people in order to be understood; **cryptic** deliberately mysterious or ambiguous and seeming to have a hidden meaning; **enigmatic** having a quality of mystery and ambiguity that makes it difficult to understand and interpret.

obscurity *n* **1 anonymity**, insignificance, unimportance, inconspicuousness, oblivion *Opposite*: fame **2 incomprehensibility**, vagueness, ambiguousness, doubt, opacity *Opposite*: clarity

obsequious *adj* **servile**, sycophantic, flattering, toadying, submissive *Opposite*: assertive

obsequiousness *n* **sycophancy**, servility, flattery, submissiveness, compliance *Opposite*: assertiveness

observable *adj* **noticeable**, visible, apparent, evident, obvious *Opposite*: imperceptible

observance *n* **1 adherence**, compliance, execution, performance, observation *Opposite*: violation **2 ritual**, ceremony, ceremonial, rite, celebration

observant *adj* **sharp-eyed**, alert, attentive, watchful, vigilant *Opposite*: unobservant

observation *n* **1 surveillance**, scrutiny, watching, inspection, examination *Opposite*: neglect **2 remark**, comment, opinion, thought, reflection

observatory *n* **building**, station, laboratory, telescope, viewpoint

observe *v* **1 detect**, perceive, witness, see, spot *Opposite*: miss **2 watch**, view, scrutinize, monitor, study *Opposite*: ignore **3 remark**, comment, say, declare, state **4 abide by**, respect, follow, comply with, heed *Opposite*: violate **5 celebrate**, keep, remember, take part in, perform *Opposite*: break

observer *n* **spectator**, witness, viewer, onlooker, bystander *Opposite*: participant

obsess *v* **preoccupy**, grip, consume, fixate, possess *Opposite*: bore

obsessed *adj* **fanatical**, gripped, preoccupied, infatuated, fixated *Opposite*: indifference

obsession *n* **mania**, fascination, fixation, passion, preoccupation *Opposite*: indifference

obsessive *adj* **compulsive**, fanatical, fixated, infatuated, neurotic *Opposite*: easygoing

obsolescence *n* **outmodedness**, unfashionableness, oldness, undesirability, uselessness *Opposite*: modernity

obsolescent *see* obsolete

obsolete *adj* **archaic**, outmoded, antiquated, passé, unfashionable *Opposite*: up-to-date

obstacle *n* **1 problem**, difficulty, hindrance, impediment, complication *Opposite*: help **2 obstruction**, barrier, blockage, blockade, impediment *Opposite*: passage

obstinacy *n* **stubbornness**, determination, pigheadedness, inflexibility, unreasonableness *Opposite*: compliance

obstinate *adj* **stubborn**, determined, pigheaded, fixed, inflexible *Opposite*: compliant

obstreperous *adj* **disruptive**, rowdy, disorderly, loud, noisy *Opposite*: demure. See COMPARE AND CONTRAST *at* **unruly**.

obstruct *v* **1 block**, barricade, impede, hold up, stop *Opposite*: clear **2 hinder**, thwart, frustrate, hamper, complicate *Opposite*: assist. See COMPARE AND CONTRAST *at* **hinder**.

obstruction *n* **obstacle**, barrier, block, blockade, barricade *Opposite*: help

obstructionism *n* **timewasting**, stalling, filibustering, sabotage, hindrance *Opposite*: helpfulness

obstructionist *adj* **stalling**, timewasting, filibustering, delaying, delay ■ *n* **staller**, timewaster, filibusterer, wrecker, saboteur

obstructive *adj* **disruptive**, uncooperative, unhelpful, obstreperous, awkward *Opposite*: helpful

obtain *v* **get**, get hold of, acquire, procure, attain *Opposite*: lose. See COMPARE AND CONTRAST *at* **get**.

obtainable *adj* **available**, accessible, reachable, attainable, at hand *Opposite*: unavailable

obtrude *v* **1 interfere**, impose, meddle, pry, interrupt **2 extend**, thrust, stick out, push out

obtrusive *adj* **1 conspicuous**, unmistakable, blatant, prominent, garish *Opposite*: inconspicuous **2 interfering**, intruding, meddlesome, forward, presumptuous

obtuse *adj* **insensitive**, dull-witted, simpleminded, imperceptive, stupid *Opposite*: astute

obverse *n* **1 front**, head, heads, side, face **2 counterpart**, complement, opposite, equivalent, opposite number ■ *adj* **1 front**, forward-facing, opposite, visible, anterior *Opposite*: reverse **2 equivalent**, complementary, opposite, other, opposing

obviate *v* **do away with**, avoid, remove, forestall, prevent

obvious *adj* **clear**, understandable, palpable,

noticeable, apparent *Opposite*: obscure

obviousness *n* **clearness**, certainty, overtness, unmistakability, conspicuousness *Opposite*: obscurity

occasion *n* **1 time**, juncture, case, instance, event **2 possibility**, opportunity, opening, season, contingency **3 reason**, cause, motive, justification, rationale ▪ *v* **cause**, motivate, give rise to, bring about, induce

occasional *adj* **infrequent**, irregular, chance, sporadic, rare *Opposite*: regular. *See* COMPARE AND CONTRAST *at* **periodic**.

occlude *v* **1 block**, stop up, close off, seal, shut off *Opposite*: free **2 cut off**, cut out, close, block off, shut *Opposite*: open

occlusion *n* **1 blocking**, obstruction, stopping up, closing off, sealing **2 cutting off**, cutting out, closure, blocking, sealing

occupancy *n* **tenancy**, tenure, habitation, possession, residence *Opposite*: vacancy

occupant *n* **inhabitant**, tenant, lodger, resident, occupier

occupation *n* **1 job**, profession, work, career, livelihood **2 activity**, pursuit, enterprise, task

occupational *adj* **work-related**, job-related, professional, industrial, working

occupied *adj* **1 busy**, engaged, employed, unavailable, working *Opposite*: free **2 in use**, full, engaged, tied down, taken *Opposite*: empty **3 conquered**, subjugated, subject, dominated, ruled *Opposite*: liberated

occupier *n* **inhabitant**, resident, tenant, occupant, lodger

occupy *v* **1 live in**, inhabit, reside in, dwell in *(literary)*, lodge *(dated)* *Opposite*: vacate **2 interest**, engage, divert, take up, entertain **3 conquer**, subjugate, dominate, rule, seize *Opposite*: liberate

occur *v* **1 happen**, take place, arise, come about, transpire **2 hit**, strike, cross your mind, appear, come to mind

occurrence *n* **1 incidence**, rate, amount, existence, manifestation **2 happening**, event, incident, episode, occasion

ocean *n* **sea**, deep, water, briny ▪ *adj* **marine**, sea, deep-sea, oceanic

oceangoing *adj* **seagoing**, sea, seaworthy, maritime, seafaring

oceanic *adj* **sea**, deep-sea, ocean, saltwater, marine

ocular *adj* **visual**, optical, ophthalmic

odd *adj* **strange**, peculiar, unusual, abnormal, anomalous *Opposite*: ordinary

oddity *n* **1 peculiarity**, quirk, foible, idiosyncrasy, twist **2 strangeness**, peculiarity, quirkiness, oddness, bizarreness *Opposite*: normality **3 eccentric**, character, original, exception, misfit **4 curiosity**, rarity, phenomenon, freak

oddments *n* **1 odds and ends**, leftovers, offcuts, bits, fragments **2 knick-knacks**, notions, sundries, curios, gewgaws

oddness *n* **strangeness**, peculiarity, mysteriousness, incongruity, weirdness *Opposite*: normality

odds *n* **chances**, probability, likelihood, balance

odds and ends *n* **remnants**, leftovers, loose ends, offcuts, fragments

odds-on *(infml)* *adv* **probably**, most likely, like enough, likely, dependably *Opposite*: unlikely

ode *n* **poem**, elegy, verse, sonnet, song *(literary)*

odious *adj* **hateful**, horrible, loathsome, revolting, detestable *Opposite*: delightful

odium *n* **abhorrence**, hatred, disgust, revulsion, hate *Opposite*: approval

odour *n* **1 scent**, perfume, stink, smell, stench **2 air**, aura, atmosphere, flavour, spirit. *See* COMPARE AND CONTRAST *at* **smell**.

odourless *adj* **unscented**, fragrance-free, neutral *Opposite*: scented

odyssey *n* **journey**, trek, crusade, pilgrimage, wanderings

oeuvre *(fml)* *n* **work**, piece, composition, opus, works

off *adj* **rotten**, rancid, bad, tainted, mouldy *Opposite*: fresh

offbeat *adj* **unusual**, unconventional, eccentric, quirky, bizarre *Opposite*: typical

off-centre *adj* **1 asymmetrical**, skewed, uneven, unbalanced, eccentric **2 off-the-wall** *(infml)*, quirky, eccentric, unconventional, odd

off chance *n* **likelihood**, probability, possibility, chance, prospect

off-colour *adj* **1 unwell**, sick, ill, unfit, under the weather *Opposite*: well **2** *(infml)* **risqué**, indecorous, suggestive, improper, indiscreet

offence *n* **1 crime**, wrongdoing, felony, fault, violation **2 insult**, affront, outrage, slight, slur **3 umbrage**, resentment, pique, indignation **4 attack**, offensive, assault, onslaught, bombardment *Opposite*: defence

offend *v* **1 hurt somebody's feelings**, upset, insult, affront, be rude to **2 commit an offence**, commit a crime, commit a felony, transgress, break the law

offended *adj* **affronted**, insulted, hurt, upset, slighted

offender *n* **criminal**, wrongdoer, reprobate, delinquent, lawbreaker

offensive *adj* **1 unpleasant**, distasteful, disgusting, odious, hateful *Opposite*: agreeable **2 insulting**, rude, impolite, provoking, provocative *Opposite*: courteous **3 aggressive**, attacking, violent, invasive, belligerent *Opposite*: peaceful

offensiveness *n* **rudeness**, impoliteness, indecency, vulgarity, abusiveness *Opposite*: politeness

offer *v* **1 proffer**, tender, present, bid **2 propose**, suggest, pose, recommend, put forward *Opposite*: withdraw ▪ *n* proposal, suggestion, bid, proposition, bargain

offering *n* contribution, gift, donation, present, submission

off-guard *adj* unready, unawares, napping, unprepared *Opposite*: ready

offhand *adj* **1** impromptu, extemporaneous, improvised, unrehearsed, spontaneous *Opposite*: premeditated **2** informal, casual, nonchalant, easygoing, indifferent *Opposite*: serious

office *n* bureau, workplace, administrative centre, headquarters, agency

office holder *n* official, officer, politician, public servant, elected official

officer *n* **1** police officer, constable, bobby (*infml*), cop (*slang*) **2** official, bureaucrat, representative, administrator, office holder

official *n* bureaucrat, administrator, representative, spokesperson, officer ▪ *adj* authorized, certified, endorsed, sanctioned, allowed *Opposite*: informal

officialdom (*infml*) *n* the powers that be, bureaucracy, administrative system, red tape (*infml*)

officiate *v* preside, manage, perform official duties, carry out official duties, solemnize

officious *adj* meddlesome, bossy, bureaucratic, self-important, overbearing

off-key *adj* out of key, tuneless, out of tune, discordant, screeching *Opposite*: melodious ▪ *adv* tunelessly, out of tune, discordantly, unmusically *Opposite*: melodiously

off-limits *adj* forbidden, prohibited, proscribed, outlawed, verboten *Opposite*: permitted

off-line *adj* off, disconnected, down *Opposite*: online

offload *v* **1** discharge, unload, deposit, dump, leave *Opposite*: load **2** pass on, get rid of, dump, deposit, devolve *Opposite*: keep **3** (*infml*) relieve of, divest, rid, free from, unburden

off-putting *adj* **1** repellent, repulsive, disgusting, distasteful, offensive *Opposite*: attractive **2** forbidding, disconcerting, upsetting, disturbing, daunting *Opposite*: comforting

offset *n* counterbalance, balance, counterpoise, equalizer, counterweight ▪ *v* counterweigh, counterbalance, make up for, counteract, compensate

offshoot *n* **1** sideshoot, sprout, sucker, branch, twig **2** derivative, subsidiary, consequence, result, outcome

offspring *n* descendants, progeny, children, issue, young

WORD BANK
❑ types of offspring only child, quadruplet, quintuplet, singleton, triplet, twin

off-the-cuff *adj* impromptu, spontaneous, improvised, unprepared, unrehearsed

off-the-peg *adj* ready-made, ready-to-wear, standard-size, mass-produced, prêt-à-porter *Opposite*: made-to-measure

off-the-shelf *adj* standard, regular, mass-produced, ordinary, run-of-the-mill *Opposite*: bespoke

off-the-wall (*infml*) *adj* bizarre, strange, eccentric, unusual, unconventional

often *adv* frequently, over and over again, time and again, repeatedly, habitually *Opposite*: seldom

ogle *v* look at, eye, leer, stare, gaze *Opposite*: ignore. *See* COMPARE AND CONTRAST *at* gaze.

ogre *n* giant, troll, tyrant, monster, fiend

oil *n* **1** lubricant, emollient, grease **2** grease, fat, lard ▪ *v* apply oil, lubricate, smear with oil, grease, loosen

WORD BANK
❑ types of cooking fat and oil butter, canola oil, corn oil, dripping, ghee, lard, margarine, olive oil, peanut oil, rape oil, sesame oil, suet, sunflower oil, vegetable oil

oily *adj* greasy, fatty, slick, slippery, oleaginous

ointment *n* gel, liniment, lotion, balm, salve

old *adj* **1** aged, elderly, mature, getting on, not getting any younger *Opposite*: young **2** from the past, ancient, from way back, long-standing, long forgotten *Opposite*: recent **3** previous, last, other, former, erstwhile *Opposite*: current

old-fashioned *adj* **1** antiquated, outdated, unfashionable, behind the times, archaic *Opposite*: up-to-date **2** fogyish, traditional, conservative, conventional, old-school *Opposite*: modern

COMPARE AND CONTRAST CORE MEANING: no longer in current use or no longer considered fashionable

old-fashioned no longer considered fashionable or suitable because of changes in taste or technology, or, nostalgically favouring or maintaining the style of a former time; **outdated** no longer relevant to modern life because it has been superseded by something better, more fashionable, or more technologically advanced; **antiquated** regarded as in need of updating or replacing, though still functioning or in use; **archaic** belonging to a much earlier period of time, often suggesting a lack of relevance to modern life; **obsolete** superseded by something new, and in some cases therefore no longer in use; **passé** dismissed as no longer current or fashionable; **antediluvian** (*infml*) extremely old-fashioned and outdated.

old hand *n* veteran, expert, professional, connoisseur, authority *Opposite*: novice

old-style *adj* traditional, outdated, outmoded, out-of-date, old *Opposite*: modern

old-time *adj* old-fashioned, outdated, outmoded, traditional, old-style *Opposite*: modern

old-world *adj* **outdated**, outmoded, quaint, traditional, old-style *Opposite*: modern

olive branch *n* **peace offering**, compromise, concession, gesture, apology

omen *n* **sign**, portent, warning, forecast, premonition

ominous *adj* **threatening**, warning, worrying, gloomy, portentous *Opposite*: promising

omission *n* **1 oversight**, lapse, slip, error, blunder **2 exclusion**, exception, absence, leaving out, hiatus *Opposite*: inclusion

omit *v* **1 leave out**, miss out, pass over, skip, skip over *Opposite*: include **2 neglect**, forget, not take the trouble, not bother, overlook *Opposite*: remember. *See* COMPARE AND CONTRAST *at* **neglect**.

omnibus *n* **compilation**, collection, anthology, edition, album

omnipotence *n* **authority**, power, all-powerfulness, supremacy, influence *Opposite*: powerlessness

omnipotent *adj* **almighty**, all-powerful, invincible, unstoppable, supreme *Opposite*: powerless

omnipresent *adj* **ubiquitous**, all-pervading, universal, ever-present, pervasive *Opposite*: absent

omniscience *n* **knowledge**, awareness, insight, wisdom, sapience *Opposite*: ignorance

omniscient *adj* **all-knowing**, all-seeing, wise, well-informed, sagacious

on *prep* **1 sitting on**, on top of, resting on, lying on, upon *Opposite*: under **2 at**, next to, by the side of, by ■ *adv* **1 happening**, taking place, scheduled, arranged, proceeding *Opposite*: off **2 without stopping**, continuously, without a break, constantly, unceasingly

on account of *prep* **owing to**, because of, due to, through, as a result of

once *adv* **1 some time ago**, formerly, previously, a long time ago, once upon a time *Opposite*: now **2 as soon as**, when, after, the minute

once-over *(infml)* *n* **examination**, inspection, check, review, survey

oncoming *adj* **approaching**, looming, nearing, advancing, onrushing

one *adj* **unique**, single, solitary, lone, individual

one and all *pron* **everyone**, everybody, all, all and sundry, ladies and gentlemen *Opposite*: nobody

one-dimensional *adj* **superficial**, lacking in depth, simplistic, simple-minded, basic

one-liner *n* **joke**, witticism, quip, bon mot, epigram

oneness *n* **1 singleness**, cohesion, coherence *Opposite*: diversity **2 agreement**, unanimity,

unity, togetherness, solidarity *Opposite*: divergence

one-off *adj* **unique**, once-in-a-lifetime, never-to-be-repeated, limited-edition, special ■ *n* **rarity**, limited edition, one in a million

onerous *adj* **difficult**, burdensome, arduous, heavy, tiring *Opposite*: easy

one-sided *adj* **biased**, unfair, prejudiced, weighted, unrepresentative *Opposite*: balanced

one-sidedness *n* **bias**, partiality, unfairness, prejudice, unrepresentativeness

onetime *adj* **former**, previous, ex, past, old *Opposite*: current

one-to-one *adj* **1 individual**, private, personal, intimate, personalized **2 corresponding**, identical, matching ■ *adv* **individually**, privately, personally, alone ■ *n* **conversation**, heart-to-heart, tête-à-tête, gossip, discussion

one-way *adj* **single**, outward *Opposite*: return

ongoing *adj* **continuing**, rolling, in progress, current, open-ended

online *adj* **connected**, on, operational, working, available *Opposite*: off-line

onlooker *n* **bystander**, spectator, viewer, observer, witness

only *adv* **merely**, simply, just, barely, no more than ■ *adj* **single**, lone, solitary, individual, one

onrush *n* **surge**, rush, wave, tide, deluge

onrushing *adj* **oncoming**, surging, rushing, approaching, nearing

on-screen *adj* **televised**, television, live, on-air, televisual

onset *n* **start**, beginning, arrival, inception *(fml)*, commencement *(fml)* *Opposite*: conclusion

onside *adj* **legal**, safe, clear, in the clear ■ *adv* **legally**, safely, legitimately

onslaught *n* **attack**, assault, offensive, ambush, blitz

on the other hand *adv* **instead**, conversely, alternatively, then again, in contrast

on the strength of *prep* **because of**, on the basis of, on account of, by reason of, by virtue of *Opposite*: notwithstanding *(fml)*

on the subject of *prep* **concerning**, with reference to, regarding, as regards, re

on the threshold of *prep* **on the brink of**, on the point of, at the start of, verging on, bordering on

onus *n* **responsibility**, burden, obligation, duty

onward *adj* **forward**, headlong *Opposite*: backward ■ *adv* **on**, forwards, ahead, headlong, straight on *Opposite*: backwards

onwards *see* **onward**

oodles *(infml)* *n* **plenty**, lots, loads *(infml)*, heaps *(infml)*, piles *(infml)*

oomph *n* **energy**, enthusiasm, life, dynamism, vivacity

ooze v 1 **seep**, leach, leak, trickle, dribble 2 **exude**, be full of, reek of, radiate, overflow with

opacity n 1 **opaqueness**, imperviousness, impenetrability, denseness, cloudiness *Opposite*: transparency 2 **obscurity**, obtuseness, impenetrability, complexity, vagueness *Opposite*: transparency

opaque adj 1 **impervious**, cloudy, muddy, milky, misty *Opposite*: transparent 2 **obscure**, unclear, incomprehensible, impenetrable, difficult *Opposite*: clear

open adj 1 **unlocked**, ajar, wide open, gaping *Opposite*: closed 2 **exposed**, uncluttered, sweeping, undeveloped, unspoilt *Opposite*: built-up 3 **accessible**, public, unrestricted, free *Opposite*: restricted 4 **approachable**, friendly, amenable, receptive, amicable *Opposite*: standoffish 5 **honest**, unguarded, direct, straight, frank *Opposite*: guarded 6 **vulnerable**, exposed, undefended, unprotected, unguarded *Opposite*: safe ■ v 1 **begin**, start, commence, initiate, launch *Opposite*: conclude 2 **unlock**, unbolt, undo, unfasten, release *Opposite*: close

open-air adj **outside**, outdoor, alfresco, uncovered *Opposite*: indoor

open-and-shut adj **simple**, clear, straightforward, clear-cut, obvious *Opposite*: ambiguous

open-ended adj **open**, flexible, undecided, unrestricted, fluid *Opposite*: fixed

opener n 1 **bottle opener**, tin opener, can opener, corkscrew 2 (infml) **starter**, introduction, icebreaker, preamble

openhanded adj **generous**, unstinting, lavish, unselfish, philanthropic *Opposite*: miserly

openhandedness n **generosity**, lavishness, unselfishness, philanthropy, bounty (literary) *Opposite*: miserliness

openhearted adj **sincere**, genuine, honest, open, kind

openheartedness n **sincerity**, genuineness, honesty, kindness, love

opening n 1 **gap**, breach, aperture, hole, fissure 2 **start**, beginning, introduction, lead-in, prologue *Opposite*: end 3 **opportunity**, chance, lucky break, break (infml)

openly adv **candidly**, explicitly, frankly, honestly, plainly *Opposite*: secretly

open-minded adj **unbiased**, unprejudiced, tolerant, liberal, progressive *Opposite*: narrow-minded

open-mindedness n **broad-mindedness**, impartiality, tolerance, liberalism, progressiveness *Opposite*: narrow-mindedness

open-mouthed adj **astonished**, amazed, astounded, horrified, aghast

openness n **honesty**, directness, frankness, sincerity, candidness *Opposite*: reticence

open out v 1 **unfold**, spread out, open, open up, stretch out *Opposite*: fold up 2 **spread out**,

radiate, separate, divide 3 **expand**, flower, spread, spread wide, get bigger

open up v 1 **unfold**, expand, spread out, open out, stretch 2 **excavate**, cut through, open, dig out, expose 3 **unwrap**, open, uncover, expose 4 **speak freely**, bare your soul, unwind, speak your mind, speak openly *Opposite*: clam up (infml) 5 **open fire**, start firing, start shooting 6 **begin trading**, open, unlock *Opposite*: close 7 (infml) **accelerate**, open the throttle, speed up, step on it, put your foot down *Opposite*: slow down

operable adj 1 **treatable**, curable, nonfatal *Opposite*: inoperable 2 **practicable**, doable, possible, feasible, workable *Opposite*: impracticable

operate v 1 **function**, work, run, go, activate 2 **trade**, work, manage, run, carry on

operation n 1 **control**, management, use, controlling, manoeuvring 2 **business**, company, venture, undertaking, outfit (infml) 3 **process**, action, act, procedure, manoeuvre 4 **campaign**, manoeuvre, procedure, raid, attack

operational adj **in use**, in operation, in order, working, active

operative adj **in effect**, functioning, working, effective, operational *Opposite*: inoperative ■ n **worker**, operator, machinist, hand, technician

operator n **worker**, operative, machinist, hand

operose (fml) adj **arduous**, taxing, difficult, strenuous, hard *Opposite*: easy

opine (fml) v **pronounce**, hold forth, discourse, lecture, preach

opinion n **view**, estimation, belief, judgment, attitude

opinionated adj **voluble**, bigoted, narrow-minded, partisan, prejudiced *Opposite*: open-minded

opinion poll n **survey**, poll, questionnaire, investigation

opponent n **adversary**, enemy, rival, challenger, antagonist *Opposite*: ally

opportune adj **favourable**, fitting, appropriate, apt, right *Opposite*: inopportune

opportunism n **resourcefulness**, unscrupulousness, cunning, deviousness, speculation

opportunist n **speculator**, freebooter, fortune hunter, buccaneer, swashbuckler

opportunistic adj **unscrupulous**, resourceful, unprincipled, devious, cunning *Opposite*: principled

opportunity n **occasion**, opening, prospect, chance, break (infml) *Opposite*: misfortune

oppose v 1 **be against**, resist, fight, contest, combat *Opposite*: support 2 **compete with**, face, compete against, do battle with, clash with

opposed adj **opposite**, different, contrasting,

divergent, conflicting *Opposite:* similar

opposing *adj* **1 opposite**, contrasting, differing, disparate, conflicting *Opposite:* similar **2 rival**, opposite, hostile, competing, antagonistic *Opposite:* allied

opposite *adj* **1 far**, other, furthest, facing, opposing *Opposite:* adjacent **2 conflicting**, contradictory, differing, reverse, contrary *Opposite:* matching ■ *n* **contrary**, reverse, converse, inverse, opposite number *Opposite:* same ■ *prep* **facing**, across from, in front of, overlooking *Opposite:* beside

opposite number *n* **counterpart**, equivalent, parallel, equal, match

opposition *n* **1 resistance**, antagonism, hostility, disapproval, disagreement *Opposite:* friendliness **2 opponent**, challenger, competitor, enemy, rival

oppress *v* **1 keep down**, coerce, tyrannize, dominate, repress *Opposite:* liberate **2 afflict**, worry, torment, depress, distress *Opposite:* relieve

oppression *n* **domination**, coercion, cruelty, tyranny, repression

oppressive *adj* **1 cruel**, harsh, domineering, tyrannical, repressive *Opposite:* fair **2 overwhelming**, crushing, depressing, distressing, stressful *Opposite:* relaxing **3 humid**, hot, close, muggy, stifling *Opposite:* fresh

oppressor *n* **autocrat**, despot, persecutor, bully, tyrant *Opposite:* liberator

opprobrious *adj* **1 scornful**, contemptuous, damning, dismissive, reproachful *Opposite:* approving **2 shameful**, humiliating, ignominious, embarrassing, belittling *Opposite:* glorious

opprobriousness *n* **1 scorn**, contempt, censoriousness, dismissiveness, reproachfulness *Opposite:* approval **2 shamefulness**, shame, humiliation, ignominy, embarrassment *Opposite:* glory

opprobrium *n* **1 scorn**, contempt, condemnation, criticism, reproach *Opposite:* approval **2 shame**, disgrace, ignominy, humiliation, embarrassment *Opposite:* glory

opt *v* **choose**, elect, decide, determine, plump for

optical *adj* **visual**, ocular, ophthalmic, photosensitive

optical illusion *n* **1 illusion**, impression, effect, visual effect, mirage **2 trick**, illusion, trick of the light, special effect, visual effect

optimal *adj* **best**, ideal, optimum, top, finest *Opposite:* worst

optimism *n* **1 hopefulness**, sanguinity, confidence, positiveness, assurance *Opposite:* pessimism **2 cheerfulness**, enthusiasm, buoyancy, sunniness, brightness *Opposite:* pessimism

optimist *n* **idealist**, romantic, utopian, visionary, hoper *Opposite:* pessimist

optimistic *adj* **hopeful**, positive, bright, cheerful, expectant *Opposite:* pessimistic

optimize *v* **enhance**, improve, adjust, heighten, elevate

optimum *n* **ideal situation**, best-case scenario, goal, ideal, best ■ *adj* **best**, ideal, optimal, top, finest *Opposite:* worst

option *n* **choice**, alternative, possibility, route, opportunity *Opposite:* imperative

optional *adj* **elective**, voluntary, discretionary, possible, free *Opposite:* compulsory

opt out *(infml)* *v* **bow out**, bail out, withdraw, get out, leave

opulence *n* **1 wealth**, affluence, riches, prosperity, fortune *Opposite:* poverty **2 lavishness**, luxury, richness, magnificence, sumptuousness *Opposite:* simplicity

opulent *adj* **1 wealthy**, lavish, luxurious, rich, magnificent *Opposite:* poor **2 abundant**, ample, lavish, profuse, rich *Opposite:* sparse

opus *n* **composition**, work, piece, production, brainchild

oracle *n* **1 prophet**, augur, soothsayer, seer, visionary **2 prophesy**, vision, revelation, foreshadowing, prediction

oral *adj* **spoken**, verbal, uttered, said, verbalized *Opposite:* written. *See* COMPARE AND CONTRAST *at* **verbal**.

orangery *n* **greenhouse**, glasshouse, hothouse, conservatory, winter garden

orate *v* **1 speak**, lecture, make a speech, take the floor, discourse **2** *(fml)* **hold forth**, preach, lecture, speak, declaim

oration *n* **speech**, discourse, address, lecture, sermon

orator *n* **speaker**, debater, lecturer, raconteur, storyteller

oratorical *adj* **rhetorical**, debating, declamatory, speechmaking, eloquent *Opposite:* halting

oratory *n* **1 debating**, discussion, rhetoric, declamation, speechifying *(infml)* **2 eloquence**, persuasiveness, cogency, skill, style **3 pomposity**, prolixity, grandiloquence, verbosity, speechifying *(infml)*

orb *n* **globe**, sphere, planet, ball, round

orbit *n* **1 path**, track, trajectory, flight path, course **2 scope**, range, compass, influence, ambit ■ *v* **circle**, circumnavigate, loop, encircle, revolve

orchard *n* **plantation**, wood, copse, grove, coppice

orchestral *adj* **instrumental**, classical, symphonic, musical

orchestrate *v* **1 score**, arrange, compose, write, rewrite **2 plan out**, work out, arrange, coordinate, organize *Opposite:* improvise

orchestration *n* **1 instrumentation**, transposition, arrangement, scoring, composition **2 planning**, organization, stage-management, arrangement, preplanning *Opposite:* improvisation

ordain *(fml)* v order, decree, proclaim, enact, command *Opposite*: suggest

ordeal n trial, torment, suffering, tribulation, test

order n 1 **instruction**, command, directive, direction, demand *Opposite*: suggestion 2 **sequence**, succession, rank, classification, arrangement *Opposite*: chaos 3 **orderliness**, neatness, tidiness, method, regulation *Opposite*: disorder 4 **stability**, calm, harmony, peace, peacefulness *Opposite*: upheaval 5 **contract**, purchase, sale, request, requisition 6 **sect**, organization, group, class, lodge ■ v 1 **command**, instruct, tell, require, charge *Opposite*: request 2 **requisition**, request, ask for, send for, send off for *Opposite*: supply 3 **arrange**, organize, regulate, classify, categorize *Opposite*: confuse

ordered adj 1 **well-ordered**, neat, tidy, methodical, well-organized *Opposite*: disorganized 2 **controlled**, regimented, consistent, steady, efficient *Opposite*: irregular

orderliness n **neatness**, order, tidiness, method, organization *Opposite*: disorderliness

orderly adj 1 **obedient**, disciplined, well-behaved, decorous, compliant *Opposite*: disorderly 2 **arranged**, tidy, methodical, neat, logical *Opposite*: disorderly

ordinance n **decree**, order, rule, regulation, law

ordinarily adv **normally**, usually, generally, customarily, in general *Opposite*: unusually

ordinariness n 1 **normality**, commonplaceness, usualness, commonness, familiarity 2 **dullness**, triteness, drabness, dreariness, predictability

ordinary adj 1 **normal**, commonplace, usual, regular, common *Opposite*: unusual 2 **dull**, trite, drab, dreary, predictable *Opposite*: extraordinary

ordination n **investiture**, consecration, ceremony, conferment, installation

ordnance n **weapons**, artillery, arms, guns, weaponry

ordure *(fml)* n **excrement**, filth, dung, manure, faeces

ore n **mineral**, rock, metal, element, aggregate

organ n 1 **body part**, tissue, structure 2 *(fml)* **agency**, organization, body, representative, voice 3 *(fml)* **publication**, mouthpiece, newspaper, magazine, periodical

organic adj 1 **carbon-based**, biological, living, animate, animal *Opposite*: inorganic 2 **gradual**, natural, spontaneous, slow, unforced *Opposite*: artificial 3 **natural**, unprocessed, unrefined, untreated, raw *Opposite*: synthetic

organism n **living thing**, creature, animal, plant, virus

organization n 1 **group**, body, society, association, party 2 **arrangement**, configuration, design, format, composition 3 **orderliness**, order, method, regulation, neatness *Opposite*: chaos

organizational adj **structural**, administrative, legislative, executive, logistic

organize v 1 **establish**, form, shape, unify, unite 2 **coordinate**, manage, control, run, set up 3 **systematize**, arrange, sort out, classify, categorize *Opposite*: disarrange

organized adj 1 **prearranged**, structured, ordered, systematized, well thought-out *Opposite*: spontaneous 2 **methodical**, logical, orderly, reasonable, sensible *Opposite*: disorganized

organizer n 1 **manager**, director, coordinator, planner, controller 2 **diary**, appointment book, PDA, personal digital assistant, daybook

orient *see* orientate

orientate v 1 **position**, turn, angle, face, place 2 **familiarize**, adjust, learn about, orient, adapt

orientation n 1 **location**, alignment, direction, positioning, angle 2 **emphasis**, focus, character, slant, thrust 3 **leaning**, tendency, proclivity, preference, inclination 4 **adjustment**, acclimatization, assimilation, acclimation, settling in 5 **initiation**, briefing, induction, training, introduction

oriented adj **concerned with**, in favour of, focused on, preoccupied with, slanted towards

orifice *(literary)* n **opening**, hole, vent, cavity, outlet

origin n **source**, derivation, provenance, cause, root

COMPARE AND CONTRAST CORE MEANING: the beginning of something

origin the beginning of something in terms of the time, place, situation, or idea from which it arose, or somebody's ancestry, social background, or country; **source** the place, person, or thing through which something has come into being or from which it has been obtained; **derivation** the origin or source of something, especially a word, phrase, or name; **provenance** the place of origin of something, or the source and ownership history of a work of art or archaeological artefact; **root** the fundamental cause, basis, or origin of something, especially a feeling or a problem.

---

original adj 1 **first**, initial, previous, fundamental, primary *Opposite*: last 2 **unique**, innovative, novel, inventive, creative *Opposite*: unoriginal ■ n **prototype**, genuine article, pattern, archetype, template *Opposite*: copy. See COMPARE AND CONTRAST at **new**.

originality n **innovation**, novelty, uniqueness, inventiveness, creativity *Opposite*: unoriginality

originally adv **first**, initially, in the beginning, formerly, at first *Opposite*: eventually

originate v 1 **begin**, derive, stem from, start, commence Opposite: finish 2 **create**, invent, initiate, instigate, inaugurate

originator n **inventor**, creator, instigator, designer, maker

ornament n 1 **knick-knack**, figurine, objet d'art, bauble, decoration 2 **embellishment**, adornment, enhancement, enrichment, trimming ■ v **adorn**, decorate, beautify, embellish, paint

ornamental adj **decorative**, attractive, for show, ornate, patterned Opposite: functional

ornamentation n **decoration**, adornment, embellishment, enhancement, garnishing

ornate adj 1 **decorative**, overelaborate, baroque, elaborate, ornamental Opposite: unadorned 2 **high-flown**, flowery, wordy, verbose, elaborate Opposite: plain

orotund (fml) adj 1 **loud**, clear, strong, ringing, stentorian Opposite: soft 2 **wordy**, verbose, grandiloquent, pompous, bombastic Opposite: humble

orphan n **child**, baby, boy, girl, waif ■ v **bereave**, leave alone, leave all alone, make an orphan

orphanage n **home**, residential home, hostel, poorhouse, workhouse

orthodox adj **conventional**, accepted, traditional, mainstream, conformist Opposite: unorthodox

orthodoxy n **accepted view**, convention, accepted belief, prevailing attitude, tenet

oscillate v 1 **swing**, move back and forth, move to and fro, move backwards and forwards, fluctuate 2 **waver**, hesitate, vacillate, blow hot and cold, dither

oscillation n **swaying**, fluctuation, vacillation, alternation, swinging

osculate (fml) v **kiss**, give a kiss, give a smacker (infml), canoodle with (infml), smooch (infml)

ossify v **petrify**, fossilize, harden, become inflexible, become fixed

ossuary (fml) n **vault**, grave, tomb, crypt, charnel house

ostensible adj **ostensive**, apparent, professed, supposed, perceived Opposite: real

ostentation n **flashiness**, showiness, display, flamboyance, pretension Opposite: modesty

ostentatious adj **flashy**, showy, flamboyant, affected, pretentious Opposite: modest

ostracism n **shunning**, snubbing, exclusion, barring, keeping out Opposite: inclusion

ostracize v **coldshoulder**, exclude, banish, shun, ignore Opposite: include

other adj **additional**, new, more, fresh, extra

otherness n **strangeness**, difference, uniqueness, distinctiveness, oddness Opposite: normality

otherwise adv **or else**, if not, else, alternatively

otiose adj **futile**, ineffectual, useless, impractical, ineffective Opposite: effective

ottoman n **divan**, couch, day bed, chaise lounge, settee

oubliette n **prison cell**, dungeon, prison, cell

ounce n **grain**, jot, scrap, small amount, modicum

oust v **expel**, throw out, get rid of, drive out, exile Opposite: appoint

ouster n **removal**, ejection, dismissal, expulsion, coup

out adv **outdoors**, out-of-doors, in the open, in the open air, alfresco Opposite: indoors ■ adj 1 **elsewhere**, not in, not at home, away, away from home Opposite: in 2 **exposed**, revealed, given away, made known, shown Opposite: hidden 3 **available**, on view, obtainable, ready, on show Opposite: unavailable 4 **unacceptable**, impossible, improbable, not worth it, not on Opposite: acceptable 5 **old-fashioned**, unfashionable, outdated, dated, passé Opposite: fashionable 6 **banned**, prohibited, disallowed, barred, prevented Opposite: legitimate 7 **unconscious**, out cold, asleep, comatose, dazed Opposite: conscious

out-and-out adj **complete**, blatant, obvious, outright, utter

outback n **wilderness**, scrubland, wilds, desert, badlands

outbid v **offer more than**, outspend, outdo, leave standing, overpay

outboard adj **external**, on the outside, outside, outward, exterior

outbrave (archaic) v **defy**, confront, brave, stand up to, face up to

outbreak n **eruption**, outburst, epidemic, occurrence, rash

outbuilding n **shed**, outhouse, lean-to, barn, shack

WORD BANK
❑ **types of outbuilding** barn, booth, byre, carport, conservatory, cowshed, garage, garden shed, gatehouse, gazebo, glasshouse, greenhouse, guardhouse, hothouse, hut, kiosk, lean-to, lodge, orangery, outhouse, pavilion, potting shed, privy (infml), sentry box, shed, stall, stand, summerhouse

outburst n **outpouring**, upsurge, surge, eruption, explosion

outcast n **untouchable**, exile, pariah, recluse, outsider

outclass v **surpass**, outshine, excel, do better than, better

outcome n **consequence**, result, ending, product, conclusion

outcrop n **rocky outcrop**, crag, ridge, bluff, boulder

outcry n 1 **protest**, disagreement, objection, chorus of disapproval, quarrel Opposite:

acceptance **2 uproar**, hullabaloo, hue and cry, turmoil, clamour

outdated *adj* **antiquated**, passé, outmoded, obsolete, dated *Opposite*: up-to-date. *See* COMPARE AND CONTRAST *at* **old-fashioned**.

outdistance *v* **outdo**, beat, do better than, outrun, outstrip

outdo *v* **exceed**, surpass, top, outdistance, outshine

outdoor *adj* **outside**, open-air, out-of-doors, alfresco *Opposite*: indoor

outdoors *adv* **out-of-doors**, outside, in the open, in the open air, alfresco *Opposite*: indoors

outer *adj* **outside**, external, on the outside, surface, superficial *Opposite*: inner

outermost *adj* **furthest**, farthest, remotest, outmost *Opposite*: innermost

outer space *n* **space**, the heavens, the universe, the solar system, the cosmos

outface *v* **1 stare out**, outstare, psych out (*infml*), stare down (*US*) *Opposite*: give in **2 brave**, stand up to, face up to, defy, confront *Opposite*: capitulate

outfall *n* **vent**, mouth, duct, channel, culvert

outfit *n* **1 suit**, clothes, clothing, ensemble, dress **2** (*infml*) **company**, team, business, group, unit ■ *v* **supply**, equip, fit out, arm, kit out

outflank *v* **1 go around**, attack from behind, attack from the rear, outmanoeuvre **2 outwit**, outmanoeuvre, outdo, bypass, outclass

outflow *n* **1 discharge**, drainage, seepage, leakage, depletion *Opposite*: influx **2 expenditure**, debit, expenses, spending, outlay *Opposite*: income

outfox *v* **defeat**, outwit, get the better of, outflank, take in

outgoing *adj* **1 outward-bound**, outbound, outward, departing, leaving *Opposite*: incoming **2 retiring**, leaving, departing, withdrawing, resigning *Opposite*: incoming **3 sociable**, friendly, gregarious, extrovert, genial *Opposite*: introvert

outgoings *n* **expenses**, expenditure, costs, overhead, outlay *Opposite*: income

outgrow *v* **1 get too large for**, grow too big for, get too big for, enlarge, grow up **2 move beyond**, be too grown-up for, be too old for, mature, develop **3 grow bigger than**, grow larger than, grow faster than, grow quicker than, outnumber

outgrowth *n* **extension**, result, development, product, consequence

outing *n* **visit**, excursion, trip, day trip, jaunt

outjockey *v* **outfox**, outdo, outwit, outmanoeuvre, outflank

outlandish *adj* **unusual**, bizarre, peculiar, strange, eccentric *Opposite*: usual

outlast *v* **outlive**, survive, live longer than, last longer than, endure

outlaw *n* **runaway**, criminal, fugitive, bandit,

desperado ■ *v* **forbid**, ban, prohibit, proscribe, veto *Opposite*: allow

outlay *n* **expenditure**, expense, cost, spending, sum *Opposite*: return ■ *v* **expend**, spend, lay out, pay out, disburse

outlet *n* **1 opening**, passage, vent, exit, channel **2 means**, channel, conduit, vent, instrument **3 department store**, shop, retailer, market, store

outline *n* **1 shape**, form, figure, contour, silhouette **2 plan**, rough draft, summary, sketch, rough idea ■ *v* **1 draw round**, sketch, draw, delineate, chart *Opposite*: fill in **2 summarize**, sketch out, delineate, run through, give a rough idea *Opposite*: expand

outlive *v* **live longer than**, outlast, survive, last longer than, endure

outlook *n* **1 viewpoint**, view, attitude, position, point of view **2 future**, prospect, time to come, time ahead **3 view**, panorama, vista

outlying *adj* **remote**, out-of-the-way, distant, faraway, far-off *Opposite*: neighbouring

outmanoeuvre *v* **get the better of**, outsmart, outfox, outwit, outflank

outmoded *adj* **1 unfashionable**, dated, passé, old-fashioned, out-of-date *Opposite*: fashionable **2 obsolete**, out of use, out of commission, archaic, antiquated

outmost *adj* **outermost**, remotest, furthest, most remote, extreme

outnumber *v* **be more numerous than**, outstrip

out-of-date *adj* **outdated**, obsolete, outmoded, old-fashioned, dated *Opposite*: up-to-date

out-of-doors *adv* **outdoors**, outside, in the open, in the open air, alfresco *Opposite*: indoors

out of the blue *adv* **unexpectedly**, without warning, all of a sudden, suddenly, surprisingly

out-of-the-way *adj* **1 distant**, off the beaten track, remote, isolated, desolate *Opposite*: accessible **2 uncommon**, unconventional, different, out of the ordinary, special *Opposite*: common

outpace *v* **outstrip**, outperform, overtake, outdo, beat

outperform *v* **outdo**, outstrip, outpace, outclass, beat *Opposite*: underperform

outpost *n* **garrison**, base, station, settlement, colony

outpouring *n* **expression**, outburst, torrent, spate, flood

output *n* **production**, productivity, amount produced, yield, harvest

outrage *n* **1 crime**, barbarity, disgrace, scandal, horror **2 indignation**, anger, rage, fury, annoyance ■ *v* **infuriate**, offend, insult, anger, enrage *Opposite*: placate

outraged *adj* **angry**, incensed, livid, infuriated, furious *Opposite*: calm

outrageous *adj* **disgraceful**, shameful, shocking, offensive, contemptible *Opposite*: commendable

outré *adj* **shocking**, eccentric, unconventional, excessive, too much

outride *v* **1 outpace**, outstrip, outclass, beat, overtake **2 survive**, last out, endure, ride out, make it through

outrider *n* **patrol**, guard, bodyguard, attendant, escort

outright *adv* **1 completely**, entirely, totally, fully, absolutely *Opposite*: partially **2 immediately**, straightaway, right away, without hesitation, at once *Opposite*: hesitantly **3 openly**, unreservedly, frankly, forthrightly, unequivocally *Opposite*: equivocally ■ *adj* **1 absolute**, complete, total, utter, out-and-out *Opposite*: partial **2 out-and-out**, clear, transparent, obvious, direct

outrun *v* **1 outpace**, outstrip, outclass, beat, overtake **2 leave behind**, flee, run faster than, elude, get away from **3 go beyond**, overrun, exceed, excel, surpass

outsell *v* **beat**, overtake, outpace, outstrip, sell more than *Opposite*: underperform

outset *n* **beginning**, start, onset, kickoff (*infml*), inception (*fml*)

outshine *v* **surpass**, outdo, outstrip, outperform, do better than

outside *adv* **1 outdoors**, in the open air, alfresco, out of doors, in the fresh air **2 beyond**, out there, elsewhere, yonder ■ *adj* **1 outdoor**, external, separate, open-air, exterior **2 external**, unknown, unfamiliar, independent, freelance **3 slight**, faint, remote, scarce, slim *Opposite*: strong ■ *prep* **beyond**, out of, further than, farther than, past *Opposite*: within ■ *n* **exterior**, outer surface, surface, external surface *Opposite*: inside

outsider *n* **stranger**, foreigner, unknown, interloper, outcast

outsize *adj* **enormous**, massive, huge, immense, gigantic

outsized *see* **outsize**

outskirts *n* **border**, fringes, periphery, bounds, outer reaches *Opposite*: centre

outsmart *v* **outwit**, outfox, outmanoeuvre, get the better of, overcome

outspoken *adj* **frank**, opinionated, honest, candid, open *Opposite*: tactful

outspokenness *n* **frankness**, honesty, candour, openness, bluntness *Opposite*: tact

outspread *adj* **extended**, spread-out, stretched, widely spread, open *Opposite*: folded ■ *v* **extend**, expand, stretch, spread, spread out *Opposite*: close in

outstanding *adj* **1 exceptional**, wonderful, stupendous, dazzling, marvellous *Opposite*: abysmal **2 unresolved**, unsettled, unpaid, remaining, owing *Opposite*: settled

outstandingly *adv* **exceptionally**, terrifically, wonderfully, stupendously, marvellously *Opposite*: abysmally

outstay *v* **outlast**, outlive, survive, stay longer than

outstretched *adj* **outspread**, extended, stretched out, spread-out, stretched *Opposite*: folded

outstrip *v* **outdo**, outshine, surpass, exceed, do better than *Opposite*: fall behind

outward *adj* **visible**, external, apparent, obvious, noticeable *Opposite*: inward

outwards *adv* **out**, outward, away, centrifugally *Opposite*: inwards

outweigh *v* **overshadow**, be more important than, prevail over, be greater than, dwarf

outwit *v* **outsmart**, outfox, outmanoeuvre, get the better of, take in

outworn *adj* **obsolete**, outmoded, out-of-date, antiquated, archaic *Opposite*: current

ovate *adj* **oval**, egg-shaped, ellipsoid

ovation *n* **standing ovation**, cheer, vote of confidence, endorsement, thumbs-up (*infml*)

over *prep* **1 throughout**, around, the length and breadth of, round, across **2 in excess of**, more than, greater than, larger than, above *Opposite*: under **3 on top of**, above, on, upon *Opposite*: beneath (*fml*) ■ *adj* **ended**, finished, done, completed, concluded

overabundance *n* **excess**, surplus, glut, superfluity, flood *Opposite*: shortage

overact *v* **ham it up**, ham, overdo it, exaggerate, overplay

overactive *adj* **feverish**, overexcited, overcharged, intense, fervid

overall *adj* **general**, complete, total, global, inclusive ■ *adv* **on the whole**, in general, generally, taken as a whole, largely *Opposite*: in particular

over and above *prep* **in addition to**, besides, as well as, added to, on top of

overarching *adj* **all-embracing**, main, all-encompassing, predominant, principal

overawe *v* **intimidate**, scare, impress, subdue

overbearing *adj* **arrogant**, domineering, bossy, imperious, pompous *Opposite*: meek

overblown *adj* **1 overdone**, excessive, exaggerated, unrestrained, immoderate *Opposite*: understated **2 pretentious**, pompous, puffed-up, extravagant *Opposite*: unassuming

overburden *v* **overload**, overtax, overstrain, burden, load

overcast *adj* **cloudy**, grey, gloomy, dark, dull *Opposite*: bright

overcharge *v* **charge too much**, take advantage of, cheat, swindle, rip off (*infml*)

overcome *v* **1 overwhelm**, overpower, incapacitate, disable, knock out **2 carry away**, affect, move to tears, reduce to tears, grip **3 surmount**, prevail over, rise above, triumph over, conquer *Opposite*: yield. *See* COMPARE AND CONTRAST *at* **defeat**.

overcompensate *v* overreact, overcorrect, overplay, give too much weight to, try too hard

overconfidence *n* arrogance, overoptimism, boldness, pride, nerve *Opposite*: caution

overconfident *adj* arrogant, full of yourself, brash, overoptimistic, bullish *(infml) Opposite*: modest

overcook *v* overdo, stew, burn, char, spoil

overcooked *adj* overdone, burnt, well done, chewy, hard *Opposite*: underdone

overcritical *adj* harsh, hypercritical, censorious, severe, critical

overcrowded *adj* filled to capacity, congested, overloaded, teeming, swarming *Opposite*: deserted

overcrowding *n* congestion, overloading, overpopulation, excess, excess numbers

overdo *v* **1** overcook, burn, stew, char, spoil **2** exaggerate, overstate, overplay, overemphasize, take to extremes *Opposite*: play down

overdone *adj* **1** overcooked, burnt, stewed, charred, spoilt *Opposite*: underdone **2** exaggerated, overstated, overplayed, overemphasized, extreme *Opposite*: restrained

overdo things *v* strain yourself, burn the candle at both ends, overtax yourself, overexert yourself, overdo it *Opposite*: relax

overdrawn *adj* in debt, in the red, overspent, insolvent, over your limit *Opposite*: in credit

overdue *adj* late, tardy, unpaid, unsettled, belated *Opposite*: early

overeat *v* overindulge, eat too much, gorge, stuff yourself, binge

overemotional *adj* emotional, sentimental, melodramatic, maudlin, histrionic *Opposite*: unemotional

overemphasize *v* exaggerate, overstate, overstress, stress, go over the top about

overenthusiasm *n* fanaticism, mania, obsessiveness, obsession, ardour

overenthusiastic *adj* overzealous, carried away, fanatical, obsessive, obsessional

overestimate *v* **1** misjudge, overrate, miscalculate, overvalue, allow too much for *Opposite*: underestimate **2** overrate, expect too much of, misjudge, miscalculate, overemphasize *Opposite*: underestimate

overexcite *v* work up, excite, get in a state, get carried away, wind up *(infml) Opposite*: calm down

overexcited *adj* carried away, high, frenzied, in a frenzy, feverish *Opposite*: calm

overexcitement *n* frenzy, mania, feverishness, anxiety, emotion

overextend *v* overstretch, overreach, go too far, bite off more than you can chew, exceed your limit

overflow *v* run over, flood, spill over, brim over, pour out ■ *n* excess, runoff, extra, surfeit, surplus *Opposite*: lack

overflowing *adj* spilling over, teeming, swarming, brimming, abundant *Opposite*: empty

overflow with *v* be full of, brim with, abound with, bubble with, be bursting at the seams with *Opposite*: lack

overgrown *adj* dense, thick, overrun, lush, untidy *Opposite*: tidy

overhang *v* project, extend, jut out, hang over, extend beyond ■ *n* projection, extension, outcrop, ledge, outcropping

overhaul *v* **1** repair, renovate, fix, refit, refurbish **2** overtake, surpass, leave behind, outdo, pass *Opposite*: fall behind ■ *n* service, refit, refurbishment

overhead *adv* above, in the air, upstairs, directly above, above your head *Opposite*: below

overheads *n* costs, outgoings, expenses, payments, business costs

overhear *v* eavesdrop, listen in, hear, eavesdrop on, listen to

overheated *adj* excited, impassioned, agitated, inflamed, hot and bothered *Opposite*: calm

overindulge *v* overeat, eat too much, stuff yourself, gorge, gorge yourself

overindulgence *n* excess, greed, intemperance, hedonism, gluttony

overindulgent *adj* excessive, greedy, immoderate, intemperate, hedonistic

overjoyed *adj* delighted, joyful, elated, ecstatic, jubilant *Opposite*: disappointed

overkill *n* excess, too much, overstatement, overegging the pudding, too much of a good thing *Opposite*: restraint

overladen *adj* overloaded, overfilled, crammed, overburdened, weighed down

overlap *v* **1** partly cover, overlie, meet, touch, cover **2** coincide, correspond, intersect, meet, come together ■ *n* **1** overlay, intersection, edge, join, connection **2** correspondence, connection, similarity, common ground, commonality

overlay *v* cover, coat, put over, overlap, drape

overload *v* overburden, overwork, tax, strain, weigh down ■ *n* excess, surplus, overwork, burden, overkill *Opposite*: lack

overloaded *adj* weighed down, weighted down, loaded, laden, full

overlook *v* **1** ignore, miss, forget, skip, neglect *Opposite*: notice **2** excuse, condone, spare, let pass, pardon *Opposite*: punish **3** give onto, be opposite, face, back onto **4** supervise, oversee, superintend, boss, observe **5** inspect, survey, examine, peruse, scan. *See* COMPARE AND CONTRAST *at* **neglect**.

overly *adv* excessively, too, desperately, exaggeratedly, exceedingly *Opposite*: slightly

overmuch adv **excessively**, too much, very much, unnecessarily, overly ■ adj **excessive**, extreme, too much, immoderate, extravagant ■ n **excess**, superfluity, surplus, overage

overnight adv **suddenly**, at once, quickly, instantly, abruptly *Opposite*: gradually ■ adj **instant**, immediate, abrupt, instantaneous, sudden *Opposite*: gradual

overpitch v **exaggerate**, overdo, overcompensate, overplay, overemphasize

overplay v **overemphasize**, exaggerate, overdo, overstress, overstate *Opposite*: underplay

overpower v 1 **subdue**, override, suppress, subjugate, conquer *Opposite*: yield 2 **overwhelm**, overshadow, floor, overcome, dumbfound

overpowering adj **overwhelming**, intense, overriding, uncontrollable, consuming *Opposite*: weak

overpoweringly adv **irresistibly**, overwhelmingly, devastatingly, strongly, intensely

overprice v **overrate**, overvalue, hike up, write up, mark up *Opposite*: underprice

overpriced adj **high-priced**, costly, extortionate, expensive, exorbitant *Opposite*: cheap

overprotect v **cosset**, fuss over, cocoon, indulge, protect *Opposite*: neglect

overrate v **overprize**, overestimate, exaggerate, overvalue *Opposite*: underrate

overrated adj **overvalued**, overestimated, hyped, puffed up, glorified *Opposite*: underrated

overreach v 1 **overdo**, bite off more than you can chew, overstretch, overextend, go too far 2 **overstrain**, overextend, overdo, overstress 3 **outwit**, outsmart, outfox, outplay, deceive

overreact v **exaggerate**, make a big deal, make something out of nothing, make a mountain out of a molehill, make a drama out of a crisis

override v 1 **disregard**, overrule, defy, flout, countermand *Opposite*: follow 2 **supersede**, dominate, prevail, predominate, overrule

overriding adj **overruling**, superseding, intervening, dominant, prevailing *Opposite*: insignificant

overrule v 1 **override**, cancel, rule against, refuse, make null and void 2 **master**, exercise authority, domineer, pull rank

overrun v **invade**, attack, assail, assault, besiege ■ n **swarming**, infested, teeming, flooded, swamped

overseas adj **foreign**, external, ultramarine *(literary)* ■ adv **abroad**, out of the country, in foreign parts

oversee v **supervise**, manage, superintend, run, direct

overseer n **supervisor**, manager, administrator, chief, boss

oversell v **exaggerate**, overvalue, overrate, hype, overstate *Opposite*: undersell

oversensitive adj **emotional**, thin-skinned, hypersensitive, vulnerable, touchy *Opposite*: thick-skinned

oversentimental adj **slushy**, mawkish, syrupy, maudlin, sad *Opposite*: callous

overshadow v **outshine**, outdo, dominate, surpass, eclipse

overshoot v **pass**, exceed, overreach, overpass, overrun *Opposite*: hit

oversight n 1 **mistake**, failure to notice, slip, omission, misunderstanding 2 **supervision**, control, overseeing, management, administration

oversimplify v **generalize**, overgeneralize, simplify, distort *Opposite*: complicate

oversize adj **extra large**, large, huge, king-size, oversized

oversized *see* **oversize**

oversleep v **sleep in**, sleep late, lie in *(infml)*

overspill n **flood**, overflow, runoff, excess, surplus ■ v **spill over**, overflow, brim over, pour out, flood

overstate v **exaggerate**, make too much of, overdo, overstress, overemphasize *Opposite*: understate

overstated adj **exaggerated**, extravagant, excessive, inflated, overelaborate *Opposite*: understated

overstatement n **exaggeration**, hyperbole, overemphasis *Opposite*: understatement

overstay v **prolong**, protract, spin out, extend

overstep v 1 **exceed**, go beyond, pass, surpass, step over 2 **transgress**, violate, disregard, disobey, contravene *Opposite*: obey

overstrain v **overstretch**, overstress, overreach, overtax, overload

overstress v 1 **overemphasize**, exaggerate, overplay, overpitch, overstate 2 **overstretch**, overstrain, overreach, overtax, overload ■ n **overstating**, overplaying, overdoing, dwelling on, going on about

overstretch v 1 **overstrain**, overstress, overreach, overdo 2 **overburden**, overtax, overload, overdo, overreach

overstrung adj **nervous**, tense, oversensitive, highly-strung, temperamental *Opposite*: placid

overstuffed adj **brimming**, overfilled, brimful, overflowing, bursting at the seams *Opposite*: empty

oversupply n **overflow**, excess, surplus, glut, superfluity ■ v **glut**, overwhelm, flood, inundate, swamp

overt adj **obvious**, unconcealed, explicit, evident, open *Opposite*: covert

overtake v 1 **pass**, go beyond, go past, overhaul, leave behind *Opposite*: fall behind 2 **hit**, sweep over, engulf, assail, strike

overtax v **strain**, overload, overdo it, overstretch, overstrain

over-the-hill adj **old**, past your prime, past your sell-by date, ancient, decrepit Opposite: up-and-coming

over-the-top (infml) adj **exaggerated**, excessive, overdone, extravagant, overblown Opposite: understated

overthrow v **conquer**, defeat, dethrone, bring down, depose Opposite: uphold

overtime n **extra pay**, extra hours, time and a half, additional hours, double time ■ adv **energetically**, tirelessly, actively, strenuously, intensely

overtone n **implication**, association, hint, undertone, connotation

overturn v **1 turn over**, knock over, tip over, upend, capsize Opposite: right **2 nullify**, abolish, invalidate, annul, reverse

overuse n **misuse**, abuse, overconsumption ■ v **overdo**, go to extremes, overplay, do to death, misuse

overused adj **overworked**, clichéd, hackneyed, commonplace, trite

overvalue v **overrate**, overprize, overestimate Opposite: undervalue

overview n **indication**, summary, outline, gestalt, synopsis

overweening adj **arrogant**, conceited, pompous, placatory, presumptuous, haughty Opposite: unassuming

overweight adj **too heavy**, heavy, big, large, weighty Opposite: underweight

overwhelm v **overpower**, overcome, engulf, devastate, crush

overwhelmed adj **1 overcome**, overawed, speechless, dazed, stunned Opposite: unimpressed **2 overpowered physically**, overcome, beaten, conquered, crushed **3 inundated**, snowed under, swamped, flooded, exhausted

overwhelming adj **irresistible**, overpowering, devastating, crushing, awe-inspiring Opposite: insignificant

overwinter v **hibernate**, lie dormant, stagnate, vegetate, lie fallow

overwork v **burn the midnight oil**, overdo it, work your fingers to the bone, overburden, overtax

overwrought adj **tense**, stressed, distraught, emotional, strained Opposite: calm

owe v **be beholden**, be obligated Opposite: repay

owed adj **owing**, unpaid, outstanding, due, payable Opposite: paid

owing adj **in arrears**, owed, due, in the red Opposite: paid

owing to prep **because of**, due to, on account of, thanks to, as a result of

owlish adj **owl-like**, serious, wise, solemn, bespectacled

own adj **individual**, private, particular, peculiar, specific ■ v **1 possess**, have, have possession of, keep, retain **2** (fml) **confess**, admit, own up, acknowledge, profess Opposite: deny

owner n **proprietor**, landlord, possessor, holder, titleholder

ownership n **possession**, rights, tenure, title, proprietorship

own goal n **self-defeating action**, blunder, mistake, misjudgment, miscalculation

own up v **confess**, admit, profess, express, utter

ox n **bull**, bullock, steer

oxidization n **reaction**, rust, tarnishing, corrosion, verdigris

oxidize v **react**, rust, tarnish, corrode, dissolve

P

PA n **public-address system**, loudspeaker, speaker, amplifier, amp

pace n **1 speed**, rapidity, swiftness, velocity, rate of knots **2 rate**, speed, tempo, time, regularity **3 step**, stride, leap, bound, hop ■ v **1 walk**, stride, march, walk back and forth, walk up and down **2 govern**, regulate, restrict, manage, limit

pacemaker n **leader**, pacesetter, pacer, innovator, trendsetter

pacific adj **1 soothing**, appeasing, conciliatory, comforting, placatory Opposite: antagonistic **2 tranquil**, peaceful, calm, untroubled, gentle Opposite: violent

pacifist n **peace lover**, conscientious objector, dove, peacemaker, peacekeeper ■ adj **pacific**, appeasing, conciliatory, placatory, comforting Opposite: antagonistic

pacify v **calm**, soothe, mollify, placate, calm down Opposite: antagonize

pack v **1 store**, arrange, put, place, sort **2 package**, wrap, wrap up, box, bundle Opposite: unpack **3 fill**, cram, stuff, jam, load **4 compact**, press, compress, squash, flatten ■ n **1 carton**, packet, box, parcel, container **2 folder**, packet, wallet, dossier, file **3 set**, bunch, group, quantity, collection **4 bag**, rucksack, backpack, haversack, daypack **5 crowd**, horde, mob, gang, bunch

package n **1 parcel**, packet, box, envelope, padded bag **2 set**, bundle, suite, raft, compendium ■ v **1 pack**, wrap, wrap up, parcel, box *Opposite*: unwrap **2 promote**, present, market, advertise, put across

packaging *n* **wrapping**, packing, wrapper, packet, box

packed *adj* **crowded**, crammed, full, full to capacity, heaving *Opposite*: empty

packet *n* **pack**, package, sachet, container, carton

pack in *v* **1 attract**, interest, excite, fill the seats, be a box office success *Opposite*: flop *(infml)* **2** *(infml)* **stop**, give up, quit, abandon, drop *Opposite*: take up

packing *n* **stuffing**, filling, filler, wadding, padding

pack up *v* **1 stop**, give up, quit, abandon, drop *Opposite*: start **2** *(infml)* **stop working**, break down, fail, seize up, jam

pact *n* **deal**, agreement, treaty, contract, accord

pad *n* **1 cushion**, cloth, wad, swab, pack **2 notepad**, sketchpad, notebook, jotter, sketchbook ▪ *v* **1 creep**, tiptoe, steal, walk, sneak **2 line**, cover, fill, stuff, wad **3 fill out**, flesh out, amplify, lengthen, expand

padding *n* **1 stuffing**, filling, wadding, lining, packing **2 verbiage**, circumlocution, periphrasis, garbage, rubbish

paddle *n* **oar**, scull, sweep, blade ▪ *v* **row**, scull, propel

page *n* **1 sheet**, piece of paper, sheet of paper, side, leaf **2 call**, beep, summons, message ▪ *v* **call**, contact, bleep, summon, beep *(US)*

pageant *n* **procession**, parade, cavalcade, display, carnival

pageantry *n* **spectacle**, display, pomp, ceremony, ritual

paid *adj* **waged**, salaried, professional, funded *Opposite*: unpaid

pain *n* **1 discomfort**, agony, aching, hurt, ache *Opposite*: pleasure **2 grief**, sorrow, anguish, ache, torture *Opposite*: joy **3** *(infml)* **nuisance**, bother, bind, menace, drag *(infml) Opposite*: pleasure ▪ *v* **sadden**, distress, upset, disturb, grieve *Opposite*: hearten

pained *adj* **hurt**, aggrieved, indignant, wounded, injured

painful *adj* **1 tender**, aching, raw, throbbing, excruciating *Opposite*: painless **2 sorrowful**, distressing, anguished, heartbreaking, upsetting *Opposite*: pleasant **3 laborious**, troublesome, awkward, laboured, tedious *Opposite*: easy **4 awful**, excruciating, dire, dreadful, agonizing *Opposite*: wonderful

painkiller *n* **analgesic**, sedative, anaesthetic, drug

painkilling *adj* **analgesic**, calming, sedative, deadening, numbing

painless *adj* **effortless**, easy, trouble-free, simple, unproblematic *Opposite*: problematic

pains *n* **care**, effort, trouble, lengths

painstaking *adj* **thorough**, careful, meticulous,

conscientious, scrupulous *Opposite*: careless. *See* COMPARE AND CONTRAST *at* **careful**.

paint *v* **1 coat**, decorate, smear, daub, splatter **2 portray**, capture, catch, show, render *(fml)*

painter *n* **artist**, watercolourist, portraitist, miniaturist

painting *n* **1 picture**, work of art, image, canvas, oil painting **2 art**, fine art, portraiture, landscape, oils

paint the town red *(infml) v* **celebrate**, have a good time, have fun, revel, go out

pair *n* **couple**, duo, twosome, brace, set ▪ *v* **pair off**, team up, join up, match up, put together *Opposite*: separate

pal *(infml) n* **friend**, comrade, mate, crony, chum *(infml)*

palatable *adj* **1 edible**, pleasant, tasty, appetizing, toothsome *Opposite*: inedible **2 acceptable**, agreeable, satisfactory, pleasant, passable *Opposite*: disagreeable

palatial *adj* **luxurious**, lavish, grand, impressive, splendid *Opposite*: miserable

palaver *n* **1 fuss**, bother, trouble, nuisance, commotion **2 chatter**, chat, gossip, talk, chit-chat *(infml)*

pale *adj* **1 light**, pastel, soft, whitish, insipid *Opposite*: dark **2 pallid**, fair, colourless, ashen, white *Opposite*: deep **3 faint**, dim, feeble, weak, watery *Opposite*: bright ▪ *v* **1 go white**, whiten, go pale, blanch, bleach *Opposite*: colour **2 diminish**, reduce, recede, lessen *Opposite*: intensify **3 lose colour**, fade, become washed out, soften, lighten *Opposite*: deepen

pall *v* **lose its attraction**, fade, diminish, wither, go sour ▪ *n* **1 cloud**, blanket, shroud, sheet, wall **2 gloom**, despair, sadness, depression, melancholy

palliative *adj* **1 analgesic**, painkilling, anaesthetic, sedative **2 soothing**, calming, relaxing, comforting, mollifying

pallid *adj* **pale**, white, ashen, pasty, colourless *Opposite*: dark

pallor *n* **paleness**, whiteness, pastiness, wanness, sallowness *Opposite*: bloom

palpable *adj* **1 intense**, tangible, physical, real, deep *Opposite*: intangible **2 obvious**, clear, demonstrable, unmistakable, evident *Opposite*: hidden

palpitate *v* **flutter**, pound, race, tremble, quiver

paltry *adj* **1 worthless**, trivial, trifling, miserable, insignificant *Opposite*: substantial **2 despicable**, wretched, mean, miserable, contemptible

pamper *v* **spoil**, indulge, coddle, mollycoddle, cosset *Opposite*: mistreat

pamphlet *n* **leaflet**, brochure, booklet, guide, tract

pan *n* **pot**, saucepan, casserole, wok, frying pan ▪ *v* *(infml)* **criticize**, berate, disparage, deride, slate *(infml) Opposite*: praise

panacea n **cure-all**, cure, solution, answer, remedy

panache n **flair**, flamboyance, style, spirit, confidence *Opposite*: awkwardness

pandemic n **epidemic**, plague, contagion, sickness, disease

pandemonium n **chaos**, bedlam, uproar, hubbub, mayhem *(infml)*

pander to v **indulge**, satisfy, gratify, bow to, go along with *Opposite*: resist

pane n **windowpane**, glass, window, sheet, panel

panel n **1 piece**, board, pane, sheet, plate **2 board**, team, jury, group, council

pang n **twinge**, spasm, paroxysm, shooting pain, cramp

panic n **fear**, anxiety, fright, terror, dread *Opposite*: calm ■ v **1 be frightened**, be terrified, lose your nerve, go to pieces, get flustered *Opposite*: calm down **2 terrify**, unnerve, scare, frighten, fluster

panicky adj **frightened**, scared, alarmed, fearful, anxious *Opposite*: calm

panic-stricken adj **terrified**, unnerved, frightened, fearful, scared out of your wits *Opposite*: calm

panoply n **display**, array, show, parade, exhibition

panorama n **view**, scene, vista, outlook, landscape

pan out *(infml)* v **turn out**, work out, develop, end up, resolve itself

pant v **gasp**, puff, wheeze, blow, gasp for air

pantomime *(infml)* n **farce**, joke, rigmarole, drama

pap n **drivel**, nonsense, rubbish, trash, garbage

paper n **1 newspaper**, daily, weekly, broadsheet, tabloid **2 document**, manuscript, thesis, dissertation, essay

paperback n **book**, softback, softcover, novel

paper over v **1 wallpaper**, cover, cover up, obscure, disguise *Opposite*: strip **2 conceal**, sweep under the carpet, hide, cover up, make light of *Opposite*: highlight

paperwork n **form-filling**, accounts, bookkeeping, correspondence, administration

papery adj **flimsy**, frail, thin, paper-thin, delicate

par n **average**, standard, norm, the usual

parable n **allegory**, fable, moral tale, folktale, tale

parade n **procession**, pageant, cavalcade, display, carnival ■ v **1 process**, march, file, strut, turn out **2 show off**, exhibit, display, trumpet, flaunt *Opposite*: hide **3 walk**, stalk, march, strut, stroll *Opposite*: skulk

paradigm n **1 model**, template, prototype, standard, pattern **2 epitome**, archetype, model, example, exemplar *(literary)* *Opposite*: antithesis

paradise n **1 heaven**, seventh heaven, nirvana, happy hunting ground *Opposite*: hell **2** *(infml)* **dream world**, wonderland, cloud nine, utopia, bliss

paradox n **inconsistency**, absurdity, irony, contradiction, contradiction in terms

paradoxical adj **inconsistent**, absurd, ironic, contradictory, illogical *Opposite*: logical

paradoxically adv **1 illogically**, absurdly, inconsistently, puzzlingly, unexpectedly *Opposite*: logically **2 strangely enough**, oddly enough, funnily enough, surprisingly, ironically

paragon n **model**, shining example, epitome, archetype, quintessence *Opposite*: rake

paragraph n **1 section**, subsection, passage, part, clause **2 article**, piece, item, story, editorial

parallel adj **similar**, equivalent, corresponding, analogous, matching *Opposite*: dissimilar ■ n **1 counterpart**, match, equal, equivalent, peer *Opposite*: opposite **2 similarity**, correspondence, equivalence, resemblance, analogy *Opposite*: dissimilarity

paramedic n **first aider**, first responder, emergency worker, rescue worker

parameter n **limit**, boundary, limitation, restriction, constraint

paramilitary adj **guerrilla**, rebel, revolutionary, terrorist ■ n **rebel**, revolutionary, terrorist, guerrilla, fighter

paramount adj **supreme**, utmost, dominant, chief, principal *Opposite*: minimal

paranoia n **fear**, suspicion, mistrust, distrust, obsession *Opposite*: confidence

paranoid adj **suspicious**, fearful, mistrustful, distrustful, obsessed *Opposite*: trusting

paraphernalia n **things**, stuff, equipment, kit, trappings

paraphrase v **rephrase**, summarize, reword, interpret, translate ■ n **summary**, rewording, précis, translation, interpretation

parasite n **1 pest**, bug, bloodsucker, insect, flea *Opposite*: host **2 leech**, scrounger *(infml)*, sponger *(infml)*, freeloader *(infml)*

WORD BANK
❏ **types of parasitic insect** bedbug, botfly, chigoe, crab louse, deer tick, flea, gadfly, harvest mite, head louse, louse, mite, sandfly, tapeworm, tick

parasitic adj **1 biting**, bloodsucking, dependent, opportunistic *Opposite*: host **2 dependent**, lazy, scrounging *(infml)*, sponging *(infml)*, freeloading *(infml)*

parasol n **sunshade**, umbrella, shade, brolly *(infml)*

parcel n **1 package**, packet, bundle, carton, box **2 tract**, plot, piece, section, portion ■ v **pack**, package, wrap, wrap up, box *Opposite*: unwrap

parcel out v **distribute**, divide, share out, give out, hand out

parcel up v **wrap up**, wrap, parcel, bundle, pack *Opposite*: unwrap

parch v **dry**, dry out, scorch, dehydrate, desiccate

parched adj 1 **dry**, arid, dried up, dried out, scorched *Opposite*: waterlogged 2 (*infml*) **thirsty**, gasping, dehydrated, dry, panting *Opposite*: refreshed. *See* COMPARE AND CONTRAST at **dry**.

pardon v 1 **forgive**, absolve, exonerate, let off, acquit *Opposite*: condemn 2 **excuse**, forgive, overlook, let pass, take no notice of *Opposite*: resent ■ n **forgiveness**, absolution, exoneration, amnesty, mercy

pare v 1 **cut**, trim, clip, cut back, tidy up *Opposite*: grow 2 **peel**, skin, strip, trim, shave

pare down v **cut back**, cut down, reduce, scale down, pare *Opposite*: increase

parentage n 1 **ancestry**, background, pedigree, origin, derivation 2 **parents**, paternity, maternity

parental adj **parent**, maternal, paternal *Opposite*: filial

parenthesis n **digression**, afterthought, addition, aside, comment

parenthood n **parentage**, fatherhood, motherhood, parenting, paternity

parenting n **childcare**, child-rearing, babycare, nurturing, child raising

parish n **community**, neighbourhood, district, village, locality

parity n **equivalence**, equality, uniformity, similarity, correspondence *Opposite*: disparity

park n **gardens**, botanical gardens, common, green, grounds ■ v (*infml*) **sit**, settle, plonk, plunk, put

parking n **car park**, parking bay, parking space, parking place, parking spot

parkland n **grassland**, land, fields, meadows, estate

parlance n **idiom**, turn of phrase, phraseology, phrasing, jargon

parley v **confer**, negotiate, talk, discuss, deliberate ■ n **conference**, meeting, discussion, negotiations, consultation

parliament n **government**, legislative body, legislature, assembly, MPs

parliamentarian n **member of parliament**, MP, politician, backbencher, legislator

parliamentary adj **governmental**, legislative, lawmaking, congressional, senatorial

parlour n **business premises**, salon, business establishment, shop, studio

parlous (*archaic*) adj **dangerous**, perilous, risky, unsafe, uncertain *Opposite*: comfortable

parochial adj **narrow**, narrow-minded, closed-minded, provincial, insular *Opposite*: broad-minded

parochialism n **narrow-mindedness**, provincialism, insularity, closed-mindedness, narrowness *Opposite*: broad-mindedness

parodist n **satirist**, humorist, imitator, lampooner, burlesquer

parody n 1 **caricature**, imitation, lampoon, satire, burlesque 2 **distortion**, travesty, misrepresentation, perversion, pale imitation *Opposite*: model ■ v 1 **distort**, pervert, misrepresent, twist 2 **lampoon**, imitate, caricature, satirize, burlesque

parole n **conditional release**, early release, bail, liberation ■ v **release on parole**, release conditionally, liberate, bail, give terms

paroxysm n 1 **outburst**, fit, frenzy, outpouring, explosion 2 **convulsion**, spasm, fit, seizure, attack

paroxysmal adj **convulsive**, violent, spasmodic, uncontrollable, involuntary

parquet n **flooring**, parquetry, floor, floorboards, inlay

parrot n **imitator**, mimic, impersonator, impressionist, copier ■ v **mimic**, imitate, copy, impersonate, echo

parrot-fashion (*infml*) adv **mindlessly**, by rote, mechanically, automatically, unthinkingly

parry v 1 **deflect**, block, fend off, shield yourself from, dodge *Opposite*: take 2 **evade**, avoid, dodge, elude, sidestep *Opposite*: answer

parse v **analyse**, describe, break down, explain, construe

parsimonious adj **thrifty**, mean, frugal, ungenerous, miserly *Opposite*: extravagant

parsimoniousness *see* **parsimony**

parsimony n **stinginess**, thrift, thriftiness, meanness, frugality *Opposite*: extravagance

parson n **cleric**, priest, minister, pastor, parish priest

parsonage n **church house**, rectory, vicarage, manse, residence

part n 1 **portion**, division, section, fraction, piece *Opposite*: whole 2 **feature**, ingredient, element, component, bit 3 **share**, portion, fragment, slice, chunk *Opposite*: whole 4 **function**, role, duty, job, position ■ v **divide**, separate, open, split, segregate *Opposite*: join

partake v 1 (*fml*) **consume**, dine, eat, drink, taste *Opposite*: abstain 2 **participate**, share, contribute, take part, play a part *Opposite*: refrain

partial adj 1 **incomplete**, fractional, limited, restricted, unfinished *Opposite*: complete 2 **biased**, prejudiced, subjective, one-sided, inequitable *Opposite*: impartial

partiality n 1 **fondness**, liking, penchant, inclination, affection *Opposite*: dislike 2 **bias**, prejudice, preference, leaning, favouritism *Opposite*: impartiality

partially adv **partly**, in part, incompletely, to

some extent, somewhat *Opposite*: completely

partial to *adj* keen on, fond of, into *(infml)*

participant *n* member, contributor, contestant, applicant, partaker *Opposite*: observer

participate *v* contribute, partake, take part, join, join in *Opposite*: observe

participation *n* contribution, input, sharing, partaking, involvement *Opposite*: observation

participatory *adj* taking part, participating, sharing, partaking, hands-on

particle *n* 1 bit, speck, spot, crumb, grain 2 iota, bit, jot, scrap, shred

parti-coloured *adj* variegated, multicoloured, pied, piebald, rainbow *Opposite*: monochrome

particular *adj* 1 specific, precise, certain, exact, actual *Opposite*: vague 2 individual, distinct, noteworthy, special, unique *Opposite*: general 3 exacting, meticulous, scrupulous, fastidious, fussy *Opposite*: relaxed

particularity *n* 1 fastidiousness, meticulousness, fussiness, carefulness, discrimination *Opposite*: carelessness 2 peculiarity, characteristic, trait, idiosyncrasy, quirk 3 individuality, distinctiveness, idiosyncrasy, singularity, originality *Opposite*: similarity

particularize *v* detail, itemize, specify, enumerate, stipulate

particularly *adv* 1 chiefly, mainly, above all, predominantly, mostly 2 exceptionally, intensely, acutely, especially, specifically *Opposite*: unexceptionally

particulars *n* details, facts, information, essentials, basics

parting *n* leaving, departure, separation, going, goodbye *Opposite*: reunion

parting shot *n* final remark, Parthian shot, last word, retort, hostile remark

partisan *n* supporter, follower, adherent, fan, member *Opposite*: opponent ■ *adj* biased, prejudiced, opinionated, one-sided, bigoted *Opposite*: impartial

partisanship *n* 1 support, devotion, membership, sponsorship, adherence 2 bias, prejudice, bigotry, narrow-mindedness, one-sidedness *Opposite*: impartiality

partition *n* 1 divider, panel, dividing wall, screen, sliding doors 2 separation, division, rift, split, dividing up ■ *v* divide, separate, wall off, fence off, split

partly *adv* partially, in part, somewhat, partway, moderately *Opposite*: wholly

partner *n* 1 spouse, wife, husband, mate, other half 2 associate, colleague, collaborator, equal, mate *Opposite*: superior ■ *v* team up, unite, join, link up, accompany

partner in crime *n* accessory, accomplice, crony, associate, sidekick *(infml)*

partnership *n* 1 affiliation, association, collaboration, companionship, alliance *Opposite*: opposition 2 company, business, firm, corporation, enterprise

part-time *adj* job-sharing, evening, weekend, freelance, casual *Opposite*: full-time

part-timer *n* part-time worker, job-sharer, freelance, freelancer, casual *Opposite*: full-timer

partway *adv* partly, partially, halfway, in part, somewhat *Opposite*: completely

party *n* 1 social gathering, gathering, festivity, revelry, event 2 faction, political party, interest group, society, splinter group 3 participant, accomplice, accessory, partaker, contributor 4 company, band, gang, crew, contingent 5 *(fml)* individual, person, one, person concerned, someone ■ *v* *(infml)* celebrate, have fun, revel, whoop it up *(infml)*, paint the town red *(infml)*

partygoer *n* celebrator, socializer, guest, sociable person, attendee

party line *n* official policy, official position, party policy, official line, dogma

party pooper *(infml)* *n* spoilsport, killjoy, bore, wet blanket *(infml)*, misery guts *(infml)*

parvenu *n* upstart, nouveau riche, social climber, arriviste, pretender

pass *v* 1 go by, overtake, exceed, outdo, surpass *Opposite*: stop 2 throw, kick, hit, toss, lob 3 hand over, give, deliver, hand, forward *Opposite*: withhold 4 elapse, go by, pass by, lapse, go 5 succeed, qualify, make the grade, excel, exceed *Opposite*: fail 6 approve, ratify, adopt, permit, accept 7 happen, occur, arise, take place, come about ■ *n* 1 permit, licence, authorization, card, documentation *Opposite*: ban 2 toss, kick, hit, throw, lob 3 passage, gorge, route, corridor, valley 4 state of affairs, state, plight, predicament, circumstances

passable *adj* 1 acceptable, adequate, good enough, all right, respectable *Opposite*: unacceptable 2 traversable, crossable, drivable, safe, penetrable *Opposite*: impassable

passage *n* 1 corridor, pathway, walkway, hall, hallway 2 way through, way, road, channel, course 3 section, part, chapter, paragraph, segment 4 migration, movement, exodus, flood, transit 5 journey, voyage, transfer, run, crossing 6 approval, enactment, passing, ratification, acceptance

passageway *n* passage, corridor, pathway, hallway, hall

pass away *v* 1 die, succumb, pass on, kick the bucket *(slang)*, depart *(fml)* 2 come to an end, finish, end, cease, terminate

pass by *v* 1 disregard, overlook, pass over, ignore, look the other way 2 overtake, go by, pass, surpass, leave behind 3 reject, turn down, decline, refuse, ignore

passé *adj* out-of-date, old, faded, aged, worn-out *Opposite*: fashionable

passenger *n* traveller, customer, fare, commuter, rail user

passer-by *n* onlooker, bystander, spectator, witness, pedestrian

pass for *v* impersonate, pass as, look like, go as, do as

passim *(fml)* *adv* here and there, throughout, frequently, in various places, in several places

passing *adj* **1** transitory, short-lived, ephemeral, fleeting, fly-by-night *Opposite*: permanent **2** cursory, quick, casual, superficial, surface *Opposite*: thorough ■ *n* **1** departure, departing, leaving, disappearance, desertion **2** death, dying, passing away, end, departure. *See* COMPARE AND CONTRAST *at* **temporary**.

passion *n* **1** fervour, ardour, obsession, infatuation, love **2** desire, hunger, thirst, appetite, craving **3** rage, fury, outburst, fever, furore. *See* COMPARE AND CONTRAST *at* **love**.

passionate *adj* **1** fervent, ardent, zealous, avid, obsessive *Opposite*: indifferent **2** fiery, quick-tempered, incensed, inflamed, enraged *Opposite*: easygoing

passionately *adv* fervently, ardently, avidly, single-mindedly, overpoweringly *Opposite*: indifferently

passionless *adj* loveless, detached, unromantic, emotionless, frigid *Opposite*: passionate

passive *adj* inert, inactive, unreceptive, reflexive, flaccid *Opposite*: active

passiveness *see* **passivity**

passivity *n* inactivity, inaction, non-participation, indifference, apathy *Opposite*: activeness

pass judgment *v* give an opinion, judge, criticize, condemn, deliver judgment

pass muster *v* measure up, be all right, check out, qualify, do

pass off *v* masquerade, pretend, misrepresent, palm off, falsify

pass on *v* convey, send, forward, impart, communicate

pass out *v* **1** faint, black out, lose consciousness, have a fainting fit, swoon *Opposite*: come to **2** distribute, hand out, give out, assign, deal out

pass over *v* ignore, neglect, discount, disregard, let go *Opposite*: consider

passport *n* **1** official document, travel document, ID, papers, permit **2** access, gateway, entry, opening, door

pass the buck *(infml)* *v* shift the blame, evade responsibility, lay something at somebody's door

pass through *v* cross, go through, lead through, traverse, move across

password *n* code word, open sesame, secret word, PIN, key

past *adj* **1** elapsed, completed, accomplished, over and done, done *Opposite*: ongoing **2** previous, historical, earlier, former, bygone *Opposite*: future ■ *n* history, earlier period, ancient times, times of yore, antiquity *Opposite*: future

paste *n* **1** adhesive, glue, gum, fixative, wallpaper paste **2** slime, goo *(infml)*, gunk *(infml)*, gloop *(infml)*, gunge *(infml)* **3** pie crust, dough, pastry ■ *v* glue, stick, gum, fix, bond

pastel *adj* pale, light, soft, muted, neutral *Opposite*: vivid ■ *n* crayon, chalk, coloured chalk, oil pastel

pasteurization *n* sterilization, heat treatment, purification, decontamination, disinfection

pasteurize *v* sterilize, heat, purify, decontaminate, disinfect

pasteurized *adj* sterilized, treated, purified, decontaminated, disinfected

pastiche *n* imitation, spoof, satire, lampoon, parody

pastime *n* hobby, interest, activity, pursuit, amusement

pasting *(infml)* *n* beating, defeat, thrashing, drubbing, pounding

past love *n* first love, ex *(infml)*, old flame *(infml)*, blast from the past *(infml)*

pastor *n* minister, priest, vicar, clergyman, cleric

pastoral *adj* rural, rustic, countryside, countrified, idyllic *Opposite*: urban

pastry *n* **1** paste, dough, pie crust **2** pie, tart, tartlet, flan, Danish pastry

pasture *n* meadow, meadowland, fallow, grassland, prairie

pasty *n* pie, Cornish pasty, meat pie, sausage roll, steak pie ■ *adj* pale, unhealthy-looking, ashen, pallid, wan

pasty-faced *adj* pasty, pale, unhealthy-looking, ashen, pallid

pat *v* **1** tap, touch, stroke, caress, massage **2** shape, smooth, mould, work, knead ■ *n* touch, tap, stroke ■ *adv* perfectly, faultlessly, fluently, impeccably, by heart

patch *n* **1** cover, reinforcement, covering, square **2** area, spot, blotch, bit, smear **3** badge, award, stripe, tag, square ■ *v* repair, cover, mend, strengthen, reinforce

patchiness *n* **1** unevenness, intermittence, bittiness, sparseness *Opposite*: evenness **2** variability, inconsistency, unreliability, irregularity, unevenness *Opposite*: consistency

patchouli *n* aromatic oil, oil, perfume, scent, essential oil

patch up *v* mend, repair, fix, strengthen, reinforce

patchwork *n* mixture, mix, collage, assortment, potpourri

patchy *adj* **1** occasional, irregular, sporadic, intermittent, sparse **2** variable, inconsistent, unreliable, erratic, unpredictable

pate *(archaic)* *n* **head**, crown, cranium, skull, bonce *(infml)*

patent *n* **copyright**, charter, right ▪ *adj* **clear**, obvious, blatant, flagrant, barefaced *Opposite*: unclear

paterfamilias *n* **father**, head of household, head, headman, paternalist

paternal *adj* **fatherly**, parental, nurturing, protective, guiding

paternalism *n* **authoritarianism**, interventionism, protectiveness, overprotectiveness, control

paternalistic *adj* **authoritarian**, patriarchal, protective, overprotective

paternity *n* **fatherhood**, parenthood, role, status, responsibility

path *n* **1 track**, trail, pathway, footpath, route **2 course**, route, way, orbit, direction

pathetic *adj* **1 pitiful**, sad, moving, tragic, doleful **2** *(infml)* **contemptible**, useless, risible, derisory, laughable. *See* COMPARE AND CONTRAST *at* **moving**.

pathfinder *n* **leader**, trailblazer, scout, pioneer, guide

pathological *adj* **1 medical**, clinical, scientific, diagnostic, immunological **2 morbid**, systemic, allergic, viral, bacteriological **3 extreme**, compulsive, uncontrolled, unreasonable, unreasoning

pathos *n* **sadness**, tragedy, bleakness, despair, anguish

pathway *n* **trail**, path, way, lane, alleyway

patience *n* **1 endurance**, staying power, stamina, persistence, perseverance *Opposite*: impatience **2 tolerance**, fortitude, serenity, imperturbability, unflappability *Opposite*: impatience

patient *adj* **1 enduring**, persistent, persevering, easygoing **2 tolerant**, long-suffering, serene, fortitudinous, imperturbable

patina *n* **1 discoloration**, tarnishing, staining, coating, verdigris **2 sheen**, shine, lustre, gloss **3 layer**, veneer, covering, coating, coat

patois *n* **1 dialect**, vernacular, idiom, language, speech **2 jargon**, slang, cant, patter, argot

pat on the back *(infml)* *n* **handshake**, round of applause, endorsement, seal of approval

patriarch *n* **1 head of family**, paterfamilias, father, head, headman *Opposite*: matriarch **2 bishop**, archbishop, prelate, leader

patriarchal *adj* **male-controlled**, male, masculine, macho

patrician *n* **aristocrat**, noble, peer, squire ▪ *adj* **aristocratic**, refined, upper-class, noble, blue-blooded

patricide *n* **1 murder**, killing, parricide, slaughter, manslaughter **2 murderer**, killer, parricide, slaughterer, homicide

patriot *n* **nationalist**, loyalist, flag-waver

patriotic *adj* **nationalistic**, loyal, jingoistic, xenophobic, chauvinistic

patriotism *n* **loyalty**, partisanship, nationalism, jingoism, xenophobia

patrol *n* **1 tour**, round, beat, circuit, perambulation **2 unit**, detachment, squad, troop, group ▪ *v* **guard**, watch, tour, make the rounds, walk the beat

patron *n* **1 sponsor**, benefactor, supporter, investor, backer **2 customer**, client, user, shopper, diner. *See* COMPARE AND CONTRAST *at* **backer**.

patronage *n* **investment**, backing, aid, sponsorship, benefaction

patronize *v* **1 be condescending to**, demean, denigrate, belittle, talk down to **2** *(fml)* **frequent**, shop at, use, utilize, visit

patronizing *adj* **condescending**, superior, denigrating, belittling, full of yourself

patter *n* **1 tapping**, drumming, beating, pitter-patter, rhythm **2 speech**, script, talk, spiel *(infml)* **3 jargon**, slang, cant, patois, argot ▪ *v* **1 tap**, drum, beat, pitter-patter, knock **2 jabber**, prattle, rattle on, rant, go on and on

pattern *n* **1 design**, decoration, shape, outline, form **2 prototype**, outline, model, example, blueprint

patterned *adj* **decorated**, spotted, lined, squared, dotted

patty *n* **1 cake**, burger, rissole **2 pie**, pasty, pastry, meat pie

paucity *n* **dearth**, scarcity, rareness, scantiness, lack

paunch *n* **stomach**, belly, gut, potbelly, pot *(infml)*

paunchy *adj* **potbellied**, portly, corpulent, fleshy, plump

pauper *n* **poor person**, down-and-out, bankrupt, indigent *(fml) Opposite*: millionaire

pause *v* **1 stop**, wait, break off, rest, stop what you're doing *Opposite*: continue **2 linger**, stop, rest, tarry, halt *Opposite*: move on **3 hesitate**, falter, waver, wait, hold back ▪ *n* **1 break**, recess, suspension, intermission, hiatus *Opposite*: continuation **2 silence**, awkward moment, hiatus, gap. *See* COMPARE AND CONTRAST *at* **hesitate**.

pave *v* **cover**, surface, floor, tile, flag

paved *adj* **cemented**, flagged, surfaced, covered, tiled

pavement *n* **path**, footpath, pathway, roadside, sidewalk *(US)*

paving *n* **flagging**, tiling, flooring, concrete, stonework

paw *n* *(infml)* **hand**, fist, mitt *(slang)* ▪ *v* **maul**, molest, fondle, stroke, pet

pawn *v* **trade in**, wager, put up, place as collateral, pledge *Opposite*: redeem

pay *v* **disburse**, reimburse, compensate, forfeit, recompense *Opposite*: receive ▪ *n* **wage**, salary, recompense, reimbursement, earnings. *See* COMPARE AND CONTRAST *at* **wage**.

payable *adj* owed, billed, due, to be paid, mature

pay back *v* repay, reimburse, pay off, settle up, restore *Opposite*: keep **2** retaliate, get even, take revenge, give tit for tat, settle scores

payback *n* **1** return, reimbursement, profit, remuneration, repayment **2** *(infml)* revenge, retaliation, retribution, vengeance, reprisal

pay cheque *n* wages, salary, pay, payment, earnings

PAYE *n* pay-as-you-earn, income tax, revenue, tax, tax at source

payee *n* recipient, beneficiary, receiver, collector, acceptor *Opposite*: payer

payer *n* spender, financier, customer, client, paymaster *Opposite*: payee

pay in *v* deposit, bank, put away, put in, save *Opposite*: withdraw

payload *n* cargo, load, freight, shipment, consignment

payment *n* sum, expense, compensation, recompense, disbursement

pay off *v* **1** settle, square, repay, pay back, reimburse **2** succeed, bear fruit, work, be effective, prosper

payoff *(infml)* *n* **1** payment, settlement, reckoning, payout, remuneration **2** bribe, graft, take, inducement, bribery

payout *n* **1** disbursement, expenditure, expenses, outgoing, charge *Opposite*: income **2** payment, pay, wages, money, cash

pay packet *n* wages, salary, paycheque, payment, earnings

payroll *n* employees, personnel, staff, workforce, workers

payslip *n* statement, slip, record, note, pay

pdq *(infml)* *adv* immediately, at once, quickly, fast, right away *Opposite*: later

peace *n* **1** concord, peacetime, harmony, armistice, reconciliation *Opposite*: war **2** harmony, calm, quiet, stillness, tranquillity *Opposite*: uproar

peaceable *adj* **1** peace-loving, amiable, agreeable, easygoing, willing to please *Opposite*: aggressive **2** tranquil, peaceful, serene, harmonious, calm *Opposite*: chaotic

peace agreement *n* treaty, truce, ceasefire, armistice, agreement

peaceful *adj* **1** quiet, serene, calm, still, peaceable *Opposite*: disordered **2** nonviolent, passive, diplomatic, peaceable, pacific *Opposite*: violent

peacekeeper *n* intermediary, mediator, go-between, diplomat, pacifist

peacekeeping *n* mediation, intermediation, diplomacy, pacification, negotiation

peacemaker *n* negotiator, arbitrator, diplomat, mediator, intermediary *Opposite*: fighter

peacemaking *n* reconciliation, conciliation, mediation, arbitration, appeasement

peace offering *n* olive branch, apology, overture, approach, gesture

peacetime *n* peace, harmony, armistice, truce, ceasefire

peach *(infml)* *n* beauty, pearl, wow *(infml)*, cracker *(infml)*, humdinger *(slang)* *Opposite*: dud *(infml)*

peachy *adj* **1** peachlike, downy, fuzzy, velvety, soft **2** *(infml)* excellent, wonderful, nice, splendid, great *Opposite*: terrible

peacock *n* egoist, exhibitionist, fop, show-off *(infml)*, dandy *(dated)*

peak *n* **1** mountain, mountaintop, summit, crest, point *Opposite*: valley **2** tip, pinnacle, zenith, top, summit *Opposite*: base ■ *v* climax, crest, top, max out *(US)* *Opposite*: dip ■ *adj* top, highest, crowning, topmost, ultimate *Opposite*: bottom

peaked *adj* pointed, sharp, pointy, spiky, tipped *Opposite*: rounded

peaky *adj* sickly-looking, pale, thin, wan, emaciated

peal *n* clangour, ringing, tolling, din, clang

peanuts *(infml)* *n* a small sum, a trifling amount, a trifle, a trifling sum, a paltry sum *Opposite*: fortune

pearl *n* treasure, precious thing, nugget, prize, gem *(infml)* *Opposite*: dud *(infml)*

pearly *adj* iridescent, lustrous, gleaming, shining, translucent *Opposite*: dull

pear-shaped *adj* bottom-heavy, broadening, widening, bulging, rotund *Opposite*: top-heavy

peasant *n* **1** farmer, labourer, farm hand, farmworker, crofter **2** country-dweller, rustic, provincial, bumpkin *(infml)*, hillbilly *(US infml)*

peat *n* mulch, moss, compost, fertilizer, turf

pebble *n* stone, nugget, grit, shingle

pebbledash *n* facing, finish, plaster, roughcast, encrustation

peccadillo *n* sin, offence, failing, indulgence, crime *Opposite*: virtue

peck *v* **1** strike, bite, jab, poke, dig **2** nibble, pick at, eat, play with, toy with *Opposite*: gobble **3** *(infml)* kiss, brush, caress, osculate *(fml)*, buss *(dated)* ■ *n* **1** bite, blow, stroke, jab, dig **2** *(infml)* kiss, brush, caress, smack, osculation *(fml)*

pecking order *n* hierarchy, class structure, social order, social structure, ladder

peckish *(infml)* *adj* hungry, famished, ravenous, starving *(infml)*, starved *(infml)* *Opposite*: full

peculiar *adj* **1** unusual, odd, strange, weird, irregular *Opposite*: normal **2** unique, idiosyncratic, local, individual, special *Opposite*: universal

peculiarity *n* **1** individuality, idiosyncrasy, distinctiveness, particularity, uniqueness **2** oddness, strangeness, weirdness, eccentricity, abnormality *Opposite*: normality

peculiarly adv 1 **uniquely**, abnormally, unusually, curiously, strangely Opposite: typically 2 **particularly**, especially, extremely, very, extraordinarily Opposite: slightly

pecuniary adj **monetary**, financial, fiscal, economic, commercial

pedagogic see pedagogical

pedagogical adj **educational**, academic, instructive, tutorial, didactic

pedagogue n **teacher**, educator, schoolteacher, instructor, tutor

pedagogy n **teaching**, education, instruction, training, tutoring

pedal n **lever**, device, control, treadle ■ v 1 **cycle**, ride, drive, steer, travel 2 **ride**, operate, propel, control, guide

pedant n **doctrinaire**, obfuscator, nitpicker, sophist, hairsplitter Opposite: dilettante

pedantic adj **finicky**, plodding, obscure, arcane, dull Opposite: dilettante

pedantry n **literalism**, laboriousness, sophistry, meticulousness, thoroughness Opposite: creativity

peddle v 1 **sell**, tout, hawk, vend, retail 2 **promote**, market, hype, espouse, advocate

pedestal n **base**, plinth, stand, dais, platform

pedestrian n **walker**, rambler, ambler, hiker, strider ■ adj **dull**, ordinary, unimaginative, uninspired, prosaic Opposite: exciting

pedestrian crossing n **crossing**, pelican crossing, crosswalk (US), zebra crossing

pedestrianized adj **traffic-free**, pedestrian, closed off

pedicure n **beauty treatment**, foot massage, cosmetic treatment, cosmetic session, chiropody treatment

pedigree n **lineage**, family background, ancestry, derivation, history ■ adj **purebred**, full-blooded, thoroughbred, noble, aristocratic

pedlar n **seller**, dealer, street trader, trader, vendor

peek v **peep**, glance, peer, steal a look, sneak a quick look Opposite: stare ■ n **look**, glance, peep, glimpse, once-over (infml) Opposite: gaze

peel v 1 **skin**, strip, pare, hull, bark 2 **flake**, come off in layers, shed, desquamate 3 **unwrap**, remove, strip off, take off ■ n **skin**, rind, peelings, covering, shell

peeler n **potato peeler**, carrot peeler, paring knife, scraper

peeling adj **flaking**, shedding, cracking, coming off, coming loose Opposite: smooth

peelings n **parings**, skin, peel, rind, shavings

peep v 1 **peek**, peer, steal a look, glance, sneak a look Opposite: gaze 2 **chirp**, twitter, tweet, chirrup, squeak ■ n 1 **peek**, glance, glimpse, look, gander (infml) 2 **sound**, utterance, noise, word

peephole n 1 **opening**, crack, hole, aperture, knothole 2 **spyhole**, eyehole, keyhole

peer n 1 **equal**, colleague, contemporary, friend, match 2 **noble**, aristocrat, lord, patrician, peer of the realm ■ v **look**, scrutinize, gaze, stare, examine Opposite: glance

peerage n 1 **peers**, aristocracy, nobility, nobles, aristocrats 2 **hereditary peerage**, life peerage, title, honour

peer group n **cohort**, coequals, generation, age group, classmates

peerless adj **incomparable**, matchless, unequalled, unrivalled, without equal Opposite: commonplace

peeve (infml) v **vex**, annoy, irritate, irk, upset Opposite: please ■ n **gripe** (infml), bugbear, irritation, vexation, nuisance Opposite: pleasure

peeved (infml) adj **annoyed**, irritated, irked, piqued, upset Opposite: pleased

peevish adj **irritable**, crabby, bad-tempered, cross, grumpy Opposite: good-tempered

peevishness n **irritability**, crabbiness, spitefulness, crossness, grumpiness

peewee (infml) adj **toy**, miniature, undersized, tiny, small Opposite: jumbo

peg n **pin**, fastener, dowel, hook, bolt ■ v 1 **fasten**, secure, attach, fix, hang Opposite: detach 2 **mark**, keep score, track, gauge, measure 3 **freeze**, fix, set, control, limit Opposite: free

pejorative (fml) adj **disapproving**, judgmental, harsh, scornful, derogatory Opposite: positive

pelican crossing n **crossing**, zebra crossing, pedestrian crossing, crosswalk (US)

pell-mell adv 1 **helter-skelter**, hurriedly, headlong, recklessly, tumultuously Opposite: carefully 2 **untidily**, higgledy-piggledy, haphazardly, chaotically, topsy-turvily Opposite: neatly

pelmet n **valance**, decoration, drapery, board, frill

pelt n **hide**, fur, skin, hair, coat ■ v 1 **bombard**, assail, assault, strafe, attack 2 **pour**, cascade, come down in sheets (infml), bucket down (infml), rain cats and dogs (infml) Opposite: drizzle

pen n **enclosure**, run, cage, coop ■ v 1 **scribble**, jot, compose, scrawl, write 2 **confine**, shut in, hold in, trap, capture Opposite: release

WORD BANK
❏ **types of pen** ballpoint, felt-tipped pen, fountain pen, highlighter, marker, quill, rollerball

penal adj **punitive**, punishing, disciplinary, corrective

penalization n **punishment**, disciplining, fining, discipline, correction Opposite: rewarding

penalize v **punish**, discipline, fine, reprimand, correct Opposite: let off

penalty n 1 **punishment**, fine, sentence, penalization **2 consequence**, disadvantage, drawback, forfeit, price *Opposite*: advantage

penance *n* **self-punishment**, reparation, forfeit, atonement, amends

penchant *n* **liking**, fondness, partiality, taste, proclivity *Opposite*: antipathy

pencil *v* **write**, draw, mark, colour, sketch

pendent *adj* **hanging**, suspended, dangling, sagging, pendulous

pending *adj* **1 undecided**, incomplete, awaiting, unresolved, pendent *(fml or literary)* *Opposite*: in hand **2 imminent**, impending, expected, approaching, forthcoming ■ *prep* **1 awaiting**, until, till **2 during**, throughout, in the course of

pendulous *adj* **1 hanging**, swinging, overhanging, drooping, loose **2 undecided**, wavering, vacillating, uncommitted, uncertain *Opposite*: decided

pendulum *n* **weight**, bob, plumb, swing

penetrate *v* **1 enter**, pass through, go through, go in, break in **2 diffuse**, seep in, soak in, infiltrate, imbue **3 work out**, solve, decipher, figure out, understand **4 grasp**, see into, perceive, figure out, comprehend

penetrating *adj* **1 all-pervading**, powerful, pungent, sharp, piercing **2 probing**, piercing, searching, questioning, inquiring **3 sharp**, intelligent, astute, perceptive, insightful *Opposite*: obtuse **4 piercing**, shrill, high-pitched, earsplitting, sharp

penetration *n* **1 diffusion**, infiltration, saturation, dispersion, dissemination **2 perception**, astuteness, understanding, discernment, comprehension **3 incursion**, access, breach, entrance, infringement

penetrative *adj* **1 penetrating**, piercing, penetrant, permeating, pervasive **2 keen**, perceptive, insightful, acute, sharp *Opposite*: unperceptive

pen friend *n* **correspondent**, letter writer, friend, acquaintance, pal *(infml)*

peninsula *n* **neck of land**, finger of land, cape, point, headland

penitence *n* **shame**, repentance, contrition, atonement, remorse *Opposite*: shamelessness

penitent *adj* **repentant**, repenting, contrite, remorseful, regretful *Opposite*: unrepentant

penitential *see* penitent

pen name *n* **pseudonym**, nom de plume, alias, nom de guerre

pennant *n* **banner**, flag, ensign, emblem, streamer

penniless *adj* **poor**, impoverished, impecunious, destitute, bankrupt *Opposite*: rich

pennon *n* **flag**, pennant, banner, standard, emblem

penny pincher *(infml)* *n* **skinflint**, miser, pinchpenny, cheapskate *(infml)*, scrooge *(infml)* *Opposite*: spendthrift

penny-pinching *(infml)* *adj* **frugal**, thrifty, tightfisted, parsimonious, tight *Opposite*: generous

pen pal *(infml)* *n* **pen friend**, correspondent, letter writer

penpusher *(infml)* *n* **bureaucrat**, clerk, writer, scribe, office worker

pension *n* **retirement pension**, retirement fund, annuity, income, retirement income

pensioner *n* **retiree**, retired person, senior citizen, senior, OAP

pensive *adj* **thoughtful**, meditative, contemplative, thinking, brooding

pensiveness *n* **thoughtfulness**, dreaminess, wistfulness, meditativeness, reflectiveness

pent-up *adj* **repressed**, stifled, unexpressed, contained, constrained *Opposite*: voiced

penultimate *adj* **last but one**, one before the last, next to last, second to last *(US)*

penumbra *n* **1 shadow**, shade, darkness **2 obscurity**, uncertainty, cloudiness, indistinctness

pen up *v* **cage**, round up, shut within, enclose, hold *Opposite*: free

penury *n* **poverty**, pennilessness, destitution, neediness, impoverishment *Opposite*: luxury

people *n* **1 nation**, community, nationality, populace, population **2 persons**, folks, individuals, public, general public **3** *(infml)* **relatives**, relations, family, folks, ancestors ■ *v* **populate**, fill, inhabit, immigrate, colonize

pep *(infml)* *n* **energy**, liveliness, vigour, perkiness, zest

pepper *v* **1 sprinkle**, shower, spray, scatter, speckle **2 intersperse**, sprinkle, interleave, infuse, scatter

pepper-and-salt *adj* **flecked**, streaked, greying, grizzled, patchy

peppery *adj* **spicy**, piquant, hot, fiery, pungent *Opposite*: mild

peppy *(infml)* *adj* **lively**, vigorous, sprightly, perky, frisky *Opposite*: lethargic

pep talk *(infml)* *n* **team talk**, speech, support, encouragement, inspiration

pep up *(infml)* *v* **spice up**, add zest, liven up, make something swing, give a bit of zing *(infml)*

per *prep* **for each**, apiece, for every, each, per capita

perambulator *(fml)* *n* **pram**, buggy, pushchair, stroller *(US)*, baby buggy *(US)*

perceive *v* **1 notice**, observe, see, take in, remark *Opposite*: ignore **2 understand**, comprehend, sense, feel, become aware of

percent *adv* **out of a hundred**, out of each hundred, in each hundred, in a hundred, per hundred ■ *n* **percentage**, part, proportion, ratio, percentile

percentage *n* **1 fraction**, proportion, ratio,

part, section **2** *(infml)* **commission**, proportion, fraction, take, profit

perceptible *adj* **noticeable**, traceable, observable, appreciable, visible *Opposite*: imperceptible

perception *n* **1 reading**, view, opinion, picture, take **2 insight**, acuity, awareness, discernment, observation

perceptive *adj* **discerning**, sensitive, insightful, keen, observant *Opposite*: insensitive

perceptiveness *n* **insight**, insightfulness, understanding, intuition, discernment

perch *v* **rest**, sit, settle, balance, alight

percipience *n* **insight**, insightfulness, perceptiveness, discernment, understanding *Opposite*: insensitivity

percipient *adj* **insightful**, perceptive, observant, discerning, understanding *Opposite*: insensitive

percolate *v* **1 drip**, filter, trickle, ooze, leach **2 seep into**, infiltrate, permeate, penetrate, get into

percolator *n* **coffeepot**, coffee maker, coffee machine

percussion *(infml)* *n* **drumming**, beating, striking, hitting, bass beat

perdition *n* **hell**, purgatory, punishment, damnation, abyss

peremptory *adj* **1 dictatorial**, authoritative, unconditional, absolute, dogmatic *Opposite*: polite **2 decisive**, no-nonsense, quick, hasty, direct *Opposite*: roundabout

perennial *adj* **recurrent**, returning, perpetual, constant, persistent *Opposite*: occasional

perestroika *n* **restructuring**, reform, reconstruction, reorganization, modernization

perfect *adj* **1 faultless**, flawless, textbook, picture-perfect, seamless *Opposite*: flawed **2 complete**, absolute, unqualified, whole, finished *Opposite*: incomplete **3 ideal**, just right, just the thing, wonderful, just what the doctor ordered *Opposite*: wrong **4 precise**, exact, accurate, on target, just right ■ *v* **1 improve**, refine, hone, tighten up, work on *Opposite*: spoil **2 achieve**, finish, complete, finalize, reach the summit of

perfection *n* **1 excellence**, rightness, faultlessness, exactness, precision **2 accomplishment**, fulfilment, completion, realization, achievement *Opposite*: abandonment

perfectionism *n* **fastidiousness**, fussiness, nitpicking, hairsplitting, pedantry *Opposite*: carelessness

perfectionist *n* **stickler**, purist, pedant, obsessive, quibbler

perfectly *adv* **1 flawlessly**, faultlessly, impeccably, effortlessly, seamlessly *Opposite*: badly **2 completely**, entirely, wholly, absolutely, utterly *Opposite*: partially

perfidious *(fml)* *adj* **disloyal**, treacherous, deceitful, dishonest, lying *Opposite*: honest

perfidy *(fml)* *n* **treachery**, disloyalty, deceit, duplicity, betrayal *Opposite*: honesty

perforate *v* **puncture**, prick, pierce, hole, go through

perforation *n* **hole**, puncture, tear, rip, slash

perform *v* **1 do**, carry out, fulfil, accomplish, execute **2 present**, act, play, put on, stage **3 function**, work, behave, act, go

COMPARE AND CONTRAST CORE MEANING: complete a task

perform complete an action or accomplish a task, especially when this requires skill or care or when it forms part of a set procedure; **do** complete an action or accomplish a task of any kind; **carry out** complete any action or task; **fulfil** do what is necessary to achieve the successful accomplishment or realization of something planned, promised, or anticipated; **discharge** *(fml)* complete duties or responsibilities successfully; **execute** put an instruction or plan into effect, or complete an action or procedure that requires skill and expertise.

performance *n* **1 presentation**, recital, act, routine, concert **2 functioning**, implementation, execution, performing, carrying out **3 feat**, deed, act, accomplishment, occurrence

performer *n* **1 player**, actor, musician, recitalist, actress *Opposite*: spectator **2 doer**, perpetrator, executor, architect, operator

perfume *n* **1 fragrance**, scent, cologne, body spray, toilet water **2 smell**, aroma, scent, odour, fragrance *Opposite*: stench ■ *v* **scent**, fragrance, imbue, freshen, lace. *See* COMPARE AND CONTRAST *at* smell.

perfumed *adj* **scented**, sweet-smelling, sweet-scented, aromatic, fragrant

perfunctory *adj* **1 unthinking**, automatic, mechanical, dutiful, obligatory *Opposite*: thoughtful **2 hasty**, superficial, quick, fleeting, hurried *Opposite*: thorough

pergola *n* **arch**, trellis, framework, arbour, structure

perhaps *adv* **maybe**, possibly, conceivably, feasibly, imaginably *Opposite*: definitely

peril *n* **danger**, threat, risk, hazard, jeopardy *Opposite*: safety

perilous *adj* **dangerous**, unsafe, hazardous, risky, death-defying *Opposite*: safe

perimeter *n* **boundary**, border, edge, limit, outskirts

period *n* **1 interval**, episode, interlude, phase, cycle **2 era**, age, epoch, stage, phase

periodic *adj* **1 episodic**, intermittent, interrupted, sporadic, occasional *Opposite*: constant **2 cyclic**, recurring, recurrent, serial, regular *Opposite*: irregular

---

COMPARE AND CONTRAST CORE MEANING: recurring over a period of time
periodic recurring or reappearing from time to time with a degree of regularity; **intermittent** occurring at irregular intervals; **occasional** occurring infrequently at irregular intervals; **sporadic** occurring irregularly and unpredictably.

---

periodical n **journal**, bulletin, magazine, review, publication

peripatetic adj **itinerant**, travelling, nomadic, wandering, roving Opposite: settled

peripheral adj 1 **outlying**, marginal, fringe, bordering, exterior Opposite: major 2 **minor**, incidental, tangential, marginal, unimportant Opposite: central

periphery n **boundary**, margin, edge, sideline, border Opposite: centre

perish (literary) v **die**, pass away, take your last breath, succumb, depart this life (fml) Opposite: live

perishable adj **unpreserved**, fresh, untreated Opposite: preserved

perished (infml) adj **cold**, freezing, frozen, shivering, perishing Opposite: boiling

perishing adj **cold**, freezing, bitter, raw, chilly Opposite: boiling

periwig n **wig**, hairpiece, toupee, rug (infml), peruke (archaic)

perjure v **lie**, bear false witness, commit perjury, fabricate, stretch the truth Opposite: tell the truth

perjury n **lying**, untruthfulness, lie, falsehood, untruth Opposite: honesty

perk n **bonus**, benefit, incentive, perquisite, extra Opposite: disadvantage

perk up v 1 **liven up**, cheer up, brighten up, wake up, awaken 2 **stick up**, stand up, prick up, cock up, pop up Opposite: droop

perky adj 1 **lively**, cheerful, energetic, jaunty, pert Opposite: despondent 2 **overconfident**, confident, self-confident, self-important, self-assured Opposite: timid

perm v **curl**, wave, kink, crimp, frizz Opposite: straighten

permanence n **perpetuity**, durability, durableness, longevity, solidity Opposite: transience

permanency see **permanence**

permanent adj **perpetual**, enduring, lasting, eternal, everlasting Opposite: temporary

permeability n **porousness**, penetrability, perviousness, absorbency, sponginess Opposite: impermeability

permeable adj **porous**, penetrable, pervious, absorbent, absorptive Opposite: impermeable

permeate v 1 **infuse**, flood, fill, infiltrate, invade 2 **filter**, seep, leak, pervade, penetrate

permeation n 1 **infusion**, pervasion, flood, infiltration, invasion 2 **filtration**, seepage, leakage, penetration, percolation

permissible adj **allowable**, allowed, permitted, acceptable, accepted Opposite: unacceptable

permission n **consent**, authorization, approval, agreement, acquiescence Opposite: embargo

permissive adj **tolerant**, lenient, liberal, accommodating, lax Opposite: strict

permit v **authorize**, allow, let, approve, consent to Opposite: forbid ■ n **licence**, document, certification, certificate, authorization

permitted adj **allowed**, allowable, permissible, acceptable, accepted Opposite: forbidden

permutation n **variation**, transformation, version, arrangement, rearrangement

pernicious adj 1 **malicious**, wicked, evil, malevolent, malign Opposite: benign 2 **destructive**, harmful, deadly, fatal, insidious Opposite: harmless

perniciousness n 1 **maliciousness**, malice, wickedness, evil, malevolence Opposite: benignity 2 **destructiveness**, harmfulness, deadliness, insidiousness, ruinousness Opposite: harmlessness

pernickety (infml) adj 1 **meticulous**, exacting, demanding, finicky, fussy Opposite: slapdash 2 **detailed**, exacting, painstaking, precise, finicky Opposite: straightforward

peroration (fml) n **speech**, oration, discourse, address, talk

peroxide n **hydrogen peroxide**, bleaching agent, bleach, tint ■ v **bleach**, tint, lighten, dye, colour

perpendicular adj **vertical**, at right angles, upright, bolt upright, erect Opposite: parallel

perpetrate v **commit**, carry out, do, be responsible for, be behind

perpetration n **commission**, enactment, transaction, action, responsibility

perpetrator n **culprit**, criminal, wrongdoer, guilty party, offender

perpetual adj **continuous**, everlasting, uninterrupted, lasting, unending Opposite: temporary

perpetuate v **continue**, preserve, prolong, carry on, spread Opposite: stop

perpetuation n **continuation**, continuance, preservation, prolongation, spread Opposite: ending

perpetuity n **eternity**, time without end, all time, infinity, permanence

perplex v **puzzle**, baffle, confuse, stun, mystify Opposite: enlighten

perplexed adj **puzzled**, baffled, confused, at a loss, stunned Opposite: comprehending

perplexing adj **puzzling**, baffling, confusing, mystifying, confounding Opposite: simple

perplexity n **puzzlement**, bafflement, confusion, bewilderment, mystification Opposite: comprehension

perquisite *(fml)* n **1 privilege**, gratuity, perk, bonus, benefit *Opposite*: disadvantage

persecute v **1 oppress**, hound, harass, maltreat, pursue *Opposite*: protect **2 pester**, harass, torment, bother, bait *Opposite*: leave alone

persecution n **1 oppression**, harassment, maltreatment, pursuit, discrimination *Opposite*: protection **2 harassment**, torment, annoyance, irritation, suffering

persecutor n **1 oppressor**, harasser, pursuer, bully, torturer *Opposite*: protector **2 pesterer**, harasser, tormentor, nuisance, baiter

perseverance n **persistence**, determination, resolve, resolution, doggedness

persevere v **persist**, continue, keep at, keep it up, keep on *Opposite*: give up

persevering adj **persistent**, determined, resolute, resolved, dogged *Opposite*: irresolute

persist v **1 persevere**, continue, keep at, keep it up, keep on *Opposite*: give up **2 continue**, endure, live on, stay, go on *Opposite*: fade away

persistence n **1 perseverance**, determination, tenacity, resolve, resolution **2 continuance**, continuation, endurance, permanence, preservation *Opposite*: transience

persistent adj **1 tenacious**, determined, obstinate, insistent, dogged *Opposite*: irresolute **2 continuing**, continual, continued, unrelenting, incessant *Opposite*: fleeting

person n **1 being**, human being, individual, creature, soul **2 body**, form, frame, figure **3** *(fml)* **appearance**, persona, personality, character, ego

persona n **1 character**, figure, person, role, part **2 identity**, role, guise, personality, character

personable adj **amiable**, friendly, pleasant, affable, agreeable *Opposite*: disagreeable

personage *(fml)* n **VIP**, celebrity, star, public figure, dignitary *Opposite*: nobody

personal adj **1 individual**, private, own, special, particular *Opposite*: public **2 offensive**, rude, derogatory, familiar, intrusive *Opposite*: complimentary

personal ad n **advertisement**, announcement, public notice, ad *(infml)*, advert *(infml)*

personal assistant n **PA**, secretary, assistant, administrative assistant, administrator

personal computer n **PC**, computer, terminal, laptop, notebook

personal effects n **belongings**, possessions, personal property, things, stuff

personality n **1 character**, nature, disposition, temperament, makeup **2 celebrity**, star, public figure, somebody, VIP *Opposite*: nobody

personalize v **1 initial**, monogram, mark, engrave, identify **2 customize**, individualize, differentiate, distinguish, specify *Opposite*: generalize

personally adv **1 for myself**, in my opinion, in my view, for my part, myself *Opposite*: generally **2 in person**, face to face, individually, myself, directly *Opposite*: indirectly

personal organizer n **1 diary**, planner, appointment book, address book, engagement book **2 hand-held computer**, electronic planner, palmtop, electronic organizer

personification n **epitome**, image, embodiment, incarnation, representation

personify v **1 epitomize**, embody, incarnate, exemplify, characterize **2 anthropomorphize**, humanize, personalize, give a human face, bring alive

personnel n **workers**, staff, employees, workforce, human resources

perspective n **1 viewpoint**, standpoint, outlook, view, perception **2 proportion**, scale, ratio, size, depth **3 vista**, view, prospect, scene, lookout

perspicacious adj **discerning**, perceptive, astute, insightful, wise *Opposite*: obtuse

perspicacity n **discernment**, perceptiveness, astuteness, shrewdness, clear-sightedness

perspiration n **sweat**, fluid, exudate, secretion, moisture

perspire v **sweat**, exude, ooze, swelter, drip

persuade v **1 encourage**, coax, influence, induce, motivate *Opposite*: dissuade **2 convince**, win over, sway, convert, bring round

persuasion n **1 persuading**, encouragement, coaxing, influence, urging **2 affiliation**, belief, order, denomination, faith

persuasive adj **convincing**, influential, winning, swaying, believable *Opposite*: unconvincing

persuasiveness n **persuasion**, influence, cogency, smoothness, eloquence

pert adj **lively**, flippant, impudent, perky, breezy

pertain to v **relate**, refer to, apply to, belong to, affect

pertinacious adj **resolute**, stubborn, obstinate, persistent, headstrong *Opposite*: malleable

pertinence n **relevance**, relatedness, appositeness, appropriateness, suitability *Opposite*: irrelevance

pertinent adj **relevant**, related, apposite, appropriate, germane *Opposite*: irrelevant

pertness n **cheekiness**, liveliness, flippancy, perkiness, breeziness

perturb v **trouble**, bother, disturb, worry, agitate

perturbation n **alarm**, worry, agitation, disquiet, trepidation *Opposite*: composure

perturbed adj **troubled**, disturbed, worried, anxious, disconcerted *Opposite*: composed

perusal n **examination**, scrutiny, inspection, checking, readthrough

peruse v **read**, examine, scan, pore over, scrutinize *Opposite*: skim

pervade v **permeate**, pass through, saturate, spread through, infuse

pervasive adj **extensive**, universal, general, inescapable, prevalent *Opposite*: localized

pervasiveness n **extensiveness**, universality, generality, ubiquity, ubiquitousness

perverse adj 1 **aberrant**, irrational, deviant, abnormal, unreasonable *Opposite*: obliging 2 **obstinate**, wilful, stubborn, headstrong, pertinacious *Opposite*: malleable

perverseness n 1 **aberrance**, irrationality, deviance, disobedience, unreasonableness 2 **wilfulness**, stubbornness, contrariness, recalcitrance *Opposite*: malleability

perversion n **distortion**, misinterpretation, twisting, corruption, misapplication

perversity n **obstinacy**, wilfulness, stubbornness, unreasonableness, contrariness *Opposite*: malleability

pervert v 1 **deprave**, corrupt, lead astray, spoil, warp 2 **distort**, misinterpret, twist, misrepresent, alter

perverted adj 1 **depraved**, corrupt, debauched, warped, degenerate 2 **distorted**, misinterpreted, twisted, garbled, changed *Opposite*: undistorted

pervious adj 1 **porous**, penetrable, absorbent, permeable *Opposite*: impervious 2 **receptive**, amenable, responsive, flexible, open *Opposite*: impervious

pessimism n **negativity**, cynicism, doubt, distrust, gloom *Opposite*: optimism

pessimist n **cynic**, doubter, worrier, nihilist, defeatist *Opposite*: optimist

pessimistic adj **negative**, cynical, doubtful, distrustful, gloomy *Opposite*: optimistic

pest n 1 **vermin**, bug, insect, fly, mosquito 2 (*infml*) **bother**, nuisance, annoyance, vexation, irritant

pester v **annoy**, harass, worry, beleaguer, disturb *Opposite*: delight

pestilence (*archaic*) n **plague**, epidemic, virus, disease, bubonic plague

pestilent adj 1 **infected**, plague-ridden, contaminated, polluted, bug-ridden *Opposite*: healthy 2 **deadly**, lethal, fatal, virulent, killer *Opposite*: mild

pet n 1 **animal**, domestic animal, domesticated animal, tame animal, companion 2 **favourite**, darling, treasure, jewel, idol 3 **dear**, love, precious, darling, dearest 4 **sulk**, huff, pique, temper, tantrum ■ adj **favourite**, special, cherished, indulged, preferred ■ v 1 **stroke**, pat, fondle, caress, nuzzle 2 **indulge**, pamper, cosset, mollycoddle, spoil

peter out v **disappear**, dwindle, fade, recede, decrease *Opposite*: grow

petite adj **small**, diminutive, short, little, tiny *Opposite*: big

petition n **request**, appeal, entreaty, requisition, application ■ v **appeal**, lobby, request, beg, plead

petitioner n **lobbyist**, activist, campaigner, requester, asker

pet name n **name**, nickname, sobriquet, diminutive, epithet

petrified adj 1 **frightened**, terrified, scared, alarmed, scared stiff *Opposite*: reassured 2 **fossilized**, hardened, solidified, fixed, calcified

petrify v 1 **frighten**, terrify, scare, alarm, fill with fear *Opposite*: reassure 2 **fossilize**, harden, solidify, ossify, fix

petrifying adj **frightening**, terrifying, horrifying, shocking, spine-chilling *Opposite*: reassuring

petrol station n **filling station**, garage, service station, gas station (*US*)

pettifogging adj **trivial**, petty, unimportant, minor, insignificant *Opposite*: important

pettiness n 1 **triviality**, unimportance, inconsequence, paltriness, irrelevance *Opposite*: importance 2 **petty-mindedness**, mean-mindedness, triviality, pettifoggery, narrow-mindedness 3 **spitefulness**, grudgingness, resentfulness, maliciousness, vindictiveness

pettish adj **peevish**, irritable, sulky, bad-tempered, petulant *Opposite*: even-tempered

petty adj 1 **trivial**, unimportant, inconsequential, insignificant, paltry *Opposite*: important 2 **petty-minded**, mean-minded, niggling, narrow-minded, trivial 3 **spiteful**, grudging, resentful, malicious, vindictive *Opposite*: generous

petty cash n **cash fund**, office fund, float, coffee fund (*US*)

petulance n **sulkiness**, crabbiness, peevishness, sullenness, moodiness *Opposite*: affability

petulant adj **sulky**, crabby, peevish, grumpy, sullen *Opposite*: affable

pew n **bench**, form, seat, bleacher (*US*)

phalanx n **group**, body, mass, unit, formation

phantasm n **ghost**, spirit, apparition, spectre, phantom

phantasmagoria n **image**, dream, hallucination, optical illusion, mirage

phantasmagoric adj **dreamlike**, bizarre, surreal, psychedelic, fantastical

phantasmagory *see* phantasmagoria

phantom n **ghost**, apparition, spirit, spectre, phantasm

Pharaoh n **ruler**, king, sovereign, monarch, emperor

pharmaceutical adj **medicinal**, medical, pharmacological, therapeutic, curative ■ n **drug**, medicine, medication, treatment, narcotic

pharmacist n **pharmacologist**, chemist, posologist, dispensing chemist, apothecary (*archaic*)

pharmacy *n* **chemist's**, dispensary, dispensing chemist's, apothecary *(archaic)*

phase *n* **stage**, point, chapter, time, segment

phenomenal *adj* **1 remarkable**, extraordinary, impressive, prodigious, outstanding *Opposite*: unremarkable **2** *(infml)* **fantastic**, wonderful, amazing, brilliant, sensational *Opposite*: moderate

phenomenon *n* **1 occurrence**, fact, experience, happening, incident **2 marvel**, wonder, singularity, miracle, spectacle **3 prodigy**, genius, bright star, enfant terrible, whiz kid *(infml)*

phial *n* **vial**, bottle, vessel, flask, flagon

philanderer *n* **flirt**, Casanova, adulterer, lady-killer, ladies' man

philanthropic *adj* **charitable**, benevolent, humanitarian, generous, big-hearted *Opposite*: misanthropic

philanthropist *n* **patron**, humanitarian, donor, sponsor, promoter *Opposite*: misanthropist

philanthropy *n* **charity**, compassion, humanity, patronage, generosity *Opposite*: misanthropy

philippic *n* **diatribe**, tirade, discourse, denunciation, insult

philistine *n* **barbarian**, boor, vulgarian *Opposite*: aesthete ■ *adj* **uncultured**, unsophisticated, uninformed, untutored, boorish *Opposite*: cultured

philistinism *n* **barbarism**, unsophistication, boorishness, ignorance

philosopher *n* **theorist**, thinker, logician, truth-seeker, academic *Opposite*: realist

philosophic *see* **philosophical**

philosophical *adj* **1 logical**, ethical, metaphysical, moral, theoretical **2 deep-thinking**, learned, thoughtful, studious, enlightened *Opposite*: shallow **3 calm**, resigned, restrained, stoical, patient *Opposite*: emotional

philosophize *v* **moralize**, speculate, theorize, pronounce, meditate

philosophy *n* **beliefs**, viewpoint, thinking, values, attitude

phlegm *n* **1 mucus**, catarrh, rheum **2 calmness**, composure, unflappability, self-possession, imperturbability *Opposite*: nervousness

phlegmatic *adj* **calm**, unemotional, composed, impassive, placid *Opposite*: nervous. *See* COMPARE AND CONTRAST *at* **impassive**.

phobia *n* **fear**, terror, dread, horror, fright

WORD BANK

❑ **types of phobia** acrophobia (fear of high places), agoraphobia (fear of public or open spaces), ailurophobia (fear of cats), arachnophobia (fear of spiders), claustrophobia (fear of confined or enclosed spaces), hydrophobia (fear of water), necrophobia (fear of death or dead bodies), nyctophobia (fear of night or darkness), photophobia (fear of light or lighted spaces), pyrophobia (fear of fire), technophobia (fear of new technology or computerization), zoophobia (fear of animals)

phobic *adj* **1 fearful**, scared, terrified, nervous, anxious *Opposite*: unconcerned **2 irrational**, neurotic, obsessed, disturbed, fixated *Opposite*: rational

phone *n* **telephone**, mobile phone, mobile, cell-phone, cellular phone ■ *v* **call**, ring, ring up, telephone, make a call

phoney *adj* **1 false**, fake, counterfeit, bogus, artificial *Opposite*: genuine **2 affected**, pretentious, insincere, deceptive, sham *Opposite*: sincere ■ *n* **fake**, impostor, hypocrite, fraud, sham

phony *see* **phoney**

photo *see* **photograph**

photocopy *n* **copy**, duplicate, reproduction, print ■ *v* **copy**, reproduce, make a copy of, run off, duplicate

photo finish *n* **close contest**, close thing, tie, neck-and-neck finish *(infml)*

photogenic *adj* **camera-friendly**, attractive, picturesque, appealing, good-looking

photograph *n* **picture**, snap, shot, snapshot, print ■ *v* **photo**, snap, shoot, get on film

photographer *n* **professional photographer**, press photographer, paparazzo, amateur photographer, photojournalist

photographic *adj* **1 pictorial**, graphic, picturesque, photogenic, camera-friendly **2 vivid**, clear, accurate, exact, detailed

photography *n* **cinematography**, filmmaking, picture making, shooting, camerawork

WORD BANK

❑ **parts of a camera** autofocus, diaphragm, exposure meter, film, filter, fisheye lens, flash, lens, lens cap, rangefinder, shutter, telephoto lens, viewfinder, zoom lens

❑ **types of photographic equipment** box camera, camera, cine camera, developer, disc camera, enlarger, headcam, microfiche, microfilm, pinhole camera, printer, projector, reflex camera, single-lens reflex, speed camera, tripod, twin-lens reflex

photojournalism *n* **photography**, news photography, reportage, camerawork, filmmaking

photo opportunity *n* **media event**, photo shoot, photo op, public-relations exercise, publicity event

photosensitive *adj* **light sensitive**, sensitive, reactive, light reactive, hypersensitive

phrasal *adj* **linguistic**, verbal, expressive, semantic, phraseological

phrase *n* **expression**, saying, idiom, axiom, slogan ■ *v* **express**, couch, put, say, put into words

phrase book *n* **glossary**, bilingual dictionary, foreign-language dictionary, dictionary, lexicon

phraseology *n* **phrasing**, wording, choice of words, word choice, terminology

phrasing *n* **wording**, turn of phrase, style, word choice, diction

physical adj 1 **bodily**, corporeal, animal, corporal, fleshly Opposite: mental 2 **substantial**, material, objective, natural, real Opposite: ethereal 3 **brute**, instinctive, visceral, instinctual, basic Opposite: refined

physical education n **sports**, gymnastics, games, exercise, aerobics

physically adv **bodily**, actually, in the flesh, really, materially Opposite: mentally

physician n **doctor**, medical doctor, doctor of medicine, general practitioner, GP

physics n **dynamics**, forces, physical processes, interactions, properties

physiognomy n **appearance**, face, features, characteristics, physical appearance

physiological adj **physical**, bodily, biological, functional

physiotherapy n **remedial exercise**, exercise, rehabilitation, physio (infml), physical therapy (US)

physique n **build**, body type, physical type, figure, form

piazza n **square**, forum, gathering place, village square, town square

picaresque adj **roguish**, mischievous, rascally, impish, villainous

pick v 1 **harvest**, gather, cut, collect, pluck 2 **select**, single out, choose, pick and choose, make a choice ■ n **best choice**, top choice, choice, cream of the crop, pick of the litter

picked adj **chosen**, selected, select, elect, hand-picked

picket n 1 **stake**, post, fence post, peg, rod 2 **striker**, protester, boycotter, blockader 3 **lookout**, sentinel, watch, sentry, guard ■ v 1 **protest**, strike, demonstrate, strike against, demonstrate at 2 **enclose**, fence, restrain, hedge in, pen in

pick holes in v **find fault with**, fault, criticize, attack, tear to shreds Opposite: praise

pickings n **earnings**, profits, takings, proceeds, spoils

pickle n 1 **chutney**, relish, pickled vegetables 2 (infml) **difficulty**, bind, predicament, plight, quandary ■ v **preserve**, marinate, cure, keep, conserve

---

WORD BANK

❏ **types of pickle** chutney, cornichon, gherkin, piccalilli, pickled cucumber, sweet pickle

---

pickled adj **preserved**, marinated, soused

pick-me-up (infml) n **refreshment**, stimulant, tonic, boost, lift

pick on v **tease**, make fun of, bully, harass, criticize

pick out v 1 **choose**, make a choice, select, pick, pull out 2 **identify**, distinguish, isolate, recognize, single out 3 **highlight**, outline, emphasize

pickpocket n **thief**, sneak thief, robber, bag-snatcher, crook (infml)

pick up v 1 **lift**, raise, hoist, raise up, elevate Opposite: put down 2 (infml) **improve**, recover, bounce back, buck up, change for the better Opposite: deteriorate 3 **give a ride to**, give a lift to, collect, come and get, call for Opposite: drop off (infml) 4 **learn**, understand, grasp, get the hang of, remember 5 **speed up**, accelerate, go faster, get better, improve Opposite: slow down 6 **restart**, take up again, continue, carry on, jump back in Opposite: drop

pick up on (infml) v **notice**, point out, focus on, single out, call attention to Opposite: miss

picky adj **fastidious**, fussy, hard to please, finicky, particular Opposite: easygoing

picnic n (infml) **nothing**, doddle (infml), walk-over (infml), cinch (infml), piece of cake (infml) ■ v **have a picnic**, eat al fresco, eat outside

pictograph n **symbol**, hieroglyph, primitive writing, character, drawing

pictographic adj **graphic**, symbolic, pictorial, illustrative, visual

pictorial adj **graphic**, symbolic, illustrative, pictographic, clear

picture n 1 **image**, depiction, portrait, representation, photograph 2 **film**, feature, flick (infml), movie (US), motion picture (US) 3 **embodiment**, epitome, perfect example, essence, personification ■ v 1 **imagine**, create in your mind, visualize, see, conceive of 2 **describe**, depict, illustrate, draw, show

picture book n **illustrated book**, children's book, story book, annual, coffee-table book

picture-postcard adj **picturesque**, attractive, pretty, chocolate-box, scenic Opposite: unattractive

picturesque adj 1 **attractive**, pretty, scenic, charming, chocolate-box Opposite: unattractive 2 **pictorial**, graphic, symbolic, pictographic, vivid

piddling (infml) adj **small**, petty, puny, paltry, trifling Opposite: enormous

pidgin n **lingua franca**, creole, patois, dialect, lingo (infml)

piebald adj **parti-coloured**, pied, skewbald, spotted, mottled Opposite: plain

piece n 1 **part**, fragment, bit, member, part of a set Opposite: whole 2 **bit**, portion, hunk, wedge, slice Opposite: whole 3 **example**, case, sample, instance, occurrence ■ v **patch**, mend, repair, restore, fix

piecemeal adv 1 **gradually**, by degrees, little by little, a little at a time, a bit at a time Opposite: together 2 **piece by piece**, bit by bit, one by one, separately, one at a time ■ adj **fragmentary**, disjointed, disconnected, disorganized, haphazard Opposite: cohesive

piece of cake (infml) n **doddle** (infml), child's play, nothing, breeze (infml), cinch (infml)

piece of music n **composition**, creation, tune, melody, work

piece of writing n **article**, essay, composition, report, discourse

piece out v **apportion**, mete out, share out, dispense, hand out

piece together v **1 work out**, reconstruct, restore, make sense of, rationalize **2 assemble**, join, fix, repair, mend *Opposite*: take apart

piecework n **freelance work**, part-time work, casual work, commission

piechart n **graph**, chart, diagram, illustration, figure

pied adj **multicoloured**, variegated, mottled, piebald, flecked *Opposite*: plain

pied-à-terre n **second home**, city apartment, holiday home, studio, town flat

pier n **dock**, wharf, berth, jetty, landing-stage

pierce v **1 bore into**, stab, impale, cut, penetrate **2 hurt**, sting, pain, wound, affront *Opposite*: heal

piercing adj **1 penetrating**, intense, sharp, loud, earsplitting *Opposite*: soothing **2 perceptive**, searching, shrewd, acute, keen *Opposite*: gentle **3 cold**, bitter, freezing, wintry, raw *Opposite*: mild

piety n **1 piousness**, devoutness, devotion, religiousness, virtue *Opposite*: impiety **2 sanctimoniousness**, moralizing, hypocrisy, smugness, self-righteousness

piffle *(infml)* n **nonsense**, garbage, rubbish, twaddle *(infml)*, bunkum *(infml) Opposite*: sense

piffling *(infml)* adj **trifling**, unimportant, trivial, insignificant, petty *Opposite*: important

pig *(infml)* n **1 glutton**, gourmand, greedy pig *(infml)*, guzzler *(infml)*, greedy guts *(infml)* **2 brute**, beast, monster, rat *(slang)*

pigeon *(infml)* n **easy target**, dupe, sitting duck *(infml)*, sucker *(infml)*, chump *(dated infml)*

pigeon-breasted adj **barrel-chested**, top-heavy, stout

pigeonhole n **1 cubbyhole**, compartment, box, shelf, slot **2 category**, class, slot, classification, compartment ▪ v **categorize**, class, classify, label, compartmentalize

piggish adj **1 greedy**, gluttonous, hoggish, self-indulgent *Opposite*: abstemious **2 stubborn**, uncooperative, obstructive, selfish, self-centred *Opposite*: considerate

piggy adj **greedy**, gluttonous, hoggish, self-indulgent, piggish *Opposite*: abstemious

piggyback adj **allied**, attached, associated, linked, added

piggy bank n **money box**, cash box, collecting box, savings box

piggy in the middle n **go-between**, pig in the middle, mediator, intermediary, negotiator

pigheaded adj **stubborn**, obstinate, mulish, dogged, single-minded *Opposite*: flexible

pigheadedness n **stubbornness**, obstinacy, mulishness, single-mindedness, intransigence *Opposite*: flexibility

pigment n **colour**, dye, stain, tint, colouring

pigmentation n **colouring**, coloration, skin-colour, pigment, colour

pig out *(infml)* v **gobble**, gorge, devour, eat, guzzle *(infml)*

pigsty n **untidy place**, mess, pit *(infml)*, tip *(infml)*, hole *(infml)*

pigswill n **slops**, pig food, scraps, mash, left-overs

pile n **1 mound**, mountain, quantity, mass, heap **2** *(infml)* **big money**, fortune, mint *(infml)*, packet *(infml)*, bomb *(infml)* **3 stake**, post, support, pillar, column **4 soft surface**, down, nap, fibre, fur ▪ v **heap**, load, stack, pile up, amass *Opposite*: scatter

pile up v **stack**, heap up, amass, mound, collect *Opposite*: scatter

pile-up *(infml)* n **crash**, car crash, collision, road accident, smash-up

pilfer v **steal**, rob, thieve, poach, take. *See* COMPARE AND CONTRAST *at* **steal**.

pilferer n **thief**, petty thief, sneak thief, robber, shoplifter

pilgrim n **hajji**, traveller, tourist, visitor, wayfarer *(literary)*

pilgrimage n **journey**, trip, visit, hajj, tour

pill n **tablet**, capsule, medication

pillage v **plunder**, sack, rob, loot, steal ▪ n **loot**, spoils, plunder, booty, prize

pillager n **plunderer**, robber, looter, raider, thief

pillar n **1 support**, column, post, prop, mast **2 rock**, mainstay, tower of strength, stalwart

pillar box n **postbox**, letterbox, mailbox *(US)*, maildrop *(US)*

pillbox n **1 box**, tin, container, étui **2 lookout post**, shelter, gun emplacement, gun shelter

pillory v **ridicule**, denounce, scorn, deride, humiliate *Opposite*: praise

pillow n **cushion**, support, pad, bolster, head rest ▪ v **protect**, support, prop up, hold up

pillowcase n **pillowslip**, slipcover, slipcase, bedding, slip

pilot v **guide**, conduct, control, navigate, lead ▪ adj **experimental**, trial, model, test, preliminary

pimple n **spot**, blemish, blackhead, boil, pustule

pimply adj **spotty**, blemished, acned *Opposite*: clear

pin n **1 brooch**, badge, stick pin **2** *(dated infml)* **iota**, tittle, pinch, bit, dash ▪ v **1 fasten**, attach, fix, secure **2 hold**, pin down, hold down, restrain, stick

pinafore n **apron**, overall, pinny *(infml)*

pinch v **1 squeeze**, nip, tweak, grasp, press **2** *(infml)* **steal**, take, make off with, pilfer, thieve ▪ n **touch**, dash, soupçon, bit, taste. *See* COMPARE AND CONTRAST *at* **steal**.

pinched adj **haggard**, gaunt, drawn, pale, thin

pinchpenny adj ungenerous, miserly, tight-fisted, mean, stingy (infml) Opposite: generous ■ n miser, skinflint, penny pincher (infml), scrooge (infml), meanie (infml)

pin down v 1 identify, determine, locate, pinpoint, isolate 2 hold down, restrain, trap, pinion, pin

pine v 1 long, yearn, ache, want, wish 2 waste away, fade, fade away, suffer, go downhill Opposite: thrive

pine cone n cone, fir cone, seed case

ping v sound, ring, ding, beep, tinkle

pinion v hold down, trap, restrain, pin down, immobilize

pink adj 1 flushed, red, rosy, glowing, blushing 2 undercooked, rare, underdone, raw

---

WORD BANK
❏ types of pink cerise, coral, fuchsia, raspberry, rose, salmon pink, shell pink, shocking pink

---

pin money n pocket money, spending money, allowance, change, small change

pinnacle n 1 summit, peak, height, top, apex Opposite: base 2 high point, peak, acme, zenith, apex Opposite: nadir

pinpoint v locate, identify, pin down, isolate, find

pinprick n hole, puncture, pinhole, perforation, prick

pins and needles n tingling, prickling, numbness

pint-size (infml) adj miniature, pocket-sized, pocket-size, little, minuscule

pioneer n innovator, inventor, forerunner, developer, creator ■ v lead the way, open up, forge, found, initiate

pioneering adj groundbreaking, revolutionary, cutting-edge, inventive, innovative

pious adj 1 devout, religious, virtuous, moral, spiritual Opposite: impious 2 self-righteous, sanctimonious, moralizing, hypocritical, smug

piousness n 1 piety, devoutness, devotion, religiousness, virtue Opposite: impiety 2 self-righteousness, sanctimoniousness, moralizing, hypocrisy, smugness

pip n 1 seed, fruit seed, stone, nut, kernel 2 spot, speck, blemish, dot, mark 3 peep, beep, bleep, ping, ding ■ v (infml) beat, defeat, pip to the post (infml)

pipe n tube, cylinder, channel, conduit, pipeline ■ v 1 supply, channel, convey, transmit, bring in 2 whistle, twitter, tweet, cheep, peep

pipe down (infml) v quiet down, keep it down, be quiet, hush, shut up (infml)

pipe dream n fantasy, aspiration, ambition, castle in the air, castle in Spain

pipeline n conduit, pipe, duct, channel, tube

pipe up v speak up, speak, make yourself heard, have your say, chip in (infml)

piping n 1 pipes, tubing, plumbing 2 edging, trimming, fringing ■ adj high-pitched, shrill, piercing, penetrating, high

piquancy n spiciness, tastiness, sharpness, tang, kick Opposite: blandness

piquant adj 1 spicy, tasty, sharp, hot, tangy Opposite: bland 2 stimulating, provocative, interesting, exciting 3 critical, biting, severe, sharp, harsh

pique n temper, resentment, annoyance, anger, ill will ■ v 1 irritate, annoy, upset, offend, bother 2 interest, intrigue, attract, stimulate, arouse Opposite: bore

piqued adj resentful, irritated, annoyed, upset, in high dudgeon

piratic adj freebooting, marauding, attacking, robbing, lawless

pirouette n spin, twirl, whirl, turn, revolution ■ v twirl, rotate, spin, turn, whirl

pit n 1 hole, ditch, well, crater, trench 2 coal mine, mine, quarry, colliery 3 dent, pock, indentation, hollow, depression 4 nadir, bottom, depths 5 (infml) untidy place, mess, dump (infml), hole (infml), pigsty (infml) ■ v set as rivals, set against, fight, oppose

pitch v 1 throw, hurl, lob, toss, fling Opposite: catch 2 erect, set up, fix, plant, put up 3 sway, move, teeter, fall, stumble 4 slope, slant, fall away, descend, dip 5 roll, lurch, plunge, rock, buck 6 propose, sell, throw, offer, deliver ■ n 1 playing field, area, terrain, field, arena 2 tone, highness, lowness, note

pitch-black adj black, inky, jet-black, black as night, dark Opposite: pale

pitch-dark adj unlit, pitch-black, dark, black, jet-black Opposite: light

pitched battle n argument, disagreement, fight, head-to-head, battle

pitcher n jug, decanter, carafe

pitchfork v 1 turn, lift, fork, toss 2 thrust, push, force, propel, drive

pitching adj rolling, lurching, plunging, rocking, bucking

piteous adj pathetic, pitiful, wretched, sad, pitiable Opposite: enviable

pitfall n drawback, snare, snag, danger, downside Opposite: advantage

pith n essence, crux, heart, nub, core

pithead n colliery, pit, coalmine, mineshaft, mine

pithiness n concision, terseness, brevity, succinctness, briefness Opposite: verbosity

pithy adj concise, terse, to the point, brief, succinct Opposite: long-winded

pitiable adj 1 contemptible, wretched, deplorable, disgraceful, miserable Opposite: admirable 2 pitiful, pathetic, unfortunate, sad, piteous Opposite: heartening

pitiful adj 1 disgraceful, deplorable, contemptible, abject, despicable Opposite: admirable 2 piteous, pathetic, pitiable,

unfortunate, sad *Opposite*: heartening
3 meagre, inadequate, derisory, small, paltry
Opposite: magnanimous

pitiless *adj* **merciless**, heartless, callous, hard,
unfeeling *Opposite*: compassionate

pitilessness *n* **mercilessness**, heartlessness,
callousness, ruthlessness, harshness *Opposite*: compassion

pit stop *n* **refuelling stop**, stop, break, servicing
stop, rest

pittance *n* **subsistence wage**, small change,
trifle, nothing, mite *Opposite*: fortune

pitted *adj* **potholed**, rutted, eroded, rough,
bumpy *Opposite*: smooth

pity *n* **1 sympathy**, compassion, mercy, mercifulness, kindliness *Opposite*: pitilessness
2 shame, disappointment, bad luck, tough
luck, letdown *Opposite*: luck ■ *v* **sympathize**,
commiserate, empathize, be there for somebody, show concern *Opposite*: blame

pitying *adj* **sympathetic**, understanding, compassionate, concerned, solicitous *Opposite*: unsympathetic

pivot *n* **hinge**, axle, axis, swivel, spindle ■
v **spin**, revolve, twist, rotate, whirl

pivotal *adj* **essential**, key, crucial, fundamental, critical *Opposite*: unimportant

pixie *n* **fairy**, elf, sprite, hobgoblin, Puck

pizzazz *(infml)* *n* **vitality**, spark, zest, style,
glamour *Opposite*: dullness

placard *n* **poster**, sign, board, advertisement,
notice

placate *v* **appease**, pacify, mollify, propitiate,
conciliate *Opposite*: enrage

placation *n* **appeasement**, pacification, mollification, conciliation, satisfaction

placatory *adj* **appeasing**, mollifying, conciliatory, calming, soothing *Opposite*: inflammatory

place *n* **1 space**, spot, position, point, area
2 location, spot, area, position, locality
3 home, house, residence, room, habitation **4 status**, rank, position, station, circumstance ■ *v* **1 assign**, hire, employ,
engage, retain *Opposite*: fire **2 position**, put,
set, lay, leave *Opposite*: jettison **3 consign**,
identify, file, locate, arrange

placebo *n* **dummy**, palliative, control, sample,
try-on *(infml)* *Opposite*: treatment

place mat *n* **table mat**, mat, cover, cloth,
coaster

placement *n* **1 siting**, positioning, location,
arrangement, situation **2 location**, settlement, assignment, situation, employment

place setting *n* **setting**, cover, place, tableware, cutlery

placid *adj* **calm**, equable, even-tempered,
imperturbable, easygoing *Opposite*: excitable

placidity *n* **calmness**, equability, serenity,
imperturbability, even-temperedness *Opposite*: excitability

plagiarism *n* **copy**, piracy, theft, bootlegging,
fraud

plagiarist *n* **copyist**, pirate, bootlegger, imitator, cheat *Opposite*: originator

plagiarize *v* **copy**, pirate, bootleg, steal, pass
off as your own *Opposite*: originate

plague *n* **1 epidemic**, disease, infection, pandemic, wave **2 curse**, affliction, scourge,
blight, visitation *Opposite*: blessing ■
v **1 afflict**, trouble, pursue, hound, harass
Opposite: bless **2 pester**, badger, bother,
harass, trouble *Opposite*: leave alone

plaid *adj* **checked**, chequered, tartan *Opposite*:
plain

plain *adj* **1 simple**, basic, unadorned, natural,
pure *Opposite*: elaborate **2 clear**, evident,
obvious, apparent, manifest *Opposite*:
obscure **3 blunt**, straightforward, direct,
frank, open *Opposite*: evasive **4 plain-featured**, ordinary, unattractive, unappealing,
homely *Opposite*: pretty ■ *n* **prairie**, savanna,
steppe, pampas. *See* COMPARE AND CONTRAST *at*
unattractive.

plain-clothes *adj* **undercover**, secret, disguised, out of uniform

plainly *adv* **1 simply**, normally, basically, naturally, purely *Opposite*: elaborately **2 clearly**,
evidently, obviously, apparently, palpably
Opposite: obscurely **3 bluntly**, straightforwardly, directly, frankly, openly *Opposite*: evasively

plainness *n* **1 simplicity**, ordinariness, naturalness, purity, bareness **2 clarity**, clearness,
palpability, tangibility, transparency *Opposite*: obscurity **3 bluntness**, straightforwardness, directness, frankness,
openness *Opposite*: evasiveness

plain-spoken *adj* **direct**, frank, blunt, forthright, bald *Opposite*: mealy-mouthed

plaint *n* **plea**, charge, accusation, complaint,
action *Opposite*: defence

plaintiff *n* **accuser**, applicant, complainant,
petitioner, litigant *Opposite*: defendant

plaintive *adj* **mournful**, lamenting, nostalgic,
sorrowful, wistful *Opposite*: cheerful

plait *v* **braid**, interweave, weave, intertwine,
crisscross *Opposite*: unravel

plan *n* **1 strategy**, scheme, project, plan of
action, tactic **2 idea**, proposal, plot, scheme,
aspiration **3 design**, diagram, layout, blueprint, outline ■ *v* **1 work out**, arrange, scheme,
plot, organize *Opposite*: improvise **2 intend**,
propose, mean, line up, schedule

plane *n* **aircraft**, aeroplane, crate *(dated infml)*,
airplane *(US)*

planet *n* **Earth**, world, globe

WORD BANK
❑ **types of planet** Earth, Jupiter, Mars, Mercury,
Neptune, Pluto, Saturn, Uranus, Venus

planned *adj* **deliberate**, intentional, prearranged, strategic, premeditated *Opposite*:
unplanned

planner n 1 **town planner**, organizer, developer, city planner, designer 2 **diary**, calendar, appointment book, wall chart, planning aid

planning n **preparation**, setting up, development, arrangement, scheduling

plant n 1 **shrub**, bush, flower, herb, pot plant 2 **factory**, works, installation, industrial unit, manufacturing plant 3 (infml) **spy**, informant, infiltrator, secret agent, mole ■ v 1 **sow**, seed, scatter, root, transplant 2 **place**, fix, stand, transplant, deposit 3 **introduce**, lodge, establish, implant, fix Opposite: erase 4 (infml) **conceal**, hide, bury

plantation n **estate**, farm, homestead, farmstead, manor

planter n **pot**, flower pot, container, window box, urn

plaque n **sign**, panel, commemoration, inscription, plate

plaster n **sticking plaster**, covering, dressing, bandage, adhesive bandage (US) ■ v **surface**, coat, cover, face, plaster over

plasterwork n **plaster**, stuccowork, stucco, pargeting, moulding

plastic adj 1 **malleable**, soft, pliable, elastic, flexible Opposite: hard 2 **artificial**, fake, synthetic, false, forced Opposite: genuine

WORD BANK
❏ **types of plastic** acetate, celluloid, epoxide, latex, melamine, neoprene, polystyrene, polythene, polyurethane, PVC, vinyl

plasticity n **malleability**, softness, pliability, elasticity, flexibility Opposite: hardness

plate n 1 **dish**, platter, salver, serving dish, bowl 2 **number plate**, registration, license plate (US) ■ v **cover**, coat, overlay, protect, shield

plateau n 1 **upland**, highland, hill, mesa, tableland 2 **level**, stage, period, phase

plated adj **coated**, overlaid, gold-plated, covered, finished Opposite: solid

platform n 1 **stage**, display place, raised area, podium, stand 2 **policy**, proposal, manifesto, programme

plating n 1 **electroplating**, silver-plating, gilding, coating, lustre 2 **armour**, armour plate, cladding, metal casing, outer casing Opposite: core

platitude n 1 **cliché**, inanity, tired expression, commonplace, banality 2 **dullness**, boredom, insipidity, triteness, plainness

platitudinous adj **clichéd**, trite, banal, corny, hackneyed Opposite: original

platonic adj **spiritual**, companionable, friendly, nonsexual, nonphysical

platoon n **squad**, legion, team, detachment, subdivision

platter n **plate**, serving dish, salver, dish, tray

plaudit n **applause**, approval, praise, positive feedback, appreciation Opposite: criticism

plausibility n **believability**, credibility, reasonableness, probability, conceivability Opposite: implausibility

plausible adj **believable**, credible, reasonable, probable, conceivable Opposite: implausible

play v **enjoy yourself**, occupy yourself, amuse yourself, have fun, frolic 2 **joke**, tease, fool around, fool about, mess about (infml) 3 **participate**, take part, join in, compete, engage in 4 **perform**, act, play-act, portray, star as ■ n 1 **recreation**, amusement, fun, diversion, games Opposite: work 2 **production**, drama, show, piece, performance

play-act (infml) v **pretend**, ham it up, put it on, put on an act, play to the gallery

playback n **replay**, rerun, reshowing, repetition, reproduction Opposite: recording

play down v **minimize**, make light of, underplay, underestimate, make little of Opposite: accentuate

player n 1 **participant**, team member, competitor, contestant 2 **actor**, thespian, performer, entertainer, play-actor

playfellow (archaic) n **friend**, playmate, mate, chum (infml), pal (infml) Opposite: enemy

playful adj 1 **lively**, bouncy, full of fun, full of life, frisky Opposite: subdued 2 **good-humoured**, lighthearted, good-natured, teasing, jokey Opposite: serious

playfulness n 1 **liveliness**, bounce, bounciness, friskiness, spirit 2 **good humour**, lightheartedness, teasing, mischief, impishness Opposite: seriousness

play games with v **deceive**, trick, confuse, mistreat, abuse

playgoer n **theatre buff**, theatregoer, spectator, punter (slang)

playground n 1 **park**, play area, community playground, adventure playground, outdoor play area (US) 2 **school yard**, school grounds, play area, recreation area, concourse Opposite: classroom

play hooky (infml) v **play truant**, truant, skip classes, miss school, absent yourself Opposite: attend

playhouse n 1 **theatre**, auditorium, studio, venue 2 **Wendy house**, tree house, den

playing field n **sports ground**, sports field, pitch, park, ground

playmate n **friend**, mate, pal (infml), chum (infml), playfellow (archaic) Opposite: enemy

play off v **oppose**, set against, pit against, go against, challenge

play-off n **final**, final round, semifinal, quarterfinal, tiebreaker

play safe v **take no risks**, hedge your bets, take care, be cautious, be careful Opposite: gamble

playschool n **playgroup**, nursery, preschool, kindergarten (US)

play the game v **toe the line**, follow the rules,

conform, comply, obey *Opposite*: act up

plaything *n* **toy**, doll, bauble, curio, knick-knack

playtime *n* **break**, interval, free time, leisure time, lunchtime

play to the gallery *v* **show off**, play up, posture, perform, play to the crowd

play up *v* 1 **exaggerate**, emphasize, embellish, highlight, draw attention to *Opposite*: play down 2 **misbehave**, act up, malfunction, go wrong *Opposite*: behave

play up to *v* **flatter**, toady, ingratiate yourself with, win the favour of, butter up *(infml)*

playwright *n* **dramatist**, writer, author, tragedian, dramaturge

play your cards close to your chest *v* be **secretive**, be a dark horse, keep quiet, keep secret, keep under wraps

plaza *n* **square**, piazza, marketplace, court, mall *(US)*

plea *n* 1 **appeal**, entreaty, prayer, request, petition *Opposite*: demand 2 **statement**, claim, defence, declaration, assertion *Opposite*: denial 3 **excuse**, pretext, reason, explanation, alibi

plea-bargain *v* **plead guilty**, do a deal, negotiate, come to an agreement, contract

plead *v* 1 **beg**, appeal, pray, entreat, request *Opposite*: demand 2 **declare**, assert, claim, state, put forward 3 **support**, defend, argue, contend, vindicate

pleading *adj* **begging**, piteous, persuasive, suppliant *(fml)*, imploring *(fml)*

pleasant *adj* 1 **enjoyable**, agreeable, pleasing, lovely, nice *Opposite*: unpleasant 2 **amiable**, friendly, congenial, likable, genial *Opposite*: nasty

pleasantness *n* 1 **appeal**, loveliness, niceness, pleasurableness, satisfaction *Opposite*: unpleasantness 2 **amiability**, friendliness, congeniality, likability, likableness *Opposite*: nastiness

pleasantries *n* **small talk**, chat, gossip, banter, conversation

pleasantry *n* **remark**, civility, banality, politeness, observation *Opposite*: insult

please *v* 1 **satisfy**, gratify, make happy, delight, thrill *Opposite*: displease 2 **like**, prefer, choose, desire, wish *Opposite*: dislike

pleased *adj* **satisfied**, happy, content, delighted, contented *Opposite*: displeased

pleasing *adj* **agreeable**, pleasant, enjoyable, lovely, nice *Opposite*: disagreeable

pleasurable *adj* **agreeable**, enjoyable, pleasing, pleasant, gratifying *Opposite*: disagreeable

pleasure *n* 1 **enjoyment**, happiness, delight, bliss, contentment *Opposite*: displeasure 2 **gratification**, indulgence, hedonism, decadence, sensuality 3 **amusement**, recreation, fun, leisure, diversion *Opposite*: work

pleat *n* **crease**, fold, tuck, gather, crimp ■ *v* **fold**, crease, tuck, gather, crimp

plebiscite *n* **referendum**, poll, vote, ballot, opinion poll

pledge *n* 1 **vow**, oath, promise, assurance, guarantee 2 **security**, deposit, guarantee, warranty, collateral ■ *v* **promise**, vow, swear, guarantee, give your word

plenary *adj (fml)* **full**, complete, entire, whole, unlimited ■ *n* **meeting**, session, general assembly, plenary meeting, plenary session

plenipotentiary *adj* **presiding**, all-powerful, in charge, officiating, supreme *Opposite*: powerless ■ *n* **minister**, minister plenipotentiary, ambassador, special envoy, envoy *Opposite*: pawn

plenteous *(literary) see* **plentiful**

plentiful *adj* **abundant**, copious, overflowing, ample, lavish *Opposite*: scarce

plenty *n* **prosperity**, abundance, copiousness, profusion, plethora *Opposite*: insufficiency ■ *adj (infml)* **ample**, a lot, lots, a load, sufficient *Opposite*: inadequate

plenum *n* **general assembly**, meeting, session, plenary meeting, plenary session

plethora *n* **overabundance**, excess, surfeit, glut, surplus *Opposite*: shortage

pliability *n* 1 **flexibility**, bendability, pliancy, softness *Opposite*: rigidity 2 **compliance**, pliancy, adaptability, flexibility, obedience *Opposite*: inflexibility

pliable *adj* 1 **flexible**, bendable, workable, pliant, plastic *Opposite*: rigid 2 **compliant**, pliant, docile, flexible, yielding *Opposite*: inflexible

COMPARE AND CONTRAST CORE MEANING: able to be bent or moulded

pliable flexible and easily bent or moulded; **ductile** describes metals that can be easily drawn out into a long continuous wire or hammered into thin sheets; **malleable** describes metals that can be hammered or pressed into various shapes without breaking or cracking; **elastic** describes substances or materials that can be stretched without breaking and then return to their original shape; **pliant** supple and springy and therefore easily bent.

pliancy *n* 1 **pliability**, flexibility, suppleness, elasticity, plasticity *Opposite*: stiffness 2 **compliance**, pliability, adaptability, flexibility, obedience *Opposite*: obstinacy

pliant *adj* 1 **supple**, springy, bendy, pliable, flexible *Opposite*: stiff 2 **compliant**, pliable, adaptable, flexible, accommodating *Opposite*: inflexible. *See* COMPARE AND CONTRAST *at* **pliable**.

plight *n* **dilemma**, trouble, predicament, difficulty, quandary

plinth *n* **pedestal**, platform, base, stand, support

plod *v* **trudge**, slog, tread, lumber, tramp *Opposite*: race

plodder n snail, toiler, slogger, idler, slow-coach (infml) Opposite: high-flier

plodding adj slow, dull, slow but sure, ponderous, tedious Opposite: rapid

plonk v place, put, put down, set down, dump ■ n (infml) wine, house wine, vin de table, vino (infml)

plop v place, put, put down, set down, plonk

plop down v flop down, sit down heavily, collapse, subside, plonk down

plot n 1 conspiracy, plan, scheme, subversion, strategy 2 story line, action, scenario, outline, narrative 3 area, section, parcel, piece, lot ■ v 1 plan, scheme, strategize, conspire, design 2 chart, map, draw, mark, map out

plotter n schemer, conspirator, conniver, contriver, strategist

plough v cultivate, till, turn over, work

plough into v crash into, bang into, drive into, run into, career into

plough on v keep at it, struggle on, persevere, plug away (infml), keep your nose to the grindstone

plough through v keep at, struggle through, plough on with, persevere, persist

plough under v bury, cover, cover over, turn over Opposite: dig up

ploy n trick, manoeuvre, strategy, plan, ruse

pluck v 1 pull, tug, pick at, grasp, take 2 pull out, remove, yank, tweak, uproot 3 pick, collect, gather, harvest 4 strum, play, twang, plunk, pick ■ n courage, determination, bravery, fortitude, nerve Opposite: cowardice. See COMPARE AND CONTRAST at courage.

pluckiness n bravery, courage, pluck, fearlessness, boldness Opposite: cowardice

pluck up courage v dare, take the plunge, brace yourself, take a deep breath, steel yourself Opposite: lose your nerve

plucky adj brave, courageous, fearless, bold, audacious Opposite: cowardly

plug n 1 stopper, cork, cap, bung, top 2 (infml) socket, outlet, power point, wall outlet, point 3 (infml) advertisement, recommendation, mention, puff, advert 4 sample, core, piece, wedge, extract 5 wad, mass, lump, wadding, padding ■ v 1 (infml) work, carry on, keep at it, keep going, persevere 2 (infml) puff, hype, sell, push, spin Opposite: run down 3 stop, cap, bung, cork, seal Opposite: unplug

plugged-in (infml) adj informed, involved, connected, in tune, in touch

plughole n outlet, bunghole, drain, hole

plug in v connect, link up, hook up (infml) Opposite: unplug

plum (infml) n reward, award, bonus, windfall, trophy ■ adj desirable, choice, covetable, prestigious, profitable

plumage n feathers, down, fluff, fuzz

plumb adv (infml) exactly, precisely, right, bang, slap (infml) ■ adj perpendicular, upright, vertical, true, aligned Opposite: horizontal ■ v 1 comprehend, understand, fathom, grasp, know 2 experience, undergo, face, suffer, go through

plumbing n drains, sanitation, drainage system, water system, heating system

plume n trail, cloud, spiral, column, curl

plummet v plunge, drop, dive, tumble, crash Opposite: climb

plummy adj 1 resonant, mellow, rich, sonorous Opposite: reedy 2 upper-class, public-school, patrician, affected, posh (infml) Opposite: common

plump adj fat, overweight, chubby, stout, fleshy Opposite: slender ■ v flop down, drop, plop down, flop, fall Opposite: stand up

plump for v choose, decide on, opt for, take, settle on

plumpness n fatness, chubbiness, fleshiness, curviness, obesity Opposite: slenderness

plump up v fatten, shake up, plump, fluff up

plunder v steal, rob, loot, pillage, raid ■ n stolen goods, loot, booty, spoils, ill-gotten gains

plunge v 1 thrust, force, throw, push, pitch 2 rush, jump, leap, lurch, throw yourself Opposite: hesitate 3 drop, dive, plummet, sink, nose-dive Opposite: soar ■ n dive, drop, plummet, nosedive, fall Opposite: climb

plunging adj 1 plummeting, dipping, dropping, tumbling, reducing Opposite: rising 2 low, low-cut, revealing, décolleté Opposite: high

plunk v twang, strum, plonk, play, pick

pluralism n variety, diversity, multiplicity, heterogeneity Opposite: homogeneity

pluralistic adj varied, mixed, diverse, multicultural, multiethnic Opposite: homogeneous

plurality n number, range, variety, multiplicity, multitude Opposite: single

plus prep in addition to, added to, as well as, along with, together with Opposite: minus ■ adj 1 desirable, positive, advantageous, favourable, good Opposite: minus 2 and above, and over, and more ■ n (infml) advantage, bonus, benefit, boon, plus point (infml) Opposite: minus

plush (infml) adj lush, luxurious, expensive, rich, lavish

plutocrat n tycoon, magnate, mogul, big shot (infml)

ply v 1 work, practise, pursue, carry out, wage 2 use, work with, apply, utilize, employ 3 supply, pile, load, provide, furnish (fml) 4 badger, hound, harass, overwhelm, bombard ■ n layer, thickness, strand, tier

p.m. adj afternoon, after lunch, evening, night Opposite: a.m.

pneumatic adj air-filled, inflated, inflatable, air Opposite: solid

poach v **1 steal**, thieve, rustle, pilfer, plunder **2 simmer**, boil, steam, braise

poacher n **thief**, rustler, robber, pilferer

pocked adj **pitted**, pockmarked, dented, cratered, scarred Opposite: unblemished

pocket n **pouch**, compartment, receptacle, sack, bag ■ v **help yourself to**, steal, appropriate, take, snaffle (infml) ■ adj **concise**, abridged, reduced, short, small

pocket money n **spending money**, pin money, expenses, extra cash, personal money

pocket-size see pocket-sized

pocket-sized adj **little**, small, handy, compact, portable Opposite: bulky

pockmark n **blemish**, scar, indentation, hollow, blotch

pockmarked adj **pitted**, pocked, dented, cratered, scarred Opposite: unblemished

pod n **shell**, husk, peapod, case, hull

podgy adj **fat**, overweight, chubby, stout, fleshy Opposite: slim

podium n **dais**, platform, stage, plinth

poem n **verse**, rhyme, ode, sonnet, elegy Opposite: prose

poet n **writer**, lyricist, rhymester, versifier, composer

poetic adj **1 lyrical**, elegiac, graceful, rhythmical, flowing Opposite: prosaic **2 sensitive**, full of feeling, profound, deep, moving Opposite: insensitive

poeticality n **lyricism**, expressivity, eloquence

poetry n **verse**, rhyme, poems, rhymes, lyrics Opposite: prose

po-faced adj **disapproving**, solemn, serious, strait-laced, humourless Opposite: jovial

pogrom n **persecution**, extermination, massacre, devastation, slaughter

poignance see poignancy

poignancy n **pathos**, sadness, tragedy, nostalgia, tenderness

poignant adj **moving**, emotional, touching, distressing, sad Opposite: unemotional. See COMPARE AND CONTRAST at **moving**.

point n **1 opinion**, fact, idea, argument, theme **2 instant**, time, stage, moment, juncture (fml) **3 aim**, meaning, central theme, intention, heart **4 purpose**, advantage, use, sense, object **5 argument**, statement, line of reasoning, thrust, viewpoint **6 detail**, item, feature, aspect, thing **7 position**, spot, place, situation, site **8 tip**, end, top, summit, peak **9 headland**, cape, promontory, spit, peninsula **10 socket**, power point, plug, contact, outlet ■ v **direct**, aim, face, indicate, draw attention to

point-blank adv **1 at close range**, straight on, dead on, close up, close to **2 frankly**, bluntly, outright, directly, directly Opposite: indirectly

pointed adj **1 sharp**, piercing, keen, pointy, jagged Opposite: blunt **2 barbed**, critical,

meaningful, incisive, sharp Opposite: mild

pointedly adv **deliberately**, purposely, intentionally, meaningfully, openly Opposite: subtly

pointer n **1 cane**, baton, stick, pole **2 needle**, indicator, hand, cursor **3 tip**, advice, hint, suggestion, warning

pointing n **mortar**, cement, grout, filling

pointless adj **useless**, futile, senseless, meaningless, worthless Opposite: useful

pointlessness n **uselessness**, futility, senselessness, meaninglessness, worthlessness Opposite: usefulness

point of view n **opinion**, attitude, standpoint, viewpoint, position

point out v **1 indicate**, show, reveal, point at, identify **2 call attention to**, draw attention to, highlight, indicate, mention Opposite: hide

point-to-point n **steeplechase**, horse race, equestrian event, cross-country racing (US)

point up v **emphasize**, draw attention to, underline, make clear, show

poise n **1 composure**, dignity, self-assurance, self-confidence, self-control Opposite: insecurity **2 grace**, bearing, deportment, good posture, composure Opposite: clumsiness ■ v **hover**, balance, float, perch, hang

poised adj **1 ready**, prepared, primed, in position, in place Opposite: unprepared **2 balanced**, suspended, hovering, on the edge, on the brink **3 composed**, dignified, self-assured, self-confident, controlled Opposite: insecure

poison n **venom**, toxin, contagion, toxic substance Opposite: antidote ■ v **1 kill**, murder, exterminate, destroy, harm **2 pollute**, taint, corrupt, contaminate, adulterate

poisoner n **murderer**, killer, exterminator, assassin, slaughterer

poisonous adj **1 toxic**, venomous, noxious, fatal, lethal Opposite: harmless **2 malicious**, evil, wicked, nasty, spiteful Opposite: kindly

poke v **1 jab**, stab, push, prod, thrust **2 protrude**, stick out, project, jut, extend **3 search through**, look through, root, browse, rummage ■ n **stab**, jab, push, prod, thrust

poke fun at v **make fun of**, ridicule, tease, mock, laugh at

poker-faced adj **expressionless**, blank, impassive, emotionless, deadpan Opposite: expressive

poky (infml) adj **small**, tiny, cramped, restricted, tight Opposite: spacious

polar adj **glacial**, Arctic, Antarctic Opposite: tropical

polarity n **division**, split, schism, divergence, polarization Opposite: convergence

polarization n **divergence**, separation, division, opposition, schism Opposite: union

polarize v **diverge**, split, drive apart, separate, create a rift in Opposite: unite

pole n 1 opposite, extreme, extremity, limit, end 2 rod, shaft, stick, post, dowel ■ v push, propel, raft, punt, shove

poleaxe v astonish, amaze, stupefy, stun, shock

polemic n argument, plea, diatribe, speech, discourse ■ adj controversial, outspoken, impassioned, uncompromising, bold Opposite: dispassionate

polemicist n debater, orator, speaker, essayist, lecturer

pole position n prime position, lead, front, advantage, catbird seat (US infml) Opposite: rear

pole-vault v jump, vault, leap, bound

police n police force, force, constabulary, law, crime squad ■ v regulate, control, keep watch over, monitor, patrol

policeman see police officer

police officer n officer, police constable, PC, copper (dated infml), bobby (dated infml)

policewoman see police officer

policy n 1 course of action, rule, strategy, plan, guiding principle 2 contract, document, certificate, statement, papers

polish v 1 shine, buff, buff up, rub, clean Opposite: tarnish 2 improve, enhance, refine, perfect, hone ■ n 1 shine, lustre, gleam, sheen, brilliance Opposite: dullness 2 refinement, skill, control, sophistication, grace

polished adj 1 refined, elegant, cultured, sophisticated, graceful Opposite: coarse 2 practised, skilful, accomplished, professional, impeccable Opposite: amateur 3 smooth, shiny, gleaming, glossy, slippery Opposite: dull

polish off v finish, finish off, dispose of, complete, eliminate Opposite: leave

polish up v 1 shine, buff, rub, clean, dust Opposite: tarnish 2 refine, improve, practise, brush up, work on Opposite: let go

polite adj 1 well-mannered, good-mannered, civil, well-bred, gracious Opposite: rude 2 refined, cultured, sophisticated, polished, elegant Opposite: coarse

politeness n good manners, graciousness, manners, civility, breeding Opposite: rudeness

politic adj tactful, diplomatic, prudent, wise, expedient Opposite: foolish

political adj 1 governmental, administrative, electoral, civil, diplomatic 2 party-political, politically aware, radical, partisan, dogmatic

political correctness n appropriateness, sensitivity, awareness, tactfulness, inclusiveness Opposite: insensitivity

politically correct adj inclusive, sensitive, tactful, inoffensive, appropriate Opposite: politically incorrect

politically incorrect adj exclusive, insensitive, inappropriate, unaware, tactless Opposite: politically correct

politician n political figure, representative, candidate, official, legislator

politicization n awareness raising, consciousness raising, lobbying

politicize v raise awareness of, put on the agenda, debate, discuss, air Opposite: depoliticize

politicking n campaigning, speechmaking, lobbying, politics, scheming

politics n 1 government, political affairs, affairs of state, policy, policymaking 2 beliefs, principles, opinions, views, theory

polity n political entity, organization, institution, state, society

poll n election, census, survey, opinion poll, sample ■ v sample, survey, question, ask, interview

pollinate v fertilize, cross-fertilize, self-fertilize, cross-pollinate, self-pollinate

pollination n fertilization, cross-fertilization, self-fertilization, cross-pollination, self-pollination

polling n voting, casting your vote, balloting, going to the polls

polling booth n cubicle, voting booth, booth, stall, box

pollutant n contaminant, impurity, toxin, poison, waste product

pollute v 1 contaminate, poison, adulterate, infest, infect Opposite: clean 2 corrupt, pervert, demoralize, violate, damage Opposite: purify

polluted adj contaminated, dirty, poisoned, adulterated, unclean Opposite: clean

polluter n contaminator, dumper, poisoner, emitter, fly-tipper Opposite: environmentalist

pollution n 1 contamination, infection, adulteration, corruption 2 contaminant, toxic waste, effluence, greenhouse gasses, smog

poltergeist n ghost, spirit, manifestation, apparition, spectre

polyglot n linguist, multilingual person, bilingual person

polygonal adj many-sided, multilateral, triangular, quadrilateral, pentagonal

polygraph n detector, lie detector, recorder, tester

polymath n fount of knowledge, Renaissance man, Renaissance woman, walking encyclopedia, mine of information Opposite: specialist

polyp n growth, tumour, cyst, nodule, swelling

polysyllabic adj long, compound, complex, multisyllabic Opposite: monosyllabic

polysyllable n long word, compound, complex word Opposite: monosyllable

polytechnic n **college**, technical college, university, tech (infml), poly (infml)

polytheism n **dualism**, animism, pantheism Opposite: monotheism

pomp n **splendour**, spectacle, display, ceremony, show Opposite: understatement

pompom n **bobble**, tassel, powder puff, decoration, detail

pomposity n **self-importance**, arrogance, pretentiousness, pretension, snobbishness Opposite: modesty

pompous adj **1 self-important**, arrogant, pretentious, snobbish, affected Opposite: modest **2 showy**, flaunting, spectacular, magnificent, grand Opposite: modest

pompousness see pomposity

poncho n **cloak**, cape, wrap

pond n **pool**, tarn, fishpond, millpond, mere (literary)

ponder v **consider**, think about, contemplate, deliberate, wonder about

ponderable adj **appreciable**, significant, considerable, substantial, weighty Opposite: insignificant

ponderous adj **1 heavy**, laborious, lumbering, weighty, unwieldy Opposite: light **2 tedious**, boring, laborious, tiresome, dull Opposite: lively

pong (infml) n **stink**, smell, whiff (infml), niff (slang), reek ■ v **smell**, stink, whiff (infml), niff (slang), reek

pongy (infml) adj **smelly**, stinky (infml), whiffy (infml), niffy (slang), cheesy Opposite: fragrant

pontiff n **pope**, bishop of Rome, Holy Father

pontifical adj **1 episcopal**, papal, prelatic **2 pompous**, self-important, pontificating, grandiose, portentous Opposite: humble

pontificate v **hold forth**, preach, go on, sound off

pontoon n **platform**, float, buoy, support, base

pony-trekking n **hacking**, horse-riding, riding, riding out, equitation (fml)

pooch (infml) n **dog**, lapdog, canine companion, canine, hound

pooh-pooh v **reject**, dismiss, spurn, scorn, scoff at Opposite: praise

pool n **1 pond**, puddle, lake, swimming pool, tarn **2 team**, band, collection, consortium, collective **3 kitty**, fund, pot (US infml) ■ v **share**, combine, bring together, put together, assemble Opposite: ration out

pooped (infml) adj **exhausted**, tired out, worn out, drained, ready to drop Opposite: invigorated

poor adj **1 destitute**, needy, poverty-stricken, impoverished, penniless Opposite: rich **2 deprived**, unfortunate, underprivileged, meagre, reduced Opposite: privileged **3 weak**, inadequate, feeble, meagre, bad Opposite: superior **4 humble**, lowly, modest, insignificant Opposite: noble

poorly adv **badly**, inadequately, weakly, feebly, scantily Opposite: well ■ adj **ill**, unwell, under the weather, sick, out of sorts Opposite: healthy

poorness n **1 poverty**, impoverishment, destitution, pennilessness, neediness Opposite: wealth **2 weakness**, inadequacy, feebleness, inferiority, poor quality Opposite: superiority

poor quality n **cheapness**, tawdriness, mediocrity, inferiority, weakness Opposite: quality

poor-quality adj **cheap**, shoddy, trashy, second-class, second-rate Opposite: first-rate

pop n **explosion**, bang, crack, report, snap ■ v **1 explode**, burst, go off, crack **2** (infml) **dash**, dart, go, call, nip (infml) **3** (infml) **put**, place, insert, drop, shove ■ adj (infml) **popular**, modern, current, accessible, easy

pope n **pontiff**, bishop of Rome, Holy Father

popeyed adj **goggle-eyed**, swollen-eyed, wide-eyed, bug-eyed (infml)

pop in (infml) v **visit**, go, stop at, look in, call in

poppet (infml) n **dear**, love, lovey (infml), darling, sweetie (infml)

poppycock (dated infml) n **nonsense**, absurdity, untruth, rubbish, twaddle (infml)

populace n **public**, population, general public, common people, lay people

popular adj **1 well-liked**, accepted, admired, in style, all the rage Opposite: unpopular **2 common**, general, prevalent, widely held, current Opposite: rare

popularity n **admiration**, approval, acceptance, fame, status Opposite: infamy

popularization n **1 promotion**, spread, commercialization, propagation, universalization **2 simplification**, vulgarization, interpretation, explanation, universalization

popularize v **1 make popular**, promote, spread, propagate, commercialize **2 simplify**, interpret, vulgarize, put in layperson's terms, explain

popularly adv **generally**, commonly, prevalently, readily, widely

populate v **inhabit**, people, settle, colonize, fill Opposite: desert

population n **inhabitants**, populace, people, residents

populist adj **mainstream**, majority, democratic, general, accessible Opposite: elitist

populous adj **crowded**, overcrowded, populated, full of people, packed Opposite: desolate

pop-up adj **spring-operated**, automatic, self-opening, folding, foldaway

porcine adj **piggy**, piggish, swinish, hoglike

pore n **hole**, opening, aperture, stoma

pore over v **examine**, scour, read, study, go over

porous *adj* **absorbent**, permeable, leaky, spongy *Opposite*: impermeable

porridge *n* **breakfast cereal**, gruel, oatmeal, oats

port *n* **seaport**, anchorage, dock, harbour, haven *(literary)*

portability *n* **movability**, transportability, transferability, lightness, compactness *Opposite*: bulkiness

portable *adj* **movable**, transportable, transferable, handy, convenient *Opposite*: fixed

portcullis *n* **gate**, door, grating, drawbridge, entry

portend *v* **foreshadow**, foretell, signify, mean, warn of

portent *n* **1 omen**, sign, presage, warning, indication **2** *(fml)* **marvel**, phenomenon, prodigy, wonder, miracle

portentous *adj* **1 significant**, important, crucial, ominous, fateful *Opposite*: trivial **2 pompous**, pretentious, self-important, haughty, arrogant *Opposite*: modest

porter *n* **gatekeeper**, doorkeeper, concierge, janitor, receptionist

portfolio *n* **1** *(fml)* **range**, collection, selection, group, set **2 case**, folder, file, wallet

portico *n* **porch**, entrance, doorway, entry, entranceway

portion *n* **1 helping**, share, slice, serving, percentage **2 fraction**, piece, bit, part, segment *Opposite*: whole ■ *v* **divide**, distribute, allocate, assign, share out

portliness *n* **stoutness**, stockiness, roundness, heaviness, heftiness *Opposite*: slimness

portly *adj* **overweight**, stout, stocky, round, heavy *Opposite*: slim

portmanteau *n* **suitcase**, case, bag, valise, holdall ■ *adj* **multiple**, combination, hybrid, blended, general-purpose

portrait *n* **picture**, representation, portrayal, likeness, photograph

portraiture *n* **portrait making**, portrait painting, photography, painting, drawing

portray *v* **depict**, represent, describe, show, interpret

portrayal *n* **representation**, interpretation, depiction, picture, description

pose *v* **1 model**, stand, sit, sit for, posture **2 impersonate**, pretend, play the part of, masquerade, profess **3 ask**, put, put forward, present, propound **4 present**, cause, create, set, establish ■ *n* **1 posture**, stance, position, attitude, carriage *(fml)* **2 pretence**, sham, fake, front, façade

poser *n* **1** *(infml)* **poseur**, show-off, exhibitionist, posturer, narcissist **2 problem**, question, puzzle, conundrum, challenge

poseur *n* **exhibitionist**, posturer, narcissist, swaggerer, peacock

posh *(infml) adj* **1 upmarket**, elegant, fashionable, expensive, luxurious *Opposite*:

downmarket 2 upper-class, well-to-do, genteel, aristocratic *Opposite*: common

posit *(fml) v* **put forward**, postulate, suggest, theorize, speculate

position *n* **1 location**, place, site, spot, point **2 posture**, stance, pose, arrangement, attitude **3 rank**, status, standing, station **4 view**, opinion, policy, stance, perception ■ *v* **put**, place, locate, stand, sit

positive *adj* **1 sure**, certain, clear, convinced, assured *Opposite*: uncertain **2 irrefutable**, definite, explicit, clear-cut, conclusive *Opposite*: dubious **3 optimistic**, confident, constructive, helpful, encouraging *Opposite*: negative

positively *adv* **1 definitely**, absolutely, completely, really, certainly **2 encouragingly**, confidently, optimistically, supportively, constructively *Opposite*: negatively

posse *(infml) n* **gang**, band, party, group, company

possess *v* **1 own**, have, hold, enjoy, keep *Opposite*: lack **2 take control**, influence, take, occupy, seize

possessed *adj* **controlled**, influenced, obsessed, crazed, overcome

possession *n* **ownership**, control, tenure, custody, proprietorship

possessions *n* **property**, belongings, wealth, goods, assets

possessive *adj* **1 domineering**, jealous, controlling, overprotective, covetous *Opposite*: trusting **2 selfish**, greedy, grasping, tight-fisted, mean *Opposite*: generous

possessiveness *n* **1 selfishness**, greed, tight-fistedness, meanness, greediness *Opposite*: generosity **2 jealousy**, jealousness, suspiciousness, overprotectiveness, insecurity

possessor *n* **owner**, holder, bearer, keeper, proprietor

possibility *n* **likelihood**, prospect, risk, chance, probability

possible *adj* **1 likely**, conceivable, imaginable, thinkable, probable *Opposite*: unlikely **2 achievable**, doable, feasible, viable, workable *Opposite*: impossible

possibly *adv* **perhaps**, maybe, probably, conceivably, feasibly *Opposite*: certainly

post *n* **1 pole**, column, stake, upright, marker **2 position**, placement, job, station, place ■ *v* **1 display**, announce, advertise, put up, publish **2 send**, dispatch, forward, airmail, mail *Opposite*: receive

postage *n* **stamp price**, postage fee, postage charge, postage cost, first-class postage

postbag *n* **1 sack**, mailbag, bag, satchel, delivery bag **2 correspondence**, mail, letters, mailbag, postal communications

postbox *n* **letterbox**, posting box, pillar box, collection box, collection point

postcard *n* **card**, picture postcard, message, note, letter

poster n 1 **picture**, print. reproduction, artwork, photograph 2 **advertisement**, placard, notice, bill, announcement

posterior adj 1 **rear**, hind, back, hindmost Opposite: front 2 (fml) **latter**, subsequent, following, next, later Opposite: former

posterity n **future generations**, later generations, generations to come, successors, future

postgraduate n **student**, postgraduate student, graduate student, PhD student, graduate

post-haste adv **fast**, immediately, right away, quickly, straight away Opposite: slowly

posthumous adj **subsequent**, retrospective, delayed, following, postmortem

posting n **placement**, relocation, position, post, military posting

postmark n **date stamp**, frank, stamp, mark, rubber stamp ■ v **frank**, stamp, date, mark, rubber-stamp

postmortem n 1 **autopsy**, postmortem examination, medical examination, examination, inquest 2 **investigation**, analysis, examination, inquest, review

postnatal adj **postpartum**, post-delivery, perinatal Opposite: antenatal

post office n 1 **PO**, GPO, sorting office, mailroom, mail depot (US) 2 **mail system**, mail service, postal service, postal communications, mail

postpone v **delay**, put off, put back, shelve, put on the back burner Opposite: bring forward

postponement n **delay**, rescheduling, rearrangement, deferment, adjournment

postscript n **afterthought**, addition, supplement, afterword, epilogue Opposite: preface

postulate v 1 **assume**, guess, hypothesize, suggest, claim 2 (fml) **nominate**, propose, select, choose, put forward

posture n **bearing**, stance, attitude, position, pose

posturing n **self-importance**, pomposity, swagger, bravado, bluster

posy n **bouquet**, bunch of flowers, spray, nosegay, arrangement

pot n **container**, pan, vessel, jar, tub ■ v 1 **shoot**, bag, catch, get, hit 2 **preserve**, seal, pickle, can, tin

potable adj **drinkable**, clean, filtered, fit to drink, drinking

potato n **tuber**, new potato, seed potato, spud (infml), tater (infml)

WORD BANK
❏ **types of processed potato** chip, crisp, croquette, French fries, fries, jacket potato, knish, latke, mash, potato cake, potato chips, potato pancake, rösti

poteen n **bootleg alcohol**, spirit, bootleg whisky, whisky, moonshine (infml)

potency n **strength**, force, power, might, vigour Opposite: weakness

potent adj 1 **strong**, effective, powerful, forceful, mighty Opposite: weak 2 **persuasive**, convincing, influential, forceful

potentate n **monarch**, ruler, leader, emperor, sovereign

potential n **ability**, capacity, possibility, makings, what it takes ■ adj **possible**, hypothetical, conceivable, likely, probable Opposite: unlikely

pothole n 1 **rut**, hole, dip, depression, fault 2 **cave**, cavern, catacomb, pit, hole

potholed adj **rutted**, pitted, holed, eroded, uneven Opposite: smooth

potholer n **speleologist**, caver, spelunker

potion n **liquid**, medicine, concoction, mixture, brew

potluck n **luck of the draw**, whatever is going, whatever is on offer, chance, whatever is available

potpourri n **miscellany**, mixture, assortment, collection, jumble

pots (infml) n **bags**, heaps (infml), piles (infml), tons (infml), loads (infml)

potshot n **shot**, pot, go, aim, try

potted adj 1 **preserved**, sealed, conserved, pickled, canned Opposite: fresh 2 (infml) **abridged**, summarized, brief, concise, shortened Opposite: full

potter v 1 **dabble**, mess, fiddle, tinker, toy 2 **go slowly**, dawdle, shuffle, amble, toddle (infml) Opposite: hurry

pottery n **ceramic objects**, earthenware, stoneware, ceramics

WORD BANK
❏ **types of pottery** bone china, ceramic, china, delft, Dresden china, earthenware, enamel, faience, Limoges, porcelain, Sèvres, stoneware, terracotta

potty (infml) adj **foolish**, irrational, eccentric, silly, ridiculous Opposite: sensible

pouch n **bag**, pocket, money bag, purse, sack

pouf n **stool**, beanbag, seat, cushion, floor cushion

poultice n **dressing**, compress, bandage, plaster

pounce v 1 **spring**, swoop, leap, jump, dive Opposite: recoil 2 **attack**, seize upon, seize, tackle, ambush ■ n **leap**, jump, spring, bound, swoop

pound n **pound sterling**, quid (infml), smacker (infml), nicker (slang) ■ v 1 **hit**, strike, batter, beat, hammer 2 **throb**, thump, beat, pulsate, pulse 3 **grind**, crush, pulverize, bruise, mash

pounding n 1 **throbbing**, thumping, pulsation, pulse, hammering 2 **beating**, thrashing, drubbing, defeat, pasting (infml)

pour v 1 decant, drizzle, dispense, discharge, transfer 2 **spill out**, gush, stream, flow, rush Opposite: trickle 3 **rain**, drench, lash, sheet down, rain cats and dogs (infml) Opposite: drizzle 4 **swarm**, crowd, teem, stream, rush Opposite: trickle

pouring adj **torrential**, heavy, sheeting down, hammering, driving Opposite: light

pour out v **reveal**, blurt out, disclose, give away, tell

pour scorn on v **disparage**, ridicule, deride, sneer at, mock

pour with rain v **pour down**, teem, come down in torrents, rain cats and dogs (infml), bucket (infml)

pout v 1 **purse your lips**, pucker, frown, scowl, glower Opposite: smile 2 **sulk**, mope, glower, scowl, grouch (infml) Opposite: smile

poverty n 1 **neediness**, destitution, hardship, deprivation, privation Opposite: affluence 2 **lack**, deficiency, scarcity, shortage, dearth Opposite: surplus

poverty-stricken adj **destitute**, in need, poor, penniless, impoverished Opposite: rich

powder n **fine particles**, dust, residue, precipitate, ash ■ v **crush**, grind, pound, pulverize, mill

powdered adj **ground**, crushed, pulverized, milled, processed Opposite: whole

powder keg n **tinderbox**, minefield, time bomb, recipe for disaster, explosive combination

powdery adj **fine**, crumbly, chalky, dusty, dry

power n 1 **ability**, capacity, faculty, potential, capability Opposite: inability 2 **strength**, force, might, energy, brawn Opposite: weakness 3 **control**, influence, authority, supremacy, rule Opposite: powerlessness 4 **authority**, right, prerogative, licence, privilege Opposite: powerlessness 5 **nation**, country, state, player, superpower

power base n **stronghold**, seat of power, headquarters, home base, base

powerful adj 1 **influential**, commanding, authoritative, controlling, prevailing Opposite: powerless 2 **strong**, mighty, brawny, muscular, sturdy Opposite: weak 3 **effective**, potent, strong, pungent, overwhelming Opposite: impotent 4 **persuasive**, compelling, forceful, effective, convincing Opposite: unimpressive

powerhouse (infml) n **driving force**, heart, centre, dynamo, live wire (infml)

powerless adj **helpless**, incapable, unable, weak, feeble Opposite: powerful

powerlessness n **helplessness**, hopelessness, weakness, feebleness, ineffectiveness

power line n **electricity cable**, overhead cable, cable, wire, overhead wire

power point n **socket**, point, electric socket, plug, hookup

practicability n **feasibility**, viability, workability, attainability, operability Opposite: impossibility

practicable adj **feasible**, realistic, possible, workable, attainable Opposite: impossible

practical adj 1 **applied**, real-world, hands-on, everyday, real Opposite: theoretical 2 **useful**, sensible, feasible, sound, workable 3 **realistic**, down-to-earth, level-headed, sensible, pragmatic Opposite: unrealistic 4 **everyday**, workaday, serviceable, functional, plain Opposite: decorative 5 **handy**, step-by-step, helpful, user-friendly, useful

practicality n 1 **usefulness**, sensibleness, feasibility, soundness, workability Opposite: uselessness 2 **realism**, common sense, levelheadedness, pragmatism, sensibleness Opposite: impracticality

practical joke n **trick**, prank, joke, lark, hoax

practically adv 1 **almost**, nearly, virtually, just about, nigh on 2 **realistically**, sensibly, rationally, reasonably, level-headedly Opposite: unrealistically

practice n 1 **repetition**, rehearsal, exercise, preparation, training 2 **habit**, custom, tradition, way, system. See COMPARE AND CONTRAST at habit.

practise v 1 **rehearse**, prepare, exercise, go through, run through Opposite: perform 2 **do**, put into practice, live out, carry out, perform Opposite: reject

practised adj **skilful**, experienced, trained, expert, adept Opposite: untrained

practitioner n **doctor**, medical practitioner, general practitioner, GP, physician

pragmatic adj **practical**, realistic, logical, rational, reasonable Opposite: idealistic

pragmatism n **practicality**, realism, logicality, rationality, reasonableness Opposite: idealism

pragmatist n **practical person**, down-to-earth person, realist, doer, rationalist Opposite: idealist

prairie n **plain**, savanna, steppe, pampas

praise n 1 **admiration**, commendation, approval, acclaim, tribute Opposite: criticism 2 **worship**, honour, adoration, devotion, thanks Opposite: vilification ■ v 1 **admire**, commend, extol, compliment, honour Opposite: criticize 2 **glorify**, honour, laud, worship, adore Opposite: vilify

praiseworthy adj **admirable**, commendable, laudable, worthy, exemplary Opposite: blameworthy

pram n **buggy**, pushchair, perambulator (fml), stroller (US), baby carriage (US)

prance v 1 **cavort**, dance, frolic, gambol, caper 2 **swagger**, strut, parade, flounce, sashay

prang (infml) v **crash**, smash, write off, bump, bash (infml)

prank n **trick**, practical joke, hoax, joke, lark

prankster n trickster, joker, practical joker, mischief-maker, imp

prate v chatter, gibber, prattle, babble, jabber

prattle v prate, gibber, chatter, jabber, babble ■ n chatter, gibber, drivel, nonsense, jabber

pray v 1 **meditate**, contemplate, say your prayers, call upon, invoke 2 **hope**, wish, cross your fingers, hope against hope, yearn 3 **request**, plead, beg, crave, ask

prayer n 1 **invocation**, meditation, contemplation, devotions, chant 2 **entreaty**, appeal, plea, request, desire

preach v 1 **give a sermon**, speak, discourse, talk, deliver an address 2 **advise**, lecture, sermonize, moralize, advocate

preacher n **minister**, pastor, missionary, lay preacher, vicar

preamble n **introduction**, preface, foreword, prelude, overture Opposite: postscript

prearrange v **organize**, set up, arrange, plan, settle upon

prearranged adj **planned**, arranged, agreed, preset, specified Opposite: chance

precarious adj **shaky**, unstable, insecure, wobbly, unsteady Opposite: stable

precaution n **protection**, safety measure, preventive measure, insurance, safeguard

precautionary adj **protective**, defensive, safety, cautionary, preventive Opposite: remedial

precede v **lead**, come first, go before, pave the way, herald Opposite: follow

precedence n **superiority**, priority, preference, primacy, antecedence

precedent n **example**, model, guide, pattern, standard

preceding adj **previous**, earlier, prior, former, past Opposite: following

precept (fml) n **principle**, teaching, rule, guideline, instruction

precinct n **district**, zone, area, sector, quarter

precincts n **grounds**, confines, area, limits, boundaries

precious adj 1 **valuable**, costly, expensive, dear, treasurable Opposite: worthless 2 **valued**, loved, beloved, important, dear Opposite: despised 3 **fastidious**, affected, overrefined, fussy, self-conscious Opposite: natural

preciousness n 1 **valuableness**, value, costliness, expensiveness, dearness Opposite: worthlessness 2 **fastidiousness**, affectation, fussiness, self-consciousness, daintiness Opposite: naturalness

precious stone n **gemstone**, jewel, stone, gem, sparkler (infml)

precipice n **rock face**, cliff, crag, sheer drop, abyss

precipitate adj 1 **rash**, impulsive, impetuous, careless, reckless Opposite: considered 2 **hurried**, hasty, swift, quick, rapid Opposite:

slow 3 **abrupt**, sudden, unexpected, surprising, unforeseen Opposite: expected ■ v **hasten**, bring on, cause, lead to, occasion Opposite: retard

precipitation n **rain**, rainfall, snow, sleet, hail

precipitous adj 1 **rash**, quick, hurried, swift, impulsive Opposite: careful 2 **steep**, sheer, abrupt, high, vertical Opposite: gentle

précis n **summary**, synopsis, résumé, abstract, sketch ■ v **summarize**, sum up, condense, outline, abridge Opposite: expand

precise adj 1 **exact**, detailed, accurate, specific, particular Opposite: vague 2 **meticulous**, scrupulous, particular, careful, fastidious Opposite: careless

precision n **exactness**, accuracy, exactitude, care, meticulousness Opposite: vagueness

preclude (fml) v **prevent**, impede, stop, rule out, exclude Opposite: permit

preclusion (fml) n **prevention**, exclusion, disqualification, prohibition, deterrence Opposite: permission

precocious adj **advanced**, developed, intelligent, bright, gifted Opposite: immature

precociousness see precocity

precocity n **talent**, cleverness, brightness, intelligence, precociousness Opposite: immaturity

precognition n **clairvoyance**, foreknowledge, premonition, foresight, second sight

preconceived adj **fixed**, set, defined, rigid, inflexible Opposite: unprejudiced

preconception n **prejudice**, bias, fixed idea, presumption, notion

precondition n **condition**, requirement, prerequisite, qualification, must

precook v **parboil**, soften, blanch

precursor n **forerunner**, ancestor, predecessor, antecedent, pioneer Opposite: successor

predate v **precede**, go before, antedate, exist before, pre-exist

predator n **marauder**, killer, hunter, pillager, raider

predatory adj **greedy**, destructive, rapacious, grasping, voracious

predecessor n **precursor**, forerunner, ancestor, antecedent, prototype Opposite: successor

predestination n **destiny**, fate, doom, kismet, lot Opposite: free will

predestine v **destine**, fate, preordain, doom, predetermine

predestined adj **fated**, destined, bound, preordained, appointed

predetermination n 1 **prearrangement**, arrangement, intention, decision, resolution 2 **predestination**, preordination, preordainment, lot, destiny Opposite: free will

predetermine v 1 **set**, programme, encode, determine, decide 2 **predestine**, destine, fate, preordain, doom

predetermined adj **1 prearranged**, programmed, encoded, fixed, determined **2 predestined**, destined, fated, bound, preordained

predicament n **difficulty**, quandary, dilemma, tight spot, tight corner

predicate (fml) v **base**, establish, found, ground, build

predict v **forecast**, foresee, envisage, expect, guess

predictability n **1 likelihood**, probability, sureness, certainty, liability Opposite: unpredictability **2 unoriginality**, banality, triteness, obviousness, staleness Opposite: originality

predictable adj **1 foreseeable**, expectable, expected, likely, probable Opposite: unlikely **2 unsurprising**, unoriginal, banal, trite, obvious Opposite: original

predictableness see predictability

predicted adj **foretold**, forecast, foreseen, prophesied, projected Opposite: unforeseen

prediction n **forecast**, guess, calculation, estimate, prophecy

predictive adj **prognostic**, extrapolative, prophetic, projecting, foretelling

predilection (fml) n **liking**, preference, fondness, partiality, penchant Opposite: dislike

predispose (fml) v **incline**, dispose, prompt, influence, prejudice

predisposed (fml) adj **inclined**, disposed, subject, liable, susceptible Opposite: unwilling

predisposition n **tendency**, disposition, inclination, penchant, bias

predominance n **1 superiority**, power, dominance, control, supremacy **2 majority**, prevalence, preponderance, numerousness Opposite: minority

predominant adj **main**, major, chief, principal, prime Opposite: minor

predominantly adv **mainly**, mostly, largely, chiefly, principally Opposite: partially

predominate v **prevail**, dominate, outweigh, preponderate, be in the majority

pre-eminence n **superiority**, authority, excellence, eminence, renown Opposite: obscurity

pre-eminent adj **distinguished**, outstanding, excellent, eminent, renowned Opposite: obscure

pre-eminently adv **to a great extent**, in large part, first and foremost, predominantly, principally Opposite: partly

pre-empt v **forestall**, anticipate, obstruct, block, prevent Opposite: react

pre-emption n **preemptive action**, preventive action, preventive measures, prevention, anticipation Opposite: reaction

pre-emptive adj **preventive**, preventative, proactive, anticipatory, blocking Opposite: reactive

preen v **groom**, smarten, clean, tidy, smooth

pre-exist v **predate**, precede, antecede, go before, prelude

pre-existing adj **previous**, prior, earlier, former, established Opposite: new

prefabricate v **manufacture**, make up, assemble, produce, mass-produce

preface n **foreword**, preamble, introduction, prologue, prelude Opposite: postscript ■ v **prefix**, precede, introduce, start, begin

prefect n **senior pupil**, monitor, captain, head boy, head girl

prefer v **favour**, have a preference, like better, wish, desire

preferable adj **better**, desirable, nicer, superior, choice Opposite: inferior

preference n **favourite**, first choice, partiality, penchant, fondness Opposite: dislike

preferential adj **special**, favoured, privileged, superior, better Opposite: disadvantageous

preferment (fml) n **promotion**, upgrading, appointment, advancement, elevation Opposite: demotion

preferred adj **favoured**, favourite, chosen, number one, in

prefigure v **anticipate**, herald, foreshadow, portend, presage

prefix v **preface**, precede, begin, start, start off

pregnancy n **1 gestation**, antenatal period, prenatal period, perinatal period, gravidity **2 significance**, importance, import, meaning

pregnant adj **1 expectant**, prenatal, gravid, expecting (infml), in the club (infml) **2 charged**, significant, weighty, meaningful, pointed

preheat v **heat**, heat up, warm, warm up, turn on Opposite: cool

prehistoric adj **1 primeval**, primitive, antediluvian, early, ancient **2 old-fashioned**, out-of-date, ancient, outmoded, antiquated Opposite: modern

prehistory n **early history**, olden days, times gone by, dawn of time, Stone Age

prejudge v **jump to conclusions**, presume, presuppose, anticipate, assume

prejudice n **1 bias**, preconception, prejudgment, predisposition, partiality Opposite: impartiality **2 bigotry**, chauvinism, narrow-mindedness, discrimination, intolerance Opposite: tolerance ■ v **influence**, bias, sway, slant, distort

prejudiced adj **biased**, intolerant, bigoted, narrow-minded, discriminatory Opposite: tolerant

prejudicial adj **harmful**, detrimental, hurtful, damaging, injurious Opposite: helpful

prelate n **archbishop**, cardinal, bishop, abbot

preliminary adj **initial**, first, opening, pilot, introductory Opposite: closing ■ n **beginning**, first round, introduction, opening, groundwork Opposite: finale

prelude n **introduction**, overture, prologue, preface, foreword *Opposite*: finale

premature adj **early**, untimely, hasty, rash, precipitate *Opposite*: overdue

premeditated adj **planned**, deliberate, intentional, calculated, thought-out *Opposite*: spontaneous

premeditation n 1 **planning**, calculation, cold-bloodedness, coldness, contemplation *Opposite*: impulsiveness 2 **reflection**, contemplation, thought, consideration, cogitation (fml) *Opposite*: spontaneity

premier adj **best**, first, leading, foremost, highest *Opposite*: worst ■ n **prime minister**, PM, first minister, president, head of state

premiere n **opening**, first night, first performance, first showing, debut

premiership n 1 **prime ministership**, presidency, leadership, term of office, tenure 2 **premier league championship**, competition, sports tournament

premise n 1 **evidence**, principle, idea, foundation, ground 2 **proposition**, supposition, hypothesis, assertion, thesis

premises n **building**, grounds, location, site, property

premium n **payment**, percentage, bonus, reward, perk ■ adj **best**, top, finest, quality, first-class *Opposite*: low-grade

premonition n 1 **intuition**, presentiment, feeling, hunch, fear 2 **warning**, omen, sign, portent, indication

premonitory adj 1 **intuitive**, predictive, clairvoyant, prophetic, precognitive 2 **warning**, prognostic, precautionary, cautionary, sobering

preoccupation n **worry**, obsession, anxiety, concern, fixation

preoccupied adj **worried**, anxious, lost in thought, elsewhere, inattentive *Opposite*: carefree

preoccupy v **worry**, concern, disturb, trouble, consume

preordained adj **inevitable**, fated, predetermined, destined, doomed

preparation n 1 **groundwork**, training, grounding, homework, research 2 **planning**, provision, arrangement, formulation, organization

preparatory adj **introductory**, foundation, preliminary, elementary, opening *Opposite*: final

prepare v 1 **get ready**, arrange, organize, plan, set up 2 **train**, groom, coach, prime, make ready 3 **make**, cook, get ready, concoct, formulate

prepared adj **ready**, set, equipped, geared up, organized

preparedness n **readiness**, preparation, alertness, attentiveness, awareness

prepare yourself v **steel yourself**, brace yourself, nerve yourself, compose yourself, get ready

prepayment n **advance payment**, down payment, payment, advance, deposit *Opposite*: debt

preponderance (fml) n 1 **majority**, mass, great number, multitude, many *Opposite*: minority 2 **dominance**, superiority, prevalence, predominance, weight

preponderant adj **greater**, more numerous, more powerful, more important, more significant *Opposite*: lesser

preponderantly adv **generally**, largely, in the main, by and large, for the most part

prepossessing (fml) adj **attractive**, pleasant, alluring, good-looking, nice-looking *Opposite*: unattractive

preposterous adj **outrageous**, absurd, ridiculous, ludicrous, unbelievable *Opposite*: sensible

preposterousness n **outrageousness**, absurdity, ridiculousness, ludicrousness, silliness *Opposite*: sensibleness

preproduction n **planning**, groundwork, organization, scheduling, planning stage

prepubescent adj **preadolescent**, preteen, preteenager, young, childish *Opposite*: adult ■ n **youngster**, preadolescent, preteenager, preteen, subteen *Opposite*: adult

prequel n **prelude**, prologue, spin-off *Opposite*: sequel

prerecord v **record**, tape, film, copy, video

prerequisite n **precondition**, requirement, condition, qualification, criterion

prerogative n **right**, privilege, due, entitlement, birthright

presage n **portent**, omen, sign, warning, signal ■ v **foretell**, foreshadow, portend, bode, augur

preschool adj **young**, toddler, infant, kindergarten, nursery

prescience n **foresight**, precognition, clairvoyance, prophecy, prediction *Opposite*: hindsight

prescient adj **prophetic**, psychic, clairvoyant, discerning, perceptive

prescribe v 1 **recommend**, suggest, advise, propose, advocate 2 **lay down**, stipulate, impose, order, set down

prescribed adj **set**, agreed, arranged, prearranged, given

prescript (fml) n **rule**, regulation, law, convention, canon

prescription n **medicine**, treatment, drug, preparation, remedy

prescriptive adj **narrow**, rigid, strict, unbending, inflexible *Opposite*: lax

prescriptiveness n **narrowness**, rigidity, strictness, inflexibility, dogmatism *Opposite*: laxity

presence n **1 attendance**, company, occurrence, incidence, existence *Opposite*: absence **2 dignity**, charisma, aura, authority, poise **3 ghost**, apparition, spirit, ghoul, manifestation

presence of mind n **nerve**, composure, level-headedness, common sense, sense

present v **1 give**, hand over, award, donate, offer *Opposite*: deny **2 show**, display, exhibit, put on view, reveal **3 cause**, represent, pose, raise, produce **4 portray**, represent, depict, cast, show **5 appear**, report, arrive, turn up, visit **6 put forward**, bring forward, introduce, announce, offer for consideration **7 exhibit**, mount, stage, put on view, organize ■ n **1 gift**, offering, grant, dowry, largesse **2 now**, here and now, present day, today, nowadays *Opposite*: past ■ *adj* **1 current**, contemporary, present-day, existing, extant *Opposite*: past **2 there**, here, in attendance, at hand, near *Opposite*: absent. *See* COMPARE AND CONTRAST *at* **give**.

presentable *adj* **1 respectable**, personable, fit to be seen, smart, well-dressed *Opposite*: scruffy **2 reasonable**, acceptable, satisfactory, good enough, passable *Opposite*: unsatisfactory

presentation n **1 performance**, exhibition, demonstration, appearance, arrangement **2 award**, donation, giving, offer, bestowal **3 talk**, lecture, seminar, speech, address

present day n **now**, here and now, present, today, nowadays *Opposite*: past

present-day *adj* **contemporary**, current, existing, present, modern *Opposite*: past

presenter n **announcer**, broadcaster, anchor, TV presenter, radio presenter

presentiment n **feeling**, intuition, foreboding, fear, sense

presently *adv* **1 soon**, shortly, in a short time, in a while, before long **2 currently**, at the moment, at present, right now, now

preservation n **1 protection**, conservation, safeguarding, defence, conservancy *Opposite*: destruction **2 maintenance**, continuation, perpetuation, keeping, upholding *Opposite*: abolition

preservative *adj* **preserving**, conserving, protective, antibacterial, antifungal *Opposite*: destructive ■ n **additive**, preserver, E number, stabilizer

preserved *adj* **1 conserved**, well-looked-after, well-maintained, well-preserved, well-kept-up *Opposite*: dilapidated **2 treated**, pickled, frozen, dried, salted *Opposite*: fresh

preserver n **protector**, guard, guardian, saviour, conserver *Opposite*: destroyer

preset *adj* **set**, predetermined, fixed, stipulated, specific

preside v **take the chair**, chair, control, supervise, head

presidency n **premiership**, leadership, term of office, tenure

president n **leader**, premier, head, head of state, chair

presidential *adj* **1 political**, constitutional, high-level, governmental, top-level **2 dignified**, authoritative, monarchic, judicious, regal

presidium n **executive committee**, committee, council, group, body

press v **1 push**, depress, force down, bear down on, compress *Opposite*: pull **2 iron**, smooth, steam, flatten, hot-press **3 pursue**, lobby, beg, entreat, enjoin **4 force**, urge, push, compel, oblige ■ n **1 journalists**, reporters, correspondents, newspapers, media **2 crowd**, horde, throng, mob, multitude

press conference n **news conference**, question and answer session, interview, conference, photo opportunity

pressed *adj* **busy**, pushed, hard-pressed, constrained, compelled

press for v **demand**, seek, urge, push for, campaign for

press-gang v **force**, coerce, bully, pressure, make

pressing *adj* **1 urgent**, important, serious, crucial, vital *Opposite*: unimportant **2 persistent**, insistent, unrelenting, unyielding, demanding *Opposite*: half-hearted

press officer n **spokesperson**, media spokesperson, press liaison officer, press agent

press on v **continue**, push on, forge ahead, keep going, carry on *Opposite*: give up

press release n **statement**, document, announcement, bulletin

press stud n **popper**, press fastener, fastening, fastener, stud

press together v **squeeze together**, force together, clamp, join together, close *Opposite*: pull apart

pressure n **1 force**, weight, heaviness, burden, compression **2 stress**, anxiety, weight, strain, tension ■ v **coerce**, force, bully, insist, compel

pressured *adj* **worried**, stressed, under pressure, overstretched, edgy *Opposite*: relaxed

pressurize v **force**, coerce, compel, make, bully

prestige n **status**, standing, stature, kudos, esteem *Opposite*: notoriety

prestigious *adj* **admired**, respected, significant, important, impressive *Opposite*: insignificant

presumably *adv* **most probably**, I assume, I imagine, in all probability, most likely

presume v **1 believe**, assume, guess, deduce, imagine *Opposite*: know **2 venture**, dare, be so bold, take the liberty, make free

presumption n **1 belief**, assumption, conjecture, supposition, presupposition **2 impertinence**, audacity, nerve, gall, impudence

presumptive *(fml) adj* **probable**, likely, plausible, convincing, reasonable *Opposite*: implausible

presumptuous *adj* **presuming**, audacious, rude, insolent, bold *Opposite*: modest

presumptuousness *n* **rudeness**, arrogance, impropriety, disrespect, inappropriateness *Opposite*: modesty

presuppose *v* **assume**, take for granted, take as read, take as fact, presume

presupposition *n* **assumption**, supposition, conjecture, belief, guess

prêt-à-porter *adj* **off-the-peg**, ready-made, ready-to-wear, mass-produced *Opposite*: made-to-measure

pretence *n* **1 trick**, con, sham, hoax, fabrication **2 claim**, suggestion, allegation, hint, supposition **3 make-believe**, fantasy, fancy, imagination, castles in the air *Opposite*: reality

pretend *v* **1 make believe**, imagine, fantasize, make up, play **2 feign**, put on, affect, profess, simulate ■ *adj* **imaginary**, make-believe, made-up, invented, false *Opposite*: real

pretender *n* **aspirant**, aspiring leader, candidate, opponent, claimant

pretend to be *v* **impersonate**, masquerade as, pose as, imitate, pass for

pretension *n* **affectation**, airs, posing, posturing, pretence *Opposite*: humility

pretentious *adj* **affected**, ostentatious, showy, exaggerated, pompous *Opposite*: down-to-earth

pretentiousness *see* **pretension**

pretext *n* **excuse**, cause, con, ploy, ruse

prettify *v* **smarten up**, do up, beautify, improve, adorn *Opposite*: mess up (*infml*)

prettiness *n* **good looks**, handsomeness, attractiveness, beauty, loveliness *Opposite*: ugliness

pretty *adj* **attractive**, beautiful, handsome, good-looking, appealing *Opposite*: unattractive ■ *adv* **rather**, fairly, reasonably, quite, moderately. *See* COMPARE AND CONTRAST *at* **good-looking**.

prevail *v* **1 triumph**, win through, succeed, be victorious, overcome *Opposite*: fail **2** (*fml*) **exist**, reign, be happening, occur, predominate

prevailing *adj* **1 current**, existing, customary, established, popular **2 usual**, main, dominant, predominant, principal *Opposite*: underlying

prevail on *v* **persuade**, convince, cajole, sway, coax into

prevalence *n* **occurrence**, commonness, pervasiveness, incidence, frequency

prevalent *adj* **common**, dominant, predominant, widespread, rampant *Opposite*: rare. *See* COMPARE AND CONTRAST *at* **widespread**.

prevaricate *v* **hedge**, evade, lie, quibble, stall *Opposite*: call a spade a spade

prevarication *n* **evasiveness**, evasion, equivocation, avoidance, hedging *Opposite*: forthrightness

prevent *v* **stop**, avert, avoid, foil, thwart *Opposite*: encourage

preventable *adj* **avoidable**, needless, unnecessary, avertible, escapable *Opposite*: inevitable

prevention *n* **1 avoidance**, deterrence, stoppage, inhibition, hindrance *Opposite*: promotion **2 obstacle**, hindrance, impediment, inhibition, restraint

preventive *adj* **anticipatory**, pre-emptive, defensive, prophylactic, deterrent ■ *n* **protection**, defence, anticipatory measure, pre-emptive measure, deterrent

preview *n* **1 showing**, performance, broadcast, screening, opening **2 trailer**, clip, foretaste, extract, coming attraction ■ *v* **1 show**, perform, broadcast, screen, promote **2 review**, describe, introduce, advertise, trail

previous *adj* **preceding**, earlier, prior, former, past *Opposite*: subsequent

prey *n* **quarry**, victim, target, kill, game *Opposite*: hunter

prey on *v* **1 live on**, live off, feed on, hunt, kill **2 worry**, preoccupy, bother, haunt, oppress **3 take advantage of**, exploit, victimize, intimidate, bully

price *n* **1 cost**, worth, fee, face value, amount **2 penalty**, cost, punishment, consequences, fine ■ *v* **set a price**, assess, estimate, rate, evaluate

priceless *adj* **1 invaluable**, inestimable, beyond price, incalculable, costly *Opposite*: worthless **2** (*infml*) **hilarious**, funny, comic, amusing, entertaining

pricey (*infml*) *adj* **costly**, expensive, dear, high-priced, exorbitant *Opposite*: cheap

prick *v* **pierce**, stab, puncture, perforate, jab ■ *n* **hole**, puncture, perforation, pinhole

prickle *n* **1 spike**, spine, barb, thorn, quill **2 itch**, tickle, sting, irritation, tingling ■ *v* **sting**, itch, tickle, prick, irritate

prickling *n* **scratchiness**, pricking, itchiness, itching, prickle

prickly *adj* **1 spiny**, thorny, barbed, bristly, spiky *Opposite*: smooth **2 itchy**, tickly, scratchy, stinging, tingling **3** (*infml*) **sensitive**, snappy, irritable, grumpy, snappish *Opposite*: impervious

pride *n* **1 arrogance**, conceit, smugness, superiority, self-importance *Opposite*: humility **2 satisfaction**, delight, gratification, enjoyment, joy **3 self-respect**, dignity, self-esteem, honour

pride and joy *n* **most prized possession**, the apple of your eye, treasure, pride, showpiece

pride yourself on *v* **be proud of**, take satisfaction in, revel in, take pride in, glory in

priest *n* **minister**, pastor, vicar, rector, presbyter

priesthood n **clergy**, ministry, cloth *Opposite*: laity

prim adj **1 prudish**, prissy, strait-laced, puritanical, moralistic *Opposite*: broad-minded **2 formal**, proper, dignified, starchy, stiff *Opposite*: informal **3 tidy**, orderly, precise, meticulous, fussy *Opposite*: messy

primacy n **pre-eminence**, importance, predominance, dominance, prevalence

primal adj **primitive**, primeval, aboriginal, primordial, prehistoric *Opposite*: new

primarily adv **first and foremost**, above all, chiefly, mainly, principally

primary adj **1 first**, initial, top, leading, foremost *Opposite*: last **2 main**, chief, most important, key, prime *Opposite*: secondary **3 basic**, core, central, fundamental, essential *Opposite*: minor

primate n **1 ape**, monkey, hominid, human **2 archbishop**, bishop, prelate, cardinal

WORD BANK

❑ **types of primate** aye-aye, baboon, Barbary ape, bonnet monkey, capuchin, chimp, chimpanzee, colobus, gibbon, gorilla, lemur, macaque, mandrill, marmoset, orang-utan, proboscis monkey, rhesus monkey, spider monkey

prime adj **1 top**, superior, superlative, best, premier *Opposite*: inferior **2 major**, main, key, chief, leading ■ n **peak**, zenith, heyday, summit, high point *Opposite*: nadir ■ v **1 prepare**, ready, get ready, make ready **2 brief**, fill in, instruct, give somebody the lowdown (infml)

primed adj **1 prepared**, ready, set, in position, poised **2 aware**, well-informed, geared up, informed, in the picture *Opposite*: unprepared

prime minister n **premier**, chief minister, head of cabinet, PM, head of government

primer n **textbook**, reader, grammar, introduction, how-to (infml)

primeval adj **1 prehistoric**, original, ancient, archaic *Opposite*: modern **2 primitive**, primordial, primal, basic, instinctive *Opposite*: considered

primitive adj **1 embryonic**, primeval, original, aboriginal, nascent *Opposite*: developed **2 simple**, basic, uncomplicated, unsophisticated, crude *Opposite*: sophisticated **3 prehistoric**, ancient, primordial, primal, archaic *Opposite*: modern

primitiveness n **1 antiquity**, ancientness, primitive stage, early stage, primeval stage **2 crudeness**, simplicity, roughness, coarseness, unsophisticatedness *Opposite*: sophistication

primness n **1 prudishness**, narrowness, shockability, oversensitivity, strait-lacedness *Opposite*: broad-mindedness **2 formality**, properness, starchiness, propriety, stiffness *Opposite*: informality **3 neatness**, tidiness, orderliness, fastidiousness, meticulousness *Opposite*: messiness

primordial adj **1 primeval**, prehistoric, primal, ancient, primitive **2 embryonic**, developing, early, nascent

primp v **fuss**, fuss over, groom, preen, adorn

prince n **leader**, leading figure, leading light, doyen, big shot (infml)

princely adj **generous**, handsome, large, significant, huge *Opposite*: measly (infml)

principal adj **main**, major, chief, most important, primary ■ n **1 head of school**, headmaster, headmistress, dean, provost **2 leader**, chief, doyenne, doyen, head *Opposite*: follower

principality n **princedom**, territory, country, domain

principally adv **mainly**, chiefly, above all, first and foremost, primarily

principle n **1 rule**, theory, notion, concept, tenet **2 code**, standard, belief, attitude, value **3 source**, wellspring, origin, cause, basis

principled adj **honourable**, righteous, upright, ethical, just *Opposite*: unethical

print n **1 pattern**, design, motif **2 reproduction**, copy, lithograph, photograph, photocopy ■ v **1 turn out**, produce, make, issue, run off **2 publish**, carry, make known, advertise, broadcast **3 stamp**, imprint, engrave, emboss

printed adj **in print**, in black and white, on paper, published, reproduced

printing n **1 production**, reproduction, lithography, offset lithography, letterpress **2 text**, lettering, words, writing, wording **3 lettering**, capitals, upper case, lower case, block lettering *Opposite*: script **4 edition**, print run, run, impression

prior adj **previous**, preceding, past, erstwhile, former *Opposite*: subsequent

prioritization n **ordering**, ranking, arranging, arrangement, listing

prioritize v **1 order**, rank, arrange, list, line up **2 concentrate on**, give precedence to, select, highlight, rank first

priority n **importance**, precedence, urgency, import, significance

prior to prep **before**, previous to, earlier than, preceding, in advance of *Opposite*: after

priory n **monastery**, convent, religious community, abbey, ashram

prise v **1 lever**, open, force, work loose, work free **2 extract**, drag out, wheedle, coax, cajole

prison n **1 jail**, detention centre, young offenders' institution, secure unit, house of correction **2 imprisonment**, confinement, solitary confinement, detention, custody

prisoner n **1 detainee**, inmate, convict, political prisoner, prisoner of war **2 captive**, hostage, kidnap victim

prissiness n **primness**, prudishness, properness, starchiness, stiffness *Opposite*: informality

prissy adj **prim**, prudish, proper, starchy, stiff Opposite: informal

pristine adj 1 **immaculate**, perfect, faultless, spotless, pure Opposite: soiled 2 **unspoiled**, untouched, primeval, original, virgin Opposite: developed

privacy n 1 **solitude**, time alone, space, seclusion, isolation Opposite: company 2 **confidentiality**, discretion, secrecy, concealment Opposite: disclosure

private adj 1 **confidential**, secret, concealed, undisclosed, classified Opposite: public 2 **secluded**, set apart, isolated, remote, cloistered 3 **privileged**, restricted, reserved, exclusive, not in the public domain Opposite: public 4 **secretive**, reserved, reticent, tight-lipped, self-contained Opposite: forthcoming

private detective n **private investigator**, private eye (infml), sleuth (infml), PI (US)

private eye (infml) see **private detective**

private investigator see **private detective**

privately adv **confidentially**, in confidence, in private, secretly, in secret Opposite: publicly

privation n **hardship**, deprivation, adversity, poverty, need

privatization n **sale**, transfer, denationalization

privatize v **sell**, transfer, denationalize, go public Opposite: nationalize

privilege n 1 **freedom**, licence, opportunity, dispensation, advantage 2 **honour**, source of pride, treat, pleasure, joy ■ v **favour**, show partiality towards, benefit Opposite: persecute

privileged adj 1 **advantaged**, lucky, fortunate, honoured Opposite: disadvantaged 2 **confidential**, private, restricted, controlled, limited Opposite: public

privy adj **in the know**, sharing in, aware of, party to, partaking of ■ n (infml) **outside toilet**, outside lavatory, outside loo, latrine, garderobe

prize n **award**, reward, trophy, medal, accolade ■ v **treasure**, cherish, value, respect, esteem

prized adj **award-winning**, high-quality, valued, respected, esteemed

prizewinning adj **award-winning**, victorious, successful, triumphant, winning Opposite: unsuccessful

pro prep **for**, in favour of, all for, in support of Opposite: against ■ n **professional**, authority, expert, specialist, ace (infml) Opposite: amateur

proactive adj **practical**, taking the initiative, hands-on, active, down to business Opposite: passive

probability n **likelihood**, prospect, odds, possibility, chance Opposite: improbability

probable adj **likely**, credible, possible, feasible, plausible Opposite: unlikely

probate n **certification**, validation, confirmation, validity

probation n **trial**, test, audition, experimentation, tryout

probationary adj **provisional**, trial, test, experimental, sample Opposite: permanent

probe n **investigation**, inquiry, review, examination, analysis ■ v **investigate**, research, delve, inquire, look into

probing adj **searching**, penetrating, analytical, inquisitive, curious Opposite: cursory

probity n **correctness**, scrupulousness, rectitude, righteousness, integrity Opposite: immorality

problem n 1 **difficulty**, setback, hitch, drawback, glitch Opposite: boost 2 **puzzle**, poser, riddle, conundrum, challenge Opposite: solution ■ adj **problematic**, tricky, unruly, badly-behaved, delinquent Opposite: easy

COMPARE AND CONTRAST CORE MEANING: something difficult to solve or understand

problem a difficult situation, matter, or person; **mystery** an event or situation that has never been fully explained or understood, or a person who is puzzling or mysterious; **puzzle** a problem whose solution requires ingenuity, or a situation that it is difficult to resolve, or somebody whose behaviour or motives are difficult to understand; **riddle** a perplexing or confusing issue; **conundrum** something puzzling, confusing, or mysterious; **enigma** somebody or something that is mysterious and hard to understand.

problematic adj **tricky**, challenging, sticky, awkward, knotty Opposite: easy

problematical see **problematic**

proboscis n **nose**, snout, feeler, trunk, antenna

procedural adj **technical**, practical, bureaucratic, routine, ritual

procedure n **process**, modus operandi, way, technique, method

proceed v **go on**, carry on, continue, ensue, advance Opposite: recede

proceedings n 1 **events**, actions, measures, trial, procedures 2 **minutes**, record, account, report, chronicle

proceeds n **profits**, income, earnings, takings, gate

process n **procedure**, course, activity, development, progression ■ v **deal with**, handle, treat, sort out, administer

procession n 1 **march**, parade, pageant, march-past, motorcade 2 **sequence**, succession, string, series, line

processional adj **ceremonial**, ritual, commemorative, celebratory, sacred

proclaim v **state publicly**, announce, declare, state, make known

proclamation n **public statement**, announcement, declaration, decree, assertion

proclivity n **liking**, appetite, taste, penchant, inclination

procrastinate v **put off**, delay, postpone, adjourn, dally *Opposite*: make a start

procrastination n **deferment**, putting off, postponement, stalling, delay *Opposite*: action

procure v **obtain**, acquire, secure, get hold of, get. *See* COMPARE AND CONTRAST *at* **get**.

procurement n **1 gaining**, obtaining, finding, locating, tracking down *Opposite*: giving up **2 buying**, purchasing, ordering, obtaining *Opposite*: selling

procurer n **buyer**, purchaser, customer, client, consumer

prod v **1 elbow**, nudge, dig, jab, push **2 urge**, stimulate, stir, prompt, provoke ■ n **nudge**, elbow, dig, jab, push

prodigal adj **wasteful**, reckless, dissolute, profligate, uncontrolled *Opposite*: cautious

prodigious adj **1 huge**, vast, copious, giant, gigantic *Opposite*: small **2 abnormal**, extraordinary, phenomenal, unusual, exceptional *Opposite*: average

prodigy n **genius**, sensation, phenomenon, wonder, star

produce v **1 create**, make, manufacture, construct, fabricate **2 give**, give off, yield, churn out, be the source of ■ n **crop**, foodstuffs, harvest, products, goods

producer n **creator**, manufacturer, maker, fabricator

product n **1 manufactured article**, commodity, artefact **2 output**, merchandise, goods, wares **3 result**, outcome, upshot, consequence, effect *Opposite*: cause **4 creation**, invention, achievement, work

production n **manufacture**, making, construction, creation, invention

productive adj **1 creative**, prolific, fecund, industrious, fruitful *Opposite*: destructive **2 useful**, helpful, constructive, beneficial, valuable *Opposite*: negative

productiveness n **usefulness**, constructiveness, use, utility, fruitfulness

productivity n **output**, efficiency, yield, production, throughput

profane adj **blasphemous**, irreverent, irreligious, disrespectful, wicked *Opposite*: sacred

profanity n **blasphemy**, oath, vulgarity, curse, swearword

profess v **1 declare**, announce, state, affirm, proclaim **2 claim**, maintain, make out, feign **3 admit**, own up, confess, acknowledge, agree

professed adj **1 declared**, acknowledged, open, stated, blatant *Opposite*: unspoken **2 supposed**, alleged, so-called, ostensible, seeming *Opposite*: proven

profession n **job**, work, occupation, line of work, career

professional adj **specialized**, qualified, proficient, skilled, trained *Opposite*: amateur ■ n **specialist**, expert, authority, pro, maven *(US) Opposite*: amateur

professionalism n **skill**, competence, expertise, proficiency, efficiency *Opposite*: incompetence

professor n **university teacher**, lecturer, fellow, don, tutor

professorial adj **academic**, pedagogical, intellectual, educational, senior

proffer v **offer**, hold out, extend, tender, volunteer *Opposite*: withdraw

proficiency n **skill**, ability, talent, expertise, aptitude *Opposite*: incompetence

proficient adj **capable**, talented, expert, gifted, adroit *Opposite*: incompetent

profile n **1 outline**, side view, shape, silhouette, contour **2 summary**, sketch, outline, report, précis ■ v **summarize**, sum up, sketch, outline, report

profit n **1 income**, earnings, revenue, proceeds, turnover *Opposite*: loss **2 advantage**, gain, benefit, use, reward *Opposite*: loss ■ v **1 earn**, bring in, make, make money on, turn a profit *Opposite*: lose **2 benefit**, gain, be of advantage to, help, aid

profitability n **1 success**, effectiveness, productivity, viability, cost-effectiveness **2 usefulness**, worth, fruitfulness, use, value *Opposite*: uselessness

profitable adj **1 lucrative**, moneymaking, gainful, commercial, cost-effective *Opposite*: unprofitable **2 advantageous**, beneficial, rewarding, useful, valuable *Opposite*: unhelpful

profiteer v **exploit**, take advantage of, make use of, racketeer, abuse ■ n **swindler**, racketeer, embezzler, crook *(infml)*, con man *(slang)*

profitmaking adj **profitable**, viable, moneymaking, economic, cost-effective *Opposite*: draining

profligacy n **wastefulness**, recklessness, dissolution, decadence, extravagance *Opposite*: parsimony

profligate adj **1 wasteful**, reckless, spendthrift, squandering, decadent *Opposite*: parsimonious **2 dissolute**, licentious, immoral, wicked, shameless

profound adj **1 deep**, thoughtful, reflective, philosophical, weighty *Opposite*: superficial **2 intense**, great, overpowering, overwhelming, extreme *Opposite*: shallow

profoundly adv **intensely**, greatly, extremely, strongly, very much

profoundness *see* **profundity**

profundity n **1 understanding**, perceptiveness, wisdom, acuity, perspicacity *Opposite*: superficiality **2 complexity**, abstruseness, difficulty, depth, intricacy *Opposite*: simplicity **3 intensity**, greatness, strength, seriousness, enormity *Opposite*: mildness **4 depth**, immensity, fathomlessness, extent, reach

profuse adj **plentiful**, copious, abundant, teeming, generous Opposite: scanty

profusion n **abundance**, large amount, excess, cornucopia, plethora Opposite: dearth

progenitor n **1 ancestor**, forebear Opposite: descendant **2 antecedent**, originator, forerunner, prototype, predecessor Opposite: copy

progeny n **offspring**, children, young, descendants, issue

prognosis n **forecast**, prediction, projection, scenario, diagnosis

prognosticate v **1 predict**, divine, foresee, foretell, forecast Opposite: recall **2 indicate**, suggest, point to, augur, signify Opposite: prove

prognostication n **1 prediction**, prognosis, projection, divination, foreseeing Opposite: recollection **2 indication**, suggestion, pointer, token, portent Opposite: proof

prognosticator n **predictor**, diviner, prophet, seer, clairvoyant

program n **setting**, option, cycle, mode, instruction ■ v **write instructions**, load instructions, write software, load software, set

programme n **1 plan**, agenda, schedule, timetable, list **2 broadcast**, production, show, transmission, game show **3 brochure**, booklet, synopsis, listing, timetable **4 system**, procedure, course, series, setup ■ v **1 schedule**, arrange, lay on, book, plan **2 train**, condition, compel, brainwash, hypnotize

programmed adj **automatic**, involuntary, planned, automated, set Opposite: spontaneous

programmer n **computer operator**, computer programmer, computer scientist, program writer, systems analyst

programming n **software design**, program design, user interface design, program writing, software development

progress n **development**, improvement, advancement, evolution, growth Opposite: regression ■ v **1 improve**, develop, advance, evolve, increase Opposite: regress **2 move forward**, advance, proceed, continue, make progress Opposite: retreat

progression n **1 development**, evolution, movement, advance, advancement Opposite: regression **2 series**, sequence, succession, string, chain

progressive adj **1 gradual**, ongoing, increasing, continuing, developing Opposite: sudden **2 liberal**, reformist, open-minded, broad-minded, radical Opposite: reactionary

progressively adv **increasingly**, more and more, with time, gradually, little by little Opposite: suddenly

progressiveness n **liberalism**, reformism, progressivism, modernism, tolerance

progressivism n **liberalism**, reformism, modernism, radicalism, leftism

prohibit v **forbid**, ban, proscribe, disallow, veto Opposite: permit

prohibited adj **forbidden**, banned, verboten, illegal, proscribed Opposite: permitted

prohibition n **ban**, exclusion, embargo, prevention, veto Opposite: permission

prohibitive adj **high-priced**, excessive, exorbitant, extortionate, unaffordable Opposite: affordable

project n **assignment**, task, undertaking, job, plan ■ v **1 forecast**, predict, estimate, foresee, foretell **2 stick out**, jut out, protrude, bulge, distend **3 throw**, launch, shoot, propel, cast **4 plan**, envisage, propose, intend, anticipate

projected adj **estimated**, planned, proposed, outlined, expected Opposite: actual

projection n **1 forecast**, prediction, plan, prognosis, estimate Opposite: outcome **2 outcrop**, protuberance, bulge, protrusion, ledge

proletarian adj **popular**, grassroots, people's, working-class, blue-collar Opposite: aristocratic

proletariat n **hoi polloi**, rank and file, grassroots, working class, workers Opposite: gentry

proliferate v **1 multiply**, thrive, flourish, boom, increase Opposite: dwindle **2 reproduce**, propagate, multiply, breed, procreate Opposite: die out

proliferation n **propagation**, explosion, spread, multiplying, production

prolific adj **1 productive**, creative, fertile, inexhaustible, high-volume Opposite: unproductive **2 (fml) abundant**, abounding, plentiful, copious, profuse Opposite: scarce

prolix adj **wordy**, verbose, long-winded, flowery, protracted Opposite: concise. See COMPARE AND CONTRAST at **wordy**.

prologue n **introduction**, preface, foreword, preamble, opening Opposite: epilogue

prolong v **extend**, lengthen, protract, draw out, spin out Opposite: curtail

prolongation n **continuation**, perpetuation, drawing out, protraction, extension Opposite: curtailment

prolonged adj **lengthy**, protracted, long, continued, extended Opposite: curtailed

prom (infml) n **promenade**, seafront, walkway, path, esplanade

promenade n **1 walkway**, seafront, path, boardwalk, esplanade **2 (fml) stroll**, walk, saunter, amble, constitutional ■ v (fml) **walk**, stroll, amble, saunter, wander

prominence n **1 fame**, importance, distinction, celebrity, eminence Opposite: obscurity **2 bump**, lump, bulge, swelling, protrusion Opposite: crater

prominent adj **1 protuberant**, protruding, projecting, bulbous, bulging *Opposite*: flat **2 noticeable**, conspicuous, obvious, blatant, flagrant *Opposite*: subtle **3 famous**, well-known, important, high-flying, top *Opposite*: obscure

promiscuous *adj* **immoral**, loose, licentious, wanton, uninhibited

promise *v* **1 assure**, swear, vow, undertake, guarantee **2 suggest**, augur, bode, look like, show all the signs ■ *n* **1 assurance**, undertaking, guarantee, contract, word *Opposite*: threat **2 potential**, possibilities, aptitude, ability, capacity

promising *adj* **1 talented**, gifted, capable, able **2 auspicious**, hopeful, likely, encouraging, favourable *Opposite*: disappointing

promisingly *adv* **favourably**, auspiciously, hopefully, well, nicely *Opposite*: disappointingly

promo *(infml)* *n* **promotion**, advertisement, publicity stunt, publicity, profile-raiser

promontory *n* **cape**, headland, peninsula, outcrop, point

promote *v* **1 advance**, upgrade, further, elevate, put forward *Opposite*: demote **2 endorse**, encourage, help, support, stimulate *Opposite*: suppress **3 advertise**, publicize, make known, market, tout *Opposite*: defame **4 further**, progress, move forward, develop, encourage *Opposite*: hinder **5 stage**, put on, organize, arrange

promoter *n* **organizer**, agent, sponsor, advocate, supporter

promotion *n* **1 upgrade**, advancement, elevation, rise, preferment *(fml)* *Opposite*: demotion **2 advertising**, marketing, publicity, publicity campaign, public relations **3 endorsement**, encouragement, help, support, stimulation **4 offer**, special promotion, deal, loss leader

promotional *adj* **publicity**, advertising, public relations, PR, positive

prompt *adj* **1 quick**, rapid, swift, without delay, speedy *Opposite*: slow **2 punctual**, on time, at the appointed time, without delay, timely *Opposite*: late ■ *v* **1 stimulate**, encourage, provoke, incite, urge *Opposite*: prevent **2 bring about**, induce, occasion, set off, trigger *Opposite*: prevent ■ *n* **stimulus**, prod, goad, reminder, aide-mémoire *(fml)*

prompting *n* **encouragement**, warning, pressure, motivation, instigation

promptness *n* **1 speed**, rapidity, swiftness, alacrity, velocity *Opposite*: slowness **2 punctuality**, timeliness, timekeeping *Opposite*: tardiness

promulgate *(fml)* *v* **1 declare**, proclaim, decree, announce, pronounce *Opposite*: withdraw **2 publicize**, spread, disseminate, circulate, transmit *Opposite*: suppress

promulgation *(fml)* *n* **1 declaration**, proclamation, decree, announcement, pronouncement *Opposite*: withdrawal **2 publicizing**, spreading, dissemination, circulation, broadcasting *Opposite*: suppression

prone *adj* **1 disposed**, predisposed, liable, inclined, likely **2 flat**, horizontal, flat out, face down, motionless *Opposite*: upright

prong *n* **point**, spike, spine, tine

pronounce *v* **1 say**, speak, utter, articulate, voice **2 state**, assert, declare, announce, decree

pronounced *adj* **marked**, noticeable, distinct, definite, obvious *Opposite*: subtle

pronouncement *n* **statement**, assertion, declaration, announcement, decree

pronto *(infml)* *adv* **straightaway**, right away, quick, quickly, at once *Opposite*: sluggishly

pronunciation *n* **articulation**, accent, elocution, intonation, enunciation

proof *n* **evidence**, testimony, verification, confirmation, attestation ■ *adj* **resistant**, resilient, impervious, immune *Opposite*: vulnerable

proofread *v* **check**, correct, check through, check over, look through

proofreader *n* **checker**, reader, editor, copy editor, corrector

prop *n* **support**, leg, crutch, buttress, pile ■ *v* **hold up**, support, prop up, sustain, buttress *Opposite*: destabilize

propaganda *n* **1 publicity**, advertising, marketing, literature, information **2 misinformation**, disinformation, party line, half-truths, cant

propagandist *n* **1 publicist**, polemicist, essayist, writer, speaker **2 partisan**, apologist, mouthpiece, sophist, spin doctor *(slang)* ■ *adj* **slanted**, distorted, one-sided, polemical, partisan

propagate *v* **1 breed**, grow, raise, reproduce, proliferate **2 spread**, broadcast, proliferate, circulate, disseminate

propagation *n* **1 breeding**, reproduction, proliferation, procreation **2 spread**, circulation, dissemination, transmission, proliferation

propagator *n* **1 spreader**, broadcaster, transmitter, communicator, diffuser **2 tray**, box, seed tray, cloche, cold frame

propel *v* **push**, drive, force, boost, thrust

propensity *n* **tendency**, inclination, partiality, bent, proclivity

proper *adj* **1 good**, correct, appropriate, suitable, right *Opposite*: wrong **2 polite**, modest, decorous, prim, genteel *Opposite*: improper **3 own**, personal, characteristic, identifiable, individual

properly *adv* **correctly**, right, appropriately, as it should be, by the book *Opposite*: incorrectly

propertied *adj* **property-owning**, land-owning, landed, affluent, moneyed *Opposite*: dispossessed

property n 1 **possessions**, belongings, goods, assets, material goods 2 **land**, home, house, estate, acreage

property owner n **proprietor**, owner, landowner, homeowner, property holder Opposite: tenant

prophecy n **prediction**, forecast, divination, foretelling, insight

prophesy v **predict**, forecast, divine, foretell, see the future

prophet n **clairvoyant**, forecaster, fortune teller, seer, prescient

prophetic adj **visionary**, farsighted, predictive, foretelling, forewarning

propinquity (fml) n **nearness**, closeness, proximity, convenience, relationship Opposite: remoteness

propitiate v **appease**, placate, mollify, pacify, soothe Opposite: provoke (infml)

propitiation (fml) n **placation**, appeasement, mollification, pacification, soothing Opposite: provocation

propitiatory adj **placatory**, conciliatory, soothing, mollifying, calming Opposite: provocative

proponent n **advocate**, supporter, exponent, protagonist, follower Opposite: opponent

proportion n 1 **amount**, quantity, part, share, percentage 2 **ratio**, comparison, relative amount, relationship

proportional adj **relative**, comparative, relational, related, proportionate

proportionate adj **balanced**, proportional, comparable, equal, equivalent

proposal n **suggestion**, offer, application, tender, bid

propose v 1 **suggest**, offer, recommend, proposition, advise 2 **intend**, plan, have in mind, aim, mean

proposer n **nominator**, supporter, sponsor, advocate, advocator

proposition n **proposal**, plan, scheme, intention, suggestion

propound v **put forward**, advocate, submit, set out, offer

proprietary adj 1 **branded**, exclusive, patented, registered, trademarked Opposite: generic 2 **private**, privately owned, privately run, privately operated, commercial 3 **protective**, jealous, territorial, possessive, suspicious

proprietor n **owner**, manager, administrator, landowner, property owner

proprietorial adj **possessive**, protective, jealous, suspicious, territorial

propriety n 1 **politeness**, decorum, modesty, good manners, respectability Opposite: impropriety 2 **correctness**, aptness, appropriateness, decency, suitability Opposite: impropriety

propulsion n **force**, forward motion, thrust, impulsion, momentum

prop up v **hold up**, support, prop, sustain, buttress Opposite: destabilize

prosaic adj 1 **straightforward**, matter-of-fact, simple, plain, ordinary 2 **banal**, mundane, everyday, dull, humdrum Opposite: extraordinary

proscribe v **ban**, bar, forbid, exclude, veto Opposite: permit

proscribed adj **prohibited**, banned, forbidden, verboten, inadmissible Opposite: permissible

proscription (fml) n **prohibition**, banning, exclusion, forbidding, interdiction

prose n **writing style**, style, text Opposite: poetry

prosecute v **put on trial**, impeach, arraign, indict, take legal action

prosecution n **trial**, action, suit, case, examination

proselytization n **preaching**, evangelization, agitation, propagandizing, campaigning

proselytize v 1 **preach**, evangelize, spread the word, make somebody see the light, convert 2 **persuade**, cajole, lecture, bend somebody's ear, talk into

proselytizer n **preacher**, evangelist, missionary, zealot, agitator

prospect n 1 **view**, scene, vision, outlook, panorama 2 **hope**, possibility, expectation, outlook, likelihood ■ v **search**, mine, dig, seek, pan

prospective adj **potential**, future, forthcoming, likely, probable

prospectus n **brochure**, list, document, booklet, leaflet

prosper v **flourish**, thrive, do well, get on, grow Opposite: decline 2 **succeed**, make money, show a profit, be in the black

prosperity n **wealth**, affluence, opulence, riches, success Opposite: poverty

prosperous adj 1 **wealthy**, affluent, rich, well-off, well-to-do Opposite: poor 2 **flourishing**, thriving, successful, booming Opposite: failing

prostrate adj 1 **flat**, face down, horizontal, level, prone Opposite: upright 2 **drained**, exhausted, desperate, powerless, at a low ebb

prostrate yourself v **bow**, genuflect, bend low, humble yourself, grovel

prostration n 1 **bowing**, kneeling, falling down, worship, adoration 2 **incapacitation**, breakdown, exhaustion, helplessness, weakness Opposite: robustness

protagonist n **character**, hero, central character, leading role, good guy (US infml)

protean adj **variable**, changeable, mutable, adjustable, fluctuating Opposite: constant

protect v **defend**, guard, keep, safeguard, look after Opposite: neglect. See COMPARE AND CONTRAST at **safeguard**.

protected adj 1 endangered, threatened, nearing extinction, dwindling Opposite: thriving 2 sheltered, safe, secure, safeguarded, shielded Opposite: exposed 3 locked, tamper-proof, inaccessible, sealed, impenetrable Opposite: open

protection n 1 safeguard, defence, guard, fortification, shield 2 security, safety, defence, asylum, sanctuary Opposite: exposure

protectionism n isolationism, protection, tariff barriers, trade barriers

protectionist n isolationist, nationalist, patriot, xenophobe ■ adj protective, isolationist, nationalist, preferential, xenophobic

protective adj defensive, caring, shielding, protecting, defending

protective covering n shell, armour, cladding, shield

protectiveness n 1 safety, security, secureness, strength, robustness 2 solicitousness, jealousy, possessiveness, suspicion 3 protectionism, isolationism, protection, tariff barriers, trade barriers

protector n 1 shield, armour, mask, apron 2 guard, guardian, minder, defender, handler

protectorate n dominion, colony, dependency, region, territory

protégé n ward, pupil, dependant, apprentice, student Opposite: protector

protest v 1 complain, object, remonstrate, dissent, dispute 2 declare, affirm, assert, insist, claim ■ n 1 complaint, objection, remonstration, dissent, dispute 2 demonstration, march, rally, campaign, dispute. See COMPARE AND CONTRAST at complain, object.

protestation n assertion, declaration, affirmation, pronouncement, disclosure

protester n activist, campaigner, demonstrator, marcher, picketer Opposite: supporter

protest march n demonstration, march, rally, protest, demo (infml)

protest rally see protest march

protocol n procedure, etiquette, conventions, code of behaviour, rules

prototype n example, sample, model, original, archetype Opposite: copy

protract v draw out, prolong, extend, spin out, drag out Opposite: shorten

protracted adj long-drawn-out, prolonged, extended, lingering, expanded Opposite: brief

protraction n 1 extension, lengthening, drawing out, continuation Opposite: shortening 2 scale drawing, plan, elevation, blueprint, diagram

protrude v stick out, jut, project, overhang, obtrude

protrusion n lump, lip, flange, overhang, outcrop

protrusive adj 1 prominent, bulging, swelling, jutting, extending Opposite: sunken 2 brash, forward, presumptuous, rude, fresh (infml) Opposite: retiring

protuberance n swelling, bulge, bump, lump, knob

protuberant adj sticking out, prominent, bulging, swelling, popping Opposite: concave

proud adj 1 pleased, satisfied, gratified, honoured, delighted Opposite: ashamed 2 impressive, stately, majestic, noble, magnificent 3 arrogant, conceited, smug, superior, self-important Opposite: humble 4 independent, self-sufficient, dignified, scrupulous, honourable 5 rewarding, satisfying, pleasurable, pleasing, uplifting 6 projecting, prominent, jutting, bulging, protrusive Opposite: sunken

---

COMPARE AND CONTRAST CORE MEANING: describing somebody who is pleased with himself or herself

proud justifiably pleased and satisfied about a situation, or self-satisfied and having an exaggerated opinion of self-worth; **arrogant** feeling or showing self-importance and contempt for others; **conceited** showing excessive satisfaction with one's personal qualities or abilities; **egotistic** having an inflated sense of self-importance, especially when this is shown through constantly talking or thinking about oneself; **vain** excessively self-satisfied, especially suggesting that somebody is overly concerned with and admires his or her own personal appearance.

---

proudly adv 1 delightedly, happily, triumphantly, joyfully Opposite: ashamedly 2 arrogantly, conceitedly, smugly, self-importantly, pompously Opposite: humbly

provable adj demonstrable, verifiable, watertight, incontestable, unarguable

prove v 1 show, establish, confirm, demonstrate, verify Opposite: disprove 2 turn out, develop, grow, grow up, be

proven adj established, confirmed, demonstrated, verified, recognized Opposite: unproven

provenance n origin, derivation, attribution, source, birthplace. See COMPARE AND CONTRAST at origin.

provender n 1 (archaic) fodder, feed, hay, forage, silage 2 (literary) food, fare, provisions, victuals, grub (infml)

proverb n maxim, axiom, adage, saying, aphorism

proverbial adj 1 well-known, axiomatic, familiar, legendary, famous 2 archetypal, clichéd, typical, regular, common Opposite: novel

provide v 1 give, supply, present, endow, grant Opposite: withhold 2 make available, deliver, offer, arrange for, run Opposite: withdraw 3 stipulate, postulate, specify, require 4 take care of, support, look after, care for, keep Opposite: neglect

provided *see* provided that

provided that *conj* **on condition that**, if, only if, as long as, so long as

providence *n* **1 wisdom**, foresight, prudence, sense, frugality **2 fate**, luck, destiny, fortune, divine intervention

provident *adj* **1 prudent**, foresighted, well-prepared, wise, careful *Opposite*: improvident **2 frugal**, thrifty, cautious, careful, sparing *Opposite*: spendthrift

providential *adj* **1 preordained**, destined, fated, God-given, divine *Opposite*: arbitrary **2 fortunate**, lucky, beneficial, advantageous, convenient *Opposite*: unfortunate. *See* COMPARE AND CONTRAST *at* **lucky**.

provider *n* **1 supplier**, source, contributor, donor, bringer *Opposite*: beneficiary **2 breadwinner**, wage-earner, earner, worker, benefactor *Opposite*: dependant

providing *conj* **on condition that**, if, only if, as long as, so long as

province *n* **1 area**, sphere, field, jurisdiction, domain **2 region**, area, state, county, prefecture

provinces *n* **outlying areas**, countryside, backwaters, hinterland, shires *Opposite*: capital

provincial *adj* **1 local**, regional, county, district, small-town *Opposite*: central **2 unsophisticated**, unfashionable, simple, outmoded, parochial *Opposite*: worldly

provincialism *n* **lack of sophistication**, lack of refinement, parochialism, narrow-mindedness, insularity *Opposite*: worldliness

provision *n* **1 delivery**, facility, running, setting up, establishment **2 anticipation**, prearrangement, forethought, wherewithal, readiness **3 stipulation**, rider, condition, proviso, if

provisional *adj* **temporary**, interim, conditional, makeshift, short-term *Opposite*: permanent

provisions *n* **supplies**, necessities, requirements, food, rations

proviso *n* **stipulation**, rider, condition, provision, if

provisory *adj* **conditional**, subject to, dependent upon, provisional, contingent *Opposite*: unconditional

provocation *n* **1 incitement**, needling, goading, baiting, niggling *Opposite*: appeasement **2 vexation**, frustration, irritation, annoyance, affront

provocative *adj* **1 challenging**, provoking, stimulating, inflammatory, incendiary *Opposite*: conciliatory **2 suggestive**, enticing, seductive, alluring, encouraging *Opposite*: forbidding

provoke *v* **1 incite**, needle, goad, bait, irritate *Opposite*: soothe **2 cause**, elicit, produce, trigger, bring about *Opposite*: prevent

provoked *adj* **irritated**, annoyed, angered, goaded, frustrated *Opposite*: unaffected

provoking *adj* **infuriating**, irritating, annoying, frustrating, maddening *Opposite*: soothing

provost *n* **principal**, director, head, chancellor, leader

prowess *n* **1 ability**, skill, expertise, competence, dexterity *Opposite*: incompetence **2 bravery**, heroism, gallantry, courage, daring *Opposite*: cowardice

prowl *v* **stalk**, lurk, skulk, lie in wait, hang about

prowler *n* **stalker**, pursuer, intruder, tormentor, Peeping Tom

proximity *n* **nearness**, closeness, juxtaposition, vicinity, immediacy *Opposite*: remoteness

proxy *n* **1 indirect means**, substitution, deputation, commission, delegation **2 substitute**, stand-in, deputy, delegate, understudy

prudence *n* **practicality**, carefulness, caution, discretion, forethought *Opposite*: imprudence

prudent *adj* **practical**, careful, cautious, sensible, discreet *Opposite*: imprudent. *See* COMPARE AND CONTRAST *at* **cautious**.

prudential *adj* **sensible**, wise, sagacious, provident, practical *Opposite*: foolish

prudery *n* **primness**, stuffiness, reserve, puritanism, prudishness *Opposite*: broadmindedness

prudish *adj* **prim**, stuffy, strait-laced, starchy, formal *Opposite*: relaxed

prudishness *see* prudery

prune *v* **1 clip**, trim, snip, cut back, cut **2 shorten**, cut, abridge, condense, tighten up *Opposite*: expand

prurient *adj* **unwholesome**, unhealthy, immodest, indecent, salacious *Opposite*: healthy

pry *v* **interfere**, poke your nose in, meddle, inquire, peer *Opposite*: leave alone

prying *adj* **interfering**, inquisitive, curious, meddling, peeping *Opposite*: incurious

PS *adv* **postscript**, addendum, afterthought, addition, stop press

psalm *n* **sacred song**, hymn, poem, canticle, prayer

Psalter *n* **book of psalms**, prayer book, breviary, hymnal, missal

pseud *n* **fraud**, fake, know-all *(infml)*, poser *(infml)*

pseudonym *n* **alias**, false name, assumed name, fictitious name, stage name

psyche *n* **1 soul**, spirit, inner self, essence, being **2 mind**, consciousness, awareness, ego, intellect

psychedelic *adj* **1 hallucinogenic**, mind-altering, mind-expanding, mood-altering, mind-blowing *(infml)* **2 coloured**, patterned, vibrant, vivid, loud *Opposite*: dull

psychic *adj* **1 mental**, cerebral, intellectual, cognitive, psychosomatic **2 supernatural**, extrasensory, mysterious, unexplained, paranormal *Opposite*: physical **3 telepathic**, clairvoyant, intuitive, second-sighted, star-gazing ■ n **clairvoyant**, spiritualist, sooth-sayer, sensitive, diviner

psychical adj **supernatural**, paranormal, spiritual, extrasensory, subliminal Opposite: physical

psychological adj **mental**, emotional, inner, spiritual, psychosomatic Opposite: physical

psychology n **mind**, thinking, mindset, makeup, sensibility

psychosomatic adj **self-induced**, mental, psychological, inner, all in the mind

psych up (infml) v **nerve**, steel, gear up, wind up, prepare

PT n **physical training**, games, physical education, PE, gymnastics

puberty n **sexual maturity**, adolescence, youth, teens

pubescent adj **pubertal**, teenage, adolescent, teen (infml)

public adj 1 **community**, civic, communal, municipal, free Opposite: private 2 **freely available**, shared, known, open, in the public domain Opposite: secret ■ n **everyone**, people, populace, community, society

publication n **book**, magazine, newspaper, journal, periodical

public disgrace n **dishonour**, disgrace, ignominy, humiliation, exposure

public figure n **celebrity**, name, personality, personage, household name

public image n **façade**, front, public face, persona, identity

publicity n **advertising**, promotion, exposure, hype, media hype

publicize v **make public**, make known, broadcast, advertise, announce Opposite: suppress

publicly adv **openly**, in public, overtly, widely, freely Opposite: secretly

public relations n **image management**, publicity, media, relations, PR

public-spirited adj **philanthropic**, charitable, altruistic, humanitarian, benevolent Opposite: selfish

publish v 1 **issue**, put out, bring out, print, distribute 2 **make public**, make known, announce, broadcast, advertise Opposite: keep secret

publisher n **producer**, originator, commissioner, editor, issuer

publishing n **publication**, printing, issuing, reproducing, dissemination

pucker v **wrinkle**, crease, gather, pull together, ruck up Opposite: smooth ■ n **gather**, wrinkle, crease, ruck, pull

puckish adj **mischievous**, playful, naughty, impish, elfin

pudding n **dessert**, sweet, afters (infml)

puddle n **pool**, slick, wet patch ■ v 1 **potter**,

mosey around, dawdle, idle, lounge about 2 **splash**, dabble, paddle, splosh, wade

pudgy (infml) adj **fat**, chubby, stubby, podgy, heavy

puerile adj **childish**, immature, infantile, foolish, silly Opposite: mature

puerility n **immaturity**, childishness, silliness, foolishness, inanity

puff n 1 **gust**, breath, draught, current, flurry 2 **cloud**, wisp, waft, billow 3 **praise**, recommendation, advertisement, publicity, blurb (slang) ■ v 1 **blow**, exhale, breathe out, breathe Opposite: inhale 2 **pant**, breathe heavily, wheeze, gasp, gasp for breath

puffed adj **out of breath**, breathless, breathing heavily, panting, gasping

puffed-up adj **pompous**, self-important, arrogant, conceited, boastful Opposite: humble

puffiness n 1 **swelling**, enlargement, inflammation, oedema, distension 2 **pomposity**, pompousness, arrogance, haughtiness, pride Opposite: humility

puffing n **wheezing**, wheeziness, breathlessness, heavy breathing, breathing ■ adj **breathless**, out of breath, panting, gasping, winded

puff out see puff up

puff up v **enlarge**, swell, inflate, expand, bulge Opposite: deflate

puffy adj **swollen**, distended, inflated, bloated, bulbous

pugilism n **boxing**, fighting, prizefighting

pugilist n **boxer**, fighter, prizefighter, pug (infml)

pugnacious adj **aggressive**, confrontational, belligerent, truculent, argumentative Opposite: peaceable

pugnaciousness see pugnacity

pugnacity n **aggression**, fierceness, forcefulness, hostility, confrontational attitude

pukka adj 1 **fine**, well-made, excellent, high-quality, first-class 2 (infml) **genuine**, authentic, real, correct, proper 3 (infml) **respectable**, high-class, upper-class, well-placed, superior

pull v 1 **drag**, heave, haul, tow Opposite: push 2 **tug**, jerk, yank, wrench, pluck 3 **attract**, draw, bring in, pull in, lure Opposite: put off 4 **strain**, sprain, damage, injure, tear 5 **remove**, extract, withdraw, draw out, pluck out Opposite: put in ■ n 1 (infml) **attraction**, appeal, power, influence, draw 2 **jerk**, tug, yank, twitch, tweak

COMPARE AND CONTRAST CORE MEANING: move something towards you or in the same direction as you

pull move something towards you or in the same direction as you; **drag** move something large or heavy with effort across a surface; **draw** pull something with a smooth movement; **haul** pull something with a steady strong movement, often involving strenuous effort; **tow** pull something along behind by means of a rope or chain; **tug** pull at something with a sharp forceful movement, without necessarily moving the object; **yank** pull something suddenly and sharply with a single strong movement.

---

pull apart v **disintegrate**, tear apart, dismantle, pull to pieces, demolish Opposite: assemble

pull back v **recoil**, shrink, shrink away, back off, retract

pull down v **demolish**, tear down, destroy, fell, flatten Opposite: build up

pulley n **winch**, hoist, block and tackle

pull in v **attract**, draw, bring in, pull, entice Opposite: put off

pull-in (dated) n **roadside café**, transport café, service area, service station

pull off (infml) v **achieve**, succeed, be successful, accomplish, carry out Opposite: fail. See COMPARE AND CONTRAST at **accomplish**.

pull out v **1 remove**, extract, withdraw, draw out, pluck out Opposite: insert **2 leave**, depart, abandon, drop out, go away Opposite: remain

pullout n **1 insert**, flier, supplement, enclosure, addendum **2 retreat**, withdrawal, departure

pull out all the stops v **do your utmost**, go all-out, move heaven and earth, make a supreme effort, do all you can

pull somebody's leg (infml) v **tease somebody**, joke, have a joke on somebody, have a laugh, tell stories

pull the plug v **end**, discontinue, close down, cut off, wind up

pull the wool over somebody's eyes v **deceive**, delude, hoodwink, swindle, con

pull through v **recover**, get better, pick up, survive, get through

pull together v **1 unite**, join forces, rally, cooperate, team up **2 organize**, arrange, assemble, draw together, bring together

pull to pieces v **1 dismantle**, pull to bits, pull apart, take to pieces, rip to pieces **2 criticize**, vilify, make short work of, make mincemeat of, rip to shreds

pull up v **1 stop**, halt, draw to a halt, brake, pull in **2 criticize**, reprimand, rebuke, take to task, have words with

pull yourself together (infml) v **compose yourself**, regain your composure, think straight, calm down, regain your self-control

pulmonary adj **pulmonic**, lung, respiratory

pulp n **1 soft tissue**, fleshy tissue, tissue, flesh **2 paste**, mush, mash, blend, soft mass ▪ v **mash**, crush, squash, pound, grind

pulpit n **1 podium**, dais, stand, lectern, reading desk **2 clergy**, church, church authorities

pulsate v **throb**, beat, pulse, thump, thud

pulsation n **throb**, beat, pulse, rhythm, pounding

pulse n **1 throb**, pulsation, rhythm, pounding,

thump **2 legume**, leguminous plant, bean, pea ▪ v **throb**, beat, pulsate, pound, palpitate

WORD BANK

❏ **types of pulse** bean, black bean, black-eyed bean, broad bean, butter bean, chickpea, French bean, garbanzo, haricot, kidney bean, lentil, lima bean, mangetout, mung bean, pea, petits pois, pinto bean, runner bean, soya bean, string bean

---

pulverization n **1 maceration**, liquidization, crushing, reduction, grinding **2** (infml) **defeat**, humiliation, thrashing, beating, whipping

pulverize v **1 grind**, crush, macerate, pulp, mash **2** (infml) **thrash**, crush, annihilate, destroy, defeat

pummel v **beat**, thump, thrash, pound, punch

pump v **1 force**, drive, impel, propel, thrust **2 question**, interrogate, quiz, probe, debrief

pump out v **produce**, give off, generate, churn out, emit

pump up v **inflate**, blow up, puff up, puff out, expand Opposite: deflate

pun n **witticism**, joke, double entendre, quip, bon mot ▪ v **play with words**, joke, quip, make a joke, banter

punch v **1 stamp**, press, perforate, cut, pierce **2 hit**, beat, strike, pummel, thump ▪ n **1 blow**, hit, thump, clout, knock **2 vigour**, drive, energy, power, verve

punch-drunk (infml) adj **dazed**, confused, bewildered, stupefied, stunned Opposite: alert

punchiness n **vigour**, energy, verve, liveliness, drive Opposite: lethargy

punch-up (infml) n **fight**, scrap (infml), brawl, set-to (infml), fistfight

punchy (infml) adj **1 pithy**, hard-hitting, forceful, terse, effective Opposite: bland **2 dazed**, confused, bewildered, stupefied, stunned Opposite: alert

punctilious adj **1 correct**, seemly, courteous, polite, civil Opposite: boorish **2 fastidious**, scrupulous, painstaking, assiduous, meticulous Opposite: sloppy (infml). See COMPARE AND CONTRAST at **careful**.

punctiliousness n **1 propriety**, courteousness, correctness, politeness, decorum Opposite: boorishness **2 fastidiousness**, precision, correctness, exactitude, efficiency Opposite: carelessness

punctual adj **on time**, in good time, prompt, on the dot Opposite: late

punctuality n **promptness**, timekeeping, reliability, regularity Opposite: lateness

punctuate v **1 mark**, edit, correct, mark up, proofread **2 interrupt**, intersperse, scatter, interpose, pepper

puncture n **hole**, perforation, wound, lesion, pinhole ▪ v **1 pierce**, stab, perforate, prick, stick in **2 undermine**, deflate, erode, ruin, destroy Opposite: inflate

pundit *n* **expert**, specialist, authority, commentator, guru

pungency *n* **spiciness**, strong flavour, bitterness, sharpness, tanginess *Opposite*: blandness **2 pithiness**, pointedness, wit, force, bite *Opposite*: mildness

pungent *adj* **1 strong**, powerful, spicy, hot, overpowering *Opposite*: bland **2 caustic**, pithy, pointed, witty, forceful *Opposite*: mild

punish *v* **chastise**, discipline, penalize, reprove, rebuke *Opposite*: commend

punishable *adj* **disciplinary**, indictable, bookable, hanging, capital

punishing *adj* **gruelling**, exhausting, demanding, tiring, arduous *Opposite*: undemanding

punishment *n* **1 sentence**, penalty, reprimand, retribution, penance *Opposite*: reward **2 rough treatment**, abuse, mistreatment, heavy use, stick *(infml)*

punitive *adj* **disciplinary**, penal, corrective, retaliatory, retributive

punk *(infml)* *adj* **inferior**, second rate, cheap, nasty, poor

punnet *n* **basket**, tray, carton, box, container

punt *n* **bet**, gamble, stake, wager, flutter ■ *v* **kick**, hit, strike, boot, shoot

puny *adj* **1 small**, weak, tiny, feeble, frail *Opposite*: robust **2 inadequate**, trifling, paltry, minor, feeble *Opposite*: considerable

pup *n* **upstart**, brat, puppy, know-all *(infml)*, smart aleck *(infml)* ■ *v* **whelp**, litter, bear, deliver, give birth

pupil *n* **acolyte**, understudy, follower, apprentice, student *Opposite*: teacher

puppet *n* **1 marionette**, dummy, doll, glove puppet, hand puppet **2 pawn**, lackey, instrument, tool, lapdog

puppy *n* **upstart**, brat, pup, smart aleck *(infml)*, know-all *(infml)*

purchase *v* **1 buy**, pay for, acquire, obtain, procure *Opposite*: sell **2 obtain**, win, gain, secure, acquire ■ *n* **1 acquisition**, buying, obtaining, procurement, securing *Opposite*: sale **2 buy**, acquisition, goods, merchandise, item **3 grip**, grasp, hold, leverage, foothold

purchaser *n* **buyer**, procurer, customer, client, consumer *Opposite*: seller

purdah *n* **1 seclusion**, withdrawal, separation, retirement, isolation **2 screen**, curtain, barrier, divider, shield

pure *adj* **1 unmixed**, one hundred per cent, genuine, real, authentic **2 uncontaminated**, unadulterated, unpolluted, clean, untainted *Opposite*: tainted **3 sheer**, complete, utter, absolute, downright **4** *(literary)* **chaste**, unsullied, uncorrupted, innocent, sinless *Opposite*: corrupt **5 clear**, vivid, strong, vibrant, rich *Opposite*: weak **6 theoretical**, abstract, fundamental, basic, higher *Opposite*: applied

purebred *adj* **thoroughbred**, pedigree, pure

purée *n* **pulp**, paste, mush, pap, sauce ■ *v* **mash**, blend, process, liquidize, pound

purely *adv* **1 entirely**, wholly, totally, thoroughly, completely *Opposite*: partly **2 merely**, only, simply, just, solely **3 chastely**, virtuously, decently, morally, innocently *Opposite*: indecently

pureness *n* **1 cleanliness**, wholesomeness, spotlessness, clarity, transparency *Opposite*: dirtiness **2 clarity**, vividness, strength, vibrancy, richness

purgative *(fml)* *n* **enema**, emetic, suppository, laxative, purge ■ *adj* **cleansing**, emetic, laxative, emptying, purging

purgatory *n* **agony**, limbo, hell, anguish, despair

purge *v* **1 get rid of**, eliminate, remove, eradicate, do away with **2** *(fml)* **pardon**, exonerate, absolve, forgive, excuse *Opposite*: castigate *(fml)* **3 wash out**, cleanse, clean, flush out, sluice ■ *n* **1 laxative**, cathartic, emetic, purgative *(fml)* **2 elimination**, removal, eradication, expulsion, ridding

purification *n* **cleansing**, sanitization, decontamination, distillation, sterilization

purifier *n* **cleanser**, filter, sterilizer, disinfectant, antiseptic

purify *v* **cleanse**, disinfect, sanitize, decontaminate, clean *Opposite*: contaminate

purist *n* **traditionalist**, perfectionist, stickler, pedant, conformist

purity *n* **1 cleanliness**, spotlessness, clarity, transparency, limpidness *Opposite*: dirtiness **2 innocence**, wholesomeness, virtue, virtuousness, chasteness

purl *n* **1 thread**, gold thread, silver thread, wire, filigree **2 border**, edge, frill, trim, fringe

purlieu *n* **1 suburb**, commuter belt, outskirts, suburbia, vicinity **2** *(fml)* **ghetto**, shanty town, slum

purloin *(fml)* *v* **steal**, walk off with, pocket, help yourself to, thieve. *See* COMPARE AND CONTRAST *at* **steal**.

purple *adj* **elaborate**, exaggerated, florid, overwritten, ornate

WORD BANK

❑ **types of purple** amethyst, aubergine, heliotrope, lavender, lilac, mauve, plum, violet

purport *v* **1 claim**, assert, allege, profess, contend **2** *(fml)* **intend**, aim, mean, plan ■ *n* **1** *(fml)* **sense**, significance, importance, meaning, implication **2** *(fml)* **purpose**, intention, aim, design, plan

purported *adj* **supposed**, claimed, alleged, ostensible, unsupported

purpose *n* **1 intention**, aim, object, objective, goal **2 determination**, resolution, resolve, persistence, perseverance *Opposite*: indifference

purpose-built *adj* **tailor-made**, custom-made, custom-built, individual, exclusive *Opposite*: standard

purposeful *adj* **focused**, determined, decisive, resolute, firm *Opposite*: indecisive

purposefulness *n* **determination**, resolution, single-mindedness, commitment, tenacity *Opposite*: aimlessness

purposeless *adj* **1 pointless**, irrational, useless, illogical, unreasonable **2 empty**, aimless, pointless, meaningless, senseless *Opposite*: meaningful

purposely *adv* **deliberately**, intentionally, on purpose, knowingly, wittingly *Opposite*: accidentally

purr *v* **vibrate**, hum, whirr, rumble, buzz

purse *n* **1 wallet**, pouch, money bag, change purse *(US)* **2 reward**, winnings, takings, prize ■ *v* **pucker**, tighten, squeeze, press, compress *Opposite*: relax

pursuance *(fml)* *n* **enactment**, undertaking, achievement, acquirement, fulfilment

pursue *v* **1 follow**, chase, hunt, trail, track **2 practise**, engage in, work at, go in for, take up. *See* COMPARE AND CONTRAST *at* **follow**.

pursuer *n* **follower**, chaser, hunter, trailer, tracker

pursuit *n* **1 chase**, hunt, search, quest, detection **2 hobby**, recreation, activity, pastime, interest

purulent *adj* **infected**, pus-filled, pussy, weeping, oozing

purvey *v* **1** *(fml)* **sell**, provide, supply, deal in, furnish *(fml)* *Opposite*: buy **2 gossip**, tattle, whisper, spread, tell

purveyor *(fml)* *n* **1 supplier**, stockist, seller, vendor, outlet **2 spreader**, gossipmonger, teller, tattler, source

pus *n* **discharge**, secretion, excretion, fluid, infection

push *v* **1 shove**, thrust, ram, press, set in motion *Opposite*: pull **2 impel**, urge, goad, force, make *Opposite*: restrain **3 advocate**, promote, advance, endorse, boost *Opposite*: oppose ■ *n* **ambition**, energy, force, impetus, motivation *Opposite*: apathy

push-button *adj* **automatic**, high-tech, remote-control, electronic *Opposite*: manual

pushcart *n* **barrow**, cart, handcart, trolley, wagon

pushchair *n* **buggy**, stroller, carriage, baby carriage *(US)*

pushed *(infml)* *adj* **1 lacking**, short, short of cash, strapped *(infml)*, hard up *(infml)* **2 hard-pressed**, pressed, busy, struggling, hard at it

push in *v* **cut in**, barge in, shove in, squeeze in, jump the queue

pushiness *n* **forcefulness**, nerve, aggressiveness, assertiveness, brashness *Opposite*: reluctance

pushing *adj* **1 approaching**, nearly, almost, just about, roughly *Opposite*: exactly **2 assertive**, forceful, aggressive, strident, brash *Opposite*: retiring

push off *v* **1** *(infml)* **go away**, leave, depart, get going, set out *Opposite*: remain **2 cast off**, shove off, embark, depart, set sail

pushover *(infml)* *n* **dupe**, soft touch, gull, target, softy *(infml)*

push through *v* **put into force**, enforce, enact, introduce, force through

pushy *(infml)* *adj* **assertive**, forceful, aggressive, strident, brash *Opposite*: retiring

pusillanimity *n* **timidity**, fear, cowardice, nervousness, hesitation *Opposite*: confidence

pusillanimous *adj* **timid**, cowardly, faint-hearted, weak, spineless *Opposite*: brave. *See* COMPARE AND CONTRAST *at* **cowardly**.

pussy *n* *(infml)* **cat**, kitten, puss *(infml)*, pussy-cat *(infml)*, kitty *(infml)* ■ *adj* **infected**, purulent, pus-filled, weeping, oozing

pussycat *n* **1 cat**, kitten, pussy *(infml)*, puss *(infml)*, kitty *(infml)* **2** *(infml)* **dear**, soft touch, pushover, softy *(infml)*, sweetie *(infml)*

pussyfoot *(infml)* *v* **1 hesitate**, waver, wander, prevaricate, procrastinate **2 tiptoe**, creep, steal, pick your way, ghost

pustule *n* **boil**, abscess, eruption, pimple, carbuncle

put *v* **place**, set, lay, position, situate *Opposite*: remove

put about *v* **spread**, circulate, tell, inform, give out *Opposite*: keep secret

put across *v* **get across**, express, transmit, articulate, explain

put a damper on *v* **deflate**, spoil, mar, subdue, depress *Opposite*: enliven

put a match to *v* **set alight**, set fire to, set on fire, light, ignite *Opposite*: put out

put an end to *v* **stop**, discontinue, halt, suspend, call a halt to *Opposite*: continue

put a premium on *v* **value**, appreciate, prize, favour, rate highly

put aside *v* **1 save**, earmark, allocate, put by, set aside **2 disregard**, ignore, close your eyes to, forget, waive **3 set down**, set aside, deposit, lay down, put down

put a spanner in the works *v* **foil**, thwart, cause, havoc, put a spoke in somebody's wheel *Opposite*: help

put a spoke in somebody's wheel *v* **foil**, thwart, frustrate, put a spanner in the works, sabotage *Opposite*: help

put a stop to *v* **put an end to**, stop, bring to an end, pull the plug on, call a halt to *Opposite*: continue

putative *adj* **1 supposed**, reputed, alleged, assumed, presumed **2 accepted**, acknowledged, recognized, known, believed

put at risk v **endanger**, jeopardize, gamble with, risk, imperil *(fml)*

put away v **1 tidy up**, pack away, clear up, tidy away, pack up *Opposite*: scatter **2** *(infml)* **consume**, eat, drink, swallow, devour **3 save**, put aside, keep, stash away, put by **4** *(infml)* **imprison**, jail, commit, confine

put back v **1 postpone**, defer, suspend, put on hold, put off **2 drink**, throw back, gulp down, swallow down **3 put away**, replace, pack away, return, clear away **4 pay back**, repay, reimburse, compensate, recompense

put back together v **mend**, repair, reassemble, rebuild, reconstruct *Opposite*: take apart

put behind you v **forget**, get over, recover from, put down to experience, get out of your system *Opposite*: brood

put by v **save**, put aside, stash away, earmark, put away

put down v **1 set down**, lay down, down, deposit, leave *Opposite*: pick up **2 enter**, write down, put in writing, record, log **3 quell**, crush, suppress, quash, repress **4** *(infml)* **ridicule**, mock, criticize, deride, disparage *Opposite*: praise **5 attribute**, ascribe, lay at the door of, impute, blame on **6 kill**, put to death, dispatch, destroy

putdown *(infml)* n **insult**, attack, gibe, criticism, dig *Opposite*: compliment

put forth *(fml)* v **1 state**, make known, publish, present, give **2 leave**, set out, depart, head off, start out

put forward v **1 state**, make known, publish, present, give **2 suggest**, propose, present, submit, offer

put in v **1 donate**, contribute, dedicate, allocate, give *Opposite*: take out **2 present**, submit, offer, make, claim *Opposite*: withdraw **3 interrupt**, break in, interpose, interject, butt in

put in an appearance v **attend**, drop in, appear, turn up, be present

put in danger v **endanger**, jeopardize, hazard, risk, compromise

put in the shade v **outshine**, be head and shoulders above, eclipse, be streets ahead of, surpass

put into v **invest in**, plough into, sink in, tie up in, devote to

put into action v **implement**, put into practice, apply, realize, carry out

put into effect v **enforce**, put into practice, exercise, apply, carry out

put into operation v **implement**, put into action, put into practice, apply, set up

put into practice v **carry out**, do, practise, realize, implement

put into words v **phrase**, articulate, formulate, express, convey

put in writing v **put down on paper**, put down in black and white, put down, confirm in writing, write down

put off v **1 postpone**, delay, defer, shelve, suspend *Opposite*: bring forward **2 disgust**, repel, offend, sicken, revolt *Opposite*: attract **3 confuse**, distract, divert, disconcert, fluster **4 hinder**, discourage, delay, obstruct, prevent

put on v **1 dress in**, wear, change into, get into, don *Opposite*: take off **2 pretend**, feign, simulate, fake, play-act **3 stage**, present, produce, mount, direct **4 gain**, add, increase, accumulate, acquire *Opposite*: lose

put-on adj **pretend**, false, fake, sham, feigned *Opposite*: genuine ■ n *(infml)* **deception**, simulation, trick, hoax, con

put on a brave front v **put a brave face on it**, keep up appearances, be brave, keep your chin up, keep a stiff upper lip *(infml)*

put on an act v **pretend**, put it on, put on a pretence, sham, feign

put on a pedestal v **elevate**, idolize, worship, admire, regard highly

put on hold v **put off**, delay, postpone, adjourn, defer

put on ice *see* put on hold

put on the back burner *see* put on hold

put on the market v **offer for sale**, put up for sale, market, advertise

put out v **1 extinguish**, douse, snuff out, stifle, snuff *Opposite*: light **2 make public**, make known, publicize, circulate, spread *Opposite*: keep secret **3 annoy**, irritate, slight, offend, exasperate *Opposite*: please

putrefaction n **decay**, decomposition, rot, breakdown, corruption

putrefy v **rot**, decay, decompose, go bad, become rancid

putrid adj **rotten**, rotting, decayed, decaying, decomposed *Opposite*: fresh

put right v **repair**, fix, mend, rectify, restore

putsch n **coup**, insurrection, uprising, revolution, revolt

put somebody's back up *(infml)* v **annoy**, irritate, get on somebody's nerves, get on the wrong side of somebody, alienate

putt v **hit**, tap, stroke, knock, push ■ n **tap**, stroke, hit, knock, push

put to death v **kill**, execute, murder, assassinate, liquidate. *See* COMPARE AND CONTRAST *at* kill.

put together v **1 assemble**, piece together, construct, build, fabricate **2 draw up**, formulate, devise, develop, prepare

put to good use v **use**, apply, exploit, exercise, make use of *Opposite*: discard

put to sleep v **knock out**, sedate, put under, numb, dope

put under v **sedate**, put to sleep, anaesthetize, put out, knock out *Opposite*: bring round

put up v **1 erect**, raise, build, construct, create *Opposite*: tear down **2 accommodate**, house, lodge, take in *Opposite*: evict **3 offer**, provide, proffer, extend, advance

put-upon *adj* **overburdened**, exploited, used, overworked, abused

put up to *v* **induce**, persuade, encourage, make, cause *Opposite*: dissuade

put up with *v* **tolerate**, endure, bear, stand, submit

put your back into *v* **try hard**, give your all, work hard, give it your best shot, give it all you've got

put your faith in *v* **trust**, rely on, count on, have confidence in, bank on

put your feet up *v* **relax**, rest, nap, lounge around, lie down

put your foot down *v* **demand**, stand firm, stand fast, be resolute, be determined

put your foot in it *(infml)* *v* **blunder**, goof, speak out of turn, be indiscreet, be tactless

put your foot in your mouth *(infml) see* **put your foot in it**

put your oar in *v* **interfere**, meddle, stick your nose in, intrude, butt in

puzzle *v* **1 mystify**, bewilder, perplex, baffle, confuse **2 wonder**, mull, brood, ponder ■ *n* **mystery**, enigma, conundrum, problem, dilemma *Opposite*: explanation. *See* COMPARE AND CONTRAST *at* **question**.

puzzled *adj* **mystified**, bewildered, perplexed, baffled, confused *Opposite*: enlightened

puzzlement *n* **bafflement**, perplexity, uncertainty, disorientation, bemusement *Opposite*: understanding

puzzle out *v* **work out**, solve, figure out, resolve, decipher

puzzler *n* **conundrum**, puzzle, mystery, riddle, brainteaser

puzzling *adj* **mystifying**, bewildering, perplexing, baffling, confusing *Opposite*: enlightening

pygmy *adj* **miniature**, small, tiny, dwarf, little

pylon *n* **tower**, mast, post, pillar

pyre *n* **fire**, bonfire, furnace

pyromaniac *n* **fire raiser**, fire setter, arsonist, torcher

Q

QC *n* **Queen's Counsel**, counsel, barrister, brief *(infml)*

quack *n* **imposter**, charlatan, fraud, fake, pretender

quackery *n* **deception**, trickery, dishonesty, fraud, deceit *Opposite*: honesty

quad *(infml) n* **quadrangle**, courtyard, yard, square, patio

quadrangle *n* **1 courtyard**, yard, square, patio, piazza **2 four-sided figure**, rectangle, oblong, quadrilateral, parallelogram

quadrilateral *n* **rectangle**, oblong, square, parallelogram, rhombus ■ *adj* **four-sided**, rectangular, square, quadrangular, quadrate

quadruped *n* **animal**, four-footed animal, tetrapod

quadruple *v* **increase fourfold**, multiply, times, magnify, augment *Opposite*: decrease

quagmire *n* **1 swamp**, marsh, bog, mire, quicksand **2 predicament**, dilemma, quandary, sticky situation, muddle

quail *v* **flinch**, recoil, cringe, baulk. *See* COMPARE AND CONTRAST *at* **recoil**.

quaint *adj* **1 old-world**, old-fashioned, picturesque, antiquated, charming *Opposite*: modern **2 strange**, peculiar, odd, curious, bizarre *Opposite*: ordinary

quake *v* **1 quail**, tremble, shudder, quaver, cower **2 shake**, tremble, quiver, shudder, shiver ■ *n (infml)* **earthquake**, tremor, seismic wave, seismic activity, temblor *(US)*

qualification *n* **1 credential**, diploma, certificate, licence **2 skill**, quality, attribute, ability, aptitude *Opposite*: failing **3 requirement**, condition, prerequisite, criterion, sine qua non **4 restriction**, reservation, modification, limitation, tempering

qualified *adj* **1 trained**, licensed, registered, certified, recognized *Opposite*: unqualified **2 suitable**, eligible, capable, competent, skilled *Opposite*: unsuitable **3 limited**, contingent, modified *Opposite*: unconditional

qualify *v* **1 be suitable**, be in the running, meet the requirements, be eligible, make the grade *Opposite*: fail **2 train**, certify, license, empower, entitle **3 restrict**, limit, modify, temper, moderate

quality *n* **1 characteristic**, feature, attribute, property, trait **2 standard**, grade, level, calibre, class **3 excellence**, superiority, distinction, merit, eminence *Opposite*: inferiority

qualm *n* **1 scruple**, pang of conscience, remorse, contrition, compunction **2 misgiving**, doubt, pang, fear, apprehensiveness

quandary *n* **dilemma**, predicament, difficulty, cleft stick, catch-22

quantifiable *adj* **calculable**, computable, measurable, assessable, determinable *Opposite*: unquantifiable

quantify *v* **calculate**, count, enumerate, measure, compute

quantitative *adj* **1 numerical**, enumerative, arithmetical, mathematical, variable **2 measurable**, quantifiable, calculable, numerical, computable *Opposite*: unquantifiable

quantity *n* **amount**, number, measure, extent, size

quantum *adj* **major**, dramatic, significant, important, considerable *Opposite*: minor

quarantine *n* **isolation**, seclusion, confinement, solitary confinement, cordon sanitaire *Opposite*: integration ■ *v* **1 isolate**, seclude, set apart, confine, separate *Opposite*: integrate **2 detain**, imprison, hold, lock up, intern *Opposite*: release

quarrel *n* **1 argument**, dispute, disagreement, row, squabble *Opposite*: reconciliation **2 complaint**, grievance, grumble, problem *(infml)*, bone to pick *(infml)* ■ *v* **argue**, row, fall out, clash, fight *Opposite*: make up

quarrelsome *adj* **argumentative**, cantankerous, irritable, petulant, confrontational *Opposite*: agreeable

quarry *n* **1 excavation**, mine, pit, diggings **2 prey**, victim, target, kill, game *Opposite*: hunter ■ *v* **mine**, dig out, extract, excavate, dig up

quarter *n* **1 fourth**, division, part, section, quadrant **2 district**, neighbourhood, sector, zone, locality ■ *v* **1 divide**, subdivide, cut up, section, split up **2 lodge**, house, billet, accommodate, put up *Opposite*: evict

quarterfinal *n* **round**, heat, leg, match, game

quarterly *adj* **three-monthly**, trimestral, four times a year ■ *n* **magazine**, periodical, journal, publication, glossy magazine

quarters *n* **rooms**, accommodation, billet, housing, lodgings *(dated)*

quash *v* **1 put down**, suppress, quell, subdue, crush *Opposite*: allow **2 nullify**, cancel, repeal, overturn, annul *Opposite*: validate

quasi *adj* **virtual**, to all intents and purposes, pseudo, would-be, self-styled *Opposite*: through and through

quatrain *n* **verse**, stanza, rhyme

quaver *v* **1 tremble**, shudder, shake, quiver, quake **2 trill**, warble, wobble, vibrate, quiver

quay *n* **dockside**, wharf, dock, pier, seafront

quayside *see* quay

queasily *adv* **nauseously**, biliously, dizzily, groggily, woozily

queasiness *n* **nausea**, sickness; biliousness, vomiting, upset stomach

queasy *adj* **1 nauseous**, sick, ill, indisposed, seasick *Opposite*: well **2 uneasy**, uncomfortable, doubtful, dubious, troubling *Opposite*: reassuring

queen *n* **1 monarch**, sovereign, ruler, crowned head, empress **2 icon**, star, prima donna, doyenne **3 epitome**, model, essence, ideal, crème de la crème

queenly *adj* **majestic**, royal, regal, dignified, stately

queen-size *adj* **large**, largish, medium-large

queer *adj* **1** *(dated)* **unusual**, unexpected, strange, surprising, funny *Opposite*: commonplace **2** *(dated)* **unwell**, sick, nauseous, queasy, faint *Opposite*: well **3** *(dated)* **eccentric**, unconventional, idiosyncratic, curious, bizarre *Opposite*: normal **4** *(dated infml)* **eccentric**, unconventional, idiosyncratic, curious, bizarre *Opposite*: normal

quell *v* **1 suppress**, put down, subdue, crush, quash *Opposite*: incite **2 allay**, assuage, alleviate, mollify, mitigate *Opposite*: aggravate

quench *v* **1 slake**, satisfy, satiate, reduce, sate *Opposite*: stimulate **2 extinguish**, put out, douse, smother, stifle *Opposite*: ignite

querulous *adj* **1 complaining**, carping, critical, difficult, hard to please *Opposite*: equable **2 whining**, cantankerous, grumbling, complaining, whingeing *(infml)* *Opposite*: good-natured

querulousness *n* **peevishness**, negativity, cantankerousness, criticalness, argumentativeness

query *n* **1 inquiry**, question, request, interrogation, demand *Opposite*: answer **2 doubt**, uncertainty, reservation, question, question mark *Opposite*: certainty ■ *v* **1 question**, cast doubt on, doubt, suspect, challenge *Opposite*: trust **2 inquire**, ask, interrogate, quiz, demand *Opposite*: answer

quest *n* **mission**, expedition, pursuit, search, hunt ■ *v* **search**, hunt, seek, chase, pursue *Opposite*: find

question *n* **1 inquiry**, query, request, interrogation, demand *Opposite*: answer **2 uncertainty**, doubt, reservation, query, question mark *Opposite*: certainty **3 issue**, subject, matter, point at issue, problem *Opposite*: resolution ■ *v* **1 interrogate**, quiz, probe, grill *(infml)*, give somebody the third degree *(infml)* *Opposite*: reply **2 query**, cast doubt on, doubt, suspect, challenge *Opposite*: trust

COMPARE AND CONTRAST CORE MEANING: ask for information

question ask for information on a particular topic, especially formally or officially; **quiz** subject somebody to persistent questions; **interrogate** question somebody systematically and intensively in a formal or official context, such as in a police investigation or court case; **grill** *(infml)* question somebody intensively; **give the third degree** *(infml)* question somebody intensively, especially in an aggressive way.

questionable *adj* **dubious**, doubtful, open to discussion, open to doubt, moot *Opposite*: indisputable

questioner *n* **interviewer**, interrogator, cross-examiner, asker, inquirer *Opposite*: interviewee

questioning *adj* **interrogative**, inquisitorial, searching, quizzical, inquiring *Opposite*: responsive

question mark *n* **doubt**, uncertainty, reservation, query, question *Opposite*: certainty

question master *n* **host**, questioner, chair, interviewer, examiner *Opposite*: contestant

questionnaire *n* **survey**, opinion poll, inquiry form, form, feedback form

queue *n* **1 line**, file, row, crocodile, column **2 tailback**, backlog, logjam ■ *v* **line up**, queue up, form a queue, get in line, wait your turn

queue-jump *v* **push in**, move ahead, leapfrog, overtake, butt in

quibble *v* **equivocate**, hedge, split hairs, nitpick, cavil *Opposite*: agree ■ *n* **objection**, cavil, equivocation, quiddity *(fml)*

quiche *n* **tart**, egg pie, flan, tartlet, pastry

quick *adj* **1 rapid**, fast, speedy, swift, nippy *Opposite*: slow **2 intelligent**, clever, bright, quick-thinking, quick-witted **3 nimble**, lively, sprightly, spry, agile *Opposite*: sluggish **4 sudden**, immediate, instant, prompt, abrupt *Opposite*: delayed **5 brief**, short, cursory, fleeting, momentary *Opposite*: lasting. *See* COMPARE AND CONTRAST *at* **intelligent**.

quicken *v* **speed up**, accelerate, hasten, pick up speed, go faster *Opposite*: slow down

quick-fire *adj* **rapid**, swift, successive, automatic, fast *Opposite*: measured

quickly *adv* **1 rapidly**, fast, speedily, swiftly, hurriedly *Opposite*: slowly **2 suddenly**, immediately, promptly, without delay, at once *Opposite*: slowly **3 briefly**, cursorily, fleetingly, momentarily, passingly *Opposite*: lastingly

quickness *n* **1 rapidity**, speed, speediness, swiftness, promptness *Opposite*: sluggishness **2 alertness**, cleverness, quick-wittedness, adroitness, sharpness

quicksand *n* **swamp**, marsh, quagmire, bog, mire

quicksilver *adj* **volatile**, mercurial, changeable, inconstant, unpredictable *Opposite*: constant

quick-tempered *adj* **fiery**, temperamental, excitable, volatile, passionate *Opposite*: calm

quick-witted *adj* **smart**, intelligent, clever, bright, sharp

quick-wittedness *n* **adroitness**, inventiveness, sharpness, intelligence, cleverness

quid pro quo *n* **deal**, trade, agreement, exchange, trade-off

quiescence *(fml) n* **inactivity**, rest, stillness, inertness, calm *Opposite*: action

quiescent *(fml) adj* **calm**, inactive, dormant, gentle, sluggish *Opposite*: active

quiet *adj* **1 silent**, noiseless, inaudible, low, soft *Opposite*: noisy **2 peaceful**, still, tranquil, uninterrupted, undisturbed *Opposite*: noisy **3 private**, discreet, unofficial, off-the-record, confidential *Opposite*: public **4 trouble-free**, straightforward, uncomplicated, simple, easy **5 relaxing**, restful, leisurely, peaceful, pleasant *Opposite*: busy **6 discreet**, modest, subtle, subdued, muted *Opposite*: showy ■ *n* **silence**, hush, peace, stillness, tranquillity *Opposite*: noise. *See* COMPARE AND CONTRAST *at* **silent**.

quieten *v* **1 fall silent**, calm down, settle down, calm, hush *Opposite*: animate **2 alleviate**, allay, soothe, assuage, quell *Opposite*: aggravate

quieten down *v* **stop talking**, fall silent, keep it down, quieten, shut up *(infml)*

quietly *adv* **1 silently**, gently, inaudibly, softly, in silence *Opposite*: loudly **2 calmly**, peacefully, tranquilly, serenely, uninterrupted *Opposite*: noisily **3 peacefully**, tranquilly, pleasantly, agreeably, restfully

quietness *n* **1 silence**, softness, quiet, noiselessness, inaudibility *Opposite*: noise **2 peace**, stillness, tranquillity, serenity, calm

quill *n* **feather**, plume, barb, spine, spike

quilt *n* **duvet**, bedspread, eiderdown, coverlet, bedcover

quintessence *n* **essence**, embodiment, epitome, personification, soul

quintessential *adj* **typical**, essential, archetypal, prototypical, model *Opposite*: atypical

quip *n* **witticism**, joke, gibe, one-liner, clever remark ■ *v* **joke**, gibe, remark, banter, retort

quirk *n* **1 twist of fate**, coincidence, accident, chance, oddity **2 idiosyncrasy**, peculiarity, foible, oddity, habit

quirky *adj* **idiosyncratic**, individual, unusual, peculiar, odd *Opposite*: normal

quit *v* **1 resign**, leave, walk out, abandon, vacate *Opposite*: stay **2 give up**, stop, relinquish, refrain from, renounce *Opposite*: take up

quite *adv* **1 fairly**, rather, moderately, relatively, reasonably *Opposite*: extremely **2 very**, entirely, completely, totally, utterly *Opposite*: slightly

quits *(infml) adj* **even**, square, settled, level, even-steven *(infml)*

quitter *(infml) n* **defeatist**, deserter, loser, pessimist, coward *Opposite*: go-getter *(infml)*

quiver *v* **tremble**, shake, shudder, shiver, quake ■ *n* **shudder**, shiver, tremble, palpitation, tremor

quivering *adj* **trembling**, quaking, quavering, unsteady, shaky *Opposite*: steady ■ *n* **pulsation**, vibration, spasm, palpitation, tremor

quixotic *adj* **romantic**, unrealistic, idealistic, impractical, dreamy *Opposite*: down-to-earth

quiz *n* **test**, puzzle, game, contest, competition ■ *v* **question**, interrogate, cross-examine, interview, examine. *See* COMPARE AND CONTRAST *at* **question**.

quizzical *adj* **questioning**, curious, puzzled, surprised, perplexed

quorum *n* **minimum**, minimum number, least, required number, lower limit

quota *n* **share**, allocation, allowance, part, ration

quotation *n* **1 quote**, citation, line, passage, extract **2 estimate**, price, figure, costing, quote

quote *v* **1 cite**, recite, repeat, refer to, mention **2 give an estimate**, estimate, bid, give a price, give a figure ■ *n* **1 quotation**, citation, line, passage, extract **2 estimate**, price, figure, costing, quotation

quotient *n* **proportion**, measure, amount, share, percentage

R

rabbi *n* **religious leader**, scholar, teacher, official, leader

rabbit *n* **bunny**, coney, cottontail ■ *v* (*infml*) **chat**, chatter, gossip, go on, run on

rabble *n* **mob**, crowd, swarm, throng, horde

rabble-rouser *n* **troublemaker**, agitator, demagogue, activist, firebrand

rabble-rousing *n* **troublemaking**, sedition, provocation, agitation, activism ■ *adj* **provocative**, inflammatory, seditious, incendiary, troublemaking

rabid *adj* **1 foaming at the mouth**, diseased, sick, ill, infected *Opposite*: well **2 fanatical**, extreme, radical, uncompromising, militant *Opposite*: lukewarm **3 intense**, fervent, ardent, violent, zealous *Opposite*: moderate

rabidly *adv* **fervently**, ardently, intensely, single-mindedly, zealously *Opposite*: moderately

race *n* **1 contest**, competition, heat, sprint, marathon **2 ethnic group**, nation, tribe, line, people (*infml*) **3 struggle**, fight, rivalry, battle, competition ■ *v* **1 compete**, take part, run, sprint, contest *Opposite*: withdraw **2 speed**, go fast, run, sprint, hurry *Opposite*: crawl

racecourse *n* **track**, turf, course, hippodrome

racer *n* **competitor**, contender, entrant, sprinter, runner

racetrack *n* **track**, stadium, running track, circuit, speedway

raceway *n* **1 channel**, race, conduit, canal, course **2 track**, circuit, course, stadium, racetrack

racial *adj* **ethnic**, cultural, tribal, national

racism *n* **racial discrimination**, discrimination, prejudice, bigotry, intolerance

racist *adj* **chauvinistic**, bigoted, xenophobic, prejudiced, discriminatory *Opposite*: tolerant

rack *n* **stand**, frame, framework, holder, shelf ■ *v* **1 afflict**, torment, plague, torture, beset *Opposite*: comfort **2 shake**, rock, devastate, play havoc with, wreck *Opposite*: restore **3 store**, shelve, stack, stow, put away *Opposite*: unpack

racket (*infml*) *n* **1 row**, noise, ruckus, din, rumpus **2 swindle**, con, fraud, sting (*infml*), fiddle (*infml*)

racketeer *n* **criminal**, swindler, hoodlum, fraudster, shark (*infml*)

rack up (*infml*) *v* **accumulate**, chalk up, score, make, achieve

rack your brains *v* **try to remember**, think hard, concentrate, make an effort, focus

raconteur *n* **narrator**, storyteller, conversationalist, after-dinner speaker, wit

racy *adj* **indecent**, risqué, indelicate, improper, sexy *Opposite*: clean

radar *n* **detector**, locater, sensor, locating system, position finder

raddled *adj* **haggard**, debauched, worn-out, dishevelled, unkempt *Opposite*: fresh

radial *adj* **circular**, outward, centrifugal, radiated, outspread

radiance *n* **1 happiness**, sparkle, joy, vivacity, joie de vivre *Opposite*: dullness **2 light**, brightness, glow, luminosity, brilliance

radiant *adj* **1 happy**, healthy, glowing, beaming, sunny *Opposite*: unhappy **2 shining**, luminous, brilliant, bright, dazzling *Opposite*: dull

radiate *v* **1 give out**, give off, emit, discharge, issue **2 exude**, emanate, glow with, bristle with, brim with **3 spread out**, branch out, diverge, spread, circulate

radiation *n* **particle emission**, energy, radioactivity, fallout, contamination

radiator *n* **heater**, room heater, storage heater, space heater

radical *adj* **1 basic**, fundamental, essential, profound, deep-seated **2 sweeping**, pervasive, thorough, far-reaching, wide-ranging *Opposite*: minor **3 revolutionary**, extreme, extremist, uncompromising, militant *Opposite*: conservative ■ *n* **extremist**, activist, militant, revolutionary, fanatic *Opposite*: conservative

radicalism *n* **extremism**, militancy, fanaticism, ardour, zealotry

radio *n* **radio set**, transistor, receiver, boom box (*infml*), wireless (*dated*)

radioactive *adj* **emitting radiation**, dangerous, harmful, hot, active

radioactivity *n* **radiation**, particle emission, energy, fallout

radio-controlled *adj* **remote-controlled**, automatic, remote

radius *n* **1 line**, distance, length **2 area**, range, circle, ambit, extent **3 scope**, area of influence, umbrella, reach, remit

raffia *n* **straw**, fibre, grass, natural fibre

raffish *adj* **1 unconventional**, dashing, rakish, disreputable, louche *Opposite*: conventional **2 showy**, ostentatious, gaudy, loud, garish *Opposite*: discreet

raffle *n* **lottery**, draw, tombola, sweepstake, drawing ■ *v* **offer**, give away, award, present, donate

raft (*infml*) *n* **bundle**, number, tranche, portfolio, range

rafter *n* **beam**, roof beam, support, joist, strut

rag *n* **1 scrap**, shred, wisp, tatter, thread **2** (*infml*) **newspaper**, paper, daily, tabloid, red-top (*infml*) ■ *v* (*dated*) **tease**, taunt, make fun of, call names, poke fun at

ragamuffin (*dated*) *n* **urchin**, waif, child

ragbag (*infml*) *n* **mixture**, mixed bag, miscellany, jumble, hotchpotch

rage *n* **fury**, wrath, anger, temper, frenzy *Opposite*: calmness ■ *v* **fume**, rant and rave, storm, seethe, thunder. *See* COMPARE AND CONTRAST *at* anger.

ragged *adj* **1 tattered**, torn, worn-out, raggedy, in tatters *Opposite*: pristine **2 unkempt**, untidy, shabby, raggedy, in rags *Opposite*: neat **3 jagged**, serrated, uneven, irregular, rough *Opposite*: even

raggedness *n* **1 untidiness**, shabbiness, scruffiness, sloppiness, messiness *Opposite*: neatness **2 unevenness**, jaggedness, roughness, irregularity, sharpness *Opposite*: smoothness

raggedy *see* ragged

raging *adj* **powerful**, intense, furious, strong, rampant *Opposite*: mild

ragtag *adj* **1 motley**, disparate, assorted, miscellaneous, multifarious **2 untidy**, shabby, unkempt, scruffy, ragged *Opposite*: neat

raid *n* **attack**, search, forced entry, break-in, incursion ■ *v* **1 storm**, attack, invade, search, break into **2 rob**, loot, plunder, hold up, burgle

raider *n* **attacker**, thief, robber, marauder, invader

rail *n* **railing**, handrail, banister, bar, support ■ *v* **protest**, complain, object, criticize, condemn *Opposite*: accept

railhead *n* **terminus**, starting point, end of the line

railing *n* **fence**, paling, barrier, balustrade, boundary line

raillery *n* **teasing**, joking, banter, repartee, kidding *Opposite*: bullying

railroad (*infml*) *v* **push**, force, steamroller, bulldoze, shove

railway *n* **1 track**, line, train track, route, railroad (*US*) **2 rail network**, rail transport system, train system, train network, railroad (*US*)

WORD BANK

❑ **types of railway** cable railway, funicular railway, light railway, metro, monorail, tramway, underground

❑ **types of rail vehicle** cable car, funicular, locomotive, metro, steam engine, TGV, train, tram, tube

❑ **parts of a train** cabin, car, carriage, coach, compartment, freight car, locomotive, luggage compartment, Pullman, restaurant car, sleeper, sleeping car, smoker, smoking car, smoking carriage, smoking compartment, steam engine, tank engine, wagon

rain *n* **1 rainfall**, drizzle, shower, torrent, precipitation **2 volley**, hail, stream, torrent, flood ■ *v* **1 pour**, drizzle, spit, pelt down, shower **2 lavish**, shower, pour, deluge, overwhelm

rainbow *n* **arc**, arch, bow ■ *adj* **multicoloured**, colourful, variegated, spectral, polychromatic *Opposite*: monochrome

rain cats and dogs (*infml*) *v* **pour with rain**, teem, pour down, come down in torrents, come down in buckets

rainfall *n* **rain**, shower, drizzle, Scotch mist, torrent *Opposite*: sunshine

rain off *v* **postpone**, cancel, put back, call off, move on *Opposite*: bring forward

rainproof *adj* **impermeable**, water-resistant, waterproof, showerproof, impervious *Opposite*: permeable

rainstorm *n* **cloudburst**, downpour, deluge, thunderstorm, shower

rainwater *n* **rain**, precipitation, rainfall, raindrops

rainy *adj* **wet**, raining, drizzling, showery, drizzly *Opposite*: dry

raise *v* **1 hoist**, lift up, uplift, elevate, move up *Opposite*: let down **2 look after**, bring up, foster, grow, breed *Opposite*: neglect **3 increase**, put up, inflate, boost, jack up *Opposite*: lower **4 build**, erect, set up, construct, put up **5 improve**, better, enhance, uplift, advance *Opposite*: deteriorate **6 mention**, bring up, present, put forward, moot *Opposite*: withdraw **7 solicit**, canvass, obtain, bring in, procure **8 lift**, end, terminate, conclude *Opposite*: impose **9 cause**, elicit, stimulate, induce, excite *Opposite*: quell

raise objections v **object**, protest about, demur, remonstrate, contest *Opposite*: agree

raise your spirits v **cheer up**, lift your spirits, gladden, hearten, buoy up *Opposite*: depress

raison d'être n **meaning**, purpose, rationale, motivation, inspiration

rajah n **king**, prince, maharajah, chief, ruler *Opposite*: subject

rake v 1 **gather**, clear up, scrape, collect, scrape up *Opposite*: scatter 2 **enfilade**, pepper, spray, shoot 3 **search through**, go through, sift, rummage, comb *Opposite*: find ■ n **reprobate**, degenerate, prodigal, profligate, squanderer *Opposite*: paragon

rake-off (*infml*) n **bribe**, kickback, favour, backhander (*infml*), sweetener (*infml*) *Opposite*: cost

rake up (*infml*) v **mention**, drag up, dredge up, bring up, dig up *Opposite*: keep mum (*infml*)

rakish adj 1 **dashing**, stylish, natty, sporty, jaunty *Opposite*: bland 2 **dissolute**, profligate, degenerate, louche, dubious *Opposite*: upright

rally n 1 **gathering**, meeting, assembly, convention, demonstration 2 **resurgence**, revival, comeback, recovery, revitalization ■ v 1 **come together**, gather, call together, bring together, unite *Opposite*: disperse 2 **revive**, improve, recover, pull through, get better *Opposite*: decline

ram v 1 **strike**, hit, bump, slam, collide with 2 **force**, stuff, jam, cram, compress

ramble v 1 **go on**, digress, go off at a tangent, ramble on, rattle on *Opposite*: focus 2 **walk**, hike, wander, roam, go for a walk ■ n **hike**, walk, roam, stroll, wander

ramble on v **go on**, ramble, digress, go off at a tangent, rattle on *Opposite*: focus

rambler n **walker**, hiker, backpacker, roamer, wanderer

rambling adj 1 **long-winded**, wordy, discursive, digressive, incoherent *Opposite*: concise 2 **spread out**, sprawling, trailing, straggling, irregular *Opposite*: compact. *See* COMPARE AND CONTRAST *at* **wordy**.

rambunctious adj **rowdy**, high-spirited, lively, disorderly, riotous *Opposite*: mellow

ramekin n **dish**, pot, container, vessel, baking dish

ramequin *see* **ramekin**

ram home v **emphasize**, stress, accentuate, drive home, underline *Opposite*: pass over

ramification n **complication**, difficulty, consequence, result, implication

ramify v 1 **branch**, divide, subdivide, fork, split *Opposite*: unite 2 **complicate**, confuse, confound, compound, intensify *Opposite*: simplify

ramp n 1 **slope**, incline, rise, upgrade, gradient 2 **hump**, ridge, bump, speed bump, rumble strip

rampage n **riot**, uproar, tumult, furor, turmoil ■ v **run riot**, riot, rage, run amok, tear

rampant adj 1 **unchecked**, unrestrained, threatening, out of control, uncontrolled *Opposite*: contained 2 **wild**, widespread, extensive, lush, rambling *Opposite*: tamed

rampart n **fortification**, embankment, bastion, wall, earthwork

ram-raid v **loot**, break in, force an entry, plunder, rob

ram-raider n **burglar**, robber, looter, thief, plunderer

ramshackle adj **rickety**, tumbledown, dilapidated, broken down, falling to pieces *Opposite*: sturdy

ranch n **farm**, smallholding, farmstead, estate, stud

rancher n **farmer**, livestock farmer, smallholder, landowner, squire

rancid adj **reeking**, fetid, sour, off, bad *Opposite*: fresh

rancidness n **sourness**, rankness, fetidness, rottenness, smelliness *Opposite*: freshness

rancorous adj **acrimonious**, bitter, malicious, resentful, vindictive *Opposite*: amicable

rancorousness *see* **rancour**

rancour n **acrimony**, bitterness, malice, resentment, vindictiveness

random adj **haphazard**, arbitrary, accidental, casual, hit and miss *Opposite*: deliberate

randomness n **haphazardness**, arbitrariness, casualness, chanciness, unpredictability *Opposite*: predictability

range n 1 **variety**, choice, series, assortment, array 2 **scope**, span, breadth, reach, extent ■ v **vary between**, fluctuate, vacillate, oscillate, alternate

ranger n 1 **wanderer**, roamer, rambler, walker, hiker 2 **park ranger**, steward, overseer, guardian, guard

rangy adj **long-legged**, tall, lanky, gangling, gangly *Opposite*: thickset

rani n **queen**, princess, maharani, consort

rank n **status**, title, category, position, level ■ v **rate**, position, place, categorize, class ■ adj 1 **sheer**, utter, complete, blatant, absolute *Opposite*: minimal 2 **vigorous**, rampant, exuberant, abundant, flourishing *Opposite*: sparse 3 (*literary*) **pungent**, fetid, stinking, smelly, bad *Opposite*: fresh

ranking n **position**, status, place, standing, rank

rankle v **irritate**, fester, gnaw, eat up, irk *Opposite*: soothe

ransack v 1 **search**, go through, rummage, turn upside down, turn out *Opposite*: find 2 **rob**, despoil, vandalize, strip, loot

ransom n **payment**, money, sum, deal, exchange ■ v **redeem**, buy back, set free, strike a deal, pay up

rant v **rage**, go on, bluster, fume, seethe *Opposite*: sweet-talk *(infml)* ■ n **outburst**, tirade, histrionics, bombast, bluster

rant and rave v **rage**, go on, keep on, bluster, shout *Opposite*: calm down

rap v **hit**, thwack, strike, tap, crack ■ n **1 blow**, tap, knock, smack, crack *Opposite*: caress **2 rebuke**, criticism, reprimand, reproach, tongue-lashing

rapacious adj **1 grasping**, greedy, avid, voracious, avaricious *Opposite*: temperate **2 destructive**, vicious, harmful, aggressive, dangerous *Opposite*: harmless

rapaciousness n **1 voraciousness**, greediness, unscrupulousness, greed, avarice **2 destructiveness**, violence, viciousness, harmfulness, aggressiveness *Opposite*: gentleness

rapid adj **swift**, quick, fast, speedy, hasty *Opposite*: slow

rapidity n **swiftness**, quickness, speed, speediness, haste *Opposite*: slowness

rapids n **fast-moving water**, white water, torrents, waterfall, fall

rap on/over the knuckles *(infml)* v **reprimand**, scold, rebuke, censure, upbraid *Opposite*: praise

rap out v **bark**, shout, snap, bawl, yell *Opposite*: whisper

rapper n **singer**, vocalist, rhymer, performer

rapport n **relationship**, bond, understanding, link, affinity *Opposite*: friction

rapprochement n **reconciliation**, reunion, understanding, settlement, compromise *Opposite*: hostility

rapt adj **1 engrossed**, fascinated, absorbed, captivated, gripped *Opposite*: bored **2 happy**, blissful, delighted, content, joyful *Opposite*: sullen

rapture n **bliss**, ecstasy, euphoria, delight, joy *Opposite*: depression

rapturous adj **delighted**, enthusiastic, thrilled, overjoyed, elated *Opposite*: unenthusiastic

rare adj **1 infrequent**, occasional, sporadic, intermittent, erratic *Opposite*: frequent **2 valuable**, unique, singular, scarce, exceptional *Opposite*: common **3 underdone**, bloody, juicy, red, pink *Opposite*: overcooked

rarefied adj **esoteric**, abstruse, exclusive, obscure, complex *Opposite*: simple

rarely adv **seldom**, infrequently, on the odd occasion, hardly ever, not often *Opposite*: often

rareness n **1 scarcity**, paucity, dearth, lack, scarceness *Opposite*: abundance **2 uniqueness**, matchlessness, exclusivity, exceptionality, individuality *Opposite*: commonness

rarified *see* **rarefied**

raring adj **enthusiastic**, eager, keen, ready, impatient *Opposite*: reluctant

rarity n **1 infrequency**, shortage, scarcity, uncommonness, fewness **2 one-off**, find, unusual object, curiosity, oddity

rascal n **1 tease**, joker, prankster, trickster, jester **2 rogue**, mischief, mischief-maker, scoundrel, scamp *(infml)*

rascally adj **1 mischievous**, impish, naughty, puckish, playful *Opposite*: well-behaved **2 dishonest**, wicked, bad, mean, untrustworthy *Opposite*: good

rash adj **impetuous**, thoughtless, hasty, impulsive, reckless *Opposite*: sensible ■ n **1 eruption**, spots, reaction, itchiness, inflammation **2 outbreak**, flush, spate, string, eruption *Opposite*: incident

rashness n **impetuousness**, thoughtlessness, haste, recklessness, foolishness *Opposite*: prudence

rasp n **file**, scraper, tool ■ v **1 scrape**, rub, grate, chafe, grind *Opposite*: smooth **2 grate**, bark, snarl, growl *Opposite*: murmur

rasping adj **harsh**, rough, grating, hoarse, jarring *Opposite*: smooth

ratchet n **notch**, tooth, cog, wheel, pawl ■ v **intensify**, inflame, step up, stir up, increase *Opposite*: lessen

rate n **1 speed**, tempo, pace, velocity **2 amount**, frequency, level, degree, proportion **3 charge**, fee, price, tariff, toll ■ v **value**, regard, rank, esteem, appraise

rather adv **1 quite**, somewhat, to a certain extent, slightly, pretty **2 very**, considerably, significantly, noticeably, extremely *Opposite*: hardly **3 sooner**, preferably, instead, by preference

ratification n **approval**, sanction, endorsement, confirmation, authorization *Opposite*: rejection

ratify v **approve**, sanction, endorse, confirm, authorize *Opposite*: reject

rating n **1 assessment**, score, evaluation, grade, ranking **2 sailor**, seaman, hand

ratio n **proportion**, relative amount, relation, percentage, share

ration n **share**, portion, allowance, quota, allotment ■ v **restrict**, control, limit, put a ceiling on, regulate *Opposite*: lavish

rational adj **1 reasonable**, sensible, logical, realistic, sound *Opposite*: illogical **2 lucid**, balanced, sane, normal, cogent *Opposite*: irrational

rationale n **reasoning**, basis, foundation, justification, motivation

rationality n **logic**, reason, shrewdness, judgment, lucidity *Opposite*: irrationality

rationalization n **1 streamlining**, restructuring, reorganization, rearrangement, reshuffling **2 justification**, explanation, reasoning, validation, excuse

rationalize v **1 adjust**, tune, level, straighten out, unravel **2 justify**, give good reason for, vindicate, excuse, explain **3 make more effi-**

cient, reduce, downsize, streamline, slim down *Opposite*: increase

ration out v distribute, share out, apportion, divide up, allot *Opposite*: pool

rations n **provisions**, supplies, food, consignment, distribution

rat on (*infml*) v **1 betray**, tell on, inform on, set up, spill the beans on (*infml*) **2 abandon**, give up on, go back on, renege on, let down *Opposite*: stick to

rattily (*infml*) adv **1 irritably**, crabbily, tetchily, grumpily (*infml*), testily (*infml*) **2 messily**, shabbily, tattily, raggedly, scruffily *Opposite*: tidily

rattle v **1 shake**, clatter, bang, crash, jangle **2 unnerve**, fluster, faze, shock, disconcert *Opposite*: calm

rattle off v **say quickly**, reel off, run through, list, recite *Opposite*: stammer

rattle on v **chatter**, go on and on, drone on, talk nineteen to the dozen, jabber *Opposite*: clam up (*infml*)

rattle through v **rush through**, dash through, make short work of, dash off (*infml*) *Opposite*: labour

rattletrap (*infml*) n **wreck**, banger (*infml*), boneshaker (*infml*), rust bucket (*infml*), heap (*slang*)

rattling adj **quick-fire**, pacey, fast, brisk, lively *Opposite*: plodding

ratty (*infml*) adj **1 irritable**, short-tempered, bad-tempered, crabby, irascible *Opposite*: easygoing **2 messy**, unkempt, shabby, seedy, tatty *Opposite*: tidy

raucous adj **loud**, harsh, rough, hoarse, disorderly *Opposite*: subdued

raucousness n **boisterousness**, wildness, disorderliness, unruliness, riotousness *Opposite*: quietness

ravage v **1 wreck**, devastate, destroy, ruin, damage *Opposite*: create **2 despoil**, pillage, plunder, sack, lay waste *Opposite*: restore

ravages n **effects**, consequences, results, aftereffects

rave v **1 rant**, rage, fume, fulminate, hold forth *Opposite*: reason **2** (*infml*) **enthuse**, praise, go on about, laud, extol *Opposite*: criticize ■ n **party**, bash, event, revelry, festivity

ravel v **tangle**, knot, twist, snag, catch *Opposite*: untangle

ravening adj **voracious**, greedy, hungry, predatory, vicious *Opposite*: sated

ravenous adj **1 hungry**, famished, starving (*infml*), starved (*infml*) *Opposite*: sated **2 greedy**, voracious, rapacious, ravening, predatory *Opposite*: generous

ravenousness n **greediness**, insatiability, hunger, greed, gluttony

raver (*infml*) n **partygoer**, hedonist, clubber, party animal (*infml*), sybarite (*literary*)

ravine n **valley**, gorge, gap, gully, canyon

raving adj **frenzied**, gibbering, crazed, raging, delirious *Opposite*: controlled

ravish v **overwhelm**, overcome, transport, overpower, delight

ravishing adj **beautiful**, stunning, gorgeous, striking, eye-catching *Opposite*: plain

raw adj **1 uncooked**, fresh, rare, red, underdone *Opposite*: cooked **2 unprocessed**, unrefined, untreated, crude, basic *Opposite*: processed **3 painful**, sore, sensitive, tender, bleeding *Opposite*: healed **4 inexperienced**, green, untrained, wet behind the ears, untried *Opposite*: experienced **5 bitter**, chilly, perishing, bleak, freezing *Opposite*: mild **6 visceral**, brutal, crude, rude, primal *Opposite*: bland

rawness n **1 inflammation**, painfulness, soreness, pain, redness **2 inexperience**, naivety, ingenuousness, innocence, immaturity *Opposite*: poise **3 cold**, chill, bitterness, iciness, chilliness *Opposite*: mildness **4 brutality**, crudeness, rudeness, primitiveness, atavism *Opposite*: polish

ray n **beam**, shaft, gleam, glimmer, flicker

raze v **destroy**, demolish, annihilate, level, flatten *Opposite*: build

razor v **shave**, cut, trim, style, clip

razzmatazz n **showiness**, flashiness, hype, razzle-dazzle, glitziness *Opposite*: dullness

re prep **on the subject of**, with regard to, with reference to, concerning, regarding

reach v **1 stretch**, touch, get hold of, grasp, extend **2 go**, move, feel, fumble, lunge **3 arrive at**, get to, attain, make, achieve **4 influence**, touch, affect, impact on, get to **5 contact**, get in touch with, access, get through to, get hold of ■ n **scope**, spread, range, orbit, grasp

reachable adj **within reach**, on hand, nearby, easy to get to, accessible *Opposite*: remote

react v **1 respond**, counter, retort, answer, reply *Opposite*: ignore **2 change**, alter, oxidize, reduce, bond

reaction n **response**, repercussion, comeback, feedback, blowback (*infml*)

reactionary adj **backward-looking**, conservative, right-wing, illiberal, unreceptive *Opposite*: progressive ■ n **conservative**, right-winger, dinosaur, diehard, extremist *Opposite*: progressive

reactivate v **restart**, reboot, galvanize, resuscitate, revitalize *Opposite*: deactivate

reactive adj **responsive**, sensitive, oversensitive, volatile, mercurial *Opposite*: phlegmatic

read v **1 understand**, comprehend, make sense of, follow **2 peruse**, scan, glance at, look at, study **3 read out**, recite, deliver, speak, declaim **4 interpret**, decipher, figure out, translate, convert **5 study**, take, do, do a degree in, research

readable adj **clear**, legible, decipherable,

understandable, comprehensible *Opposite*: illegible

reader *n* **booklover**, bibliophile, bookworm *(infml)*

readership *n* **circulation**, audience, distribution, market share, niche

readily *adv* **1 willingly**, gamely, eagerly, voluntarily, gladly *Opposite*: grudgingly **2 promptly**, unhesitatingly, quickly, straightaway, at once *Opposite*: belatedly **3 without difficulty**, easily, effortlessly, with no trouble, smoothly *Opposite*: painfully

readiness *n* **1 willingness**, gameness, eagerness, keenness, enthusiasm *Opposite*: unwillingness **2 promptness**, speediness, quickness, alacrity, skill *Opposite*: delay

reading *n* **1 understanding**, comprehension, construing, interpretation, analysis **2 recitation**, recital, rendition, performance, presentation

readjust *v* **1 get used to**, settle, settle in, accommodate, come to terms with **2 rearrange**, realign, modify, calibrate, rectify *Opposite*: leave alone

readjustment *n* **rearrangement**, change, modification, alteration, reformation

read out *v* **announce**, recite, deliver, declaim, reel off

read-out *n* **1 data**, information, figures, statistics, details **2 display**, retrieval, record, screen, monitor

read up *v* **study**, find out about, look into, investigate, research

ready *adj* **1 prepared**, set, all set, complete, standing by *Opposite*: unprepared **2 likely to**, about to, on the verge of, on the point of, liable to *Opposite*: unlikely **3 willing**, eager, prepared, disposed, keen *Opposite*: unwilling **4 quick**, prompt, apt, timely, swift *Opposite*: slow **5 perceptive**, discerning, attentive, wide-awake, astute *Opposite*: dull ■ *v* **prepare**, set, arrange, prime, make plans for

ready-made *adj* **off-the-peg**, prêt-à-porter, retail, high-street, convenient *Opposite*: personalized

ready-to-wear *see* **ready-made**

reaffirm *v* **repeat**, reassert, confirm, reiterate, endorse *Opposite*: contradict

reaffirmation *n* **restatement**, repetition, reiteration, endorsement, confirmation *Opposite*: contradiction

reagent *n* **substance**, component, element, chemical, mixture

real *adj* **1 actual**, factual, material, tangible, physical *Opposite*: nonexistent **2 genuine**, original, authentic, bona fide, valid *Opposite*: false **3 sincere**, unfeigned, genuine, frank, heartfelt *Opposite*: artificial

realign *v* **readjust**, straighten, manipulate, rearrange, restore *Opposite*: disarrange

realignment *n* **readjustment**, rearrangement, shift, repositioning, relocation

realism *n* **practicality**, pragmatism, level-headedness, common sense, sanity *Opposite*: impracticality

realist *n* **pragmatist**, doer, experimenter, radical, stoic *Opposite*: idealist

realistic *adj* **1 practical**, sensible, pragmatic, down-to-earth, level-headed *Opposite*: impractical **2 convincing**, lifelike, representative, truthful, accurate *Opposite*: unnatural

reality *n* **1 realism**, authenticity, truth, certainty, veracity *Opposite*: idealism **2 actuality**, the everyday, experience, existence, life *Opposite*: make-believe

realizable *adj* **achievable**, attainable, realistic, viable, possible *Opposite*: unattainable

realization *n* **1 understanding**, comprehension, consciousness, awareness, recognition *Opposite*: ignorance **2 achievement**, fulfilment, accomplishment, carrying out, attainment *Opposite*: failure

realize *v* **1 understand**, comprehend, become conscious, appreciate, grasp *Opposite*: misunderstand **2 achieve**, fulfil, accomplish, carry out, bring to fruition *Opposite*: fail. *See* COMPARE AND CONTRAST *at* **accomplish**.

real-life *adj* **actual**, true, factual, real, realistic *Opposite*: imaginary

reallocate *v* **redistribute**, reshuffle, reorganize, transfer, rationalize

really *adv* **1 actually**, in fact, in truth, in reality, truly **2 very**, thoroughly, truly, genuinely, sincerely *Opposite*: hardly

realm *n* **1 scope**, area, range, domain, sphere **2 kingdom**, monarchy, dominion, empire, land

realness *n* **reality**, actuality, authenticity, genuineness, sincerity

realty *n* **real property**, land, property, estate, real estate *(US)*

real world *n* **reality**, life, everyday, the world, actuality *Opposite*: ivory tower

real-world *adj* **practical**, actual, everyday, real, real-life *Opposite*: imaginary

ream *n* **quantity**, amount, pack, pile

reanimate *v* **revive**, restore, reawaken, awaken, resuscitate *Opposite*: deaden

reap *v* **1 gather**, harvest, garner, collect, pick *Opposite*: sow **2 obtain**, acquire, gain, earn, secure *Opposite*: lose

reaper *n* **gatherer**, harvester, cutter, gleaner, mower

reappear *v* **come back**, recur, resurface, return, come again *Opposite*: disappear

reappearance *n* **recurrence**, repetition, re-emergence, return, comeback *Opposite*: disappearance

reappraisal *n* **reassessment**, re-evaluation, re-examination, review, reconsideration

reappraise v **reassess**, re-evaluate, check, reconsider, re-examine

rear v **raise**, bring up, care for, nurture, take care of Opposite: neglect ■ n **back**, stern, tail, tail end, back end Opposite: front

rearguard n tail end, rear, back end, tail, back Opposite: vanguard

rear its head v **appear**, loom, turn up, materialize, rise up Opposite: disappear

rearm v **1 arm**, equip, provide, supply, sell **2 re-equip**, build up, upgrade, reinforce, fortify Opposite: disarm

rearmament n **1 equipment**, armament, provision, supply, sale **2 buildup**, re-equipment, upgrade, fortification, reinforcement Opposite: disarmament

rearmost adj **backmost**, last, final, ultimate, hinder Opposite: foremost

rearrange v **1 reorder**, reorganize, reposition, move, move around Opposite: leave **2 reschedule**, change the date, postpone, delay, adjourn

rearrangement n **1 reorganization**, reordering, movement, change, relocation **2 rescheduling**, postponement, change of date, delay, adjournment

rearwards adv **backwards**, towards the back, behind, back, to the rear Opposite: forwards ■ adj **backward**, behind, back, to the rear, over your shoulder Opposite: forward

reason n **1 justification**, explanation, basis, grounds, cause **2 motive**, cause, aim, end, goal **3 thought**, judgment, logic, sense, mind **4 sanity**, right mind, mind, wits, senses Opposite: insanity ■ v **1 think**, rationalize, deduce, work out, figure out **2 argue**, debate, discuss, influence, persuade. See COMPARE AND CONTRAST at **deduce**.

reasonable adj **1 sensible**, rational, acceptable, practical, realistic Opposite: unreasonable **2 inexpensive**, affordable, cheap, moderate, economical Opposite: expensive **3 not bad**, quite good, passable, tolerable, all right Opposite: appalling. See COMPARE AND CONTRAST at **valid**.

reasonableness n **sensibleness**, rationality, equanimity, fairness, common sense Opposite: irrationality

reasonably adv **1 sensibly**, rationally, judiciously, level-headedly, soundly Opposite: irrationally **2 quite**, fairly, moderately, rather, relatively Opposite: extremely

reasoned adj **rational**, coherent, logical, lucid, analytic Opposite: illogical

reasoning n **analysis**, logic, calculation, reckoning, interpretation

reassemble v **1 put back together**, reconstruct, rebuild, repair, mend Opposite: take apart **2 meet again**, reconvene, reunite, get back together, congregate Opposite: disperse

reassert v **restate**, reaffirm, repeat, reiterate, confirm Opposite: abandon

reassertion n **reaffirmation**, restatement, repetition, reiteration, confirmation Opposite: abandonment

reassess v **reconsider**, review, re-evaluate, re-examine, have another look at

reassessment n **reconsideration**, review, re-evaluation, check, revision

reassurance n **comfort**, assurance, support, encouragement, hope Opposite: discouragement

reassure v **assure**, comfort, support, encourage, set your mind at rest Opposite: discourage

reassuring adj **encouraging**, comforting, supportive, cheering, heartening Opposite: discouraging

reawaken v **stir up**, revive, bring back, rekindle, resuscitate Opposite: obliterate

rebadge v **give another name**, change the name of, rename, retitle, rebrand

rebarbative (fml) adj **unpleasant**, unattractive, objectionable, annoying, forbidding Opposite: pleasant

rebate n **refund**, repayment, return, discount, reimbursement Opposite: supplement

rebel n **protester**, objector, campaigner, agitator, radical Opposite: loyalist ■ v **1 revolt**, rise up, mutiny, resist, mount the barricades Opposite: comply with **2 protest**, campaign, agitate, defy, dissent Opposite: obey

rebellion n **revolt**, uprising, insurgence, upheaval, mutiny Opposite: compliance

rebellious adj **1 revolutionary**, militant, armed, treacherous, mutinous Opposite: law-abiding **2 disobedient**, unruly, insubordinate, recalcitrant, defiant Opposite: obedient

rebelliousness n **1 revolution**, insurrection, sedition, mutiny, treachery Opposite: compliance **2 disobedience**, unruliness, recalcitrance, insubordination, defiance Opposite: obedience

rebirth n **1 regeneration**, renewal, restoration, revitalization, rejuvenation Opposite: degeneration **2 revival**, renaissance, reawakening, renascence, return Opposite: disappearance

reboot v **restart**, start up again, open again, boot up

reborn adj **born again**, recreated, regenerated, renewed, revitalized

rebound v **1 spring back**, recoil, ricochet, jump back, return **2 recover**, bounce back, rally, pick up, return to normal

rebuff v **reject**, snub, refuse, repulse, slight Opposite: accept ■ n **rejection**, refusal, snub, slight, denial Opposite: acceptance

rebuild v **1 reconstruct**, build, restructure, re-erect, remake Opposite: destroy **2 restore**, renovate, recreate, reconstitute, do up Opposite: neglect

rebuke v **reprimand**, reprove, censure,

reproach, take to task *Opposite*: praise ■
n **reproach**, reproof, censure, reprimand,
scolding *Opposite*: compliment

rebut *v* **refute**, disprove, deny, invalidate, contradict *Opposite*: accept

rebuttal *n* **refutation**, disproof, denial, negation, contradiction *Opposite*: endorsement

recalcitrance *n* **resistance**, noncooperation,
stubbornness, obstinacy, obduracy *Opposite*: cooperation

recalcitrant *adj* **unruly**, refractory, disobedient, wayward, headstrong *Opposite*:
cooperative. *See* COMPARE AND CONTRAST *at* unruly.

recall *v* **1 remember**, bring to mind, evoke,
call to mind, recollect *Opposite*: forget **2 call
back**, call in, take back, withdraw, take out
■ *n* **memory**, recollection, remembrance, reminiscence *Opposite*: amnesia

recant *v* **take back**, renounce, repudiate,
disavow, retract *Opposite*: avow *(fml)*

recantation *n* **denial**, withdrawal, repudiation, retraction, revocation *Opposite*:
affirmation

recap *v* **sum up**, summarize, go over, run
through, review ■ *n* **summary**, outline,
summing up, review, restatement

recapitulate *(fml)* *v* **sum up**, recap, summarize,
run through, review

recapitulation *(fml)* *n* **recap**, summary, restatement, review, outline

recapture *v* **1 regain**, retake, take back,
reclaim, repossess **2 summon up**, recall,
evoke, bring back, recollect

recast *v* **1 reorganize**, re-present, re-form,
modify, alter **2 reassign**, reallocate, reselect,
redistribute

recede *v* **1 move away**, retreat, go back, withdraw, draw back *Opposite*: advance **2 diminish**, lessen, decline, wane, fade *Opposite*:
increase

receding *adj* **retreating**, withdrawing, disappearing, ebbing, declining *Opposite*:
growing

receipt *n* **1 acknowledgment**, proof of purchase,
slip, voucher, chit *(dated) Opposite*: invoice
2 receiving, reception, delivery, unloading,
acceptance *Opposite*: dispatch

receive *v* **1 get**, obtain, accept, take, have
Opposite: dispatch **2 hear**, catch, sense,
gather, grasp **3 entertain**, have round, greet,
welcome, meet

receivership *n* **bankruptcy**, insolvency, liquidation, failure, ruin

recent *adj* **new**, of late, fresh, current, topical
Opposite: old

recently *adv* **lately**, only just, in recent times,
a moment ago, a short time ago

receptacle *n* **container**, vessel, holder, repository, magazine

reception *n* **1 welcome**, greeting, reaction,
response, treatment **2 party**, function, drinks

party, cocktail party, gathering **3 signal**,
clarity, picture, sound **4 receipt**, receiving,
delivery, unloading, acceptance *Opposite*:
dispatch

receptionist *n* **receiver**, welcomer, greeter,
telephonist, switchboard operator

receptive *adj* **1 open**, amenable, accessible,
interested, approachable *Opposite*: hostile
2 alert, sensitive, responsive, sharp, bright
Opposite: slow

receptiveness *n* **1 approachability**, friendliness, openness, accessibility, interest *Opposite*: hostility **2 alertness**, sensitivity,
responsiveness, acuteness, brightness *Opposite*: slowness

receptivity *see* **receptiveness**

recess *n* **1 alcove**, nook, indentation, niche,
bay **2 break**, vacation, time off, rest, retreat

recession *n* **depression**, slump, downturn, collapse, decline *Opposite*: boom

recessionary *adj* **falling**, declining, failing, in
slump, in depression *Opposite*: booming

recessive *adj* **1 receding**, falling, retreating,
ebbing, declining *Opposite*: growing
2 latent, suppressed, dormant, hidden,
masked *Opposite*: dominant

recharge *v* **renew**, refresh, boost, revive, revitalize *Opposite*: drain

recherché *adj* **rare**, exotic, obscure, exquisite,
unusual *Opposite*: ordinary

recidivism *n* **reoffending**, backsliding, lapse,
regression, degeneracy

recidivist *n* **reoffender**, hardened criminal,
repeat offender, backslider, lawbreaker

recipe *n* **formula**, guidelines, instructions,
method, steps

recipient *n* **receiver**, beneficiary, heir,
addressee, inheritor *Opposite*: donor

reciprocal *adj* **mutual**, joint, shared, equal,
common *Opposite*: one-sided

reciprocate *v* **give in return**, respond, return,
give back, counter

reciprocation *n* **giving in return**, correspondence, exchange, trade, interchange

reciprocity *n* **mutual benefit**, mutuality,
exchange, trade, trade-off *Opposite*: isolation

recital *n* **performance**, concert, presentation,
reading, recitation

recitation *n* **recital**, reading, performance,
narration, presentation

recitative *n* **declamation**, narrative, oratorio,
opera, singing

recite *v* **1 declaim**, narrate, perform, rehearse,
speak publicly **2 list**, enumerate, reel off,
regurgitate, itemize

reckless *adj* **irresponsible**, wild, thoughtless,
uncontrolled, out of control *Opposite*: cautious

reckon *v* **1 calculate**, add up, total, tot up,
count **2 regard**, consider, judge, rate,

deem *(fml)* **3 think**, believe, suppose, imagine, feel *Opposite*: know

reckonable *adj* **calculable**, countable, quantifiable, finite, measurable *Opposite*: incalculable

reckoning *n* **1 calculation**, estimate, weighing up, computation, arithmetic **2 opinion**, judgment, view, estimation

reckon on *(infml)* *v* **depend**, rely, count on, bank on, be prepared for

reckon with *v* **allow for**, bargain for, be prepared for, expect, anticipate

reclaim *v* **get back**, regain, retrieve, recover, repossess

reclamation *n* **recovery**, retrieval, repossession, recuperation, renovation

recline *v* **lie down**, lie back, stretch out, loll, lounge *Opposite*: stand

recluse *n* **hermit**, loner, outsider, lone wolf, solitary

reclusive *adj* **isolated**, cloistered, solitary, withdrawn, secluded *Opposite*: sociable

recognition *n* **1 identification**, detection, distinguishing, perception, differentiation **2 credit**, gratitude, acknowledgment, thanks, appreciation *Opposite*: blame **3 acceptance**, admission, concession, acknowledgement *Opposite*: denial

recognizable *adj* **familiar**, identifiable, decipherable, detectable, distinguishable *Opposite*: unfamiliar

recognize *v* **1 know**, identify, distinguish, make out, be familiar with **2 acknowledge**, credit, cherish, value, have appreciation for **3 accept**, acknowledge, appreciate, understand, admit *Opposite*: deny

recognized *adj* **1 documented**, familiar, known, standard, predictable *Opposite*: unknown **2 established**, acclaimed, professional, accepted, important

recoil *v* **shrink**, withdraw, quail, wince, flinch *Opposite*: confront ■ *n* **shrinking**, wince, withdrawal, start, retreat

COMPARE AND CONTRAST CORE MEANING: draw back in fear or distaste
recoil draw back suddenly or react mentally in fear, horror, disgust, or distaste; **flinch** draw back physically because of fear or pain, or avoid confronting something unpleasant; **quail** tremble or cower with fear or apprehension; **shrink** move away physically from something because of fear or disgust, or feel reluctance to do something because of fear or apprehension; **wince** make an involuntary movement away from something in response to a stimulus such as pain or embarrassment.

recollect *v* **remember**, recall, call to mind, summon up, think of *Opposite*: forget

recollection *n* **memory**, recall, remembrance, reminiscence, calling to mind

recommence *v* **begin again**, restart, resume, take up again, continue

recommend *v* **1 suggest**, advocate, propose, advise, urge *Opposite*: oppose **2 endorse**, commend, vouch for, mention, put in a good word for *Opposite*: criticize

COMPARE AND CONTRAST CORE MEANING: put forward ideas to somebody deciding on a course of action
recommend put forward a course of action as being worthy of acceptance in the circumstances; **advise** give advice in a relatively open and objective way; **advocate** support or speak in favour of something; **counsel** *(fml or literary)* advise somebody on a particular course of action; **suggest** propose something in a tentative way as a possible course of action for somebody else to consider.

recommendation *n* **1 reference**, endorsement, commendation, blessing, approval *Opposite*: disparagement **2 advice**, proposal, suggestion, counsel *(fml or literary)*

recompense *v* **reward**, compensate, repay, pay, remunerate *Opposite*: charge ■ *n* **payment**, reward, remuneration, repayment, return *Opposite*: cost

reconcile *v* **settle**, bring together, square, reunite, resolve *Opposite*: fall out

reconciliation *n* **settlement**, understanding, squaring off, resolution, compromise *Opposite*: conflict

recondite *adj* **obscure**, abstruse, complex, out-of-the-way, little known *Opposite*: mainstream. *See* COMPARE AND CONTRAST *at* **obscure**.

recondition *v* **overhaul**, service, tune, clean, repair. *See* COMPARE AND CONTRAST *at* **renew**.

reconnaissance *n* **investigation**, scouting, inspection, exploration, survey

reconnect *v* **connect up**, rewire, rejoin, join up, put together again *Opposite*: sever

reconnection *n* **connecting again**, connecting up, rejoining, rewiring, recombination *Opposite*: severance

reconnoitre *v* **explore**, scout, investigate, survey, search ■ *n* **investigation**, reconnaissance, exploration, survey, scouting

reconsider *v* **reassess**, re-evaluate, review, think again, go back over

reconsideration *n* **reassessment**, re-evaluation, review, re-examination

reconstitute *v* **1 reconstruct**, rebuild, re-form, put back together, build again *Opposite*: take apart **2 alter**, change, reorganize, modify, revise *Opposite*: maintain

reconstitution *n* **1 reconstruction**, rebuilding, re-formation, putting back together, building again *Opposite*: breakup **2 alteration**, modification, reorganization, revision, change

reconstruct *v* **rebuild**, renovate, recreate, redo, restructure *Opposite*: take apart

reconstructed *adj* **rebuilt**, recreated, reassembled, restored, renovated *Opposite*: original

reconstruction *n* **rebuilding**, renovation, reform, modernization, renewal

reconvene v resume, come together again, call together again, gather again, call again

record n 1 account, report, archive, chronicle, document 2 past performance, track record, reputation, background, history 3 personal best, top score, high, world record, best ■ v 1 note down, make a note, keep a note, take notes, keep details 2 make a recording, tape, video, film, pick up

recording n footage, video recording, copy, soundtrack, tape

recount v tell, narrate, relate, report, describe

re-count n verification, second opinion, check ■ v count again, verify, tally up, check

recoup v get back, earn, make back, recover, regain Opposite: lose

recourse n option, alternative, remedy, way out, choice

recover v 1 get well, get better, pull through, recuperate, make progress Opposite: deteriorate 2 get back, claim, regain, recuperate, recoup Opposite: lose

recovery n 1 revival, upturn, recuperation, mending, healing Opposite: deterioration 2 retrieval, salvage, recapture, repossession, regaining Opposite: loss

re-create v reproduce, copy, redesign, reinvent, reconstruct. See COMPARE AND CONTRAST at copy.

recreation n 1 leisure, hobby, pastime, exercise, play Opposite: work 2 regeneration, rebirth, reformation, restoration, restitution Opposite: exhaustion

recreational adj leisure, spare time, fun, frivolous, entertaining

recreation room n playroom, games room, den (US)

recrimination n accusation, blame, reproach, allegation, retort Opposite: appeasement

recriminatory adj counter-accusatory, accusing, retaliatory, counterattacking Opposite: placatory

recrudescence n reactivation, recurrence, breaking out again, repetition, happening again

recruit v employ, take on, enlist, engage, conscript Opposite: fire (infml) ■ n employee, trainee, beginner, novice, newcomer Opposite: old hand

recruitment n staffing, employment, enrolment, conscription, enlistment Opposite: dismissal

rectangular adj four-sided, quadrilateral, quadrangular, oblong

rectification n correction, improvement, adjustment, minor adjustment, modification

rectify v put right, set right, correct, remedy, cure Opposite: damage

rectilinear adj straight-lined, with straight lines, direct, unbending, uncurving Opposite: serpentine

rectitude n 1 righteousness, morality, goodness, correctness, decency Opposite: immorality 2 (fml) correctness, rightness, precision, accuracy, exactness

rector n 1 minister, cleric, parson, priest, vicar 2 principal, head, director, chancellor, dean

rectory n vicarage, manse, church house, residence

recumbent (literary) adj lying down, leaning, lying back, reclining, resting Opposite: upright

recuperate v 1 convalesce, build up your strength, recover, get better, get well Opposite: deteriorate 2 get back, retrieve, reclaim, recover, recapture Opposite: lose

recuperation n 1 convalescence, healing, recovery, getting better, restoration Opposite: deterioration 2 retrieval, recovery, repossession, salvage, reclamation Opposite: loss

recuperative adj curative, restorative, invigorating, convalescent, healing

recur v happen again, persist, return, come back, reappear Opposite: cease

recurrence n reappearance, return, repetition, relapse Opposite: cessation

recurrent adj repeated, persistent, frequent, periodic, intermittent Opposite: finished

recurring see recurrent

recurvate adj curved, bowed, arched, rounded, bent Opposite: straight

recycle v reprocess, salvage, reuse, recover, reutilize Opposite: throw away

red-blooded adj vigorous, strong, robust, hearty, lusty Opposite: weak

red-carpet adj preferential, VIP, no-expense-spared, special, favoured

redden v flush, blush, colour, glow Opposite: redden

redecorate v revamp, spruce up, refurbish, restore, repaint

redeem v 1 cash in, cash, trade in, exchange, convert Opposite: keep 2 compensate for, make up for, make amends for, restore, redress 3 release, liberate, free, emancipate, deliver Opposite: arrest

redeemable adj exchangeable, valid, good, convertible, equivalent Opposite: irredeemable

redeeming adj saving, good, positive, abiding, compensatory

redemption n 1 salvation, rescue, release, liberation, emancipation Opposite: downfall 2 improvement, recovery, renovation, reclamation, refurbishment Opposite: deterioration 3 exchange, use, conversion, trade-in, buying back

redemptive adj liberating, redeeming, saving, rescuing, delivering

redeploy v redistribute, divert, post, send, dispatch

redeployment n **redistribution**, posting, reorganization, relocation, rearrangement

redevelop v **improve**, revitalize, renovate, revamp, restore *Opposite*: neglect

redevelopment n **improvement**, renovation, revitalization, revamping, restoration *Opposite*: neglect

red-faced adj 1 **blushing**, flushed, embarrassed, hot and bothered, sweating 2 **ruddy**, weather-beaten, rosy, florid, rubicund (*literary*)

redheaded adj **auburn**, chestnut-haired, auburn-haired, ginger, strawberry blonde

red herring n **decoy**, trick, ploy, lure, diversion

red-hot adj **burning**, boiling, scalding, fiery, scorching (*infml*) *Opposite*: cold

redirect v **forward**, send, readdress, send on, transmit

redirection n **sending on**, resending, rerouting, transferral, forwarding

rediscover v **find again**, revive, experience again, remember, relive

rediscovery n **finding again**, discovering again, reawakening, seeing afresh, rekindling

redistribute v **reallocate**, reorder, sort out, restructure, rearrange

redistribution n **redeployment**, rearrangement, relocation, reorganization, restructuring

red-letter day n **special day**, day to remember, occasion, event, turning point

red light n 1 **traffic light**, warning signal, warning light, stop light, stop sign *Opposite*: green light 2 (*infml*) **rejection**, disapproval, refusal, no, prohibition *Opposite*: approval

redness n 1 **blush**, flush, rosiness, glow, pinkness *Opposite*: pallor 2 **soreness**, rawness, tenderness, inflammation, painfulness

redo v **rebuild**, do from scratch, do again, recreate, start again

redolence n **suggestion**, hint, trace, evocation, reminiscence

redolent adj 1 **suggestive**, reminiscent, evocative, indicative, recalling 2 **scented**, aromatic, fragrant, sweet-smelling, perfumed

redouble v **intensify**, renew, increase, multiply, amplify *Opposite*: reduce

redoubtable adj **formidable**, impressive, terrible, mighty, fearsome *Opposite*: unimpressive

redraft n **rewrite**, reworking, alteration, modification, change ■ v **rewrite**, reword, rework, revise, rephrase

redress n **compensation**, reparation, damages, recompense, reimbursement ■ v 1 **restore**, level out, equalize, right, rectify 2 **reimburse**, repay, pay damages, pay reparations, remunerate

red tape (*infml*) n **formalities**, bureaucracy, paperwork, official procedure, rules and regulations

reduce v 1 **decrease**, lessen, diminish, cut, trim down *Opposite*: increase 2 **downgrade**, cut down, demote, degrade, slash *Opposite*: upgrade 3 **lose weight**, slim, slim down, go on a diet, diet

reduced adj **cheap**, bargain, cut-price, low-price, on sale

reduction n **discount**, decrease, lessening, drop, saving *Opposite*: increase

redundancy n **unemployment**, job loss, dismissal, severance, termination *Opposite*: employment

redundant adj 1 **laid off**, let go, out of work, out of a job, jobless *Opposite*: employed 2 **superfluous**, outmoded, disused, surplus, unneeded *Opposite*: needed

reduplicate v **repeat**, double, copy, redo, recast

reduplication n **repetition**, copying, imitation, doubling, duplication

reed n **cane**, stalk, stem

reediness n **squeakiness**, shrillness, stridency, screechiness, squawkiness *Opposite*: sonority

re-educate v **retrain**, reskill, re-equip, requalify, reinstruct

re-education n **retraining**, reskilling, re-equipping, requalification, reinstruction

reedy adj 1 **high-pitched**, thin, shrill, high, feeble *Opposite*: full-bodied 2 **thin**, narrow, slim, skinny, long *Opposite*: squat

reef n **ridge**, bar, bank, mound, range

reek v 1 **stink**, smell, pong (*infml*) 2 **show signs**, smack, smell, suggest, be redolent of ■ n **stench**, stink, smell, odour, whiff. *See* COMPARE AND CONTRAST *at* **smell**.

reel n **roll**, spool, cylinder, bobbin, roller ■ v 1 **lurch**, stagger, totter, stumble, wobble 2 **wind**, whirl, spin, go round and round, revolve

re-elect v **vote in again**, reappoint, reconfirm, endorse, reinstall

re-election n **reappointment**, endorsement, confirmation

reel off v **recite**, rattle off, list, repeat, go through

re-enter v **return**, retrace one's steps, go back into, withdraw into, retire into *Opposite*: leave

re-entry n **return**, going back into, going into again, going in again

re-establish v **establish again**, create again, regenerate, reinvent, rebuild

re-examination n **reappraisal**, reconsideration, reassessment, re-evaluation, rechecking

re-examine v **reconsider**, go back over, review, reassess, check

ref (*infml*) n **referee**, umpire, arbitrator, adjudicator, mediator

refectory n **cafeteria**, dining hall, mess hall, lunchroom (*US*)

refer v 1 **consult**, check, turn to, look up, examine 2 **mention**, denote, talk about, bring up, speak of 3 **signify**, mean, indicate, suggest, insinuate 4 **send to**, direct to, pass on to, consign to, turn over to 5 **apply to**, relate to, concern, belong, be relevant to

referee n **umpire**, arbitrator, judge, arbiter, adjudicator *Opposite*: partisan ■ v **arbitrate**, adjudicate, umpire, mediate, judge

reference n 1 **orientation**, position, situation, location, locus 2 **allusion**, mention, suggestion, indication, citation 3 **recommendation**, testimonial, character reference, endorsement, commendation

referendum n **vote**, poll, plebiscite, survey, ballot

referral n **transfer**, recommendation, appointment, medical appointment

refill v **replenish**, top up, fill up, restock, stock up *Opposite*: empty

refine v 1 **purify**, process, treat, filter, distil *Opposite*: contaminate 2 **improve**, polish, perfect, hone, enhance *Opposite*: coarsen

refined adj 1 **sophisticated**, advanced, superior, polished, distinguished *Opposite*: coarse 2 **purified**, processed, treated, filtered, distilled

refinement n 1 **modification**, alteration, minor change, improvement, enhancement 2 **sophistication**, finesse, class, maturity, delicacy *Opposite*: vulgarity

refining n 1 **purifying**, sanitizing, decontaminating, cleansing, filtering *Opposite*: adulterating 2 **improving**, cultivating, educating, taming, enlightening *Opposite*: coarsening ■ adj **improving**, educating, cultivating, civilizing, enlightening *Opposite*: coarsening

refit v **overhaul**, renovate, re-equip, service, repair ■ n **overhaul**, re-equipping, repair, refurbishment, service

reflate v **expand**, increase, stimulate, spur on, build up *Opposite*: deflate

reflation n **expansion**, increase, stimulation, boost, advance *Opposite*: deflation

reflect v 1 **reproduce**, mirror, imitate, replicate, redirect 2 **be a sign of**, reveal, expose, suggest, signal 3 **think**, consider, ponder, mull over, contemplate

reflection n 1 **indication**, sign, manifestation, suggestion, expression 2 **consideration**, thinking, thought, contemplation, meditation *Opposite*: impulse 3 **mirror image**, likeness, echo, image, replication

reflective adj **thoughtful**, pensive, wistful, meditative, contemplative *Opposite*: impulsive

reflex n **reaction**, impulse, instinct, spontaneous effect, response

reflexive adj **automatic**, impulsive, spontaneous, involuntary, instinctive *Opposite*: premeditated

reform v **improve**, restructure, revolutionize, remodel, modernize ■ n **improvement**, reorganization, restructuring, modification, transformation

re-form v **recreate**, reconstruct, re-fashion, rebuild, remake

reformation n **improvement**, renovation, reorganization, restructuring, overhaul

reformatory n **institution**, detention centre, secure unit, jail, prison

reformed adj **rehabilitated**, transformed, changed, converted, renewed

reformer n **improver**, campaigner, activist, crusader, agitator *Opposite*: conservative

refract v **bend**, divert, change course, detour, deflect

refraction n **bending**, change of direction, change of course, diversion, detour

refractory adj **headstrong**, stubborn, rebellious, obstinate, wayward *Opposite*: placid

refrain v **desist**, abstain, hold back, leave off, cease *Opposite*: persist ■ n **chorus**, strain, theme

refresh v **revive**, cool down, enliven, invigorate, rejuvenate *Opposite*: wear out

refresher n **reminder**, revision, update, review

refreshing adj **stimulating**, uplifting, inspirational, invigorating, energizing *Opposite*: draining

refreshment n **drink**, food, nourishment, sustenance, nutriment

refreshments n **food and drink**, snacks, drinks, nibbles, hors d'oeuvres

refrigerate v **keep cold**, store at a low temperature, cool, ice, chill *Opposite*: heat

refrigeration n **cooling**, chilling, preservation, freezing, conserving

refuel v **refill**, replenish, top up, restock, resupply *Opposite*: run down

refuge n **haven**, sanctuary, shelter, harbour, protection

refugee n **person in exile**, immigrant, migrant, expatriate, exile

refund v **repay**, reimburse, give back, pay back, compensate *Opposite*: keep ■ n **repayment**, reimbursement, money back, compensation, recompense *Opposite*: payment

refurbish v **renovate**, restore, refit, fix up, spruce up

refurbishment n **restoration**, renovation, overhaul, renewal, repair

refusal n **negative response**, snub, denial, rejection, negation *Opposite*: acceptance

refuse v **say no**, decline, reject, snub, rebuff *Opposite*: accept ■ n **waste**, garbage, rubbish, litter, debris

refutation n **repudiation**, disproof, negation, rejection, contradiction *Opposite*: confirmation

refute *v* **disprove**, contest, rebut, counter, repudiate *Opposite*: prove

regain *v* **recover**, get back, recuperate, recoup, reclaim *Opposite*: lose

regal *adj* **royal**, majestic, noble, imperial, stately

regale *v* **entertain**, amuse, delight, divert

regalia *n* **symbols of office**, ceremonial objects, ceremonial dress, insignia

regard *v* **1 look upon**, stare, observe, gaze at, view **2 consider**, hold, think, see, view **3 relate to**, concern, touch on, connect with, have to do with ▪ *n* **1 respect**, esteem, favour, admiration, honour *Opposite*: disregard **2** *(fml)* **look**, stare, gaze, glance

COMPARE AND CONTRAST CORE MEANING: appreciation of the worth of somebody or something **regard** a mixture of liking and appreciation of somebody or something; **admiration** warm approval and appreciation of somebody or something, often suggesting a desire to copy or resemble somebody; **esteem** a high opinion and appreciation of somebody or something; **favour** a liking and preference for somebody or something; **respect** a strong acknowledgment and appreciation of somebody's abilities and achievements; **reverence** a feeling of deep respect and devotion combined with a slight sense of awe; **veneration** a profound feeling of respect and awe.

regarding *prep* **concerning**, about, on the subject of, on the topic of, as regards

regardless *adv* **anyway**, anyhow, no matter what, whatever happens, nevertheless

regardless of *prep* **in spite of**, despite, apart from, not considering, notwithstanding

regatta *n* **boat race**, race, gala, competition, contest

regenerate *v* **renew**, restore, revive, redevelop, reinforce *Opposite*: degenerate

regeneration *n* **renewal**, rebirth, revival, renaissance, rejuvenation

regenerative *adj* **growing back**, reformative, recreating, re-forming, recovering *Opposite*: degenerative

regent *n* **substitute**, proxy, replacement, protector

regime *n* **1 government**, command, rule, administration, management **2 routine**, system, regimen, treatment, course of therapy

regimen *n* **routine**, schedule, treatment, regime, course of therapy

regiment *n* **military unit**, troop, squadron, battalion, brigade ▪ *v* **1 control strictly**, regulate, oppress, suppress, order *Opposite*: liberate **2 organize systematically**, arrange, order, file, organize

regimental *adj* **strict**, rigid, disciplined, harsh, ordered *Opposite*: lax

regimentation *n* **control**, regulation, oppression, suppression, organization

regimented *adj* **1 controlled**, disciplined, restricted, strict, rigid *Opposite*: undisciplined **2 well-ordered**, neatly arranged, organized, systematic, structured *Opposite*: disordered

region *n* **area**, district, county, section, province

regional *adj* **local**, area, district, provincial, county *Opposite*: national

regionalism *n* **1 regional loyalty**, regional prejudice, decentralization, home loyalty, area loyalty **2 linguistic feature**, local expression, dialect word

register *n* **list**, record, catalogue, roll, index ▪ *v* **1 enter**, list, record, catalogue, keep details **2 enrol**, join, sign up, matriculate, enlist **3 reach**, touch, record, measure, indicate **4 reveal**, disclose, show, convey, score *Opposite*: hide

registrar *n* **1 public official**, recorder, public administrator, record-keeper, clerk **2 administrative officer**, school administrator, university official, administrator, bursar **3 senior hospital doctor**, specialist, consultant

registration *n* **1 registering**, recording, record-keeping, cataloguing, listing **2 enrolment**, enlisting, signing up, signing on, course enrolment

registry *n* **records office**, register office, archive, administrative office, office

regress *v* **1 relapse**, revert, lapse, backslide, retrogress *Opposite*: progress **2 go back**, lose headway, lose ground, retreat, move back *Opposite*: advance

regression *n* **1 recession**, retreat, retrogression, return *Opposite*: advance **2 reversion**, deterioration, relapse, worsening, getting worse *Opposite*: progression

regressive *adj* **reverting**, returning, going back, degenerating, deteriorating *Opposite*: progressive

regret *v* **1 be sorry**, be apologetic, apologize for, be repentant, feel sorry **2** *(fml)* **be disappointed**, be unhappy, lament, be remorseful, express grief ▪ *n* **1 remorse**, guilt, repentance, compunction, pang of conscience *Opposite*: shamelessness **2 disappointment**, sorrow, unhappiness, grief, distress *Opposite*: contentment

regretful *adj* **1 apologetic**, remorseful, repentant, sorry, penitent *Opposite*: unapologetic **2 disappointed**, unhappy, sorrowful, sad *Opposite*: content

regrettable *adj* **unfortunate**, deplorable, lamentable, undesirable, unwelcome *Opposite*: fortunate

regroup *v* **re-form**, recover, rearrange, recuperate, reorder *Opposite*: scatter

regular *adj* **1 even**, steady, unvarying, consistent, systematic *Opposite*: irregular

2 recurring, recurrent, frequent, repeated, fixed *Opposite*: intermittent **3 ordered**, methodical, even, consistent, reliable *Opposite*: inconsistent **4 usual**, normal, standard, ordinary, customary *Opposite*: unusual ■ *n* **soldier**, combatant, legionnaire, squaddie *(slang)*, GI *(US)*

regularity *n* **orderliness**, symmetry, uniformity, consistency, constancy *Opposite*: inconsistency

regularize *v* **standardize**, normalize, make conform, legalize, regulate

regulate *v* **1 control**, order, adjust, set, synchronize *Opposite*: deregulate **2** *(fml)* **direct**, control, guide, manage, handle

regulation *n* **1 rule**, directive, guideline, parameter, instruction **2 control**, adjustment, adaptation, alteration, management

regulator *n* **1 device**, valve, mechanism, controller, rheostat **2 watchdog**, controller, supervisory body, manager, supervisor

regulatory *adj* **controlling**, supervisory, governing, monitoring, directing

regurgitate *v* **1 bring up**, vomit, spew up, spit up, throw up *(infml)* *Opposite*: ingest **2 repeat**, rehearse, go over, do again, reiterate

regurgitation *n* **1 bringing up**, vomiting, sicking up, spitting out, spewing **2 repetition**, rehearsal, restating, churning out, recitation

rehabilitate *v* **1 restore**, recover, mend, repair, re-establish **2 assimilate**, acclimatize, re-educate, naturalize, reorient

rehabilitation *n* **reintegration**, restoration, therapy, recuperation, convalescence

rehash *v* **rework**, reuse, do again, go over, repeat

rehearsal *n* **practice**, preparation, trial, run-through, dummy run *Opposite*: performance

rehearse *v* **practise**, go over, run through, prepare, train

rehearsed *adj* **practised**, prepared, learned, studied, planned out *Opposite*: ad-lib

reheat *v* **heat up**, warm up, warm through, warm, heat

rehouse *v* **move**, transfer, relocate, resettle

reign *n* **rule**, sovereignty, control, supremacy, sway ■ *v* **rule**, hold sway, govern, control, lead

reimburse *v* **repay**, pay back, give money back, compensate, refund

reimbursement *n* **repayment**, compensation, recompense, settlement, damages

rein *n* **bridle**, restraint, harness, leash, lead

reincarnate *v* **revive**, bring back, revitalize, rejuvenate, reawaken

reincarnation *n* **re-embodiment**, rebirth, re-creation, reawakening, restoration

reinforce *v* **1 strengthen**, support, underpin, buttress, bolster *Opposite*: underplay

2 emphasize, underline, highlight, add force to, boost *Opposite*: weaken

reinforcement *n* **1 strengthening**, support, underpinning, fortification, buttressing *Opposite*: weakening **2 emphasis**, underlining, underscoring, corroboration, backup *Opposite*: underplaying

rein in *v* **hold back**, cut back, restrain, reduce, decrease *Opposite*: unleash

reinstate *v* **restore**, return, give back, re-establish, put back

reinstatement *n* **restoration**, return, recall, replacement, re-establishment

reinsurance *n* **provision**, extra cover, protection

reinsure *v* **take out extra cover**, transfer, make extra provision

reintroduce *v* **introduce again**, bring into effect again, reinstate, restore, re-establish

reintroduction *n* **reinstatement**, restoration, re-establishment

reinvigorated *adj* **revitalized**, refreshed, restored, recharged, fresh *Opposite*: exhausted

reissue *v* **rerelease**, redistribute, recirculate, republish, send out again ■ *n* **new issue**, reprint, rerelease, new edition, new copy

reiterate *v* **repeat**, go over, restate, stress, reinforce

reiteration *n* **repetition**, replication, restatement, echo, recap

reject *v* **refuse**, rebuff, decline, snub, throw out *Opposite*: accept

rejection *n* **refusal**, denial, rebuff, denunciation, refutation *Opposite*: acceptance

rejig *(infml)* *v* **rearrange**, alter, readjust, reorganize, change

rejoice *(literary)* *v* **celebrate**, be pleased about, cheer, exult, be glad *Opposite*: lament

rejoin *(fml)* *v* **reply**, answer, respond, retort, return

rejoinder *(fml)* *n* **response**, answer, reply, comeback, retort. *See* COMPARE AND CONTRAST *at* **answer**.

rejuvenate *v* **revitalize**, invigorate, revive, make younger, revivify

rejuvenation *n* **revitalization**, reinvigoration, regeneration, renewal, renovation

rekindle *v* **renew**, reawaken, revive, regenerate, relight *Opposite*: kill

relapse *v* **go back to**, revert, deteriorate, degenerate, fall back *Opposite*: improve ■ *n* **deterioration**, decline, degeneration, reversion, waning *Opposite*: improvement

relate *v* **1 connect**, link, associate, correlate, link up **2 interact**, get on, form a relationship, connect, cooperate **3 tell**, narrate, speak about, recount, relay

related *adj* **connected**, linked, associated, correlated, interrelated *Opposite*: unconnected

relating to *prep* about, regarding, re, apropos of, in relation to

relation *n* family member, relative, next of kin

relations *n* 1 kith and kin, kin, family members, relatives, family 2 relationships, dealings, associations, affairs, contact

relationship *n* association, connection, affiliation, rapport, liaison

relative *adj* comparative, qualified, virtual *Opposite*: absolute ■ *n* family member, relation, next of kin

relative to *prep* in relation to, compared with, proportionate to, corresponding to

relativism *n* contingency, belief, doctrine *Opposite*: absolutism

relativist *n* equivocator, fence sitter, agnostic, waverer, vacillator ■ *adj* contingent, dependent, relative

relativity *n* relativeness, dependence, contingency

relax *v* 1 loosen, slacken, ease, let up on, let out *Opposite*: tense 2 rest, put your feet up, take it easy, have a break, lie down 3 unwind, calm down, slow down, let go, loosen up 4 lessen, decrease, diminish, lower, ease *Opposite*: increase

relaxation *n* 1 recreation, leisure, entertainment, rest, repose 2 reduction, lessening, easing, slackening, moderation *Opposite*: increase

relaxed *adj* 1 tranquil, calm, comfortable, stress-free, unperturbed *Opposite*: tense 2 lenient, easygoing, untroubled, casual, laid-back *(infml) Opposite*: strict

relaxing *adj* calming, soothing, comforting, peaceful, tranquil *Opposite*: harrowing

relay *v* communicate, pass on, transmit, spread, convey

release *v* 1 let go, free, discharge, liberate, let loose *Opposite*: hold 2 make public, make available, announce, publish, circulate *Opposite*: withhold ■ *n* 1 relief, discharge, freedom, liberation, emancipation *Opposite*: arrest 2 announcement, issue, statement, publication, proclamation

relegate *v* demote, downgrade, transfer, consign, refer *Opposite*: promote

relegation *n* demotion, sending down, transfer down, lowering of rank, downgrade *Opposite*: promotion

relent *v* give in, cave in, change your mind, concede, yield *Opposite*: stand firm

relentless *adj* 1 ceaseless, unremitting, persistent, endless, steady 2 remorseless, merciless, pitiless, ruthless, heartless

relentlessness *n* 1 ceaselessness, unremittingness, persistence, intensity, steadiness 2 remorselessness, mercilessness, pitilessness, ruthlessness, harshness

relevance *n* significance, bearing, application, importance, weight *Opposite*: irrelevance

relevant *adj* pertinent, applicable, germane, related, appropriate *Opposite*: unrelated

reliability *n* dependability, consistency, steadfastness, trustworthiness *Opposite*: untrustworthiness

reliable *adj* dependable, consistent, steadfast, unswerving, unfailing *Opposite*: unreliable

reliance *n* dependence, confidence, trust, belief, faith *Opposite*: independence

reliant *adj* dependent, needful, conditional, subject to, contingent *Opposite*: independent

relic *n* historical object, artefact, remnant, remains, vestige

relief *n* 1 assistance, aid, help, reinforcement, support 2 respite, release, reprieve, break, liberation

relieve *v* 1 ease, release, alleviate, reduce, mitigate *Opposite*: exacerbate 2 take the place of, take over for, substitute for, stand in for, replace 3 dismiss, release, let go, discharge, get rid of *Opposite*: appoint

relieved *adj* reassured, thankful, calmed, pleased, comforted *Opposite*: worried

religion *n* faith, belief, creed, conviction, denomination

religious *adj* 1 theological, sacred, holy, consecrated, church *Opposite*: secular 2 spiritual, devout, pious, holy, observant *Opposite*: irreligious 3 thorough, conscientious, dutiful, faithful, reliable *Opposite*: unreliable

religiousness *n* devoutness, piousness, spirituality, sense of God, faithfulness

relinquish *v* give up, surrender, hand over, abandon, renounce *Opposite*: retain

reliquary *n* repository, casket, container, shrine

relish *v* enjoy, delight in, savour, take pleasure in, like *Opposite*: dislike ■ *n* enjoyment, delight, pleasure, elation, appreciation *Opposite*: displeasure

relive *v* experience again, go through again, live through again, remember, recall *Opposite*: forget

reload *v* refill, fill, load again, replenish, recharge *Opposite*: unload

relocate *v* move, change place, reposition, transfer, displace *Opposite*: remain

relocation *n* transfer, moving, rearrangement, repositioning, replacement

reluctance *n* unwillingness, lack of enthusiasm, disinclination, hesitancy, foot-dragging *(infml) Opposite*: enthusiasm

reluctant *adj* unwilling, unenthusiastic, disinclined, loath, hesitant *Opposite*: enthusiastic. *See* COMPARE AND CONTRAST *at* unwilling

rely *v* depend on, bank on, count on, trust, be sure of *Opposite*: distrust

remain *v* 1 stay, stay put, stay behind, stay on, linger *Opposite*: leave 2 continue, keep on, endure, persist, go on *Opposite*: stop

remainder *n* rest, residue, remnants, remains, leftovers

remaining adj residual, outstanding, left over, excess, lingering

remains n 1 leftovers, remnants, relics, remainder, ruins 2 dead body, corpse, cadaver, ashes, carcass

remake n new version, cover version, cover, new edition, re-creation ■ v produce again, recreate, re-form, change the format, reshape

remand v return to custody, return to prison, commit to custody, imprison, jail ■ n return to custody, return to prison, committal to custody, custody, prison

remark n comment, statement, observation, aside, mention ■ v say, comment, state, observe, pronounce

remarkable adj extraordinary, amazing, notable, outstanding, noteworthy Opposite: ordinary

remarry v get married again, marry again, get wed again, re-wed, wed again (fml or literary)

rematch n replay, a second go, another game

remedial adj corrective, counteractive, helpful, educative, curative Opposite: precautionary

remedy n 1 solution, cure, answer, antidote, resolution 2 medicine, medication, preparation, mixture, therapy ■ v 1 cure, relieve, improve, alleviate, ease 2 resolve, deal with, correct, improve, make better Opposite: exacerbate

remember v 1 keep in mind, bear in mind, retain, memorize, learn Opposite: forget 2 recall, think of, recollect, dredge up, hark back to Opposite: forget

remembrance n commemoration, memory, tribute, recollection, reminiscence

remind v 1 be reminiscent, strike a chord, take you back, jog your memory, ring a bell (infml) 2 repeat, retell, prompt, recap, run by again

reminder n 1 cue, notice, prompt, recap, aide-mémoire (fml) 2 souvenir, token, memento, knick-knack, keepsake

reminisce v recall, talk about, hark back to, muse over, evoke

reminiscence n 1 nostalgia, recollection, looking back, musing, rumination 2 memory, recollection, reminder

reminiscent adj suggestive, evocative, resonant, redolent, similar

remiss adj careless, negligent, lax, slipshod, slapdash Opposite: diligent

remission n reduction, decrease, lessening, diminution, cutback

remissive adj pardoning, forgiving, absolving, exonerating

remit v 1 send, forward, dispatch, pay, settle 2 submit, refer, pass on Opposite: handle 3 slacken, decrease, lessen, diminish, cancel Opposite: increase ■ n responsibility, concern, sphere of activity, job, brief

remittance n 1 payment, transfer of funds,

transmittal, fee, transfer 2 release, dispatch, discharge (fml)

remix v produce a new version of, rehash, reproduce, alter, change ■ n new recording, different version, new version, latest version, revised version

remnant n remainder, remains, relic, residue, trace

remodel v alter, modify, modernize, adapt, adjust

remonstrance n 1 argument, evidence, backup, proof, case 2 protest, complaint, objection, petition, dispute

remonstrate v argue, protest, object, oppose, complain Opposite: agree. See COMPARE AND CONTRAST at object.

remorse n regret, sorrow, repentance, penitence, guilt

remorseful adj regretful, repentant, penitent, contrite, apologetic Opposite: unrepentant

remorseless adj 1 pitiless, ruthless, merciless, callous, cruel Opposite: merciful 2 inexorable, implacable, indefatigable, unbending, unyielding

remote adj 1 distant, isolated, inaccessible, far-flung, far-off Opposite: nearby 2 aloof, detached, withdrawn, reserved, cool Opposite: approachable 3 slight, outside, slim, unlikely, improbable Opposite: likely

remotely adv 1 slightly, tenuously, marginally, minimally, a little Opposite: closely 2 at all, in the least, the least bit, the slightest bit Opposite: greatly

remoteness n 1 isolation, seclusion, distance, solitude, inaccessibility Opposite: closeness 2 aloofness, detachment, reserve, inaccessibility, coolness Opposite: approachability 3 slightness, improbability, faintness, slimness Opposite: likelihood

remount v get on again, get back on, mount again, ride again, get back in the saddle

removable adj detachable, not fixed, can be removed, changeable, transferable Opposite: attached

removal n taking away, elimination, exclusion, subtraction, deletion Opposite: addition

remove v 1 take away, get rid of, eliminate, do away with, eradicate Opposite: add 2 take off, detach, cut off, amputate, disconnect

remunerate v pay, reward, compensate, recompense, repay

remuneration n payment, fee, salary, wage, compensation. See COMPARE AND CONTRAST at wage.

renaissance n rebirth, new start, new beginning, resurgence, revitalization Opposite: decline

rename v give a new name, retitle, rechristen, nickname, change the name of

renascent adj becoming active, budding, burgeoning, appearing, becoming popular

rend v **tear**, tear apart, rip, come apart, split *Opposite*: mend. *See* COMPARE AND CONTRAST *at* **tear**.

render v 1 *(fml)* **provide**, give, deliver, submit, make available 2 *(fml)* **portray**, represent, depict, execute, translate 3 *(fml)* **decide**, decree, judge, adjudicate, declare 4 **make**, cause, cause to become 5 **melt down**, reduce, condense, concentrate, boil down *Opposite*: solidify

rendering n 1 **portrayal**, depiction, picture, image, portrait 2 **version**, translation, interpretation, interpreting, execution 3 **plaster coating**, plaster, pebbledash, coating, cladding

rendezvous n 1 **engagement**, meeting, appointment, tryst, assignation 2 **meeting place**, meeting point, assembly point, location, site ■ v **meet**, come together, make contact, get together, assemble

rendition n **version**, interpretation, performance, rendering, execution

renegade n **apostate**, traitor, rebel, turncoat, betrayer *Opposite*: loyalist

renege v **go back on**, break your word, break a promise, back out, default

renew v 1 **return to**, reintroduce, repeat, restart, begin again 2 **rekindle**, revitalize, rejuvenate, refresh, revive 3 **recondition**, renovate, refurbish, revamp, restore

---

COMPARE AND CONTRAST CORE MEANING: improve the condition of something

renew replace something worn or broken; **recondition** bring something such as a machine or appliance back to a good condition or working state by means of repairs or replacement of parts; **renovate** bring something such as a building back to a former better state by means of repairs, redecoration, or refurbishment; **restore** bring something back to an original state after it has been damaged or fallen into a bad condition; **revamp** improve the appearance or condition of something.

---

renewal n **regeneration**, restitution, rekindling, revitalization, rejuvenation

renounce v 1 **relinquish**, surrender, hand over, give up, abdicate *Opposite*: accept 2 **disavow**, repudiate, reject, abandon, forsake *Opposite*: embrace

renovate v **renew**, recondition, modernize, refurbish, repair *Opposite*: wear out. *See* COMPARE AND CONTRAST *at* **renew**.

renovation n **facelift**, revamp, makeover, restoration, redecoration

renown n **fame**, celebrity, notoriety, prominence, popularity *Opposite*: obscurity

renowned adj **famous**, well-known, celebrated, prominent, popular *Opposite*: unknown

rent n 1 **rental**, rent payment, hire charge, fee, payment 2 **hole**, tear, rip, split, slash ■ v **let**, hire out, lend out, rent out, charter

rental n **rent payment**, fee, payment, hire charge, charge

renunciation n 1 **repudiation**, abandonment, denial, renouncement, rejection *Opposite*: acceptance 2 **surrender**, disowning, relinquishment, abdication

reorder v **rearrange**, reorganize, regroup, restructure, move around

reorganization n **reform**, restructuring, reshuffle, redeployment, reformation

reorganize v **regroup**, move around, reorder, rearrange, restructure

rep *(infml)* n **representative**, agent, courier, delegate, deputy

repaint v **redecorate**, renovate, touch up, patch up, freshen up

repair v **mend**, fix, patch up, restore, darn *Opposite*: damage ■ n **overhaul**, reparation, restoration, patch-up, mending

reparation n **amends**, compensation, damages, recompense, reimbursement

repartee n **banter**, wit, wordplay, badinage, raillery

repast *(literary)* n **meal**, banquet, feast, buffet, collation

repatriate v **send home**, deport, send back, banish, exile

repatriation n **sending home**, going home, deportation, return, exile

repay v **pay**, pay back, reimburse, refund, pay off

repayment n **payment**, refund, reimbursement, settlement, compensation

repeal v **cancel**, revoke, rescind, annul, nullify *Opposite*: enact

repeat v 1 **reiterate**, recap, go over, echo, retell 2 **do again**, replicate, duplicate, show again, copy ■ n **recurrence**, replication, reiteration, duplication, reappearance

repeated adj **recurrent**, frequent, recurring, repetitive, constant *Opposite*: rare

repel v 1 **disgust**, nauseate, repulse, make you feel sick 2 **keep away**, fend off, drive back, keep at bay, deter *Opposite*: attract

repellent adj 1 **disgusting**, revolting, nauseating, repulsive, repugnant *Opposite*: attractive 2 **impervious**, impermeable, resistant, proof, tight

repent v **regret**, be sorry, apologize, ask forgiveness, feel sorrow

repentance n **regret**, sorrow, remorse, penitence, atonement *Opposite*: shamelessness

repentant adj **regretful**, remorseful, apologetic, penitent, rueful *Opposite*: unrepentant

repercussion n **consequence**, effect, upshot, impact, aftermath

repertoire n **repertory**, collection, selection, series, stock

repertory n 1 **staging**, production, performance **2 theatre company**, theatre group, company, repertory theatre, theatre **3 repertoire**, selection, series, stock, range

repetition *n* recurrence, replication, duplication, reiteration, reappearance

repetitious *adj* boring, monotonous, tedious, dull, repetitive *Opposite*: innovative

repetitive *see* repetitious

repetitively *adv* repeatedly, continually, over and over again, cyclically, frequently *Opposite*: infrequently

rephrase *v* restate, retell, say differently, express in other words, put another way

replace *v* **1 substitute**, trade, use instead, exchange, switch **2 replenish**, put back, restore, return, reinstate

replacement *n* substitute, stand-in, substitution, proxy, surrogate *Opposite*: original

replay *v* play again, rerun, repeat, retell, reiterate ■ *n* rerun, repetition, reiteration, echo, repeat

replenish *v* replace, refill, fill, stock up, top up *Opposite*: deplete

replenishment *n* replacement, refill, top up, renewal

replete *adj* **1 full**, complete, supplied, abounding, brimming *Opposite*: lacking **2 sated**, satisfied, satiated, full, full up *Opposite*: hungry

repletion *n* fullness, surfeit, glut, satiety

replica *n* copy, reproduction, imitation, model, facsimile *Opposite*: original

replicate *v* duplicate, repeat, copy, imitate, reproduce. *See* COMPARE AND CONTRAST *at* copy.

replication *n* repetition, duplication, imitation, copying, reproduction

reply *v* respond, answer, retort, answer back, react *Opposite*: ask ■ *n* response, account, answer, retort, riposte *Opposite*: question. *See* COMPARE AND CONTRAST *at* answer.

report *v* **1 give an account**, tell, state, describe, give details **2 register**, check in, present yourself, turn up, show up ■ *n* **1 tale**, statement, description, testimony, story **2 loud noise**, bang, boom, crash, explosion

reportage *n* news coverage, reporting, coverage, mention, analysis

reportedly *adv* allegedly, supposedly, apparently, seemingly, so they say *Opposite*: actually

reporter *n* foreign correspondent, special correspondent, journalist, correspondent, writer

repose *n* **1 inactivity**, sleep, rest, relaxation, restfulness *Opposite*: activity **2 calmness**, peace, stillness, tranquillity, calm *Opposite*: agitation ■ *v* **(fml)** relax, rest, take it easy, recline, put your feet up

reposition *v* shift, transpose, move, relocate

repositioning *n* transposition, relocation, moving, move

repository *n* **1 store**, container, storage area, storage place, receptacle **2 source**, fountain, mine, storehouse, origin

repossess *v* recoup, take back, reclaim, recover, recuperate

repossession *n* recovery, reclamation, retrieval, taking back, seizure

repot *v* transplant, transfer, replant, pot, pot on

reprehensible *adj* wrong, bad, disgraceful, shameful, inexcusable *Opposite*: praiseworthy

reprehension *n* criticism, censure, condemnation, telling off, admonition *Opposite*: praise

reprehensive *adj* condemnatory, reproachful, accusing, reproving, critical *Opposite*: praiseworthy

represent *v* **1 act for**, speak for, stand for, stand in for **2 stand for**, symbolize, correspond to, signify, exemplify *Opposite*: misrepresent

representation *n* **1 picture**, image, symbol, depiction, illustration **2 statement**, complaint, submission, argument **3 account**, version, portrayal, description, interpretation

representational *adj* realistic, representative, figurative, depictive, mimetic *Opposite*: abstract

representative *n* **1 envoy**, delegate, agent, spokesperson, diplomat **2 agent**, courier, delegate, deputy, rep **(infml)** ■ *adj* **1 symbolic**, descriptive, illustrative, evocative, expressive **2 illustrative**, typical, characteristic, demonstrative, archetypal

repress *v* **1 curb**, block, suppress, contain, keep inside *Opposite*: express **2 dominate**, subdue, overpower, subjugate, quell

repressed *adj* **1 stifled**, bottled-up, suppressed, blocked, curbed *Opposite*: expressed **2 intimidated**, crushed, suppressed, subjugated, overpowered *Opposite*: liberated

repression *n* suppression, subjugation, domination, authoritarianism, tyranny

repressive *adj* oppressive, suppressive, tyrannical, authoritarian, brutal *Opposite*: liberal

reprieve *v* let off, pardon, grant a stay of execution, acquit, stay *Opposite*: punish ■ *n* official pardon, stay of execution, amnesty, pardon, acquittal

reprimand *v* chastise, reproach, lecture, scold, admonish *Opposite*: praise ■ *n* rebuke, admonishment, warning, dressing-down, reproof

reprint *v* reissue, print again, publish again, produce again, republish ■ *n* reissue, copy, edition

reprisal *n* retaliation, revenge, act of vengeance, punishment, payback **(infml)**

reprise *n* reappearance, echo, recap, repeat,

repetition ■ v **repeat**, reinterpret, re-enact, re-present

reproach v **admonish**, accuse, reprove, criticize, scold *Opposite*: praise ■ n **criticism**, censure, reprimand, blame, accusation *Opposite*: praise

reproachful adj **censorious**, accusing, disapproving, reproving, critical *Opposite*: approving

reprobate n **degenerate**, rascal, troublemaker, sinner, wrongdoer

reprocess v **process again**, reuse, recycle, recover, reclaim

reproduce v **1 copy**, replicate, duplicate, repeat, imitate **2 have children**, produce offspring, produce young, breed, give birth. *See* COMPARE AND CONTRAST *at* copy.

reproduction n **1 copy**, imitation, replica, duplicate, facsimile *Opposite*: original **2 breeding**, procreation, propagation, generation, multiplication ■ adj **imitation**, replica, fake, faux *Opposite*: genuine

reproductive adj **generative**, multiplicative, procreative, procreant, propagative

reproof n **criticism**, blame, accusation, rebuke, scolding *Opposite*: compliment

reprove v **criticize**, take to task, accuse, rebuke, scold *Opposite*: praise

reproving adj **disapproving**, condemnatory, reproachful, admonitory, censorious *Opposite*: approving

reptilian adj **cold-blooded**, unfriendly, emotionless, inhuman, stony *Opposite*: warm

republic n **state**, nation, democracy *Opposite*: monarchy

republican n **antiroyalist**, antimonarchist *Opposite*: monarchist ■ adj **pro-republic**, antiroyalist, antimonarchist *Opposite*: monarchist

republicanism n **antimonarchism**, antiroyalism, political belief *Opposite*: monarchism

repudiate v **1 reject**, renounce, retract, disavow, turn your back on *Opposite*: acknowledge **2 deny**, refute, contradict, gainsay, disclaim *Opposite*: accept

repudiation n **1 retraction**, renunciation, rejection, abandonment, disavowal *(fml) Opposite*: acknowledgment **2 denial**, refutation, negation, disclaimer, contradiction *Opposite*: acceptance

repugnance n **disgust**, revulsion, hatred, hate, abhorrence *Opposite*: attraction. *See* COMPARE AND CONTRAST *at* dislike.

repugnant adj **1 offensive**, objectionable, distasteful, unacceptable, obnoxious *Opposite*: agreeable **2 disgusting**, revolting, nauseating, repulsive, hideous *Opposite*: attractive

repulse v **1 repel**, drive away, force away, hold back, hold off *Opposite*: yield **2 disgust**, sicken, nauseate, repel, appal **3 reject**, rebuff, resist, spurn, snub *Opposite*: welcome

repulsed adj **disgusted**, nauseated, revolted, repelled, sickened *Opposite*: attracted

repulsion n **disgust**, revulsion, nausea, loathing, repugnance *Opposite*: attraction

repulsive adj **disgusting**, revolting, nauseating, hideous, vile *Opposite*: attractive

repulsiveness n **hideousness**, repugnance, foulness, abhorrence, vileness *Opposite*: attractiveness

reputable adj **highly regarded**, trustworthy, well-thought-of, sound, upright *Opposite*: disreputable

reputation n **standing**, status, name, character, repute *(fml)*

repute *(fml) see* reputation

reputed adj **supposed**, alleged, presumed, apparent, believed *Opposite*: actual

request v **ask for**, apply for, call for, entreat, invite *Opposite*: demand ■ n **appeal**, call, application, entreaty, invitation *Opposite*: demand

requiem n **1 service**, Mass, funeral, funeral Mass, service for the dead **2 funeral music**, lament, dirge, funeral hymn, funeral song

require v **1 need**, necessitate, want, have need of, entail **2 oblige**, compel, demand, expect, force

required adj **necessary**, obligatory, compulsory, mandatory, essential *Opposite*: optional

requirement n **obligation**, condition, prerequisite, must, necessity *Opposite*: option

requisite *(fml)* adj **necessary**, mandatory, vital, essential, indispensable *Opposite*: optional. *See* COMPARE AND CONTRAST *at* necessary.

requisition n **demand**, request, application, summons ■ v **1 take over**, commandeer, seize, take possession of, appropriate *Opposite*: relinquish **2 demand**, apply for, call for, request, put in for

reread v **revise**, look back over, check through, go through, read again

rerun v **replay**, repeat, play again, air again, show again ■ n **repeat**, repeat showing, replay

reschedule v **postpone**, rearrange, defer, reorganize, suspend *Opposite*: bring forward

rescheduling n **postponement**, deferment, putting off, rearrangement, rearranging

rescind v **withdraw**, annul, cancel, repeal, overturn *Opposite*: authorize

rescue v **save**, free, set free, liberate, release *Opposite*: abandon ■ n **release**, liberation, saving, salvage *Opposite*: capture

rescuer n **saviour**, champion, liberator, salvation, redeemer *Opposite*: captor

research n **investigation**, study, exploration, examination, enquiries ■ v **investigate**, study, explore, do research, delve into

researcher *n* **investigator**, academic, scholar, scientist, student

resemblance *n* **similarity**, likeness, semblance, sameness, alikeness *Opposite*: difference

resemble *v* **look like**, bear a resemblance to, be similar to, be like, look a lot like *Opposite*: differ

resembling *adj* **like**, similar to, not unlike, close to, reminiscent of

resent *v* **1 begrudge**, bear a grudge, feel bitter about, have hard feelings about, feel aggrieved *Opposite*: accept **2 dislike**, not like, hate, be offended by, show antipathy towards *Opposite*: like

resentful *adj* **angry**, bitter, indignant, offended, aggrieved

resentment *n* **anger**, bitterness, dislike, hatred, antipathy. *See* COMPARE AND CONTRAST *at* **anger**.

reservation *n* **1 advance booking**, booking, registration, reserved seat, arrangement **2 protected area**, sanctuary, refuge, game reserve, game park **3 unwillingness**, reluctance, hesitation, distance, aloofness *Opposite*: enthusiasm **4 condition**, proviso, rider, corollary, stipulation

reservations *n* **misgivings**, doubts, hesitation, questions, uncertainties

reserve *v* **1 set aside**, keep, keep back, hold back, put to one side *Opposite*: use **2 book**, retain, put your name down for, make a reservation *Opposite*: cancel ■ *n* **1 store**, cache, hoard, stock, emergency supply **2 reservation**, park, game park, protected area, game reserve **3 substitute**, stand-in, fallback, replacement, locum

reserved *adj* **1 booked**, retained, taken, engaged *Opposite*: free **2 earmarked**, kept, set aside, held in reserve, kept back *Opposite*: used **3 aloof**, reticent, standoffish, snobbish, distant *Opposite*: outgoing

reserves *n* **1 assets**, funds, contingency fund, financial resources, capital **2 stocks**, supplies, hoard, resources, stores

reservist *n* **soldier**, reserve, reserve member, part-time soldier, Territorial

reservoir *n* **tank**, pool, basin, lake, artificial lake

reset *v* **rearrange**, reorganize, retune, change, right

resettle *v* **relocate**, transfer, transplant, emigrate, immigrate

resettlement *n* **relocation**, immigration, emigration, migration, transfer

reshape *v* **redesign**, reform, rewrite, restructure, reformat

reshuffle *n* **reorganization**, rearrangement, rationalization, reallocation, reordering ■ *v* **reorganize**, rearrange, rationalize, reallocate, reorder

reside *v* **1 live**, live in, inhabit, have your home, be a resident of **2 exist in**, be inherent in, be located in, be a feature of, be present in

residence *n* **house**, home, seat, habitation, dwelling *(fml)*

residency *n* **placement**, position, job, post, internship

resident *n* **occupant**, inhabitant, denizen, tenant, occupier

residential *adj* **domestic**, suburban, housing, domiciliary *Opposite*: business

residual *adj* **left over**, remaining, lingering, left behind, outstanding

residue *n* **remains**, remainder, rest, deposit, scum

resign *v* **leave**, leave your job, quit, walk out, give notice *Opposite*: sign on

resignation *n* **1 notice**, notification, letter of resignation **2 acceptance**, acquiescence, acknowledgment, submission, forbearance *(fml)* *Opposite*: defiance

resigned *adj* **reconciled**, accepting, acquiescent, submissive, stoic *Opposite*: resistant

resign yourself *v* **accept**, acknowledge, give in to, yield to, reconcile yourself *Opposite*: resist

resilience *n* **1 buoyancy**, spirit, hardiness, toughness, resistance *Opposite*: defeatism **2 pliability**, flexibility, elasticity, suppleness, bounciness *Opposite*: rigidity

resilient *adj* **1 hardy**, strong, tough, robust, buoyant *Opposite*: defeatist **2 elastic**, pliable, flexible, supple, resistant *Opposite*: rigid

resin *n* **mastic**, gum, balm, kauri gum, gamboge

resinous *adj* **sticky**, viscous, tacky, gummy

resist *v* **1 fight**, battle, struggle, fight back, attack *Opposite*: surrender **2 oppose**, defy, stand firm, contest, challenge *Opposite*: accept **3 withstand**, survive, endure, weather, be proof against *Opposite*: succumb **4 keep from**, avoid, refuse, refrain, withstand *Opposite*: give in

resistance *n* **1 confrontation**, fight, battle, fighting, struggle *Opposite*: surrender **2 opposition**, defiance, challenge, endurance *Opposite*: acceptance

resistant *adj* **1 opposed**, dead set against, unwilling, defiant, challenging *Opposite*: accepting **2 resilient**, hardy, unaffected, impervious, tough *Opposite*: weak

resistor *n* **regulator**, rheostat, controller

resit *n* **retake**, re-examination, re-test, repeat ■ *v* **take again**, retake, repeat, sit again

resolute *adj* **firm**, staunch, unyielding, stubborn, unbendable *Opposite*: irresolute

resoluteness *n* **firmness**, determination, steadfastness, staunchness, single-mindedness *Opposite*: indecisiveness

resolution *n* **1 decree**, declaration, decision, motion, ruling **2 promise**, pledge, oath, vow

3 resolve, determination, steadfastness, tenacity, firmness *Opposite*: indecision **4 solution**, answer, end, upshot, outcome

resolve v **1 make up your mind**, decide, determine, make a decision, undertake **2 solve**, get to the bottom of, sort out, put an end to, settle ■ *n* **resolution**, determination, steadfastness, tenacity, doggedness *Opposite*: indecision

resolved *adj* **determined**, set, resolute, fixed, committed *Opposite*: undecided

resonance *n* **1 timbre**, character, quality, tone, reverberation **2 significance**, meaning, importance, suggestion, echo

resonant *adj* **1 booming**, ringing, echoing, reverberating, resounding *Opposite*: tinny **2 significant**, meaningful, important, evocative, indicative *Opposite*: insignificant

resonate v **reverberate**, vibrate, resound, ring, echo

resort *n* **option**, recourse, alternative, course of action, possibility

resort to v **turn to**, give in to, have recourse to, fall back on, avail yourself of

resound v **echo**, resonate, boom, ring, reverberate

resounding *adj* **1 loud**, booming, echoing, ringing, resonant *Opposite*: weak **2 unqualified**, categorical, unambiguous, definite, unquestionable *Opposite*: qualified

resource *n* **reserve**, supply, source, means, store

resourceful *adj* **ingenious**, imaginative, inventive, practical, quick-witted *Opposite*: unimaginative

resourcefulness *n* **ingenuity**, imagination, inventiveness, wits, originality

resources *n* **capital**, income, possessions, wealth, property

respect *n* **1 admiration**, high opinion, regard, esteem, reverence *Opposite*: disrespect **2 detail**, regard, matter, particular, point ■ v **1 value**, revere, think a lot of, esteem, defer to *Opposite*: disrespect **2 show consideration for**, appreciate, regard, have a high regard for, recognize *Opposite*: disregard **3 follow**, abide by, comply with, obey, acknowledge *Opposite*: deny. *See* COMPARE AND CONTRAST *at* regard.

respectability *n* **decency**, propriety, uprightness, decorum, morality *Opposite*: indecency

respectable *adj* **1 reputable**, highly regarded, well-thought-of, decent, good *Opposite*: disreputable **2 adequate**, decent, reasonable, acceptable, satisfactory *Opposite*: inadequate

respected *adj* **reliable**, authoritative, distinguished, venerable, esteemed

respectful *adj* **deferential**, reverential, reverent, humble, dutiful *Opposite*: disrespectful

respectfulness *n* **deference**, respect, regard, consideration, honour *Opposite*: contemptuousness

respecting *prep* **with regard to**, regarding, with respect to, in respect of, relating to

respective *adj* **own**, individual, particular, separate, corresponding

respects *n* **compliments**, good wishes, greetings, salutations *(fml)*

respiration *n* **breathing**, inhalation, exhalation

respirator *n* **breathing apparatus**, ventilator, gas mask, oxygen mask

respiratory *adj* **breathing**, lung, respirational

WORD BANK
❏ **parts of a respiratory system** air sac, airway, alveolus, bronchial tube, bronchiole, bronchus, larynx, lung, pharynx, throat, trachea, vocal cords, voice box, windpipe

respire v **breathe**, take breaths, inhale, exhale

respite *n* **1 interval**, break, breathing space, lull, relief **2 reprieve**, delay, adjournment, hiatus, break

resplendent *adj* **splendid**, dazzling, magnificent, glorious, brilliant *Opposite*: unimpressive

respond v **1 reply**, answer, retort, answer back, rejoin *(fml)* **2 react**, act in response, take action, counter, act *Opposite*: ignore

respondent *n* **defendant**, accused, plaintiff

response *n* **reply**, answer, retort, comeback, reaction. *See* COMPARE AND CONTRAST *at* answer.

responsibility *n* **1 accountability**, duty, charge, concern, obligation *Opposite*: irresponsibility **2 blame**, liability, guilt, answerability, fault **3 task**, remit, brief, assignment, concern

responsible *adj* **1 accountable**, in charge, in control, in authority, answerable **2 to blame**, liable, guilty, at fault, blamable **3 dependable**, conscientious, trustworthy, reliable, sensible *Opposite*: irresponsible

responsive *adj* **receptive**, open, approachable, reactive, quick to respond *Opposite*: sluggish

responsively *adv* **sensitively**, quick-wittedly, instinctively, positively, favourably

responsiveness *n* **receptiveness**, openness, reaction, sensitivity, awareness *Opposite*: sluggishness

rest *n* **1 break**, respite, time out, relaxation, recreation **2 remainder**, residue, leftovers, remnants, surplus **3 stand**, support, holder, rack, frame ■ v **1 relax**, take it easy, have a rest, take a break, have a break **2 lie**, lean, lay, place, put

restart v **1 resume**, take up, start again, pick up, start over *(US)* **2 revive**, resurrect, save, renew, reopen *Opposite*: wind down

restate v **repeat**, reaffirm, reiterate, say again, regurgitate

rested adj **refreshed**, relaxed, restored, reinvigorated, revitalized Opposite: exhausted

restful adj **soothing**, relaxing, soporific, calming, peaceful Opposite: stimulating

restitution n 1 **compensation**, recompense, reimbursement, amends, repayment 2 **restoration**, return, reinstatement

restive see **restless**

restiveness n **restlessness**, impatience, agitation, edginess, nervousness Opposite: calmness

restless adj **fidgety**, agitated, edgy, impatient, on edge Opposite: relaxed

restlessness n **agitation**, impatience, restiveness, edginess Opposite: calmness

restock v **refill**, replenish, top up, fill up, replace

rest on v **hinge on**, turn on, depend on, rely, hang on

restoration n 1 **reinstatement**, re-establishment, return, restitution, reinstallation Opposite: abolition 2 **refurbishment**, renovation, repair, renewal, rebuilding

restorative adj **healing**, uplifting, invigorating, soothing, recuperative Opposite: draining

restore v 1 **reinstate**, re-establish, bring back, return, give back 2 **refurbish**, renovate, repair, renew, recondition. See COMPARE AND CONTRAST at renew.

restrain v 1 **hold back**, prevent, stop, keep, deter 2 **control**, bring under control, keep under control, keep in check, check 3 **confine**, detain, jail, lock up, imprison Opposite: free

restrained adj **reserved**, controlled, in control of yourself, self-possessed, calm Opposite: demonstrative

restraining order n **injunction**, court order, gagging order, stay

restraint n 1 **self-control**, control, command, self-possession, self-discipline Opposite: self-indulgence 2 **limit**, limitation, curb, ceiling, restriction 3 **captivity**, arrest, imprisonment, confinement, detention Opposite: freedom 4 **belt**, chain, shackle, fetter, bond

restrict v **limit**, confine, put a ceiling on, curb, control Opposite: loosen

restricted adj 1 **limited**, controlled, constrained, regulated, delimited Opposite: open 2 **classified**, top-secret, secret, confidential, privileged Opposite: public

restriction n **limit**, constraint, restraint, control, ceiling

restrictive adj **preventive**, obstructive, limiting, deterring, restraining Opposite: free

restructure v **rearrange**, reorganize, reform, reshuffle, redistribute

restructuring n **rearrangement**, reorganization, shake-up, reform, reshuffle

result n 1 **consequence**, outcome, upshot, effect, product 2 **mark**, grade, score, outcome 3 **calculation**, solution, answer, findings, conclusion ■ v 1 **cause**, bring about, give rise to, occasion, lead to 2 **ensue**, be caused by, stem, rise, be brought about by

resultant adj **subsequent**, ensuing, resulting, consequential, follow-on

resulting adj **subsequent**, resultant, ensuing, consequential, follow-on

resume v 1 **recommence**, start again, continue, begin again, pick up where you left off Opposite: stop 2 **return**, go back, reoccupy, take up again

résumé n **précis**, review, outline, rundown, summary

resumption n **recommencement**, continuation, carrying on, renewal, reopening

resurface v 1 **float up**, come up, break the surface, rise Opposite: sink 2 **reappear**, come back, rematerialize, re-emerge, return 3 **coat**, cover, skim, overlay, surface

resurgence n **revival**, renaissance, rebirth, resurrection, recovery Opposite: disappearance

resurgent adj **burgeoning**, growing, rising, increasing, reviving

resurrect v 1 **resuscitate**, bring back to life, raise from the dead, restore to life, revive Opposite: kill 2 **save**, breathe new life into, revive, revivify, restart

resurrection n **revival**, renaissance, rebirth, revivification, reappearance

resuscitate v 1 **give the kiss of life to**, give artificial respiration to, bring round, save Opposite: asphyxiate 2 **breathe new life into**, revive, revivify, resurrect, boost

resuscitation n 1 **artificial respiration**, cardiac massage, revival, recovery 2 **restoration**, resurgence, renewal, revival, revitalization

retail n **trade**, selling, marketing, merchandising, wholesale ■ v **sell**, trade, put on the market, put up for sale, vend

retailer n 1 **shop**, store, retail outlet 2 **seller**, vendor, merchant, trader, dealer

retain v 1 **keep**, keep hold of, hold on to, hold, hang on to Opposite: let go 2 **recall**, recollect, keep in mind, remember, hold Opposite: forget

retainer n **deposit**, down payment, fee, payment

retake v 1 **take back**, recapture, regain, reconquer, win back 2 **repeat**, redo, resit ■ n **resit**, exam, examination, repeat

retaliate v **hit back**, strike back, get even, even the score, react Opposite: forgive

retaliation n **reprisal**, revenge, vengeance, retribution Opposite: forgiveness

retaliatory adj **tit-for-tat**, reciprocal, reactive, punitive, revengeful Opposite: forgiving

retard v **delay**, slow down, hold up, hold back, hinder Opposite: speed up

retardation n **delay**, check, obstruction, hindrance, obstacle *Opposite*: acceleration

retarded adj **underdeveloped**, slow, stunted, arrested, lagging *Opposite*: accelerated

retch v **vomit**, gag, be sick, heave (*infml*), throw up (*infml*)

retell v **repeat**, restate, go over, reiterate, recite

retention n **1 holding**, retaining, preservation, withholding, maintenance *Opposite*: release **2 remembering**, memorizing, recalling, memory, recollection *Opposite*: forgetting

retentive adj **retaining**, absorbent, spongy

rethink v **reconsider**, change your mind, change direction, change tack, change course ■ n **reconsideration**, change of mind, change of heart, second thoughts, volte-face

reticence n **1 reserve**, silence, uncommunicativeness, discretion, restraint *Opposite*: openness **2 shyness**, bashfulness, reserve, quietness, modesty *Opposite*: boldness

reticent adj **reserved**, discreet, restrained, unforthcoming, uncommunicative *Opposite*: talkative. *See* COMPARE AND CONTRAST *at* **silent**.

retinue n **entourage**, followers, attendants, servants, aides

retire v **1 give up work**, stop working, step down, be pensioned off, be superannuated **2 go to bed**, call it a day, turn in (*infml*), hit the sack (*infml*), hit the hay (*infml*) **3 leave**, take your leave, withdraw, go away, go off

retired adj **superannuated**, pensioned off, discharged, emeritus, emerita *Opposite*: working

retirement n **1 superannuation**, departure, leaving, giving up work, stepping down **2 withdrawal**, retreat, sequestration, seclusion

retiring adj **reticent**, self-effacing, unassuming, shy, reserved

retort v **reply**, answer, respond, counter, rejoin (*fml*) ■ n **reply**, response, riposte, answer, squelch (*slang*). *See* COMPARE AND CONTRAST *at* **answer**.

retouch v **touch up**, correct, restore, renovate, improve

retrace v **review**, redo, go back over, repeat

retract v **1 draw in**, draw back, pull in, pull back, withdraw *Opposite*: extend **2 deny**, take back, withdraw, apologize, recant *Opposite*: stand by

retractable adj **telescopic**, folding, collapsible

retraction n **withdrawal**, refutation, disclaimer, denial, negation *Opposite*: confirmation

retreat n **1 departure**, withdrawal, flight, evacuation *Opposite*: advance **2 haven**, hideaway, sanctuary, refuge, shelter ■ v **move away**, move back, draw back, back away, run away *Opposite*: advance

retrench v **cut back**, economize, save, save money, tighten your belt

retrenchment n **cutback**, economizing, cuts, cost-cutting, belt-tightening

retribution n **vengeance**, revenge, reprisal, reckoning, justice

retributive adj **punitive**, retaliatory, vengeful, punishing, revengeful

retrieval n **recovery**, repossession, rescue, reclamation, salvage *Opposite*: loss

retrieve v **save**, get back, recover, regain, repossess *Opposite*: lose

retro adj **period**, old-fashioned, dated, historical, passé

retrograde adj **1 backward**, reversing, rearward *Opposite*: forward **2 regressive**, declining, worsening, getting worse, deteriorating *Opposite*: improving

retrogress v **1 regress**, decline, revert, degenerate, worsen *Opposite*: progress **2 move backwards**, reverse, go back, retreat, draw back *Opposite*: move forward

retrogression n **decline**, regression, return, relapse, deterioration *Opposite*: progression

retrogressive adj **1 regressive**, reverting, degenerating, worsening, getting worse *Opposite*: progressive **2 reversing**, retreating, withdrawing, moving back, drawing back

retrospect n **recollection**, remembrance, review, reconsideration, survey *Opposite*: prospect

retrospective adj **1 reviewing**, reflective, surveying, reconsidering **2 retroactive**, backdated, ex post facto **3 backward-looking**, nostalgic, retrograde, traditional, conservative *Opposite*: forward-thinking ■ n **exhibition**, show, presentation, showcase, display

retrospectively adv **on reflection**, in retrospect, with hindsight, with the benefit of hindsight, on second thoughts

return v **1 revisit**, come back, go again, come again, go back *Opposite*: depart **2 send back**, take back, replace, restore *Opposite*: retain **3 resume**, go back, revert, revisit, begin again *Opposite*: stop **4 repay**, pay back, refund, reimburse, give back *Opposite*: keep ■ n **1 coming back**, reappearance, reoccurrence, arrival, homecoming *Opposite*: departure **2 profit**, earnings, yield, revenue, proceeds

returns n **revenue**, earnings, yield, proceeds, takings *Opposite*: outlay

reunification n **reunion**, reconsolidation, amalgamation, recombination, reintegration

reunify v **reunite**, come together, rejoin, bring together, reintegrate

reunion n **1 gathering**, meeting, event, get-together (*infml*) **2 reunification**, reintegration, recombination, reconsolidation

reunite v **reunify**, unite, bring together, unify, come together *Opposite*: split

reusable adj **refillable**, returnable, recyclable, green, ecofriendly *Opposite*: disposable

reuse v recycle, reclaim, reprocess, salvage Opposite: discard

rev n revolution, cycle, rotation, turn, revolution per minute ■ v race, roar, scream, increase power, accelerate

revaluation n revision, reappraisal, reassessment, readjustment, redefinition

revalue v 1 raise, increase, up, enhance, augment (fml) Opposite: devalue 2 reappraise, re-evaluate, adjust, reset, change

revamp v restore, make over, renew, refurbish, give a facelift ■ n facelift, refurbishment, restoration, renovation, overhaul. See COMPARE AND CONTRAST at **renew**.

reveal v 1 make known, disclose, divulge, expose, make public Opposite: conceal 2 expose, uncover, show, bare, bring to light Opposite: cover up

revealing adj 1 skimpy, see-through, figure-hugging, close-fitting, tight-fitting 2 enlightening, illuminating, telling, telltale, informative Opposite: obscure

revealingly adv tellingly, significantly, interestingly, importantly, conspicuously

reveille n 1 wake-up call, early-morning call, bugle call Opposite: lights out 2 early morning, daybreak, dawn, sunrise, the crack of dawn Opposite: dusk

revel v 1 delight, enjoy, take pleasure in, luxuriate, bask 2 make merry, celebrate, have fun, socialize, let your hair down (infml) ■ n celebration, party, festivities, carnival, merrymaking

revelation n 1 exposé, exposure, disclosure, leak, admission 2 surprise, shock, eye opener

reveller n partygoer, roisterer, merrymaker, pleasure-seeker, celebrator

revelry n festivities, revels, celebrations, partying, merriment

revenge n retaliation, vengeance, retribution, settling of scores, reprisal ■ v requite, avenge, even the score, get your own back, retaliate

revenue n income, proceeds, profits, returns, takings Opposite: expenses

reverberate v echo, resound, ring, vibrate, resonate

reverberating adj resounding, echoing, resonant, rich, rumbling

reverberation n echo, sound, noise, boom

reverberations n aftershock, aftereffects, impact, shock

revere v admire, respect, look up to, hold in the highest regard, be in awe of Opposite: despise

revered adj 1 respected, valued, illustrious, distinguished, esteemed Opposite: vilified 2 holy, sacred, blessed, venerated, hallowed Opposite: vilified

reverence n respect, admiration, worship, veneration, regard Opposite: contempt. See COMPARE AND CONTRAST at **regard**.

reverend adj 1 (fml) respected, revered, venerated, worthy, noble 2 ecclesiastical, clerical, priestly (literary), ministerial ■ n vicar, priest, cleric, minister, parson

reverent see reverential

reverential adj respectful, deferential, worshipful, humble, awed Opposite: disrespectful

reverie n daydream, dream, trance, musing, contemplation

reversal n 1 turnaround, U-turn, volte-face, about-turn, about-face (US) 2 setback, hitch, problem, reverse, blow

reverse v 1 overturn, turn round, undo, annul, invalidate Opposite: carry out 2 move backwards, back up, drive backwards, go backwards, retreat Opposite: advance 3 transpose, switch, invert, reorder, rearrange ■ n 1 contrary, opposite, antithesis, converse 2 back, rear, underneath, other side, opposite side Opposite: front 3 setback, reversal, hitch, problem, misfortune ■ adj opposite, contrary, converse, inverse Opposite: same

reversible adj 1 rescindable, revocable, alterable, adjustable, changeable Opposite: irreversible 2 two-sided, dual-purpose, multipurpose, double-sided, two-in-one

reversion n 1 return, decline, deterioration, degeneration, retreat 2 reversal, turnaround, about-turn, U-turn, volte-face

revert v 1 return, go back, take a step back, relapse, regress 2 go back, revisit, go over again, take another look at, return 3 regress, change back, return, mutate, degenerate 4 lapse, backslide, go back to your old ways, slip back, reoffend 5 be returned, pass, pass back, return, go back

review v 1 reconsider, re-examine, reassess, go over, check 2 appraise, evaluate, assess, look at, examine ■ n 1 publication, magazine, journal, periodical 2 appraisal, evaluation, assessment, examination, analysis 3 reconsideration, re-examination, reassessment, check, re-evaluation

reviewer n critic, commentator, assessor, referee

revile v insult, abuse, scorn, condemn, censure Opposite: praise

revise v 1 amend, modify, adjust, alter, change 2 study, brush up, go over, look over, go through

revision n 1 amendment, reconsideration, modification, adjustment, alteration 2 study, revising, homework

revisionism n reassessment, reconsideration, reinterpretation, pragmatism, alteration

revisionist adj pragmatic, heretical, progressive, modernizing, controversial ■ n pragmatist, modernizer, heretic, liberal

revisit v 1 return to, go back to, come back to, retreat to, re-enter Opposite: abandon

2 reconsider, re-examine, reassess, re-evaluate, rethink

revitalization n **renewal**, renaissance, revival, new life, recovery Opposite: decline

revitalize v **refresh**, invigorate, revive, rejuvenate, regenerate Opposite: wear out

revitalizing adj **energizing**, vitalizing, stimulating, uplifting, invigorating

revival n **1 revitalization**, renewal, restoration, stimulation, reinforcement Opposite: disappearance **2 resuscitation**, recovery, waking, bringing round, coming to Opposite: relapse

revive v **1 resuscitate**, come round, recover, come to, bring round Opposite: lose consciousness **2 recover**, pick up, perk up, resume, develop Opposite: die down **3 revitalize**, renew, breathe life into, restore, refresh Opposite: kill **4 put on**, stage, restage, perform, redo

revivify v **rejuvenate**, breathe new life into, refresh, resurrect, resuscitate Opposite: exhaust

revocation n **cancellation**, withdrawal, reversal, overturning, annulment Opposite: enactment

revoke v **cancel**, annul, rescind, withdraw, retract

revolt v **1 rebel**, rise up, mutiny, riot **2 repel**, repulse, sicken, nauseate, turn your stomach Opposite: attract ■ n **rebellion**, revolution, uprising, upheaval, insurgency

revolted adj **nauseated**, appalled, horror-struck, horror-stricken, dismayed Opposite: charmed

revolting adj **disgusting**, repellent, repulsive, sickening, nauseating Opposite: appealing

revolution n **1 rebellion**, revolt, uprising, upheaval, insurgency **2 transformation**, conversion, alteration, upheaval, development **3 rotation**, turn, spin, cycle, circle

revolutionary adj **1 rebellious**, radical, insurgent, mutinous, anarchist **2 radical**, groundbreaking, world-shattering, innovative, avant-garde Opposite: conventional ■ n **rebel**, radical, insurgent, rioter, mutineer

revolutionize v **transform**, transfigure, reform, alter, change Opposite: maintain

revolve v **rotate**, turn, spin, circle, orbit

revolving adj **rotating**, turning, spinning, circling, gyrating

revue n **variety show**, show, skit, sketch show, satire

revulsion n **disgust**, repulsion, repugnance, distaste, dislike Opposite: attraction

reward n **recompense**, payment, repayment, return, remuneration Opposite: penalty ■ v **recompense**, pay, repay, remunerate, compensate Opposite: penalize

rewarding adj **satisfying**, worthwhile, gratifying, pleasing, fulfilling Opposite: disappointing

rewind v **wind back**, spool back, reverse

rewire v **redo**, renovate, renew, refurbish, revamp

reword v **rephrase**, redraft, rewrite, rework, revise

rework v **amend**, revise, alter, modify, change

rewrite v **redraft**, rephrase, reword, rework, revise ■ n **revision**, amendment, alteration, modification

rhapsodic adj **ecstatic**, enthusiastic, lyrical, rapturous, fervent Opposite: unenthusiastic

rhapsodize v **enthuse**, be ecstatic, eulogize, go on about, go over the top (infml)

rhapsody n **ecstasy**, rapture, bliss, enthusiasm, eagerness Opposite: gloom

rheostat n **control**, regulator, resistor, controller

rhetoric n **1 oratory**, public speaking, speech-making, speechifying (infml) **2 bombast**, pomposity, grandiloquence, fustian, loftiness **3 language**, expression, style, idiom, words

rhetorical adj **1 bombastic**, pompous, pretentious, periphrastic, voluble **2 oratorical**, verbal, linguistic, stylistic

rhetorician n **orator**, speaker, public speaker, debater, advocate

rheumatic adj **stiff**, aching, sore, inflexible, rigid Opposite: flexible

rhinestone n **paste**, strass, diamanté

rhizome n **stem**, shoot, root, tuber, corm

rhomboid see rhombus

rhombus n **diamond**, lozenge, parallelogram, rhomboid

rhyme n **1 assonance**, consonance, rhyming **2 poem**, verse, nursery rhyme, jingle, limerick

rhyme or reason n **sense**, logic, meaning, pattern

rhythm n **1 beat**, pace, tempo, time, measure **2 regularity**, pattern, progression, sequence

rhythmic adj **1 recurring**, regular, periodic, recurrent **2 musical**, cadenced, metrical

rib n **beam**, strut, spoke, spine, spar ■ v (infml) **tease**, make fun of, laugh at, mock, kid

ribald adj **coarse**, vulgar, bawdy, rude, lewd Opposite: refined

ribaldry n **coarseness**, vulgarity, bawdiness, rudeness, lewdness Opposite: refinement

ribbed adj **grooved**, corrugated, ridged, bumpy, uneven

ribbon n **1 band**, tie, trimming, decoration, tape **2 strip**, stretch, band, length **3 decoration**, award, honour, badge of honour, medal

rich adj **1 wealthy**, well-off, affluent, prosperous, moneyed Opposite: poor **2 full**, abounding, plentiful, stuffed, heavy Opposite: lacking **3 opulent**, gorgeous, lush, luxuriant, splendid Opposite: shabby **4 heavy**, indigestible, calorific, cloying, unhealthy *Opposite*: light **5 productive**, fertile, abundant, plentiful, fruitful *Opposite*: infertile **6 intense**, deep, strong, full, powerful *Opposite*: weak **7** (*infml*) **ironic**, amusing, irritating, annoying, ridiculous

riches *n* resources, treasures, reserves, materials, raw materials

richly *adv* **1 opulently**, luxuriantly, luxuriously, splendidly, ornately *Opposite*: shabbily **2 thoroughly**, fully, completely, totally, deeply *Opposite*: barely

richness *n* **1 prosperity**, fortune, affluence, wealth *Opposite*: poverty **2 opulence**, luxury, sumptuousness, splendour, luxuriousness *Opposite*: shabbiness **3 fertility**, fruitfulness, productivity, lushness, fullness *Opposite*: infertility **4 intensity**, depth, strength, fullness, power *Opposite*: weakness

rick *v* twist, pull, sprain, crick, put out

rickety *adj* shaky, unsteady, unstable, rocky, unbalanced *Opposite*: firm

ricochet *v* recoil, rebound, glance off, bounce off, reflect ■ *n* **rebound**, recoil, reverberation, reflection, echo

rictus *n* grimace, grin, fixed expression, contortion

rid *v* **1** (*archaic*) **free**, clear, purge, liberate, cleanse **2 get rid of**, dispense with, do away with, divest, drop

riddle *n* puzzle, conundrum, question, brainteaser, problem ■ *v* **1 pierce**, perforate, puncture, pepper, damage **2 sift**, screen, sieve, separate. *See* COMPARE AND CONTRAST *at* **problem**.

ride *v* **1 gallop**, canter, trot, jockey **2 travel**, journey, go, be carried, be conveyed *Opposite*: walk **3 depend on**, rest on, centre on, rely on, be contingent on ■ *n* trip, outing, jaunt, journey, cycle

ride out *v* endure, brave, stick out, survive, live through *Opposite*: succumb

rider *n* proviso, qualification, provision, condition, stipulation

ride up *v* roll up, slide up, wriggle up, move up, wrinkle *Opposite*: fall down

ridge *n* crest, point, edge, rim, elevation ■ *v* fold, crumple, crinkle, crease, wrinkle

ridicule *v* belittle, mock, deride, scorn, scoff at ■ *n* mockery, scorn, derision, laughter, mimicry

COMPARE AND CONTRAST CORE MEANING: belittle by making fun of somebody or something
ridicule make fun of somebody or something in a cruel contemptuous way; **deride** trivialize somebody or something; **laugh at** make scornful fun of somebody or their behaviour; **mock** treat somebody or something with scorn, often by cruel mimicking; **send up** (*infml*) parody or mimic somebody or something.

ridiculous *adj* ludicrous, preposterous, absurd, silly, outlandish *Opposite*: sensible

ridiculousness *n* ludicrousness, preposterousness, absurdity, irrationality, outlandishness *Opposite*: sense

riding *n* show jumping, racing, hunting, dressage, cross-country

rife *adj* **1 widespread**, common, endemic, extensive, prevalent *Opposite*: rare **2 full**, abounding, bursting, laden, loaded *Opposite*: lacking. *See* COMPARE AND CONTRAST *at* **widespread**.

riff *n* phrase, refrain, melody, tune, groove ■ *v* play, jam, improvise, strum, perform

riffle *v* **1 flick through**, turn the pages of, peruse, glance at, scan **2 shuffle**, mix, mix up, randomize, jumble up **3 ripple**, roughen, undulate, get choppy, ruffle ■ *n* flick, quick look, glance, perusal, skim

rifle *v* ransack, search, search through, rummage, go through

rift *n* **1 crack**, hole, fissure, split, crevice **2 disagreement**, difference, conflict, falling-out, quarrel

rig *v* **1 fix**, engineer, arrange, prepare, fit **2 improvise**, fix up, invent, set up, assemble *Opposite*: plan **3 manipulate**, falsify, mock up, fix, set up ■ *n* **1 oil rig**, platform, derrick **2** (*infml*) **dress**, clothes, clothing, outfit, rigout (*infml*)

rigging *n* ropes, chains, wires, supports, pulleys

right *adj* **1 correct**, accurate, true, exact, precise *Opposite*: wrong **2 appropriate**, respectable, fitting, proper, desirable *Opposite*: inappropriate **3 just**, proper, fair, moral, honourable *Opposite*: immoral **4 well**, healthy, in shape, fit, very well *Opposite*: ill ■ *adv* **1 correctly**, exactly, accurately, precisely, directly *Opposite*: inexactly **2 appropriately**, as it should be, acceptably, suitably, properly *Opposite*: unsuitably **3** (*infml*) **utterly**, entirely, completely, absolutely, totally ■ *n* **1 truth**, honesty, goodness, morality, fairness *Opposite*: wrong **2 entitlement**, privilege, due, birthright, justification ■ *v* redress, rectify, amend, remedy, correct

right-angled *adj* angled, square, perpendicular, ninety-degree, right-angle

righteous *adj* virtuous, moral, good, just, blameless *Opposite*: sinful

righteousness *n* virtue, morality, justice, decency, uprightness *Opposite*: wickedness

rightful *adj* fair, correct, legal, due, just *Opposite*: unlawful

rightfulness *n* truth, fairness, correctness, legality, lawfulness

right hand *n* assistant, aide, deputy, lieutenant, helper

right-hand *adj* **1 right**, rightward, starboard *Opposite*: left-hand **2 trusted**, important, reliable, principal, main

right-handed *adj* clockwise, left to right, circular, round, helical *Opposite*: left-handed

rightio (dated infml) see **righto**

rightist adj **right-wing**, conservative, traditionalist

rightly adv 1 **correctly**, truly, exactly, accurately, precisely Opposite: wrongly 2 **justly**, fittingly, justifiably, suitably, rightfully Opposite: unreasonably 3 (infml) **for certain**, without a shadow of a doubt, for sure, certainly, positively

right-minded adj **reasonable**, sensible, fairminded, decent, rational

rightness n 1 **rectitude**, correctness, faultlessness, truth, precision 2 **aptness**, suitability, appropriateness, timeliness, properness Opposite: inappropriateness

righto (dated infml) adv **right**, all right, okay (infml), OK (infml), okeydokey (infml)

right-wing adj **conservative**, rightist, traditionalist Opposite: left-wing

right-winger n **conservative**, rightist, traditionalist Opposite: liberal

rigid adj 1 **unbending**, inflexible, stiff, firm, set Opposite: floppy 2 **severe**, strict, harsh, stern, inflexible Opposite: lax

rigidity n 1 **stiffness**, inflexibility, hardness, firmness, rigour Opposite: floppiness 2 **inflexibility**, firmness, severity, strictness, stringency Opposite: laxity

rigmarole n 1 **explanation**, account, excuse, palaver, verbiage 2 **fuss**, bother, ritual, business, hassle (infml)

rigorous adj 1 **hard**, severe, harsh, demanding, laborious Opposite: mild 2 **exact**, thorough, precise, meticulous, painstaking Opposite: slapdash

rigorousness n 1 **strictness**, discipline, severity, harshness, difficulty Opposite: leniency 2 **exactness**, thoroughness, discipline, meticulousness, scrupulousness Opposite: negligence

rigour n 1 **severity**, strictness, harshness, intransigence, dogmatism Opposite: flexibility 2 **thoroughness**, consistency, exactitude, precision, meticulousness Opposite: negligence 3 **hardship**, difficulty, adversity, hard time, difficult time Opposite: mildness 4 **stiffness**, rigidity, unresponsiveness, stiffening, rigor mortis Opposite: flexibility

rig out (infml) v 1 **equip**, provide, prepare, arrange, fit out 2 **dress up**, kit out, clothe, get up (infml), attire (fml)

rig up v **improvise**, cobble together, set up, assemble, fix up Opposite: plan

rile (infml) v **anger**, enrage, annoy, irritate, irk Opposite: placate

rim n **edge**, border, lip, perimeter, circumference Opposite: centre

rime n **frost**, hoar frost, ice

rind n **peel**, skin, husk, crust, coat Opposite: flesh

ring n 1 **circle**, loop, hoop, band, halo 2 **group**, band, gang, organization, team 3 **impression**, semblance, appearance, feel, air 4 **call**, phone call, telephone call, buzz (infml), bell (infml) ■ v 1 **encircle**, enclose, circle, surround 2 **peal**, tinkle, chime, toll, ding-dong 3 **call**, phone, telephone, give a ring, ring up 4 **resonate**, resound, ring out, reverberate, echo

ring a bell (infml) v **strike a chord**, jog somebody's memory, sound familiar, be reminiscent, remind

ring-fence v **set aside**, isolate, restrict, stipulate, protect ■ n 1 **restriction**, limitation, specification, separation, reservation 2 **fence**, barrier, boundary, perimeter, border

ringleader n **gang leader**, leader of the pack, agitator, instigator, inciter

ringlet n **curl**, lock, twist, coil, spiral

ringmaster n **master of ceremonies**, MC, host, chair, chairperson

ring off v **hang up**, put the receiver down, finish, go Opposite: hang on

ring out v **be heard**, sound, rise, pierce the silence, blast out

ringside adj **front row**, grandstand, touchline, unimpeded, unobstructed

ring up v **call**, phone, telephone, ring, give a tinkle

rink n **arena**, floor, space, area

rinse n 1 **wash**, clean, bathe, sluice, dip 2 **solution**, colourant, dye, tint, bleach

riot n 1 **uprising**, insurrection, disturbance, unrest, demonstration 2 (infml) **laugh** (infml), scream (infml), gas (infml), hoot (slang) ■ v **mutiny**, demonstrate, run riot, rebel, protest

rioter n **demonstrator**, rebel, revolutionary, insurgent, protester

riotous adj 1 **violent**, disorderly, unruly, uncontrolled, uproarious Opposite: peaceful 2 **wild**, debauched, uncontrolled, out of control, hedonistic Opposite: subdued

riotously adv 1 **hilariously**, madly, sidesplittingly, screamingly, wildly 2 **raucously**, rowdily, wildly, rambunctiously, noisily Opposite: quietly

rip v 1 **tear**, split, cleave, shred, scratch Opposite: mend 2 **snatch**, tear, seize, grab, pluck Opposite: give 3 **speed**, tear, dash, rush, fly Opposite: amble ■ n **tear**, split, scratch, cleft, slash. See COMPARE AND CONTRAST at **tear**.

ripcord n **cord**, line, string, cable, rope

ripe adj 1 (infml) **pungent**, strong, sour, strong-smelling, off Opposite: sweet 2 **mature**, ready, grown, fully grown, matured Opposite: unripe 3 **ready**, suitable, prepared, crying out, disposed

ripen v **mature**, season, grow, develop, evolve

ripeness n **maturity**, readiness, mellowness, age

rip off (infml) v **overcharge**, cheat, swindle, dupe, deceive

rip-off (infml) n **swindle**, con, cheat, diddle (infml), swizz (infml)

riposte n **reply**, retort, comeback, response, answer ▪ v **retort**, reply, come back, return, counter. See COMPARE AND CONTRAST at **answer**.

ripple v **undulate**, swell, flow, move, rise and fall ▪ n **wave**, undulation, swell, current, wrinkle Opposite: stillness

rip-roaring (infml) adj **exciting**, uproarious, boisterous, rollicking, energetic Opposite: boring

rip up v **tear up**, shred, pull apart, chew up, pull to pieces Opposite: piece together

rise v **1 stand up**, get up, get to your feet, arise (literary) Opposite: sit down **2 go up**, increase, climb, mount, get higher Opposite: drop **3 rebel**, revolt, mutiny, rise up, riot Opposite: conform **4 originate**, begin, start, come out of, be set in motion Opposite: end **5 emerge**, come up, appear, arise, be apparent Opposite: disappear **6 wake up**, get up, get out of bed, arise, awaken Opposite: retire ▪ n **1 increase**, growth, upsurge, intensification, escalation Opposite: decrease **2 growth**, spread, development, expansion, advance Opposite: decline **3 hill**, slope, incline, acclivity, elevation Opposite: hollow **4 climb**, ascent, elevation Opposite: fall **5 increase**, promotion, advance, elevation

rise above v **surmount**, overcome, conquer, triumph over, surpass

rise and fall n **swell**, undulation, ripple, movement, rolling Opposite: stability

rise to (infml) v **respond**, meet, shine, succeed, perform

rise to the bait v **respond**, react, get angry, be provoked, answer Opposite: ignore

rise up v **1 rebel**, revolt, riot, rise, mutiny **2 emerge**, stand up, float up, soar, arise (literary) Opposite: sink

risibility n **1** (fml) **humorousness**, sense of humour, happiness, wit, humour Opposite: soberness **2 ridiculousness**, ludicrousness, absurdity, laughableness, stupidity Opposite: seriousness

risible adj **1 laughable**, ludicrous, absurd, ridiculous, stupid Opposite: serious **2** (fml) **humorous**, good-humoured, happy, cheerful, cheery Opposite: sombre

rising adj **increasing**, growing, going up, mounting, getting higher Opposite: falling ▪ n **uprising**, rebellion, revolt, mutiny, riot

risk n **1 danger**, jeopardy, peril, hazard, menace Opposite: safety **2 possibility**, chance, danger, hazard, gamble ▪ v **1 endanger**, jeopardize, lay bare, expose, imperil (fml) Opposite: protect **2 chance**, hazard, attempt, gamble, venture Opposite: play safe

riskiness n **hazardousness**, perilousness, precariousness, dangerousness, audaciousness Opposite: safety

risky adj **dangerous**, hazardous, chancy, precarious, perilous Opposite: safe

risqué adj **racy**, rude, lewd, salacious, naughty Opposite: decorous

rite n **1 ritual**, ceremony, formal procedure, service, sacrament **2 custom**, habit, practice, routine, procedure

ritual n **1 rite**, ceremony, service, formal procedure, sacrament **2 custom**, habit, practice, routine, procedure ▪ adj **1 ceremonial**, procedural, ceremonious, sacramental, formal **2 customary**, habitual, usual, normal, expected

ritualistic adj **ceremonial**, formalized, formulaic, ritualized, sacred

rival n **1 competitor**, opponent, adversary, contender, challenger Opposite: ally **2 equal**, match, counterpart, peer, equivalent ▪ v **1 match**, equal, be the equal of, be similar to, compare with **2 oppose**, compete with, challenge, go up against, be against **3 outdo**, surpass, exceed, beat, top ▪ adj **competing**, opposing, challenging, contending, enemy

rivalry n **competition**, opposition, contention, competitiveness, enmity Opposite: cooperation

river n **stream**, waterway, tributary, canal, watercourse

riverside n **waterside**, water's edge, bank, shore

rivet n **pin**, nail, fastener, press stud, bolt ▪ v **1** (infml) **fascinate**, enthral, entrance, interest, mesmerize Opposite: bore **2 fasten**, hold, pin, bolt, nail

riveting (infml) adj **fascinating**, enthralling, exciting, spellbinding, entrancing Opposite: boring

rivulet n **stream**, burn, gully, brook (literary), creek (US)

RNA n **nucleic acid**, ribonucleic acid, genetic material

road n **street**, thoroughfare, lane, way

WORD BANK

❑ **types of major road** A-road, artery, avenue, boulevard, bypass, clearway, dual carriageway, flyover, main road, motorway, parkway, ring road, toll road, trunk road, turnpike

❑ **types of minor road** access road, access strip, alley, alleyway, B-road, backstreet, blind alley, byroad, byway, cart track, corniche, cul-de-sac, dead end, dirt track, driveway, esplanade, frontage road, lane, mews, parade, path, promenade, service road, side street, slip road, street, track

---

roadblock n **barricade**, barrier, sentry post, obstruction, blockade

roadhouse (dated) n **hotel**, pub, bar, transport café, tavern

road show n **1 radio show**, live broadcast, open-air broadcast, broadcast, tour **2 campaign**, publicity campaign, advertising campaign, media circus (infml), dog-and-pony show (US)

road sign n **sign**, signpost, notice, stop sign, one-way sign

road-test v **try out**, test, test drive, trial, run

roadway n **road**, street, thoroughfare, highway

roadworks n **road repairs**, carriageway repairs, maintenance work, construction work, repair work

roadworthiness n **safety**, soundness, reliability, working order

roadworthy adj **safe**, fit, legal, driveable, suitable

roam v **wander**, rove, travel, journey, stray *Opposite*: settle

roamer n **wanderer**, traveller, rover, itinerant, nomad

roaming adj **wandering**, roving, itinerant, nomadic, peripatetic *Opposite*: stationary

roaring adj 1 **busy**, thriving, prosperous, active *Opposite*: slack 2 **noisy**, loud, deafening, boisterous, thunderous *Opposite*: quiet

roast v **bake**, cook, heat

roasting (infml) adj **boiling**, hot, red-hot, sweltering, burning up *Opposite*: cool

rob v 1 **steal from**, take from, hold up, raid, mug 2 **deprive**, cheat, strip, drain, fleece (infml)

robber n **thief**, burglar, pickpocket, shoplifter, mugger

robbery n **theft**, burglary, break-in, mugging, stealing

robe n **dressing gown**, negligée, housecoat, bathrobe, gown

robot n **automaton**, android, machine, computer, mechanical device

robotic adj 1 **mechanical**, mechanized, automated, automatic, cybernetic 2 **machine-like**, mechanical, unresponsive, unfeeling, humourless *Opposite*: warm

robotics n **cybernetics**, automation, engineering, manufacturing, science

robust adj **healthy**, vigorous, hearty, strong, tough *Opposite*: weak

robustness n **heftiness**, sturdiness, strength, toughness, forcefulness *Opposite*: weakness

rock n 1 **stone**, boulder, pebble 2 **pillar**, mainstay, tower of strength, stalwart ■ v 1 **sway**, swing, shake, move up and down, pitch 2 (infml) **astound**, shock, shake, stun, disturb

rock bottom n **the lowest**, the bottom, the depths, all-time low, nadir

rocker n 1 **biker**, greaser, Hell's Angel, motorcyclist, youth 2 (infml) **rock star**, rock musician, rock singer, rock and roller, pop star 3 (infml) **rock fan**, groupie (infml), headbanger (slang)

rockery n **garden**, rock garden, alpine garden, terrace

rocket v 1 **speed**, whiz, hurtle, fly, zoom 2 (infml) **shoot up**, soar, increase rapidly, go through the roof (infml), go sky-high (infml) *Opposite*: plummet

rock face n **cliff face**, face, precipice, crag, cliff

rock garden n **garden**, rockery, alpine garden, terrace

rock-hard adj **solid**, firm, cast-iron, hard as nails, like granite *Opposite*: soft

rockiness n **shakiness**, unsteadiness, uncertainty, insecurity, instability *Opposite*: steadiness

rock-solid adj 1 **firm**, unshakable, solid, rigid, unyielding *Opposite*: shaky 2 **durable**, unbreakable, strong, firm, enduring *Opposite*: breakable

rock-strewn adj **stony**, rocky, gravelly, pebbly, rough *Opposite*: smooth

rocky adj 1 **stony**, rock-strewn, pebbly, gravelly 2 **difficult**, troubled, uncertain, not easy, hard *Opposite*: easy 3 **shaky**, unsteady, wobbly, unsound, insecure *Opposite*: stable

rod n **bar**, pole, stick, shaft, dowel

rodeo n **competition**, display, festival, meet, fair

rogue n **scoundrel**, rascal, reprobate, ne'er-do-well (dated), cad (dated)

roguery n 1 **dishonesty**, deceit, unscrupulousness, double-dealing, sharp practice *Opposite*: honesty 2 **mischief**, mischievousness, playfulness, naughtiness, tricks

roguish adj 1 **dishonest**, deceitful, unscrupulous, double-dealing, criminal *Opposite*: honest 2 **mischievous**, naughty, impish, wicked, malicious

roguishness n 1 **unscrupulousness**, dishonesty, deceit, double-dealing, sharp practice *Opposite*: honesty 2 **mischievousness**, mischief, playfulness, naughtiness, tricks

roister v 1 **revel**, make merry, celebrate, drink, party (infml) 2 **brag**, boast, show off, swagger, gloat

roisterer n 1 **reveller**, partygoer, merrymaker, pleasure-seeker, celebrator 2 **braggart**, boaster, show-off (infml), loudmouth (infml), bigmouth (infml)

role n 1 **part**, character, person, title role, starring role 2 **position**, function, responsibility, job, task

role model n **example**, model, paradigm, exemplar (literary)

role-play v **act**, act out, enact, play, imagine

role-playing n **acting**, acting out, game-playing, imagination, play-acting

roll v 1 **bowl**, trundle, troll, set rolling, roll along 2 **revolve**, turn, turn over, turn round, spin ■ n **reel**, cylinder, spool, tube, bolt

roll call n **attendance check**, register check, checkup, check, monitoring

roller n **breaker**, wave, whitecap

roller-skate v **skate**, blade, Rollerblade

rollicking adj **boisterous**, rowdy, loud, carefree, swashbuckling ■ n (infml) **reprimand**, scolding, dressing-down, telling-off (infml), talking-to (infml)

roll in v arrive, enter, land, roll up, appear Opposite: leave

rolling adj 1 **undulating**, rising and falling, gently sloping Opposite: steep 2 **progressing**, continuing, ongoing, continuous, constant

roll out v **introduce**, launch, inaugurate, issue, bring out

roll out the red carpet v **treat like royalty**, give a hero's welcome, lionize, make a fuss of, welcome

roll up v 1 **appear**, turn up, ride up, show up, roll in Opposite: leave 2 **turn up**, push back, furl Opposite: unroll

roman adj 1 **upright**, straight, plain Opposite: italic 2 **in classical style**, classical, ancient

romance n 1 **relationship**, love affair, affair, involvement, fling (infml) 2 **love**, passion, amorousness, ardour, sex 3 **allure**, excitement, adventure, nostalgia, feeling 4 **fascination**, enthusiasm, passion, love, love affair 5 **love story**, romantic story, romantic tale, weepie (infml), tearjerker (infml) Opposite: tragedy 6 **adventure story**, adventure, tale, story, narrative 7 **fantasy**, story, tall tale, fiction, daydream ■ v 1 **tell stories**, fantasize, romanticize 2 **be romantic**, act romantically, swoon, daydream, be in love 3 **court** (dated), woo (literary), pay court to (dated) 4 **have an affair**, have a love affair with, have a relationship with, date, have a fling with

romantic adj 1 **loving**, passionate, tender, amorous, adoring Opposite: platonic 2 **idealistic**, dreamy, quixotic, impractical, starry-eyed Opposite: prosaic

romanticism n **idealization**, fantasy, nostalgia, soft focus, rose-tinted glasses

romanticize v 1 **idealize**, glamorize, sentimentalize, put on a pedestal, view through rose-tinted spectacles 2 **daydream**, swoon, gush, dream, rhapsodize

Romeo n **Don Juan**, Casanova, seducer, wolf, womanizer

romp v 1 **cavort**, frolic, horse around, caper, prance 2 **sail**, steam, coast, cruise, whiz Opposite: struggle 3 (infml) **win**, coast, excel yourself, surpass yourself, walk it (infml) Opposite: lose ■ n 1 **frolic**, frisk, gambol, run, scramble 2 (infml) **page-turner**, thriller, chiller, potboiler Opposite: bore 3 (infml) **foregone conclusion**, one-horse race, piece of cake (infml), cinch (infml), walkover (infml)

roofed adj **covered**, enclosed, vaulted, topped Opposite: open

roofing n **tiling**, slating, tiles, slates, thatch

rooftop n **roof**, top, tiles, slates, gable

room n 1 **space**, extent, span, capacity, volume 2 **compartment**, apartment (fml), chamber (literary) 3 **scope**, opportunity, possibility, occasion, chance

---

WORD BANK

❑ **types of room in public buildings** antechamber, anteroom, ballroom, banqueting hall, boardroom, cell, changing room, classroom, cloakroom, dining hall, dormitory, dressing room, entrance hall, foyer, gallery, games room, hall, lavatory, library, lobby, lounge, meeting room, office, powder room, reception room, refectory, rest room, schoolroom, stateroom, surgery, vault, waiting room, ward

❑ **types of room in the home** atelier, attic, bathroom, bedchamber (literary), bedroom, boudoir, boxroom, day room, den, dining room, drawing room, family room, garret, guestroom, kitchen, kitchenette, laundry room, living room, loft, parlour, playroom, recreation room, salon, scullery, sitting room, sleeping quarters, spare room, study, sun lounge, toilet, utility room

---

roominess n **spaciousness**, largeness, capaciousness, generousness, sizableness Opposite: smallness

roommate n **flatmate**, housemate, lodger, cotenant, roomie (US infml)

rooms n **housing**, quarters, place, accommodation, lodgings (dated)

roomy adj **spacious**, large, generous, sizable, capacious Opposite: cramped

roost v **settle**, rest, stay, perch, sleep

root n 1 **stem**, rhizome, tuber, radicle, radix 2 **origin**, cause, source, basis, starting place ■ v 1 **dig**, grub, rootle, forage, delve 2 **search**, delve, rifle, burrow, rummage 3 **cheer**, shout, applaud, yell, clap Opposite: jeer. See COMPARE AND CONTRAST at origin.

rooted adj **entrenched**, ingrained, fixed, deep-rooted, deep-seated

rootless adj **drifting**, freewheeling, roving, nomadic, itinerant Opposite: rooted

root out v 1 **eradicate**, remove, get rid of, do away with, eliminate 2 **find**, discover, locate, turn up, unearth Opposite: hide

roots n **origins**, ancestry, background, heritage, pedigree

rope n **cord**, line, cable, lead, twine ■ v **tie**, fasten, lash, secure, attach Opposite: untie

ropy (infml) adj 1 **poor**, shoddy, trashy, cheap and nasty, rubbishy Opposite: excellent 2 **ill**, unwell, sick, bad, off-colour Opposite: healthy

rose n 1 **design**, rosette, ornament, representation, emblem 2 **sprinkler**, jet, nozzle, spray, attachment 3 **ceiling rose**, fitting, boss, connector, socket

roseate adj **reddish**, rose, fuchsia, magenta, rose-coloured

rosebud n **bud**, bloom, rose, flower, blossom

rose-coloured adj **optimistic**, idealistic, assured, sanguine, trusting Opposite: pessimistic

rose-tinted see **rose-coloured**

rosette n 1 **badge**, decoration, prize 2 **ornament**, design, rose, shape, representation

rosiness n **blush**, flush, pinkness, redness, glow

roster n **rota**, list, schedule, roll, register

rostrum n **platform**, podium, stage, dais, stand

rosy adj 1 **pink**, reddish, pinkish, rose, roseate 2 **blushing**, flushed, glowing, healthy, ruddy Opposite: pale 3 **promising**, auspicious, successful, happy, favourable Opposite: unpromising 4 **optimistic**, idealistic, unrealistic, hopeful, encouraging Opposite: pessimistic

rot v **decompose**, decay, putrefy, disintegrate, go off ■ n 1 **decay**, deterioration, putrefaction, decomposition, corrosion 2 (infml) **nonsense**, balderdash, rubbish, garbage, twaddle (infml) Opposite: sense

rota n **roster**, list, schedule, register, roll

rotary adj **rotating**, turning, revolving, rotational, gyratory

rotate v 1 **turn**, revolve, go, spin, swivel 2 **replace**, switch, alternate, exchange, swap (infml) 3 **take turns**, alternate, interchange, switch, swap (infml)

rotation n 1 **revolution**, turning, spin, gyration 2 **replacement**, switching, cycle, sequence 3 **alternation**, variation, interchange

rote n **repetition**, memorization, routine, habit, rotation

rotisserie n **spit**, skewer, brochette, grill, barbecue

rotor n **blade**, propeller, aerofoil

rotten adj 1 **decayed**, putrid, bad, decomposed, rotted Opposite: fresh 2 (infml) **awful**, bad, nasty, terrible, unpleasant Opposite: pleasant 3 (infml) **inferior**, poor, bad, dreadful, incompetent Opposite: good 4 (infml) **unwell**, ill, sick, off-colour, poorly (infml) Opposite: healthy 5 (infml) **unhappy**, uncomfortable, guilty, embarrassed, bad Opposite: happy 6 **unfair**, unethical, immoral, unprincipled, dishonest Opposite: just ■ adv (infml) **terribly**, unduly, excessively, overly, outrageously Opposite: slightly

rottenness n 1 **decay**, mouldiness, dry rot, wet rot, badness Opposite: freshness 2 (infml) **unpleasantness**, awfulness, dreadfulness, hideousness, ghastliness Opposite: pleasantness 3 (infml) **beastliness**, nastiness, cruelness, cruelty, horridness Opposite: goodness

rotter (dated infml) n **scoundrel**, liar, swindler, cheat, cad (dated) Opposite: angel

rotting adj **decomposing**, decaying, putrid, bad, contaminated Opposite: fresh

rotund adj **overweight**, stout, fat, plump, corpulent Opposite: slender

rotunda n **pavilion**, tower, dome, cupola

rotundity n **roundness**, sphericalness, rotundness, overweight, stoutness Opposite: slenderness

rouge (dated) n **blusher**, lipstick, makeup, face paint, colouring ■ v **make up**, redden, highlight, paint, beautify

rough adj 1 **uneven**, bumpy, irregular, jagged, lumpy Opposite: even 2 **coarse**, shaggy, hairy, bristly, bushy Opposite: smooth 3 **turbulent**, stormy, tempestuous, squally, wild Opposite: calm 4 **rugged**, wild, uncultivated, rocky, hilly Opposite: cultivated 5 **violent**, forceful, tough, physical, forcible Opposite: gentle 6 **boorish**, unrefined, rough-and-ready, coarse, crude Opposite: refined 7 **harsh**, grating, jarring, discordant, rasping Opposite: melodious 8 **approximate**, sketchy, vague, estimated, imprecise Opposite: exact 9 (infml) **unwell**, sickly, ill, out of sorts, seedy (infml) Opposite: well 10 **difficult**, trying, challenging, unpleasant, uncomfortable Opposite: easy 11 **rowdy**, boisterous, noisy, violent, tough Opposite: quiet ■ n **outline**, sketch, summary, draft, mock-up

roughage n **bulk**, cellulose, bran, fibre

rough-and-ready adj 1 **crude**, simple, basic, primitive, serviceable Opposite: sophisticated 2 **down-to-earth**, unpretentious, honest, rough-hewn, kind-hearted Opposite: refined

rough-and-tumble n **hurly-burly**, cut and thrust, infighting, sparring, fracas

roughcast n **coating**, cladding, facing, plasterwork, rendering

rough copy n **outline**, sketch, summary, draft, rough

roughen v **coarsen**, toughen, scratch, abrade, rough Opposite: soften

rough-hewn adj 1 **rough**, unfinished, undressed, incomplete 2 **crude**, basic, primitive, simple, rough Opposite: polished 3 **rugged**, rough, unrefined, coarse, crude

roughhouse (infml) n **rowdiness**, boisterousness, rough-and-tumble, horseplay, roughness

roughneck (infml) n **thug**, hoodlum, rowdy, yobbo (infml), hooligan (infml)

roughness n 1 **unevenness**, coarseness, bumpiness, irregularity, jaggedness Opposite: smoothness 2 **coarseness**, shagginess, hairiness, bristliness, bushiness Opposite: smoothness 3 **turbulence**, storminess, tempestuousness, wildness Opposite: calmness 4 **ruggedness**, wildness, rockiness, hilliness, cragginess Opposite: gentleness 5 **violence**, force, toughness, power, brutality Opposite: gentleness 6 **brusqueness**, rudeness, gruffness, harshness, coarseness Opposite: refinement 7 **harshness**, discordance, astringency, gruffness, raucousness Opposite: smoothness 8 **vagueness**, sketchiness, ambiguity, inexactness, haziness Opposite: exactness 9 **rowdiness**, boisterousness, noisiness, violence, toughness Opposite: quietness

rough out v **draft**, outline, prepare, sketch, block out Opposite: finalize

rough up (infml) v **maltreat**, mistreat, abuse, batter, manhandle Opposite: take care of

round n **circle**, disc, slice, ring, band ■ v **turn**, circumnavigate, negotiate, skirt round, skirt ■ prep **surrounding**, around, about, encircling, encompassing ■ adv **around**, about, near, on all sides

round about prep **around**, about, circa, say, in the region of

roundabout n 1 **merry-go-round**, carousel, ride, attraction 2 **traffic island**, traffic junction, junction, intersection, crossroads ■ adj **indirect**, oblique, circuitous, winding, meandering Opposite: direct

rounded adj **curved**, smoothed, smooth-edged, round, curvy Opposite: pointed

round-eyed adj **open-mouthed**, amazed, gaping, staring, fascinated

roundly adv **severely**, forcefully, completely, utterly, bluntly

roundness n **roundedness**, plumpness, chubbiness Opposite: slenderness

round-shouldered adj **stooping**, hunched, slouching, bent, bent over Opposite: erect

round table n **discussion**, negotiation, debate, forum, meeting

round-the-clock adj **24-hour**, day-and-night, 24/7, continuous, constant

round trip n **both ways**, return journey, return trip, return, circuit

round up v **capture**, gather together, collect, arrest, amass Opposite: disperse

round-up n 1 **assembly**, capture, hunt, herding, rodeo Opposite: release 2 **summary**, rundown, review, summing up, recap

rouse v 1 **stir**, wake up, revive, awaken, disturb Opposite: lull 2 **stir up**, provoke, incite, move, galvanize Opposite: lull

rousing adj **stirring**, inspiring, moving, exciting, stimulating Opposite: soothing

rout n 1 **retreat**, flight, stampede, surrender, collapse Opposite: advance 2 **defeat**, massacre, landslide, thrashing, beating Opposite: victory 3 **tumult**, disorder, riot, disturbance, hubbub ■ v **beat back**, overpower, overwhelm, beat, defeat Opposite: retreat

route n 1 **road**, path, way, track, itinerary 2 **course**, means, method, way, direction ■ v **direct**, send, transmit, move, channel

routine n 1 **procedure**, practice, habit, custom, sequence 2 **tedium**, monotony, mundaneness, dullness, dreariness Opposite: variety ■ adj 1 **usual**, standard, everyday, normal, customary Opposite: unusual 2 **monotonous**, dull, tedious, repetitive, humdrum Opposite: exciting. See COMPARE AND CONTRAST at habit.

rove v **wander**, roam, range, meander, travel

rover n **wanderer**, traveller, rolling stone, nomad, drifter

roving adj 1 **roaming**, travelling, wandering, rambling, nomadic Opposite: stationary 2 **erratic**, wandering, fickle, capricious, inconsistent Opposite: steady

row n 1 **line**, chain, string, file, queue 2 **disagreement**, dispute, quarrel, controversy, argument Opposite: agreement 3 **noise**, rumpus, din, commotion, racket (infml) Opposite: lull ■ v 1 **paddle**, scull, punt, take the oars, propel 2 **fight**, quarrel, have a row, disagree, argue Opposite: agree

rowdiness n **disorderliness**, unruliness, noisiness, loudness, raucousness Opposite: restraint

rowdy adj **disorderly**, unruly, noisy, loud, raucous Opposite: restrained

rower n **oarsperson**, sculler, coxswain, cox

royal adj 1 **regal**, imperial, majestic, stately, noble 2 **magnificent**, splendid, noble, excellent, grand Opposite: ordinary

royalist n **monarchist**, traditionalist, constitutionalist, conservative, loyal subject Opposite: republican

royals n **royalty**, crowned heads, monarchs, sovereigns, royal family

royalty n 1 **royals**, crowned heads, monarchs, sovereigns, royal family 2 **fee**, payment, percentage, credit, token

RP n **Received Pronunciation**, BBC English, the Queen's English, Standard English, British English

RSI n **repetitive strain injury**, tenosynovitis, carpal tunnel syndrome, industrial injury, work-related injury

rub v 1 **massage**, stroke, caress, knead, pat 2 **polish**, wipe, buff, shine, clean 3 **chafe**, hurt, gall, irritate, scrape Opposite: soothe

rubber n **India rubber**, foam rubber, neoprene, gum, elastic

rubberneck (infml) v **stare**, gaze, gape, goggle, ogle. See COMPARE AND CONTRAST at gaze.

rubbernecking (infml) n **staring**, gazing, gaping, ogling, gawking (infml)

rubber stamp n **stamping device**, stamp, seal, stamper, signet

rubber-stamp v **approve**, sanction, pass, let through, nod through (infml) Opposite: veto

rubbery adj **tough**, elastic, chewy, hard, overcooked Opposite: tender

rubbing n 1 **impression**, brass rubbing, copy, reproduction, relief 2 **friction**, scraping, abrasion, resistance, chafing 3 **soreness**, chafing, irritation, blistering, saddle sores

rubbish n 1 **refuse**, debris, litter, waste, junk (infml) 2 **nonsense**, drivel, garbage, claptrap (infml), hogwash (infml) ■ v (infml) **pooh-pooh**, criticize, dismiss, ridicule, disparage Opposite: praise

rubbish bin n **dustbin**, bin, wheelie bin, waste bin, waste paper bin

rubbishy adj **inferior**, poor quality, poor, bad, dodgy (infml) Opposite: quality

rubble n **debris**, ruins, wreckage, remains, bricks

rub down v **1 finish**, wipe down, sand, scour, prepare **2 massage**, rub, go over, oil, stroke **3 dry**, rub, dry off, towel dry, towel

rub out v **erase**, delete, wipe, expunge, efface

rubric n **1 title**, heading, header, head, introduction **2 rules**, instructions, guidelines, directions, rulebook **3 custom**, tradition, practice, system, convention **4 class**, category, classification, division, type

rub up the wrong way v **irritate**, annoy, make somebody's hackles rise, infuriate, offend

ruched adj **pleated**, gathered, frilled, frilly, edged Opposite: plain

ruck n **1 mass**, pile, heap, accumulation, conglomeration **2 crease**, wrinkle, crumple, fold, rumple ■ v **wrinkle**, crease, fold, crumple, gather Opposite: smooth

rucksack n **backpack**, haversack, knapsack, frame rucksack, daypack

ruckus n **commotion**, disturbance, rumpus, riot, uproar

ruction n **quarrel**, fight, dispute, disturbance, row

ructions n **rumpus**, fuss, uproar, dispute, controversy

ruddiness n **redness**, rosiness, glow, blush, flush Opposite: pallor

ruddy adj **reddish**, rosy, flushed, glowing, healthy-looking Opposite: pale

rude adj **1 impolite**, discourteous, insolent, bad-mannered, ill-mannered Opposite: polite **2 foul**, crude, offensive, vulgar, foulmouthed Opposite: polite

rudeness n **impoliteness**, insolence, discourtesy, offensiveness, vulgarity Opposite: politeness

rudimentary adj **basic**, elementary, simple, fundamental, primary Opposite: advanced

rudiments n **basics**, essentials, fundamentals, principles, beginnings

rue v **regret**, lament, repent, deplore, feel sorry about

rueful adj **regretful**, remorseful, apologetic, repentant, contrite Opposite: cheerful

ruffian (dated) n **thug**, tough guy, gangster, hooligan (infml), hood (US slang)

ruffle v **1 disturb**, tousle, rumple, upset, dishevel Opposite: smooth **2 perturb**, upset, annoy, disrupt, distress Opposite: calm

rug n **1 carpet**, mat, hearth rug, sheepskin, runner **2** (infml) **wig**, toupee, hairpiece, periwig **3 blanket**, car rug, throw, cover, bedspread

rugged adj **1 rocky**, rough, craggy, uneven, jagged Opposite: rolling **2 strong-featured**, craggy, chiselled, weathered, furrowed **3 strong**, hardy, tough, robust, resilient Opposite: weak **4 testing**, demanding, difficult, harsh, tough Opposite: easy **5 well-built**, sturdy, tough, robust, strong Opposite: flimsy

ruggedness n **1 roughness**, rockiness, harshness, jaggedness, cragginess Opposite: smoothness **2 strong features**, cragginess, handsomeness, manliness, masculinity Opposite: roundness **3 toughness**, resilience, stamina, endurance, strength Opposite: weakness **4 unforgiving nature**, difficulty, harshness, toughness, severity Opposite: gentleness **5 resilience**, sturdiness, toughness, robustness, strength Opposite: flimsiness

rug rat (US infml) n **child**, infant, toddler, sprog (slang)

ruin n **1 remains**, wreck, debris, wreckage, shell **2 devastation**, shambles, decay, destruction, collapse Opposite: regeneration **3 decline**, downfall, defeat, fall, disaster Opposite: improvement ■ v **damage**, wreck, spoil, destroy, devastate Opposite: mend

ruination n **1 destruction**, loss, ruin, calamity, devastation Opposite: salvation **2 undoing**, downfall, ruin, curse, destruction Opposite: making

ruined adj **1 tumbledown**, crumbling, derelict, abandoned, uninhabited Opposite: renovated **2 bankrupt**, insolvent, out of business, broke (infml), cleaned out (infml) Opposite: solvent

ruinous adj **disastrous**, damaging, harmful, devastating, catastrophic Opposite: advantageous

rule n **1 instruction**, law, regulation, decree, statute **2 regime**, power, control, leadership, reign ■ v **govern**, reign, run, administrate, have power over Opposite: follow

rulebook n **manual**, rules, instructions, directory, rubric

rule out v **1 exclude**, dismiss, reject, discount, discard Opposite: consider **2 prevent**, exclude, ban, prohibit, forbid Opposite: facilitate

ruler n **monarch**, sovereign, leader, head of state, potentate Opposite: subject

WORD BANK
❏ **types of ruler** chief, chieftain, emir, emperor, empress, governor, head of state, king, maharajah, maharani, Pharoah, president, queen, rajah, rani, regent, sultan, tsar, tsarina, tsaritsa

rule the roost v **be in control**, be in charge, reign supreme, lord it, hold sway

ruling adj **presiding**, reigning, governing, dominant, sovereign Opposite: subordinate ■ n **decision**, verdict, edict, judgment, declaration

ruling body n **council**, administration, government, assembly, legislative body

rum (dated infml) adj **odd**, strange, extraordinary, weird, bizarre Opposite: usual

rumble v **grumble**, thunder, crash, growl, roll

rumbling (infml) n **indication**, early sign, beginning, warning sign, rumour

rumbustious adj **boisterous**, exuberant, swashbuckling, swaggering, rambunctious Opposite: reticent

ruminate v **1 chew**, graze, browse, crop, pasture **2 ponder**, think over, reflect, chew over, meditate

rumination n **1 chewing**, grazing, browsing, chewing the cud **2 reflection**, pondering, contemplation, musing, thought

ruminative adj **thoughtful**, pensive, reflective, contemplative, speculative Opposite: blithe

rummage v **search**, look through, grope, fumble, poke around

rumour n **1 unconfirmed report**, claim, report, tale, allegation Opposite: fact **2 speculation**, opinion, gossip, talk, tittle-tattle ■ v **say**, believe, allege, claim, speculate Opposite: confirm

rumoured adj **supposed**, thought, whispered, alleged, believed Opposite: true

rumour mill n **grapevine**, network, newsmongers, gossips, tattlers

rumourmonger n **gossip**, telltale, scandalmonger, gossipmonger, tattletale (US)

rump n **hindquarters**, back end, rear, buttocks, rear end

rumple v **wrinkle**, crumple, crease, crinkle, pucker Opposite: tidy

rumpled adj **crumpled**, creased, untidy, messy, bedraggled Opposite: tidy

rumpus n **disturbance**, commotion, furore, brouhaha, fuss

run v **1 sprint**, jog, lope, scuttle, scamper **2 compete**, enter, participate, take part, contend **3 operate**, function, process **4 manage**, administer, govern, administrate, lead **5 flow**, stream, trickle, course, pour out **6 proceed**, happen, go, progress, move along **7 move**, pass, cast, throw **8 continue**, extend, reach, stretch, go ■ n **1 outing**, trip, ride, excursion, visit **2 sequence**, series, chain, string, list **3 course**, route, route, lane, path **4 enclosure**, pen, cage, coop, paddock **5 sprint**, race, lope, dart, dash

runabout n **wanderer**, rover, rolling stone, nomad, traveller

run after v **pursue**, chase, go after, follow, hound

run along v **go away**, go, leave, depart, take leave Opposite: stay

run amok v **go berserk**, be in a frenzy, run riot, go on the rampage, rampage

run a risk v **take a risk**, play a dangerous game, sail close to the wind, court disaster, play Russian roulette

run around v **associate**, spend time, keep company, hang out (infml), hang (slang)

run away v **escape**, flee, run off, abscond, elope

runaway n **escapee**, absentee, absconder, fugitive ■ adj (infml) **bestselling**, blockbusting, hit, roaring, huge

runaway success n **big hit**, smash, smash hit, blockbuster (infml), barnburner (US infml)

run by v **explain**, describe, tell, impart, acquaint

run down v **1 bring to an end**, close down, wind up, shut down, peter out Opposite: start **2 belittle**, criticize, knock, disparage, put down Opposite: praise

rundown n **background**, details, information, lowdown (infml), info (infml)

run-down adj **1 exhausted**, tired, weak, wearied, worn-out Opposite: energetic **2 under the weather**, worn out, tired, weary, washed out Opposite: well **3 dilapidated**, ramshackle, shabby, neglected, derelict Opposite: well-kept

rune n **character**, letter, symbol, sign, hieroglyph

rung n **step**, stair, tread, stage

run-in (infml) n **argument**, confrontation, quarrel, clash, disagreement

run into v **1 come across**, bump into, meet by chance, encounter **2 hit**, bump into, crash into, collide with, run over Opposite: miss

runner n **1 sprinter**, jogger, racer, contender, competitor **2 candidate**, contender, entrant, participant, competitor **3 messenger**, courier, gofer (infml)

runner-up n **second place**, person in second place, silver medallist, second to finish, next best person

running n **management**, administration, organization, operation, controlling ■ adv **in a row**, consecutively, on the trot, successively, in succession

runny adj **liquid**, fluid, gooey, soft, thin Opposite: set

run off v **flee**, escape, run away, decamp, scarper (slang)

run-of-the-mill adj **mediocre**, ordinary, middling, average, undistinguished Opposite: extraordinary

run on v **go on**, carry on, continue, keep going Opposite: stop

run out v **end**, expire, come to an end, finish

run over v **1 crush**, hit, squash, flatten, collide with **2 explain**, summarize, go over, run through, cover

run rings around v **outshine**, beat, outdo, outstrip, outperform

run rings round see **run rings around**

run riot v **run amok**, go on the rampage, riot, go berserk, rampage

runt n **smallest**, weakest, littlest

run the gauntlet v **undergo**, experience, face, suffer, endure

run through v **1 use up**, exhaust, eat through, go through, deplete Opposite: conserve

2 review, go over, examine, consider, look over **3 pervade**, spread through, underlie, permeate **4 rehearse**, practise, try out, go through **5 infect**, contaminate, pollute

run-through n **1 rehearsal**, practice, dry run, test run, test **2 review**, survey, summary, overview, résumé

run up v **1 accumulate**, amass, collect, incur, build up Opposite: discharge **2 sew**, create, make, put together

run-up n **1 approach**, advance, run **2 buildup**, introduction, lead-in

runway n **landing strip**, airstrip, landing field, taxiway, flight strip

rupture n **1 break**, crack, tear, split, fissure **2 disagreement**, falling-out, split, breakup, separation ■ v **break**, crack, burst, come apart, rip apart

rural adj **country**, rustic, pastoral, bucolic, countryside Opposite: urban

ruse n **trick**, dodge, subterfuge, wile, con

rush v **1 hurry**, precipitate, hasten, dash, bolt **2 run**, hurry, dash, sprint, flash Opposite: dawdle ■ n **1 blast**, current, gale, gust, blow **2 haste**, hurry, urgency, flash

rushed adj **hurried**, quick, swift, hasty Opposite: leisurely

rushes n **unedited prints**, dailies, first prints, raw footage, footage

rust n **corrosion**, oxidation, erosion, corruption, decomposition ■ v **corrode**, oxidize, tarnish, erode, decompose

rustic adj **rural**, country, pastoral, bucolic, countryside Opposite: urban

rustle v **crunch**, crackle, whisper, swish

rustler n **thief**, poacher, robber, horse thief, cattle thief

rustle up (infml) v **prepare**, concoct, put together, make, produce

rustproof adj **nonrusting**, rust-free, rust-proofed, stainless-steel, corrosion-proof ■ v **seal**, make rustproof, waterproof, coat, paint

rusty adj **1 corroded**, oxidized, tarnished, eroded **2 out of practice**, out of form, unpractised, unaccustomed, off form

rut n **furrow**, groove, channel, runnel, pothole

ruthless adj **cruel**, callous, brutal, pitiless, merciless Opposite: merciful

ruthlessness n **callousness**, cruelty, mercilessness, brutality, heartlessness Opposite: mercy

rutted adj **uneven**, furrowed, potholed, bumpy Opposite: smooth

RV n **recreational vehicle**, camper, motor caravan, mobile home, trailer

S

sabbatical n **study leave**, leave, time off, retreat, leave of absence

sabotage n **disruption**, damage, vandalism, interference, interruption ■ v **disrupt**, damage, vandalize, interfere with, interrupt

saboteur n **vandal**, terrorist, ecowarrior, computer hacker, hunt saboteur

sabre rattling n **display of force**, bravado, empty, threats, bluffing

sac n **bag**, sack, pouch, case, pod

saccharine adj **1 sugary**, sickly, sweet, syrupy, treacly Opposite: sour **2 sentimental**, slushy, gushy, mawkish, cloying Opposite: unsentimental

sacerdotal adj **clerical**, ecclesiastic, religious, spiritual, priestly (literary)

sachet n **envelope**, packet, pouch

sack n **1 bag**, brown bag, gunnysack, carryall, pouch **2** (infml) **dismissal**, termination, layoff, discharge, pink slip (US) ■ v **1** (infml) **dismiss**, lay off, throw out, give somebody notice, give somebody their cards Opposite: employ

2 ransack, plunder, destroy, pillage, tear apart

sacking (infml) n **dismissal**, discharge, job loss, notice, layoff

sacrament n **rite**, ceremony, ritual, service, mass

sacred adj **holy**, blessed, consecrated, hallowed, revered Opposite: secular

sacrifice n **price**, toll, cost, loss, expense ■ v **give up**, forgo, forfeit, let go, surrender

sacrilege n **blasphemy**, desecration, profanity, irreverence, violation Opposite: reverence

sacrilegious adj **blasphemous**, profane, irreverent, heretical, impious Opposite: pious

sacrosanct adj **1 sacred**, revered, holy, sanctified **2 inviolable**, untouchable, off limits, protected

sad adj **1 unhappy**, miserable, depressed, down, low Opposite: happy **2 depressing**, gloomy, miserable, cheerless, distressing Opposite: cheerful

sadden v **depress**, distress, upset, dismay, pain Opposite: cheer

saddlebag n **basket**, bag, pannier, carrier, holdall

saddle with v **burden**, lumber, encumber, weigh down, land

sadistic adj **cruel**, nasty, callous, heartless, vicious Opposite: kind

sadly adv **1 unhappily**, miserably, gloomily, wretchedly, dejectedly Opposite: happily **2 unfortunately**, unluckily, regrettably, alas Opposite: luckily

sadness n **unhappiness**, misery, depression, dejection, despondency Opposite: happiness

safari n **trek**, expedition, trip, search, quest

safe adj **1 harmless**, benign, innocuous, innocent, nonviolent Opposite: dangerous **2 secure**, protected, sheltered, in safe hands, out of harm's way Opposite: unsafe **3 unharmed**, undamaged, uninjured, unhurt, unscathed **4 reliable**, dependable, trustworthy, careful, cautious Opposite: unsafe ■ n **strongbox**, lockbox, safe-deposit box, vault

safeguard n **protection**, precaution, defence, safety measure, safety device Opposite: hazard ■ v **defend**, protect, preserve, guard, shield Opposite: endanger

---

COMPARE AND CONTRAST CORE MEANING: keep safe from actual or potential damage or attack

safeguard take steps to prevent somebody or something from being harmed or damaged; **protect** keep somebody or something from any kind of harm or damage; **defend** deter an actual or threatened attack; **guard** work to prevent damage, loss, or attack by being vigilant and taking defensive measures; **shield** prevent harm, damage, or attack by using a physical barrier or by intervening in a protective way.

---

safeguarding n **protection**, preservation, conservation, defence, maintenance Opposite: destruction

safe haven n **refuge**, asylum, haven, sanctuary

safe house n **hideout**, hideaway, retreat, refuge, hidey-hole (infml)

safekeeping n **protection**, care, security, custody, safety

safe place n **refuge**, safe haven, hideaway, haven, sanctuary

safety n **care**, security, protection, shelter, wellbeing Opposite: danger

safety belt n **seat belt**, strap, restraint, harness, safety harness

safety net n **safety device**, safeguard, fail-safe, guard, shield

safety valve n **1 fail-safe**, valve, safety device, safety precaution, overflow **2 release**, channel, outlet

sag v **droop**, wilt, slump, flag, drop ■ n **drop**, slump, dip, fall, depression

saga n **epic**, account, chronicle, tale, legend

sagacious adj **wise**, knowledgeable, learned, erudite, perceptive Opposite: foolish

sagaciousness (fml) see sagacity

sagacity n **wisdom**, knowledge, erudition, perceptiveness, intelligence Opposite: stupidity

sagging adj **drooping**, wilting, flaccid, floppy, slumped

saggy see sagging

said adj **1 alleged**, supposed, assumed **2 previously mentioned**, above, aforesaid (fml), aforementioned (fml)

sail v **1 set sail**, navigate, cruise, voyage, put out to sea **2 glide**, float, flow, drift, fly

sailing n **boating**, cruising, yachting, navigation

sailor n **seafarer**, mariner, navigator, deckhand, salt (infml)

sail through v **do well**, do with ease, pass with flying colours, breeze through Opposite: fail

saintliness n **virtue**, goodness, piety, holiness, devoutness Opposite: evil

saintly adj **virtuous**, good, holy, pious, devout Opposite: evil

salaam n **greeting**, salutation, bow, nod, acknowledgment ■ v **greet**, bow, salute, nod, acknowledge

salacious adj **risqué**, indecent, crude, improper, obscene

salad days (dated) n **youth**, prime, heyday

salaried adj **remunerated**, on the payroll, on the books, paid, compensated

salary n **income**, pay, wage, payment, remuneration. See COMPARE AND CONTRAST at wage.

sale n **1 transaction**, deal, selling, retailing, vending Opposite: purchase **2 auction**, clearance sale, garage sale, jumble sale, car boot sale

saleable adj **vendible**, marketable, commercial, commercially viable

sales assistant n **salesperson**, shop assistant, cashier, floorwalker

salesperson n **1 seller**, trader, marketer, vendor, hawker **2 sales assistant**, shop assistant, cashier, floorwalker

sales representative n **salesperson**, seller, trader, marketer, vendor

salient adj **noticeable**, striking, prominent, outstanding, relevant Opposite: minor

saline adj **salty**, salt, brackish, briny, salted

saliva n **spittle**, spit, drool, dribble, slobber

salivate v **drool**, dribble, slobber, slaver

sallow adj **yellow**, sickly, wan, washed-out, ashen

sally n **1 attack**, sortie, breakout, breakthrough, raid **2 rush**, charge, dash, push ■ v **1 attack**, charge, raid, strike **2 go forth**, go out, venture forth, venture out, set out Opposite: retreat

salon n 1 **soiree**, gathering, rendezvous, meeting, group 2 **beauty salon**, hair salon, hairdresser's, barbershop, barber's

salt away v **hoard**, save, squirrel away, put by, set aside Opposite: fritter away

salt water n **brine**, sea water, saline

salty adj **salt**, saline, brackish, salted, briny Opposite: sweet

salubrious (fml) adj **healthy**, wholesome, respectable, decent, hygienic Opposite: insalubrious (fml)

salutary adj **beneficial**, helpful, useful, valuable, constructive

salutation n **greeting**, acknowledgment, welcome, gesture, salute

salute v **acknowledge**, greet, welcome, gesture, wave ■ n **sign of respect**, salutation, greeting, acknowledgment, signal

salvage v **save**, recover, rescue, retrieve, reclaim

salvation n **redemption**, rescue, recovery, escape, deliverance (fml) Opposite: ruination

salve n **lotion**, ointment, balm, balsam, liniment Opposite: irritant ■ v **appease**, soothe, comfort, mollify, calm Opposite: irritate

salver n **tray**, platter, plate, serving dish, dish

salvo n **barrage**, bombardment, round, torrent, hail

same adj 1 **identical**, alike, matching, similar, equal Opposite: different 2 **unchanged**, constant, consistent, uniform, even Opposite: changed

sameness n 1 **similarity**, likeness, resemblance, uniformity, equivalence Opposite: difference 2 **monotony**, repetitiveness, uniformity, consistency, evenness Opposite: variety

samey (infml) adj **repetitive**, unvaried, unchanging, monotonous, similar Opposite: varied

samovar n **tea urn**, urn, teapot, jug, kettle

sample n **example**, taster, model, trial, illustration ■ v **test**, try, appraise, try out, check out

sampler n 1 **technician**, tester, analyst, quality control analyst, laboratory technician 2 **selection**, sample, cross section, sampling, representative selection 3 **sample**, tryout, example, taste, illustration 4 **embroidery**, sewing, needlework, handwork

sampling n **sample**, specimen, cross section, selection, test group

sanatorium n **clinic**, hospital, infirmary, hospice, spa

sanctified adj **sacred**, holy, blessed, consecrated, hallowed Opposite: desecrated

sanctify v **bless**, consecrate, hallow, dedicate, purify Opposite: desecrate

sanctimonious adj **self-righteous**, smug, pious, pompous, self-satisfied Opposite: humble

sanctimoniousness n **self-righteousness**, smugness, pomposity, superiority

sanction n 1 **authorization**, permission, approval, agreement, consent Opposite: prohibition 2 **support**, approval, encouragement, agreement, affirmation 3 **restriction**, penalty, ban, punishment, injunction ■ v **authorize**, permit, approve, allow, pass Opposite: veto

sanctity n **holiness**, blessedness, sacredness, inviolability, purity Opposite: profanity

sanctuary n 1 **refuge**, asylum, shelter, safe haven, haven 2 **safety**, protection, refuge, asylum, shelter 3 **reserve**, reservation, national park, nature reserve, preserve (US)

sanctum n 1 **holy of holies**, sanctum sanctorum, temple, altar, shrine 2 **retreat**, den, refuge, study, hideaway

sand n 1 **shingle**, grit, gravel, powder, silt 2 **beach**, strand, shore, dune, shoreline ■ v **rub down**, smooth, sandpaper, polish, rub

sandbank n **sandbar**, dune, mound, bank, hummock

sandbar n **sandbank**, ridge, shallows, shoal

sandpaper v **rub down**, smooth, sand, polish, rub

sandwich n **snack**, roll, sarnie (infml), butty (infml), toasty (infml) ■ v **squeeze in**, squash in, pack in, cram, slot in

WORD BANK

❏ **types of sandwich** club sandwich, double-decker, open sandwich, panini, sub (infml), submarine, wrap

sane adj 1 **well-balanced**, compos mentis, rational, stable, healthy Opposite: insane 2 **sensible**, reasonable, rational, sound, wise Opposite: irrational

saneness see sanity

sang-froid n **self-possession**, calmness, poise, aplomb, self-assurance Opposite: anxiety

sanguinary (fml) adj 1 **bloody**, gory, brutal, grim, gruesome 2 **bloodthirsty**, murderous, ruthless, savage, cruel

sanguine adj **confident**, optimistic, cheerful, hopeful, positive Opposite: pessimistic

sanitary adj **hygienic**, clean, healthy, wholesome, sterile Opposite: insanitary

sanitation n **hygiene**, cleanliness, cleanness, public health, health

sanitize v 1 **purify**, fumigate, disinfect, clean, cleanse Opposite: contaminate 2 **censor**, clean up, bowdlerize, water down

sanity n 1 **rationality**, lucidity, reason, stability, saneness Opposite: insanity 2 **reasonableness**, sense, rationality, soundness, wisdom Opposite: unreasonableness

sap n 1 **juice**, fluid, liquid, latex 2 **energy**, vitality, health, strength, life ■ v 1 **dig down**, burrow, bore, tunnel, mine 2 **weaken**, drain, undermine, deplete, eat away *Opposite*: boost

sapient *adj* **wise**, learned, educated, intelligent, knowing *Opposite*: ignorant

sapling *n* **tree**, seedling, plantlet, sprout, scion

sarcasm *n* **irony**, mockery, cynicism, derision, acerbity

sarcastic *adj* **ironic**, mocking, sardonic, cynical, caustic

---

COMPARE AND CONTRAST CORE MEANING: describes remarks that are designed to hurt or mock

sarcastic contemptuous, scornful, or mocking and intended to hurt or belittle; **ironic** deliberately stating the opposite of the truth, usually with the intention of being amusing; **sardonic** mocking and cynical or disdainful, though not deliberately hurtful; **satirical** using ridicule, especially in a work of art, to criticize somebody's or something's faults, especially in the arts or politics; **caustic** harsh and bitter and intended to mock, offend, or belittle.

---

sarcophagus *n* **coffin**, tomb, casket *(US)*

sardonic *adj* **mocking**, scornful, ironic, sarcastic, derisive. *See* COMPARE AND CONTRAST *at* **sarcastic**.

sarsen *n* **rock**, boulder, stone, cairn, block

sartorial *adj* **dress**, fashion, clothing

sash *n* **band**, ribbon, belt, cummerbund, tie

sashay *v* **flounce**, sway, strut, prance, swagger

satchel *n* **bag**, shoulder bag, haversack, school bag, briefcase

sate *v* **fill up**, fill, satiate, stuff, gorge

sated *adj* **full**, satiated, gorged, bursting, satisfied *Opposite*: hungry

satellite *n* **1 dependency**, protectorate, colony, overseas territory, subject population **2 satellite television**, satellite TV, satellite broadcasting, digital television, digital TV

satiate *v* **1 glut**, fill, satisfy, sate, fill up **2 gratify**, satisfy, quench, sate, slake

satiated *adj* **1 full**, satisfied, replete, sated, full up *Opposite*: unsatisfied **2 gratified**, satisfied, quenched, sated, slaked

satiety *n* **fullness**, surfeit, glut, repletion

satiny *adj* **lustrous**, luminous, shiny, radiant, glossy *Opposite*: dull

satire *n* **1 mockery**, irony, sarcasm, ridicule, wit **2 parody**, lampoon, burlesque, caricature, travesty

satirical *adj* **mocking**, ironic, sardonic, humorous, sarcastic. *See* COMPARE AND CONTRAST *at* **sarcastic**.

satirist *n* **humorist**, wit, joker, satirizer, comic

satirize *v* **mock**, ridicule, parody, lampoon, deride

satisfaction *n* **1 contentment**, pleasure, happiness, joy, enjoyment *Opposite*: dissatisfaction **2 gratification**, consummation, fulfilment **3 approval**, liking, taste, contentment, agreement *Opposite*: dissatisfaction **4 redress**, reparation, compensation, settlement, repayment

satisfactory *adj* **acceptable**, reasonable, pleasing, fitting, agreeable *Opposite*: unsatisfactory

satisfied *adj* **content**, pleased, happy, gratified, fulfilled *Opposite*: dissatisfied

satisfy *v* **1 content**, please, gratify, mollify, placate *Opposite*: dissatisfy **2 gratify**, satiate, quench, sate, slake **3 convince**, assure, persuade, reassure, win over **4 fulfil**, comply with, meet, suit, fill

satisfying *adj* **1 pleasing**, gratifying, fulfilling, rewarding, enjoyable *Opposite*: dissatisfying **2 filling**, sustaining, nourishing, substantial, satiating *Opposite*: insufficient

saturate *v* **1 soak**, drench, wet through, douse, steep *Opposite*: dry out **2 oversupply**, overwhelm, overload, flood, inundate

saturated *adj* **1 soaked**, soaking, drenched, wet through, wet *Opposite*: dry **2 packed**, full, brimming, brimful, overfull *Opposite*: empty

saturation *n* **1 wetness**, soaking, drenching, wetting, moistening *Opposite*: dryness **2 fullness**, capacity, overload, satiety, permeation

saturnalia *n* **orgy**, celebration, bacchanalia, revel, party

saturnine *adj* **melancholy**, morose, gloomy, sad, sullen *Opposite*: cheerful

sauce *(infml)* *n* **impudence**, impertinence, rudeness, insolence, nerve

---

WORD BANK

❏ **types of seasonings, sauces, and dips** aioli, apple sauce, barbecue sauce, béarnaise, béchamel, brown sauce, catsup, chilli sauce, coulis, dressing, French dressing, gravy, guacamole, hollandaise, horseradish, hummus, ketchup, marinade, mayonnaise, mint sauce, raita, Russian dressing, salad cream, salsa, satay, soy sauce, stock, tabasco, tahini, taramasalata, tartare sauce, Thousand Island dressing, vinegar, vinaigrette, wasabi, Worcester sauce

---

saucepan *n* **pan**, pot, cooking pot

saucer *n* **plate**, bowl, dish

saucy *adj* **impudent**, smart, rude, impertinent *(fml)*, cheeky

saunter *v* **stroll**, walk, amble, meander, ramble *Opposite*: hurry ■ *n* **walk**, stroll, amble, ramble, meander

sauté *v* **fry**, stir-fry, pan-fry, brown

savage *adj* **1 violent**, unrestrained, vicious, fierce, ferocious *Opposite*: gentle **2 severe**, harsh, drastic, stringent, ruthless *Opposite*: mild **3 undomesticated**, wild, ferocious, fierce, feral *Opposite*: tame ■ *v* **1 attack**, brutalize, mug, maul, mangle **2 criticize**, tear apart, maul, destroy, attack *Opposite*: praise

savagery *n* **cruelty**, violence, barbarity, viciousness, barbarism *Opposite*: gentleness

savanna n **grassland**, pampas, plains, prairie

savant n **guru**, philosopher, thinker, pundit, expert

save v **1 rescue**, recover, salvage, bail out, revive Opposite: abandon **2 accumulate**, bank, salt away, collect Opposite: spend **3 keep back**, set aside, put aside, put away, hold back Opposite: use up **4 avoid**, prevent, stop, avert, bar ■ prep **but**, except, apart from, with the exception of, excluding Opposite: including

save for prep **but**, except, apart from, with the exception of, excluding

saver n **investor**, collector, hoarder, gatherer, squirrel (infml)

saving n **economy**, reduction, cutback, discount, cut Opposite: increase

saving grace n **merit**, advantage, strong point, strong suit, virtue Opposite: failing

savings n **investments**, reserves, nest egg, funds, hoard Opposite: expenditure

saviour n **redeemer**, rescuer, knight in shining armour, liberator, deliverer

savoir-faire n **confidence**, style, flair, poise, sense

savour v **enjoy**, relish, appreciate, delight in, cherish ■ n **taste**, smell, flavour, aroma, tang

savourless adj **tasteless**, insipid, bland, flavourless Opposite: flavourful

savourlessness n **tastelessness**, insipidity, blandness, flavourlessness Opposite: tastiness

savoury adj **1 salty**, salt, spicy, piquant, pungent Opposite: sweet **2 respectable**, pleasant, acceptable, nice, wholesome Opposite: unsavoury **3 appetizing**, tasty, flavoursome, palatable, delicious Opposite: insipid

savvy (infml) n **shrewdness**, practicality, knowledge, perception, understanding Opposite: ignorance

saw n **saying**, proverb, adage, maxim, motto ■ v **cut**, slice, sever, divide, chop

say v **1 speak**, utter, articulate, declare, pronounce **2 convey**, indicate, reveal, give away, tell ■ n **input**, voice, opinion, view, pennyworth ■ adv **approximately**, roughly, about, around, give or take Opposite: exactly

saying n **proverb**, adage, maxim, axiom, motto

say-so (infml) n **authorization**, authority, permission, approval, agreement Opposite: veto

say sorry v **apologize**, excuse yourself, crawl, grovel, beg forgiveness

say yes v **agree**, accept, consent, acquiesce, assent Opposite: refuse

say your piece v **speak out**, speak up, protest, take a stand, make a stand Opposite: hold back

scab n **crust**, layer, skin, shell, covering

scabbard n **sheath**, case, covering, cover, casing

scabby adj **mangy**, scaly, diseased, shabby, dirty Opposite: unblemished

scabrous adj **rough**, flaky, scaly, mangy, leprous Opposite: smooth

scads (infml) n **lots**, scores, tons (infml), heaps (infml), buckets (infml) Opposite: none

scaffold n **1 support**, framework, frame, platform, shell **2 gallows**, gibbet, halter, noose

scaffolding n **support**, framework, frame, platform, shell

scalawag (dated infml) see scallywag

scald v **1 burn**, blister, singe, sear, injure **2 sterilize**, boil, steam, autoclave, heat Opposite: contaminate **3 bring to the boil**, boil, heat, warm, simmer Opposite: chill

scalding adj **1 boiling**, piping hot, baking, burning, blistering Opposite: icy **2 scathing**, blistering, critical, fierce, scornful Opposite: complimentary

scale n **1 weighing machine**, balance, scales, weighbridge, measure **2 gradation**, tier, band, ratio, progression **3 extent**, size, range, gamut, degree **4 deposit**, crust, fur, covering, plaque **5 plate**, flake, skin, scab, scurf ■ v **1 ascend**, climb, mount, go up, clamber up **2 peel**, pare, skin, exfoliate, flake

scale down v **reduce**, decrease, lower, cut back, cut down Opposite: scale up

scale up v **increase**, expand, extend, raise, step up Opposite: scale down

scallop n **pinking**, edging, scalloping, piping, border

scallywag (dated infml) n **mischief-maker**, scamp (infml), rascal, monkey (infml), imp

scaly adj **flaking**, peeling, crusty, encrusted, scabby Opposite: smooth

scamp (infml) n **rogue**, imp, urchin, rascal, monkey (infml) Opposite: angel

scamper v **scurry**, scuttle, run, hurry, dash Opposite: dawdle

scan v **1 scrutinize**, examine, look into, pore over, inspect **2 skim**, skim through, glance at, glance over, browse Opposite: study **3 examine**, photograph, visualize, image, X-ray ■ n **1 perusal**, skim, examination, inspection, look **2 image**, X-ray, CT scan, MRI scan, PET scan

scandal n **1 disgrace**, shame, dishonour, humiliation, outrage **2 gossip**, tittle-tattle, rumour, talk, rumourmongering

scandalize v **horrify**, outrage, shock, disgust, dismay Opposite: impress

scandalmonger n **gossip**, rumourmonger, gossipmonger, newsmonger, snoop (infml)

scandalous adj **shocking**, outrageous, disgraceful, immoral, shameful Opposite: admirable

scant adj **slight**, limited, negligible, little, scarce Opposite: extensive

scanty adj 1 insufficient, inadequate, meagre, little, scarce Opposite: abundant 2 revealing, flimsy, light, low-cut, tight

scapegoat n stooge, victim, accused, culprit, fall guy (slang) ■ v blame, incriminate, condemn, accuse, reproach Opposite: exonerate

scar n 1 mark, blemish, mutilation, scratch, wound 2 effect, wound, trauma, hurt, after-effect ■ v 1 damage, mark, blemish, mutilate, disfigure 2 traumatize, hurt, affect, damage, mark

scarce adj 1 in short supply, limited, insufficient, inadequate, scant Opposite: abundant 2 rare, uncommon, unusual, infrequent, threatened Opposite: common

scarcely adv barely, hardly, not quite, only just, just Opposite: fully

scarceness see scarcity

scarcity n 1 shortage, lack, dearth, insufficiency, scarceness Opposite: abundance 2 rarity, uncommonness, infrequency, lack, want Opposite: commonness

scare v frighten, terrify, startle, alarm, panic Opposite: reassure ■ n fright, shock, start, jolt, alarm Opposite: reassurance

scarecrow n figure, effigy, guy, mannequin

scared adj frightened, afraid, fearful, terrified, nervous Opposite: fearless

scaremonger n alarmist, doomsayer, troublemaker, rumourmonger, newsmonger Opposite: optimist

scare off v frighten away, drive away, chase off, scare away, frighten Opposite: welcome

scarf n muffler, headscarf, bandana, cravat, shawl

scarify v 1 (infml) scare, frighten, alarm, worry, startle Opposite: reassure 2 lacerate, scratch, score, cut, incise

scariness n menace, creepiness (infml), spookiness (infml) Opposite: reassurance

scarp n escarpment, ridge, cliff, bluff, crag

scarred adj 1 mutilated, disfigured, marked, injured, wounded 2 damaged, defaced, blemished, marked, scratched

scary (infml) adj frightening, chilling, terrifying, petrifying, daunting Opposite: reassuring

scat (infml) v run away, run off, escape, flee, abscond

scathing adj scornful, mocking, derisive, sarcastic, contemptuous Opposite: complimentary

scatter v 1 throw, strew, fling, sprinkle, distribute Opposite: collect 2 disperse, spread out, spread, flee, take flight Opposite: gather

COMPARE AND CONTRAST CORE MEANING: spread around

scatter spread things around physically, especially in a random widespread manner; **broadcast** spread or transmit information, especially by means of radio or television, or scatter seeds over the ground; **distribute** allocate, share, or give out something in a structured or organized way, or spread something over a particular surface or area; **disseminate** spread ideas, information, or attitudes such as goodwill.

scatterbrained adj absent-minded, vague, forgetful, woolly-headed, careless Opposite: focused

scattered adj 1 dispersed, distributed, strewn, sprinkled, disseminated Opposite: concentrated 2 infrequent, isolated, discrete, separate, occasional Opposite: frequent

scattering n handful, sprinkling, trickle, bit, smattering

scattershot adj disorganized, indiscriminate, random, chaotic, slapdash Opposite: focused

scatty (infml) adj empty-headed, forgetful, absent-minded, scatterbrained, dizzy (infml) Opposite: organized

scavenge v hunt, forage, search, rummage, sift

scenario n situation, state of affairs, state, setup, circumstances

scene n 1 act, division, part, section, passage 2 setting, site, place, background, backdrop 3 sight, prospect, picture, panorama, view 4 fuss, commotion, exhibition, incident, spectacle

scenery n 1 set, backdrop, backcloth, background, decor 2 landscape, panorama, vista, outlook, view

scenic adj picturesque, beautiful, attractive, lovely, charming Opposite: unsightly

scent n 1 smell, odour, aroma, perfume, bouquet 2 trail, trace, track, spoor 3 perfume, fragrance, cologne, toilet water, eau de cologne 4 hint, trace, air, whiff, suggestion ■ v 1 predict, foresee, foretell, sense, feel 2 sniff, smell, detect, sense, pick up 3 imbue, perfume, fill, infuse, suffuse. See COMPARE AND CONTRAST at smell.

scented adj perfumed, fragrant, aromatic, sweet-smelling, fragranced Opposite: odourless

sceptic n cynic, disbeliever, doubter, doubting Thomas, questioner Opposite: believer

sceptical adj cynical, disbelieving, doubtful, doubting, unconvinced Opposite: convinced. See COMPARE AND CONTRAST at doubtful.

scepticism n cynicism, disbelief, doubt, incredulity, uncertainty Opposite: conviction

sceptre n staff, staff of office, mace, rod, insignia

schedule n agenda, timetable, diary, calendar, list ■ v arrange, plan, timetable, programme, book Opposite: cancel

scheduled adj arranged, planned, timetabled, programmed, listed Opposite: unplanned

schema n plan, diagram, scheme, schematic, representation

schematize v **systematize**, arrange, structure, organize, draft *Opposite*: disarrange

scheme n 1 **plot**, plan, conspiracy, ploy, ruse 2 **plan**, method, stratagem, idea, proposal 3 **arrangement**, system, structure, outline, organization *Opposite*: chaos 4 **diagram**, plan, schematic, graphic, representation ■ v **plot**, conspire, intrigue, connive, plan

schemer n **plotter**, conspirator, conniver, traitor, intriguer

scheming adj **devious**, calculating, conniving, conspiratorial, treacherous *Opposite*: honest

schism n **split**, break, division, rupture, rift *Opposite*: union

schismatic adj **factional**, divisive, clashing, conflicting, controversial *Opposite*: unifying

schlep (infml) v **lug**, haul, heave, drag, cart ■ n **trek**, trudge, hike, bore, bind

schmaltz (infml) n **sentimentality**, slush, mush, corniness, mawkishness

schmaltzy (infml) adj **sentimental**, cloying, sugary, saccharine, slushy

scholar n **academic**, researcher, don, professor, doctor

scholarly adj **learned**, academic, erudite, intellectual, educated *Opposite*: lowbrow

scholarship n 1 **grant**, bursary, studentship, subsidy, allowance 2 **learning**, erudition, study, knowledge, research *Opposite*: ignorance

scholastic adj **educational**, academic, pedagogic, school, college

school n **group**, set, coterie, brotherhood, sisterhood *Opposite*: individual ■ v **train**, instruct, educate, discipline, teach

WORD BANK

❏ **types of school** academy, boarding school, comprehensive, faith school, grammar school, high school, infant school, junior school, middle school, nursery school, prep school, preschool, primary school, private school, public school, senior high, state school, trade school

schoolchild n **pupil**, student, scholar, schoolboy, schoolgirl

schooling n **education**, teaching, training, instruction, tuition

school of thought n **philosophy**, doctrine, ideology, outlook, attitude

science n **discipline**, knowledge, skill, learning, scholarship

scientific adj **technical**, methodical, systematic, logical, precise *Opposite*: unscientific

scintilla n **jot**, iota, scrap, shred, speck

scintillate v 1 **sparkle**, glitter, gleam, flash, glint 2 **fascinate**, dazzle, charm, shine, sparkle *Opposite*: bore

scintillating adj **sparkling**, dazzling, brilliant, bright, glittering *Opposite*: dull

scintillation n **sparkling**, glittering, gleaming, flashing, glinting *Opposite*: dullness

scion n 1 **cutting**, graft, shoot, implant, implantation 2 **offspring**, child, heir, descendant, son *Opposite*: parent

scoff v 1 **jeer**, sneer, mock, ridicule, make fun of *Opposite*: praise 2 (infml) **eat**, gobble, stuff your face, bolt, wolf *Opposite*: nibble

scoffing adj **mocking**, jeering, sneering, dismissive, contemptuous

scold v **rebuke**, admonish, reprimand, reproach, discipline *Opposite*: praise

scolding n **admonishment**, reprimand, reproach, rebuke, caution *Opposite*: praise

sconce n **light fixture**, bracket, wall lamp, candleholder, light fitting

scoop n 1 **ladle**, dipper, serving spoon, server, soup ladle 2 (infml) **news story**, story, exclusive, revelation, exposé ■ v 1 **dig**, hollow, scrape, shovel, excavate *Opposite*: fill 2 **lift**, gather up, pick up, raise, take *Opposite*: drop

scoot (infml) v 1 **go away**, leave, scat (infml), make yourself scarce (infml), skedaddle (slang) *Opposite*: arrive 2 **move quickly**, rush, hurry, scurry, dash *Opposite*: dawdle

scope n 1 **possibility**, choice, room, opportunity, space *Opposite*: constraint 2 **range**, extent, capacity, span, reach

scorch v **burn**, singe, sear, char, blacken

scorched adj 1 **burnt**, singed, seared, charred, blackened 2 **dried**, dry as a bone, dry, parched, baked *Opposite*: drenched

scorching (infml) adj **boiling**, baking, sweltering, sizzling (infml), blazing *Opposite*: freezing

score n 1 **total**, tally, mark, result, count 2 **notch**, cut, slash, groove, nick ■ v 1 **achieve**, chalk up, attain, make, gain 2 **keep count**, keep a tally, keep score, count, tot up 3 **cut into**, slash, notch, nick, slice 4 **scratch**, etch, carve, mark, scrape

scoreboard n **display**, board, panel, notice board

scorecard n **tally**, scoresheet, record, card

scores n **lots**, tons (infml), heaps (infml), buckets (infml), piles (infml) *Opposite*: none

scoresheet n **sheet**, scorecard, tally, record

scorn n **contempt**, disdain, disrespect, derision, scornfulness *Opposite*: admiration ■ v 1 **show contempt for**, despise, disdain, belittle, deride *Opposite*: admire 2 **reject**, spurn, rebuff, turn down, refuse *Opposite*: choose

scorned adj 1 **despised**, disdained, belittled, derided, disparaged *Opposite*: admired 2 **rejected**, spurned, rebuffed, turned down, refused *Opposite*: chosen

scornful adj **contemptuous**, disdainful, disrespectful, mocking, derisive *Opposite*: admiring

scornfulness n **contempt**, disdain, disrespect, mockery, derision

scotch v **stop**, spoil, foil, scuttle, scupper *Opposite*: initiate

scot-free adv **unpunished**, without punishment, with impunity, lightly, easily

scoundrel n **rogue**, rascal, villain, cheat, crook *(infml) Opposite*: hero

scour v 1 **scrub**, rub, clean, wash, polish *Opposite*: dirty 2 **search**, comb, hunt, go over with a fine-tooth comb, rake through

scourge n **bane**, blight, plague, curse, menace *Opposite*: blessing ■ v **plague**, curse, afflict, terrorize, torment *Opposite*: bless

scout n **lookout**, spy, watch, undercover agent, detective ■ v 1 **search**, hunt, scout around, look around, cast around *Opposite*: find 2 **check out**, reconnoitre, survey, investigate, spy out

scout around v **search**, hunt, scout, look around, cast around

scowl n **glare**, frown, glower, grimace, stare *Opposite*: smile ■ v **look daggers**, glare, frown, glower, grimace *Opposite*: smile

scrabble v 1 **scratch**, dig, scrape, claw, pick 2 **grope**, fumble, clutch, rummage, rootle

scragginess n **scrawniness**, boniness, gauntness, skinniness, thinness *Opposite*: plumpness

scraggly adj **messy**, untidy, dishevelled, unkempt, tangled *Opposite*: tidy

scraggy adj **scrawny**, skinny, bony, gaunt, thin *Opposite*: plump. *See* COMPARE AND CONTRAST *at* thin.

scram *(infml)* v **run off**, run away, get out, get away, bolt

scramble v 1 **climb**, clamber, crawl, scrabble, struggle *Opposite*: descend 2 **move quickly**, rush, run, scuttle, jostle *Opposite*: plod 3 **mix up**, jumble, mix, muddle, confuse *Opposite*: unscramble ■ n 1 **ascent**, climb, clamber, hike *Opposite*: descent 2 **rush**, run, stampede, commotion, dash *Opposite*: calm

scrap n 1 **piece**, bit, fragment, slip, wisp 2 *(infml)* **fight**, scuffle, tussle, row, clash ■ v 1 **cancel**, abandon, get rid of, do away with, give up *Opposite*: adopt 2 **scuffle**, fight, tussle, spar, brawl

scrape v 1 **rub**, scratch, scuff, abrade, scour 2 **graze**, scratch, scuff, mark, abrade ■ n 1 *(infml)* **fight**, brawl, clash, fracas, scuffle 2 *(infml)* **predicament**, plight, problem, fix *(infml)*, pickle *(infml)* 3 **scratch**, scuff, graze, mark, abrasion

scrape by v **make do**, survive, make ends meet, get by, scratch a living *Opposite*: prosper

scrape out v **hollow out**, scoop out, gouge out, carve out, gouge *Opposite*: fill

scrape together v **collect**, amass, put by, put aside, scrape up *Opposite*: disperse

scrapheap n **rubbish dump**, junkyard, landfill, tip

scrappy adj 1 **fragmentary**, fragmented, bitty, patchy, piecemeal *Opposite*: complete 2 **disjointed**, inconsistent, disconnected, incoherent, patchy *Opposite*: uniform 3 *(infml)* **plucky**, courageous, determined, spirited, spunky *(infml) Opposite*: timid 4 *(infml)* **argumentative**, contrary, confrontational, hotheaded, quarrelsome *Opposite*: docile

scraps n **leftovers**, scrapings, slops, crumbs, leavings

scratch v 1 **scrape**, graze, grate, rub, cut 2 **itch**, rub, scrape, worry at 3 **cancel**, abandon, forget, scrap, leave out *Opposite*: keep 4 **pull out**, drop out, bow out, withdraw, abandon *Opposite*: continue ■ n **cut**, scrape, graze, score, nick

scratched adj **scuffed**, scored, scraped, marked, damaged

scratch together v **collect**, amass, put by, put aside, scratch up *Opposite*: disperse

scratchy adj **itchy**, prickly, tickly, irritating, uncomfortable *Opposite*: soft

scrawl v **scribble**, doodle, pencil, write, draw ■ n **illegible writing**, scribble, doodle, graffiti, squiggle

scrawled adj **indecipherable**, illegible, incomprehensible, scribbled, untidy *Opposite*: neat

scrawniness n **gauntness**, skinniness, boniness, scragginess, thinness *Opposite*: plumpness

scrawny adj **scraggy**, skinny, bony, gaunt, thin *Opposite*: plump. *See* COMPARE AND CONTRAST *at* thin.

scream n 1 **shriek**, yell, cry, yelp, shout *Opposite*: murmur 2 *(infml)* **laugh** *(infml)*, riot *(infml)*, gas *(infml)*, card *(dated infml)*, hoot *(slang)* ■ v **shout**, shriek, yell, cry, screech *Opposite*: whisper

scree n **rock debris**, talus, rubble, gravel, stones

screech n **scream**, shriek, squeal, cry, yelp *Opposite*: whisper ■ v **shriek**, scream, squeal, cry, yelp *Opposite*: whisper

screen n 1 **partition**, divider, panel, shield, guard 2 **shade**, awning, canopy, shelter, curtain 3 **monitor**, display, VDU, computer screen, television ■ v 1 **test**, inspect, examine, diagnose, check 2 **hide**, conceal, cover, protect, shelter *Opposite*: reveal 3 **partition**, separate, divide, mark off, curtain *Opposite*: open out 4 **broadcast**, put on, show, transmit, project 5 **vet**, select, assess, investigate, test

screening n 1 **show**, showing, viewing, programme, projection 2 **broadcast**, showing, transmission, run, airing 3 **inspection**, testing, examination, diagnosis, checking 4 **selection**, vetting, assessment, investigation, inspection

screenplay n **script**, dialogue, scenario, text, writing

screenwriter n **scriptwriter**, writer, dramatist, author, playwright

screw v 1 **twist**, rotate, coil, turn, wind *Opposite*: unscrew 2 **attach**, bolt, fasten, fix, secure 3 **crumple**, twist, distort, contort, crinkle *Opposite*: smooth

screw up v **muster**, gather, summon, call up, pluck up *Opposite*: lose

scribble v 1 **scrawl**, jot, write, dash off *(infml)* 2 **draw**, doodle, scrawl, squiggle ▪ n 1 **doodle**, scrawl, jotting, squiggle, design 2 **writing**, handwriting, scrawl, lettering

scribbled *adj* **scrawled**, jotted, untidy, illegible, indecipherable *Opposite*: neat

scribe n **transcriber**, copyist, clerk, illuminator

scrimmage n **struggle**, tussle, fray, scrum, ruckus ▪ v **fight**, battle, skirmish, scuffle, brawl

scrimp v **economize**, save, skimp, draw in your horns, tighten your belt *Opposite*: squander

script n 1 **screenplay**, text, dialogue, words, libretto 2 **writing**, calligraphy, handwriting, hand, cursive

scriptwriter n **writer**, author, playwright, screenwriter, dramatist

scroll n **roll**, parchment, document, certificate, manuscript

scrooge *(infml)* n **miser**, skinflint, niggard, pinchpenny, cheapskate *(infml)*

scrounge *(infml)* v 1 **beg**, borrow, solicit, sponge *(infml)*, cadge *(infml)* *Opposite*: give 2 **scavenge**, rummage, forage, go through, search

scrounger *(infml)* n **beggar**, borrower, cadger *(infml)*, sponger *(infml)*, freeloader *(infml)* *Opposite*: donor

scrub v 1 **clean**, rub, scour, polish, brush *Opposite*: dirty 2 *(infml)* **cancel**, delete, erase, forget about, scratch *Opposite*: schedule ▪ n 1 **undergrowth**, brush, bush, brushwood, vegetation 2 **rub**, clean, scour, polish, brush

scruffy *adj* **untidy**, shabby, tatty, unkempt, dishevelled *Opposite*: tidy

scrum n **tussle**, fray, scuffle, scrimmage, struggle

scrummy *(infml) see* **scrumptious**

scrumptious *(infml) adj* **delicious**, delectable, mouthwatering, tasty, delightful *Opposite*: revolting

scrunch v **crumple**, crush, crunch, crease, wrinkle *Opposite*: smooth

scruple n **misgiving**, doubt, qualm, compunction, hesitation

scrupulous *adj* 1 **conscientious**, meticulous, thorough, careful, rigorous *Opposite*: sloppy 2 **trustworthy**, reliable, dependable, trusty, upright. *See* COMPARE AND CONTRAST *at* **careful**.

scrupulousness n 1 **honesty**, reliability, dependability, trustworthiness, decency 2 **conscientiousness**, meticulousness, thoroughness, carefulness, rigour

scrutinize v **examine**, inspect, study, pore over, analyse *Opposite*: skim

scrutiny n **examination**, inspection, study, analysis, search

scud v **speed**, sweep, fly, sail, rush *Opposite*: crawl

scuff v **scrape**, wear away, rub, graze, scratch ▪ n **scratch**, scrape, graze, abrasion

scuffle n **fight**, brawl, punch-up, fracas, fray ▪ v **wrestle**, fight, come to blows, exchange blows, scrap

scull n **oar**, paddle, blade, sweep ▪ v **row**, paddle, propel, canoe

sculpt v **carve**, shape, mould, form, fashion

sculpture n **statue**, statuette, figure, figurine, carving

scum n **froth**, foam, impurities, filth, crust

scupper v **wreck**, stymie, thwart, ruin, spoil

scurf n 1 **dandruff**, dander, dead skin, flakes 2 **encrustation**, scale, crust, deposit, coat

scurrilous *adj* **scandalous**, slanderous, libellous, defamatory, outrageous *Opposite*: complimentary

scurry v **dash**, scuttle, scamper, dart, rush *Opposite*: saunter

scuttle v 1 **destroy**, stymie, thwart, spoil, ruin 2 **scurry**, scamper, dart, dash, rush *Opposite*: saunter

scythe v **cut**, cut down, hack, slice, sweep

sea n **ocean**, deep, depths, briny *Opposite*: dry land ▪ *adj* **maritime**, aquatic, oceanic, marine, nautical *Opposite*: land

seaboard n **coast**, coastline, shore, seashore, shoreline *Opposite*: interior

sea change n **transformation**, metamorphosis, shift, turnaround, U-turn

seacoast *see* **seaboard**

seafaring *adj* **maritime**, nautical, oceangoing, seagoing, marine

seafront n **waterfront**, promenade, esplanade, boardwalk, beach

seagoing *see* **seafaring**

seal n 1 **closure**, cover, stopper, lid, cap 2 **stamp**, hallmark, impression, signet, sigil ▪ v 1 **close**, fasten, stick, close up, shut *Opposite*: open 2 **guarantee**, settle, finalize, wrap up, confirm

sea lane n **seaway**, shipping lane, sea route, channel, corridor

sealed *adj* 1 **closed**, stuck down, wrapped, taped up *Opposite*: unsealed 2 **impenetrable**, hermetically sealed, vacuum-packed, airtight, watertight *Opposite*: unsealed

seal off v **close off**, cordon off, fence off, isolate, quarantine *Opposite*: open

seam n 1 **join**, joint, closure, ridge 2 **layer**, stratum, vein, lode

seaman n **sailor**, mariner, seafarer, navigator, deckhand

seamless *adj* 1 **unified**, all-in-one, one-piece, whole, continuous *Opposite*: joined 2 **smooth**, perfect, faultless, uniform, unified

seamy *adj* **unpleasant**, degenerate, sordid, squalid, seedy *Opposite*: wholesome

seaport *n* **harbour**, port, coastal town, anchorage, dock

sear *v* **burn**, scorch, solder, singe, char

search *v* **examine**, rifle, comb, look for, seek ■ *n* **examination**, hunt, quest, pursuit, exploration

searching *adj* **thorough**, penetrating, incisive, probing, pointed *Opposite*: superficial

searchlight *n* **light**, spotlight, beam, lamp, torch

search out *v* **discover**, uncover, find out, find, research

search party *n* **searchers**, rescue party, rescuers, rescue patrol, emergency workers

search through *v* **sift through**, sort through, rummage, hunt through, ransack

searing *adj* **1 blistering**, sweltering, scorching (*infml*), sizzling (*infml*), roasting (*infml*) *Opposite*: freezing **2 intense**, shooting, stabbing, agonizing, excruciating *Opposite*: mild

seashore *n* **coastline**, shore, shoreline, coast, seacoast

seasick *adj* **sick**, nauseous, queasy, travelsick, ill

seaside *n* **beach**, seafront, seashore, coast, shore

season *n* **period**, term, spell, time, time of year ■ *v* **flavour**, spice, spike, pepper, salt

seasonable *adj* **appropriate**, fitting, timely, opportune, suitable *Opposite*: unseasonable

seasonal *adj* **1 cyclical**, periodic, cyclic, recurrent, spring *Opposite*: year-round **2 limited**, sporadic, intermittent, temporary, casual *Opposite*: permanent

seasoned *adj* **experienced**, veteran, hardened, tested, weathered *Opposite*: inexperienced

seasoning *n* **flavouring**, flavour, zest, zing (*infml*)

seat *n* **1 chair**, bench, couch, pew, stool **2 base**, HQ, contro. centre, headquarters, centre ■ *v* **1 place**, sit, sit down, set, install **2 accommodate**, hold, sit, contain, take

seating *n* **seats**, chairs, spaces, places, places to sit

WORD BANK

❑ **types of seating** armchair, beach chair, bench, Boston rocker, bucket seat, carver, chair, chaise longue, chesterfield, couch, deck chair, easy chair, highchair, ladder-back, lounger, love seat, pew, recliner, rocking chair, settee, sofa, stall, stool, sunlounger, swivel chair, Windsor chair, wing chair

sea wall *n* **dike**, jetty, breakwater, groyne, embankment

seaway *n* **channel**, sea lane, shipping lane, sea route, canal

secede *v* **withdraw**, break away, break from, disaffiliate, pull out *Opposite*: affiliate

secession *n* **withdrawal**, departure, separation, retreat, retirement

seclude *v* **isolate**, separate, keep away, keep apart, remove

secluded *adj* **private**, sheltered, quiet, isolated, out-of-the-way *Opposite*: public

seclusion *n* **privacy**, shelter, isolation, quiet, solitude

second *adj* **additional**, another, next, subsequent, following ■ *n* **moment**, minute, instant, trice, flash *Opposite*: age ■ *v* **1 support**, agree with, endorse, subscribe, uphold *Opposite*: oppose **2 transfer**, assign, post, attach, send

secondary *adj* **1 subordinate**, minor, inferior, lesser, tributary *Opposite*: primary **2 derived**, derivative, resulting, resultant, consequent *Opposite*: original

second-class *adj* **second-rate**, mediocre, indifferent, middling, second best *Opposite*: first-class

seconder *n* **supporter**, endorser, backer, advocate, assenter

second-guess *v* **predict**, guess, foretell, anticipate, work out

second-hand *adj* **used**, hand-me-down, nearly new *Opposite*: new ■ *adv* **indirectly**, circuitously, through the grapevine *Opposite*: directly

secondly *adv* **then**, furthermore, in addition, what is more, also *Opposite*: firstly

second name *n* **surname**, family name, last name

second-rate *adj* **inadequate**, mediocre, unsatisfactory, poor, below standard *Opposite*: first-rate

second sight *n* **clairvoyance**, foresight, foreknowledge, precognition, intuition

second thoughts *n* **reconsideration**, pangs, doubts, qualms, misgivings

secrecy *n* **concealment**, confidentiality, privacy, mystery, silence *Opposite*: openness

secret *adj* **1 clandestine**, covert, stealthy, surreptitious, furtive *Opposite*: open **2 confidential**, private, classified, top-secret, restricted *Opposite*: public ■ *n* **confidence**, skeleton in the cupboard, mystery, riddle, enigma

COMPARE AND CONTRAST CORE MEANING: conveying a desire or need for concealment
secret intentionally withheld from general knowledge; **clandestine** describes an activity that needs to be concealed, usually because it is illegal or unauthorized; **covert** not intended to be known, seen, or found out, suggesting a lack of honesty or openness; **furtive** cautious and careful in order to escape notice; **stealthy** quiet, slow, and cautious in order to escape notice; **surreptitious** done in a concealed or underhand way to escape notice.

secret agent *n* **spy**, undercover agent, double agent, mole, infiltrator

secretary *n* **clerical worker**, PA, personal assistant, administrative assistant, office assistant

secretary-general *n* **chief executive officer**, CEO, head, chief, chair

secrete *v* **1 hide**, hide away, conceal, stow, squirrel away *Opposite*: display **2 exude**, ooze, emit, produce, squirt *Opposite*: absorb

secretion *n* **discharge**, excretion, exudation, emission, ooze

secretive *adj* **private**, mysterious, enigmatic, guarded, reticent *Opposite*: open

secretly *adv* **clandestinely**, covertly, in secret, surreptitiously, furtively *Opposite*: openly

sect *n* **1 group**, clique, faction, camp, party **2 religious group**, religious persuasion, denomination, cult, movement

sectarian *adj* **1 religious**, denominational, sectional, factional **2 dogmatic**, intolerant, bigoted, biased, partisan *Opposite*: tolerant

section *n* **part**, unit, piece, segment, slice *Opposite*: whole ■ *v* **divide**, divide up, partition, split, segment *Opposite*: combine

sector *n* **1 part**, division, subdivision, segment, portion *Opposite*: whole **2 area**, zone, region, quarter, district

secular *adj* **earthly**, worldly, nonspiritual, profane, lay *Opposite*: spiritual

secure *adj* **1 safe**, protected, safe and sound, safe as houses, sheltered *Opposite*: vulnerable **2 confident**, assured, self-confident, sure of yourself, self-assured *Opposite*: insecure **3 fixed firmly**, closed, fastened, locked *Opposite*: unfastened **4 dependable**, reliable, safe, stable, steady *Opposite*: unreliable ■ *v* **1 fix**, fasten, make fast, position, attach *Opposite*: loosen **2 make safe**, safeguard, fortify, lock, lock up **3 obtain**, acquire, get, get hold of, capture *Opposite*: lose **4 guarantee**, ensure, give security, indemnify, assure. *See* COMPARE AND CONTRAST *at* get.

securely *adv* **firmly**, steadily, tightly, strongly, safely

security *n* **1 safety**, refuge, sanctuary, haven, safekeeping *Opposite*: danger **2 precautions**, safety measures, defence, protection **3 confidence**, wellbeing, self-assurance, reassurance, self-confidence *Opposite*: insecurity **4 guarantee**, collateral, surety, insurance, indemnity

sedate *adj* **1 dignified**, calm, cool, demure, serene *Opposite*: boisterous **2 staid**, unexciting, dull, slow-moving, slow *Opposite*: exciting ■ *v* **anaesthetize**, tranquillize, drug, put under sedation, knock out *Opposite*: revive

sedateness *n* **1 dignity**, calmness, coolness, demureness, composedness **2 staidness**, dullness, slowness

sedation *n* **calm**, restfulness, drowsiness, torpor, tranquillity *Opposite*: excitement

sedative *n* **tranquillizer**, narcotic, barbiturate, downer *(slang)* *Opposite*: stimulant ■ *adj* **tranquillizing**, calming, soothing, relaxing, soporific *Opposite*: stimulating

sedentary *adj* **sitting**, inactive, deskbound, desk *Opposite*: active

sediment *n* **residue**, deposit, dregs, remains, grounds

sedition *n* **1 incitement to rebellion**, agitation, treason, subversion, rabble-rousing **2 rebellion**, mutiny, defiance, unrest, civil disobedience

seditious *adj* **rebellious**, subversive, treasonable, disloyal, mutinous *Opposite*: loyal

seduce *v* **1 entice**, lead astray, lure, allure, tempt **2 persuade**, wheedle, inveigle, talk into, coax

see *v* **1 perceive**, observe, distinguish, notice, witness **2 understand**, realize, perceive, grasp, appreciate *Opposite*: misunderstand **3 meet**, visit, pay a visit to, go to see, call on **4 find out**, establish, investigate, look into, check **5 imagine**, picture, envisage, predict, foresee **6 make sure**, see to it, ensure, make certain, guarantee **7 consider it**, think about it, weigh it up, give it some thought, think it over **8 date**, escort, accompany, go with, go out with **9 look at**, refer to, consult, view, regard

see about *v* **take care of**, look into, investigate, find out about, attend to *Opposite*: leave alone

seed *n* **1 kernel**, pip, spore, germ, stone **2 source**, beginning, start, starting point, nucleus ■ *v* **sow**, plant, broadcast, scatter *Opposite*: harvest

seed capital *see* seed money

seediness *n* **1 dinginess**, grubbiness, shabbiness, squalor, tattiness **2** *(infml)* **sickliness**, paleness, roughness *(infml)*

seedling *n* **sprout**, sapling, plantlet, slip, twig

seed money *n* **startup funds**, pump priming funds, venture capital, initial investment, working capital

seedy *adj* **1 dingy**, sordid, shabby, squalid, sleazy *Opposite*: respectable **2** *(infml)* **unwell**, ill, sick, poorly *(infml)*, pale *Opposite*: healthy

see eye to eye *v* **agree**, see things the same way, have the same opinion, be of the same mind *Opposite*: disagree

seeing *conj* **considering**, bearing in mind, as, since, in view of

see into *v* **discern**, understand, penetrate, comprehend, figure out

see in your mind's eye *v* **imagine**, picture, visualize, envision, see

seek *v* **1 search for**, try to find, hunt for, pursue, seek out *Opposite*: find **2 strive for**, try for, go after, pursue, work towards *Opposite*: achieve **3 ask for**, enquire about, request *Opposite*: obtain

seek out v look for, seek, search for, try to find, hunt for Opposite: find

seek to v try to, aspire to, endeavour to, aim to, attempt to Opposite: succeed

seem v appear, give the impression, seem like, look, look as if

seeming adj apparent, outward, ostensible, surface, superficial Opposite: real

seemingly adv 1 by all accounts, on the face of it, to all appearances, rumour has it, or so it seems Opposite: actually 2 apparently, outwardly, ostensibly, superficially, externally Opposite: really

seemly adj appropriate, decorous, fitting, fit, decent Opposite: unseemly

see off v 1 say goodbye to, bid farewell to, send off, take to the station, take to the airport Opposite: welcome 2 (infml) get rid of, get shot of (infml), chase off, chase away, force to go Opposite: invite 3 defeat, beat, withstand, fend off, put paid to (infml)

see out v 1 stay, last, last out, live out, survive 2 show to the door, show out, say goodbye to, accompany, go with Opposite: usher in

seep v leak, ooze, trickle, dribble, soak

seepage n leakage, leak, outflow, waste, escape

seer n prophet, soothsayer, clairvoyant, oracle, fortune-teller

see red (infml) v lose your temper, go berserk, be enraged, fly into a rage, rage Opposite: calm down

seesaw v alternate, go up and down, oscillate, fluctuate, swing Opposite: stabilize

seethe v 1 boil, bubble, froth, foam, churn 2 fume, rage, be furious, be livid, boil with rage Opposite: calm down 3 teem, swarm, be alive with, be crawling with

seething adj 1 fuming, furious, livid, beside yourself, enraged Opposite: calm 2 boiling, bubbling, foaming, on the boil, simmering Opposite: still 3 bustling, busy, frantic, heaving, teeming Opposite: quiet

see through v 1 understand, get to the bottom of, be wise to, know inside out, read like a book 2 persevere with, persist at, stick at, stay with, carry out Opposite: quit

see-through adj transparent, translucent, sheer, diaphanous, gauzy Opposite: opaque

see to v deal with, sort out, handle, take care of, manage

see to it v make sure, see, ensure, make certain, guarantee

segment n section, part, piece, slice, sector Opposite: whole ■ v divide, split, subdivide, section, portion

segmentation n division, subdivision, separation, splitting up, dissection Opposite: integration

segregate v separate, separate out, isolate, keep apart, set apart Opposite: integrate

segregation n separation, isolation, exclusion, setting apart, apartheid Opposite: integration

seize v 1 take hold of, grab, grab hold of, get hold of, snatch Opposite: relinquish 2 appropriate, confiscate, take away, sequester, remove Opposite: return 3 take control of, capture, take, take over, annex Opposite: lose 4 arrest, capture, take into custody, apprehend, take hostage Opposite: release 5 take advantage of, grab, jump at, take

seize up v 1 grind to a halt, jam, fail, stop working, stall 2 stiffen, stiffen up, freeze up, stick, cramp

seizure n 1 attack, fit, spasm, convulsion 2 capture, arrest, abduction, apprehension Opposite: release 3 appropriation, confiscation, commandeering, annexation, capture Opposite: return

seldom adv not often, hardly ever, rarely, infrequently, occasionally Opposite: often

select v choose, pick, pick out, decide on, opt for Opposite: deselect ■ adj 1 choice, top quality, first-class, excellent, first-rate Opposite: inferior 2 exclusive, elite, privileged, cliquey, restricted

selected adj carefully chosen, designated, nominated, particular, certain Opposite: all

selection n range, assortment, collection, choice, variety

selective adj discerning, discriminating, discriminatory, careful, choosy (infml) Opposite: indiscriminate

selectivity n discrimination, discernment, choosiness (infml)

selector n chooser, picker, committee member, jury member, panel member

self n personality, nature, character, psyche, identity

self-abasement n humbling, humiliation, mortification, prostration, eating humble pie Opposite: self-aggrandizement

self-absorbed adj full of yourself, self-regarding, self-centred, narcissistic, egocentric Opposite: considerate

self-absorption n self-preoccupation, egotism, egoism, egocentricity, self-centredness Opposite: generosity

self-acting adj self-operating, automatic, automated, mechanized, mechanical

self-aggrandizement n ambition, self-promotion, self-importance, self-glorification, self-glory

self-assertive adj confident, self-confident, forceful, assured, aggressive Opposite: timid

self-assurance n confidence, self-confidence, self-possession, poise, assurance Opposite: timidity

self-assured adj confident, self-confident, poised, assured, self-possessed Opposite: timid

self-centred adj selfish, self-interested, egocentric, egotistic, egoistic *Opposite*: altruistic

self-centredness n selfishness, self-interest, egocentricity, egotism, egoism *Opposite*: altruism

self-coloured adj uniform, plain, single-colour, unpatterned *Opposite*: patterned

self-conceit n smugness, arrogance, swollen head, boastfulness, conceit *Opposite*: modesty

self-confessed adj admitted, by your own admission, self-proclaimed, acknowledged, known *Opposite*: closet

self-confidence n confidence, self-assurance, self-possession, poise, assurance *Opposite*: insecurity

self-confident adj confident, self-assured, self-possessed, poised, assured *Opposite*: insecure

self-congratulation n self-satisfaction, smugness, self-praise, self-glorification, self-flattery *Opposite*: self-hatred

self-conscious adj ill at ease, awkward, uncomfortable, embarrassed, insecure *Opposite*: self-confident

self-contained adj independent, self-sufficient, self-reliant, autonomous *Opposite*: dependent

self-contradictory adj inconsistent, self-contradicting, contradictory, illogical, unreasonable *Opposite*: consistent

self-control n self-discipline, discipline, willpower, restraint, strength of mind *Opposite*: self-indulgence

self-critical adj self-deprecatory, self-deprecating, self-effacing, reticent, humble

self-defence n self-protection, self-preservation, defence, resistance

self-denial n abstinence, abstemiousness, frugality, asceticism, self-discipline *Opposite*: self-indulgence

self-deprecating adj self-critical, self-deprecatory, self-effacing, modest, humble *Opposite*: boastful

self-deprecation n self-criticism, self-depreciation, self-effacement, modesty, humility *Opposite*: boasting

self-determination n autonomy, self-rule, self-government, freedom, independence

self-discipline n self-control, discipline, willpower, restraint, strength of mind *Opposite*: self-indulgence

self-doubt n uncertainty, lack of confidence, insecurity, self-loathing, self-hatred *Opposite*: self-confidence

self-effacing adj modest, quiet, meek, diffident, unassuming *Opposite*: brash

self-employed adj freelance, your own boss, working for yourself, independent, freelancing *Opposite*: employed

self-esteem n confidence, self-confidence,

self-worth, sense of worth, self-respect *Opposite*: insecurity

self-evident adj obvious, clear, plain, manifest, undeniable *Opposite*: unclear

self-explanatory adj clear, easy to understand, easy to follow, understandable, transparent *Opposite*: unclear

self-expression n creativity, making a statement, assertiveness, individualism, expressing yourself

self-fertilization n self-fertilizing, self-pollination, self-pollinating, autogamy, hermaphroditism *Opposite*: cross-fertilization

self-flattery n self-congratulation, self-satisfaction, self-praise, self-glorification, self-aggrandizement *Opposite*: self-abasement

self-glorification n self-promotion, self-congratulation, self-satisfaction, self-praise, self-flattery *Opposite*: self-deprecation

self-governing adj autonomous, independent, sovereign, self-determining, self-sufficient *Opposite*: dependent

self-government n autonomy, independence, self-governance, sovereignty, self-rule *Opposite*: dependence

self-gratification n self-indulgence, hedonism, pleasure-seeking, high living, selfishness *Opposite*: self-sacrifice

self-hatred n self-contempt, self-loathing, self-disgust, self-denigration, self-dislike *Opposite*: self-love

self-help n support, mutual support, group support, help, counselling

self-image n opinion of yourself, self-perception, self-esteem, self-regard, self-respect

self-immolation n suicide, self-sacrifice, hara-kiri, suttee, martyrdom

self-importance n arrogance, pride, egotism, haughtiness, pomposity *Opposite*: humility

self-important adj arrogant, pompous, conceited, egotistic, bumptious *Opposite*: humble

self-imposed adj chosen, voluntary, self-inflicted, self-induced, of your own free will *Opposite*: enforced

self-incrimination n self-accusation, self-implication, confession, admission of guilt, self-blame

self-indulgence n 1 decadence, indulgence, hedonism, pleasure, luxury *Opposite*: restraint 2 self-pity, childishness, selfishness, self-centredness, self-absorption *Opposite*: restraint

self-indulgent adj 1 decadent, indulgent, hedonistic, epicurean, luxurious *Opposite*: restrained 2 self-pitying, wallowing, childish, selfish, self-centred *Opposite*: restrained

self-interest n selfishness, self-centredness, egotism, self-regard, egocentricity *Opposite*: altruism

self-interested adj selfish, self-centred, self-seeking, egocentric, egoistic *Opposite*: altruistic

selfish *adj* **self-centred**, self-seeking, self-interested, egotistic, egoistic *Opposite*: selfless

selfishness *n* **self-centredness**, self-interest, egotism, egoism, egocentricity *Opposite*: selflessness

selfless *adj* **unselfish**, self-sacrificing, altruistic, generous, noble *Opposite*: selfish

selflessness *n* **unselfishness**, self-sacrifice, altruism, generosity, gallantry *Opposite*: selfishness

self-love *n* **egotism**, selfishness, egocentricity, narcissism, egoism *Opposite*: modesty

self-motivated *adj* **energetic**, dynamic, keen, enthusiastic, driven *Opposite*: unmotivated

self-obsessed *adj* **self-centred**, egocentric, egomaniacal, egotistical, narcissistic

self-opinionated *adj* **1 overconfident**, sure of yourself, cocksure, self-confident, opinionated *Opposite*: diffident **2 conceited**, vain, full of yourself, self-satisfied, bigheaded *(infml) Opposite*: self-deprecating

self-opinioned *see* **self-opinionated**

self-pity *n* **self-indulgence**, misery, unhappiness, defeatism, self-absorption *Opposite*: cheerfulness

self-pitying *adj* **self-absorbed**, wallowing, defeatist, sorry for yourself, miserable *Opposite*: happy-go-lucky

self-possessed *adj* **confident**, self-assured, self-confident, assured, poised *Opposite*: insecure

self-possession *n* **confidence**, self-assurance, self-confidence, assurance, poise *Opposite*: insecurity

self-preservation *n* **self-protection**, self-defence, survival, preservation instinct, survival instinct

self-promotion *n* **self-aggrandizement**, self-importance, self-glorification, self-glory, self-praise *Opposite*: self-deprecation

self-regard *n* **1 self-interest**, self-centredness, selfishness, egotism, egocentricity *Opposite*: altruism **2 self-respect**, self-esteem, self-worth, dignity, pride *Opposite*: self-hatred

self-regarding *adj* **selfish**, self-centred, egocentric, egotistic, self-absorbed *Opposite*: selfless

self-reliance *n* **independence**, self-sufficiency, autonomy, self-confidence, self-assurance *Opposite*: dependence

self-reliant *adj* **independent**, self-sufficient, autonomous, self-confident, self-assured *Opposite*: dependent

self-reproach *n* **self-criticism**, remorse, contrition, shame, guilt *Opposite*: self-congratulation

self-respect *n* **self-esteem**, self-confidence, confidence, dignity, pride *Opposite*: self-hatred

self-restraint *n* **self-control**, self-discipline, discipline, willpower, moderation *Opposite*: abandon

self-righteous *adj* **sanctimonious**, smug, self-satisfied, complacent, pious *Opposite*: humble

self-righteousness *n* **sanctimoniousness**, smugness, complacency, piety, superciliousness *Opposite*: humility

self-rule *n* **self-government**, independence, self-determination, autonomy, self-governance *Opposite*: dependence

self-sacrifice *n* **altruism**, unselfishness, selflessness, self-denial, martyrdom *Opposite*: selfishness

self-sacrificing *adj* **altruistic**, unselfish, selfless, noble, self-denying *Opposite*: selfish

selfsame *adj* **very same**, identical, very, exact, same *Opposite*: different

self-satisfaction *n* **smugness**, complacency, self-righteousness, conceit, arrogance *Opposite*: self-doubt

self-satisfied *adj* **smug**, pleased with yourself, self-righteous, conceited, arrogant

self-seeking *adj* **selfish**, self-centred, self-regarding, egocentric, egoistic *Opposite*: selfless

self-serving *adj* **selfish**, egotistic, self-centred, narcissistic, egocentric *Opposite*: altruistic

self-styled *adj* **self-appointed**, self-proclaimed, so-called, professed, would-be *Opposite*: certified

self-sufficiency *n* **independence**, autonomy, self-reliance, self-support *Opposite*: dependence

self-sufficient *adj* **independent**, autonomous, self-reliant, self-supporting, self-financing *Opposite*: dependent

self-supporting *adj* **self-sufficient**, self-financing, profitable, healthy, successful *Opposite*: struggling

self-will *n* **determination**, obstinacy, stubbornness, pigheadedness, wilfulness *Opposite*: weakness

self-willed *adj* **headstrong**, obstinate, determined, stubborn, pigheaded *Opposite*: weak-willed

self-worth *n* **self-esteem**, self-respect, self-confidence, pride, dignity

sell *v* **1 vend**, wholesale, trade, retail, flog *(infml) Opposite*: buy **2 put up for sale**, market, offer, deal in, auction *Opposite*: buy **3 be bought**, go, be snapped up, be popular, be in demand **4 persuade people to buy**, market, promote, advertise, traffic in

seller *n* **vendor**, retailer, wholesaler, supplier, merchant *Opposite*: buyer

selling *n* **vending**, sales, marketing, trade, retailing *Opposite*: buying

sell out *v* **1 run out**, be out of stock, be snapped up, go, be unavailable *Opposite*: stock up

2 give in, give up, sell your soul, betray your principles, be co-opted

sellout n **1 box-office hit**, hit, smash hit, smash, bestseller *Opposite*: flop *(infml)* **2** *(infml)* **betrayal**, treachery, disloyalty, apostasy, co-optation *Opposite*: loyalty

semblance n **1 trace**, shred, fragment, measure, modicum **2 appearance**, impression, air, resemblance, façade

semiconscious adj **half-conscious**, half-awake, half-asleep, surfacing, dazed

semidarkness n **twilight**, half-light, dusk, dimness, gloom

semifinal n round, heat, leg, match, game

seminal adj **influential**, important, formative, pivotal, inspirational *Opposite*: insignificant

seminar n **1 meeting**, session, round table, discussion, conference **2 discussion group**, tutorial, class, evening class, talk

seminary n theological college, divinity school, college, training college, academy

senate n **governing body**, legislature, congress, parliament, diet

senator n **senate member**, politician, representative, legislator, congresswoman

send v **1 direct**, refer, guide, show, lead **2 post**, transmit, dispatch, forward, consign *Opposite*: receive **3 transmit**, project, broadcast, disseminate, give off **4 propel**, hurl, fling, throw, fire *Opposite*: bring

send down v expel, rusticate, suspend, banish, dismiss

send for v request, summon, call for, order, assemble *Opposite*: dismiss

send off v dispatch, send, post, send away, transmit *Opposite*: receive

sendoff n **goodbye**, farewell, leaving party, leaving do, valediction *(fml)* *Opposite*: welcome

send on v forward, redirect, readdress, transfer, pass on *Opposite*: return

send over the edge v derange, unhinge, unsettle, stress out *(infml)*

send packing *(infml)* v dismiss, expel, evict, turn out, throw out *Opposite*: welcome

send to Coventry v ostracize, ignore, freeze out, give the cold shoulder to, exclude

send up v **1 raise**, elevate, heighten, boost, bump up *(infml)* *Opposite*: lower **2** *(infml)* **lampoon**, satirize, mock, parody, ridicule

sendup *(infml)* n **parody**, lampoon, takeoff, impersonation, caricature

senile adj **confused**, disorientated, forgetful, failing, absent-minded

senior adj **1 older**, elder, oldest, eldest, firstborn *Opposite*: junior **2 high-ranking**, high-grade, superior, higher, leading *Opposite*: junior ■ n **1 elder**, first-born, elder sibling, big brother, big sister *Opposite*: junior **2 boss**, superior, chief, manager, leader *Opposite*: junior

senior citizen n **pensioner**, OAP, retired person, retiree

seniority n superiority, supremacy, precedence, priority, position

sensation n **1 feeling**, sense, impression, awareness, consciousness *Opposite*: numbness **2 commotion**, stir, fuss, uproar, rumpus *Opposite*: lull **3 phenomenon**, miracle, wonder, marvel, spectacle

sensational adj **1 outstanding**, excellent, dramatic, amazing, extraordinary *Opposite*: predictable **2 startling**, shocking, scandalous, melodramatic, lurid *Opposite*: understated **3** *(infml)* **amazing**, astounding, marvellous, exciting, thrilling *Opposite*: boring

sensationalism n **exaggeration**, overstatement, luridness, scandal, melodrama *Opposite*: understatement

sensationalist adj **startling**, shocking, scandalous, melodramatic, lurid *Opposite*: understated

sense n **1 feeling**, sensation, awareness, perception **2 appreciation**, impression, consciousness, awareness, feeling **3 intelligence**, brains, intellect, wisdom, sagacity *Opposite*: folly **4 purpose**, point, reason, function, end **5 opinion**, view, viewpoint, consensus, mood **6 gist**, substance, drift, nub, idea **7 meaning**, denotation, significance, signification, implication ■ v **1 detect**, identify, distinguish, recognize, know **2 perceive**, feel, have a feeling, get the impression, discern *Opposite*: observe **3 intuit**, guess, suspect, pick up, feel

senseless adj **1 stupid**, silly, foolish, mindless, idiotic *Opposite*: sensible **2 unconscious**, comatose, numb, deadened, knocked out *Opposite*: conscious **3 pointless**, ridiculous, absurd, meaningless, futile *Opposite*: worthwhile

senselessness n **1 stupidity**, silliness, foolishness, madness, idiocy *Opposite*: sense **2 pointlessness**, ridiculousness, absurdity, irrationality, meaninglessness

sensibility n **responsiveness**, deep feeling, emotional response, receptivity, susceptibility *Opposite*: insensitivity

sensible adj **1 level-headed**, sane, rational, reasonable, shrewd *Opposite*: foolish **2 practical**, serviceable, workable, functional, utilitarian *Opposite*: impractical **3** *(fml)* **aware**, conscious, mindful, cognizant *(fml)*. *See* COMPARE AND CONTRAST *at* **aware**.

sensibleness n **rationality**, level-headedness, reasonableness, shrewdness, wisdom *Opposite*: foolishness

sensitive adj **1 responsive**, receptive, susceptible, aware, perceptive *Opposite*: indifferent **2 delicate**, irritable, susceptible, allergic, difficult *Opposite*: robust **3 subtle**, delicate, complex, searching, penetrating *Opposite*: superficial **4 thoughtful**, sympathetic, understanding, perceptive, considerate *Opposite*: unsympathetic **5 thin-skinned**, easily upset, easily hurt, hypersensitive, vulnerable *Opposite*: impervious **6 secret**, confidential, classified, top secret, restricted *Opposite*: public **7 awkward**, tricky, difficult, sticky, delicate *Opposite*: straightforward **8 precise**, exact, delicate, finely tuned, responsive *Opposite*: imprecise

sensitivity *n* **compassion**, sympathy, understanding, kindliness, warmth *Opposite*: indifference

sensitize *v* **1 alert**, make aware, inform, explain, brief *Opposite*: desensitize **2 expose**, make sensitive, irritate, trigger, induce *Opposite*: desensitize

sensor *n* **device**, measuring device, instrument, radar, beam

sensual *adj* **1 sexual**, erotic, voluptuous, fleshly, carnal *Opposite*: ascetic **2 sensory**, carnal, bodily, physical, corporeal *Opposite*: intellectual

sensuous *adj* **sumptuous**, opulent, rich, deep, intense *Opposite*: ascetic

sentence *n* **judgment**, verdict, ruling, decree, condemnation ■ *v* **pass judgment on**, condemn, punish, send to prison, pronounce judgment on *Opposite*: acquit

sententious *adj* **moralizing**, moralistic, judgmental, critical, censorious *Opposite*: approving

sentient *adj* **1 conscious**, animate, flesh-and-blood, alive, living *Opposite*: inanimate **2 emotional**, responsive, sensate, perceptive, feeling *Opposite*: intellectual

sentiment *n* **1 feeling**, emotion, response, reaction, attitude **2 sentimentality**, mawkishness, gush, romanticism, corn *(infml)*

sentimental *adj* **mawkish**, romantic, slushy, mushy, maudlin *Opposite*: cynical

sentimentality *n* **mawkishness**, corniness, slushiness, mushiness, romanticism *Opposite*: cynicism

sentimentalize *v* **gush**, emotionalize, romanticize, wax lyrical *(literary)*

sentinel *see* **sentry**

sentry *n* **guard**, patrol, lookout, watch, sentinel

separable *adj* **divisible**, distinguishable, detachable, removable, discrete *Opposite*: inseparable

separate *adj* **1 unconnected**, disconnected, individual, independent, unattached *Opposite*: connected **2 distinct**, discrete, detached, loose, dispersed *Opposite*: attached ■ *v* **1 split up**, split, divorce, part, part company **2 divide**, part, disconnect, undo, split *Opposite*: unite **3 break away**, secede, branch out, break free, break *Opposite*: join

separately *adv* **1 independently**, alone, individually, one at a time, singly *Opposite*: together **2 distinctly**, unconnectedly, disjointedly, discretely, severally *Opposite*: together

separateness *n* **distinctness**, disconnectedness, separation, distinctiveness, difference

separate off *v* **divide**, divide off, split off, detach, sever

separate out *v* **strain**, filter, pass through a filter, sieve, extract *Opposite*: cohere *(fml)*

separation *n* **1 parting**, departure, goodbye, farewell, leave-taking *(literary) Opposite*: meeting **2 division**, severance, taking apart, partition, disjunction *Opposite*: unification **3 split-up**, split, divorce, estrangement, rift

separatist *n* **dissenter**, secessionist, protester, rebel, freedom fighter

separator *n* **1 divider**, barrier, partition, dividing wall, screen **2 sieve**, strainer, filter, extractor, centrifuge *Opposite*: blender

septic *adj* **poisoned**, infected, festering, gangrenous, diseased *Opposite*: healthy

sepulchral *adj* **funereal**, sombre, sad, dismal, melancholy *Opposite*: cheery

sepulchre *n* **vault**, tomb, grave, crypt, burial chamber

sequel *n* **1 consequence**, development, result, outcome, upshot *Opposite*: prelude **2 follow-on**, continuation, conclusion, follow-up *Opposite*: prequel

sequence *n* **1 series**, succession, run, progression, chain **2 order**, arrangement, classification, categorization, system *Opposite*: disarray

sequential *adj* **1 in sequence**, consecutive, in order, successive, chronological *Opposite*: jumbled **2 consequent**, resulting, resultant, ensuing, following *Opposite*: previous

sequentially *adv* **in sequence**, in succession, successively, in order, consecutively *Opposite*: out of order

sequester *v* **1 confiscate**, requisition, appropriate, impound, seize *Opposite*: restore **2** *(fml)* **isolate**, separate, segregate, cut off, set apart

sequestrate *v* **confiscate**, seize, appropriate, repossess, impound *Opposite*: release

sequestration *n* **confiscation**, appropriation, impounding, seizure, requisitioning *Opposite*: restoration

sequin *n* **spangle**, bead, bauble, star, decoration

serenade *v* **sing**, croon, court, entertain, divert

serendipitous *adj* **fortunate**, lucky, happy, fortuitous, providential. *See* COMPARE AND CONTRAST at **lucky**.

serendipity *n* **fate**, destiny, karma, providence, luck *Opposite*: design

serene *adj* **1 calm**, composed, unruffled, cool, unflustered *Opposite*: agitated **2 tranquil**, calm, peaceful, still, quiet *Opposite*: bustling

serenity *n* **1 composure**, coolness, peace of mind, poise, equanimity *Opposite*: panic **2 tranquillity**, calmness, peacefulness, quietude, quietness *Opposite*: bustle

serial *adj* sequential, successive, consecutive, ongoing, in order *Opposite*: random

series *n* sequence, succession, run, chain, string

serious *adj* 1 dangerous, acute, life-threatening, critical, grave *Opposite*: minor 2 important, momentous, significant, crucial, vital *Opposite*: trivial 3 thought-provoking, meaningful, intense, deep, profound *Opposite*: lightweight 4 thoughtful, grave, solemn, sombre, stern *Opposite*: lighthearted 5 earnest, sincere, genuine, honest, resolute *Opposite*: flippant

seriously *adv* 1 badly, dangerously, critically, fatally, acutely *Opposite*: slightly 2 earnestly, truly, sincerely, genuinely, honestly *Opposite*: jokingly 3 (*infml*) extremely, very, really, totally, utterly

serious-minded *adj* earnest, sensible, sedate, steady, determined *Opposite*: frivolous

seriousness *n* 1 importance, significance, gravity, weightiness, momentousness *Opposite*: triviality 2 earnestness, sincerity, genuineness, honesty, resoluteness *Opposite*: flippancy

sermon *n* 1 talk, address, homily, discourse, oration *Opposite*: conversation 2 lecture, harangue, homily, talking-to (*infml*), ticking-off (*infml*) *Opposite*: praise

sermonize *v* preach, pontificate, moralize, hold forth, lecture *Opposite*: flatter

serpent *n* traitor, liar, cheat, sneak, troublemaker *Opposite*: friend

serpentine *adj* winding, meandering, twisting, sinuous, bending *Opposite*: straight

serrated *adj* jagged, toothed, notched, ragged, saw-toothed *Opposite*: smooth

servant *n* domestic, retainer, help *Opposite*: employer

WORD BANK
❏ **types of servant** butler, chambermaid, cleaner, cook, factotum, flunky, footman, lackey, maid, maidservant, major-domo, valet

serve *v* 1 supply, dish up, serve up, hand out, hand round 2 wait on, wait at table, wait, attend, tend 3 function, work, operate, act, perform 4 work for, help, aid, attend, assist

service *n* 1 help, assistance, aid, use, benefit *Opposite*: disservice 2 facility, provision, package, deal, amenity 3 ceremony, ritual, rite, sacrament, mass 4 overhaul, examination, check, tune-up, maintenance ■ *v* repair, overhaul, examine, tune, check

serviceable *adj* 1 durable, hard-wearing, strong, stout, tough *Opposite*: flimsy 2 working, operative, functional, in working order, usable *Opposite*: broken 3 effective, helpful, practical, useful, practicable *Opposite*: impractical

services *n* 1 service station, motorway facilities, motorway service station, service area,

filling station 2 service industries, service sector, service jobs, customer services *Opposite*: manufacturing 3 public amenities, civic amenities, amenities, public services, council services 4 armed forces, forces, military, armed services, security forces

servile *adj* submissive, abject, fawning, subservient, sycophantic *Opposite*: proud

serving *n* portion, helping, plateful, ration, quota

serving dish *n* platter, salver, plate, tray, dish

servitude *n* 1 slavery, bondage, serfdom, enslavement, vassalage *Opposite*: freedom 2 subjection, subjugation, subordination, dependence, dependency *Opposite*: liberty

session *n* 1 meeting, sitting, assembly, conference, gathering 2 term, period, semester, trimester, quarter 3 shift, stint, go, spell, phase

set *v* 1 put, place, locate, position, situate *Opposite*: pick up 2 establish, fix, agree on, appoint, decide *Opposite*: change 3 adjust, regulate, synchronize, align, programme 4 become hard, harden, go hard, solidify, congeal *Opposite*: liquefy ■ *n* 1 scenery, stage set, film set, setting, location 2 collection, group, arrangement, array, series *Opposite*: individual 3 circle, group, clique, gang, crowd ■ *adj* 1 established, usual, customary, traditional, conventional *Opposite*: changing 2 inflexible, obstinate, determined, resolute, resolved *Opposite*: flexible 3 ready, prepared, fit, primed, organized *Opposite*: unprepared 4 firm, congealed, solid, hard, fixed *Opposite*: liquid

set about *v* begin, tackle, start, launch into, get down to

set against *v* 1 compare, contrast, consider, set side by side, oppose 2 pit against, turn against, set as rivals, set in opposition, alienate *Opposite*: bring together

set alight *v* kindle, light, ignite, set light to, set fire to *Opposite*: put out

set apart *v* 1 reserve, put aside, keep on one side, set aside, separate 2 distinguish, differentiate, single out, make something stand out, mark out

set aside *v* 1 reserve, save, keep back, put to one side, lay by *Opposite*: use up 2 reject, discard, annul, break free from, shake off

set back *v* delay, hinder, hold up, impede, slow down *Opposite*: facilitate

setback *n* hindrance, holdup, delay, impediment, stumbling block *Opposite*: boost

set down *v* 1 put down, lay down, place, deposit, put 2 write down, report, record, chronicle, write out

set eyes on *v* catch sight of, observe, notice, sight, spot

set fire to *v* kindle, light, ignite, set light to, set alight *Opposite*: put out

set foot in *v* enter, go in, come into, show your face, turn up

set forth *(fml)* v **state**, describe, express, lay down, present

set free v **1 liberate**, free, release, discharge, let go *Opposite*: imprison **2 untie**, unloose, unshackle, unleash, let loose *Opposite*: tie up

set in v **come to stay**, be here to stay, take root, become established, become entrenched *Opposite*: pass

set in motion v **start**, initiate, begin, kick-start, set off *Opposite*: stop

set off v **1 start out**, set out, go, depart, leave *Opposite*: arrive **2 detonate**, explode, light, ignite, trigger *Opposite*: defuse **3 start**, begin, commence, start off, burst out *Opposite*: finish **4 initiate**, instigate, launch, inaugurate, begin **5 draw attention to**, display, bring out, highlight, enhance

set on v **attack**, set upon, assault, lay into, terrorize

set on fire v **kindle**, light, ignite, set alight, set fire to *Opposite*: put out

set out v **1 leave**, set off, depart, go, move off *Opposite*: arrive **2 embark on**, start, begin, commence, set off *Opposite*: finish **3 plan**, aim, intend, determine, design **4 display**, lay out, arrange, present, show **5 explain**, specify, define, describe, detail

set phrase n **expression**, phrase, idiom, turn of phrase, saying

set right v **correct**, rectify, right, put right, put to rights

set store by v **deem important**, value, esteem, prize, regard highly

sett n **paving stone**, paving slab, paver, stone, slab

settee n **sofa**, couch, chaise lounge, divan, futon

setting n **location**, surroundings, scenery, situation, background

settle v **1 resolve**, reconcile, clear up, straighten out, mend **2 stay**, inhabit, put down roots, set up house, establish yourself **3 land**, perch, alight, roost, come to rest *Opposite*: take off **4 become peaceful**, become calm, settle down, calm down, relax *Opposite*: fluster **5 pay**, defray, discharge, clear, foot *Opposite*: owe **6 sink**, drop, descend, fall, go to the bottom *Opposite*: rise

settled adj **established**, stable, solid, firm, steady *Opposite*: unsettled

settle down v **1 become less restless**, quieten down, relax, calm down, snuggle down *Opposite*: agitate **2 sink**, drop, descend, fall, stabilize *Opposite*: rise

settle for v **agree to**, accept, make do with, take, be happy with *Opposite*: refuse

settle in v **1 adapt**, acclimatize, adjust, get used to it, find your feet **2 get comfortable**, snuggle down, ensconce yourself, bed down, get comfy

settlement n **1 resolution**, conclusion, completion, decision, agreement **2 payment**, defrayal, clearance, clearing, reimbursement *Opposite*: receipt **3 community**, village, town, township, colony

settle on v **choose**, pick, select, decide on, agree on *Opposite*: reject

settler n **colonizer**, colonist, pioneer, pilgrim, immigrant

settle up v **pay the bill**, pay, pay up, settle the debt, settle your account *Opposite*: quibble

set to v **1 get on with it**, put your shoulder to the wheel, make a start, get started, start work **2 come to blows**, start fighting, lay into, grapple, tussle

set-to *(infml)* n **confrontation**, quarrel, altercation, disagreement, row *Opposite*: reconciliation

set up v **1 establish**, inaugurate, found, institute, launch **2 erect**, raise, build, construct, put up **3** *(infml)* **frame**, trap, entrap, trick, con

setup n **1 system**, arrangement, format, situation, structure **2** *(infml)* **frame**, trap, trick, deception, con

set upon v **attack**, assault, lay into, assail, pounce on *Opposite*: defend

seventh heaven n **bliss**, ecstasy, heaven, nirvana, cloud nine *Opposite*: despair

sever v **1 cut**, split, separate, undo, disunite *Opposite*: unite **2 cut off**, chop off, lop off, shear off, slice off *Opposite*: attach

several adj **some**, quite a lot of, a number of, numerous, many

severally adv **separately**, individually, singly, one at a time, one by one *Opposite*: together

severance n **1 separation**, detachment, disconnection, division, taking apart *Opposite*: joining **2 compensation**, redundancy pay, redundancy money, severance pay, golden handshake *(infml)*

severe adj **1 harsh**, stern, strict, cruel, brutal *Opposite*: gentle **2 acute**, grave, critical, mortal, serious *Opposite*: slight **3 plain**, simple, spartan, unadorned, unembellished *Opposite*: ornate

severity n **1 harshness**, sternness, strictness, cruelty, brutality *Opposite*: gentleness **2 gravity**, seriousness, acuteness, dangerousness, awfulness *Opposite*: insignificance **3 plainness**, simplicity, starkness, bareness, austerity *Opposite*: opulence

sew v **stitch**, seam, baste, tack, hem *Opposite*: unpick

sewer n **drain**, septic tank, cesspit, cesspool, open drain

sewing n **stitching**, embroidery, tapestry, needlework, needlepoint

sew up v **1 stitch up**, sew, stitch, darn, repair *Opposite*: unpick **2 settle**, clinch, tie up, finalize, finish

sex n **gender**, sexual category, masculinity, femininity

sexy *adj* **1 erotic**, sensual, sexual, suggestive, pleasurable **2 voluptuous**, curvaceous, sensuous, alluring, attractive

shabbiness *n* **1 scruffiness**, untidiness, dilapidation, seediness, raggedness *Opposite*: elegance **2 inconsiderateness**, unfairness, meanness, disrespect, negligence *Opposite*: decency

shabby *adj* **1 scruffy**, untidy, ragged, tattered, worn out *Opposite*: elegant **2 inconsiderate**, unjust, mean, dishonourable, contemptible *Opposite*: decent

shack *n* **hut**, shanty, hovel, lean-to, shed

shackle *v* **1 fetter**, manacle, handcuff, chain, put in irons *Opposite*: free **2 constrain**, restrict, impede, hamper, hinder *Opposite*: facilitate

shackles *n* **fetters**, manacles, chains, restraints, irons

shade *n* **1 shadow**, dark, darkness, gloom, gloominess *Opposite*: light **2 blind**, screen, awning, canopy, cover **3 hue**, tint, tinge, colour, tone **4 hint**, trace, suggestion, touch, dash ■ *v* **1 cover**, shield, protect, screen, veil *Opposite*: expose **2 darken**, eclipse, blot out, shadow, block out *Opposite*: brighten **3 fill in**, hatch, colour, colour in, block in

shades *n* (*infml*) ■ **sunglasses**, sunspecs (*infml*), dark glasses, tinted lenses

shadiness *n* **1 dishonesty**, crookedness, underhandedness, shiftiness, suspiciousness *Opposite*: honesty **2 dimness**, dark, darkness, shadowiness, obscurity *Opposite*: brightness

shadow *n* **1 silhouette**, outline, shape, figure, form **2 shade**, dark, darkness, gloom, gloominess *Opposite*: light **3 hint**, trace, suggestion, touch, shade **4 constant companion**, alter ego, sidekick, other self, double **5 private investigator**, private detective, private eye (*infml*), sleuth (*infml*), PI (*US*) **6 follower**, stalker, pursuer, tracker, tail (*infml*) **7 ghost**, spectre, spirit, wraith, apparition ■ *v* **1 follow**, trail, track, stalk, observe **2 darken**, eclipse, blot out, shade *Opposite*: brighten. *See* COMPARE AND CONTRAST *at* follow.

shadows *n* **shade**, dark, darkness, obscurity, dimness *Opposite*: light

shadowy *adj* **1 indistinct**, obscure, vague, indistinguishable, unclear *Opposite*: distinct **2 dim**, dark, murky, gloomy, poorly lit *Opposite*: bright **3 ghostly**, spectral, ethereal, sinister, mysterious *Opposite*: material

shady *adj* **1 out of the sun**, in the shade, shaded, under the trees, cool *Opposite*: sunny **2 dishonest**, underhand, shifty, suspicious, devious *Opposite*: aboveboard

shagginess *n* **hairiness**, dishevelment, untidiness, bushiness, scruffiness *Opposite*: neatness

shaggy *adj* **hairy**, unkempt, dishevelled, bushy, unshaven *Opposite*: tidy

shake *v* **1 wobble**, judder, jolt, jerk, bounce **2 tremble**, quiver, quake, shudder, shiver **3 agitate**, stir, blend, mix **4 unsettle**, unnerve, disturb, distress, upset *Opposite*: reassure **5 brandish**, flourish, flaunt, wave, wield ■ *n* **1 tremor**, vibration, judder, wobble, lurch **2 shudder**, quiver, quake, tremble, shiver **3 waggle**, wave, flourish, twirl

shake off *v* **1 get rid of**, get away from, lose, elude, leave behind **2 recover from**, recuperate from, get over, get rid of *Opposite*: succumb

shake-out *n* **transformation**, radical change, upheaval, overhaul, reorganization

shake up *v* **1 transform**, overhaul, change drastically, revamp, rethink *Opposite*: leave alone **2 upset**, disturb, distress, shock, alarm *Opposite*: calm down **3 mix**, blend, combine, agitate, shake

shake-up *n* **transformation**, radical change, upheaval, overhaul, reorganization

shakiness *n* **1 tremor**, shaking, trembling, shake, jerkiness *Opposite*: control **2 wobbliness**, instability, flimsiness, fragility, insubstantiality *Opposite*: sturdiness **3 uncertainty**, precariousness, instability, unreliability, weakness *Opposite*: reliability

shaking *n* **vibration**, jolting, juddering, rocking, rattling

shaky *adj* **1 wobbly**, unstable, unsteady, insecure, rickety *Opposite*: steady **2 trembling**, shaking, quivering, quaking, shuddering *Opposite*: composed **3 unsupported**, unsound, questionable, dubious, doubtful *Opposite*: dependable

shallow *adj* **1 low**, thin, light, narrow, surface *Opposite*: deep **2 superficial**, trivial, slight, insubstantial, petty *Opposite*: profound

sham *n* **1 pretence**, charade, con, fraud **2 impostor**, charlatan, con, fake, fraud ■ *adj* **fake**, mock, bogus, imitation, pretended *Opposite*: bona fide ■ *v* **pretend**, fake, put it on, act, play *Opposite*: real

shamble *v* **shuffle**, amble, waddle, drag your feet, walk *Opposite*: stride

shambles *n* **1 fiasco**, disaster, failure, mess, botch (*infml*) *Opposite*: success **2 mess**, muddle, tip, dump, chaos

shambling *adj* **awkward**, ungainly, clumsy, uncoordinated, lumbering *Opposite*: graceful

shambolic (*infml*) *adj* **disorganized**, chaotic, messy, haphazard, confused *Opposite*: orderly

shame *n* **disgrace**, embarrassment, dishonour, humiliation, mortification *Opposite*: pride ■ *v* **embarrass**, discredit, disgrace, humiliate, mortify *Opposite*: honour

shamefaced *adj* **ashamed**, embarrassed, abashed, sheepish, hangdog *Opposite*: proud

shameful *adj* **disgraceful**, reprehensible, dishonourable, discreditable, shocking *Opposite*: honourable

shameless *adj* brazen, barefaced, unabashed, blatant, unashamed *Opposite*: ashamed

shamelessness *n* lack of remorse, brazenness, hardheartedness, boldness, impudence *Opposite*: repentance

shank *n* stem, shaft, trunk, rod, bar

shape *n* 1 form, figure, outline, silhouette, profile 2 character, nature, form, identity, structure ■ *v* 1 model, mould, whittle, manipulate, smooth 2 sway, determine, cause, influence, affect

---

WORD BANK
❏ **types of angular shape** box, cross, cube, diamond, dodecahedron, dogleg, lozenge, oblong, parallelogram, pentagon, polygon, pyramid, quadrangle, quadrilateral, rectangle, rhomboid, rhombus, square, star, tetragon, tetrahedron, trapezium, trapezoid, triangle
❏ **types of rounded shape** arc, arch, ball, bend, bow, bulb, circle, circlet, coil, cone, crescent, curl, curve, cylinder, dome, figure of eight, globe, heart, helix, hemisphere, hoop, horseshoe, kidney, loop, orb, oval, ring, round, semicircle, sphere, spheroid, spiral, teardrop

---

shapeless *adj* baggy, loose-fitting, formless, ill-defined, amorphous *Opposite*: defined

shapelessness *n* amorphousness, formlessness, bagginess, fluidity *Opposite*: definition

shapely *adj* well-formed, attractive, well-rounded, well-proportioned, pleasing

shape up *v* 1 develop, progress, improve, come along, come together 2 improve, pull yourself together, get it together, reform, mend your ways

shard *n* sliver, splinter, spike, shaving, chip

share *v* 1 split, go halves, divide, divide up, divvy (*infml*) 2 distribute, allocate, assign, apportion, allot 3 communicate, let somebody in on, impart, reveal, disclose ■ *n* part, portion, segment, cut, stake *Opposite*: whole

shared *adj* common, communal, joint, mutual, collective

share out *v* divide up, give out, parcel out, distribute, allot

sharp *adj* 1 pointed, razor-sharp, tapered, pointy, jagged *Opposite*: blunt 2 quick, intelligent, razor-sharp, incisive, astute *Opposite*: dull 3 abrupt, sudden, quick, brusque, urgent *Opposite*: gentle 4 shrill, piercing, loud, high-pitched, strident *Opposite*: soft 5 harsh, severe, snappy, sarcastic, snappish *Opposite*: gentle 6 severe, acute, strong, hard, intense *Opposite*: mild 7 sour, tangy, acid, acrid, pungent *Opposite*: sweet 8 clear, well-defined, definite, clear-cut, distinct *Opposite*: imprecise ■ *adv* exactly, precisely, on the dot, promptly, punctually

sharpen *v* 1 hone, whet, grind, file, strop *Oppo-*

site: blunt 2 improve, hone, perfect, brush up, refine *Opposite*: worsen

sharp-eyed *adj* 1 observant, watchful, alert, vigilant, attentive *Opposite*: unobservant 2 eagle-eyed, with good eyesight, with good vision, with eyes like a hawk, hawk-eyed *Opposite*: short-sighted

sharpish (*infml*) *adv* quickly, fast, straightaway, right away, immediately *Opposite*: eventually

sharply *adv* 1 abruptly, suddenly, all at once, hard, tight *Opposite*: gently 2 harshly, severely, cuttingly, unkindly, snappishly *Opposite*: gently 3 alarmingly, steeply, greatly, dramatically, suddenly *Opposite*: gradually 4 briskly, abruptly, suddenly, smartly, swiftly *Opposite*: slowly 5 extremely, clearly, distinctly, acutely, deeply *Opposite*: subtly 6 clearly, distinctly, strikingly, obviously, eye-catchingly *Opposite*: hazily

sharpness *n* 1 acuity, perceptiveness, intelligence, quickness, keenness *Opposite*: slowness 2 harshness, severity, unkindness, snappishness, terseness *Opposite*: gentleness 3 clarity, definition, distinctness, contrast, intensity *Opposite*: haziness 4 acidity, sourness, bitterness, tanginess, pungency *Opposite*: sweetness

sharp-sighted *adj* 1 eagle-eyed, with good eyesight, with good vision, with eyes like a hawk, hawk-eyed 2 observant, watchful, alert, vigilant, attentive *Opposite*: unobservant

sharp-tongued *adj* sarcastic, caustic, harsh, mean, brusque *Opposite*: gentle

sharp-witted *adj* quick, sharp, quick-witted, acute, bright

shatter *v* 1 smash, break, smash to smithereens, splinter, fragment 2 destroy, wreck, crush, blast, demolish *Opposite*: build up

shattered *adj* 1 devastated, crushed, traumatized, horrified, suffering 2 tired, exhausted, all in, spent, prostrate *Opposite*: lively

shattering *adj* devastating, crushing, shocking, earthshattering, cataclysmic *Opposite*: wonderful

shatterproof *adj* indestructible, unbreakable, nonbreaking, resistant, strengthened

shave *v* cut off, shear, cut, trim, clip

shaving *n* chip, splinter, flake, shred, sliver *Opposite*: chunk

shawl *n* wrap, stole, scarf, rebozo, cloak

sheaf *n* bundle, cluster, clump, wad, stack

shear *v* cut off, shave, clip, trim, crop

sheath *n* cover, case, casing, covering, scabbard

sheathe *v* 1 put away, replace, retract, stash (*infml*) *Opposite*: take out 2 envelop, swathe, cloak, wrap, drape

sheathing n **casing**, covering, outer layer, jacket, shield

shed v 1 **radiate**, emit, disperse, cast, project 2 **cast off**, slough off, get rid of, moult, lose

shed light on v **clarify**, explain, illuminate, elucidate, clear up

sheen n **shine**, polish, lustre, gloss, gleam

sheep n 1 **ewe**, ram, lamb 2 **conformist**, follower, traditionalist, lemming, yes man Opposite: individualist

sheepish adj **ashamed**, shamefaced, embarrassed, hangdog, guilty Opposite: unashamed

sheepishness n **shame**, embarrassment, guilt, awkwardness, self-consciousness

sheer adj 1 **pure**, complete, absolute, utter, unalloyed 2 **steep**, vertical, perpendicular, precipitous, abrupt Opposite: gentle 3 **fine**, transparent, translucent, thin, diaphanous Opposite: thick ■ adv **vertically**, straight up, plumb, precipitously, steeply

sheerness n **fineness**, thinness, translucence, transparency, gauziness Opposite: thickness

sheet n 1 **piece**, page, leaf, folio, slip 2 **expanse**, mass, area, layer

sheet down v **pour**, rain heavily, rain cats and dogs (infml), tip down (infml), chuck it down (infml)

sheik n **leader**, ruler, chief, chieftain, head

shelf n 1 **ledge**, sill, projection, bookshelf, mantelpiece 2 **layer**, ridge, step, ledge, rock shelf

shell n 1 **case**, casing, covering, shield, crust 2 **husk**, skeleton, carcass, remains 3 **bomb**, explosive, missile, mortar, projectile ■ v **bombard**, shoot at, fire at, open fire on, shoot down

shellfish n **crustacean**, mollusc, seafood

WORD BANK
❏ types of shellfish abalone, clam, cockle, crab, crayfish, langoustine, lobster, mussel, oyster, prawn, scallop, shrimp, whelk, winkle

shell out (infml) v **pay out**, pay up, pay, spend, give

shelter n 1 **protection**, cover, refuge, retreat, haven 2 **housing**, accommodation, living quarters, lodging, somewhere to stay ■ v 1 **protect**, shield, cover, defend, harbour 2 **take shelter**, take refuge, take cover, hide

sheltered adj 1 **protected**, privileged, comfortable, shielded, cosy Opposite: harsh 2 **secluded**, protected, shielded, isolated, insulated Opposite: exposed

shelve v **put on hold**, put on ice, defer, abandon, cancel

shenanigans (infml) n 1 **trickery**, mischief, trouble, carry-on (infml), to-do (infml) 2 **playfulness**, joking around, pranks, tricks, tomfoolery (infml)

shepherd v **marshal**, drive, guide, steer, pilot

sherd see **shard**

shield n **protection**, armour, defence, safeguard, buffer ■ v **protect**, guard, defend, shelter, safeguard Opposite: expose. See COMPARE AND CONTRAST at **safeguard**.

shielded adj **protected**, safeguarded, isolated, defended, sheltered Opposite: exposed

shift v 1 **move**, budge, vary, transfer, change 2 (infml) **remove**, get rid of, loosen, lift, clean 3 (infml) **hurry up**, get a move on (infml), buck up (infml dated), get moving, hurry Opposite: slow down ■ n 1 **move**, swing, modification, alteration, change 2 **stint**, spell, scheduled time, period, turn. See COMPARE AND CONTRAST at **change**.

shifting adj **unstable**, ever-changing, fluctuating, fluid, flowing Opposite: fixed

shiftless adj **lazy**, idle, good-for-nothing, indolent, slothful Opposite: industrious

shifty adj **suspicious**, suspect, dubious, dishonest, untrustworthy Opposite: trustworthy

shilly-shally v 1 **waver**, dilly-dally, dither, hesitate, vacillate Opposite: decide 2 **waste time**, hang around, hang about, dawdle, delay Opposite: forge ahead

shimmer v **sparkle**, glisten, shine, glitter, gleam

shimmering adj **iridescent**, sparkling, shining, gleaming, glistening

shindig (infml) n **party**, bash, jamboree, do (infml), get-together (infml)

shine v 1 **excel**, be good at, stand out, have a gift for, be skilled at Opposite: bomb (infml) 2 **glow**, gleam, glimmer, sparkle, glitter 3 **polish**, burnish, wax, buff, buff up ■ n **polish**, lustre, gloss, gleam

shining adj **outstanding**, excellent, admirable, brilliant, superb Opposite: poor

shiny adj **glossy**, gleaming, glittery, polished, shimmering Opposite: dull

ship n **vessel**, craft, boat ■ v **send**, transport, distribute, dispatch, convey

WORD BANK
❏ types of historical vessel clipper, flagship, galleon, galley, Indiaman, longboat, longship, man-of-war, tall ship, windjammer
❏ types of military vessel aircraft carrier, battle cruiser, battleship, cruiser, cutter, destroyer, frigate, gunboat, minesweeper, submarine, warship
❏ types of motor vessel barge, cabin cruiser, canal boat, coaster, container ship, cutter, dredger, factory ship, ferry, ferryboat, freighter, houseboat, hovercraft, hydrofoil, icebreaker, launch, lifeboat, lighter, lightship, motorboat, powerboat, speedboat, steamboat, steamer, tanker, trawler, tug
❏ types of sailing vessel barque, brig, brigantine, catamaran, catboat, dhow, felucca, junk, ketch, sailing boat, schooner, sloop, smack, trimaran, yacht
❏ types of small vessel canoe, dinghy, dory,

dugout, gondola, kayak, life raft, narrow boat, pedalo, pirogue, punt, raft, rowing boat, sampan, scull, skiff

❏ **parts of a sailing vessel** boom, bowsprit, gaff, gaffsail, jib, mainsail, mainstay, mast, mizzen, pennant, sheet, shroud, spanker, spinnaker, topsail

❏ **parts of a ship or boat** bilge, bow, bridge, cabin, capstan, crow's nest, deck, engine room, forecastle, galley, gunwale, helm, hold, hull, keel, outboard motor, outrigger, poop, prow, rowlock, rudder, stateroom, stern, superstructure, tiller

shipment *n* **consignment**, delivery, batch, load, cargo

shipping *n* **delivery**, transportation, distribution, carriage, freight

shipshape *adj* **in order**, neat, tidy, organized, spick-and-span *Opposite*: untidy

shirk *v* **evade**, avoid, dodge, duck, get out of *Opposite*: accept

shirker *n* **lazy person**, slacker, idler, loafer, malingerer *Opposite*: worker

shiver *v* **shake**, tremble, quiver, quake, shudder ■ *n* **quiver**, shudder, tremor, tremble, quake

shoal *n* **sandbar**, sandbank, ridge, shallows

shock *n* **1 surprise**, jolt, blow, bombshell, kick in the teeth **2 distress**, numbness, devastation, disbelief, astonishment ■ *v* **1 stun**, alarm, surprise, frighten, astonish *Opposite*: calm **2 traumatize**, upset, devastate, shake up, alarm *Opposite*: reassure **3 scandalize**, outrage, appal, offend, horrify

shocked *adj* **1 surprised**, stunned, dazed, upset, shaken *Opposite*: indifferent **2 scandalized**, outraged, appalled, offended *Opposite*: indifferent

shocking *adj* **1 outrageous**, scandalous, offensive, disgraceful, reprehensible *Opposite*: acceptable **2 distressing**, startling, upsetting, disturbing, worrying *Opposite*: comforting **3** *(infml)* **dreadful**, awful, bad, appalling, lamentable *Opposite*: pleasant

shockingly *adv* **1 outrageously**, scandalously, disgracefully, reprehensibly, unpardonably *Opposite*: acceptably **2 startlingly**, distressingly, upsettingly, disturbingly, worryingly *Opposite*: comfortingly **3 dreadfully**, awfully, appallingly, lamentably, horribly

shock wave *n* **1 repercussion**, reaction, shock, effect **2 tremor**, shudder, shock, trembling, agitation

shoddy *adj* **1 careless**, slapdash, inferior, cheap, substandard *Opposite*: fine **2 inconsiderate**, mean, unkind, dishonest, rotten *Opposite*: considerate

shoelace *n* **cord**, lace, bootlace, tie, fastener

shoo away *v* **chase off**, drive away, frighten away, scare off *Opposite*: invite

shoot *v* **1 fire**, let off, open fire, fire off, fire at **2 kill**, slaughter, shoot down, bring down, gun down *(infml)* **3 spurt**, squirt, burst, jet,

gush **4 film**, photograph, take, snap, capture **5 aim**, point, direct, cast, score **6 start to grow**, produce buds, develop, appear, sprout **7** *(infml)* **dart**, dash, run, race, speed ■ *n* **new growth**, branch, leaf bud, outgrowth, stem

shoot down *v* **1 kill**, slaughter, destroy, murder, bring down **2 attack**, tear to shreds, pick holes in, pillory, criticize

shooting *n* **1 gunfire**, shelling, bombardment, fire, firing **2 killing**, murder, assassination, execution, slaying

shoot up *v* **appear**, soar, rocket, spring up, mushroom *Opposite*: plummet

shop *n* **1 store**, outlet, showroom, emporium **2 spree**, shopping spree, shopping expedition, walk round the shops, binge **3 workshop**, plant, factory, garage, yard ■ *v* **go shopping**, buy groceries, go window-shopping, go on a spree, go to the shops

WORD BANK

❏ **types of food outlet** bakery, butcher's, chip shop, deli, delicatessen, drive-through, farmers' market, fishmonger's, greengrocer's, grocer's, grocery store, refreshment stand, supermarket, sweetshop, takeaway

❏ **types of retail outlet** bazaar, beauty salon, bookshop, boutique, chain store, charity shop, chemist, corner shop, covered market, department store, discount store, dispensary, duty-free, filling station, flea market, garden centre, hair salon, hairdresser's, hypermarket, kiosk, mall, mart, newsstand, nursery, petrol station, pharmacy, post office, saleroom, service station, superstore, warehouse

shopkeeper *n* **retailer**, seller, salesperson, merchant, trader

shoplift *v* **steal**, rob, pilfer, thieve, pocket

shoplifting *n* **stealing**, theft, thieving, pilfering, pinching *(infml)*

shopper *n* **customer**, consumer, buyer, purchaser, bargain hunter

shopping *n* **errands**, spending, shop, weekly shop, clothes shopping

shopping centre *n* **shopping precinct**, arcade, pedestrian precinct, shopping complex, mall *(US)*

shore *n* **coast**, beach, seashore, coastline, seaboard

shoreline *n* **beach**, shore, seashore, water's edge, coastline

shore up *v* **prop up**, support, hold up, buttress, bolster

shorn of *adj* **deprived of**, stripped of, minus, less, lacking

short *adj* **1 small**, little, petite, tiny, diminutive *Opposite*: tall **2 brief**, quick, rapid, fleeting, passing *Opposite*: lengthy **3 concise**, succinct, condensed, brief, to the point *Opposite*: long **4 curt**, brusque, snappy, abrupt, unfriendly *Opposite*: friendly ■ *adv* **midstream**, abruptly, suddenly, sharply *Oppo-*

site: gradually ■ *n (infml)* **drink**, tot, nip, measure, shot *(infml)*

shortage *n* **lack**, scarcity, deficiency, dearth, famine *Opposite*: excess. *See* COMPARE AND CONTRAST *at* lack.

short break *n* **break**, rest, holiday, weekend away, midweek break

shortcoming *n* **inadequacy**, failing, fault, deficiency, limitation *Opposite*: virtue

short course *n* **crash course**, intensive course, introductory course, refresher course

shorten *v* **cut down**, cut, cut back, curtail, abbreviate *Opposite*: lengthen

shortfall *n* **deficit**, loss, underperformance, gap, lack *Opposite*: excess

short form *n* **abbreviation**, shortening, contraction, acronym, ellipsis

short-handed *adj* **short-staffed**, understaffed, short

short-list *v* **select**, choose, pick out, cream off, narrow down

short-lived *adj* **brief**, fleeting, transitory, passing, short *Opposite*: long-lasting. *See* COMPARE AND CONTRAST *at* temporary.

shortly *adv* **1 soon**, before long, in a while, in a minute, in a moment *Opposite*: later **2 curtly**, brusquely, abruptly, briskly, tersely *Opposite*: pleasantly

shortness *n* **1 smallness**, tininess, squatness, dumpiness *Opposite*: tallness **2 quickness**, rapidity, speed, transience *Opposite*: length **3 briefness**, brevity, terseness, conciseness, concision *Opposite*: length **4 curtness**, brusqueness, abruptness, briskness, terseness *Opposite*: pleasantness

short of *prep* **apart from**, other than, without, bar *Opposite*: including

short-sighted *adj* **1 myopic**, nearsighted *(US)* *Opposite*: farsighted **2 ill-considered**, thoughtless, unthinking, imprudent, ill-advised *Opposite*: farsighted

short-sightedness *n* **thoughtlessness**, imprudence, rashness, hastiness *Opposite*: far-sightedness

short-staffed *adj* **short-handed**, understaffed, understrength

short story *n* **novella**, tale, story, fable, parable *Opposite*: epic

short-tempered *adj* **quick-tempered**, irritable, impatient, irascible, touchy

short-term *adj* **temporary**, immediate, instant, short-range, interim *Opposite*: long-term

shot *n* **1 gunshot**, potshot, round, volley, report **2 bullet**, cannonball, slug, gunshot, buckshot **3 picture**, photo, photograph, snapshot, snap **4 try**, go, attempt, turn, crack *(infml)* **5 injection**, jab *(infml)*, inoculation, vaccination **6** *(infml)* **measure**, drink, glass, tot, slug *(infml)*

shot in the arm *n* **boost**, fillip, spur, kick-start, stimulus

shot in the dark *n* **guess**, conjecture, speculation, potshot, attempt

should *v* **ought to**, had better, have a duty to, be duty-bound to, must

shoulder *v* **bear**, take on, accept, assume, carry *Opposite*: refuse

shout *v* **yell**, cry, scream, bellow, screech *Opposite*: whisper ■ *n* **cry**, yell, scream, bellow, screech *Opposite*: whisper

shout at *v* **yell at**, scold, reprimand, haul over the coals, berate *Opposite*: praise

shove *v* **1 push**, thrust, heave, propel, jostle *Opposite*: pull **2 put**, throw, toss, slap, sling ■ *n* **thrust**, push, heave, jolt

shovel *n* **spade**, scoop, trowel, tool ■ *v* **scoop**, move, dig, spoon, heap

show *v* **1 present**, display, exhibit, expose, disclose *Opposite*: hide **2 stand out**, stick out, show up, appear, surface **3 accompany**, take, guide, direct, point **4 prove**, illustrate, demonstrate, confirm, indicate *Opposite*: disprove **5 demonstrate**, illustrate, explain, teach, point out ■ *n* **1 demonstration**, display, expression, illustration, appearance **2 performance**, musical, cabaret, play, film **3 fair**, fête, exhibition, trade show, county show

show business *n* **the stage**, theatre, the boards, films, movies

showcase *n* **1 glass case**, cabinet, display case, display cabinet, vitrine **2 platform**, vehicle, setting, stage

showdown *n* **confrontation**, head-to-head, face-off, row, fight

shower *n* **1 wash**, dip, rinse, spray **2 cascade**, burst, deluge, hail, spray **3 cloudburst**, downpour, storm, rainstorm, flurry ■ *v* **1 wash**, clean up, freshen up, rinse **2 rain**, rain down, pour, pour down, spit **3 overwhelm**, inundate, flood, deluge, bombard

showery *adj* **rainy**, wet, changeable, damp, spitting *Opposite*: dry

showground *n* **arena**, ring, enclosure, field, ground

showing *n* **presentation**, performance, viewing, screening, display

showing off *n* **bravado**, boastfulness, boasting, bragging, posturing

show off *v* **1 boast**, brag, shoot your mouth off, sing your own praises, pose **2 display**, flaunt, parade, flourish, flash *(infml)* *Opposite*: hide

show-off *(infml)* *n* **boaster**, braggart, bragger, exhibitionist, know-all *(infml)*

showpiece *n* **centrepiece**, pride and joy, focus, attraction, pièce de résistance

showroom *n* **shop**, outlet, store

show up *v* **1** *(infml)* **come**, turn up, arrive, put in an appearance, appear **2 highlight**, emphasize, point up, bring to light, reveal *Opposite*: hide **3 stand out**, stick out, show, catch your eye, come to light **4 embarrass**, humiliate, put somebody to shame, mortify, shame

showy *adj* **1 impressive**, attractive, eye-catching, splendid, magnificent *Opposite*: modest **2 ostentatious**, flashy, gaudy, garish, tasteless *Opposite*: restrained

show your face *v* **turn up**, appear, put in an appearance, come, arrive *Opposite*: hide

shred *n* **scrap**, strip, bit, piece, sliver *Opposite*: whole ■ *v* **slice**, cut up, tear up, rip up, grate

shrewd *adj* **astute**, sharp, smart, perceptive, discerning *Opposite*: naive

shrewdness *n* **astuteness**, sharpness, smartness, perceptiveness, discernment *Opposite*: naivety

shriek *n* **screech**, scream, yell, cry, yelp *Opposite*: whisper

shrill *adj* **piercing**, high-pitched, strident, penetrating, harsh *Opposite*: low

shrine *n* **memorial**, monument, tomb, grave, sanctuary

shrink *v* **1 contract**, shrivel, wither, telescope, shorten *Opposite*: grow **2 fall**, drop, decrease, decline, diminish *Opposite*: rise **3 cower**, cringe, flinch, recoil, draw back *Opposite*: stand your ground. *See* COMPARE AND CONTRAST *at* recoil.

shrinkage *n* **reduction**, decrease, decline, contraction, fall *Opposite*: growth

shrink back *v* **recoil**, cringe, shrink away, shy away, flinch *Opposite*: advance

shrink from *v* **recoil from**, baulk at, avoid, shirk, shun *Opposite*: welcome

shrivel *v* **shrink**, wither, dry up, contract, curl up *Opposite*: expand

shroud *n* **covering**, cover, blanket, layer, cloak

shrub *n* **bush**, plant, tree, flowering shrub

> **WORD BANK**
> ❏ **types of shrub or bush** azalea, bramble, briar, broom, camellia, elder, forsythia, gardenia, gorse, hawthorn, heather, hydrangea, laurel, lavender, lilac, magnolia, privet, pussy willow, rhododendron, rose, sagebrush, witch hazel

shrubbery *n* **bushes**, undergrowth, border, herbaceous border, hedging

shrug off *v* **dismiss**, pooh-pooh, ignore, treat lightly, make light of

shrunken *adj* **wasted**, emaciated, dried up, withered, shrivelled *Opposite*: bloated

shudder *v* **shake**, tremble, shiver, wince, quake ■ *n* **tremble**, shake, shiver, tremor, judder

shuffle *v* **1 scuffle**, hobble, trundle, shamble, lumber **2 mix up**, jumble up, muddle up, rearrange, reorder

shun *v* **avoid**, turn away from, spurn, reject, eschew *Opposite*: court

shunt *v* **1 push**, shove, move, shift, propel **2** (*infml*) **hit**, collide with, smash into, bump into ■ *n* **1** (*infml*) **collision**, crash, smash, accident, prang (*infml*) **2 shove**, thrust, jolt, push

shush (*infml*) *v* **silence**, hush, quieten, quieten down, shut up (*infml*)

shut *v* **1 close**, close up, push to, fasten, secure *Opposite*: open **2 close down**, close, close up shop, shut down, go out of business *Opposite*: start up

shutdown *n* **closure**, cessation, stoppage, halt, end

shut off *v* **1 switch off**, turn off, close off, close down, shut down *Opposite*: turn on **2 isolate**, cut off, separate, seclude, set apart

shut out *v* **lock out**, keep out, exclude, keep off, debar *Opposite*: let in

shuttle *v* **go back and forth**, travel between, ply between, commute, ferry

shut up *v* **1** (*infml*) **be quiet**, fall silent, quieten down, clam up (*infml*), pipe down (*infml*) **2 confine**, imprison, cage, shut in, lock in *Opposite*: let loose **3** (*infml*) **silence**, hush, gag, muzzle, cut off **4 close**, close up, lock, lock up, secure *Opposite*: open up

shut up shop *v* **1 stop**, call it a day, turn in, close, shut *Opposite*: start up **2 close down**, shut down, go out of business, go bankrupt, go to the wall *Opposite*: start up

shy *adj* **1 introverted**, retiring, withdrawn, timid, bashful *Opposite*: outgoing **2 cautious**, wary, nervous, afraid, fearful *Opposite*: confident

shy away *v* **retreat**, shrink, recoil, flinch, back off

shyness *n* **introversion**, timidity, bashfulness, inhibition, reticence *Opposite*: boldness

sick *adj* **1 ill**, unwell, bad, under the weather, off-colour *Opposite*: well **2 nauseous**, queasy, bilious, dizzy, green around the gills (*infml*) **3 bored**, up to here, sick to death, sick to the back teeth, sick and tired (*infml*) **4** (*infml*) **tasteless**, in bad taste, gruesome, bizarre, sickening ■ *n* (*infml*) **vomit**, spew, puke (*infml*), chunder (*infml*), bile (*literary*)

sickbay *n* **infirmary**, sanatorium, sickroom, hospital

sicken *v* **nauseate**, turn your stomach, repel, disgust, make sick

sickening *adj* **1 disgusting**, nauseating, stomach-churning, shocking, appalling *Opposite*: appealing **2** (*infml*) **annoying**, maddening, irritating, infuriating, disappointing *Opposite*: pleasing

sickly *adj* **1 unhealthy**, weak, ill, unwell, pale *Opposite*: healthy **2 cloying**, overpowering, disgusting, suffocating, nauseating *Opposite*: appealing **3 saccharine**, sentimental, cloying, sickly-sweet, mawkish *Opposite*: tough

sickly-sweet *adj* **saccharine**, cloying, mawkish, sentimental, nauseating

sickness *n* **1 illness**, disease, virus, condition, bad health *Opposite*: health **2 nausea**, vomiting, queasiness, biliousness, throwing up (*infml*)

sick up (infml) v **vomit**, spew, throw up (infml), puke (slang), hurl (slang)

side n 1 **surface**, face, elevation, wall, plane 2 **part**, area, region, section, segment 3 **edge**, boundary, flank, bank, periphery 4 **aspect**, facet, feature, quality, characteristic 5 **team**, squad, line-up, group, gang

side effect n **unexpected result**, secondary effect, by-product, consequence, knock-on effect

sidekick (infml) n **assistant**, helper, associate, subordinate, partner Opposite: boss

sideline n **hobby**, pastime, offshoot, secondary activity, second job Opposite: career ■ v 1 **put aside**, shelve, put off, slow pedal, put on the back burner Opposite: promote 2 **relegate**, demote, exclude, downgrade, lay off Opposite: promote

sidelong adj **sideways**, oblique, slanting, indirect, askew Opposite: direct

sidesplitting adj **hilarious**, riotous, uproarious, rollicking, funny Opposite: dull

sidestep v **avoid**, evade, dodge, duck, bypass

side street n **alley**, back street, lane, side road

sidetrack v **distract**, deflect, divert, change the subject, get off the point

side view n **cross section**, profile, section, side, aspect

sideways adj **oblique**, slanting, indirect, sidelong, slanted Opposite: straight ■ adv **to one side**, to the left, to the right, askew, askance Opposite: straight

side with v **back**, support, take somebody's side, be in somebody's camp, take somebody's part Opposite: oppose

sidle v **edge**, creep, slither, snake, inch

siege n **blockade**, cordon, barrier, barricade, obstruction

siesta n **rest**, nap, sleep, catnap, snooze (infml)

sift v 1 **sieve**, filter, separate, put through a sieve, strain 2 **sort through**, go through, go through with a fine-tooth comb, examine, select

sigh v 1 **exhale**, heave a sigh, moan, groan, breathe Opposite: inhale 2 **yearn**, long, hanker, pine, want Opposite: dislike ■ n **exhalation**, moan, groan, complaint, lament

sight n 1 **vision**, eyesight, ability to see 2 **view**, spectacle, prospect, picture, scene ■ v **notice**, catch sight of, spot, see, glimpse Opposite: miss

sighted adj **seeing**, keen-sighted, partially sighted, long-sighted, eagle-eyed Opposite: blind

sights n **tourist attractions**, places of interest, highlights, wonders, marvels

sightseeing n **tourism**, visiting the attractions, going to places of interest, seeing the sights, exploration

sightseer n **tourist**, visitor, holidaymaker, day tripper, tripper (infml) Opposite: resident

sign n 1 **symbol**, mark, emblem, insignia, logo 2 **signal**, indication, symptom, warning, clue 3 **notice**, poster, road sign, hoarding, placard 4 **trace**, track, trail, footprint, mark 5 **omen**, warning, portent, premonition, indication ■ v 1 **autograph**, sign your name, initial, authorize, endorse 2 **employ**, contract, hire, engage, take on Opposite: dismiss 3 **make signs**, signal, gesture, motion, indicate

signal n **sign**, indication, gesture, indicator, motion ■ v 1 **communicate**, indicate, suggest, intimate, hint 2 **gesture**, gesticulate, motion, sign, beckon 3 **indicate**, mark, herald, portend, announce

signally adv **completely**, notably, totally, absolutely, one hundred per cent

signatory n **party**, participant, guarantor, the undersigned, cosignatory

signature n **name**, autograph, cross, mark, initials

signboard n **sign**, signpost, notice, hoarding, road sign

significance n 1 **importance**, impact, substance, weight, magnitude Opposite: meaninglessness 2 **meaning**, implication, import, worth, connotation

significant adj 1 **meaningful**, knowing, meaning, suggestive, expressive Opposite: blank 2 **important**, major, noteworthy, momentous, substantial Opposite: insignificant 3 **considerable**, large, major, big, sizable Opposite: paltry

significantly adv 1 **considerably**, appreciably, drastically, notably, radically 2 **meaningfully**, knowingly, suggestively, pointedly, expressively Opposite: innocently

significant other n **partner**, lover, spouse, other half, better half

signification n **meaning**, sense, gist, signification, denotation

signify v **mean**, indicate, show, imply, suggest

signing n 1 **ratification**, validation, adoption, passing, authorization Opposite: rejection 2 **new employee**, new player, new arrival, recruit, acquisition

sign on v **enlist**, sign up, enrol, put your name down, register

signpost n 1 **signboard**, sign, notice, marker, road sign 2 **indication**, suggestion, pointer, marker, sign ■ v **flag**, mark, indicate, label, designate Opposite: conceal

sign up v 1 **recruit**, employ, sign, take somebody on, contract Opposite: fire 2 **enlist**, join, enrol, become a member, put your name down Opposite: quit

silage n **fodder**, feed, grass, forage

silence n 1 **quietness**, quiet, hush, stillness, peace Opposite: noise 2 **muteness**, taciturnity, reticence, reserve, uncommunicativeness Opposite: chatter ■ v 1 **make quiet**, quieten, hush, muzzle, shut up (infml)

2 stop, put an end to, gag, stifle, suppress *Opposite*: encourage

silent *adj* **1 still**, hushed, soundless, noiseless, quiet *Opposite*: noisy **2 mute**, tongue-tied, uncommunicative, taciturn, reticent *Opposite*: talkative **3 unspoken**, unvoiced, voiceless, tacit, wordless *Opposite*: spoken

COMPARE AND CONTRAST CORE MEANING: not speaking or not saying much

silent not speaking or communicating at any particular time, especially through choice, or not inclined to speak much; **quiet** not inclined to speak much, often because of shyness; **reticent** unwilling to communicate very much, talk freely, or reveal all the facts; **taciturn** habitually reserved in speech and manner; **uncommunicative** not willing to say much, especially not to reveal information, or tending not to say much.

silhouette *n* **outline**, shape, shadow, profile, line

silken *adj* **smooth**, soft, silky, silky-smooth, glossy *Opposite*: coarse

silky *adj* **1 glossy**, smooth, soft, silken, silky-smooth *Opposite*: rough **2 smooth**, honeyed, mellifluous, sweet, unctuous *Opposite*: harsh

sill *n* **ledge**, shelf, ridge, projection, windowsill

silliness *n* **1 stupidity**, ridiculousness, childishness, madness, idiocy *Opposite*: sense **2 triviality**, meaninglessness, mindlessness, puerility, inanity *Opposite*: importance

silly *adj* **1 stupid**, ridiculous, impractical, childish, asinine *Opposite*: sensible **2 trivial**, meaningless, mindless, puerile, senseless *Opposite*: important

silt *n* **deposit**, mud, sediment, sludge, residue

silver-tongued *adj* **eloquent**, smooth-talking, grandiloquent, fluent, flattering *Opposite*: tongue-tied

silvery *adj* **silver**, grey, hoary, shiny

similar *adj* **alike**, like, comparable, parallel, analogous *Opposite*: dissimilar

similarity *n* **resemblance**, comparison, likeness, parallel, correspondence *Opposite*: difference

similarly *adv* **1 alike**, in the same way, comparably, analogously, relatedly *Opposite*: differently **2 likewise**, also, in the same way, correspondingly, equally *Opposite*: on the contrary

similitude *(fml) n* **similarity**, resemblance, likeness, sameness, semblance *Opposite*: difference

simmer *v* **1 boil**, bubble, cook **2 seethe**, rumble, bubble, boil, fester

simmer down *v* **cool down**, calm down, settle down, regain your self-control, compose yourself *Opposite*: blow your top *(infml)*

simper *v* **smirk**, grimace, sneer, look smug, look coy *Opposite*: frown ▪ *n* **grimace**, smirk,

sneer, smug look, coy look *Opposite*: frown

simple *adj* **1 easy**, straightforward, uncomplicated, trouble-free, effortless *Opposite*: difficult **2 plain**, minimal, unadorned, unfussy, down-to-earth *Opposite*: fancy **3 humble**, modest, unassuming, unpretentious, meek *Opposite*: pretentious **4 guileless**, ingenuous, naive, unsophisticated, green *Opposite*: sophisticated

simple-minded *adj* **1 simplistic**, crude, basic, one-dimensional, unsophisticated *Opposite*: subtle **2 naive**, childlike, unsophisticated, artless, guileless *Opposite*: sophisticated

simplicity *n* **1 ease**, straightforwardness, effortlessness, easiness, lack of complication *Opposite*: difficulty **2 plainness**, minimalism, cleanness, lack of adornment, austerity **3 humility**, modesty, unpretentiousness, meekness, unassumingness *Opposite*: pride **4 guilelessness**, naivety, ingenuousness, lack of sophistication, artlessness *Opposite*: sophistication

simplified *adj* **cut down**, basic, easy, abridged, shortened *Opposite*: complex

simplify *v* **make simpler**, make easier, make straightforward, abridge, shorten *Opposite*: complicate

simplistic *adj* **naive**, unsophisticated, crude, basic, one-dimensional *Opposite*: sophisticated

simply *adv* **1 just**, only, merely, purely, basically **2 easily**, straightforwardly, in basic terms, in simple terms, in words of one syllable *Opposite*: elaborately **3 plainly**, minimally, cleanly, austerely, unpretentiously *Opposite*: elaborately **4 frankly**, absolutely, obviously, undeniably, unquestionably **5 modestly**, humbly, unassumingly, meekly, unpretentiously *Opposite*: proudly **6 naively**, guilelessly, ingenuously, candidly, innocently *Opposite*: knowingly

simulate *v* **1 replicate**, reproduce, imitate, suggest, copy **2 fake**, pretend, feign, put on, sham **3 mimic**, ape, copy, imitate, parrot

simulated *adj* **1 virtual**, cyber-, computer-generated **2 fake**, imitation, pretend, counterfeit, sham *Opposite*: genuine

simulation *n* **imitation**, reproduction, replication, recreation, mock-up

simulator *n* **simulant**, emulator, trainer

simultaneous *adj* **concurrent**, immediate, instantaneous, real-time, synchronized *Opposite*: separate

sin *n* **1 crime**, misdemeanour, transgression, misdeed, wrongdoing *Opposite*: good deed **2 wickedness**, iniquity, depravity, immorality, debauchery *Opposite*: goodness ▪ *v* **transgress**, do wrong, commit a crime, lapse, be led astray

since *conj* **as**, because, given that, seeing as, in view of the fact that ▪ *adv* **meanwhile**, in the meantime, subsequently, later, then

sincere adj **1 honest**, open, frank, natural, straight Opposite: disingenuous **2 heartfelt**, genuine, real, true, truthful Opposite: insincere

sincerity n **genuineness**, honesty, earnestness, naturalness, unaffectedness Opposite: insincerity

sinecure n **easy ride**, plum job, soft option, cushy job (infml), cushy number (infml)

sine qua non n **prerequisite**, essential condition, precondition, requirement, necessity

sinewy adj **wiry**, lean, strong, muscly, brawny Opposite: frail

sinful adj **wicked**, bad, evil, corrupt, errant Opposite: virtuous

sing v **1 croon**, chant, hum, warble, carol **2 resonate**, buzz, hum, purr, vibrate

singe v **scorch**, burn, char, sear

singer n **vocalist**, songster, lead singer, soloist, chorister

singing n **vocals**, songs, vocal music, chanting, warbling ■ adj **vocal**, choral, melodic, whistling, humming Opposite: instrumental

single adj **1 solitary**, on its own, lone, sole, solo **2 particular**, distinct, separate, specific, definite Opposite: general **3 unmarried**, unattached, lone, free Opposite: attached ■ n **record**, song, track, release

single-handed adj **unassisted**, unaided, lone, solo, unaccompanied Opposite: assisted ■ adv **by yourself**, on your own, alone, without help, without assistance

single-minded adj **focused**, dedicated, resolute, dogged, driven Opposite: unfocused

single-mindedness n **sense of purpose**, concentration, application, attention, focus Opposite: aimlessness

single out v **pick out**, choose, select, identify, pull out

singly adv **individually**, alone, one by one, one at a time, piecemeal Opposite: together

sing out v **call out**, pipe up, speak up, speak out, shout

sing the praises of v **eulogize**, acclaim, praise, lionize, extol Opposite: criticize

singular adj **remarkable**, extraordinary, particular, outstanding, curious

singularity n **distinctiveness**, individuality, originality, uniqueness, peculiarity

sing your own praises v **boast**, swagger, swank, try to make an impression, brag

sinister adj **menacing**, ominous, threatening, evil, disturbing

sink v **1 go under**, go down, go under the surface, be submerged, go downwards Opposite: float **2 fall**, descend, drop, decline, go down Opposite: rise **3 dig**, drill, mine, bore ■ n **basin**, bowl, hand basin, washbasin

sink in v **go in**, enter, penetrate, diffuse, permeate

sinuous adj **lithe**, supple, twisting, winding, graceful

sip v **taste**, drink, swallow, sup Opposite: gulp ■ n **drink**, swallow, taste, drop, mouthful

siphon v **draw off**, tap, drain off

siren n **alarm**, alert, warning, alarm bell, danger signal

sister n **1 nun**, holy sister, religious, vestal (literary) **2 friend**, supporter, ally, associate ■ adj **fellow**, parallel, associated, corresponding, equivalent

sit v **1 be seated**, sit down, take a seat, take the weight off your feet, take a pew Opposite: stand **2 assemble**, meet, convene, be in session Opposite: disperse **3 be placed**, be positioned, lie, rest, be on top of

sit around v **kill time**, do nothing, lounge around, hang about, hang around

sit down v **be seated**, take a seat, take the weight off your feet, park yourself, take a pew Opposite: stand up

sit-down (infml) n **rest**, break, respite, breather (infml)

site n **place**, location, spot, position ■ v **put**, position, place, situate, locate

sit-in n **protest**, demonstration, rally, vigil, demo (infml)

sitting n **session**, meeting, hearing

situate v **place**, set, put, locate, position

situated (fml) adj **located**, positioned, set, placed, sited

situation n **1 state of affairs**, circumstances, state, condition, status quo **2 location**, position, site, place, setting **3** (fml) **job**, post, position

sixth sense n **intuition**, feeling, hunch, ESP

sizable adj **substantial**, generous, good-sized, ample, large Opposite: small

size n **dimension**, mass, bulk, amount, extent

sizeable see sizable

size up v **assess**, look somebody up and down, take stock of, evaluate, appraise

sizzle v **crackle**, spit, hiss, sputter

sizzling (infml) adj **boiling**, red-hot, baking, blistering, sweltering Opposite: freezing

skate over (infml) v **skim over**, dismiss, pass over, skirt around, fail to deal with Opposite: dwell on

skein n **hank**, ball, bundle, length, coil

skeletal adj **thin**, emaciated, skinny, gaunt, wasted Opposite: obese

skeleton n **1 frame**, bones, carcass **2 plan**, outline, framework, sketch, bare bones (infml) ■ adj **minimum**, basic, essential, minimal Opposite: full

sketch n **draft**, plan, drawing, rough copy, rough ■ v **draw**, outline, draft, delineate, block in

sketchy adj **vague**, unclear, hazy, imprecise, woolly Opposite: detailed

skew v 1 tilt, slant, twist, angle, slope *Opposite*: straighten 2 **distort**, bias, slant, twist, spin

skewed adj 1 tilted, slanted, twisted, crooked, askew *Opposite*: straight 2 **distorted**, biased, slanted, prejudiced, partial *Opposite*: objective

skewer n spit, brochette, spike, spear, needle ■ v impale, spear, spike, pierce, stab

skewwhiff (infml) adj crooked, lopsided, tilted, cockeyed, slanted *Opposite*: straight

skid v slip, slide, slew, slither, spin out

skilful adj clever, adroit, dexterous, skilled, expert *Opposite*: incompetent

skill n ability, talent, cleverness, dexterity, expertise. *See* COMPARE AND CONTRAST *at* ability.

skilled adj accomplished, expert, capable, able, trained *Opposite*: untrained

skim v 1 glide, fly, float, soar 2 scan, speedread, browse, glance at, flick through *Opposite*: peruse

skim off v cull, cream off, hive off, handpick, choose

skimp v stint, withhold, hold back on, be sparing with, pinch *Opposite*: lavish

skimpy adj meagre, insufficient, scanty, inadequate, sparse *Opposite*: generous

skin n 1 hide, pelt, fur, coat 2 casing, covering, membrane, crust, coating ■ v 1 peel, pare, excoriate, desquamate 2 graze, scrape, flay, scuff

skin-deep adj superficial, on the surface, on the outside, shallow, artificial

skinflint n miser, pinchpenny, cheapskate (infml), penny pincher (infml), scrooge (infml)

skinniness n gauntness, scrawniness, thinness, boniness, leanness *Opposite*: plumpness

skinny adj thin, lean, undernourished, emaciated, scrawny *Opposite*: fat. *See* COMPARE AND CONTRAST *at* thin.

skin tone n skin colour, complexion, skin, facial appearance, flesh colour

skip v 1 hop, bounce, prance, gambol, caper 2 omit, leave out, miss out, miss, pass over 3 (infml) avoid, miss, cut (infml), bunk off (infml) *Opposite*: attend

skip off (infml) v run away, make a sharp exit, do a runner, do a moonlight flit, duck out *Opposite*: stay put

skipper (infml) n captain, boss, chief, head, person in charge

skirmish n battle, fight, engagement, scuffle, clash ■ v clash, fight, scuffle, tussle, scrap. *See* COMPARE AND CONTRAST *at* fight.

skirt v 1 border, edge, adjoin, abut, neighbour 2 go around, avoid, evade, bypass, edge past 3 skim over, pass over, avoid, evade, bypass *Opposite*: tackle

WORD BANK
❏ **types of skirt** dirndl, hobble skirt, kilt, maxi skirt, miniskirt, pencil skirt, sarong, tutu, wraparound

skit n parody, satire, spoof, sketch, burlesque

skittish adj 1 wary, jumpy, edgy, nervous, uneasy 2 playful, lively, frisky, excited, restless

skiver (infml) n shirker, layabout, lazybones (infml), idler, freeloader (infml) *Opposite*: gogetter (infml)

skulduggery n trickery, tricks, dishonesty, cheating, mischief *Opposite*: honesty

skulk v lurk, loiter, creep, prowl, lie in wait

skull (infml) n mind, brain, head, noggin, noddle (dated infml)

sky n heaven, blue, atmosphere, firmament (literary)

sky-high adj excessive, very high, elevated, exorbitant, over-the-top

skyjack v hijack, seize, take over, take control of, capture

skyline n horizon, distance, prospect, vista

skyrocket (infml) v rise steeply, go through the ceiling, climb sharply, shoot up, hit the roof (infml) *Opposite*: plummet

skyscraper n multistorey building, tower, highrise building

skyward adv heavenward, upward, up, above, aloft ■ adj upward, heavenward, aloft

skywards *see* skyward

slab n lump, chunk, block, hunk, piece

slack adj 1 loose, limp, relaxed, baggy, floppy *Opposite*: taut 2 careless, inattentive, idle, inefficient, unprofessional *Opposite*: diligent 3 slow-moving, slow, dull, quiet, sluggish *Opposite*: brisk

slacken v loosen, relax, release, slacken off *Opposite*: tighten

slacker n idler, loafer, shirker, lazybones (infml), skiver (infml)

slackness n 1 looseness, limpness, bagginess, floppiness, droopiness *Opposite*: tautness 2 carelessness, negligence, laxity, inattention, laziness *Opposite*: meticulousness

slake v quench, satisfy, satiate, sate, extinguish *Opposite*: exacerbate

slam (infml) v criticize, berate, disparage, deride, slate (infml) *Opposite*: praise

slander n 1 defamation, character assassination, disparagement, vilification, calumny (fml) 2 slur, smear, slight, insult, libel ■ v insult, malign, slur, smear, disparage *Opposite*: compliment. *See* COMPARE AND CONTRAST *at* malign.

slanderous adj libellous, defamatory, insulting, malicious, disparaging

slang n jargon, vernacular, colloquial speech, dialect, argot

slanging match *n* **argument**, shouting match, spat, quarrel, row

slant *v* **incline**, lean, skew, slope, tilt ■ *n* **1 angle**, incline, diagonal, pitch, gradient **2 viewpoint**, angle, attitude, point of view, perspective

slanted *adj* **biased**, prejudiced, one-sided, partial, unfair *Opposite*: balanced

slanting *adj* **angled**, at an angle, sloping, on a slope, oblique *Opposite*: level

slantways *adv* **diagonally**, crossways, crosswise, at an angle, obliquely *Opposite*: straight

slantwise *see* **slantways**

slap *n* **smack**, blow, spank, cuff, clout ■ *v* **hit**, smack, spank, cuff, swipe

slapdash *adj* **careless**, messy, clumsy, hasty, hurried *Opposite*: meticulous

slaphappy *adj* **slapdash**, careless, haphazard, hit-and-miss, irresponsible *Opposite*: meticulous

slapstick *n* **knockabout**, farce, clowning, burlesque, comedy

slash *v* **1 cut**, hack, slice, gash, slit **2 reduce**, cut, lower, drop, decrease *Opposite*: increase ■ *n* **laceration**, gash, slit, tear, rip

slat *n* **plank**, board, lath

slate *(infml)* *v* **criticize**, censure, disparage, pan *(infml)*, find fault with

slaughter *v* **kill**, murder, massacre, butcher, slay *(fml or literary)* ■ *n* **killing**, murder, massacre, carnage, butchery. *See* COMPARE AND CONTRAST *at* **kill**.

slaver *v* **drool**, slobber, dribble, salivate

slay *(fml or literary)* *v* **kill**, murder, assassinate, massacre, eliminate

sleaze *n* **corruption**, dishonesty, malpractice, scandal, foul play *Opposite*: probity

sleazy *adj* **1 seedy**, sordid, squalid, grubby, grotty **2 corrupt**, immoral, dishonest, shady, slimy *Opposite*: honest

sleek *adj* **smooth**, shiny, glossy, silky, lustrous

sleep *n* **slumber**, nap, doze, siesta, catnap ■ *v* **be asleep**, slumber, be dead to the world, nap, doze

sleepily *adv* **drowsily**, dozily, woozily, wearily, blearily *Opposite*: alertly

sleep in *v* **oversleep**, sleep late, stay in bed, snooze on, ignore the alarm

sleepiness *n* **drowsiness**, tiredness, lethargy, somnolence, lassitude *Opposite*: alertness

sleepless *adj* **1 wakeful**, restless, disturbed, unsleeping, awake **2 alert**, active, vigilant, attentive, ready

sleeplessness *n* **1 insomnia**, wakefulness, restlessness **2 alertness**, vigilance, readiness, liveliness

sleepy *adj* **1 drowsy**, tired, lethargic, heavy-eyed, sluggish *Opposite*: alert **2 quiet**, dull, slow, inactive, peaceful *Opposite*: lively

sleet *n* **slush**, snow, frozen rain

sleeve *n* **cover**, jacket, protective cover, envelope, dust jacket

sleight of hand *n* **dexterity**, skill, adroitness, cunning, trickery

slender *adj* **1 slim**, slight, lean, trim, thin *Opposite*: fat **2 small**, slim, meagre, slight, little *Opposite*: considerable. *See* COMPARE AND CONTRAST *at* **thin**.

slenderness *n* **thinness**, slimness, skinniness, fineness, narrowness *Opposite*: stoutness

sleuth *v* **1 investigate**, look for clues, spy, look into things, check things out **2 track**, tail, follow, pursue, stalk ■ *n* *(infml)* **detective**, private detective, Sherlock Holmes, investigator, private eye *(infml)*

slew *v* **veer**, swing, slide, skid, swerve

slice *n* **1 piece**, sliver, wedge, portion, segment **2 share**, cut, portion, part, percentage ■ *v* **cut**, share, carve, divide, cut up

slick *adj* **1 polished**, professional, efficient, glossy, smooth **2 glib**, shoddy, superficial, untrustworthy, shallow, facile **3 slippery**, smooth, glossy, shiny, glassy

slide *v* **1 glide**, slither, slip, skim, skate **2 go down**, fall, decrease, diminish, drop *Opposite*: rise

slight *adj* **1 small**, minor, unimportant, trivial, insignificant *Opposite*: considerable **2 slim**, delicate, thin, feeble, slender *Opposite*: stocky ■ *n* **snub**, insult, slur, smear, rebuff ■ *v* **insult**, offend, snub, scorn, affront

slightly *adv* **somewhat**, to some extent, a little, a touch, marginally *Opposite*: considerably

slim *adj* **1 thin**, trim, slender, slight, lean *Opposite*: fat **2 faint**, slim, remote, poor, slight *Opposite*: considerable ■ *v* **diet**, go on a diet, lose weight, watch your weight, reduce *(US)*. *See* COMPARE AND CONTRAST *at* **thin**.

slim down *v* **reduce**, streamline, rationalize, cut, cut back *Opposite*: expand

slime *n* **paste**, mucus, gunge *(infml)*, goo *(infml)*, gunk *(infml)*

slimming *adj* **1 low-fat**, light, diet, low-calorie, healthy *Opposite*: fattening **2 flattering**, becoming, thinning *Opposite*: unflattering

slimness *n* **1 narrowness**, fineness, slightness, thinness, flatness *Opposite*: bulkiness **2 slenderness**, leanness, svelteness, trimness, thinness *Opposite*: plumpness

slimy *adj* **1 greasy**, oily, slippery, slick **2 smarmy**, oily, grovelling, sycophantic, unctuous

sling *v* **1 throw**, toss, lob, fling, hurl **2 hang**, suspend, dangle, drape, hook up

slink *v* **creep**, sneak, tiptoe, steal, skulk

slip *v* **1 trip**, fall, lose your balance, lose your footing, tumble **2 slide**, glide, slither, skid, skate **3 sneak**, steal, creep, flit, slink ■ *n* **blunder**, mistake, error, omission, gaffe. *See* COMPARE AND CONTRAST *at* **mistake**.

slip back v **revert**, relapse, lapse, slide back, return

slippery adj 1 **greasy**, oily, slick, icy, slimy Opposite: dry 2 **sneaky**, shifty, crafty, devious, dishonest Opposite: trustworthy

slipshod adj **careless**, shoddy, slapdash, slack, sloppy (infml) Opposite: thorough

slip up (infml) v **make a mistake**, go wrong, get it wrong, blunder, trip up

slip-up (infml) n **blunder**, slip, mistake, error, omission

slit v **cut**, slash, gash, nick, tear ■ n **opening**, cut, slash, gash, slot. See COMPARE AND CONTRAST at **tear**.

slither v **slide**, glide, slink, slip, skid

sliver n **slice**, shaving, splinter, flake, shard

slobber v **drool**, dribble, salivate, slaver

slog v 1 **plod**, trudge, tramp, trek, hike 2 **work**, labour, toil, grind, struggle ■ n 1 **trek**, hike, tramp, trail, marathon 2 **drag**, effort, strain, grind, struggle

slogan n **motto**, saying, jingle, catch phrase, watchword

slop v **spill**, slosh, splatter, splash, swill

slope n **gradient**, incline, hill, rise, angle ■ v **incline**, slant, tilt, lean, rise

slope off (infml) v **slink**, creep, sneak, skulk, steal away

sloppy adj 1 **messy**, untidy, disordered, chaotic, slovenly Opposite: tidy 2 (infml) **slack**, shoddy, careless, poor, slipshod Opposite: meticulous 3 (infml) **sentimental**, slushy, romantic, corny, gushing

slosh v **spill**, slop, splatter, splash, swill

slot n 1 **slit**, hole, opening, niche, space 2 **time**, window, opening, space, period ■ v **position**, locate, fit, insert, slip

sloth n **laziness**, idleness, indolence, apathy, sluggishness Opposite: liveliness

slothful adj **lazy**, idle, sluggish, inactive, indolent Opposite: energetic

slothfulness see **sloth**

slot in v **fit in**, squeeze in, accommodate, accept, see

slouch v **slump**, droop, stoop, sprawl, lounge ■ n (infml) **idler**, loafer, slacker, shirker, freeloader (infml)

slovenly adj **careless**, dishevelled, untidy, messy, unkempt

slow adj 1 **sluggish**, unhurried, measured, deliberate, dawdling Opposite: fast 2 **time-consuming**, drawn-out, protracted, lengthy, lingering Opposite: quick ■ v **slow down**, decelerate, brake, reduce, slacken

slow down v 1 **decelerate**, slow up, slow, brake, reduce speed Opposite: speed up 2 **hold up**, hold back, delay, slow, retard Opposite: speed up

slowly adv **gradually**, unhurriedly, bit by bit, little by little, at a snail's pace Opposite: quickly

slowness n **leisureliness**, sluggishness, deliberateness, gradualness Opposite: fastness

slow up v 1 **hold up**, hold back, delay, slow, retard Opposite: speed up 2 **decelerate**, slow down, slow, brake, reduce speed

sludge n **mud**, slush, mire, muck, slop

slug n 1 **bullet**, shot, shell, cartridge, pellet 2 (infml) **shot**, gulp, swallow, mouthful, glassful Opposite: sip 3 **blow**, hit, thump, punch, whack ■ v 1 (infml) **swallow**, gulp, down, drink, swill Opposite: sip 2 **hit**, thump, strike, punch, whack

sluggish adj **inactive**, lethargic, slow, listless, slothful Opposite: energetic

sluggishness n **lethargy**, slowness, listlessness, sloth, laziness Opposite: alertness

sluice n **channel**, conduit, race, drain, gutter ■ v **clean**, flush, rinse, hose, wash

slum n **shanty town**, favela, purlieu (fml), colonia (US)

slumber v **sleep**, drowse, doze, be dead to the world, catnap ■ n 1 **sleep**, doze, nap, catnap, siesta 2 **rest**, inactivity, inertia, torpor, laziness

slump v 1 **collapse**, fall, sink, tumble, lurch 2 **slouch**, bend, hunch, droop, sprawl 3 **decrease**, decline, collapse, plummet, crash Opposite: rise ■ n **recession**, crash, collapse, decline, plummet Opposite: rise

slur v 1 **speak**, run together, blend, overlap, overrun 2 **demean**, smear, insult, slight, besmirch ■ n **smear**, disgrace, insult, slight, stain

slurp v **gulp**, suck, drink, swallow, down ■ n **mouthful**, swallow, drink, sip, gulp

slurred adj **indistinct**, inaudible, unclear, garbled, incoherent Opposite: distinct

slush n **sludge**, mud, mire, muck, slurry

slushy adj 1 **snowy**, icy, wet, mushy, sloppy Opposite: dry 2 **sentimental**, mushy, corny, syrupy, mawkish Opposite: unsentimental

sly adj 1 **crafty**, cunning, clever, skilful, knowing 2 **evasive**, wily, devious, furtive, underhand Opposite: honest

slyness n 1 **craftiness**, cunning, skill, artfulness, cleverness Opposite: clumsiness 2 **sneakiness**, evasiveness, furtiveness, dishonesty, underhandedness Opposite: openness

smack v 1 **hit**, clout, slap, cuff, spank 2 **suggest**, imply, hint at, look like, sound like ■ n 1 **slap**, blow, clout, cuff, spank 2 **taste**, flavour, tang, bite, savour

small adj 1 **little**, minute, tiny, diminutive, miniature Opposite: big 2 **unimportant**, trivial, slight, lesser, minor Opposite: major

small arms n **weapons**, guns, firearms, side arms, pistols

smallholding n **farm**, croft, plot, allotment

smallness n **tininess**, littleness, minuteness, compactness Opposite: largeness

smalls *(infml)* n **underwear**, underclothes, underclothing, undies *(infml)*

small-scale *adj* **1 limited**, modest, moderate, minor, unimportant *Opposite*: large-scale **2 little**, small, miniature, minuscule, tiny *Opposite*: large-scale

small screen *(infml)* n **television**, telly *(infml)*, TV *(infml)*, box *(slang)*, goggle-box *(dated infml)*

small talk n **chat**, conversation, pleasantries, gossip, chatter

small-time *(infml)* adj **petty**, unimportant, local, minor, insignificant *Opposite*: major

smarmy *adj* **sycophantic**, oily, slimy, grovelling, unctuous

smart *adj* **1 elegant**, tidy, stylish, chic, well-dressed *Opposite*: shabby **2 clever**, intelligent, bright, sharp, quick *Opposite*: stupid **3 insolent**, rude, facetious, clever, disrespectful **4 fashionable**, chic, glamorous, stylish, voguish **5 lively**, brisk, vigorous, energetic, quick ■ *v* **sting**, burn, hurt, chafe, tingle. *See* COMPARE AND CONTRAST *at* **intelligent**.

smart aleck *(infml)* n **know-all** *(infml)*, clever Dick *(infml)*, clever clogs *(infml)*, smartypants *(infml)*, wiseacre *(infml)*

smarten *v* **1 spruce up**, clean up, revamp, do up, redecorate *Opposite*: let go **2 speed up**, accelerate, quicken, increase, pick up *Opposite*: slow

smarten up *v* **1 spruce up**, clean up, revamp, do up, redecorate *Opposite*: let go **2 brighten up**, liven up, cheer up, enliven, energize *Opposite*: stagnate

smartly *adv* **1 stylishly**, nattily, neatly, tidily, elegantly *Opposite*: untidily **2 vigorously**, briskly, energetically, quickly, rapidly **3 intelligently**, cleverly, ably, knowledgeably *Opposite*: stupidly

smartness *n* **neatness**, tidiness, elegance, stylishness, chicness *Opposite*: untidiness

smarty-pants *(infml)* n **know-all** *(infml)*, clever clogs *(infml)*, clever Dick *(infml)*, smart aleck *(infml)*, wiseacre *(infml)*

smash *v* **shatter**, break, demolish, destroy, crush *Opposite*: repair ■ *n* **1 crash**, bang, crunch **2 blow**, chop, punch, kick, volley **3 accident**, crash, collision, pile-up *(infml)*, wreck *(US)*

smasher *(infml)* n **beauty**, cracker *(infml)*, ace *(infml)*, knockout *(infml)*, looker *(infml)*

smashing *(infml)* adj **wonderful**, marvellous, great, brilliant *(infml)*, terrific *(infml)* *Opposite*: dreadful

smash up *v* **wreck**, write off, damage, ruin, trash *(infml)*

smash-up *n* **crash**, collision, accident, prang *(infml)*, pile-up *(infml)*

smattering *n* **bit**, modicum, dash, iota, little *Opposite*: lot

smear *v* **1 spread**, coat, daub, cover, wipe **2 sully**, discredit, disgrace, besmirch, tarnish *Opposite*: praise ■ *n* **1 mark**, smudge, blotch, stain, blot **2 slur**, insult, slight, affront, slander

smear campaign *n* **mudslinging**, whispering campaign, muckraking, defamation, slander

smell *v* **1 stink**, reek, pong *(infml)*, whiff *(infml)* **2 sniff**, sense, get a whiff of, suspect, taste ■ *n* **odour**, aroma, perfume, scent, fragrance

---

COMPARE AND CONTRAST CORE MEANING: the way something smells

smell a neutral, pleasant, or unpleasant quality detected by the nerves of the nose; **odour** a neutral or unpleasant smell; **aroma** a distinctive pleasant smell, especially one related to cooking or food; **bouquet** a characteristic pleasant smell, usually associated with fine wines; **scent** a pleasant, sweet smell, for example the smell of flowers, or the characteristic smell given off by a particular animal; **perfume** a sweet, pleasant, and heady smell, especially the smell of flowers or plants; **fragrance** a sweet pleasant smell, especially a delicate or subtle one; **stink** a strong unpleasant smell; **stench** a strong unpleasant smell, especially one associated with burning or decay; **reek** a strong unpleasant smell.

---

smelly *adj* **stinking**, reeking, foul, malodorous, putrid *Opposite*: fragrant

smelt *v* **1 melt**, melt down, liquefy, flux **2 found**, cast, produce, manufacture

smidge *(infml)* see **smidgen**

smidgen *(infml)* n **dash**, drop, bit, splash, morsel

smile *v* **grin**, beam, smirk, leer, sneer *Opposite*: frown ■ *n* **beam**, grin, smirk, leer *Opposite*: frown

smiley *adj* **smiling**, happy, cheery, sunny, cheerful *Opposite*: miserable ■ *n* **emoticon**, smiley face, symbol, sign-off *(US)*

smirk *n* **grin**, leer, sneer, simper ■ *v* **sneer**, leer, grin, simper

smithereens *(infml)* n **pieces**, bits, fragments, shards

smitten *(literary)* adj **in love**, besotted, enamoured, head over heels in love, infatuated *Opposite*: indifferent

smog *n* **pollution**, smoke, fog, haze

smoke *n* **fumes**, smog, poisonous gas, firedamp, chokedamp ■ *v* **burn**, be on fire, smoulder

smoke alarm *n* **smoke detector**, fire alarm, sensor

smoke detector see **smoke alarm**

smoke out *v* **1 drive out**, force out, turn out, eject, expel *Opposite*: bring in **2 bring to light**, reveal, expose, unearth, discover *Opposite*: conceal

smoker *n* **1 cigarette smoker**, pipe smoker, cigar smoker, chain-smoker, heavy smoker **2 smoking compartment**, smoking car, smoking carriage

smoke screen n 1 **cloud of smoke**, wall of smoke, smoke 2 **cover-up**, cover, camouflage, screen, mask

smoky adj **misty**, murky, cloudy, foggy, hazy Opposite: clear

smooch (infml) v **kiss**, cuddle, hug, hold each other close, caress ■ n **cuddle**, kiss, hug, caress, embrace

smooth adj 1 **flat**, even, level, horizontal, plane Opposite: uneven 2 **easy**, flowing, effortless, efficient 3 **charming**, suave, persuasive, glib, silver-tongued Opposite: gauche 4 **soft**, silky, downy, velvety, shiny Opposite: rough ■ v **flatten**, smooth out, level, iron, press Opposite: crumple

smooth down v **flatten**, iron out, paste down, smooth out, even out Opposite: scrunch

smoothie n 1 (infml) **charmer**, smooth talker, smooth character, fast talker, poser (infml) 2 **drink**, fruit juice, milk shake, yogurt drink

smoothly adv **easily**, effortlessly, efficiently, well, slickly Opposite: awkwardly

smoothness n 1 **flatness**, evenness, levelness Opposite: unevenness 2 **ease**, effortlessness, efficiency Opposite: awkwardness 3 **charm**, suaveness, persuasiveness, glibness, slickness 4 **softness**, silkiness, velvetiness, sleekness Opposite: roughness

smooth out v 1 **flatten**, iron out, paste down, smooth down, even out Opposite: crease 2 **ease**, calm, defuse, soothe, smooth over Opposite: stir up

smooth over v **ease**, calm, defuse, soothe, smooth out Opposite: stir up

smooth talk n **flattery**, nonsense, rubbish, garbage, sweet talk (infml) Opposite: sincerity

smooth-tongued adj **smooth-talking**, silver-tongued, eloquent, persuasive, convincing

smoothy see smoothie

smother v 1 **suffocate**, stifle, choke, asphyxiate 2 **overwhelm**, overpower, oppress, suffocate, stifle 3 **suppress**, repress, stifle, hold back, restrain Opposite: express

smoulder v 1 **burn**, smoke, glow 2 **fume**, seethe, glower, burn, boil 3 **lurk**, fester, rumble, linger, persist

smudge n **blotch**, smear, stain, mark, splodge ■ v **smear**, blur, distort, blot, smirch

smug adj **self-satisfied**, superior, self-righteous, arrogant, conceited Opposite: humble

smuggle v **handle contraband**, traffic, run, sneak in, bring in

smugness n **complacency**, arrogance, self-satisfaction, conceit, self-righteousness Opposite: humility

smut n 1 **obscenity**, dirt, filth, pornography, erotica 2 **soot**, smudge, ash, grime, dirt

smutty adj 1 **obscene**, dirty, pornographic, filthy, explicit 2 **sooty**, smudged, grimy, dirty, grubby Opposite: pristine 3 **crude**, foul-mouthed, indelicate, tasteless, loutish

snaffle (infml) v **steal**, rob, pilfer, pocket, take

snag n **problem**, hitch, difficulty, obstacle, hurdle Opposite: solution ■ v **catch**, rip, tear

snail mail (infml) n **postal service**, post, surface mail, airmail, mail

snake n **sea snake**, water snake, serpent (literary) ■ v **wind**, bend, twist, meander, turn

WORD BANK

❑ **types of non-poisonous snake** anaconda, blacksnake, boa, boa constrictor, garter snake, grass snake, king snake, python, rat snake, water snake, whip snake

❑ **types of poisonous snake** adder, asp, cobra, copperhead, coral snake, diamondback, fer-de-lance, horned viper, mamba, pit viper, puff adder, rattler, rattlesnake, ringhals, sea snake, sidewinder, taipan, viper, water moccasin

snaky adj **winding**, windy, bendy, twisting, meandering Opposite: straight

snap v 1 **break**, crack, shatter, give way, come apart 2 **retort**, bark, shout, yell, speak sharply 3 **bite**, nip, bite at ■ adj **sudden**, spur-of-the-moment, impulsive, spontaneous, instant Opposite: considered

snappish adj **irritable**, snappy, bad-tempered, short-tempered, sharp Opposite: good-natured

snappy adj 1 **irritable**, bad-tempered, short-tempered, sharp, curt Opposite: good-natured 2 (infml) **lively**, brisk, interesting, stimulating, to the point Opposite: dull 3 **hasty**, quick, fast, speedy, rapid Opposite: slow 4 (infml) **stylish**, chic, fashionable, smart, elegant Opposite: dowdy

snapshot n 1 **photo**, photograph, picture, snap, portrait 2 **view**, glimpse, outline, idea, thumbnail sketch

snap up v **grab**, seize, pounce on, take up

snare n **trap**, noose, gin, lasso ■ v **catch**, trap, capture, ensnare, entrap

snarl v 1 **growl**, roar, bellow 2 **speak angrily**, bark, growl, snap, rasp

snarl up v **jam up**, back up, grind to a halt, come to a standstill, reach gridlock Opposite: free up

snarl-up n **blockage**, holdup, jam, traffic jam, logjam

snatch v 1 **grab**, grasp, seize, take 2 **steal**, run off with, pinch (infml), filch (infml), nick (slang)

snazzy (infml) adj **flashy**, bright, colourful, loud, ostentatious Opposite: drab

sneak v 1 **slip**, steal, creep, slink, tiptoe 2 **tell tales**, inform, tell, grass (slang), snitch (slang) ■ n **informer**, telltale, snitch (slang), grass (slang)

sneakiness n **slyness**, furtiveness, stealth, deviousness, cunning Opposite: openness

sneaking adj **niggling**, uneasy, nagging, uncomfortable, worrying

sneak preview n advance showing, premiere, preview, screening, advance screening

sneak thief n pickpocket, shoplifter, burglar, thief, robber

sneak up on v 1 creep up on, steal up on, come up on, come up behind, surprise 2 catch napping, catch unawares, take by surprise, surprise, creep up on

sneaky adj sly, devious, shifty, underhand, mean Opposite: honest

sneer v scorn, scoff, turn your nose up at, mock, deride

sneering adj scornful, contemptuous, disdainful, sarcastic, arrogant Opposite: admiring

sneeze n sniff, sniffle, snuffle, splutter, snort ■ v sniffle, sniff, snuffle, splutter, snort

snicker v whinny, neigh, snort, snuffle, bray

snide adj sarcastic, mean, unpleasant, malicious, spiteful Opposite: pleasant

sniff v 1 snuffle, breathe, inhale Opposite: exhale 2 smell, scent, get a whiff of, catch the scent of ■ n breath, snort, snuffle, lungful, inhalation

sniff at v turn your nose up at, sneer at, hold in contempt, look down on, scorn Opposite: accept

sniffle v 1 sniff, snuffle, snivel, snort, splutter 2 whimper, snivel, cry, weep, sob

sniff out (infml) v discover, find, unearth, track down, detect

sniffy (infml) adj contemptuous, haughty, disdainful, scornful, superior Opposite: humble

snifter (infml) n drink, nightcap, tot, splash, nip

snigger v laugh, smirk, mock, deride, sneer ■ n laugh, sneer, snort, snicker (US)

snip v cut, shear, slice, nick, trim ■ n (infml) bargain, good deal, good buy, steal (infml), giveaway (infml)

sniper n gunman, marksman, assassin, rifleman, shooter

snippet n extract, piece, bit, scrap

snippy (infml) adj irritable, snappy, grumpy, crabby, sharp Opposite: good-tempered

snivel v sob, sniff, cry, weep, whimper

snob n social climber, name-dropper, elitist

snobbery n arrogance, superciliousness, condescension, pretentiousness, conceit Opposite: humility

snobbish adj high and mighty, superior, arrogant, condescending, supercilious Opposite: humble

snobbishness see snobbery

snobby see snobbish

snooker (infml) v thwart, stymie, put paid to (infml), obstruct, hinder Opposite: assist

snoop (infml) n spy, poke around, watch, sneak, pry Opposite: mind your own business ■ n spy, sneak, meddler, intruder, eavesdropper

snooty (infml) adj 1 high and mighty, condescending, hoity-toity, supercilious, snobbish Opposite: humble 2 exclusive, select, posh (infml)

snooze (infml) v doze, sleep, doze off, nap, nod off Opposite: wake up ■ n sleep, doze, nap, catnap, siesta

snore v snort, breathe heavily, snuffle, wheeze

snorkel v swim, dive, scuba dive

snort v grunt, exhale, breathe out, inhale, draw in

snout n nose, muzzle, proboscis, schnozzle (US slang)

snow n sleet, snowflake, slush, hail, ice

snowball v increase, mount, balloon, swell, grow quickly Opposite: decrease

snowbound adj snowed in, snowed up, cut off, isolated, shut in

snowfall n snowstorm, blizzard, whiteout, flurry

snowstorm n blizzard, whiteout, snowfall, flurry

snow under v inundate, swamp, bury, overwhelm, overload

snowy adj snow-white, hoary, white

snub v ignore, coldshoulder, slight, look right through, cut Opposite: acknowledge ■ n rebuff, slight, rejection, rebuke, insult

snub-nosed adj button-nosed, pug-nosed, retroussé

snuff v 1 extinguish, put out, douse, snuff out, blow out Opposite: light 2 (infml) destroy, kill, eliminate, abolish, eradicate Opposite: save

snuffle v sniff, sniffle, snort, snivel, splutter ■ n snort, sniff, sniffle, snivel, splutter

snug adj 1 cosy, warm, comfortable, homely, inviting Opposite: uncomfortable 2 close, well-fitting, neat, close-fitting, tight Opposite: loose

snuggle v nestle, nuzzle, cuddle, burrow, huddle

so adv consequently, as a result, therefore, subsequently, accordingly

soak v 1 immerse, steep, marinate, infuse, saturate 2 drench, douse, saturate, wet, drown Opposite: dry out

soaked adj wet through, saturated, sodden, waterlogged, drenched Opposite: dry

soaking adj drenched, soaked, soaking wet, sopping wet, sopping Opposite: dry

so-and-so (infml) n whatchamacallit (infml), thingamajig (infml), thingummy (infml), thingamabob (infml), whatshisname (infml)

soap n 1 cleanser, detergent, shampoo, soap powder, washing powder 2 (infml) serial, soap opera, series, programme ■ v cleanse, lather, wash, wash down, shampoo

soap opera n serial, series, soap (infml)

soap powder *n* **detergent**, washing powder, soap, soapsuds, cleanser

soapsuds *n* foam, lather, suds, froth, bubbles

soar *v* **1 fly**, ascend, climb, wheel, circle *Opposite*: plummet **2 rise**, rocket, climb, mount, go through the roof *Opposite*: plummet

soaring *adj* **rising**, mounting, climbing, spiralling, increasing *Opposite*: plummeting

sob *v* **moan**, cry, weep, snivel, sniffle

sobbing *n* **crying**, weeping, howling, tears, snivelling

sober *adj* **1 abstemious**, clear-headed, temperate, teetotal, moderate **2 serious**, sombre, solemn, thoughtful, calm *Opposite*: frivolous **3 dull**, sombre, drab, dreary, staid *Opposite*: bright **4 rational**, judicious, level-headed, clear-headed, sensible *Opposite*: speculative

soberness *n* **1 seriousness**, solemnity, sombreness, gravity, glumness *Opposite*: frivolity **2 dullness**, sombreness, drabness, plainness, simplicity *Opposite*: brightness **3 rationality**, judiciousness, level-headedness, clear-headedness, lucidity

sobriety *n* **1 abstemiousness**, abstinence, temperance, moderation, soberness **2 seriousness**, sombreness, solemnity, thoughtfulness, calm *Opposite*: flippancy

sobriquet *n* **nickname**, pet name, term of endearment, alias, assumed name

sob story *(infml)* *n* **tale of woe**, hard-luck story, sorry tale, sad story

so-called *adj* **supposed**, alleged, ostensible, purported, self-styled

sociability *n* **1 gregariousness**, companionability, conviviality, hospitality **2 friendliness**, pleasantness, amiability, affability, geniality

sociable *adj* **1 gregarious**, companionable, convivial, good company, hospitable *Opposite*: retiring **2 friendly**, outgoing, amiable, warm, affable *Opposite*: unsociable

social *adj* **communal**, community, common, societal, public ■ *n* **party**, gathering, get-together *(infml)*, do *(infml)*

social climber *n* **hanger-on**, sycophant, toady, snob, socialite

socialism *n* **collectivism**, social democracy, public ownership, communism, communalism

socialist *n* **collectivist**, social democrat, communist, communalist

socialite *n* **trendsetter**, one of the beautiful people, one of the glitterati, member of café society, social climber

socialize *v* **meet people**, go out, get out, mix, mingle

socially *adv* **1 communally**, publicly, within society, generally, collectively **2 in public**, in a social context, with other people, in a crowd **3 as a friend**, outside of work, informally, on a social basis

societal *adj* **social**, group, shared, general, common

society *n* **1 civilization**, culture, humanity, the social order, the world **2 people**, the public, the general public, the populace, the population **3 association**, union, group, guild, league **4 high society**, the upper classes, polite society, the upper crust *(infml)*

sock *(infml)* *n* **hit**, punch, thump, whack, thwack ■ *v* **hit**, punch, thump, whack, thwack

socket *n* **1 hole**, opening, hollow **2 power point**, outlet, plug *(infml)*

sod *n* **turf**, clod, grass, earth

sodden *adj* **saturated**, soaking, soaked, soaking wet, sopping *Opposite*: dry

sofa *n* **settee**, couch, chaise longue, day bed, futon

so far *adv* **up to now**, thus far, hitherto, until now, to date

soft *adj* **1 yielding**, squashy, spongy, pliable, elastic *Opposite*: hard **2 smooth**, silky, supple, velvety *Opposite*: rough **3 low**, mellifluous, melodious, faint, muted *Opposite*: loud **4 gentle**, flowing, delicate, subtle, understated *Opposite*: harsh **5 dim**, diffused, mellow, subtle, gentle *Opposite*: bright **6 lenient**, lax, easy, forgiving, overindulgent *Opposite*: strict **7 tender**, sensitive, gentle, kind, sympathetic *Opposite*: hardhearted **8 wet**, spineless, weak, soppy *(infml)*, pathetic *(infml)*

soft-boiled *adj* **soft-hearted**, soft, sympathetic, sentimental, indulgent *Opposite*: hard-boiled *(infml)*

soften *v* **1 make softer**, relax, make pliable *Opposite*: harden **2 alleviate**, lessen, reduce, diminish, mitigate *Opposite*: exacerbate **3 moderate**, relax, temper, tone down, assuage

soft furnishings *n* **upholstery**, curtains, rugs, cushions, fabrics

soft-hearted *adj* **sympathetic**, kind, caring, warm, good-natured *Opposite*: hardhearted

softie *see* **softy**

softly *adv* **1 tenderly**, delicately, gently, kindly, sympathetically *Opposite*: severely **2 quietly**, gently, mellifluously, melodiously, faintly *Opposite*: harshly **3 dimly**, gently, lightly, subtly, faintly *Opposite*: brightly

softly-softly *adj* **cautious**, discreet, tentative, vigilant, mindful *Opposite*: heavy-handed

softness *n* **1 gentleness**, smoothness, quietness, faintness *Opposite*: harshness **2 pliability**, suppleness, flexibility, elasticity, malleability

soft-pedal *(infml)* *v* **play down**, downplay, make light of, underplay, minimize *Opposite*: emphasize

soft sell *(infml)* *n* **persuasion**, persuasiveness, subtlety, sweet-talking *(infml)*, soft-soaping *(infml)*

soft-soap (infml) v **flatter**, play up to, lay it on thick, sweet-talk (infml), butter up (infml)

soft-spoken adj **quiet**, gentle, calm, tranquil, serene Opposite: loud

soft spot n **weakness**, partiality, affection, weak spot, liking

soft touch n **easy prey**, easy target, pushover (infml), sucker (infml), softy (infml)

softy (infml) n **soft touch**, easy target, easy prey, sucker (infml)

soggy adj **damp**, wet, moist, mushy, squelchy Opposite: dry

soigné adj **well-groomed**, well turned-out, neat, elegant, chic Opposite: dowdy

soil n 1 **earth**, dirt, topsoil, mud, dust 2 **territory**, land, country, ground ■ v **dirty**, get dirty, foul, muddy, stain Opposite: cleanse

soiled adj **dirty**, grubby, muddy, stained, filthy Opposite: clean. See COMPARE AND CONTRAST at **dirty**.

soiree n **party**, celebration, dinner party, evening, gathering

soirée see **soiree**

sojourn (literary) n **visit**, stay, stop, stopover ■ v **stay**, stop, remain, dwell (literary), abide (archaic)

solace n **comfort**, consolation, support, relief, help Opposite: aggravation

solarium n **conservatory**, sun lounge, suntrap, greenhouse

solder v **join**, fuse, weld, bond, connect

soldier n 1 **fighter**, combatant, warrior, regular, legionnaire Opposite: noncombatant 2 **private**, sapper, gunner, corporal, sergeant 3 **worker**, supporter, campaigner, crusader, workhorse

soldier of fortune n **mercenary**, adventurer, hired gun (slang) Opposite: regular

soldier on v **persevere**, continue, carry on, keep on, keep going Opposite: give up

sole adj 1 **only**, solitary, single, individual, singular 2 **exclusive**, private, unique, special, individual

solecism n **error**, mistake, blunder, slip, gaffe

solely adv **exclusively**, only, merely, just, uniquely

solemn adj 1 **earnest**, sincere, serious, firm, grave Opposite: flippant 2 **sombre**, grave, serious, sober, sad Opposite: cheerful 3 **formal**, official, ceremonial, ritual, sacred

solemnity n **sombreness**, gravity, seriousness, soberness, sadness

solemnize v **celebrate**, honour, make official, formalize, sanctify

solicit v 1 **ask for**, beg, seek, petition for, plead for Opposite: grant 2 **ask**, petition, lobby, plead with, implore (fml)

solicitor n **lawyer**, advocate, legal representative, attorney (US)

solicitous adj **considerate**, caring, attentive, concerned, kind Opposite: uncaring

solicitousness n **concern**, attentiveness, consideration, care, kindness

solicitude n 1 **concern**, attentiveness, consideration, care, kindness Opposite: negligence 2 **anxiety**, concern, worry, unease, apprehension Opposite: serenity

solid adj 1 **hard**, rock-hard, rock-solid, concrete, firm Opposite: soft 2 **dense**, unbroken, continuous, closed, blocked Opposite: hollow 3 **pure**, genuine, unadulterated, one hundred per cent, unmixed 4 **sturdy**, strong, secure, firm, stable Opposite: weak 5 **unanimous**, universal, widespread, popular, general Opposite: patchy 6 **reliable**, dependable, sound, trustworthy, level-headed Opposite: unreliable ■ n 1 **object**, thing, artefact, item, entity 2 **figure**, pyramid, tetrahedron, sphere, icosahedron

solidarity n **unity**, harmony, cohesion, commonality, camaraderie Opposite: discord

solidify v **harden**, go hard, coagulate, congeal, set Opposite: dissolve

solidity n **hardness**, firmness, sturdiness, strength, toughness Opposite: softness

solidness see **solidity**

soliloquy n **monologue**, speech, declamation, oration, dramatic monologue

solitaire n **single stone**, gemstone, jewel, diamond, precious stone

solitary adj 1 **lone**, single, sole, individual, solo Opposite: accompanied 2 **private**, unsociable, unsocial, self-contained, self-sufficient Opposite: sociable 3 **isolated**, desolate, out-of-the-way, secluded, unfrequented

solitary confinement n **isolation**, imprisonment, confinement, detention, custody

solitude n **loneliness**, privacy, isolation, seclusion, separateness

solo adj **single**, unaccompanied, lone Opposite: joint ■ adv **alone**, on your own, singly, by yourself Opposite: together

soloist n **artist**, artiste, musician, singer, vocalist Opposite: accompanist

solubility n **dissolvability**, deliquescence Opposite: insolubility

soluble adj 1 **dissolvable**, deliquescent Opposite: insoluble 2 **solvable**, answerable, fathomable, resolvable, decipherable Opposite: insoluble

solution n 1 **answer**, key, explanation, resolution, way out Opposite: problem 2 **mix**, mixture, liquid, blend, cocktail

solvable adj **soluble**, resolvable, fathomable, answerable, decipherable Opposite: insoluble

solve v **resolve**, crack, answer, explain, get to the bottom of

solvency n **creditworthiness**, affluence, wealth, soundness, comfort Opposite: insolvency

solvent *adj* **in the black**, in credit, in funds, in the money, in clover *Opposite*: insolvent

sombre *adj* **1 depressing**, dull, gloomy, drab, dingy *Opposite*: bright **2 muted**; dark, dull, solemn, funereal *Opposite*: bright **3 depressed**, gloomy, sad, melancholy, funereal *Opposite*: cheerful

some *adv* **approximately**, about, around, roughly, more or less *Opposite*: exactly ■ *adj* **1 a number of**, a quantity of, a little, a few, several *Opposite*: all **2 certain**, particular, selected, specific

somebody *pron* **some person**, someone *Opposite*: nobody ■ *n* **celebrity**, someone, name, superstar, bigwig *(infml) Opposite*: nobody

someday *adv* **one day**, sooner or later, sometime, soon, in the future *Opposite*: never

somehow *adv* **one way or another**, someway, by hook or by crook, come what may, come hell or high water

someone *see* **somebody**

somersault *n* **tumble**, forward roll, flip-flop, cartwheel, flip ■ *v* **turn over**, tumble, flip over, cartwheel, flip

something *adv* **a little**, somewhat, to some degree, rather, slightly *Opposite*: completely

sometime *adv* **at some point**, someday, at some time, in the future, one day *Opposite*: never ■ *adj* **(fml) former**, onetime, previous, earlier, ex *(infml) Opposite*: current

sometimes *adv* **occasionally**, now and then, every now and then, every so often, now and again *Opposite*: always

someway *adv* **somehow**, one way or another, in some way, by some means, by hook or by crook

somewhat *adv* **rather**, fairly, slightly, to some extent, to a certain extent

somewhere *adv* **wherever**, anywhere, anyplace *(US infml)*, someplace *(US infml)*

somnolent *adj* **sleepy**, drowsy, dozy, half asleep, half awake

son *n* **child**, lad, boy, kid *(infml)*

son et lumière *n* **entertainment**, spectacle, light show, tableau, spectacular

song *n* **1 tune**, melody, air, refrain, jingle **2 birdsong**, call, warble, warbling, cry

song and dance *(infml) n* **fuss**, drama, commotion, palaver, hysterics

songbook *n* **anthology**, collection, hymn book, book, hymnal

songster *n* **singer**, vocalist, lead singer, soloist, chanteuse

songwriter *n* **composer**, lyricist, songsmith, librettist

sonic *adj* **auditory**, aural, audible, sound

sonic boom *n* **boom**, shock wave, noise, rumble, roar

sonnet *n* **poem**, verse, rhyme

sonny *(infml) n* **lad**, young man, my boy, my lad, sonny boy *(infml)*

sonny boy *(infml) see* **sonny**

sonority *n* **resonance**, fullness, roundness, richness, reverberation

sonorous *adj* **loud**, deep, resonant, echoing, booming *Opposite*: thin

soon *adv* **almost immediately**, quickly, rapidly, shortly, presently *Opposite*: eventually

sooner *adv* **1 earlier**, faster, more quickly, more rapidly, nearer *Opposite*: later **2 rather**, more readily, more willingly, preferably, as soon *Opposite*: reluctantly

soot *n* **dust**, powder, grime, ashes, dirt

soothe *v* **1 ease**, relieve, alleviate, reduce, palliate *Opposite*: aggravate **2 calm**, pacify, quieten, appease, mollify *Opposite*: excite

soothing *adj* **calming**, comforting, restful, gentle, peaceful *Opposite*: irritating

soothsayer *n* **fortune-teller**, oracle, seer, astrologer, clairvoyant

sooty *adj* **dirty**, grimy, black, filthy, dusty *Opposite*: clean

sop *n* **concession**, offering, bribe, pacifier, gesture

sophisticate *v* **educate**, school, mould, acculturate, tutor ■ *n* **socialite**, trendsetter, connoisseur, aesthete, cognoscente *Opposite*: hoi polloi

sophisticated *adj* **1 urbane**, cultured, chic, erudite, refined *Opposite*: gauche **2 clever**, advanced, high-level, complex, erudite *Opposite*: crude

sophistication *n* **1 refinement**, style, chic, urbanity, elegance *Opposite*: naivety **2 complexity**, cleverness, erudition, difficulty, intricacy *Opposite*: crudeness

sophistry *n* **casuistry**, fallaciousness, illogicality, sophism, dishonesty *Opposite*: logic

soporific *adj* **1 sleep-inducing**, calming, tranquillizing, narcotic, hypnotic *(infml) Opposite*: energizing **2 tedious**, boring, interminable, turgid, endless *Opposite*: stimulating

sopping *adj* **drenched**, soaked, dripping, sodden, saturated *Opposite*: dry

soppy *adj* **1 (infml) sentimental**, mawkish, soft, slushy, corny *Opposite*: unsentimental **2 soaked**, wet, sopping wet, sopping, dripping *Opposite*: dry

soprano *n* **singer**, vocalist, soloist, chanteuse, diva ■ *adj* **high**, high-pitched, shrill, piercing, soaring *Opposite*: bass

sop up *v* **soak up**, mop up, sponge, absorb, wipe

sorbet *n* **water ice**, fruit ice, ice, sherbet *(US)*

sorcerer *n* **wizard**, magician, enchanter, magus, witch

sorceress *n* **witch**, enchantress, sibyl, magician, necromancer *(literary)*

sorcery *n* **witchcraft**, wizardry, magic, black magic, enchantment

sordid adj 1 base, disreputable, sleazy, repugnant, disgusting *Opposite*: uplifting 2 squalid, distasteful, disgusting, low, dirty *Opposite*: pleasant

sordidness n 1 baseness, sleaze, unpleasantness, repugnance, wretchedness *Opposite*: pleasantness 2 squalor, grime, filth, squalidness, grubbiness *Opposite*: cleanliness

sore adj 1 painful, uncomfortable, tender, stinging, aching *Opposite*: comfortable 2 annoying, sensitive, embarrassing, controversial, difficult *Opposite*: uncontroversial 3 (infml) angry, cross, mad, annoyed, upset *Opposite*: pleased ■ n wound, abscess, lesion, eruption, blister

sorely (fml) adv deeply, truly, greatly, very much, really *Opposite*: not at all

soreness n tenderness, pain, discomfort, distress, agony

sorrow n grief, mourning, sadness, distress, sorrowfulness *Opposite*: joy

sorrowful adj 1 distressed, sad, mournful, grief-stricken, unhappy *Opposite*: joyful 2 distressing, tragic, sad, solemn, unhappy *Opposite*: happy

sorrowing adj sad, mournful, grief-stricken, distressed, unhappy *Opposite*: joyful

sorry adj 1 apologetic, regretful, remorseful, repentant, sad *Opposite*: glad 2 pitiful, miserable, wretched, forlorn, pathetic *Opposite*: fine

sort n 1 category, kind, class, type, genus 2 (infml) personality type, person, character, type, individual ■ v arrange, classify, rank, place, sort out *Opposite*: mix up. *See* COMPARE AND CONTRAST *at* **type**.

sorted (infml) adj organized, arranged, in hand, under control, dealt with

sortie n 1 attack, manoeuvre, foray, incursion, inroad *Opposite*: retreat 2 excursion, trip, outing, journey, jaunt

sort out v 1 resolve, deal with, solve, iron out, fix 2 put in order, arrange, file, disentangle, tidy up *Opposite*: mix up 3 separate, distinguish, segregate, sort, divide 4 (infml) punish, reprimand, scold, deal with, rebuke *Opposite*: reward

SOS n distress signal, cry for help, call for help, alarm, flare

so-so (infml) adj average, fair, mediocre, unremarkable, indifferent *Opposite*: exceptional

sought-after adj desirable, coveted, in demand, exclusive, fashionable *Opposite*: unpopular

souk n bazaar, market, marketplace, flea market, emporium

soul n 1 spirit, consciousness, psyche, will, essence 2 depth, personality, atmosphere, emotion, passion 3 individual, person, anyone, someone, example 4 soul music, gospel, R & B, rhythm and blues, blues

soul-destroying adj demoralizing, depressing, disheartening, unfulfilling, boring *Opposite*: uplifting

soulful adj expressive, affecting, sad, moving, poignant *Opposite*: emotionless

soulfulness n expressiveness, sadness, poignancy, emotion, mournfulness

soulless adj bleak, utilitarian, characterless, inexpressive, insensitive *Opposite*: soulful

soul mate n friend, mate, bosom friend, boon companion, confidant

soul-searching n thought, consideration, contemplation, introspection, assessment

sound n 1 noise, resonance, hum, echo, thud *Opposite*: silence 2 strait, channel, inlet, fjord ■ v 1 seem, appear, look 2 go off, ring out, explode, ring, wail 3 announce, declare, signal, express, ring out ■ adj 1 whole, healthy, unblemished, perfect, normal *Opposite*: infirm 2 sensible, good, firm, unassailable, reliable *Opposite*: unsound 3 complete, comprehensive, wide-ranging, all-encompassing, thorough *Opposite*: superficial 4 firm, rigorous, good, hard, severe *Opposite*: half-hearted

WORD BANK

❏ **types of animal sound** baa, bark, bay, bleat, bray, caterwaul, croak, growl, grunt, howl, mew, miaow, moo, neigh, oink, purr, roar, snarl, squeak, squeal, whinny, woof, yap, yelp

❏ **types of bird sound** caw, cheep, chirp, chirrup, cluck, cock-a-doodle-doo, coo, hoot, peep, quack, screech, squawk, trill, tweet, twitter, warble

❏ **types of human sound** babble, bawl, bellow, boo, catcall, chatter, chortle, chuckle, cry, gasp, giggle, groan, grunt, howl, hum, moan, murmur, mutter, peep, scream, screech, shout, shriek, sigh, slurp, sniffle, snigger, splutter, squeal, titter, wail, wheeze, whimper, whine, whisper, whistle, whoop, yell

❏ **types of continuous sound** beep, bleep, boom, burble, buzz, chug, crackle, creak, drone, gurgle, hiss, honk, hoot, hum, purl (literary), purr, rasp, rattle, roar, rumble, rustle, sizzle, sonic boom, swish, swoosh, throb, thunder, toot, whirr, whiz, whoosh

❏ **types of impact sound** bang, beat, bong, bonk (infml), bump, clang, clank, clap, clash, clatter, click, clip-clop, clop, clunk, crack, crash, patter, pitter-patter, plop, plunk, pop, ratatat-tat, rattle, slam, smash, splash, splat, squelch, squish, tap, thud, thump, thwack, tick, ticktock, wham

❏ **types of ringing sound** chime, chink, clink, ding, ding-a-ling, ding-dong, honk, hoot, jangle, jingle, knell, peal, ping, pip, ring, ting, tinkle, toll, tootle (infml)

sound bite n comment, announcement, statement, declaration, response

sound effect n sound, recording, effect, special effect

sounding board n confidant, confidante, close friend, best friend, intimate

soundings n **enquiries**, investigations, research, surveys, market research

soundless adj **silent**, noiseless, still, quiet, mute Opposite: noisy

soundly adv **1 deeply**, well, like a log, peacefully, fast Opposite: fitfully **2 thoroughly**, roundly, severely, firmly, decisively

soundness n **1 wholeness**, completeness, health, healthiness, fitness Opposite: infirmity **2 reliability**, unassailability, security, accuracy, dependability Opposite: unreliability **3 completeness**, comprehensiveness, thoroughness, depth, range Opposite: superficiality **4 thoroughness**, firmness, severity, rigorousness Opposite: half-heartedness

sound off (infml) v **hold forth**, go on, have your say, speak up, speak out

sound out v **investigate**, test, explore, survey, look into

soundproof adj **impenetrable**, insulated, lined, padded, sealed ■ v **insulate**, line, seal, pad, protect

sound system n **hi-fi**, stereo, music centre, stereo system, audio system

soundtrack n **1 recording**, music, dialogue, sound, sound effects **2 music**, album, LP, tape, CD

soupçon n **hint**, touch, speck, morsel, modicum Opposite: surfeit

soup up (infml) v **boost**, enhance, tune up, modify, upgrade

sour adj **1 acid**, tart, bitter, acerbic, vinegary Opposite: sweet **2 bad**, rancid, off, curdled, fetid Opposite: fresh **3 bitter**, disagreeable, unpleasant, bad-tempered, resentful Opposite: agreeable ■ v **1 curdle**, go sour, go off, ferment, turn **2 taint**, ruin, harm, spoil, embitter Opposite: improve

source n **1 basis**, foundation, origin, cause, font **2 informant**, spokesperson, informer, supplier, stool pigeon (slang) **3 resource**, supply, fund, mine, well **4 natural spring**, upwelling, fount, fountain Opposite: estuary ■ v **obtain**, find, track down, trace, track. See COMPARE AND CONTRAST at **origin**.

sour grapes n **resentment**, jealousy, bitterness, ill feeling, envy

sourly adv **1 tartly**, bitterly, drily, acridly, acidly Opposite: sweetly **2 disagreeably**, unpleasantly, bitterly, resentfully, spitefully Opposite: agreeably

sourness n **1 acidity**, tartness, bitterness, tang, acridness Opposite: sweetness **2 bitterness**, resentment, acrimony, unpleasantness, hostility Opposite: pleasantness

sourpuss (infml) n **complainer**, grumbler, whiner, grouch (infml), moaner (infml)

souse v **1 pickle**, marinade, soak, steep, preserve **2 soak**, steep, douse, saturate, immerse

souvenir n **memento**, reminder, keepsake, knick-knack, remembrance

sovereign n **monarch**, ruler, potentate, king, queen Opposite: subject ■ adj **1 independent**, autonomous, self-governing, free, self-determining **2 supreme**, dominant, ascendant, predominant, absolute **3 outstanding**, superior, supreme, excellent, matchless

sovereignty n **1 dominion**, control, rule, power, authority **2 independence**, autonomy, self-government, freedom, self-determination

sow v **spread**, propagate, disseminate, scatter, strew Opposite: reap

spa n **1 health resort**, thalassotherapy centre, sanatorium, health spa, health farm **2 whirlpool bath**, plunge pool, Turkish bath, sauna, hot tub

space n **1 solar system**, galaxy, outer space, deep space, universe **2 interval**, time, period, pause, window **3 area**, place, seat, bay, plot **4** (infml) **leeway**, freedom, autonomy, liberty, latitude ■ v **spread out**, move apart, space out, set apart

space-age adj **hi-tech**, automated, up-to-the-minute, state-of-the-art, new

space capsule n **spacecraft**, spaceship, rocket, capsule, vehicle

spacecraft n **spaceship**, space rocket, rocket, rocket ship (US)

WORD BANK

❏ **types of spacecraft** biosatellite, lander, launch vehicle, lunar module, multistage rocket, orbital space station, orbiter, rocket, rover, satellite, space capsule, spacelab, space probe, space rocket, space shuttle, space station

❏ **parts of a spacecraft** booster rocket, bus, cabin, command module, drogue parachute, footpad, grain, life-support system, nose cone, plasma engine, pod, retropack, rocket engine, shroud, solar cell, stage, thruster

---

spaceflight n **flight**, rocket flight, shuttle flight, space travel, orbiting

space platform see **space station**

space probe n **rover**, lander, spacecraft, satellite, probe

spacer n **insertion**, insert, piece, part, bar

spaceship n **1 space capsule**, space shuttle, lunar module, ship, capsule **2 flying saucer**, alien craft, UFO, unidentified flying object

space station n **space platform**, orbital space station, spacelab, extraterrestrial base

spacewalk n **extravehicular activity**, EVA, moonwalk

spacing n **1 space**, arrangement, layout, spaces, gaps **2 arranging**, positioning, placing, ordering, spacing out

spacious adj **roomy**, airy, large, open, expansive Opposite: cramped

spade n **garden spade**, shovel, scoop, snow shovel ■ v **dig**, shovel, scoop, excavate, fill in

spadework n **groundwork**, research, drudgery, preliminaries, preparatory work

spam *n* junk mail, unsolicited mail, mail, direct mail, junk *(infml)* ■ *v* e-mail, post, block, send, distribute

span *n* 1 distance, width, length, extent, area 2 time, duration, period, limit ■ *v* cross, cover, reach over, extend over, bridge

spangle *n* sequin, bead, bauble, star ■ *v* 1 sprinkle, stud, pepper, dot, spot 2 sparkle, glitter, shine, glisten, twinkle

spank *v* whack, smack, slap, hit, strike

spanking *n* smacking, smack, slap, thrashing, beating ■ *adj* 1 remarkable, excellent, outstanding, wonderful, marvellous *Opposite*: ordinary 2 vigorous, brisk, rapid, fast, lively *Opposite*: weak

spar *n* pole, arm, boom, mast, rod ■ *v* 1 scuffle, fight, box, exchange blows, scrap 2 argue, fence, dispute, squabble, bicker *Opposite*: agree

spare *v* 1 show mercy to, free, release, save, pardon *Opposite*: condemn 2 afford, do without, get by without, manage without, give up *Opposite*: need ■ *adj* 1 replacement, extra, auxiliary, additional, emergency *Opposite*: main 2 sparse, thin, mean, insubstantial, frugal *Opposite*: abundant

spare part *n* reserve, extra, stand-by, part, replacement

spare time *n* free time, leisure time, time off, downtime *(US)*

sparing *adj* 1 frugal, parsimonious, economical, careful, thrifty *Opposite*: generous 2 meagre, sparse, limited, restricted, insufficient *Opposite*: plentiful

spark *n* 1 flash, flicker, sparkle, arc, glint 2 stimulus, catalyst, incentive, spur, trigger ■ *v* 1 sparkle, flicker, glimmer, glint, glow 2 generate, produce, inspire, initiate, set off

sparkle *v* 1 shine, glitter, glisten, flash, flicker 2 fizzle, bubble, fizz, ferment, effervesce 3 excel, scintillate, shine, come into your own, come to life ■ *n* 1 life, vivacity, energy, enthusiasm, gusto *Opposite*: apathy 2 effervescence, carbonation, bubbles, aeration, gassiness

sparkler *(infml)* *n* gem, diamond, gemstone, jewel, precious stone

sparkling *adj* 1 glittering, glistening, twinkling, iridescent, spangled *Opposite*: dull 2 vivacious, witty, brilliant, scintillating, vibrant *Opposite*: dull 3 fizzy, effervescent, carbonated, bubbly, aerated *Opposite*: still

sparkly *see* sparkling

spark off *v* generate, produce, inspire, initiate, set off

sparky *adj* lively, spirited, enthusiastic, bubbly, feisty *(infml)* *Opposite*: lifeless

sparring partner *n* opponent, adversary, sworn enemy, counterpart, opposite number

sparse *adj* thin, spare, scant, light, scarce *Opposite*: dense

sparseness *n* thinness, scarceness, scarcity, meagreness, bareness

spartan *adj* frugal, simple, basic, bare, severe *Opposite*: luxurious

spasm *n* shudder, contraction, seizure, ripple, paroxysm

spasmodic *adj* fitful, irregular, intermittent, occasional, sporadic *Opposite*: continuous

spat *n* quarrel, fight, row, argument, tiff

spate *n* flood, rash, epidemic, wave, sequence

spatial *adj* three-dimensional, 3-D, longitudinal, latitudinal, altitudinal

spatter *v* 1 shower, spray, sprinkle, scatter, splash 2 spray, splatter, shower, mark, splash

spawn *n* 1 roe, frogspawn, fish eggs, eggs, seed 2 brood, issue, offspring, progeny, young ■ *v* 1 lay, deposit, produce 2 reproduce, give birth, procreate, breed, hatch 3 create, generate, produce, initiate, set off

spay *v* neuter, sterilize, castrate, operate on, geld

speak *v* 1 chatter, talk, verbalize, articulate, chat *Opposite*: shut up *(infml)* 2 say, tell, express, state, voice 3 be fluent in, converse in, speak a language 4 address, lecture, preach, give a talk, give a lecture

speaker *n* 1 utterer, chatterer, reciter, talker 2 orator, lecturer, narrator, spokesman, spokeswoman

speak for *v* speak on behalf of, represent, act on behalf of, stand for, argue for

speaking *n* speech, language, communication, discourse, talking

speak out *v* 1 be frank, speak your mind, say your piece, have your say, speak up *Opposite*: equivocate 2 talk loudly, raise your voice, exclaim, shout, speak up *Opposite*: mutter

speak to *v* 1 get in touch with, contact, approach, talk to, address 2 reprimand, discipline, reprove, talk to, have a word with 3 *(fml)* discuss, consider, go into, deal with, address

speak up *v* 1 speak out, exclaim, talk loudly, raise your voice, shout *Opposite*: mutter 2 be frank, speak your mind, say your piece, have your say, protest *Opposite*: equivocate

speak up for *v* support, back, argue for, defend, approve *Opposite*: attack

speak your mind *v* be frank, not beat about the bush, speak up, speak out, make yourself heard *Opposite*: equivocate

spear *n* lance, spike, javelin, assegai, harpoon ■ *v* impale, spike, stab, pierce, gouge

spearhead *n* driving force, forefront, head, lead, leader ■ *v* lead, front, head, organize, direct

special *adj* 1 superior, distinct, different, exceptional, distinctive *Opposite*: ordinary 2 individual, specific, particular, distinct, one *Opposite*: general

special consideration n **dispensation**, concession, allowance, indulgence, preference

special delivery n **express**, courier, premium rate, overnight delivery, registered post

special education n **special needs education**, literacy tuition, numeracy tuition, specialist tuition, specialist support

specialism n **1 specialization**, narrowing down, concentration, focusing in, gaining expertise **2 speciality**, area of expertise, subject, sphere, forte

specialist n **authority**, expert, consultant, doyen, whiz *(infml)*

speciality n **specialism**, area of expertise, subject, sphere, forte

specialization n **1 narrowing down**, concentration, focusing in, gaining expertise, gaining in-depth knowledge *Opposite*: diversification **2 adaptation**, change, mutation, selection, evolution

specialize v **concentrate**, focus, dedicate yourself to, major in *Opposite*: diversify

specialized adj **particular**, dedicated, focused, specific, expert *Opposite*: generalized

specially adv **1 particularly**, in particular, especially, specifically, expressly *Opposite*: generally **2 personally**, individually, to order

species n **class**, type, kind, sort, genus. *See* COMPARE AND CONTRAST *at* **type**.

specific adj **1 exact**, precise, detailed, explicit, definite *Opposite*: vague **2 particular**, peculiar, exclusive, special, restricted *Opposite*: general **3 distinctive**, particular, express, identifiable, certain *Opposite*: indefinite ■ n **detail**, particular, aspect, feature, fact *Opposite*: generality

specification n **requirement**, condition, plan, order, arrangement

specified adj **1 stated**, quantified, definite, spelt out, detailed *Opposite*: unstated **2 stipulated**, required, postulated, restricted, insisted on *Opposite*: optional

specify v **1 state**, identify, spell out, detail, give *Opposite*: suggest **2 stipulate**, agree, lay down, postulate, issue

specious adj **false**, hollow, erroneous, baseless, inaccurate *Opposite*: valid

speciousness n **falsity**, hollowness, inaccuracy, falseness, deceptiveness *Opposite*: validity

speck n **1 dot**, fleck, spot, dab, blob **2 particle**, fragment, crumb, iota, scrap ■ v **dot**, fleck, spot, speckle, stipple

speckle n **fleck**, mark, speck, spot, dot ■ v **mark**, fleck, dust, stipple, dot

speckled adj **spotted**, freckled, dotted, stippled, dappled

specs *(infml) see* **spectacles**

spectacle n **1 sight**, scene, vision, marvel, phenomenon **2 display**, show, demonstration, exhibition, event

spectacles n **glasses**, goggles, specs *(infml)*

spectacular adj **1 stunning**, impressive, amazing, fantastic, fabulous *Opposite*: humdrum **2 remarkable**, huge, great, enormous, mighty *Opposite*: unimpressive ■ n **show**, display, performance, extravaganza, special

spectacularly adv **extremely**, enormously, hugely, monumentally, prodigiously *Opposite*: mildly

spectate v **watch**, look on, observe, take in, look *Opposite*: participate

spectator n **viewer**, watcher, observer, onlooker, bystander *Opposite*: participant

spectral adj **ghostly**, phantom, ethereal, supernatural, ghostlike *Opposite*: real

spectre n **1 ghost**, apparition, phantom, spirit, spook **2 threat**, menace, shadow, danger, possibility

spectrum n **range**, band, field, gamut, variety

speculate v **1 wonder**, guess, conjecture, hypothesize, reason *Opposite*: know **2 consider**, contemplate, reflect on, ponder, deliberate *Opposite*: decide **3 gamble**, take risks, hazard, risk, venture

speculation n **conjecture**, rumour, opinion, gossip, assumption *Opposite*: fact

speculative adj **1 tentative**, approximate, rough, exploratory, provisional *Opposite*: definite **2 hypothetical**, notional, theoretical, academic, abstract *Opposite*: proven **3 dangerous**, risky, unpredictable, uncertain, dicey *(infml) Opposite*: safe

speculator n **risk-taker**, investor, entrepreneur, opportunist, adventurer

speech n **1 language**, talking, verbal communication, dialogue, words **2 tongue**, idiom, dialect, vernacular, native tongue **3 lecture**, oration, sermon, talk, homily

speechify *(infml)* v **pontificate**, lecture, pronounce, preach, hold forth

speechless adj **astonished**, astounded, amazed, dumbstruck, wordless

speechmaker n **speaker**, orator, raconteur, preacher, lecturer

speed n **1 pace**, rate, velocity, momentum, tempo **2 haste**, hurry, swiftness, speediness, hustle *Opposite*: slowness ■ v **race**, fly, zoom, break the speed limit, drive too fast *Opposite*: crawl

speedily adv **quickly**, promptly, soon, hastily, hurriedly *Opposite*: slowly

speediness n **1 quickness**, promptness, hastiness, rapidity, speed *Opposite*: slowness **2 fastness**, swiftness, nimbleness, rapidness, fleetness *(literary) Opposite*: sluggishness

speeding adj **fast-moving**, hurtling, flying, moving, fast *Opposite*: slow

speed limit n **maximum speed**, top speed, permitted speed, limit, restriction

speedometer n speedo, clock, gauge, recorder

speed-read v skim, scan, read

speed trap n radar trap, police trap, traffic control

speed up v accelerate, get faster, get moving, get going, hurry up Opposite: slow down

speedway n track, course, circuit, racetrack

speedy adj 1 quick, immediate, prompt, early, fast Opposite: slow 2 fast-moving, speeding, swift, nimble, fast Opposite: slow

spell v signify, mean, bring, predict, imply ■ n 1 incantation, curse, enchantment, hex, evil eye 2 influence, fascination, thrall, glamour, enchantment 3 (infml) bout, interlude, stretch, session, time period

spellbinding adj mesmerizing, enthralling, entrancing, fascinating, captivating Opposite: boring

spellbound adj enthralled, fascinated, awestruck, rapt, captivated Opposite: distracted

spell-check v check, check over, check through, correct, proofread

spell out v make obvious, explain in simple terms, make clear, explain, interpret Opposite: obfuscate

spend v 1 use, use up, waste, fritter, squander Opposite: save 2 devote, apply, employ, fill, occupy 3 pay, expend, pay out, splurge, lay out

spending n expenditure, expenses, costs, payments, outgoings Opposite: earnings

spending money n cash, money, ready cash, pin money, pocket money Opposite: savings

spendthrift n wastrel, squanderer, waster, prodigal, profligate Opposite: miser ■ adj wasteful, extravagant, improvident, prodigal, reckless Opposite: miserly

spent adj 1 exhausted, tired, washed-out, worn-out, shattered Opposite: fresh 2 consumed, used up, expended, paid, paid out Opposite: saved 3 finished, over, done, completed, over and done with Opposite: new

sperm n 1 semen, seed, ejaculate 2 cell, gamete, spermatozoon

spermatozoon n sperm, cell, gamete

spew v 1 disgorge, discharge, vomit, send out, churn out 2 pour out, pour forth, gush, flow, stream Opposite: dribble ■ n vomit, sick (infml), puke (slang)

sphere n 1 ball, globe, orb, bubble 2 area, speciality, subject, field, area of interest 3 sphere of influence, compass, scope, range, domain

spherical adj sphere-shaped, globular, rotund, circular, round

sphinxlike adj enigmatic, mysterious, cryptic, bemusing, baffling Opposite: transparent

spice n 1 seasoning, flavouring, additive 2 interest, excitement, flavour, colour, a little something Opposite: blandness ■ v 1 season, flavour, enhance, lace 2 enliven, liven up,

ginger up, lace, add zest to Opposite: tone down

spick-and-span adj 1 tidy, clean, neat, immaculate, spotless Opposite: untidy 2 in perfect condition, immaculate, as new, in tiptop condition, in mint condition Opposite: used

spicy adj hot, spiced, curried, piquant, peppery Opposite: mild

spidery adj 1 thin, spindly, angular, squiggly, jerky Opposite: bold 2 gangling, spindly, lanky, skinny, thin Opposite: plump

spiel (infml) n patter, speech, lecture, talk, waffle (infml) ■ v prattle, pitch, go on, hold forth, jabber

spigot n 1 stopper, plug, bung, cork, peg 2 projection, end, tip, point, spike

spike n point, barb, spear, thorn, spine ■ v 1 spear, impale, pierce, skewer, run through (literary) 2 (infml) thwart, confound, frustrate, dash, quash Opposite: foster

spiked adj spiky, sharp, pointed, hobnailed, jagged Opposite: smooth

spiky adj prickly, thorny, sharp, bristly, spiny Opposite: smooth

spill v slop, drip, leak, trickle, dribble Opposite: absorb ■ n 1 leak, spillage, escape, discharge, overflow 2 (infml) tumble, fall, roll, trip, stumble

spillage n 1 spilling, spill, discharge, emission, leak 2 wastage, waste, loss, spill, slick

spill over v 1 overflow, brim over, leak out, run over, spill out 2 spread, extend, overflow, advance, creep

spill the beans (infml) v let the cat out of the bag, give the game away, tell, confess, let on Opposite: keep secret

spin v turn, rotate, revolve, gyrate, whirl ■ n 1 gyration, rotation, turn, whirl, swirl 2 drive, outing, run, trip, jaunt 3 (infml) point of view, viewpoint, slant, angle, bias

spinal adj back, backbone, vertebral

spinal column n spine, back, backbone, vertebrae, vertebral column

spindle n 1 rod, bar, shaft, axle, pole 2 leg, baluster, support, vertical, upright

spindly adj skinny, gangly, lanky, thin, frail Opposite: sturdy

spin doctor (infml) n PR expert, propagandist, publicist, representative, marketing expert

spindrift n spray, sea spray, foam, mist, vapour

spine n spinal column, vertebral column, backbone, back, vertebrae

spine-chilling *adj* **bloodcurdling**, chilling, terrifying, petrifying, frightening *Opposite*: comforting

spineless *adj* **gutless**, cowardly, weak, timid, spiritless *Opposite*: courageous. *See* COMPARE AND CONTRAST *at* **cowardly**.

spinelessness *n* **weakness**, gutlessness, cowardice, feebleness, faint-heartedness *Opposite*: courage

spine-tingling *adj* **hair-raising**, thrilling, frightening, gripping, exciting *Opposite*: soothing

spinner *n* **rotator**, whirler, whirligig, turner, gyrator

spinney *n* **wood**, thicket, copse, coppice, grove

spin-off *v* **derive**, result, develop, grow, follow on ■ *n* **by-product**, derivative, offshoot, extra, bonus

spin out *v* **drag out**, prolong, keep going, draw out, eke out *Opposite*: cut

spiny *adj* **barbed**, prickly, spiky, bristly, thorny *Opposite*: smooth

spiral *v* **1 escalate**, increase, get worse, run away, rise *Opposite*: plummet **2 fly**, rise, ascend, descend, soar

spire *n* **tip**, spike, pinnacle, point, top *Opposite*: base

spirit *n* **1 soul**, inner self, life force, chi, essence *Opposite*: body **2 will**, strength, courage, character, strength of mind **3 disposition**, temperament, attitude, nature, temper **4 feeling**, attitude, mood, tendency, atmosphere **5 ghost**, soul, ghoul, phantom, apparition ■ *v* **remove**, take away, whisk off, steal, abduct

spirited *adj* **forceful**, determined, strong-willed, vigorous, energetic *Opposite*: lacklustre

spiritless *adj* **spineless**, gutless, cowardly, sad, dejected *Opposite*: energetic

spirits *n* **emotional state**, frame of mind, state of mind, mental state, feelings

spiritual *adj* **1 religious**, holy, sacred, divine, heavenly *Opposite*: secular **2 mental**, emotional, psychological, temperamental, internal *Opposite*: physical

spiritualist *n* **medium**, clairvoyant, seer, psychic, mystic

spirituality *n* **holiness**, sanctity, religiousness, otherworldliness, unworldliness

spit *v* **1 expectorate**, splutter, hawk, expel, gob *(slang) Opposite*: swallow **2 sputter**, sizzle, pop, spatter, spurt **3 utter**, splutter, hiss, mutter, say **4 rain**, shower, drizzle, mizzle, sprinkle *(US)* **5 impale**, skewer, spear, spike, run through *(literary)* ■ *n* **1 saliva**, spittle, sputum, dribble **2 skewer**, rotisserie, brochette, rod, broach

spit and polish *(infml) n* **meticulousness**, tidiness, cleanliness, orderliness, neatness

spite *n* **malice**, ill will, ill feeling, vindictiveness, meanness *Opposite*: goodwill

spiteful *adj* **malicious**, vindictive, mean, nasty, vicious *Opposite*: kind

spitefulness *see* **spite**

spitting image *(infml) n* **double**, twin, clone, image, spit *Opposite*: opposite

spittle *n* **saliva**, spit, sputum, dribble

splash *v* **1 plop**, slop, spatter, spray, slap **2 splatter**, get water on, wet, dash, spray *Opposite*: dab **3 wallow**, wade, plop, flap, flop *Opposite*: glide

splashy *adj* **1 gaudy**, garish, bright, bold, colourful *Opposite*: drab **2** *(infml)* **showy**, ostentatious, flamboyant, flashy, bold *Opposite*: restrained

splat *n* **smack**, splash, plop, slop, slap

splatter *v* **splash**, spatter, bespatter, dash, spray

splay *v* **1 spread**, spread out, spread wide, open, open out *Opposite*: close up **2 turn out**, turn outwards, twist, bend, distort ■ *adj* **outspread**, splayed, splayed-out, spread, spread-out ■ *n* **slope**, bevel, slant, angle, incline

spleen *n* **ill temper**, anger, irritation, annoyance, grumpiness *Opposite*: contentment

splendid *adj* **1 magnificent**, grand, superb, impressive, fine *Opposite*: unimpressive **2 excellent**, marvellous, wonderful, fabulous, great

splendiferous *adj* **magnificent**, splendid, superlative, wonderful, superb *Opposite*: abysmal

splendour *n* **1 magnificence**, glory, grandeur, brilliance, impressiveness *Opposite*: drabness **2 wonder**, marvel, glory, triumph, miracle

splenetic *adj* **bad-tempered**, spiteful, irritable, peevish, waspish *Opposite*: good-tempered

splice *v* **join**, intertwine, interweave, merge, fix together *Opposite*: split ■ *n* **seam**, join, connection, link, joint

spline *n* **1 key**, tooth, blade, fin, projection **2 connecting strip**, connector, connection, joining strip, link

splint *v* **immobilize**, strap, bind, bandage, secure

splinter *n* **fragment**, particle, piece, shard, sliver ■ *v* **fall apart**, crack, disintegrate, come apart, break up *Opposite*: mend

splinter group *n* **faction**, sect, offshoot, subset, minority

split *v* **1 divide**, rip, tear, crack, come apart *Opposite*: join **2 cause a rift in**, breach, divide, partition ■ *n* **1 tear**, hole, rip, crack, fissure **2 difference**, breach, breakup, divergence, rift *Opposite*: reconciliation **3 splitting**, ripping, tearing, cracking, rupture **4 crack**, division, rift, rent, break. *See* COMPARE AND CONTRAST *at* **tear**.

split hairs *v* **quibble**, equivocate, be pedantic, argue, mince matters

split-level *adj* **two-tier**, twin-tier, twin-level, two-level

split on *(infml)* *v* **inform**, tell on, give away, blow the whistle on, betray *Opposite:* protect

split second *n* **instant**, moment, flash, the twinkling of an eye, second

split-second *adj* **instant**, instantaneous, immediate, prompt, high-speed *Opposite:* tardy

splitting *adj* **excruciating**, unbearable, piercing, intense, severe *Opposite:* slight

split up *v* **part**, break up, split, go your separate ways, end things *Opposite:* unite

split-up *n* **breakup**, separation, dissolution, ending, divorce *Opposite:* marriage

splodge *see* **splotch**

splotch *n* **spot**, stain, mark, blot, blotch ■ *v* **mark**, stain, spot, blemish, blot

splurge *v* **1 spend**, fritter, waste, squander, run through *Opposite:* save **2** *(infml)* **indulge**, binge, wallow, spoil, treat ■ *n* **1** *(infml)* **bout**, spree, binge, orgy, session **2** *(infml)* **display**, exhibition, show, parade, demonstration

splutter *v* **choke**, gasp, cough, spit, stutter

spoil *v* **1 ruin**, blemish, blot, blight, impair *Opposite:* improve **2 indulge**, pander to, be soft on, pamper, cosset *Opposite:* neglect **3 decay**, go rotten, rot, go bad, go off

spoilage *n* **1 decay**, rot, decomposition, degeneration, putrefaction **2 waste**, wastage, loss, leakage, spillage

spoiled *adj* **1 ruined**, damaged, decayed, rotted, rotten *Opposite:* fresh **2 overindulged**, ruined, wilful, self-centred, brattish *Opposite:* neglected

spoils *n* **1 plunder**, loot, booty, haul, pickings **2 reward**, prize, gain, profit, earnings

spoilsport *n* **killjoy**, stuffed shirt, dog in the manger, curmudgeon, wet blanket *(infml)*

spoilt *see* **spoiled**

spoke *n* **1 rod**, bar, rib, strut, shaft **2 rung**, step, foothold, strut, bar

spoken *adj* **verbal**, vocal, oral, articulated, vocalized *Opposite:* written. *See* COMPARE AND CONTRAST *at* **verbal**.

spokesperson *n* **representative**, speaker, voice, spokesman, spokeswoman

sponge *n* *(infml)* **parasite**, hanger-on, idler, user, sponger *(infml)* ■ *v* **clean**, wipe, wash, rub, mop

sponger *(infml)* *n* **parasite**, hanger-on, idler, user, scrounger *(infml) Opposite:* donor

spongy *adj* **1 soft**, springy, malleable, elastic, flexible *Opposite:* firm **2 absorbent**, porous, osmotic, permeable, penetrable *Opposite:* impermeable **3 soggy**, squishy, moist, sodden, waterlogged *Opposite:* dry

sponsor *n* **backer**, guarantor, patron, promoter, champion ■ *v* **back**, support, pay for, subsidize, fund. *See* COMPARE AND CONTRAST *at* **backer**.

sponsorship *n* **backing**, support, protection, patronage, funding

spontaneity *n* **impulsiveness**, naturalness, artlessness, extemporaneity, freedom *Opposite:* constraint

spontaneous *adj* **impulsive**, unprompted, spur-of-the-moment, natural, artless *Opposite:* planned

spoof *n* **1 hoax**, prank, deception, trick, bluff **2 parody**, satire, skit, burlesque, caricature ■ *v* **1 deceive**, fool, trick, bluff, hoax **2 satirize**, burlesque, parody, caricature, take off *(infml)*

spook *n* **1 spy**, mole, double agent, sleuth *(infml)*, snoop *(infml)* **2** *(infml)* **ghost**, wraith, phantom, spectre, apparition ■ *v* **startle**, surprise, shock, alarm, agitate *Opposite:* soothe

spooky *adj* **1 strange**, amazing, odd, unnerving, extraordinary *Opposite:* normal **2** *(infml)* **frightening**, ghostly, unnerving, mysterious, eerie *Opposite:* reassuring

spool *n* **reel**, coil, pin, bobbin ■ *v* **wind**, reel, coil, roll

spoon *v* **serve**, ladle, spoon over, spoon out, serve up

spoonerism *n* **slip of the tongue**, mistake, error, Freudian slip, tongue twister

spoon-feed *v* **1 feed**, nourish, take care of, look after, care for *Opposite:* neglect **2 mollycoddle**, coddle, overindulge, wait on hand and foot, do everything for *Opposite:* neglect

spoonful *n* **spoon**, portion, serving, teaspoonful, dessertspoonful

spoor *n* **trail**, track, paw prints, hoof marks, footmarks ■ *v* **track**, stalk, follow, trail, hunt

sporadic *adj* **irregular**, intermittent, infrequent, periodic, erratic *Opposite:* regular. *See* COMPARE AND CONTRAST *at* **periodic**.

spore *n* **reproductive structure**, dormant bacterium, bacterium, microorganism

sporran *n* **pouch**, purse, bag

sport *n* **1 diversion**, game, amusement, hobby, pastime *Opposite:* work **2** *(fml)* **joking**, clowning, teasing, fooling around, fooling about ■ *v* *(infml)* **wear**, don, display, exhibit, show off

---

WORD BANK

❏ **types of ball game** American football, Australian Rules, baseball, basketball, cricket, football, hockey, hurling, lacrosse, netball, polo, rounders, rugby, Rugby League, Rugby Union, shinty, softball, water polo

❏ **types of combat sport** aikido, boxing, fencing, judo, karate, kendo, kickboxing, kung fu, sumo, tae kwon do, wrestling

❏ **types of court game** badminton, jai alai, pelota, rackets, squash, table tennis, tennis, volleyball

❏ **types of extreme sport** barefoot waterskiing, basejumping, bungee jumping, in-line skating, mountain biking, mountain boarding, skateboarding, skysurfing, sport climbing, street luge, stunt bicycling, wakeboarding

❏ **types of sports equipment** ball, bat, bowl, club,

cue, discus, football, glove, helmet, hockey stick, javelin, lacrosse stick, mallet, mitt, pad, puck, racket, shot, shuttlecock, spikes, tee, wicket ❏ **types of target ball game** billiards, boules, bowling, bowls, croquet, golf, pool, snooker ❏ **types of track and field** cross-country, decathlon, discus, hammer throw, heptathlon, high jump, javelin, long jump, marathon, modern pentathlon, pole vault, relay race, shot put, sprint, steeplechase, triathlon, triple jump ❏ **types of winter sport** alpine skiing, biathlon, bobsleigh, cross-country skiing, curling, downhill, figure skating, ice dancing, ice hockey, langlauf, Nordic skiing, skiing, ski jump, slalom, snowboarding, speed skating, toboggan, XC skiing

sporting *adj* **fair**, generous, honourable, decent, honest *Opposite*: dishonest

sporting chance *n* **fair chance**, good chance, decent chance, fair shot, reasonable chance

sports *adj* **1 sporting**, games, athletic **2 casual**, informal, leisure, outdoor, leisurewear

sportscast *n* **sports broadcast**, sports update, sports programme, televised sports event, televised match

sportscaster *n* **sports broadcaster**, sports presenter, sports commentator, sports reporter, sports correspondent

sports ground *n* **stadium**, arena, pitch, field, ground

sportsperson *n* **competitor**, player, contestant, athlete

sporty *adj* **1 athletic**, active, good at sport, fit, muscular **2 flashy**, stylish, jaunty, natty, snazzy *(infml) Opposite*: formal

spot *n* **1 mark**, blemish, stain, smudge, speck **2** *(infml)* **predicament**, mess, difficulty, awkward situation, quandary **3 pimple**, pustule, boil, blackhead, whitehead **4 place**, location, site, setting, corner **5 bit**, soupçon, touch, dash, tad *(infml)* **6 advertisement**, commercial, promotion, ad *(infml)*, advert *(infml)* ◼ *v* **1 notice**, spy, recognize, catch a glimpse of, catch sight of *Opposite*: miss **2 stain**, dirty, blemish, smudge, speck *Opposite*: clean

spot check *n* **inspection**, check, search, examination, visit

spot-check *v* **inspect**, check, search, examine, double-check

spotless *adj* **1 immaculate**, spick-and-span, clean, clean as a new pin, pristine *Opposite*: dirty **2 unblemished**, flawless, perfect, faultless, impeccable *Opposite*: flawed

spotlessly *adv* **immaculately**, extremely, perfectly, absolutely, very

spotlessness *n* **1 cleanliness**, cleanness, pristineness, immaculateness, neatness *Opposite*: dirtiness **2 flawlessness**, wholesomeness, innocence, stainlessness, irreproachability *Opposite*: imperfection

spotlight *n* **attention**, limelight, fuss, focus, interest *Opposite*: anonymity ◼ *v* **highlight**, point up, draw attention to, underline, focus on *Opposite*: obscure

spot-on *(infml) adj* **1 exactly right**, dead right, bang on *(infml)*, accurate, correct *Opposite*: wrong **2 ideal**, just right, perfect, just what we need, just what the doctor ordered *Opposite*: disastrous

spotted *adj* **dotted**, marked, speckled, dappled, mottled *Opposite*: plain

spotty *adj* **1 mottled**, patterned, blotchy, spotted, dotted **2 blemished**, pockmarked, covered with spots, pimpled, pimply *Opposite*: unblemished

spouse *n* **other half**, wife, husband, next of kin, partner

spout *v* **1 spew out**, shoot out, discharge, spurt, emit *Opposite*: retain **2 talk**, utter, pontificate, ramble on, sermonize ◼ *n* **1 jet**, fountain, stream, column, spurt **2 tube**, pipe, nozzle, outlet, spray

sprain *v* **twist**, pull, injure, rick, strain

sprawl *v* **1 slump**, collapse, lounge, loll, slouch *Opposite*: curl up **2 spread out**, cover, extend over, stretch over, trail *Opposite*: shrink ◼ *n* **stretch**, mass, extension, spread, straggle

sprawling *adj* **extensive**, rambling, expansive, straggling, straggly *Opposite*: contained

spray *n* **1 gush**, squirt, mist, jet, fountain **2 atomizer**, aerosol, spray can, pump dispenser, sprayer **3 sprig**, bouquet, stem, posy, buttonhole ◼ *v* **1 scatter**, squirt, send out, spew, spurt **2 cover**, drench, squirt, mist, dose

spray can *n* **aerosol**, atomizer, spray, pump dispenser, sprayer

spray gun *n* **spray**, atomizer, airbrush, sprayer, diffuser

spread *v* **1 open out**, unfold, place, lay out, put out *Opposite*: furl **2 increase**, extend, multiply, reach, stretch *Opposite*: shrink **3 last**, continue, go on, carry on, persist **4 broadcast**, disseminate, circulate, publish, propagate **5 apply**, put on, smear, daub, butter *Opposite*: remove **6 disperse**, distribute, share out, allot, divide *Opposite*: collect ◼ *n* **1 range**, extent, increase, coverage, span **2 variety**, range, selection, array, assortment **3 ranch**, estate, farm, plantation, station **4** *(infml)* **feast**, banquet, binge, meal, supper

spread-eagled *adj* **sprawled**, sprawling, prone, prostrate, face down *Opposite*: erect

spread out *v* **1 move apart**, divide up, split up *Opposite*: amass **2 extend**, cover, spread, go as far as, stretch **3 share out**, share, divide up, split up

spreadsheet *n* **worksheet**, database, table

spree *n* **1 binge**, extravaganza, fling, orgy, splurge *(infml)* **2 jaunt**, outing, trip, excursion, break

sprig *n* **spray**, twig, stem, branch, shoot

sprightly *adj* **energetic**, active, spry, lively, agile *Opposite*: lethargic

spring *v* **jump**, leap, bounce, pounce, launch

yourself ■ n 1 **coil**, spiral, helix, mainspring, hairspring 2 **elasticity**, springiness, bounce, give, flexibility *Opposite*: rigidity 3 **leap**, bound, jump, bounce, vault 4 **springtime**, season, seedtime, springtide (literary) 5 **source**, upwelling, fount, fountain, water source

spring back v ricochet, recoil, shrink

springboard n catalyst, facilitator, spur, trigger, launch pad *Opposite*: brake

spring-clean v scour, scrub, wash down, dust down, clean out *Opposite*: dirty

springtime n season, spring, seedtime, springtide (literary)

spring up v appear, emerge, pop up, come into existence, mushroom *Opposite*: disappear

springy adj bouncy, elastic, supple, pliable, soft *Opposite*: unyielding

sprinkle v 1 shake over, dust, scatter, cover 2 **intersperse**, pepper, strew, scatter, litter ■ n **sprinkling**, shake, dusting, scattering, scatter

sprinkler n 1 sprayer, irrigator, waterer, spray, hose 2 **nozzle**, rose, showerhead, spray, diffuser

sprinkling n scattering, dash, shake, pinch, bit *Opposite*: heap

sprint n dash, burst, race, run, cycle race *Opposite*: marathon ■ v **hurry**, run, dash, race, gallop *Opposite*: dawdle

sprinter n runner, racer, competitor

sprite n fairy, nymph, elf, dryad, leprechaun

sprocket n tooth, cog, notch, projection, sprocket wheel

sprout v 1 **grow**, shoot, develop, bud, spring *Opposite*: wither 2 **spring up**, spring, emerge, appear, pop up ■ n **shoot**, bud, leaf, young branch, new growth

spruce adj smart, neat, dapper, trim, elegant *Opposite*: scruffy

spruce up v smarten, smarten up, tidy, neaten, improve *Opposite*: mess up (infml)

spry adj sprightly, lively, active, agile, energetic *Opposite*: slow

spud (infml) n **potato**, tater (infml), murphy (dated infml)

spunk (infml) n **pluck**, spirit, toughness, determination, nerve *Opposite*: cowardice

spunky (infml) adj **plucky**, spirited, tough, determined, energetic *Opposite*: cowardly

spur n 1 **incentive**, stimulus, incitement, provocation, motive *Opposite*: disincentive 2 **ridge**, mountainside, projection, edge, saddle 3 **branch**, limb, shoot, offshoot, outgrowth 4 **spike**, point, barb, spine ■ v **urge**, encourage, incite, prompt, stimulate *Opposite*: discourage. See COMPARE AND CONTRAST at motive.

spurious adj false, bogus, fake, forged, counterfeit *Opposite*: genuine

spurn v reject, snub, slight, rebuff, repulse *Opposite*: accept

spur-of-the-moment adj **spontaneous**, impulsive, unplanned, impromptu, unpremeditated *Opposite*: planned

spurt n 1 **jet**, spray, squirt, gush, spout *Opposite*: trickle 2 **increase**, burst, surge, rush, swell ■ v **gush**, spray, burst, jet, erupt *Opposite*: trickle

sputter v 1 **pop**, splutter, spit, sizzle, crackle 2 **splutter**, gasp, spit, stammer, snort

sputum n mucus, phlegm, saliva, spit, spittle

spy n **secret agent**, undercover agent, double agent, mole, infiltrator ■ v 1 **watch**, eavesdrop, listen in, observe, scrutinize 2 **work undercover**, pry, reconnoitre, snoop (infml), nose around (infml) 3 **spot**, glimpse, notice, observe, see 4 **discover**, search out, detect, find out, observe *Opposite*: overlook 5 **investigate**, poke around, explore, search, research

spyhole n peephole, slot, chink, opening, window

spying n **undercover work**, intelligence work, espionage, eavesdropping, infiltration

spy out v discover, uncover, seek out, sniff out, nose out *Opposite*: overlook

squabble n quarrel, row, tiff, dispute, argument *Opposite*: reconciliation ■ v **argue**, bicker, quarrel, disagree, have words *Opposite*: make up

squad n group, team, crew, company, gang

squad car n police car, patrol car, panda car, cruiser (US)

squadron n regiment, troop, team, squad, company

squalid adj 1 **filthy**, dirty, foul, nasty, fetid *Opposite*: clean 2 **seedy**, repulsive, sordid, sleazy, low *Opposite*: charming. See COMPARE AND CONTRAST at dirty.

squall n storm, gust of wind, windstorm, gust, shower

squally adj stormy, gusty, blustery, wild, inclement *Opposite*: fine

squalor n 1 **filth**, dirt, dirtiness, foulness, grime *Opposite*: cleanliness 2 **nastiness**, sordidness, unpleasantness, degradation, immorality *Opposite*: charm

squander v waste, spend, throw away, fritter away, dissipate *Opposite*: save

square n 1 **four-sided figure**, quadrangle, tetragon, rectangle, parallelogram 2 **plaza**, open area, marketplace, place, parade ■ adj 1 **foursided**, right-angled, rectangular, quadrangular, tetragonal 2 **fair**, honest, genuine, just, straight *Opposite*: dishonest ■ v 1 **shape**, form, file down, sharpen, even up 2 **adjust**, align, realign, set straight, straighten *Opposite*: unbalance 3 **pay off**, settle, clear, pay, balance 4 **agree**, harmonize, accord, fit, tally *Opposite*: conflict ■ adv 1 **at right angles**, directly, straight 2 (infml) **fairly**, honestly, openly, straightforwardly, straight

squarely adv directly, exactly, evenly, head-on, straight *Opposite*: indirectly

square meal n **nourishment**, hot meal, proper meal, food, sustenance Opposite: nibble

square up v 1 **settle up**, even up, settle your debts, settle the bill, pay up 2 **work out**, turn out fine, sort itself out, be arranged, be organized Opposite: go wrong 3 **face up to**, confront, look something in the eye, tackle, take on Opposite: evade 4 **put up your fists**, make a stand, put up a fight, stand your ground, take up the gauntlet Opposite: run away

squash v 1 **crush**, flatten, compress, pulp, mash Opposite: reshape 2 **cram**, squeeze, wedge, force, jam Opposite: coax 3 **overcome**, stop, conquer, suppress, quash Opposite: encourage ■ n **squeeze**, crush, congestion, crowd, jam

squashy adj **soft**, yielding, spongy, springy, mushy Opposite: firm

squat v **crouch**, sit on your heels, hunker down, bend Opposite: stand ■ adj **short**, thickset, thick, stubby, stocky Opposite: tall

squatter n **unlawful tenant**, unlawful resident, resident, trespasser

squawk v 1 **screech**, call, cry, squeal, shriek 2 (infml) **complain**, protest, whine, wail, grumble ■ n (infml) **protest**, complaint, whine, wail, grumble

squeak v **squeal**, whine, yelp, shrill, pipe

squeak through (infml) v **scrape through**, scrape by, manage, achieve, do

squeaky adj **high-pitched**, shrill, whiny, noisy, creaky

squeaky-clean adj 1 **virtuous**, righteous, pure, honourable, unimpeachable Opposite: corrupt 2 **clean**, clean as a new pin, spotless, dirt-free, pristine

squeal n **screech**, yelp, shriek, yell, cry ■ v **yell**, cry, shriek, yelp, howl

squeamish adj 1 **nauseous**, queasy, sick, woozy 2 **prudish**, delicate, easily upset, easily offended, puritanical Opposite: strong 3 **fastidious**, particular, scrupulous, fussy, uncompromising Opposite: easygoing

squeamishness n 1 **queasiness**, nauseousness, sickness, qualmishness, seediness (infml) 2 **delicacy**, prudishness, prudery, shockability, puritanism Opposite: toughness

squeeze v 1 **press**, squash, compress, constrict, pinch 2 **find time for**, make time for, make room for, fit in, slot in 3 **grip**, hold on, grasp, hug, clutch Opposite: release 4 **hug**, embrace, cuddle, enfold, clasp Opposite: release 5 **crush**, squash, cram, crowd, jam Opposite: coax 6 **extract**, wring, expel, drive out, mangle 7 **pressurize**, put pressure on, harass, oppress, lean on (infml)

squeeze out v **exclude**, express, force out, freeze out, ostracize

squelch v 1 **squish**, splash, splosh, suck, gurgle 2 **crush**, squash, flatten, trample, squish

squelchy adj **soggy**, squishy, wet, squidgy, watery Opposite: dry

squidgy adj 1 **soggy**, squelchy, slimy, mushy, marshy Opposite: dry 2 **squashy**, spongy, springy, pliable, soft Opposite: firm

squiggle n **scribble**, wavy line, doodle, ornamentation, flourish

squiggly adj **wavy**, curvy, wobbly, bumpy, scribbly Opposite: straight

squint v **narrow your eyes**, peer, peek, look, glance ■ n **peep**, peer, quick look, glance, glimpse ■ adj (infml) **crooked**, lopsided, cross-eyed, off balance, uneven Opposite: straight ■ adv (infml) **lopsidedly**, askew, crookedly, unevenly Opposite: straight

squire n 1 **landowner**, lord, landlord, owner, proprietor Opposite: tenant 2 **attendant**, retainer, steward, man, servant

squirm v 1 **wriggle**, writhe, twist, turn, fidget 2 **feel shame**, feel embarrassment, feel remorse, feel guilty, feel awkward

squirrel n (infml) **hoarder**, collector, accumulator, saver, magpie (infml) ■ v **hoard**, collect, accumulate, store, put aside Opposite: throw out

squirt v **spurt**, shoot, jet, gush, spray ■ n **spurt**, jet, fountain, stream, spray

squish v 1 **squeeze**, crush, squash, squelch, pinch 2 **splash**, squelch, splosh, suck, gurgle

squishy adj **squelchy**, soggy, soft, mushy, squidgy Opposite: firm

stab v **knife**, wound, pierce, cut, spear ■ n 1 **pang**, twinge, ache, pain, prick 2 (infml) **attempt**, go, try, shot, guess

stabbing n **knife attack**, assault, wounding, attack ■ adj **sharp**, acute, piercing, shooting, intense

stability n **constancy**, steadiness, firmness, solidity, permanence Opposite: instability

stabilization n **steadying**, steadiness, maintenance, balance, equilibrium Opposite: change

stabilize v **become stable**, even out, become constant, calm, calm down Opposite: change

stab in the back (infml) v **betray**, let down, be disloyal to, sell out, wound ■ n **betrayal**, wound, attack, act of disloyalty, act of treachery

stable adj 1 **steady**, unchanging, even, constant, firm Opposite: changeable 2 **secure**, fixed, firm, permanent, rigid Opposite: unstable 3 **calm**, steady, even, settled, level-headed Opposite: erratic ■ n 1 **stall**, shed, stabling 2 **team**, gang, string, group, lineup

staccato adj **clipped**, disjointed, disconnected, faltering, monosyllabic

stack n 1 **pile**, heap, mass, mound, mountain 2 **chimney**, smokestack, flue ■ v **pile**, load, heap, mound, amass

stacked adj **loaded**, weighted, set, slanted, fixed

stacks (infml) n **lots**, masses, piles (infml), tons (infml), loads (infml) Opposite: a few

stadium n **sports ground**, arena, pitch, ground, field

staff n **1 employees**, personnel, workers, workforce, team **2 rod**, cane, pole, wand, stick ■ v **operate**, run, work, control, supervise

stage n **1 phase**, period, step, point, leg **2 platform**, rostrum, stand, scaffold, podium **3 theatre**, arena, playhouse, the boards ■ v **put on**, perform, present, show, play

stagecoach n **carriage**, horse-drawn carriage, cart

stage door n **back door**, side door, entrance, way in, exit

stage fright n **first-night nerves**, fear, panic, nerves (infml)

stage-manage v **engineer**, contrive, manipulate, devise, set up

stage name n **pseudonym**, alias, assumed name, professional name

stage whisper n **aside**, mutter, murmur Opposite: shout

stagey see stagy

stagflation n **slump**, recession, downturn, stagnation, inflation Opposite: growth

stagger v **1 reel**, lurch, sway, totter, wobble **2 astound**, amaze, shock, stun, surprise **3 alternate**, vary, zigzag, rotate, space out Opposite: overlap

staggered adj **1 stunned**, shocked, amazed, astounded, taken aback Opposite: unaffected **2 alternated**, spread out, spaced out, zigzagged

staggering adj **astounding**, amazing, confounding, overwhelming, stunning

staging n **performance**, dramatization, production, enactment, presentation

staging post n **stopover**, halt, stop, break, halfway house

stagnant adj **1 still**, motionless, stationary, standing, immobile Opposite: moving **2 sluggish**, inactive, inert, torpid, dull Opposite: active

stagnate v **1 stand still**, come to a halt, grind to a halt, be idle, languish Opposite: progress **2 fester**, rot, deteriorate, go off, decay **3 vegetate**, be inactive, idle, be idle, sit around

stagnation n **inactivity**, inaction, inertia, torpor, sluggishness Opposite: movement

stagy adj/theatrical, dramatic, histrionic, exaggerated, artificial Opposite: unaffected

staid adj **sedate**, serious, grave, sober, dull Opposite: exciting

stain n **1 mark**, blemish, spot, blot, imperfection **2 tint**, dye, colour, pigment **3 stigma**, slur, disgrace, dishonour, blemish ■ v **1 blemish**, tarnish, soil, discolour, mark **2 disgrace**, sully, taint, debase, dishonour Opposite: honour

stained adj **discoloured**, marked, blemished, tainted, tarnished

stair n **1 step**, tread, rung **2 staircase**, stairway, flight of steps, set of steps, flight of stairs

stairs n **staircase**, stair, stairway, flight of steps, set of steps

stairwell n **hall**, entrance hall, vestibule, shaft

stake n **1 bet**, wager, ante, risk, venture **2 post**, pale, pole, palisade, picket **3 investment**, claim, share, involvement, concern **4 prize**, winnings, purse, stakes ■ v **risk**, gamble, bet, venture, hazard

stakeholder n **investor**, shareholder, backer, sponsor, participant

stake out v **1 mark out**, demarcate, delimit, chalk out, measure out **2 establish**, clarify, define, limit, restrict **3** (infml) **spy on**, watch, keep under surveillance, keep watch on, keep an eye on

stakeout (infml) n **close watch**, watch, observation, investigation, examination

stakes n **1 risk**, risk factor, danger, element of danger **2 reward**, prize, recompense, incentive, winnings

stale adj **1 decayed**, sour, old, musty, hard Opposite: fresh **2 hackneyed**, worn-out, tired, overused, boring Opposite: original

stalemate n **impasse**, deadlock, standoff, logjam, standstill

staleness n **1 mustiness**, mouldiness, decay, flatness, sourness Opposite: freshness **2 unoriginality**, overuse, insipidness

stalk n **stem**, shoot, twig, branch, trunk ■ v **follow**, trail, track, pursue, shadow

stalker n **prowler**, pursuer, shadow, tracker, follower

stall n **1 booth**, stand, arcade, shop, kiosk **2 compartment**, pen, coop, shed, cubicle ■ v **1 stop**, cut out, freeze, pause, halt Opposite: keep going **2 delay**, put off, defer, postpone, suspend Opposite: advance **3 play for time**, prevaricate, equivocate, hedge, hesitate

stalwart adj **1 strong**, muscular, athletic, brawny, sturdy Opposite: feeble **2 resolute**, vigorous, determined, committed, unfaltering Opposite: uncommitted **3 brave**, courageous, daring, fearless, bold Opposite: cowardly

stamina n **staying power**, endurance, energy, resilience, resistance Opposite: frailty

stammer v **stumble**, stutter, falter, hesitate, pause ■ n **stutter**, hesitant speech, speech impediment

stamp n **1 mark**, imprint, mould, cast, hallmark **2 character**, kind, make, sort, type ■ v **1 trample**, stomp, crush, squash, plod Opposite: tiptoe **2 imprint**, engrave, inscribe, fix, impress

stampede n **rush**, mad dash, flight, rout, pandemonium ■ v **rush**, hurry, run, dash, sprint

stamping ground (infml) n **patch**, haunt, place, home, territory

stamp out v **eradicate**, banish, destroy,

remove, eliminate *Opposite*: cultivate

stance n 1 **attitude**, position, stand, standpoint, view 2 **posture**, deportment, bearing, attitude, carriage *(fml)*

stanch *see* **staunch**

stand v 1 **rise**, get up, stand up, get to your feet, be on your feet *Opposite*: sit 2 **place**, situate, position, set, put 3 **erect**, mount, hoist, put up, stick up 4 **remain**, halt, stop, continue, exist 5 **tolerate**, endure, put up with, abide, bear ■ n 1 **attitude**, opinion, stance, position, viewpoint 2 **stop**, standstill, stay, rest, halt 3 **stall**, counter, booth, kiosk, tent 4 **platform**, rostrum, stage, place, post 5 **rack**, frame, support, holder, shelf

standard n 1 **criterion**, benchmark, touchstone, paradigm, yardstick 2 **norm**, average, mean, par, level 3 **flag**, banner, ensign, pennant, streamer ■ *adj* **normal**, typical, average, usual, ordinary *Opposite*: unusual

standard-bearer n **leader**, ringleader, prime mover, spearhead, director

standardize v **regulate**, homogenize, normalize, even out, regiment *Opposite*: vary

standard of living n **level of comfort**, means, level of affluence, wealth, lifestyle

standards n **principles**, values, morals, ethics, ideals

stand by v **support**, stick by, back, stick up for, side with *Opposite*: abandon

stand-by n 1 **reserve**, deputy, stand-in, double, understudy 2 **substitute**, replacement, spare, backup, reserve ■ *adj* 1 **reserve**, fallback, replacement, stand-in, deputy 2 **last-minute**, late *Opposite*: reserved

stand down v **resign**, step down, quit, bow out, give up

stand firm v **persevere**, stand your ground, hold on, hold out, dig in your heels *Opposite*: yield

stand for v 1 **put up with**, tolerate, abide, withstand, stand 2 **mean**, signify, represent, denote, symbolize 3 **advocate**, promote, support, champion, endorse

stand in v **fill in**, substitute, deputize, take somebody's place, do somebody's work

stand-in n **replacement**, understudy, deputy, substitute, reserve

stand in for v **take the place of**, deputize for, substitute for, cover for, do the work of

standing n 1 **rank**, status, position, reputation, station 2 **duration**, existence, continuance, age, tenure ■ *adj* 1 **established**, settled, fixed, immovable, durable *Opposite*: temporary 2 **standing**, vertical, upright, upended, perpendicular *Opposite*: horizontal

standing order n **rule**, order, instruction, protocol, procedure

standing stone n **obelisk**, menhir, dolmen, megalith, column

standoff n **stalemate**, impasse, deadlock, logjam, standstill

standoffish *adj* **distant**, aloof, superior, unapproachable, cold *Opposite*: affable

stand out v 1 **be obvious**, be prominent, show up, be conspicuous, stick out 2 **project**, jut, protrude, jut out, stick out

standpipe n **water pipe**, tap, emergency pipe, water supply, hydrant

standpoint n **point of view**, position, stance, angle, viewpoint

standstill n **halt**, stop, stoppage, full stop, cessation

stand up v 1 **rise**, stand, get to your feet, get up, arise *(literary)* *Opposite*: sit down 2 **endure**, last, survive, continue, hold out

standup *adj* 1 **intense**, fierce, furious, blazing, violent *Opposite*: mild 2 **erect**, upright, standing, upstanding, vertical *Opposite*: flat 3 **solo**, improvised, off-the-cuff, impromptu, ad lib *Opposite*: rehearsed

stand up to v **face**, brave, take on, meet head-on, confront *Opposite*: avoid

stand your ground v **stand firm**, persist, persevere, reserve, hold out *Opposite*: give in

stanza n **verse**, section, stave, couplet, triplet

staple n **clip**, fastener, nail, tack, pin ■ v **fasten**, affix, clip, attach, secure ■ *adj* **main**, chief, principal, essential, primary *Opposite*: minor

star n **celebrity**, superstar, personality, icon ■ v 1 **feature**, showcase, head the cast, top the bill, play the lead 2 **do well**, excel, shine, succeed, stand out

WORD BANK
❑ **types of star** binary star, black hole, brown dwarf, dark star, dwarf star, galaxy, giant star, nebula, nova, pulsar, quasar, red giant, sun, supernova, white dwarf

star billing n **top billing**, star status, top of the bill, main attraction, star turn

starboard *adj* **right-hand**, right, right-side *Opposite*: port

starchy *adj* **stiff**, solemn, prudish, prim, austere *Opposite*: relaxed

star-crossed *adj* **ill-fated**, unlucky, ill-starred, doomed, unfortunate *Opposite*: lucky

stardom n **fame**, celebrity, prominence, renown, glory *Opposite*: anonymity

stardust n **romance**, dreaminess, sentiment, emotion, feeling

stare v **gaze**, gape, look intently, ogle, glare *Opposite*: ignore ■ n **intent look**, gaze, gape, glare, glower. *See* COMPARE AND CONTRAST *at* gaze.

stare out v **outstare**, stare at, look at, gaze at, stare down (US)

star in v **play the lead in**, feature in, act in, play in, head the cast

stark *adj* 1 **bleak**, bare, barren, desolate, austere *Opposite*: opulent 2 **complete**, utter, absolute, sheer, downright *Opposite*: partial 3 **plain**, unambiguous, simple, blunt, unadulterated Opposite: ambiguous ■ adv **completely**, utterly, entirely, wholly, fully Opposite: partially

starkness n 1 **austerity**, bleakness, harshness, severity, sparseness Opposite: opulence 2 **frankness**, unambiguity, blatancy, harshness, bluntness Opposite: ambiguity

starlet n **actor**, rising young star, new talent, star of tomorrow, star in the making

starlight n **glow**, gleam, sheen, twinkle, sparkle

starlit adj **starry**, bright, glowing, gleaming, twinkling Opposite: dark

starry adj **glittery**, shiny, bright, sparkly, brilliant Opposite: dull

starry-eyed adj **dreamy**, optimistic, idealistic, head-in-the-clouds, happy Opposite: cynical

starship n **spaceship**, space shuttle, space station, flying saucer

star sign n **sign of the zodiac**, birth sign, sun sign, sign, astrological sign

WORD BANK
❑ **types of star sign** Aquarius, Aries, Cancer, Capricorn, Gemini, Leo, Libra, Pisces, Sagittarius, Scorpio, Taurus, Virgo

star-studded adj **star-spangled**, all-star, celebrity, big-name, glittering Opposite: unknown

star system n **constellation**, galaxy, Milky Way, solar system

start v 1 **begin**, commence, start off, get going, set off Opposite: finish 2 **create**, found, begin, establish, set up Opposite: close 3 **set out**, leave, set off, depart, get going Opposite: arrive 4 **jump**, recoil, flinch, shrink, twitch ■ n 1 **beginning**, birth, foundation, onset, dawn Opposite: end 2 **lead**, advantage, edge, boon, gain 3 **twitch**, jump, jerk, flinch, jolt 4 **shock**, fright, surprise, turn

starter n **hors d'oeuvre**, first course, entrée, appetizer, meze

starting point n 1 **basis**, base, foundation, point of departure, beginning 2 **starting line**, starting block, starting grid, starting post, starting gate Opposite: finishing line

startle v **surprise**, disconcert, shock, alarm, frighten

startled adj **surprised**, disconcerted, alarmed, astonished, amazed

startling adj **surprising**, astonishing, amazing, astounding, staggering Opposite: comforting

start off v 1 **begin**, commence, get going, start out, start Opposite: finish 2 **set off**, start out, be off, get going, start Opposite: arrive

start on v 1 **begin**, tackle, deal with, embark on, get going on Opposite: finish 2 (infml) **scold**, harass, pester, nag, annoy

start out v 1 **start off**, start, begin, set off, get going Opposite: arrive 2 **intend**, mean, plan, propose, expect

start up v 1 **switch on**, turn on, fire up, power up, ignite Opposite: turn off 2 **set up**, open, begin, launch, create Opposite: close down 3 **pipe up**, resound, be heard, begin, start Opposite: quieten down 4 **leap up**, jump up, stand up, get up, rise Opposite: sit down

star turn n **main attraction**, star attraction, big name, top of the bill, top act

starvation n **hunger**, malnourishment, undernourishment, famishment, famine

starve v **have nothing to eat**, go hungry, famish, be malnourished, go short of food Opposite: eat

starved adj 1 **deprived**, bereft, devoid, lacking, without 2 (infml) **ravenous**, hungry, famished, starving (infml) Opposite: replete

starving (infml) adj **ravenous**, hungry, famished, starved (infml) Opposite: replete

stash n **supply**, hideaway, hoard, mass, pile ■ v (infml) **hide**, hoard, put away, put by, stockpile

stasis n **stability**, motionlessness, status quo, continuity, inertia Opposite: change

state n 1 **condition**, situation, position, status, circumstances 2 (infml) **confusion**, turmoil, disarray, disorder, chaos 3 **federation**, kingdom, nation, land, territory 4 **grandeur**, ceremony, pomp, splendour, glory ■ adj 1 **public**, government, municipal, state-run, state-owned 2 **formal**, official, stately, imperial, royal ■ v **utter**, affirm, declare, assert, express

statecraft n **government**, management, governance, administration, direction

stateless adj **homeless**, nationless, displaced, refugee, outlawed

stateliness n **grandeur**, pomp, glory, dignity, majesty

stately adj **grand**, splendid, dignified, imperial, majestic Opposite: modest

stately home n **mansion**, manor, hall, country house, great house

statement n 1 **declaration**, announcement, report, account, speech 2 **record**, account, receipt, invoice

state of affairs n **situation**, set of circumstances, condition, setup, position

state of mind n **mood**, temper, attitude, feelings, spirits

state-of-the-art adj **advanced**, high-tech, cutting-edge, up-to-the-minute, up-to-date Opposite: antiquated

state-owned adj **public**, public-sector, state, state-run, nationalized Opposite: private

stateroom n **first-class compartment**, first-class cabin, sleeping compartment, berth, sleeper

state secret n **confidential matter**, affair of state, top-secret matter, confidential information, classified material

static adj 1 **still**, motionless, stationary, inert, standing Opposite: moving 2 **unchanging**, constant, invariable, unvarying *Opposite*: dynamic

station *n* **1 position**, place, post, location, situation **2 rank**, class, status, position, level ■ *v* **post**, base, position, place, situate

stationary *adj* **motionless**, still, immobile, inactive, fixed *Opposite*: moving

stationery *n* **writing materials**, writing implements, pen and paper, writing paper, notepaper

statistic *n* **number**, figure, digit, piece of data, measurement

statistics *n* **figures**, data, numbers, information

statuary *n* **sculptures**, statues, figures, monuments, busts

statue *n* **figurine**, figure, sculpture, effigy, statuette

statuesque *adj* **stately**, elegant, graceful, majestic, dignified *Opposite*: ungainly

statuette *see* **statue**

stature *n* **1 build**, height, physique, figure, tallness **2 standing**, importance, prominence, status, rank

status *n* **1 rank**, position, standing, grade, station **2 eminence**, prestige, prominence, importance, significance **3 category**, condition, class, type, stage

status quo *n* **current situation**, existing state of affairs, present circumstances, how things stand

status symbol *n* **asset**, must-have, prize possession

statute *n* **decree**, act, ruling, edict, order

statute book *n* **body of law**, record, legislation, legal code, law book

statute law *n* **written law**, law, constitution, legislation

statutory *adj* **constitutional**, legislative, legal

staunch *v* **stop**, stem, halt, hold back, curb ■ *adj* **loyal**, faithful, steadfast, reliable, dependable *Opposite*: wavering

stave *n* **1 plank**, slat, board, lath, band **2 bar**, rung, tread, step, crosspiece **3 stanza**, verse, section, couplet, triplet

stave off *v* **fend off**, keep at bay, hold off, delay, deflect

stay *v* **1 remain**, wait, hang about, continue, keep on *Opposite*: go **2 reside**, live, inhabit, settle, dwell *(literary)* **3 stop**, halt, delay, defer, put off ■ *n* **1 visit**, break, holiday, stopover, vacation **2 halt**, stop, delay, deferment, adjournment

staying power *n* **stamina**, endurance, determination, doggedness, vigour *Opposite*: frailty

stay on *v* **remain**, stay, stay put, stay behind, stay out *Opposite*: leave

stay out *v* **be out**, not come home, not come back, stop out *(infml)*

stay put *v* **remain**, stay, stay still, tarry, hang on *Opposite*: move

stay up *v* **stop up**, burn the candle at both ends, stay up till all hours, burn the midnight oil, make a night of it

steadfast *adj* **1 unwavering**, unfaltering, resolute, committed, dedicated *Opposite*: wavering **2 loyal**, trusty, dependable, faithful, trustworthy *Opposite*: inconstant *(literary)*

steadfastness *n* **1 resoluteness**, commitment, dedication, persistence, determination *Opposite*: wavering **2 loyalty**, faithfulness, trustworthiness, devotion, dependability *Opposite*: disloyalty

steadily *adv* **progressively**, gradually, increasingly, little by little, bit by bit *Opposite*: suddenly

steadiness *n* **1 control**, stability, firmness, balance, equilibrium *Opposite*: unsteadiness **2 calmness**, composure, equanimity, serenity, reliability *Opposite*: excitability **3 regularity**, uniformity, constancy

steady *adj* **1 stable**, firm, fixed, solid, sturdy *Opposite*: rickety **2 continual**, constant, perpetual, never-ending, ceaseless *Opposite*: intermittent **3 even**, regular, uniform, unchanging, unvarying *Opposite*: irregular **4 calm**, cool, collected, composed, unruffled *Opposite*: excitable ■ *v* **stabilize**, secure, fix, support, strengthen *Opposite*: undermine

steal *v* **1 pilfer**, misappropriate, embezzle, take, pocket **2 creep**, sneak, slip, slink, tiptoe ■ *n* *(infml)* **bargain**, good deal, good buy, giveaway *(infml)*, snip *(infml)* *Opposite*: rip-off *(infml)*

COMPARE AND CONTRAST CORE MEANING: the taking of property unlawfully

steal take something that belongs to somebody else, illegally or without the owner's permission; **pinch** *(infml)* steal something; **nick** *(slang)* steal something; **filch** *(infml)* steal something furtively and opportunistically, usually a small item or something of little value; **purloin** *(fml)* steal something, sometimes used humorously or euphemistically; **pilfer** steal small items of little value, especially habitually; **embezzle** take for personal use money or property that has been given on trust by others, without their knowledge; **misappropriate** take something, especially money, dishonestly or in order to use it for an improper or illegal purpose.

stealing *n* **theft**, robbery, burglary, thieving, pilfering

stealth *n* **furtiveness**, surreptitiousness, sneakiness, slyness, craftiness *Opposite*: openness

stealthy *adj* **furtive**, surreptitious, sly, silent, cautious *Opposite*: blatant. *See* COMPARE AND CONTRAST *at* **secret**.

steam *n* **vapour**, condensation, haze, mist, fog

steamroller *v* **1 compress**, bulldoze, flatten, crush, squash **2 crush**, squash, demolish, destroy, overwhelm **3 force**, compel, coerce, bludgeon, bully

steam up v mist up, fog up, cloud, cloud over, mist over

steamy adj 1 humid, muggy, damp, sticky, hot and sticky 2 misted up, misty, fogged up, foggy, steamed up Opposite: clear

steel v strengthen, toughen, harden, fortify, brace

steely adj 1 hard, strong, tough, sturdy, rugged Opposite: soft 2 determined, resolute, unyielding, unbending, rigid Opposite: irresolute

steel yourself v brace yourself, harden your heart, pluck up your courage, prepare yourself, compose yourself

steep adj 1 sheer, vertical, sharp, precipitous, abrupt Opposite: gentle 2 (infml) unreasonable, extreme, excessive, expensive, dear Opposite: reasonable ■ v 1 soak, immerse, drench, submerge, suffuse 2 imbue, permeate, infuse

steeple n tower, spire, turret, bell tower, belfry

steeply adv sharply, precipitously, abruptly, suddenly Opposite: gently

steepness n sharpness, abruptness, gradient, sheerness Opposite: gentleness

steer v 1 control, drive, pilot, navigate, manoeuvre 2 direct, guide, point, conduct, lead. See COMPARE AND CONTRAST at **guide**.

steerage n third class, bottom deck, tourist class, lower deck

steering committee n steering group, board, panel, team, commission

stellar adj 1 astral, astronomical, astrophysical, solar, planetary Opposite: earthly 2 all-star, star-studded, star-spangled, starry, celebrity Opposite: unknown

stem n stalk, shoot, trunk, twig, branch ■ v stop, staunch, halt, curtail, restrict Opposite: accelerate

stem from v arise from, originate from, come from, derive from, develop from

stench n stink, reek, unpleasant smell, foul smell, pong (infml) Opposite: fragrance. See COMPARE AND CONTRAST at **smell**.

stencil n 1 template, cutout, guide, plate, pattern 2 pattern, design, lettering, motif, border ■ v 1 decorate, adorn, paint, ornament 2 apply, paint, work, draw, trace

stentorian adj loud, powerful, booming, thunderous, deafening Opposite: quiet

step n 1 pace, footstep, stride 2 move, movement, action, measure 3 stage, phase, period 4 stair, rung, tread ■ v walk, tread, march, pace, move

step down v 1 stand down, resign, retire, bow out, withdraw Opposite: stay on 2 decrease, reduce, lower, lessen, restrict Opposite: step up

step in v intervene, intercede, interpose, interrupt, get involved

stepladder n ladder, steps, portable ladder, folding ladder, stairs

step out v 1 go out, step outside, nip out, leave, absent yourself Opposite: stay put 2 march, tear along, rush, stride, dash Opposite: crawl

steppe n prairie, grassland, plain, savanna, pampas

stepping stone n 1 stone, boulder, rock, foothold, bridge 2 stage, step, means of access, stage of progress, stage of advancement

step up v increase, intensify, improve, maximize, accelerate Opposite: lower

stereophonic adj stereo, audio, binaural, hi-fi, high-fidelity

stereotype v typecast, label, pigeonhole, categorize, pack

stereotypical adj conventional, orthodox, formulaic, banal, hackneyed Opposite: original

sterile adj 1 germ-free, disinfected, antiseptic, sterilized, spotlessly clean Opposite: dirty 2 infertile, unproductive, barren Opposite: fertile 3 bare, fruitless, unfruitful, unproductive, desolate Opposite: verdant 4 dull, unimaginative, banal, unstimulating Opposite: creative

sterility n 1 barrenness, unfruitfulness, unproductiveness, desolation, bareness Opposite: fruitfulness 2 infertility, barrenness, childlessness, unproductiveness, impotence Opposite: fertility 3 cleanness, antisepsis, disinfection, decontamination, purity Opposite: contamination 4 dullness, unimaginativeness, lack of imagination, lack of creativity, banality Opposite: creativity

sterilization n 1 purification, cleansing, disinfection, fumigation, decontamination 2 neutering, castration, gelding, spaying

sterilize v 1 disinfect, bleach, make germ-free, fumigate, sanitize 2 neuter, spay, geld, castrate

sterilizer n disinfectant, germicide, antiseptic, bactericide, sanitizer

sterling adj 1 genuine, authentic, true, pure, real Opposite: spurious 2 excellent, exceptional, matchless, incomparable, worthy Opposite: mediocre

stern adj 1 strict, harsh, severe, austere, unsympathetic Opposite: easygoing 2 grim, forbidding, formidable, dour, serious Opposite: cheerful

sternness n 1 severity, strictness, harshness, firmness, austerity Opposite: leniency 2 grimness, seriousness, sombreness, gravity, humourlessness Opposite: cheerfulness

stet v let it stand, restore, retain, undo, ignore Opposite: delete

stew n (infml) difficult situation, state (infml), flap (infml), tizzy (infml), lather (infml) ■ v 1 simmer, boil slowly, braise, casserole, parboil 2 be upset, be troubled, be agitated, worry, trouble

stick n twig, cane, baton, rod, staff ■ v 1 spear,

stab, penetrate, pierce, spike **2 attach**, glue, fix, fasten, join *Opposite*: detach **3** *(infml)* **put**, lay, place, set, deposit **4** *(infml)* **push**, put, thrust, shove, poke *Opposite*: withdraw

stick around *(infml)* v **linger**, wait, stay, remain, hang about *(infml) Opposite*: leave

stick at v **persist at**, continue with, persist, persevere with, see through *Opposite*: give up

stick by v **remain loyal to**, stay loyal to, remain faithful to, support, adhere to *Opposite*: let down

sticker n **label**, sticky label, sign, marker, bumper sticker

stickiness n **tackiness**, gluiness, gumminess, adhesiveness, pastiness

sticking plaster n **plaster**, dressing, bandage, pad, corn plaster

sticking point n **stumbling block**, bone of contention, impasse, obstacle, deadlock

stick-in-the-mud *(infml)* n **reactionary**, diehard, fogy, fuddy-duddy *(infml)*, stuffed shirt *(infml) Opposite*: daredevil

stickler n **pedant**, nitpicker, perfectionist, martinet, hard taskmaster

stick out v **1 extend**, poke out, jut out, push out, thrust out **2 put up with**, endure, bear, weather, see through *Opposite*: give up

stick to v **1 follow**, obey, abide by, stand by, remain faithful to *Opposite*: abandon **2 adhere**, cling, follow, cling to, hold

stick together v **stay close**, remain unified, remain loyal, remain friendly, concur *Opposite*: split up

stick up v **1 protrude**, point upwards, point up, stand up, bristle *Opposite*: hang down **2 point up**, cock, prick up, make vertical, raise up

stick up for v **support**, defend, stand up for, stand by, argue for

stick with v **1 persist with**, continue with, persevere with, see through, stay with *Opposite*: give up **2 stay loyal to**, remain loyal to, remain faithful to, stay close to, stay with *Opposite*: abandon

sticky adj **1 tacky**, gluey, gummy, adhesive, pasty **2** *(infml)* **difficult**, tricky, delicate, awkward, sensitive **3 muggy**, humid, close, clammy, sultry *Opposite*: dry

sticky wicket *(infml)* n **tricky situation**, awkward situation, difficult situation, difficult problem, embarrassing problem

stiff adj **1 rigid**, firm, inflexible, unbending, unbendable *Opposite*: limp **2 severe**, harsh, drastic, stringent, excessive *Opposite*: lenient **3 formal**, stuffy, standoffish, aloof, pompous *Opposite*: relaxed **4 strong**, vigorous, powerful, robust, intense *Opposite*: weak **5 demanding**, exacting, arduous, testing, tough *Opposite*: easy **6 aching**, painful, arthritic, tender, sore

stiffen v **1 harden**, thicken, solidify, congeal,

become rigid *Opposite*: soften **2 strengthen**, make stronger, reinforce, toughen, brace *Opposite*: weaken

stiffly adv **rigidly**, firmly, inflexibly, unbendingly, tautly

stiff-necked adj **obstinate**, arrogant, stubborn, proud, haughty *Opposite*: yielding

stiffness n **1 rigidity**, firmness, inflexibility, tautness, hardness *Opposite*: limpness **2 severity**, harshness, stringency, excessiveness, extremity *Opposite*: leniency **3 formality**, stuffiness, standoffishness, aloofness, pomposity *Opposite*: informality **4 strength**, vigour, power, robustness, intensity *Opposite*: weakness **5 difficulty**, arduousness, laboriousness, rigorousness, toughness *Opposite*: ease

stifle v **1 smother**, asphyxiate, throttle, suffocate, choke **2 suppress**, repress, restrain, curb, hold back *Opposite*: let out

stifling adj **1 hot**, boiling, airless, muggy, close *Opposite*: cool **2 oppressive**, repressive, overpowering, restrictive, inhibiting *Opposite*: liberating

stigma n **shame**, disgrace, dishonour, humiliation

stigmatize v **brand**, slur, defame, mark out, pillory

still adj **1 motionless**, immobile, unmoving, at rest, at a standstill *Opposite*: moving **2 flat**, nonsparkling, uncarbonated ▪ v **calm**, allay, dispel, banish, quieten *Opposite*: stir up ▪ adv **even now**, in spite of everything, even so, nevertheless, nonetheless

stillborn adj **1 born dead**, dead at birth, miscarried, aborted, dead **2 ineffectual**, useless, ineffective, unsuccessful, abortive *Opposite*: successful

stillness n **motionlessness**, immobility, silence, quietness, tranquillity *Opposite*: movement

stilt n **post**, column, support, pillar, pole

stilted adj **affected**, stiff, wooden, mannered, unnatural *Opposite*: natural

stimulant n **stimulating substance**, tonic, pick-me-up *(infml)*, upper *(slang)*, pep pill *(dated) Opposite*: sedative ▪ adj **stimulating**, tonic, restorative, intoxicant, energizing *Opposite*: sedative

stimulate v **1 rouse**, arouse, kindle, excite, inspire *Opposite*: dampen **2 quicken**, accelerate, increase, invigorate, promote *Opposite*: slow down

stimulating adj **1 inspiring**, encouraging, motivating, interesting, thought-provoking *Opposite*: boring **2 invigorating**, refreshing, energizing, rousing *Opposite*: relaxing

stimulation n **inspiration**, motivation, encouragement, stimulus, incentive

stimulus n **incentive**, spur, inducement, impetus, provocation

sting v **smart**, prick, tingle, throb, hurt

stinging adj **hurtful**, cutting, harsh, hard, cruel

stingy *(infml)* *adj* **miserly**, ungenerous, parsimonious, sparing, grudging *Opposite*: generous

stink *v* **smell horrible**, reek, smell, hum *(infml)*, pong *(infml)* ■ *n* 1 **stench**, smell, horrible smell, unpleasant odour, reek *Opposite*: perfume 2 *(infml)* **fuss**, scandal, uproar, rumpus, commotion. *See* COMPARE AND CONTRAST *at* smell.

stinker *n* **problem**, nightmare, shocker *(infml)*, horror *(infml)*, poser *(infml)* *Opposite*: delight

stinking *adj* **foul-smelling**, reeking, smelly, stinky, rotten

stink out *v* **make smelly**, permeate, pervade, overpower, fill with a smell *Opposite*: deodorize

stinky *adj* 1 **smelly**, stinking, foul-smelling, putrid, rotten *Opposite*: fragrant 2 **nasty**, unfair, dishonest, devious, mean-spirited *Opposite*: pleasant

stint *n* **spell**, stretch, time, shift, period

stint on *v* **be sparing with**, be mean with, be parsimonious with, be frugal with, ration

stipend *n* **allowance**, salary, payment, pay, wage. *See* COMPARE AND CONTRAST *at* wage.

stipendiary *adj* **paid**, salaried, remunerated ■ *n* **earner**, wage earner, breadwinner, payee, employee

stipple *v* **dab**, paint, dot, speckle, fleck

stippled *adj* **mottled**, dappled, speckled, spotted, flecked

stipulate *v* **specify**, lay down, instruct, order, require

stipulation *n* **condition**, requirement, proviso, demand, specification

stir *v* 1 **mix**, blend, swirl, fold, whip 2 **rouse**, wake up, move, budge, shift 3 **awaken**, arouse, revive, call to mind, bring back 4 **motivate**, incite, provoke, excite, inspire 5 **agitate**, cause feeling, disturb, trouble, upset ■ *n* **commotion**, disturbance, fuss, uproar, hue and cry

stir-crazy *(infml)* *adj* **mentally unsettled**, restless, frantic, distraught, agitated

stir-fry *v* **fry**, pan-fry, sauté

stirrer *(infml)* *n* **troublemaker**, agitator, agent provocateur, firebrand, mischief-maker *Opposite*: peacemaker

stirring *adj* **rousing**, inspiring, moving, emotive, exciting *Opposite*: uninspiring

stirrup *n* **foot support**, strap, loop, ring

stir up *v* **awaken**, reawaken, bring back, kindle, inflame *Opposite*: calm

stitch *v* 1 **sew**, sew up, stitch up, darn, baste 2 **suture**, sew up, close

stitching *n* **sewing**, stitches, seam, needlework, embroidery

stock *n* 1 **supply**, stockpile, hoard, reserve, accumulation 2 **livestock**, farm animals, domestic animals, cattle, sheep ■ *adj* **standard**, typical, routine, run-of-the-mill, ordi-

nary ■ *v* **keep**, have a supply of, have available, carry, supply

stockade *n* 1 **barrier**, fence, enclosure, palisade, paling 2 **enclosure**, fort, pen, fenced area, enclosed area

stockbroker *n* **securities broker**, broker, investment analyst, financial adviser, trader

stock car *n* **racing car**, dragster, hot rod *(slang)*

stock cube *n* **concentrate**, vegetable extract, meat extract, bouillon cube *(US)*

stock exchange *n* **stock market**, trading, bourse, exchange, money market

stockholder *n* **investor**, shareholder, stakeholder, bondholder

stocking filler *n* **Christmas present**, Christmas gift, small present, small gift, extra

stockings *n* **leg coverings**, nylons, hose, tights, leggings

stock-in-trade *n* 1 **basic resource**, staple, commodity 2 **goods**, equipment, stock, merchandise, wares

stockist *n* **seller**, shop, store, wholesaler, retailer

stock market *n* **financial market**, stock exchange, exchange, market, bourse

stockpile *n* **supply**, hoard, accumulation, store, stock ■ *v* **store up**, stock up on, store, squirrel away, collect. *See* COMPARE AND CONTRAST *at* collect.

stockroom *n* **storeroom**, storehouse, store, warehouse

stocks *n* **shares**, bonds, holdings

stock-still *adv* **motionless**, completely still, absolutely still, immobile, without moving *Opposite*: moving

stocktaking *n* 1 **evaluation**, assessment, appraisal, reassessment, reappraisal 2 **inventory**, listing, itemizing, counting, checking

stock up *v* **stockpile**, hoard, save up, collect, lay in *Opposite*: finish off

stocky *adj* **thickset**, sturdy, solid, stout, squat *Opposite*: slight

stockyard *n* **yard**, enclosure, farmyard, farm, enclosed yard

stodge *(infml)* *n* 1 **heavy food**, solid food, filling food, starchy food, substantial food 2 **something dull**, something stuffy, something boring, dull subject, turgidity

stodgy *(infml)* *adj* 1 **heavy**, filling, starchy, indigestible, hard to digest *Opposite*: light 2 **dull**, turgid, uninteresting, unexciting, stuffy *Opposite*: lively

stoic *n* **impassive person**, patient person, fatalist, ascetic, unfeeling person ■ *adj* **long-suffering**, impassive, resigned, enduring, tolerant *Opposite*: excitable. *See* COMPARE AND CONTRAST *at* impassive.

stoical *see* stoic

stoicism *n* **impassiveness**, endurance,

patience, indifference, fortitude *Opposite*: excitability

stoke *v* 1 **put fuel on**, add fuel to, fuel, stoke up 2 **strengthen**, intensify, stir up, stoke up, encourage

stoke up *see* **stoke**

stole *n* **garment**, shawl, wrap, scarf, pashmina

stolid *adj* **impassive**, unresponsive, dull, emotionless, insensitive *Opposite*: emotional. *See* COMPARE AND CONTRAST *at* **impassive**.

stomachache *n* **stomach pain**, colic, indigestion, cramp, stitch

stomach-churning *see* **stomach-turning**

stomach pump (*infml*) *n* **suction pump**, suction device, aspirator, siphon, syringe

stomach-turning *adj* **sickening**, nauseating, revolting, disgusting, repulsive

stomp *v* **tread heavily**, stamp, tramp, clump, plod

stone-cold *adj* **very cold**, chilly, icy, frozen, freezing *Opposite*: boiling ∎ *adv* (*infml*) **completely**, absolutely, utterly, totally, dead

stone-dead *adj* **lifeless**, cold, dead as a dodo, dead as a doornail, deceased (*fml*) *Opposite*: alive

stoneground *adj* **ground**, milled, crushed, powdered

stone's throw *n* **short distance**, stonecast, no distance, short way, hop, skip, and jump

stonewall (*infml*) *v* 1 **evade**, obstruct, avoid, refuse, rebuff *Opposite*: cooperate 2 **delay**, hold off, hold back, stall

stonewashed *adj* **faded**, worn, distressed, washed-out, acid-washed

stonework *n* **masonry**, brickwork, walls

stony *adj* 1 **rocky**, flinty, pebbly, rock-strewn, shingly 2 **pitiless**, unfeeling, unsympathetic, unyielding, flinty *Opposite*: compassionate 3 (*infml*) **penniless**, impoverished, impecunious, broke (*infml*), poor *Opposite*: well-off

stony-broke (*infml*) *adj* **penniless**, impoverished, impecunious, poor, bankrupt *Opposite*: well-off

stony-faced *adj* **expressionless**, unemotional, unfriendly, blank, cold *Opposite*: smiling

stony-hearted *adj* **hardhearted**, unfeeling, pitiless, unsympathetic, hard *Opposite*: softhearted

stooge *n* **straight partner**, comic actor, comedian, butt, foil

stool *n* **seat**, chair, footrest, ottoman (*US*)

stoop *v* 1 **bend down**, bend forwards, bend over, bend, lean forwards *Opposite*: straighten up 2 **lower yourself**, condescend, deign, debase yourself, patronize

stop *v* 1 **discontinue**, end, bring to an end, bring to a close, bring to a standstill *Opposite*: begin 2 **prevent**, impede, hinder, prohibit, obstruct *Opposite*: permit 3 **end**, finish, come to an end, be over, break off *Opposite*: begin

4 pause, interrupt, break off, stop off, take a break *Opposite*: continue **5 block**, block up, block off, obstruct, plug ∎ *n* **halt**, break, rest, stopover, stay

stop by *v* **drop in**, call by, call, call in, visit

stopcock *n* **valve**, tap, cock, spigot, stopper

stopgap *n* **temporary solution**, substitute, makeshift, expedient, temporary measure

stop off *v* **call**, call in, stop by, stop, drop in

stop out (*infml*) *v* **stay out**, stay out late, come home late, stay away, sleep over

stopover *n* **break in your journey**, stop, halt, pause, stop-off

stoppage *n* 1 **strike**, work stoppage, industrial action, wildcat strike, go-slow 2 **blockage**, obstruction, obstacle, barrier

stoppage time *n* **injury time**, timeout, extra time, overtime, extension

stopped *adj* 1 **stationary**, still, at a standstill, immobile, motionless *Opposite*: moving 2 **clogged**, blocked, congested, backed up, stopped up *Opposite*: open **3 not working**, out of order, out of commission, worn-out, crashed *Opposite*: working

stopper *n* **plug**, bung, cork, top, lid

stop press *n* **late news**, recent news, last-minute news, news flash, postscript

stop up *v* **plug**, plug up, block, block up, block off

stop working *v* **break down**, break, fail, seize up, pack up (*infml*) *Opposite*: function

storage *n* 1 **storing**, stowage, stowing, packing, loading 2 **storage space**, storage capacity, storage area, stowage, room

WORD BANK

❏ **types of storage space** armoury, arms depot, arsenal, attic, barn, basement, bunker, cellar, depository, depot, dump, garage, gasometer, granary, hangar, hayloft, hold, landfill, larder, loft, luggage compartment, magazine, morgue, mortuary, pantry, rubbish dump, shed, silo, strongroom, treasury, warehouse, water tower, weapon store, woodshed

store *v* **put away**, stow, keep, deposit, put in storage ∎ *n* 1 **supply**, stockpile, hoard, accumulation, collection 2 **shop**, outlet, emporium, showroom, depository 3 **warehouse**, depository, depot, stockroom, repository

stores *n* **supplies**, provisions, equipment, goods, food

store up *v* **amass**, hoard, save, accumulate, stockpile

storey *n* **floor**, level, section, division, landing

storm *n* 1 **tempest**, squall, gale, hurricane, tornado 2 **outburst**, outbreak, explosion, eruption, wave ∎ *v* 1 **capture**, carry, take by storm, take, overmaster (*literary*) 2 **rage**, fume, rant and rave, thunder, bluster 3 **stamp**, stomp, stalk, flounce, march

stormbound *adj* **housebound**, confined, isolated, cut off, snowed in

storm cloud *n* sign of violence, omen, herald, harbinger, danger signal

storm drain *n* drain, storm-water sewer, gutter, channel, drainage system

stormproof *adj* storm-resistant, protected, strong, tough, waterproof

storm-tossed *adj* choppy, stormy, rough, battered, wild *Opposite*: calm

stormy *adj* 1 squally, rainy, thundery, blustery, windy *Opposite*: calm 2 tempestuous, violent, turbulent, unsettled, volatile *Opposite*: placid

story *n* 1 tale, narrative, account, legend, chronicle 2 account, report, version, statement, description 3 (*infml*) lie, untruth, falsehood, barefaced lie, fib (*infml*) 4 article, piece, feature, report, item

storybook *adj* fairy-tale, fictional, make-believe, mythical, fanciful *Opposite*: real

story line *n* plot, narrative, story, theme, scenario

storyteller *n* 1 narrator, teller of tales, teller, relater, raconteur 2 (*infml*) liar, prevaricator, deceiver, fabricator, fibber (*infml*)

stoup *n* basin, vessel, bowl, receptacle, chalice

stout *adj* 1 thickset, heavy, solid, plump, chubby *Opposite*: slender 2 brave, firm, stalwart, determined, resolute *Opposite*: faint-hearted 3 sturdy, strong, solid, substantial, tough *Opposite*: flimsy

stouthearted *adj* courageous, brave, resolute, bold, valiant *Opposite*: cowardly

stoutness *n* 1 fatness, heaviness, solidity, plumpness, chubbiness *Opposite*: slenderness 2 sturdiness, solidity, strength, heftiness, toughness *Opposite*: flimsiness 3 bravery, firmness, stalwartness, determination, resoluteness

stow *v* put away, tidy away, put, pack, store

stowage *n* stowing, storage, packing, loading, putting away

stowaway *n* fare-dodger, runaway, escapee, escaper, fugitive

straddle *v* 1 be astride, bestride, sit astride, stand astride 2 span, include, overlap, link, connect

strafe *v* bombard, attack, fire at, shell, blitz ■ *n* aerial attack, bombardment, air attack, blitz, shelling

straggle *v* 1 lag, lag behind, trail, trail behind, fall behind 2 spread untidily, spread out, sprawl, extend, spread 3 stray, ramble, maunder, meander, rove *Opposite*: keep up

straggler *n* dawdler, laggard, loiterer, lingerer, slowcoach (*infml*) *Opposite*: leader

straggly *adj* untidy, unkempt, messy, dishevelled, tousled *Opposite*: tidy

straight *adj* 1 candid, frank, direct, open, honest *Opposite*: devious 2 level, upright, horizontal, vertical, perpendicular *Opposite*: askew 3 honest, straightforward, fair, law-abiding, aboveboard *Opposite*: dishonest 4 consecutive, successive, uninterrupted, in a row, running 5 undiluted, neat, plain, unmixed, unadulterated *Opposite*: diluted 6 tidy, neat, in order, orderly, organized *Opposite*: untidy ■ *adv* 1 as the crow flies, in a straight line, directly, from A to B, by the shortest possible route *Opposite*: indirectly 2 directly, without delay, immediately, at once, instantly *Opposite*: later

straightaway *adv* immediately, at once, without delay, right away, promptly *Opposite*: later

straighten *v* 1 make straight, straighten out, unbend, uncurl, flatten *Opposite*: bend 2 make level, level, set straight, straighten up, adjust 3 tidy, tidy up, order, arrange, organize

straighten out *v* 1 make straight, straighten, unbend, uncurl, flatten *Opposite*: bend 2 put right, sort out, set right, settle, rectify *Opposite*: confuse

straighten up *v* align, justify, straighten, level, make flush

straight-faced *adj* deadpan, poker-faced, expressionless, blank, serious *Opposite*: smiling

straightforward *adj* 1 frank, forthright, candid, direct, honest *Opposite*: devious 2 easy, simple, facile, uncomplicated, clear-cut *Opposite*: complicated

straightforwardness *n* 1 frankness, candour, honesty, truthfulness, openness *Opposite*: deviousness 2 ease, facility, simplicity, clarity, easiness *Opposite*: difficulty

straight-out (*infml*) *adj* blunt, unrestrained, direct, frank, honest *Opposite*: restrained

straight-talking *adj* blunt, direct, frank, candid, forthright *Opposite*: evasive

strain *v* 1 make a great effort, try hard, struggle, labour, endeavour 2 damage, injure, hurt, pull, sprain 3 drain, sieve, filter, sift, separate 4 tax, overburden, overload, burden, overtax ■ *n* 1 nervous tension, tension, stress, worry, anxiety 2 exertion, effort, tension, struggle, force 3 injury, sprain, wrench, crick 4 breed, species, type, form, sort

strained *adj* 1 tense, forced, artificial, awkward, laboured *Opposite*: natural 2 stressed, tense, worried, nervous, nervy (*infml*) *Opposite*: calm

strait *n* passage, channel, canal, sound

straitened *adj* impoverished, severe, distressed, difficult, pinched *Opposite*: comfortable

straitjacket *n* restriction, limitation, restraint, shackles, constraint *Opposite*: freedom

strait-laced *adj* prudish, puritanical, prim, moralistic, strict *Opposite*: broad-minded

strand *n* 1 thread, filament, fibre, string, wire 2 lock, tress, wisp, curl 3 element, component, constituent, aspect, feature ■ *v* cut off, maroon, trap, leave high and dry, abandon *Opposite*: rescue

strange adj **1 odd**, bizarre, outlandish, eccentric, weird Opposite: normal **2 unfamiliar**, foreign, alien, unknown, mysterious Opposite: familiar **3 inexplicable**, surprising, funny, astonishing, perplexing Opposite: unsurprising

strangely adv **1 oddly**, bizarrely, outlandishly, eccentrically, weirdly Opposite: normally **2 inexplicably**, surprisingly, funnily, astonishingly, perplexingly Opposite: unsurprisingly

strangeness n **1 weirdness**, peculiarity, eccentricity, abnormality, incongruity Opposite: normality **2 lack of familiarity**, newness, foreignness, mysteriousness

stranger n **foreigner**, alien, outsider, visitor, guest Opposite: acquaintance

strangle v **1 choke**, strangulate, throttle, garrotte, asphyxiate **2 stifle**, repress, suppress, inhibit, smother Opposite: express

stranglehold n **1 strong hold**, throttlehold, iron grip, grip, lock **2 power**, dominion, control, sway, domination

strangulate v **strangle**, throttle, choke, smother, asphyxiate

strangulation n **strangling**, throttling, choking, smothering, asphyxiation

strap n **band**, fastening, belt, strip, leash ■ v **fasten**, belt, secure, lash, buckle

straphanger (infml) n **passenger**, traveller, commuter, rider

strapline n **subheading**, subhead, heading, head, title

strapped (infml) adj **needy**, wanting, short of money, impecunious, impoverished Opposite: flush (infml)

strapping (infml) adj **robust**, broad-shouldered, burly, well-built, sturdy Opposite: delicate

stratagem n **trick**, ruse, ploy, wile, subterfuge

strategic adj **planned**, tactical, calculated, deliberate, premeditated Opposite: unplanned

strategist n **tactician**, planner, policymaker, plotter, schemer

strategy n **plan**, scheme, policy, approach, tactic

stratum (fml) n **layer**, band, level, division, section

straw n **grass**, hay, stubble, chaff

straw poll n **poll**, opinion poll, show of hands, referendum, questionnaire

stray v **wander away**, wander off, go astray, get lost, drift ■ adj **lost**, wandering, abandoned, homeless, vagrant

streak n **1 line**, band, strip, stripe, vein **2 element**, side, trait, characteristic, quality **3 run**, stretch, roll ■ v **1 mark**, stripe, stain, line, fleck **2 move fast**, fly, flash, zoom, whiz

streaky adj **stripy**, striped, striated, banded, lined

stream n **1 watercourse**, river, beck, torrent,

rivulet **2 jet**, spurt, torrent, cascade Opposite: drip **3 flood**, torrent, barrage, onslaught ■ v **flow**, pour out, flood, gush, spill

streamer n **flag**, banner, bunting, ribbon, decoration

streamline v **rationalize**, modernize, update, reorganize, restructure

streamlined adj **1 sleek**, smooth, slick, aerodynamic **2 efficient**, rationalized, modernized, updated, reorganized Opposite: cumbersome

street credibility n **coolness**, credibility, sophistication, fashionableness, street cred (infml)

streetwise (infml) adj **astute**, quick-witted, sharp-witted, smart, sharp Opposite: inexperienced

strength n **1 power**, force, might, potency, muscle Opposite: weakness **2 strong point**, strong suit, forte, asset, métier Opposite: weakness **3 intensity**, concentration, dilution, depth, potency

strengthen v **make stronger**, reinforce, fortify, brace, toughen Opposite: weaken

strength of mind n **resolve**, determination, strength, fortitude, willpower Opposite: weakness

strenuous adj **1 taxing**, arduous, exhausting, demanding, hard Opposite: light **2 active**, energetic, determined, spirited, tireless Opposite: half-hearted. See COMPARE AND CONTRAST at **hard**.

stress n **1 strain**, anxiety, worry, tension, trauma **2 emphasis**, importance, weight, accent, urgency ■ v **emphasize**, lay emphasis on, underline, underscore, accentuate. See COMPARE AND CONTRAST at **worry**.

stressed adj **harassed**, worried, strained, tense, anxious Opposite: relaxed

stressed out (infml) see **stressed**

stressful adj **demanding**, taxing, worrying, traumatic, tense Opposite: relaxing

stress out (infml) v **worry**, bother, get to, harass, perturb Opposite: relax

stretch v **1 extend**, elongate, enlarge, widen, broaden Opposite: shrink **2 spread out**, extend, unfold, spread, unroll **3 be elastic**, give, expand, yield ■ n **1 give**, bounce, spring, elasticity Opposite: rigidity **2 section**, expanse, bit, area, sweep **3 spell**, period, stint, time, run

stretch a point v **1 make allowances**, bend the rules, turn a blind eye, make an exception **2 exaggerate**, overstate, inflate, amplify, embroider Opposite: understate

stretched adj **1 extended**, outstretched, elongated, expanded, lengthened Opposite: contracted **2 strained**, overextended, pushed, fraught, busy Opposite: relaxed

stretch out v **recline**, lie back, bask, lounge, sprawl

stretchy adj elastic, flexible, springy, pliable Opposite: rigid

strew v 1 scatter, throw, disperse, distribute, spread Opposite: gather 2 litter, cover, fill, sprinkle, dot

striation n pattern, marking, corrugation, incision, ridge

stricken adj 1 troubled, tormented, wracked, disturbed, traumatized 2 laid low, afflicted, suffering, affected, wracked Opposite: well 3 injured, damaged, wounded, hurt, struck

strict adj 1 severe, firm, stern, harsh, stringent Opposite: lenient 2 exact, precise, accurate, narrow, meticulous Opposite: inaccurate

strictness n 1 severity, firmness, sternness, harshness, stringency Opposite: leniency 2 exactitude, precision, accuracy, narrowness, meticulousness Opposite: inaccuracy

stricture (fml) n 1 criticism, attack, rebuke, telling off, censure 2 restriction, restraint, limit, constraint, limitation

stride v step, walk, pace, tread, march ■ n 1 pace, step, tread, gait, walk 2 advance, progress, development, improvement, headway

strident adj 1 loud, harsh, grating, shrill, raucous Opposite: soft 2 vociferous, forceful, persuasive, clamorous, baying Opposite: gentle

strife n trouble, conflict, discord, contention, fighting Opposite: harmony

strike v 1 hit, beat, smack, thump, clout 2 collide with, hit, crash into, smash into, bump into Opposite: miss 3 occur to, come to mind, dawn on, hit, come to 4 attack, launch an attack, fall on, set on, hit 5 discover, hit upon, light on, stumble across, chance upon 6 take industrial action, stop work, come out, down tools, walk out 7 reach, arrive at, attain, achieve, arrange ■ n 1 raid, attack, assault, foray, air strike 2 industrial action, go-slow, walkout, work-to-rule, work stoppage

strike down v 1 knock down, floor, fell, bring down, knock out 2 afflict, lay low, infect, affect, make ill 3 kill, bring down, murder, assassinate, slaughter

strike it rich v hit the jackpot, come into money, make your fortune, laugh all the way to the bank, rake it in (infml)

strike off v delete, cross off, remove, withdraw Opposite: include

strike out v 1 cross out, delete, score out, strike through, cancel 2 set out, leave, depart, go, move off Opposite: arrive 3 attack, lash out, set on, assail

striker n 1 picket, picketer, demonstrator, protester 2 forward, attacker, winger

strike up v start, begin, commence, initiate, make a start Opposite: stop

strike while the iron's hot v take the opportunity, grab the chance, make the most of it, make hay while the sun shines (infml)

striking adj 1 conspicuous, noticeable, marked, remarkable, salient Opposite: inconspicuous 2 good-looking, handsome, attractive, eye-catching, beautiful

striking distance n stone's throw, short distance, a hairsbreadth, hop, skip, and jump, spitting distance (infml)

string n 1 cord, thread, filament, twine, rope 2 sequence, series, run, chain, succession

string along (infml) v 1 deceive, mislead, lead on, lead up the garden path, send on a wild-goose chase 2 tag along, hang around, go along, go along for the ride, join in 3 agree, go along with, be of one mind, concur, approve Opposite: disagree

stringency n severity, strictness, rigour, harshness, inflexibility Opposite: flexibility

stringent adj severe, strict, rigorous, stern, harsh Opposite: lax

stringer n journalist, reporter, correspondent, columnist, writer

stringy adj tough, chewy, sinewy, gristly, fibrous Opposite: tender

strip v 1 undress, strip off, doff, shed, peel off Opposite: dress 2 deprive, take away, divest, deny, rid Opposite: furnish (fml) ■ n band, sliver, shred, ribbon, slip

stripe n band of colour, strip, band, line, streak

stripped adj bare, exposed, unprotected, uncovered, unvarnished Opposite: coated

stripped-down adj lean, spare, sparse, minimalist, utilitarian

strive v struggle, endeavour, go all out, do your best, do your utmost

stroke n 1 hit, blow, knock, rap, lash 2 rub, caress, fondle, pat ■ v caress, fondle, pat, rub

stroll v walk, amble, saunter, ramble, go for a constitutional ■ n saunter, walk, amble, turn, wander

strong adj 1 powerful, burly, brawny, muscular, sturdy Opposite: weak 2 robust, sturdy, stout, solid, durable Opposite: fragile 3 glaring, dazzling, bright, stark, brilliant Opposite: dim 4 keen, staunch, dedicated, firm, fanatical Opposite: indifferent 5 convincing, sound, clear, clear-cut, persuasive Opposite: weak 6 fervent, great, intense, deep, deep-seated Opposite: weak 7 intense, concentrated, pungent, piquant, spicy Opposite: insipid

strong-arm (infml) adj coercive, forcible, violent, physical, forceful Opposite: peaceable ■ v coerce, compel, force, frighten, bully

strongbox n safe-deposit box, cash box, safe, coffer, vault

stronghold n fortress, refuge, bastion, citadel, sanctuary

strong-minded adj 1 determined, dogged, persevering, persistent, resolute *Opposite*: weak-willed **2 confident**, clear-thinking, certain, intelligent, decisive

strong-mindedness *n* **1 determination**, doggedness, perseverance, persistence, resoluteness *Opposite*: vacillation **2 confidence**, strength, strength of character, character, clarity *Opposite*: weakness

strong point *n* **strength**, forte, asset, métier, strong suit *Opposite*: weakness

strong suit *see* **strong point**

strong-willed *adj* **resolute**, determined, strong-minded, iron-willed, unbending *Opposite*: weak

strop *(infml)* *n* **bad mood**, bad temper, huff, pet, rage

stroppiness *(infml)* *n* **awkwardness**, uncooperativeness, obstreperousness, difficultness, unhelpfulness

stroppy *(infml)* *adj* **awkward**, uncooperative, obstreperous, difficult, unhelpful *Opposite*: amiable

structural *adj* **1 physical**, mechanical, organizational, operational **2 basic**, important, essential, fundamental, underlying

structure *n* **1 construction**, assembly, building, edifice, erection *(fml)* **2 arrangement**, organization, construction, configuration, makeup ■ *v* **arrange**, construct, configure, put together, make up

structured *adj* **1 organized**, planned, controlled, designed, arranged *Opposite*: unstructured **2 defined**, coordinated, well-defined, designed, formal *Opposite*: amorphous

struggle *v* **1 strive**, try, strain, fight, work hard *Opposite*: coast **2 fight**, grapple, tussle, wrestle, battle **3 writhe**, wriggle, thrash about, brawl, scuffle ■ *n* **1 tussle**, fight, brawl, scuffle, skirmish **2 effort**, exertion, labour, toil, work

strum *v* **play**, thrum, improvise, jam, twang

strut *v* **swagger**, march, parade, prance, walk ■ *n* **support**, rod, brace, crosspiece, girder

stub *n* **stump**, end, remains, remnant, counterfoil ■ *v* **hit**, bump, bang, knock, bash *(infml)*

stubble *n* **1 stalks**, stems, rubbish, debris, refuse **2 whiskers**, five o'clock shadow, growth, beard, moustache

stubborn *adj* **1 persistent**, dogged, tenacious, persevering, determined *Opposite*: half-hearted **2 obstinate**, immovable, inflexible, wilful, mulish *Opposite*: flexible

stubbornness *n* **1 persistence**, tenacity, perseverance, doggedness, stalwartness **2 obstinacy**, inflexibility, obduracy, pigheadedness, mulishness *Opposite*: flexibility

stubby *adj* **short**, broad, thick, stumpy, squat *Opposite*: slender

stub out *v* **extinguish**, put out, snuff

stuck *adj* **1 wedged**, fixed, trapped, caught, jammed *Opposite*: loose **2 baffled**, mystified, puzzled, without an answer, at a complete loss

stuck-up *(infml)* *adj* **snobbish**, arrogant, conceited, superior, self-important *Opposite*: unassuming

stud *n* **knob**, boss, rivet, nail, screw ■ *v* **1 fit with studs**, decorate, fasten, rivet, secure **2 dot**, pepper, sprinkle, scatter, speckle

student *n* **scholar**, pupil, schoolboy, schoolgirl, schoolchild *Opposite*: teacher

student loan *n* **loan**, government loan, educational loan, subsidized loan

studied *adj* **deliberate**, intentional, calculated, considered, premeditated *Opposite*: spontaneous

studio *n* **1 workplace**, workshop, workroom, atelier, pottery **2 academy**, conservatory, dance school, ballet school, dance academy

studious *adj* **1 thoughtful**, serious, reflective, bookish, scholarly *Opposite*: frivolous **2 diligent**, painstaking, careful, assiduous, industrious *Opposite*: careless

study *v* **1 learn**, take in, revise, read, swot *(infml)* **2 investigate**, research, experiment, examine, consider ■ *n* **1 learning**, education, training, revision, schoolwork **2 investigation**, examination, survey, review, inquiry **3 report**, findings, conclusions, research paper, analysis

stuff *v* **fill**, pack, cram, ram, jam ■ *n* **1 material**, substance, matter, raw material **2 things**, objects, paraphernalia, articles, mess **3 possessions**, belongings, things, kit, tackle

stuffed *adj* **1 filled**, lined, packed, jammed, crammed **2** *(infml)* **full**, fit to burst, replete, sated, satiated *Opposite*: hungry

stuffed shirt *(infml)* *n* **fogy**, old fogy, killjoy, spoilsport, fuddy-duddy *(infml)*

stuffiness *n* **1 airlessness**, staleness, closeness, mugginess, fug *Opposite*: freshness **2 formality**, conventionality, staidness, stand-offishness, pomposity *Opposite*: informality

stuff up *(infml)* *v* **make a mess of**, botch *(infml)*, mess up *(infml)*, foul up *(infml)*, blow it *(slang)* *Opposite*: sort out

stuffy *adj* **1 airless**, stale, smelly, hot, warm *Opposite*: fresh **2 strait-laced**, old-fashioned, conventional, formal, pompous *Opposite*: informal **3 congested**, blocked up, stuffed up, clogged up, bunged up *(infml)* *Opposite*: clear

stultify *v* **1 bore**, dull, numb, deaden, put off *Opposite*: stimulate **2 make a fool of**, belittle, ridicule, humiliate, set up *(infml)* **3 cancel out**, block, render useless, pre-empt, vitiate *Opposite*: advance

stumble *v* **1 trip**, trip up, lose your footing, lose your balance, falter **2 stagger**, lurch, sway, blunder, roll **3 hesitate**, stop and start, hem and haw, falter, stammer **4 come across**, find, discover, happen on, chance on ■ *n* **1 blunder**, trip, stagger, false step, mishap **2 mistake**, hesitation, slip, blunder, slip-up *(infml)*. See COMPARE AND CONTRAST at **hesitate.**

stumbling block *n* **obstacle**, problem, difficulty, sticking point, obstruction *Opposite*: aid

stump *n* **base**, stub, butt, end, remains ■ *v* **baffle**, puzzle, perplex, mystify, nonplus *Opposite*: enlighten

stump up *(infml)* *v* **come up with**, pay, provide, put in, contribute *Opposite*: withhold

stumpy *adj* **squat**, stubby, short, thickset, broad *Opposite*: lanky

stun *v* **1 knock out**, paralyse, numb, daze, put out of action *Opposite*: bring round **2 shock**, upset, dumbfound, daze, amaze

stunner *(infml)* *n* **star**, smash, sensation, hit, triumph

stunning *adj* **spectacular**, striking, fabulous, splendid, superb *Opposite*: unimpressive

stunningly *adv* **extremely**, spectacularly, strikingly, fabulously, remarkably *Opposite*: moderately

stunt *v* **inhibit**, restrict, arrest, hold back, impede *Opposite*: assist ■ *n* **feat**, exploit, act, deed, show

stunted *adj* **underdeveloped**, undersized, small, short, little

stupefaction *n* **confusion**, befuddlement, bemusement, perplexity, bewilderment

stupefied *adj* **1 confused**, fuddled, punch-drunk, stunned, befuddled *Opposite*: clear-headed **2 amazed**, astonished, astounded, stunned, dazed

stupefy *v* **1 amaze**, astonish, astound, surprise, stagger **2 confuse**, befuddle, bewilder, stun, perplex *Opposite*: enlighten

stupendous *adj* **1 astonishing**, astounding, amazing, surprising, stunning *Opposite*: unremarkable **2 fantastic**, wonderful, out of this world, marvellous, great *Opposite*: awful **3 huge**, vast, large, colossal, enormous *Opposite*: tiny

stupendously *adv* **tremendously**, impressively, amazingly, exceptionally, remarkably *Opposite*: slightly

stupid *adj* **1 unintelligent**, dull, brainless, obtuse, witless *Opposite*: intelligent **2 foolish**, fatuous, inane, nonsensical, silly *Opposite*: sensible **3 unwise**, senseless, ill-advised, imprudent, injudicious *Opposite*: wise

stupidity *n* **foolishness**, foolhardiness, silliness, inanity, folly *Opposite*: sense

stupor *n* **1 torpor**, lethargy, inertness, limpness, blankness *Opposite*: activeness **2 daze**, dream, trance, shock, numbness *Opposite*: consciousness

sturdiness *n* **strength**, solidity, durability, toughness, hardiness *Opposite*: weakness

sturdy *adj* **1 well-built**, strong, robust, powerful, muscular *Opposite*: frail **2 well-made**, durable, robust, tough, hard-wearing *Opposite*: rickety **3 resolute**, decisive, determined, strenuous, enthusiastic *Opposite*: feeble

stutter *v* **stammer**, trip over your tongue, falter, stumble, hesitate *Opposite*: enunciate ■ *n* **stammer**, speech disorder, impediment, impairment, speech impediment

sty *n* **cyst**, swelling, lump, boil, sore

style *n* **1 design**, type, sort, form, variety **2 method**, approach, way, manner, fashion **3 flair**, panache, chic, bravura, stylishness *Opposite*: gracelessness **4 luxury**, luxuriousness, extravagance, lavishness, opulence ■ *v* **1 fashion**, design, shape, cut, adapt **2** *(fml)* **name**, call, nickname, label, term

stylish *adj* **fashionable**, sophisticated, chic, modish, smart *Opposite*: unfashionable

stylishness *n* **style**, flair, chic, panache, smartness *Opposite*: dowdiness

stylistic *adj* **formal**, technical, literary, musical, artistic *Opposite*: spontaneous

stylize *v* **formalize**, abstract, schematize, systematize, outline

stylized *adj* **conventional**, artificial, formalized, formal, unnatural *Opposite*: natural

stymie *v* **hinder**, prevent, block, thwart, confound *Opposite*: enable ■ *n* **impasse**, dead end, stalemate, standstill, deadlock *Opposite*: breakthrough

suave *adj* **urbane**, smooth, polished, polite, sophisticated *Opposite*: awkward

subcategory *n* **subsection**, subclass, subgroup, subdivision

subconscious *adj* **unconscious**, intuitive, hidden, unintentional, involuntary *Opposite*: deliberate

subcontract *v* **delegate**, farm out, contract out, commission, mandate

subculture *n* **subgroup**, culture, grouping, group, subdivision

subcutaneous *adj* **hypodermic**, hypodermal, intravenous, internal, dermatological

subdirectory *n* **division**, subdivision, directory, file, storage space

subdivide *v* **divide**, section, segment, split, cut *Opposite*: unify

subdivision *n* **1 section**, part, division, sector, tract **2 division**, sectioning, segmenting, separation, splitting up *Opposite*: unification

subdue *v* **1 restrain**, suppress, hold back, control, discipline **2 pacify**, calm, calm down, soothe, mollify **3 subjugate**, conquer, vanquish, defeat, overpower

subdued *adj* **1 passive**, cowed, submissive, quiet, unresponsive *Opposite*: uplifted **2 gentle**, low, restrained, muted, subtle *Opposite*: loud

subeditor *n* **assistant editor**, editorial assistant, assistant, deputy editor, sub *(infml)*

subgroup n subcategory, subsection, subclass, subdivision, smaller group

subhuman adj bestial, animal, inhuman, inhumane, wicked

subject n 1 topic, theme, focus, subject matter, area under discussion 2 subordinate, vassal, liege, dependent, citizen Opposite: sovereign 3 field, speciality, study, discipline, area

---

COMPARE AND CONTRAST CORE MEANING: what is under discussion

subject a matter that is under discussion or investigation; **topic** a matter dealt with in a text or discussion; **subject matter** the material dealt with in a film, discussion, or other medium; **matter** the material that is dealt with in speech or writing, as opposed to its presentation; **theme** a distinct, recurring, and unifying idea in music, literature, art, or film; **burden** (literary) the main argument or recurrent theme in music or literature.

---

subjection n domination, subjugation, overpowering, enslavement, oppression

subjective adj 1 slanted, biased, prejudiced, skewed, one-sided Opposite: objective 2 individual, particular, idiosyncratic, independent, personal Opposite: general

subjectively adv personally, individually, instinctively, intuitively, emotionally Opposite: objectively

subjectivity n bias, prejudice, partisanship, partiality Opposite: objectivity

subject matter n topic, theme, subject, focus, question. See COMPARE AND CONTRAST at subject.

subject to v cause to experience, cause to undergo, expose to, put through, make susceptible ■ adj conditional on, dependent on, depending on, bound by, answerable to Opposite: unrelated

subjugate v conquer, vanquish, subdue, defeat, overpower Opposite: liberate

sublimate v channel, redirect, transfer, direct, reroute

sublimation n redirection, transferral, direction, rerouting, division

sublime adj 1 inspiring, inspirational, uplifting, awe-inspiring, moving Opposite: ridiculous 2 (infml) excellent, superb, splendid, marvellous, wonderful

subliminal adj subconscious, unconscious, hidden, concealed, unintentional Opposite: conscious

submerge v 1 plunge, immerse, dip, sink, duck 2 suppress, conceal, hide, stifle Opposite: reveal

submerged adj underwater, flooded, inundated, waterlogged, sunken

submission n 1 obedience, compliance, capitulation, surrender, acquiescence Opposite: resistance 2 proposal, suggestion, plan, tender, offer

submissive adj obedient, passive, compliant, acquiescent, subservient Opposite: assertive

submit v 1 present, propose, tender, offer, suggest Opposite: withdraw 2 give in, yield, agree to, acquiesce, resign yourself to Opposite: resist. See COMPARE AND CONTRAST at yield.

subnormal adj substandard, second-rate, poor, inferior, below average Opposite: superior

subordinate adj secondary, lesser, subsidiary, inferior, lower Opposite: main ■ n assistant, junior, underling, minion, aide Opposite: boss

subordination n relegation, demotion, reduction, subservience

suborn v incite, bribe, induce, entice, corrupt

subpoena n summons, order, call ■ v summon, compel, require, order, command

subscribe v 1 donate to, give to, pledge, promise, contribute 2 agree with, approve of, support, condone, hold with Opposite: disagree

subscription n payment, donation, contribution

subsequent adj following, succeeding, ensuing, successive, consequent Opposite: preceding

subservient adj obedient, compliant, acquiescent, docile, deferential Opposite: assertive

subset n subsection, subdivision, subgroup, subcategory, subclass

subside v 1 collapse, cave in, fall down, drop, sink Opposite: rise 2 diminish, lessen, decrease, dwindle, wane Opposite: build up

subsidence n subsiding, sinking, settling, dropping, collapsing

subsidiary adj 1 supplementary, auxiliary, ancillary, additional, contributory Opposite: main 2 subordinate, lesser, secondary, junior, lower Opposite: major ■ n branch, division, holding, company, firm

subsidize v finance, fund, sponsor, back, support

subsidy n funding, financial backing, grant, support, aid

subsist v exist, survive, live, make ends meet, keep going

subsistence n survival, existence, maintenance, sustenance

subspecies n category, strain, genus, sort, class

substance n 1 material, matter, stuff, ingredient, body 2 core, essence, import, gist, nub 3 affluence, property, money, means, wealth Opposite: poverty

substandard adj inferior, second-rate, poor, subnormal, below average Opposite: superior

substantial adj considerable, large, extensive, significant, important Opposite: small

substantially adv considerably, significantly, noticeably, markedly, greatly Opposite: insignificantly

substantiate v **validate**, authenticate, verify, corroborate, prove *Opposite*: disprove

substantiation n **corroboration**, confirmation, validation, authentication, support

substantive adj **1 practical**, applicable, functional, utilitarian *Opposite*: impractical **2 essential**, fundamental, basic, central, elementary *Opposite*: secondary **3 independent**, autonomous, separate, individual *Opposite*: dependent **4 substantial**, decent, considerable, respectable, significant *Opposite*: insignificant

substantively adv **1 practically**, functionally, applicably **2 essentially**, fundamentally, basically, centrally, elementarily **3 independently**, autonomously, individually, separately **4 substantially**, considerably, significantly, noticeably, markedly *Opposite*: insignificantly

substitute v **1 replace with**, exchange, use instead, switch, swap *(infml)* **2 stand in for**, fill in for, take the place of, relieve, deputize for ■ n **alternative**, replacement, stand-in, locum, surrogate

substitution n **replacement**, switch, exchange, changeover, change

subsume v **include**, incorporate, count, list, consider

subterfuge n **trick**, ploy, ruse, stratagem, manoeuvre

subterranean adj **1 underground**, deep, below ground, buried, hidden **2 secret**, clandestine, underground, covert, arcane *Opposite*: open

subtext n **implication**, hidden agenda, suggestion, connotation, intimation

subtitle n **caption**, legend, surtitle, supertitle

subtle adj **1 slight**, faint, fine, thin, imperceptible *Opposite*: coarse **2 understated**, delicate, indirect, elusive, refined *Opposite*: blunt **3 intelligent**, experienced, sensitive, shrewd, perceptive *Opposite*: obtuse **4 cunning**, sly, crafty, devious, tricky *Opposite*: ingenuous

subtleness n **1 delicacy**, subtlety, refinement, intricacy, elusiveness *Opposite*: bluntness **2 intelligence**, experience, sensitivity, shrewdness, perceptiveness **3 cunning**, deviousness, slyness, craftiness, trickiness *Opposite*: ingenuousness **4 slightness**, faintness, fineness

subtlety n **1 delicacy**, subtleness, refinement, intricacy, elusiveness *Opposite*: blatancy **2 detail**, nicety, fine point, nuance **3 sensitivity**, delicacy, tact, discernment, finesse

subtract v **take away**, take from, take off, deduct, withdraw *Opposite*: add

subtraction n **deduction**, removal, withdrawal, debit, deletion *Opposite*: addition

suburb n **conurbation**, district, environs, commuter belt, development *Opposite*: centre

suburban adj **outlying**, peripheral, out-of-

town, outer, residential *Opposite*: central

suburbia n **suburbs**, commuter belt, conurbation, environs, outskirts *Opposite*: centre

subvention *(fml)* n **1 grant**, subsidy, payment, donation, endowment **2 aid**, support, backing, sponsorship, funding

subversion n **rebellion**, sedition, treason, mutiny, insurrection *Opposite*: compliance

subversive adj **dissident**, rebellious, revolutionary, insubordinate, seditious *Opposite*: law-abiding ■ n **traitor**, collaborator, mutineer, revolutionary, insubordinate *Opposite*: patriot

subvert v **undermine**, overthrow, destabilize, sabotage, disrupt *Opposite*: support

subway n **underpass**, tunnel, passageway

subzero adj **freezing**, bitter, icy, ice-cold, glacial *Opposite*: tropical

succeed v **1 achieve**, accomplish, hit the target, turn out well, be successful *Opposite*: fail **2 do well**, get ahead, prosper, be successful, thrive *Opposite*: fail **3 follow**, come after, replace, supersede, supplant *Opposite*: precede

succeeding adj **following**, subsequent, ensuing, next, successive *Opposite*: preceding

success n **1 achievement**, accomplishment, victory, triumph, feat *Opposite*: failure **2 hit**, winner, sensation, star, triumph *Opposite*: failure

successful adj **1 fruitful**, positive, effective, efficacious *(fml)* *Opposite*: unsuccessful **2 prosperous**, up-and-coming, well-off, wealthy, rich *Opposite*: poor **3 flourishing**, thriving, booming, profitable, lucrative *Opposite*: ailing

succession n **series**, sequence, chain, run, string *Opposite*: individual

successive adj **consecutive**, succeeding, following, sequential, uninterrupted *Opposite*: single

successor n **heir**, inheritor, replacement, beneficiary *Opposite*: predecessor

success story n **success**, winner, sensation, hit, triumph

succinct adj **concise**, pithy, brief, to the point, laconic *Opposite*: long-winded

succinctness n **concision**, pithiness, conciseness, brevity, briefness *Opposite*: verbosity

succulence n **juiciness**, lusciousness, tenderness, moistness, tastiness *Opposite*: dryness

succulent adj **juicy**, moist, tender, luscious, delicious *Opposite*: dry

succumb v **1 give way**, yield, give in, submit, surrender *Opposite*: withstand **2 die**, pass away, perish, depart, expire *(fml)*. *See* COMPARE AND CONTRAST *at* yield.

such as *adv* **for example**, like, namely, viz, as

suck *v* **1 draw**, pull on, lap, slurp, drink **2 extract**, draw, pull, force, take out **3 pull**, draw, force, sweep, bear ▪ *n* **slurp**, draw, pull, drink, taste

sucker *(infml)* *n* **gull**, dupe, pushover *(infml)*, mug *(slang)*, mark *(slang)* ▪ *v* **trick**, con, fool, gull, dupe

suck in *v* **1 involve**, implicate, entangle, embroil, draw in *Opposite*: exclude **2 breathe in**, inhale, draw in, take in, pull in

suck up *v* **1 absorb**, soak up, take up, sop up *Opposite*: exude **2** *(infml)* **ingratiate yourself**, flatter, grovel, toady, crawl *(infml)*

suction *n* **force**, pressure, pull, draw, drag

sudden *adj* **unexpected**, abrupt, rapid, swift, hasty *Opposite*: gradual

suddenly *adv* **unexpectedly**, abruptly, rapidly, swiftly, all of a sudden *Opposite*: gradually

suddenness *n* **unexpectedness**, quickness, abruptness, rapidity, swiftness

suds *n* **lather**, bubbles, foam, froth, spume *(literary)*

sue *v* **1** *(fml)* **petition**, beg, plead, appeal, implore *(fml)* **2 litigate**, prosecute, indict, file a suit, charge

suffer *v* **1 feel pain**, hurt, agonize, ache, smart **2 undergo**, experience, bear, endure, go through **3 tolerate**, endure, bear, put up with, stand **4 deteriorate**, fall off, be impaired, drop off *(infml)*

sufferance *n* **1 tolerance**, toleration, acquiescence, allowance, permission *Opposite*: prohibition **2 endurance**, stamina, staying power, stoicism, fortitude

sufferer *n* **invalid**, victim, patient, case, martyr

suffering *n* **1 pain**, distress, agony, torment, affliction **2 sorrow**, grief, misery, woe, anguish

suffice *(fml)* *v* **be sufficient**, do, serve, suit

sufficiency *n* **right amount**, adequacy, abundance, plenty *Opposite*: insufficiency

sufficient *adj* **adequate**, enough, satisfactory, necessary, appropriate *Opposite*: inadequate

suffocate *v* **smother**, choke, stifle, throttle, asphyxiate

suffuse *v* **spread through**, pervade, fill, saturate, flood

sugar *n* *(infml)* **honey**, sweetheart, darling, dearest, precious ▪ *v* **sweeten**, dress up, disguise, titivate, improve

sugary *adj* **1 sweet**, syrupy, sickly, sugared, sweetened *Opposite*: bitter **2 sentimental**, mawkish, gushy, mushy, syrupy *Opposite*: dry

suggest *v* **1 propose**, put forward, advise, recommend, advocate *Opposite*: veto **2 imply**, insinuate, intimate, indicate, hint *Opposite*: state **3 remind**, bring to mind, call to mind, evoke, conjure up. *See* COMPARE AND CONTRAST *at* **recommend**.

suggestibility *n* **susceptibility**, openness, vulnerability, credulousness, credulity *Opposite*: strong-mindedness

suggestible *adj* **susceptible**, impressionable, gullible, credulous, malleable *Opposite*: strong-minded

suggestion *n* **1 proposal**, proposition, submission, recommendation, idea *Opposite*: order **2 implication**, hint, insinuation, intimation, indication *Opposite*: statement **3 evocation**, air, aura, hint, trace

suggestive *adj* **1 evocative**, redolent, reminiscent, indicative, expressive **2 improper**, indelicate, indecent, lewd, risqué

suicidal *adj* **1** *(infml)* **desperate**, cheerless, hopeless, unhappy, miserable **2 dangerous**, treacherous, perilous, reckless, madcap *Opposite*: sensible

suicide *n* **1 death**, self-destruction, self-immolation **2 recklessness**, rashness, perversity, irresponsibility, madness

suit *n* **costume**, ensemble, dress suit, trouser suit, uniform ▪ *v* **1 go with**, match, fit, be fitting, agree with *Opposite*: clash **2 flatter**, become, show up, enhance

WORD BANK
❏ **types of suit** all-in-one, black tie, boiler suit, business suit, catsuit, dress suit, jumpsuit, overalls, pinstripe suit, trouser suit, white tie, zoot suit

suitability *n* **appropriateness**, aptness, fittingness, fitness, correctness *Opposite*: unsuitability

suitable *adj* **appropriate**, apposite, fit, apt, right *Opposite*: inappropriate

suitcase *n* **case**, luggage, baggage, bag, valise

suite *n* **set**, collection, group, complement

suited *adj* **right**, matched, well-matched, appropriate, apposite *Opposite*: wrong

sulk *v* **mope**, be in a mood, feel sorry for yourself, be in a huff, pout *Opposite*: rejoice *(literary)* ▪ *n* **bad temper**, mood, temper, huff, bad mood

sulkiness *n* **moodiness**, resentfulness, temper, bad temper, moroseness *Opposite*: joviality

sulky *adj* **morose**, angry, resentful, sullen, unsociable *Opposite*: jovial

sullen *adj* **surly**, morose, hostile, bad-tempered, dour *Opposite*: friendly

sullenness *n* **surliness**, hostility, bad temper, moodiness, moroseness *Opposite*: friendliness

sullied *adj* **tainted**, dishonoured, discredited, corrupt, disgraced

sully *v* **tarnish**, taint, smear, denigrate, spoil *Opposite*: praise

sulphurous *adj* **acrid**, reeking, stinking, foul, bitter

sultry *adj* **hot**, humid, muggy, stifling, oppressive *Opposite*: fresh

sum *n* **1 figure**, amount, quantity, entirety, totality **2 calculation**, addition, computation, summation

summarily *adv* **instantly**, immediately, instantaneously, abruptly, suddenly *Opposite*: eventually

summarize *v* **sum up**, précis, abridge, recap, go over *Opposite*: elaborate

summary *n* **précis**, synopsis, digest, sum-up, outline *Opposite*: exposition ■ *adj* **1 swift**, rapid, instant, immediate, instantaneous *Opposite*: considered **2 short**, brief, concise, abridged, succinct

summation *n* **1 addition**, calculation, computation, sum **2 sum total**, total, sum, final total, grand total **3 summary**, summing up, synopsis, outline, précis

summer *n* **1 summertime**, dog days, midsummer, solstice *Opposite*: winter **2 warm weather**, sun, sunshine, warmth, heat **3 prime**, best time, summertime, best years, golden age

summerhouse *n* **gazebo**, pagoda, hut, shed, shelter

summertime *see* **summer**

summery *adj* **warm**, balmy, sunny, hot *Opposite*: wintry

summit *n* **1 peak**, top, pinnacle, apex, acme *Opposite*: base **2 conference**, meeting, summit meeting, talks

summon *v* **1 call**, send for, call for, call upon, beckon *Opposite*: dismiss **2 convene**, call together, get together, gather, assemble *Opposite*: dismiss **3 muster**, rouse, find, activate, rally *Opposite*: demobilize

summons *n* **order**, writ, directive, command, subpoena

sumptuous *adj* **costly**, lavish, splendid, opulent, spectacular *Opposite*: meagre

sumptuousness *n* **luxuriousness**, luxury, lavishness, splendour, opulence

sums *(infml)* *n* **mathematics**, arithmetic, maths, calculation

sum total *n* **whole**, totality, entirety, aggregate, summation

sum up *v* **summarize**, recap, synopsize, encapsulate, abridge *Opposite*: elaborate

sunbaked *adj* **hardened**, dried, sun-dried, heated, cracked

sunbathe *v* **sun yourself**, bask, tan, catch some rays *(slang)*

sunbeam *n* **ray**, beam, shaft, sunlight, sunshine *Opposite*: moonbeam

Sunday best *n* **best clothes**, finery, formal wear, best bib and tucker *(infml)*

sundown *n* **sunset**, nightfall, twilight, dusk, evening *Opposite*: sunrise

sun-dried *adj* **dried**, preserved, dried up, dehydrated, jerked *Opposite*: fresh

sundries *n* **miscellany**, miscellanea, hotchpotch, assortment, odds and ends

sundry *adj* **various**, miscellaneous, assorted, varied, different *Opposite*: uniform

sunglasses *n* **dark glasses**, sunspecs *(infml)*, shades *(infml)*

sunk *adj* **1 ruined**, dashed, in trouble, defeated, destroyed *Opposite*: successful **2 depressed**, downcast, downhearted, dejected, in the dumps *Opposite*: happy

sunken *adj* **1 submerged**, underwater, immersed **2 hollow**, gaunt, deep-set, cadaverous, pinched **3 recessed**, lower, settled, dipped, depressed *Opposite*: raised

sunless *adj* **dark**, cloudy, overcast, murky, gloomy *Opposite*: sunny

sunlight *n* **sunshine**, daylight, light, rays, sunbeams

sunlit *adj* **sunny**, bright, light, sundrenched, bathed in light *Opposite*: dark

sunnily *adv* **cheerfully**, cheerily, happily, genially, gaily *Opposite*: gloomily

sunny *adj* **1 sunlit**, bright, luminous, brilliant, cloudless *Opposite*: dark **2 cheerful**, cheery, bright, bright and breezy, positive *Opposite*: gloomy

sunrise *n* **dawn**, daybreak, break of day, first light, daylight *Opposite*: sunset

sunscreen *see* **suntan lotion**

sunset *n* **sundown**, dusk, evening, night, nightfall *Opposite*: sunrise

sunshade *n* **parasol**, umbrella, garden umbrella, beach umbrella, awning

sunshine *n* **sunlight**, light, rays, sunbeams, brightness *Opposite*: rainfall

sunspecs *see* **sunglasses**

sunspot *(infml)* *n* **resort**, tourist spot, holiday resort, beach resort

suntan cream *see* **suntan lotion**

suntan lotion *n* **sun lotion**, sun cream, suntan cream, sunscreen, sunblock

suntanned *adj* **brown**, tanned, bronzed, sunburnt *Opposite*: pale

suntan oil *see* **suntan lotion**

sup *v* **spoon**, sip, drink, partake of, lap *Opposite*: gulp ■ *n* **mouthful**, sip, swallow, drink, draught *Opposite*: gulp

super *adj* **1** *(infml)* **wonderful**, fantastic, great, marvellous, fabulous *Opposite*: awful **2 superior**, better, enhanced, improved, outstanding *Opposite*: inferior

superabundant *adj* **overabundant**, in excess, excessive, extra, abounding *Opposite*: insufficient

superannuated *adj* **1 retired**, pensioned off, discharged, elderly, aged *Opposite*: working **2 out-of-date**, antiquated, out of fashion, outmoded, passé *Opposite*: fashionable **3 worn out**, worn, unusable, used up, useless *Opposite*: new

superb *adj* **excellent**, outstanding, wonderful, splendid, fabulous *Opposite*: abysmal

superbug n supergerm, germ, microorganism, pathogen, bug (infml)

supercharge v 1 boost, modify, charge, power up, amplify Opposite: downgrade 2 charge, overdo, load, overload, hype Opposite: understate

supercilious adj arrogant, contemptuous, disdainful, pompous, superior Opposite: humble

superciliousness n arrogance, contemptuousness, contempt, condescension, haughtiness Opposite: humility

supercool (infml) adj cool, modern, contemporary, fashionable, trendy (infml) Opposite: passé

super-duper (infml) adj excellent, marvellous, colossal, impressive, pleasing Opposite: inferior

superego n conscience, integrity, scruples, sense of propriety, sense of judgment

superficial adj 1 shallow, trivial, trifling, unimportant, paltry Opposite: profound 2 surface, shallow, external, exterior, on the surface Opposite: deep 3 insincere, shallow, artificial, phoney, apparent Opposite: sincere 4 cursory, sketchy, rapid, hasty, quick Opposite: thorough

superficiality n shallowness, triviality, frivolity, levity, paltriness Opposite: profundity

superficially adv 1 apparently, seemingly, supposedly, outwardly, ostensibly Opposite: wholly 2 cursorily, sketchily, rapidly, hastily, casually Opposite: thoroughly

superfine adj 1 delicate, fine, light, sheer, fragile Opposite: coarse 2 superior, first-class, first-rate, high-quality, best Opposite: inferior

superfluity n 1 oversupply, excess, overabundance, surfeit, surplus Opposite: insufficiency 2 luxury, extra, frill, trifle, indulgence Opposite: necessity

superfluous adj extra, surplus, redundant, unnecessary, unessential Opposite: basic

supergrass (infml) n informer, grass (slang), squealer (slang), rat (slang)

superhero n champion, crusader, rescuer, fighter, protector

superhuman adj phenomenal, prodigious, staggering, heroic, exceptional Opposite: normal

superimpose v place over, overlay, lay over, apply to, cover

superintend v supervise, manage, oversee, administer, control Opposite: ignore

superintendent n manager, supervisor, administrator, officer, controller Opposite: underling

superior adj 1 better, better-quality, advanced, improved, enhanced Opposite: inferior 2 excellent, high-class, top-quality, exclusive, first-class Opposite: second-rate

3 higher, upper, over, above Opposite: lower 4 condescending, arrogant, disdainful, supercilious, aloof Opposite: humble 5 larger, greater, bigger, higher, more Opposite: smaller ■ n boss, manager, chief, elder, better Opposite: inferior

superiority n 1 advantage, dominance, lead, pre-eminence, power Opposite: inferiority 2 condescension, arrogance, haughtiness, disdain, aloofness Opposite: humility

superiority complex n superiority, inflated ego, self-importance, disdain, superciliousness Opposite: inferiority complex

superlative adj excellent, unmatched, unbeatable, untouchable, best Opposite: unremarkable

supernatural adj paranormal, mystic, mystical, ghostly, ghostlike Opposite: natural

WORD BANK
❑ **types of supernatural being** banshee, brownie, elf, fairy, fairy godmother, fay (literary), genie, imp, jinni, pixie, poltergeist, sprite

supernumerary adj 1 extra, excessive, superfluous, spare, surplus Opposite: necessary 2 substitute, extra, auxiliary, ancillary, standby Opposite: permanent

superpower n world power, giant, power bloc, global force, global influence

supersaver n discount, special offer, concession

supersede v succeed, take over, overtake, supplant, replace Opposite: precede

superstar n star, megastar, celebrity, icon, luminary Opposite: nobody

superstition n fallacy, false notion, delusion, misconception, fantasy

superstitious adj credulous, gullible, illogical, irrational, delusory Opposite: rational

superstructure n 1 structure, construction, elevation, frame, framework Opposite: foundation 2 idea, concept, system, structure, argument Opposite: premise

supertitle n surtitle, caption, legend

supervene (fml) v 1 interrupt, charge in, butt in, appear, turn up 2 ensue, follow, supersede, succeed, pursue

supervise v oversee, manage, administer, control, run Opposite: neglect

supervision n 1 management, direction, administration, regulation, command Opposite: neglect 2 care, custody, guardianship, protection, guidance

supervision order n charge, order, authorization, mandate, appointment

supervisor n manager, administrator, superintendent, controller, overseer Opposite: underling

supervisory adj managerial, administrative, superintendent, managing, controlling Opposite: subordinate

supine *adj* **1 flat**, horizontal, flat on one's back, prostrate, prone *Opposite*: standing **2 lethargic**, passive, inactive, apathetic, listless *Opposite*: vigorous

supplant *v* **oust**, displace, succeed, replace, unseat *Opposite*: install

supple *adj* **1 lithe**, agile, mobile, double-jointed, sinuous *Opposite*: stiff **2 bendable**, elastic, plastic, pliant, pliable *Opposite*: rigid

supplement *n* **1 addition**, extra, complement, enhancement, increase *Opposite*: deduction **2 section**, insert, appendix, attachment, rider ■ *v* **add**, complement, accompany, enhance, improve *Opposite*: deduct

supplemental *see* **supplementary**

supplementary *adj* **extra**, additional, added, add-on, top-up *Opposite*: deducted

suppleness *n* **litheness**, agility, mobility, flexibility, limberness *Opposite*: stiffness

suppliant (*fml*) *adj* **prayerful**, petitionary, begging, pleading, supplicant (*fml*) *Opposite*: beneficent ■ *n* **petitioner**, applicant, aspirant, suitor, beggar *Opposite*: benefactor

supplicant (*fml*) *n* **petitioner**, applicant, suitor, aspirant, beggar *Opposite*: donor

supplicate (*fml*) *v* **appeal**, petition, request, beg, entreat *Opposite*: grant

supplication (*fml*) *n* **appeal**, request, entreaty, petition, plea *Opposite*: concession

supplier *n* **provider**, trader, seller, dealer, contractor *Opposite*: consumer

supplies *n* **provisions**, materials, goods, food, stores

supply *v* **provide**, give, make available, sell, bring *Opposite*: receive ■ *n* **amount**, quantity, fund, reserve, stock *Opposite*: dearth

support *v* **1 hold up**, reinforce, prop up, maintain, shore up *Opposite*: weaken **2 sustain**, provide for, keep, take care of, look after *Opposite*: neglect **3 help**, encourage, back up, aid, be there for *Opposite*: abandon **4 favour**, champion, back, follow, espouse *Opposite*: oppose **5 corroborate**, confirm, verify, bear witness, prove *Opposite*: deny **6** (*literary*) **bear**, hold, carry, sustain, take ■ *n* **1 prop**, foundation, scaffold, brace, stanchion **2 sustenance**, provision, care, funding, funds *Opposite*: abandonment **3 corroboration**, confirmation, verification, authentication, substantiation *Opposite*: denial **4 assistance**, encouragement, backing, help, aid

supporter *n* **follower**, fan, enthusiast, devotee, ally *Opposite*: detractor

support group *n* **encounter group**, forum, self-help group, therapy group, circle

supporting *adj* **secondary**, backup, subsidiary, supportive, auxiliary *Opposite*: primary

supportive *adj* **helpful**, caring, sympathetic, compassionate, reassuring *Opposite*: unhelpful

support system *n* **friends**, network, helpers, group, support

suppose *v* **1 presume**, assume, understand, believe, expect **2 imagine**, pretend, consider, theorize, hypothesize

supposed *adj* **1 hypothetical**, theoretical, imaginary, fictional, made-up *Opposite*: actual **2 thought**, believed, assumed, alleged, understood *Opposite*: known

supposedly *adv* **allegedly**, evidently, apparently, theoretically, hypothetically *Opposite*: actually

supposing *conj* **assuming**, suppose, let's say, let's assume, say

supposition *n* **1 belief**, guess, idea, theory, possibility *Opposite*: fact **2 guesswork**, inference, hypothesis, speculation, conjecture *Opposite*: knowledge

suppress *v* **1 hold back**, repress, stifle, restrain, contain *Opposite*: express **2 overpower**, overwhelm, overturn, conquer, defeat *Opposite*: submit **3 muffle**, withhold, censor, smother, quash *Opposite*: publicize

suppression *n* **1 repression**, containment, control, restraint, inhibition *Opposite*: expression **2 conquest**, defeat, destruction, overthrow, clampdown **3 withholding**, cover-up, concealment, censorship, veil of secrecy *Opposite*: revelation

suppurate *v* **discharge pus**, fester, weep, ooze, seep

supranational *adj* **multinational**, international, cosmopolitan, worldwide, universal *Opposite*: local

supremacist *n* **chauvinist**, racist, xenophobe, bigot, sexist

supremacy *n* **1 pre-eminence**, ascendancy, primacy, superiority, domination *Opposite*: inferiority **2 reign**, sovereignty, rule, authority, power

supreme *adj* **1 highest**, best, ultimate, superlative, utmost *Opposite*: worst **2 sovereign**, dominant, uppermost, first, highest

supremely *adv* **extremely**, completely, enormously, absolutely, superlatively

supremo (*infml*) *n* **leader**, head, chief, authority, expert

surcharge *v* **charge extra**, charge again, charge more, tack on, levy again ■ *n* **extra charge**, supplement, extra, price, hidden extra

sure *adj* **1 unquestionable**, undisputable, certain, definite, guaranteed *Opposite*: uncertain **2 certain**, in no doubt, convinced, positive, confident *Opposite*: uncertain **3 dependable**, reliable, effective, trustworthy, trusty *Opposite*: unreliable

sure-fire (*infml*) *adj* **guaranteed**, dependable, safe, assured, foolproof *Opposite*: doubtful

sure-footed *adj* **1 agile**, skilled, confident, skilful, nimble *Opposite*: clumsy **2 confident**, competent, unerring, capable, infallible

surely *adv* **1 certainly**, definitely, of course,

without doubt, unquestionably *Opposite*: doubtfully **2 confidently**, assuredly, with conviction, with confidence, with assurance *Opposite*: insecurely

sureness *n* **certainty**, certitude, confidence, assurance, firm belief *Opposite*: uncertainty

sure thing (*infml*) *n* **certainty**, safe bet, odds-on chance, winner, cert (*infml*)

surety *n* **security**, indemnity, guarantee, warranty, bond

surf *n* **waves**, breakers, rollers, whitecaps, spray

surface *n* **outside**, top, exterior, façade, side *Opposite*: inside ▪ *adj* **superficial**, shallow, external, exterior, outward *Opposite*: inner ▪ *v* **1 rise**, float up, come up, go up, emerge *Opposite*: sink **2 appear**, reappear, turn up, show up, pop up **3 become known**, come to light, come out, come out in the open, emerge **4 coat**, cover, skim, overlay, resurface

surface mail *n* **overland mail**, regular mail, first-class mail, second-class mail, registered mail *Opposite*: airmail

surfeit *n* **excess**, surplus, glut, flood, oversupply *Opposite*: deficit

surge *v* **rush**, rush forward, flow, pour, gush ▪ *n* **flow**, outpouring, gush, rush, heave

surgeon *n* **doctor**, physician, medical practitioner, specialist, neurosurgeon

surgical *adj* **1 medical**, clinical, operating, invasive **2 precise**, exact, accurate, definite, meticulous *Opposite*: imprecise

surly *adj* **gruff**, brusque, abrupt, short, curt *Opposite*: friendly

surmise *v* **guess**, deduce, infer, construe, gather *Opposite*: know ▪ *n* **guesswork**, deduction, inference, conclusion, assumption *Opposite*: knowledge

surmount *v* **1 overcome**, prevail, conquer, triumph, get through *Opposite*: fail **2** (*fml*) **scale**, climb, top, clear, ascend *Opposite*: descend

surmountable *adj* **manageable**, conquerable, resolvable, controllable, winnable *Opposite*: intractable

surname *n* **last name**, family name, cognomen *Opposite*: first name

surpass *v* **exceed**, better, outdo, outshine, improve on *Opposite*: trail

surplus *n* **excess**, extra, spare, leftovers, remainder *Opposite*: shortfall ▪ *adj* **extra**, excess, spare, remaining, additional *Opposite*: essential

surprise *v* **1 startle**, alarm, astonish, astound, amaze **2 catch unawares**, catch napping, take by surprise, burst in on, intrude on ▪ *n* **1 shock**, revelation, bolt from the blue, disclosure, bombshell (*infml*) **2 astonishment**, amazement, wonder, disbelief, shock

surprised *adj* **astonished**, astounded, amazed, taken aback, staggered

surprising *adj* **astonishing**, astounding, amazing, shocking, startling *Opposite*: expected

surprisingly *adv* **1 astonishingly**, astoundingly, amazingly, unexpectedly, unpredictably **2 to my surprise**, to my amazement, out of the blue, without warning, without prior notice

surreal *adj* **strange**, weird, odd, unreal, dreamlike *Opposite*: ordinary

surrender *v* **1 give in**, give up, admit defeat, lay down your arms, yield *Opposite*: hold out **2 relinquish**, give up, hand over, part with, forfeit *Opposite*: retain ▪ *n* **admission of defeat**, submission, laying down of arms, capitulation, renunciation *Opposite*: perseverance. *See* COMPARE AND CONTRAST *at* **yield**.

surreptitious *adj* **furtive**, secret, sneaky, sly, covert *Opposite*: open. *See* COMPARE AND CONTRAST *at* **secret**.

surreptitiousness *n* **secrecy**, covertness, discretion, concealment, stealth *Opposite*: openness

surrogacy *n* **substitution**, proxy, standing in, surrogateship, replacement

surrogate *n* **substitute**, replacement, proxy, stand-in, deputy

surround *v* **1 enclose**, encircle, encase, enfold, envelop **2 besiege**, lay siege to, encircle, hem in ▪ *n* **border**, mount, edge, edging, frame

surrounding *adj* **nearby**, close, adjacent, neighbouring, immediate *Opposite*: distant

surroundings *n* **environs**, surrounds, setting, environment, background

surtax *n* **surcharge**, tax, levy, extra, supplement *Opposite*: relief

surtitle *n* **supertitle**, caption, legend

surveillance *n* **observation**, investigation, scrutiny, reconnaissance, shadowing

survey *n* **1 analysis**, appraisal, scrutiny, evaluation, assessment **2 inspection**, examination, investigation, review, inquiry ▪ *v* **1 look at**, consider, peruse, regard, think about **2 examine**, study, inspect, assess, analyse **3 plot**, chart, map out, measure, graph *Opposite*: sketch

surveyor *n* **inspector**, assessor, examiner, reviewer, evaluator

survival *n* **existence**, endurance, being, subsistence, persistence *Opposite*: death

survive *v* **1 live**, live on, endure, carry on, go on *Opposite*: perish **2 outlive**, outlast, live through *Opposite*: die

surviving *adj* **living**, alive, enduring, persisting, remaining *Opposite*: gone

survivor *n* **fighter**, stayer, sticker, toughie (*infml*)

susceptibility *n* **1 vulnerability**, defencelessness, weakness, exposure, predisposition *Opposite*: imperviousness **2 sensitivity**, receptiveness, openness, touchiness, impressionableness *Opposite*: hardness

susceptible adj **1 sensitive**, receptive, open, impressionable, swayable Opposite: impervious **2 vulnerable**, at risk, liable, prone, disposed Opposite: invulnerable

suspect v **1 think**, believe, suppose, imagine, guess **2 doubt**, distrust, mistrust, have doubts, disbelieve Opposite: trust ■ n **accused**, defendant, respondent ■ adj **suspicious**, doubtful, dubious, unsure, questionable Opposite: trustworthy

suspend v **1 hang**, hang up, dangle, swing, string up **2 interrupt**, check, break off, adjourn, hold Opposite: resume **3 postpone**, put on hold, defer, delay, stay Opposite: bring forward

suspended adj **1 hanging**, floating, hovering, dangling, strung up **2 postponed**, put off, deferred, adjourned, held over Opposite: advanced **3 barred**, banned, proscribed, excluded Opposite: allowed

suspended sentence n **deferred sentence**, deferment, sentence, punishment, judgment

suspense n **1 anticipation**, expectation, expectancy, excitement, tension Opposite: flatness **2 uncertainty**, unsureness, doubt, insecurity, confusion Opposite: knowledge **3 anxiety**, apprehension, tension, fear, nervousness Opposite: calm

suspension n **interruption**, holdup, check, postponement, delay Opposite: resumption

suspicion n **1 doubt**, question, inkling, misgiving, feeling Opposite: certainty **2 mistrust**, apprehension, distrust, disbelief, wariness Opposite: trust **3 hint**, suggestion, trace, touch, tinge

suspicious adj **1 suspect**, dubious, shady, shifty, untrustworthy Opposite: trustworthy **2 doubtful**, distrustful, mistrustful, apprehensive, wary Opposite: sure

suss (infml) v **solve**, figure out, work out, crack, decipher

sustain v **1 withstand**, bear, tolerate, endure, weather Opposite: buckle **2 experience**, undergo, suffer, incur, contract **3 maintain**, continue, carry on, keep up, keep going Opposite: quit **4 nourish**, keep going, feed, nurture Opposite: deplete **5 support**, hold up, prop up, keep up, maintain

sustainable adj **1 maintainable**, bearable, justifiable, workable, defensible **2 ecological**, environmental, green, natural, balanced Opposite: unsustainable

sustained adj **continued**, constant, continual, continuous, nonstop Opposite: temporary

sustenance n **nourishment**, food, nutrition, provisions, rations Opposite: deprivation

susurrate v **rustle**, whisper, murmur, breathe

suture n **seam**, join, junction, joint, closure ■ v **sew**, sew up, stitch, stitch up, close Opposite: cut

suzerain n **superpower**, colonial power, ruling nation

svelte adj **lithe**, graceful, slender, willowy, sylphlike Opposite: stocky

Svengali n **manipulator**, controller, guru, charmer, guide

swab n **gauze**, lint, cloth, wipe, pad ■ v **wipe**, clean, cleanse, moisten, wash

swaddle v **wrap**, bandage, wrap up, swathe, envelop Opposite: unwrap

swag n **1 curtain**, drape, hanging, drapery **2 festoon**, garland, chain

swagger v **strut**, parade, flounce, prance, sweep Opposite: creep ■ n **boastfulness**, arrogance, bluster, conceit, boasting Opposite: timidity

swaggering adj **1 boastful**, boasting, blustering, bragging, vaunting Opposite: modest **2 self-important**, self-satisfied, strutting, smug, arrogant Opposite: self-effacing

swallow v **1 ingest**, consume, take in, down, eat Opposite: vomit **2 gulp**, sip, gulp down, gobble up Opposite: regurgitate **3 destroy**, engulf, swallow up, take over, gobble up **4 suppress**, repress, choke back, hold back, hide Opposite: express **5 retract**, take back, back down, recant, eat your words **6** (infml) **believe**, accept, fall for, credit, buy (US infml) Opposite: reject ■ n **gulp**, sip, nip, mouthful, swig (infml)

swamp n **wetland**, marsh, bog, mire, fen ■ v **1 flood**, inundate, deluge, engulf, drown Opposite: drain **2 overwhelm**, snow under, overload, inundate, flood

swampland n **swamps**, marshes, marshland, bog, wetland

swampy adj **marshy**, boggy, muddy, slushy, squelchy Opposite: dry

swan (infml) v **wander**, drift, float, laze, idle

swank (infml) n **1 bragger**, swaggerer, exhibitionist, boaster, show-off (infml) **2 ostentation**, show, display, affectation, exhibitionism ■ v **show off**, swagger, strut, parade, boast

swanky (infml) adj **upmarket**, glamorous, highclass, stylish, elegant Opposite: downmarket

swan song n **farewell**, final act, last act, curtain, finale Opposite: debut

swap (infml) v **exchange**, trade, barter, do a deal, change ■ n **changeover**, substitution, exchange, switch, interchange

swap over v **switch**, change over, change round, interchange, change places

sward n **turf**, grass, grassland, green, lawn

swarm n **1 group**, cloud, flight **2 horde**, crowd, throng, flock, bevy ■ v **1 crowd**, throng, mass, flock, pile **2 teem**, be overrun, bristle, be alive with, be full **3 group**, hover, circle, fly, rise

swarming adj **crawling**, teeming, brimming, overrun, crowded Opposite: empty

swarthy adj **dark**, weather-beaten, dark-complexioned, leathery, tanned Opposite: pale

swashbuckler n 1 **adventurer**, daredevil, swash, buccaneer, pirate 2 **action movie**, pirate film, period film, action film, adventure movie

swashbuckling adj 1 **daring**, adventurous, heroic, exciting, cavalier Opposite: timid 2 **strutting**, swaggering, boasting, blustery, blustering Opposite: modest

swat v **swipe**, slap, hit, smack, thwack

swatch n **sample**, batch, strip, snip, piece

swathe v 1 **wrap**, cover, bandage, bind, entwine Opposite: unwrap 2 **enfold**, envelop, drape, cloak, shroud Opposite: expose ■ n **strip**, ribbon, band, wrapping, bandage

sway v 1 **swing**, waver, oscillate, move to and fro, rock 2 **bend**, lean, veer, slant, tilt 3 **influence**, bias, affect, control, persuade ■ n **power**, influence, control, authority, command Opposite: subjection

swear v 1 **affirm**, assert, declare, claim, maintain 2 **vow**, pledge, promise, give your word, attest 3 **curse**, blaspheme, damn, utter profanities, execrate (literary or fml) Opposite: bless

swear by v **trust**, rely on, depend on, have faith in, put your faith in Opposite: doubt

swear in v **inaugurate**, install, initiate, induct, administer an oath to Opposite: discharge

swear off v **give up**, renounce, abstain from, desist from, stop

swearword n **expletive**, four-letter word, curse, oath, bad language

sweat v 1 (infml) **worry**, fret, panic, be anxious, be concerned Opposite: relax 2 **perspire**, swelter, wilt, drip

sweat out v **wait out**, see through, endure, see out, stick out Opposite: give up on

sweaty adj 1 **perspiring**, covered with sweat, clammy, damp, sticky Opposite: dry 2 **hot**, boiling, warm, sticky, sultry Opposite: cool

sweep v 1 **brush**, clean up, tidy up, clear away, brush off 2 **speed**, zoom, race, fly, dash Opposite: creep 3 **carry**, move, seize, grab, take 4 **arc**, arch, bend, bow, curve ■ n 1 (infml) **sweepstake**, lottery, draw, raffle, game of chance 2 **arc**, arch, bend, bow, swing 3 **scope**, range, extent, stretch, span

sweep aside v **dismiss**, ignore, brush aside, have done with, reject Opposite: consider

sweep away v 1 **bowl over**, astonish, carry away, astound, overwhelm 2 **brush**, sweep up, clean up, clear up, remove

sweeping adj 1 **far-reaching**, comprehensive, all-encompassing, extensive, across-the-board Opposite: restricted 2 **indiscriminate**, generalized, general, broad, blanket Opposite: specific

sweep somebody off his/her feet v **attract**, enchant, charm, allure, beguile Opposite: turn off (infml)

sweepstake n **lottery**, draw, raffle, game of chance, prize draw

sweep up v **brush**, tidy up, clean, pick up, clean up

sweet adj 1 **sugary**, syrupy, saccharine, sweetened, honeyed Opposite: bitter 2 **fresh**, pure, wholesome Opposite: foul 3 **sweet-smelling**, fragrant, perfumed, scented, odorous (literary) Opposite: smelly 4 **melodious**, melodic, harmonious, musical, tuneful Opposite: harsh 5 **satisfying**, gratifying, enjoyable, rewarding, pleasing Opposite: unrewarding 6 **kind**, thoughtful, considerate, pleasant, amiable Opposite: inconsiderate 7 **lovable**, charming, engaging, appealing, attractive Opposite: unappealing ■ n 1 **bonbon**, chew, mint, confection, confectionery 2 **dessert**, pudding, afters (infml)

sweeten v 1 **make sweeter**, add sugar to, sugarcoat, sugar, honey 2 **enhance**, improve, better, intensify, heighten 3 **pacify**, mollify, appease, soothe, soften up Opposite: aggravate

sweetener n 1 **sweet substance**, sugar, saccharine, aspartame 2 (infml) **bribe**, inducement, carrot, honey, molasses

sweetening n **sweet substance**, sweetener, sugar, saccharine, aspartame

sweetheart n **darling**, dear, dearest, beloved, pet

sweetie (infml) see **sweetheart**

sweetie pie (infml) see **sweetheart**

sweetness n 1 **sugariness**, syrupiness, saccharinity Opposite: sourness 2 **charm**, cuteness, appeal, attractiveness, delightfulness 3 **kindness**, thoughtfulness, consideration, pleasantness, amiability Opposite: unkindness 4 **freshness**, pureness, purity, wholesomeness 5 **melodiousness**, harmony, pleasantness, mellifluousness Opposite: harshness 6 **fragrance**, sweet smell, perfume 7 **lovableness**, charm, appeal, attraction

sweetness and light n **pleasantness**, harmony, peace, friendliness, concord Opposite: unpleasantness

sweet nothings n **romantic words**, romantic phrases, loving words, endearments, pillow talk

sweet-smelling adj **aromatic**, perfumed, fragrant, sweet-scented, fresh Opposite: smelly

sweet talk (infml) n **flattery**, smooth talk, cajolery, flannel (infml), blarney (infml)

sweet-talk (infml) v **charm**, flatter, smooth-talk, persuade, cajole Opposite: bully

sweet tooth n **craving**, taste, fondness, liking, relish

swell v 1 **puff up**, puff out, swell up, bulge, bloat Opposite: deflate 2 **increase**, grow, enlarge, inflate, expand Opposite: decrease 3 **add to**, increase, enhance, improve, expand Opposite: diminish ■ n 1 **wave**, undulation, billow, breaker, surge 2 (dated infml) **fop**, fashion plate, clotheshorse (infml), dandy (dated), beau (archaic)

swelling n **bulge**, bump, puffiness, inflammation, distension

swelter v **feel hot**, sweat, perspire, overheat, burn Opposite: shiver

sweltering adj **boiling**, baking, burning up, red-hot, blistering Opposite: freezing

swerve v **veer**, veer off, turn sharply, swing over, change direction

swift adj **quick**, speedy, fast, rapid, prompt

swiftness n **rapidity**, quickness, fastness, pace, speed Opposite: slowness

swig (infml) v **drink**, swill, toss off, take a drop, guzzle (infml) ■ n **mouthful**, draught, nip, drink

swill v **1 rinse**, sluice, wash out, wash down, swab **2 gulp down**, swig (infml), guzzle (infml), knock back (infml), quaff (literary) ■ n **pig food**, slops, pigswill, mash, scraps

swim v **1 bathe**, go for a dip, go swimming **2 spin**, whirl, reel, sway

swimming baths (dated) see **swimming pool**

swimmingly adv **successfully**, well, smoothly, easily, like a house on fire Opposite: laboriously

swimming pool n **pool**, plunge pool, baths, lido, swimming baths (dated)

swindle v **cheat**, con, dupe, trick, double-cross ■ n **fraud**, hoax, embezzlement, confidence trick, con

swindler n **cheat**, trickster, charlatan, fraud, embezzler

swine n **hog**, boar, pig

swing v **1 dangle**, hang, hang down, be suspended, sway **2 swerve**, veer, reel, pivot, rotate **3 rock**, fluctuate, move back and forth, sway, move backwards and forwards **4** (infml) **manage**, succeed in, accomplish, arrange, bring off ■ n **swipe**, smack, slap, thump, blow

swing at v **hit**, hit out at, lash out, strike, thump

swingeing adj **severe**, harmful, punishing, harsh, draconian Opposite: mild

swing round v **wheel round**, spin round, wheel around, turn round, swivel round

swipe v **1** (infml) **steal**, pilfer, make off with, walk off with, run off with **2 hit**, swing at, lash out, hit out at, strike ■ n **1 blow**, hit, swing, slap, smack **2** (infml) **critical remark**, cutting remark, dig, putdown (infml) Opposite: compliment

swipe card n **plastic card**, magnetic card, smart card, key card, credit card

swirl v **whirl**, twirl, spin, eddy, churn ■ n **twirl**, whirl, spin, eddy

swish v **hiss**, whoosh, whistle, whisper, rustle ■ adj (infml) **smart**, upmarket, fashionable, posh (infml), classy (infml) Opposite: downmarket

switch n **1 control**, lever, button, knob, key **2 change**, shift, adjustment, difference,

modification **3 exchange**, substitution, changeover, replacement, trade **4 whip**, lash, crop, cat-o'-nine-tails

switchback n **bend**, twist, zigzag, hairpin, turn

switch off v **1 shut down**, stop, deactivate, disconnect, cut Opposite: switch on **2** (infml) **relax**, unwind, stop worrying, stop paying attention, chill out (infml)

switch on v **turn on**, start, start up, activate, connect Opposite: switch off

swivel v **spin**, rotate, revolve, pivot, turn round

swollen adj **distended**, inflamed, engorged, puffy, puffed-up

swollen head n **conceit**, self-conceit, pride, vanity, arrogance Opposite: modesty

swollen-headed adj **conceited**, full of yourself, vain, self-important, puffed up Opposite: modest

swoon v **pass out**, faint, black out, lose consciousness, faint away ■ n **faint**, blackout, loss of consciousness, unconsciousness

swoop v **pounce**, jump, leap, dive, fly down

swoosh v **rustle**, swish, rush, swirl, whiz

swordplay n **sword fighting**, fencing, duelling, foil fencing, combat

sworn adj **confirmed**, affirmed, avowed (fml)

swot (infml) v **study**, revise, cram (infml), mug up (infml), bone up (infml)

sybarite n **voluptuary**, sensualist, hedonist, epicurean, pleasure-lover Opposite: spartan

sycophancy n **servility**, obsequiousness, flattery, fawning, toadying

sycophant n **toady**, flatterer, minion, yes man, bootlicker (infml)

sycophantic adj **ingratiating**, flattering, kowtowing, obsequious, apple-polishing (US slang)

syllabus n **course outline**, curriculum, programme, programme of study, prospectus

sylph n **nymph**, sprite, fairy, dryad, naiad

sylphlike adj **slender**, willowy, lithe, slim, graceful Opposite: hefty

symbiosis n **cooperation**, interdependence, relationship, association, synergy Opposite: independence

symbiotic adj **mutually beneficial**, interdependent, synergetic, cooperative, reciprocal Opposite: independent

symbol n **1 sign**, representation, character, figure, mark **2 emblem**, image, badge, logo

symbolic adj **representative**, figurative, emblematic, representational

symbolism n **imagery**, allegory, representation

symbolize v **represent**, be a symbol of, be a sign of, signify, stand for

symmetrical adj **balanced**, even, equal, proportioned, regular Opposite: asymmetric

symmetry n **regularity**, balance, equilibrium,

evenness, proportion *Opposite*: asymmetry

sympathetic *adj* **1 understanding**, concerned, kind, kindly, compassionate *Opposite*: unfeeling **2 approving**, in agreement, in accord, supportive, well-disposed *Opposite*: against **3 agreeable**, congenial, likable, friendly, amiable *Opposite*: disagreeable

sympathize *v* empathize, feel sorry for, commiserate, express sympathy, understand

sympathizer *n* partisan, backer, follower, adherent, well-wisher *Opposite*: opponent

sympathy *n* **1 understanding**, compassion, kindness, consideration, empathy *Opposite*: incomprehension **2 pity**, commiseration, condolences **3 approval**, agreement, support, backing

symphonic *adj* **musical**, orchestral, instrumental, classical, philharmonic

symposium *n* **conference**, seminar, meeting, convention

symptom *n* **indication**, sign, warning sign, indicator

symptomatic *adj* **indicative**, suggestive, characteristic

synchronize *v* **harmonize**, coordinate, orchestrate, bring into line, match

synchronized *adj* **coordinated**, harmonized, corresponding, matched, in time

syncopate *v* **modify**, play, shift, swing, stress

syncopation *n* **shift of accent**, modification, accent, stress, rhythm

syndicate *n* **association**, collective, consortium, organization, group

syndrome *n* **condition**, disease, pattern, set of symptoms, disorder

synergy *n* **working together**, interaction, cooperation, combined effect, collaboration

synonym *n* **alternative word**, alternative expression, other word, substitute, replacement

synonymous *adj* **identical**, the same, one and the same, equal, tantamount *Opposite*: different

synopsis *n* **outline**, rundown, précis, summing up, summary

syntax *n* **grammar**, sentence structure, language rules, composition, word order

synthesis *n* **1 mixture**, amalgamation, combination, blend, fusion *Opposite*: separation **2 production**, creation, making, manufacture

synthesize *v* **1 manufacture**, create, make, produce **2 fuse**, blend, combine, amalgamate, integrate *Opposite*: separate

synthetic *adj* **1 artificial**, fake, mock, imitation, faux *Opposite*: real **2 insincere**, sham, bogus, put on, phoney *Opposite*: genuine

syrup *n* **golden syrup**, treacle, molasses, sauce, maple syrup

syrupy *adj* **1 sugary**, thick, treacly, sweet **2 sentimental**, sickly, mawkish, cloying, schmaltzy *(infml)*

system *n* **1 scheme**, arrangement, classification, structure, organism **2 method**, technique, procedure, routine, approach **3 orderliness**, regularity, method, logic *Opposite*: disorder

systematic *adj* **methodical**, orderly, organized, efficient, logical *Opposite*: disorganized

systematize *v* **arrange**, order, regulate, sort, classify

systemic *adj* **universal**, complete, general

T

tab *n* tag, flap, label, ticket, stub

tabernacle *n* **chest**, cabinet, container, case, box

table *n* **1 bench**, board, desk, counter, stand **2 food**, fare, diet, provision, menu **3 chart**, graph, diagram, spreadsheet, record ■ *v* **propose**, put forward, submit, suggest, enter *Opposite*: withdraw

WORD BANK
❑ **types of table** bedside table, card table, coffee table, console, davenport, desk, dining table, dressing table, end table, escritoire, gateleg table, occasional table, Pembroke table, picnic table, rolltop desk, tea table, trestle table, vanity table, worktable, writing desk

tableau *n* **display**, picture, montage, scene, representation

tablecloth *n* **cover**, cloth, covering

tableland *n* **plain**, flatland, prairie, plateau, upland *Opposite*: lowland

table mat *n* **place mat**, coaster, mat, pad, trivet

tablet *n* **1 pill**, capsule, lozenge **2 slab**, block, bar, cake, lump

tableware *n* **crockery**, plates, dishes, dinner service, tea service

tabloid *n* **paper**, newspaper, red-top *(infml)*, rag *(infml)* ■ *adj* **sensationalist**, shocking, lurid, scandalous, yellow

taboo *adj* **1 offensive**, unmentionable, unthinkable, distasteful, off-limits **2 forbidden**, banned, prohibited, barred, proscribed *Opposite*: acceptable ■ *n* **ban**, prohibition, bar, restriction, interdict ■ *v* **forbid**, ban, prohibit, bar, proscribe *Opposite*: allow

tabular *adj* **flat**, level, smooth, even, horizontal

tabulate *v* **tabularize**, chart, arrange, organize, present

tabulation *n* **tabularization**, arrangement, organization, presentation, formulation

tacit *adj* **unspoken**, implicit, inferred, implied, understood *Opposite*: explicit

taciturn *adj* **reserved**, uncommunicative, reticent, silent, quiet *Opposite*: garrulous. *See* COMPARE AND CONTRAST *at* **silent**.

taciturnity *n* **reserve**, uncommunicativeness, reticence, silence, quietness *Opposite*: garrulousness

tack *n* **1 nail**, pin, screw, staple, clip **2 approach**, tactic, line, method, policy **3 direction**, path, bearing, course, way ■ *v* **1 pin**, nail, fasten, attach, affix *Opposite*: unfasten **2 append**, add on, tag on, stick on, attach *Opposite*: remove

tackiness *(infml)* *n* **tastelessness**, bad taste, vulgarity, cheapness, nastiness *Opposite*: tastefulness

tackle *n* **1 challenge**, attack, block, confrontation, throw **2 equipment**, apparatus, kit, outfit, tools ■ *v* **1 undertake**, begin, embark upon, attempt, engage in **2 confront**, challenge, face, speak to, collar **3 block**, stop, throw, seize, grab

tacky *adj* **1 sticky**, messy, gluey, gummy, adhesive *Opposite*: dry **2** *(infml)* **tasteless**, in bad taste, vulgar, cheap, nasty *Opposite*: tasteful

tact *n* **diplomacy**, discretion, sensitivity, delicacy, thoughtfulness *Opposite*: tactlessness

tactful *adj* **diplomatic**, discreet, sensitive, delicate, thoughtful *Opposite*: tactless

tactic *n* **method**, approach, course, ploy, policy

tactical *adj* **strategic**, planned, premeditated, pre-emptive, psychological *Opposite*: accidental

tactician *n* **strategist**, negotiator, planner, schemer, diplomat

tactics *n* **strategy**, planning, campaign, manoeuvres, devices

tactile *adj* **1 tangible**, palpable, perceptible, physical, concrete *Opposite*: intangible **2 demonstrative**, physical, affectionate, touchy-feely *(infml) Opposite*: reserved

tactless *adj* **insensitive**, undiplomatic, indiscreet, indelicate, thoughtless *Opposite*: tactful

tactlessness *n* **insensitivity**, indiscretion, indelicacy, thoughtlessness, inconsiderateness *Opposite*: tact

tad *(infml)* *n* **bit**, little, touch, mite, dash *Opposite*: lot

tag *n* **label**, ticket, tab, docket, identifier ■ *v* **1 mark**, label, ticket, docket, identify **2 append**, tack on, add on, attach, stick on *Opposite*: remove

tag along *v* **link up**, join in, follow, accompany, go with

tail *(infml)* *n* **follower**, shadow, stalker, pursuer, tracker ■ *v* **follow**, trail, track, shadow, stalk

tailback *n* **traffic jam**, queue, line, gridlock, logjam

tail end *n* **end**, close, ending, conclusion, finish *Opposite*: start

tailgate *v* **dog**, hound, be hard on the heels of, follow, pursue

tail light *n* **rear light**, tail lamp, brake light, stoplight *(US) Opposite*: headlight

tail off *v* **fade**, peter out, dwindle, decrease, fall away *Opposite*: build up

tailor *v* **1 make**, make to measure, cut, fashion, mould **2 adapt**, customize, custom-build, modify, fit

tailored *adj* **1 custom-made**, bespoke, made-to-measure, tailor-made, handmade *Opposite*: off-the-peg **2 fitted**, shaped, well-cut, figure-hugging, close-fitting *Opposite*: casual **3 adapted**, customized, custom-built, modified, altered

tailor-made *adj* **1 perfect**, ideal, right, suitable, appropriate *Opposite*: wrong **2 made-to-measure**, bespoke, custom-made, tailored, handmade *Opposite*: off-the-peg

tailpiece *n* **end**, end piece, finale, finial, coda

tailspin *n* **1 nosedive**, dive, spin, spiral, descent **2** *(infml)* **panic**, flap, turmoil, flat spin, whirl

taint *v* **contaminate**, pollute, stain, spoil, infect *Opposite*: enhance ■ *n* **stain**, blemish, blot, defect, fault

tainted *adj* **contaminated**, polluted, stained, spoiled, soiled *Opposite*: pure

take *v* **1 remove**, appropriate, acquire, grab, seize *Opposite*: give **2 carry**, transfer, fetch, bring, transport *Opposite*: leave **3 conquer**, capture, win, seize, secure *Opposite*: lose **4 grasp**, grab, seize, catch, catch on to *Opposite*: drop **5 choose**, select, procure, receive, buy *Opposite*: leave **6 accompany**, bring, escort, guide, lead **7 undertake**, adopt, accept, take on, assume *Opposite*: refuse **8 bear**, stand, endure, tolerate, suffer *Opposite*: reject **9 support**, hold up, hold, bear, manage **10 contain**, hold, accept, accommodate, house **11 study**, learn, read, do, take up *Opposite*: teach **12 consider**, look at, discuss, examine, think about *Opposite*: disregard **13 require**, need, demand, use, accept *Opposite*: reject **14 derive**, draw, experience, feel, extract **15 presume**, assume, believe, consider, perceive **16 succeed**, work, stick, root, come off *(infml) Opposite*: fail **17 subtract**, deduct, take away, take off, remove *Opposite*: add ■ *n* **1 receipts**, takings, earnings, income, revenue *Opposite*: expenditure **2 shot**, sequence, scene **3 impression**, interpretation, opinion, view, point of view

take aback *v* **surprise**, stun, shock, nonplus, knock for six *(infml)*

take a back seat *v* **hold back**, restrain yourself, rein back, stay out of it

take a break *v* rest, relax, take time out, come up for air, pause *Opposite*: press on

take a breather *(infml) see* **take a break**

take account of *v* allow for, take into consideration, bear in mind, make allowances for, keep in mind *Opposite*: ignore

take a chance *v* gamble, venture, risk it, chance it, stick your neck out *Opposite*: play safe

take action *v* act, do something, take the plunge, take the bull by the horns, get stuck in

take a dim view of *v* disapprove of, not think much of, frown on, object to, dislike *Opposite*: approve

take advantage of somebody *v* exploit, use, mistreat, abuse, take for a ride

take advantage of something *v* make the most of, cash in on, profit from, exploit, make use of

take a fancy to *v* like, approve of, take a liking to, be fond of, love *Opposite*: dislike

take after *v* resemble, act like, imitate, look like, bear a resemblance to *Opposite*: differ

take a gamble *v* gamble, venture, risk it, chance it, stick your neck out *Opposite*: play safe

take amiss *v* take the wrong way, take exception, take umbrage, take offence, be put out *Opposite*: understand

take an oath *v* promise, swear, pledge, vow, give your word

take apart *v* **1** dismantle, take to bits, take to pieces, break up, pull apart *Opposite*: assemble **2** *(infml)* criticize, censure, condemn, lash, pan *(infml) Opposite*: praise

take as read *v* accept, believe, take at face value, take for granted, assume *Opposite*: challenge

take at face value *v* believe, accept, take as read, take for granted, rely on *Opposite*: question

take a turn for the worse *v* go from bad to worse, deteriorate, decline, slip, relapse *Opposite*: improve

take away *v* **1** remove, cart off, carry off, carry away, take off *Opposite*: bring **2** subtract, deduct, take, take off *Opposite*: add

takeaway *adj* ready-made, precooked, prepared, to go, carryout ■ *n* ready-made meal, fast food, carryout, takeout *(US)*, ready meal

take back *v* **1** withdraw, retract, recant, renounce, disclaim *Opposite*: stick to **2** regain, recapture, retake, recover, retrieve *Opposite*: give back **3** return, exchange, refund, redeem, trade in *Opposite*: keep **4** reinstate, reaccept, bring back, welcome back, have back *Opposite*: dismiss **5** remind, transport, jog your memory, put you in mind of, make you think of

take by storm *v* **1** capture, overwhelm, storm, seize, conquer **2** captivate, enthral, bowl over, impress, charm

take by surprise *v* surprise, burst in on, catch napping, take unawares, catch unawares

take care *v* **1** be careful, pay attention, mind out, look out, watch out **2** make sure, ensure, make certain, confirm, check *Opposite*: neglect

take care of *v* **1** look after, care for, nurse, tend, support *Opposite*: neglect **2** deal with, see to, handle, manage, do *Opposite*: neglect

take charge *v* assume responsibility, take over, hold the fort, take the reins, take up the baton *Opposite*: step down

take control *see* **take charge**

take cover *v* hide, take shelter, shelter, take refuge, conceal yourself *Opposite*: emerge

take down *v* **1** note, jot down, write down, make a note of, record **2** dismantle, demolish, knock down, pull down, take apart *Opposite*: put up **3** humiliate, humble, deflate, embarrass, mortify *Opposite*: puff up

take effect *v* happen, function, work, operate, succeed

take exception *v* take offence, take umbrage, be put out, object, disapprove *Opposite*: welcome

take five *(infml) v* take a break, take time out, take a rest, rest, relax *Opposite*: keep on

take flight *v* run away, run off, flee, take off, decamp *Opposite*: stay put

take for a ride *v* cheat, deceive, swindle, trick, con

take for granted *v* **1** assume, presume, take as read, expect, count on **2** undervalue, underrate, hold cheap, hold in contempt, disregard *Opposite*: appreciate

take heart *v* cheer up, perk up, brighten up, take comfort, snap out of it *Opposite*: lose heart

take home *v* make, be paid, net, earn, get

take-home pay *n* net income, net salary, net wages, net pay, net income after deductions

take in *v* **1** absorb, understand, comprehend, grasp, assimilate *Opposite*: ignore **2** include, contain, comprise, encompass, cover *Opposite*: exclude **3** deceive, dupe, fool, mislead, trick **4** let in, receive, admit, entertain, accommodate *Opposite*: bar **5** reduce, alter, shrink, shorten, draw in *Opposite*: let out

take in hand *v* deal with, cope with, tackle, get to grips with, take on

take into consideration *v* allow for, take into account, bear in mind, make allowances for, keep in mind *Opposite*: ignore

take into custody *v* arrest, detain, imprison, confine, hold *Opposite*: release

take in your stride *v* deal with, cope with, accept, take on board, manage

take issue with *v* disagree, differ, beg to differ, oppose, challenge *Opposite*: agree

take it easy v 1 **relax**, unwind, put your feet up, laze about, laze around *Opposite*: toil 2 **calm down**, relax, simmer down, keep your shirt on, lighten up (infml) *Opposite*: explode

take legal action v go to court, sue, press charges, prosecute, litigate

taken adj **occupied**, in use, engaged, spoken for, busy *Opposite*: free

take no notice of v **ignore**, disregard, pay no attention, pay no heed, close your eyes *Opposite*: notice

take off v 1 **remove**, discard, strip off, slip out of, peel off *Opposite*: put on 2 **deduct**, subtract, take away, take, remove *Opposite*: add 3 (infml) **parody**, imitate, mimic, impersonate, satirize 4 **cancel**, suspend, discontinue, abolish, do away with *Opposite*: reinstate 5 **launch**, depart, leave, lift off, fly off *Opposite*: land 6 (infml) **leave**, go, depart, disappear, set out *Opposite*: stay 7 (infml) **succeed**, flourish, bloom, boom, prosper *Opposite*: flop (infml). *See* COMPARE AND CONTRAST *at* imitate.

takeoff n 1 **departure**, ascent, launch, lift off, start *Opposite*: touchdown 2 (infml) **imitation**, impersonation, impression, parody, skit

take offence v take exception, take umbrage, take amiss, take the wrong way, be put out

take on v 1 **undertake**, assume, deal with, accept, adopt *Opposite*: refuse 2 **employ**, hire, engage, sign, bring on board *Opposite*: fire 3 **adopt**, acquire, gain, display, show *Opposite*: lose 4 **face**, confront, oppose, fight, vie with *Opposite*: avoid

take on board v 1 **understand**, grasp, comprehend, realize, absorb *Opposite*: deny 2 **accept**, include, accommodate, implement, allow for *Opposite*: reject

take out v 1 **remove**, extract, pull out, bring out, fish out *Opposite*: insert 2 **arrange**, organize, set up, obtain, acquire *Opposite*: cancel 3 **ask out**, invite out, accompany, treat, take *Opposite*: stand up 4 **vent**, direct, aim, express, relieve

take over v 1 **take possession of**, annex, capture, hijack, seize *Opposite*: cede (fml) 2 **take control**, take charge, take the reins, step in, assume responsibility *Opposite*: step down

takeover n **coup**, overthrow, seizure, appropriation, occupation *Opposite*: secession

take part v **join in**, participate, play, play a part, cooperate *Opposite*: opt out (infml)

take place v **happen**, occur, have effect, go on, come about

take pleasure in v **delight in**, enjoy, be taken with, love, take great delight in *Opposite*: hate

take possession of v **take over**, take control of, sequester, impound, occupy *Opposite*: abandon

take precedence v **have priority**, outweigh, come first, come before, predominate

take prisoner v **capture**, take captive, take hostage, seize, imprison *Opposite*: release

taker n **customer**, client, patron, purchaser, buyer

take root v **set in**, develop, start, grow, settle in *Opposite*: die off

take shape v **form**, develop, crystallize, take form, shape up *Opposite*: dissolve

take steps v **make a start**, proceed, start, take action, do something

take stock v **reflect**, weigh up, sum up, think over, count your blessings

take the blame v **take responsibility**, face the music, own up, get it in the neck (infml), carry the can (infml) *Opposite*: get away with

take the bull by the horns v **take the plunge**, bite the bullet, grasp the nettle, take the initiative, jump in *Opposite*: hold back

take the edge off v **dampen**, blunt, dilute, relieve, mitigate *Opposite*: heighten

take the lead v **blaze a trail**, set a trend, originate, break new ground, break through *Opposite*: fall behind

take the mickey (infml) v **tease**, make fun of, laugh at, bait, kid

take the place of v **replace**, succeed, displace, supersede, take over from

take the plunge v **dive in**, jump in, throw caution to the wind, take the bull by the horns, bite the bullet *Opposite*: hold back

take the rough with the smooth v **take the bad with the good**, make the best of things, make the best of a bad job, look on the bright side, keep your chin up *Opposite*: crack up (infml)

take to v 1 **warm to**, take a fancy to, take a liking to, fall for, get on with *Opposite*: dislike 2 **begin**, start, commence, take up, go in for *Opposite*: stop

take to court v **prosecute**, sue, take legal action, press charges, file a suit

take to pieces v **take apart**, take to bits, dismantle, disassemble, strip down *Opposite*: put together

take to task v **reprimand**, scold, rebuke, reprove, haul over the coals *Opposite*: praise

take to your heels v **run away**, run off, flee, run, show a clean pair of heels *Opposite*: stay put

take unawares v **surprise**, catch on the hop, catch out, catch off guard, take by surprise

take up v 1 **start**, go in for, adopt, engage in, assume *Opposite*: give up 2 **continue**, resume, go on, pick up, carry on *Opposite*: leave off 3 **raise**, lift, pick up, gather up, hoist *Opposite*: put down 4 **shorten**, raise, lift, pin up, gather up *Opposite*: let down 5 **occupy**, fill, cover, absorb, consume

take-up n **acceptance**, reception, use, participation, response

take up the baton v **take control**, take charge,

take over, take the reins, step in *Opposite*: step down

take up the gauntlet *v* **accept a challenge**, take on, confront, stand up to *Opposite*: run away

taking *adj* **captivating**, attractive, enchanting, pleasing, winning *Opposite*: unattractive

takings *n* **earnings**, income, proceeds, profits, receipts *Opposite*: expenditure

tale *n* **1 account**, fiction, romance, anecdote, legend **2 lie**, untruth, rumour, falsehood, story *Opposite*: truth

talent *n* **aptitude**, flair, gift, bent, knack

COMPARE AND CONTRAST CORE MEANING: the natural ability to do something well
talent a natural ability to do something well that can be developed by training; **gift** a natural ability, especially an artistic ability, or a social skill; **aptitude** a natural ability to do or learn something, especially one that is not yet fully developed; **flair** a natural ability to do something well, especially creative or artistic ability; **bent** a natural ability, inclination, or liking for something; **knack** an intuitive ability to do something well, especially one that might not be developed by training; **genius** exceptional intellectual or creative ability.

talented *adj* **gifted**, accomplished, able, brilliant, artistic

taleteller *n* **informer**, turncoat, snitch *(slang)*, stool pigeon *(slang)*, rat *(slang)*

talisman *n* **stone**, jewel, amulet, charm, trinket

talk *v* **1 communicate**, speak, chat, gossip, chatter **2 converse**, debate, compare notes, have a word, have a discussion **3 confess**, betray, turn over, inform, crack ■ *n* **1 conversation**, exchange, dialogue, tête-à-tête, heart-to-heart **2 lecture**, speech, address, discourse, oration **3 gossip**, conversation, rumour, chatter, speculation **4 language**, words, vocabulary, jargon, speech

talkative *adj* **chatty**, verbose, garrulous, voluble, loquacious *Opposite*: reticent

COMPARE AND CONTRAST CORE MEANING: talking a lot
talkative willing to talk readily and at length; **chatty** talking freely about unimportant things in a friendly way; **gossipy** talking with relish about other people and their lives, often unkindly or maliciously; **garrulous** excessively or pointlessly talkative; **loquacious** tending to talk a great deal.

talkativeness *n* **chattiness**, verbosity, garrulousness, volubility, fluency *Opposite*: reticence

talk back *v* **argue**, answer back, defy, retort, quibble

talker *n* **communicator**, conversationalist, speaker, gossip, chatterer

talking *n* **1 speaking**, conversation, chat, chatting, gossip **2 debate**, words, discussion, negotiation, conference

talking point *n* **topic of conversation**, debating point, issue, question, hot topic

talking-to *(infml)* *n* **dressing-down**, reprimand, lecture, tongue-lashing, scolding

talk into *v* **persuade**, coax, induce, convince, move *Opposite*: talk out of

talk out of *v* **dissuade**, sway, put off, discourage, deter *Opposite*: talk into

talk over *v* **discuss**, negotiate, debate, review, go into

talks *n* **negotiations**, discussions, summit, dialogue, conference

tall *adj* **1 high**, big, giant, lofty, lanky *Opposite*: short **2 difficult**, hard, complicated, demanding, trying *Opposite*: easy **3 incredible**, unbelievable, unlikely, far-fetched, exaggerated *Opposite*: likely

tallness *n* **height**, loftiness, size, lankiness, stature *Opposite*: shortness

tall story *see* tall tale

tall tale *n* **cock-and-bull story**, unlikely story, tale, tall story, fairy tale

tally *v* **1 match**, correspond, agree, check, equate *Opposite*: clash **2 compute**, count, reckon, score, total ■ *n* **score**, count, total, reckoning, calculation

talon *n* **claw**, nail, fingernail, hook, spur

tame *adj* **1 domestic**, domesticated, broken, trained, disciplined *Opposite*: wild **2 docile**, meek, compliant, subdued, unresisting *Opposite*: rebellious **3 bland**, dull, insipid, boring, unexciting *Opposite*: exciting ■ *v* **1 domesticate**, break in, train, discipline, pacify **2 repress**, suppress, overcome, subjugate, subdue

tameness *n* **1 docility**, meekness, compliance, submissiveness, obedience *Opposite*: rebelliousness **2 blandness**, dullness, insipidness, flatness, tedium *Opposite*: excitement

tamp *v* **fill**, pack, stuff, cram, compress

tamper *v* **1 interfere**, meddle, monkey with, fool with, tinker **2 corrupt**, rig, influence, manipulate, bribe

tampon *n* **plug**, pad, wad, swab, compress

tan *n* **suntan**, sunburn, colour, bronze, brownness ■ *v* **1 bronze**, go brown, brown, toast, burn **2 treat**, preserve, process, dye, wash

tang *n* **trace**, hint, smack, suggestion, flavour

tangent *n* **line**, curve, angle, refraction, curvature

tangential *adj* **peripheral**, lateral, oblique, divergent, indirect *Opposite*: central

tangibility *n* **1 palpability**, perceptibility, physicality, reality, solidity *Opposite*: intangibility **2 actuality**, reality, clarity, plainness, obviousness *Opposite*: intangibility

tangible *adj* **1 palpable**, touchable, perceptible, concrete, physical *Opposite*: intangible **2 actual**, substantial, real, certain, evident *Opposite*: intangible

tangle *v* **1 knot**, twist, snarl, interweave, intertwine *Opposite*: untangle **2 snag**, catch, snarl, snare, hook *Opposite*: undo **3 trap**, catch, ensnare, entangle, enmesh *Opposite*: release **4 come up against**, confront, mess with, square up, oppose *Opposite*: avoid ■ *n* **1 mass**, jumble, knot, mesh, web **2 mess**, jam, difficulty, mix-up, complication

tangled *adj* **1 knotted**, twisted, snarled, interwoven, intertwined *Opposite*: straight **2 complicated**, confused, knotty, complex, messy *Opposite*: straightforward

tangy *adj* **pungent**, sharp, strong, piquant, tasty *Opposite*: bland

tank *n* **cistern**, boiler, reservoir, container, chamber

tankard *n* **mug**, beer mug, jug, stein, toby jug

tanker *n* **transporter**, freighter, lorry, truck

tanned *adj* **brown**, bronzed, suntanned, dark, sunburnt *Opposite*: pale

tantalize *v* **tease**, entice, torment, torture, tempt *Opposite*: turn off *(infml)*

tantalizing *adj* **teasing**, enticing, tormenting, tempting, provocative *Opposite*: boring

tantamount *adj* **equal**, equivalent, the same as, synonymous, as good as *Opposite*: different

tantrum *n* **outburst**, fit of temper, fit, frenzy, fret

tap *n* **1 blow**, rap, knock, bang, beat **2 stopper**, plug, bung, cork **3 valve**, stopcock, spout, spigot, faucet *(US)* ■ *v* **1 rap**, knock, bang, beat, strike **2 draw off**, draw out, extract, run off, release *Opposite*: block up **3 bug**, listen in on, record, monitor, intercept **4** *(infml)* **use**, utilize, draw on, draw off, exploit

tape *n* **1 ribbon**, strip, string, tie, band **2 adhesive tape**, sticky tape, insulating tape, masking tape, packing tape **3 cassette**, cassette tape, video, videotape, video cassette **4 tape measure**, measuring tape, measure, tapeline ■ *v* **1 record**, tape-record, copy, save, video *Opposite*: erase **2 stick**, fasten, attach, secure, bind *Opposite*: detach

tape measure *n* **tape**, measuring tape, measure, rule, ruler

taper *v* **1 narrow**, come to a point, thin down, dwindle, elongate *Opposite*: widen **2 reduce**, phase out, taper off, tail off, diminish *Opposite*: increase ■ *n* **1 candle**, torch, light, flame **2 narrowing**, point, thinning down, dwindling, elongation

tape-record *v* **tape**, record, copy, save, video

tapered *adj* **1 tapering**, narrowing, pointed, elongated, shaped *Opposite*: flared **2 gradually reduced**, phased out, tailed off, diminished, decreased

tapering *adj* **tapered**, narrowing, pointed, elongated, shaped *Opposite*: widening

tapestry *n* **wall hanging**, drapery, arras

tar *n* **asphalt**, Tarmac, pitch, macadam, blacktop *(US)*

tardiness *n* **lateness**, delay, belatedness, unpunctuality *Opposite*: punctuality

tardy *adj* **late**, delayed, overdue, belated, unpunctual *Opposite*: punctual

target *n* **1 board**, mark, bull's eye, bull, goal **2 aim**, objective, object, focus, end **3 butt**, victim, scapegoat, foil, recipient ■ *v* **1 aim at**, aim for, focus on, home in on, seek out **2 direct**, aim, point, level, train

tariff *n* **1 tax**, duty, due, excise, levy **2 price**, price list, rate, charge, cost

Tarmac *n* **tar**, asphalt, pitch, macadam, bitumen

tarn *n* **lake**, pool, pond, loch, lagoon

tarnish *v* **1 dull**, discolour, stain, smear, smudge *Opposite*: clean **2 sully**, damage, stain, taint, blot *Opposite*: enhance

tarnished *adj* **1 dull**, discoloured, stained, smeared, smudged *Opposite*: shiny **2 sullied**, damaged, stained, tainted, blotted *Opposite*: enhanced

tarpaulin *n* **canvas**, cover, sheet, sheeting, tarp *(infml)*

tarry *v* **1 remain**, stay, stay put, visit, sojourn *(literary)* **2 linger**, loiter, dawdle, hang around, hesitate

tart *adj* **1 sharp**, acid, acidic, sour, bitter *Opposite*: sweet **2 acerbic**, biting, sharp, sour, acid *Opposite*: kind ■ *n* **pie**, tartlet, pastry, quiche, flan

tartan *n* **pattern**, plaid, check

tartar *n* **plaque**, deposit, residue, coating, scale

tartness *n* **1 sharpness**, acidity, sourness, bitterness *Opposite*: sweetness **2 acerbity**, sharpness, sourness, acidity, bitterness *Opposite*: kindness

tart up *(infml)* *v* **smarten up**, tidy up, decorate, do up, make up

task *n* **job**, chore, duty, mission, commission

task force *n* **team**, unit, squad, detail, crew

tassel *n* **bobble**, tuft, fringe, braid, edging

taste *n* **1 sense of taste**, palate, discrimination, sensitivity, perception **2 flavour**, tang, savour, hint, smack **3 try**, sample, test, bite, nibble **4 liking**, preference, leaning, penchant, fondness *Opposite*: dislike **5 discrimination**, discernment, judgment, tastefulness, good taste ■ *v* **1 discern**, pick up, recognize, get, feel **2 sample**, try, test, eat, bite *Opposite*: devour **3 experience**, sample, preview, get a taste of, get a hint of

tasteful *adj* **discerning**, discriminating, sophisticated, refined, stylish *Opposite*: tasteless

tastefulness *n* **discernment**, discrimination, judgment, taste, sophistication *Opposite*: tastelessness

tasteless *adj* **1 bland**, flavourless, flat, insipid, weak *Opposite*: tasty **2 in bad taste**, in poor taste, cheap, flashy, loud *Opposite*: tasteful **3 vulgar**, crude, foul-mouthed, boorish, gross

tastelessness *n* **1 blandness**, flavourlessness, flatness, insipidness, weakness *Opposite*: tastiness **2 bad taste**, poor taste, cheapness, flashiness, loudness *Opposite*: tastefulness

taster n 1 **analyst**, sampler, buyer, specialist, connoisseur 2 **preview**, foretaste, appetizer, sample, excerpt

tastiness n **deliciousness**, flavour, yumminess, juiciness, succulence *Opposite*: tastelessness

tasty adj **delicious**, flavoursome, mouth-watering, appetizing, succulent *Opposite*: tasteless

tat (infml) n **rubbish**, junk (infml), jumble, scrap, seconds

tater (infml) n **potato**, spud (infml), murphy (dated infml)

tattered adj **torn**, ragged, tatty, dilapidated, frayed *Opposite*: smart

tatters n **rags**, shreds, bits, pieces, strips

tattiness n **shabbiness**, scruffiness, rag-gedness, dilapidation, untidiness *Opposite*: smartness

tattle v **gossip**, tittle-tattle, prattle, chat, chatter *Opposite*: keep secret (infml) ■ n 1 **gossip**, tattler, telltale, informer, informant 2 **tittle-tattle**, gossip, prattle, chat, chatter *Opposite*: fact

tattler n **gossip**, tattle, sneak, telltale, informer

tattoo n 1 **design**, pattern, picture, decoration, mark 2 **signal**, summons, call, recall, order 3 **parade**, display, tournament, show, pageant

tatty adj **shabby**, worn, scruffy, dog-eared, down-at-heel *Opposite*: smart

taunt v **mock**, tease, jeer, sneer, goad *Opposite*: compliment ■ n **insult**, gibe, sneer, affront, criticism *Opposite*: compliment

taunting adj **mocking**, provocative, provoking, teasing, spiteful *Opposite*: kind

taut adj 1 **tight**, stretched, rigid, stiff, tense *Opposite*: slack 2 **worried**, anxious, stressed, tense, nervous *Opposite*: calm

tauten v **tighten**, stretch, stiffen, pull tight, tense *Opposite*: slacken

tautness n **tightness**, tension, pull, stretch, rigidity *Opposite*: slackness

tautological adj **repetitious**, repetitive, inele-gant, reiterative, redundant

tautology n **repetition**, reiteration, duplication, redundancy, superfluity

tavern (archaic) n **inn**, pub, local, bar, watering hole (infml)

tawdriness n **cheapness**, gaudiness, flashi-ness, showiness, tastelessness *Opposite*: tastefulness

tawdry adj **cheap**, gaudy, flashy, showy, taste-less *Opposite*: tasteful

tax n **duty**, levy, toll, excise, tariff ■ v 1 **charge**, hit, burden, cream off, deduct *Opposite*: exempt 2 **strain**, overtax, overstretch, stretch, overload *Opposite*: relieve 3 **accuse**, reproach, blame, confront, present

taxable adj **chargeable**, assessable, dutiable, rateable, payable *Opposite*: tax-exempt

taxation n 1 **fiscal policy**, tax policy, tax system, revenue system, taxes 2 **duty**, levy, toll, dues, excise

tax-exempt adj **exempt from taxation**, exempt, untaxed, tax-free, duty-free *Opposite*: taxable

taxing adj **demanding**, tough, difficult, strenu-ous, challenging *Opposite*: effortless

taxonomy n **classification**, nomenclature, taxo-nomic system, catalogue, categorization

tea n **drink**, infusion, tisane, brew, decoction

tea break n **break**, coffee break, rest, refresh-ment break, elevenses

teach v 1 **impart**, communicate, show, explain, clarify *Opposite*: learn 2 **educate**, tutor, train, instruct, coach *Opposite*: learn

COMPARE AND CONTRAST CORE MEANING: impart knowledge or skill in something

teach impart knowledge or skill to somebody by instruction or example; **educate** increase the knowledge or develop the abilities of somebody by formal teaching or training, especially in a school or college context; **train** teach the skills necessary for a particular task or job by means of instruction, observation, and practice; **instruct** teach somebody a subject, methodology, or skill, not necessarily in a school or college context; **coach** give special tuition to one person or a small group of people, especially in preparation for an exam, or teach sports, artistic, or life skills; **tutor** give somebody individual tuition in a particular subject or skill; **school** train somebody in a par-ticular skill or area of expertise in a thorough and detailed way; **drill** teach something by means of repeated exercises and practice.

teacher n **educator**, tutor, instructor, coach, trainer *Opposite*: student

teaching n 1 **education**, lessons, instruction, coaching, training *Opposite*: learning 2 **phi-losophy**, ideas, principles, beliefs, thinking

team n 1 **side**, squad, players, lineup, crew 2 **group**, band, crew, gang, panel

team-mate n **colleague**, co-player, partner, fellow player

teamster n **driver**, carter, charioteer, handler, trainer

team up v **join forces**, collaborate, cooperate, work together, get together *Opposite*: split up

teamwork n **cooperation**, collaboration, joint effort, solidarity, communication

tear v 1 **rip**, rend, split, gash, slash *Opposite*: join 2 **sprain**, rip, pull, injure, damage 3 **snatch**, rip, grab, wrench, pluck *Opposite*: coax 4 **dash**, rush, hurry, rip, streak *Oppo-site*: saunter ■ n 1 **slit**, rip, split, slash, gash *Opposite*: join 2 **teardrop**, drop, droplet, drip, bead

COMPARE AND CONTRAST CORE MEANING: pull apart forcibly
tear pull something apart, either by accident or on purpose, leaving jagged edges; **rend** pull something apart violently; **rip** tear something with a sudden rough splitting action, accompanied by a distinctive noise, especially accidentally; **split** divide something into two parts with a single movement, usually by force.

tear apart v 1 **destroy**, fragment, wreck, separate, dismantle *Opposite*: reunite 2 **distress**, disturb, devastate, pain, hurt *Opposite*: reassure

tear away v **drag away**, pull away, haul away, depart, leave *Opposite*: linger

tearaway n **delinquent**, troublemaker, hoodlum, hooligan (*infml*), yob (*infml*)

tear down v **demolish**, rip down, pull down, destroy, remove *Opposite*: construct

teardrop n **tear**, drop, droplet, drip, bead

tearful adj 1 **in tears**, crying, weeping, sobbing, howling 2 **sad**, emotional, unhappy, mournful, melancholy *Opposite*: cheerful

tear into v **lay into**, attack, go for, round on, set on *Opposite*: praise

tear-jerker (*infml*) n **sentimental story**, drama, tragedy, sad story, weepie (*infml*) *Opposite*: comedy

tear up v **rip up**, shred, destroy, rip to pieces, rip to shreds

tease v 1 **joke**, laugh, mock, kid, taunt 2 **torment**, harass, pester, bother, annoy *Opposite*: pet 3 **tantalize**, arouse, lead somebody on, encourage, excite *Opposite*: satisfy ■ n **joker**, clown, mocker, teaser, tormentor

teaser n 1 **puzzle**, puzzler, brainteaser, tough one, mystery 2 **tease**, joker, clown, mocker, leg-puller (*infml*)

tea service n **tea set**, cups and saucers, china, porcelain, crockery

tea set *see* **tea service**

teasing adj 1 **playful**, mocking, tongue-in-cheek, mischievous, jokey *Opposite*: serious 2 **provocative**, coy, flirtatious, suggestive, tempting *Opposite*: straightforward ■ n **playfulness**, banter, repartee, raillery, leg-pulling (*infml*) *Opposite*: seriousness

tea-time n **dinnertime**, suppertime, mealtime, time for tea, time for dinner

technical adj 1 **technological**, scientific, industrial, mechanical 2 **practical**, mechanical, procedural, methodological, methodical 3 **nominal**, official, strict, narrow, literal *Opposite*: loose 4 **specialized**, precise, official, professional, specialist *Opposite*: general

technicality n **detail**, small point, trifle

technician n **specialist**, expert, operator, mechanic, engineer

technique n **method**, system, practice, modus operandi, procedure

technological adj **technical**, scientific, industrial, high-tech

technologist n **scientist**, engineer, technician, boffin (*infml*), maven (*US*)

technology n 1 **equipment**, machinery, tools 2 **skill**, knowledge, expertise, know-how (*infml*)

tedious adj **boring**, dull, dreary, monotonous, mind-numbing *Opposite*: interesting

tediousness n **boredom**, dullness, dreariness, monotony, tedium *Opposite*: excitement

tedium *see* **tediousness**

teem v 1 **swarm**, crowd, abound, be full, be stuffed 2 **pour**, pelt, stream, rain, rain cats and dogs (*infml*) *Opposite*: drizzle

teeming adj **swarming**, packed, crowded, heaving, crawling *Opposite*: empty

teen (*infml*) adj **teenage**, adolescent, youth, young, juvenile ■ n **teenager**, adolescent, young person, youth, youngster

teenage adj **adolescent**, young, youth, juvenile, teen (*infml*)

teenager n **adolescent**, young person, youth, youngster, young adult. *See* COMPARE AND CONTRAST *at* **youth**.

teens n **adolescence**, youth, young adulthood

teeny (*infml*) adj **tiny**, small, little, minute, wee *Opposite*: enormous

tee off v **drive off**, start, begin, commence, initiate

teeter v **totter**, stagger, wobble, shake, dodder

teething troubles n **problems**, glitches, difficulties, snags, hitches

teetotal adj **dry**, nondrinking, abstemious, abstinent, sober

telecaster n **broadcaster**, presenter, announcer, commentator, newsreader

telecommuter n **homeworker**, teleworker, freelancer, outworker

telecommuting n **working from home**, freelancing, outworking

telegram n **wire**, cable, message, telegraph, telex

telegraph v **send by wire**, send a message, cable, wire, transmit

telegraphic adj **concise**, abbreviated, condensed, truncated, succinct *Opposite*: verbose

telemarketing *see* **telesales**

telepathic adj **clairvoyant**, psychic, telekinetic, extrasensory, subconscious

telepathy n **thought transference**, ESP, extrasensory perception, mind-reading, sixth sense

telephone v **phone**, call, give somebody a call, ring, buzz (*infml*)

telephone call n **call**, ring, phone call, bell (*infml*), buzz (*infml*)

telesales n telephone sales, marketing, sales, telemarketing

telescopic adj 1 **magnifying**, enlarging, tele-photo, zoom 2 **collapsible**, retractable, fold-away, foldup, compactible

telethon n fundraiser, phone-in, charity appeal, broadcast appeal, solicitation

televise v broadcast, emit, relay, put out, put on

television n telly, TV (infml), small screen (infml), box (slang), goggle-box (dated infml)

teleworker n telecommuter, homeworker, free-lancer, outworker

teleworking n telecommuting, freelancing, out-working, homeworking

tell v 1 **inform**, let know, say, advise, notify Opposite: keep in the dark 2 **relate**, narrate, recount, describe, report 3 **express**, say, voice, communicate, state 4 **instruct**, order, direct, command, charge 5 **distinguish**, recognize, differentiate, identify, discriminate Opposite: confuse 6 **divulge**, disclose, expose, reveal, inform Opposite: keep secret

tell against v count against, go against, work against, weigh against

tell apart v distinguish, differentiate, tell one from another, identify, tell the difference between

teller n cashier, banker, bank clerk

telling adj 1 revealing, informative, significant, telltale, indicative Opposite: uninformative 2 **effective**, expressive, important, significant, influential Opposite: ineffective

telling-off (infml) n reprimand, scolding, dressing-down, lecture, tongue-lashing Opposite: praise

tell lies v lie, tell untruths, tell stories, dissemble, perjure yourself Opposite: tell the truth

tell off (infml) v reprimand, scold, rebuke, give a talking-to, haul over the coals Opposite: commend

tell stories v tell lies, lie, tell untruths, prevaricate, fabricate

telltale adj revealing, informative, betraying, significant, divulging Opposite: uninformative ■ n informer, sneak, gossip, blabbermouth (infml), snitch (slang)

tell the truth v be honest, give your word, be straight with, be open, be truthful Opposite: lie

temerity n nerve, audacity, gall, boldness, impudence Opposite: reticence

temp n temporary worker, office temporary, fill-in, stand-in, temporary secretary ■ v do temporary work, fill in, stand in

temper n 1 **anger**, rage, bad mood, bad humour, mood 2 **disposition**, temperament, state of mind, frame of mind, humour ■ v **moderate**, mitigate, alleviate, soften, lighten Opposite: intensify

temperament n nature, character, personality, disposition, temper

temperamental adj **unpredictable**, erratic, unreliable, undependable, up and down Opposite: consistent

temperance n 1 **teetotalism**, sobriety, abstinence, abstemiousness, soberness Opposite: intemperance 2 **self-control**, restraint, self-restraint, moderation, self-denial Opposite: indulgence

temperate adj 1 **restrained**, self-controlled, controlled, measured, reasonable Opposite: intemperate 2 **moderate**, mild, clement, pleasant, comfortable Opposite: extreme

tempered adj hardened, toughened, hard, annealed, strengthened

tempest n 1 (literary) **storm**, gale, thunderstorm, hurricane, cyclone Opposite: calm 2 **uproar**, commotion, tumult, upheaval, disturbance

tempestuous adj 1 **stormy**, rough, turbulent, intemperate, inclement Opposite: calm 2 **emotional**, passionate, intense, hysterical, violent Opposite: relaxed

template n pattern, master, stencil, model, prototype

tempo n beat, speed, pulse, rhythm, measure

temporal adj 1 **chronological**, time-based, sequential, progressive, historical Opposite: spatial 2 **worldly**, earthly, secular, lay, profane Opposite: spiritual

temporary adj passing, transitory, short-lived, fleeting, ephemeral Opposite: permanent

---

COMPARE AND CONTRAST CORE MEANING: lasting only a short time

temporary lasting or designed to last for a short time; **fleeting** very brief or rapid; **passing** superficial and not long-lasting; **transitory** existing only for a short time; **ephemeral** lasting for a short time and leaving no permanent trace; **evanescent** (literary) disappearing after a short time and soon forgotten; **short-lived** lasting only for a short time.

---

temporize v delay, defer, procrastinate, take your time, hesitate Opposite: set to

tempt v 1 **lure**, allure, entice, attract, excite Opposite: repel 2 **invite**, attract, appeal, draw, move Opposite: put off

temptation n 1 **desire**, craving, urge, impulse, compulsion Opposite: repulsion 2 **persuasion**, coaxing, inducement, enticement, invitation Opposite: repulsion 3 **lure**, enticement, attraction, offer, invitation

tempted adj of a mind to, attracted, interested, curious, drawn Opposite: uninterested

tempting adj alluring, enticing, attractive, appealing, inviting Opposite: unappealing

tenable adj reasonable, acceptable, defensible, plausible, rational Opposite: untenable

tenacious adj stubborn, obstinate, resolute, firm, persistent Opposite: irresolute

tenacity n stubbornness, obstinacy, resolve,

firmness, persistence *Opposite*: irresolution

tenancy *n* **occupancy**, rental, contract, lease, tenure *Opposite*: ownership

tenant *n* **renter**, occupier, occupant, resident, lodger *Opposite*: landlord

tend *v* **1 have a habit of**, have a tendency to, incline, lean towards, be disposed **2 incline**, veer, lean, bend, verge **3 look after**, care for, take care of, cultivate, attend to *Opposite*: neglect **4 be in charge of**, manage, keep an eye on, watch over, watch

tendency *n* **1 propensity**, bent, leaning, inclination, predisposition **2 trend**, drift, movement, bias, current

tendentious *adj* **provocative**, opinionated, biased, partisan, subjective *Opposite*: impartial

tender *adj* **1 sensitive**, delicate, sore, raw, painful **2 loving**, caring, affectionate, fond, kind *Opposite*: rough **3 young**, youthful, immature, inexperienced, impressionable *Opposite*: seasoned ■ *n* **proposal**, proposition, bid, offer, submission ■ *v* **offer**, proffer, present, give, hand in *Opposite*: withdraw

tenderfoot *(infml)* *n* **novice**, recruit, raw recruit, newcomer, beginner *Opposite*: old hand

tenderhearted *adj* **soft-hearted**, compassionate, sympathetic, kind, soft *Opposite*: hardhearted

tenderheartedness *n* **soft-heartedness**, compassion, sympathy, tenderness, kindness *Opposite*: hardheartedness

tenderize *v* **beat**, smash, hit, soak, steep

tenderness *n* **1 sympathy**, gentleness, kindness, kind-heartedness, fondness *Opposite*: unkindness **2 sensitivity**, soreness, rawness, painfulness, inflammation

tendril *n* **1 stem**, vine, shoot, frond, branch **2** *(literary)* **twist**, coil, wisp, lock, curl

tenement *n* **block of flats**, apartment block, high-rise, housing project *(US)*

tenet *n* **principle**, theory, idea, assumption, belief

tenor *n* **mood**, tone, gist, drift, meaning

tense *adj* **1 anxious**, nervous, stressed, worried, edgy *Opposite*: relaxed **2 taut**, tight, rigid, stiff, strained *Opposite*: loose

tensile *adj* **ductile**, stretchy, stretchable, workable, malleable *Opposite*: rigid

tension *n* **1 worry**, nervousness, anxiety, stress, strain *Opposite*: relaxation **2 conflict**, ill feeling, friction, hostility, mistrust *Opposite*: ease **3 tautness**, tightness, stiffness, strain, pressure *Opposite*: relaxation

tent *n* **shelter**, marquee, bivouac, camp, pavilion

tentacle *n* **limb**, organ, appendage, feeler, antenna

tentative *adj* **1 hesitant**, cautious, faltering,

unsure, timid *Opposite*: sure **2 provisional**, exploratory, speculative, unconfirmed, indefinite *Opposite*: definite

tenuous *adj* **weak**, shaky, unsubstantiated, questionable, feeble *Opposite*: convincing

tenure *n* **1 tenancy**, freehold, occupancy, occupation, lease *Opposite*: ownership **2** *(fml)* **term**, duration, span, period, time

tepid *adj* **1 lukewarm**, hand hot, blood hot, warmish, warm *Opposite*: icy **2 unenthusiastic**, half-hearted, lukewarm, indifferent, apathetic *Opposite*: enthusiastic

tercentenary *n* **300th anniversary**, anniversary, commemoration, celebration, festival

term *n* **1 word**, expression, phrase, name, idiom **2** *(fml)* **period**, time, stretch, tenure, span ■ *v* **call**, name, label, dub, designate

terminal *adj* **fatal**, incurable, deadly, mortal, lethal *Opposite*: curable ■ *n* **1 station**, airport, rail terminal, passenger terminal, terminus **2 workstation**, visual display unit, VDU, computer, monitor. *See* COMPARE AND CONTRAST *at* deadly.

terminally *adv* **fatally**, incurably, mortally, lethally, critically

terminate *v* **end**, finish, come to an end, conclude, stop *Opposite*: start

termination *(fml)* *n* **end**, finish, close, expiry, conclusion *Opposite*: start

terminology *n* **terms**, language, expressions, vocabulary, jargon

terminus *n* **last stop**, station, end of the line, depot, garage

terms *n* **1 footing**, rapport, relations, relationship, standing **2 conditions**, stipulations, provisos, provisions, requisites **3 language**, expressions, vocabulary, terminology, jargon

terrace *n* **walkway**, promenade, patio, veranda, porch *(US)*

terraced *adj* **1 in terraces**, stepped, ridged, tiered, split-level **2 adjoining**, attached, joined *Opposite*: detached

terrain *n* **land**, topography, territory, ground, landscape

terrestrial *adj* **1 earthly**, worldly, global, telluric *Opposite*: extraterrestrial **2 landdwelling**, surface-dwelling, land, earthbound

terrible *adj* **1 extreme**, severe, serious, grave, intense *Opposite*: mild **2 horrible**, horrifying, horrific, horrendous, frightful *Opposite*: pleasant **3 awful**, dreadful, rotten, appalling, poor *Opposite*: wonderful

terribly *adv* **1 very**, extremely, tremendously, exceedingly, incredibly *Opposite*: slightly **2 awfully**, appallingly, offensively, intolerably, horribly *Opposite*: pleasantly

terrific *adj* **1 enormous**, great, huge, massive, tremendous *Opposite*: insignificant **2** *(infml)* **wonderful**, marvellous, excellent, remarkable, superb *Opposite*: awful

terrifically *adv* **very**, extremely, tremendously, exceedingly, incredibly *Opposite*: slightly

terrified *adj* **frightened**, horrified, scared, scared stiff, petrified *Opposite*: unafraid

terrify *v* **frighten**, horrify, scare, petrify, shock *Opposite*: comfort

terrifying *adj* **frightening**, petrifying, chilling, startling, alarming *Opposite*: reassuring

territorial *adj* **1 regional**, local, land, provincial, national **2 defensive**, protective, possessive, assertive, jealous

territory *n* **1 land**, terrain, ground, area, region **2 country**, land, state, province, region **3 field**, subject, speciality, area, terrain **4 patch**, beat, domain, pitch, property

terror *n* **1 fear**, horror, dread, fright, alarm *Opposite*: security **2** (*infml*) **nuisance**, troublemaker, imp, pest (*infml*), horror (*infml*)

terrorism *n* **intimidation**, terror, resistance, guerrilla warfare, sabotage

terrorist *n* **guerrilla**, partisan, freedom fighter, saboteur, nonstate actor

terrorize *v* **terrify**, frighten, scare, threaten, intimidate *Opposite*: reassure

terror-stricken *adj* **terrified**, petrified, scared to death, scared stiff, frightened out of your wits *Opposite*: calm

terse *adj* **1 abrupt**, curt, short, brusque, clipped *Opposite*: expansive **2 concise**, brief, succinct, pithy, short and sweet *Opposite*: wordy

terseness *n* **1 abruptness**, curtness, shortness, brusqueness, snappishness *Opposite*: expansiveness **2 concision**, brevity, succinctness, pithiness, economy *Opposite*: verbosity

test *n* **1 examination**, exam, quiz, trial, assessment **2 trial run**, trial, test drive, run-through, practice **3 proof**, evidence, sign, criterion, yardstick **4 ordeal**, hardship, tribulation, torment, difficulty ■ *v* **try**, try out, put to the test, examine, quiz

testament *n* **evidence**, witness, testimony, proof, demonstration

test drive *n* **trial run**, trial, drive, run, spin

test-drive *v* **try out**, try, take for a spin, put something through its paces, drive

tested *adj* **verified**, tried, confirmed, established, experienced *Opposite*: untried

tester *n* **sample**, trial size, free sample, free gift

testify *v* **1 give evidence**, bear witness, appear, swear, state **2** (*fml*) **prove**, show, confirm, bear out, indicate *Opposite*: disprove

testimonial *n* **1 recommendation**, reference, endorsement, confirmation, statement **2 tribute**, honour, reward, celebration, acknowledgement

testimony *n* **1 evidence**, statement, declaration, deposition, affidavit **2 indication**, demonstration, testament, evidence, witness

testiness (*infml*) *n* **irritability**, grumpiness, impatience, touchiness, crabbiness

testing *adj* **challenging**, difficult, taxing, tough, trying *Opposite*: easy

test match *n* **international**, match, game, cricket match, rugby match

testy (*infml*) *adj* **irritable**, grumpy, impatient, touchy, crabby *Opposite*: even-tempered

tetchiness (*infml*) *see* **testiness**

tetchy (*infml*) *see* **testy**

tether *n* **rope**, chain, lead, rein, tie ■ *v* **tie up**, tie, hitch, fasten, secure *Opposite*: release

text *n* **1 manuscript**, transcript, typescript, writing, script **2 passage**, piece, article, extract, content **3 textbook**, schoolbook, reader, primer, manual ■ *v* **communicate**, contact, correspond, send a text message, write

textbook *n* **text**, schoolbook, reader, primer, manual ■ *adj* **model**, classic, typical, prime, definitive *Opposite*: atypical

textile *n* **fabric**, cloth, material, piece goods, yard goods

textual *adj* **written**, word-based, documented, documentary, stylistic

texture *n* **feel**, touch, surface, consistency, quality

textured *adj* **surfaced**, raised, rough, coarse, bumpy *Opposite*: smooth

thank *v* **express thanks**, show gratitude, express gratitude, show appreciation, be grateful

thankful *adj* **1 grateful**, appreciative, gratified, obliged, beholden *Opposite*: ungrateful **2 pleased**, glad, relieved, happy, satisfied *Opposite*: dissatisfied

thankfully *adv* **1 gratefully**, appreciatively, with gratitude, with thanks *Opposite*: ungratefully **2** (*infml*) **luckily**, happily, mercifully, fortunately, as luck would have it

thankfulness *n* **gratitude**, thanks, appreciation, appreciativeness, recognition *Opposite*: ingratitude

thankless *adj* **unappreciated**, unrewarding, unacknowledged, taken for granted, difficult *Opposite*: rewarding

thanks *n* **gratitude**, appreciation, thankfulness, appreciativeness, recognition *Opposite*: ingratitude

thanks to *prep* **because of**, on account of, due to, owing to, as a result of

thatch *n* **1 roofing**, roof, straw, rushes, reeds **2 thick hair**, hair, shock, mop, tresses

thaw *v* **melt**, defrost, soften, liquefy, warm up *Opposite*: freeze

theatre *n* **1 playhouse**, auditorium, theatre-in-the-round, cinema, hall **2 drama**, plays, dramatic art, the stage, acting **3 sphere**, focus, realm, scene, site

theatregoer *n* **playgoer**, drama-lover, thespian, spectator, literati (*fml*)

theatrical *adj* **1 dramatic**, acting, stage, dramaturgical **2 melodramatic**, dramatic, histrionic, exaggerated, affected *Opposite*: restrained

theft *n* **robbery**, stealing, burglary, shoplifting, holdup

theism *n* **faith**, belief, religion, piety *Opposite*: atheism

theme *n* **1 subject**, topic, idea, subject matter, matter **2 melody**, music, refrain, leitmotif, theme tune. *See* COMPARE AND CONTRAST *at* **subject**.

then *adv* **1 at that time**, at that moment, at that point, at that juncture, then and there *Opposite*: now **2 next**, afterwards, subsequently, later, and **3 in that case**, so, therefore **4 on the other hand**, but then, then again, but then again, nonetheless **5 and**, in addition, too, also, besides

theological *adj* **religious**, scriptural, doctrinal, dogmatic, spiritual

theology *n* **divinity**, religion, religious studies, doctrine, dogmatics

theorem *n* **proposition**, formula, deduction, statement, proposal

theoretical *adj* **theoretic**, hypothetical, academic, notional, imaginary *Opposite*: concrete

theorist *n* **philosopher**, thinker, theoretician, theorizer, academic

theorize *v* **hypothesize**, conjecture, imagine, conceive, put forward

theory *n* **1 philosophy**, model, concept, system, scheme **2 hypothesis**, premise, presumption, conjecture, supposition

therapeutic *adj* **1 curative**, remedial, corrective, restorative, medicinal *Opposite*: preventive **2 healing**, relaxing, calming, satisfying, helpful *Opposite*: stressful

therapist *n* **psychoanalyst**, psychotherapist, analyst, psychiatrist, counsellor

therapy *n* **treatment**, rehabilitation, healing, help, remedy

thereabouts *adv* **around there**, around then, near there, in that area, or so

thereafter *adv* **after that**, from that time on, afterwards, subsequently, then *Opposite*: previously

the real McCoy (*infml*) *n* **the real thing**, the genuine article, the very thing, the real deal (*US*)

thereby *adv* **so**, in that way, by this means, in so doing, in this manner

therefore *adv* **consequently**, so, and so, then, as a result

thereupon (*fml*) *adv* **immediately**, directly, consequently, subsequently, accordingly

thermal *adj* **warm**, hot, tepid, volcanic *Opposite*: cool ■ *n* **warm air**, current, updraught

thermostat *n* **regulator**, control, device, bimetallic strip, sensor

thesaurus *n* **vocabulary list**, word list, lexicon

thesis *n* **1 dissertation**, paper, essay, composition, treatise **2 proposition**, theory, notion, hypothesis, idea *Opposite*: antithesis

thespian *n* **actor**, actress, player, artiste, personality

thick *adj* **1 deep**, broad, fat, wide, chunky *Opposite*: thin **2 viscous**, syrupy, gooey, glutinous, heavy *Opposite*: runny **3 dense**, profuse, bushy, impenetrable, copious *Opposite*: thin **4 filled**, full, covered, crowded, teeming *Opposite*: empty **5 pronounced**, impenetrable, distinct, extreme, marked *Opposite*: slight **6 indistinct**, slurred, muffled, hoarse, gruff *Opposite*: clear

thicken *v* **congeal**, stiffen, set, solidify, clot *Opposite*: thin

thicket *n* **copse**, coppice, grove, covert, undergrowth *Opposite*: clearing

thickness *n* **1 viscosity**, stiffness, body, texture, stodginess *Opposite*: fluidity **2 width**, breadth, depth, wideness, chunkiness *Opposite*: thinness

thickset *adj* **stocky**, heavy, hefty, bulky, solid *Opposite*: slight

thick-skinned *adj* **1 unsympathetic**, insensitive, callous, unfeeling, tactless *Opposite*: sensitive **2 impervious**, unconcerned, unmoved, tough, hardened *Opposite*: thin-skinned

thief *n* **robber**, burglar, shoplifter, pickpocket, bandit

thieve *v* **steal**, rob, shoplift, raid, burgle *Opposite*: return

thimble *n* **cover**, cap, protector

thin *adj* **1 narrow**, fine, slim, threadlike, slender *Opposite*: thick **2 skinny**, slim, slender, bony, lean *Opposite*: fat **3 watery**, weak, dilute, diluted, runny *Opposite*: thick **4 sheer**, gauzy, diaphanous, light, fine *Opposite*: thick **5 reedy**, high, tinny, shrill, squeaky *Opposite*: resonant ■ *v* **water down**, dilute, thin out, weaken, disperse *Opposite*: condense

---

COMPARE AND CONTRAST CORE MEANING: without much flesh, the opposite of fat

thin having little body fat; **lean** muscular and fit-looking, without excess fat; **slim** pleasingly thin and well-proportioned; **slender** gracefully and attractively thin; **emaciated** unhealthily thin, usually because of illness or starvation; **scraggy** or **scrawny** unpleasantly or unhealthily thin and bony; **skinny** extremely thin.

---

thing *n* **1 object**, article, item, entity, gadget **2 occurrence**, event, incident, phenomenon, matter **3 detail**, point, idea, issue, feature **4** (*infml*) **obsession**, fixation, mania, craze, preoccupation

thingamabob (*infml*) *n* **thing**, whatsit (*infml*), thingamajig (*infml*), thingummy (*infml*), thingy (*infml*)

thingamajig (*infml*) *see* **thingamabob**

things *n* **belongings**, clothes, possessions, equipment, stuff

thingumabob (infml) see **thingamabob**

thingumajig (infml) see **thingamabob**

thingummy (infml) see **thingamabob**

thingy (infml) see **thingamabob**

think v 1 reason, contemplate, reflect, ponder, deliberate Opposite: act 2 believe, feel, consider, judge, agree Opposite: doubt

thinker n philosopher, theorist, intellectual, academic, scholar Opposite: doer

thinking adj rational, thoughtful, intelligent, discerning, intellectual Opposite: unthinking ■ n thoughts, philosophy, idea, theory, accepted wisdom

think over v reflect, deliberate, ponder, weigh up, chew over Opposite: forget

think-tank n committee, body, advisory board, group of experts, commission

think the world of v have a high regard for, think highly of, like, have a high opinion of, look up to

think through v consider, contemplate, ponder, mull over, weigh up

think twice v think carefully, be careful, be wary, take heed, consider

think up v invent, devise, come up with, create, dream up

thinner n solvent, diluent, diluter, stripper, cleaner

thinness n 1 narrowness, fineness, slenderness, slimness, shallowness Opposite: thickness 2 skinniness, emaciation, leanness, boniness, lankiness Opposite: fatness

thin-skinned adj sensitive, hypersensitive, easily upset, emotional, touchy Opposite: thick-skinned

third party n intermediary, go-between, arbitrator

third-rate adj poor quality, inferior, mediocre, poor, shoddy Opposite: first-class

thirst n 1 dehydration, dryness, thirstiness, thirsting 2 craving, desire, longing, hunger, eagerness Opposite: apathy ■ v desire, crave, want, ache, pine

thirsty adj 1 dehydrated, dry, parched, thirsting, gasping 2 desiring, craving, eager, keen, hungry Opposite: apathetic

thong n string, cord, band, strap, belt

thorn n prickle, barb, spike, spine, point

thorny adj 1 tricky, problematic, awkward, controversial, knotty Opposite: uncontroversial 2 prickly, barbed, spiky, spiny, pointed

thorough adj 1 methodical, careful, systematic, painstaking, meticulous Opposite: careless 2 full, detailed, systematic, exhaustive, in-depth Opposite: careless 3 absolute, complete, total, out-and-out, utter Opposite: partial. See COMPARE AND CONTRAST at careful.

thoroughbred adj pedigree, purebred, pure

thoroughfare n main road, through road,

street, road, way Opposite: backstreet

thoroughgoing adj 1 full, detailed, systematic, exhaustive, in-depth Opposite: careless 2 complete, thorough, absolute, total, out-and-out Opposite: partial

thoroughly adv 1 methodically, carefully, systematically, painstakingly, meticulously Opposite: carelessly 2 completely, absolutely, totally, utterly, from top to bottom Opposite: partially

thoroughness n care, attention to detail, meticulousness, scrupulousness, diligence Opposite: carelessness

though conj although, while, even if, even though, despite the fact that ■ adv however, and yet, yet, nevertheless, nonetheless

thought n 1 consideration, contemplation, thinking, attention, reflection 2 idea, notion, brain wave, inspiration, concept 3 ideas, philosophy, thinking, notions, accepted wisdom

thoughtful adj 1 considerate, kind, caring, unselfish, selfless Opposite: thoughtless 2 pensive, meditative, contemplative, brooding, reflective 3 careful, meticulous, painstaking, thorough, deep Opposite: superficial

thoughtfulness n 1 consideration, kindness, care, unselfishness, selflessness Opposite: thoughtlessness 2 pensiveness, meditation, contemplation, reflection, thought 3 care, attention to detail, attention, thought, carefulness Opposite: superficiality

thoughtless adj 1 inconsiderate, unkind, uncaring, selfish, insensitive Opposite: thoughtful 2 careless, heedless, reckless, negligent, unthinking Opposite: prudent

thoughtlessness n 1 inconsideration, unkindness, selfishness, insensitivity, tactlessness Opposite: thoughtfulness 2 carelessness, heedlessness, recklessness, negligence, inattention Opposite: prudence

thought-provoking adj stimulating, challenging, provocative, interesting, inspiring Opposite: dull

thoughts n opinion, view, point of view, feelings, judgment

thrash v 1 beat, whip, give a hiding, spank, smack 2 defeat, beat, trounce, whip, paste Opposite: lose 3 toss, writhe, flail, squirm, roll

thrashing n 1 beating, whipping, spanking, battering, lashing 2 defeat, rout, downfall, conquest, beating Opposite: victory

thrash out v hammer out, resolve, solve, discuss, debate

thread n 1 cotton, cord, yarn, strand, fibre 2 idea, drift, gist, sequence, story line ■ v 1 string, wind, loop, lace, pass through 2 make your way, pick your way, edge through, squeeze through, negotiate

threadbare adj 1 worn, worn-out, shabby, ragged, thin Opposite: new 2 well-worn, trite, hackneyed, clichéd, banal *Opposite*: original

threat *n* **1 warning**, menace, intimidation **2 danger**, risk, hazard, menace, peril *Opposite*: promise

threaten *v* **1 intimidate**, bully, menace, warn, terrorize *Opposite*: reassure **2 endanger**, jeopardize, menace, compromise, cloud *Opposite*: guard **3 loom**, lurk, hover, portend, creep up

threatened *adj* **endangered**, at risk, in peril, vulnerable, dying out *Opposite*: safe

threatening *adj* **1 intimidating**, bullying, menacing, hostile, aggressive *Opposite*: reassuring **2 ominous**, menacing, foreboding, inauspicious, sinister *Opposite*: reassuring

three-dimensional *adj* **1 three-D**, solid, deep *Opposite*: two-dimensional **2 believable**, realistic, convincing, lifelike, true-to-life *Opposite*: two-dimensional

thresh *v* winnow, flail, separate, beat, rub

threshold *n* **1 doorway**, door, doorstep, entrance, entry **2 starting point**, verge, brink, edge, dawn *Opposite*: end **3 level**, limit, maximum, ceiling, outside

thrift *n* **frugality**, economy, carefulness, caution, prudence *Opposite*: extravagance

thrifty *adj* frugal, economical, careful, cautious, prudent *Opposite*: extravagant

thrill *v* **excite**, electrify, exhilarate, delight, inspire *Opposite*: bore ■ *n* **adventure**, delight, joy, pleasure, quiver *Opposite*: bore

thrilled *adj* **excited**, electrified, exhilarated, ecstatic, elated *Opposite*: disappointed

thriller *n* **whodunit**, murder mystery, crime novel, detective story, page-turner

thrilling *adj* **exciting**, electrifying, exhilarating, delightful, inspiring *Opposite*: boring

thrive *v* **1 be healthy**, grow well, flourish, bloom, blossom *Opposite*: decline **2 be successful**, flourish, prosper, boom, bloom *Opposite*: fail

thriving *adj* **flourishing**, prosperous, booming, blooming, blossoming *Opposite*: failing

throaty *adj* **husky**, hoarse, croaky, gruff, guttural *Opposite*: piping

throb *v* **pound**, thump, pulsate, pulse, thud ■ *n* **pounding**, thump, pulsation, pulse, rhythm

thrombosis *n* **coagulation**, clotting, blockage, occlusion

throne *n* **1 seat**, chair, cathedra **2 power**, authority, sovereignty, command, rule

throng *n* **multitude**, mass, crowd, horde, swarm *Opposite*: few ■ *v* **crowd**, pack, jam, cram, inundate *Opposite*: disperse

throttle *v* **1 regulate**, control, adjust, correct, check **2 strangle**, choke, garrotte, strangulate, suffocate **3 silence**, gag, muzzle, stifle, subdue

through *prep* **1 across**, past, throughout, within, round **2 during**, throughout, during the course of, in **3 via**, out of, by way of, by

means of **4 because of**, owing to, due to, as a result of

through and through *adv* **completely**, totally, entirely, utterly, at heart *Opposite*: partially

throughout *prep* **through**, during, all over, during the course of, in

throughput *n* **amount**, quantity, data, material, output

throw *v* **1 fling**, toss, hurl, pitch, lob *Opposite*: catch **2 drop**, leave, put, cast, toss **3 project**, cast, direct, send out, beam **4 move**, flick, switch, connect, disconnect **5 organize**, arrange, host, give, hold **6** (*infml*) **confuse**, puzzle, bewilder, perplex, baffle ■ *n* **1 toss**, lob, heave, pitch, fling **2 rug**, cover, blanket, shawl, coverlet

---

COMPARE AND CONTRAST CORE MEANING: send something through the air

throw cause something to go through the air using a physical movement; **chuck** (*infml*) throw something in a reckless or aimless way; **fling** throw something fast using a lot of force; **heave** (*infml*) throw something large or heavy with effort in a particular direction; **hurl** throw something with great force; **toss** throw something small or light in a casual or careless way; **cast** throw something to a particular place or into a particular thing, or throw a fishing line or net.

---

throw away *v* **1 discard**, throw out, get rid of, dispose of, dump *Opposite*: keep **2 waste**, squander, fritter away, ruin, spoil *Opposite*: make the most of

throwaway *adj* **1 disposable**, paper, plastic **2 wasteful**, profligate, extravagant, careless, improvident *Opposite*: frugal **3 off-the-cuff**, casual, offhand, passing, spontaneous *Opposite*: intended

throwback *n* **reversion**, regression, resemblance, relic, retrogression

throw in *v* **1 add**, drop in, include, mention, refer to **2 include**, add, give, tack on, add on

throw in the towel (*infml*) *v* **give in**, surrender, give up, admit defeat, concede *Opposite*: stand firm

throw off *v* **1 shake off**, shed, shrug off, get rid of, discard *Opposite*: keep **2 elude**, evade, escape, give somebody the slip, shake off

throw out *v* **1 discard**, throw away, get rid of, dispose of, dump *Opposite*: keep **2 expel**, eject, show the door, dismiss, kick out (*infml*) *Opposite*: welcome **3 dismiss**, reject, disallow, turn down, refuse *Opposite*: pass

throw up *v* **1 cause**, create, produce, bring to light, pose *Opposite*: conceal **2** (*infml*) **abandon**, give up, relinquish, resign, throw away *Opposite*: keep **3** (*infml*) **vomit**, be sick, gag, retch, spew

throw yourself into *v* **engross yourself in**, immerse yourself in, bury yourself in, devote yourself to, commit to

thrum *v* **strum**, pluck, twang, play, brush

thrust v 1 **push**, shove, force, propel, prod 2 **stretch**, extend, stretch out, reach, reach out ∎ n 1 **shove**, push, prod, lunge, drive 2 **attack**, assault, offensive, push, drive 3 **point**, gist, meaning, focus, direction 4 **power**, force, propulsion, momentum, impetus

thug n **brute**, criminal, mugger, hoodlum, gangster

thumb v flick through, flip through, leaf through, skim, browse through *Opposite*: pore over

thumbs-down (infml) n **disapproval**, rejection, denial, no, veto *Opposite*: thumbs-up (infml)

thumbs-up (infml) n **approval**, acceptance, agreement, endorsement, ratification *Opposite*: thumbs-down (infml)

thump v **punch**, hit, whack, pummel

thumping (infml) adj **large**, huge, enormous, impressive ∎ adv **very**, exceptionally, extremely, inordinately, really

thunder n **din**, boom, rumble, roar, clap ∎ v 1 **boom**, roar, resound, rumble, clap 2 **shout**, bellow, boom, roar, yell *Opposite*: whisper

thunderbolt n 1 **thunderclap**, clap of thunder, thunder, crash of thunder 2 **shock**, surprise, bolt from the blue, eye opener, kick in the face

thunderclap see **thunderbolt**

thundering (dated infml) adj **great**, impressive, large, extreme, big ∎ adv **very**, extremely, enormously, hugely, inordinately

thunderous adj **deafening**, loud, roaring, booming, crashing

thunderstorm n **storm**, downpour, deluge, rainstorm, cloudburst

thunderstruck adj **incredulous**, amazed, taken aback, stunned, shocked

thus (fml) adv 1 **therefore**, consequently, as a result, so, accordingly 2 **like this**, in this way, in this manner, as follows, like so

thus far adv **up till now**, up to now, yet, so far, hitherto

thwack n **smack**, clap, knock, rap, whack ∎ v **hit**, strike, whack, smack, slap

thwart v **frustrate**, spoil, prevent, foil, ruin *Opposite*: aid

tic n **twitch**, spasm, convulsion, fit, paroxysm

tick (infml) n **moment**, second, minute, instant, trice

ticket n 1 **permit**, travel document, voucher, receipt, coupon 2 **label**, tag, tab, marker, sticker

ticking-off (infml) n **reprimand**, rebuke, scolding, dressing-down, telling-off (infml) *Opposite*: commendation

tickle v 1 **prickle**, irritate, scratch, itch 2 **amuse**, entertain, delight, please, make somebody laugh

tickler (infml) n **puzzle**, riddle, problem, enigma, poser

ticklish adj **tricky**, delicate, thorny, awkward, problematic *Opposite*: straightforward

tickly adj **prickly**, itchy, irritating, scratchy

tick off (infml) v **rebuke**, scold, reprimand, reprove, haul over the coals

tidal wave n 1 **tsunami**, bore, eagre 2 **surge**, wave, swell, deluge

tiddly (infml) adj **minute**, small, teeny (infml), weeny (infml), titchy (infml) *Opposite*: ginormous (infml)

tide n **current**, flow, surge, wave, drift

tidiness n **neatness**, trimness, orderliness, order, regulation

tidy adj 1 **neat**, orderly, shipshape, in order, organized *Opposite*: untidy 2 **smart**, immaculate, well-groomed, well-turned-out, dapper *Opposite*: untidy 3 **large**, fair, considerable, sizable, reasonable *Opposite*: small ∎ v **neaten**, tidy up, clear up, straighten, arrange

tie v 1 **bind**, fasten, secure, attach, lash *Opposite*: untie 2 **be equal**, draw, finish equal, finish even, be neck and neck (infml) ∎ n 1 **bond**, link, connection, relation, join 2 **draw**, dead heat, equal finish, stalemate

tiebreaker n **deciding game**, tie-break, decider

tie in v **connect**, associate, relate, link, join *Opposite*: disconnect

tie-in n **link**, relationship, connection, linkup, association

tie in knots v **confuse**, muddle, mix up, baffle, bewilder

tier n **row**, level, layer, stage, rank

tie the knot (infml) v **get married**, marry, wed, walk down the aisle, get hitched (infml)

tie up v 1 **lash**, truss, fasten, lace, tie *Opposite*: untie 2 **complete**, clinch, finalize, resolve, end

tie-up n **link**, connection, linkup, association, relationship

tiff n **quarrel**, argument, row, falling-out, squabble

tight adj 1 **taut**, stretched, tense, firm, stiff *Opposite*: loose 2 **close-fitting**, body-hugging, skintight, snug, fitted *Opposite*: baggy 3 **firm**, fixed, strong, unyielding, tough *Opposite*: weak 4 **strict**, stringent, harsh, firm, tough *Opposite*: lax 5 **mean**, tightfisted, parsimonious, niggardly, stingy (infml) *Opposite*: generous 6 **difficult**, problematic, awkward, tricky, tough *Opposite*: easy

tighten v **make tighter**, tauten, constrict, stiffen, squeeze *Opposite*: loosen

tighten your belt v **cut back**, economize, retrench, draw in your horns, scrimp and save

tightfisted adj **miserly**, mean, tight, grasping, parsimonious *Opposite*: generous

tightfistedness n **scrimping**, meanness, stinginess, tightness, miserliness *Opposite*: generosity

tight-fitting *adj* tight, close-fitting, snug, figure-hugging, skintight *Opposite:* baggy

tightknit *adj* closely connected, integrated, united, interwoven, intertwined

tight-lipped *adj* silent, uncommunicative, reticent, withdrawn, taciturn *Opposite:* loquacious

tightness *n* tension, tautness, stiffness, rigidity *Opposite:* looseness

tight spot *n* tight corner, difficult position, tricky situation, predicament, quandary

till *n* cash register, cash box, box, drawer, tray ▪ *v* plough, dig, cultivate, turn over, rake

tilt *v* tip, slope, slant, lean, list *Opposite:* straighten up ▪ *n* slope, slant, angle, gradient, incline

tilted *adj* slanted, slanting, sloping, sloped, lopsided *Opposite:* level

timber *n* wood, logs, planks, lumber *(US)*

timbre *n* tone, pitch, resonance, sound, quality

time *n* 1 period, while, spell, stretch, stint 2 occasion, instance, moment, point, instant 3 era, age, epoch, period, season 4 tempo, rhythm, beat, speed, measure ▪ *v* 1 count, measure, clock, calculate, record 2 schedule, programme, timetable, plan, arrange

WORD BANK

❑ **types of time period** calendar month, fortnight, leap year, lunar month, midweek, month, quarter, semester, trimester, week, weekend, year

time bomb *n* tinderbox, volcano, accident waiting to happen, flashpoint

time-consuming *adj* laborious, slow, inefficient, long, onerous *Opposite:* timesaving

time-honoured *adj* traditional, customary, habitual, age-old, respected *Opposite:* recent

time lag *n* lapse, interlude, gap, interval, pause

timeless *adj* eternal, ageless, enduring, undying, everlasting *Opposite:* ephemeral

timelessness *n* agelessness, endurance, endlessness, changelessness, immutability *Opposite:* transience

timely *adj* opportune, well-timed, appropriate, apt, judicious *Opposite:* untimely

time off *n* leisure, free time, spare time, leave, holiday

timepiece *n* chronometer, timer, clock

timesaving *adj* quick, streamlined, efficient, effective, improved *Opposite:* timeconsuming

timescale *n* timetable, schedule, programme, time, period

timeserver *n* opportunist, weathercock, waverer, equivocator, vacillator *Opposite:* stalwart

time span *n* duration, period, extent, length, span

timetable *n* schedule, agenda, plan, programme, calendar ▪ *v* schedule, arrange, plan, organize, programme

timeworn *adj* 1 shabby, tattered, threadbare, worn, well-worn *Opposite:* brand-new 2 hackneyed, overworked, stale, trite, stock *Opposite:* original

timid *adj* nervous, shy, fearful, timorous, diffident *Opposite:* bold

timidity *n* nervousness, shyness, fearfulness, timorousness, diffidence *Opposite:* boldness

timing *n* judgment, technique, skill, effectiveness, control

timorous *adj* nervous, fearful, timid, frightened, scared *Opposite:* brave

timorousness *n* nervousness, fearfulness, timidity, shyness, fear *Opposite:* bravery

tin *n* 1 can, tin can, canister, container, cylinder 2 box, container, caddy, biscuit tin, cake tin

tincture *n* 1 solution, essence, distillate, extract, distillation 2 tinge, tint, hint, nuance, tone

tinder *n* kindling, firewood, brushwood, sticks, twigs

tinderbox *n* flashpoint, crucible, volcano, no-go area, accident waiting to happen

ting *v* ding, ting-a-ling, ring, ping, tinkle

tinge *n* hint, touch, dash, drop, trace ▪ *v* tint, colour, stain, shade, mix

tingle *v* prickle, sting, itch, tickle, prick ▪ *n* sting, prickle, itch, tickle, prick

tingling *adj* prickly, itchy, scratchy, burning, stinging

tinker *v* 1 fiddle, tamper, interfere, fool around, play 2 repair, mend, fix, put right

tinkle *v* ring, jingle, clink, chink, ding ▪ *n* (infml) call, ring, phone, phone call, telephone call

tinny *adj* 1 thin, high, metallic, shrill, ringing *Opposite:* resonant 2 shoddy, cheap, worthless, inferior, poor

tinsel *n* 1 metallic thread, glitter, streamer, spangle, decoration 2 showiness, glitz, flashiness, pretentiousness, glitter

tint *n* 1 shade, colour, hue, touch, trace 2 rinse, dye, colourant, streak, highlight ▪ *v* dye, colour, shade, streak, rinse

tiny *adj* miniature, minuscule, small, little *Opposite:* enormous

tip *v* 1 tilt, slope, slant, lean, list *Opposite:* straighten up 2 knock over, pour, empty, spill, knock 3 give, slip, reward, pay, bribe ▪ *n* 1 slope, slant, angle, gradient, incline 2 rubbish dump, civic amenity point, landfill, garbage dump *(US)* 3 (infml) hovel, pigsty, dump (infml), hole (infml), pigpen *(US)* 4 gratuity, gift, reward, bonus, extra 5 warning, clue, pointer, prompt, hint 6 hint, suggestion, idea, pointer

tip off *v* warn, inform, advise, forewarn, tip the wink (infml)

tip-off (infml) *n* warning, clue, hint, pointer, prompt

tipster n **adviser**, consultant, analyst, informant, informer

tiptoe v **creep**, sneak, steal, skulk, glide Opposite: stamp

tiptop (infml) adj **first-rate**, excellent, superb, first-class, superlative Opposite: dreadful

tirade n **outburst**, rant, diatribe, harangue, lecture

tire v **exhaust**, wear out, drain, fatigue, enervate

tired adj **1 weary**, sleepy, drowsy, fatigued, exhausted Opposite: energetic **2 bored**, weary, sick, jaded, dissatisfied **3 overused**, trite, hackneyed, clichéd, old Opposite: fresh

tiredness n **weariness**, sleepiness, fatigue, drowsiness, exhaustion Opposite: energy

tireless adj **untiring**, diligent, determined, unstinting, assiduous Opposite: weary

tirelessness n **diligence**, determination, assiduousness, indefatigability, industriousness Opposite: weariness

tiresome adj **annoying**, irritating, tedious, wearisome, dull

tiring adj **exhausting**, strenuous, arduous, wearing, demanding

tissue n **1 soft tissue**, fleshy tissue, flesh, matter, material **2 web**, net, network, mass, series

titan n **giant**, superman, superwoman, genius Opposite: nobody

titanic adj **colossal**, monumental, immense, gigantic, massive Opposite: insignificant

titbit n **1 morsel**, taste, bite, dainty, delicacy **2 gossip**, snippet, scrap, scandal, news

titch (infml) n **little person**, pip squeak (infml), shorty, tiddler (infml) Opposite: bruiser (infml)

titchy (infml) adj **tiny**, minute, weeny (infml), teeny (infml), teeny-weeny (infml) Opposite: massive

tit for tat n **retaliation**, blow for blow, revenge, reprisal, vengeance

tithe n **church tax**, tax, duty, contribution, portion

titivate v **do up**, dress up, adorn, decorate, beautify

titivation n **adornment**, embellishment, beautification, prettification, enhancement

title n **1 name**, heading, label, designation **2 championship**, trophy, cup, award **3 ownership**, entitlement, deed, right, claim ■ v **call**, name, label, designate, refer to

titled adj **noble**, aristocratic, patrician, blue-blooded, upper-class

title deed n **title**, deed, document, proof of ownership, ownership

titleholder n **1 champion**, winner, reigning champion, cupholder **2 owner**, proprietor, possessor, vendor, holder

title page n **front page**, title, opening page, frontispiece

tittle-tattle n **gossip**, scandal, hearsay, tale, word of mouth ■ v **gossip**, chatter, prattle, yak (infml), chinwag (infml)

titular adj **nominal**, in name only, supposed, ostensible, so-called Opposite: actual

tizzy (infml) n **panic**, dither, flap (infml), lather (infml), state (infml)

T-junction n **junction**, intersection, fork, road junction

toady n **flatterer**, sycophant, groveller, creep (infml), crawler (infml) ■ v **grovel**, fawn, flatter, kowtow, crawl (infml)

toadying n **obsequiousness**, sycophancy, servility, flattery, fawning ■ adj **obsequious**, sycophantic, servile, flattering, fawning

to all intents and purposes adv **practically**, in practice, virtually, as good as, pretty much (infml)

toast n **1 salute**, tribute, pledge, health **2 darling**, favourite, delight, sweetheart ■ v **1 grill**, brown, crisp, heat, cook **2 drink to**, pledge, salute, drink the health of

toasty adj **warm**, snug, cosy, pleasant Opposite: chilly

toboggan n **sleigh**, sledge, bobsleigh, luge, sled (US) ■ v **1 sleigh**, sledge, luge, sled (US) **2 slip**, slide, hurtle, tumble

tocsin n **alarm**, warning, bell, siren, signal

today adv **nowadays**, these days, currently, now, at the moment Opposite: yesteryear

toddle v **1 totter**, patter, pad, waddle **2** (infml) **walk**, stroll, amble

toddler n **child**, baby, tot (infml), kid (infml)

to-do (infml) n **fuss**, commotion, bother, scene, kerfuffle (infml)

toehold n **start**, advantage, jumping-off point, beginning, entry

toff (infml) n **aristocrat**, aristo (infml), nob (infml), swell (dated infml), dandy (dated)

together adv **1 jointly**, as one, mutually, in concert, collectively Opposite: alone **2 simultaneously**, at once, at the same time, concurrently, all together Opposite: separately ■ adj (infml) **composed**, calm, collected, organized, cool Opposite: flustered

togetherness n **closeness**, intimacy, devotedness, friendship, inseparability Opposite: estrangement

together with prep **as well as**, accompanied by, with, alongside, in addition to

toggle n **1 fastener**, peg, button, buckle, clasp **2 switch**, key, command, button, lever ■ v **change**, change over, switch, move, transfer

togs (infml) n **clothes**, outfit, dress, clothing, kit

toil n **work**, labour, drudgery, slog, hard work Opposite: relaxation ■ v **labour**, strive, work, slog, slave Opposite: take it easy

toilet n **1 lavatory**, chamber pot, urinal, latrine, water closet **2 public convenience**, powder room, ladies, gents, WC **3** *(fml)* **washing**, dressing, grooming, bathing, toilette

toiletry *n* **beauty product**, skincare product, cosmetic product

---

WORD BANK

❑ **types of toiletry** aftershave, bath salts, body scrub, body milk, body wash, bubble bath, cleanser, cleansing cream, cologne, conditioner, cotton wool, dental floss, deodorant, eau de cologne, eau de toilette, face cream, face scrub, facial mask, foam bath, hair gel, hair mousse, hair spray, hand cream, moisturizer, mouthwash, night cream, perfume, shampoo, shaving cream, shower gel, soap, talcum powder, toilet water, toner, toothpaste

---

toilette *(literary) n* **dressing**, grooming, bathing, getting dressed, preparations

toilet water *n* **cologne**, eau de cologne, eau de toilette, scent, aftershave

token *n* **1 mark**, demonstration, sign, symbol, indication **2 voucher**, coupon, slip, coin **3 keepsake**, remembrance, souvenir, reminder, memento ■ *adj* **symbolic**, nominal, perfunctory, empty

tolerable *adj* **1 bearable**, acceptable, endurable, supportable *(literary) Opposite*: unbearable **2 reasonable**, average, passable, fair, adequate *Opposite*: intolerable

tolerance *n* **broad-mindedness**, acceptance, open-mindedness, lenience, charity *Opposite*: intolerance

tolerant *adj* **accepting**, easygoing, lenient, broad-minded, open-minded *Opposite*: intolerant

tolerate *v* **stand**, bear, abide, put up with, endure *Opposite*: forbid

toleration *n* **allowance**, acceptance, open-mindedness, broad-mindedness, liberality *Opposite*: prejudice

toll *n* **1 fee**, tax, levy, payment, duty **2 peal**, ring, ding-dong, clang, ding-a-ling

tollbooth *n* **barrier**, gate, kiosk, booth, ticket office

tollgate *n* **barrier**, gate, entrance, exit

tomb *n* **burial chamber**, catacomb, grave, burial place, crypt

tombola *n* **lottery**, draw, raffle, game of chance

tomboyish *adj* **boyish**, unladylike, mannish, boisterous, unruly

tombstone *n* **headstone**, gravestone, monument

tome *n* **book**, volume, digest, work

tomfoolery *(infml) n* **silliness**, horseplay, mischief, clowning, fooling around *Opposite*: sensibleness

ton *(infml) n* **mass**, mountain, lot, ocean, stack *(infml)*

tonality *n* **tone**, timbre, pitch, sound, sound quality *Opposite*: atonality

tone *n* **1 sound**, pitch, quality, timbre **2 quality**,

manner, character, attitude, tendency **3 character**, atmosphere, feel, ambience **4 colour**, hue, tint, tinge, shade

tone down *v* **dilute**, moderate, soften, restrain, modulate *Opposite*: intensify

toneless *adj* **colourless**, expressionless, monotonous, neutral, monochrome *Opposite*: vibrant

tone up *v* **firm up**, strengthen, get in shape, exercise

tongue *n* **language**, patois, dialect, speech, idiom. *See* COMPARE AND CONTRAST *at* **language**.

tongue-in-cheek *adj* **lighthearted**, ironic, insincere, flippant, whimsical *Opposite*: serious

tongue-tied *adj* **speechless**, shy, awkward, silent, inarticulate *Opposite*: talkative

tonic *n* **boost**, fillip, stimulant, shot in the arm, livener

tonnage *n* **weight**, heaviness, capacity, size

tons *adv* **a lot**, a great deal, lots, loads *(infml)*, heaps *(infml)* ■ *n (infml)* **lots**, plenty, oodles *(infml)*, loads *(infml)*, piles *(infml)*

too *adv* **1 also**, as well, in addition, besides, moreover **2 excessively**, overly, extremely, exceedingly, overmuch *Opposite*: insufficiently

tool *n* **instrument**, implement, device, means, utensil

WORD BANK

❑ **types of carpentry tool** awl, bradawl, drill, hammer, jigsaw, mallet, plane, sander, saw, vice
❑ **types of cosmetic tool** comb, curling tongs, emery board, hair dryer, hairbrush, nail clippers, nail file, nail scissors, nailbrush, razor, shaving brush, tweezers
❑ **types of general tool** bellows, blowtorch, crowbar, file, grease gun, jack, jemmy, lathe, machine tool, pincers, pliers, plumb line, plunger, poker, pump, punch, rasp, screwdriver, socket spanner, socket wrench, soldering iron, spade, spanner, tongs, trowel
❑ **types of medical instrument** forceps, lancet, probe, scalpel, speculum, stethoscope, syringe

---

tooth *n* **1 fang**, tusk, chopper *(slang)* **2 indentation**, projection, tine, cog, prong

---

WORD BANK

❑ **types of tooth** baby tooth, bucktooth *(infml)*, canine, chopper, cuspid, denture, eyetooth, fang, incisor, milk tooth, molar, premolar, wisdom tooth

---

toothless *adj* **powerless**, useless, impotent, ineffective, ineffectual *Opposite*: effective

toothsome *adj* **delicious**, palatable, tasty, appetizing, mouthwatering *Opposite*: unappetizing

tootle *(infml) v* **1 drive slowly**, go slowly, pootle, meander, wend your way *Opposite*: dash **2 hoot**, toot, sound, honk, beep ■ *n* **drive**, pootle, meander, crawl *Opposite*: dash

top *n* **1 pinnacle**, summit, peak, apex, crown

Opposite: bottom **2 cork**, lid, cap, cover, stopper ■ *adj* **1 highest**, topmost, maximum, uppermost *Opposite*: bottom **2 best**, first, chief, principal, important ■ *v* **outdo**, surpass, better, improve on, cap

WORD BANK

❏ **types of sweater or cardigan** cardigan, crew neck, jersey, jumper, polo neck, pullover, sweater, turtleneck, twinset, V neck

❏ **types of top** basque, blouse, bodice, body warmer, bolero, boob tube *(slang)*, bustier, gilet, halter, jerkin, polo shirt, shirt, smock, surplice, sweatshirt, T-shirt, tabard, tank top, tee, tunic, vestment, waistcoat

top-class *adj* **best**, world-class, first-class, first-rate, top-flight

top drawer *n* **1 cream**, crème de la crème, elite, pick, best **2 aristocracy**, nobility, high society, gentry, upper class

top-drawer *adj* **1 top-flight**, best, first-rate, first-class, premium **2 upper class**, high class, noble, titled, aristocratic

top-flight *adj* **top-drawer**, best, first-rate, first-class, premium

top-heavy *adj* **unbalanced**, unstable, uneven, disproportionate, lopsided

topic *n* **theme**, subject, matter, issue, subject matter. *See* COMPARE AND CONTRAST *at* subject.

topical *adj* **up-to-date**, interesting, current, newsworthy, contemporary

topicality *n* **interest**, relevance, newsworthiness, current interest, contemporaneity

top-level *adj* **highest**, most senior, most important, most powerful

topmost *adj* **highest**, uppermost, top, peak *Opposite*: bottommost

topnotch *(infml) adj* **top-class**, first-rate, superior, first-class, excellent *Opposite*: inferior

top-of-the-range *adj* **best**, most expensive, exclusive, premium, premier *Opposite*: basic

topographical *adj* **geographical**, structural, natural, landscape, environmental

topography *n* **features**, landscape, geography, structure, countryside

topping *n* **top layer**, coating, glaze, garnish, frosting *Opposite*: filling

topple *v* **1 fall over**, tip over, collapse, fall, tumble **2 bring down**, overthrow, depose, oust, remove

top-quality *adj* **choice**, select, fine, rare

top-ranking *adj* **high-ranking**, senior, important, powerful, high-level

top-rated *adj* **favourite**, popular, well-liked, top, top ten *Opposite*: unpopular

tops *(infml) adv* **at most**, as a maximum, at the most, max *(slang)*

top-secret *adj* **undercover**, covert, secret, clandestine, restricted

topsoil *n* **soil**, earth, loam, dirt, peat

topspin *n* **forward spin**, spin, momentum, force, impetus

topsy-turvy *adj* **confused**, disordered, chaotic, in disarray, upside down *Opposite*: orderly

top up *v* **1 refill**, replenish, refuel, freshen **2 make up**, augment, complete, chip in *(infml)*

top-up *n* **1 supplement**, increase, increment, extra, addition **2 refill**, fill-up, replenishment, extra serving, extra measure

tor *n* **peak**, crag, outcrop, rock face

torch *n* **penlight**, light, lamp, lantern, flash *(US infml)* ■ *v (infml)* **burn down**, set on fire, set light to, put a match to, set fire to

torchlight *n* **beam**, light, illumination, lamplight

torment *v* **annoy**, tease, plague, persecute, taunt *Opposite*: comfort ■ *n* **1 anguish**, suffering, agony, distress, pain *Opposite*: pleasure **2 nuisance**, bane, plague, annoyance, irritation *Opposite*: delight

tormented *adj* **anguished**, tortured, distressed, grief-stricken, plagued

tormenter *see* tormentor

tormentor *n* **oppressor**, tyrant, persecutor, bully, teaser

torn *adj* **1 ripped**, frayed, ragged, tattered, shabby **2 undecided**, uncertain, in a quandary, in a dilemma, unable to decide *Opposite*: decided

tornado *n* **hurricane**, whirlwind, cyclone, storm, windstorm

torpedo *(infml) v* **ruin**, destroy, wreck, spoil, thwart

torpid *adj* **lazy**, languorous, listless, sluggish, apathetic *Opposite*: energetic

torpor *n* **inactivity**, inertia, indolence, languor, lethargy *Opposite*: excitement

torque *n* **rotating force**, rotation, twisting, turning, turning force

torrent *n* **1 rush**, flood, flow, deluge, gush *Opposite*: trickle **2 outburst**, flood, flow, tide, stream

torrential *adj* **heavy**, pouring, driving, lashing, drenching *Opposite*: light

torrid *adj* **1 hot**, stifling, sweltering, boiling, burning *Opposite*: cool **2 passionate**, amorous, impassioned, erotic, steamy *(infml)*

torsion *n* **twisting**, turning, turning force, rotation, spin

tort *n* **wrongful act**, unlawful act, illegal act, offence, misdemeanour

tortuous *adj* **1 twisting**, winding, convoluted, circuitous, indirect *Opposite*: direct **2 complex**, complicated, intricate, difficult, involved *Opposite*: simple **3 devious**, deceitful, crafty, sly, artful *Opposite*: straightforward

torture *v* **torment**, afflict, persecute, brutalize, punish ■ *n* **agony**, torment, anguish, pain, suffering

torturer n intimidator, bully, pesterer, harasser, teaser

tosh (infml) n rubbish, nonsense, stuff and nonsense, twaddle (infml), bunkum (infml)

toss v 1 throw, pitch, fling, lob, hurl 2 mix, stir, blend, mix up ∎ n lob, throw, pitch, heave, fling. See COMPARE AND CONTRAST at throw.

toss-up n even chance, chance, risk, fifty-fifty, luck of the draw

tot n 1 dram, finger, thimbleful, snifter (infml) 2 (infml) toddler, child, baby, small child, kid (infml)

total n sum, whole, entirety, full amount, totality ∎ adj 1 entire, whole, full, complete, aggregate Opposite: partial 2 absolute, unmitigated, complete, unreserved, out-and-out ∎ v 1 add up, count up, tot up; calculate, sum 2 amount to, add up to, come to, equal, make

totalitarian adj authoritarian, tyrannous, one-party, oppressive, autocratic Opposite: democratic

totalitarianism n despotism, absolutism, tyranny, autocracy, authoritarianism

totality n entirety, whole, total, sum, full amount Opposite: part

totally adv completely, entirely, absolutely, wholly, fully Opposite: partly

tote (infml) v 1 carry, cart, lug, haul, heave 2 brandish, carry, hold, wield, bear

totem n 1 ritual object, sacred symbol, icon, charm, talisman 2 symbol, representation, emblem, image, icon

totemic adj symbolic, emblematic, iconic, representative

totter v walk unsteadily, stagger, wobble, teeter, stumble

tot up v add up, add together, count up, total, calculate

touch n 1 pat, tap, stroke, fondle, feel 2 trace, bit, dash, drop, hint 3 style, facility, gift, knack, ability ∎ v 1 handle, feel, finger, tap, stroke 2 converge, meet, come into contact, join, contact Opposite: separate 3 move, affect, upset, stir, touch a chord 4 match, come close to, meet, rival, equal

touch-and-go adj uncertain, unpredictable, doubtful, unknown, risky Opposite: certain

touch down v land, alight, come down, set down, arrive Opposite: take off

touchdown n 1 landing, descent, arrival Opposite: blastoff 2 score, try, point

touched adj affected, moved, warmed, heartened, impressed Opposite: unmoved

touchiness n irritability, impatience, grumpiness, cantankerousness, moodiness Opposite: composure

touching adj moving, poignant, stirring, tender, pitiful. See COMPARE AND CONTRAST at moving.

touch on v deal with, refer to, mention, treat, allude to

touchstone n criterion, standard, benchmark, yardstick, hallmark

touch up v retouch, restore, freshen, freshen up, refurbish

touchy adj 1 sensitive, quick-tempered, impatient, petulant, cantankerous Opposite: even-tempered 2 delicate, sensitive, tricky, awkward, ticklish

touchy-feely (infml) adj demonstrative, expressive, effusive, unreserved, emotional Opposite: undemonstrative

tough adj 1 durable, strong, sturdy, robust, hardy Opposite: weak 2 hard, chewy, stringy, stiff, leathery Opposite: tender 3 threatening, rough, hard, harsh, dangerous Opposite: pleasant 4 difficult, hard, demanding, exacting, arduous Opposite: easy 5 severe, strict, rigid, inflexible, stern Opposite: lenient. See COMPARE AND CONTRAST at hard.

toughen v strengthen, harden, build up, reinforce, fortify Opposite: weaken

toughened adj hardened, reinforced, strengthened, fortified, unbreakable

tough-minded adj realistic, determined, tough, single-minded, resilient Opposite: weak-willed

toughness n 1 durability, hardiness, robustness, roughness, stoutness Opposite: flimsiness 2 hardness, chewiness, stringiness, stiffness Opposite: tenderness 3 roughness, harshness, hardness, danger Opposite: pleasantness 4 difficulty, arduousness, strenuousness, challenge, trickiness Opposite: ease 5 severity, strictness, rigidity, inflexibility, firmness Opposite: leniency

toupee n wig, hairpiece, hair extension

tour n trip, excursion, expedition, outing, journey ∎ v sightsee, explore, visit, travel around, go around

tourism n travel, holiday business, leisure industry, service sector, travel industry

tourist n traveller, sightseer, visitor, holidaymaker, day tripper

touristy adj crowded, busy, much-frequented, popular, overvisited Opposite: quiet

tournament n contest, competition, event, tourney, game

tourniquet n band, strap, bandage

tousle v tangle, ruffle, rumple, dishevel, disorder Opposite: tidy

tousled adj dishevelled, messy, tangled, ruffled, windswept Opposite: tidy

tout v advertise, hype, flaunt, push, publicize Opposite: understate ∎ n seller, hawker, peddler, vendor

tow v pull, drag, draw, haul, lug. See COMPARE AND CONTRAST at pull.

towards prep 1 in the direction of, to, near, just before 2 regarding, concerning, for, about, on

towel n cloth, bath towel, bath sheet, hand

towel, guest towel ■ v **dry**, rub down, rub, wipe, dab

tower v 1 **loom**, overlook, be head and shoulders above, soar, rise 2 **surpass**, exceed, excel, top, transcend

towering adj **high**, tall, soaring, lofty, immense Opposite: short

tower of strength (infml) n **rock**, mainstay, anchor, helper, advocate

town n **municipality**, city, settlement, township, metropolis. See COMPARE AND CONTRAST at **city**.

townie (infml) n **town dweller**, city dweller, urbanite, city slicker

townsfolk n **townspeople**, populace, residents, inhabitants

township n **small town**, urban area, settlement, town, hamlet

townspeople n **townsfolk**, populace, residents, inhabitants

towpath n **path**, footpath, bridleway, canal path, track

towrope n **towline**, rope, line, cable, cord

toxic adj **poisonous**, deadly, lethal, noxious, contaminated Opposite: harmless

toxicity n **poisonousness**, venomousness, deadliness, noxiousness, harmfulness Opposite: harmlessness

toxin n **poison**, pollutant, contaminant, venom

toy with v 1 **flirt with**, tease, philander 2 **play with**, fiddle with, fidget with, handle, finger 3 **think about**, consider, ponder, contemplate, entertain Opposite: dismiss

trace v 1 **draw**, outline, copy, mark out, sketch 2 **find**, locate, discover, hunt down, track down ■ n 1 **sign**, indication, evidence, remnant, residue 2 **suggestion**, hint, dash, drop, touch

tracery n **decoration**, pattern, design, interlacing, ornamentation

track n 1 **trail**, footprints, footsteps, path, trace 2 **path**, pathway, road, way, trail ■ v **follow**, hunt down, chase, pursue, stalk

track down v **find**, hunt down, catch, capture, discover

tracker n **trailer**, follower, chaser, hunter, shadow

tract n 1 **area**, territory, zone, region, expanse 2 **pamphlet**, article, treatise, leaflet

tractability n 1 **docility**, controllability, manageability, obedience, manipulability Opposite: intractability 2 **malleability**, pliability, workability, ductility, elasticity Opposite: intractability

tractable adj 1 **docile**, controllable, manageable, obedient, manipulable Opposite: intractable 2 **malleable**, pliable, workable, ductile, elastic Opposite: intractable

traction n 1 **adhesive friction**, grip, purchase, adhesion 2 **power**, tractive force, pull, tow, tug

trade n 1 **commerce**, business, industry, market, dealings 2 **occupation**, job, employment, line of work, profession 3 **customers**, public, patrons, custom, clientele ■ v 1 **deal**, buy and sell, do business, operate, traffic 2 **exchange**, barter, negotiate, swap (infml), dicker (infml)

trade fair n **exhibition**, exposition, fair, display, show

trade in v **exchange**, redeem, give in part payment, barter, swap (infml)

trade-in n **part exchange**, exchange, deal, transaction, swap (infml)

trademark n 1 **symbol**, logo, emblem, brand 2 **characteristic**, feature, trait, attribute, facet

trade name n **brand name**, brand, trademark, name, registered trademark

trade-off n **compromise**, balance, adjustment, interchange, transaction

trader n **dealer**, buyer, seller, broker, agent

tradition n **custom**, institution, ritual, habit, convention Opposite: innovation. See COMPARE AND CONTRAST at **habit**.

traditional adj **usual**, conventional, customary, established, fixed Opposite: progressive

traditionalism n **conventionalism**, conservatism, conformity, orthodoxy, fundamentalism Opposite: progressivism

traditionalist n **conservative**, purist, fundamentalist, conformist Opposite: progressive ■ adj **traditional**, conservative, purist, old-school, orthodox Opposite: progressive

traduce v **criticize**, disparage, malign, run down, defame Opposite: praise

traffic n 1 **road traffic**, traffic flow, circulation, stream of traffic, rush-hour traffic 2 **transportation**, movement, passage, toing and froing, travel 3 **trade**, commerce, business, dealings, transactions ■ v 1 **have dealings**, deal in, trade, trade in, transfer 2 **smuggle**, run, handle

traffic jam n **tailback**, bottleneck, gridlock, holdup

tragedy n **disaster**, calamity, catastrophe, misfortune, heartbreak Opposite: joy

tragic adj **sad**, disastrous, catastrophic, heartbreaking, heartrending Opposite: joyous

tragicomic adj **bittersweet**, poignant, affecting, moving

trail v 1 **tug**, drag, pull, draw, tow Opposite: push 2 **follow**, track, tail, shadow, trace 3 **drop back**, lag behind, fall behind, straggle, follow on Opposite: lead ■ n 1 **path**, track, way, road, footpath 2 **track**, footprints, footsteps, paw marks, paw prints

trail away v **fade**, disappear, grow faint, die away, diminish Opposite: intensify

trailblazer n **pioneer**, leader, innovator, entrepreneur, architect

trailer n clip, preview, ad (infml), promo (infml), advert (infml)

train n 1 **procession**, file, convoy, line 2 **sequence**, chain, succession, string, series ■ v 1 **teach**, coach, educate, instruct, tutor 2 **exercise**, work out, keep fit, keep in shape 3 **aim**, direct, focus, point, line up. See COMPARE AND CONTRAST at **teach**.

trained adj **skilled**, qualified, proficient, accomplished, competent

trainee n **apprentice**, learner, novice, beginner Opposite: trainer

trainer n **coach**, teacher, guide, instructor, mentor Opposite: trainee

training n 1 **tuition**, education, schooling, teaching, guidance 2 **exercise**, working out, keep fit, physical activity, drill

traipse (infml) v **trudge**, tramp, plod, slog, trek

trait n **mannerism**, peculiarity, attribute, characteristic, feature

traitor n **conspirator**, collaborator, turncoat, defector, deserter Opposite: loyalist

traitorous adj **disloyal**, faithless, duplicitous, deceitful, treacherous Opposite: loyal

trajectory n **route**, course, flight, path, line

trammel n **restriction**, limitation, hindrance, curb, constraint ■ v 1 **confine**, limit, restrain, restrict, hinder 2 **ensnare**, snare, catch, net, entangle

tramp n 1 **vagrant**, homeless person, beggar, vagabond, hobo 2 **traipse**, march, trek, hike, trudge ■ v **trudge**, trek, hike, traipse, march

trample v **crush**, flatten, walk on, stamp on, step on

trance n **dream**, daze, spell, stupor, reverie Opposite: alertness

tranquil adj 1 **calm**, serene, peaceful, still, relaxing Opposite: noisy 2 **composed**, calm, cool, unruffled, unperturbed Opposite: agitated

tranquillity n 1 **calm**, serenity, stillness, peacefulness, hush Opposite: turmoil 2 **composure**, equanimity, calmness, coolness, self-possession Opposite: panic

tranquillize v **sedate**, calm, put out, put under, knock out

transact v **carry out**, conduct, manage, handle, perform

transaction n **deal**, business, contract, matter, operation

transatlantic adj **transoceanic**, intercontinental, long-haul

transcend v **rise above**, go beyond, exceed, go above, excel

transcendence n 1 **divine existence**, otherworldliness, state of grace, perfection, wholeness Opposite: mundaneness 2 **superiority**, greatness, excellence, pre-eminence, loftiness Opposite: inferiority

transcendent adj 1 **superior**, excellent, supreme, great, unequalled Opposite: inferior 2 **divine**, perfect, heavenly, supernatural, otherworldly Opposite: earthy 3 **mystical**, awe-inspiring, uplifting, inspirational, inspiring

transcendental adj 1 **mystical**, awe-inspiring, uplifting, inspirational, inspiring 2 **divine**, perfect, heavenly, supernatural, otherworldly

transcontinental adj **pancontinental**, coast-to-coast, continent-wide

transcribe v **copy out**, write out, copy, set down, write down

transcript n **record**, copy, text, transcription

transcription see transcript

transect v **divide**, bisect, cut, split, cut across

transfer v 1 **move**, transport, relocate, remove, shift 2 **transmit**, convey, hand on, hand over, turn over ■ n 1 **transmission**, handover, assignment, allocation, transference 2 **relocation**, removal, move, resettlement, displacement

transference n **transfer**, conversion, devolution, conveyance, transmission

transfiguration n **metamorphosis**, transformation, makeover, change, conversion

transfigure v **change**, metamorphose, transform, convert, transmute

transfix v 1 **fascinate**, mesmerize, engross, spellbind, hypnotize 2 **stab**, spike, gore, run through, pierce

transform v **alter**, convert, change, transmute, renovate. See COMPARE AND CONTRAST at **change**.

transformation n **alteration**, conversion, revolution, renovation, makeover

transgress v **misbehave**, disobey, go astray, lapse, sin Opposite: behave

transgression n **wrongdoing**, misbehaviour, disobedience, lapse, sin

transgressor n **wrongdoer**, lawbreaker, sinner, offender, criminal

transience n **briefness**, brevity, impermanence, transitoriness, shortness Opposite: permanence

transient adj **fleeting**, brief, passing, transitory, temporary Opposite: permanent

transit n **transportation**, transfer, transport, travel, shipment

transition n **changeover**, shift, change, alteration, move

transitional adj **intermediate**, in-between, interim, provisional, temporary Opposite: permanent

transitory adj **fleeting**, passing, brief, temporary, momentary Opposite: permanent. See COMPARE AND CONTRAST at **temporary**.

translate v 1 **interpret**, decode, decipher, explain, render (fml) 2 **convert**, transform, transmute, turn, change

translation n **conversion**, paraphrase, version, rendition, interpretation

translator *n* interpreter, decoder, decipherer, converter

transliterate *v* transcribe, convert, translate, transmute, transform

transliteration *n* transcription, conversion, translation, transformation, rendering

translucence *n* 1 transparency, sheerness, filminess, limpidity, translucency *Opposite*: opacity 2 **glow**, luminosity, brightness, luminescence, luminousness *Opposite*: dullness

translucent *adj* 1 transparent, semitransparent, see-through, lucid, clear *Opposite*: opaque 2 **glowing**, luminous, radiant, shining, lustrous *Opposite*: dull

transmigrate *v* wander, migrate, travel, shift, drift *Opposite*: settle

transmigration *n* migration, wandering, travelling, movement, shifting

transmissible *adj* communicable, infectious, contagious, catching

transmission *n* 1 spread, communication, diffusion, conduction 2 **programme**, show, broadcast

transmit *v* 1 convey, hand on, spread, communicate, diffuse 2 put on the air, send out, put out, broadcast

transmittable *adj* communicable, infectious, catching, contagious

transmittance *n* transmission, diffusion, conduction, transfer, transferral

transmutation *n* transfiguration, transmogrification, change, transformation, alteration

transmute *v* transfigure, transmogrify, transform, alter, change. *See* COMPARE AND CONTRAST *at* change.

transnational *adj* international, multinational, transcontinental, intercontinental, global ■ *n* multinational, conglomerate, corporation

transparency *n* 1 clearness, limpidity, translucence, filminess, sheerness *Opposite*: opacity 2 **slide**, photograph, photo, shot *Opposite*: print 3 **clarity**, plainness, obviousness, directness, unambiguousness *Opposite*: ambiguousness

transparent *adj* 1 see-through, clear, translucent, crystal clear *Opposite*: opaque 2 **obvious**, clear, apparent, plain, evident *Opposite*: unclear

transpire *v* happen, occur, take place, come about, go on

transplant *v* remove, relocate, move, transfer, shift

transplantation *n* relocation, movement, transfer, replacement, uprooting

transport *v* convey, move, bring, carry, transfer ■ *n* 1 conveyance, carriage, transportation, transference, passage 2 **vehicle**, means of transport, conveyance, means of transport

transportable *adj* mobile, portable, movable, travel, transferable

transportation *n* transport, conveyance, carriage, transference, passage

transporter *n* carrier, haulier, courier, shipper, delivery service

transpose *v* 1 invert, switch, reverse, exchange, swap *(infml)* 2 **move**, transfer, rearrange, alter, reorder

transposition *n* 1 reversal, inversion, switch, exchange, substitution 2 **rearrangement**, reordering, recasting, relocation, shuffle

transubstantiation *(fml)* *n* conversion, transformation, metamorphosis, mutation, alteration

transverse *adj* crosswise, at right angles, sloping, oblique, slanting

trap *n* ruse, trick, snare, deception, con ■ *v* 1 catch, ensnare, entrap, ambush, corner *Opposite*: release 2 **trick**, deceive, dupe, con, ensnare

trap door *n* hatch, flap, small door, entrance, doorway

trapped *adj* 1 shut in, locked in, stuck, surrounded, hemmed in *Opposite*: released 2 **stuck**, caught, jammed, stuck fast, wedged *Opposite*: free

trappings *n* accessories, accoutrements, paraphernalia, trimmings, frills

trash *n* nonsense, rubbish, drivel, gibberish, double talk ■ *v (infml)* wreck, destroy, ruin, damage, smash

trashy *adj* cheap, worthless, tasteless, shabby, rubbishy *Opposite*: quality

trauma *n* shock, upset, disturbance, ordeal, suffering

traumatic *adj* shocking, disturbing, upsetting, distressing, harrowing

traumatize *v* shock, upset, distress, devastate, disturb

traumatized *adj* disturbed, shocked, upset, troubled, distressed *Opposite*: unaffected

travail *n* hard work, toil, effort, exertion, labour

travel *v* journey, tour, take a trip, voyage, trek ■ *adj* portable, lightweight, foldaway, collapsible, transportable

traveller *n* 1 itinerant, New Age traveller, nomad, rover, wanderer 2 **explorer**, voyager, tourist, holidaymaker, trekker

travelogue *n* travel piece, talk, lecture, travel programme

travels *n* voyage, journey, trip, exploration, trekking

travel-sick *adj* queasy, nauseous, unwell, ill, seasick

traverse *v* cross, pass through, negotiate, navigate, go across

travesty *n* charade, caricature, sham, parody, mockery

trawl *v* 1 fish, catch fish, go fishing 2 **hunt**, search, rummage around, sift, look through ■ *n* search, investigation, hunt, rummage, scan

tray n 1 **salver**, platter, serving dish, plate, baking tray 2 **receptacle**, container, in-tray, out-tray, in-box (US)

treacherous adj 1 **unfaithful**, traitorous, disloyal, deceitful, false Opposite: loyal 2 **dangerous**, hazardous, precarious, unsafe, perilous Opposite: safe

treachery n **deceit**, treason, deceitfulness, sedition, disloyalty Opposite: loyalty

treacly adj 1 **sticky**, glutinous, gooey, gluey, syrupy 2 **sentimental**, mawkish, romanticized, romantic, slushy

tread v 1 **trample**, crush, squash, flatten, stomp 2 **walk**, step, stride, tramp, pace ■ n **step**, footstep, footfall, tramp, stamp

treadle n foot pedal, lever, control

treadmill n **daily grind**, routine, drudgery, toil, slog

treason n **sedition**, treachery, disloyalty, subversion, betrayal Opposite: allegiance

treasonable adj **traitorous**, treacherous, subversive, disloyal, rebellious

treasure n 1 **wealth**, riches, money, valuables, cache 2 **star**, paragon, pearl, prize, gem (infml) ■ v **cherish**, value, prize, adore, hold dear Opposite: neglect

treasured adj **dear**, precious, loved, cherished, beloved

treasurer n **banker**, bursar, bookkeeper, accountant, financial officer

treat v 1 **regard**, consider, think of, behave towards, act towards 2 **care for**, take care of, doctor, cure, nurse 3 **pay for**, pick up the check, pick up the tab, pay the bill, give 4 **indulge**, spoil, pamper, make a fuss of 5 **deal with**, go into, discuss, handle, touch on ■ n **luxury**, extravagance, indulgence, delight, pleasure Opposite: necessity

treatise n **dissertation**, discourse, essay, thesis, paper

treatment n 1 **cure**, healing, care, therapy, medicine Opposite: placebo 2 **handling**, behaviour, conduct, dealing, management

treaty n **agreement**, accord, contract, pact, truce

treble adj 1 **triple**, three times, thrice, threefold 2 **high-pitched**, high, shrill, piping ■ v **increase**, triple, increase threefold, increase by three, multiply

tree n 1 **sapling**, bush, shrub 2 **diagram**, tree diagram, family tree, hierarchy, pyramid

treetop n **crown**, canopy, foliage

trek v **hike**, walk, ramble, march, tramp ■ n **walk**, hike, ramble, journey, march

trellis n **lattice**, grille, fence, fencing, frame

tremble v **shiver**, shake, shudder, quiver, judder ■ n **shake**, shiver, shudder, quake, quiver

trembling n **shaking**, vibrating, quivering, shuddering, wobbling ■ adj 1 **unsteady**, vibrating, quivering, shuddering, quaking

Opposite: still 2 **timorous**, tremulous, nervous, terrified, fearful Opposite: confident

tremendous adj 1 **great**, incredible, fabulous, terrific, marvellous Opposite: awful 2 **huge**, great, enormous, vast, immense Opposite: tiny

tremendously adv **very**, extremely, greatly, enormously, vastly Opposite: slightly

tremor n 1 **shake**, tremble, vibration, quiver, shiver 2 **earthquake**, shock, quake (infml)

tremulous adj 1 **unsteady**, quivering, trembling, quavering, shaky Opposite: steady 2 **timid**, timorous, trembling, shy, fearful Opposite: confident

trench n **ditch**, channel, drain, dugout, trough

trenchancy n **incisiveness**, forcefulness, acerbity, brutality, directness Opposite: gentleness

trenchant adj **incisive**, cutting, sharp, biting, acerbic Opposite: mild

trend n 1 **tendency**, drift, leaning, inclination, movement 2 **fashion**, style, look, craze, vogue

trendsetter n **innovator**, pacesetter, modernizer, leader, leading light Opposite: imitator

trendsetting adj **influential**, innovative, cutting-edge, leading, new Opposite: conventional

trendy (infml) adj **fashionable**, in, up-to-the-minute, cool, stylish Opposite: unfashionable

trepidation n **fear**, anxiety, unease, nervousness, apprehension Opposite: equanimity

trespass v **intrude**, infringe, encroach, invade, interlope

trespasser n **intruder**, squatter, interloper, snooper (infml) Opposite: guest

tress n **lock**, strand, curl, tuft, wisp

tresses n **locks** (literary), hair, curls, ringlets

trestle n **support**, bracket, stand, frame, framework

triad n **trio**, threesome, triangle, troika, triumvirate

trial n 1 **test**, examination, experiment, tryout, audition 2 **hearing**, court case, court-martial, prosecution, legal proceedings 3 **ordeal**, hardship, suffering, trouble, misery ■ adj **experimental**, probationary, pilot, provisional, test

triangle n **threesome**, trio, three-way relationship, triad, trinity

triangular adj **three-sided**, trilateral, three-cornered, wedge-shaped, deltoid

tribal adj **ethnic**, family, ancestral, familial, group

tribe n 1 **people**, ethnic group, community, society, population 2 (infml) **family**, clan, people (infml)

tribulation *n* **misfortune**, trial, suffering, ordeal, distress

tribunal *n* **1 court**, court of law, law court **2 board**, panel, committee, body

tributary *n* **branch**, arm, offshoot, river, stream

tribute *n* **1 compliment**, mark of respect, honour, praise, acknowledgment **2 tax**, duty, excise, toll, payment

trice *n* **instant**, flash, moment, twinkling, no time

trick *n* **1 deception**, ploy, ruse, hoax, dodge **2 joke**, prank, stunt, caper **3 knack**, technique, skill, secret **4 habit**, mannerism, trait, characteristic, way ■ *v* **deceive**, cheat, mislead, trap, fool ■ *adj* **fake**, false, artificial, bogus, hoax *Opposite*: real

trickery *n* **1 deception**, deceit, fraud, scam *(slang)*, sting *(US slang)* **2 dishonesty**, deception, deceit, fraudulence, chicanery

trickiness *n* **1 difficulty**, complication, delicacy, awkwardness, intricacy *Opposite*: simplicity **2 craftiness**, slipperiness, deviousness, slyness, duplicity *Opposite*: honesty

trickle *v* **drip**, drop, seep, dribble, ooze *Opposite*: flood ■ *n* **dribble**, drop, drip *Opposite*: flood

trickster *n* **cheat**, swindler, charlatan, fraud, slippery customer

tricky *adj* **1 complicated**, delicate, awkward, thorny, problematic *Opposite*: simple **2 devious**, sly, deceitful, crafty, cunning *Opposite*: straight

trier *n* **1 tester**, experimenter, taster, volunteer, guinea pig **2 sticker**, fighter, striver, struggler, stayer *Opposite*: defeatist

trifle *n* **1 nothing**, frippery, triviality **2 smidgen**, bit, little, drop, touch

trifling *adj* **trivial**, petty, small, tiny, silly *Opposite*: significant

trigger *v* **activate**, set off, cause, generate, start *Opposite*: halt

trigger-happy *(infml)* *adj* **rash**, violent, dangerous, wild, unpredictable

trigger off *v* **activate**, set off, cause, generate, start *Opposite*: halt

trill *v* **warble**, quaver, shrill, tweet, vibrate

trillion *(infml)* *n* **lots**, tons *(infml)*, loads *(infml)*, masses *(infml)*, stacks *(infml)*

trilogy *n* **series**, sequence, set, cycle, trio

trim *v* **1 clip**, cut, shear, pare, prune *Opposite*: lengthen **2 cut back**, prune, decrease, lower, shave *Opposite*: augment *(fml)* **3 decorate**, adorn, embroider, embellish, edge ■ *adj* **1 tidy**, orderly, smart, spruce, dapper *Opposite*: messy **2 slim**, fit, shapely, sleek, slender *Opposite*: bulky ■ *n* **decoration**, adornment, frill, edge, border

trimming *n* **decoration**, adornment, frill, garnish, extra

trimmings *n* **1 side dishes**, extras, accompaniments **2 extras**, accompaniments, addons, accessories, embellishments **3 clippings**, parings, bits, pieces, nail clippings

trimness *n* **1 neatness**, tidiness, smartness, spruceness, orderliness **2 slenderness**, slimness, compactness, sleekness, thinness

trinity *n* **threesome**, trio, triad, troika, triplet

trinket *n* **ornament**, charm, knick-knack, bauble, gewgaw

trio *n* **threesome**, triad, troika, trinity, triangle

trip *n* **1 journey**, tour, excursion, expedition, outing **2 slip**, stumble, tumble, fall ■ *v* **1 stumble**, trip up, slip, tumble, falter **2 skip**, hop, prance, caper, dance

tripartite *adj* **three-way**, three-party, multilateral, triple

tripe *(infml)* *n* **rubbish**, nonsense, garbage, drivel, trash *Opposite*: fact

triple *adj* **1 tripartite**, three-way, three-layered, triple-decker *Opposite*: single **2 treble**, threefold, multiple *Opposite*: single ■ *v* **treble**, triplicate, multiply by three, increase, boost *Opposite*: reduce

triplet *n* **trio**, triad, threesome, troika

tripper *(infml)* *n* **tourist**, day tripper, holidaymaker, visitor, excursionist *(dated)*

trip up *v* **1 stumble**, trip, slip, tumble, fall **2 trap**, trick, confuse, disconcert, unsettle

trite *adj* **commonplace**, stale, tired, pedestrian, worn *Opposite*: original

triteness *n* **dullness**, tiredness, staleness, corniness, banality *Opposite*: originality

triumph *n* **1 victory**, achievement, conquest, accomplishment, coup *Opposite*: failure **2 rejoicing**, pride, elation, delight, satisfaction *Opposite*: sorrow ■ *v* **succeed**, prevail, win, overcome, be victorious *Opposite*: lose

triumphal *adj* **ceremonial**, commemorative, victory, heroic, celebratory

triumphant *adj* **1 winning**, victorious, glorious, dominant, proud **2 exultant**, celebratory, jubilant, elated, delighted *Opposite*: sorrowful

triumph over *v* **overcome**, defeat, beat, prevail over, get the better of

triumvirate *n* **trio**, threesome, triad, troika, triplet

trivet *n* **stand**, support, rest, tripod

trivia *n* **minutiae**, trivialities, froth, nonsense, trifles *Opposite*: essentials

trivial *adj* **unimportant**, small, inconsequential, slight, trifling *Opposite*: crucial

triviality *n* **1 unimportance**, inconsequence, worthlessness, insignificance, pettiness *Opposite*: importance **2 trifle**, nothing, frippery

trivialize *v* **play down**, belittle, underestimate, make light of, tone down *Opposite*: highlight

troika *n* **trio**, triumvirate, threesome, triad, triplet

troll v 1 **fish**, angle, trail, spin, lure 2 **amble**, wander, saunter, drift, walk ■ n **giant**, ogre, hobgoblin, goblin, monster

troop n **crowd**, horde, throng, multitude, herd ■ v 1 **move**, gather, rally, come together, get together 2 **march**, parade, stream, trudge, traipse

trophy n **cup**, award, medal, crown, title

tropical adj **hot**, steamy, humid, sultry, stifling Opposite: temperate

trot v **jog**, run, hurry, scurry, scamper Opposite: saunter

troubadour n **minstrel**, musician, poet, wandering minstrel, bard (literary)

trouble n 1 **problem**, difficulty, dilemma, nuisance, snag Opposite: ease 2 **worry**, concern, distress, anxiety, care 3 **complaint**, ailment, disease, illness, malady Opposite: good health 4 **effort**, bother, inconvenience, work, thought 5 **strife**, unrest, disorder, disturbance, discontent Opposite: accord ■ v 1 **concern**, worry, distress, agitate, harass 2 **bother**, put out, inconvenience, disturb, burden 3 **make an effort**, take pains, exert yourself, bother Opposite: hang back. See COMPARE AND CONTRAST at bother.

troubled adj 1 **anxious**, concerned, bothered, worried, disturbed Opposite: calm 2 **problematic**, tricky, awkward, difficult Opposite: easy

trouble-free adj **easy**, simple, painless, straightforward, uncomplicated Opposite: troublesome

troublemaker n **mischief-maker**, menace, agitator, firebrand, rabble-rouser Opposite: conciliator

troubleshooter n 1 **technician**, engineer, mechanic, problem solver, expert 2 **mediator**, consultant, ombudsman, adviser, counsellor

troublesome adj 1 **worrying**, upsetting, bothersome, wearisome, difficult Opposite: trouble-free 2 **disorderly**, rowdy, unruly, uncooperative, undisciplined Opposite: well-behaved

trough n 1 **manger**, crib, rack, holder 2 **channel**, furrow, trench, gutter, ditch 3 **depression**, low, low pressure area Opposite: ridge

trounce v **beat**, thrash, rout, crush, overwhelm. See COMPARE AND CONTRAST at defeat.

trouncing n **routing**, thrashing, crushing, drubbing, beating

troupe n **company**, cast, band, ensemble, group

trousseau n **bridal goods**, bottom drawer, hope chest (US)

truancy n **absence**, nonattendance, absenteeism, malingering, skiving (infml) Opposite: attendance

truant n **absentee**, malingerer, shirker, skiver (infml) ■ v **shirk**, go AWOL, malinger, skive (infml), bunk off (infml)

truce n **ceasefire**, armistice, treaty, peace, respite

truculence n **defiance**, belligerence, sullenness, insolence, impertinence Opposite: enthusiasm

truculent adj **hostile**, belligerent, defiant, quarrelsome, argumentative Opposite: easygoing

trudge v **tramp**, traipse, slog, plod, trek ■ n **slog**, trek, hike, march, haul

true adj 1 **factual**, accurate, right, correct, proper Opposite: false 2 **real**, genuine, actual, valid, authentic Opposite: fake 3 **faithful**, dedicated, constant, loyal, sincere Opposite: unfaithful

true-blue adj **right-wing**, traditional, conservative, diehard, old-school

true-life adj **genuine**, realistic, real-life, real, true

true to life adj **realistic**, convincing, accurate, authentic, lifelike Opposite: unrealistic

truism n **axiom**, cliché, maxim, adage, saying

truly adv 1 **really**, in fact, beyond doubt, actually, indeed 2 **sincerely**, faithfully, honestly, in all honesty, genuinely Opposite: insincerely 3 **very**, greatly, really, indeed, exceptionally

trump v **outdo**, go one better, call somebody's bluff, undermine, outmanoeuvre

trumped-up adj **false**, fake, conviction, madeup, fabricated Opposite: genuine

truncate v **shorten**, abbreviate, trim, cut, prune Opposite: lengthen

trundle v 1 **roll**, roll along, rattle, labour, wheel 2 **traipse**, trail, saunter, lumber, wander

trunk n **stem**, bole, stalk

trunks n **swimming trunks**, bathing trunks, shorts

truss v **bind**, tie up, tie, tether, string

trust n 1 **faith**, belief, hope, conviction, confidence Opposite: distrust 2 **custody**, care, protection, responsibility, guard ■ v 1 **have faith in**, believe, rely on, depend on, confide in Opposite: distrust 2 **hope**, believe, expect, assume, suppose Opposite: despair 3 **entrust**, confide, assign, consign, commit

trustee n 1 **fund manager**, fund administrator, director 2 **representative**, deputy, agent, executor, guardian

trustfulness n **unwariness**, credulity, innocence, lack of caution, trustingness Opposite: wariness

trusting adj **gullible**, credulous, unquestioning, believing, naive Opposite: suspicious

trustworthiness n **honesty**, dependability, reliability, fidelity, constancy Opposite: dishonesty

trustworthy adj **dependable**, reliable, responsible, truthful, honest Opposite: corrupt

trusty adj **faithful**, dependable, reliable, constant, loyal Opposite: unreliable

truth n 1 **fact**, certainty, reality, actuality, veracity *Opposite*: untruth 2 **honesty**, integrity, fidelity, sincerity

truthful adj 1 **honest**, straight, frank, open, straightforward *Opposite*: dishonest 2 **correct**, true, reliable, accurate, exact *Opposite*: false

truthfulness n 1 **honesty**, truth, candour, frankness, openness *Opposite*: dishonesty 2 **accuracy**, reliability, correctness, exactitude, faithfulness *Opposite*: inaccuracy

try v 1 **attempt**, endeavour, strive, aim, seek 2 **test**, sample, taste, appraise, evaluate 3 **strain**, vex, tax, exasperate, annoy *Opposite*: soothe 4 **judge**, put on trial, hear, take to court ■ n **attempt**, effort, go, stab *(infml)*, crack *(infml)*

trying adj **annoying**, tiresome, irritating, wearisome, frustrating *Opposite*: soothing

try out v **test**, sample, check out, experiment with, appraise

tryout n **trial**, test, evaluation, audition, assessment

tryst n **assignation**, rendezvous, meeting, date, encounter

try your hand v **experiment**, try out, have a shot, make an attempt, have a go *(infml)*

tub n 1 **container**, carton, pot, drum, barrel 2 **bath**, hip bath, hot tub, plunge bath, bathtub

tubby *(infml)* adj **plump**, podgy, chubby, portly, overweight *Opposite*: skinny

tube n **pipe**, cylinder, hose, conduit, duct

tuber n **storage organ**, rhizome, root, underground stem

tubing n **tubes**, pipes, plumbing

tubular adj **tube-shaped**, cylindrical, tube-like, hollow

tuck v 1 **insert**, put, push, slip, place *Opposite*: remove 2 **pleat**, fold, dart, gather, pucker ■ n 1 **pleat**, fold, dart, gather, pucker 2 **food**, nosh *(infml)*, grub *(infml)*, tucker *(infml)*

tucker *(infml)* n **food**, tuck, nosh *(infml)*, grub *(infml)*, chow *(slang)*

tuft n **clump**, tussock, cluster, bunch, truss

tug v **pull**, tow, haul, heave, jerk *Opposite*: push ■ n **yank**, heave, pull, jerk, haul *Opposite*: push. *See* COMPARE AND CONTRAST *at* pull.

tug of war n **tussle**, power struggle, struggle, battle, wrangle *Opposite*: agreement

tuition n **instruction**, teaching, schooling, training, education

tumble v 1 **fall over**, fall down, stumble, trip up, topple *Opposite*: stand up 2 **plummet**, drop, nose-dive, plunge, dive *Opposite*: rise

tumbledown adj **ramshackle**, rickety, rundown, derelict, dilapidated

tumbler n 1 **glass**, tall glass, beaker, whisky glass, highball glass *(US)* 2 **acrobat**, gymnast, aerialist, trapeze artist, entertainer

tummy *(infml)* n **stomach**, abdomen, paunch, pot, gut

tumour n **growth**, lump, cancer, polyp

tumult n **uproar**, commotion, clamour, hubbub, hullabaloo *Opposite*: peace

tumultuous adj 1 **unrestrained**, unbridled, riotous, boisterous, rowdy *Opposite*: restrained 2 **turbulent**, confused, chaotic, agitated *Opposite*: calm

tune n **melody**, song, air, jingle, harmony ■ v **adjust**, fine-tune, change, alter, modify

tuneful adj **melodic**, melodious, harmonious, musical, pleasant *Opposite*: discordant

tuneless adj **unmusical**, droning, monotone, atonal, monotonous *Opposite*: tuneful

tune-up n **service**, overhaul, fine-tune, check, maintenance

tunnel n 1 **channel**, passageway, subway, shaft, underpass *Opposite*: bridge 2 **burrow**, hole, warren, earth, sett ■ v **excavate**, burrow, dig, mine, channel

turbid adj 1 **muddy**, cloudy, opaque, dirty, murky *Opposite*: clear 2 **confused**, muddled, disorganized, scrambled, chaotic *Opposite*: clear

turbulence n 1 **commotion**, confusion, turmoil, disorder, unrest *Opposite*: calm 2 **violence**, rowdiness, unruliness, riotousness, restlessness 3 **storminess**, tempestuousness, choppiness, blusteriness

turbulent adj 1 **confused**, unstable, chaotic, tumultuous, in turmoil *Opposite*: orderly 2 **violent**, rowdy, unruly, riotous, quarrelsome *Opposite*: peaceful 3 **stormy**, tempestuous, raging, choppy, blustery *Opposite*: settled

tureen n **bowl**, serving dish, dish, casserole

turf n 1 **lawn**, grass, pasture, meadow, verdure 2 *(infml)* **area of expertise**, sphere of influence, field, territory, orbit 3 *(infml)* **territory**, patch, beat, neighbourhood, home turf

turgid adj **pompous**, boring, dull, hard going, stilted *Opposite*: amusing

turmoil n **chaos**, disorder, confusion, uproar, tumult *Opposite*: order

turn v 1 **twist**, revolve, rotate, go around, spin 2 **direct**, aim, point, focus, set 3 **bend**, change direction, bear, veer, meander 4 **go**, become, alter, convert, transform 5 **curdle**, go sour, sour, spoil, go off ■ n 1 **bend**, corner, junction, fork, curve 2 **rotation**, revolution, twist, spin, twirl 3 **fright**, scare, shock, start, jolt 4 **fit**, seizure, attack, funny turn, spasm 5 **ride**, spin, jaunt, trip, outing 6 **errand**, favour, good turn, service, good deed 7 **performance**, act, skit, sketch, party piece 8 **go**, try, chance, opportunity, shot *(infml)*

turn a blind eye to v **overlook**, ignore, take no notice of, disregard, excuse *Opposite*: condemn

turnabout n **reversal**, sea change, U-turn, turnround, change

turn against v turn on, reject, rebuff, spurn, exclude

turn away v dismiss, reject, repel, rebuff, refuse Opposite: welcome

turn away from v reject, give up, abandon, abjure, relinquish Opposite: take up

turn back v 1 go back, retrace your steps, return Opposite: continue 2 fold back, fold down, fold over, turn down, turn over

turncoat n traitor, deserter, defector, collaborator, double agent

turn down v 1 refuse, decline, reject, disallow, veto Opposite: accept 2 lessen, lower, decrease, reduce, muffle Opposite: turn up

turned-out adj groomed, dressed, presented, clad, got up (infml)

turn in v 1 hand in, hand over, give in, remit, submit 2 inform on, blow the whistle on, betray, report, hand over 3 (infml) go to bed, go to sleep, hit the sack (infml), hit the hay (infml) Opposite: rise

turning n 1 turn-off, junction, exit, minor road, ramp Opposite: entrance 2 joinery, carpentry, woodwork, carving, cabinetmaking

turning point n crossroads, defining moment, decisive moment, crisis, watershed

turn off v 1 switch off, deactivate, shut down, disable, stop Opposite: turn on 2 relax, unwind, switch off, wind down, take it easy Opposite: gear up 3 (infml) disgust, irritate, bore, deter, displease Opposite: attract

turn-off n turning, exit, junction, minor road, turn

turn of phrase n way with words, way of putting things, way of speaking, style, manner

turn on v 1 switch on, start, activate, get going, set in motion Opposite: turn off 2 depend on, rest on, hinge on, centre on, hang on 3 attack, go for, round on, lay into, set upon Opposite: defend 4 (infml) arouse, excite, interest, enthuse, stimulate Opposite: turn off

turn out v 1 turn off, switch off, deactivate, shut down, disable Opposite: turn on 2 attend, turn up, show up, appear, put in an appearance 3 evict, throw out, empty, eject, expel Opposite: welcome 4 end up, work out, come out, transpire, result 5 produce, make, manufacture, churn out, assemble

turnout n crowd, audience, attendance, gathering

turn over v 1 capsize, flip over, overturn, upturn, turn turtle 2 mull over, think about, go over, consider, reflect on 3 hand over, hand in, give in, remit, submit Opposite: hold onto

turnover n 1 incomings, income, gross revenue, business, revenue Opposite: costs 2 throughput, sales, trade, business, buying and selling 3 staff renewal rate, hiring and firing rate, staff resignation rate, staff resignations, staff turnover

turn round v 1 complete, finish, accomplish, process 2 improve, boost, increase, bump up (infml)

turnround n 1 dispatch, processing, completion 2 reversal, sea change, U-turn, turnabout, change

turnstile n gate, barrier, entrance, park entrance, kissing gate

turn the corner v get better, start to improve, look up, be on the turn, be out of danger

turn to v consult, refer to, fall back on, resort to, rely on

turn turtle v capsize, flip over, turn over, overturn, upturn

turn up v 1 increase, amplify, intensify, boost, step up Opposite: turn down 2 come to light, surface, appear, reappear, materialize Opposite: disappear 3 find, uncover, unearth, dig up, discover Opposite: conceal 4 arrive, appear, attend, put in an appearance, come

turn your back on v ignore, abandon, leave behind, put behind you, forsake Opposite: take care of

turn your nose up at v scorn, disdain, sneer at, sniff at, reject Opposite: accept

turn your stomach v sicken, disgust, repel, revolt, nauseate Opposite: attract

turpitude (fml) n immorality, wickedness, depravity, baseness, improbity

turret n tower, battlement, steeple, bartizan

tussle v fight, brawl, scuffle, clash, struggle ■ n brawl, fight, struggle, scuffle, clash

tutelage n instruction, guidance, teaching, coaching, expert hand

tutor n teacher, instructor, don, professor, lecturer ■ v teach, educate, instruct, school, coach. See COMPARE AND CONTRAST at teach.

tutorial n class, lesson, seminar, lecture, discussion group

TV (infml) n television, telly, small screen (infml), box (slang), goggle-box (dated infml)

twaddle (infml) n nonsense, balderdash, rubbish, drivel, garbage Opposite: sense

twang n accent, drawl, intonation, inflection, resonance ■ v reverberate, vibrate, ping, plunk

tweak v 1 pinch, nip, jerk, twist, tug 2 (infml) fine-tune, correct, adjust, modify, regulate ■ n nip, pinch, twist, jerk, tug

twee adj cutesy, bijou, quaint, dainty, sweet

tweedy adj casual, informal, sporty, horsey, outdoor

tweet v chirp, peep, chirrup, twitter, cheep

twenty-four/seven adv around the clock, all the time, constantly, always

twice adv two times, double, twofold

twiddle v fidget, fiddle, play, toy, handle

twig n branch, shoot, stem, stick ■ v (infml) understand, grasp, comprehend, realize, discern

twilight n dusk, nightfall, evening, sunset, sundown Opposite: dawn

twilit *adj* **dusky**, shady, shadowy, moonlit, crepuscular *(literary) Opposite*: sunlit

twin *n* **double**, doppelgänger, clone, identical twin, Siamese twin ■ *adj* **1 identical**, matching, alike, indistinguishable, like *Opposite*: different **2 dual**, double, twofold, paired *Opposite*: single ■ *v* **pair**, link, join, match, associate

twine *n* **string**, thread, cord, yarn ■ *v* **coil**, twist, wind, loop, snake

twinge *n* **pang**, pain, stitch, ache, wrench

twinkle *v* **shine**, sparkle, glimmer, gleam, flicker ■ *n* **sparkle**, gleam, glimmer, flicker, shine

twinkling *n* **flash**, second, moment, split second, instant

twirl *v* **1 wind**, coil, twist, curl, bend **2 spin**, rotate, whirl, turn, revolve ■ *n* **1 coil**, spiral, twist, loop **2 whirl**, spin, revolution, rotation, turn

twist *v* **1 wind**, coil, curl, bend, twirl **2 rotate**, turn, screw, unscrew, wind **3 sprain**, pull, hurt, injure, turn **4 distort**, misrepresent, alter, manipulate, warp *Opposite*: clarify **5 meander**, snake, wind, curve, bend **6 contort**, screw up, grimace, crumple, writhe ■ *n* **1 rotation**, screw, wind, turn **2 spiral**, coil, kink, curl, bend **3 development**, change, turn, incident, event

twisted *adj* **1 warped**, perverse, sick, perverted, abnormal *Opposite*: wholesome **2 misshapen**, distorted, warped, bent, deformed *Opposite*: straight

twisting *adj* **winding**, meandering, bendy, twisty, windy

twist somebody's arm *v* **compel**, force, pressure, coerce, persuade

twisty *adj* **winding**, tortuous, meandering, bendy, snaking *Opposite*: straight

twit *(dated) n* **fool**, buffoon, dupe, sucker *(infml)*, boob *(infml)*

twitch *v* **jerk**, jolt, shudder, yank, convulse ■ *n* **tic**, spasm, jerk, jolt, convulsion

twitcher *(infml) n* **birdwatcher**, ornithologist, birder *(US)*

twitchiness *n* **jitteriness**, jumpiness, restlessness, uneasiness, nervousness

twitchy *(infml) adj* **nervous**, fidgety, on edge, agitated, jumpy *Opposite*: still

two-dimensional *adj* **1 flat**, flattened, plane, smooth, level *Opposite*: three-dimensional **2 superficial**, shallow, oversimplified, formulaic, cardboard *Opposite*: complex

two-faced *adj* **hypocritical**, false, insincere, deceitful, double dealing *Opposite*: genuine

twofold *adj* **double**, dual, twin

twosome *n* **pair**, duo, couple, two of a kind

two-time *v* **1 betray**, mislead, deceive, double-cross, take in **2 be unfaithful**, cheat, deceive, play away *(infml)*, cuckold *(archaic)*

two-tone *adj* **stripy**, striped, light-and-dark, two-toned *Opposite*: plain

two-way *adj* **reciprocal**, cooperative, shared, mutual, collaborative

tycoon *n* **magnate**, mogul, business person, industrialist

tyke *n* **child**, imp, urchin, tearaway, monkey *(infml)*

type *n* **1 kind**, sort, category, class, genre **2 font**, typeface, lettering, print, style ■ *v* **key**, input, enter, key in ■ *n* *(infml)* **character**, individual, person, sort

---

COMPARE AND CONTRAST CORE MEANING: a group having a common quality or qualities

type a group of individuals or items with strongly marked and readily defined similarities; **kind** a group of individuals or items connected by shared characteristics; **sort** a general word used in the same way as *kind*; **category** a set of things that are classified together because of common characteristics; **class** used in the same way as *category*; **species** a specific group of animals, plants, insects, or other organisms, used in formal taxonomic classification; **genre** a particular style of painting, writing, dance, or other art form.

---

typecast *v* **stereotype**, pigeonhole, categorize, limit, restrict

typeface *n* **script**, type, font, lettering, print

typhoon *n* **storm**, cyclone, tornado, hurricane, tropical storm

typical *adj* **1 characteristic**, archetypal, distinctive, representative, emblematic *Opposite*: uncharacteristic **2 usual**, normal, standard, mainstream, average *Opposite*: unusual

typify *v* **characterize**, epitomize, symbolize, exemplify, personify

typo *(infml) n* **misprint**, typographical error, keyboarding error, error, mistake *Opposite*: correction

typography *n* **1 design**, typesetting, formatting, layout, composition **2 print style**, font, type, lettering, script

tyrannical *adj* **oppressive**, dictatorial, autocratic, despotic, authoritarian

tyrannize *v* **oppress**, dictate, bully, domineer, intimidate

tyranny *n* **oppression**, dictatorship, autocracy, domination, despotism

tyrant *n* **oppressor**, dictator, bully, autocrat, despot

tyro *n* **novice**, beginner, learner, newcomer, trainee *Opposite*: veteran. *See* COMPARE AND CONTRAST *at* **beginner**.

U

ubiquitous *adj* **omnipresent**, universal, pervasive, global, abundant

UFO *n* **flying saucer**, spaceship, spacecraft

ugliness *n* **1 unattractiveness**, unsightliness, hideousness, repulsiveness *Opposite*: attractiveness **2 violence**, hostility, cruelty, viciousness, malice *Opposite*: friendliness **3 unpleasantness**, dreadfulness, horridness, obnoxiousness, foulness

ugly *adj* **1 unattractive**, hideous, unsightly, revolting, repulsive *Opposite*: attractive **2 nasty**, threatening, dangerous, intimidating, menacing *Opposite*: friendly **3 unpleasant**, horrible, dreadful, horrid, obnoxious *Opposite*: nice. *See* COMPARE AND CONTRAST *at* **unattractive**.

ulcer *n* **boil**, abscess, pustule, carbuncle, sore

ulterior *adj* **hidden**, concealed, secret, underhand, unknown *Opposite*: transparent

ulterior motive *n* **hidden agenda**, hidden intention, design, scheme

ultimate *adj* **1 final**, last, eventual, decisive, definitive *Opposite*: first **2 fundamental**, basic, essential, supreme, extreme *Opposite*: superficial

ultimately *adv* **in the end**, eventually, in due course, finally, at last *Opposite*: initially

ultimatum *n* **challenge**, demand, requirement, petition, stipulation

ultra *adj* **extreme**, radical, revolutionary, excessive, extremist *Opposite*: mainstream

ultramodern *adj* **avant-garde**, progressive, modernistic, radical, futuristic *Opposite*: old-fashioned

umbrage *n* **offence**, exception, resentment, affront, slight

umbrella *n* **1 parasol**, sunshade, brolly *(infml)* **2 aegis**, auspices, authority, protection, support

umpire *n* **referee**, adjudicator, arbitrator, arbiter, mediator ■ *v* **adjudicate**, referee, arbitrate, judge, mediate

umpteen *(infml) adj* **countless**, numerous, innumerable, millions of, myriad

unabashed *adj* **unashamed**, unembarrassed, shameless, bold, brazen *Opposite*: abashed

unabated *adj* **persistent**, undiminished, relentless, unrelieved, unrelenting *Opposite*: reduced

unable *adj* **powerless**, incapable, impotent, inept, incompetent *Opposite*: able

unabridged *adj* **full-length**, complete, whole, entire, uncut *Opposite*: abridged

unacceptable *adj* **intolerable**, insupportable, undesirable, objectionable, deplorable *Opposite*: acceptable

unaccommodating *adj* **unhelpful**, awkward, uncooperative, difficult, disobliging *Opposite*: helpful

unaccompanied *adj* **alone**, by yourself, on your own, lone, solitary

unaccomplished *adj* **1 unfinished**, incomplete, uncompleted, unfulfilled, undone *Opposite*: accomplished **2 unskilful**, amateurish, unpolished, inexpert, untalented *Opposite*: accomplished

unaccountable *adj* **inexplicable**, puzzling, strange, unfathomable, baffling *Opposite*: explicable

unaccounted-for *adj* **missing**, lost, absent, gone, disappeared

unaccustomed *adj* **1 unused**, not used, inexperienced, unfamiliar, unacquainted *Opposite*: accustomed **2 unfamiliar**, unusual, different, new, strange *Opposite*: accustomed

unachievable *adj* **unattainable**, impracticable, impossible, unfeasible, inaccessible *Opposite*: achievable

unacquainted *adj* **ignorant**, unaccustomed, unaware, uninformed, unknowledgeable *Opposite*: knowledgeable

unadorned *adj* **plain**, bare, austere, simple, unembellished *Opposite*: ornate

unadulterated *adj* **pure**, untouched, untainted, complete, unmodified *Opposite*: tainted

unadventurous *adj* **cautious**, conservative, careful, timid, shy *Opposite*: daredevil

unaffected *adj* **1 unchanged**, unaltered, unmoved, impervious, impassive *Opposite*: different **2 genuine**, natural, unpretentious, sincere, modest *Opposite*: pretentious

unafraid *adj* **fearless**, bold, confident, brave, courageous *Opposite*: afraid

unaided *adv* **unassisted**, independently, by yourself, of your own accord, on your own *Opposite*: jointly

unalleviated *adj* **constant**, unrelieved, unremitting, unmitigated, inexorable *Opposite*: intermittent

unalloyed *adj* **pure**, sheer, absolute, total, utter *Opposite*: partial

unalterable *adj* **unchangeable**, fixed, irreversible, final, set *Opposite*: impermanent

unambiguous *adj* **unmistakable**, clear-cut,

explicit, definite, decided *Opposite*: vague

unambitious *adj* **apathetic**, unaspiring, unenterprising, unassertive, lazy *Opposite*: ambitious

unanimous *adj* **common**, agreed, undisputed, undivided, united *Opposite*: undecided

unannounced *adj* **unexpected**, impromptu, spontaneous, surprise *Opposite*: arranged

unanswerable *adj* **unfathomable**, insoluble, unresolvable, unsolvable, inexplicable

unanticipated *adj* **surprising**, unexpected, unlooked-for, unforeseen, unsuspected *Opposite*: expected

unapologetic *adj* **impenitent**, unrepentant, unreformed, unremorseful, without regret *Opposite*: penitent

unappealing *adj* **unattractive**, unpleasant, disagreeable, uninviting, unlikable *Opposite*: appealing. *See* COMPARE AND CONTRAST *at* **unattractive**.

unappetizing *adj* **unattractive**, unpleasant, unenticing, uninviting, unpalatable *Opposite*: appetizing

unapproachable *adj* **distant**, unfriendly, aloof, cold, standoffish *Opposite*: approachable

unarguable *adj* **beyond doubt**, incontestable, incontrovertible, indisputable, beyond question *Opposite*: arguable

unarmed *adj* **unprotected**, defenceless, exposed, vulnerable, weaponless *Opposite*: armed

unashamed *adj* **unembarrassed**, unapologetic, blatant, brazen, barefaced *Opposite*: ashamed

unasked *adj* **1 unsolicited**, uninvited, unsought, unexpected, unimaginable *Opposite*: expected **2 uninvited**, unwelcome, excluded, unexpected, left out

unassailable *adj* **1 incontrovertible**, unquestionable, impregnable, irrefutable, indisputable *Opposite*: tenuous **2 invincible**, unbeatable, impregnable, indomitable, invulnerable *Opposite*: vulnerable

unassisted *adj* **unaided**, single-handed, solo, lone *Opposite*: assisted

unassuming *adj* **modest**, humble, self-effacing, unassertive, meek *Opposite*: arrogant

unattached *adj* **free**, uncommitted, single, unmarried, separated *Opposite*: attached

unattainable *adj* **unachievable**, impossible, unfeasible, inaccessible, unreachable *Opposite*: attainable

unattractive *adj* **unappealing**, ugly, nasty, unpleasant, distasteful *Opposite*: attractive

COMPARE AND CONTRAST CORE MEANING: not pleasant to look at

unattractive not pleasant in appearance; **unsightly** spoiling an appearance which would otherwise be quite attractive; **ugly** very unpleasant to look at; **hideous** extremely unpleasant to look at; **homely** (*mainly US*) describes somebody who is not attractive; **plain** describes somebody, especially a woman, who is not attractive.

unattractiveness *n* **ugliness**, unpleasantness, unsightliness, distastefulness, repulsiveness *Opposite*: attractiveness

unauthorized *adj* **illegal**, unlawful, unofficial, unsanctioned, unlicensed *Opposite*: legitimate

unavailability *n* **unobtainability**, inaccessibility, unattainability, unreachability, absence *Opposite*: availability

unavailable *adj* **1 unobtainable**, inaccessible, unattainable, unreachable, absent *Opposite*: available **2 engaged**, busy, occupied, unobtainable *Opposite*: available

unavailing *adj* **vain**, unsuccessful, futile, failed, ineffective *Opposite*: successful

unavoidability *n* **inevitability**, inescapability, certainty, necessity, obligation

unavoidable *adj* **inevitable**, inescapable, obvious, manifest, obligatory *Opposite*: avoidable

unaware *adj* **ignorant**, uninformed, oblivious, unconscious, unmindful *Opposite*: conscious

unawares *adv* **by surprise**, off guard, unexpectedly, on the hop (*infml*)

unbalance *v* **disturb**, unhinge, derange, distort, destabilize *Opposite*: stabilize

unbalanced *adj* **1 uneven**, lopsided, unequal, crooked, top-heavy *Opposite*: even **2 unstable**, disturbed, unhinged, deranged *Opposite*: well-balanced **3 biased**, one-sided, inequitable, prejudiced, unfair *Opposite*: impartial

unbearable *adj* **intolerable**, agonizing, excruciating, awful, insufferable *Opposite*: tolerable

unbeatable *adj* **invincible**, supreme, unassailable, unconquerable, peerless *Opposite*: vulnerable

unbeaten *adj* **undefeated**, unsurpassed, successful, triumphant, victorious

unbecoming *adj* **improper**, inappropriate, incorrect, unsuitable, unflattering *Opposite*: fitting

unbelief *n* **nonbelief**, scepticism, incredulity, agnosticism, atheism *Opposite*: faith

unbelievable *adj* **1 implausible**, incredible, farfetched, fantastic, unlikely *Opposite*: plausible **2 incredible**, amazing, extraordinary, astonishing, great *Opposite*: ordinary

unbelievably *adv* **extraordinarily**, incredibly, extremely, very, exceptionally *Opposite*: unremarkably

unbeliever *n* **nonbeliever**, sceptic, atheist, agnostic, freethinker *Opposite*: believer

unbelieving *adj* **incredulous**, sceptical, doubting, suspicious, questioning *Opposite*: credulous

unbend *v* **straighten**, release, free, relax, loosen *Opposite*: bend

unbending *adj* **inflexible**, fixed, rigid,

adamant, obdurate *Opposite*: flexible

unbiased *adj* **impartial**, balanced, dispassionate, neutral, unprejudiced *Opposite*: partial

unbind *v* untie, release, free, undo, liberate *Opposite*: bind

unblemished *adj* **flawless**, perfect, untarnished, pure, blameless *Opposite*: flawed

unblock *v* clear, unclog, free, clear out, clean out *Opposite*: block

unbolt *v* unfasten, unlock, open, unscrew, release *Opposite*: lock

unbounded *adj* limitless, unrestrained, abundant, boundless, uncontrolled *Opposite*: limited

unbowed *adj* undefeated, defiant, stubborn, determined, relentless *Opposite*: defeated

unbreakable *adj* indestructible, strong, permanent, indissoluble, firm *Opposite*: fragile

unbridled *adj* unrestrained, uncontrolled, uninhibited, unconcealed, unchecked *Opposite*: contained

unbroken *adj* continuous, constant, uninterrupted, steady, complete *Opposite*: intermittent

unburden *(fml) v* relieve, divest, free, release, let go *Opposite*: brood

unbutton *v* undo, open, unfasten *Opposite*: fasten

uncalled-for *adj* unjustified, unwarranted, undeserved, unprovoked, gratuitous *Opposite*: justifiable

uncanny *adj* eerie, weird, strange, mysterious, supernatural

uncared-for *adj* **neglected**, unloved, untended, unkempt, unattended *Opposite*: cherished

uncaring *adj* hardhearted, unfeeling, heartless, indifferent, cold *Opposite*: caring

unceasing *adj* constant, continuous, interminable, never-ending, perpetual *Opposite*: sporadic

unceremonious *adj* abrupt, hasty, rushed, terse, rude *Opposite*: gracious

uncertain *adj* **1** unsure, vague, doubtful, hesitant, undecided *Opposite*: sure **2 indeterminate**, inexact, undefined, indefinite, ambiguous *Opposite*: exact. *See* COMPARE AND CONTRAST *at* **doubtful**.

uncertainty *n* doubt, indecision, hesitation, vagueness, ambiguity *Opposite*: confidence

unchain *v* release, unlock, unfetter, unshackle, liberate *Opposite*: chain

unchangeable *adj* fixed, unalterable, unvarying, constant, unchanged *Opposite*: changeable

unchanged *adj* **unaffected**, unmoved, untouched *Opposite*: affected

unchanging *adj* static, fixed, invariable, unchangeable, rigid *Opposite*: flexible

uncharacteristic *adj* unusual, atypical, abnormal, out of character, unexpected *Opposite*: typical

uncharitable *adj* mean, unkind, hurtful, spiteful, cruel *Opposite*: generous

uncharted *adj* unexplored, new, unfamiliar, unmapped, unknown *Opposite*: familiar

unchecked *adj* unimpeded, unrestrained, unhindered, unrestricted, unconstrained *Opposite*: restricted

uncivil *adj* rude, discourteous, impolite, insulting, bad-mannered *Opposite*: courteous

uncivilized *adj* **1** primitive, barbaric, uncultured, unsophisticated, crude *Opposite*: civilized **2 remote**, distant, far-off, isolated, unreachable *Opposite*: reachable **3 coarse**, impolite, discourteous, unrefined, vulgar *Opposite*: polite

unclasp *v* unfasten, undo, open, unbuckle, untie *Opposite*: fasten

unclassified *adj* **1** random, unsystematic, disorganized, unorganized, uncategorized *Opposite*: organized **2 open**, public, released, unconcealed, accessible *Opposite*: secret

unclean *adj* **1** impure, dirty, contaminated, polluted, infected *Opposite*: pure **2 unchaste**, sinful, impure, unworthy, immoral *Opposite*: chaste. *See* COMPARE AND CONTRAST *at* **dirty**.

uncleanness *n* **1** dirtiness, filthiness, impurity, griminess, squalor *Opposite*: cleanness **2 unchasteness**, sinfulness, impurity, unworthiness, immorality *Opposite*: chasteness

unclear *adj* **1** indistinct, hazy, indeterminate, blurred, indistinguishable *Opposite*: clear **2 uncertain**, doubtful, undecided, unsure, in doubt *Opposite*: definite. *See* COMPARE AND CONTRAST *at* **obscure**.

unclench *v* relax, release, open, let go, slacken *Opposite*: tighten

unclog *v* unblock, clear, free, release, clean out *Opposite*: block

unclothe *v* undress, strip, uncover, disrobe *(fml) Opposite*: dress

unclothed *adj* bare, naked, uncovered, undressed, nude *Opposite*: dressed

uncoil *v* unravel, unwind, undo, untwist, release *Opposite*: twist

uncomfortable *adj* **1** painful, tight, rough, scratchy, itchy *Opposite*: comfortable **2 embarrassing**, awkward, difficult, tricky, unpleasant *Opposite*: enjoyable **3 uneasy**, awkward, ill at ease, embarrassed, tense *Opposite*: relaxed

uncommitted *adj* casual, uninterested, indifferent, unattached, free *Opposite*: committed

uncommon *adj* rare, unusual, infrequent, scarce, special *Opposite*: common

uncommunicative *adj* reserved, reticent, taciturn, silent, withdrawn *Opposite*: talkative. *See* COMPARE AND CONTRAST *at* silent.

uncomplaining *adj* accepting, tolerant, long-suffering, patient, accommodating *Opposite*: intolerant

uncomplicated *adj* simple, straightforward, unfussy, basic, unsophisticated *Opposite*: complex

uncomplimentary *adj* disparaging, derogatory, unflattering, negative, rude *Opposite*: complimentary

uncompromising *adj* inflexible, rigid, adamant, unbending, obdurate *Opposite*: flexible

unconcealed *adj* obvious, open, evident, apparent, blatant *Opposite*: hidden

unconcern *n* indifference, apathy, disregard, nonchalance, disinterest *Opposite*: anxiety

unconcerned *adj* indifferent, unworried, nonchalant, undaunted, undisturbed *Opposite*: anxious

unconditional *adj* unqualified, total, categorical, absolute, unrestricted *Opposite*: qualified

unconditioned *adj* unrestricted, limitless, undefined, unlimited, open-ended *Opposite*: restricted

unconfident *adj* insecure, unsure, nervous, apprehensive, self-doubting *Opposite*: self-assured

unconfined *adj* free, liberated, released, loose, at large *Opposite*: restricted

unconfirmed *adj* unverified, unsubstantiated, unproven, unofficial, unsupported *Opposite*: verified

uncongenial *adj* disagreeable, unfriendly, unwelcoming, unpleasant, inhospitable *Opposite*: friendly

unconnected *adj* separate, unrelated, independent, distinct, isolated *Opposite*: linked

unconquerable *adj* unbeatable, unassailable, unattainable, insurmountable, indomitable *Opposite*: vulnerable

unconscionable *adj* 1 unacceptable, shocking, horrifying, immoral, reprehensible *Opposite*: acceptable 2 unreasonable, beyond the pale, irrational, ridiculous, illogical *Opposite*: reasonable

unconscious *adj* 1 comatose, insentient, insensible, out cold, cataleptic *Opposite*: awake 2 unaware, oblivious, ignorant, unwitting, insensible *Opposite*: aware 3 unintentional, automatic, mechanical, instinctive, involuntary *Opposite*: deliberate ■ *n* id, superego, ego, self, psyche

unconsciousness *n* oblivion, sleep, nothingness, insentience, catalepsy *Opposite*: consciousness

unconsidered *adj* hasty, unthinking, impulsive, reactive, imprudent *Opposite*: considered

unconstitutional *adj* illegal, unauthorized, unlawful, undemocratic, unofficial *Opposite*: lawful

unconstrained *adj* unimpeded, free, unrestrained, unrestricted, unhindered *Opposite*: restricted

unconstructive *adj* unhelpful, negative, unenthusiastic, uncooperative, ineffectual *Opposite*: constructive

uncontaminated *adj* pure, clean, unadulterated, antiseptic, sterilized *Opposite*: contaminated

uncontrollable *adj* 1 irrepressible, uncontainable, overpowering, wild, overwhelming 2 unruly, disobedient, out of control, unmanageable, disorderly *Opposite*: well-behaved

uncontrolled *adj* unrestrained, abandoned, wild, hysterical, uninhibited *Opposite*: restrained

uncontroversial *adj* undisputed, uncontentious, uncontended, unquestionable, indisputable *Opposite*: controversial

unconventional *adj* eccentric, unusual, alternative, avant-garde, strange *Opposite*: conventional

unconventionality *n* eccentricity, originality, nonconformity, oddness, quirkiness *Opposite*: conventionality

unconvinced *adj* sceptical, incredulous, disbelieving, unimpressed, unmoved *Opposite*: convinced

unconvincing *adj* implausible, unimpressive, weak, feeble, unsuccessful *Opposite*: persuasive

uncooked *adj* raw, rare, fresh, unprepared *Opposite*: cooked

uncooperative *adj* unhelpful, disobliging, awkward, obstinate, contrary *Opposite*: amenable

uncoordinated *adj* clumsy, ungainly, awkward, ungraceful, inept *Opposite*: graceful

uncork *v* 1 open, break open, unplug, break into, pop open *Opposite*: plug 2 unleash, release, give vent to, pour out, set free *Opposite*: hold in

uncorrupted *adj* unadulterated, unspoiled, uncontaminated, chaste, pure *Opposite*: corrupted

uncounted *adj* innumerable, countless, numerous, myriad, incalculable *Opposite*: few

uncouple *v* undo, disengage, separate, detach, unyoke *Opposite*: join

uncouth *adj* rude, uncivilized, bad-mannered, ill-mannered, foul-mouthed *Opposite*: polite

uncouthness *n* rudeness, vulgarity, bad manners, crudeness, coarseness *Opposite*: politeness

uncover *v* expose, discover, reveal, unearth, find out *Opposite*: conceal

uncovered *adj* **exposed**, bare, open, naked, revealed *Opposite*: concealed

uncovering *n* **exposure**, discovery, disclosure, revelation *Opposite*: concealment

uncritical *adj* **indiscriminating**, accepting, credulous, naive, gullible *Opposite*: discriminating

unction *n* **1 balm**, ointment, salve, oil, lotion **2 earnestness**, fervour, zeal, passion, enthusiasm

unctuous *adj* **1 ingratiating**, sycophantic, slimy, smarmy, obsequious *Opposite*: arrogant **2 oily**, greasy, fatty, slippery, slimy

uncultivated *adj* **1 unrefined**, unsophisticated, coarse, uncultured, unpolished *Opposite*: refined **2 fallow**, untilled, unplanted, unfarmed *Opposite*: cultivated

uncultured *adj* **unrefined**, philistine, boorish, unsophisticated, uncultivated *Opposite*: refined

uncurl *v* **straighten**, straighten out, uncoil, flatten, unwind *Opposite*: curl

uncut *adj* **unabridged**, complete, full-length, unedited, uncensored *Opposite*: abridged

undamaged *adj* **unspoiled**, untouched, unharmed, unhurt, intact *Opposite*: spoiled

undaunted *adj* **fearless**, unconcerned, unworried, carefree, undisturbed *Opposite*: scared

undeceive *v* **inform**, tell, notify, enlighten, disabuse *Opposite*: deceive

undecided *adj* **1 in two minds**, in doubt, dithering, vacillating, uncertain *Opposite*: decided **2 unresolved**, open, unclear, vague, ambivalent *Opposite*: certain

undecipherable *adj* **illegible**, unreadable, inexplicable, mysterious, unfathomable *Opposite*: clear

undecorated *adj* **plain**, simple, unornamented, austere, spartan *Opposite*: ornate

undefeated *adj* **unbeaten**, reigning, unvanquished, unconquered, unbowed *Opposite*: defeated

undefended *adj* **unguarded**, unprotected, unfortified, deserted, defenceless *Opposite*: defended

undefiled *adj* **unsullied**, pure, unpolluted, unblemished, unstained *Opposite*: defiled (*fml*)

undefined *adj* **indeterminate**, vague, approximate, open-ended, indefinite *Opposite*: defined

undemanding *adj* **easy**, straightforward, light, simple, unchallenging *Opposite*: demanding

undemocratic *adj* **inequitable**, unfair, autocratic, high-handed, dictatorial *Opposite*: democratic

undemonstrative *adj* **unemotional**, restrained, phlegmatic, stoical, impassive *Opposite*: demonstrative

undeniable *adj* **irrefutable**, indisputable, incontestable, incontrovertible, unquestionable *Opposite*: questionable

undependable *adj* **unreliable**, unpredictable, variable, erratic, fickle *Opposite*: dependable

under *prep* **1 below**, in, underneath, beneath (*fml*) *Opposite*: above **2 below**, less than *Opposite*: over

underachieve *v* **disappoint**, flounder, drift, drop out, underperform *Opposite*: excel

underage *adj* **juvenile**, immature, youthful, young, callow

underclothes *n* **underwear**, underclothing, underthings, undies (*infml*)

underclothing *see* underclothes

undercover *adj* **secret**, hidden, covert, disguised, clandestine *Opposite*: open

undercurrent *n* **1 current**, tide, undertow, pull, stream **2 feeling**, hint, undertow, suggestion, connotation

undercut *v* **undermine**, destabilize, detract, weaken, damage *Opposite*: strengthen

underdeveloped *adj* **immature**, small, undersized, weak, unused

underdog *n* **loser**, small fry, runner up, second best, little guy

underdone *adj* **rare**, bloody, pink, undercooked *Opposite*: overdone

underemphasize *v* **play down**, understate, underplay, minimize, underrate *Opposite*: overemphasize

underestimate *v* **undervalue**, underrate, misjudge, miscalculate *Opposite*: overestimate

underfed *adj* **malnourished**, starving, frail, weak, undernourished *Opposite*: well-fed

undergo *v* **experience**, feel, suffer, endure, undertake *Opposite*: avoid

underground *adj* **1 subterranean**, below ground, covered, buried, deep **2 subversive**, secretive, dissident, alternative, covert *Opposite*: open

undergrowth *n* **bushes**, scrub, brushwood, vegetation, understorey

underhand *adj* **deceitful**, dishonest, sneaky, mean, sly *Opposite*: open ■ *adv* **deceitfully**, dishonestly, sneakily, slyly, craftily *Opposite*: openly

underhanded *see* underhand

underlie *v* **lie beneath**, lie behind, motivate, cause, inspire

underline *v* **underscore**, emphasize, highlight, feature, stress *Opposite*: ignore

underling *n* **minion**, inferior, subject, junior, subordinate *Opposite*: superior

underlying *adj* **fundamental**, original, causal, primary, basic

undermine *v* **weaken**, dent, chip away at, challenge, destabilize *Opposite*: bolster

underneath *prep* **under**, below, beneath (*fml*) *Opposite*: on top of ■ *n* **base**, bottom, underside, footing, foundation *Opposite*: top

undernourished *adj* **malnourished**, underfed,

starved, hungry, famished *Opposite*: well-fed

undernourishment *n* **malnutrition**, starvation, hunger, famine

underperform *v* **fail**, underachieve, disappoint, flounder, drift *Opposite*: excel

underpin *v* **1 shore up**, prop up, reinforce, support, buttress *Opposite*: undermine **2 support**, lie beneath, underlie, give support to, bolster *Opposite*: weaken

underpinning *n* **foundation**, reinforcement, groundwork, keystone, bedrock

underplay *v* **make light of**, minimize, understate, play down, talk down *Opposite*: overplay

underprice *v* **cheapen**, undersell, underrepresent, understate *Opposite*: overprice

underprivileged *adj* **disadvantaged**, deprived, poor, needy, neglected *Opposite*: well-off

underprop *v* **underpin**, shore up, prop up, jack up, reinforce *Opposite*: undermine

underrate *v* **undervalue**, underestimate, think little of, devalue, misjudge *Opposite*: overrate

underrated *adj* **undervalued**, underestimated, unappreciated, unrecognized, misunderstood *Opposite*: overrated

underrepresent *v* **understate**, undersell, lessen, play down, make light of *Opposite*: overemphasize

underscore *v* **underline**, highlight, emphasize, accentuate, call attention to *Opposite*: ignore

undersea *adj* **submarine**, underwater, bathyal, bathypelagic

undersell *v* **understate**, play down, make light of, denigrate, cheapen *Opposite*: oversell

undershrub *n* **subshrub**, bush, plant

underside *n* **base**, bottom, underneath, basement, foundation

undersized *adj* **puny**, underdeveloped, small, short, stunted *Opposite*: extra-large

understand *v* **1 comprehend**, appreciate, know, recognize, realize **2 sympathize**, empathize, identify, appreciate

understandable *adj* **comprehensible**, clear, logical, reasonable, fathomable *Opposite*: incomprehensible

understanding *adj* **sympathetic**, empathetic, considerate, thoughtful, kind *Opposite*: unsympathetic ■ *n* **1 agreement**, arrangement, deal, contract, settlement **2 sympathy**, empathy, identification, consideration, kindness *Opposite*: indifference **3 grasp**, perception, intellect, mind, wit *Opposite*: ignorance **4 interpretation**, construction, personal feeling, estimation, perception

understate *v* **play down**, minimize, devalue, belittle, make little of *Opposite*: exaggerate

understated *adj* **modest**, inconspicuous, discreet, unfussy, minimalist *Opposite*: exaggerated

understatement *n* **irony**, dryness, sarcasm, underestimation *Opposite*: exaggeration

understood *adj* **unspoken**, tacit, silent, unstated, unwritten *Opposite*: explicit

understorey *n* **forest floor**, bushes, underwood, brush, scrub

understrength *adj* **1 understaffed**, short-handed, short-staffed, short, down **2 dilute**, weak, thin, diluted, watered down

understudy *n* **substitute**, cover, stand-by, stand-in, replacement

undertake *v* **take on**, assume, start, commence, embark on *Opposite*: relinquish

undertaker *n* **funeral director**, embalmer, mortician *(US)*

undertaking *n* **responsibility**, task, job, enterprise, commission

under-the-counter *adj* **illegal**, unofficial, illicit, wrongful, criminal *Opposite*: aboveboard

under-the-table *adj* **underhand**, unofficial, secret, surreptitious, sneaky *Opposite*: aboveboard

underthings *n* **underwear**, underclothes, underclothing, undies *(infml)*

undertone *n* **hint**, suggestion, trace, tinge, undercurrent *Opposite*: overtone

undertow *n* **current**, undercurrent, tide, pull, stream

undervalue *v* **underrate**, underestimate, play down, devalue, belittle *Opposite*: overrate

underwater *adj* **1 submerged**, sunken, flooded, subaquatic, subsurface *Opposite*: dry **2 undersea**, submarine, sunken, submerged, marine

underway *adj* **happening**, in progress, ongoing, on the go, proceeding

underwear *n* **underclothes**, underclothing, underthings, undies *(infml)*

WORD BANK

❑ **types of lower-body underwear** bloomers *(dated)*, boxer shorts, briefs, camiknickers, corset, crinoline, drawers, foundation garment, garter, girdle, G-string, jockstrap, knee-highs, knickers, leg-warmer, long johns, nylons, panties, pants, petticoat, slip, sock, stockings, support stockings, thigh-highs, thong, tights, underpants, underskirt
❑ **types of upper body underwear** basque, body, body stocking, bodysuit, bra, camisole, chemise, string vest, teddy, undershirt, vest

---

underweight *adj* **skinny**, skin-and-bone, scrawny, half-starved, underfed *Opposite*: overweight

underworld *n* **gangland**, criminal world, nether world ■ *adj* **criminal**, gangland, illicit, illegal, unlawful *Opposite*: legal

underwrite *v* **guarantee**, countersign, back, endorse, fund

underwriter *n* **sponsor**, backer, supporter, guarantor, financier

undeserved *adj* **unwarranted**, unmerited, unearned, unfair, unjustifiable *Opposite*: deserved

undesirable *adj* **unwanted**, unwelcome, uninvited, objectionable, disagreeable *Opposite*: desirable

undetectable *adj* **untraceable**, indiscernible, unnoticeable, imperceptible, invisible *Opposite*: obvious

undetermined *adj* **1 hesitating**, undecided, irresolute, unsettled, vacillating *Opposite*: decided **2 unresolved**, indeterminate, indefinite, undecided, incalculable *Opposite*: definite **3 unknown**, undiscovered, unidentified, unheard of, unfamiliar *Opposite*: known

undeveloped *adj* **immature**, young, embryonic, unripe, emergent *Opposite*: mature

undeviating *adj* **unswerving**, firm, solid, absolute, total *Opposite*: shaky

undies *(infml) n* **underwear**, underclothes, underclothing, underthings

undignified *adj* **unseemly**, unbecoming, indecorous, improper, humiliating *Opposite*: dignified

undiluted *adj* **straight**, neat, unadulterated, unmixed, full-strength *Opposite*: diluted

undiplomatic *adj* **tactless**, crass, thoughtless, indiscreet, inconsiderate *Opposite*: diplomatic

undirected *adj* **purposeless**, aimless, directionless, pointless, wandering *Opposite*: purposeful

undisciplined *adj* **unmanageable**, out of control, wild, unruly, disobedient *Opposite*: well-behaved

undisclosed *adj* **secret**, unnamed, hidden, unrevealed, unidentified *Opposite*: known

undisguised *adj* **unconcealed**, plain, straightforward, open, public *Opposite*: concealed

undisposed *adj* **unwilling**, loath, reluctant, unprepared, hesitant *Opposite*: disposed

undisputed *adj* **acknowledged**, undoubted, certain, undeniable, unquestionable *Opposite*: questionable

undistinguished *adj* **ordinary**, everyday, run-of-the-mill, commonplace, nothing special *Opposite*: unusual

undistorted *adj* **factual**, truthful, exact, accurate, straight *Opposite*: inaccurate

undisturbed *adj* **1 uninterrupted**, in peace, unbroken, unobstructed *Opposite*: interrupted **2 untouched**, intact, whole, flawless, undamaged *Opposite*: damaged **3 peaceful**, serene, composed, at peace, at ease *Opposite*: anxious

undivided *adj* **complete**, entire, whole, total, full *Opposite*: partial

undo *v* **1 unfasten**, untie, unbutton, loosen, disengage *Opposite*: fasten **2 cancel out**, cancel, nullify, invalidate, render null and void

undoing *n* **downfall**, ruin, ruination, collapse, destruction *Opposite*: making

undone *adj* **1 uncompleted**, unfinished, incomplete, half-done, unconcluded *Opposite*: done **2 unfastened**, open, gaping, unzipped, unbuttoned **3 ruined**, in trouble, lost, in deep water, destroyed *Opposite*: fine

undoubted *adj* **certain**, sure, absolute, definite, indubitable *Opposite*: doubtful

undreamed-of *adj* **unexpected**, unhoped-for, unimaginable, unanticipated, unlooked-for *Opposite*: anticipated

undress *v* **strip off**, strip, unclothe, remove your clothes, bare *Opposite*: dress

undressed *adj* **naked**, bare, nude, stripped, with nothing on *Opposite*: dressed. *See* COMPARE AND CONTRAST *at* **naked**.

undue *adj* **unwarranted**, excessive, unnecessary, unjustified, unjustifiable *Opposite*: justified

undulant *(fml) see* **undulating**

undulate *v* **roll**, ripple, rise and fall, swell, heave

undulating *adj* **rolling**, rising and falling, swelling, heaving, surging

undulation *n* **wave**, ripple, furrow, crinkle, wrinkle

unduly *adv* **excessively**, overly, disproportionately, unjustifiably, undeservedly *Opposite*: justifiably

undying *adj* **unending**, never-ending, endless, perpetual, eternal *Opposite*: inconstant

unearned *adj* **undeserved**, unwarranted, unmerited, unjustified, uncalled-for

unearth *v* **1 dig up**, exhume, disinter, excavate, extract *Opposite*: bury **2 disclose**, reveal, expose, publicize, bring to light *Opposite*: cover up

unearthly *adj* **1 eerie**, weird, bizarre, strange, macabre *Opposite*: normal **2 unreasonable**, inappropriate, outrageous, ridiculous, absurd *Opposite*: acceptable

unease *n* **anxiety**, nervousness, restlessness, awkwardness, uneasiness *Opposite*: calm. *See* COMPARE AND CONTRAST *at* **worry**.

uneasiness *n* **anxiety**, nervousness, restlessness, awkwardness, unease *Opposite*: calmness

uneasy *adj* **anxious**, nervous, troubled, uncomfortable, ill at ease *Opposite*: calm

uneconomic *adj* **1 unprofitable**, not viable, lossmaking, profitless *Opposite*: profitable **2 inefficient**, wasteful, uneconomical, improvident, extravagant *Opposite*: efficient

uneconomical *adj* **inefficient**, wasteful, extravagant, uneconomic, profligate *Opposite*: efficient

unedited *adj* **complete**, unabridged, unexpurgated, uncut, full-length *Opposite*: edited

uneducated *adj* **unschooled**, untaught, ignorant, illiterate, uninformed *Opposite*: educated

unembellished *adj* **1 unadorned**, plain, without ornamentation, simple, straightforward *Opposite*: fancy **2 factual**, unembroidered, undistorted, truthful, straightforward *Opposite*: fictional

unembroidered *adj* **factual**, unembellished, undistorted, truthful, unvarnished *Opposite*: florid

unemotional *adj* **impassive**, dispassionate, undemonstrative, unresponsive, detached *Opposite*: emotional

unemployed *adj* **jobless**, out of work, out of a job, unwaged, laid off *Opposite*: employed

unemployment *n* **joblessness**, job loss, redundancy, idleness *Opposite*: employment

unending *adj* **endless**, never-ending, eternal, everlasting, interminable *Opposite*: finite

unendurable *adj* **insufferable**, unbearable, intolerable, insupportable, excruciating *Opposite*: bearable

unenlightened *adj* **1 prejudiced**, ignorant, narrow, narrow-minded, closed-minded *Opposite*: enlightened **2 unaware**, uninformed, ignorant, oblivious, unacquainted *Opposite*: informed

unenthusiastic *adj* **apathetic**, indifferent, unresponsive, lukewarm, half-hearted *Opposite*: enthusiastic

unenviable *adj* **undesirable**, disagreeable, unpleasant, uninviting, objectionable *Opposite*: enviable

unequal *adj* **1 uneven**, unbalanced, lopsided, asymmetrical, disproportionate *Opposite*: equal **2 unfair**, inequitable, one-sided, mismatched, unbalanced *Opposite*: fair **3 unsatisfactory**, unfit, unable, incapable, inadequate

unequalled *adj* **unrivalled**, matchless, unsurpassed, incomparable, unique *Opposite*: ordinary

unequivocal *adj* **clear**, plain, unambiguous, unmistakable, explicit

unerring *adj* **certain**, sure, absolute, positive, definite *Opposite*: faulty

unessential *adj* **dispensable**, superfluous, unnecessary, inessential, replaceable *Opposite*: essential

unethical *adj* **unprincipled**, immoral, wrong, bad, unscrupulous *Opposite*: ethical

uneven *adj* **1 rough**, jagged, bumpy, patchy, irregular *Opposite*: level **2 unequal**, unbalanced, lopsided, asymmetrical, disproportionate *Opposite*: equal **3 mismatched**, one-sided, unfair, unbalanced, disproportionate *Opposite*: fair

unevenness *n* **1 roughness**, jaggedness, bumpiness, patchiness *Opposite*: evenness **2 inequality**, one-sidedness, disparity *Opposite*: equality **3 asymmetry**, disproportion, irregularity *Opposite*: symmetry

uneventful *adj* **boring**, monotonous, ordinary, humdrum, dull *Opposite*: exciting

unexceptionable *adj* **inoffensive**, unobjectionable, faultless, irreproachable, acceptable *Opposite*: exceptionable *(fml)*

unexceptional *adj* **undistinguished**, nondescript, anonymous, modest, indifferent *Opposite*: extraordinary

unexcited *adj* **calm**, restrained, subdued, unresponsive, impassive *Opposite*: excited

unexciting *adj* **dull**, boring, tedious, monotonous, humdrum *Opposite*: exciting

unexpected *adj* **unforeseen**, unanticipated, unpredicted, surprising, startling *Opposite*: expected

unexplained *adj* **mysterious**, unsolved, inexplicable, impenetrable, arcane *Opposite*: apparent

unexpressed *adj* **unstated**, unspoken, unsaid, unknown *Opposite*: articulated

unfailing *adj* **reliable**, certain, dependable, trustworthy, constant *Opposite*: erratic

unfair *adj* **1 unjust**, inequitable, iniquitous, unwarranted, unmerited *Opposite*: fair **2 unethical**, dishonest, dishonourable, deceitful, underhand *Opposite*: honest **3 partial**, one-sided, biased, prejudicial, discriminating *Opposite*: fair

unfairness *n* **1 injustice**, wrongness, wrong, iniquitousness, unreasonableness *Opposite*: fairness **2 underhandedness**, dishonesty, dishonourableness, deceitfulness, fraudulence *Opposite*: honesty **3 partiality**, one-sidedness, bias, prejudice, discrimination *Opposite*: fairness

unfaithful *adj* **disloyal**, false, untrue, adulterous, treacherous *Opposite*: faithful

unfaithfulness *n* **disloyalty**, infidelity, falseness, adultery, treachery *Opposite*: faithfulness

unfaltering *adj* **untiring**, indefatigable, tireless, unflagging, persistent *Opposite*: faltering

unfamiliar *adj* **1 unknown**, new, untried, strange, alien *Opposite*: familiar **2 unacquainted**, unaccustomed, unaware, unversed, unskilled *Opposite*: familiar

unfamiliarity *n* **1 newness**, strangeness, unusualness, foreignness, exoticism *Opposite*: familiarity **2 unaccustomedness**, inexperience, ignorance, unawareness, lack of experience *Opposite*: familiarity

unfashionable *adj* **out-of-date**, outmoded, dated, old-fashioned, behind the times *Opposite*: trendy *(infml)*

unfasten *v* **undo**, unhook, unlock, disengage, detach *Opposite*: fasten

unfastened *adj* **undone**, loosened, untied, unbuttoned, unzipped *Opposite*: fastened

unfathomable *adj* **1 deep**, profound, bottomless, unsounded, unplumbed *Opposite*: shallow **2 incomprehensible**, impenetrable, inscrutable, unknowable, indecipherable *Opposite*: straightforward

unfavourable *adj* **1 disapproving**, negative, uncomplimentary, opposed, hostile *Opposite*: approving **2 harmful**, adverse, bad, detrimental, disadvantageous *Opposite*: beneficial

unfeasible *adj* **impracticable**, impractical, unworkable, unachievable, out of the question *Opposite*: feasible

unfeeling *adj* **unsympathetic**, hardhearted, callous, cruel, heartless *Opposite*: sympathetic

unfetter *v* **release**, liberate, free, unchain, unshackle *Opposite*: fetter

unfettered *adj* **freed**, unencumbered, unconstrained, unregulated, autonomous *Opposite*: constrained

unfilled *adj* **empty**, vacant, void, unoccupied, untaken *Opposite*: full

unfinished *adj* **incomplete**, uncompleted, fragmentary, partial, ongoing *Opposite*: finished

unfit *adj* **1 unsuitable**, inappropriate, unsuited, inapt, unacceptable *Opposite*: suitable **2 unqualified**, incompetent, inept, useless, incapable *Opposite*: competent **3 out of shape**, out of condition, unhealthy, weak, puny *Opposite*: fit

unfitted *adj* **unsuited**, unequipped, unprepared, unsuitable, unqualified *Opposite*: fitted

unfitting *adj* **unsuitable**, inappropriate, unbecoming, out of place, unseemly *Opposite*: fitting

unfix *v* **detach**, loosen, disengage, separate, undo *Opposite*: attach

unflagging *adj* **untiring**, indefatigable, tireless, unfaltering, persistent *Opposite*: weak

unflappability *n* **calmness**, coolness, patience, composure, control *Opposite*: excitability

unflappable *adj* **composed**, calm, unflustered, collected, imperturbable *Opposite*: anxious

unflattering *adj* **1 unbecoming**, unattractive, unappealing, ugly *Opposite*: becoming **2 critical**, uncomplimentary, faultfinding, unfavourable *Opposite*: complimentary

unfledged *adj* **inexperienced**, naive, innocent, fresh, immature *Opposite*: experienced

unflinching *adj* **unwavering**, constant, steady, undaunted, persistent *Opposite*: wavering

unflustered *adj* **composed**, calm, unflappable, collected, imperturbable *Opposite*: agitated

unfocused *adj* **1 blurred**, unclear, fuzzy, indistinct, bleary *Opposite*: clear **2 ill-defined**, nonspecific, imprecise, woolly, vague *Opposite*: focused

unfold *v* **1 open out**, open up, unfurl, spread out, display *Opposite*: fold up **2 explain**, clarify, make known, disclose, reveal *Opposite*: conceal **3 develop**, evolve, grow, progress, advance *Opposite*: deteriorate

unforced *adj* **voluntary**, natural, spontaneous, unwitting, unprompted *Opposite*: forced

unforeseeable *adj* **unexpected**, unanticipated, undreamed-of, unpredictable, surprise *Opposite*: predictable

unforeseen *adj* **unexpected**, unanticipated, unpredicted, surprising, startling *Opposite*: expected

unforgettable *adj* **memorable**, remarkable, treasured, cherished, haunting *Opposite*: unremarkable

unforgivable *adj* **unpardonable**, inexcusable, indefensible, unjustifiable, intolerable *Opposite*: understandable

unforgiving *adj* **1 intolerant**, merciless, pitiless, remorseless, vindictive *Opposite*: tolerant **2 demanding**, exacting, taxing, challenging, hard *Opposite*: easy

unformed *adj* **1 shapeless**, formless, indistinct, imprecise, amorphous *Opposite*: distinct **2 undeveloped**, immature, green, callow, underdeveloped *Opposite*: mature

unformulated *adj* **vague**, indistinct, unclear, hazy, nebulous *Opposite*: clear

unforthcoming *adj* **uncommunicative**, reticent, taciturn, standoffish, distant *Opposite*: voluble

unfortunate *adj* **1 unlucky**, luckless, unsuccessful, unhappy, ill-fated *Opposite*: lucky **2 disastrous**, calamitous, doomed, hopeless, fateful *Opposite*: fortunate **3 inappropriate**, inopportune, ill-timed, tactless, untimely *Opposite*: timely ■ *n* **wretch**, underdog, loser, lame duck, weakling

unfortunately *adv* **1 unluckily**, unhappily, regrettably, sadly, alas *Opposite*: fortunately **2 inappropriately**, inopportunely, tactlessly, ill-advisedly, regrettably *Opposite*: appropriately

unfounded *adj* **groundless**, unsupported, baseless, unsubstantiated, speculative *Opposite*: proven

unfreeze *v* **relax**, rescind, repeal, release, liberate *Opposite*: freeze

unfrequented *adj* **lonely**, neglected, isolated, quiet, desolate *Opposite*: busy

unfriendliness *n* **aloofness**, surliness, coldness, coolness, frostiness *Opposite*: friendliness

unfriendly *adj* **1 aloof**, distant, surly, cold, frosty *Opposite*: friendly **2 unfavourable**, ill-disposed, inimical, hostile, inauspicious *Opposite*: well-disposed

unfruitful *adj* **1 unsuccessful**, unprofitable, unproductive, unrewarding, fruitless *Opposite*: profitable **2 infertile**, sterile, barren, bare, fruitless *Opposite*: fertile

unfurl *v* **open out**, open up, unfold, spread out, expand *Opposite*: fold up

unfurnished *adj* **bare**, empty, unequipped, unfitted *Opposite*: furnished

unfussy *adj* **understated**, simple, uncomplicated, modest, plain *Opposite*: fussy

ungainliness *n* **1 gracelessness**, awkwardness, clumsiness, inelegance, gaucheness *Opposite*: gracefulness **2 awkwardness**, unwieldiness, cumbersomeness, heaviness, clumsiness *Opposite*: convenience

ungainly *adj* **1 graceless**, awkward, clumsy, inelegant, ungraceful *Opposite*: graceful **2 awkward**, unwieldy, cumbersome, inconvenient, heavy *Opposite*: convenient

ungenerous *adj* **1 miserly**, tightfisted, parsimonious, mean, grudging *Opposite*: generous **2 mean-spirited**, nasty, mean, unkind, cruel *Opposite*: kind

unglued *adj* **1 separated**, detached, parted, disconnected, divided *Opposite*: whole **2** (*infml*) **upset**, angry, disconcerted, hysterical, unnerved *Opposite*: calm

ungodly *adj* **1 impious**, irreligious, irreverent, blasphemous, profane *Opposite*: pious **2 wicked**, sinful, immoral, corrupt, depraved *Opposite*: virtuous **3** (*infml*) **unreasonable**, unearthly, late, unsocial, ridiculous *Opposite*: reasonable

ungovernable *adj* **uncontrollable**, out of control, unmanageable, unruly, anarchic *Opposite*: controllable

ungraceful *adj* **1 clumsy**, ungainly, graceless, uncoordinated, lumbering *Opposite*: elegant **2 rude**, impolite, discourteous, gruff, brusque *Opposite*: polite

ungracious *adj* **ill-mannered**, discourteous, rude, impolite, bad-mannered *Opposite*: gracious

ungrateful *adj* **1 unappreciative**, thankless, churlish, unmindful, ungracious *Opposite*: grateful **2 unpleasant**, unrewarding, thankless, unsatisfying *Opposite*: rewarding

ungratefully *adv* **unappreciatively**, churlishly, thanklessly, ungraciously *Opposite*: gratefully

ungratefulness *n* **unappreciativeness**, ingratitude, churlishness, thanklessness, ungraciousness *Opposite*: gratitude

unguarded *adj* **1 unprotected**, undefended, unshielded, unfortified, defenceless *Opposite*: guarded **2 unwary**, careless, indiscreet, thoughtless, imprudent *Opposite*: guarded

unguent *n* **ointment**, salve, balm, oil, unction

unhampered *adj* **unrestricted**, unimpeded, unhindered, unconstrained, free *Opposite*: restricted

unhappily *adv* **1 sadly**, miserably, discontentedly, despondently, dejectedly *Opposite*: happily **2 unfortunately**, unluckily, regrettably, alas, sadly *Opposite*: luckily

unhappiness *n* **sadness**, sorrow, grief, misery, discontent *Opposite*: happiness

unhappy *adj* **1 sad**, miserable, discontented, despondent, dejected *Opposite*: happy **2 unfortunate**, ill-fated, hopeless, doomed, fateful *Opposite*: fortunate **3 inappropriate**,

ill-chosen, infelicitous, tactless, unfortunate *Opposite*: well-chosen **4 displeased**, annoyed, upset, angry, disappointed *Opposite*: pleased

unharmed *adj* **uninjured**, unhurt, unscathed, undamaged, unscratched *Opposite*: harmed

unhealthy *adj* **1 sick**, unfit, out of condition, out of shape, sickly *Opposite*: well **2 harmful**, detrimental, injurious, damaging, unwholesome *Opposite*: healthy **3 corrupt**, unwholesome, morbid, unnatural, ghoulish *Opposite*: wholesome

unheard *adj* **unheeded**, disregarded, ignored, overlooked, unnoticed

unheard-of *adj* **1 unknown**, unfamiliar, new, obscure, undiscovered *Opposite*: well-known **2 unprecedented**, exceptional, extraordinary, novel, unusual *Opposite*: ordinary **3 offensive**, rude, disgusting, repulsive, shocking *Opposite*: inoffensive

unhelpful *adj* **1 uncooperative**, contrary, awkward, unaccommodating, obstructive *Opposite*: helpful **2 useless**, unconstructive, impractical, unnecessary, negative *Opposite*: useful

unhelpfulness *n* **1 uncooperativeness**, unsupportiveness, contrariness, impracticality *Opposite*: helpfulness **2 uselessness**, negativity, pointlessness, needlessness, worthlessness *Opposite*: usefulness

unhesitating *adj* **prompt**, unreserved, wholehearted, confident, forthright *Opposite*: tentative

unhindered *adj* **unimpeded**, unconstrained, unrestricted, unobstructed, unchecked

unhinge *v* **unbalance**, derange, madden, drive insane, disturb

unhinged *adj* **unbalanced**, deranged, disturbed, irrational, crackers (*infml*) *Opposite*: sane

unhitch *v* **unfasten**, untie, undo, uncouple, detach *Opposite*: fasten

unholy *adj* **1 unconsecrated**, unhallowed, unblessed, profane, secular *Opposite*: consecrated **2 ungodly**, blasphemous, secular, immoral, evil *Opposite*: holy **3 outrageous**, ungodly, disgraceful, scandalous, shocking

unhook *v* **undo**, release, uncouple, detach, disengage *Opposite*: hook

unhoped-for *adj* **unexpected**, unanticipated, surprising, undreamed-of, unforeseen *Opposite*: expected

unhopeful *adj* **doubtful**, despondent, gloomy, dejected, pessimistic *Opposite*: hopeful

unhurried *adj* **slow**, easygoing, dawdling, calm, deliberate *Opposite*: hurried

unhurt *adj* **uninjured**, unharmed, undamaged, unscathed, safe *Opposite*: hurt

unhygienic *adj* **insanitary**, unclean, polluted, unhealthy, foul *Opposite*: hygienic

unidentified *adj* **nameless**, anonymous, faceless, unnamed, unknown *Opposite*: known

unidentified flying object *see* **UFO**

unification *n* **amalgamation**, union, merger, alliance, association *Opposite*: split

unified *adj* **united**, combined, amalgamated, incorporated, integrated *Opposite*: disjointed

uniform *n* **livery**, dress, costume, garb, attire *(fml) Opposite*: mufti ▪ *adj* **1 unchanging**, unvarying, even, unbroken, undeviating *Opposite*: uneven **2 consistent**, standardized, homogeneous, harmonized, regular *Opposite*: inconsistent **3 identical**, like, alike, similar, equal *Opposite*: different

uniformity *n* **consistency**, regularity, standardization, homogeneity, evenness *Opposite*: inconsistency

unify *v* **unite**, join, amalgamate, merge, combine *Opposite*: separate

unilateral *adj* **one-sided**, independent, autonomous, autarchic, individual *Opposite*: joint

unimaginable *adj* **inconceivable**, unbelievable, incredible, unthinkable, indescribable *Opposite*: conceivable

unimaginative *adj* **dull**, boring, insipid, bland, uninspired *Opposite*: imaginative

unimpaired *adj* **undamaged**, unaffected, unhindered, perfect, operational *Opposite*: impaired

unimpassioned *adj* **unemotional**, cool, detached, sober, calm *Opposite*: impassioned

unimpeachable *adj* **faultless**, flawless, impeccable, irreproachable, blameless *Opposite*: blameworthy

unimpeded *adj* **without hindrance**, unhindered, unhampered, unchecked, unconstrained *Opposite*: hindered

unimportance *n* **insignificance**, inconsequentiality, irrelevance, slightness, triviality *Opposite*: importance

unimportant *adj* **inconsequential**, slight, insignificant, trivial, trifling *Opposite*: important

unimpressed *adj* **unenthusiastic**, uninspired, unconvinced, unmoved, indifferent *Opposite*: enthusiastic

unimpressive *adj* **uninspiring**, indifferent, mediocre, unimposing, insignificant *Opposite*: impressive

unimproved *adj* **unchanged**, unaltered, natural, original, unworked *Opposite*: improved

unincorporated *adj* **independent**, separate, distinct, stand-alone, autonomous *Opposite*: incorporated

unindustrialized *adj* **undeveloped**, farming, agricultural, rural *Opposite*: industrialized

uninformative *adj* **unhelpful**, vague, uncommunicative, unproductive, useless *Opposite*: informative

uninformed *adj* **ignorant**, uneducated, unaware, unacquainted, unfamiliar *Opposite*: informed

uninhabitable *adj* **derelict**, dilapidated, ramshackle, tumbledown, run-down *Opposite*: habitable

uninhabited *adj* **unoccupied**, unpopulated, deserted, abandoned, unpeopled *Opposite*: inhabited

uninhibited *adj* **1 unrestrained**, outgoing, unconstrained, candid, open *Opposite*: shy **2 wanton**, abandoned, dissolute, licentious, immodest *Opposite*: restrained

uninitiated *adj* **inexperienced**, unskilled, unversed, unqualified, untrained *Opposite*: experienced

uninjured *adj* **unhurt**, unharmed, undamaged, intact, safe *Opposite*: hurt

uninspired *adj* **bland**, insipid, boring, dull, unimaginative *Opposite*: inspired

uninspiring *adj* **dull**, lacklustre, lifeless, boring, tame *Opposite*: inspiring

uninstructed *adj* **untaught**, unschooled, uneducated, uninformed, untutored *Opposite*: educated

unintelligent *adj* **stupid**, foolish, silly, inane, daft *(infml) Opposite*: clever

unintelligible *adj* **incomprehensible**, inarticulate, incoherent, garbled, jumbled *Opposite*: intelligible

unintended *see* **unintentional**

unintentional *adj* **accidental**, inadvertent, unplanned, chance, involuntary *Opposite*: intentional

uninterested *adj* **indifferent**, apathetic, blasé, impassive, unconcerned *Opposite*: concerned

uninteresting *adj* **boring**, dull, unexciting, tedious, monotonous *Opposite*: interesting

uninterrupted *adj* **continuous**, continual, nonstop, incessant, never-ending *Opposite*: sporadic

uninvited *adj* **unwelcome**, unwanted, undesirable, unsought, unsolicited *Opposite*: welcome

uninviting *adj* **unappealing**, unattractive, bleak, unpalatable, disgusting *Opposite*: attractive

uninvolved *adj* **1 detached**, removed, aloof, unconcerned, indifferent *Opposite*: involved **2 uncomplicated**, straightforward, easy, simple, plain *Opposite*: convoluted **3 single**, footloose and fancy free, unmarried, unattached, free *Opposite*: attached *(infml)*

union *n* **1 amalgamation**, combination, blending, coming together, joining together *Opposite*: separation **2 coalition**, alliance, association, confederacy, confederation **3 agreement**, harmony, accord, unity, unison *Opposite*: discord **4 marriage**, matrimony, wedlock, bond, wedding *Opposite*: divorce

unique *adj* **sole**, single, one-off, exclusive, exceptional *Opposite*: common

uniqueness *n* **individuality**, exclusivity, exceptionality, inimitability, distinctiveness *Opposite*: commonness

unison *n* **agreement**, harmony, accord, unity, union *Opposite*: discord

unit *n* **1 component**, element, part, piece, item **2 corps**, detachment, group, company, troop

unite *v* **1 join**, fuse, mix, bond, come together *Opposite*: separate **2 marry**, wed, hitch, bond, tie

united *adj* **joint**, combined, amalgamated, unified, cohesive *Opposite*: separated

unitize *v* **1 bring together**, unite, combine, centralize, condense *Opposite*: separate **2 separate**, take apart, break up, divide up, disassemble *Opposite*: join

unity *n* **agreement**, harmony, accord, unison, union *Opposite*: disarray

universal *adj* **worldwide**, widespread, general, common, collective *Opposite*: local. *See* COMPARE AND CONTRAST *at* **widespread**.

universalism *n* **breadth**, amplitude, diversity, gamut, spectrum

universe *n* **cosmos**, world, creation, life, space

university *n* **institution of higher education**, college, academia, academy, academe *(fml)*

unjust *adj* **unfair**, undue, undeserved, unmerited, unwarranted *Opposite*: just

unjustifiable *adj* **indefensible**, unwarrantable, inexcusable, unforgivable, unpardonable *Opposite*: justifiable

unjustified *adj* **unfounded**, baseless, unfair, unwarranted, unpardonable *Opposite*: justified

unjustly *adv* **unfairly**, unreasonably, partially, one-sidedly, discriminatorily *Opposite*: fairly

unkempt *adj* **dishevelled**, untidy, rumpled, tousled, messy *Opposite*: tidy

unkind *adj* **nasty**, mean, cruel, callous, heartless *Opposite*: kind

unkindness *n* **nastiness**, meanness, cruelty, callousness, heartlessness *Opposite*: kindness

unknot *v* **untie**, undo, unpick, disentangle, unstitch *Opposite*: knot

unknowable *adj* **incomprehensible**, enigmatic, mysterious, indecipherable, arcane *Opposite*: comprehensible

unknowing *adj* **1 unwitting**, ingenuous, naive, innocent, ignorant *Opposite*: knowing **2 unintentional**, accidental, inadvertent, unintended, unplanned *Opposite*: deliberate

unknown *adj* **1 unidentified**, indefinite, mysterious, unheard of, nameless *Opposite*: known **2 unfamiliar**, strange, foreign, alien, undiscovered *Opposite*: familiar ■ *n* **nonentity**, nobody, newcomer, beginner, stranger *Opposite*: celebrity

unlaboured *adj* **effortless**, easy, painless, trouble-free, carefree *Opposite*: laboured

unlace *v* **undo**, unfasten, unthread, unknot, untie *Opposite*: lace

unlatch *v* **open**, undo, unfasten, unlock, unbolt *Opposite*: latch

unlawful *adj* **illegal**, illicit, illegitimate, wrongful, nonlegal *Opposite*: lawful

---

COMPARE AND CONTRAST CORE MEANING: not in accordance with laws or rules

unlawful not permitted by the law or by the rules of an organization or religion, or not recognized as valid by those laws or rules; **illegal** contravening a specific written statute, rule, or law, especially a criminal law; **illicit** not permitted by the law, suggesting especially that something is considered morally wrong or unacceptable; **wrongful** (often used in civil lawsuits) unjust, unfair, or against conscience, but not punishable by criminal law; **nonlegal** not established or affected under common law or legislation.

---

unlearned *adj* **uneducated**, illiterate, unschooled, unlettered, untutored *Opposite*: educated

unleash *v* **set free**, give a free rein to, allow to run free, allow to run riot, uncheck *Opposite*: control

unless *prep* **if not**, if, except, save, but for

unlettered *adj* **uneducated**, illiterate, unschooled, untaught, untutored *Opposite*: educated

unlicensed *adj* **uninhibited**, unrestricted, unrestrained, abandoned, immoral *Opposite*: inhibited

unlike *adj* **different**, dissimilar, nothing like, distinct, contrasting *Opposite*: like

unlikelihood *n* **improbability**, doubtfulness, implausibility, dubiousness, questionability *Opposite*: likelihood

unlikely *adj* **1 improbable**, doubtful, dubious, questionable *Opposite*: likely **2 implausible**, dubious, doubtful, suspect, incongruous *Opposite*: credible

unlimited *adj* **limitless**, infinite, unrestricted, unrestrained, boundless *Opposite*: limited

unlisted *adj* **private**, ex-directory, unpublished, confidential, secret *Opposite*: listed

unlit *adj* **dark**, darkened, dim, pitch-black, murky *Opposite*: bright

unload *v* **unpack**, drop off, drop, deliver, empty *Opposite*: load

unlock *v* **1 undo**, release, unchain, open, unbolt *Opposite*: lock **2 solve**, reveal, answer, expose, get to the bottom of

unlooked-for *adj* **unexpected**, undreamed-of, unanticipated, uninvited, unsolicited *Opposite*: expected

unloose *v* **set free**, release, let out, unleash, let off the lead *Opposite*: tie up

unlovely *adj* **unattractive**, objectionable, obnoxious, nasty, ugly *Opposite*: attractive

unluckiness *n* **bad luck**, misfortune, ill luck, mishap *Opposite*: luck

unlucky *adj* **1 unsuccessful**, wretched, hapless,

unfortunate, tragic *Opposite*: lucky **2 inauspicious**, fateful, ill-fated, doomed, star-crossed *Opposite*: fortunate

unmake *v* **1 undo**, take apart, reverse, deconstruct, dismantle *Opposite*: put back **2 demote**, fire, sack, replace, expel

unmanageable *adj* **uncontrollable**, unruly, riotous, out of control, out of hand *Opposite*: manageable

unmanliness *n* **weakness**, cowardliness, timidity, fearfulness, apprehension *Opposite*: manliness

unmanly *adj* **weak**, cowardly, timid, fearful, apprehensive *Opposite*: manly

unmannered *adj* **1 rude**, boorish, impolite, crude, coarse *Opposite*: well-mannered **2 unaffected**, easy, natural, genuine, simple *Opposite*: affected

unmannerly *adj* **rude**, impolite, ill-mannered, bad-mannered, disrespectful *Opposite*: polite

unmarked *adj* **spotless**, unblemished, pristine, immaculate, perfect *Opposite*: marked

unmarried *adj* **single**, unattached, bachelor, spinster, free *Opposite*: married

unmask *v* **expose**, blow the whistle on, reveal, unveil, debunk *Opposite*: conceal

unmatched *adj* **supreme**, matchless, unrivalled, consummate, unparalleled

unmeant *adj* **unintended**, accidental, inadvertent, unplanned, unintentional *Opposite*: deliberate

unmentionable *adj* **taboo**, offensive, prohibited, forbidden, restricted *Opposite*: respectable ■ *n* **taboo**, no-go area, anathema, no-no (*infml*)

unmerciful *adj* **1 cruel**, severe, harsh, hard, unsparing *Opposite*: merciful **2 excessive**, unrelenting, extreme, remorseless, unremitting

unmerited *adj* **undeserved**, unwarranted, unjustified, unearned, unjust *Opposite*: fair

unmindful *adj* **unaware**, oblivious, unconscious, careless, heedless *Opposite*: mindful

unmistakable *adj* **obvious**, definite, distinctive, unambiguous, unique *Opposite*: ambiguous

unmitigated *adj* **sheer**, pure, absolute, unadulterated, unalloyed

unmodified *adj* **original**, unchanged, basic, untouched *Opposite*: modified

unmotivated *adj* **apathetic**, unenthusiastic, indifferent, shiftless, uninterested *Opposite*: keen

unmovable *adj* **inflexible**, rigid, stubborn, obstinate, obdurate *Opposite*: flexible

unmoved *adj* **indifferent**, unaffected, unresponsive, insensitive, impassive *Opposite*: touched. *See* COMPARE AND CONTRAST *at* **impassive**.

unmoving *adj* **still**, motionless, inactive, lifeless, inert *Opposite*: moving

unmusical *adj* **unmelodic**, dissonant, discordant, jarring, harsh *Opposite*: musical

unnamed *adj* **unidentified**, anonymous, unspecified, nameless, unknown *Opposite*: named

unnatural *adj* **1 abnormal**, aberrant, atypical, unusual, perverted *Opposite*: normal **2 strange**, odd, peculiar, atypical, irregular *Opposite*: typical **3 supernatural**, weird, bizarre, paranormal, uncanny *Opposite*: ordinary **4 artificial**, contrived, affected, insincere, pretend *Opposite*: natural

unnecessary *adj* **needless**, pointless, redundant, superfluous, gratuitous *Opposite*: necessary

unneeded *adj* **extra**, superfluous, unnecessary, surplus, unwanted *Opposite*: necessary

unnerve *v* **alarm**, frighten, scare, upset, nonplus *Opposite*: calm

unnerved *adj* **frightened**, scared, alarmed, unsettled, anxious *Opposite*: calm

unnerving *adj* **frightening**, unsettling, demoralizing, intimidating, upsetting *Opposite*: comforting

unnoticeable *adj* **invisible**, imperceptible, unremarkable, inconspicuous, hidden *Opposite*: conspicuous

unnoticed *adj* **unobserved**, overlooked, ignored, unseen, disregarded

unnumbered *adj* **1 numberless**, numerous, myriad, countless, many *Opposite*: few **2 unidentified**, unmarked, untagged, uncounted

unobjectionable *adj* **inoffensive**, agreeable, pleasant, innocuous, harmless *Opposite*: unpleasant

unobservant *adj* **inattentive**, unperceptive, incurious, negligent, careless *Opposite*: observant

unobserved *adj* **unnoticed**, ignored, overlooked, unseen, disregarded *Opposite*: evident

unobstructed *adj* **clear**, free, unhindered, passable, open *Opposite*: barred

unobtainable *adj* **unavailable**, unattainable, inaccessible, out of stock *Opposite*: available

unobtrusive *adj* **inconspicuous**, unremarkable, modest, bland, discreet *Opposite*: conspicuous

unoccupied *adj* **1 inactive**, at a loose end, idle, unemployed, out of work *Opposite*: busy **2 vacant**, free, untenanted, empty, disused *Opposite*: occupied. *See* COMPARE AND CONTRAST *at* **vacant**.

unofficial *adj* **unauthorized**, unsanctioned, informal, unendorsed, private *Opposite*: official

unopposed *adj* **unchallenged**, unobstructed, unrestricted, unhampered, unimpeded *Opposite*: challenged

unorganized *adj* **1 chaotic**, disorganized,

muddled, messy, disorderly *Opposite*: well-organized **2 careless**, disorganized, unprepared, sloppy, slapdash *Opposite*: methodical

unoriginal *adj* derivative, copied, imitative, clichéd, banal *Opposite*: original

unoriginality *n* derivativeness, triteness, staleness, imitativeness, banality *Opposite*: originality

unorthodox *adj* unconventional, nonconformist, untraditional, unusual, eccentric *Opposite*: orthodox

unpack *v* unload, take out, empty, undo, empty out *Opposite*: pack up

unpaid *adj* **1** unsettled, outstanding, overdue, due, owed *Opposite*: paid **2 voluntary**, amateur, honorary, free *Opposite*: paid

unpalatable *adj* **1** inedible, indigestible, disgusting, revolting, foul-tasting *Opposite*: tasty **2 unacceptable**, unpleasant, painful, disagreeable, harsh *Opposite*: acceptable

unparalleled *adj* unmatched, supreme, matchless, beyond compare, unequalled *Opposite*: mediocre

unpardonable *adj* unforgivable, indefensible, inexcusable, deplorable, reprehensible *Opposite*: understandable

unpeg *v* undo, unfasten, untie, detach, release *Opposite*: fasten

unperceptive *adj* undiscerning, unobservant, insensitive, obtuse, indiscriminate *Opposite*: perceptive

unperturbed *adj* calm, at peace, tranquil, collected, composed *Opposite*: anxious

unpick *v* unravel, untangle, untie, undo, disentangle

unplanned *adj* **1** unintended, accidental, unintentional, unexpected, inadvertent *Opposite*: planned **2 spontaneous**, impromptu, ad hoc, unprepared, spur-of-the-moment *Opposite*: planned

unpleasant *adj* **1** disagreeable, nasty, unlikable, horrible, horrid *Opposite*: pleasant **2 unfriendly**, hostile, cold, unkind, spiteful *Opposite*: friendly

unpleasantness *n* **1** disagreeableness, nastiness, horribleness, horridness, distastefulness *Opposite*: pleasantness **2 ill feeling**, trouble, fuss, bother, upset *Opposite*: harmony **3 unfriendliness**, spitefulness, nastiness, unkindness, offensiveness *Opposite*: friendliness **4 disagreement**, conflict, argument, quarrel, dispute *Opposite*: agreement

unplug *v* **1** unblock, clear, free, clean, release **2 disconnect**, switch off, undo, take out, remove *Opposite*: plug in

unplumbed *adj* mysterious, unfathomable, enigmatic, unexplored, unknowable *Opposite*: known

unpolluted *adj* clean, pure, uncontaminated, untainted, fresh *Opposite*: contaminated

unpopular *adj* disliked, hated, out of favour,

shunned, detested *Opposite*: popular

unpopulated *adj* abandoned, deserted, depopulated, uninhabited, empty *Opposite*: overcrowded

unpractised *adj* inexperienced, unrehearsed, unschooled, untrained, unfamiliar *Opposite*: practised

unprecedented *adj* unparalleled, extraordinary, record, first-time, unique *Opposite*: ordinary

unpredictability *n* randomness, impulsiveness, volatility, fickleness, changeableness *Opposite*: predictability

unpredictable *adj* random, erratic, changeable, impulsive, volatile *Opposite*: predictable

unpredicted *adj* surprising, unexpected, shocking, astonishing, unforeseen *Opposite*: predicted

unprejudiced *adj* fair, neutral, tolerant, unbiased, evenhanded *Opposite*: biased

unpremeditated *adj* unplanned, unintended, impulsive, spur-of-the-moment, sudden *Opposite*: premeditated

unprepared *adj* **1** unready, unsuspecting, ill-equipped, unqualified, untrained *Opposite*: prepared **2 improvised**, unrehearsed, ad hoc, impromptu, spontaneous *Opposite*: rehearsed

unprepossessing *adj* ugly, unattractive, plain, unpleasant, uninviting *Opposite*: attractive

unpretentious *adj* modest, unassuming, unaffected, natural, self-effacing *Opposite*: pretentious

unpretentiousness *n* modesty, humility, humbleness, simplicity, artlessness *Opposite*: grandiosity

unprincipled *adj* dishonest, corrupt, amoral, immoral, devious *Opposite*: honest

unprintable *adj* rude, foul, offensive, shocking, coarse *Opposite*: inoffensive

unproblematic *adj* easy, smooth, straightforward, trouble-free, simple *Opposite*: tricky

unprocessed *adj* natural, whole, unrefined, untreated, crude

unproductive *adj* **1** fruitless, infertile, barren, sterile, blocked *Opposite*: fertile **2 idle**, lazy, slow, wasteful, inefficient *Opposite*: productive

unprofessional *adj* **1** unethical, unprincipled, immoral, dishonourable, wrong *Opposite*: ethical **2 amateurish**, amateur, slack, inexpert, shoddy *Opposite*: expert

unprofitable *adj* **1** lossmaking, unsuccessful, running at a loss, nonpaying, insolvent *Opposite*: profitable **2 unhelpful**, useless, pointless, futile, fruitless *Opposite*: helpful

unpromising *adj* gloomy, bleak, discouraging, doubtful, off-putting *Opposite*: encouraging

unprompted *adj* spontaneous, unforced, impulsive, off your own bat *(infml)*, willing *Opposite*: forced

unpronounceable adj unsayable, difficult, impossible

unpronounced adj silent, mute, unvoiced, unspoken, unsaid Opposite: voiced

unprotected adj defenceless, undefended, open to attack, insecure, vulnerable Opposite: secure

unproven adj unverified, unconfirmed, untried, untested, undocumented Opposite: proven

unprovoked adj gratuitous, wanton, senseless, motiveless, uncalled-for Opposite: provoked

unqualified adj 1 untrained, unprofessional, ill-equipped, inexpert, untaught Opposite: trained 2 definite, unreserved, absolute, complete, utter Opposite: qualified

unquantifiable adj immeasurable, uncountable, unidentifiable, indefinable, indeterminate Opposite: quantifiable

unquestionable adj indisputable, incontestable, absolute, undeniable, categorical Opposite: arguable

unquestioned adj undisputed, accepted, unchallenged, automatic, logical Opposite: questionable

unquestioning adj unthinking, wholehearted, obedient, absolute, automatic Opposite: reluctant

unquiet adj 1 noisy, turbulent, loud, rowdy, boisterous Opposite: quiet 2 anxious, unsettled, restless, agitated, fidgety Opposite: calm

unravel v 1 undo, untie, unknot, loosen, disentangle Opposite: tie 2 solve, clear up, resolve, sort out, get to the bottom of 3 fail, go wrong, fall apart, collapse, crumble Opposite: come together

unreadable adj 1 illegible, incomprehensible, indecipherable, scrawled, scribbled Opposite: legible 2 impenetrable, dense, tedious, turgid, boring Opposite: readable 3 blank, expressionless, impassive, poker-faced, inscrutable

unreal adj 1 false, artificial, imitation, fake, pretend Opposite: genuine 2 imaginary, dreamlike, illusory, fantastic, weird Opposite: real

unrealistic adj impractical, idealistic, impracticable, improbable, unlikely Opposite: practical

unreality n 1 strangeness, incongruity, oddness, weirdness, abnormality Opposite: reality 2 fantasy, delusion, fancy, self-delusion, illusion Opposite: reality

unreasonable adj 1 irrational, perverse, arbitrary, unreasoning, awkward Opposite: rational 2 excessive, exorbitant, immoderate, extravagant, extreme Opposite: reasonable

unreasonableness n 1 irrationality, arbitrariness, awkwardness, perverseness, difficultness Opposite: rationality 2 excessiveness, injustice, exorbitance, extrav-

agance, unfairness Opposite: reasonableness

unreceptive adj disinclined, ill-disposed, unwilling, resistant, unteachable Opposite: receptive

unreconstructed adj 1 old-fashioned, unchanging, unrepentant, dyed-in-the-wool, traditional 2 unchanged, unaltered, unvaried, unmodified, original

unrefined adj 1 unprocessed, untreated, raw, crude, untouched Opposite: refined 2 vulgar, unsophisticated, uncultured, crude, coarse Opposite: sophisticated

unreformed adj unapologetic, unrepentant, dyed-in-the-wool, inveterate, diehard Opposite: reformed

unrehearsed adj unprepared, impromptu, off-the-cuff, spontaneous, impulsive Opposite: prepared

unrelated adj 1 unconnected, separate, distinct, dissimilar, disparate Opposite: linked 2 irrelevant, beside the point, extraneous, unconnected, impertinent (fml) Opposite: relevant

unrelenting adj remorseless, relentless, insistent, merciless, pitiless Opposite: yielding

unreliability n 1 undependability, untrustworthiness, unpredictability, changeableness, irregularity Opposite: dependability 2 inaccuracy, fallibility, untrustworthiness, flimsiness, dubiousness Opposite: reliability

unreliable adj 1 undependable, fly-by-night, variable, unpredictable, changeable Opposite: dependable 2 inaccurate, fallacious, flimsy, threadbare, untrue Opposite: reliable

unrelieved adj constant, unbroken, chronic, unmitigated, unalleviated Opposite: intermittent

unremarkable adj ordinary, everyday, commonplace, average, typical Opposite: remarkable

unremitting adj constant, incessant, continuous, chronic, unrelenting Opposite: intermittent

unremorseful adj unrepentant, unapologetic, impenitent, unashamed, shameless Opposite: apologetic

unrepentant adj impenitent, unapologetic, unashamed, shameless, unremorseful Opposite: remorseful

unreserved adj 1 unqualified, total, complete, utter, absolute Opposite: qualified 2 open, demonstrative, candid, frank, extrovert Opposite: reserved

unresolved adj unsettled, unanswered, uncertain, vague, pending Opposite: settled

unresponsive adj unfeeling, insensitive, indifferent, impassive, uncaring Opposite: responsive

unresponsiveness n unfeelingness, insensitivity, indifference, impassiveness, coldness Opposite: responsiveness

unrest n 1 **discontent**, turbulence, strife, conflict, disturbance *Opposite*: calm 2 **anxiousness**, anxiety, disquiet, worry, uneasiness *Opposite*: peace

unrestrained adj **uncontrolled**, wild, unrestricted, abandoned, uninhibited *Opposite*: restrained

unrestricted adj **open**, unobstructed, unhindered, unlimited, unhampered *Opposite*: restricted

unrevealed adj **secret**, hidden, unknown, mysterious, clandestine *Opposite*: known

unrewarding adj **thankless**, fruitless, unfulfilling, unsatisfactory, difficult *Opposite*: satisfying

unrighteous adj 1 **sinful**, wicked, evil, irreligious, unholy *Opposite*: righteous 2 **unjust**, unfair, ill-deserved, unkind, wrong *Opposite*: just

unripe adj **immature**, green, young, fresh, undeveloped *Opposite*: ripe

unrivalled adj **unequalled**, unique, singular, unsurpassed, extraordinary *Opposite*: ordinary

unroll v **open**, unfurl, stretch out, spread out, unfold *Opposite*: roll up

unruffled adj **calm**, tranquil, unmoved, in control, at ease *Opposite*: flustered

unruliness n **boisterousness**, disruptiveness, disorderliness, rowdiness, recalcitrance *Opposite*: orderliness

unruly adj **boisterous**, disruptive, disorderly, rowdy, wild *Opposite*: orderly

---

COMPARE AND CONTRAST CORE MEANING: not submitting to control

unruly boisterous, disruptive, and difficult to control or discipline; **intractable** (fml) strongwilled and rebellious, refusing to be controlled or to submit to discipline; **recalcitrant** obstinate and defiant in refusing to submit to discipline or control; **obstreperous** noisy, difficult to control, and uncooperative; **wilful** stubbornly disregarding the opinions or advice of others; **wild** showing a general lack of control or restraint; **wayward** disobedient and uncontrollable.

---

unrushed adj **unhurried**, slow, leisurely, calm, gentle *Opposite*: hurried

unsafe adj **dangerous**, insecure, hazardous, risky, perilous *Opposite*: secure

unsaid adj **tacit**, unspoken, implicit, silent, unstated *Opposite*: spoken

unsatisfactory adj **inadequate**, unacceptable, substandard, disappointing, insufficient *Opposite*: acceptable

unsatisfied adj **displeased**, discontented, unhappy, unfulfilled, disgruntled *Opposite*: pleased

unsavoury adj 1 **unpleasant**, disagreeable, revolting, disgusting, repellent *Opposite*: pleasant 2 **immoral**, unpleasant, villainous, shady, unacceptable *Opposite*: wholesome

unscathed adj **unharmed**, intact, unhurt, untouched, safe *Opposite*: injured

unschooled adj **uneducated**, untaught, untutored, untrained, illiterate *Opposite*: educated

unscientific adj **intuitive**, instinctive, irrational, unempirical, seat-of-the-pants (infml) *Opposite*: systematic

unscramble v **decode**, sort out, decipher, work out, make out *Opposite*: encode

unscrew v **take off**, remove, detach, loosen, undo *Opposite*: tighten

unscripted adj **unplanned**, unexpected, impromptu, impulsive, unscheduled

unscrupulous adj **dishonest**, unprincipled, corrupt, immoral, deceitful *Opposite*: honest

unscrupulousness n **dishonesty**, corruptness, crookedness, immorality, deviousness *Opposite*: honesty

unseal v **open**, uncap, unstop, break open, unscrew *Opposite*: seal

unseasonable adj 1 **unusual**, abnormal, unexpected, odd, strange *Opposite*: seasonable 2 **untimely**, inopportune, ill-timed, inconvenient, unwelcome *Opposite*: seasonable

unseat v **depose**, oust, overthrow, dethrone, remove *Opposite*: enthrone (fml)

unseemliness n **impropriety**, tastelessness, uncouthness, loutishness, rudeness *Opposite*: propriety

unseemly adj **inappropriate**, rude, uncouth, improper, indecorous *Opposite*: proper

unseen adj **hidden**, unnoticed, unobserved, invisible, concealed *Opposite*: noticeable

unselective adj **indiscriminating**, undiscerning, blanket, haphazard, random *Opposite*: discerning

unselfish adj **selfless**, generous, noble, magnanimous, liberal *Opposite*: selfish

unselfishness n **selflessness**, generosity, magnanimity, kindness, consideration *Opposite*: selfishness

unsentimental adj **unemotional**, impassive, unfeeling, hard-bitten, tough *Opposite*: sentimental

unsettle v **worry**, disturb, upset, disconcert, unnerve *Opposite*: soothe

unsettled adj 1 **anxious**, worried, disturbed, upset, disconcerted *Opposite*: calm 2 **changeable**, variable, unpredictable, uncertain, changing *Opposite*: settled 3 **undecided**, unresolved, undetermined, open-ended, arguable *Opposite*: decided

unsettling adj **upsetting**, worrying, disturbing, disconcerting, disquieting *Opposite*: soothing

unshackle v **release**, unchain, let loose, set free, liberate *Opposite*: chain

unshakable adj **steadfast**, resolute, constant, unwavering, entrenched *Opposite*: wavering

unshaped adj unformed, formless, shapeless, amorphous, indistinct Opposite: shaped

unsheathe v draw, pull, remove, extract, uncover

unsightliness n ugliness, hideousness, horridness, unpleasantness, nastiness Opposite: attractiveness

unsightly adj unattractive, ugly, hideous, unpleasant, unprepossessing Opposite: attractive. See COMPARE AND CONTRAST at **unattractive**.

unskilful adj inept, unskilled, untrained, untalented, incompetent Opposite: skilful

unskilled adj inexpert, amateurish, untrained, uneducated, unqualified Opposite: trained

unsmiling adj stern, severe, serious, dour, grim-faced Opposite: cordial

unsnag v disentangle, clear, free, untangle, release Opposite: snag

unsnarl v disentangle, clear, free, untangle, unblock Opposite: tangle

unsociable adj unfriendly, antisocial, aloof, shy, standoffish Opposite: friendly

unsolicited adj unwelcome, unwanted, uninvited, unsought, spontaneous Opposite: requested

unsolvable adj impenetrable, unknowable, impossible, unfathomable, insoluble Opposite: soluble

unsolved adj unexplained, unresolved, mysterious, baffling Opposite: resolved

unsophisticated adj 1 unworldly, naive, inexperienced, ingenuous, simple Opposite: sophisticated 2 crude, simple, unrefined, basic, primitive Opposite: advanced

unsought adj unsolicited, spontaneous, uninvited, uncalled-for, unwanted

unsound adj 1 ill, frail, unwell, unhealthy, sick Opposite: well 2 unsafe, unstable, rickety, in poor condition, ramshackle Opposite: secure 3 illogical, specious, flawed, fallacious, erroneous Opposite: logical

unsparing adj 1 merciless, harsh, cruel, unforgiving, severe Opposite: merciful 2 generous, munificent, openhanded, liberal, charitable Opposite: frugal

unspeakable adj 1 indescribable, inexpressible, unutterable, undefinable, overwhelming 2 awful, disgusting, appalling, foul, revolting

unspeakably adv 1 indescribably, inexpressibly, unutterably, undefinably, unbelievably 2 terribly, awfully, appallingly, horribly, horrendously

unspeaking adj silent, mute, wordless, still, speechless Opposite: verbose

unspecified adj unnamed, indefinite, vague, indeterminate, undetermined Opposite: specific

unspiritual adj earthly, worldly, mundane, material, irreligious Opposite: spiritual

unspoilt adj 1 pristine, pure, perfect, untouched, unharmed Opposite: marred 2 uncorrupted, natural, innocent, pure, wholesome Opposite: spoiled

unspoken adj tacit, understood, silent, implicit, undeclared Opposite: explicit

unsporting adj dishonest, unfair, dishonourable, disreputable, mean-spirited Opposite: sporting

unsportsmanlike adj dirty, dishonest, nasty, foul, unethical Opposite: exemplary

unspotted adj 1 unstained, clean, spotless, unblemished, pristine Opposite: spotted 2 pure, moral, unblemished, faultless, righteous Opposite: impure 3 unobserved, unseen, unnoticed, unperceived, undiscovered Opposite: seen

unstable adj 1 unbalanced, uneven, wobbly, rickety, ramshackle Opposite: steady 2 volatile, unpredictable, unsteady, erratic, unhinged Opposite: stable

unstated adj unspecified, unspoken, tacit, understood, implicit Opposite: specified

unsteadiness n 1 tremulousness, instability, shakiness, precariousness, treacherousness Opposite: stability 2 changeability, erraticism, variability, unreliability, irregularity Opposite: constancy

unsteady adj 1 wobbly, shaky, unstable, uneven, rickety Opposite: stable 2 changeable, erratic, variable, unreliable, irregular Opposite: constant

unstick v release, free, take off, take down, take apart Opposite: stick

unstinting adj generous, charitable, openhanded, liberal, unsparing Opposite: stingy (infml)

unstipulated adj unspecified, unstated, unmentioned, undeclared Opposite: specified

unstop v unblock, free, clear, unplug, open up Opposite: stop

unstoppable adj irresistible, overwhelming, overpowering, persistent, unrelenting Opposite: avoidable

unstrained adj cloudy, milky, opaque, murky Opposite: clear

unstrap v undo, remove, unbuckle, unshackle, unleash Opposite: tie up

unstressed adj relaxed, carefree, at ease, cool, calm Opposite: stressed

unstructured adj formless, shapeless, amorphous, free Opposite: structured

unstudied adj unaffected, natural, genuine, sincere, relaxed Opposite: affected

unsubstantiated adj unconfirmed, unproven, unsupported, uncorroborated Opposite: proven

unsuccessful adj ineffective, failed, vain, unproductive, abortive Opposite: successful

unsuitability n inappropriateness, inaptness,

unbecomingness, incongruity, incompatibility *Opposite*: appropriateness

unsuitable *adj* inappropriate, unbecoming, unfitting, inapt, unbefitting *Opposite*: appropriate

unsullied *adj* pure, clean, unblemished, faultless, untarnished *Opposite*: tarnished

unsung *adj* unacknowledged, silent, unrecognized, anonymous, nameless *Opposite*: renowned

unsupported *adj* uncorroborated, unconfirmed, unsubstantiated, unverified, unfounded *Opposite*: supported

unsure *adj* 1 uncertain, doubtful, unconvinced, dubious, suspicious *Opposite*: certain 2 unconfident, hesitant, shy, insecure, irresolute *Opposite*: confident. *See* COMPARE AND CONTRAST *at* doubtful.

unsurpassed *adj* unrivalled, unmatched, supreme, incomparable, unequalled *Opposite*: ordinary

unsurprising *adj* predictable, foreseeable, expected, anticipated, foreseen *Opposite*: surprising

unsurprisingly *adv* of course, naturally, obviously, expectedly, predictably *Opposite*: surprisingly

unsuspected *adj* unanticipated, unpredicted, unknown, unimagined, surprise *Opposite*: known

unsuspecting *adj* unwary, gullible, credulous, innocent, unsuspicious *Opposite*: wary

unsustainable *adj* unjustifiable, unmaintainable, unverifiable, untenable, indefensible *Opposite*: sustainable

unswerving *adj* unwavering, staunch, reliable, trusty, solid *Opposite*: wavering

unsymmetrical *adj* asymmetrical, uneven, irregular, lopsided *Opposite*: symmetrical

unsympathetic *adj* unfeeling, uncaring, insensitive, cold, indifferent *Opposite*: caring

unsystematic *adj* haphazard, random, chaotic, disorganized, disorderly *Opposite*: organized

untainted *adj* unpolluted, undamaged, unblemished, unspoiled, pure *Opposite*: tainted

untaken *adj* available, unclaimed, unoccupied, free, spare *Opposite*: taken

untangle *v* unravel, disentangle, untie, unpick, straighten out *Opposite*: tangle

untapped *adj* unused, unexploited, untouched, available, intact *Opposite*: used

untarnished *adj* unblemished, clean, spotless, shining, unsullied *Opposite*: blemished

untaught *adj* untutored, uneducated, untrained, natural, born *Opposite*: trained

untenable *adj* indefensible, unsustainable, weak, unsound, shaky *Opposite*: watertight

untested *adj* 1 inexperienced, unproven, inexpert, new, raw *Opposite*: experienced 2 experimental, untried, unapproved, unverified, unproven *Opposite*: reliable

untether *v* release, untie, unstrap, unchain, free *Opposite*: tie up

unthinkable *adj* 1 absurd, ridiculous, unlikely, impossible, improbable *Opposite*: likely 2 unimaginable, impossible, fantastic, unbelievable, incredible *Opposite*: conceivable

unthinking *adj* 1 careless, thoughtless, tactless, undiplomatic, inconsiderate *Opposite*: thoughtful 2 instinctive, automatic, mechanical, intuitive, impulsive *Opposite*: calculated

unthreatened *adj* secure, safe, safe and sound, protected, impregnable *Opposite*: threatened

untidiness *n* 1 mess, disorder, muddle, disarray, jumble *Opposite*: order 2 shabbiness, scruffiness, raggedness *Opposite*: smartness

untidy *adj* 1 messy, in a mess, disorderly, muddled, jumbled *Opposite*: neat 2 unkempt, ragged, shabby, scruffy, bedraggled *Opposite*: smart

untie *v* 1 unknot, unfasten, loosen, undo, unravel *Opposite*: fasten 2 release, free, set free, unleash, let loose *Opposite*: tie up

until *prep* up until, while waiting for, pending, till, up to

untimely *adj* 1 ill-timed, inconvenient, inappropriate, unfortunate, inopportune *Opposite*: timely 2 premature, early, precocious, advance *Opposite*: late

untiring *adj* tireless, determined, dogged, indefatigable, constant *Opposite*: faltering

untold *adj* 1 indescribable, inexpressible, indefinable, ineffable *(fml)* 2 uncountable, countless, innumerable, myriad, numberless *Opposite*: few

untouchable *adj* unattainable, matchless, superlative, superior, unrivalled *Opposite*: ordinary

untouched *adj* 1 unhurt, intact, unharmed, undamaged, safe and sound *Opposite*: injured 2 unaffected, indifferent, unmoved, unimpressed, unconcerned *Opposite*: affected

untoward *adj* 1 annoying, unpleasant, inconvenient, troublesome, awkward *Opposite*: pleasant 2 inappropriate, unfitting, unseemly, improper, unbecoming *Opposite*: appropriate

untrained *adj* untaught, inexpert, untutored, unqualified, inexperienced *Opposite*: trained

untrammelled *adj* unrestricted, free, unhindered, unimpeded, liberated *Opposite*: restrained

untreated *adj* unprocessed, unrefined, natural, raw, crude *Opposite*: treated

untried *adj* untested, inexperienced, unproven, new, novel *Opposite*: tested

untroubled *adj* **peaceful**, calm, tranquil, undisturbed, unflustered *Opposite*: troubled

untrue *adj* **1 false**, incorrect, wrong, fallacious, untruthful *Opposite*: true **2 cheating**, unfaithful, disloyal, treacherous, two-faced *Opposite*: faithful

untrustworthiness *n* **unreliability**, dishonesty, deceitfulness, disloyalty, treachery *Opposite*: dependability

untrustworthy *adj* **unreliable**, dishonest, deceitful, disloyal, treacherous *Opposite*: dependable

untruth *n* **lie**, falsehood, fiction, fabrication, deceit *Opposite*: truth. *See* COMPARE AND CONTRAST *at* **lie**.

untruthful *adj* **lying**, mendacious, dishonest, deceitful, false *Opposite*: truthful

untruthfulness *n* **dishonesty**, deceit, lies, falsehood, fabrication *Opposite*: truthfulness

untutored *adj* **untaught**, uneducated, untrained, unschooled, unqualified *Opposite*: educated

unusable *adj* **useless**, out of commission, unworkable, inoperative, broken *Opposite*: usable

unused *adj* **1 new**, brand-new, fresh, pristine *Opposite*: used **2 idle**, vacant, unemployed, unexploited, fallow **3 unaccustomed**, unfamiliar, unacquainted, inexperienced *Opposite*: familiar

unusual *adj* **1 uncommon**, rare, infrequent, scarce, unfamiliar *Opposite*: common **2 strange**, odd, curious, extraordinary, abnormal *Opposite*: ordinary

unutterable *adj* **unspeakable**, indescribable, inexpressible, indefinable, ineffable *(fml)*

unvarnished *adj* **plain**, straight, honest, unembellished, literal *Opposite*: embellished

unvarying *adj* **unwavering**, constant, unchanging, consistent, inflexible *Opposite*: varying

unveil *v* **1 uncover**, unwrap, bare, expose *Opposite*: cover **2 reveal**, expose, make public, divulge, show *Opposite*: conceal

unveiling *n* **1 opening**, launch, presentation, inauguration, debut *Opposite*: closure **2 revelation**, disclosure, exposure, uncovering, release *Opposite*: cover-up

unventilated *adj* **airless**, stuffy, unaired, close, stale *Opposite*: airy

unverified *adj* **unconfirmed**, unsupported, unsubstantiated, uncorroborated, unproven *Opposite*: verified

unvoiced *adj* **unspoken**, silent, secret, hidden, mute *Opposite*: spoken

unwaged *adj* **unemployed**, jobless, out of work, redundant, on the dole *(infml)* *Opposite*: employed

unwanted *adj* **1 surplus**, superfluous, unnecessary, discarded, redundant *Opposite*: necessary **2 unwelcome**, unsolicited, annoying, undesirable, uninvited *Opposite*: welcome

unwariness *n* **incautiousness**, unguardedness, rashness, carelessness, gullibility *Opposite*: wariness

unwarrantable *adj* **uncalled-for**, indefensible, unjustifiable, unforgivable, inexcusable

unwarranted *adj* **unjustified**, undeserved, unnecessary, gratuitous, needless *Opposite*: justified

unwary *adj* **imprudent**, unguarded, rash, careless, unsuspecting *Opposite*: wary

unwashed *adj* **dirty**, grubby, grimy, sordid, squalid *Opposite*: clean

unwavering *adj* **firm**, staunch, solid, steadfast, untiring *Opposite*: irresolute

unwearied *adj* **unflagging**, tireless, indefatigable, uncomplaining, unceasing

unwelcome *adj* **unwanted**, undesirable, annoying, unsolicited, uninvited *Opposite*: welcome

unwelcoming *adj* **hostile**, unfriendly, standoffish, unreceptive, inhospitable *Opposite*: friendly

unwell *adj* **ill**, sick, under the weather, out of sorts *Opposite*: well, poorly *(infml)*

unwholesome *adj* **unpleasant**, distasteful, objectionable, nasty, disagreeable *Opposite*: pleasant

unwholesomeness *n* **1 foulness**, insalubriousness, noxiousness, unhealthiness, harmfulness *Opposite*: wholesomeness **2 coarseness**, indecency, vulgarity, foulness, profanity *Opposite*: wholesomeness

unwieldy *adj* **awkward**, heavy, bulky, cumbersome, clumsy *Opposite*: manageable

unwilling *adj* **reluctant**, disinclined, grudging, loath, unenthusiastic *Opposite*: willing

---

COMPARE AND CONTRAST CORE MEANING: lacking the desire to do something

unwilling not prepared to do something; **reluctant** showing no enthusiasm for doing something and only doing it if forced; **disinclined** showing a lack of enthusiasm for something rather than a strong objection to it; **averse** *(fml)* strongly opposed to or disliking something; **hesitant** not keen to do something because of uncertainty or lack of confidence; **loath** having reservations about doing something.

---

unwillingness *n* **reluctance**, disinclination, refusal, indisposition, aversion *Opposite*: willingness

unwind *v* **1 undo**, loosen, unravel, untwist, disentangle *Opposite*: wind **2 relax**, wind down, slow down, calm down, kick back *Opposite*: work up

unwise *adj* **foolish**, imprudent, rash, ill-advised, injudicious *Opposite*: prudent

unwitting *adj* **1 unaware**, unsuspecting, ignorant, innocent, unconscious *Opposite*: knowing **2 accidental**, involuntary, unintentional, coincidental, inadvertent *Opposite*: deliberate

unwonted *adj* **unusual**, atypical, uncharacteristic, singular, unexpected *Opposite*: customary

unworkable *adj* **impracticable**, unusable, unfeasible, ineffectual, impractical *Opposite*: viable

unworldliness *n* **innocence**, naivety, simplicity, ingenuousness, callowness *Opposite*: worldliness

unworldly *adj* **inexperienced**, callow, green, ingenuous, artless *Opposite*: experienced

unworried *adj* **calm**, untroubled, at ease, unruffled, unflustered *Opposite*: perturbed

unworthiness *n* **1 worthlessness**, contemptibility, pitifulness, unfitness **2 shamefulness**, dishonour, discredit, shame, disgrace

unworthy *adj* **1 undeserving**, worthless, contemptible, pitiful, unfit *Opposite*: deserving **2 shameful**, degrading, dishonourable, disgraceful, disreputable *Opposite*: reputable

unwrap *v* **undo**, unpack, remove, open, tear open *Opposite*: wrap

unwritten *adj* **1 spoken**, oral, unrecorded, vocal, unprinted *Opposite*: written **2 understood**, accepted, traditional, tacit, known

unyielding *adj* **1 firm**, unbending, obstinate, steadfast, obdurate *Opposite*: acquiescent **2 inflexible**, rigid, stiff, unbending, solid *Opposite*: flexible

unyoke *v* **untie**, separate, disjoin, unhook, loose *Opposite*: join

unzip *v* **1 undo**, unfasten, open, disengage, free **2 open**, expand, access, decompress *Opposite*: compress

up *adj* **1 awake**, out of bed, up and about, active, up and doing *Opposite*: asleep **2 happy**, positive, optimistic, hopeful, cheerful *Opposite*: down **3 winning**, in the lead, ahead, leading *Opposite*: behind

up-and-coming *adj* **emerging**, rising, budding, promising, talented *Opposite*: over-the-hill

up-and-down *adj* **1 moody**, temperamental, changeable, tempestuous, turbulent *Opposite*: equable **2 rising and falling**, bobbing, bouncing

upbeat *(infml) adj* **optimistic**, cheerful, positive, buoyant, bubbly *Opposite*: downbeat *(infml)*

upbraid *v* **scold**, reproach, tear a strip off, chastise, reprimand *Opposite*: praise

upbringing *n* **education**, childhood, background, rearing, nurture

update *v* **1 inform**, bring up-to-date, keep informed, keep posted, fill in **2 modernize**, revise, renew, bring up-to-date, renovate

upend *v* **turn over**, tip up, tip over, upset, topple *Opposite*: right

up-front *(infml) adj* **straightforward**, honest, frank, plain-spoken, open *Opposite*: coy

upgrade *v* **1 promote**, advance, elevate, raise, move up *Opposite*: demote **2 improve**, update, renew, modernize, renovate *Opposite*: downgrade ■ *n* **1 promotion**, advancement, elevation, exaltation *Opposite*: demotion **2 improvement**, upgrading, renovation, modernization, enhancement

upgrading *n* **1 promotion**, advancement, step up, advance, progression *Opposite*: demotion **2 improvement**, renovation, modernization, transformation, enhancement

upheaval *n* **disturbance**, turmoil, disorder, confusion, cataclysm *Opposite*: peace

upheave *v* **lift up**, raise, thrust up, elevate, lift *Opposite*: drop

uphill *adj* **1 climbing**, ascending, rising, mounting *Opposite*: downhill **2 difficult**, hard, arduous, demanding, tough *Opposite*: easy

uphold *v* **support**, sustain, maintain, defend, endorse

upholster *v* **cover**, pad, stuff, fill, decorate

upholstery *n* **fabric**, furnishings, covers, furniture, material

upkeep *n* **maintenance**, repairs, keep, conservation, preservation

upland *n* **moorland**, high ground, highland, plateau, tableland *Opposite*: lowland

uplift *v* **1 elevate**, raise, hoist, lift *Opposite*: drop **2 inspire**, enrich, improve, move, hearten *Opposite*: depress

uplifting *adj* **inspiring**, elevating, improving, enriching, heartening *Opposite*: depressing

uplighter *n* **standard lamp**, lamp, floor lamp *(US)*

upmarket *adj* **expensive**, high-class, smart, chic, exclusive *Opposite*: downmarket

upper *adj* **higher**, greater, better, superior *Opposite*: lower

upper circle *n* **gallery**, loggia, balcony, circle, dress circle

upper class *n* **aristocracy**, nobility, noblesse, gentry, elite *Opposite*: lower class

upper-class *adj* **aristocratic**, noble, blue-blooded, highborn *(literary) Opposite*: lower-class

upper crust *see* upper class

uppercut *n* **blow**, punch, hit, haymaker *(slang)*

upper hand *n* **advantage**, initiative, ascendancy, edge, control *Opposite*: disadvantage

uppermost *adj* **1 highest**, top, topmost, upmost *Opposite*: bottom **2 primary**, main, principal, chief, greatest *Opposite*: last

uppity *adj* **1** *(infml)* **presumptuous**, pretentious, snobbish, haughty, bumptious *Opposite*: humble **2** *(dated infml)* **stubborn**, difficult, cantankerous, irritable, tetchy *(infml) Opposite*: flexible

uprate *v* **increase**, raise, upgrade, up, adjust *Opposite*: decrease

upright *adj* **1 standing**, straight, vertical, erect *Opposite*: horizontal **2 righteous**, moral, honourable, decent, honest *Opposite*: immoral

uprightness *n* **righteousness**, morality, honourableness, decency, honesty *Opposite*: immorality

uprising *n* **rebellion**, revolution, revolt, rising, unrest

uproar *n* **disturbance**, noise, chaos, pandemonium, upheaval *Opposite*: quiet

uproarious *adj* **hilarious**, funny, riotous, raucous, boisterous

uproot *v* **1 pull up**, deracinate, dig up, rip up *Opposite*: plant **2 displace**, evacuate, move on, relocate, deracinate *Opposite*: settle

uprush *n* **rush**, surge, updraught, draught, blast

upset *v* **1 spill**, knock over, tip over, overturn, upend *Opposite*: right **2 disturb**, disrupt, reorder, reverse, mix up *Opposite*: order **3 distress**, hurt, disturb, sadden, trouble *Opposite*: please ■ *n* **1 defeat**, disappointment, affront, letdown, shock **2 surprise**, shock, confusion, disarray, disruption ■ *adj* **sad**, disturbed, unhappy, hurt, disappointed *Opposite*: composed

upset stomach *n* **indigestion**, stomachache, heartburn, bellyache *(infml)*, tummy ache *(infml)*

upsetting *adj* **distressing**, disturbing, hurtful, offensive, disappointing *Opposite*: pleasing

upshot *n* **result**, outcome, consequence, effect, end

upside *n* **advantage**, benefit, plus *(infml)*, positive *(infml)* *Opposite*: disadvantage

upside-down *adj* **1 upturned**, wrong way up, wrong side up, overturned, on its head *Opposite*: upright **2 in a mess**, in a state *(infml)*, messy, untidy, topsy-turvy *Opposite*: orderly

upstage *v* **outdo**, outmanoeuvre, put somebody's nose out of joint, outshine, surpass

upstanding *adj* **virtuous**, honest, decent, respectable, honourable *Opposite*: degenerate

upstart *n* **nobody**, unknown, parvenu, arriviste, nonentity *Opposite*: grandee

upstretched *adj* **raised**, upraised, upturned, outstretched, extended *Opposite*: hanging down

upsurge *n* **increase**, rise, surge, gain, expansion *Opposite*: decrease

upswing *n* **increase**, improvement, upturn, turnround, upsurge *Opposite*: downswing

uptake *n* **1 acceptance**, approval, interest, commitment, agreement *Opposite*: refusal **2 understanding**, comprehension, perception, appreciation, apprehension *Opposite*: incomprehension

up-tempo *adj* **exciting**, lively, fast, rapid, frenetic *Opposite*: dull

uptight *(infml)* *adj* **tense**, bothered, anxious, wound up, neurotic *Opposite*: calm

up-to-date *adj* **1 informed**, in touch, conversant, in the know, au fait **2 current**, latest, new, brand-new, modern *Opposite*: old-fashioned **3 fashionable**, cool, chic, trendy *(infml)*, à la mode *(dated)* *Opposite*: passé

up-to-the-minute *adj* **latest**, current, contemporary, state-of-the-art, contemporaneous *Opposite*: out-of-date

upturn *v* **overturn**, capsize, tip over, upset, turn turtle *Opposite*: right ■ *n* **improvement**, recovery, revival, growth, expansion *Opposite*: slump

upward *adj* **1 ascendant**, mounting, skyward, uphill, ascending *Opposite*: downward **2 rising**, improving, increasing, growing, expanding *Opposite*: downward

upwards *adv* **up**, uphill, higher, skyward, in the air

upwelling *n* **upsurge**, surge, burst, outburst, outpouring

upwind *adj* **windward**, exposed, open, bare, windy *Opposite*: leeward

up with *adj* **abreast**, up-to-date, familiar, conversant, au fait

urban *adj* **city**, town, built-up, municipal, inner-city *Opposite*: rural

urbane *adj* **sophisticated**, refined, courteous, suave, polished *Opposite*: unsophisticated

urbanite *n* **metropolitan**, cosmopolitan, citizen, resident, townie *(infml)* *Opposite*: rustic

urbanity *n* **sophistication**, refinement, courteousness, courtesy, suaveness *Opposite*: uncouthness

urbanization *n* **development**, suburbanization, expansion, sprawl, spread

urban myth *n* **myth**, folktale, tale, tall story, fable

urban sprawl *n* **urbanization**, development, suburbia, sprawl, expansion

urchin *n* **imp**, rascal, tyke, brat, tearaway

urge *v* **1 advise**, recommend, exhort, prevail on, press *Opposite*: dissuade **2 advocate**, commend, promote, back, support *Opposite*: downplay **3 encourage**, drive, push, force, impel *Opposite*: discourage ■ *n* **need**, wish, impulse, desire, inclination *Opposite*: disinclination

urgency *n* **1 need**, exigency, importance, necessity, hurry *Opposite*: unimportance **2 earnestness**, insistence, perseverance, firmness, resolve *Opposite*: vacillation

urgent *adj* **1 vital**, crucial, pressing, imperative, burning *Opposite*: trivial **2 earnest**, insistent, persuasive, pleading, demanding *Opposite*: half-hearted

urgently *adv* **immediately**, straightaway, instantly, at once, directly *Opposite*: whenever

urn *n* **vase**, container, vessel, pot, jug

usable *adj* **functional**, practical, serviceable, working, functioning *Opposite*: unusable

usage *n* **1 treatment**, handling, control, management, running **2 practice**, procedure, custom, norm, tradition

use *v* **1 employ**, make use of, utilize, exercise, bring into play *Opposite*: forgo **2 consume**, expend, spend, exhaust, use up *Opposite*: conserve **3 manipulate**, exploit, take advantage of, mistreat, abuse **4 behave toward**, handle, treat, manipulate, manage **5 benefit from**, make use of, enjoy, avail yourself of, tap ■ *n* **1 expenditure**, consumption, wear and tear, wastage, depletion *Opposite*: saving **2 treatment**, handling, manipulation, exploitation, management **3 employment**, application, utilization, exploitation, consumption *Opposite*: disuse **4 purpose**, function, application, service, role **5 usefulness**, help, assistance, benefit, aid *Opposite*: harm

COMPARE AND CONTRAST CORE MEANING: put something to use

use put something into action or service; **employ** make use of something such as a tool or a resource in a particular way; **make use of** use what is readily available, especially in a sensible or economical way; **utilize** find a practical or unintended use for something.

used *adj* **1 second-hand**, castoff, hand-me-down, recycled *Opposite*: new **2 expended**, old, worn, worn out, consumed *Opposite*: remaining **3 exploited**, taken advantage of, misused, manipulated, abused

used to *adj* **1 accustomed**, hardened, inured, schooled, conditioned *Opposite*: unaccustomed **2 familiar**, at home, au fait, at ease, easy *Opposite*: unfamiliar

useful *adj* **1 practical**, helpful, serviceable, of use, constructive *Opposite*: useless **2 convenient**, valuable, beneficial, advantageous, expedient *Opposite*: disadvantageous

usefulness *n* **1 practicality**, helpfulness, worth, utility, convenience *Opposite*: uselessness **2 valuableness**, convenience, advantageousness, expediency, suitability

useless *adj* **1 unusable**, impractical, unserviceable, inoperable, unworkable *Opposite*: useful **2 unsuccessful**, futile, ineffectual, unavailing, worthless *Opposite*: successful **3** *(infml)* **inept**, hopeless, incompetent, inefficient, ineffectual *Opposite*: effective

uselessness *n* **1 impracticality**, unusableness, inoperability, unworkability, inadequacy *Opposite*: usefulness **2 unsuccessfulness**, pointlessness, futility, ineffectualness, ineffectiveness *Opposite*: worth **3** *(infml)* **ineptness**, hopelessness, ineffectiveness, incompetence, inefficiency *Opposite*: effectiveness

user *n* **operator**, worker, employer, manipulator, handler

user-friendliness *n* **accessibility**, manageability, handiness, manipulability, convenience *Opposite*: inaccessibility

user-friendly *adj* **accessible**, comprehensible, intelligible, manipulable, manageable *Opposite*: inaccessible

use up *v* **expend**, consume, exhaust, wear out, deplete *Opposite*: conserve

usher *n* **attendant**, escort, guide, leader, conductor ■ *v* **escort**, conduct, guide, steer, pilot

usher in *v* **herald**, introduce, lead to, announce, signal *Opposite*: see out

usual *adj* **1 normal**, typical, common, standard, natural *Opposite*: exceptional **2 habitual**, routine, everyday, customary, familiar *Opposite*: irregular

COMPARE AND CONTRAST CORE MEANING: often done, used, bought, or consumed

usual normal, common, or typical; **customary** conforming to regular or typical practice; **habitual** done so often or repeatedly that the behaviour or practice has become ingrained; **routine** normal, regular, and usual in every way, even predictable, repetitive, and monotonous; **wonted** *(fml)* usual or typical.

usually *adv* **normally**, typically, customarily, generally, by and large *Opposite*: exceptionally

usurp *v* **seize**, appropriate, take over, assume, commandeer *Opposite*: surrender

usury *n* **moneylending**, overcharging, extortion, daylight robbery *(infml)*, highway robbery *(US infml)*

utensil *n* **tool**, instrument, implement, appliance, device

WORD BANK

❑ **types of utensil** beater, bottle opener, can opener, corkscrew, drainer, garlic press, grater, juice extractor, lemon squeezer, liquidizer, mill, mincer, mortar, nutcracker, opener, peeler, pestle, sieve, soup ladle, spatula, strainer, tin-opener, whisk

utilitarian *adj* **practical**, useful, serviceable, functional, down-to-earth *Opposite*: useless

utility *n* **1 usefulness**, practicality, efficiency, handiness, helpfulness *Opposite*: uselessness **2 convenience**, service, benefit, worth, advantage *Opposite*: worthlessness

utilization *n* **use**, application, employment, deployment, operation

utilize *v* **use**, apply, employ, operate, develop *Opposite*: forgo. *See* COMPARE AND CONTRAST *at* **use**.

utmost *adj* **1 greatest**, highest, extreme, chief, supreme *Opposite*: least **2 farthest**, extreme, most distant, farthermost, remotest

utopia *n* **ideal**, paradise, never-never land, heaven, Shangri-la

utopian *adj* **1 ideal**, perfect, ultimate, best, model **2 idealistic**, naive, impracticable, impractical, unworkable *Opposite*: pragmatic ■ *n* **idealist**, romantic, visionary, dreamer, purist *Opposite*: pragmatist

utter *v* **say**, speak, pronounce, express, state ■ *adj* **absolute**, total, complete, sheer, downright *Opposite*: partial

utterance *n* **1 word**, sound, note, noise, exclamation *Opposite*: silence **2 statement**, speech, remark, declaration, announcement

U-turn *n* **1 turn**, rotation, revolution, about-turn, volte-face **2 change**, reversal, climbdown, volte face, about-turn

V

vacancy *n* **job**, post, situation *(fml)*, position, opening

vacant *adj* **1 empty**, available, unoccupied, not in use, void *Opposite*: occupied **2 blank**, empty, expressionless, indifferent, vacuous *Opposite*: alert

---

COMPARE AND CONTRAST CORE MEANING: lacking contents or occupants

vacant without occupants or contents, often temporarily; **unoccupied** not lived in by anybody, or currently without occupants; **empty** not containing or holding anything, or without occupants; **void** having no contents, or having no incumbent, occupant, or holder.

---

vacate *v* **1 empty**, evacuate, clear out, free, divest *Opposite*: fill **2 leave**, relinquish, check out, give up, depart *Opposite*: occupy

vacation *n* **holiday**, break, trip, rest, retreat

vaccinate *v* **inoculate**, immunize, protect, jab *Opposite*: expose

vaccination *n* **inoculation**, injection, immunization, jab *(infml)*, shot *(infml)*

vaccine *n* **inoculation**, injection, serum, preparation, shot *(infml)*

vacillate *v* **waver**, hesitate, chop and change, dither, think twice *Opposite*: decide. *See* COMPARE AND CONTRAST *at* **hesitate**.

vacillating *adj* **irresolute**, indecisive, hesitant, dithering, fickle *Opposite*: resolute

vacillation *n* **indecisiveness**, irresoluteness, indecision, irresolution, hesitancy *Opposite*: resolution

vacuity *(fml)* *n* **mindlessness**, blankness, vacantness, inaneness, stupidity *Opposite*: intelligence

vacuous *adj* **stupid**, unintelligent, inane, vacant, mindless *Opposite*: intelligent

vacuum *n* **void**, space, emptiness, nothingness, blankness

vagabond *n* **vagrant**, tramp, beggar, drifter, traveller *Opposite*: resident

vagary *n* **whim**, fancy, notion, mood, quirk *Opposite*: choice

vagrancy *n* **homelessness**, penury, destitution, rootlessness, begging *Opposite*: residence

vagrant *n* **vagabond**, tramp, beggar, drifter, hobo *Opposite*: resident ■ *adj* **nomadic**, itinerant, wandering, roaming, roving *Opposite*: settled

vague *adj* **1 unclear**, imprecise, indefinite, ambiguous, equivocal *Opposite*: definite **2 indistinct**, unclear, indistinguishable, hazy, fuzzy *Opposite*: clear **3 absent-minded**, abstracted, distracted, distant, unclear *Opposite*: alert

vagueness *n* **1 nebulousness**, imprecision, indistinctness, ambiguity, elusiveness *Opposite*: precision **2 abstraction**, absent-mindedness, pensiveness, dreaminess *Opposite*: attentiveness **3 haziness**, fuzziness, formlessness, imprecision, blurredness *Opposite*: clarity

vain *adj* **1 proud**, conceited, narcissistic, arrogant, self-important *Opposite*: humble **2 useless**, ineffective, otiose, unsuccessful, hopeless *Opposite*: successful **3 empty**, hollow, idle, pointless, futile *Opposite*: reliable

---

COMPARE AND CONTRAST CORE MEANING: without substance or unlikely to be carried though

vain failing to have or unlikely to have the intended or desired result; **empty** lacking substance, sincerity, or truthfulness; **hollow** not sincere or genuine; **idle** unlikely to be carried out or impossible to put into effect.

---

valediction *(fml)* *n* **farewell**, goodbye, sendoff, adieu *(literary)*, leave-taking *(literary)*

valedictory *(fml)* *n* **farewell**, goodbye, parting, leave-taking *(literary)* *Opposite*: welcome ■ *adj* **parting**, farewell, goodbye, final, last *Opposite*: welcoming

valet *v* **clean**, clean out, vacuum, tidy, polish

valetudinarian *n* **1 convalescent**, patient, invalid, valetudinary **2 hypochondriac**, neurotic, valetudinary ■ *adj* **sickly**, feeble, unhealthy, frail, weak *Opposite*: healthy

valiant *adj* **brave**, courageous, heroic, fearless, noble *Opposite*: cowardly

valid *adj* **1 reasonable**, sound, rational, justifiable, legitimate *Opposite*: unjustifiable **2 lawful**, legal, binding, effective, in force *Opposite*: illegal **3 usable**, acceptable, authorized, endorsed, official *Opposite*: unusable **4 convincing**, compelling, sound, persuasive, cogent *Opposite*: unconvincing

COMPARE AND CONTRAST CORE MEANING: worthy of acceptance or credence
valid having a solid foundation or justification; **cogent** forceful and convincing to the intellect and reason; **convincing** likely to overcome doubts and win the support of those who hear it; **reasonable** acceptable and according to common sense; **sound** based on good sense and acceptable reasoning and worthy of approval.

validate *v* **1 prove**, substantiate, confirm, authenticate, corroborate *Opposite*: disprove **2 authorize**, certify, endorse, ratify, legalize *Opposite*: invalidate

validation *n* **1 authentication**, proof, endorsement, confirmation, corroboration **2 authorization**, endorsement, ratification, certification, legalization *Opposite*: invalidation

validity *n* **1 legality**, authority, legitimacy, authenticity, lawfulness **2 cogency**, rationality, legitimacy, soundness, strength *Opposite*: weakness

valley *n* **gorge**, dale, basin, vale (*literary*), dell (*literary*) *Opposite*: hill

valorous *adj* **noble**, brave, courageous, heroic, fearless *Opposite*: cowardly

valour *n* **boldness**, courage, bravery, heroism, fearlessness *Opposite*: cowardice

valuable *adj* **1 costly**, expensive, priceless, dear, important *Opposite*: inexpensive **2 invaluable**, helpful, important, valued, useful *Opposite*: worthless **3 cherished**, valued, appreciated, respected, treasured

valuation *n* **estimate**, assessment, evaluation, appraisal, survey

value *n* **1 worth**, price, cost, rate, charge **2 benefit**, importance, worth, significance, usefulness *Opposite*: insignificance ■ *v* **1 rate**, assess, estimate, evaluate, appraise **2 prize**, appreciate, respect, esteem, treasure *Opposite*: scorn

valued *adj* **appreciated**, respected, esteemed, treasured, cherished

valueless *adj* **inconsequential**, worthless, insignificant, paltry, miserable *Opposite*: valuable

values *n* **principles**, standards, morals, ethics, ideals

valve *n* **regulator**, controller, stopcock, tap, spigot

vampire *n* **parasite**, hanger-on, predator, sponge, freeloader (*infml*)

vamp up *v* **repair**, rework, revamp, do up, modernize

van *n* **forefront**, front, lead, head, vanguard

vandal *n* **criminal**, trespasser, delinquent, thug, hooligan (*infml*)

vandalism *n* **damage**, destruction, defacement, wreckage, sabotage

vandalize *v* **destroy**, damage, deface, wreck, break

vane *n* **blade**, slat, fin, plate, strip

vanguard *n* **1 front line**, front, advance guard *Opposite*: rearguard **2 forefront**, front, lead, head, cutting edge

vanish *v* **1 disappear**, evaporate, go missing, fade away, peter out *Opposite*: appear **2 become extinct**, die out, disappear, cease to exist, be exterminated

vanished *adj* **disappeared**, missing, died out, gone, extinct *Opposite*: present

vanity *n* **1 pride**, narcissism, self-importance, conceit, arrogance *Opposite*: humility **2 futility**, emptiness, uselessness, pointlessness, worthlessness *Opposite*: value

vanquish *v* **defeat**, conquer, subjugate, crush, subdue *Opposite*: surrender. *See* COMPARE AND CONTRAST *at* defeat.

vantage point *n* **1 viewpoint**, viewing platform, belvedere, lookout, crow's nest **2 standpoint**, viewpoint, angle, point of view, perspective

vapid *adj* **1 lifeless**, uninteresting, unexciting, vacuous, tame *Opposite*: lively **2 flavourless**, insipid, tasteless, weak, tame *Opposite*: tasty

vaporize *v* **1 turn to vapour**, evaporate, boil away, boil, heat *Opposite*: condense **2 vanish**, disappear, evaporate, fade away, go away **3 destroy**, annihilate, burn, incinerate, burn away *Opposite*: preserve

vaporizer *n* **nebulizer**, atomizer, aerosol, spray, inhaler

vaporous *adj* **1 gaseous**, smoky, misty, steamy, foggy **2 volatile**, unstable, unpredictable, explosive, flammable *Opposite*: stable **3 insubstantial**, ephemeral, impermanent, evanescent, nebulous *Opposite*: solid **4 fanciful**, ridiculous, implausible, fantastic, unreal *Opposite*: real **5 murky**, hazy, cloudy, obscure, dim *Opposite*: clear

vapour *n* **1 gas**, air, ether **2 clouds**, fumes, smoke, water vapour, miasma **3 aerosol**, spray, mist

variability *n* **1 erraticism**, inconsistency, capriciousness, changeability, unpredictability *Opposite*: predictability **2 unevenness**, patchiness, irregularity, inconsistency *Opposite*: consistency **3 flexibility**, adaptability, fickleness, inconstancy, mutability *Opposite*: fixedness

variable *adj* **1 varying**, changing, fluctuating, changeable, erratic *Opposite*: constant **2 uneven**, patchy, up-and-down, irregular, inconsistent *Opposite*: consistent **3 mutable**, adjustable, flexible, capricious, inconstant *Opposite*: fixed

variance *n* **1 alteration**, modification, adjustment, change **2 divergence**, disparity, difference, discrepancy, inconsistency *Opposite*: consistency **3 conflict**, clash, dissent, dispute, difference of opinion *Opposite*: agreement

variant *adj* **irregular**, different, optional, modified, abnormal ■ *n* **variation**, alternative, deviation, modification, departure

variation *n* **1 variant**, adaptation, reworking, departure, alteration **2 difference**, disparity, dissimilarity, distinction, discrepancy *Opposite*: similarity

varied *adj* **heterogeneous**, diverse, wide-ranging, mixed, different *Opposite*: homogeneous

variegated *adj* **spotted**, mottled, pied, dappled, speckled *Opposite*: uniform

variety *n* **1 diversity**, change, variability, variation *Opposite*: monotony **2 type**, kind, form, sort, category **3 collection**, diversity, assortment, selection, multiplicity

variety show *n* **show**, revue, cabaret, entertainment, performance

various *adj* **1 numerous**, many, a number of, several, countless *Opposite*: few **2 a variety of**, a range of, an assortment of, a mixture of, different *Opposite*: same

varnish *n* **lacquer**, paint, finish, glaze, coating ■ *v* **paint**, glaze, finish, polish, lacquer

vary *v* **1 change**, alter, fluctuate, adjust, adapt *Opposite*: standardize **2 diverge**, differ, be different, contrast, fluctuate *Opposite*: conform. *See* COMPARE AND CONTRAST *at* **change**.

vase *n* **rose bowl**, urn, jug, pot, container

vast *adj* **massive**, huge, enormous, gigantic, immense *Opposite*: small

vastly *adv* **much**, greatly, infinitely, immensely, immeasurably *Opposite*: slightly

vastness *n* **massiveness**, incalculability, limitlessness, immensity, hugeness

vat *n* **container**, cask, barrel, tank, drum

vault *n* **1 arch**, dome, cupola **2 crypt**, cellar, mausoleum, undercroft, burial chamber **3 strongroom**, treasury, safe, treasure house ■ *v* **jump**, leap, spring, hurdle, bound

vaulted *adj* **curved**, domed, arched

vaunt *v* **puff**, boast, brag, show off, hype *Opposite*: play down

vaunted *adj* **hyped**, praised, promoted, advertised, flaunted *Opposite*: downplayed

vector *n* **course**, trajectory, path, flight path, route

veer *v* **change course**, turn, swing, swerve, bend

vegan *n* **fruitarian**, vegetarian, veggie *(infml)*

vegetable *adj* **plant**, herbal, vegetal

WORD BANK
❑ **types of root vegetable** beet, beetroot, carrot, cassava, celeriac, mangel-wurzel, new potato, pak choi, parsnip, potato, rutabaga, sugar beet, swede, sweet potato, turnip, yam
❑ **types of vegetable** artichoke, asparagus, aubergine, brassica, broccoli, Brussels sprout, cabbage, cauliflower, corn on the cob, courgette, fennel, garlic, greens, kale, leek, marrow, okra, onion, pumpkin, spinach, squash, sweetcorn, Swiss chard

vegetarian *n* **fruitarian**, vegan, lacto-vegetarian, ovolactovegetarian, veggie *(infml)*

vegetate *v* **sit around**, stagnate, twiddle your thumbs, kill time, loaf

vegetation *n* **plants**, plant life, flora, ground cover, bedding

veggie *(infml)* *n* **lactovegetarian**, fruitarian, vegetarian, ovolactovegetarian, vegan

vehemence *n* **forcefulness**, intensity, fervour, passion, violence *Opposite*: indifference

vehement *adj* **fervent**, passionate, heated, violent, intense *Opposite*: apathetic

vehicle *n* **1 means of transport**, transport, conveyance **2 medium**, means of expression, channel, means, mouthpiece

WORDBANK
❑ **types of commercial or industrial vehicle** articulated lorry, backhoe, black cab, breakdown lorry, bulldozer, cab, combine, combine harvester, crane, digger, dumper truck, earthmover, hackney cab, hackney carriage, hearse, juggernaut, lorry, minicab, pick-up, removal van, roadroller, snowplough, steamroller, tanker, taxi, tractor, transporter, truck, van
❑ **types of leisure vehicle** all-terrain vehicle, bobsleigh, cablecar, camper, campervan, caravan, chair lift, dogsled, dune buggy, go-cart, golf cart, land yacht, luge, mobile home, motor home, sledge, sleigh, snowmobile, toboggan, trailer
❑ **types of military vehicle** amphibian, armoured car, jeep, tank
❑ **types of public service vehicle** ambulance, bus, charabanc, coach, dustcart, fire engine, minibus, panda car *(infml)*, police car, shuttle, squad car
❑ **types of control** accelerator, brake, choke, clutch, gas gauge, gear lever, horn, pedal, rev counter, speedometer, steering wheel, wheel
❑ **types of internal feature** air bag, back seat, booster seat, cab, child seat, cup holder, dashboard, driving seat, glove compartment, headrest, passenger seat, rearview mirror, seat belt, sound system, sun visor
❑ **types of external feature** brake light, bumper, exhaust pipe, fog light, hazard light, headlight, high beam, hubcap, indicator, kick-start, mud flap, mudguard, number plate, plate, roof rack, sidelight, silencer, tail light, turn signal, tyre, wheel, windscreen wiper, wing mirror
❑ **parts of an external structure** aerofoil, axle, bodywork, bonnet, boot, chassis, coachwork, fin, grille, hull, side mirror, spoiler, sunroof, tailgate, windscreen, wing

veil *n* **mask**, blanket, shroud, covering, curtain ■ *v* **cover**, conceal, hide, mask, cloak *Opposite*: reveal

veiled *adj* **1 indirect**, oblique, obscure, covert, roundabout *Opposite*: overt **2 masked**, cloaked, shrouded, covered, hooded *Opposite*: uncovered

vein *n* **1 layer**, seam, lode, stratum, deposit **2 mood**, frame of mind, manner, strain, attitude **3 streak**, strip, stripe, line

veined *adj* **patterned**, marbled, lined, streaked

veld *n* **grassland**, savanna, prairie, plain

veldt *see* **veld**

velocity *n* **speed**, rate, rapidity, swiftness, pace

velvety *adj* **soft**, smooth, silky, downy, furry *Opposite*: rough

venal *adj* **1 corruptible**, mercenary, bribable, bent, unprincipled *Opposite*: honest **2 corrupt**, degenerate, decadent, lawless, amoral *Opposite*: aboveboard

vend *v* **sell**, trade, deal in, hawk, flog *(infml)*

vendetta *n* **1 feud**, blood feud, quarrel, dispute, grudge **2 campaign**, crusade, war, battle, hate campaign

vending machine *n* **slot machine**, dispenser, snack machine, coin-operated machine

vendor *n* **seller**, retailer, dealer, supplier, merchant

veneer *n* **1 covering**, facing, finish, surface, layer **2 appearance**, semblance, pretence, guise, show ■ *v* **cover**, finish, conceal, plate

venerable *adj* **respected**, esteemed, honoured, revered, admired *Opposite*: disreputable

venerate *v* **revere**, worship, adore, idolize, esteem *Opposite*: disrespect

veneration *n* **worship**, adoration, reverence, honour, respect *Opposite*: disdain. *See* COMPARE AND CONTRAST *at* regard.

vengeance *n* **revenge**, retribution, reprisal, retaliation, punishment

vengeful *adj* **vindictive**, implacable, unforgiving, revengeful, resentful *Opposite*: merciful

venial *adj* **forgivable**, excusable, pardonable, understandable, minor *Opposite*: unforgivable

venom *n* **1 poison**, toxin, bane *Opposite*: antidote **2 malice**, spite, rancour, spleen, acrimony *Opposite*: affection

venomous *adj* **1 poisonous**, deadly, toxic, noxious, lethal *Opposite*: harmless **2 malicious**, spiteful, virulent, bitter, rancorous

vent *n* **opening**, outlet, aperture, escape, exhaust ■ *v* **express**, give vent to, find expression for, voice, release *Opposite*: suppress

ventilate *v* **1 air**, aerate, air out, freshen **2 publicize**, make public, make known, air, express

ventilation *n* **air circulation**, airing, aeration

ventilator *n* **1 fan**, vent, opening, flue, aperture **2 life support machine**, respirator, breathing apparatus, iron lung

venture *n* **1 undertaking**, course, endeavour, project, mission **2 business enterprise**, undertaking, scheme, project, endeavour ■ *v* **1 hazard**, dare, undertake, brave, try **2 offer**, put forward, volunteer, express, say **3 presume**, dare, be so bold, take the liberty, have the audacity

venturesome *(fml) adj* **1 daring**, adventurous, enterprising, bold, brave *Opposite*: cautious **2 hazardous**, chancy, dangerous, risky, perilous *Opposite*: safe

venue *n* **site**, place, location, scene, setting

veracious *adj* **honest**, truthful, genuine, principled, dependable *Opposite*: dishonest

veracity *n* **1 truth**, accuracy, reliability, genuineness, authenticity *Opposite*: falsity **2 truthfulness**, honesty, integrity, uprightness, reliability *Opposite*: dishonesty

veranda *n* **terrace**, balcony, porch, loggia, gallery

verbal *adj* **spoken**, oral, vocal, unwritten, voiced *Opposite*: unspoken

---

COMPARE AND CONTRAST CORE MEANING: expressed in words

verbal using words, especially spoken words, rather than pictures or physical action; **spoken** expressed with the voice; **oral** expressed in spoken form rather than in writing.

---

verbalization *n* **articulation**, expression, speech, voicing

verbalize *v* **express**, articulate, voice, put into words, speak

verbatim *adj* **exact**, word for word, precise, literal, word-perfect *Opposite*: imprecise ■ *adv* **word for word**, exactly, precisely, to the letter, literally *Opposite*: approximately

verbiage *n* **empty words**, claptrap *(infml)*, waffle *(infml)*, gobbledegook *(infml)*

verbose *adj* **wordy**, prolix, long-winded, talkative, bombastic *Opposite*: taciturn. *See* COMPARE AND CONTRAST *at* wordy.

verbosity *n* **long-windedness**, garrulousness, wordiness, prolixity, loquaciousness *Opposite*: succinctness

verdant *adj* **green**, lush, luxuriant, fertile, leafy

verdict *n* **decision**, judgment, finding, result, outcome

verdigris *n* **patina**, tarnish, corrosion, greenness, coloration

verdure *n* **greenery**, lushness, vegetation, flora, plant life

verge *n* **edge**, border, threshold, approach, limit ■ *v* **be near to**, approach, border on, come close to, near

verge on *see* **verge**

verifiable *adj* **demonstrable**, provable, confirmable, certifiable, showable *Opposite*: moot

verification *n* **confirmation**, corroboration, proof, substantiation, authentication *Opposite*: contradiction

verified *adj* **confirmed**, proved, shown, tested, substantiated *Opposite*: unconfirmed

verify *v* **confirm**, bear out, prove, authenticate, validate *Opposite*: disprove

verisimilitude *(fml)* *n* **truth**, credibility, authenticity, reliability, plausibility *Opposite*: falsity

veritable *adj* **absolute**, real, genuine, out-and-out, authentic *Opposite*: false

verity *(fml)* *n* **truth**, fact, principle, reality, sincerity

verminous *adj* **infested**, pest-ridden, louse-ridden, rat-infested, crawling

vernacular *n* **dialect**, language, patois, argot, colloquial speech

versatile *adj* **1 adaptable**, flexible, resourceful, multitalented, all-round *Opposite*: inflexible **2 multipurpose**, adaptable, handy, useful, nifty *(infml)* *Opposite*: inflexible

versatility *n* **1 adaptability**, flexibility, resourcefulness *Opposite*: inflexibility **2 usefulness**, handiness, niftiness *(infml)*

verse *n* **1 stanza**, canto, section, unit **2 poetry**, rhyme, blank verse, free verse, doggerel *Opposite*: prose

versed *adj* **experienced**, competent, conversant, proficient, knowledgeable *Opposite*: inexperienced

version *n* **1 account**, description, report, side, story **2 form**, type, variety, kind, sort **3 adaptation**, edition, translation, rendering

versus *prep* **1 against**, contra, in competition with **2 as opposed to**, contrasted with, set against, against, as against

vertebrate *n* **animal**, mammal, bird, reptile, amphibian *Opposite*: invertebrate

vertex *n* **apex**, summit, height, pinnacle, apogee *Opposite*: base

vertical *adj* **perpendicular**, upright, erect, straight up, straight down *Opposite*: horizontal

vertiginous *adj* **high**, dizzying, tall, lofty, exposed

vertigo *n* **dizziness**, giddiness, unsteadiness, faintness, lightheadedness

verve *n* **vitality**, energy, dynamism, vigour, dash *Opposite*: lethargy

very *adv* **extremely**, incredibly, awfully, exceptionally, exceedingly *Opposite*: a bit *(infml)* ■ *adj* **actual**, self-same, same, identical, exact

vessel *n* **1 container**, pot, bowl, jug, pitcher **2 boat**, ship, craft

vest *v* **devolve**, consign, entrust, assign, lodge

vested interest *n* **1 special interest**, interest, concern, stake, investment **2 stakeholder**, supporter, shareholder

vestibule *n* **entrance hall**, foyer, lobby, antechamber, atrium

vestige *n* **trace**, sign, mark, indication, hint

vestigial *adj* **1 residual**, remaining, imperceptible, token **2 nonfunctioning**, functionless, stunted, degenerate, atrophic *Opposite*: functional

vestment *n* **1 robe**, garment, dress, habit, uniform **2 surplice**, chasuble, cope, vesture *(archaic)*

vet *v* **examine**, check, scrutinize, research, inspect

veteran *n* **expert**, old hand, past master, trouper, old-timer *Opposite*: novice

veto *n* **1 rejection**, refusal, bar, disallowance, prevention *Opposite*: approval **2 prohibition**, ban, sanction, embargo, order *Opposite*: release ■ *v* **1 reject**, turn down, bar, disallow, refuse *Opposite*: approve **2 prohibit**, ban, forbid, outlaw, proscribe *Opposite*: permit

vex *v* **1 annoy**, displease, irk, irritate, anger *Opposite*: pacify **2 agitate**, distress, trouble, bother, torment *Opposite*: placate **3 confound**, confuse, perplex, puzzle, tease *Opposite*: enlighten

vexation *n* **annoyance**, upset, displeasure, bother, irritation *Opposite*: satisfaction

vexatious *adj* **annoying**, upsetting, irritating, troublesome, bothersome *Opposite*: placatory

vexed *adj* **1 irritated**, provoked, annoyed, upset, angry *Opposite*: calm **2 debated**, controversial, contentious, fractious, problematic *Opposite*: uncomplicated

vexing *adj* **annoying**, puzzling, frustrating, worrying, worrisome *Opposite*: easy

via *prep* **by way of**, through, by

viability *n* **practicability**, feasibility, practicality, capability, sustainability *Opposite*: impracticality

viable *adj* **practicable**, worthwhile, feasible, practical, sustainable *Opposite*: impossible

vial *n* **ampoule**, vessel, container, flask, bottle

vibrancy *n* **vitality**, vivacity, animation, enthusiasm, effervescence *Opposite*: lethargy

vibrant *adj* **1 pulsating**, energetic, vibrating, effervescent, alive *Opposite*: listless **2 bright**, dazzling, vivid, brilliant, flamboyant *Opposite*: dull

vibrate *v* **shake**, quiver, tremble, shudder, judder

vibration *n* **shaking**, quivering, trembling, shuddering, juddering *Opposite*: stillness

vicarage *n* **rectory**, manse, church house, parsonage, residence

vicarious *adj* **1 displaced**, indirect, remote, removed, distanced *Opposite*: direct **2 empathetic**, sympathetic, assumed, imagined, adopted **3 delegated**, surrogate, substitute, proxy, deputized

vice *n* **1 depravity**, iniquity, evil, wickedness, immorality *Opposite*: goodness **2 defect**, failing, flaw, imperfection, fault *Opposite*: strength

vicinal *adj* **1 neighbouring**, adjacent, nearby, close, proximate *Opposite*: distant **2 local**, district, municipal, regional, provincial *Opposite*: international

vicinity n **neighbourhood**, environs, locality, district, area

vicious adj 1 **ferocious**, savage, wild, brutish, fierce Opposite: gentle 2 **spiteful**, malicious, mean, rancorous, backbiting Opposite: kind

vicious circle n **catch-22**, no-win situation, impasse, stalemate

viciousness n 1 **ferociousness**, savagery, wildness, brutishness, ferocity Opposite: gentleness 2 **maliciousness**, meanness, spitefulness, rancorousness, venomousness Opposite: kindness

vicissitudes n **changes**, variations, vagaries, ups and downs, fluctuations

victim n 1 **fatality**, casualty, sufferer, injured party 2 **dupe**, butt, target, object, prey

victimization n **persecution**, discrimination, oppression, ill-treatment, harassment Opposite: favouritism

victimize v **persecute**, discriminate against, harass, oppress, pick on Opposite: favour

victor n **winner**, champion, conqueror, medallist, prizewinner Opposite: loser

victorious adj **winning**, triumphant, champion, prizewinning, successful Opposite: losing

victory n **conquest**, triumph, win, success Opposite: defeat

victuals n **food**, provisions, supplies, foodstuffs, food and drink

video v **videotape**, record, tape, film, capture

WORD BANK
❏ **types of video equipment** camcorder, DVD, palmcorder, video camera, video cassette, video cassette recorder, videodisk, video recorder, videotape

---

video display terminal n **screen**, monitor, interface, terminal, viewer

videotape v **record**, video, tape, film, capture

vie v **compete**, contend, contest, strive, fight Opposite: collaborate

view n 1 **sight**, vision, observation, examination, scrutiny 2 **scene**, picture, spectacle, prospect, vista 3 **opinion**, interpretation, assessment, understanding ■ v 1 **look at**, see, regard, observe, notice 2 **inspect**, examine, look over, look at, observe 3 **consider**, regard, think of, perceive, look on

viewable adj 1 **available**, on view, on display, accessible 2 **fit**, presentable, acceptable, all right, appropriate Opposite: inappropriate

viewer n **watcher**, spectator, onlooker, ogler, observer

viewing n 1 **watching**, inspecting, seeing, observing, looking 2 **programming**, broadcasts, programmes, broadcasting, showing

viewpoint n 1 **point of view**, view, perspective, standpoint, position 2 **vantage point**, viewing platform, belvedere, lookout, crow's nest

vigil n **night watch**, watch, wake

vigilance n **watchfulness**, attentiveness, observance, care, caution Opposite: inattentiveness

vigilant adj **watchful**, alert, attentive, on your guard, wary Opposite: inattentive. See COMPARE AND CONTRAST at **cautious**.

vignette n 1 **design**, decoration, illustration, frontispiece, picture 2 **essay**, article, piece, monograph 3 **picture**, painting, drawing, photograph, print 4 **scene**, extract, clip, fragment, snippet

vigorous adj **robust**, active, strong, energetic, dynamic Opposite: feeble

vigour n 1 **vitality**, energy, robustness, strength, heartiness Opposite: lethargy 2 **intensity**, forcefulness, force, ferocity, gusto Opposite: feebleness 3 **potency**, strength, life, robustness, stamina Opposite: weakness

vile adj 1 **disgusting**, loathsome, revolting, repulsive, repellent Opposite: admirable 2 **evil**, wicked, shameful, depraved, base Opposite: good 3 **unpleasant**, horrid, horrible, dreadful, awful Opposite: pleasant. See COMPARE AND CONTRAST at **mean**.

vileness n 1 **evil**, depravity, wickedness, lowness, degradation Opposite: goodness 2 **unpleasantness**, dreadfulness, awfulness, horridness, horribleness Opposite: pleasantness 3 **repulsiveness**, loathsomeness, hatefulness, despicableness

vilification n **maliciousness**, abuse, disparagement, criticism, backbiting Opposite: acclaim

vilify v **malign**, abuse, denigrate, belittle, disparage Opposite: compliment. See COMPARE AND CONTRAST at **malign**.

village n **hamlet**, rural community, settlement

villager n **country dweller**, rustic, country cousin (dated)

villain n **scoundrel**, rogue, desperado, heavy, baddie (infml) Opposite: hero

villainous adj 1 **wicked**, criminal, heinous, depraved, iniquitous Opposite: good 2 **unpleasant**, undesirable, obnoxious, offensive, unreliable Opposite: pleasant

villainy n **wickedness**, wrongdoing, evil, foul play, badness Opposite: goodness

vim (infml) n **vitality**, energy, exuberance, verve, vigour Opposite: lethargy

vindicate v 1 **justify**, maintain, claim, support, defend 2 **clear**, exonerate, absolve, acquit, exculpate (fml) Opposite: implicate

vindication n 1 **exoneration**, absolution, acquittal, exculpation (fml) Opposite: implication 2 **justification**, evidence, proof, assertion

vindictive adj 1 **vengeful**, unforgiving, revengeful, rancorous, implacable Opposite: forgiving 2 **spiteful**, malicious, mean, cruel, hurtful Opposite: kind

vindictiveness n 1 **spite**, malice, cruelty, nastiness, unkindness Opposite: kindness 2 **vengefulness**, bitterness, rancour, resentment

vine *n* climber, creeper, liana

vinegary *adj* **1** sour, astringent, acidic, acid, tart *Opposite*: sweet **2** irritable, sour, bitter, embittered, unpleasant *Opposite*: pleasant

vintage *n* era, time, age, epoch, period ■ *adj* **1** classic, typical, traditional, essential, prime *Opposite*: atypical **2** out-of-date, dated, antique, old, outmoded *Opposite*: new

vinyl *n* LPs, records, discs, singles, albums

violate *v* **1** disregard, infringe, defy, breach, disobey *Opposite*: obey **2** disrupt, disturb, interrupt, encroach upon, intrude upon *Opposite*: respect **3** defile, desecrate, spoil, destroy, ruin *Opposite*: venerate

violation *n* **1** infringement, breach, contravention, defiance, disobedience *Opposite*: obedience **2** disruption, intrusion, encroachment, disturbance, interruption *Opposite*: respect **3** defilement, desecration, destruction, ruin, abuse *Opposite*: veneration

violence *n* **1** physical force, pugnaciousness, pugnacity, aggression, fighting *Opposite*: passivity **2** ferocity, strength, force, fierceness, viciousness *Opposite*: gentleness

violent *adj* **1** pugnacious, aggressive, brutal, cruel, sadistic *Opposite*: peaceful **2** fierce, ferocious, vehement, vicious, forceful *Opposite*: gentle

VIP *n* dignitary, name, luminary, star, celebrity

viperish *adj* malicious, spiteful, nasty, unkind, malevolent *Opposite*: kind

virtual *adj* **1** near, practical, effective, fundamental, essential *Opposite*: actual **2** computer-generated, simulated, cybernetic

virtually *adv* **1** in effect, effectively, essentially, fundamentally, to all intents and purposes **2** almost, nearly, near, nigh on, close to

virtual reality *n* computer modelling, simulated reality, computer simulation, simulation, VR

virtue *n* **1** goodness, righteousness, integrity, honesty, morality *Opposite*: wickedness **2** asset, feature, quality, advantage, benefit *Opposite*: disadvantage

virtuosity *n* skill, technique, brilliance, flair, talent

virtuoso *n* **1** musician, bravura player, artist, maestro **2** wunderkind, genius, prodigy, ace (*infml*), wizard (*infml*)

virtuous *adj* good, righteous, worthy, honourable, moral *Opposite*: bad

virulent *adj* **1** infectious, contagious, poisonous, lethal, strong *Opposite*: weak **2** malicious, bitter, vituperative, venomous, fierce *Opposite*: kind

virus *n* **1** illness, infection, sickness, disease **2** computer virus, Trojan horse, worm

visa *n* endorsement, pass, entry permit, documents, papers

visage *n* look, appearance, aspect, form, mien (*fml*)

vis-à-vis *prep* **1** regarding, in relation to, in respect of, re, with reference to **2** versus, compared with, contrasted with, in comparison with, opposite to

viscera *n* internal organs, intestines, entrails, guts, bowels

visceral *adj* instinctual, instinctive, intuitive, gut, primitive *Opposite*: reasoned

viscid *adj* thick, sticky, gooey, gluey, treacly *Opposite*: runny

viscosity *n* viscidness, thickness, stickiness, gluiness, gooeyness *Opposite*: fluidity

viscous *adj* viscid, thick, sticky, glutinous, gelatinous *Opposite*: runny

visibility *n* **1** discernibility, perceptibility, conspicuousness, luminosity *Opposite*: invisibility **2** prominence, familiarity, profile, image, high profile

visible *adj* **1** noticeable, observable, perceptible, evident, in evidence *Opposite*: invisible **2** prominent, high-profile, familiar, ubiquitous

vision *n* **1** eyesight, sight, ability to see **2** concept, mental picture, idea, image, visualization **3** revelation, prophecy, dream, hallucination, apparition **4** foresight, imagination, forethought, prescience, farsightedness

visionary *adj* **1** inventive, creative, farseeing, prescient, original *Opposite*: unimaginative **2** unrealistic, impracticable, quixotic, fanciful, unworkable *Opposite*: practicable ■ *n* prophet, dreamer, thinker, seer

visit *v* **1** call on, call in on, drop in on, go to see, pay a visit **2** go to, stay in, stay at, stop with, stop at ■ *n* **1** social call, official visit, call, duty call **2** stay, stopover, holiday, break, trip

visitation *n* **1** visit, examination, inspection, check, checkup **2** punishment, curse, calamity, blight, catastrophe

visitor *n* caller, guest, tourist, sightseer

visitor centre *n* tourist centre, information office, inquiry office, information point, help point

visor *n* screen, blind, eyeshade

vista *n* view, panorama, outlook, scene, landscape

visual *adj* **1** graphic, pictorial, filmic, painterly, photographic **2** concrete, visible, discernible, observable, evident **3** optical, chromatic, ophthalmic, ocular ■ *n* graphic, visual aid, illustration, picture, photograph

visual aid *n* model, film, video, chart, illustration

visualization *n* **1** imagining, conjuring up, picturing, conception **2** mental image, mental picture, vision, hallucination, image **3** positive thinking, therapy, cognitive therapy, meditation, image creation

visualize *v* imagine, envisage, picture, see in your mind's eye, dream of

vital adj 1 **important**, crucial, fundamental, critical, necessary Opposite: unimportant 2 **energetic**, vigorous, vivacious, dynamic, vibrant Opposite: lifeless. See COMPARE AND CONTRAST at necessary.

vitality n **liveliness**, energy, vivacity, vigour, life Opposite: lethargy

vitalize v **animate**, energize, buoy up, bolster, hearten Opposite: deaden

vitally adv **extremely**, indispensably, enormously, absolutely, really

vitreous adj **enamel**, vitric, vitriform, glasslike, glassy

vitriol n **hatred**, bitterness, venom, spleen, sarcasm Opposite: love

vitriolic adj **spiteful**, venomous, hurtful, acerbic, bitter Opposite: kind

vituperation n 1 **outburst**, attack, criticism, censuring, condemnation 2 **abuse**, venom, vitriol, savaging, mauling

vituperative adj **insulting**, abusive, offensive, malicious, slanderous

vivacious adj **vibrant**, lively, bubbly, cheerful, spirited Opposite: languid

vivacity n **high-spiritedness**, liveliness, animation, verve, vivaciousness Opposite: lethargy

vivid adj 1 **intense**, rich, gaudy, bright, glowing Opposite: dull 2 **fresh**, distinct, clear, crystal clear, lucid Opposite: vague 3 **striking**, powerful, strong, clear, intense Opposite: understated 4 **active**, lively, creative, ingenious, original Opposite: prosaic

vividness n 1 **richness**, gaudiness, colourfulness, brightness, vibrancy Opposite: dullness 2 **freshness**, distinctness, clarity, lucidity, clearness Opposite: vagueness 3 **power**, strength, clarity, intensity 4 **liveliness**, creativity, ingeniousness, flamboyance, intensity Opposite: banality

vocabulary n 1 **language**, words, terms, expressions, terminology 2 **dictionary**, glossary, lexicon, word list. See COMPARE AND CONTRAST at language.

vocal adj 1 **uttered**, verbal, voiced, spoken, unwritten Opposite: silent 2 **outspoken**, frank, insistent, vociferous, voluble Opposite: quiet

vocalist n **singer**, lead vocalist, backing vocalist, lead singer, backing singer

vocalize v **express**, voice, articulate, give voice to, put into words

vocals n **lyrics**, words, singing, chorus

vocation n 1 **career**, profession, job, occupation, work 2 **aptitude**, inclination, talent, bent, urge

vocational adj **occupational**, professional, job-related, career, work

vociferous adj **clamorous**, vocal, loud, voluble, raucous Opposite: quiet

vogue n **fashion**, trend, craze, rage, mode

voguish adj 1 **fashionable**, elegant, chic, stylish, modish Opposite: unfashionable 2 **passing**, in vogue, in, up-to-the-minute, popular Opposite: unpopular

voice n 1 **speech**, singing, vocal sound, power of speech 2 **opinion**, say, right of speech, expression, declaration ■ v 1 **express**, assert, declare, proclaim, opine (fml) 2 **pronounce**, articulate, utter, declare, intone (fml)

voiced adj **stated**, enunciated, spoken, uttered, expressed

voiceless adj 1 **silent**, unspeaking, mute, taciturn, wordless Opposite: speaking 2 **unrepresented**, disenfranchised, invisible, ignored, forgotten Opposite: represented

voiceover n **narration**, commentary, narrative

void adj 1 **annulled**, cancelled, invalid, null and void, negated (fml) Opposite: valid 2 **empty**, vacant, unoccupied, not in use, occupied ■ n **empty space**, emptiness, vacuum, hollowness, abyss ■ v **cancel**, annul, render null and void, vacate, reject. See COMPARE AND CONTRAST at vacant.

volatile adj 1 **unstable**, precarious, changeable, dangerous, hazardous Opposite: stable 2 **unpredictable**, explosive, hot-blooded, impulsive, fickle Opposite: placid

volatility n 1 **instability**, precariousness, changeability, explosiveness Opposite: stability 2 **unpredictability**, explosiveness, hot-bloodedness, impulsiveness, fickleness Opposite: placidity

volition n **wish**, will, decision, choice, desire Opposite: coercion

volley n **torrent**, shower, stream, cascade, barrage ■ v **lob**, hit, strike, kick

volte-face n **about-turn**, U-turn, reversal, change of direction, change of heart

voluble adj **talkative**, fluent, articulate, verbose, loquacious Opposite: taciturn

volume n 1 **quantity**, amount, degree, size, level 2 **capacity**, size, dimensions, measurements, bulk 3 **book**, tome, work 4 **part**, section, edition

voluminous adj **big**, huge, large, capacious, roomy Opposite: small

voluntarily adv **willingly**, of your own accord, happily, gladly, freely Opposite: reluctantly

voluntary adj 1 **unpaid**, charitable, volunteer Opposite: professional 2 **intended**, intentional, controlled, deliberate, chosen Opposite: involuntary

volunteer n **helper**, unpaid worker, candy striper (US) ■ v 1 **offer**, come forward, agree, step up, undertake 2 **give**, offer, tell, advise, inform

vomit v 1 **be sick**, be nauseous, be nauseated, gag, retch 2 **expel**, spew out, spew forth, eject, send out ■ n **sick**, vomitus, barf (infml), chunder (infml), puke (slang)

voracious adj **insatiable**, avid, hungry, ravenous, gluttonous Opposite: sated

voraciousness *see* **voracity**

voracity *n* **greed**, greediness, gluttony, hunger, rapaciousness

vortex *n* **1 whirlpool**, whirlwind, waterspout, tornado, cyclone **2 quagmire**, morass, maelstrom, turbulence, whirlwind

vote *n* **ballot**, election, division, secret ballot, show of hands ■ *v* **choose**, cast your vote, elect, opt for, support *Opposite*: abstain

voter *n* **elector**, constituent, supporter, backer

votive *adj* **1 ritual**, prayerful, supplicatory *(fml)*, precatory *(fml)* **2 promised**, pledged, vowed, contractual, agreed

voucher *n* **coupon**, ticket, receipt, chit *(dated)*, check *(US)*

vouch for *v* **speak for**, support, guarantee, back up, stand up for

vouchsafe *v* **1 give**, grant, offer, bestow *(fml)* **2** *(fml)* **promise**, agree, allow, permit, consent

vow *n* **promise**, oath, pledge, guarantee, declaration ■ *v* **swear**, promise, guarantee, undertake, declare

voyage *n* **journey**, trip, expedition, passage, crossing ■ *v* **journey**, sail, cruise, travel

voyager *n* **traveller**, explorer, adventurer, tourist, vacationer *(US)*

vulgar *adj* **1 rude**, offensive, crude, bad, earthy *Opposite*: decent **2 tasteless**, brash, common, kitsch, ostentatious *Opposite*: tasteful **3 bad-mannered**, uncouth, discourteous, unrefined, rude *Opposite*: polite

vulgarism *n* **1 obscenity**, swear word, four-letter word, expletive, rude word **2 colloquialism**, popular expression, idiom, common term

vulgarity *n* **1 rudeness**, offensiveness, crudeness, crudity, earthiness *Opposite*: decency **2 bad manners**, uncouthness, rudeness, loutishness, boorishness *Opposite*: politeness **3 tastelessness**, brashness, ostentatiousness, commonness, kitsch *Opposite*: tastefulness **4 swearword**, curse, bad language, four-letter word, rude word

vulnerability *n* **susceptibility**, weakness, defencelessness, helplessness, exposure *Opposite*: invincibility

vulnerable *adj* **susceptible**, weak, defenceless, helpless, exposed *Opposite*: invincible

vulturine *adj* **opportunistic**, exploitative, greedy, avaricious, grasping

W

wackiness *(infml)* *n* **zaniness**, silliness, wildness, eccentricity, oddness *Opposite*: conventionality

wacky *(infml)* *adj* **silly**, zany, madcap, way out, off the wall *Opposite*: conventional

wad *n* **1 bundle**, roll, sheaf, stack, pile **2 lump**, mass, cushion, clump, chunk **3 twist**, chew, portion, gob *(slang)* ■ *v* **1 plug**, lag, stuff, fill, pad **2 compress**, scrunch, squeeze, compact, screw

wadding *n* **padding**, lining, insulation, lagging, filling

waddle *v* **toddle**, sway, shuffle, wobble

wade *v* **paddle**, stride, walk, splash

wade through *v* **plough through**, struggle through, battle through, tackle, deal with

wafer-thin *adj* **thin**, paper-thin, slim

waffle *(infml)* *v* **go on**, ramble, make small talk, blabber, babble ■ *n* **nonsense**, rubbish, drivel, balderdash, gobbledegook *(infml)*

waft *v* **drift**, float, glide, sail, fan ■ *n* **puff**, breath, gust, breeze, draught

wag *v* **wave to and fro**, move from side to side, flap, wiggle, waggle ■ *n* **1 wiggle**, waggle, shake, twitch, wave **2** *(dated)* **wit**, humorist, comedian, comic, joker

wage *n* **salary**, pay, earnings, income, take-home pay ■ *v* **carry on**, conduct, pursue, engage in, fight

COMPARE AND CONTRAST CORE MEANING: money given for work done

wage a fixed regular payment made on an hourly, weekly, or daily basis, especially to manual workers; **salary** a fixed regular annual sum, usually paid on a monthly basis, especially to clerical or professional workers; **pay** a wage or salary; **fee** a payment made to a professional person by a client; **remuneration** payment for work, goods, or services; **emolument** *(fml)* any payment for work; **honorarium** money given in exchange for services for which there is normally no fixed charge; **stipend** a regular payment or allowance for living expenses, especially one made to a member of the clergy or a student.

wage earner *n* **breadwinner**, provider, earner, worker, supporter

wage packet *n* **wage**, salary, pay packet, wages, earnings

wager *n* **bet**, gamble, stake, ante, flutter *(infml)* ■ *v* **bet**, gamble, stake, risk, venture

wages *n* **salary**, pay, earnings, income, take-home pay

wage war on *v* **oppose**, combat, resist, fight, do battle

waggish *(dated)* adj **humorous**, witty, mischievous, droll, jocular

waggishness *(dated)* n **humorousness**, wit, mischievousness, mischief, drollness

waggle v **wiggle**, wag, shake, wave to and fro, move from side to side

waif n **stray**, soul, urchin, orphan, ragamuffin *(dated)*

wail v 1 **howl**, moan, weep, yowl, keen 2 **complain**, fuss, whine, kick up a fuss *(infml)*, kick up a storm *(infml)* ■ n 1 **howl**, moan, yowl, scream, cry 2 **complaint**, protest, whine, fuss

wainscot n **panelling**, wainscoting, cladding, lining

waistline n **waist**, middle, midriff

wait v 1 **stay**, remain, hang around, linger, stop 2 **delay**, pause, hold your fire, postpone, hang on *Opposite*: begin 3 **expect**, anticipate, await, wait on ■ n **delay**, pause, interval, postponement, gap

waiter n **server**, attendant, maître d', head waiter, maître d'hôtel

waiting area n **concourse**, foyer, meeting point, waiting room, reception

wait on v 1 **care for**, serve, mother, nurse, take care of 2 *(infml)* **expect**, anticipate, await, wait for

waive v **surrender**, give up, relinquish, put aside, ignore *Opposite*: retain

waiver n 1 **disclaimer**, relinquishment, renunciation, abdication, abandonment 2 **contract**, agreement, bond

wake v 1 **wake up**, awaken, stir, come round, come to 2 **arouse**, stir, awaken, rouse, kindle *Opposite*: stifle

wakeful adj 1 **restless**, disturbed, sleepless, unable to sleep, insomniac *Opposite*: drowsy 2 **alert**, vigilant, on guard, attentive, aware *Opposite*: inattentive

wakefulness n 1 **restlessness**, sleeplessness, insomnia, tossing and turning, restiveness *Opposite*: drowsiness 2 **alertness**, vigilance, attentiveness, awareness, watchfulness *Opposite*: inattentiveness

waken *see* **wake up**

wake up v 1 **wake**, awaken, stir, come round, come to *Opposite*: go to sleep 2 **liven up**, come to life, come alive, revive, animate

walk v **go on foot**, stroll, amble, saunter, march ■ n 1 **stroll**, saunter, march, amble, promenade *(fml)* 2 **gait**, pace, tread, stride, way of walking

walkabout *(infml)* n **walk**, stroll, saunter, amble, tour

walk a tightrope v **tread dangerously**, invite trouble, ask for trouble, ask for it, skate on thin ice

walk away v 1 **abandon**, leave, withdraw, abdicate, back down from 2 **win**, triumph, sail through, succeed, walk it *(infml)*

walk down the aisle v **get married**, marry, tie the knot *(infml)*, get hitched *(infml)*, get spliced *(slang)*

walker n **hiker**, rambler, stroller

walking adj **outdoor**, hiking, rambling, cross-country, heavy-duty

walking stick n **cane**, stick, bamboo, staff

walk in on v **barge in**, march in, interrupt, intrude, butt in

walk off v **turn your back**, walk away, leave, go, quit *Opposite*: remain

walk off with v **steal**, embezzle, pocket, appropriate, take

walk-on n **bit part**, cameo, minor part, extra, nonspeaking part

walk out v 1 **leave**, storm out, go off in a huff, flounce out, take yourself off *(infml)* 2 **go on strike**, down tools, take industrial action, stop work

walkout n **strike**, stoppage, protest, industrial action

walk out on *(infml)* v **leave**, abandon, leave in the lurch, go, desert

walk over *(infml)* v **defeat**, beat, overpower, trounce, thrash

walkover *(infml)* n **easy victory**, child's play, runaway, runaway victory, pushover *(infml)* *Opposite*: challenge

walk through v **rehearse**, practise, run through

walkway n 1 **path**, footpath, pathway, pavement, alley 2 **aisle**, corridor, passage, passageway

wall n **partition**, divider, screen, panel, bulkhead

wallet n **folder**, file, case, holder

wallop *(infml)* v 1 **thump**, smack, thwack, strike, hit 2 **defeat**, beat, trounce, whip, destroy ■ n 1 **blow**, thump, bash, smack, thwack 2 **fizz**, punch, clout, pizazz *(infml)*, buzz *(infml)*

walloping *(infml)* n 1 **beating**, thrashing, hiding *(infml)* 2 **defeat**, drubbing, rout, hiding *(infml)* ■ adj **huge**, enormous, gigantic, stupendous, massive ■ adv **extremely**, very, tremendously, inordinately, stupendously

wallow v **flounder**, stumble, lurch, stagger, welter

wallow in v **enjoy**, bask in, revel in, relish, make the most of

wallpaper n **wall covering**, paper, lining paper

wall-to-wall *(infml)* adj **omnipresent**, all-pervasive, nonstop, ceaseless, never-ending

waltz n *(infml)* **cinch** *(infml)*, piece of cake *(infml)*, breeze *(infml)*, pushover *(infml)*, walkover *(infml)* ■ v 1 **walk**, stroll, swan, breeze, saunter 2 **romp**, sail, steam, whizz, cruise

wan adj 1 **pallid**, ashen, ashy, drawn, washed-out 2 **listless**, feeble, weak, down, depressed *Opposite*: strong

wand n **baton**, stick, rod, pointer

wander v 1 **stroll**, meander, walk, ramble, roam 2 **drift**, stray, digress, lose the point, lose the thread ■ n **walk**, stroll, ramble, mosey (infml), mooch (slang)

wanderer n **nomad**, vagrant, itinerant, traveller, rover

wandering adj **itinerant**, nomadic, peripatetic, travelling, drifting Opposite: settled

wanderlust n **desire to travel**, itchy feet, travel bug

wane v **diminish**, decrease, decline, get smaller, fade Opposite: wax (literary)

wangle (infml) v **engineer**, contrive, obtain, get, fix (infml)

waning adj **fading**, declining, weakening, diminishing, disappearing Opposite: increasing

wannabe (infml) n **hopeful**, aspirant, imitator, clone, camp follower ■ adj **aspiring**, aspirational, would-be, hopeful, budding

want v 1 **desire**, wish for, long for, crave, covet 2 **need**, require, lack, be short of, miss ■ n 1 **lack**, absence, shortage, scarcity, dearth 2 **poverty**, famine, hunger, need, neediness

COMPARE AND CONTRAST CORE MEANING: seek to have, do, or achieve something

want feel a need or desire for something; **desire** want something very strongly; **wish** have a strong, sometimes unrealistic, desire to have or to do something; **long** have a strong desire for somebody or something, especially something difficult to achieve; **yearn** want something very much, especially with a feeling of sadness when it seems unlikely that it can ever be obtained; **covet** have a strong desire to possess something that belongs to somebody else, or (fml) want something very much; **crave** want something very much, especially when this desire is physical.

wanted adj **required**, sought, sought after, hunted, desired

wanting adj **deficient**, inadequate, imperfect, not good enough, not up to standard Opposite: adequate ■ prep **without**, lacking, in need of, short of, minus

wanton adj 1 **gratuitous**, motiveless, meaningless, reckless, needless Opposite: justifiable 2 **immoral**, immodest, abandoned, licentious, lustful Opposite: restrained 3 **malevolent**, malicious, cruel, vicious, nasty Opposite: benign 4 **excessive**, extravagant, unrestrained, heedless, unreasonable Opposite: restrained

wantonness n **depravity**, debauchery, immorality, shamelessness, impiety Opposite: restraint

wants n **needs**, requirements, desires, requests, wishes

war n 1 **warfare**, hostilities, fighting, combat, action Opposite: peace 2 **campaign**, battle, struggle, fight, conflict 3 **competition**, rivalry, feud, battle, struggle. See COMPARE AND CONTRAST at **fight**.

warble v **sing**, trill, pipe up, chirrup, sing out

war cry n **battle cry**, rallying call, call to arms

warden n **custodian**, curator, keeper, steward, superintendent

warder n **prison officer**, jailer, custodian, guard, screw (slang)

ward off v **defend against**, protect against, deflect, hold off, keep at bay

wardrobe n **clothes**, clothing, apparel, gear (infml), attire (fml)

wares n **goods**, merchandise, produce, products, commodities

warfare n 1 **fighting**, conflict, combat, action, hostilities 2 **rivalry**, feud, competition, contest, struggle

warhorse n **campaigner**, warrior, stalwart, old hand, master

wariness n **caution**, suspicion, care, circumspection, guardedness Opposite: carelessness

warlike adj 1 **belligerent**, aggressive, bellicose, confrontational, hostile Opposite: friendly 2 **martial**, military, militaristic, warring, war

warlock n **sorcerer**, wizard, enchanter, witch, necromancer (literary)

warlord n **military leader**, general, chieftain, guerrilla leader, commander

warm adj 1 **temperate**, tepid, balmy, hot, lukewarm Opposite: cool 2 **kind**, kindly, warmhearted, kind-hearted, friendly Opposite: unfriendly 3 **cosy**, inviting, restful, cheerful, cheery Opposite: unwelcoming 4 **lively**, passionate, ardent, fiery, enthusiastic Opposite: cool 5 **sincere**, heartfelt, deep, earnest, wholehearted ■ v 1 **heat**, heat up, reheat, warm up, melt Opposite: cool 2 **take to**, become fond of, take a liking to, take a fancy to, get on with Opposite: cool off 3 **become enthusiastic about**, get going on, get fired up about, get excited, become enthused ■ n **warmth**, warmness, heat Opposite: cold

warm-blooded adj **passionate**, impetuous, enthusiastic, ardent, emotional Opposite: cold-blooded

warm-hearted adj **kindly**, tender, kind, sympathetic, affectionate Opposite: cold-hearted

warm-heartedness n **tenderness**, kindness, sympathy, affection, love Opposite: cold-heartedness

warmness see **warmth**

warmonger n **hawk**, belligerent, jingo, jingoist, aggressor Opposite: peacemaker

warmongering n **sabre rattling**, belligerence, aggression, jingoism, hawkishness Opposite: peacemaking

warmth n 1 **warmness**, heat, hotness Opposite: cold 2 **balminess**, temperateness, high temperature, warmness Opposite: coldness 3 **friendliness**, cordiality, warm-heartedness, kind-heartedness, warmness Opposite: cold-heartedness 4 **enthusiasm**, eagerness, earnestness, ardour, fervour *Opposite*: apathy

warm up *v* **1** limber up, loosen up, get loose, stretch *Opposite*: cool off **2 warm**, heat, heat up, reheat, warm through *Opposite*: cool off

warm-up *n* **exercises**, limbering up, loosening up, preparation

warn *v* **1** caution, advise, inform, notify, tell **2 alert**, forewarn, advise, tell, notify

warning *n* **1 threat**, indication, portent, wake-up call, forewarning **2 notice**, caution, caveat, word of warning, advice ■ *adj* **cautionary**, threatening, cautioning

warn off *v* deter, discourage, dissuade, put off, scare off

war of words *n* argument, row, slanging match, disagreement, fight

warp *v* **1** distort, twist, deform, bend, buckle *Opposite*: straighten **2 change**, pervert, damage, distort, misrepresent ■ *n* twist, bend, distortion, deviation, alteration

warped *adj* **1** misshapen, distorted, deformed, twisted, bent **2 changed**, damaged, distorted, misrepresented, confused **3 partial**, biased, one-sided, prejudiced, skewed *Opposite*: impartial

warrant *n* **authorization**, permit, licence, authority, certification ■ *v* **1 merit**, deserve, necessitate, call for, demand **2 guarantee**, affirm, certify, secure, assure

warranty *n* guarantee, contract, pledge, assurance

warren *n* **1 hole**, earth, habitat, burrow, lair **2 maze**, labyrinth, catacomb

warring *adj* belligerent, combatant, fighting, sparring, opposing *Opposite*: friendly

warrior *n* soldier, fighter, combatant, trooper

wart *n* lump, growth, verruca

war-torn *adj* war-ravaged, frontline, battle-weary, war-scarred, battle-scarred *Opposite*: peaceful

wary *adj* watchful, cautious, suspicious, distrustful, mistrustful *Opposite*: careless. *See* COMPARE AND CONTRAST *at* **cautious**.

wash *v* **1** clean, bathe, rinse, sponge down, wash down **2 bathe**, bath, clean up, wash up (US) **3 flow over**, splash, lap, swish, pound **4 erode**, wash away, carry away, bear away, sweep away ■ *n* **1 shower**, shampoo, sponge, rinse, wash-down **2 layer**, film, coat, overlay, coating **3 stain**, tint, rinse, suffusion, colouring

washable *adj* colourfast, easy-care, noniron, preshrunk, unfading

washbasin *n* hand basin, basin, bowl, sink, washbowl

washbowl *see* **washbasin**

wash down *v* clean, rinse, sluice, sponge down, hose down

washed-out *adj* **1 wan**, pallid, ashen, ashy, drawn **2 exhausted**, tired out, used up, drained, all in *Opposite*: energetic

washed-up *(infml) adj* **unsuccessful**, finished, defeated, through, failed *Opposite*: successful

washer *n* seal, gasket, liner, ring, lining

washing *n* **1** laundry, dirty linen, dirty clothes, wash **2 wash**, weekly wash, clothes wash **3 coat**, coating, film, layer, overlay

wash out *v* wash, rinse, flush, swill, hose

washout *(infml) n* **failure**, dead loss, disaster, disappointment, flop *(infml) Opposite*: success

wash over *v* flow over, engulf, sweep over, overwhelm, come over

wash your hands of *v* disown, abandon, refuse to have anything to do with, absolve yourself, ignore

waspish *adj* **1 irritable**, touchy, irascible, cantankerous, peevish *Opposite*: affable **2 malignant**, spiteful, malicious, nasty, vindictive *Opposite*: friendly

waspishness *n* **1 irritability**, touchiness, irascibility, cantankerousness, peevishness *Opposite*: affability **2 spitefulness**, spite, malice, maliciousness, nastiness *Opposite*: friendliness

waspy *see* **waspish**

wastage *n* waste, surplus, excess, leftovers

waste *v* **1 squander**, fritter away, misuse, dissipate, throw away *Opposite*: save **2 ravage**, devastate, ruin, spoil, despoil **3 atrophy**, wither, become emaciated, waste away, weaken *Opposite*: strengthen ■ *n* litter, rubbish, grey water, garbage (US), trash (US) ■ *adj* **1 excess**, surplus, unwanted, discarded, remaining **2 uncultivated**, barren, bare, fallow *Opposite*: cultivated

waste away *v* wither, waste, atrophy, become emaciated, weaken *Opposite*: strengthen

wasted *adj* **1 missed**, misused, lost, unexploited, unused **2 ravaged**, withered, shrunken, atrophied, emaciated *Opposite*: healthy **3 futile**, fruitless, unproductive, worthless, useless *Opposite*: worthwhile

wasteful *adj* extravagant, careless, uneconomical, profligate, lavish *Opposite*: frugal

wastefulness *n* extravagance, carelessness, profligacy, improvidence, lavishness *Opposite*: frugality

wasteland *n* wilds, wilderness, desert, badlands, wastes

wastes *see* **wasteland**

watch *v* **1 observe**, look at, stare at, gaze at, survey *Opposite*: ignore **2 pay attention to**, beware, mind, be cautious about, consider **3 spy on**, stalk, keep under observation, keep an eye on, keep under surveillance **4 look after**, keep an eye on, mind, guard, watch over *Opposite*: neglect ■ *n* guard, lookout, sentry, sentinel

watchdog *n* ombudsman, supervisory body, regulator, overseer

watcher *n* **observer**, onlooker, spectator, viewer, witness

watchful *adj* **observant**, attentive, alert, vigilant, on the alert *Opposite*: inattentive

watchfulness *n* **alertness**, attention, vigilance, caution, care *Opposite*: inattentiveness

watchman *n* **night watchman**, guard, security guard, custodian, caretaker

watch out *v* **1 be careful**, look out, be alert, be wary, take care **2 look out**, look, wait, watch, be on the lookout

watch over *v* **supervise**, look after, keep an eye on, guard, mind *Opposite*: neglect

watchtower *n* **lookout tower**, lookout post, observation tower, crow's nest

watchword *n* **motto**, slogan, maxim, byword, catch phrase

watch your step *v* **be careful**, take care, watch out, look out, pay attention

watch your weight *v* **be on a diet**, diet, slim, watch what you eat, cut down

water *n* **1 liquid**, rainwater, seawater, mineral water, tap water **2 fill with tears**, stream, run, fill up, well ■ *v* **1 soak**, spray, irrigate, drench, sprinkle

water bird *n* **waterfowl**, freshwater bird, duck

waterborne *adj* **1 aquatic**, floating, marine, riverine **2 transmissible**, contagious, catching

watercourse *n* **1 ditch**, conduit, drain, culvert **2 waterway**, channel, stream, river, rivulet

water down *v* **1 dilute**, thin down, weaken, attenuate *Opposite*: thicken **2 soften**, reduce, moderate, mitigate, regulate *Opposite*: beef up *(infml)*

watered-down *adj* **1 diluted**, dilute, thin, weak, insipid *Opposite*: concentrated **2 moderated**, weakened, vapid, qualified, toned-down *Opposite*: unqualified

waterfall *n* **cascade**, cataract, falls, weir, force

waterfowl *n* **water bird**, freshwater bird, duck

waterfront *n* **harbour**, lakefront, seafront, oceanfront, water's edge

water hole *n* **oasis**, pool, pond, water source, spring

watering hole *n* **1 oasis**, pool, pond, water hole, wallow **2** *(infml)* **bar**, pub, club

waterless *adj* **dry**, arid, parched, dehydrated

water line *n* **1 load line**, Plimsoll line, Plimsoll mark, watermark **2 tidemark**, watermark, high watermark, floodmark, tideline

waterlogged *adj* **sodden**, sopping, drenched, wet, soaking *Opposite*: dry

watermark *n* **1 mark**, imprint, logo, emblem **2 water line**, load line, Plimsoll line, Plimsoll mark **3 tidemark**, water line, high watermark, floodmark, tideline

waterproof *adj* **water-resistant**, rainproof, watertight, impermeable *Opposite*: permeable

watershed *n* **turning point**, defining moment,

breaking point, seminal moment, crisis

waterside *n* **riverbank**, shore, bank, water's edge, waterfront ■ *adj* **waterfront**, beachfront, seaside, lakeside, riverside

watertight *adj* **1 sealed**, waterproof, impermeable, rainproof *Opposite*: permeable **2 incontrovertible**, unassailable, sound, firm, irrefutable *Opposite*: weak

waterway *n* **watercourse**, canal, river, channel, stream

waterworks *n* **tears**, crying, weeping, sobbing, blubbering *(infml)*

watery *adj* **1 wet**, soggy, squelchy, boggy, moist *Opposite*: dry **2 watered-down**, thin, weak, runny, dilute *Opposite*: thick **3 feeble**, faint, weak, wan, hazy *Opposite*: forceful **4 bland**, tasteless, insipid, weak, diluted *Opposite*: strong

wave *v* **1 gesticulate**, gesture, signal, beckon **2 brandish**, flourish, wield, wag, shake **3 flutter**, flap, sway, undulate, move to and fro ■ *n* **1 breaker**, roller, dumper, ripple, surge **2 upsurge**, groundswell, tendency, trend, movement **3 gesture**, signal, sign **4 rash**, spate, outbreak, epidemic, series **5 current**, surge, impulse, oscillation, undulation **6 curl**, kink, undulation, ringlet

waver *v* **1 dither**, hesitate, be indecisive, be irresolute, vacillate **2 tremble**, shake, flutter, flicker, shudder. *See* COMPARE AND CONTRAST *at* hesitate

wavering *n* **fluctuation**, vacillation, indecisiveness, irresolution, uncertainty *Opposite*: resolution ■ *adj* **1 indecisive**, uncertain, undecided, vacillating, uncommitted *Opposite*: decisive **2 flickering**, shaky, trembling, quivering, unsteady

waviness *n* **curliness**, unevenness, undulation, corrugation, sinuosity

wavy *adj* **curly**, curvy, crimped, undulating *Opposite*: straight

wax *n* **beeswax**, candle wax, tallow ■ *v* **1 polish**, shine, buff, put a shine on, buff up **2** *(literary)* **become**, turn, grow, start to be **3** *(literary)* **expand**, increase, enlarge, get bigger, grow *Opposite*: wane

waxen *adj* **pale**, pallid, ashen, ashy, wan

waxiness *n* **greasiness**, fattiness, slipperiness, shininess, slickness

waxwork *n* **figure**, manikin, model, effigy, replica

way *n* **1 method**, means, technique, mode, system **2 custom**, style, practice, tradition, discipline **3 route**, road, direction, path **4 street**, avenue, lane, path, pathway

waylay *v* **accost**, intercept, surprise, ambush, lie in wait for

way of life *n* **lifestyle**, customs, habits, traditions

way of thinking *n* **ideas**, beliefs, opinion, philosophy, position

way-out *adj* **1** *(infml)* **unusual**, peculiar, odd,

strange, weird *Opposite*: conventional
2 *(dated infml)* **excellent,** wonderful, terrific,
fantastic, great

ways *n* **habits,** conduct, customs, behaviour,
traditions

ways and means *n* **methods,** approaches,
means, devices, systems

wayside *n* **roadside,** verge, kerb, edge, hard
shoulder

wayward *adj* **wilful,** naughty, unruly, errant,
disobedient *Opposite*: well-behaved. *See*
COMPARE AND CONTRAST *at* **unruly.**

waywardness *n* **wilfulness,** naughtiness, disobedience, unruliness, rebelliousness *Opposite*: obedience

weak *adj* **1 feeble,** frail, infirm, debilitated,
puny *Opposite*: robust **2 tired,** faint, enervated, exhausted, drained *Opposite*: strong
3 delicate, insubstantial, flimsy, wispy,
fragile *Opposite*: sturdy **4 vulnerable,**
defenceless, helpless, unprotected,
unguarded *Opposite*: invulnerable **5 powerless,** ineffectual, toothless, inadequate,
feeble *Opposite*: powerful **6 cowardly,** spineless, faint-hearted, timid, weak-willed
Opposite: bold **7 faint,** feeble, low, dim, soft
Opposite: strong **8 watery,** diluted, insipid,
bland, tasteless *Opposite*: strong **9 unconvincing,** half-hearted, ineffectual, feeble,
implausible *Opposite*: convincing

COMPARE AND CONTRAST CORE MEANING: lacking
physical strength or energy
weak not physically fit or mentally strong; **feeble**
lacking physical or mental strength or health; **frail**
in a physically weak state as a result of illness or
advanced years; **infirm** lacking strength as a result
of long illness or advanced years; **debilitated** with
strength and energy temporarily diminished as a
result of illness or physical exertion; **decrepit**
(*infml*) made weak by advanced years; **enervated**
made weak and tired by physical or mental exertion.

weaken *v* **1 grow weaker,** deteriorate, fail,
decline, wane *Opposite*: strengthen **2 give in,**
cave in, give way, yield, vacillate *Opposite*:
stand firm **3 damage,** destabilize, detract
from, shake, undermine *Opposite*: bolster
4 dilute, water down, thin, adulterate *Opposite*: strengthen **5 enfeeble,** exhaust, enervate, debilitate, sap *Opposite*: fortify

weakened *adj* **debilitated,** enfeebled, deteriorated, declining, faded

weakening *n* **deterioration,** decline, damage,
destabilization, undermining *Opposite*:
strengthening

weak-kneed *adj* **spineless,** cowardly, weak,
feeble, submissive *Opposite*: courageous

weakness *n* **1 flaw,** fault, Achilles' heel, weak
spot, weak point *Opposite*: strength **2 frailty,**
feebleness, flimsiness, fragility, debility
Opposite: robustness **3 powerlessness,** vulnerability, defencelessness, helplessness,

impotence *Opposite*: strength **4 fondness,**
liking, taste, soft spot, penchant *Opposite*:
dislike **5 faintness,** softness, dimness, paleness, feebleness *Opposite*: strength **6 wateriness,** blandness, lack of flavour, insipidness
Opposite: strong flavour

weak point *see* **weak spot**

weak spot *n* **weakness,** Achilles heel, failing,
fault, limitation

weak-willed *adj* **irresolute,** spineless, vacillating, easily led, spiritless *Opposite*: resolute

weal *n* **swelling,** welt, wound, mark, contusion
(fml)

wealth *n* **1 riches,** prosperity, affluence,
means, assets *Opposite*: poverty **2 large
quantity,** abundance, cornucopia, variety,
choice *Opposite*: dearth

wealthy *adj* **rich,** well-off, well-to-do, affluent,
prosperous *Opposite*: poor

weapon *n* **1 armament,** firearm, missile, gun
2 defence, deterrent, big stick

weaponry *n* **arms,** armaments, arsenal,
weapons, ordnance

weapon store *n* **arsenal,** armoury, storeroom,
store, cache

wear *v* **1 be dressed in,** dress in, show off, have
on, put on **2 display,** bear, carry, hold, show
3 rub, fray, scuff, grind, wear out ■ *n* **1 deterioration,** wear and tear, friction, abrasion,
scuffing **2 dress,** clothing, clothes, garments,
uniform

wear and tear *n* **deterioration,** wear, attrition,
abrasion, erosion

wear away *v* **erode,** wear down, wear out, eat
at, eat away at

wear down *v* **overcome,** weaken, erode, wear
away, wear out

weariness *n* **1 tiredness,** exhaustion, fatigue,
lethargy, inertia *Opposite*: energy **2 apathy,**
disillusionment, jadedness, disenchantment
Opposite: enthusiasm

wearing *adj* **tiring,** exhausting, trying, tiresome, wearisome *Opposite*: refreshing

wearisome *adj* **tiresome,** boring, tedious,
trying, thankless *Opposite*: stimulating

wear off *v* **weaken,** fade, lessen, diminish,
disappear *Opposite*: increase

wear out *v* **1 exhaust,** tire out, fatigue, sap,
drain *Opposite*: invigorate **2 use up,** run
down, fray, deplete, trash *(infml)* *Opposite*:
renovate

weary *adj* **1 tired,** tired out, all in, worn out,
exhausted *Opposite*: fresh **2 disillusioned,**
disenchanted, jaded, worn down, fed up
(infml) *Opposite*: enthusiastic ■ *v* **drain,** sap,
exhaust, tire, lose patience

wearying *adj* **tiresome,** wearisome, tiring,
exhausting, wearing

wear yourself out *v* **tire yourself out,** exhaust
yourself, run yourself into the ground,

overdo it, burn the candle at both ends

weather n **climate**, meteorological conditions, climatic conditions, elements ∎ v **1 endure**, withstand, sit out, ride out, last out *Opposite*: succumb **2 erode**, corrode, season, toughen, harden

weather-beaten adj **worn**, battered, wind-swept, weathered, gnarled

weather-bound adj **delayed**, held up, fog-bound, snowbound, postponed

weathercock *see* **weather vane**

weathered adj **worn**, battered, windswept, weather-beaten, gnarled

weatherproof adj **watertight**, waterproof, rain-proof, stormproof, windproof

weather vane n **wind indicator**, wind gauge, weathercock, anemometer, windsock

weave v **1 interlace**, lace, intertwine, plait, knit *Opposite*: unpick **2 invent**, create, compose, construct, fabricate **3 zigzag**, stagger, wind, twist, crisscross ∎ n **pile**, texture, nap

web n **network**, mesh, net, tissue, grid

webbing n **lattice**, trellis, netting, network, strap work

wed v **1 get married**, walk down the aisle, say "I do", get hitched *(infml)*, tie the knot *(infml)* *Opposite*: split up **2 join in matrimony**, marry, join in wedlock, unite **3 join**, link, unite, marry, merge *Opposite*: separate **4** *(fml or literary)* **marry**, take in marriage, espouse *(archaic)* *Opposite*: divorce

wedded adj **1 marital**, conjugal, married, matrimonial, connubial *(literary)* **2 committed**, devoted, linked, connected, attached *Opposite*: unattached

wedding n **marriage**, wedding ceremony, marriage ceremony, nuptials *(fml)*

wedge n **segment**, block, chock, sliver, hunk ∎ v **1 lodge**, hold, fix, jam, block *Opposite*: dislodge **2 cram**, pack, jam, ram, stuff

wedlock n **matrimony**, marriage, married state

wee adj **small**, minute, petite, little, tiny *Opposite*: big

weed v **hoe**, tidy, pick over, clear

WORD BANK
❏ **types of weed** bindweed, burdock, chickweed, dandelion, dock, goosegrass, ground elder, nettle, ragwort, shepherd's purse, stinging nettle, thistle

weed out v **remove**, extract, discard, get rid of, eliminate *Opposite*: select

weedy adj **weak**, puny, thin, scraggy, feeble *Opposite*: strong

weekend v **stay**, holiday, take a break, visit, vacation *(US)*

weekender n **tourist**, holidaymaker, visitor, sightseer, vacationer *(US)*

weensy *(infml)* *see* **weeny**

weeny *(infml)* adj **tiny**, little, small, wee, minute *Opposite*: huge

weep v **1 cry**, sob, wail, snivel, boohoo **2 leak**, suppurate, seep, exude, ooze

weepie *(infml)* n **movie**, film, melodrama, tear-jerker *(infml)*

weepy adj **1 oversentimental**, slushy, mushy, syrupy, overemotional **2** *(infml)* **tearful**, emotional, sad, miserable, sensitive

weigh v **consider**, ponder, weigh up, think about, evaluate

weigh against v **count against**, tell against, militate against, countervail

weigh down v **1 worry**, depress, get down, trouble, burden *Opposite*: hearten **2 overload**, load down, burden, charge, encumber

weight n **1 heaviness**, mass, bulk, weightiness, heft *(US)* **2 burden**, load, encumbrance **3 influence**, power, substance, significance, import

weighted adj **biased**, prejudiced, slanted, subjective, one-sided *Opposite*: impartial

weightiness n **1 weight**, heaviness, mass, bulk, heft *(US)* **2 gravity**, seriousness, importance, heaviness, import

weighting n **allowance**, premium, increment

weightless adj **light**, feathery, insubstantial, ethereal, airy *Opposite*: heavy

weighty adj **1 heavy**, big, substantial, hefty, bulky *Opposite*: insubstantial **2 important**, serious, grave, solemn, momentous *Opposite*: frivolous

weigh up v **assess**, evaluate, consider, examine, size up

weir n **dam**, barrage, dike, barrier, wall

weird adj **strange**, odd, bizarre, peculiar, unusual *Opposite*: normal

welcome adj **1 at home**, comfortable, at ease, relaxed, comfy *(infml)* *Opposite*: unwelcome **2 longed-for**, long-awaited, timely, opportune, heaven-sent *Opposite*: untimely **3 appreciated**, pleasurable, delightful, pleasing, pleasant *Opposite*: unwelcome ∎ n **greeting**, reception, salutation, salute, hospitality *Opposite*: farewell ∎ v **1 greet**, receive, hail, meet, salute *Opposite*: snub **2 accept**, appreciate, approve, jump at, be grateful for *Opposite*: reject

welcoming adj **friendly**, warm, hospitable, convivial, openhearted *Opposite*: unwelcoming

weld v **fuse**, join, repair, solder, link *Opposite*: separate ∎ n **repair**, join, link, joint, bond

welfare n **wellbeing**, interests, happiness, good, safety *Opposite*: harm

well n **1 shaft**, bore, borehole, pit **2 spring**, fountain, artesian well, source, water supply ∎ v **1 spring up**, brim, surge, rise, gush *Opposite*: subside **2 grow**, rise, swell, intensify, increase *Opposite*: subside ∎ adv **1 pleasingly**, splendidly, perfectly, pleasantly, nicely *Opposite*: badly **2 properly**, ethically, acceptably, correctly, suitably *Opposite*: improperly **3 competently**, ably, skilfully, capably, satisfactorily *Opposite*: badly **4 justly**, appropriately, fairly, fittingly, justifiably *Opposite*: unfairly **5 comfortably**, easily, agreeably **6 favourably**, highly, admiringly, kindly, positively *Opposite*: unfavourably **7 thoroughly**, fully, carefully, completely, meticulously *Opposite*: partially **8 clearly**, precisely, in detail, distinctly, perfectly *Opposite*: poorly **9 familiarly**, intimately, closely, personally, deeply *Opposite*: slightly **10 anyway**, anyhow, in any case, to cut a long story short, now then **11 good-naturedly**, good-humouredly, cheerfully, jovially, genially ■ *adj* **1 healthy**, glowing, fit, fighting fit, on form *Opposite*: unwell **2 satisfactory**, all right, good, lucky, fortunate *Opposite*: unsatisfactory

well-adjusted *adj* **stable**, normal, level-headed, well-balanced, sane *Opposite*: maladjusted

well-advised *adj* **sensible**, prudent, wise, judicious, shrewd *Opposite*: ill-advised

well-appointed *adj* **well-equipped**, well-resourced, fully furnished, well-furnished, luxurious

well-argued *adj* **clear**, clearly stated, cogent, sensible, lucid *Opposite*: illogical

well-balanced *adj* **1 sensible**, rational, stable, judicious, well-adjusted *Opposite*: unstable **2 harmonious**, balanced, well-proportioned, proportionate, coordinated *Opposite*: unbalanced

well-behaved *adj* **good**, obedient, dutiful, well-mannered, polite *Opposite*: disobedient

wellbeing *n* **happiness**, comfort, security, good, welfare

well-beloved *adj* **1 loved**, cherished, desired, beloved, adored *Opposite*: hated **2 respected**, honoured, venerated, revered, esteemed *Opposite*: disgraced

wellborn *adj* **aristocratic**, blue-blooded, noble, patrician, highborn *(literary) Opposite*: lowly

well-bred *adj* **polite**, well-mannered, mannerly, courteous, refined *Opposite*: common

well-built *adj* **sturdy**, strong, muscular, muscly, burly *Opposite*: puny

well-chosen *adj* **choice**, appropriate, apposite, apt, relevant *Opposite*: inappropriate

well-defined *adj* **distinct**, sharp, definite, clear, precise *Opposite*: vague

well-designed *adj* **1 elegant**, stylish, well-made, chic, classy *(infml)* **2 handy**, ingenious, clever, useful, neat

well-developed *adj* **1 well-built**, strong, toned, finely honed, muscular *Opposite*: puny **2 sophisticated**, well-rounded, strong, mature, acute *Opposite*: underdeveloped

well-disposed *adj* **approving**, friendly, kindly, sympathetic, benevolent *Opposite*: hostile

well-dressed *adj* **smart**, chic, stylish, elegant, well turned-out *Opposite*: scruffy

well-educated *adj* **cultured**, erudite, knowledgeable, well-read, learned *Opposite*: ignorant

well-endowed *adj* **1 affluent**, wealthy, well-to-do, rich, moneyed *Opposite*: poor **2 gifted**, skilled, talented, able, skilful

well-equipped *adj* **well-appointed**, well-resourced, well-furnished, luxurious, lavish *Opposite*: spartan

well-established *adj* **firm**, deep-rooted, unshakable, fixed, ingrained *Opposite*: shaky

well-expressed *adj* **eloquent**, persuasive, fluent, expressive, articulate *Opposite*: inarticulate

well-fed *adj* **1 healthy**, well-nourished, thriving, flourishing **2 overweight**, fat, obese, bulky, stout *Opposite*: thin

well-founded *adj* **logical**, understandable, justifiable, substantiated, sound *Opposite*: illogical

well-groomed *adj* **well-turned-out**, well-dressed, smart, dapper, spruce *Opposite*: unkempt

well-grounded *adj* **1 knowledgeable**, well-informed, au fait, conversant, well-acquainted *Opposite*: ignorant **2 well-founded**, logical, understandable, justifiable, substantiated *Opposite*: illogical

well-heeled *(infml) adj* **wealthy**, well-off, comfortable, rich, affluent *Opposite*: poor

well-informed *adj* **knowledgeable**, informed, in the know, up-to-date, educated *Opposite*: uneducated

well-intentioned *adj* **well-meant**, well-meaning, kindly, goodhearted, benevolent *Opposite*: malicious

well-kept *adj* **1 neat**, tidy, well-maintained, orderly, ordered *Opposite*: untidy **2 preserved**, safe, cherished, treasured, confidential

well-known *adj* **famous**, renowned, eminent, familiar, recognized *Opposite*: unknown

well-mannered *adj* **polite**, mannerly, decent, decorous, courteous *Opposite*: impolite

well-matched *adj* **compatible**, suited, complementary, well-suited, suitable *Opposite*: incompatible

well-meaning *adj* **well-intentioned**, kind, kindly, goodhearted, benevolent *Opposite*: malicious

well-meant *adj* **well-intentioned**, kind, kindly, kind-hearted, goodhearted *Opposite*: malicious

well-nigh *adv* **nearly**, almost, nigh on, practically, just about *Opposite*: totally

well-off *adj* **1 wealthy**, rich, comfortable, affluent, prosperous *Opposite*: poor **2 lucky**, fortunate, in luck, privileged, blessed *Opposite*: unfortunate

well-oiled *adj* **1 efficient**, smooth-running, well-organized, effective, well-ordered *Opposite*: inefficient

well-ordered *adj* **tidy**, regimented, disciplined, efficient, well-organized *Opposite*: inefficient

well-organized *adj* **efficient**, disciplined, well-ordered, regimented, ordered *Opposite*: inefficient

well-paid *adj* **lucrative**, profitable, productive, rewarding, remunerative

well-preserved *adj* **youthful**, fresh-looking, young-looking, girlish, boyish *Opposite*: wizened

well-read *adj* **knowledgeable**, educated, cultured, erudite, well-educated *Opposite*: uninformed

well-rounded *adj* **1 experienced**, seasoned, accomplished, well-versed, mature *Opposite*: inexperienced **2 comprehensive**, varied, wide, balanced, broad *Opposite*: narrow **3 shapely**, pleasing, well-formed, attractive, curvaceous *Opposite*: unattractive

well-spoken *adj* **articulate**, eloquent, refined, fluent, coherent *Opposite*: inarticulate

well-suited *adj* **compatible**, well-matched, complementary, of a kind, suited *Opposite*: incompatible

well-thought-of *adj* **respected**, esteemed, highly regarded, reputable, admired *Opposite*: despised

well-thought-out *adj* **well-planned**, well-organized, clever, ingenious, elegant *Opposite*: disorganized

well-timed *adj* **timely**, opportune, propitious, felicitous, appropriate *Opposite*: untimely

well-to-do *adj* **wealthy**, rich, well-off, affluent, prosperous *Opposite*: poor

well-tried *adj* **tried and tested**, established, well-founded, acknowledged, well-known *Opposite*: untried

well-turned *adj* **1 shapely**, graceful, elegant, well-formed, pretty *Opposite*: inelegant **2 eloquent**, well-crafted, well-expressed, articulate, witty *Opposite*: clumsy

well-turned-out *adj* **neat**, smart, spruce, dapper, well-dressed *Opposite*: unkempt

well up *v* **surge**, gush forth, spring up, spill over, emanate *Opposite*: subside

well-versed *adj* **knowledgeable**, familiar, experienced, informed, well-read *Opposite*: ignorant

well-wisher *n* **supporter**, sympathizer, friend, guardian angel *(infml) Opposite*: detractor

well-worn *adj* **1 worn**, worn out, ragged, threadbare, frayed *Opposite*: brand-new **2 hackneyed**, timeworn, unoriginal, banal, overworked *Opposite*: original

welt *n* **weal**, swelling, ridge, wound, mark

welter *n* **flurry**, jumble, mass, confusion, muddle ∎ *v* **wallow**, roll, pitch and toss

wend *v* **proceed**, go, travel, move, journey *Opposite*: stay put

western *n* **cowboy film**, spaghetti western, horse opera

wet *adj* **1 damp**, soaked, soaking, drenched, sodden *Opposite*: dry **2 rainy**, showery, drizzly, damp, misty *Opposite*: dry ∎ *n* **1 moisture**, wetness, liquid, damp, dampness *Opposite*: dry **2 wet weather**, rain, drizzle, damp, dampness *Opposite*: dry ∎ *v* **make wet**, dampen, moisten, soak, saturate *Opposite*: dry

wet blanket *(infml) n* **spoilsport**, killjoy, party pooper *(infml)*, stick-in-the-mud *(infml)*, stuffed shirt *(infml)*

wetland *n* **marsh**, swamp, fen, bog, marshes *Opposite*: desert

wetness *n* **dampness**, damp, humidity, condensation, moisture *Opposite*: dryness

whack *v* **hit**, thump, slap, strike, clout ∎ *n* **thump**, blow, slap, thwack, clout

whacked *(infml) adj* **tired**, tired out, shattered, exhausted, worn-out *Opposite*: fresh

whacking *(infml) adj* **huge**, enormous, massive, gigantic, mammoth *Opposite*: piddling *(infml)*

wharf *n* **quay**, quayside, jetty, pier, dock

whatchamacallit *(infml) n* **whatnot**, thingamabob *(infml)*, thingumajig *(infml)*, thingy *(infml)*, thingummy *(infml)*

whatever *pron* **anything**, everything, all, no matter what, whatsoever ∎ *adv* **at all**, whatsoever, of any kind

whatsoever *adj* **at all**, whatever, of any kind

wheedle *v* **1 coax**, cajole, inveigle, charm, persuade *Opposite*: bully **2 coax out**, winkle out, get out, draw out, obtain

wheel *v* **1 roll**, trundle, manoeuvre, move **2 turn**, veer, swing, circle, swivel

wheel around *v* **swivel around**, swing around, turn round, spin around, turn full circle

wheel clamp *n* **clamp**, lock, immobilizer, Denver boot *(US)*

wheel-clamp *v* **clamp**, immobilize, secure, lock

wheeler-dealer *(infml) n* **fixer**, negotiator, dealer, trader

wheeze *v* **1 breathe heavily**, gasp, rasp, pant, rattle **2 speak hoarsely**, whisper, hiss, rasp, pant

wheeziness *n* **breathlessness**, hoarseness, gasping, puffing, panting

wheezy *adj* **breathless**, hoarse, short of breath, out of breath, husky

whelp *n* **cub**, pup, puppy, baby, offspring ∎ *v* **give birth**, bear young, pup, cub, litter

whenever *conj* **every time**, each time, each and every time, on every occasion, when

whereabouts *n* **location**, situation, position, site, place

whereas *conj* **while**, where, but, however, although

whereupon *(fml)* conj **at which point**, at which, as a result of which, so, and so

wherewithal n **means**, ability, resources, money, finances

whet v **1 sharpen**, hone, grind, file *Opposite*: blunt **2 stimulate**, arouse, augment, rouse, kindle *Opposite*: quell

whiff n **1 smell**, aroma, scent, odour, reek **2 trace**, vestige, sign, hint, suggestion ■ v *(infml)* **reek**, pong *(infml)*, smell, stink, hum *(infml)*

whiffy *(infml)* adj **smelly**, stinking, foul-smelling, fetid, pongy *(infml)* *Opposite*: fragrant

while conj **1 as**, at the same time as, even as, during which **2 but**, however, in contrast, whereas **3 even though**, though, although, despite the fact, whereas ■ n **time**, period, interval, little, bit

while away v **pass**, spend, idle, fritter away, kill

whim n **impulse**, urge, notion, quirk, caprice

whimper v **cry**, whine, sob, snivel, moan

whimsical adj **1 fanciful**, quirky, unusual, imaginative, original *Opposite*: practical **2 amusing**, playful, humorous, witty, quaint *Opposite*: serious **3 erratic**, unpredictable, random, impulsive, capricious *Opposite*: dependable

whimsy n **1 quaintness**, oddity, oddness, eccentricity, quirkiness *Opposite*: seriousness **2 fancy**, flight of fancy, whim, caprice, fantasy

whine v **1 whimper**, cry, wail, moan, bleat **2 grumble**, complain, gripe *(infml)*, moan *(infml)*, bellyache *(infml)* *Opposite*: accept **3 wail**, moan, howl, drone, hum ■ n **complaint**, wail, whimper, cry, moan *(infml)*. *See* COMPARE AND CONTRAST *at* **complain**.

whiner n **grumbler**, complainer, whinger *(infml)*, moaner *(infml)*, grouch *(infml)*

whinge *(infml)* v **whine**, complain, bleat *(infml)*, moan *(infml)*, bellyache *(infml)* *Opposite*: accept

whinger *(infml)* n **complainer**, grumbler, whiner, malcontent, moaner *(infml)*

whinny v **neigh**, whicker, nicker

whip v **1 flog**, thrash, beat, lash, flagellate **2 whisk**, beat, cream, aerate, stir **3** *(infml)* **steal**, take, rob, thieve, pinch *(infml)* ■ n **lash**, crop, cat-o'-nine-tails, switch

whiplash n **blow**, stroke, lash, hit, impact

whip-round *(infml)* n **collection**, appeal, kitty, fund

whip up v **1 stir up**, drum up, incite, provoke, arouse *Opposite*: pacify **2** *(infml)* **rattle off**, prepare, concoct, cook, produce

whirl v **spin**, twirl, reel, rotate, turn ■ n **1 rotation**, spin, twirl, turn, flick **2 flurry**, bustle, hustle, commotion, tumult

whirlpool n **eddy**, vortex, swirl, current, waterspout

whirlwind n **tornado**, hurricane, cyclone, waterspout, vortex ■ adj **rapid**, short-lived, tumultuous, brief, swift *Opposite*: leisurely

whirr v **hum**, purr, buzz, whine, drone

whisk v **1 beat**, whip, cream, aerate, stir **2 take**, bundle, bustle, hustle, whip *Opposite*: drag

whisker n **fraction**, inch, millimetre, hair's-breadth

whiskers n **facial hair**, sideburns, moustache, muttonchops, stubble

whisper v **murmur**, sigh, mutter, breathe, utter *Opposite*: shout ■ n **rumour**, word, gossip, tale, hint *Opposite*: fact

whistle v **screech**, shrill, shriek, hoot, toot

whistle-blower n **informer**, mole, telltale, snitch *(slang)*, grass *(slang)*

whistle-stop adj **barnstorming**, whirlwind, lightning, rapid, speedy *Opposite*: relaxed

whit *(dated)* n **iota**, bit, jot, grain, speck

white adj **1 snowy**, silver, silvery, bleached, grey *Opposite*: black **2 pale**, pallid, ashen, wan, washed-out *Opposite*: flushed **3 frosty**, snowy, hoary, icy, frozen

WORD BANK
❏ **types of white** cream, eggshell, ivory, magnolia, off-white, oyster, pearl, platinum, silver, snow white

whitecap n **crest**, surf, breaker, white horses, wave

white-collar adj **professional**, managerial, management, salaried, office *Opposite*: blue-collar

white-hot adj **1 incandescent**, glowing, white, luminescent, hot *Opposite*: ice-cold **2 intense**, fevered, frenetic, frenzied, excited *Opposite*: lethargic

white-knuckle adj **exhilarating**, frightening, terrifying, exciting, roller-coaster *Opposite*: safe

whiten v **blanch**, whitewash, bleach, fade, pale *Opposite*: darken

whiteness n **paleness**, milkiness, lightness, pallor, wanness *Opposite*: ruddiness

whiteout n **blizzard**, snowstorm, storm

whitewash n **1 distemper**, lime, whitening, paint **2 cover-up**, deception, conspiracy, plot, concealment *Opposite*: exposure **3** *(infml)* **defeat**, rout, one-horse race, trouncing, beating *Opposite*: triumph ■ v **1 paint**, decorate, distemper, cover, smear **2 misrepresent**, cover up, conceal, explain away, gloss over *Opposite*: expose **3 trounce**, defeat, beat, rout, outclass *Opposite*: succumb

white water n **1 rapids**, torrents, foam, spray, current **2 shallows**, shoals, sandbanks, sandbar

whittle v **carve**, shape, fashion, shave, sculpt

whittle away v **eat into**, erode, eat away at, reduce, consume *Opposite*: build up

whittle down v cut down, trim, pare down, reduce, diminish Opposite: increase

whiz v 1 whirr, hum, hiss, buzz, rattle 2 dash, go, nip (infml), pop (infml), zip (infml) Opposite: dawdle ■ n (infml) **expert**, prodigy, genius, whiz kid (infml), bright spark (infml)

whiz kid (infml) n **prodigy**, expert, genius, wizard (infml), whiz (infml)

whodunit n **mystery**, thriller, cliffhanger

whole adj 1 **entire**, complete, full, in one piece, total Opposite: partial 2 **intact**, in one piece, unbroken, undivided, unspoiled Opposite: broken 3 **unimpaired**, healthy, sound, fit, well Opposite: unhealthy 4 **healed**, cured, healthy, restored, rehabilitated Opposite: ill ■ n 1 **sum total**, aggregate, total, unit, entity 2 **entirety**, totality, unity, everything, all Opposite: part

wholehearted adj **enthusiastic**, passionate, unreserved, total, unstinting Opposite: grudging

wholeness n **completeness**, entirety, totality, unity, fullness

wholesale adj **extensive**, comprehensive, across-the-board, indiscriminate, blanket Opposite: partial ■ adv **indiscriminately**, extensively, comprehensively, generally, broadly Opposite: partially

wholesaler n **trader**, retailer, supplier, dealer, vendor

wholesome adj 1 **healthy**, healthful, nutritious, good, nourishing Opposite: unwholesome 2 **decent**, moral, clean, honest, clean-living Opposite: unwholesome 3 **sensible**, open, honest, commonsensical, practical Opposite: unhelpful 4 **fit**, healthy, fresh-faced, clean-cut, ruddy Opposite: unhealthy

wholesomeness n 1 **freshness**, healthiness, healthfulness, naturalness, goodness Opposite: unwholesomeness 2 **morality**, uprightness, decency, integrity, virtuousness Opposite: immorality 3 **common sense**, sense, practicality, good sense, openness Opposite: impracticality 4 **healthiness**, fitness, glow, ruddiness, haleness Opposite: unwholesomeness

wholly adv 1 **completely**, entirely, totally, altogether, utterly Opposite: partially 2 **solely**, exclusively, only, just, absolutely Opposite: generally

whoop v cry out, shout, scream, howl, hoot

whoosh n dash, zoom, rush, spurt, surge ■ v 1 **rush**, zoom, burst, whistle, whiz Opposite: dawdle 2 **zoom**, whistle, swish, hiss, roar

whopper (infml) n 1 **monster**, giant, elephant, Goliath, leviathan 2 **lie**, untruth, tale, fabrication, falsehood Opposite: truth

whopping (infml) n **thrashing**, defeat, drubbing, pasting (infml), licking (infml) ■ adj **enormous**, gigantic, monstrous, huge, big Opposite: tiny

whorl n spiral, coil, curl, twist, swirl

whys and wherefores n reasons, ins and outs, details, the full picture, motives

wicked adj 1 **evil**, bad, wrong, depraved, immoral Opposite: good 2 **mischievous**, naughty, roguish, impish, teasing Opposite: respectful 3 **mean**, cutting, acerbic, sharp, malicious Opposite: gentle 4 (infml) **distressing**, dreadful, awful, atrocious, severe Opposite: excellent

wickedness n 1 **evil**, badness, iniquity, sin, impiety Opposite: goodness 2 **impishness**, cheekiness, naughtiness, mischievousness

wicker n cane, rattan, wickerwork, bamboo

wicket n **gate**, door, opening, aperture, entrance

wide adj 1 **broad**, ample, large, thick, spacious Opposite: narrow 2 **extensive**, varied, widespread, inclusive, eclectic Opposite: narrow 3 **baggy**, roomy, loose, loose-fitting, capacious Opposite: tight ■ adv **off course**, off target, off the mark, wide of the mark, out

wide-awake (infml) adj **fully awake**, alert, bright-eyed and bushy-tailed, perky, watchful Opposite: asleep

wide-eyed adj 1 **amazed**, astonished, open-mouthed, dumbfounded, flabbergasted (infml) Opposite: impassive 2 **naive**, innocent, inexperienced, green, credulous Opposite: knowing

widely adv **extensively**, broadly, generally, far and wide, commonly Opposite: narrowly

widen v **broaden**, extend, expand, enlarge, make wider Opposite: narrow

wide-open adj 1 **open wide**, gaping, yawning, cavernous, agape (literary) 2 **unpredictable**, undecided, anybody's guess, unsettled, in the balance Opposite: settled 3 **vulnerable**, unprotected, exposed, unguarded, at risk Opposite: protected

wide-ranging adj **extensive**, widespread, comprehensive, across-the-board, inclusive Opposite: narrow

widespread adj **extensive**, prevalent, general, common, rife Opposite: limited

COMPARE AND CONTRAST CORE MEANING: occurring over a wide area

widespread existing or happening in many places, or affecting many people; **prevalent** occurring commonly or widely as a dominant feature; **rife** full of or severely affected by something undesirable that occurs frequently or in great numbers over a wide area, especially when it appears to be uncontrollable; **epidemic** spreading more quickly and more extensively than expected; **universal** affecting the whole world or everyone in the world.

width n breadth, thickness, girth, size, measurement

wield v 1 **exercise**, exert, use, have, employ 2 **brandish**, manipulate, handle, ply, carry Opposite: conceal

wife n **spouse**, partner, mate, consort *Opposite*: husband

wig v *(dated infml)* **berate**, lambaste, lecture, take to task, dress down ■ n **toupee**, hairpiece, periwig, extension, rug *(infml)*

wiggle v **wriggle**, waggle, twist, jiggle, squirm ■ n **jiggle**, shake, wriggle, twist, waggle

wiggly adj **undulating**, wavy, curved, curvy, curving *Opposite*: straight

wigwam n **tepee**, tent, yurt, hut, lodge

wild adj **1 untamed**, undomesticated, uncultivated, natural, feral *Opposite*: tame **2 rough**, desolate, barren, remote, uninhabited *Opposite*: gentle **3 stormy**, blustery, squally, tempestuous, windswept *Opposite*: calm **4 enthusiastic**, eager, mad, excited, thrilled *Opposite*: unenthusiastic **5 rowdy**, undisciplined, riotous, unruly, rough *Opposite*: orderly **6 overwhelmed**, overcome, overpowered, devastated, destroyed **7 untidy**, dishevelled, unkempt, tousled, messy *Opposite*: tidy **8** *(infml)* **outrageous**, madcap, foolish, unconventional, irrational *Opposite*: sensible. *See* COMPARE AND CONTRAST *at* **unruly**.

wilderness n **wilds**, rough country, wasteland, desert, outback

wildlife n **flora and fauna**, nature, natural world, environment, biota

wildness n **1 roughness**, remoteness, desolation, barrenness, harshness **2 rowdiness**, lack of control, lack of discipline, unruliness, roughness *Opposite*: orderliness **3 dishevelment**, messiness, scruffiness, untidiness, unruliness *Opposite*: tidiness **4** *(infml)* **recklessness**, madness, foolishness, passion, waywardness

wiles n **tricks**, trickery, guile, deceit, artifice *(fml)*

wilful adj **1 deliberate**, determined, intentional, conscious, malicious *Opposite*: unwitting **2 stubborn**, obstinate, headstrong, perverse, obstreperous *Opposite*: compliant. *See* COMPARE AND CONTRAST *at* **unruly**.

wilfulness n **1 premeditation**, consciousness, deliberateness, maliciousness, malevolence **2 stubbornness**, obstinacy, perverseness, perversity, obstreperousness *Opposite*: compliance

wiliness n **cunning**, wiles, craftiness, guile, craft *Opposite*: ingenuousness

will n **1 mind**, brain, consciousness, thoughts, thought processes **2 determination**, resolve, willpower, motivation, spirit **3 desire**, inclination, wish, longing, determination **4** *(fml)* **bidding**, command, dictate, wish, desire ■ v **want**, wish, yearn, desire, long

willies *(infml)* n **shakes**, goose pimples, jitters *(infml)*, creeps *(infml)*, shivers *(infml)*

willing adj **1 prepared**, ready, set, agreeable, disposed *Opposite*: unwilling **2 eager**, keen, enthusiastic, game, helpful *Opposite*: reluctant

willingly adv **1 freely**, readily, gladly, happily, cheerfully *Opposite*: unwillingly **2 eagerly**, enthusiastically, keenly, cooperatively, readily *Opposite*: reluctantly

willingness n **1 readiness**, inclination, will, preparedness, disposition *Opposite*: unwillingness **2 enthusiasm**, alacrity, motivation, eagerness, keenness *Opposite*: reluctance

willowy adj **1 graceful**, slim, elegant, lissom, svelte *Opposite*: stocky **2 flexible**, bendable, malleable, springy, supple *Opposite*: stiff

willpower n **determination**, resolve, resolution, iron will, strength of will *Opposite*: weakness

willy-nilly adv **regardless**, anyway, in any case, like it or not, unceremoniously ■ adj **haphazard**, random, unsystematic, arbitrary, unselective *Opposite*: methodical

wilt v **droop**, shrivel, wither, fade, wane *Opposite*: flourish

wily adj **crafty**, cunning, guileful, sly, devious *Opposite*: ingenuous

win v **1 come first**, succeed, triumph, be victorious, be successful *Opposite*: lose **2 gain**, earn, secure, attain, collect *Opposite*: lose ■ n **victory**, success, triumph, landslide, conquest *Opposite*: defeat

wince n **1 grimace**, scowl, flinch, gasp, cringe *Opposite*: smile **2 recoil**, flinch, cringe, jump, start ■ v **1 grimace**, scowl, shudder, flinch, gasp *Opposite*: smile **2 recoil**, flinch, jump, cringe, shrink. *See* COMPARE AND CONTRAST *at* **recoil**.

winch n **hoist**, windlass, pulley, crane, capstan ■ v **raise**, hoist, lift, lift up, pull

wind n **current of air**, breeze, gale, squall, gust ■ v **1 coil**, twist, encircle, roll, wrap around *Opposite*: unwind **2 snake**, meander, bend, curve, twist

---

WORD BANK

❏ **types of wind** antitrade, bise, chinook, cyclone, foehn, harmattan, hurricane, khamsin, levanter, mistral, monsoon, northeaster, northwester, Santa Ana, simoom, sirocco, southeaster, southwester, tornado, trade wind, tramontana, typhoon, westerly

---

windbreak n **shelter**, panel, barrier, screen, fence

wind down v **relax**, unwind, rest, loosen up, hang loose *(infml)*

winded adj **breathless**, out of breath, short of breath, panting, gasping

windfall n **bonus**, handout, bonanza, payout, dividend

winding adj **zigzagging**, snaky, snaking, twisting, curving *Opposite*: straight

windlass n **winch**, hoist, crane, capstan, pulley

window n **1 pane**, windowpane, glass, glazing **2 gap**, space, opening, hole **3 opportunity**, period, chance, slot, window of opportunity **4 dialogue box**, box, frame, display, interface

---

WORD BANK

❏ **types of window** bay window, casement, dormer window, fanlight, French window, lancet window, picture window, porthole, rose window, sash window, skylight

❏ **parts of a window** ledge, pane, sill, window ledge, windowpane, windowsill

---

windowpane *n* pane, window, glass, glazing

windowsill *n* ledge, window ledge, sill, shelf

windstorm *n* storm, wind, gale, hurricane, cyclone

windswept *adj* desolate, windy, barren, inhospitable, exposed *Opposite*: sheltered

wind up *v* **1** end, conclude, bring to an end, complete, finish *Opposite*: start off **2** liquidate, close down, close, shut down, terminate *(fml)* **3** *(infml)* tease, have somebody on, kid, fool, pull somebody's leg *(infml)* **4** *(infml)* infuriate, enrage, madden, annoy, irritate *Opposite*: amuse

wind-up *n* *(infml)* joke, trick, prank, practical joke, tease ■ *adj* clockwork, mechanical, spring-operated, manual

windy *adj* **1** blustery, breezy, stormy, gusty, squally *Opposite*: still **2** *(infml)* wordy, voluble, verbose, pompous, bombastic *Opposite*: meek

wing *n* **1** annexe, extension, part, arm, section **2** division, subdivision, arm, section, department ■ *v* **1** fly, head, speed, race, whiz **2** injure, wound, hurt, maim, shoot

wink *v* flash, twinkle, sparkle, glitter, glint

winkle out *v* extract, worm, draw out, prise, wheedle

winner *n* **1** victor, champion, conqueror, leader, frontrunner *(infml)* *Opposite*: loser **2** success, hit, sensation, triumph, sure thing *(infml)* *Opposite*: failure

winning *adj* **1** successful, triumphant, victorious, best, champion **2** charming, captivating, endearing, persuasive, engaging *Opposite*: unprepossessing

winnings *n* prize money, prize, money, earnings, receipts

winnow *v* examine, go through, sort through, pick over, inspect

win over *v* convince, persuade, convert, win round, bring round

winsome *adj* charming, fetching, sweet, lovely, attractive

winter *n* **1** wintertime, midwinter, depth of winter *Opposite*: summer **2** end, twilight, close, closing, ending

wintriness *n* chilliness, coldness, bitterness, iciness, bleakness *Opposite*: warmth

wintry *adj* chilly, cold, bracing, freezing, nippy *Opposite*: summery

wipe *v* **1** rub, polish, mop, swab, clean **2** erase, remove, delete, obliterate, destroy **3** smear, spread, rub, distribute, streak

wipe out *(infml)* *v* annihilate, destroy, eradicate, obliterate, exterminate *Opposite*: protect

wipe the floor with *(infml)* *v* defeat, beat hollow, thrash, trounce, outclass

wipe the slate clean *(infml)* *v* make a fresh start, start afresh, forgive and forget, bury the hatchet, let bygones be bygones

wire *n* flex, cable, lead, line, filament ■ *v* connect, hook up, install, equip

wired *adj* **1** strengthened, supported, reinforced, held together, bound **2** *(infml)* online, on the Net, on the Web, connected **3** *(infml)* energetic, excited, wound up, hyperactive

wiretap *v* tap, bug, monitor, listen in on, eavesdrop ■ *n* tap, monitor, bug *(infml)*

wiriness *n* **1** leanness, slimness, thinness, muscularity, strength *Opposite*: fatness **2** coarseness, stiffness, bristliness, roughness, scratchiness *Opposite*: softness

wiry *adj* **1** lean, slim, thin, muscular, sinewy *Opposite*: fat **2** coarse, stiff, bristly, rough, scratchy *Opposite*: soft

wisdom *n* understanding, sense, knowledge, insight, perception *Opposite*: foolishness

wise *adj* **1** astute, intelligent, clever, prudent, sensible *Opposite*: foolish **2** knowledgeable, learned, informed, erudite, aware *Opposite*: ignorant **3** shrewd, cunning, crafty, devious, wily

wisecrack *(infml)* *n* witticism, quip, riposte, gibe, retort ■ *v* joke, quip, gibe, retort, gag

wish *v* **1** want, desire, crave, require, covet **2** demand, ask, request, ask for, bid ■ *n* **1** desire, aspiration, hope, yearning, longing *Opposite*: disinclination **2** request, demand, bidding, command, requirement. *See* COMPARE AND CONTRAST *at* want.

wishful thinking *n* delusion, fantasy, self-delusion, self-deception, idealism *Opposite*: reality

wishy-washy *(infml)* *adj* **1** indecisive, irresolute, weak, feeble, spineless *Opposite*: decisive **2** watery, insipid, bland, tasteless, weak *Opposite*: strong

wisp *n* strand, scrap, tendril, thread, lock

wispy *adj* flimsy, fine, thin, light, slight *Opposite*: substantial

wistful *adj* pensive, melancholy, thoughtful, reflective, contemplative *Opposite*: satisfied

wistfulness *n* melancholy, pensiveness, reminiscence, nostalgia, dreaminess *Opposite*: contentment

wit *n* **1** wittiness, jocularity, facetiousness, fun, humour *Opposite*: seriousness **2** comedian, humorist, comic, joker, satirist **3** intelligence, smartness, cleverness, intellect, keenness *Opposite*: stupidity

witch *n* enchantress, sorceress, magician, occultist, necromancer *(literary)*

witch doctor *n* shaman, healer, soothsayer, medium, druid

with *prep* **1 together with**, along with, in conjunction with, beside, alongside *Opposite*: without **2 in addition to**, plus, including, as well as, and *Opposite*: without

withdraw *v* **1 remove**, take out, extract, pull out, draw *Opposite*: insert **2 retract**, renounce, disavow, revoke, take back *Opposite*: confirm **3 leave**, depart, retire, pull out, retreat *Opposite*: remain

withdrawal *n* **1 removal**, extraction, drawing, taking out, taking away *Opposite*: insertion **2 retraction**, renunciation, revocation, disclaimer, abjuration *Opposite*: confirmation **3 retreat**, departure, leaving, abandonment, retirement *Opposite*: arrival **4 alienation**, depression, isolation, detachment

withdrawn *adj* **reserved**, inhibited, solitary, introverted, introvert *Opposite*: outgoing

wither *v* **1 shrivel**, wilt, dry up, shrink, droop *Opposite*: bloom **2 weaken**, waste away, decline, fade, wane *Opposite*: strengthen **3 crush**, mortify, humiliate, abash, put down

withering *adj* **contemptuous**, scornful, sarcastic, sneering, arrogant *Opposite*: complimentary

with hindsight *adv* **in retrospect**, retrospectively, looking back, from experience

withhold *v* **hold back**, keep back, refuse, deny, suppress *Opposite*: give

within *adv* **inside**, in, indoors, in the interior *Opposite*: outside

within an ace of *prep* **within reach of**, a hair's-breadth from, a stone's throw from, on the verge of

with-it *(dated infml) adj* **cool**, fashionable, up-to-date, modern, modish

with one accord *(fml) adv* **simultaneously**, as one, in unison, together, unanimously

with one voice *see* **with one accord**

without *prep* **devoid of**, lacking, minus, in default of, sans *(literary) Opposite*: with

without fail *adv* **for certain**, reliably, like clockwork, unfailingly, dependably

without further ado *adv* **immediately**, at once, straightaway, forthwith, without delay

with reason *adv* **rightly**, with good cause, justifiably, justly, properly *Opposite*: unjustifiably

with reference to *see* **with regard to**

with regard to *prep* **regarding**, as regards, relating to, in connection with, concerning

with respect to *see* **with regard to**

withstand *v* **endure**, survive, resist, bear, weather *Opposite*: succumb

witless *adj* **foolish**, stupid, mindless, unintelligent, silly *Opposite*: sensible

witness *n* **observer**, spectator, bystander, onlooker, watcher ■ *v* **1 see**, observe, view, perceive, watch **2 countersign**, endorse, sign, attest, authenticate

wits *n* **reason**, shrewdness, acumen, faculties, mind

witter *(infml) v* **prattle**, gabble, go on, rattle on, chatter

wittering *(infml) n* **chatter**, babble, prattle, gabble, blather *(infml)*

witticism *n* **quip**, joke, riposte, gibe, one-liner

wittiness *n* **cleverness**, sharpness, keenness, comedy, sense of humour *Opposite*: dullness

wittingly *adv* **knowingly**, consciously, purposely, on purpose, intentionally *Opposite*: unwittingly

witty *adj* **amusing**, droll, humorous, funny, entertaining *Opposite*: dull

wiz *(infml) n* **expert**, prodigy, genius, wizard *(infml)*, ace *(infml)*

wizard *n* **1 sorcerer**, warlock, magician, shaman, witch doctor **2** *(infml)* **expert**, prodigy, genius, virtuoso, boffin *(infml)*

wizardry *n* **1 sorcery**, magic, divination, shamanism, spells **2 skill**, expertise, genius, brilliance, accomplishment

wizened *adj* **wrinkled**, lined, wrinkly, withered, crinkly *Opposite*: smooth

wobble *v* **1 shake**, vibrate, tremble, bob, quiver **2 quaver**, wave, shake, vary, oscillate **3 dither**, waver, vacillate, shilly-shally, hesitate *Opposite*: take the plunge

wobbliness *n* **1 shakiness**, unsteadiness, instability, ricketiness, rockiness *Opposite*: steadiness **2** *(infml)* **weakness**, unsteadiness, shakiness, trembling, reeling *Opposite*: steadiness

wobbly *adj* **1 unstable**, unsteady, rickety, rocky, shaky *Opposite*: steady **2** *(infml)* **weak**, trembling, woozy, dizzy, unsteady *Opposite*: fit

wodge *(infml) n* **lump**, chunk, pile, heap, handful *Opposite*: fragment

woe *n* **1 affliction**, misfortune, calamity, disaster, trouble *Opposite*: joy **2 grief**, distress, anguish, affliction, sadness *Opposite*: happiness

woebegone *adj* **miserable**, anguished, despairing, sad, wretched *Opposite*: cheerful

woeful *adj* **1 unhappy**, doleful, sad, sorrowful, mournful *Opposite*: cheerful **2 distressing**, traumatic, harrowing, tragic, unpleasant **3 pathetic**, pitiful, regrettable, bad, inadequate *Opposite*: wonderful

wok *n* **pan**, frying pan, skillet

wolf *n* *(infml)* **Casanova**, Don Juan, Romeo, womanizer, Lothario *(literary)* ■ *v* **gobble**, bolt, gulp down, devour, gorge *Opposite*: nibble

woman *n* **female**, lady, matron *Opposite*: man

womanhood *n* **1 adulthood**, maturity, independence *Opposite*: manhood **2 women**, womankind, females, womenfolk *Opposite*: mankind

womankind *n* **women**, womanhood, females, womenfolk *Opposite*: mankind

womanly *adj* **female**, feminine *Opposite*: manly

wonder n 1 **surprise**, astonishment, awe, amazement, admiration 2 **miracle**, phenomenon, marvel, sensation, curiosity ∎ v 1 **speculate**, doubt, question, conjecture, ponder 2 **marvel**, admire, gaze at, be amazed

wonderful adj 1 **magnificent**, superb, amazing, astonishing, fantastic Opposite: awful 2 **delightful**, pleasing, great, brilliant, perfect

wonderland n **utopia**, paradise, heaven, never-never land, nirvana

wonderment n **amazement**, astonishment, awe, surprise, bewilderment

wonky (infml) adj 1 **unreliable**, unsteady, insecure, wobbly, shaky Opposite: steady 2 **askew**, wrong, uneven, bent, off-centre Opposite: level

wont (fml) adj **accustomed**, used, in the habit of, inclined, liable Opposite: unaccustomed ∎ n **habit**, custom, tendency, preference, practice. See COMPARE AND CONTRAST at **habit**.

woo (literary) v **court**, persuade, encourage, entice, pursue Opposite: discourage

wood n 1 **timber**, firewood, logs, planks, kindling 2 **forest**, woodland, copse, covert, coppice

woodcarving n 1 **carving**, sculpture, woodwork, art, craft 2 **sculpture**, figure, embellishment, adornment, feature

woodcut n 1 **block**, carving, design, matrix 2 **print**, engraving, picture, illustration, portrait

wooded adj **forested**, woody, timbered, arboreal, sylvan (literary)

wooden adj 1 **wood**, timber, woody, ligneous 2 **stilted**, inexpressive, stiff, emotionless, deadpan Opposite: expressive 3 **dull**, toneless, flat Opposite: resonant

woodland n **forest**, wood, woods, timberland

woods n **wood**, forest, woodland, copse, covert

woodshed n **shed**, outbuilding, outhouse, garden shed, lean-to

woodwork n 1 **carpentry**, joinery, cabinetmaking, turning 2 **fittings**, doors, window frames, skirting boards, skirting 3 (infml) **goalpost**, crossbar, upright, goal, post

WORD BANK
❑ **types of woodwork** cabinetmaking, carpentry, carving, joinery, marquetry, woodcarving

woody adj **forested**, wooded, timbered, woodland, arboreal

woof v **bark**, yap, yelp

woolgather v **daydream**, dream, be miles away, fantasize, be lost in thought

woollen adj **knitted**, woven, wool, woolly, crocheted

woollens n **clothing**, sweaters, jumpers, cardigans

woolliness n **vagueness**, vagueness, haziness, haziness, obscurity

woolly adj 1 **woollen**, knitted, woven, wool, crocheted 2 **vague**, confused, unfocused, unclear, ill-defined Opposite: clear

woozy adj **dizzy**, faint, lightheaded, unsteady, nauseous Opposite: clear-headed

word n 1 **term**, expression, name 2 **chat**, conversation, talk, discussion, announcement 3 **information**, news, communication, gen (infml), info (infml) 4 **rumour**, report, whisper, gossip, tittle-tattle 5 **promise**, assurance, guarantee, oath, pledge 6 **command**, order, authorization, say-so (infml), go-ahead (infml) 7 **password**, code word, magic word, key word ∎ v **express**, phrase, couch, utter, articulate

word for word adv **verbatim**, in the same words, faithfully, exactly, precisely Opposite: loosely

word-for-word adj **verbatim**, faithful, exact, precise, accurate Opposite: loose

wordiness n **long-windedness**, verbosity, loquaciousness, prolixity Opposite: succinctness

wording n **phrasing**, words, language, phraseology, diction

wordless adj **silent**, mute, nonverbal, mimed, gestured

word list n **vocabulary**, glossary, dictionary, thesaurus, lexicon

word-perfect adj 1 **verbatim**, word for word, perfect, impeccable, consummate Opposite: unprepared 2 **correct**, accurate, exact, precise, literal

wordplay n **punning**, puns, repartee, wit, banter

WORD BANK
❑ **types of wordplay** acrostic, anagram, logogram, malapropism, palindrome, pun, spoonerism, telestich

words n 1 **argument**, disagreement, difference of opinion, dispute, confrontation 2 **lyrics**, verses, chorus, libretto, text

wordy adj **verbose**, long-winded, rambling, loquacious, prolix Opposite: concise

COMPARE AND CONTRAST CORE MEANING: too long or not concisely expressed

wordy using an excessive number of words in writing or speech; **verbose** expressed in language that is wordy and not precise; **long-winded** tediously wordy in speech or writing; **rambling** excessively long with many changes of subject, making it difficult to follow; **prolix** tiresomely wordy; **diffuse** lacking organization and conciseness.

work n 1 **labour**, employment, job, vocation, occupation Opposite: unemployment 2 **effort**, exertion, labour, toil, slog Opposite: leisure 3 **composition**, design, creation, opus, masterpiece ∎ v 1 **toil**, labour, slog, drudge 2 **perform**, bring about, produce, effect (fml) 3 **succeed**, be successful, thrive, work out,

come off (infml) **4 operate**, control, drive, run, function

workable adj **practical**, practicable, feasible, doable Opposite: impracticable

workaday adj **everyday**, ordinary, plain, homespun, commonplace Opposite: extraordinary

work against v **counteract**, cancel out, oppose, run counter to, interfere with Opposite: support

workaholic n **overachiever**, type A, workhorse (infml) Opposite: idler

workbench n **bench**, worktop, work surface, worktable

workbook n **exercise book**, schoolbook, notebook, jotter, notepad

worked up (infml) adj **agitated**, upset, excited, worried, hot and bothered Opposite: calm

worker n **employee**, member of staff, hand, operative, wage earner

work force n **personnel**, staff, employees, workers, human resources

workhorse (infml) n **hard worker**, good worker, rock, mainstay, pillar

working adj **1 operational**, functioning, effective, running Opposite: broken **2 employed**, occupied, at work, in work, salaried Opposite: unemployed

working class n **manual workers**, hoi polloi, the masses, proletariat, wage-earners Opposite: aristocracy

working group n **task force**, team, working party, committee, unit

working out n **exercising**, physical exercise, exercise, training, physical training

working party see **working group**

workings n **mechanism**, machinery, works, moving parts

workload n **amount of work**, assignment, job, load, capacity

workmate n **colleague**, coworker, fellow worker

work of art n **1 objet d'art**, creation, painting, sculpture, picture **2 masterpiece**, beauty, tour de force, pièce de résistance, work of genius Opposite: disaster (infml)

work on v **1 develop**, hone, build up, work up, perfect **2 influence**, sway, persuade, pressurize, pressure

work out v **1 exercise**, train, drill **2 solve**, figure out, decipher, resolve, deduce **3 understand**, comprehend, make sense of, fathom, conceive **4 plan**, devise, outline, sketch, arrange. See COMPARE AND CONTRAST at **deduce**.

workout n **1 exercise session**, exercises, training, aerobics, callisthenics **2 test**, road test, trial, run

workplace n **place of work**, workshop, workstation, work, office

workroom n **room**, workshop, study, office, studio

works n **1 factory**, plant, installation, industrial unit, manufacturing plant **2 mechanism**, workings, machinery, moving parts **3** (infml) **everything**, the whole thing, the lot, all of it, the whole kit and caboodle (infml)

worksheet n **1 homework sheet**, handout, test, quiz, question sheet **2 schedule**, job sheet, log, record

workshy adj **lazy**, idle, indolent, slothful, apathetic

workspace n **working area**, workstation, workplace, booth, cubicle

workstation n **workplace**, workspace, computer terminal

work surface n **surface**, worktop, workbench, workspace, work unit

worktop n **counter**, bench, work surface

work to rule v **go slow**, take industrial action, slow down

work-to-rule n **go-slow**, industrial action, slowdown (US)

work up v **1 develop**, work on, hone, improve, refine **2 agitate**, upset, disturb, provoke, irritate Opposite: calm

workup n **diagnosis**, examination, checkup, medical

world n **1 Earth**, planet, globe **2 biosphere**, ecosphere, creation, all God's creatures, flora and fauna **3 humankind**, humanity, the human race **4 domain**, realm, sphere, circle, area

world-beater n **champion**, superstar, one in a million, star, classic

world-class adj **first-rate**, first-class, superlative, outstanding, topnotch (infml)

world-famous adj **famous**, renowned, popular, acclaimed, notorious Opposite: unknown

worldliness n **1 materialism**, consumerism, acquisitiveness, greed, secularism **2 experience**, knowledge, sophistication, worldly wisdom

worldly adj **1 material**, temporal, earthly, materialistic, human **2 experienced**, sophisticated, mature, knowing, worldly wise Opposite: naive

worldly goods n **possessions**, belongings, assets, property

worldly-wise adj **sophisticated**, experienced, mature, knowing, worldly Opposite: naive

world-weariness n **discontent**, melancholy, boredom, ennui

world-weary adj **jaded**, discontented, bored, melancholic

worldwide adj **universal**, international, all-inclusive, wide-reaching, global Opposite: local

worm-eaten adj **1 wormy**, worm-infested, holey, rotten, decaying **2 dilapidated**, ramshackle, tumbledown, rickety

worm out v **elicit**, find out, coax out, ferret out, inveigle

worn *adj* **damaged**, shabby, tatty, dog-eared, dilapidated

worried *adj* **concerned**, anxious, apprehensive, nervous, bothered *Opposite*: unconcerned

worrier *n* **pessimist**, neurotic, fidget, worry-guts *(infml)*, fusspot *(infml)*

worrisome *adj* **troublesome**, worrying, annoying, irritating, bothersome

worry *v* **1 be anxious**, fret, be troubled, be concerned, be bothered **2 annoy**, pester, bother, trouble, disturb **3 touch**, pick, interfere with, claw at, tear at ■ *n* **anxiety**, unease, disquiet, discomfort, care

COMPARE AND CONTRAST CORE MEANING: a troubled mind

worry a troubled state of mind resulting from concern about current or potential difficulties; **unease** a feeling of anxiousness or lack of satisfaction with a situation; **care** a state of troubled anxiety; **anxiety** nervous apprehension about a future event or a general fear of possible misfortune; **angst** nonspecific chronic anxiety about the human condition or the state of the world; **stress** the worry and nervous apprehension related to a particular situation or event, for example a job or the process of moving house.

worrying *adj* **perturbing**, disturbing, upsetting, disquieting, nerve-racking *Opposite*: reassuring

worse *adj* **not as good as**, inferior, of inferior quality, poorer, of poorer quality *Opposite*: better

worsen *v* **1 get worse**, deteriorate, degenerate, go downhill, degrade *Opposite*: improve **2 make something worse**, exacerbate, aggravate, impair, inflame *Opposite*: improve

worsening *n* **deterioration**, aggravation, degeneration, decline *Opposite*: improvement

worship *v* **adore**, love, revere, adulate, deify ■ *n* **adoration**, love, reverence, respect, devotion

worshipful *adj* **reverential**, respectful, reverent, deferential, adoring

worshipper *n* **celebrant**, adorer, venerator, participant, believer

worst *adj* **nastiest**, vilest, poorest, wickedest, foulest *Opposite*: best

worth *n* **1 value**, price, cost, rate **2 merit**, appeal, significance, attraction, importance **3 wealth**, means, assets, value, substance

worthiness *n* **1 merit**, value, worth, praiseworthiness **2 dullness**, earnestness, boringness

worthless *adj* **1 valueless**, of no value, of little worth, insignificant, useless *Opposite*: valuable **2 empty**, hollow, meaningless, futile, pointless

worthlessness *n* **1 insignificance**, unimportance, irrelevance, triviality *Opposite*: value **2 pointlessness**, meaninglessness, futility, emptiness, hollowness

worthwhile *adj* **valuable**, useful, meaningful, sensible, advisable *Opposite*: worthless

worthy *adj* **1 commendable**, praiseworthy, laudable, admirable, valuable **2 well-intentioned**, well-meaning, earnest, pedestrian, dull

would-be *adj* **hopeful**, aspiring, prospective, budding, potential

wound *n* **injury**, lesion, cut, gash, sore ■ *v* **1 injure**, hurt, harm, damage, mutilate **2 offend**, upset, hurt, injure, distress

wounded *adj* **1 injured**, hurt, suffering **2 offended**, hurt, upset, distressed, aggrieved

wounding *adj* **hurtful**, cutting, acerbic, sharp *Opposite*: kind

wow *(infml)* *n* **winner**, smash, triumph, sensation, knockout *(infml)* *Opposite*: flop *(infml)*

wraith *n* **ghost**, phantom, apparition, spirit, spectre

wrangle *v* **argue**, dispute, quarrel, bicker, squabble ■ *n* **dispute**, argument, quarrel, squabble, disagreement

wrap *v* **1 enfold**, drape, swathe, cover, envelop **2 wrap up**, gift wrap, package *Opposite*: unwrap ■ *n* **1 shawl**, cloak, stole, cape **2 wrapping**, packaging, casing, covering

wrapper *n* **covering**, wrapping, wrap, cover, packaging

wrapping *n* **packaging**, covering, casing, wrap, cover

wrap up *v* **1 wrap**, gift wrap, parcel, package *Opposite*: unwrap **2 dress warmly**, muffle up, bundle up *(infml)* **3** *(infml)* **conclude**, complete, finish, finish off, end *Opposite*: begin

wrath *n* **anger**, rage, fury, madness, ire *(fml)*. See COMPARE AND CONTRAST *at* anger.

wrathful *adj* **furious**, angry, irate, enraged, fuming

wreak *v* **cause**, do, inflict, create, bring about

wreath *n* **garland**, circlet, headdress, laurel

wreathe *v* **1 adorn**, cover, garland, swathe, festoon **2 twist**, writhe, coil, wind

wreck *v* **destroy**, ruin, demolish, break, shatter ■ *n* **ruin**, remains, wreckage, shell, hulk

wreckage *n* **ruins**, remains, debris, wreck, rubble

wrecked *adj* **1 broken**, smashed, damaged, ruined, cracked **2** *(infml)* **exhausted**, worn-out, bushed *(infml)*, done in *(infml)*

wrench *v* **1 strain**, injure, hurt, pull, sprain **2 pull**, tug, haul, heave, jerk ■ *n* **1 injury**, sprain, strain, crick **2 pull**, tug, haul, heave, jerk

wrest *v* **1 gain**, take, seize, grasp **2 grab**, snatch, tug, pull

wrestle *v* **struggle**, fight, grapple, tussle, brawl

wretch *n* **1 unfortunate**, victim, languisher, sufferer, poor thing **2 rogue**, rascal, imp, horror *(infml)*, scallywag *(dated infml)* **3** *(fml)* **scoundrel**, rascal, rogue, villain, blackguard

wretched *adj* **1 miserable**, desolate, heartbroken, pitiful, dejected *Opposite*: happy **2 harsh**, hard, deprived, inferior, grim *Opposite*: comfortable **3 worthless**, base, despicable, inadequate, inferior *Opposite*: noble **4 irritating**, annoying, infuriating, frustrating, exasperating

wriggle *v* **wiggle**, writhe, turn, squirm, twist

wring *v* **squeeze**, twist, mangle, press, compress

wrinkle *n* **crease**, crinkle, line, fold, furrow ■ *v* **screw**, crumple, crinkle, crease, fold *Opposite*: smooth

wrinkled *adj* **1 crumpled**, creased, crinkly, rucked, rumpled *Opposite*: smooth **2 wrinkly**, wizened, weathered, lined, furrowed *Opposite*: smooth

wrinkly *see* **wrinkled**

writ *n* **summons**, court order, injunction, restraining order

write *v* **1 inscribe**, put pen to paper, transcribe, engrave, carve **2 write down**, put in writing, note down, enter, record **3 compose**, create, script, author, devise **4 send a letter to**, drop a line to, correspond with, contact, get in touch with

write down *v* **record**, note down, jot down, set down, put in writing

write off *v* **1** (*infml*) **cancel**, forget, disregard, set aside, abandon **2 wreck**, ruin, destroy, demolish, total (*US slang*)

writer *n* **author**, novelist, playwright, poet, journalist

write-up *n* **report**, article, piece, review, critique

writhe *v* **squirm**, wriggle, twist, struggle, thrash

writing *n* **1 script**, symbols, inscription, marks, characters **2 text**, literature, prose, journalism, copy

written *adj* **on paper**, printed, in black and white, in print

wrong *adj* **1 incorrect**, mistaken, erroneous, off beam, wide of the mark *Opposite*: right **2 immoral**, wicked, dishonest, illegal, sinful *Opposite*: right **3 amiss**, not right, unsuitable, improper, inappropriate *Opposite*: suitable ■ *n* **sin**, crime, injury, harm, damage ■ *v* **insult**, injure, wound, harm, ill-treat

wrongdoer *n* **criminal**, offender, sinner, reprobate, outlaw

wrongdoing *n* **bad behaviour**, unlawful activity, crime, offence, misconduct

wrong-foot *v* **catch out**, surprise, take unawares, take by surprise, trip up

wrongful *adj* **illegal**, unlawful, unfair, unjust, criminal *Opposite*: rightful. *See* COMPARE AND CONTRAST *at* **unlawful**.

wrong-headed *adj* **1 unreasonable**, obstinate, stubborn, perverse **2 irrational**, unreasoning, unthinking, ill-considered, ill-conceived

wrought-up *adj* **tense**, nervous, agitated, excited, on edge

wry *adj* **ironic**, cynical, sardonic, dry, droll

wryness *n* **humour**, irony, satire, dryness, drollness

XYZ

xenophobia *n* **chauvinism**, racial intolerance, dislike of foreigners, nationalism, prejudice *Opposite*: tolerance

xenophobic *adj* **chauvinistic**, intolerant, nationalistic, prejudiced, racist *Opposite*: tolerant

yak (*infml*) *v* **chatter**, chat, talk, gossip, natter

yammer (*infml*) *v* **chatter**, chat, talk, gossip, natter

yank *v* **pull**, tug, jerk, wrench, snatch ■ *n* **tug**, pull, jerk, wrench, heave. *See* COMPARE AND CONTRAST *at* **pull**.

yap *v* **1 bark**, yelp, bay, woof **2** (*infml*) **chatter**, chat, talk, gossip

yard *n* **1 patio**, courtyard, terrace, back yard **2 enclosure**, work area, storage area

yardstick *n* **measure**, index, gauge, benchmark, standard

yarn *n* **1 thread**, fibre, wool **2** (*infml*) **story**, tale, tall story, shaggy dog story, anecdote

yawn *v* **1 stretch**, stretch yourself, rub your eyes, sigh, nod **2 gape**, split, fly open, gap, crack *Opposite*: close up ■ *n* **bore**, nonevent, waste of time, mind-numbing experience, drag (*infml*) *Opposite*: laugh

yawning *adj* **deep**, cavernous, gaping, wide, open *Opposite*: narrow

yearbook *n* **annual**, annual report, almanac

yearly *adj* **annual**, twelve-monthly, year on year ■ *adv* **annually**, every year, once a year

yearn *v* **desire**, long, crave, ache, hanker. *See* COMPARE AND CONTRAST *at* **want**.

yearning *n* **desire**, longing, yen, hunger, thirst

year-round *adj* **constant**, continual, continuous, perennial *Opposite*: seasonal

years *n* **an age**, an inordinate length of time, aeons, ages (*infml*), centuries (*infml*)

yell v **shout**, scream, shriek, roar, bellow ■ n **shriek**, shout, scream, roar, bellow

yell at v **scold**, shout at, tear off a strip, rebuke, lash

yelp v **bark**, yap, cry, squeal, squeak

yen n **urge**, desire, wish, longing, yearning

yes adv **affirmative**, sure, certainly, absolutely, of course Opposite: no ■ n **affirmative**, positive response, nod, aye, thumbs-up (infml) Opposite: no

yesteryear n **past**, long ago, former times, days gone by, olden days Opposite: today

yet adv **1 up till now**, so far, thus far, hitherto, until now **2 however**, nevertheless, nonetheless, still, in spite of that

yield v **1 produce**, bear, generate, bring in, return **2 give in**, submit, surrender, succumb, capitulate Opposite: resist **3 give up**, concede, grant, relinquish, resign Opposite: keep ■ n **1 harvest**, crop, produce, vintage **2 profit**, earnings, income, revenue, return

COMPARE AND CONTRAST CORE MEANING: give way

yield give way to something such as force, pressure, entreaty, or persuasion; **capitulate** cease to resist a superior force, especially one that seems invincible, sometimes without having offered strong opposition; **submit** accept somebody else's authority or will, especially reluctantly or under pressure; **succumb** give in to something due to weakness or the failure to offer effective opposition; **surrender** give way to the power of another person and stop offering resistance, usually after active opposition.

yielding adj **1 soft**, elastic, springy, squashy, resilient Opposite: firm **2 compliant**, acquiescent, docile, accommodating, tractable Opposite: stubborn

yob (infml) n **thug**, vandal, hoodlum, yobbo (infml), hooligan (infml)

yoke n **repression**, oppression, burden, bondage, encumbrance

yomp (infml) v **trudge**, march, clump, stomp, clomp

young adj **1 youthful**, little, juvenile, adolescent, immature Opposite: old **2 new**, early, undeveloped, fledgling, beginning Opposite: established ■ n **offspring**, children, babies, litter, brood

WORD BANK

❏ **types of young animal** bullock, calf, colt, cub, fawn, foal, heifer, joey, kid, kitten, lamb, leveret, piglet, pup, puppy, whelp, yearling

❏ **types of young bird** chick, cygnet, duckling, eaglet, eyas, fledgling, gosling, nestling, owlet, pullet, squab

younger generation n **young people**, youth, teenagers, adolescents, youngsters

young person n **teenager**, adolescent, youngster, juvenile, child Opposite: adult

youngster n **child**, young person, teenager, youth, adolescent Opposite: adult. See COMPARE AND CONTRAST at youth.

youth n **1 childhood**, adolescence, formative years, infancy, early life Opposite: adulthood **2 child**, teenager, youngster, minor, young person Opposite: adult

COMPARE AND CONTRAST CORE MEANING: somebody who is young

youth a man or boy who is in his teens or early twenties; **child** a young person between birth and the onset of puberty; **kid** (infml) a child or young person; **teenager** somebody between the ages of thirteen and nineteen; **youngster** somebody who is young, or somebody younger than others mentioned or present.

youthful adj **1 young**, childlike, childish, boyish, girlish Opposite: old **2 vigorous**, energetic, lively, enthusiastic, active Opposite: sluggish

youthfulness n **1 youth**, freshness, newness, childishness, first flush of youth Opposite: age **2 enthusiasm**, energy, radiance, vigour, liveliness Opposite: sluggishness

yowl v **howl**, squall, squeal, wail, caterwaul

yucky (infml) adj **nasty**, revolting, horrid, unpleasant, disgusting Opposite: yummy (infml)

yummy (infml) adj **delicious**, tasty, mouthwatering, delectable, luscious Opposite: yucky (infml)

zany adj **unconventional**, madcap, crazy (infml), wacky (infml)

zap (infml) v **1 destroy**, kill, annihilate, exterminate, delete **2 change channels**, switch channels, flick through, cruise, surf **3 whiz**, zoom, tear, rip, shoot Opposite: dawdle

zappy (infml) adj **lively**, forceful, striking, eye-catching, energetic

zeal n **enthusiasm**, passion, fanaticism, fervour, ardour Opposite: apathy

zealot n **extremist**, fanatic, bigot, evangelist, dogmatist Opposite: moderate

zealous adj **enthusiastic**, keen, passionate, fervent, ardent Opposite: apathetic

zenith n **peak**, summit, pinnacle, top, acme Opposite: nadir

zeppelin n **airship**, dirigible, blimp, aircraft, balloon

zero n **nothing**, nil, nought, zilch (infml)

zest n **1 enthusiasm**, keenness, gusto, relish, appetite Opposite: apathy **2 taste**, tang, piquancy, bite, spice

zestful adj **enthusiastic**, keen, passionate, dynamic, energetic Opposite: apathetic

zigzag v **wind**, meander, crisscross, weave, snake

zilch (infml) n **nothing**, zero, nil, nought

zillion (infml) n **squillion**, million, billion, shedload, truckload